Real-world examples are key to the applied approach of this book. The seventh edition of Microeconomics incorporates more than 100 detailed examples into the flow of the text. The following is a list of these examples:

# Microeconomics

## SEVENTH EDITION

# Microeconomics

SEVENTH
EDITION

Robert S. Pindyck

*Massachusetts Institute of Technology*

Daniel L. Rubinfeld

*University of California, Berkeley*

PEARSON
Prentice
Hall

*Pearson Educational International*

**Editorial Director:** Sally Yagan
**AVP/Editor in Chief:** Eric Svendsen
**AVP/Executive Editor:** Chris Rogers
**VP/Director of Development:** Steve Deitmer
**Senior Development Editor:** Ron Librach
**Product Development Manager:** Ashley Santora
**Assistant Editor:** Susie Abraham
**Marketing Manager:** Andrew Watts
**Marketing Assistant:** Ian Gold
**Permissions Project Manager:** Charles Morris
**Senior Managing Editor:** Judy Leale
**Associate Managing Editor:** Suzanne DeWorken
**Senior Operations Specialist:** Arnold Vila
**Art Director:** Kenny Beck
**Text and Cover Designer:** Maureen Eide
**Cover Illustration:** Corin Skidds
**Director, Image Resource Center:** Melinda Patelli
**Manager, Rights and Permissions:** Zina Arabia
**Manager, Visual Research:** Beth Brenzel
**Image Permission Coordinator:** Annette Linder
**Composition:** GGS Book Services PMG
**Full-Service Project Management:** Jeanine Furino/GGS Book Services PMG
**Printer/Binder:** Courier Kendallville
**Typeface:** 10/11 Palatino

Credits and acknowledgments borrowed from other sources and reproduced, with permission, in this textbook appear on appropriate page within text (or on pages 723–724).

If you purchased this book within the United States or Canada you should be aware that it has been wrongfully imported without the approval of the Publisher or the Author.

**Copyright © 2009, 2005, 2001, 1998, 1995 by Pearson Education, Inc., Upper Saddle River, New Jersey, 07458.** Pearson Prentice Hall. All rights reserved. Printed in the United States of America. This publication is protected by Copyright and permission should be obtained from the publisher prior to any prohibited reproduction, storage in a retrieval system, or transmission in any form or by any means, electronic, mechanical, photocopying, recording, or likewise. For information regarding permission(s), write to: Rights and Permissions Department.

**Pearson Prentice Hall**™ is a trademark of Pearson Education, Inc.
**Pearson**® is a registered trademark of Pearson plc
**Prentice Hall**® is a registered trademark of Pearson Education, Inc.

Pearson Education Ltd., London
Pearson Education Singapore, Pte. Ltd
Pearson Education, Canada, Inc.
Pearson Education–Japan
Pearson Education Australia PTY, Limited

Pearson Education North Asia, Ltd., Hong Kong
Pearson Educación de Mexico, S.A. de C.V.
Pearson Education Malaysia, Pte. Ltd
Pearson Education Upper Saddle River, New Jersey

10 9 8 7
ISBN-13: 978-0-13-713335-2
ISBN-10: 0-13-713335-9

*To our daughters,*

Maya, Talia, and Shira
Sarah and Rachel

# ABOUT THE AUTHORS

FIGURE 0.1    Authors of Microeconomics

The authors, back again for a new edition, reflect on their years of successful textbook collaboration. Pindyck is on the right and Rubinfeld on the left.

Revising a textbook every three or four years takes considerable work, so Pindyck asked, "Why bother? The last edition was clearly written and students loved it." "Don't be silly," replied Rubinfield. "Remember what our publisher said—the old edition was getting stale, and we need some new and jazzy examples." "I guess that makes sense," replied Pindyck, "but do you think it has anything to do with the used book market?" Rubinfield paused. "Could be, but remember that 7 is our lucky number."

Robert S. Pindyck is the Bank of Tokyo-Mitsubishi Ltd. Professor of Economics and Finance in the Sloan School of Management at M.I.T. Daniel L. Rubinfeld is the Robert L. Bridges Professor of Law and Professor of Economics at the University of California, Berkely, and Visiting Professor of Law at NYU. Both received their Ph.D's from M.I.T., Pindyck in 1971 and Rubinfeld in 1972. Professor Pindyck's research and writing have covered a variety of topics in microeconomics, including the effects of uncertainty on firm behavior and market structure, the determinants of market power, the behavior of natural resource, commodity, and financial markets, and criteria for investment decisions. Professor Rubinfeld, who served as chief economist at the Department of Justice in 1997 and 1998, is the author of a variety of articles relating to antitrust, competition policy, law and economics, law and statistics, and public economics.

Pindyck and Rubinfeld are also co-authors of *Econometric Models and Economic Forecasts*, another best-selling textbook that may yet be turned into a feature film. Always looking for ways to earn some extra spending money, the two authors recently enrolled as human subjects in a double-blind test of a new hair restoration medication. Rubinfeld strongly suspects that he is being given the placebo.

This is probably more than you want to know about these authors, but for further information, see their websites: **http://web.mit.edu/rpindyck/www** and **http://www.law.berkeley.edu/faculty/rubinfeldd**.

# BRIEF CONTENTS

# CONTENTS

## 11 Pricing with Market Power   391

## 12 Monopolistic Competition and Oligopoly   443

## LIST OF EXAMPLES

# PREFACE

For students who care about how the world works, microeconomics is one of the most relevant and interesting subjects they can study. A good grasp of microeconomics is vital for managerial decision making, for designing and understanding public policy, and more generally for appreciating how a modern economy functions.

We wrote this book, *Microeconomics*, because we believe that students need to be exposed to the new topics that have come to play a central role in microeconomics over the years—topics such as game theory and competitive strategy, the roles of uncertainty and information, and the analysis of pricing by firms with market power. We also felt that students need to be shown how microeconomics can help us to understand what goes on in the world and how it can be used as a practical tool for decision making. Microeconomics is an exciting and dynamic subject, but students need to be given an appreciation of its relevance and usefulness. They want and need a good understanding of how microeconomics can actually be used outside the classroom.

To respond to these needs, the seventh edition of *Microeconomics* provides a treatment of microeconomic theory that stresses its relevance and application to both managerial and public policy decision making. This applied emphasis is accomplished by including 118 extended examples that cover such topics as the analysis of demand, cost, and market efficiency; the design of pricing strategies; investment and production decisions; and public policy analysis. Because of the importance that we attach to these examples, they are included in the flow of the text. (A complete list is included on the endpapers inside the front cover.)

The coverage in this edition of *Microeconomics* incorporates the dramatic changes that have occurred in the field in recent years. There has been growing interest in game theory and the strategic interactions of firms (Chapters 12 and 13), in the role and implications of uncertainty and asymmetric information (Chapters 5 and 17), in the pricing strategies of firms with market power (Chapters 10 and 11), and in the design of policies to deal efficiently with externalities such as environmental pollution (Chapter 18). These topics, which receive only limited attention in most books, are covered extensively here.

That the coverage in *Microeconomics* is comprehensive and up-to-date does not mean that it is "advanced" or difficult. We have worked hard to make the exposition clear and accessible as well as lively and engaging. We believe that the study of microeconomics should be enjoyable and stimulating. We hope that our book reflects this belief. Except for appendices and footnotes, *Microeconomics* uses no calculus. As a result, it should be suitable for students with a broad range of backgrounds. (Those sections that are more demanding are marked with an asterisk and can be easily omitted.)

# CHANGES IN THE SEVENTH EDITION

Each new edition of this book has built on the success of prior editions by adding a number of new topics, by adding and updating examples, and by improving the exposition of existing materials.

The seventh edition continues that tradition. We have expanded and updated Chapter 18 (Externalities and Public Goods), so that it now includes a more thorough and up-to-date treatment of environmental economics, a topic that has been receiving increasing coverage in many intermediate microeconomics courses. In particular, we have rewritten and improved the clarity of the sections on externalities, included a new section on stock externalities (of the kind that arise with greenhouse gases and global warming), and added an example on pollution control in China. We have also introduced new material on alternative forms of organizations in Chapter 8, substantially revised and updated our coverage of behavioral economics in Chapter 5, and improved the exposition of some of the core material on production and cost in Chapters 6, 7, and 8, including the mathematical appendix to Chapter 7. In Chapter 14, we added new material to clarify the distinction between monopsony power and bargaining power. In addition, we have added several new examples, replaced a number of older examples with new ones, and updated most of the other examples.

These improvements aside, we have maintained our prior chapter organization. This should make it easy for those who have been loyal users in the past to make the transition to the new edition. As always, we have attempted to make the text as clear, accessible, and engaging as possible.

The layout of this edition is similar to that of the prior edition. This has allowed us to continue to define key terms in the margins (as well as in the Glossary at the end of the book), and also to use the margins to include Concept Links that relate newly developed ideas to concepts introduced previously in the text.

# ALTERNATIVE COURSE DESIGNS

This new edition of *Microeconomics* offers instructors considerable flexibility in course design. For a one-quarter or one-semester course stressing the basic core material, we would suggest using the following chapters and sections of chapters: 1 through 6, 7.1-7.4, 8 through 10, 11.1-11.3, 12, 14, 15.1-15.4, 18.1-18.2, and 18.5. A somewhat more ambitious course might also include parts of Chapters 5 and 16 and additional sections in Chapters 7 and 9. To emphasize uncertainty and market failure, an instructor should also include substantial parts of Chapters 5 and 17.

Depending on one's interests and the goals of the course, other sections could be added or used to replace the materials listed above. A course emphasizing modern pricing theory and business strategy would include all of Chapters 11, 12, and 13 and the remaining sections of Chapter 15. A course in managerial economics might also include the appendices to Chapters 4, 7, and 11, as well as the appendix on regression analysis at the end of the book. A course stressing welfare economics and public policy should include Chapter 16 and additional sections of Chapter 18.

Finally, we want to stress that those sections or subsections that are more demanding and/or peripheral to the core material have been marked with an asterisk. These sections can easily be omitted without detracting from the flow of the book.

# SUPPLEMENTARY MATERIALS

Ancillaries of an exceptionally high quality are available to instructors and students using this book. The *Instructor's Manual*, prepared by Duncan M. Holthausen of North Carolina State University provides detailed solutions to all end-of-chapter Questions for Review and Exercises. The seventh edition contains many entirely new review questions and exercises, and a number of exercises have been revised and updated. The new instructor's manual has been revised accordingly. Each chapter also contains Teaching Tips to summarize key points.

The *Test Bank*, prepared by Douglas J. Miller of the University of Missouri, contains approximately 2,000 multiple-choice and short-answer questions with solutions. All of this material has been thoroughly reviewed, accuracy checked, and revised for this edition. The print version of the Test Bank is designed for use with the new *TestGen* test-generating software. This computerized package allows instructors to custom-design, save, and generate classroom tests. The test program permits instructors to edit, add, or delete questions from the test banks; edit existing graphics and create new graphics; analyze test results; and organize a database of tests and student results. This new software allows for greater flexibility and ease of use. It provides many options for organizing and displaying tests, along with a search and sort feature.

The *PowerPoint Lecture Presentation* has been completely revised for this edition by Fernando and Yvonn Quijano of Dickinson State University. Instructors can edit the detailed outlines to create their own full-color, professional-looking presentations and customized handouts for students. The PowerPoint Presentation is downloadable from the Instructor Resources link at **www.prenhall.com/pindyck**.

A set of four-color *Acetates* of selected figures and tables from the text is available for instructors using the seventh edition.

The *Study Guide*, prepared by Valerie Suslow of the University of Michigan and Jonathan Hamilton of the University of Florida, provides a wide variety of review materials and exercises for students. Each chapter contains a list of important concepts, chapter highlights, a concept review, problem sets, and a self-test quiz. Worked-out answers and solutions are provided for all exercises, problem sets, and self-test questions.

**Online Resources** The *Companion Website* (**http://www.prenhall.com/pindyck**) is a content-rich website with exercises, activities, and resources related specifically to the seventh edition of *Microeconomics*. The *Online Study Guide* offers students another opportunity to sharpen their problem-solving skills and to assess their understanding of text material. It contains a set of both multiple-choice and essay quizzes. Each question submitted by the student is graded and immediate feedback is provided for correct and incorrect answers. The online study guide also allows students to e-mail results to up to four e-mail addresses. The website also provides current events articles and exercises related to topics in the book. These exercises help show students the relevance of economics in today's world. They may also direct students to appropriate updated economics-related websites to gather data and analyze specific economic problems.

For instructors, the Companion Website provides a *Syllabus Manager*. This feature allows instructors to enhance their lectures with all the resources available with this text. Instructors can post their syllabus to the site and download supplements and lecture aids. Instructors should log in under Instructor Resources in order to access this material.

# ACKNOWLEDGMENTS

As the saying goes, it takes a village to revise a textbook. Because the seventh edition of *Microeconomics* has been the outgrowth of years of experience in the classroom, we owe a debt of gratitude to our students and to the colleagues with whom we often discuss microeconomics and its presentation. We have also had the help of capable research assistants. For the first six editions of the book, these included Peter Adams, Walter Athier, Phillip Gibbs, Salar Jahedi Jamie Jue, Rashmi Khare, Masaya Okoshi, Kathy O'Regan, Karen Randig, Subi Rangan, Deborah Senior, Ashesh Shah, Nicola Stafford, and Wilson Tai. Kathy Hill helped with the art, while Assunta Kent, Mary Knott, and Dawn Elliott Linahan provided secretarial assistance with the first edition. We especially want to thank Lynn Steele and Jay Tharp who provided considerable editorial support for the second edition. Mark Glickman and Steve Wiggins assisted with the examples in the third edition, while Andrew Guest, Jeanette Sayre, and Lynn Steele provided valuable editorial support for the third, fourth, and fifth editions, as did Brandi Henson and Jeanette Sayre for the sixth edition.

Writing this book has been both a painstaking and enjoyable process. At each stage we received exceptionally fine guidance from teachers of microeconomics throughout the country. After the first draft of the first edition of the book had been edited and reviewed, it was discussed at a two-day focus group meeting in New York. This provided an opportunity to get ideas from instructors with a variety of backgrounds and perspectives. We would like to thank the following focus group members for advice and criticism: Carl Davidson of Michigan State University; Richard Eastin of the University of Southern California; Judith Roberts of California State University, Long Beach; and Charles Strein of the University of Northern Iowa.

We would like to thank the reviewers who provided comments and ideas that have contributed significantly to the seventh edition of *Microeconomics*:

Ashley Ahrens, Mesa State College
Anca Alecsandru, Louisiana State University
Albert Assibey-Mensah, Kentucky State University
Charles A. Bennett, Gannon University
Maharukh Bhiladwalla, Rutgers University
Raymonda Burgman, DePauw University
H. Stuart Burness, University of New Mexico
Peter Calcagno, College of Charleston
Eric Chiang, Florida Atlantic University
Tom Cooper, Georgetown College
Robert Crawford, Marriott School, Brigham Young University
Julie Cullen, University of California, San Diego
Richard Eastin, University of Southern California
Michael Enz, Western New England College
John Francis, Auburn University, Montgomery
Delia Furtado, University of Connecticut
Craig Gallet, California State University, Sacramento
Michele Glower, Lehigh University
Tiffani Gottschall, Washington & Jefferson College
Adam Grossberg, Trinity College
Bruce Hartman, California State University, The California Maritime Academy
Daniel Henderson, Binghamton University

Wayne Hickenbottom, University of Texas at Austin
Stella Hofrenning, Augsburg College
Duncan M. Holthausen, North Carolina State University
Brian Jacobsen, Wisconsin Lutheran College
Jonatan Jelen, New York University
Changik Jo, Anderson University
Mahbubul Kabir, Lyon College
Brian Kench, University of Tampa
Paul Koch, Olivet Nazarene University
Dennis Kovach, Community College of Allegheny County
Sang Lee, Southeastern Louisiana University
Peter Marks, Rhode Island College
Douglas J Miller, University of Missouri-Columbia
Laudo Ogura, Grand Valley State University
Ozge Ozay, University of Utah
Jonathan Powers, Knox College
Lucia Quesada, Universidad Torcuato Di Telia
Benjamin Rashford, Oregon State University
Fred Rodgers, Medaille College
William Rogers, University of Missouri-Saint Louis
Menahem Spiegel, Rutgers University
Houston Stokes, University of Illinois at Chicago
Mira Tsymuk, Hunter College, CUNY
Thomas Watkins, Eastern Kentucky University
David Wharton, Washington College
Beth Wilson, Humboldt State University

We would also like to thank all those who reviewed the first six editions at various stages of their evolution:

Nii Adote Abrahams, Missouri Southern State College
Jack Adams, University of Arkansas, Little Rock
Sheri Aggarwal, Dartmouth College
Ted Amato, University of North Carolina, Charlotte
John J. Antel, University of Houston
Kerry Back, Northwestern University
Dale Ballou, University of Massachusetts, Amherst
William Baxter, Stanford University
Gregory Besharov, Duke University
Victor Brajer, California State University, Fullerton
James A. Brander, University of British Columbia
David S. Bullock, University of Illinois
Jeremy Bulow, Stanford University
Winston Chang, State University of New York, Buffalo
Henry Chappel, University of South Carolina
Larry A. Chenault, Miami University
Harrison Cheng, University of Southern California
Kwan Choi, Iowa State University
Charles Clotfelter, Duke University
Kathryn Combs, California State University, Los Angeles
Richard Corwall, Middlebury College
John Coupe, University of Maine at Orono
Jacques Cremer, Virginia Polytechnic Institute and State University

Carl Davidson, Michigan State University
Gilbert Davis, University of Michigan
Arthur T. Denzau, Washington University
Tran Dung, Wright State University
Richard V. Eastin, University of Southern California
Maxim Engers, University of Virginia
Carl E. Enomoto, New Mexico State University
Ray Farrow, Seattle University
Gary Ferrier, Southern Methodist University
Roger Frantz, San Diego State University
Patricia Gladden, University of Missouri
Otis Gilley, Louisiana Tech University
William H. Greene, New York University
Thomas A. Gresik, Notre Dame University
John Gross, University of Wisconsin at Milwaukee
Jonathan Hamilton, University of Florida
Claire Hammond, Wake Forest University
James Hartigan, University of Oklahoma
George Heitman, Pennsylvania State University
George E. Hoffer, Virginia Commonwealth University
Robert Inman, The Wharton School, University of Pennsylvania
Joyce Jacobsen, Rhodes College
B. Patrick Joyce, Michigan Technological University
David Kaserman, Auburn University
Michael Kende, INSEAD, France
Philip G. King, San Francisco State University
Tetteh A. Kofi, University of San Francisco
Anthony Krautman, DePaul University
Leonard Lardaro, University of Rhode Island
Robert Lemke, Florida International University
Peter Linneman, University of Pennsylvania
Leonard Loyd, University of Houston
R. Ashley Lyman, University of Idaho
James MacDonald, Rensselaer Polytechnical Institute
Wesley A. Magat, Duke University
Anthony M. Marino, University of Southern Florida
Lawrence Martin, Michigan State University
John Makum Mbaku, Weber State University
Richard D. McGrath, College of William and Mary
David Mills, University of Virginia, Charlottesville
Richard Mills, University of New Hampshire
Jennifer Moll, Fairfield University
Michael J. Moore, Duke University
W. D. Morgan, University of California at Santa Barbara
Julianne Nelson, Stern School of Business, New York University
George Norman, Tufts University
Daniel Orr, Virginia Polytechnic Institute and State University
Christos Paphristodoulou, Mälardalen University
Sharon J. Pearson, University of Alberta, Edmonton
Ivan P'ng, University of California, Los Angeles
Michael Podgursky, University of Massachusetts, Amherst
Charles Ratliff, Davidson College
Judith Roberts, California State University, Long Beach

Geoffrey Rothwell, Stanford University
Nestor Ruiz, University of California, Davis
Edward L. Sattler, Bradley University
Roger Sherman, University of Virginia
Nachum Sicherman, Columbia University
Sigbjørn Sødal, Agder University College
Houston H. Stokes, University of Illinois, Chicago
Richard W. Stratton, University of Akron
Charles T. Strein, University of Northern Iowa
Charles Stuart, University of California, Santa Barbara
Valerie Suslow, University of Michigan
Theofanis Tsoulouhas, North Carolina State
Abdul Turay, Radford University
Sevin Ugural, Eastern Mediterranean University
Nora A. Underwood, University of California, Davis
Nikolaos Vettas, Duke University
David Vrooman, St. Lawrence University
Michael Wasylenko, Syracuse University
Robert Whaples, Wake Forest University
Lawrence J. White, New York University
Michael F. Williams, University of St. Thomas
Arthur Woolf, University of Vermont
Chiou-nan Yeh, Alabama State University
Peter Zaleski, Villanova University
Joseph Ziegler, University of Arkansas, Fayetteville

Apart from the formal review process, we are especially grateful to Jean
Andrews, Paul Anglin, J. C. K. Ash, Ernst Berndt, George Bittlingmayer,
Severin Borenstein, Paul Carlin, Whewon Cho, Setio Angarro Dewo, Frank
Fabozzi, Joseph Farrell, Frank Fisher, Jonathan Hamilton, Robert Inman, Joyce
Jacobsen, Stacey Kole, Preston McAfee, Jeannette Mortensen, John Mullahy,
Krishna Pendakur, Jeffrey Perloff, Ivan P'ng, A. Mitchell Polinsky, Judith
Roberts, Geoffrey Rothwell, Garth Saloner, Joel Schrag, Daniel Siegel, Thomas
Stoker, David Storey, James Walker, and Michael Williams, who were kind
enough to provide comments, criticisms, and suggestions as the various edi-
tions of this book developed.

There were a number of people who offered helpful comments, corrections,
and suggestions for the seventh edition. We owe special thanks to Avinash
Dixit, Paul Joskow, and Bob Inman. We also want to thank the following people
for their comments and corrections: Smita Brunnermeier, Ralf Faber, Tom
Friedland, Volker Grzimek, Phillip L. Hersch, Shirley Hsiao, Narayan D.
Lelgiri, Shahram Manouchehri, Jungbein Moon, Abdul Qayum, Jacques
Siegers, Jörg Spenkuch, Menahem Spiegel, Alex Thomas, and Shine Wu.

Among those who offered helpful comments, corrections, and suggestions for
the Seventh Edition were Steve Allen, Smita Brunnermeier, Tom Friedland,
Phillip L. Hersh, Shirley Hsiao, Narayan D. Lelgiri, Shahram Manouchehri,
Jungbein Moon, Jacques Siegers, Menahem Spiegel, Alex Thomes, and Shine Wu.

Chapter 5 of this seventh edition contains new and updated material on
behavioral economics, whose genesis owes much to the thoughtful comments
of George Akerlof. We also want to thank Jay Kim, Maciej Kotowski, Smita
Brunnerneier, Tammy McGavock, and Shira Pindyck for their superb research
assistance on this edition, and Matt Hartman and Ida Ng for their outstanding
editorial assistance, and for carefully reviewing the page proofs of this edition.

We also wish to express our sincere thanks for the extraordinary effort those at Macmillan and Prentice Hall made in the development of the various editions of our book. Throughout the writing of the first edition, Bonnie Lieberman provided invaluable guidance and encouragement; Ken MacLeod kept the progress of the book on an even keel; Gerald Lombardi provided masterful editorial assistance and advice; and John Molyneux ably oversaw the book's production.

In the development of the second edition, we were fortunate to have the encouragement and support of David Boelio, and the organizational and editorial help of two Macmillan editors, Caroline Carney and Jill Lectka. The second edition also benefited greatly from the superb development editing of Gerald Lombardi, and from John Travis, who managed the book's production.

Jill Lectka and Denise Abbott were our editors for the third edition, and we benefited greatly from their input. We thank Valerie Ashton, John Sollami, and Sharon Lee for their superb handling of the production of the third edition.

Leah Jewell was our editor for the fourth edition; her patience, thoughtfulness, and perseverance were greatly appreciated. We also thank our Production Editor, Dee Josephson, for managing the production process so effectively, and our Design Manager, Patricia Wosczyk, for her help with the book's design.

We appreciate the outstanding efforts of our Senior Development Editor, Ron Librach; Associate Managing Editor, Suzanne DeWorken; Art Director, Kenny Beck; Project Manager with GGS Book Services PMG, Jeanine Furino; Editor in Chief, Eric Svendsen; Executive Editor, Chris Rogers; Assistant Editor, Susie Abraham; Editorial Assistant, Vanessa Bain; and Marketing Manager, Andy Watts.

We owe a special debt of thanks to Catherine Lynn Steele, whose superb editorial work carried us through five editions of this book. Lynn passed away on December 10, 2002. We will miss her very much.

*R.S.P.*
*D.L.R.*

# PART•ONE

## Introduction: Markets and Prices

Part 1 surveys the scope of microeconomics and introduces some basic concepts and tools. Chapter 1 discusses the range of problems that micro-economics addresses, and the kinds of answers it can provide. It also explains what a market is, how we determine the boundaries of a market, and how we measure market price.

Chapter 2 covers one of the most important tools of microeconomics: supply-demand analysis. We explain how a competitive market works and how supply and demand determine the prices and quantities of goods and services. We also show how supply-demand analysis can be used to deter-mine the effects of changing market conditions, including government intervention.

# Preliminaries

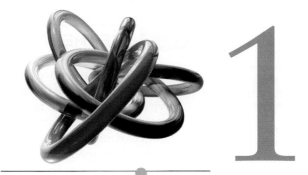

Economics is divided into two main branches: microeconomics and macroeconomics. **Microeconomics** deals with the behavior of individual economic units. These units include consumers, workers, investors, owners of land, business firms—in fact, any individual or entity that plays a role in the functioning of our economy.[1] Microeconomics explains how and why these units make economic decisions. For example, it explains how consumers make purchasing decisions and how their choices are affected by changing prices and incomes. It also explains how firms decide how many workers to hire and how workers decide where to work and how much work to do.

Another important concern of microeconomics is how economic units interact to form larger units—markets and industries. Microeconomics helps us to understand, for example, why the American automobile industry developed the way it did and how producers and consumers interact in the market for automobiles. It explains how automobile prices are determined, how much automobile companies invest in new factories, and how many cars are produced each year. By studying the behavior and interaction of individual firms and consumers, microeconomics reveals how industries and markets operate and evolve, why they differ from one another, and how they are affected by government policies and global economic conditions.

By contrast, **macroeconomics** deals with aggregate economic quantities, such as the level and growth rate of national output, interest rates, unemployment, and inflation. But the boundary between macroeconomics and microeconomics has become less and less distinct in recent years. The reason is that macroeconomics also involves the analysis of markets—for example, the aggregate markets for goods and services, labor, and corporate bonds. To understand how these aggregate markets operate, we must first understand the behavior of the firms, consumers, workers, and investors who constitute them. Thus macroeconomists have become increasingly concerned with the microeconomic foundations of aggregate economic phenomena, and much of macroeconomics is actually an extension of microeconomic analysis.

---

[1]The prefix *micro-* is derived from the Greek word meaning "small." However, many of the individual economic units that we will study are small only in relation to the U.S. economy as a whole. For example, the annual sales of General Motors, IBM, or Microsoft are larger than the gross national products of many countries.

• **microeconomics**  Branch of economics that deals with the behavior of individual economic units—consumers, firms, workers, and investors—as well as the markets that these units comprise.

• **macroeconomics**  Branch of economics that deals with aggregate economic variables, such as the level and growth rate of national output, interest rates, unemployment, and inflation.

# 1.1 THE THEMES OF MICROECONOMICS

The Rolling Stones once said: "You can't always get what you want." This is true. For most people (even Mick Jagger), that there are limits to what you can have or do is a simple fact of life learned in early childhood. For economists, however, it can be an obsession.

Much of microeconomics is about *limits*—the limited incomes that consumers can spend on goods and services, the limited budgets and technical know-how that firms can use to produce things, and the limited number of hours in a week that workers can allocate to labor or leisure. But microeconomics is also about *ways to make the most of these limits*. More precisely, it is about *the allocation of scarce resources*. For example, microeconomics explains how consumers can best allocate their limited incomes to the various goods and services available for purchase. It explains how workers can best allocate their time to labor instead of leisure, or to one job instead of another. And it explains how firms can best allocate limited financial resources to hiring additional workers versus buying new machinery, and to producing one set of products versus another.

In a planned economy such as that of Cuba, North Korea, or the former Soviet Union, these allocation decisions are made mostly by the government. Firms are told what and how much to produce, and how to produce it; workers have little flexibility in choice of jobs, hours worked, or even where they live; and consumers typically have a very limited set of goods to choose from. As a result, many of the tools and concepts of microeconomics are of limited relevance in those countries.

## Trade-Offs

In modern market economies, consumers, workers, and firms have much more flexibility and choice when it comes to allocating scarce resources. Microeconomics describes the *trade-offs* that consumers, workers, and firms face, and *shows how these trade-offs are best made*.

The idea of making optimal trade-offs is an important theme in microeconomics—one that you will encounter throughout this book. Let's look at it in more detail.

**Consumers**  Consumers have limited incomes, which can be spent on a wide variety of goods and services, or saved for the future. *Consumer theory*, the subject matter of Chapters 3, 4, and 5 of this book, describes how consumers, based on their preferences, maximize their well-being by trading off the purchase of more of some goods for the purchase of less of others. We will also see how consumers decide how much of their incomes to save, thereby trading off current consumption for future consumption.

**Workers**  Workers also face constraints and make trade-offs. First, people must decide whether and when to enter the workforce. Because the kinds of jobs—and corresponding pay scales—available to a worker depend in part on educational attainment and accumulated skills, one must trade off working now (and earning an immediate income) for continued education (and the hope of earning a higher future income). Second, workers face trade-offs in their choice of employment. For example, while some people choose to work for large corporations that offer job security but limited potential for advancement, others prefer to work for small companies where there is more opportunity for advancement but less security. Finally, workers must sometimes decide how many hours per week they wish to work, thereby trading off labor for leisure.

**Firms** Firms also face limits in terms of the kinds of products that they can produce, and the resources available to produce them. General Motors, for example, is very good at producing cars and trucks, but it does not have the ability to produce airplanes, computers, or pharmaceuticals. It is also constrained in terms of financial resources and the current production capacity of its factories. Given these constraints, GM must decide how many of each type of vehicle to produce. If it wants to produce a larger total number of cars and trucks next year or the year after, it must decide whether to hire more workers, build new factories, or do both. The *theory of the firm*, the subject matter of Chapters 6 and 7, describes how these trade-offs can best be made.

## Prices and Markets

A second important theme of microeconomics is the role of *prices*. All of the trade-offs described above are based on the prices faced by consumers, workers, or firms. For example, a consumer trades off beef for chicken based partly on his or her preferences for each one, but also on their prices. Likewise, workers trade off labor for leisure based in part on the "price" that they can get for their labor—i.e., the *wage*. And firms decide whether to hire more workers or purchase more machines based in part on wage rates and machine prices.

Microeconomics also describes how prices are determined. In a centrally planned economy, prices are set by the government. In a market economy, prices are determined by the interactions of consumers, workers, and firms. These interactions occur in *markets*—collections of buyers and sellers that together determine the price of a good. In the automobile market, for example, car prices are affected by competition among Ford, General Motors, Toyota, and other manufacturers, and also by the demands of consumers. The central role of markets is the third important theme of microeconomics. We will say more about the nature and operation of markets shortly.

## Theories and Models

Like any science, economics is concerned with the *explanations* of observed phenomena. Why, for example, do firms tend to hire or lay off workers when the prices of their raw materials change? How many workers are likely to be hired or laid off by a firm or an industry if the price of raw materials increases by, say, 10 percent?

In economics, as in other sciences, explanation and prediction are based on *theories*. Theories are developed to explain observed phenomena in terms of a set of basic rules and assumptions. The *theory of the firm*, for example, begins with a simple assumption—firms try to maximize their profits. The theory uses this assumption to explain how firms choose the amounts of labor, capital, and raw materials that they use for production and the amount of output they produce. It also explains how these choices depend on the *prices* of inputs, such as labor, capital, and raw materials, and the prices that firms can receive for their outputs.

Economic theories are also the basis for making predictions. Thus the theory of the firm tells us whether a firm's output level will increase or decrease in response to an increase in wage rates or a decrease in the price of raw materials. With the application of statistical and econometric techniques, theories can be used to construct models from which quantitative predictions can be made.

A *model* is a mathematical representation, based on economic theory, of a firm, a market, or some other entity. For example, we might develop a model of a particular firm and use it to predict *by how much* the firm's output level will change as a result of, say, a 10-percent drop in the price of raw materials.

Statistics and econometrics also let us measure the *accuracy* of our predictions. For example, suppose we predict that a 10-percent drop in the price of raw materials will lead to a 5-percent increase in output. Are we sure that the increase in output will be exactly 5 percent, or might it be somewhere between 3 and 7 percent? Quantifying the accuracy of a prediction can be as important as the prediction itself.

No theory, whether in economics, physics, or any other science, is perfectly correct. The usefulness and validity of a theory depend on whether it succeeds in explaining and predicting the set of phenomena that it is intended to explain and predict. Theories, therefore, are continually tested against observation. As a result of this testing, they are often modified or refined and occasionally even discarded. The process of testing and refining theories is central to the development of economics as a science.

When evaluating a theory, it is important to keep in mind that it is invariably imperfect. This is the case in every branch of science. In physics, for example, Boyle's law relates the volume, temperature, and pressure of a gas.[2] The law is based on the assumption that individual molecules of a gas behave as though they were tiny, elastic billiard balls. Physicists today know that gas molecules do not, in fact, always behave like billiard balls, which is why Boyle's law breaks down under extremes of pressure and temperature. Under most conditions, however, it does an excellent job of predicting how the temperature of a gas will change when the pressure and volume change, and it is therefore an essential tool for engineers and scientists.

The situation is much the same in economics. For example, because firms do not maximize their profits all the time, the theory of the firm has had only limited success in explaining certain aspects of firms' behavior, such as the timing of capital investment decisions. Nonetheless, the theory does explain a broad range of phenomena regarding the behavior, growth, and evolution of firms and industries, and has thus become an important tool for managers and policymakers.

## Positive versus Normative Analysis

Microeconomics is concerned with both *positive* and *normative* questions. Positive questions deal with explanation and prediction, normative questions with what *ought* to be. Suppose the U.S. government imposes a quota on the import of foreign cars. What will happen to the price, production, and sales of cars? What impact will this policy change have on American consumers? On workers in the automobile industry? These questions belong to the realm of **positive analysis**: statements that describe relationships of cause and effect.

• **positive analysis** Analysis describing relationships of cause and effect.

Positive analysis is central to microeconomics. As we explained above, theories are developed to explain phenomena, tested against observations, and used to construct models from which predictions are made. The use of economic theory for prediction is important both for the managers of firms and for public

---

[2]Robert Boyle (1627–1691) was a British chemist and physicist who discovered experimentally that pressure ($P$), volume ($V$), and temperature ($T$) were related in the following way: $PV = RT$, where $R$ is a constant. Later, physicists derived this relationship as a consequence of the kinetic theory of gases, which describes the movement of gas molecules in statistical terms.

policy. Suppose the federal government is considering raising the tax on gasoline. The change would affect the price of gasoline, consumers' purchasing choices for small or large cars, the amount of driving that people do, and so on. To plan sensibly, oil companies, automobile companies, producers of automobile parts, and firms in the tourist industry would all need to estimate the impact of the change. Government policymakers would also need quantitative estimates of the effects. They would want to determine the costs imposed on consumers (perhaps broken down by income categories); the effects on profits and employment in the oil, automobile, and tourist industries; and the amount of tax revenue likely to be collected each year.

Sometimes we want to go beyond explanation and prediction to ask such questions as "What is best?" This involves **normative analysis**, which is also important for both managers of firms and those making public policy. Again, consider a new tax on gasoline. Automobile companies would want to determine the best (profit-maximizing) mix of large and small cars to produce once the tax is in place. Specifically, how much money should be invested to make cars more fuel-efficient? For policymakers, the primary issue is likely to be whether the tax is in the public interest. The same policy objectives (say, an increase in tax revenues and a decrease in dependence on imported oil) might be met more cheaply with a different kind of tax, such as a tariff on imported oil.

• **normative analysis**
Analysis examining questions of what ought to be.

Normative analysis is not only concerned with alternative policy options; it also involves the design of particular policy choices. For example, suppose it has been decided that a gasoline tax is desirable. Balancing costs and benefits, we then ask what is the optimal size of the tax.

Normative analysis is often supplemented by value judgments. For example, a comparison between a gasoline tax and an oil import tariff might conclude that the gasoline tax will be easier to administer but will have a greater impact on lower-income consumers. At that point, society must make a value judgment, weighing equity against economic efficiency. When value judgments are involved, microeconomics cannot tell us what the best policy is. However, it can clarify the trade-offs and thereby help to illuminate the issues and sharpen the debate.

## 1.2 WHAT IS A MARKET?

We can divide individual economic units into two broad groups according to function—*buyers* and *sellers*. Buyers include consumers, who purchase goods and services, and firms, which buy labor, capital, and raw materials that they use to produce goods and services. Sellers include firms, which sell their goods and services; workers, who sell their labor services; and resource owners, who rent land or sell mineral resources to firms. Clearly, most people and most firms act as both buyers and sellers, but we will find it helpful to think of them as simply buyers when they are buying something and sellers when they are selling something.

Together, buyers and sellers interact to form *markets*. A **market** is *the collection of buyers and sellers that, through their actual or potential interactions, determine the price of a product or set of products*. In the market for personal computers, for example, the buyers are business firms, households, and students; the sellers are Hewlett-Packard, Lenovo, Dell, Apple, and a number of other firms. Note that a market includes more than an *industry. An industry is a collection of firms that sell the same or closely related products*. In effect, an industry is the supply side of the market.

• **market** Collection of buyers and sellers that, through their actual or potential interactions, determine the price of a product or set of products.

• **market definition**
Determination of the buyers, sellers, and range of products that should be included in a particular market.

Economists are often concerned with **market definition**—with determining which buyers and sellers should be included in a particular market. When defining a market, *potential* interactions of buyers and sellers can be just as important as *actual* ones. An example of this is the market for gold. A New Yorker who wants to buy gold is unlikely to travel to Zurich to do so. Most buyers of gold in New York will interact only with sellers in New York. But because the cost of transporting gold is small relative to its value, buyers of gold in New York *could* purchase their gold in Zurich if the prices there were significantly lower.

• **arbitrage** Practice of buying at a low price at one location and selling at a higher price in another.

Significant differences in the price of a commodity create a potential for **arbitrage**: buying at a low price in one location and selling at a higher price somewhere else. The possibility of arbitrage prevents the prices of gold in New York and Zurich from differing significantly and creates a world market for gold.

Markets are at the center of economic activity, and many of the most interesting issues in economics concern the functioning of markets. For example, why do only a few firms compete with one another in some markets, while in others a great many firms compete? Are consumers necessarily better off if there are many firms? If so, should the government intervene in markets with only a few firms? Why have prices in some markets risen or fallen rapidly, while in other markets prices have hardly changed at all? And which markets offer the best opportunities for an entrepreneur thinking of going into business?

## Competitive versus Noncompetitive Markets

• **perfectly competitive market** Market with many buyers and sellers, so that no single buyer or seller has a significant impact on price.

In this book, we study the behavior of both competitive and noncompetitive markets. A **perfectly competitive market** has many buyers and sellers, so that no single buyer or seller has a significant impact on price. Most agricultural markets are close to being perfectly competitive. For example, thousands of farmers produce wheat, which thousands of buyers purchase to produce flour and other products. As a result, no single farmer and no single buyer can significantly affect the price of wheat.

Many other markets are competitive enough to be treated as if they were perfectly competitive. The world market for copper, for example, contains a few dozen major producers. That number is enough for the impact on price to be small if any one producer goes out of business. The same is true for many other natural resource markets, such as those for coal, iron, tin, or lumber.

Other markets containing a small number of producers may still be treated as competitive for purposes of analysis. For example, the U.S. airline industry contains several dozen firms, but most routes are served by only a few firms. Nonetheless, because competition among those firms is often fierce, for some purposes airline markets can be treated as competitive. Finally, some markets contain many producers but are *noncompetitive*; that is, individual firms can jointly affect the price. The world oil market is one example. Since the early 1970s, that market has been dominated by the OPEC cartel. (A *cartel* is a group of producers that acts collectively.)

## Market Price

• **market price** Price prevailing in a competitive market.

Markets make possible transactions between buyers and sellers. Quantities of a good are sold at specific prices. In a perfectly competitive market, a single price—the **market price**—will usually prevail. The price of wheat in Kansas City and the price of gold in New York are two examples. These prices are usually easy to measure. For example, you can find the price of corn, wheat, or gold each day in the business section of a newspaper.

In markets that are not perfectly competitive, different firms might charge different prices for the same product. This might happen because one firm is trying to win customers from its competitors, or because customers have brand loyalties that allow some firms to charge higher prices than others. For example, two brands of laundry detergent might be sold in the same supermarket at different prices. Or two supermarkets in the same town might sell the same brand of laundry detergent at different prices. In cases such as this, when we refer to the market price, we will mean the price averaged across brands or supermarkets.

The market prices of most goods will fluctuate over time, and for many goods the fluctuations can be rapid. This is particularly true for goods sold in competitive markets. The stock market, for example, is highly competitive because there are typically many buyers and sellers for any one stock. As anyone who has invested in the stock market knows, the price of any particular stock fluctuates from minute to minute and can rise or fall substantially during a single day. Likewise, the prices of commodities such as wheat, soybeans, coffee, oil, gold, silver, and lumber can rise or fall dramatically in a day or a week.

## Market Definition—The Extent of a Market

As we saw, *market definition* identifies which buyers and sellers should be included in a given market. However, to determine which buyers and sellers to include, we must first determine the **extent of a market**—its *boundaries*, both *geographically* and in terms of the *range of products* to be included in it.

When we refer to the market for gasoline, for example, we must be clear about its geographic boundaries. Are we referring to downtown Los Angeles, southern California, or the entire United States? We must also be clear about the range of products to which we are referring. Should regular-octane and high-octane premium gasoline be included in the same market? Gasoline and diesel fuel?

For some goods, it makes sense to talk about a market only in terms of very restrictive geographic boundaries. Housing is a good example. Most people who work in downtown Chicago will look for housing within commuting distance. They will not look at homes 200 or 300 miles away, even though those homes might be much cheaper. And homes (together with the land they are sitting on) 200 miles away cannot be easily moved closer to Chicago. Thus the housing market in Chicago is separate and distinct from, say, that in Cleveland, Houston, Atlanta, or Philadelphia. Likewise, retail gasoline markets, though less limited geographically, are still regional because of the expense of shipping gasoline over long distances. Thus the market for gasoline in southern California is distinct from that in northern Illinois. On the other hand, as we mentioned earlier, gold is bought and sold in a world market; the possibility of arbitrage prevents the price from differing significantly from one location to another.

We must also think carefully about the range of products to include in a market. For example, there is a market for single-lens reflex (SLR) digital cameras, and many brands compete in that market. But what about compact "point-and-shoot" digital cameras? Should they be considered part of the same market? Probably not, because they are typically used for different purposes and so do not compete with SLR cameras. Gasoline is another example. Regular- and premium-octane gasolines might be considered part of the same market because most consumers can use either. Diesel fuel, however, is not

**• extent of a market** Boundaries of a market, both geographical and in terms of range of products produced and sold within it.

part of this market because cars that use regular gasoline cannot use diesel fuel, and vice versa.[3]

Market definition is important for two reasons:

- A company must understand who its actual and potential competitors are for the various products that it sells or might sell in the future. It must also know the product boundaries and geographical boundaries of its market in order to set price, determine advertising budgets, and make capital investment decisions.

- Market definition can be important for public policy decisions. Should the government allow a merger or acquisition involving companies that produce similar products, or should it challenge it? The answer depends on the impact of that merger or acquisition on future competition and prices; often this can be evaluated only by defining a market.

---

### EXAMPLE 1.1    Markets for Prescription Drugs

The development of a new drug by a pharmaceutical company is an expensive venture. It begins with large expenditures on research and development, then requires various stages of laboratory and clinical testing, and, if the new drug is finally approved, marketing, production, and sales. At that point, the firm faces the important problem of determining the price of the new drug.

Pricing depends on the preferences and medical needs of the consumers who will be buying the drug, the characteristics of the drug, and the number and characteristics of *competing* drugs. Pricing a new drug, therefore, requires a good understanding of the market in which it will be sold.

In the pharmaceutical industry, market boundaries are sometimes easy to determine, and sometimes not so easy to determine. Markets are usually defined in terms of *therapeutic classes* of drugs. For example, there is a market for *antiulcer drugs* that is very clearly defined. For some time, there were four competitors in the market: Tagamet, Zantac, Axid, and Pepcid. All four drugs work in roughly the same way: They cause the stomach to produce less hydrochloric acid. They differ slightly in terms of their side effects and their interactions with other drugs that a patient might be taking, but in most cases they could be readily substituted for each other.[4]

Another example of a clearly defined pharmaceutical market is the market for *anticholesterol* drugs. There are several major products in the U.S. market: the leading brand is Pfizer's Lipitor, followed by Vytorin (Merck), Pravachol (Bristol-Myers Squibb), Zocor (also Merck), and Lescol (Novartis). These drugs all do pretty much the same thing (reduce blood cholesterol levels) and work in pretty

---

[3]How can we determine the extent of a market? Since the market is where the price of a good is established, one approach focuses on market prices. We ask whether product prices in different geographic regions (or for different product types) are approximately the same, or whether they tend to move together. If either is the case, we place them in the same market. For a more detailed discussion, see George J. Stigler and Robert A. Sherwin, "The Extent of the Market," *Journal of Law and Economics* 27 (October 1985): 555–85.

[4]As we will see in Example 10.1, more recently Prilosec, Prevacid, and then Nexium entered the market. These are also antiulcer drugs, but work on a different biochemical mechanism.

much the same way. While their side effects and interactions differ somewhat, they are all close substitutes. Thus when Pfizer sets the price of Lipitor, it must be concerned not only with the willingness of patients (and their insurance companies) to pay, but also with the prices and characteristics of the competing drugs. Likewise, a drug company that is considering whether to develop a new anticholesterol drug knows that if it commits itself to the investment and succeeds, it will have to compete with the other existing drugs. The company can use this information to project its potential revenues from the new drug, and thereby evaluate the investment.

Sometimes, however, pharmaceutical market boundaries are more ambiguous. Consider *painkillers*, a category that includes aspirin, acetaminophen (sold under the brand name Tylenol but also sold generically), ibuprofen (sold under such brand names as Motrin and Advil but also sold generically), naproxen (sold by prescription but also sold over the counter by the brand name Aleve), and Voltaren (a more powerful prescription drug produced by Novartis). There are many types of painkillers, and some work better than others for certain types of pain (e.g., headaches, arthritis, muscle aches, etc.). Side effects likewise differ. While some types of painkillers are used more frequently for certain symptoms or conditions, there is considerable spillover. For example, depending on the severity of the pain and the pain tolerance of the patient, a toothache might be treated with any of the painkillers listed above. This substitutability makes the boundaries of the painkiller market difficult to define.

---

**EXAMPLE 1.2**     The Market for Sweeteners

In 1990, the Archer-Daniels-Midland Company (ADM) acquired the Clinton Corn Processing Company (CCP).[5] ADM was a large company that produced many agricultural products, one of which was high-fructose corn syrup (HFCS). CCP was another major U.S. corn syrup producer. The U.S. Department of Justice (DOJ) challenged the acquisition on the grounds that it would lead to a dominant producer of corn syrup with the power to push prices above competitive levels. Indeed, ADM and CCP together accounted for over 70 percent of U.S. corn syrup production.

ADM fought the DOJ decision, and the case went to court. The basic issue was whether corn syrup represented a distinct market. If it did, the combined market share of ADM and CCP would have been about 40 percent, and the DOJ's concern might have been warranted. ADM, however, argued that the correct market definition was much broader—a market for sweeteners which included sugar as well as corn syrup. Because the ADM–CCP combined share of a sweetener market would have been quite small, there would be no concern about the company's power to raise prices.

ADM argued that sugar and corn syrup should be considered part of the same market because they are used interchangeably to sweeten a vast array of food products, such as soft drinks, spaghetti sauce, and pancake syrup. ADM also showed that as the level of prices for corn syrup and sugar fluctuated, industrial food producers would change the proportions of each sweetener that they used in their products. In October 1990, a federal judge agreed with ADM's argument

---

[5]This example is based on F. M. Scherer, "Archer-Daniels-Midland and Clinton Corn Processing," Case C16-92-1126, John F. Kennedy School of Government, Harvard University, 1992.

that sugar and corn syrup were both part of a broad market for sweeteners. The acquisition was allowed to go through.

Sugar and corn syrup continue to be used interchangeably to satisfy Americans' strong taste for sweetened foods. In 2004, per-capita consumption of sweeteners in the U.S. was about 140 pounds per person, of which sugar accounted for 62 pounds and corn syrup 78 pounds.

## 1.3 REAL VERSUS NOMINAL PRICES

We often want to compare the price of a good today with what it was in the past or is likely to be in the future. To make such a comparison meaningful, we need to measure prices relative to an *overall price level*. In absolute terms, the price of a dozen eggs is many times higher today than it was 50 years ago. Relative to prices overall, however, it is actually lower. Therefore, we must be careful to correct for inflation when comparing prices across time. This means measuring prices in *real* rather than *nominal* terms.

• **nominal price** Absolute price of a good, unadjusted for inflation.

The **nominal price** of a good (sometimes called its "current-dollar" price) is its absolute price. For example, the nominal price of a pound of butter was about $0.87 in 1970, $1.88 in 1980, about $1.99 in 1990, and about $3.40 in 2007. These are the prices you would have seen in supermarkets in those years. The **real price** of a good (sometimes called its "constant-dollar" price) is the price relative to an aggregate measure of prices. In other words, it is the price adjusted for inflation.

• **real price** Price of a good relative to an aggregate measure of prices; price adjusted for inflation.

For consumer goods, the aggregate measure of prices most often used is the **Consumer Price Index (CPI)**. The CPI is calculated by the U.S. Bureau of Labor Statistics by surveying retail prices, and is published monthly. It records how the cost of a large market basket of goods purchased by a "typical" consumer changes over time. Percentage changes in the CPI measure the rate of inflation in the economy.

• **Consumer Price Index** Measure of the aggregate price level.

Sometimes we are interested in the prices of raw materials and other intermediate products bought by firms, as well as in finished products sold at wholesale to retail stores. In this case, the aggregate measure of prices often used is the **Producer Price Index (PPI)**. The PPI is also calculated by the U.S. Bureau of Labor Statistics and published monthly, and records how, on average, prices at the wholesale level change over time. Percentage changes in the PPI measure cost inflation and predict future changes in the CPI.

• **Producer Price Index** Measure of the aggregate price level for intermediate products and wholesale goods.

So which price index should you use to convert nominal prices to real prices? It depends on the type of product you are examining. If it is a product or service normally purchased by consumers, use the CPI. If instead it is a product normally purchased by businesses, use the PPI.

Because we are examining the price of butter in supermarkets, the relevant price index is the CPI. After correcting for inflation, do we find that the price of butter was more expensive in 2007 than in 1970? To find out, let's calculate the 2007 price of butter in terms of 1970 dollars. The CPI was 38.8 in 1970 and rose to about 205.8 in 2007. (There was considerable inflation in the United States during the 1970s and early 1980s.) In 1970 dollars, the price of butter was

$$\frac{38.8}{205.8} \times \$3.40 = \$0.64$$

In real terms, therefore, the price of butter was lower in 2007 than it was in 1970.[6] Put another way, the nominal price of butter went up by about 290 percent, while the CPI went up 430 percent. Relative to the aggregate price level, butter prices fell.

In this book, we will usually be concerned with real rather than nominal prices because consumer choices involve analyses of price comparisons. These relative prices can most easily be evaluated if there is a common basis of comparison. Stating all prices in real terms achieves this objective. Thus, even though we will often measure prices in dollars, we will be thinking in terms of the real purchasing power of those dollars.

---

**EXAMPLE 1.3**　The Price of Eggs and the Price of a College Education

In 1970, Grade A large eggs cost about 61 cents a dozen. In the same year, the average annual cost of a college education at a private four-year college, including room and board, was about $2530. By 2007, the price of eggs had risen to $1.64 a dozen, and the average cost of a college education was $27,560. In real terms, were eggs more expensive in 2007 than in 1970? Had a college education become more expensive?

Table 1.1 shows the nominal price of eggs, the nominal cost of a college education, and the CPI for 1970–2007. (The CPI is based on 1983 = 100.) Also shown are the *real* prices of eggs and college education in 1970 dollars, calculated as follows:

$$\text{Real price of eggs in 1980} = \frac{\text{CPI}_{1970}}{\text{CPI}_{1980}} \times \text{nominal price in 1980}$$

$$\text{Real price of eggs in 1990} = \frac{\text{CPI}_{1970}}{\text{CPI}_{1990}} \times \text{nominal price in 1990}$$

and so forth.

**TABLE 1.1**　The Real Price of Eggs and of a College Education[7]

|  | 1970 | 1980 | 1990 | 2000 | 2007 |
|---|---|---|---|---|---|
| Consumer Price Index | 38.8 | 82.4 | 130.7 | 172.2 | 205.8 |
| **Nominal Prices** | | | | | |
| Grade A Large Eggs | $0.61 | $0.84 | $1.01 | $0.91 | $1.64 |
| College Education | $2530 | $4912 | $12,018 | $20,186 | $27,560 |
| **Real Prices ($1970)** | | | | | |
| Grade A Large Eggs | $0.61 | $0.40 | $0.30 | $0.21 | $0.31 |
| College Education | $2530 | $2313 | $3568 | $4548 | $5196 |

The table shows clearly that the real cost of a college education rose (by 105 percent) during this period, while the real cost of eggs fell (by 49 percent). It is

---

[6]Two good sources of data on the national economy are the *Economic Report of the President* and the *Statistical Abstract of the United States*. Both are published annually and are available from the U.S. Government Printing Office.

[7]You can get data on the cost of a college education by visiting the National Center for Educational Statistics and download the Digest of Education Statistics at **http://nces.ed.gov**. Historical and current data on the average retail price of eggs can be obtained from the Bureau of Labor Statistics (BLS) at **http://www.bls.gov**, by selecting CPI—Average Price Data.

these relative changes in prices that are important for the choices that consumers make, not the fact that both eggs and college cost more in nominal dollars today than they did in 1970.

In the table, we calculated real prices in terms of 1970 dollars, but we could just as easily have calculated them in terms of dollars of some other base year. For example, suppose we want to calculate the real price of eggs in *1990 dollars*. Then:

$$\text{Real price of eggs in 1970} = \frac{\text{CPI}_{1990}}{\text{CPI}_{1970}} \times \text{nominal price in 1970}$$

$$= \frac{130.7}{38.8} \times 0.61 = 2.05$$

$$\text{Real price of eggs in 2007} = \frac{\text{CPI}_{1990}}{\text{CPI}_{2007}} \times \text{nominal price in 2007}$$

$$= \frac{130.7}{205.8} \times 1.64 = 1.04$$

$$\text{Percentage change in real price} = \frac{\text{real price in 2007} - \text{real price in 1970}}{\text{real price in 1970}}$$

$$= \frac{1.04 - 2.05}{2.05} = -0.49$$

Notice that the percentage decline in real price is 49 percent whether we use 1970 dollars or 1990 dollars as the base year.

---

**EXAMPLE 1.4**     The Minimum Wage

The federal minimum wage—first instituted in 1938 at a level of 25 cents per hour—has been increased periodically over the years. From 1991 through 1995, for example, it was $4.25 an hour. Congress voted to raise it to $4.75 in 1996 and then to $5.15 in 1997. Legislation in 2007 to increase the minimum wage yet again would raise it to $6.55 an hour in 2008 and $7.25 in 2009.[8]

Figure 1.1 shows the minimum wage from 1938 through 2010, both in nominal terms and in 2000 constant dollars. Note that although the legislated minimum wage has steadily increased, in real terms the minimum wage today is not much different from what is was in the 1950s.

Nonetheless, the 2007 decision to increase the minimum wage was a difficult one. Although the higher minimum wage would provide a better standard of living for those workers who had been paid below the minimum, some analysts feared that it would also lead to increased unemployment among young and unskilled workers. The decision to increase the minimum wage, therefore, raises both normative and positive issues. The normative issue is whether any loss of teenage and low-skilled jobs is outweighed by two factors: (1) the direct benefits to those workers who now earn more as a result; and (2) any indirect benefits to other workers whose wages might be increased along with the wages of those at the bottom of the pay scale.

---

[8]Some states also have minimum wages that are higher than the federal minimum wage. For example, in 2007 the minimum wage in Massachusetts was $7.50 per hour, in New York it was $7.15, and in California it was $7.50 and scheduled to increase to $8.00 in 2008. You can learn more about the minimum wage at **http://www.dol.gov**.

**FIGURE 1.1  The Minimum Wage**

In nominal terms, the minimum wage has increased steadily over the past 70 years. However, in real terms its expected 2010 level is below that of the 1970s.

An important positive issue is how many fewer workers (if any) would be able to get jobs with a higher minimum wage. As we will see in Chapter 14, this issue is still hotly debated. Statistical studies have suggested that an increase in the minimum wage of about 10 percent would increase teenage unemployment by 1 to 2 percent. (The actual increase from $5.15 to $7.25 represents a 41-percent increase.) However, one review of the evidence questions whether there are any significant unemployment effects.[9]

# 1.4  WHY STUDY MICROECONOMICS?

We think that after reading this book you will have no doubt about the importance and broad applicability of microeconomics. In fact, one of our major goals is to show you how to apply microeconomic principles to actual decision-making problems. Nonetheless, some extra motivation early on never hurts. Here are two examples that not only show the use of microeconomics in practice, but also provide a preview of this book.

## Corporate Decision Making: Ford's Sport Utility Vehicles

In 1991, the Ford Motor Company introduced the Explorer, which became the best-selling sport utility vehicle (SUV) in the United States. In 1997, Ford introduced the Expedition, a larger and roomier SUV. This car was also a big success

---

[9]The first study is David Neumark and William Wascher, "Employment Effects of Minimum and Subminimum Wages: Panel Data on State Minimum Wage Laws," *Industrial and Labor Relations Review* 46 (October 1992): 55–81. A review of the literature appears in David Card and Alan Krueger, *Myth and Measurement: The New Economics of the Minimum Wage* (Princeton: Princeton University Press, 1995).

and contributed significantly to Ford's profits. By 2002, Ford was offering six SUV models and manufacturing over a half dozen others through its subsidiaries. In the period 2005 to 2007, higher gas prices and growing concerns about global warming took a toll on all SUV sales, and Ford's profits turned to losses. In response, Ford worked on developing new and smaller cars. But Ford also modified its SUV models, making them lighter and more fuel efficient.

The design and efficient production of Ford's SUVs involved not only some impressive engineering, but a lot of economics as well. First, Ford had to think carefully about how the public would react to the design and performance of its new products. How strong would demand be initially, and how fast would it grow? How would demand depend on the prices that Ford charged? Understanding consumer preferences and trade-offs and predicting demand and its responsiveness to price are essential to Ford and every other automobile manufacturer. (We discuss consumer preferences and demand in Chapters 3, 4, and 5.)

Next, Ford had to be concerned with the cost of manufacturing these cars. How high would production costs be? How would costs depend on the number of cars produced each year? How would union wage negotiations and the prices of steel and other raw materials affect costs? How much and how fast would costs decline as managers and workers gained experience with the production process? And to maximize profits, how many of these cars should Ford plan to produce each year? (We discuss production and cost in Chapters 6 and 7 and the profit-maximizing choice of output in Chapter 8.)

Ford also had to design a pricing strategy and consider how competitors would react to it. For example, should Ford charge a low price for the basic stripped-down version of the Explorer but high prices for individual options, such as leather seats? Or would it be more profitable to make these options "standard" items and charge a higher price for the whole package? Whatever strategy Ford chose, how were competitors likely to react? Would DaimlerChrysler try to undercut Ford by lowering the price of its Jeep Grand Cherokee? Might Ford be able to deter DaimlerChrysler or GM from lowering prices by threatening to respond with its own price cuts? (We discuss pricing in Chapters 10 and 11 and competitive strategy in Chapters 12 and 13.)

Because its SUV product line required large investments in new capital equipment, Ford had to consider both the risks and possible outcomes of its decisions. Some of this risk was due to uncertainty over the future price of gasoline (higher gasoline prices would reduce the demand for heavy vehicles). Some was due to uncertainty over the wages that Ford would have to pay its workers. What would happen if world oil prices doubled or tripled, or if the U.S. government imposed a heavy tax on gasoline? How much bargaining power would unions have, and how might union demands affect wage rates? How should Ford take these uncertainties into account when making investment decisions? (Commodity markets and the effects of taxes are discussed in Chapters 2 and 9. Labor markets and union power are discussed in Chapter 14. Investment decisions and the role of uncertainty are discussed in Chapters 5 and 15.)

Ford also had to worry about organizational problems. Ford is an integrated firm in which separate divisions produce engines and parts and then assemble finished cars. How should managers of different divisions be rewarded? What price should the assembly division be charged for engines that it receives from another division? Should all parts be obtained from the upstream divisions, or should some be purchased from outside firms?

(We discuss internal pricing and organizational incentives for the integrated firm in Chapters 11 and 17.)

Finally, Ford had to think about its relationship to the government and the effects of regulatory policies. For example, all of Ford's cars must meet federal emissions standards, and production-line operations must comply with health and safety regulations. How might these regulations and standards change over time? How might they affect costs and profits? (We discuss the role of government in limiting pollution and promoting health and safety in Chapter 18.)

## Public Policy Design: Automobile Emission Standards for the Twenty-First Century

In 1970, the Federal Clean Air Act imposed strict tailpipe emission standards on new automobiles. These standards have become increasingly stringent—the 1970 levels of nitrogen oxides, hydrocarbons, and carbon monoxide emitted by automobiles had been reduced by about 90 percent by 1999. Now, as the number of cars on the roads keeps increasing, the government must consider how stringent these standards should be in the coming years.

The design of a program like the Clean Air Act involves a careful analysis of the ecological and health effects of auto emissions. But it also involves a good deal of economics. First, the government must evaluate the monetary impact of the program on consumers. Emission standards affect the cost both of purchasing a car (catalytic converters would be necessary, which would raise the cost of cars) and of operating it (gas mileage would be lower, and converters would have to be repaired and maintained). Because consumers ultimately bear much of this added cost, it is important to know how it affects their standards of living. This means analyzing consumer preferences and demand. For example, would consumers drive less and spend more of their income on other goods? If so, would they be nearly as well off? (Consumer preferences and demand are discussed in Chapters 3 and 4.)

To answer these questions, the government must determine how new standards will affect the cost of producing cars. Might automobile producers minimize cost increases by using new lightweight materials? (Production and cost are discussed in Chapters 6 and 7.) Then the government needs to know how changes in production costs will affect the production levels and prices of new automobiles. Are the additional costs absorbed by manufacturers or passed on to consumers in the form of higher prices? (Output determination is discussed in Chapter 8 and pricing in Chapters 10 through 13.)

Finally, the government must ask why the problems related to air pollution are not solved by our market-oriented economy. The answer is that much of the cost of air pollution is external to the firm. If firms do not find it in their self-interest to deal adequately with auto emissions, what is the best way to alter their incentives? Should standards be set, or is it more economical to impose air pollution fees? How do we decide what people will pay to clean up the environment when there is no explicit market for clean air? Is the political process likely to solve these problems? The ultimate question is whether the auto emissions control program makes sense on a cost-benefit basis. Are the aesthetic, health, and other benefits of clean air worth the higher cost of automobiles? (These problems are discussed in Chapter 18.)

These are just two examples of how microeconomics can be applied in the arenas of private and public-policy decision making. You will discover many more applications as you read this book.

# SUMMARY

1. Microeconomics is concerned with the decisions made by individual economic units—consumers, workers, investors, owners of resources, and business firms. It is also concerned with the interaction of consumers and firms to form markets and industries.

2. Microeconomics relies heavily on the use of theory, which can (by simplification) help to explain how economic units behave and to predict what behavior will occur in the future. Models are mathematical representations of theories that can help in this explanation and prediction process.

3. Microeconomics is concerned with positive questions that have to do with the explanation and prediction of phenomena. But microeconomics is also important for normative analysis, in which we ask what choices are best—for a firm or for society as a whole. Normative analyses must often be combined with individual value judgments because issues of equity and fairness as well as of economic efficiency may be involved.

4. A *market* refers to a collection of buyers and sellers who interact, and to the possibility for sales and purchases that result from that interaction. Microeconomics involves the study of both perfectly competitive markets, in which no single buyer or seller has an impact on price, and noncompetitive markets, in which individual entities can affect price.

5. The market price is established by the interaction of buyers and sellers. In a perfectly competitive market, a single price will usually prevail. In markets that are not perfectly competitive, different sellers might charge different prices. In this case, the market price refers to the average prevailing price.

6. When discussing a market, we must be clear about its extent in terms of both its geographic boundaries and the range of products to be included in it. Some markets (e.g., housing) are highly localized, whereas others (e.g., gold) are global in nature.

7. To account for the effects of inflation, we measure real (or constant-dollar) prices, rather than nominal (or current-dollar) prices. Real prices use an aggregate price index, such as the CPI, to correct for inflation.

# QUESTIONS FOR REVIEW

1. It is often said that a good theory is one that can be refuted by an empirical, data-oriented study. Explain why a theory that cannot be evaluated empirically is not a good theory.

2. Which of the following two statements involves positive economic analysis and which normative? How do the two kinds of analysis differ?
   a. Gasoline rationing (allocating to each individual a maximum amount of gasoline that can be purchased each year) is poor social policy because it interferes with the workings of the competitive market system.
   b. Gasoline rationing is a policy under which more people are made worse off than are made better off.

3. Suppose the price of regular-octane gasoline were 20 cents per gallon higher in New Jersey than in Oklahoma. Do you think there would be an opportunity for arbitrage (i.e., that firms could buy gas in Oklahoma and then sell it at a profit in New Jersey)? Why or why not?

4. In Example 1.3, what economic forces explain why the real price of eggs has fallen while the real price of a college education has increased? How have these changes affected consumer choices?

5. Suppose that the Japanese yen rises against the U.S. dollar—that is, it will take more dollars to buy a given amount of Japanese yen. Explain why this increase simultaneously increases the real price of Japanese cars for U.S. consumers and lowers the real price of U.S. automobiles for Japanese consumers.

6. The price of long-distance telephone service fell from 40 cents per minute in 1996 to 22 cents per minute in 1999, a 45-percent (18 cents/40 cents) decrease. The Consumer Price Index increased by 10 percent over this period. What happened to the real price of telephone service?

# EXERCISES

1. Decide whether each of the following statements is true or false and explain why:
   a. Fast-food chains like McDonald's, Burger King, and Wendy's operate all over the United States. Therefore, the market for fast food is a national market.
   b. People generally buy clothing in the city in which they live. Therefore, there is a clothing market in, say, Atlanta that is distinct from the clothing market in Los Angeles.
   c. Some consumers strongly prefer Pepsi and some strongly prefer Coke. Therefore, there is no single market for colas.

2. The following table shows the average retail price of butter and the Consumer Price Index from 1980 to 2000, scaled so that the CPI = 100 in 1980.

| | 1980 | 1985 | 1990 | 1995 | 2000 |
|---|---|---|---|---|---|
| CPI | 100 | 130.58 | 158.56 | 184.95 | 208.98 |
| Retail price of butter (salted, grade AA, per lb.) | $1.88 | $2.12 | $1.99 | $1.61 | $2.52 |

a. Calculate the real price of butter in 1980 dollars. Has the real price increased/decreased/stayed the same from 1980 to 2000?

b. What is the percentage change in the real price (1980 dollars) from 1980 to 2000?

c. Convert the CPI into 1990 = 100 and determine the real price of butter in 1990 dollars.

d. What is the percentage change in real price (1990 dollars) from 1980 to 2000? Compare this with your answer in (b). What do you notice? Explain.

3. At the time this book went to print, the minimum wage was $5.85. To find the current value of the CPI, go to **http://www.bls.gov/cpi/home.htm**. Click on Consumer Price Index-All Urban Consumers (Current Series) and select U.S. All items. This will give you the CPI from 1913 to the present.

a. With these values, calculate the current real minimum wage in 1990 dollars.

b. Stated in real 1990 dollars, what is the percentage change in the real minimum wage from 1985 to the present?

# The Basics of Supply and Demand

2

One of the best ways to appreciate the relevance of economics is to begin with the basics of supply and demand. Supply-demand analysis is a fundamental and powerful tool that can be applied to a wide variety of interesting and important problems. To name a few:

- Understanding and predicting how changing world economic conditions affect market price and production
- Evaluating the impact of government price controls, minimum wages, price supports, and production incentives
- Determining how taxes, subsidies, tariffs, and import quotas affect consumers and producers

We begin with a review of how supply and demand curves are used to describe the *market mechanism*. Without government intervention (e.g., through the imposition of price controls or some other regulatory policy), supply and demand will come into equilibrium to determine both the market price of a good and the total quantity produced. What that price and quantity will be depends on the particular characteristics of supply and demand. Variations of price and quantity over time depend on the ways in which supply and demand respond to other economic variables, such as aggregate economic activity and labor costs, which are themselves changing.

We will, therefore, discuss the characteristics of supply and demand and show how those characteristics may differ from one market to another. Then we can begin to use supply and demand curves to understand a variety of phenomena—for example, why the prices of some basic commodities have fallen steadily over a long period while the prices of others have experienced sharp fluctuations; why shortages occur in certain markets; and why announcements about plans for future government policies or predictions about future economic conditions can affect markets well before those policies or conditions become reality.

Besides understanding *qualitatively* how market price and quantity are determined and how they can vary over time, it is also important to learn how they can be analyzed *quantitatively*. We will see how simple "back of the envelope" calculations can be used to analyze and predict evolving market conditions. We will also show how markets respond both to domestic and international macroeconomic fluctuations and to the effects of government interventions. We will try to convey this understanding through simple examples and by urging you to work through some exercises at the end of the chapter.

21

## 2.1 SUPPLY AND DEMAND

The basic model of supply and demand is the workhorse of microeconomics. It helps us understand why and how prices change, and what happens when the government intervenes in a market. The supply-demand model combines two important concepts: a *supply curve* and a *demand curve*. It is important to understand precisely what these curves represent.

### The Supply Curve

• **supply curve** Relationship between the quantity of a good that producers are willing to sell and the price of the good.

The **supply curve** shows the quantity of a good that producers are willing to sell at a given price, holding constant any other factors that might affect the quantity supplied. The curve labeled $S$ in Figure 2.1 illustrates this. The vertical axis of the graph shows the price of a good, $P$, measured in dollars per unit. This is the price that sellers receive for a given quantity supplied. The horizontal axis shows the total quantity supplied, $Q$, measured in the number of units per period.

The supply curve is thus a relationship between the quantity supplied and the price. We can write this relationship as an equation:

$$Q_S = Q_S(P)$$

Or we can draw it graphically, as we have done in Figure 2.1.

Note that the supply curve in Figure 2.1 slopes upward. In other words, the higher the price, *the more that firms are able and willing to produce and sell*. For example, a higher price may enable current firms to expand production by hiring extra workers or by having existing workers work overtime (at greater cost to the firm). Likewise, they may expand production over a longer period of time by increasing

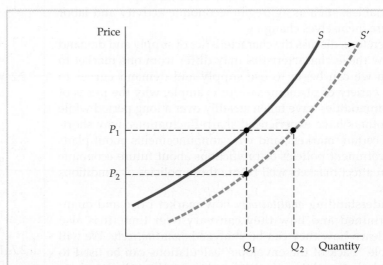

**FIGURE 2.1 The Supply Curve**

The supply curve, labeled $S$ in the figure, shows how the quantity of a good offered for sale changes as the price of the good changes. The supply curve is upward sloping: The higher the price, the more firms are able and willing to produce and sell. If production costs fall, firms can produce the same quantity at a lower price or a larger quantity at the same price. The supply curve then shifts to the right (from $S$ to $S'$).

the size of their plants. A higher price may also attract new firms to the market. These newcomers face higher costs because of their inexperience in the market and would therefore have found entry uneconomical at a lower price.

**Other Variables That Affect Supply** The quantity supplied can depend on other variables besides price. For example, the quantity that producers are willing to sell depends not only on the price they receive but also on their production costs, including wages, interest charges, and the costs of raw materials. The supply curve labeled $S$ in Figure 2.1 was drawn for particular values of these other variables. A change in the values of one or more of these variables translates into a shift in the supply curve. Let's see how this might happen.

The supply curve $S$ in Figure 2.1 says that at a price $P_1$, the quantity produced and sold would be $Q_1$. Now suppose that the cost of raw materials *falls*. How does this affect the supply curve?

Lower raw material costs—indeed, lower costs of any kind—make production more profitable, encouraging existing firms to expand production and enabling new firms to enter the market. If at the same time the market price stayed constant at $P_1$, we would expect to observe a greater quantity supplied. Figure 2.1 shows this as an increase from $Q_1$ to $Q_2$. When production costs *decrease*, output *increases* no matter what the market price happens to be. *The entire supply curve thus shifts to the right*, which is shown in the figure as a shift from $S$ to $S'$.

Another way of looking at the effect of lower raw material costs is to imagine that the quantity produced stays fixed at $Q_1$ and then ask what price firms would require to produce this quantity. Because their costs are lower, they would accept a lower price—$P_2$. This would be the case no matter what quantity was produced. Again, we see in Figure 2.1 that the supply curve must shift to the right.

We have seen that the response of quantity supplied to changes in price can be represented by movements *along the supply curve*. However, the response of supply to changes in other supply-determining variables is shown graphically as a *shift of the supply curve itself*. To distinguish between these two graphical depictions of supply changes, economists often use the phrase *change in supply* to refer to shifts in the supply curve, while reserving the phrase *change in the quantity supplied* to apply to movements along the supply curve.

## The Demand Curve

The **demand curve** shows how much of a good consumers are willing to buy as the price per unit changes. We can write this relationship between quantity demanded and price as an equation:

$$Q_D = Q_D(P)$$

• **demand curve** Relationship between the quantity of a good that consumers are willing to buy and the price of the good.

or we can draw it graphically, as in Figure 2.2. Note that the demand curve in that figure, labeled $D$, slopes *downward*: Consumers are usually ready to buy more if the price is lower. For example, a lower price may encourage consumers who have already been buying the good to consume larger quantities. Likewise, it may allow other consumers who were previously unable to afford the good to begin buying it.

Of course the quantity of a good that consumers are willing to buy can depend on other things besides its price. *Income* is especially important. With greater incomes, consumers can spend more money on any good, and some consumers will do so for most goods.

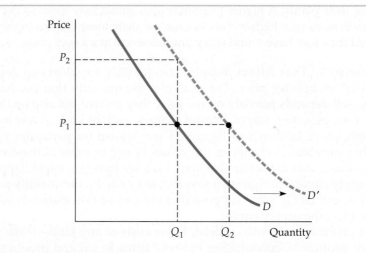

**FIGURE 2.2 The Demand Curve**

The demand curve, labeled $D$, shows how the quantity of a good demanded by consumers depends on its price. The demand curve is downward sloping; holding other things equal, consumers will want to purchase more of a good as its price goes down. The quantity demanded may also depend on other variables, such as income, the weather, and the prices of other goods. For most products, the quantity demanded increases when income rises. A higher income level shifts the demand curve to the right (from $D$ to $D'$).

**Shifting the Demand Curve** Let's see what happens to the demand curve if income levels increase. As you can see in Figure 2.2, if the market price were held constant at $P_1$, we would expect to see an increase in the quantity demanded—say, from $Q_1$ to $Q_2$, as a result of consumers' higher incomes. Because this increase would occur no matter what the market price, the result would be a *shift to the right of the entire demand curve*. In the figure, this is shown as a shift from $D$ to $D'$. Alternatively, we can ask what price consumers would pay to purchase a given quantity $Q_1$. With greater income, they should be willing to pay a higher price—say, $P_2$ instead of $P_1$ in Figure 2.2. Again, *the demand curve will shift to the right*. As we did with supply, we will use the phrase *change in demand* to refer to shifts in the demand curve, and reserve the phrase *change in the quantity demanded* to apply to movements along the demand curve.[1]

**Substitute and Complementary Goods** Changes in the prices of related goods also affect demand. Goods are **substitutes** when an increase in the price of one leads to an increase in the quantity demanded of the other. For example, copper and aluminum are substitute goods. Because one can often be substituted for the other in industrial use, *the quantity of copper demanded will increase if the price of aluminum increases*. Likewise, beef and chicken are substitute goods because most consumers are willing to shift their purchases from one to the other when prices change.

Goods are **complements** when an increase in the price of one leads to a decrease in the quantity demanded of the other. For example, automobiles and

• **substitutes** Two goods for which an increase in the price of one leads to an increase in the quantity demanded of the other.

• **complements** Two goods for which an increase in the price of one leads to a decrease in the quantity demanded of the other.

---

[1]Mathematically, we can write the demand curve as

$$Q_D = D(P, I)$$

where $I$ is disposable income. When we draw a demand curve, we are keeping $I$ fixed.

gasoline are complementary goods. Because they tend to be used together, a decrease in the price of gasoline increases the quantity demanded for automobiles. Likewise, computers and computer software are complementary goods. The price of computers has dropped dramatically over the past decade, fueling an increase not only in purchases of computers, but also purchases of software packages.

We attributed the shift to the right of the demand curve in Figure 2.2 to an increase in income. However, this shift could also have resulted from either an increase in the price of a substitute good or a decrease in the price of a complementary good. Or it might have resulted from a change in some other variable, such as the weather. For example, demand curves for skis and snowboards will shift to the right when there are heavy snowfalls.

## 2.2 THE MARKET MECHANISM

The next step is to put the supply curve and the demand curve together. We have done this in Figure 2.3. The vertical axis shows the price of a good, $P$, again measured in dollars per unit. This is now the price that sellers receive for a given quantity supplied, and the price that buyers will pay for a given quantity demanded. The horizontal axis shows the total quantity demanded and supplied, $Q$, measured in number of units per period.

**Equilibrium** The two curves intersect at the **equilibrium**, or **market-clearing, price** and quantity. At this price ($P_0$ in Figure 2.3), the quantity supplied and the quantity demanded are just equal (to $Q_0$). The **market mechanism** is the tendency in a free market for the price to change until the market *clears*—i.e., until the quantity supplied and the quantity demanded are equal. At this point, because there is neither excess demand nor excess supply, there is no pressure for the price to change further. Supply and demand might not always be in equilibrium, and

• **equilibrium** (or **market-clearing) price** Price that equates the quantity supplied to the quantity demanded.

• **market mechanism** Tendency in a free market for price to change until the market clears.

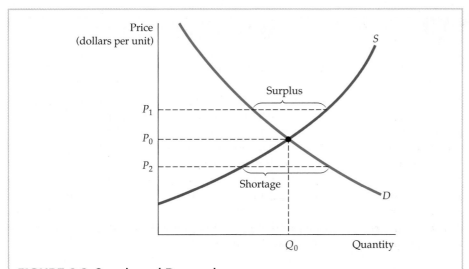

**FIGURE 2.3 Supply and Demand**

The market clears at price $P_0$ and quantity $Q_0$. At the higher price $P_1$, a surplus develops, so price falls. At the lower price $P_2$, there is a shortage, so price is bid up.

some markets might not clear quickly when conditions change suddenly. The *tendency*, however, is for markets to clear.

To understand why markets tend to clear, suppose the price were initially above the market-clearing level—say, $P_1$ in Figure 2.3. Producers will try to produce and sell more than consumers are willing to buy. A **surplus**—a situation in which the quantity supplied exceeds the quantity demanded—will result. To sell this surplus—or at least to prevent it from growing—producers would begin to lower prices. Eventually, as price fell, quantity demanded would increase, and quantity supplied would decrease until the equilibrium price $P_0$ was reached.

> • **surplus** Situation in which the quantity supplied exceeds the quantity demanded.

The opposite would happen if the price were initially below $P_0$—say, at $P_2$. A **shortage**—a situation in which the quantity demanded exceeds the quantity supplied—would develop, and consumers would be unable to purchase all they would like. This would put upward pressure on price as consumers tried to outbid one another for existing supplies and producers reacted by increasing price and expanding output. Again, the price would eventually reach $P_0$.

> • **shortage** Situation in which the quantity demanded exceeds the quantity supplied.

**When Can We Use the Supply-Demand Model?** When we draw and use supply and demand curves, we are assuming that at any given price, a given quantity will be produced and sold. This assumption makes sense only if a market is at least roughly *competitive*. By this we mean that both sellers and buyers should have little *market power*—i.e., little ability *individually* to affect the market price.

Suppose instead that supply were controlled by a single producer—a monopolist. In this case, there will no longer be a simple one-to-one relationship between price and the quantity supplied. Why? Because a monopolist's behavior depends on the shape and position of the demand curve. If the demand curve shifts in a particular way, it may be in the monopolist's interest to keep the quantity fixed but change the price, or to keep the price fixed and change the quantity. (How this could occur is explained in Chapter 10.) Thus when we work with supply and demand curves, we implicitly assume that we are referring to a competitive market.

## 2.3 CHANGES IN MARKET EQUILIBRIUM

We have seen how supply and demand curves shift in response to changes in such variables as wage rates, capital costs, and income. We have also seen how the market mechanism results in an equilibrium in which the quantity supplied equals the quantity demanded. Now we will see how that equilibrium changes in response to shifts in the supply and demand curves.

Let's begin with a shift in the supply curve. In Figure 2.4, the supply curve has shifted from $S$ to $S'$ (as it did in Figure 2.1), perhaps as a result of a decrease in the price of raw materials. As a result, the market price drops (from $P_1$ to $P_3$), and the total quantity produced increases (from $Q_1$ to $Q_3$). This is what we would expect: Lower costs result in lower prices and increased sales. (Indeed, gradual decreases in costs resulting from technological progress and better management are an important driving force behind economic growth.)

Figure 2.5 shows what happens following a rightward shift in the demand curve resulting from, say, an increase in income. A new price and quantity result after demand comes into equilibrium with supply. As shown in Figure 2.5, we would expect to see consumers pay a higher price, $P_3$, and firms produce a greater quantity, $Q_3$, as a result of an increase in income.

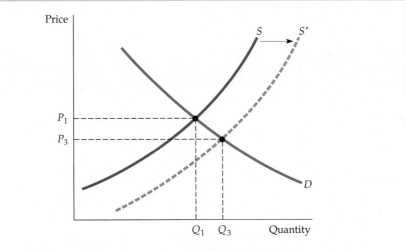

**FIGURE 2.4 New Equilibrium Following Shift in Supply**

When the supply curve shifts to the right, the market clears at a lower price $P_3$ and a larger quantity $Q_3$.

In most markets, both the demand and supply curves shift from time to time. Consumers' disposable incomes change as the economy grows (or contracts, during economic recessions). The demands for some goods shift with the seasons (e.g., fuels, bathing suits, umbrellas), with changes in the prices of related goods (an increase in oil prices increases the demand for natural gas), or simply with changing tastes. Similarly, wage rates, capital costs, and the prices of raw materials also change from time to time, and these changes shift the supply curve.

Supply and demand curves can be used to trace the effects of these changes. In Figure 2.6, for example, shifts to the right of both supply and demand result in a

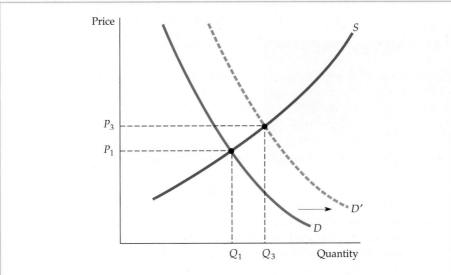

**FIGURE 2.5 New Equilibrium Following Shift in Demand**

When the demand curve shifts to the right, the market clears at a higher price $P_3$ and a larger quantity $Q_3$.

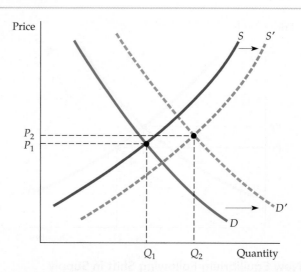

**FIGURE 2.6 New Equilibrium Following Shifts in Supply and Demand**

Supply and demand curves shift over time as market conditions change. In this example, rightward shifts of the supply and demand curves lead to a slightly higher price and a much larger quantity. In general, changes in price and quantity depend on the amount by which each curve shifts and the shape of each curve.

slightly higher price (from $P_1$ to $P_2$) and a much larger quantity (from $Q_1$ to $Q_2$). In general, price and quantity will change depending both on how much the supply and demand curves shift and on the shapes of those curves. To predict the sizes and directions of such changes, we must be able to characterize quantitatively the dependence of supply and demand on price and other variables. We will turn to this task in the next section.

**EXAMPLE 2.1** The Price of Eggs and the Price of a College Education Revisited

In Example 1.3 (page 13), we saw that from 1970 to 2007, the real (constant-dollar) price of eggs fell by 49 percent, while the real price of a college education rose by 105 percent. What caused this large decline in egg prices and large increase in the price of college?

We can understand these price changes by examining the behavior of supply and demand for each good, as shown in Figure 2.7. For eggs, the mechanization of poultry farms sharply reduced the cost of producing eggs, shifting the supply curve downward. At the same time, the demand curve for eggs shifted to the left as a more health-conscious population changed its eating habits and tended to avoid eggs. As a result, the real price of eggs declined sharply while total annual consumption increased (from 5300 million dozen to 7400 million dozen).

As for college, supply and demand shifted in the opposite directions. Increases in the costs of equipping and maintaining modern classrooms, laboratories, and libraries, along with increases in faculty salaries, pushed the supply curve up. At the

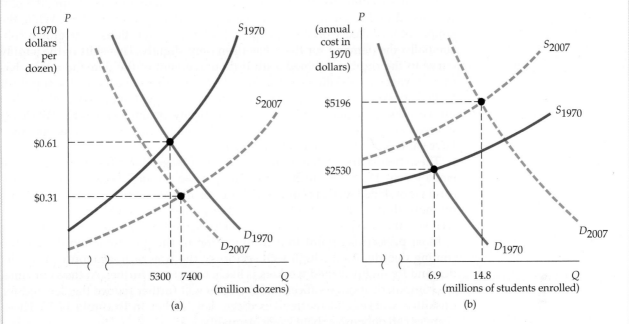

**FIGURE 2.7 (a) Market for Eggs (b) Market for College Education**

**(a)** The supply curve for eggs shifted downward as production costs fell; the demand curve shifted to the left as consumer preferences changed. As a result, the real price of eggs fell sharply and egg consumption rose. **(b)** The supply curve for a college education shifted up as the costs of equipment, maintenance, and staffing rose. The demand curve shifted to the right as a growing number of high school graduates desired a college education. As a result, both price and enrollments rose sharply.

same time, the demand curve shifted to the right as a larger percentage of a growing number of high school graduates decided that a college education was essential. Thus, despite the increase in price, 2007 found nearly 15 million students enrolled in undergraduate college degree programs, compared with 6.9 million in 1970.

**EXAMPLE 2.2**      **Wage Inequality in the United States**

Although the U.S. economy has grown vigorously over the past two decades, the gains from this growth have not been shared equally by all. The wages of skilled high-income workers have grown substantially, while the wages of unskilled low-income workers have, in real terms, actually fallen slightly. Overall, there has been growing inequality in the distribution of earnings, a phenomenon which began around 1980 and has accelerated in recent years. For example, from 1978 to 2005, people in the top 20 percent of the income distribution experienced an increase in their average real (inflation-adjusted) pretax household income of 50 percent, while those in the bottom 20 percent saw their average real pretax income increase by only 6 percent.[2]

---

[2]In *after-tax* terms, the growth of inequality has been even greater; the average real after-tax income of the bottom 20 percent of the distribution *fell* over this period. For historical data on income inequality in the United States, see the Historical Income Inequality Tables at the U.S. Census Bureau Web site: **http://www.census.gov/**.

Why has income distribution become so much more unequal during the past two decades? The answer is in the supply and demand for workers. While the supply of unskilled workers—people with limited educations—has grown substantially, the demand for them has risen only slightly. This shift of the supply curve to the right, combined with little movement of the demand curve, has caused wages of unskilled workers to fall. On the other hand, while the supply of skilled workers—e.g., engineers, scientists, managers, and economists—has grown slowly, the demand has risen dramatically, pushing wages up. (We leave it to you as an exercise to draw supply and demand curves and show how they have shifted, as was done in Example 2.1.)

These trends are evident in the behavior of wages for different categories of employment. From 1980 to 2007, for example, the real (inflation-adjusted) weekly earnings of skilled workers (such as finance, insurance, and real estate workers) rose by more than 35 percent. Over the same period, the weekly real incomes of relatively unskilled workers (such as retail trade workers) rose by only 10 percent.[3]

Most projections point to a continuation of this phenomenon during the coming decade. As the high-tech sectors of the American economy grow, the demand for highly skilled workers is likely to increase further. At the same time, the computerization of offices and factories will further reduce the demand for unskilled workers. (This trend is discussed further in Example 14.7.) These changes can only exacerbate wage inequality.

| EXAMPLE 2.3 | The Long-Run Behavior of Natural Resource Prices |
| --- | --- |

Many people are concerned about the earth's natural resources. At issue is whether our energy and mineral resources are likely to be depleted in the near future, leading to sharp price increases that could bring an end to economic growth. An analysis of supply and demand can give us some perspective.

The earth does indeed have only a finite amount of mineral resources, such as copper, iron, coal, and oil. During the past century, however, the prices of these and most other natural resources have declined or remained roughly constant relative to overall prices. Figure 2.8, for example, shows the price of copper in real terms (adjusted for inflation), together with the quantity consumed from 1880 to 2007. (Both are shown as an index, with 1880 = 1.) Despite short-term variations in price, no significant long-term increase has occurred, even though annual consumption is now about 100 times greater than in 1880. Similar patterns hold for other mineral resources, such as iron, oil, and coal.[4]

---

[3]For detailed earnings data, visit the Detailed Statistics section of the web site of the Bureau of Labor Statistics (BLS): **http://www.bls.gov/**. Select Employment, Hours, and Earnings from the Current Employment Statistics survey (National).

[4]The index of U.S. copper consumption was around 102 in 1999 and 2000 but then dropped off significantly due to falling demand from 2001 to 2006. Consumption data (1880–1899) and price data (1880–1969) in Figure 2.8 are from Robert S. Manthy, *Natural Resource Commodities—A Century of Statistics* (Baltimore: Johns Hopkins University Press, 1978). More recent price (1970–2007) and consumption data (1970–2007) are from the U.S. Geological Survey—Minerals Information, Copper Statistics and Information (**http://minerals.usgs.gov/**).

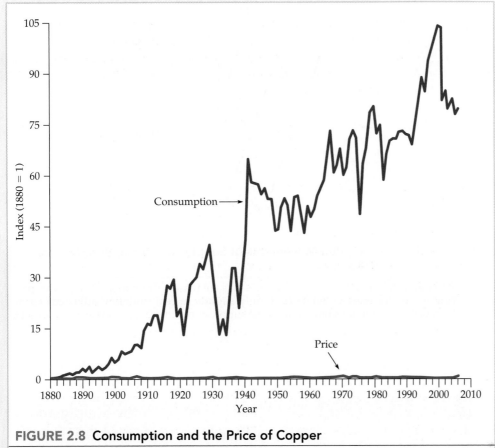

**FIGURE 2.8 Consumption and the Price of Copper**

Although annual consumption of copper has increased about a hundredfold, the real (inflation-adjusted) price has not changed much.

As you can see from Figure 2.9, the demands for these resources grew along with the world economy. But as demand grew, production costs fell. The decline in costs was due, first, to the discovery of new and bigger deposits that were cheaper to mine, and then to technical progress and the economic advantage of mining and refining on a large scale. As a result, the supply curve shifted over time to the right. Over the long term, because increases in supply were greater than increases in demand, price often fell, as shown in Figure 2.9.

This is not to say that the prices of copper, iron, and coal will decline or remain constant forever. After all, these resources are *finite*. But as prices begin to rise, consumption will likely shift, at least in part, to substitute materials. Copper, for example, has already been replaced in many applications by aluminum and, more recently, in electronic applications by fiber optics. (See Example 2.8 for a more detailed discussion of copper prices.)

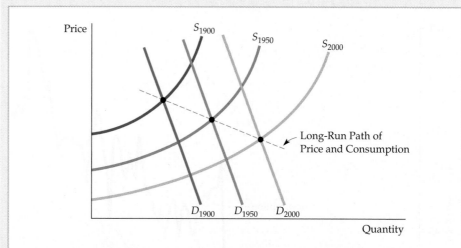

**FIGURE 2.9 Long-Run Movements of Supply and Demand for Mineral Resources**

Although demand for most resources has increased dramatically over the past century, prices have fallen or risen only slightly in real (inflation-adjusted) terms because cost reductions have shifted the supply curve to the right just as dramatically.

---

**EXAMPLE 2.4** The Effects of 9/11 on the Supply and Demand for New York City Office Space

The September 11, 2001, terrorist attack on the World Trade Center (WTC) complex damaged or destroyed 21 buildings, accounting for 31.2 million square feet (msf) of Manhattan office space—nearly 10 percent of the city's entire inventory. Just prior to the attack, the Manhattan office vacancy rate was 8.0 percent, and the average asking rent was $52.50 per square foot (psf). Given the huge unexpected reduction in the quantity of office space supplied, we might expect the equilibrium rental price of office space to increase and, as a result, the equilibrium quantity of rented office space to decrease. And because it takes time to construct new office buildings and restore damaged ones, we might also expect the vacancy rate to decline sharply.

Surprisingly, however, the vacancy rate in Manhattan *increased* from 8.0 percent in August 2001 to 9.3 percent in November 2001. Moreover, the average rental price *fell* from $52.50 to $50.75 per square foot. In downtown Manhattan, the location of the Trade Center, the changes were even more dramatic: The vacancy rate rose from 7.5 percent to 10.6 percent, and the average rental price fell nearly 8 percent, to $41.81. What happened? Rental prices fell because the demand for office space fell.

Figure 2.10 describes the market for office space in downtown Manhattan. The supply and demand curves before 9/11 appear as $S_{Aug}$ and $D_{Aug}$. The equilibrium price and quantity of downtown Manhattan office space were $45.34 psf and 76.4 msf, respectively. The reduction in supply from August until November is indicated by a leftward shift in the supply curve (from $S_{Aug}$ to $S'_{Nov}$); the result is a higher equilibrium price $P'$ and a lower equilibrium quantity, $Q'$. This is the outcome that most forecasters predicted for the months following September 11.

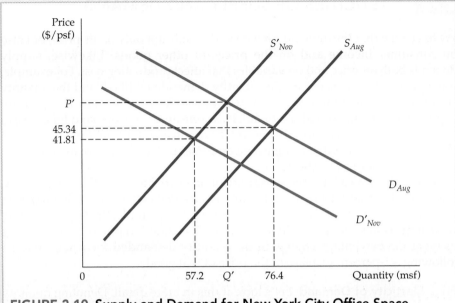

**FIGURE 2.10 Supply and Demand for New York City Office Space**

Following 9/11 the supply curve shifted to the left, but the demand curve also shifted to the left, so that the average rental price fell.

Many forecasters, however, failed to predict the significant *decrease* in demand for office space complementing the loss in supply. First, many firms, both displaced and non-displaced, chose not to relocate downtown because of quality-of-life concerns (i.e., the WTC ruins, pollution, disabled transportation, and aging inventory). Firms displaced by the attack were also forced to reevaluate their office-space needs, and they ultimately repurchased a little more than 50 percent of their original office space in Manhattan. Others left Manhattan but stayed in New York City; still others moved to New Jersey.[5] Furthermore, in late 2001, the U.S. economy was experiencing an economic slowdown (exacerbated by the events of September 11) that further reduced the demand for office space. Therefore, the cumulative decrease in demand (a shift from $D_{Aug}$ to $D'_{Nov}$) actually caused the average rental price of downtown Manhattan office space to decrease rather than increase in the months following September 11. By November, even though the price had fallen to $41.81, there were 57.2 msf on the market.

There is evidence that office real estate markets in other major U.S. cities experienced similar surges in vacancy rates following 9/11. For instance, in Chicago, not only did vacancy rates increase in downtown office buildings, this increase was significantly more pronounced in properties in or near landmark buildings that are considered preferred targets for terrorist attacks.[6]

The Manhattan commercial real estate market bounced back strongly after 2001. In 2007, the office vacancy rate in Manhattan was 5.8 percent, its lowest figure since 9/11 and the average asking rent was over $74 psf.

---

[5]See Jason Bram, James Orr, and Carol Rapaport, "Measuring the Effects of the September 11 Attack on New York City," Federal Reserve Bank of New York, *Economic Policy Review*, November, 2002.

[6]See Alberto Abadie and Sofia Dermisi, "Is Terrorism Eroding Agglomeration Economies in Central Business Districts? Lessons from the Office Real Estate Market in Downtown Chicago," National Bureau of Economic Research, Working Paper 12678, November, 2006.

## 2.4 ELASTICITIES OF SUPPLY AND DEMAND

We have seen that the demand for a good depends not only on its price, but also on consumer income and on the prices of other goods. Likewise, supply depends both on price and on variables that affect production cost. For example, if the price of coffee increases, the quantity demanded will fall and the quantity supplied will rise. Often, however, we want to know *how much* the quantity supplied or demanded will rise or fall. How sensitive is the demand for coffee to its price? If price increases by 10 percent, how much will the quantity demanded change? How much will it change if income rises by 5 percent? We use *elasticities* to answer questions like these.

• **elasticity** Percentage change in one variable resulting from a 1-percent increase in another.

An **elasticity** measures the sensitivity of one variable to another. Specifically, it is a number that tells us *the percentage change that will occur in one variable in response to a 1-percent increase in another variable*. For example, the *price elasticity of demand* measures the sensitivity of quantity demanded to price changes. It tells us what the percentage change in the quantity demanded for a good will be following a 1-percent increase in the price of that good.

**Price Elasticity of Demand**  Let's look at this in more detail. Denoting quantity and price by $Q$ and $P$, we write the **price elasticity of demand**, $E_p$, as

• **price elasticity of demand** Percentage change in quantity demanded of a good resulting from a 1-percent increase in its price.

$$E_p = (\%\Delta Q)/(\%\Delta P)$$

where $\%\Delta Q$ simply means "percentage change in $Q$" and $\%\Delta P$ means "percentage change in $P$." (The symbol $\Delta$ is the Greek capital letter *delta*; it means "the change in." So $\Delta X$ means "the change in the variable $X$," say, from one year to the next.) The percentage change in a variable is just *the absolute change in the variable divided by the original level of the variable*. (If the Consumer Price Index were 200 at the beginning of the year and increased to 204 by the end of the year, the percentage change—or annual rate of inflation—would be $4/200 = .02$, or 2 percent.) Thus we can also write the price elasticity of demand as follows:[7]

$$E_P = \frac{\Delta Q/Q}{\Delta P/P} = \frac{P}{Q}\frac{\Delta Q}{\Delta P} \tag{2.1}$$

The price elasticity of demand is usually a negative number. When the price of a good increases, the quantity demanded usually falls. Thus $\Delta Q/\Delta P$ (the change in quantity for a change in price) is negative, as is $E_p$. Sometimes we refer to the *magnitude* of the price elasticity—i.e., its absolute size. For example, if $E_p = -2$, we say that the elasticity is 2 in magnitude.

When the price elasticity is greater than 1 in magnitude, we say that demand is *price elastic* because the percentage decline in quantity demanded is greater than the percentage increase in price. If the price elasticity is less than 1 in magnitude, demand is said to be *price inelastic*. In general, the price elasticity of demand for a good depends on the availability of other goods that can be substituted for it. When there are close substitutes, a price increase will cause the consumer to buy less of the good and more of the substitute. Demand will then be highly price elastic. When there are no close substitutes, demand will tend to be price inelastic.

---

[7]In terms of infinitesimal changes (letting the $\Delta P$ become very small), $E_p = (P/Q)(dQ/dP)$.

**Linear Demand Curve** Equation (2.1) says that the price elasticity of demand is the change in quantity associated with a change in price ($\Delta Q/\Delta P$) times the ratio of price to quantity ($P/Q$). But as we move down the demand curve, $\Delta Q/\Delta P$ may change, and the price and quantity will always change. Therefore, the price elasticity of demand must be measured *at a particular point on the demand curve* and will generally change as we move along the curve.

This principle is easiest to see for a **linear demand curve**—that is, a demand curve of the form

$$Q = a - bP$$

As an example, consider the demand curve

$$Q = 8 - 2P$$

For this curve, $\Delta Q/\Delta P$ is constant and equal to –2 (a $\Delta P$ of 1 results in a $\Delta Q$ of –2). However, the curve does *not* have a constant elasticity. Observe from Figure 2.11 that as we move down the curve, the ratio $P/Q$ falls; the elasticity therefore decreases in magnitude. Near the intersection of the curve with the price axis, $Q$ is very small, so $E_p = -2(P/Q)$ is large in magnitude. When $P = 2$ and $Q = 4$, $E_p = -1$. At the intersection with the quantity axis, $P = 0$ so $E_p = 0$.

Because we draw demand (and supply) curves with price on the vertical axis and quantity on the horizontal axis, $\Delta Q/\Delta P = (1/\text{slope of curve})$. As a result, for any price and quantity combination, the steeper the slope of the curve, the less elastic is demand. Figure 2.12 shows two special cases. Figure 2.12(a) shows a demand curve reflecting **infinitely elastic demand**: Consumers will buy as much as they can at a single price $P^*$. For even the smallest increase in price above this level, quantity demanded drops to zero, and for any decrease in price, quantity demanded increases without limit. The demand curve in Figure 2.12(b), on the other hand, reflects **completely inelastic demand**: Consumers will buy a fixed quantity $Q^*$, no matter what the price.

* **linear demand curve** Demand curve that is a straight line.

* **infinitely elastic demand** Principle that consumers will buy as much of a good as they can get at a single price, but for any higher price the quantity demanded drops to zero, while for any lower price the quantity demanded increases without limit.

* **completely inelastic demand** Principle that consumers will buy a fixed quantity of a good regardless of its price.

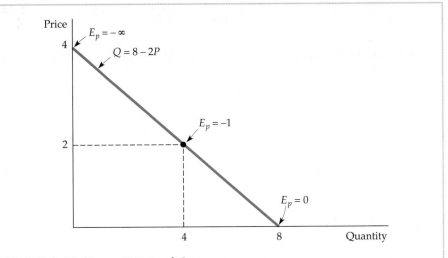

**FIGURE 2.11 Linear Demand Curve**

The price elasticity of demand depends not only on the slope of the demand curve but also on the price and quantity. The elasticity, therefore, varies along the curve as price and quantity change. Slope is constant for this linear demand curve. Near the top, because price is high and quantity is small, the elasticity is large in magnitude. The elasticity becomes smaller as we move down the curve.

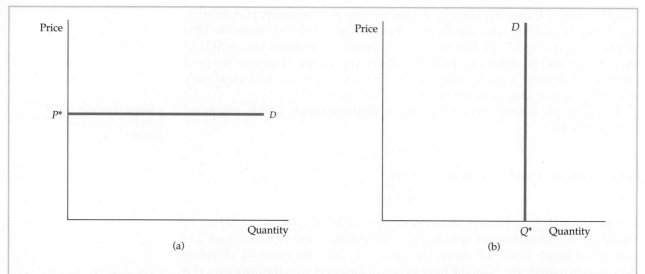

**FIGURE 2.12** (a) Infinitely Elastic Demand    (b) Completely Inelastic Demand

**(a)** For a horizontal demand curve, $\Delta Q/\Delta P$ is infinite. Because a tiny change in price leads to an enormous change in demand, the elasticity of demand is infinite. **(b)** For a vertical demand curve, $\Delta Q/\Delta P$ is zero. Because the quantity demanded is the same no matter what the price, the 3elasticity of demand is zero.

**Other Demand Elasticities** We will also be interested in elasticities of demand with respect to other variables besides price. For example, demand for most goods usually rises when aggregate income rises. The **income elasticity of demand** is the percentage change in the quantity demanded, $Q$, resulting from a 1-percent increase in income $I$:

• **income elasticity of demand** Percentage change in the quantity demanded resulting from a 1-percent increase in income.

$$E_I = \frac{\Delta Q/Q}{\Delta I/I} = \frac{I}{Q}\frac{\Delta Q}{\Delta I} \qquad (2.2)$$

The demand for some goods is also affected by the prices of other goods. For example, because butter and margarine can easily be substituted for each other, the demand for each depends on the price of the other. A **cross-price elasticity of demand** refers to the percentage change in the quantity demanded for a good that results from a 1-percent increase in the price of another good. So the elasticity of demand for butter with respect to the price of margarine would be written as

• **cross-price elasticity of demand** Percentage change in the quantity demanded of one good resulting from a 1-percent increase in the price of another.

$$E_{Q_b P_m} = \frac{\Delta Q_b/Q_b}{\Delta P_m/P_m} = \frac{P_m}{Q_b}\frac{\Delta Q_b}{\Delta P_m} \qquad (2.3)$$

where $Q_b$ is the quantity of butter and $P_m$ is the price of margarine.

In this example, the cross-price elasticities will be positive because the goods are *substitutes*: Because they compete in the market, a rise in the price of margarine, which makes butter cheaper relative to margarine, leads to an increase in the quantity of butter demanded. (Because the demand curve for butter will shift to the right, the price of butter will rise.) But this is not always the case. Some goods are *complements*: Because they tend to be used together, an increase in the price of one tends to push down the consumption of the other. Take gasoline and motor oil. If the price of gasoline goes up, the quantity of gasoline demanded falls—motorists will drive less. And because people are driving less, the demand for motor oil also falls. (The entire demand curve for motor oil shifts to the left.) Thus, the cross-price elasticity of motor oil with respect to gasoline is negative.

**Elasticities of Supply** Elasticities of supply are defined in a similar manner. The **price elasticity of supply** is the percentage change in the quantity supplied resulting from a 1-percent increase in price. This elasticity is usually positive because a higher price gives producers an incentive to increase output.

> • **price elasticity of supply** Percentage change in quantity supplied resulting from a 1-percent increase in price.

We can also refer to elasticities of supply with respect to such variables as interest rates, wage rates, and the prices of raw materials and other intermediate goods used to manufacture the product in question. For example, for most manufactured goods, the elasticities of supply with respect to the prices of raw materials are negative. An increase in the price of a raw material input means higher costs for the firm; other things being equal, therefore, the quantity supplied will fall.

## Point versus Arc Elasticities

So far, we have considered elasticities at a particular point on the demand curve or the supply curve. These are called *point elasticities*. The **point elasticity of demand**, for example, is *the price elasticity of demand at a particular point on the demand curve* and is defined by Equation (2.1). As we demonstrated in Figure 2.11 using a linear demand curve, the point elasticity of demand can vary depending on where it is measured along the demand curve.

> • **point elasticity of demand** Price elasticity at a particular point on the demand curve.

There are times, however, when we want to calculate a price elasticity over some portion of the demand curve (or supply curve) rather than at a single point. Suppose, for example, that we are contemplating an increase in the price of a product from $8.00 to $10.00 and expect the quantity demanded to fall from 6 units to 4. How should we calculate the price elasticity of demand? Is the price increase 25 percent (a $2 increase divided by the original price of $8), or is it 20 percent (a $2 increase divided by the new price of $10)? Is the percentage decrease in quantity demanded 33 1/3 percent (2/6) or 50 percent (2/4)?

There is no correct answer to such questions. We could calculate the price elasticity using the original price and quantity. If so, we would find that $E_p$ = (−33 1/3 percent/25 percent) = −1.33. Or we could use the new price and quantity, in which case we would find that $E_p$ = (−50 percent/20 percent) = −2.5. The difference between these two calculated elasticities is large, and neither seems preferable to the other.

**Arc Elasticity of Demand** We can resolve this problem by using the **arc elasticity of demand**: *the elasticity calculated over a range of prices*. Rather than choose either the initial or the final price, we use an average of the two, $\overline{P}$; for the quantity demanded, we use $\overline{Q}$. Thus the arc elasticity of demand is given by

> • **arc elasticity of demand** Price elasticity calculated over a range of prices.

$$\text{Arc elasticity:} \quad E_p = (\Delta Q/\Delta P)(\overline{P}/\overline{Q}) \qquad \textbf{(2.4)}$$

In our example, the average price is $9 and the average quantity 5 units. Thus the arc elasticity is

$$E_p = (-2/\$2)(\$9/5) = -1.8$$

The arc elasticity will always lie somewhere (but not necessarily halfway) between the point elasticities calculated at the lower and the higher prices.

Although the arc elasticity of demand is sometimes useful, economists generally use the word "elasticity" to refer to a *point* elasticity. Throughout the rest of this book, we will do the same, unless noted otherwise.

**EXAMPLE 2.5** The Market for Wheat

Wheat is an important agricultural commodity, and the wheat market has been studied extensively by agricultural economists. During recent decades, changes in the wheat market had major implications for both American farmers and U.S. agricultural policy. To understand what happened, let's examine the behavior of supply and demand beginning in 1981.

From statistical studies, we know that for 1981 the supply curve for wheat was approximately as follows:[8]

$$Supply: \quad Q_S = 1800 + 240P$$

where price is measured in nominal dollars per bushel and quantities in millions of bushels per year. These studies also indicate that in 1981, the demand curve for wheat was

$$Demand: \quad Q_D = 3550 - 266P$$

By setting the quantity supplied equal to the quantity demanded, we can determine the market-clearing price of wheat for 1981:

$$Q_S = Q_D$$
$$1800 + 240P = 3550 - 266P$$
$$506P = 1750$$
$$P = \$3.46 \text{ per bushel}$$

To find the market-clearing quantity, substitute this price of $3.46 into either the supply curve equation or the demand curve equation. Substituting into the supply curve equation, we get

$$Q = 1800 + (240)(3.46) = 2630 \text{ million bushels}$$

What are the price elasticities of demand and supply at this price and quantity? We use the demand curve to find the price elasticity of demand:

$$E_P^D = \frac{P}{Q}\frac{\Delta Q_D}{\Delta P} = \frac{3.46}{2630}(-266) = -0.35$$

[8]For a survey of statistical studies of the demand and supply of wheat and an analysis of evolving market conditions, see Larry Salathe and Sudchada Langley, "An Empirical Analysis of Alternative Export Subsidy Programs for U.S. Wheat," *Agricultural Economics Research* 38:1 (Winter 1986). The supply and demand curves in this example are based on the studies they surveyed.

Thus demand is inelastic. We can likewise calculate the price elasticity of supply:

$$E_P^S = \frac{P}{Q} \frac{\Delta Q_S}{\Delta P} = \frac{3.46}{2630}(240) = 0.32$$

Because these supply and demand curves are linear, the price elasticities will vary as we move along the curves. For example, suppose that a drought caused the supply curve to shift far enough to the left to push the price up to $4.00 per bushel. In this case, the quantity demanded would fall to 3550 − (266)(4.00) = 2486 million bushels. At this price and quantity, the elasticity of demand would be

$$E_P^D = \frac{4.00}{2486}(-266) = -0.43$$

The wheat market has evolved over the years, in part because of changes in demand. The demand for wheat has two components: domestic (demand by U.S. consumers) and export (demand by foreign consumers). During the 1980s and 1990s, domestic demand for wheat rose only slightly (due to modest increases in population and income). Export demand, however, fell sharply. There were several reasons. First and foremost was the success of the Green Revolution in agriculture: Developing countries like India, which had been large importers of wheat, became increasingly self-sufficient. In addition, European countries adopted protectionist policies that subsidized their own production and imposed tariff barriers against imported wheat.

In 2007, demand and supply were

$$Demand: \quad Q_D = 2900 - 125P$$

$$Supply: \quad Q_S = 1460 + 115P$$

Once again, equating quantity supplied and quantity demanded yields the market-clearing (nominal) price and quantity:

$$1460 + 115P = 2900 - 125P$$
$$P = \$6.00 \text{ per bushel}$$
$$Q = 1460 + (115)(6) = 2150 \text{ million bushels}$$

Thus the price of wheat (in nominal terms) rose considerably since 1981. In fact, nearly all of this increase occurred during 2005 to 2007. (In 2002, for example, the price of wheat was only $2.78 per bushel.) The causes? Dry weather in 2005, even dryer weather in 2006, and heavy rains in 2007 combined with increased export demand. You can check to see that, at the 2007 price and quantity, the price elasticity of demand was −0.35 and the price elasticity of supply 0.32. Given these low elasticities, it is not surprising that the price of wheat rose so sharply.[9]

[9]These are short-run elasticity estimates from Economics Research Service (ERS) of the U.S. Department of Agriculture (USDA). For more information, consult the following publications: William Lin, Paul C. Westcott, Robert Skinner, Scott Sanford, and Daniel G. De La Torre Ugarte, *Supply Response Under the 1996 Farm Act and Implications for the U.S. Field Crops Sector* (Technical Bulletin No. 1888, ERS, USDA, July 2000, **http://www.ers.usda.gov/**); and James Barnes and Dennis Shields, *The Growth in U.S. Wheat Food Demand* (Wheat Situation and Outlook Yearbook, WHS-1998, **http://www.ers.usda.gov/**).

The price of wheat was actually greater than $3.46 in 1981 because the U.S. government bought wheat through its price-support program. In addition, throughout the 1980s and 1990s, farmers received direct subsidies for the wheat they produced. In 1996, Congress passed the Freedom to Farm bill designed to eliminate crop subsidies and acreage limitations for wheat and other agricultural products. Since that time, however, emergency aid to farmers and direct loan payments have effectively maintained the price subsidies originally "phased out" by the 1996 bill. In May 2002, Congress passed another bill subsidizing farmers over the next 10 years, at a projected cost to taxpayers of $190 billion.

We discuss how such agricultural policies work and evaluate the costs and benefits for consumers, farmers, and the federal budget in Chapter 9.

## 2.5 SHORT-RUN VERSUS LONG-RUN ELASTICITIES

When analyzing demand and supply, we must distinguish between the short run and the long run. In other words, if we ask how much demand or supply changes in response to a change in price, we must be clear about *how much time is allowed to pass before we measure the changes in the quantity demanded or supplied.* If we allow only a short time to pass—say, one year or less—then we are dealing with the *short run*. When we refer to the *long run* we mean that enough time is allowed for consumers or producers to *adjust fully* to the price change. In general, short-run demand and supply curves look very different from their long-run counterparts.

### Demand

For many goods, demand is much more price elastic in the long run than in the short run. For one thing, it takes time for people to change their consumption habits. For example, even if the price of coffee rises sharply, the quantity demanded will fall only gradually as consumers begin to drink less. In addition, the demand for a good might be linked to the stock of another good that changes only slowly. For example, the demand for gasoline is much more elastic in the long run than in the short run. A sharply higher price of gasoline reduces the quantity demanded in the short run by causing motorists to drive less, but it has its greatest impact on demand by inducing consumers to buy smaller and more fuel-efficient cars. But because the stock of cars changes only slowly, the quantity of gasoline demanded falls only slowly. Figure 2.13(a) shows short-run and long-run demand curves for goods such as these.

**Demand and Durability** On the other hand, for some goods just the opposite is true—demand is more elastic in the short run than in the long run. Because these goods (automobiles, refrigerators, televisions, or the capital equipment purchased by industry) are *durable*, the total stock of each good owned by consumers is large relative to annual production. As a result, a small change in the total stock that consumers want to hold can result in a large percentage change in the level of purchases.

Suppose, for example, that the price of refrigerators goes up 10 percent, causing the total stock of refrigerators that consumers want to hold to drop 5 percent. Initially, this will cause purchases of new refrigerators to drop much more than 5 percent. But eventually, as consumers' refrigerators depreciate (and units must

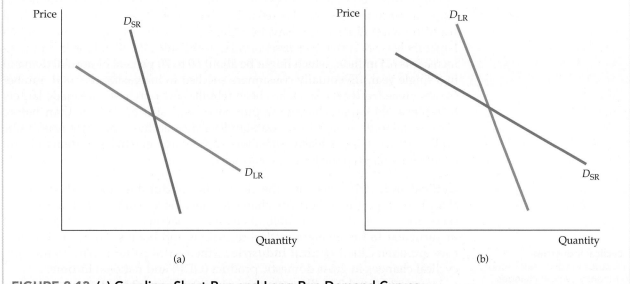

**FIGURE 2.13** **(a) Gasoline: Short-Run and Long-Run Demand Curves**
**(b) Automobiles: Short-Run and Long-Run Demand Curves**

**(a)** In the short run, an increase in price has only a small effect on the quantity of gasoline demanded. Motorists may drive less, but they will not change the kinds of cars they are driving overnight. In the longer run, however, because they will shift to smaller and more fuel-efficient cars, the effect of the price increase will be larger. Demand, therefore, is more elastic in the long run than in the short run. **(b)** The opposite is true for automobile demand. If price increases, consumers initially defer buying new cars; thus annual quantity demanded falls sharply. In the longer run, however, old cars wear out and must be replaced; thus annual quantity demanded picks up. Demand, therefore, is less elastic in the long run than in the short run.

be replaced), the quantity demanded will increase again. In the long run, the total stock of refrigerators owned by consumers will be about 5 percent less than before the price increase. In this case, while the long-run price elasticity of demand for refrigerators would be −.05/.10 = −0.5, the short-run elasticity would be much larger in magnitude.

Or consider automobiles. Although annual U.S. demand—new car purchases—is about 10 to 12 million, the stock of cars that people own is around 130 million. If automobile prices rise, many people will delay buying new cars. The quantity demanded will fall sharply, even though the total stock of cars that consumers might want to own at these higher prices falls only a small amount. Eventually, however, because old cars wear out and must be replaced, the quantity of new cars demanded picks up again. As a result, the long-run change in the quantity demanded is much smaller than the short-run change. Figure 2.13(b) shows demand curves for a durable good like automobiles.

**Income Elasticities** Income elasticities also differ from the short run to the long run. For most goods and services—foods, beverages, fuel, entertainment, etc.—the income elasticity of demand is larger in the long run than in the short run. Consider the behavior of gasoline consumption during a period of strong economic growth during which aggregate income rises by 10 percent. Eventually people will increase gasoline consumption because they can afford to take more trips and perhaps own larger cars. But this change in consumption takes time, and demand initially increases only by a small amount. Thus, the long-run elasticity will be larger than the short-run elasticity.

For a durable good, the opposite is true. Again, consider automobiles. If aggregate income rises by 10 percent, the total stock of cars that consumers will want to own will also rise—say, by 5 percent. But this change means a much larger increase in *current purchases* of cars. (If the stock is 130 million, a 5-percent increase is 6.5 million, which might be about 60 to 70 percent of normal demand in a single year.) Eventually consumers succeed in increasing the total number of cars owned; after the stock has been rebuilt, new purchases are made largely to replace old cars. (These new purchases will still be greater than before because a larger stock of cars outstanding means that more cars need to be replaced each year.) Clearly, the short-run income elasticity of demand will be much larger than the long-run elasticity.

**Cyclical Industries** Because the demands for durable goods fluctuate so sharply in response to short-run changes in income, the industries that produce these goods are quite vulnerable to changing macroeconomic conditions, and in particular to the business cycle—recessions and booms. Thus, these industries are often called **cyclical industries**—their sales patterns tend to magnify cyclical changes in gross domestic product (GDP) and national income.

Figures 2.14 and 2.15 illustrate this principle. Figure 2.14 plots two variables over time: the annual real (inflation-adjusted) rate of growth of GDP and the annual real rate of growth of investment in producers' durable equipment (i.e., machinery and other equipment purchased by firms). Note that although the

• **cyclical industries**
Industries in which sales tend to magnify cyclical changes in gross domestic product and national income.

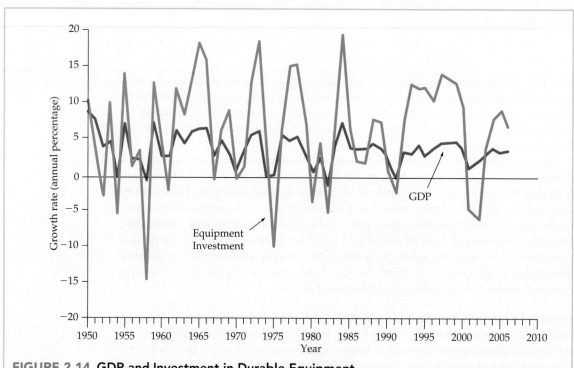

**FIGURE 2.14 GDP and Investment in Durable Equipment**

Annual growth rates are compared for GDP and investment in durable equipment. Because the short-run GDP elasticity of demand is larger than the long-run elasticity for long-lived capital equipment, changes in investment in equipment magnify changes in GDP. Thus capital goods industries are considered "cyclical."

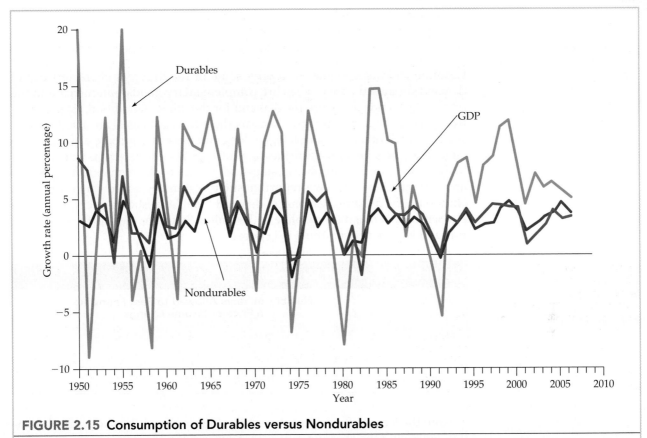

**FIGURE 2.15 Consumption of Durables versus Nondurables**

Annual growth rates are compared for GDP, consumer expenditures on durable goods (automobiles, appliances, furniture, etc.), and consumer expenditures on nondurable goods (food, clothing, services, etc.). Because the stock of durables is large compared with annual demand, short-run demand elasticities are larger than long-run elasticities. Like capital equipment, industries that produce consumer durables are "cyclical" (i.e., changes in GDP are magnified). This is not true for producers of nondurables.

durable equipment series follows the same pattern as the GDP series, the changes in GDP are magnified. For example, in 1961–1966 GDP grew by at least 4 percent each year. Purchases of durable equipment also grew, but by much more (over 10 percent in 1963–1966). Equipment investment likewise grew much more quickly than GDP during 1993–1998. On the other hand, during the recessions of 1974–1975, 1982, 1991, and 2001, equipment purchases fell by much more than GDP.

Figure 2.15 also shows the real rate of growth of GDP, along with the annual real rates of growth of spending by consumers on durable goods (automobiles, appliances, etc.) and nondurable goods (food, fuel, clothing, etc.). Note that while both consumption series follow GDP, only the durable goods series tends to magnify changes in GDP. Changes in consumption of nondurables are roughly the same as changes in GDP, but changes in consumption of durables are usually several times larger. This is why companies such as General Motors and General Electric are considered "cyclical": Sales of cars and electrical appliances are strongly affected by changing macroeconomic conditions.

EXAMPLE 2.6 The Demand for Gasoline and Automobiles

Gasoline and automobiles exemplify some of the different characteristics of demand discussed above. They are complementary goods—an increase in the price of one tends to reduce the demand for the other. In addition, their respective dynamic behaviors (long-run versus short-run elasticities) are just the opposite from each other. For gasoline, the long-run price and income elasticities are larger than the short-run elasticities; for automobiles, the reverse is true.

There have been a number of statistical studies of the demands for gasoline and automobiles. Here we report elasticity estimates based on several that emphasize the dynamic response of demand.[10] Table 2.1 shows price and income elasticities of demand for gasoline in the United States for the short run, the long run, and just about everything in between.

| TABLE 2.1 Demand for Gasoline | | | | | |
|---|---|---|---|---|---|
| | **Number of Years Allowed to Pass Following a Price or Income Change** | | | | |
| **Elasticity** | **1** | **2** | **3** | **5** | **10** |
| Price | −0.2 | −0.3 | −0.4 | −0.5 | −0.8 |
| Income | 0.2 | 0.4 | 0.5 | 0.6 | 1.0 |

Note the large differences between the long-run and the short-run elasticities. Following the sharp increases that occurred in the price of gasoline with the rise of the OPEC oil cartel in 1974, many people (including executives in the automobile and oil industries) claimed that the quantity of gasoline demanded would not change much—that demand was not very elastic. Indeed, for the first year after the price rise, they were right. But demand did eventually change. It just took time for people to alter their driving habits and to replace large cars with smaller and more fuel-efficient ones. This response continued after the second sharp increase in oil prices that occurred in 1979–1980. It was partly because of this response that OPEC could not maintain oil prices above $30 per barrel, and prices fell. The oil and gasoline price increases that occurred in 2005–2007 likewise led to a gradual demand response.

Table 2.2 shows price and income elasticities of demand for automobiles. Note that the short-run elasticities are much larger than the long-run elasticities. It should be clear from the income elasticities why the automobile industry is so highly cyclical. For example, GDP fell by nearly 3 percent in real

[10]For gasoline and automobile demand studies and elasticity estimates, see R. S. Pindyck, *The Structure of World Energy Demand* (Cambridge, MA: MIT Press, 1979); Carol Dahl and Thomas Sterner, "Analyzing Gasoline Demand Elasticities: A Survey," *Energy Economics* (July 1991); Molly Espey, "Gasoline Demand Revised: An International Meta-Analysis of Elasticities," *Energy Economics* (July 1998); David L. Greene, James R. Kahn, and Robert C. Gibson, "Fuel Economy Rebound Effects for U.S. Household Vehicles," *The Energy Journal* 20 (1999); Daniel Graham and Stephen Glaister, "The Demand for Automobile Fuel: A Survey of Elasticities," *Journal of Transport Economics and Policy* 36 (January 2002); and Ian Parry and Kenneth Small, "Does Britain or the United States Have the Right Gasoline Tax?" *American Economic Review* 95 (2005).

| TABLE 2.2 | Demand for Automobiles | | | | |
|---|---|---|---|---|---|
| | **Number of Years Allowed to Pass Following a Price or Income Change** | | | | |
| **Elasticity** | **1** | **2** | **3** | **5** | **10** |
| Price | −1.2 | −0.9 | −0.8 | −0.6 | −0.4 |
| Income | 3.0 | 2.3 | 1.9 | 1.4 | 1.0 |

(inflation-adjusted) terms during the 1982 recession, but automobile sales fell by about 8 percent in real terms. Auto sales recovered, however, during 1983–1985. They also fell by about 8 percent during the 1991 recession (when GDP fell 2 percent), but began to recover in 1993, and rose sharply during 1995–1999.

## Supply

Elasticities of supply also differ from the long run to the short run. For most products, long-run supply is much more price elastic than short-run supply: Firms face *capacity constraints* in the short run and need time to expand capacity by building new production facilities and hiring workers to staff them. This is not to say that the quantity supplied will not increase in the short run if price goes up sharply. Even in the short run, firms can increase output by using their existing facilities for more hours per week, paying workers to work overtime, and hiring some new workers immediately. But firms will be able to expand output much more when they have the time to expand their facilities and hire larger permanent workforces.

For some goods and services, short-run supply is completely inelastic. Rental housing in most cities is an example. In the very short run, there is only a fixed number of rental units. Thus an increase in demand only pushes rents up. In the longer run, and without rent controls, higher rents provide an incentive to renovate existing buildings and construct new ones. As a result, the quantity supplied increases.

For most goods, however, firms can find ways to increase output even in the short run—if the price incentive is strong enough. However, because various constraints make it costly to increase output rapidly, it may require large price increases to elicit small short-run increases in the quantity supplied. We discuss these characteristics of supply in more detail in Chapter 8.

**Supply and Durability** For some goods, supply is more elastic in the short run than in the long run. Such goods are durable and can be recycled as part of supply if price goes up. An example is the *secondary supply* of metals: the supply from *scrap metal*, which is often melted down and refabricated. When the price of copper goes up, it increases the incentive to convert scrap copper into new supply, so that, initially, secondary supply increases sharply. Eventually, however, the stock of good-quality scrap falls, making the melting, purifying, and refabricating more costly. Secondary supply then contracts. Thus the long-run price elasticity of secondary supply is smaller than the short-run elasticity.

Figures 2.16(a) and 2.16(b) show short-run and long-run supply curves for primary (production from the mining and smelting of ore) and secondary copper production. Table 2.3 shows estimates of the elasticities for each component of

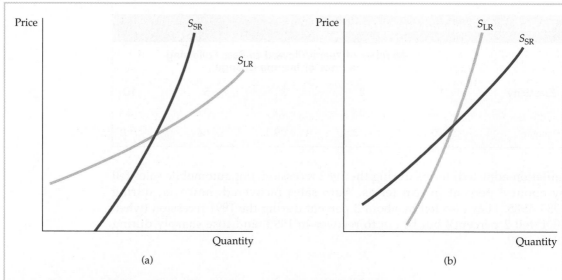

**FIGURE 2.16 Copper: Short-Run and Long-Run Supply Curves**

Like that of most goods, the supply of primary copper, shown in part (**a**), is more elastic in the long run. If price increases, firms would like to produce more but are limited by capacity constraints in the short run. In the longer run, they can add to capacity and produce more. Part (**b**) shows supply curves for secondary copper. If the price increases, there is a greater incentive to convert scrap copper into new supply. Initially, therefore, secondary supply (i.e., supply from scrap) increases sharply. But later, as the stock of scrap falls, secondary supply contracts. Secondary supply is therefore less elastic in the long run than in the short run.

supply and for total supply, based on a weighted average of the component elasticities.[11] Because secondary supply is only about 20 percent of total supply, the price elasticity of total supply is larger in the long run than in the short run.

| TABLE 2.3 Supply of Copper | | |
| --- | --- | --- |
| **Price Elasticity of:** | **Short-Run** | **Long-Run** |
| Primary supply | 0.20 | 1.60 |
| Secondary supply | 0.43 | 0.31 |
| Total supply | 0.25 | 1.50 |

**EXAMPLE 2.7**  The Weather in Brazil and the Price of Coffee in New York

Droughts or subfreezing weather occasionally destroy or damage many of Brazil's coffee trees. Because Brazil is by far the world's largest coffee producer the result is a decrease in the supply of coffee and a sharp run-up in its price.

In July 1975, for example, a frost destroyed most of Brazil's 1976–1977 coffee crop. (Remember that it is winter in Brazil when it is summer in the northern

---

[11]These estimates were obtained by aggregating the regional estimates reported in Franklin M. Fisher, Paul H. Cootner, and Martin N. Baily, "An Econometric Model of the World Copper Industry," *Bell Journal of Economics* 3 (Autumn 1972): 568–609.

hemisphere.) As Figure 2.17 shows, the price of a pound of coffee in New York went from 68 cents in 1975 to $1.23 in 1976 and $2.70 in 1977. Prices fell but then jumped again in 1986, after a seven-month drought in 1985 ruined much of Brazil's crop. Finally, starting in June 1994, freezing weather followed by a drought destroyed nearly half of Brazil's crop. As a result, the price of coffee in 1994–1995 was about double its 1993 level. By 2002, however, the price had dropped to its lowest level in 30 years. (Researchers predict that over the next 50 years, global warming may eliminate as much as 60 percent of Brazil's coffee-growing areas, resulting in a major decline in coffee production and an increase in prices. Should that happen, we will discuss it in the twentieth edition of this book.)

**FIGURE 2.17  Price of Brazilian Coffee**

When droughts or freezes damage Brazil's coffee trees, the price of coffee can soar. The price usually falls again after a few years, as demand and supply adjust.

The important point in Figure 2.17 is that any run-up in price following a freeze or drought is usually short-lived. Within a year, price begins to fall; within three or four years, it returns to its earlier levels. In 1978, for example, the price of coffee in New York fell to $1.48 per pound, and by 1983, it had fallen in real (inflation-adjusted) terms to within a few cents of its prefreeze 1975 price.[12] Likewise, in 1987 the price of coffee fell to below its predrought 1984 level, and then continued declining until the 1994 freeze.

Coffee prices behave this way because both demand and supply (especially supply) are much more elastic in the long run than in the short run.

---

[12]During 1980, however, prices temporarily went just above $2.00 per pound as a result of export quotas imposed under the International Coffee Agreement (ICA). The ICA is essentially a cartel agreement implemented by the coffee-producing countries in 1968. It has been largely ineffective and has seldom had an effect on the price. We discuss cartel pricing in detail in Chapter 12.

Figure 2.18 illustrates this fact. Note from part (a) of the figure that in the very short run (within one or two months after a freeze), supply is completely inelastic: There are simply a fixed number of coffee beans, some of which have been damaged by the frost. Demand is also relatively inelastic. As a result of the frost, the supply curve shifts to the left, and price increases sharply, from $P_0$ to $P_1$.

In the intermediate run—say, one year after the freeze—both supply and demand are more elastic, supply because existing trees can be harvested more intensively (with some decrease in quality), and demand because consumers have had time to change their buying habits. As part (b) shows, although the intermediate-run supply curve also shifts to the left, price has come down from $P_1$ to $P_2$. The quantity supplied has also increased somewhat from the short run, from $Q_1$ to $Q_2$. In the long run shown in part (c), price returns to its normal level because growers have had time to replace trees damaged by the freeze. The long-run supply curve, then, simply reflects the cost of producing coffee, including the costs of land, of planting and caring for the trees, and of a competitive rate of profit.[13]

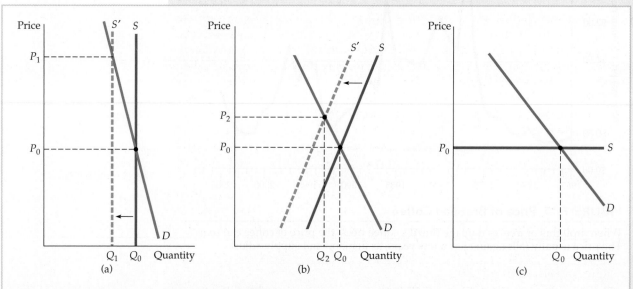

### FIGURE 2.18 Supply and Demand for Coffee

(a) A freeze or drought in Brazil causes the supply curve to shift to the left. In the short run, supply is completely inelastic; only a fixed number of coffee beans can be harvested. Demand is also relatively inelastic; consumers change their habits only slowly. As a result, the initial effect of the freeze is a sharp increase in price, from $P_0$ to $P_1$. **(b)** In the intermediate run, supply and demand are both more elastic; thus price falls part of the way back, to $P_2$. **(c)** In the long run, supply is extremely elastic; because new coffee trees will have had time to mature, the effect of the freeze will have disappeared. Price returns to $P_0$.

---

[13]You can learn more about the world coffee market from the Foreign Agriculture Service of the U.S. Department of Agriculture by visiting their Web site at **http://www.fas.usda.gov/htp/tropical/coffee.html**. Another good source of information is **http://www.nationalgeographic.com/coffee**.

# *2.6 UNDERSTANDING AND PREDICTING THE EFFECTS OF CHANGING MARKET CONDITIONS

So far, our discussion of supply and demand has been largely qualitative. To use supply and demand curves to analyze and predict the effects of changing market conditions, we must begin attaching numbers to them. For example, to see how a 50-percent reduction in the supply of Brazilian coffee may affect the world price of coffee, we must determine actual supply and demand curves and then calculate the shifts in those curves and the resulting changes in price.

In this section, we will see how to do simple "back of the envelope" calculations with linear supply and demand curves. Although they are often approximations of more complex curves, we use linear curves because they are easier to work with. It may come as a surprise, but one can do some informative economic analyses on the back of a small envelope with a pencil and a pocket calculator.

First, we must learn how to "fit" linear demand and supply curves to market data. (By this we do not mean *statistical fitting* in the sense of linear regression or other statistical techniques, which we will discuss later in the book.) Suppose we have two sets of numbers for a particular market: The first set consists of the price and quantity that generally prevail in the market (i.e., the price and quantity that prevail "on average," when the market is in equilibrium or when market conditions are "normal"). We call these numbers the *equilibrium price* and *quantity* and denote them by $P^*$ and $Q^*$. The second set consists of the price elasticities of supply and demand for the market (at or near the equilibrium), which we denote by $E_S$ and $E_D$, as before.

These numbers may come from a statistical study done by someone else; they may be numbers that we simply think are reasonable; or they may be numbers that we want to try out on a "what if" basis. Our goal is to *write down the supply and demand curves that fit (i.e., are consistent with) these numbers.* We can then determine numerically how a change in a variable such as GDP, the price of another good, or some cost of production will cause supply or demand to shift and thereby affect market price and quantity.

Let's begin with the linear curves shown in Figure 2.19. We can write these curves algebraically as follows:

$$Demand: \quad Q = a - bP \tag{2.5a}$$

$$Supply: \quad Q = c + dP \tag{2.5b}$$

Our problem is to choose numbers for the constants $a$, $b$, $c$, and $d$. This is done, for supply and for demand, in a two-step procedure:

• **Step 1:** Recall that each price elasticity, whether of supply or demand, can be written as

$$E = (P/Q)(\Delta Q/\Delta P)$$

where $\Delta Q/\Delta P$ is the change in quantity demanded or supplied resulting from a small change in price. For linear curves, $\Delta Q/\Delta P$ is constant. From equations

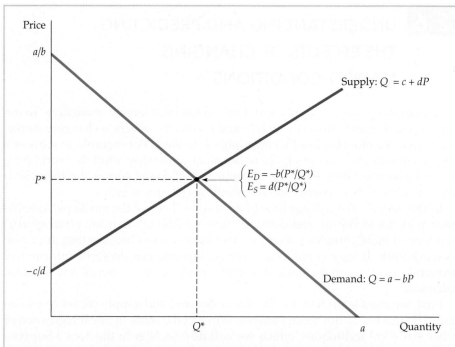

**FIGURE 2.19 Fitting Linear Supply and Demand Curves to Data**

Linear supply and demand curves provide a convenient tool for analysis. Given data for the equilibrium price and quantity $P^*$ and $Q^*$, as well as estimates of the elasticities of demand and supply $E_D$ and $E_S$, we can calculate the parameters $c$ and $d$ for the supply curve and $a$ and $b$ for the demand curve. (In the case drawn here, $c < 0$.) The curves can then be used to analyze the behavior of the market quantitatively.

(2.5a) and (2.5b), we see that $\Delta Q/\Delta P = d$ for supply and $\Delta Q/\Delta P = -b$ for demand. Now, let's substitute these values for $\Delta Q/\Delta P$ into the elasticity formula:

$$\text{Demand:} \quad E_D = -b(P^*/Q^*) \qquad \textbf{(2.6a)}$$

$$\text{Supply:} \quad E_S = d(P^*/Q^*) \qquad \textbf{(2.6b)}$$

where $P^*$ and $Q^*$ are the equilibrium price and quantity for which we have data and to which we want to fit the curves. Because we have numbers for $E_S$, $E_D$, $P^*$, and $Q^*$, we can substitute these numbers in equations (2.6a) and (2.6b) and solve for $b$ and $d$.

- **Step 2:** Since we now know $b$ and $d$, we can substitute these numbers, as well as $P^*$ and $Q^*$, into equations (2.5a) and (2.5b) and solve for the remaining constants $a$ and $c$. For example, we can rewrite equation (2.5a) as

$$a = Q^* + bP^*$$

and then use our data for $Q^*$ and $P^*$, together with the number we calculated in Step 1 for $b$, to obtain $a$.

Let's apply this procedure to a specific example: long–run supply and demand for the world copper market. The relevant numbers for this market are as follows:

Quantity $Q^* = 12$ million metric tons per year (mmt/yr)

Price $P^* = \$2.00$ per pound

Elasticity of suppy $E_S = 1.5$

Elasticity of demand $E_D = -0.5$.

(The price of copper has fluctuated during the past few decades between $0.60 and more than $3.50, but $2.00 is a reasonable average price for 2005–2007.)

We begin with the supply curve equation (2.5b) and use our two–step procedure to calculate numbers for $c$ and $d$. The long–run price elasticity of supply is 1.5, $P^* = \$2.00$, and $Q^* = 12$.

- **Step 1:** Substitute these numbers in equation (2.6b) to determine $d$:

$$1.5 = d(2/12) = d/6$$

So that $d = (1.5)(6) = 9$

- **Step 2:** Substitute this number for $d$, together with the numbers for $P^*$ and $Q^*$, into equation (2.5b) to determine $c$:

$$12 = c + (9)(2.00) = c + 18$$

so that $c = 12 - 18 = -6$. We now know $c$ and $d$, so we can write our supply curve:

*Supply:* $\quad Q = -6 + 9P$

We can now follow the same steps for the demand curve equation (2.5a). An estimate for the long–run elasticity of demand is −0.5.[14] First, substitute this number, as well as the values for $P^*$ and $Q^*$, into equation (2.6a) to determine $b$:

$$-0.5 = -b(2/12) = -b/6$$

so that $b = (0.5)(6) = 3$. Second, substitute this value for $b$ and the values for $P^*$ and $Q^*$ in equation (2.5a) to determine $a$:

$$12 = a - (3)(2) = a - 6$$

so that $a = 12 + 6 = 18$. Thus, our demand curve is

*Demand:* $\quad Q = 18 - 3P$

To check that we have not made a mistake, let's set the quantity supplied equal to the quantity demanded and calculate the resulting equilibrium price:

$$Supply = -6 + 9P = 18 - 3P = Demand$$
$$9P + 3P = 18 + 6$$

or $P = 24/12 = 2.00$, which is indeed the equilibrium price with which we began.

Although we have written supply and demand so that they depend only on price, they could easily depend on other variables as well. Demand, for

---

[14]See Claudio Agostini, "Estimating Market Power in the U.S. Copper Industry," *Review of Industrial Organization* 28 (2006).

example, might depend on income as well as price. We would then write demand as

$$Q = a - bP + fI, \qquad (2.7)$$

where $I$ is an index of aggregate income or GDP. For Example, $I$ might equal 1.0 in a base year and then rise or fall to reflect percentage increases or decreases in aggregate income.

For our copper market example, a reasonable estimate for the long–run income elasticity of demand is 1.3. For the linear demand curve (2.7), we can then calculate $f$ by using the formula for the income elasticity of demand: $E = (I/Q)(\Delta Q/\Delta I)$. Taking the base value of $I$ as 1.0, we have

$$1.3 = (1.0/12)(f)$$

Thus $f = (1.3)(12)/(1.0) = 15.6$. Finally, substituting the values $b = 3$, $f = 15.6$, $P^* = 2.00$, and $Q^* = 12$ in equation (2.7), we can calculate that $a$ must equal 2.4.

We have seen how to fit linear supply and demand curves to data. Now, to see how these curves can be used to analyze markets, let's look at Example 2.8, which deals with the behavior of copper prices, and Example 2.9, which concerns the world oil market.

### EXAMPLE 2.8    The Behavior of Copper Prices

After reaching a level of about $1.00 per pound in 1980, the price of copper fell sharply to about 60 cents per pound in 1986. In real (inflation-adjusted) terms, this price was even lower than during the Great Depression 50 years earlier. Prices increased in 1988–1989 and in 1995, largely as a result of strikes by miners in Peru and Canada that disrupted supplies, but then fell again from 1996 through 2003. Prices increased sharply, however, during 2005–2007. Figure 2.20 shows the behavior of copper prices during 1965–2007 in both real and nominal terms.

Worldwide recessions in 1980 and 1982 contributed to the decline of copper prices; as mentioned above, the income elasticity of copper demand is about 1.3. But copper demand did not pick up as the industrial economies recovered during the mid-1980s. Instead, the 1980s saw a steep decline in demand.

The price decline through 2003 occurred for two reasons. First, a large part of copper consumption is for the construction of equipment for electric power generation and transmission. But by the late 1970s, the growth rate of electric power generation had fallen dramatically in most industrialized countries. In the United States, for example, the growth rate fell from over 6 percent per annum in the 1960s and early 1970s to less than 2 percent in the late 1970s and 1980s. This decline meant a big drop in what had been a major source of copper demand. Second, in the 1980s, other materials, such as aluminum and fiber optics, were increasingly substituted for copper.

Why did the price increase sharply in 2005–2007? First, the demand for copper from China and other Asian countries began increasing dramatically, replacing the demand from Europe and the U.S. Chinese copper consumption, for example, increased by 32 percent from 2002 to 2006. Second, because prices had dropped so much from 1996 through 2003, producers in the U.S., Canada, and

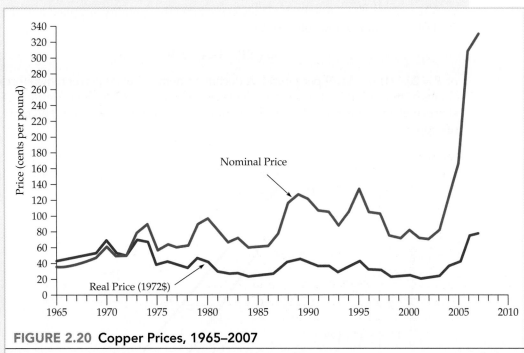

**FIGURE 2.20 Copper Prices, 1965–2007**

Copper prices are shown in both nominal (no adjustment for inflation) and real (inflation-adjusted) terms. In real terms, copper prices declined steeply from the early 1970s through the mid-1980s as demand fell. In 1988–1990, copper prices rose in response to supply disruptions caused by strikes in Peru and Canada but later fell after the strikes ended. Prices declined during the 1996–2002 period but then increased sharply during 2005–2007.

Chile closed unprofitable mines and cut production. Between 2000 and 2003, for example, U.S. mine production of copper declined by 23 percent.[15]

One might expect the high prices of 2005–2007 to stimulate investments in new mines and increases in production, and that is indeed what has happened. Arizona, for example, experienced a copper boom as Phelps Dodge opened a major new mine in 2007.[16] By 2007, producers began to worry that prices would decline again, either as a result of these new investments or because demand from Asia would level off or even drop.

What would a decline in demand do to the price of copper? To find out, we can use the linear supply and demand curves that we just derived. Let's calculate the effect on price of a 20-percent decline in demand. Because we are not concerned here with the effects of GDP growth, we can leave the income term, $fI$, out of the demand equation.

We want to shift the demand curve to the left by 20 percent. In other words, we want the quantity demanded to be 80 percent of what it would be otherwise for every value of price. For our linear demand curve, we simply multiply the right–hand side by 0.8:

$$Q = (0.8)(18 - 3P) = 14.4 - 2.4P$$

[15]Our thanks to Patricia Foley, Executive Director of the American Bureau of Metal Statistics, for supplying the data on China. Other data are from the Monthly Reports of the U.S. Geological Survey Mineral Resources Program—**http://minerals.usgs.gov/minerals/pubs/copper**.

[16]The boom created hundreds of new jobs, which in turn led to increases in housing prices: "Copper Boom Creates Housing Crunch," *The Arizona Republic*, July 12, 2007.

Supply is again $Q = -6 + 9P$. Now we can equate the quantity supplied and the quantity demanded and solve for price:

$$-6 + 9P = 14.4 - 2.4P$$

or $P = 20.4/11.4 = \$1.79$ per pound. A decline in demand of 20 percent, therefore, entails a drop in price of roughly 21 cents per pound, or 10.5 percent. Figure 2.21 shows how this shift in the demand curve affects the equilibrium price and quantity of copper.[17]

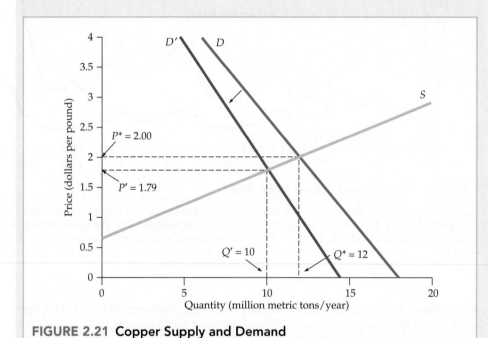

**FIGURE 2.21 Copper Supply and Demand**

The shift in the demand curve corresponding to a 20-percent decline in demand leads to a 10.5-percent decline in price.

---

**EXAMPLE 2.9**  ·  Upheaval in the World Oil Market

Since the early 1970s, the world oil market has been buffeted by the OPEC cartel and by political turmoil in the Persian Gulf. In 1974, by collectively restraining output, OPEC (the Organization of Petroleum Exporting Countries) pushed world oil prices well above what they would have been in a competitive market. OPEC could do this because it accounted for much of

---

[17]Note that because we have multiplied the demand function by 0.8—i.e., reduced the quantity demanded at every price by 20 percent—the new demand curve is not parallel to the old one. Instead, the curve rotates downward at its intersection with the price axis.

world oil production. During 1979–1980, oil prices shot up again, as the Iranian revolution and the outbreak of the Iran-Iraq war sharply reduced Iranian and Iraqi production. During the 1980s, the price gradually declined, as demand fell and competitive (i.e., non-OPEC) supply rose in response to price. Prices remained relatively stable during 1988–2001, except for a temporary spike in 1990 following the Iraqi invasion of Kuwait. Prices increased again in 2002–2003 as a result of a strike in Venezuela and then the war with Iraq in the spring of 2003; they continued to increase during 2005–2007 as a result of rising oil demand in Asia and reductions in OPEC output. Figure 2.22 shows the world price of oil from 1970 to 2007, in both nominal and real terms.

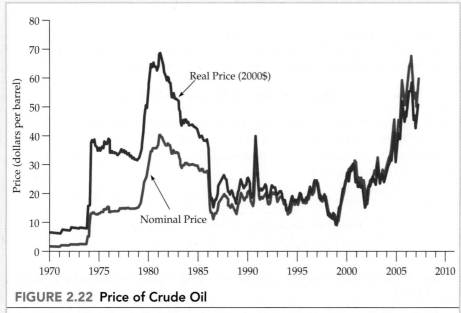

**FIGURE 2.22  Price of Crude Oil**

The OPEC cartel and political events caused the price of oil to rise sharply at times. It later fell as supply and demand adjusted.

The Persian Gulf is one of the less stable regions of the world—a fact that has led to concern over the possibility of new oil supply disruptions and sharp increases in oil prices. What would happen to oil prices—in both the short run and longer run—if a war or revolution in the Persian Gulf caused a sharp cutback in oil production? Let's see how simple supply and demand curves can be used to predict the outcome of such an event.

Because this example is set in 2005–2007, all prices are measured in 2005 dollars. Here are some rough figures:

- 2005–7 world price = $50 per barrel
- World demand and total supply = 34 billion barrels per year (bb/yr)
- OPEC supply = 14 bb/yr
- Competitive (non-OPEC) supply = 20 bb/yr

The following table gives price elasticity estimates for oil supply and demand:[18]

|  | Short Run | Long Run |
|---|---|---|
| World demand: | −0.05 | −0.40 |
| Competitive supply: | 0.10 | 0.40 |

You should verify that these numbers imply the following for demand and competitive supply in the *short run*:

$$\text{Short-run demand:} \qquad D = 35.5 - 0.03P$$
$$\text{Short-run competitive supply:} \qquad S_C = 18.0 + 0.04P$$

Of course, *total* supply is competitive supply *plus* OPEC supply, which we take as constant at 14 bb/yr. Adding this 14 bb/yr to the competitive supply curve above, we obtain the following for the total short-run supply:

$$\text{Short-run total supply:} \qquad S_T = 32 + 0.04P$$

You should verify that the quantity demanded and the total quantity supplied are equal at an equilibrium price of $50 per barrel.

You should also verify that the corresponding demand and supply curves for the *long run* are as follows:

$$\text{Long-run demad:} \qquad D = 47.5 - 0.27P$$
$$\text{Long-run competitive supply:} \qquad S_C = 12 + 0.16P$$
$$\text{Long-run total supply:} \qquad S_T = 26 + 0.16P$$

Again, you can check that the quantities supplied and demanded equate at a price of $50.

Saudi Arabia is one of the world's largest oil producers, accounting for roughly 3 bb/yr, which is nearly 10 percent of total world production. What would happen to the price of oil if, because of war or political upheaval, Saudi Arabia stopped producing oil? We can use our supply and demand curves to find out.

For the *short run*, simply subtract 3 from total supply:

$$\text{Short-run demand:} \qquad D = 35.5 - 0.03P$$
$$\text{Short-run total supply:} \qquad S_T = 29 + 0.04P$$

By equating this total quantity supplied with the quantity demanded, we can see that in the short run, the price will nearly double to $92.86 per barrel. Figure 2.23 shows this supply shift and the resulting short-run increase in price. The initial

[18]For the sources of these numbers and a more detailed discussion of OPEC oil pricing, see Robert S. Pindyck, "Gains to Producers from the Cartelization of Exhaustible Resources," *Review of Economics and Statistics* 60 (May 1978): 238–51; James M. Griffin and David J. Teece, *OPEC Behavior and World Oil Prices* (London: Allen and Unwin, 1982); and John C. B. Cooper, "Price Elasticity of Demand for Crude Oil: Estimates for 23 Countries," *O\*rganization of the Petroleum Exporting Countries Review* (March 2003).

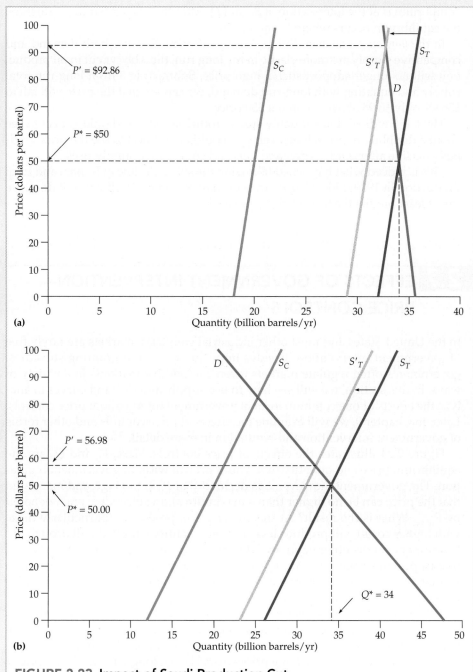

**FIGURE 2.23 Impact of Saudi Production Cut**

The total supply is the sum of competitive (non-OPEC) supply and the 14 bb/yr of OPEC supply. Part **(a)** shows the short-run supply and demand curves. If Saudi Arabia stops producing, the supply curve will shift to the left by 3 bb/yr. In the short-run, price will increase sharply. Part **(b)** shows long-run curves. In the long run, because demand and competitive supply are much more elastic, the impact on price will be much smaller.

equilibrium is at the intersection of $S_T$ and $D$. After the drop in Saudi production, the equilibrium occurs where $S'_T$ and $D$ cross.

In the *long run*, however, things will be different. Because both demand and competitive supply are more elastic in the long run, the 3 bb/yr cut in oil production will no longer support such a high price. Subtracting 3 from long-run total supply and equating with long-run demand, we can see that the price will fall to $56.98, only $6.98 above the initial $50 price.

Thus, if Saudi Arabia suddenly stops producing oil, we should expect to see about a doubling in price. However, we should also expect to see the price gradually decline afterward, as demand falls and competitive supply rises.

This is indeed what happened following the sharp decline in Iranian and Iraqi production in 1979–1980. History may or may not repeat itself, but if it does, we can at least predict the impact on oil prices.[19]

## 2.7 EFFECTS OF GOVERNMENT INTERVENTION— PRICE CONTROLS

In the United States and most other industrial countries, markets are rarely free of government intervention. Besides imposing taxes and granting subsidies, governments often regulate markets (even competitive markets) in a variety of ways. In this section, we will see how to use supply and demand curves to analyze the effects of one common form of government intervention: price controls. Later, in Chapter 9, we will examine the effects of price controls and other forms of government intervention and regulation in more detail.

Figure 2.24 illustrates the effects of price controls. Here, $P_0$ and $Q_0$ are the equilibrium price and quantity that would prevail without government regulation. The government, however, has decided that $P_0$ is too high and mandated that the price can be no higher than a maximum allowable *ceiling price*, denoted by $P_{max}$. What is the result? At this lower price, producers (particularly those with higher costs) will produce less, and the quantity supplied will drop to $Q_1$. Consumers, on the other hand, will demand more at this low price; they would like to purchase the quantity $Q_2$. Demand therefore exceeds supply, and a shortage develops—i.e., there is *excess demand*. The amount of excess demand is $Q_2 - Q_1$.

This excess demand sometimes takes the form of queues, as when drivers lined up to buy gasoline during the winter of 1974 and the summer of 1979. In both instances, the lines were the result of price controls; the government prevented domestic oil and gasoline prices from rising along with world oil prices. Sometimes excess demand results in curtailments and supply rationing, as with natural gas price controls and the resulting gas shortages of the mid-1970s, when industrial consumers closed factories because gas supplies were cut off. Sometimes it spills over into other markets, where it artificially increases demand. For example, natural gas price controls caused potential buyers of gas to use oil instead.

---

[19]You can obtain recent data and learn more about the world oil market by accessing the Web sites of the American Petroleum Institute at **www.api.org** or the U.S. Energy Information Administration at **www.eia.doe.gov**.

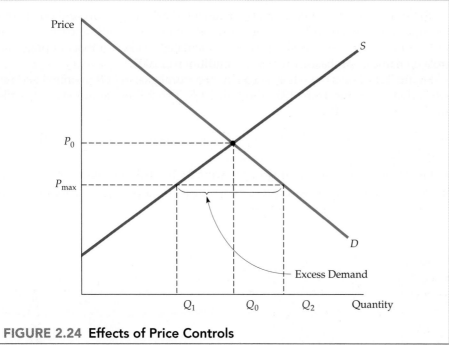

**FIGURE 2.24 Effects of Price Controls**

Without price controls, the market clears at the equilibrium price and quantity $P_0$ and $Q_0$. If price is regulated to be no higher than $P_{max}$, the quantity supplied falls to $Q_1$, the quantity demanded increases to $Q_2$, and a shortage develops.

Some people gain and some lose from price controls. As Figure 2.24 suggests, producers lose: They receive lower prices, and some leave the industry. Some but not all consumers gain. While those who can purchase the good at a lower price are better off, those who have been "rationed out" and cannot buy the good at all are worse off. How large are the gains to the winners and how large are the losses to the losers? Do total gains exceed total losses? To answer these questions, we need a method to measure the gains and losses from price controls and other forms of government intervention. We discuss such a method in Chapter 9.

**EXAMPLE 2.10**   Price Controls and Natural Gas Shortages

In 1954, the federal government began regulating the wellhead price of natural gas. Initially the controls were not binding; the ceiling prices were above those that cleared the market. But in about 1962, when these ceiling prices did become binding, excess demand for natural gas developed and slowly began to grow. In the 1970s, this excess demand, spurred by higher oil prices, became severe and led to widespread curtailments. Soon ceiling prices were far below prices that would have prevailed in a free market.[20]

---

[20]This regulation began with the Supreme Court's 1954 decision requiring the then Federal Power Commission to regulate wellhead prices on natural gas sold to interstate pipeline companies. These price controls were largely removed during the 1980s, under the mandate of the Natural Gas Policy Act of 1978. For a detailed discussion of natural gas regulation and its effects, see Paul W. MacAvoy and Robert S. Pindyck, *The Economics of the Natural Gas Shortage* (Amsterdam: North-Holland, 1975); R. S. Pindyck, "Higher Energy Prices and the Supply of Natural Gas," *Energy Systems and Policy* 2(1978): 177–209; and Arlon R. Tussing and Connie C. Barlow, *The Natural Gas Industry* (Cambridge, MA: Ballinger, 1984).

Today, producers and industrial consumers of natural gas, oil, and other commodities are concerned that the government might respond, once again, with price controls if prices rise sharply. Let's calculate the likely impact of price controls on natural gas, based on market conditions in 2007.

Figure 2.25 shows the wholesale price of natural gas, in both nominal and real (2000 dollars) terms, from 1950 through 2007. The following numbers describe the U.S. market in 2007:

- The (free-market) wholesale price of natural gas was $6.40 per mcf (thousand cubic feet);
- Production and consumption of gas were 23 Tcf (trillion cubic feet);
- The average price of crude oil (which affects the supply and demand for natural gas) was about $50 per barrel.

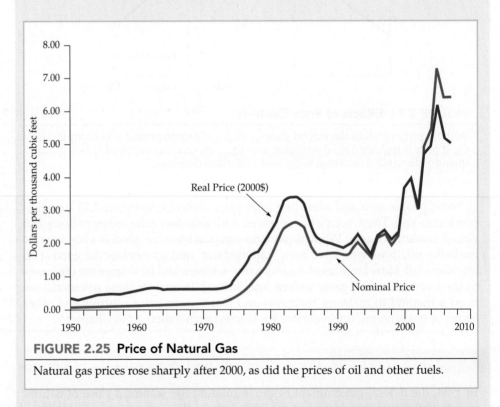

**FIGURE 2.25 Price of Natural Gas**

Natural gas prices rose sharply after 2000, as did the prices of oil and other fuels.

A reasonable estimate for the price elasticity of supply is 0.2. Higher oil prices also lead to more natural gas production because oil and gas are often discovered and produced together; an estimate of the cross-price elasticity of supply is 0.1. As for demand, the price elasticity is about –0.5, and the cross-price elasticity with respect to oil price is about 1.5. You can verify that the following linear supply and demand curves fit these numbers:

$$\text{Supply}: \quad Q = 15.90 + 0.72P_G + 0.05P_O$$
$$\text{Demand}: \quad Q = 0.02 - 1.8P_G + 0.69P_O$$

where $Q$ is the quantity of natural gas (in Tcf), $P_G$ is the price of natural gas (in dollars per mcf), and $P_O$ is the price of oil (in dollars per barrel). You can also verify, by equating the quantities supplied and demanded and substituting $50 for $P_O$, that these supply and demand curves imply an equilibrium free-market price of $6.40 for natural gas.

Suppose the government determines that the free-market price of $6.40 per mcf is too high, decides to impose price controls, and sets a maximum price of $3.00 per mcf. What impact would this have on the quantity of gas supplied and the quantity demanded?

Substitute $3.00 for $P_G$ in both the supply and demand equations (keeping the price of oil, $P_O$, fixed at $50). You should find that the supply equation gives a quantity supplied of 20.6 Tcf and the demand equation a quantity demanded of 29.1 Tcf. Therefore, these price controls would create an excess demand (i.e., shortage) of 29.1 − 20.6 = 8.5 Tcf. In Example 9.1 we'll show how to measure the resulting gains and loses to producers and consumers.

# SUMMARY

1. Supply-demand analysis is a basic tool of microeconomics. In competitive markets, supply and demand curves tell us how much will be produced by firms and how much will be demanded by consumers as a function of price.
2. The market mechanism is the tendency for supply and demand to equilibrate (i.e., for price to move to the market-clearing level), so that there is neither excess demand nor excess supply.
3. Elasticities describe the responsiveness of supply and demand to changes in price, income, or other variables. For example, the price elasticity of demand measures the percentage change in the quantity demanded resulting from a 1-percent increase in price.
4. Elasticities pertain to a time frame, and for most goods it is important to distinguish between short-run and long-run elasticities.

5. If we can estimate, at least roughly, the supply and demand curves for a particular market, we can calculate the market-clearing price by equating the quantity supplied with the quantity demanded. Also, if we know how supply and demand depend on other economic variables, such as income or the prices of other goods, we can calculate how the market-clearing price and quantity will change as these other variables change. This is a means of explaining or predicting market behavior.
6. Simple numerical analyses can often be done by fitting linear supply and demand curves to data on price and quantity and to estimates of elasticities. For many markets, such data and estimates are available, and simple "back of the envelope" calculations can help us understand the characteristics and behavior of the market.

# QUESTIONS FOR REVIEW

1. Suppose that unusually hot weather causes the demand curve for ice cream to shift to the right. Why will the price of ice cream rise to a new market-clearing level?
2. Use supply and demand curves to illustrate how each of the following events would affect the price of butter and the quantity of butter bought and sold: (a) an increase in the price of margarine; (b) an increase in the price of milk; (c) a decrease in average income levels.
3. If a 3-percent increase in the price of corn flakes causes a 6-percent decline in the quantity demanded, what is the elasticity of demand?
4. Explain the difference between a shift in the supply curve and a movement along the supply curve.

5. Explain why for many goods, the long-run price elasticity of supply is larger than the short-run elasticity.
6. Why do long-run elasticities of demand differ from short-run elasticities? Consider two goods: paper towels and televisions. Which is a durable good? Would you expect the price elasticity of demand for paper towels to be larger in the short run or in the long run? Why? What about the price elasticity of demand for televisions?
7. Are the following statements true or false? Explain your answers.
   a. The elasticity of demand is the same as the slope of the demand curve.
   b. The cross-price elasticity will always be positive.

c. The supply of apartments is more inelastic in the short run than the long run.

8. Suppose the government regulates the prices of beef and chicken and sets them below their market-clearing levels. Explain why shortages of these goods will develop and what factors will determine the sizes of the shortages. What will happen to the price of pork? Explain briefly.

9. The city council of a small college town decides to regulate rents in order to reduce student living expenses. Suppose the average annual market-clearing rent for a two-bedroom apartment had been $700 per month and that rents were expected to increase to $900 within a year. The city council limits rents to their current $700-per-month level.

a. Draw a supply and demand graph to illustrate what will happen to the rental price of an apartment after the imposition of rent controls.

b. Do you think this policy will benefit all students? Why or why not?

10. In a discussion of tuition rates, a university official argues that the demand for admission is completely price inelastic. As evidence, she notes that while the university has doubled its tuition (in real terms) over the past 15 years, neither the number nor quality of students applying has decreased. Would you accept this argument? Explain briefly. (*Hint*: The official makes an assertion about the demand for admission, but does she actually observe a demand curve? What else could be going on?)

11. Suppose the demand curve for a product is given by

$$Q = 10 - 2P + P_S$$

where $P$ is the price of the product and $P_S$ is the price of a substitute good. The price of the substitute good is $2.00.

a. Suppose $P = $1.00$. What is the price elasticity of demand? What is the cross-price elasticity of demand?

b. Suppose the price of the good, $P$, goes to $2.00. Now what is the price elasticity of demand? What is the cross-price elasticity of demand?

12. Suppose that rather than the declining demand assumed in Example 2.8, a decrease in the cost of copper production causes the supply curve to shift to the right by 40 percent. How will the price of copper change?

13. Suppose the demand for natural gas is perfectly inelastic. What would be the effect, if any, of natural gas price controls?

# EXERCISES

1. Suppose the demand curve for a product is given by $Q = 300 - 2P + 4I$, where $I$ is average income measured in thousands of dollars. The supply curve is $Q = 3P - 50$.

a. If $I = 25$, find the market-clearing price and quantity for the product.

b. If $I = 50$, find the market-clearing price and quantity for the product.

c. Draw a graph to illustrate your answers.

2. Consider a competitive market for which the quantities demanded and supplied (per year) at various prices are given as follows:

| Price (Dollars) | Demand (Millions) | Supply (Millions) |
|---|---|---|
| 60 | 22 | 14 |
| 80 | 20 | 16 |
| 100 | 18 | 18 |
| 120 | 16 | 20 |

a. Calculate the price elasticity of demand when the price is $80 and when the price is $100.

b. Calculate the price elasticity of supply when the price is $80 and when the price is $100.

c. What are the equilibrium price and quantity?

d. Suppose the government sets a price ceiling of $80. Will there be a shortage, and if so, how large will it be?

3. Refer to Example 2.5 (page 38) on the market for wheat. In 1998, the total demand for U.S. wheat was $Q = 3244 - 283P$ and the domestic supply was $Q_S = 1944 + 207P$. At the end of 1998, both Brazil and Indonesia opened their wheat markets to U.S. farmers. Suppose that these new markets add 200 million bushels to U.S. wheat demand. What will be the free-market price of wheat and what quantity will be produced and sold by U.S. farmers?

4. A vegetable fiber is traded in a competitive world market, and the world price is $9 per pound. Unlimited quantities are available for import into the United States at this price. The U.S. domestic supply and demand for various price levels are shown as follows:

| Price | U.S. Supply (Million Lbs) | U.S. Demand (Million Lbs) |
|---|---|---|
| 3 | 2 | 34 |
| 6 | 4 | 28 |
| 9 | 6 | 22 |
| 12 | 8 | 16 |
| 15 | 10 | 10 |
| 18 | 12 | 4 |

a. What is the equation for demand? What is the equation for supply?

b. At a price of $9, what is the price elasticity of demand? What is it at a price of $12?

c. What is the price elasticity of supply at $9? At $12?

d. In a free market, what will be the U.S. price and level of fiber imports?

*5. Much of the demand for U.S. agricultural output has come from other countries. In 1998, the total demand for wheat was $Q = 3244 - 283P$. Of this, total domestic demand was $Q_D = 1700 - 107P$, and domestic supply was $Q_S = 1944 + 207P$. Suppose the export demand for wheat falls by 40 percent.

a. U.S. farmers are concerned about this drop in export demand. What happens to the free-market price of wheat in the United States? Do farmers have much reason to worry?

b. Now suppose the U.S. government wants to buy enough wheat to raise the price to $3.50 per bushel. With the drop in export demand, how much wheat would the government have to buy? How much would this cost the government?

6. The rent control agency of New York City has found that aggregate demand is $Q_D = 160 - 8P$. Quantity is measured in tens of thousands of apartments. Price, the average monthly rental rate, is measured in hundreds of dollars. The agency also noted that the increase in $Q$ at lower $P$ results from more three-person families coming into the city from Long Island and demanding apartments. The city's board of realtors acknowledges that this is a good demand estimate and has shown that supply is $Q_S = 70 + 7P$.

a. If both the agency and the board are right about demand and supply, what is the free-market price? What is the change in city population if the agency sets a maximum average monthly rent of $300 and all those who cannot find an apartment leave the city?

b. Suppose the agency bows to the wishes of the board and sets a rental of $900 per month on all apartments to allow landlords a "fair" rate of return. If 50 percent of any long-run increases in apartment offerings comes from new construction, how many apartments are constructed?

7. In 1998, Americans smoked 470 billion cigarettes, or 23.5 billion packs of cigarettes. The average retail price was $2 per pack. Statistical studies have shown that the price elasticity of demand is −0.4, and the price elasticity of supply is 0.5. Using this information, derive linear demand and supply curves for the cigarette market.

8. In Example 2.8 we examined the effect of a 20-percent decline in copper demand on the price of copper, using the linear supply and demand curves developed in Section 2.6. Suppose the long-run price elasticity of copper demand were −0.75 instead of −0.5.

a. Assuming, as before, that the equilibrium price and quantity are $P^* = \$2$ per pound and $Q^* = 12$ million metric tons per year, derive the linear demand curve consistent with the smaller elasticity.

b. Using this demand curve, recalculate the effect of a 20-percent decline in copper demand on the price of copper.

9. In Example 2.8 (page 52), we discussed the recent increase in world demand for copper, due in part to China's rising consumption.

a. Using the original elasticities of demand and supply (i.e. $E_S = 1.5$ and $E_D = -0.5$), calculate the effect of a 20-percent *increase* in copper demand on the price of copper.

b. Now calculate the effect of this increase in demand on the equilibrium quantity, $Q^*$.

c. As we discussed in Example 2.8, the U.S. production of copper declined between 2000 and 2003. Calculate the effect on the equilibrium price and quantity of *both* a 20-percent increase in copper demand (as you just did in part a) *and* of a 20-percent decline in copper supply.

10. Example 2.9 (page 54) analyzes the world oil market. Using the data given in that example:

a. Show that the short-run demand and competitive supply curves are indeed given by

$$D = 35.5 - 0.03P$$
$$S_C = 18 + 0.04P$$

b. Show that the long-run demand and competitive supply curves are indeed given by

$$D = 47.5 - 0.27P$$
$$S_C = 12 + 0.16P$$

c. In Example 2.9 we examined the impact on price of a disruption of oil from Saudi Arabia. Suppose that instead of a decline in supply, OPEC production *increases* by 2 billion barrels per year (bb/yr) because the Saudis open large new oil fields. Calculate the effect of this increase in production on the supply of oil in both the short run and the long run.

11. Refer to Example 2.10 (page 59), which analyzes the effects of price controls on natural gas.

a. Using the data in the example, show that the following supply and demand curves describe the market for natural gas in 2005–2007:

$$\textit{Supply}: \quad Q = 15.90 + 0.72P_G + 0.05P_O$$
$$\textit{Demand}: \quad Q = 0.02 - 1.8P_G + 0.69P_O$$

Also, verify that if the price of oil is $50, these curves imply a free-market price of $6.40 for natural gas.

b. Suppose the regulated price of gas were $4.50 per thousand cubic feet instead of $3.00. How much excess demand would there have been?

c. Suppose that the market for natural gas remained unregulated. If the price of oil had increased from $50 to $100, what would have happened to the free-market price of natural gas?

*12. The table below shows the retail price and sales for instant coffee and roasted coffee for 1997 and 1998.

   a. Using these data alone, estimate the short-run price elasticity of demand for roasted coffee. Derive a linear demand curve for roasted coffee.

   b. Now estimate the short-run price elasticity of demand for instant coffee. Derive a linear demand curve for instant coffee.

   c. Which coffee has the higher short-run price elasticity of demand? Why do you think this is the case?

| Year | Retail Price of Instant Coffee ($/Lb) | Sales of Instant Coffee (Million Lbs) | Retail Price of Roasted Coffee ($/Lb) | Sales of Roasted Coffee (Million Lbs) |
|---|---|---|---|---|
| 1997 | 10.35 | 75 | 4.11 | 820 |
| 1998 | 10.48 | 70 | 3.76 | 850 |

# PART · TWO

## Producers, Consumers, and Competitive Markets

Part 2 presents the theoretical core of microeconomics.

Chapters 3 and 4 explain the principles underlying consumer demand. We see how consumers make consumption decisions, how their preferences and budget constraints determine their demands for various goods, and why different goods have different demand characteristics. Chapter 5 contains more advanced material that shows how to analyze consumer choice under uncertainty. We explain why people usually dislike risky situations and show how they can reduce risk and choose among risky alternatives. We also discuss aspects of consumer behavior that can only be explained by delving into the psychological aspects of how people make decisions.

Chapters 6 and 7 develop the theory of the firm. We see how firms combine inputs, such as capital, labor, and raw materials, to produce goods and services in a way that minimizes the costs of production. We also see how a firm's costs depend on its rate of production and production experience. Chapter 8 then shows how firms choose profit-maximizing rates of production. We also see how the production decisions of individual firms combine to determine the competitive market supply curve and its characteristics.

Chapter 9 applies supply and demand curves to the analysis of competitive markets. We show how government policies, such as price controls, quotas, taxes, and subsidies, can have wide-ranging effects on consumers and producers, and we explain how supply-demand analysis can be used to evaluate these effects.

# Consumer Behavior

# 3

A decade ago, General Mills decided to introduce a new breakfast cereal product. The new brand, Apple-Cinnamon Cheerios, offered a sweetened and more flavorful variant on General Mills' classic Cheerios product. But before Apple-Cinnamon Cheerios could be extensively marketed, the company had to resolve an important problem: *How high a price should it charge?* No matter how good the cereal was, its profitability would depend on the company's pricing decision. Knowing that consumers would pay more for a new product was not enough. The question was *how much more*. General Mills, therefore, had to conduct a careful analysis of consumer preferences to determine the demand for Apple-Cinnamon Cheerios.

General Mills' problem in determining consumer preferences mirrors the more complex problem faced by the U.S. Congress in evaluating the federal Food Stamps program. The goal of the program is to give low-income households coupons that can be exchanged for food. But there has always been a problem in the program's design that complicates its assessment: To what extent do food stamps provide people with *more* food, as opposed to simply subsidizing the purchase of food that they would have bought anyway? In other words, has the program turned out to be little more than an income supplement that people spend largely on nonfood items instead of a solution to the nutritional problems of the poor? As in the cereal example, we need an analysis of consumer behavior. In this case, the federal government must determine how spending on food, as opposed to spending on other goods, is affected by changing income levels and prices.

Solving these two problems—one involving corporate policy and the other public policy—requires an understanding of the **theory of consumer behavior**: the explanation of how consumers allocate incomes to the purchase of different goods and services.

## Consumer Behavior

How can a consumer with a limited income decide which goods and services to buy? This is a fundamental issue in microeconomics—one that we address in this chapter and the next. We will see how consumers allocate their incomes across goods and explain how these allocation decisions determine the demands for various goods and services. In turn, understanding consumer purchasing decisions will help us to understand how changes in income and prices affect the demand for goods and services and why the demand for some products is more sensitive than others to changes in prices and income.

• **theory of consumer behavior** Description of how consumers allocate incomes among different goods and services to maximize their well-being.

Consumer behavior is best understood in three distinct steps:

1. **Consumer Preferences:** The first step is to find a practical way to describe the reasons people might prefer one good to another. We will see how a consumer's *preferences* for various goods can be described graphically and algebraically.

2. **Budget Constraints:** Of course, consumers also consider *prices*. In Step 2, therefore, we take into account the fact that consumers have limited incomes which restrict the quantities of goods they can buy. What does a consumer do in this situation? We find the answer to this question by putting consumer preferences and budget constraints together in the third step.

3. **Consumer Choices:** Given their preferences and limited incomes, consumers choose to buy combinations of goods that maximize their satisfaction. These combinations will depend on the prices of various goods. Thus, understanding consumer choice will help us understand *demand*— i.e., how the quantity of a good that consumers choose to purchase depends on its price.

These three steps are the basics of consumer theory, and we will go through them in detail in the first three sections of this chapter. Afterward, we will explore a number of other interesting aspects of consumer behavior. For example, we will see how one can determine the nature of consumer preferences from actual observations of consumer behavior. Thus, if a consumer chooses one good over a similarly priced alternative, we can infer that he or she prefers the first good. Similar kinds of conclusions can be drawn from the actual decisions that consumers make in response to changes in the prices of the various goods and services that are available for purchase.

At the end of this chapter, we will return to the discussion of real and nominal prices that we began in Chapter 1. We saw that the Consumer Price Index can provide one measure of how the well-being of consumers changes over time. In this chapter, we delve more deeply into the subject of purchasing power by describing a range of indexes that measure changes in purchasing power over time. Because they affect the benefits and costs of numerous social-welfare programs, these indexes are significant tools in setting government policy in the United States.

**What Do Consumers Do?** Before proceeding, we need to be clear about our assumptions regarding consumer behavior, and whether those assumptions are realistic. It is hard to argue with the proposition that consumers have preferences among the various goods and services available to them, and that they face budget constraints which put limits on what they can buy. But we might take issue with the proposition that consumers decide which combinations of goods and services to buy so as to maximize their satisfaction. Are consumers as rational and informed as economists often make them out to be?

We know that consumers do not always make purchasing decisions rationally. Sometimes, for example, they buy on impulse, ignoring or not fully accounting for their budget constraints (and going into debt as a result). Sometimes consumers are unsure about their preferences or are swayed by the consumption decisions of friends and neighbors, or even by changes in mood. And even if consumers do behave rationally, it may not always be feasible for them to account fully for the multitude of prices and choices that they face daily.

Economists have recently been developing models of consumer behavior that incorporate more realistic assumptions about rationality and decision making. This area of research, called *behavioral economics*, has drawn heavily from findings in psychology and related fields. We will discuss some key results from behavioral economics in Chapter 5. At this point we simply want to make it clear that our basic model of consumer behavior necessarily makes some simplifying assumptions. But we also want to emphasize that this model has been extremely successful in explaining much of what we actually observe regarding consumer choice and the characteristics of consumer demand. As a result, this model is a basic "workhorse" of economics. It is used widely, not only in economics, but also in related fields such as finance and marketing.

## 3.1 CONSUMER PREFERENCES

Given both the vast number of goods and services that our industrial economy provides for purchase and the diversity of personal tastes, how can we describe consumer preferences in a coherent way? Let's begin by thinking about how a consumer might compare different groups of items available for purchase. Will one group of items be preferred to another group, or will the consumer be indifferent between the two groups?

### Market Baskets

We use the term *market basket* to refer to such a group of items. Specifically, a **market basket** is a list with specific quantities of one or more goods. A market basket might contain the various food items in a grocery cart. It might also refer to the quantities of food, clothing, and housing that a consumer buys each month. Many economists also use the word *bundle* to mean the same thing as market basket.

• **market basket** (or **bundle**)
List with specific quantities of one or more goods.

How do consumers select market baskets? How do they decide, for example, how much food versus clothing to buy each month? Although selections may occasionally be arbitrary, as we will soon see, consumers usually select market baskets that make them as well off as possible.

Table 3.1 shows several market baskets consisting of various amounts of food and clothing purchased on a monthly basis. The number of food items can be measured in any number of ways: by total number of containers, by number of packages of each item (e.g., milk, meat, etc.), or by number of pounds or grams. Likewise, clothing can be counted as total number of pieces, as number of pieces

| TABLE 3.1 Alternative Market Baskets | | |
|---|---|---|
| **Market Basket** | **Units of Food** | **Units of Clothing** |
| A | 20 | 30 |
| B | 10 | 50 |
| D | 40 | 20 |
| E | 30 | 40 |
| G | 10 | 20 |
| H | 10 | 40 |

*Note:* We will avoid the use of the letters *C* and *F* to represent market baskets, whenever market baskets might be confused with the number of units of food and clothing.

of each type of clothing, or as total weight or volume. Because the method of measurement is largely arbitrary, we will simply describe the items in a market basket in terms of the total number of *units* of each commodity. Market basket *A*, for example, consists of 20 units of food and 30 units of clothing, basket *B* consists of 10 units of food and 50 units of clothing, and so on.

To explain the theory of consumer behavior, we will ask whether consumers *prefer* one market basket to another. Note that the theory assumes that consumers' preferences are consistent and make sense. We explain what we mean by these assumptions in the next subsection.

## Some Basic Assumptions about Preferences

The theory of consumer behavior begins with three basic assumptions about people's preferences for one market basket versus another. We believe that these assumptions hold for most people in most situations.

1. **Completeness:** Preferences are assumed to be *complete*. In other words, consumers can compare and rank all possible baskets. Thus, for any two market baskets *A* and *B*, a consumer will prefer *A* to *B*, will prefer *B* to *A*, or will be indifferent between the two. By *indifferent* we mean that a person will be equally satisfied with either basket. Note that these preferences ignore costs. A consumer might prefer steak to hamburger but buy hamburger because it is cheaper.

2. **Transitivity:** Preferences are *transitive*. Transitivity means that if a consumer prefers basket *A* to basket *B* and basket *B* to basket *C*, then the consumer also prefers *A* to *C*. For example, if a Porsche is preferred to a Cadillac and a Cadillac to a Chevrolet, then a Porsche is also preferred to a Chevrolet. Transitivity is normally regarded as necessary for consumer consistency.

3. **More is better than less:** Goods are assumed to be desirable—i.e., to be *good*. Consequently, *consumers always prefer more of any good to less*. In addition, consumers are never satisfied or satiated; *more is always better, even if just a little better*.[1] This assumption is made for pedagogic reasons; namely, it simplifies the graphical analysis. Of course, some goods, such as air pollution, may be undesirable, and consumers will always prefer less. We ignore these "bads" in the context of our immediate discussion of consumer choice because most consumers would not choose to purchase them. We will, however, discuss them later in the chapter.

These three assumptions form the basis of consumer theory. They do not explain consumer preferences, but they do impose a degree of rationality and reasonableness on them. Building on these assumptions, we will now explore consumer behavior in greater detail.

## Indifference Curves

We can show a consumer's preferences graphically with the use of *indifference curves*. An **indifference curve** *represents all combinations of market baskets that provide a consumer with the same level of satisfaction*. That person is therefore *indifferent* among the market baskets represented by the points graphed on the curve.

• **indifference curve** Curve representing all combinations of market baskets that provide a consumer with the same level of satisfaction.

---

[1]Thus some economists use the term *nonsatiation* to refer to this third assumption.

Given our three assumptions about preferences, we know that a consumer can always indicate either a preference for one market basket over another or indifference between the two. We can then use this information to rank all possible consumption choices. In order to appreciate this principle in graphic form, let's assume that there are only two goods available for consumption: food $F$ and clothing $C$. In this case, all market baskets describe combinations of food and clothing that a person might wish to consume. As we have already seen, Table 3.1 provides some examples of baskets containing various amounts of food and clothing.

In order to graph a consumer's indifference curve, it helps first to graph his or her individual preferences. Figure 3.1 shows the same baskets listed in Table 3.1. The horizontal axis measures the number of units of food purchased each week; the vertical axis measures the number of units of clothing. Market basket $A$, with 20 units of food and 30 units of clothing, is preferred to basket $G$ because $A$ contains more food *and* more clothing (recall our third assumption that more is better than less). Similarly, market basket $E$, which contains even more food and even more clothing, is preferred to $A$. In fact, we can easily compare all market baskets in the two shaded areas (such as $E$ and $G$) to $A$ because they contain either more or less of both food and clothing. Note, however, that $B$ contains more clothing but less food than $A$. Similarly, $D$ contains more food but less clothing than $A$. Therefore, comparisons of market basket $A$ with baskets $B$, $D$, and $H$ are not possible without more information about the consumer's ranking.

This additional information is provided in Figure 3.2, which shows an indifference curve, labeled $U_1$, that passes through points $A$, $B$, and $D$. This curve indicates that the consumer is indifferent among these three market baskets. It tells us that in moving from market basket $A$ to market basket $B$, the consumer feels neither better nor worse off in giving up 10 units of food to obtain 20 additional

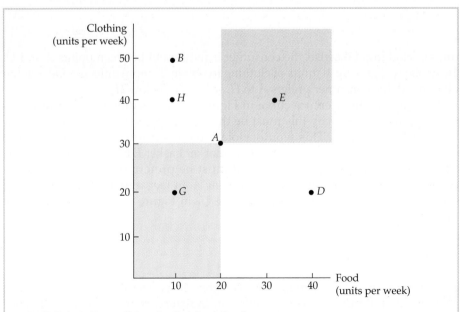

**FIGURE 3.1 Describing Individual Preferences**

Because more of each good is preferred to less, we can compare market baskets in the shaded areas. Basket $A$ is clearly preferred to basket $G$, while $E$ is clearly preferred to $A$. However, $A$ cannot be compared with $B$, $D$, or $H$ without additional information.

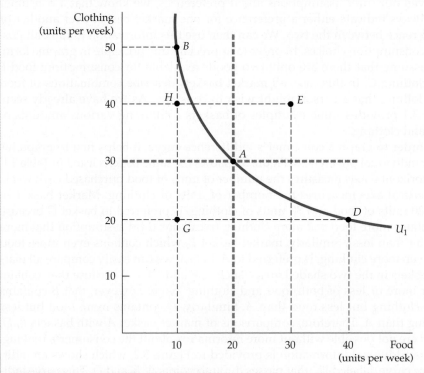

**FIGURE 3.2 An Indifference Curve**

The indifference curve $U_1$ that passes through market basket $A$ shows all baskets that give the consumer the same level of satisfaction as does market basket $A$; these include baskets $B$ and $D$. Our consumer prefers basket $E$, which lies above $U_1$, to $A$, but prefers $A$ to $H$ or $G$, which lie below $U_1$.

units of clothing. Likewise, the consumer is indifferent between points $A$ and $D$: He or she will give up 10 units of clothing to obtain 20 more units of food. On the other hand, the consumer prefers $A$ to $H$, which lies below $U_1$.

Note that the indifference curve in Figure 3.2 slopes downward from left to right. To understand why this must be the case, suppose instead that it sloped upward from $A$ to $E$. This would violate the assumption that more of any commodity is preferred to less. Because market basket $E$ has more of both food and clothing than market basket $A$, it must be preferred to $A$ and therefore cannot be on the same indifference curve as $A$. In fact, any market basket lying *above and to the right of* indifference curve $U_1$ in Figure 3.2 is preferred to any market basket on $U_1$.

## Indifference Maps

• **indifference map** Graph containing a set of indifference curves showing the market baskets among which a consumer is indifferent.

To describe a person's preferences for *all* combinations of food and clothing, we can graph a set of indifference curves called an **indifference map**. Each indifference curve in the map shows the market baskets among which the person is indifferent. Figure 3.3 shows three indifference curves that form part of an indifference map (the entire map includes an infinite number of such curves). Indifference curve $U_3$ generates the highest level of satisfaction, followed by indifference curves $U_2$ and $U_1$.

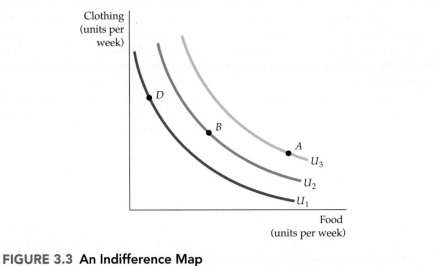

**FIGURE 3.3 An Indifference Map**

An indifference map is a set of indifference curves that describes a person's preferences. Any market basket on indifference curve $U_3$, such as basket $A$, is preferred to any basket on curve $U_2$ (e.g., basket $B$), which in turn is preferred to any basket on $U_1$, such as $D$.

Indifference curves cannot intersect. To see why, we will assume the contrary and see how the resulting graph violates our assumptions about consumer behavior. Figure 3.4 shows two indifference curves, $U_1$ and $U_2$, that intersect at $A$. Because $A$ and $B$ are both on indifference curve $U_1$, the consumer must be indifferent between these two market baskets. Because both $A$ and $D$ lie on

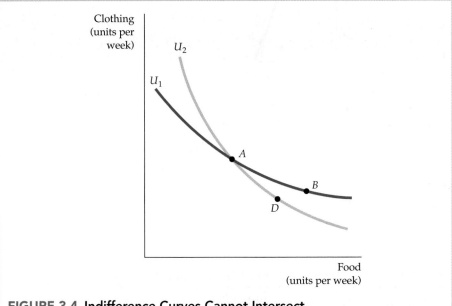

**FIGURE 3.4 Indifference Curves Cannot Intersect**

If indifference curves $U_1$ and $U_2$ intersect, one of the assumptions of consumer theory is violated. According to this diagram, the consumer should be indifferent among market baskets $A$, $B$, and $D$. Yet $B$ should be preferred to $D$ because $B$ has more of both goods.

indifference curve $U_2$, the consumer is also indifferent between these market baskets. Consequently, using the assumption of transitivity, the consumer is also indifferent between $B$ and $D$. But this conclusion can't be true: Market basket $B$ must be preferred to $D$ because it contains more of both food and clothing. Thus, intersecting indifference curves contradicts our assumption that more is preferred to less.

Of course, there are an infinite number of nonintersecting indifference curves, one for every possible level of satisfaction. In fact, every possible market basket (each corresponding to a point on the graph) has an indifference curve passing through it.

## The Shape of Indifference Curves

Recall that indifference curves are all downward sloping. In our example of food and clothing, when the amount of food increases along an indifference curve, the amount of clothing decreases. The fact that indifference curves slope downward follows directly from our assumption that more of a good is better than less. If an indifference curve sloped upward, a consumer would be indifferent between two market baskets even though one of them had more of *both* food and clothing.

As we saw in Chapter 1, people face trade-offs. The shape of an indifference curve describes how a consumer is willing to substitute one good for another. Look, for example, at the indifference curve in Figure 3.5. Starting at

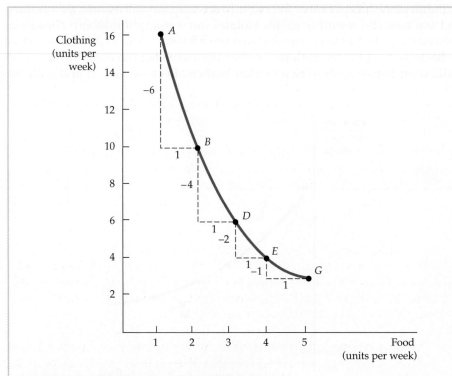

**FIGURE 3.5 The Marginal Rate of Substitution**

The magnitude of the slope of an indifference curve measures the consumer's marginal rate of substitution (MRS) between two goods. In this figure, the MRS between clothing ($C$) and food ($F$) falls from 6 (between $A$ and $B$) to 4 (between $B$ and $D$) to 2 (between $D$ and $E$) to 1 (between $E$ and $G$). When the MRS diminishes along an indifference curve, the curve is convex.

market basket *A* and moving to basket *B*, we see that the consumer is willing to give up 6 units of clothing to obtain 1 extra unit of food. However, in moving from *B* to *D*, he is willing to give up only 4 units of clothing to obtain an additional unit of food; in moving from *D* to *E*, he will give up only 2 units of clothing for 1 unit of food. The more clothing and the less food a person consumes, the more clothing he will give up in order to obtain more food. Similarly, the more food that a person possesses, the less clothing he will give up for more food.

## The Marginal Rate of Substitution

To quantify the amount of one good that a consumer will give up to obtain more of another, we use a measure called the **marginal rate of substitution (MRS)**. *The MRS of food F for clothing C is the maximum amount of clothing that a person is willing to give up to obtain one additional unit of food.* Suppose, for example, the MRS is 3. This means that the consumer will give up 3 units of clothing to obtain 1 additional unit of food. If the MRS is 1/2, the consumer is willing to give up only 1/2 unit of clothing. Thus, the MRS measures *the value that the individual places on 1 extra unit of a good in terms of another.*

Look again at Figure 3.5. Note that clothing appears on the vertical axis and food on the horizontal axis. When we describe the MRS, we must be clear about which good we are giving up and which we are getting more of. To be consistent throughout the book, we will define the MRS in terms of *the amount of the good on the vertical axis that the consumer is willing to give up in order to obtain 1 extra unit of the good on the horizontal axis.* Thus, in Figure 3.5 the MRS refers to the amount of clothing that the consumer is willing to give up to obtain an additional unit of food. If we denote the *change* in clothing by $\Delta C$ and the change in food by $\Delta F$, the MRS can be written as $-\Delta C/\Delta F$. We add the negative sign to make the marginal rate of substitution a positive number (remember that $\Delta C$ is always negative; the consumer *gives up* clothing to obtain additional food).

Thus the MRS at any point is equal in magnitude to the slope of the indifference curve. In Figure 3.5, for example, the MRS between points *A* and *B* is 6: The consumer is willing to give up 6 units of clothing to obtain 1 additional unit of food. Between points *B* and *D*, however, the MRS is 4: With these quantities of food and clothing, the consumer is willing to give up only 4 units of clothing to obtain 1 additional unit of food.

**Convexity**  Also observe in Figure 3.5 that the MRS falls as we move down the indifference curve. This is not a coincidence. This decline in the MRS reflects an important characteristic of consumer preferences. To understand this, we will add an additional assumption regarding consumer preferences to the three that we discussed earlier in this chapter (see page 70):

4. **Diminishing marginal rate of substitution:** Indifference curves are usually *convex*, or bowed inward. The term *convex* means that the slope of the indifference curve *increases* (i.e., becomes less negative) as we move down along the curve. In other words, *an indifference curve is convex if the MRS diminishes along the curve.* The indifference curve in Figure 3.5 is convex. As we have seen, starting with market basket *A* in Figure 3.5 and moving to basket *B*, the MRS of food *F* for clothing *C* is $-\Delta C/\Delta F = -(-6)/1 = 6$. However, when we start at basket *B* and move from *B* to *D*, the MRS falls to 4. If we start at basket *D* and move to *E*, the MRS is 2. Starting at *E* and

---

• **marginal rate of substitution (MRS)**  Maximum amount of a good that a consumer is willing to give up in order to obtain one additional unit of another good.

moving to *G*, we get an MRS of 1. As food consumption increases, the slope of the indifference curve falls in magnitude. Thus the MRS also falls.[2]

Is it reasonable to expect indifference curves to be convex? Yes. As more and more of one good is consumed, we can expect that a consumer will prefer to give up fewer and fewer units of a second good to get additional units of the first one. As we move down the indifference curve in Figure 3.5 and consumption of food increases, the additional satisfaction that a consumer gets from still more food will diminish. Thus, he will give up less and less clothing to obtain additional food.

Another way of describing this principle is to say that consumers generally prefer balanced market baskets to market baskets that contain all of one good and none of another. Note from Figure 3.5 that a relatively balanced market basket containing 3 units of food and 6 units of clothing (basket *D*) generates as much satisfaction as another market basket containing 1 unit of food and 16 units of clothing (basket *A*). It follows that a balanced market basket containing, for example, 6 units of food and 8 units of clothing will generate a higher level of satisfaction.

## Perfect Substitutes and Perfect Complements

The shape of an indifference curve describes the willingness of a consumer to substitute one good for another. An indifference curve with a different shape implies a different willingness to substitute. To see this principle, look at the two somewhat extreme cases illustrated in Figure 3.6.

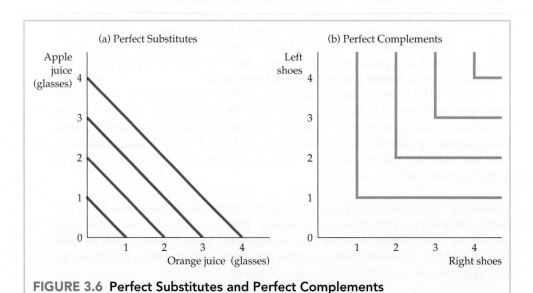

**FIGURE 3.6 Perfect Substitutes and Perfect Complements**

In **(a)**, Bob views orange juice and apple juice as perfect substitutes: He is always indifferent between a glass of one and a glass of the other. In **(b)**, Jane views left shoes and right shoes as perfect complements: An additional left shoe gives her no extra satisfaction unless she also obtains the matching right shoe.

[2]With nonconvex preferences, the MRS increases as the amount of the good measured on the horizontal axis increases along any indifference curve. This unlikely possibility might arise if one or both goods are addictive. For example, the willingness to substitute an addictive drug for other goods might increase as the use of the addictive drug increased.

Figure 3.6(a) shows Bob's preferences for apple juice and orange juice. These two goods are perfect substitutes for Bob because he is entirely indifferent between having a glass of one or the other. In this case, the MRS of apple juice for orange juice is 1: Bob is always willing to trade 1 glass of one for 1 glass of the other. In general, we say that two goods are **perfect substitutes** when the marginal rate of substitution of one for the other is a constant. Indifference curves describing the trade-off between the consumption of the goods are straight lines. The slope of the indifference curves need not be –1 in the case of perfect substitutes. Suppose, for example, that Dan believes that one 16-megabyte memory chip is equivalent to two 8-megabyte chips because both combinations have the same memory capacity. In that case, the slope of Dan's indifference curve will be –2 (with the number of 8-megabyte chips on the vertical axis).

Figure 3.6(b) illustrates Jane's preferences for left shoes and right shoes. For Jane, the two goods are perfect complements because a left shoe will not increase her satisfaction unless she can obtain the matching right shoe. In this case, the MRS of left shoes for right shoes is zero whenever there are more right shoes than left shoes; Jane will not give up any left shoes to get additional right shoes. Correspondingly, the MRS is infinite whenever there are more left shoes than right because Jane will give up all but one of her excess left shoes in order to obtain an additional right shoe. Two goods are **perfect complements** when the indifference curves for both are shaped as right angles.

**Bads** So far, all of our examples have involved products that are "goods"—i.e., cases in which more of a product is preferred to less. However, some things are **bads**: *Less of them is preferred to more.* Air pollution is a bad; asbestos in housing insulation is another. How do we account for bads in the analysis of consumer preferences?

The answer is simple: We redefine the product under study so that consumer tastes are represented as a preference for less of the bad. This reversal turns the bad into a good. Thus, for example, instead of a preference for air pollution, we will discuss the preference for clean air, which we can measure as the degree of reduction in air pollution. Likewise, instead of referring to asbestos as a bad, we will refer to the corresponding good, the removal of asbestos.

With this simple adaptation, all four of the basic assumptions of consumer theory continue to hold, and we are ready to move on to an analysis of consumer budget constraints.

> In § 2.1, we explain that two goods are *substitutes* when an increase in the price of one leads to an increase in the quantity demanded of the other.

• **perfect substitutes** Two goods for which the marginal rate of substitution of one for the other is a constant.

> In §2.1 we explain that goods are *complements* when an increase in the price of one leads to a decrease in the quantity demanded of the other.

• **perfect complements** Two goods for which the MRS is zero or infinite; the indifference curves are shaped as right angles.

• **bad** Good for which less is preferred rather than more.

---

**EXAMPLE 3.1** Designing New Automobiles (I)

Suppose you worked for the Ford Motor Company and had to help plan new models to introduce. Should the new models emphasize interior space or handling? Horsepower or gas mileage? To decide, you would want to know how people value the various attributes of a car, such as power, size, handling, gas mileage, interior features, and so on. The more desirable the attributes, the more people would be willing to pay for a car. However, the better the attributes, the more the car will cost to manufacture. A car with a more powerful engine and more interior space, for example, will cost more to produce than a car with a smaller engine and less space. How should Ford trade off these different attributes and decide which ones to emphasize?

The answer depends in part on the cost of production, but it also depends on consumer preferences. To find out how much people are willing to pay for various attributes, economists and marketing experts look at the prices that people actually do pay for a wide range of models with a range of attributes. For example, if the only difference between two cars is interior space, and if the car with 2 additional cubic feet sells for $1000 more than its smaller counterpart, then interior space will be valued at $500 per cubic foot. By evaluating car purchases over a range of buyers and a range of models, one can estimate the values associated with various attributes, while accounting for the fact that these valuations may diminish as more and more of each attribute is included in a car. One way to obtain such information is by conducting surveys in which individuals are asked about their preferences for various automobiles with different combinations of attributes. Another way is to statistically analyze past consumer purchases of cars whose attributes varied.

One recent statistical study looked at a wide range of Ford models with varying attributes.[3] Figure 3.7 describes two sets of indifference curves, derived from an analysis that varies two attributes: *interior size* (measured in cubic feet) and *acceleration* (measured in horsepower) *for typical consumers of Ford automobiles*. Figure 3.7(a) describes the preferences of typical owners of Ford Mustang coupes. Because they tend to place greater value on acceleration than size, Mustang owners have a high marginal rate of substitution for size versus acceleration; in other words, they are willing to give up quite a bit of size to get better acceleration. Compare these preferences to those of Ford Explorer owners, shown in Figure 3.7(b). They have a lower MRS and will consequently give up a considerable amount of acceleration to get a car with a roomier interior.

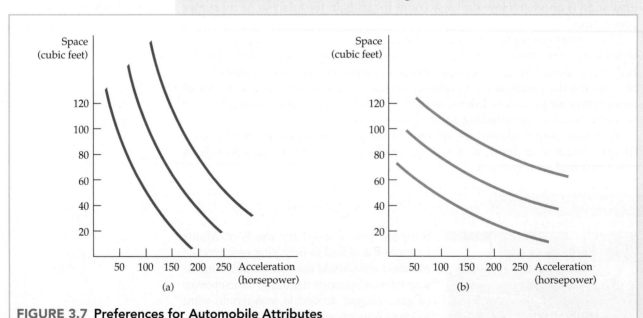

**FIGURE 3.7 Preferences for Automobile Attributes**

Preferences for automobile attributes can be described by indifference curves. Each curve shows the combination of acceleration and interior space that give the same satisfaction. Owners of Ford Mustang coupes **(a)** are willing to give up considerable interior space for additional acceleration. The opposite is true for owners of Ford Explorers **(b)**.

[3]Amil Petrin, "Quantifying the Benefits of New Products: The Case of the Minivan," *Journal of Political Economy* 110 (2002): 705–729. We wish to thank Amil Petrin for providing some of the empirical information in this example.

**Utility** You may have noticed a convenient feature of the theory of consumer behavior as we have described it so far: *It has not been necessary to associate a numerical level of satisfaction with each market basket consumed.* For example, with respect to the three indifference curves in Figure 3.3 (page 73), we know that market basket $A$ (or any other basket on indifference curve $U_3$) gives more satisfaction than any market basket on $U_2$, such as $B$. Likewise, we know that the market baskets on $U_2$ are preferred to those on $U_1$. The indifference curves simply allow us to describe consumer preferences graphically, building on the assumption that consumers can rank alternatives.

We will see that consumer theory relies only on the assumption that consumers can provide relative rankings of market baskets. Nonetheless, it is often useful to assign *numerical values* to individual baskets. Using this numerical approach, we can describe consumer preferences by assigning scores to the levels of satisfaction associated with each indifference curve. The concept is known as utility. In everyday language, the word *utility* has rather broad connotations, meaning, roughly, "benefit" or "well-being." Indeed, people obtain "utility" by getting things that give them pleasure and by avoiding things that give them pain. In the language of economics, the concept of **utility** refers to *the numerical score representing the satisfaction that a consumer gets from a market basket.* In other words, utility is a device used to simplify the ranking of market baskets. If buying three copies of this textbook makes you happier than buying one shirt, then we say that the three books give you more utility than the shirt.

• **utility** Numerical score representing the satisfaction that a consumer gets from a given market basket.

**Utility Functions** A **utility function** is a formula that assigns a level of utility to each market basket. Suppose, for example, that Phil's utility function for food ($F$) and clothing ($C$) is $u(F,C) = F + 2C$. In that case, a market basket consisting of 8 units of food and 3 units of clothing generates a utility of $8 + (2)(3) = 14$. Phil is therefore indifferent between this market basket and a market basket containing 6 units of food and 4 units of clothing $[6 + (2)(4) = 14]$. On the other hand, either market basket is preferred to a third containing 4 units of food and 4 units of clothing. Why? Because this last market basket has a utility level of only $4 + (4)(2) = 12$.

• **utility function** Formula that assigns a level of utility to individual market baskets.

We assign utility levels to market baskets so that if market basket $A$ is preferred to basket $B$, the number will be higher for $A$ than for $B$. For example, market basket $A$ on the highest of three indifference curves $U_3$ might have a utility level of 3, while market basket $B$ on the second-highest indifference curve $U_2$ might have a utility level of 2; on the lowest indifference curve $U_1$, basket $D$ has a utility level of 1. Thus the utility function provides the same information about preferences that an indifference map does: Both order consumer choices in terms of levels of satisfaction.

Let's examine one particular utility function in some detail. The *utility function* $u(F,C) = FC$ tells us that the level of satisfaction obtained from consuming $F$ units of food and $C$ units of clothing is the product of $F$ and $C$. Figure 3.8 shows indifference curves associated with this function. The graph was drawn by initially choosing one particular market basket—say, $F = 5$ and $C = 5$ at point $A$. This market basket generates a utility level $U_1$ of 25. Then the indifference curve (also called an *isoutility* curve) was drawn by finding all market baskets for which $FC = 25$ (e.g., $F = 10$, $C = 2.5$ at point $B$; $F = 2.5$, $C = 10$ at point $D$). The second indifference curve, $U_2$, contains all market baskets for which $FC = 50$ and the third, $U_3$, all market baskets for which $FC = 100$.

It is important to note that the numbers attached to the indifference curves are for convenience only. Suppose the utility function were changed to $u(F,C) = 4FC$. Consider any market basket that previously generated a utility level of 25—say,

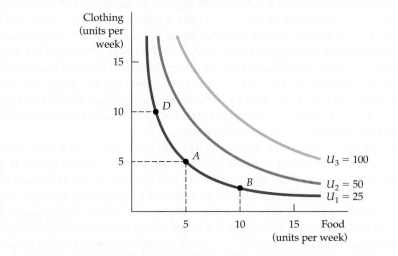

**FIGURE 3.8** Utility Functions and Indifference Curves

A utility function can be represented by a set of indifference curves, each with a numerical indicator. This figure shows three indifference curves (with utility levels of 25, 50, and 100, respectively) associated with the utility function $FC$.

$F = 5$ and $C = 5$. Now the level of utility has increased, by a factor of 4, to 100. Thus the indifference curve labeled 25 looks the same, although it should now be labeled 100 rather than 25. In fact, the only difference between the indifference curves associated with the utility function $4FC$ and the utility function $FC$ is that the curves are numbered 100, 200, and 400, rather than 25, 50, and 100. It is important to stress that the utility function is simply a way of *ranking* different market baskets; the *magnitude* of the utility difference between any two market baskets does not really tell us anything. The fact that $U_3$ has a level of utility of 100 and $U_2$ has a level of 50 does not mean that market baskets on $U_3$ generate twice as much satisfaction as those on $U_2$. This is so because we have no means of objectively measuring a person's satisfaction or level of well-being from the consumption of a market basket. Thus whether we use indifference curves or a measure of utility, we know only that $U_3$ is better than $U_2$ and that $U_2$ is better than $U_1$. We do not, however, know by *how much* one is preferred to the other.

**Ordinal versus Cardinal Utility** The three indifference curves in Figure 3.3 (page 73) provide a ranking of market baskets that is ordered, or *ordinal*. For this reason, a utility function that generates a ranking of market baskets is called an **ordinal utility function**. The ranking associated with the ordinal utility function places market baskets in the order of most to least preferred. However, as explained above, it does not indicate by *how much* one is preferred to another. We know, for example, that any market basket on $U_3$, such as $A$, is preferred to any on $U_2$, such as $B$. However, the *amount* by which $A$ is preferred to $B$ (and $B$ to $D$) is not revealed by the indifference map or by the ordinal utility function that generates it.

When working with ordinal utility functions, we must be careful to avoid a trap. Suppose that Juan's ordinal utility function attaches a utility level of 5 to a copy of this textbook; meanwhile Maria's utility function attaches a level of 10. Will Maria be happier than Juan if each of them gets a copy of this book? We

• **ordinal utility function** Utility function that generates a ranking of market baskets in order of most to least preferred.

don't know. Because these numerical values are arbitrary, interpersonal comparisons of utility are impossible.

When economists first studied utility and utility functions, they hoped that individual preferences could be quantified or measured in terms of basic units and could therefore provide a ranking that allowed for interpersonal comparisons. Using this approach, we could say that Maria gets twice as much satisfaction as Juan from a copy of this book. Or if we found that having a second copy increased Juan's utility level to 10, we could say that his happiness has doubled. If the numerical values assigned to market baskets did have meaning in this way, we would say that the numbers provided a *cardinal* ranking of alternatives. A utility function that describes *by how much* one market basket is preferred to another is called a **cardinal utility function**. Unlike ordinal utility functions, a cardinal utility function attaches to market baskets numerical values that cannot arbitrarily be doubled or tripled without altering the differences between the values of various market baskets.

Unfortunately, we have no way of telling whether a person gets twice as much satisfaction from one market basket as from another. Nor do we know whether one person gets twice as much satisfaction as another from consuming the same basket. (Could *you* tell whether you get twice as much satisfaction from consuming one thing versus another?) Fortunately, this constraint is unimportant. Because our objective is to understand consumer behavior, all that matters is knowing how consumers rank different baskets. Therefore, we will work only with ordinal utility functions. This approach is sufficient for understanding both how individual consumer decisions are made and what this knowledge implies about the characteristics of consumer demand.

**• cardinal utility function**
Utility function describing by how much one market basket is preferred to another.

---

**EXAMPLE 3.2**     Can Money Buy Happiness?

Economists use the term *utility* to represent a measure of the satisfaction or happiness that individuals get from the consumption of goods and services. Because a higher income allows one to consume more goods and services, we say that utility increases with income. But does greater income and consumption really translate into greater happiness? Research comparing various measures of happiness suggests that the answer is a qualified yes.[4]

In one study, an ordinal scale for happiness was derived from the answer to the following question. "How satisfied are you at present with your life, all things considered?"[5] Possible responses ran on a scale from 0 (completely dissatisfied) to 10 (completely satisfied). Income was found to be a very strong predictor of happiness (another strong predictor was whether a person was employed or not). On average, as income increased by one percent, the satisfaction score increased one half a point. Knowing that there is a positive relationship between utility or satisfaction and income, it is reasonable to assign utility values to the

---

[4]For a review of the relevant literature which underlies this example, see Raphael DiTella and Robert MacCulloch, "Some Uses of Happiness Data in Economics," *Journal of Economic Perspectives* 20 (Winter 2006): 25–46.

[5]Paul Frijters, John P. Haisken-Denew, and Michael A. Shields, "Money Does Matter! Evidence from Increasing Real Income and Life Satisfaction in East Germany Following Reunification," *American Economic Review* 94 (June 2004): 730–40.

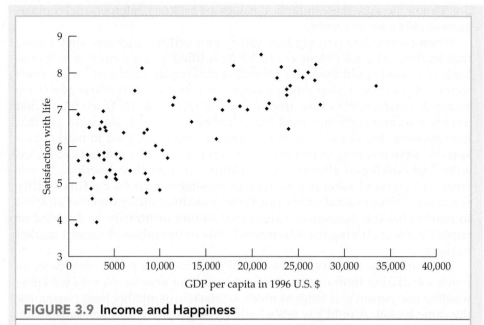

**FIGURE 3.9 Income and Happiness**

A cross-country comparison shows that individuals living in countries with higher GDP per capita are on average happier than those living in countries with lower per-capita GDP.

baskets of goods and services that consumers buy. Whether that relationship is cardinal or ordinal remains an ongoing debate.

Let's take this inquiry one step further. Can one compare levels of happiness *across* as well as *within* countries? Once again, the evidence says yes. In a separate survey of individuals in 67 countries, a team of researchers asked: "All things considered, how satisfied are you with your life as a whole these days?" Responses were given on a ten-point scale, with 1 representing the most dissatisfied and 10 the most satisfied.[6] Income was measured by each country's per-capita gross domestic product in U.S. dollars. Figure 3.9 shows the results, with each data point representing a different country. You can see that as we move from poor countries with incomes below $5000 per capita to those with incomes closer to $10,000 per capita, satisfaction increases substantially. Once we move past the $10,000 level, the index scale of satisfaction increases at a lower rate.

Comparisons across countries are difficult because there are likely to be many other factors that explain satisfaction besides income (e.g., health, climate, political environment, human rights, etc.). Moreover, it is possible that the relationship between income and satisfaction goes two ways: Although higher incomes generate more satisfaction, greater satisfaction offers greater motivation for individuals to work hard and generate higher incomes. Interestingly, even when studies account for other factors, the positive relationship between income and satisfaction remains.

---

[6]Ronald Inglehart et al., *European and World Values Surveys Four-Wave Integrated Data File, 1981–2004 (2006)*. Available online: **http://www.worldvaluessurvey.org**.

## 3.2 BUDGET CONSTRAINTS

So far, we have focused only on the first element of consumer theory— consumer preferences. We have seen how indifference curves (or, alternatively, utility functions) can be used to describe how consumers value various baskets of goods. Now we turn to the second element of consumer theory: the **budget constraints** that consumers face as a result of their limited incomes.

• **budget constraints** Constraints that consumers face as a result of limited incomes.

### The Budget Line

To see how a budget constraint limits a consumer's choices, let's consider a situation in which a woman has a fixed amount of income, $I$, that can be spent on food and clothing. Let $F$ be the amount of food purchased and $C$ be the amount of clothing. We will denote the prices of the two goods $P_F$ and $P_C$. In that case, $P_F F$ (i.e., price of food times the quantity) is the amount of money spent on food and $P_C C$ the amount of money spent on clothing.

The **budget line** indicates *all combinations of F and C for which the total amount of money spent is equal to income*. Because we are considering only two goods (and ignoring the possibility of saving), our hypothetical consumer will spend her entire income on food and clothing. As a result, the combinations of food and clothing that she can buy will all lie on this line:

• **budget line** All combinations of goods for which the total amount of money spent is equal to income.

$$P_F F + P_C C = I \qquad (3.1)$$

Suppose, for example, that our consumer has a weekly income of $80, the price of food is $1 per unit, and the price of clothing is $2 per unit. Table 3.2 shows various combinations of food and clothing that she can purchase each week with her $80. If her entire budget were allocated to clothing, the most that she could buy would be 40 units (at a price of $2 per unit), as represented by market basket $A$. If she spent her entire budget on food, she could buy 80 units (at $1 per unit), as given by market basket $G$. Market baskets $B$, $D$, and $E$ show three additional ways in which her $80 could be spent on food and clothing.

Figure 3.10 shows the budget line associated with the market baskets given in Table 3.2. Because giving up a unit of clothing saves $2 and buying a unit of food costs $1, the amount of clothing given up for food along the budget line must be the same everywhere. As a result, the budget line is a straight line from point $A$ to point $G$. In this particular case, the budget line is given by the equation $F + 2C = \$80$.

| TABLE 3.2   Market Baskets and the Budget Line | | | |
|---|---|---|---|
| Market Basket | Food (F) | Clothing (C) | Total Spending |
| A | 0 | 40 | $80 |
| B | 20 | 30 | $80 |
| D | 40 | 20 | $80 |
| E | 60 | 10 | $80 |
| G | 80 | 0 | $80 |

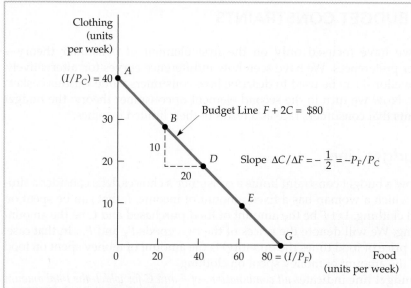

**FIGURE 3.10 A Budget Line**

A budget line describes the combinations of goods that can be purchased given the consumer's income and the prices of the goods. Line *AG* (which passes through points *B*, *D*, and *E*) shows the budget associated with an income of $80, a price of food of $P_F = \$1$ per unit, and a price of clothing of $P_C = \$2$ per unit. The slope of the budget line (measured between points *B* and *D*) is $-P_F/P_C = -10/20 = -1/2$.

The intercept of the budget line is represented by basket *A*. As our consumer moves along the line from basket *A* to basket *G*, she spends less on clothing and more on food. It is easy to see that the extra clothing which must be given up to consume an additional unit of food is given by the ratio of the price of food to the price of clothing ($\$1/\$2 = 1/2$). Because clothing costs $2 per unit and food only $1 per unit, 1/2 unit of clothing must be given up to get 1 unit of food. In Figure 3.10, the slope of the line, $\Delta C/\Delta F = -1/2$, measures the relative cost of food and clothing.

Using equation (3.1), we can see how much of *C* must be given up to consume more of *F*. We divide both sides of the equation by $P_C$ and then solve for *C*:

$$C = (I/P_C) - (P_F/P_C)F \qquad (3.2)$$

Equation (3.2) is the equation for a straight line; it has a vertical intercept of $I/P_C$ and a slope of $-(P_F/P_C)$.

The slope of the budget line, $-(P_F/P_C)$, is *the negative of the ratio of the prices of the two goods*. The magnitude of the slope tells us the rate at which the two goods can be substituted for each other without changing the total amount of money spent. The vertical intercept $(I/P_C)$ represents the maximum amount of *C* that can be purchased with income *I*. Finally, the horizontal intercept $(I/P_F)$ tells us how many units of *F* can be purchased if all income were spent on *F*.

## The Effects of Changes in Income and Prices

We have seen that the budget line depends both on income and on the prices of the goods, $P_F$ and $P_C$. But of course prices and income often change. Let's see how such changes affect the budget line.

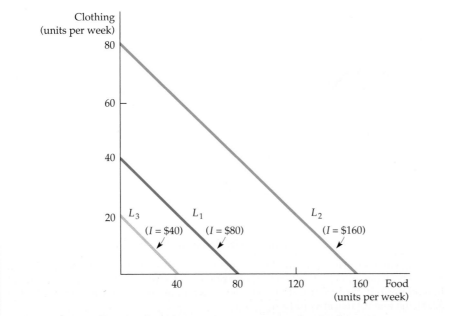

**FIGURE 3.11 Effects of a Change in Income on the Budget Line**

A change in income (with prices unchanged) causes the budget line to shift parallel to the original line ($L_1$). When the income of \$80 (on $L_1$) is increased to \$160, the budget line shifts outward to $L_2$. If the income falls to \$40, the line shifts inward to $L_3$.

**Income Changes** What happens to the budget line when income changes? From the equation for the straight line (3.2), we can see that a change in income alters the vertical intercept of the budget line but does not change the slope (because the price of neither good changed). Figure 3.11 shows that if income is doubled (from \$80 to \$160), the budget line shifts outward, from budget line $L_1$ to budget line $L_2$. Note, however, that $L_2$ remains parallel to $L_1$. If she desires, our consumer can now double her purchases of both food and clothing. Likewise, if her income is cut in half (from \$80 to \$40), the budget line shifts inward, from $L_1$ to $L_3$.

**Price Changes** What happens to the budget line if the price of one good changes but the price of the other does not? We can use the equation $C = (I/P_C) - (P_F/P_C)F$ to describe the effects of a change in the price of food on the budget line. Suppose the price of food falls by half, from \$1 to \$0.50. In that case, the vertical intercept of the budget line remains unchanged, although the slope changes from $-P_F/P_C = -\$1/\$2 = -\$1/2$ to $-\$0.50/\$2 = -\$1/4$. In Figure 3.12, we obtain the new budget line $L_2$ by rotating the original budget line $L_1$ outward, pivoting from the $C$-intercept. This rotation makes sense because a person who consumes only clothing and no food is unaffected by the price change. However, someone who consumes a large amount of food will experience an increase in his purchasing power. Because of the decline in the price of food, the maximum amount of food that can be purchased has doubled.

On the other hand, when the price of food doubles from \$1 to \$2, the budget line rotates inward to line $L_3$ because the person's purchasing power has diminished. Again, a person who consumed only clothing would be unaffected by the food price increase.

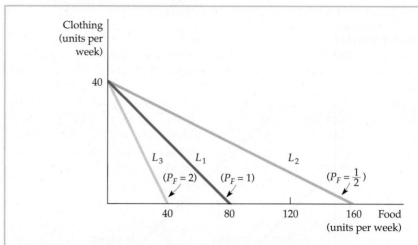

**FIGURE 3.12 Effects of a Change in Price on the Budget Line**

A change in the price of one good (with income unchanged) causes the budget line to rotate about one intercept. When the price of food falls from $1.00 to $0.50, the budget line rotates outward from $L_1$ to $L_2$. However, when the price increases from $1.00 to $2.00, the line rotates inward from $L_1$ to $L_3$.

What happens if the prices of both food and clothing change, but in a way that leaves the *ratio* of the two prices unchanged? Because the slope of the budget line is equal to the ratio of the two prices, the slope will remain the same. The intercept of the budget line must shift so that the new line is parallel to the old one. For example, if the prices of both goods fall by half, then the slope of the budget line does not change. However, both intercepts double, and the budget line is shifted outward.

This exercise tells us something about the determinants of a consumer's *purchasing power*—her ability to generate utility through the purchase of goods and services. Purchasing power is determined not only by income, but also by prices. For example, our consumer's purchasing power can double either because her income doubles *or* because the prices of all the goods that she buys fall by half.

Finally, consider what happens if everything doubles—the prices of both food and clothing *and* the consumer's income. (This can happen in an inflationary economy.) Because both prices have doubled, the ratio of the prices has not changed; neither, therefore, has the slope of the budget line. Because the price of clothing has doubled along with income, the maximum amount of clothing that can be purchased (represented by the vertical intercept of the budget line) is unchanged. The same is true for food. Therefore, inflationary conditions in which all prices and income levels rise proportionately will not affect the consumer's budget line or purchasing power.

## 3.3 CONSUMER CHOICE

Given preferences and budget constraints, we can now determine how individual consumers choose how much of each good to buy. We assume that consumers make this choice in a rational way—that they choose goods to *maximize the satisfaction they can achieve, given the limited budget available to them.*

The maximizing market basket must satisfy two conditions:

1. *It must be located on the budget line.* To see why, note that any market basket to the left of and below the budget line leaves some income unallocated—income which, if spent, could increase the consumer's satisfaction. Of course, consumers can—and often do—save some of their incomes for future consumption. In that case, the choice is not just between food and clothing, but between consuming food or clothing now and consuming food or clothing in the future. At this point, however, we will keep things simple by assuming that all income is spent now. Note also that any market basket to the right of and above the budget line cannot be purchased with available income. Thus, the only rational and feasible choice is a basket on the budget line.

2. *It must give the consumer the most preferred combination of goods and services.*

These two conditions reduce the problem of maximizing consumer satisfaction to one of picking an appropriate point on the budget line.

In our food and clothing example, as with any two goods, we can graphically illustrate the solution to the consumer's choice problem. Figure 3.13 shows how the problem is solved. Here, three indifference curves describe a consumer's preferences for food and clothing. Remember that of the three curves, the outermost curve, $U_3$, yields the greatest amount of satisfaction, curve $U_2$ the next greatest amount, and curve $U_1$ the least.

Note that point $B$ on indifference curve $U_1$ is not the most preferred choice, because a reallocation of income in which more is spent on food and less on

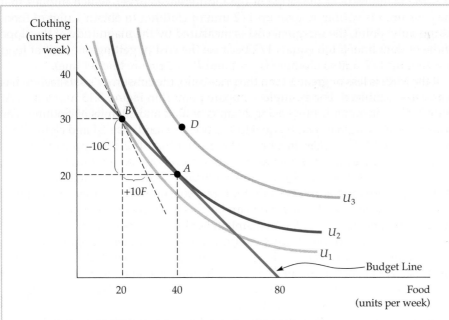

**FIGURE 3.13 Maximizing Consumer Satisfaction**

A consumer maximizes satisfaction by choosing market basket $A$. At this point, the budget line and indifference curve $U_2$ are tangent, and no higher level of satisfaction (e.g., market basket $D$) can be attained. At $A$, the point of maximization, the MRS between the two goods equals the price ratio. At $B$, however, because the MRS [− (−10/10) = 1] is greater than the price ratio (1/2), satisfaction is not maximized.

clothing can increase the consumer's satisfaction. In particular, by moving to point $A$, the consumer spends the same amount of money and achieves the increased level of satisfaction associated with indifference curve $U_2$. In addition, note that baskets located to the right and above indifference curve $U_2$, like the basket associated with $D$ on indifference curve $U_3$, achieve a higher level of satisfaction but cannot be purchased with the available income. Therefore, $A$ maximizes the consumer's satisfaction.

We see from this analysis that the basket which maximizes satisfaction must lie on the highest indifference curve that touches the budget line. Point $A$ is the point of tangency between indifference curve $U_2$ and the budget line. At $A$, the slope of the budget line is exactly equal to the slope of the indifference curve. Because the MRS ($-\Delta C / \Delta F$) is the negative of the slope of the indifference curve, we can say that satisfaction is maximized (given the budget constraint) at the point where

$$\text{MRS} = P_F / P_C \tag{3.3}$$

This is an important result: Satisfaction is maximized when *the marginal rate of substitution* (of $F$ for $C$) *is equal to the ratio of the prices* (of $F$ to $C$). Thus the consumer can obtain maximum satisfaction by adjusting his consumption of goods $F$ and $C$ so that the MRS equals the price ratio.

The condition given in equation (3.3) illustrates the kinds of optimization conditions that arise in economics. In this instance, satisfaction is maximized when the **marginal benefit**—the benefit associated with the consumption of one additional unit of food—is equal to the **marginal cost**—the cost of the additional unit of food. The marginal benefit is measured by the MRS. At point $A$, it equals $1/2$ (the magnitude of the slope of the indifference curve), which implies that the consumer is willing to give up $1/2$ unit of clothing to obtain 1 unit of food. At the same point, the marginal cost is measured by the magnitude of the slope of the budget line; it too equals $1/2$ because the cost of getting one unit of food is giving up $1/2$ unit of clothing ($P_F = 1$ and $P_C = 2$ on the budget line).

If the MRS is less or greater than the price ratio, the consumer's satisfaction has not been maximized. For example, compare point $B$ in Figure 3.13 to point $A$. At point $B$, the consumer is purchasing 20 units of food and 30 units of clothing. The price ratio (or marginal cost) is equal to $1/2$ because food costs \$1 and clothing \$2. However, the MRS (or marginal benefit) is greater than $1/2$; it is approximately 1. As a result, the consumer is able to substitute 1 unit of food for 1 unit of clothing without loss of satisfaction. Because food is cheaper than clothing, it is in her interest to buy more food and less clothing. If our consumer purchases 1 less unit of clothing, for example, the \$2 saved can be allocated to two units of food, even though only one unit is needed to maintain her level of satisfaction.

The reallocation of the budget continues in this manner (moving along the budget line), until we reach point $A$, where the price ratio of $1/2$ just equals the MRS of $1/2$. This point implies that our consumer is willing to trade one unit of clothing for two units of food. Only when the condition MRS $= 1/2 = P_F / P_C$ holds is she maximizing her satisfaction.

The result that the MRS equals the price ratio is deceptively powerful. Imagine two consumers who have just purchased various quantities of food and clothing. If both are maximizing, you can tell the value of each person's MRS by looking at the prices of the two goods. What you cannot tell, however, is the quantity of each good purchased, because that decision is determined by their individual preferences. If the two consumers have different tastes, they will consume different quantities of food and clothing, even though each MRS is the same.

• **marginal benefit** Benefit from the consumption of one additional unit of a good.

• **marginal cost** Cost of one additional unit of a good.

EXAMPLE 3.3 Designing New Automobiles (II)

Our analysis of consumer choice allows us to see how different preferences of consumer groups for automobiles can affect their purchasing decisions. Following up on Example 3.1 (page 77), we consider two groups of consumers planning to buy new cars. Suppose that each consumer has an overall car budget of $20,000, but has decided to allocate $10,000 to interior size and acceleration and $10,000 to all the other attributes of a new car. Each group, however, has different preferences for size and acceleration.

Figure 3.14 shows the car-buying budget constraint faced by individuals in each group. Those in the first group, who are typical of Ford Mustang coupe owners with preferences similar to those in Figure 3.7 (a page 78), prefer acceleration to size. By finding the point of tangency between a typical individual's indifference curve and the budget constraint, we see that consumers in this group would prefer to buy a car whose acceleration was worth $7000 and whose size was worth $3000. Individuals in the second group, who are typical of Ford Explorer users, would prefer cars with $2500 worth of acceleration and $7500 worth of size.[7]

We have simplified matters for this example by considering only two attributes. In practice, an automobile company will use marketing and statistical studies to learn how different groups of consumers value a broad set of attributes.

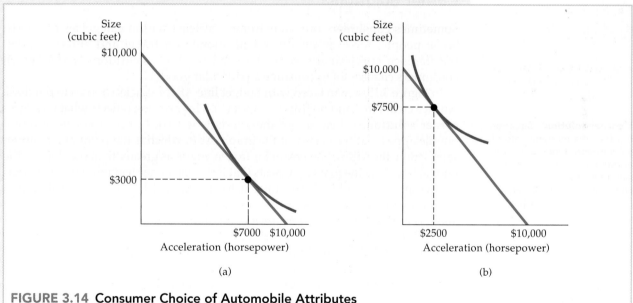

(a)            (b)

**FIGURE 3.14** **Consumer Choice of Automobile Attributes**

The consumers in **(a)** are willing to trade off a considerable amount of interior space for some additional acceleration. Given a budget constraint, they will choose a car that emphasizes acceleration. The opposite is true for consumers in **(b)**.

---

[7]The first set of indifference curves for the Ford Mustang coupe will be of the following form: $U$ (level of utility) $= b_0$ (constant) $+ b_1{}^*S$ (space in cubic feet) $* b_2{}^*S^2 + b_3{}^*H$ (horsepower) $+ b_4{}^*H^2 + b_5{}^*O$ (a list of other attributes). Each indifference curve represents the combinations of $S$ and $H$ that generate the same level of utility. The comparable relationship for the Ford Explorer will have the same form, but different $b$'s.

Combined with information about how these attributes will affect manufacturing costs, the company can design a production and marketing plan.

In the context of our example, one potentially profitable option is to appeal to both groups of consumers by manufacturing a model emphasizing acceleration to a slightly lesser degree than preferred by those in Figure 3.14(a). A second option is to produce a relatively large number of cars that emphasize size and a smaller number emphasizing acceleration.

Knowledge about the preferences of each group (i.e., the actual indifference curves), along with information about the number of consumers in each, would help the firm make a sensible business decision. In fact, an exercise similar to the one we've described here was carried out by General Motors in a survey of a large number of automobile buyers.[8] Some of the results were expected. For example, households with children tended to prefer functionality over style and so tended to buy minivans rather than sedans and sporty cars. Rural households, on the other hand, tended to purchase pickups and all-wheel drives. More interesting was the strong correlation between age and attribute preferences. Older consumers tended to prefer larger and heavier cars with more safety features and accessories (e.g., power windows and steering). Further, younger consumers preferred greater horsepower and more stylish cars.

## Corner Solutions

Sometimes consumers buy in extremes, at least within categories of goods. Some people, for example, spend no money on travel and entertainment. Indifference curve analysis can be used to show conditions under which consumers choose not to consume a particular good.

In Figure 3.15, a man faced with budget line $AB$ for snacks chooses to purchase only ice cream ($IC$) and no frozen yogurt ($Y$). This decision reflects what is called a **corner solution**. When one of the goods is not consumed, the consumption bundle appears at the corner of the graph. At $B$, which is the point of maximum satisfaction, the MRS of ice cream for frozen yogurt is greater than the slope of the budget line. This inequality suggests that if the consumer had more frozen yogurt to give up, he would gladly trade it for additional ice cream. At this point, however, our consumer is already consuming all ice cream and no frozen yogurt, and it is impossible to consume *negative* amounts of frozen yogurt.

*When a corner solution arises, the consumer's MRS does not necessarily equal the price ratio.* Unlike the condition expressed in equation (3.3), the necessary condition for satisfaction to be maximized when choosing between ice cream and frozen yogurt in a corner solution is given by the following inequality.[9]

$$\text{MRS} \geq P_{IC}/P_Y \qquad (3.4)$$

This inequality would, of course, be reversed if the corner solution were at point $A$ rather than $B$. In either case, we can see that the marginal benefit–marginal

• **corner solution** Situation in which the marginal rate of substitution of one good for another in a chosen market basket is not equal to the slope of the budget line.

---

[8]The survey design and the results are described in Steven Berry, James Levinsohn, and Ariel Pakes, "Differentiated Products Demand Systems from a Combination of Micro and Macro Data: The New Car Market," *Journal of Political Economy*, 112 (February 2004): 68–105.

[9]Strict equality could hold if the slope of the budget constraint happened to equal the slope of the indifference curve—a condition that is unlikely.

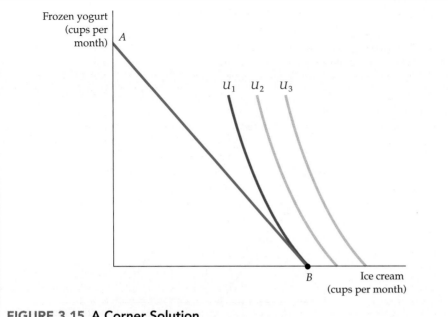

**FIGURE 3.15 A Corner Solution**

When the consumer's marginal rate of substitution is not equal to the price ratio for all levels of consumption, a corner solution arises. The consumer maximizes satisfaction by consuming only one of the two goods. Given budget line $AB$, the highest level of satisfaction is achieved at $B$ on indifference curve $U_1$, where the MRS (of ice cream for frozen yogurt) is greater than the ratio of the price of ice cream to the price of frozen yogurt.

cost equality that we described in the previous section holds only when positive quantities of all goods are consumed.

An important lesson here is that predictions about how much of a product consumers will purchase when faced with changing economic conditions depend on the nature of consumer preferences for that product and related products and on the slope of the consumer's budget line. If the MRS of ice cream for frozen yogurt is substantially greater than the price ratio, as in Figure 3.15, then a small decrease in the price of frozen yogurt will not alter the consumer's choice; he will still choose to consume only ice cream. But if the price of frozen yogurt falls far enough, the consumer could quickly choose to consume a lot of frozen yogurt.

**EXAMPLE 3.4**     A College Trust Fund

Jane Doe's parents have provided a trust fund for her college education. Jane, who is 18, can receive the entire trust fund on the condition that she spend it only on education. The fund is a welcome gift but perhaps not as welcome as an unrestricted trust. To see why Jane feels this way, consider Figure 3.16, in which dollars per year spent on education are shown on the horizontal axis and dollars spent on other forms of consumption on the vertical.

The budget line that Jane faces before being awarded the trust is given by line $PQ$. The trust fund expands the budget line outward as long as the full amount of the fund, shown by distance $PB$, is spent on education. By accepting the trust

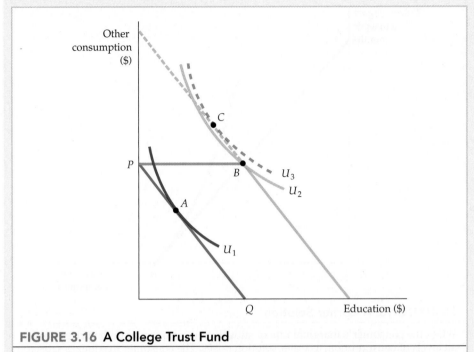

**FIGURE 3.16 A College Trust Fund**

When given a college trust fund that must be spent on education, the student moves from $A$ to $B$, a corner solution. If, however, the trust fund could be spent on other consumption as well as education, the student would be better off at $C$.

fund and going to college, Jane increases her satisfaction, moving from $A$ on indifference curve $U_1$ to $B$ on indifference curve $U_2$.

Note that $B$ represents a corner solution because Jane's marginal rate of substitution of education for other consumption is lower than the relative price of other consumption. Jane would prefer to spend a portion of the trust fund on other goods in addition to education. Without restriction on the trust fund, she would move to $C$ on indifference curve $U_3$, decreasing her spending on education (perhaps going to a junior college rather than a four-year college) but increasing her spending on items that she enjoys more than education.

Recipients usually prefer unrestricted to restricted trusts. Restricted trusts are popular, however, because they allow parents to control children's expenditures in ways that they believe are in the children's long-run best interests.

## 3.4 REVEALED PREFERENCE

In Section 3.1, we saw how an individual's preferences could be represented by a series of indifference curves. Then in Section 3.3, we saw how preferences, given budget constraints, determine choices. Can this process be reversed? If we know the choices that a consumer has made, can we determine his or her preferences?

We can if we have information about a sufficient number of choices that have been made when prices and income levels varied. The basic idea is simple. *If a consumer chooses one market basket over another, and if the chosen market*

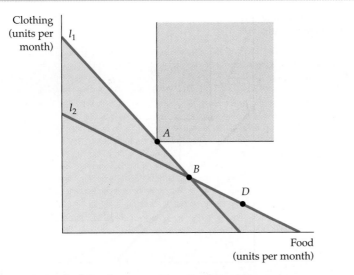

**FIGURE 3.17 Revealed Preference: Two Budget Lines**

If an individual facing budget line $l_1$ chose market basket $A$ rather than market basket $B$, $A$ is revealed to be preferred to $B$. Likewise, the individual facing budget line $l_2$ chooses market basket $B$, which is then revealed to be preferred to market basket $D$. Whereas $A$ is preferred to all market baskets in the green-shaded area, all baskets in the pink-shaded area are preferred to $A$.

*basket is more expensive than the alternative, then the consumer must prefer the chosen market basket.*

Suppose that an individual, facing the budget constraint given by line $l_1$ in Figure 3.17, chooses market basket $A$. Let's compare $A$ to baskets $B$ and $D$. Because the individual could have purchased basket $B$ (and all baskets below line $l_1$) and did not, we say that $A$ is *preferred to* $B$.

It might seem at first glance that we cannot make a direct comparison between baskets $A$ and $D$ because $D$ is not on $l_1$. But suppose the relative prices of food and clothing change, so that the new budget line is $l_2$ and the individual then chooses market basket $B$. Because $D$ lies on budget line $l_2$ and was not chosen, $B$ is preferred to $D$ (and to all baskets below line $l_2$). Because $A$ is preferred to $B$ and $B$ is preferred to $D$, we conclude that $A$ is preferred to $D$. Furthermore, note in Figure 3.17 that basket $A$ is preferred to all of the baskets that appear in the green-shaded areas. However, because food and clothing are "goods" rather than "bads," all baskets that lie in the pink-shaded area in the rectangle above and to the right of $A$ are preferred to $A$. Thus, the indifference curve passing through $A$ must lie in the unshaded area.

Given more information about choices when prices and income levels vary, we can get a better fix on the shape of the indifference curve. Consider Figure 3.18. Suppose that facing line $l_3$ (which was chosen to pass through $A$), the individual chooses market basket $E$. Because $E$ was chosen even though $A$ was equally expensive (it lies on the same budget line), $E$ is preferred to $A$, as are all points in the rectangle above and to the right of $E$. Now suppose that facing line $l_4$ (which passes through $A$), the individual chooses market basket $G$. Because $G$ was chosen and $A$ was not, $G$ is preferred to $A$, as are all market baskets above and to the right of $G$.

We can go further by making use of the assumption that indifference curves are convex. In that case, because $E$ is preferred to $A$, all market baskets above

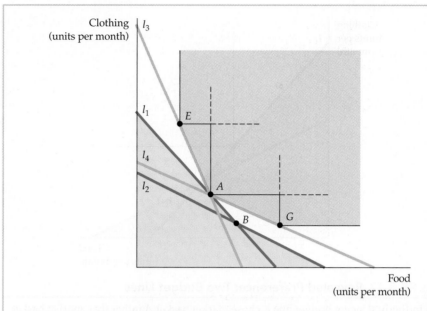

**FIGURE 3.18 Revealed Preference: Four Budget Lines**

Facing budget line $l_3$ the individual chooses $E$, which is revealed to be preferred to $A$ (because $A$ could have been chosen). Likewise, facing line $l_4$, the individual chooses $G$ which is also revealed to be preferred to $A$. Whereas $A$ is preferred to all market baskets in the green-shaded area, all market baskets in the pink-shaded area are preferred to $A$.

and to the right of line $AE$ in Figure 3.18 must be preferred to $A$. Otherwise, the indifference curve passing through $A$ would have to pass through a point above and to the right of $AE$ and then fall below the line at $E$—in which case the indifference curve would not be convex. By a similar argument, all points on $AG$ or above are also preferred to $A$. Therefore, the indifference curve must lie within the unshaded area.

The revealed preference approach is valuable as a means of checking whether individual choices are consistent with the assumptions of consumer theory. As Example 3.5 shows, revealed preference analysis can help us understand the implications of choices that consumers must make in particular circumstances.

**EXAMPLE 3.5** Revealed Preference for Recreation

A health club has been offering the use of its facilities to anyone who is willing to pay an hourly fee. Now the club decides to alter its pricing policy by charging both an annual membership fee and a lower hourly fee. Does this new financial arrangement make individuals better off or worse off than they were under the old arrangement? The answer depends on people's preferences.

Suppose that Roberta has $100 of income available each week for recreational activities, including exercise, movies, restaurant meals, and so on. When the

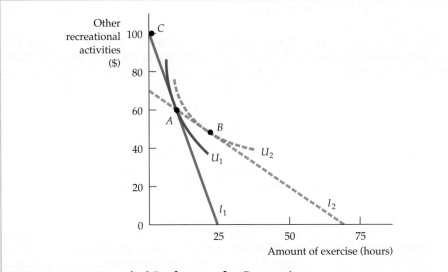

**FIGURE 3.19 Revealed Preference for Recreation**

When facing budget line $l_1$, an individual chooses to use a health club for 10 hours per week at point $A$. When the fees are altered, she faces budget line $l_2$. She is then made better off because market basket $A$ can still be purchased, as can market basket $B$, which lies on a higher indifference curve.

health club charged a fee of $4 per hour, Roberta used the facility 10 hours per week. Under the new arrangement, she is required to pay $30 per week but can use the club for only $1 per hour.

Is this change beneficial for Roberta? Revealed preference analysis provides the answer. In Figure 3.19, line $l_1$ represents the budget constraint that Roberta faced under the original pricing arrangement. In this case, she maximized her satisfaction by choosing market basket $A$, with 10 hours of exercise and $60 of other recreational activities. Under the new arrangement, which shifts the budget line to $l_2$, she could still choose market basket $A$. But because $U_1$ is clearly not tangent to $l_2$, Roberta will be better off choosing another basket, such as $B$, with 25 hours of exercise and $45 worth of other recreational activities. Because she would choose $B$ when she could still choose $A$, she prefers $B$ to $A$. The new pricing arrangement therefore makes Roberta better off. (Note that $B$ is also preferred to $C$, which represents the option of not using the health club at all.)

We could also ask whether this new pricing system—called a *two-part tariff*—will increase the club's profits. If all members are like Roberta and more use generates more profit, then the answer is yes. In general, however, the answer depends on two factors: the preferences of all members and the costs of operating the facility. We discuss the two-part tariff in detail in Chapter 11, where we study ways in which firms with market power set prices.

## 3.5 MARGINAL UTILITY AND CONSUMER CHOICE

In Section 3.3, we showed graphically how a consumer can maximize his or her satisfaction, given a budget constraint. We do this by finding the highest indifference curve that can be reached, given that budget constraint. Because the highest indifference curve also has the highest attainable level of utility, it is natural to recast the consumer's problem as one of maximizing utility subject to a budget constraint.

The concept of utility can also be used to recast our analysis in a way that provides additional insight. To begin, let's distinguish between the total utility obtained by consumption and the satisfaction obtained from the last item consumed. **Marginal utility (MU)** measures *the additional satisfaction obtained from consuming one additional unit of a good*. For example, the marginal utility associated with a consumption increase from 0 to 1 unit of food might be 9; from 1 to 2, it might be 7; from 2 to 3, it might be 5.

These numbers imply that the consumer has **diminishing marginal utility**: As more and more of a good is consumed, consuming additional amounts will yield smaller and smaller additions to utility. Imagine, for example, the consumption of television: Marginal utility might fall after the second or third hour and could become very small after the fourth or fifth hour of viewing.

We can relate the concept of marginal utility to the consumer's utility-maximization problem in the following way. Consider a small movement down an indifference curve in Figure 3.8 (page 80). The additional consumption of food, $\Delta F$, will generate marginal utility $MU_F$. This shift results in a total increase in utility of $MU_F \Delta F$. At the same time, the reduced consumption of clothing, $\Delta C$, will lower utility per unit by $MU_C$, resulting in a total loss of $MU_C \Delta C$.

Because all points on an indifference curve generate the same level of utility, the total gain in utility associated with the increase in $F$ must balance the loss due to the lower consumption of $C$. Formally,

$$0 = MU_F(\Delta F) + MU_C(\Delta C)$$

Now we can rearrange this equation so that

$$-(\Delta C/\Delta F) = MU_F/MU_C$$

But because $-(\Delta C/\Delta F)$ is the MRS of $F$ for $C$, it follows that

$$MRS = MU_F/MU_C \tag{3.5}$$

Equation (3.5) tells us that the MRS is the ratio of the marginal utility of $F$ to the marginal utility of $C$. As the consumer gives up more and more of $C$ to obtain more of $F$, the marginal utility of $F$ falls and that of $C$ increases, so MRS decreases.

We saw earlier in this chapter that when consumers maximize their satisfaction, the MRS of $F$ for $C$ is equal to the ratio of the prices of the two goods:

$$MRS = P_F/P_C \tag{3.6}$$

Because the MRS is also equal to the ratio of the marginal utilities of consuming $F$ and $C$ (from equation 3.5), it follows that

$$MU_F/MU_C = P_F/P_C$$

or

$$MU_F/P_F = MU_C/P_C \tag{3.7}$$

Equation (3.7) is an important result. It tells us that utility maximization is achieved when the budget is allocated so that *the marginal utility per dollar of expenditure is the same for each good*. To see why this principle must hold, suppose that a person gets more utility from spending an additional dollar on

• **marginal utility (MU)** Additional satisfaction obtained from consuming one additional unit of a good.

• **diminishing marginal utility** Principle that as more of a good is consumed, the consumption of additional amounts will yield smaller additions to utility.

food than on clothing. In this case, her utility will be increased by spending more on food. As long as the marginal utility of spending an extra dollar on food exceeds the marginal utility of spending an extra dollar on clothing, she can increase her utility by shifting her budget toward food and away from clothing. Eventually, the marginal utility of food will decrease (because there is diminishing marginal utility in its consumption) and the marginal utility of clothing will increase (for the same reason). Only when the consumer has satisfied the **equal marginal principle**—i.e., *has equalized the marginal utility per dollar of expenditure across all goods*—will she have maximized utility. The equal marginal principle is an important concept in microeconomics. It will reappear in different forms throughout our analysis of consumer and producer behavior.

• **equal marginal principle**
Principle that utility is maximized when the consumer has equalized the marginal utility per dollar of expenditure across all goods.

---

**EXAMPLE 3.6**　　Marginal Utility and Happiness

In Example 3.2 (page 81), we saw that money (i.e., a higher income) can buy happiness, at least to a degree. But what, if anything, does research on consumer satisfaction tell us about the relationship between happiness and the concepts of utility and marginal utility? Interestingly, that research is consistent with a pattern of diminishing marginal utility of income, both in the U.S. and across countries. To see why, let's re-examine Figure 3.9 (page 82) in Example 3.2. The data suggest that as incomes increase from one country to the next, satisfaction, happiness, or utility (we are using the three words interchangeably) all increase as per-capita income increases. The *incremental* increase in satisfaction, however, declines as income increases. If one is willing to accept that the satisfaction index resulting from the survey is a cardinal index, then the results are consistent with a diminishing marginal utility of income.

The results for the U.S. are qualitatively very similar to those for the 67 countries that make up the data for Figure 3.9. Figure 3.20 calculates the mean level of life satisfaction for nine separate income groups in the population; the lowest has a mean income of $6,250, the next a mean income of $16,250, and so on until the highest group, whose mean income is $87,500. The solid curve is the one that best fits the data. Once again, we can see that reported happiness increases with income, but at a diminishing rate.

These results offer strong support for the modern theory of economic decision making that underlies this text, but they are still being carefully scrutinized. For example, they do not account for the fact that satisfaction tends to vary with age, with younger people often expressing less satisfaction than older folks. Or we can look at this a different way. Students have something positive to look forward to as they get older and wiser.

A second issue arises when we compare the results of happiness studies over time. Per-capita incomes in the U.S., U.K., Belgium, and Japan have all risen substantially over the past 20 years. Average happiness, however, has remained relatively unchanged. (Denmark, Germany, and Italy did show some increased satisfaction.) One plausible interpretation is that happiness is a relative, not absolute, measure of well-being. As a country's income increases over time, its citizens increase their expectations; in other words, they aspire to having higher incomes. To the extent that satisfaction is tied to whether those aspirations are met, satisfaction may not increase as income grows over time.

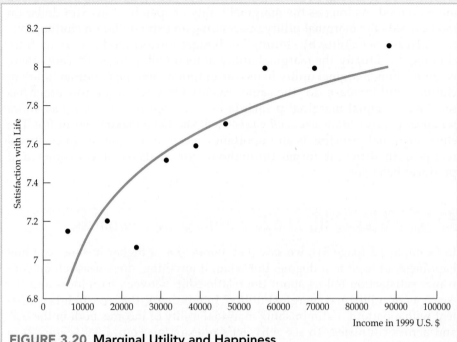

**FIGURE 3.20 Marginal Utility and Happiness**

A comparison of mean levels of satisfaction with life across income classes in the United States shows that happiness increases with income, but at a diminishing rate.

---

**EXAMPLE 3.7**   Gasoline Rationing

In times of war and other crises, governments often impose price controls on critical products. In 1974 and 1979, for example, the U.S. government imposed price controls on gasoline. As a result, motorists wanted to buy more gasoline than was available at controlled prices, and gasoline had to be rationed. Nonprice rationing is an alternative way of dealing with shortages that some people consider fairer than relying on uncontested market forces. Under a market system, those with higher incomes can outbid those with lower incomes to obtain goods that are in scarce supply. Under one form of rationing, everyone has an equal chance to purchase a rationed good.

In the United States, gasoline was allocated by long lines at the gas pump: While those who were willing to give up their time waiting got the gas they wanted, others did not. By guaranteeing every eligible person a minimum amount of gasoline, rationing can provide some people with access to a product that they could not otherwise afford. But rationing hurts others by limiting the amount of gasoline that they can buy.[10]

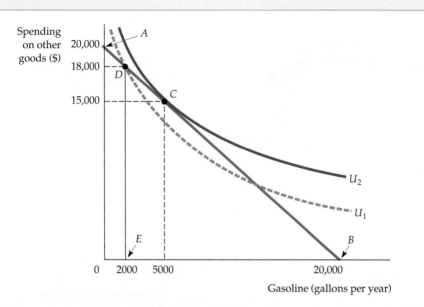

**FIGURE 3.21 Inefficiency of Gasoline Rationing**

When a good is rationed, less is available than consumers would like to buy. Consumers may be worse off. Without gasoline rationing, up to 20,000 gallons of gasoline are available for consumption (at point $B$). The consumer chooses point $C$ on indifference curve $U_2$, consuming 5000 gallons of gasoline. However, with a limit of 2000 gallons of gasoline under rationing (at point $E$), the consumer moves to $D$ on the lower indifference curve $U_1$.

We can see this principle clearly in Figure 3.21, which applies to a woman with an annual income of $20,000. The horizontal axis shows her annual consumption of gasoline, the vertical axis her remaining income after purchasing gasoline. Suppose the controlled gasoline price is $1 per gallon. Because her income is $20,000, she is limited to the points on budget line $AB$, which has a slope of –1. At $1 per gallon, she might wish to buy 5000 gallons of gasoline per year and spend $15,000 on other goods, represented by $C$. At this point, she would have maximized her utility (by being on the highest possible indifference curve $U_2$), given her budget constraint of $20,000.

With rationing, however, our consumer can purchase only 2000 gallons of gasoline. Thus, she now faces budget line $ADE$, a line that is no longer a straight line because purchases above 2000 gallons are not possible. The figure shows that her choice to consume at $D$ involves a lower level of utility, $U_1$, than would be achieved without rationing, $U_2$, because she is consuming less gasoline and more of other goods than she would otherwise prefer.

It is clear that at the rationed price the woman would be better off if her consumption were not constrained. But is she better off under a rationing system than she would be if there were no rationing at all? The answer, not surprisingly, depends on what the competitive market price of gasoline would have been

---

[10]For a more extensive discussion of gasoline rationing, see H. E. Frech III and William C. Lee, "The Welfare Cost of Rationing-by-Queuing Across Markets: Theory and Estimates from the U.S. Gasoline Crises," *Quarterly Journal of Economics* (1987): 97–108.

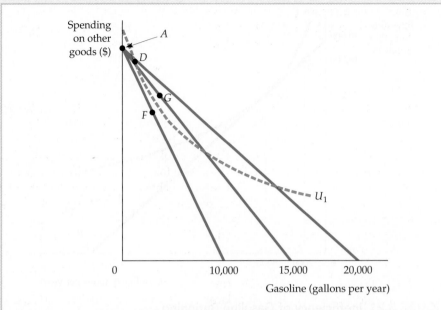

**FIGURE 3.22 Comparing Gasoline Rationing to the Free Market**

If the price of gasoline in a competitive market is $2.00 per gallon and the maximum consumption of gasoline is 10,000 gallons per year, the woman is better off under rationing (which holds the price at $1.00 per gallon), since she chooses the market basket at point $F$, which lies below indifference curve $U_1$ (the level of utility achieved under rationing). However, she would prefer a free market if the competitive price were $1.50 per gallon, since she would select market basket $G$, which lies above indifference curve $U_1$.

without rationing. As Figure 3.22 illustrates, the woman would be better off under rationing if the market price were $2.00 per gallon; in this case, the maximum consumption of gasoline would be 10,000 gallons per year, and she would choose point F which lies below indifference curve $U_1$ (the level of utility reached under rationing). However, she would be worse off under rationing if the market price was $1.50; in this case, the maximum consumption of gasoline would be 15,000 gallons per year, and she would choose point $G$, which lies above indifference curve $U_1$.

---

In §1.3, we introduced the *Consumer Price Index* as a measure of the cost of a "typical" consumer's entire market basket. As such, changes in the CPI also measure the rate of inflation.

• **cost-of-living index** Ratio of the present cost of a typical bundle of consumer goods and services compared with the cost during a base period.

# *3.6 COST-OF-LIVING INDEXES

The Social Security system has been the subject of heated debate for some time now. Under the present system, a retired person receives an annual benefit that is initially determined at the time of retirement and is based on his or her work history. The benefit then increases from year to year at a rate equal to the rate of increase of the Consumer Price Index (CPI). Does the CPI accurately reflect the cost of living for retirees? Is it appropriate to use the CPI as we now do—as a **cost-of-living index** for other government programs, for private union pensions, and for private wage agreements? On a similar note, we might ask whether the Producer Price Index (PPI) accurately measures the change over time in the cost of production. The answers to these questions lie in the economic theory of consumer behavior. In this section, we describe the theoretical underpinnings of cost indexes such as the CPI, using an example that describes the hypothetical price changes that students and their parents might face.

> In §1.3, we explained that the *Producer Price Index* provides a measure of the aggregate price level for intermediate products and wholesale goods.

## Ideal Cost-of-Living Index

Let's look at two sisters, Rachel and Sarah, whose preferences are identical. When Sarah began her college education in 1995, her parents gave her a "discretionary" budget of $500 per quarter. Sarah could spend the money on food, which was available at a price of $2.00 per pound, and on books, which were available at a price of $20 each. Sarah bought 100 pounds of food (at a cost of $200) and 15 books (at a cost of $300). Ten years later, in 2005, when Rachel (who had worked during the interim) is about to start college, her parents promise her a budget that is equivalent in buying power to the budget given to her older sister. Unfortunately, prices in the college town have increased, with food now $2.20 per pound and books $100 each. By how much should the discretionary budget be increased to make Rachel as well off in 2005 as her sister Sarah was in 1995? Table 3.3 summarizes the relevant data and Figure 3.23 provides the answer.

The initial budget constraint facing Sarah in 1995 is given by line $l_1$ in Figure 3.23; her utility-maximizing combination of food and books is at point $A$ on indifference curve $U_1$. We can check that the cost of achieving this level of utility is $500, as stated in the table:

$$\$500 = 100 \text{ lbs. of food} \times \$2.00/\text{lb.} + 15 \text{ books} \times \$20/\text{book}$$

As Figure 3.23 shows, to achieve the same level of utility as Sarah while facing the new higher prices, Rachel requires a budget sufficient to purchase the food-book consumption bundle given by point $B$ on line $l_2$ (and tangent to indifference curve $U_1$), where she chooses 300 lbs. of food and 6 books. Note that in doing so, Rachel has taken into account the fact that the price of books has increased relative to food. Therefore, she has substituted toward food and away from books.

The cost to Rachel of attaining the same level of utility as Sarah is given by

$$\$1260 = 300 \text{ lbs. of food} \times \$2.20/\text{lb.} + 6 \text{ books} \times \$100/\text{book}$$

The ideal *cost-of-living adjustment* for Rachel is therefore $760 (which is $1260 minus the $500 that was given to Sarah). The ideal cost-of-living index is

$$\$1260/\$500 = 2.52$$

Our index needs a base year, which we will set at 1995 = 100, so that the value of the index in 2005 is 252. A value of 252 implies a 152 percent increase in the cost of living, whereas a value of 100 would imply that the cost of living has not changed.

| TABLE 3.3 Ideal Cost-of-Living Index | | |
|---|---|---|
| | **1995 (Sarah)** | **2005 (Rachel)** |
| Price of books | $20/book | $100/book |
| Number of books | 15 | 6 |
| Price of food | $2.00/lb. | $2.20/lb. |
| Pounds of food | 100 | 300 |
| Expenditure | $500 | $1260 |

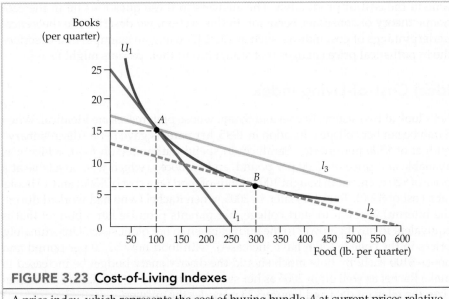

**FIGURE 3.23 Cost-of-Living Indexes**

A price index, which represents the cost of buying bundle *A* at current prices relative to the cost of bundle *A* at base-year prices, overstates the ideal cost-of-living index.

• **ideal cost-of-living index**
Cost of attaining a given level of utility at current prices relative to the cost of attaining the same utility at base-year prices.

This **ideal cost-of-living index** represents *the cost of attaining a given level of utility at current (2005) prices relative to the cost of attaining the same utility at base (1995) prices.*

## Laspeyres Index

Unfortunately, such an ideal cost-of-living index would entail large amounts of information. We would need to know individual preferences (which vary across the population) as well as prices and expenditures. Actual price indexes are therefore based on consumer *purchases*, not preferences. A price index that uses a *fixed consumption bundle in the base period* is called a Laspeyres price index. The **Laspeyres price index** answers the question: *What is the amount of money at current-year prices that an individual requires to purchase the bundle of goods and services that was chosen in the base year divided by the cost of purchasing the same bundle at base-year prices?*

• **Laspeyres price index**
Amount of money at current year prices that an individual requires to purchase a bundle of goods and services chosen in a base year divided by the cost of purchasing the same bundle at base-year prices.

The Laspeyres price index was illustrated in Figure 3.23. Calculating a Laspeyres cost-of-living index for Rachel is a straightforward process. Buying 100 pounds of food and 15 books in 2005 would require an expenditure of $1720 ($100 \times \$2.20 + 15 \times \$100$). This expenditure allows Rachel to choose bundle *A* on budget line $l_3$ (or any other bundle on that line). Line $l_3$ was constructed by shifting line $l_2$ outward until it intersected point *A*. Note that $l_3$ is the budget line that allows Rachel to purchase, at current 2005 prices, the same consumption bundle that her sister purchased in 1995. To compensate Rachel for the increased cost of living, we must increase her discretionary budget by $1220. Using 100 as the base in 1995, the Laspeyres index is therefore

$$100 \times \$1720/\$500 = 344$$

**Comparing Ideal Cost-of-Living and Laspeyres Indexes** In our example, the Laspeyres price index is clearly much higher than the ideal price index. Does a Laspeyres index always overstate the true cost-of-living index? The answer is yes, as you can see from Figure 3.23. Suppose that Rachel was given the budget associated with line $l_3$ during the base year of 1995. She could choose bundle *A*, but clearly she could achieve a higher level of utility if she purchased more food and fewer books (by moving to the right on line $l_3$). Because $A$ and $B$ generate equal utility, it follows that Rachel is better off receiving a Laspeyres cost-of-living adjustment rather than an ideal adjustment. The Laspeyres index overcompensates Rachel for the higher cost of living, and the Laspeyres cost-of-living index is, therefore, greater than the ideal cost-of-living index.

This result holds generally. Why? Because *the Laspeyres price index assumes that consumers do not alter their consumption patterns as prices change.* By changing consumption, however—increasing purchases of items that have become relatively cheaper and decreasing purchases of relatively more expensive items—consumers can achieve the same level of utility without having to consume the same bundle of goods that they did before the price change.

## Paasche Index

Another commonly used cost-of-living index is the **Paasche index**. Unlike the Laspeyres index, which focuses on the cost of buying a base-year bundle, the Paasche index focuses on the cost of buying the *current year's bundle*. In particular, the Paasche index answers another question: *What is the amount of money at current-year prices that an individual requires to purchase the current bundle of goods and services divided by the cost of purchasing the same bundle in the base year?*

**Comparing the Laspeyres and Paasche Indexes** It is helpful to compare the Laspeyres and the Paasche cost-of-living indexes.

- **Laspeyres index:** The amount of money at current-year prices that an individual requires to purchase the bundle of goods and services that was *chosen in the base year* divided by the cost of purchasing the same bundle at base-year prices.

- **Paasche index:** The amount of money at current-year prices that an individual requires to purchase the bundle of goods and services *chosen in the current year* divided by the cost of purchasing the same bundle in the base year.

Both the Laspeyres (LI) and Paasche (PI) indexes are **fixed-weight indexes**: The quantities of the various goods and services in each index remain unchanged. For the Laspeyres index, however, the quantities remain unchanged at *base-year* levels; for the Paasche they remain unchanged at *current-year* levels. Suppose generally that there are two goods, food ($F$) and clothing ($C$). Let:

$P_{Ft}$ and $P_{Ct}$ be current-year prices

$P_{Fb}$ and $P_{Cb}$ be base-year prices

$F_t$ and $C_t$ be current-year quantities

$F_b$ and $C_b$ be base-year quantities

We can write the two indexes as:

$$\text{LI} = \frac{P_{Ft}F_b + P_{Ct}C_b}{P_{Fb}F_b + P_{Cb}C_b}$$

$$\text{PI} = \frac{P_{Ft}F_t + P_{Ct}C_t}{P_{Fb}F_t + P_{Cb}C_t}$$

Just as the Laspeyres index will overstate the ideal cost of living, the Paasche will understate it because it assumes that the individual will buy the current-year bundle in the base period. In actuality, facing base-year prices, consumers would have been able to achieve the same level of utility at a lower cost by changing their consumption bundles. Because the Paasche index is a ratio of the

• **Paasche index** Amount of money at current-year prices that an individual requires to purchase a current bundle of goods and services divided by the cost of purchasing the same bundle in a base year.

• **fixed-weight index** Cost-of-living index in which the quantities of goods and services remain unchanged.

cost of buying the current bundle divided by the cost of buying the current bundle at baseyear prices, overstating the cost of the base-year bundle (the denominator in the ratio) will cause the Paasche index itself to be understated.

To illustrate the Laspeyres-Paasche comparison, let's return to our earlier example and focus on Sarah's choices of books and food. For Sarah (who went to college in 1995), the cost of buying the base-year bundle of books and food at current-year prices is $1720 (100 lbs. × $2.20/lb. + 15 books × $100/book). The cost of buying the same bundle at base-year prices is $500 (100 lbs × $2/lb. + 15 books × $20/book). The Laspeyres price index, LI, is therefore 100 × $1720/$500 = 344, as reported previously. In contrast, the cost of buying the current-year bundle at current-year prices is $1260 (300 lbs. × $2.20/lb. + 6 books × $100/book). The cost of buying the same bundle at base-year prices is $720 (300 lbs × $2/lb. + 6 books × $20/book). Consequently, the Paasche price index, PI, is 100 × $1260/$720 = 175. As expected, the Paasche index is lower than the Laspeyres index and lower than the ideal index of 252.

## Price Indexes in the United States: Chain Weighting

Historically, both the CPI and the PPI were measured as Laspeyres price indexes. The overall CPI was calculated each month by the U.S. Bureau of Labor Statistics as the ratio of the cost of a typical bundle of consumer goods and services to the cost during a base period. A CPI for a particular category of goods and services (e.g., housing) would utilize a bundle of goods and services from that category. Similar calculations were done for the PPI using bundles of intermediate and wholesale goods.

We have seen that the Laspeyres index overstates the amount needed to compensate individuals for price increases. With respect to Social Security and other government programs, this means that using the CPI with base weights to adjust retirement benefits would tend to overcompensate most recipients and would thus require greater government expenditure.

While economists have known of this problem for years, it was not until the energy-price shocks of the 1970s, more recent fluctuations in food prices, and concerns surrounding federal deficits that dissatisfaction with the Laspeyres index grew. It was estimated, for example, that a failure to account for changes in computer-buying patterns in response to a sharp decrease in computer prices had caused the CPI to overstate the cost of living substantially.

• **chain-weighted price index** Cost-of-living index that accounts for changes in quantities of goods and services.

For this reason, the U.S. government changed the construction of the CPI and the PPI, switching from a simple Laspeyres index to an index in which the base weights are updated every few years. A **chain-weighted price index** is a cost-of-living index that accounts for changes in quantities of goods and services over time. Chain weighting was not new to the U.S. It had been adopted in 1995 as an improvement to the GDP Deflator, a Paasche price index used to deflate measures of gross domestic product (GDP) in order to obtain an estimate of real GDP (GDP adjusted for inflation).[11] Using chain-weighted versions of the CPI, PPI, and GDP deflator has reduced the biases associated with the use of simple Laspeyres and Paasche indexes, but because the weights are changed only infrequently, the biases have not been eliminated.[12]

---

[11]For the latest changes in the CPI and PPI, see **http://www.bls.gov/cpi** and **http://www.bls.gov/ppi**. For information about the calculation of real GDP, see **http://www.bea.gov**.

[12]Failures to account adequately for the appearance of new goods and improvements in the quality of exisiting goods are additional sources of bias with respect to the CPI and PPI.

| EXAMPLE 3.8 | The Bias in the CPI |
|---|---|

In the past decade, there has been growing public concern about the solvency of the Social Security system. At issue is the fact that retirement benefits are linked to the Consumer Price Index. Because the CPI was a Laspeyres index that could overstate the cost of living substantially, Congress has asked several economists to look into the matter.

A commission chaired by Stanford University professor Michael Boskin concluded that the CPI overstated inflation by approximately 1.1 percentage points—a significant amount given the relatively low rate of inflation in the United States in recent years.[13] According to the commission, approximately 0.4 percentage points of the 1.1-percentage-point bias was due to the failure of the Laspeyres price index to account for changes in the current year mix of consumption of the products in the base-year bundle. The remainder of the bias was due to the failure of the index to account for the growth of discount stores (approximately 0.1 percentage points), for improvements in the quality of existing products, and, most significantly, for the introduction of new products (0.6 percentage points).

The bias in the CPI was particularly acute when evaluating the costs of medical care. From 1986 to 1996, the average increase in the CPI was 3.6 percent, but the medical component of the CPI increased at an average annual rate of 6.5 percent per year. Thus, one estimate placed the total bias of the medical insurance part of the CPI at approximately 3.1 percentage points annually. This bias has enormous policy implications as the nation struggles to contain medical-care costs and provide health care to an aging population.[14]

If the bias in the CPI were to be eliminated, in whole or in part, the cost of a number of federal programs would decrease substantially (as would, of course, the corresponding benefits to eligible recipients in the programs). In addition to Social Security, affected programs would include federal retirement programs (for railroad employees and military veterans), Supplemental Security Income (income support for the poor), food stamps, and child nutrition. According to one study, a 1-percentage-point reduction in the CPI would increase national savings and thereby reduce the national debt by approximately $95 billion per year in year 2000 dollars.[15]

In addition, the effect of any CPI adjustments would not be restricted to the expenditure side of the federal budget. Because personal income tax brackets are inflation-adjusted, a CPI adjustment decreasing the rate of measured price increase would necessitate a smaller upper adjustment in tax brackets and, consequently, increase federal tax revenues.

---

[13]Michael J. Boskin, Ellen R. Dulberger, Robert J. Gordon, Zvi Griliches, and Dale W. Jorgenson, "The CPI Commission: Findings and Recommendations," *American Economic Review* 87 (May 1997): 78–93.

[14]For more information, see Chapters 1 and 2 of *Measuring the Prices of Medical Treatments*, Jack E. Triplett, Editor; Washington, D.C.: Brookings Institution Press, 1999 (**http://brookings. nap.edu/**).

[15]Michael F. Bryan and Jagadeesh Gokhale, "The Consumer Price Index and National Savings," *Economic Commentary* (October 15, 1995) at **http://www.clev.frb.org/**. The data have been adjusted upward using the GDP deflator.

# SUMMARY

1. The theory of consumer choice rests on the assumption that people behave rationally in an attempt to maximize the satisfaction that they can obtain by purchasing a particular combination of goods and services.

2. Consumer choice has two related parts: the study of the consumer's preferences and the analysis of the budget line that constrains consumer choices.

3. Consumers make choices by comparing market baskets or bundles of commodities. Preferences are assumed to be complete (consumers can compare all possible market baskets) and transitive (if they prefer basket A to B, and B to C, then they prefer A to C). In addition, economists assume that more of each good is always preferred to less.

4. Indifference curves, which represent all combinations of goods and services that give the same level of satisfaction, are downward-sloping and cannot intersect one another.

5. Consumer preferences can be completely described by a set of indifference curves known as an indifference map. An indifference map provides an ordinal ranking of all choices that the consumer might make.

6. The marginal rate of substitution (MRS) of F for C is the maximum amount of C that a person is willing to give up to obtain 1 additional unit of F. The MRS diminishes as we move down along an indifference curve. When there is a diminishing MRS, indifference curves are convex.

7. Budget lines represent all combinations of goods for which consumers expend all their income. Budget lines shift outward in response to an increase in consumer income. When the price of one good (on the horizontal axis) changes while income and the price of the other good do not, budget lines pivot and rotate about a fixed point (on the vertical axis).

8. Consumers maximize satisfaction subject to budget constraints. When a consumer maximizes satisfaction by consuming some of each of two goods, the marginal rate of substitution is equal to the ratio of the prices of the two goods being purchased.

9. Maximization is sometimes achieved at a corner solution in which one good is not consumed. In such cases, the marginal rate of substitution need not equal the ratio of the prices.

10. The theory of revealed preference shows how the choices that individuals make when prices and income vary can be used to determine their preferences. When an individual chooses basket A even though he or she could afford B, we know that A is preferred to B.

11. The theory of the consumer can be presented by two different approaches. The indifference curve approach uses the ordinal properties of utility (that is, it allows for the ranking of alternatives). The utility function approach obtains a utility function by attaching a number to each market basket; if basket A is preferred to basket B, A generates more utility than B.

12. When risky choices are analyzed or when comparisons must be made among individuals, the cardinal properties of the utility function can be important. Usually the utility function will show diminishing marginal utility: As more and more of a good is consumed, the consumer obtains smaller and smaller increments of utility.

13. When the utility function approach is used and both goods are consumed, utility maximization occurs when the ratio of the marginal utilities of the two goods (which is the marginal rate of substitution) is equal to the ratio of the prices.

14. An ideal cost-of-living index measures the cost of buying, at current prices, a bundle of goods that generates the same level of *utility* as was provided by the bundle of goods consumed at base-year prices. The Laspeyres price index, however, represents the cost of buying the bundle of goods chosen in the base year at current prices relative to the cost of buying *the same bundle* at base-year prices. The CPI, even with chain weighting, overstates the ideal cost-of-living index. By contrast, the Paasche index measures the cost at current-year prices of buying a bundle of goods chosen in the current year divided by the cost of buying the same bundle at base-year prices. It thus understates the ideal cost-of-living index.

# QUESTIONS FOR REVIEW

1. What are the four basic assumptions about individual preferences? Explain the significance or meaning of each.

2. Can a set of indifference curves be upward sloping? If so, what would this tell you about the two goods?

3. Explain why two indifference curves cannot intersect.

4. Jon is always willing to trade one can of Coke for one can of Sprite, or one can of Sprite for one can of Coke.

   a. What can you say about Jon's marginal rate of substitution?

   b. Draw a set of indifference curves for Jon.

   c. Draw two budget lines with different slopes and illustrate the satisfaction-maximizing choice. What conclusion can you draw?

5. What happens to the marginal rate of substitution as you move along a convex indifference curve? A linear indifference curve?

6. Explain why an MRS between two goods must equal the ratio of the price of the goods for the consumer to achieve maximum satisfaction.

7. Describe the indifference curves associated with two goods that are perfect substitutes. What if they are perfect complements?

8. What is the difference between ordinal utility and cardinal utility? Explain why the assumption of cardinal utility is not needed in order to rank consumer choices.

9. Upon merging with the West German economy, East German consumers indicated a preference for Mercedes-Benz automobiles over Volkswagens. However, when they converted their savings into deutsche marks, they flocked to Volkswagen dealerships. How can you explain this apparent paradox?

10. Draw a budget line and then draw an indifference curve to illustrate the satisfaction-maximizing choice associated with two products. Use your graph to answer the following questions.
    a. Suppose that one of the products is rationed. Explain why the consumer is likely to be worse off.
    b. Suppose that the price of one of the products is fixed at a level below the current price. As a result, the consumer is not able to purchase as much as she would like. Can you tell if the consumer is better off or worse off?

11. Based on his preferences, Bill is willing to trade four movie tickets for one ticket to a basketball game. If movie tickets cost $8 each and a ticket to the basketball game costs $40, should Bill make the trade? Why or why not?

12. Describe the equal marginal principle. Explain why this principle may not hold if increasing marginal utility is associated with the consumption of one or both goods.

13. The price of computers has fallen substantially over the past two decades. Use this drop in price to explain why the Consumer Price Index is likely to overstate substantially the cost-of-living index for individuals who use computers intensively.

14. Explain why the Paasche index will generally understate the ideal cost-of-living index.

# EXERCISES

1. In this chapter, consumer preferences for various commodities did not change during the analysis. In some situations, however, preferences do change as consumption occurs. Discuss why and how preferences might change over time with consumption of these two commodities:
   a. cigarettes.
   b. dinner for the first time at a restaurant with a special cuisine.

2. Draw indifference curves that represent the following individuals' preferences for hamburgers and soft drinks. Indicate the direction in which the individuals' satisfaction (or utility) is increasing.
   a. Joe has convex indifference curves and dislikes both hamburgers and soft drinks.
   b. Jane loves hamburgers and dislikes soft drinks. If she is served a soft drink, she will pour it down the drain rather than drink it.
   c. Bob loves hamburgers and dislikes soft drinks. If he is served a soft drink, he will drink it to be polite.
   d. Molly loves hamburgers and soft drinks, but insists on consuming exactly one soft drink for every two hamburgers that she eats.
   e. Bill likes hamburgers, but neither likes nor dislikes soft drinks.
   f. Mary always gets twice as much satisfaction from an extra hamburger as she does from an extra soft drink.

3. If Jane is currently willing to trade 4 movie tickets for 1 basketball ticket, then she must like basketball better than movies. True or false? Explain.

4. Janelle and Brian each plan to spend $20,000 on the styling and gas mileage features of a new car. They can each choose all styling, all gas mileage, or some combination of the two. Janelle does not care at all about styling and wants the best gas mileage possible. Brian likes both equally and wants to spend an equal amount on each. Using indifference curves and budget lines, illustrate the choice that each person will make.

5. Suppose that Bridget and Erin spend their incomes on two goods, food ($F$) and clothing ($C$). Bridget's preferences are represented by the utility function $U(F,C) = 10FC$, while Erin's preferences are represented by the utility function $U(F,C) = .20F^2C^2$.
   a. With food on the horizontal axis and clothing on the vertical axis, identify on a graph the set of points that give Bridget the same level of utility as the bundle (10, 5). Do the same for Erin on a separate graph.
   b. On the same two graphs, identify the set of bundles that give Bridget and Erin the same level of utility as the bundle (15, 8).
   c. Do you think Bridget and Erin have the same preferences or different preferences? Explain.

6. Suppose that Jones and Smith have each decided to allocate $1000 per year to an entertainment budget in the form of hockey games or rock concerts. They both like hockey games and rock concerts and will choose to consume positive quantities of both goods. However, they differ substantially in their preferences for these two forms of entertainment. Jones prefers hockey games to rock concerts, while Smith prefers rock concerts to hockey games.

**a.** Draw a set of indifference curves for Jones and a second set for Smith.

**b.** Using the concept of marginal rate of substitution, explain why the two sets of curves are different from each other.

**7.** The price of DVDs (*D*) is $20 and the price of CDs (*C*) is $10. Philip has a budget of $100 to spend on the two goods. Suppose that he has already bought one DVD and one CD. In addition, there are 3 more DVDs and 5 more CDs that he would really like to buy.

**a.** Given the above prices and income, draw his budget line on a graph with CDs on the horizontal axis.

**b.** Considering what he has already purchased and what he still wants to purchase, identify the three different bundles of CDs and DVDs that he could choose. For this part of the question, assume that he cannot purchase fractional units.

**8.** Anne has a job that requires her to travel three out of every four weeks. She has an annual travel budget and can travel either by train or by plane. The airline on which she typically flies has a frequent-traveler program that reduces the cost of her tickets according to the number of miles she has flown in a given year. When she reaches 25,000 miles, the airline will reduce the price of her tickets by 25 percent for the remainder of the year. When she reaches 50,000 miles, the airline will reduce the price by 50 percent for the remainder of the year. Graph Anne's budget line, with train miles on the vertical axis and plane miles on the horizontal axis.

**9.** Debra usually buys a soft drink when she goes to a movie theater, where she has a choice of three sizes: the 8-ounce drink costs $1.50, the 12-ounce drink $2.00, and the 16-ounce drink $2.25. Describe the budget constraint that Debra faces when deciding how many ounces of the drink to purchase. (Assume that Debra can costlessly dispose of any of the soft drink that she does not want.)

**10.** Antonio buys five new college textbooks during his first year at school at a cost of $80 each. Used books cost only $50 each. When the bookstore announces that there will be a 10 percent increase in the price of new books and a 5 percent increase in the price of used books, Antonio's father offers him $40 extra.

**a.** What happens to Antonio's budget line? Illustrate the change with new books on the vertical axis.

**b.** Is Antonio worse or better off after the price change? Explain.

**11.** Consumers in Georgia pay twice as much for avocados as they do for peaches. However, avocados and peaches are the same price in California. If consumers in both states maximize utility, will the marginal rate of substitution of peaches for avocados be the same for consumers in both states? If not, which will be higher?

**12.** Ben allocates his lunch budget between two goods, pizza and burritos.

**a.** Illustrate Ben's optimal bundle on a graph with pizza on the horizontal axis.

**b.** Suppose now that pizza is taxed, causing the price to increase by 20 percent. Illustrate Ben's new optimal bundle.

**c.** Suppose instead that pizza is rationed at a quantity less than Ben's desired quantity. Illustrate Ben's new optimal bundle.

**13.** Brenda wants to buy a new car and has a budget of $25,000. She has just found a magazine that assigns each car an index for styling and an index for gas mileage. Each index runs from 1 to 10, with 10 representing either the most styling or the best gas mileage. While looking at the list of cars, Brenda observes that on average, as the style index increases by one unit, the price of the car increases by $5000. She also observes that as the gas-mileage index rises by one unit, the price of the car increases by $2500.

**a.** Illustrate the various combinations of style (*S*) and gas mileage (*G*) that Brenda could select with her $25,000 budget. Place gas mileage on the horizontal axis.

**b.** Suppose Brenda's preferences are such that she always receives three times as much satisfaction from an extra unit of styling as she does from gas mileage. What type of car will Brenda choose?

**c.** Suppose that Brenda's marginal rate of substitution (of gas mileage for styling) is equal to $S/(4G)$. What value of each index would she like to have in her car?

**d.** Suppose that Brenda's marginal rate of substitution (of gas mileage for styling) is equal to $(3S)/G$. What value of each index would she like to have in her car?

**14.** Connie has a monthly income of $200 that she allocates among two goods: meat and potatoes.

**a.** Suppose meat costs $4 per pound and potatoes $2 per pound. Draw her budget constraint.

**b.** Suppose also that her utility function is given by the equation $U(M, P) = 2M + P$. What combination of meat and potatoes should she buy to maximize her utility? (*Hint:* Meat and potatoes are perfect substitutes.)

**c.** Connie's supermarket has a special promotion. If she buys 20 pounds of potatoes (at $2 per pound), she gets the next 10 pounds for free. This offer applies only to the first 20 pounds she buys. All potatoes in excess of the first 20 pounds (excluding bonus potatoes) are still $2 per pound. Draw her budget constraint.

**d.** An outbreak of potato rot raises the price of potatoes to $4 per pound. The supermarket ends its promotion. What does her budget constraint look like now? What combination of meat and potatoes maximizes her utility?

**15.** Jane receives utility from days spent traveling on vacation domestically (*D*) and days spent traveling on vacation in a foreign country (*F*), as given by the utility function $U(D,F) = 10DF$. In addition, the price of a day spent traveling domestically is $100, the price of a day spent traveling in a foreign country is $400, and Jane's annual travel budget is $4000.

   **a.** Illustrate the indifference curve associated with a utility of 800 and the indifference curve associated with a utility of 1200.

   **b.** Graph Jane's budget line on the same graph.

   **c.** Can Jane afford any of the bundles that give her a utility of 800? What about a utility of 1200?

   ***d.** Find Jane's utility-maximizing choice of days spent traveling domestically and days spent in a foreign country.

**16.** Julio receives utility from consuming food ($F$) and clothing ($C$) as given by the utility function $U(F,C) = FC$. In addition, the price of food is $2 per unit, the price of clothing is $10 per unit, and Julio's weekly income is $50.

   **a.** What is Julio's marginal rate of substitution of food for clothing when utility is maximized? Explain.

   **b.** Suppose instead that Julio is consuming a bundle with more food and less clothing than his utility maximizing bundle. Would his marginal rate of substitution of food for clothing be greater than or less than your answer in part a? Explain.

**17.** The utility that Meredith receives by consuming food $F$ and clothing $C$ is given by $U(F,C) = FC$. Suppose that Meredith's income in 1990 is $1200 and that the prices of food and clothing are $1 per unit for each. By 2000, however, the price of food has increased to $2 and the price of clothing to $3. Let 100 represent the cost of living index for 1990. Calculate the ideal and the Laspeyres cost-of-living index for Meredith for 2000. (*Hint:* Meredith will spend equal amounts on food and clothing with these preferences.)

# Individual and Market Demand

Chapter 3 laid the foundation for the theory of consumer demand. We discussed the nature of consumer preferences and saw how, given budget constraints, consumers choose market baskets that maximize utility. From here it's a short step to analyzing demand and showing how the demand for a good depends on its price, the prices of other goods, and income.

Our analysis of demand proceeds in six steps:

1. We begin by deriving the demand curve for an individual consumer. Because we know how changes in price and income affect a person's budget line, we can determine how they affect consumption choice. We will use this information to see how the quantity of a good demanded varies in response to price changes as we move along an individual's demand curve. We will also see how this demand curve shifts in response to changes in the individual's income.

2. With this foundation, we will examine the effect of a price change in more detail. When the price of a good goes up, individual demand for it can change in two ways. First, because it has now become more expensive relative to other goods, consumers will buy less of it and more of other goods. Second, the higher price reduces the consumer's purchasing power. This reduction is just like a reduction in income and will lead to a reduction in consumer demand. By analyzing these two distinct effects, we will better understand the characteristics of demand.

3. Next, we will see how individual demand curves can be aggregated to determine the market demand curve. We will also study the characteristics of market demand and see why the demands for some kinds of goods differ considerably from the demands for others.

4. We will go on to show how market demand curves can be used to measure the benefits that people receive when they consume products, above and beyond the expenditures they make. This information will be especially important later, when we study the effects of government intervention in a market.

5. We then describe the effects of *network externalities*—i.e., what happens when a person's demand for a good also depends on the demands of *other* people. These effects play a crucial role in the demands for many high-tech products, such as computer hardware and software, and telecommunications systems.

6. Finally, we will briefly describe some of the methods that economists use to obtain empirical information about demand.

## 4.1 INDIVIDUAL DEMAND

This section shows how the demand curve of an individual consumer follows from the consumption choices that a person makes when faced with a budget constraint. To illustrate these concepts graphically, we will limit the available goods to food and clothing, and we will rely on the utility-maximization approach described in Section 3.3 (page 86).

> In §3.3, we explain how a consumer chooses the market basket on the highest indifference curve that touches the consumer's budget line.

### Price Changes

We begin by examining ways in which the consumption of food and clothing changes when the price of food changes. Figure 4.1 shows the consumption choices that a person will make when allocating a fixed amount of income between the two goods.

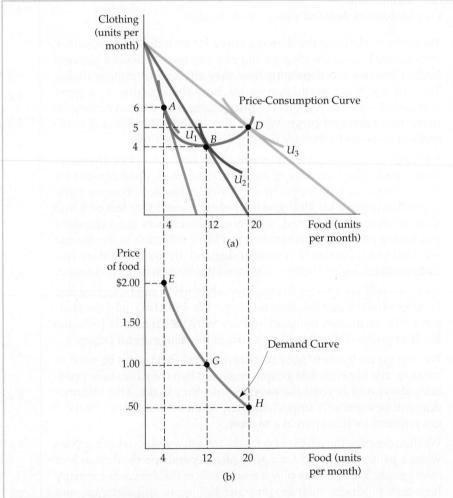

**FIGURE 4.1 Effect of Price Changes**

A reduction in the price of food, with income and the price of clothing fixed, causes this consumer to choose a different market basket. In **(a)**, the baskets that maximize utility for various prices of food (point $A$, $2; $B$, $1; $D$, $0.50) trace out the price-consumption curve. Part **(b)** gives the demand curve, which relates the price of food to the quantity demanded. (Points $E$, $G$, and $H$ correspond to points $A$, $B$, and $D$, respectively).

Initially, the price of food is $1, the price of clothing $2, and the consumer's income $20. The utility-maximizing consumption choice is at point *B* in Figure 4.1(a). Here, the consumer buys 12 units of food and 4 units of clothing, thus achieving the level of utility associated with indifference curve $U_2$.

Now look at Figure 4.1(b), which shows the relationship between the price of food and the quantity demanded. The horizontal axis measures the quantity of food consumed, as in Figure 4.1(a), but the vertical axis now measures the price of food. Point *G* in Figure 4.1(b) corresponds to point *B* in Figure 4.1(a). At *G*, the price of food is $1, and the consumer purchases 12 units of food.

Suppose the price of food increases to $2. As we saw in Chapter 3, the budget line in Figure 4.1(a) rotates inward about the vertical intercept, becoming twice as steep as before. The higher relative price of food has increased the magnitude of the slope of the budget line. The consumer now achieves maximum utility at *A*, which is found on a lower indifference curve, $U_1$. (Because the price of food has risen, the consumer's purchasing power—and thus attainable utility—has fallen.) At *A*, the consumer chooses 4 units of food and 6 units of clothing. In Figure 4.1(b), this modified consumption choice is at *E*, which shows that at a price of $2, 4 units of food are demanded.

> In §3.2, we explain how the budget line shifts in response to a price change.

Finally, what will happen if the price of food *decreases* to 50 cents? Because the budget line now rotates outward, the consumer can achieve the higher level of utility associated with indifference curve $U_3$ in Figure 4.1(a) by selecting *D*, with 20 units of food and 5 units of clothing. Point *H* in Figure 4.1(b) shows the price of 50 cents and the quantity demanded of 20 units of food.

## The Individual Demand Curve

We can go on to include all possible changes in the price of food. In Figure 4.1(a), the **price-consumption curve** traces the utility-maximizing combinations of food and clothing associated with every possible price of food. Note that as the price of food falls, attainable utility increases and the consumer buys more food. This pattern of increasing consumption of a good in response to a decrease in price almost always holds. But what happens to the consumption of clothing as the price of food falls? As Figure 4.1(a) shows, the consumption of clothing may either increase or decrease. The consumption of both food *and* clothing can increase because the decrease in the price of food has increased the consumer's ability to purchase both goods.

> • **price-consumption curve**
> Curve tracing the utility-maximizing combinations of two goods as the price of one changes.

An **individual demand curve** relates the quantity of a good that a single consumer will buy to the price of that good. In Figure 4.1(b), the individual demand curve relates the quantity of food that the consumer will buy to the price of food. This demand curve has two important properties:

> • **individual demand curve**
> Curve relating the quantity of a good that a single consumer will buy to its price.

1. *The level of utility that can be attained changes as we move along the curve.* The lower the price of the product, the higher the level of utility. Note from Figure 4.1(a) that a higher indifference curve is reached as the price falls. Again, this result simply reflects the fact that as the price of a product falls, the consumer's purchasing power increases.

2. *At every point on the demand curve, the consumer is maximizing utility by satisfying the condition that the marginal rate of substitution (MRS) of food for clothing equals the ratio of the prices of food and clothing.* As the price of food falls, the price ratio and the MRS also fall. In Figure 4.1(b), the price ratio falls from 1 ($2/$2) at *E* (because the curve $U_1$ is tangent to a budget line with a slope of −1 at *A*) to 1/2 ($1/$2) at *G*, to 1/4 ($0.50/$2)

> In §3.1, we introduce the marginal rate of substitution (MRS) as a measure of the maximum amount of one good that the consumer is willing to give up in order to obtain one unit of another good.

at *H*. Because the consumer is maximizing utility, the MRS of food for clothing decreases as we move down the demand curve. This phenomenon makes intuitive sense because it tells us that the relative value of food falls as the consumer buys more of it.

The fact that the MRS varies along the individual's demand curve tells us something about how consumers value the consumption of a good or service. Suppose we were to ask a consumer how much she would be willing to pay for an additional unit of food when she is currently consuming 4 units. Point *E* on the demand curve in Figure 4.1(b) provides the answer: $2. Why? As we pointed out above, because the MRS of food for clothing is 1 at *E*, one additional unit of food is worth one additional unit of clothing. But a unit of clothing costs $2, which is, therefore, the value (or marginal benefit) obtained by consuming an additional unit of food. Thus, as we move down the demand curve in Figure 4.1(b), the MRS falls. Likewise, the value that the consumer places on an additional unit of food falls from $2 to $1 to $0.50.

## Income Changes

We have seen what happens to the consumption of food and clothing when the price of food changes. Now let's see what happens when income changes.

The effects of a change in income can be analyzed in much the same way as a price change. Figure 4.2(a) shows the consumption choices that a consumer will make when allocating a fixed income to food and clothing when the price of food is $1 and the price of clothing $2. As in Figure 4.1(a), the quantity of clothing is measured on the vertical axis and the quantity of food on the horizontal axis. Income changes appear as changes in the budget line in Figure 4.2(a). Initially, the consumer's income is $10. The utility-maximizing consumption choice is then at *A*, at which point she buys 4 units of food and 3 units of clothing.

This choice of 4 units of food is also shown in Figure 4.2(b) as *E* on demand curve $D_1$. Demand curve $D_1$ is the curve that would be traced out if we held income fixed at $10 *but varied the price of food*. Because we are holding the price of food constant, we will observe only a single point *E* on this demand curve.

What happens if the consumer's income is increased to $20? Her budget line then shifts outward parallel to the original budget line, allowing her to attain the utility level associated with indifference curve $U_2$. Her optimal consumption choice is now at *B*, where she buys 10 units of food and 5 units of clothing. In Figure 4.2(b) her consumption of food is shown as *G* on demand curve $D_2$. $D_2$ is the demand curve that would be traced out if we held income fixed at $20 but varied the price of food. Finally, note that if her income increases to $30, she chooses *D*, with a market basket containing 16 units of food (and 7 units of clothing), represented by *H* in Figure 4.2(b).

We could go on to include all possible changes in income. In Figure 4.2(a), the **income-consumption curve** traces out the utility-maximizing combinations of food and clothing associated with every income level. The income-consumption curve in Figure 4.2 slopes upward because the consumption of both food and clothing increases as income increases. Previously, we saw that a change in the price of a good corresponds to *a movement along a demand curve*. Here, the situation is different. Because each demand curve is measured for a particular level of income, any change in income must lead to *a shift in the demand curve itself*. Thus *A* on the income-consumption curve in Figure 4.2(a) corresponds to *E* on demand curve $D_1$ in Figure 4.2(b); *B* corresponds to *G* on a different demand curve $D_2$. The upward-sloping income-consumption curve implies that an

• **income-consumption curve**
Curve tracing the utility-maximizing combinations of two goods as a consumer's income changes.

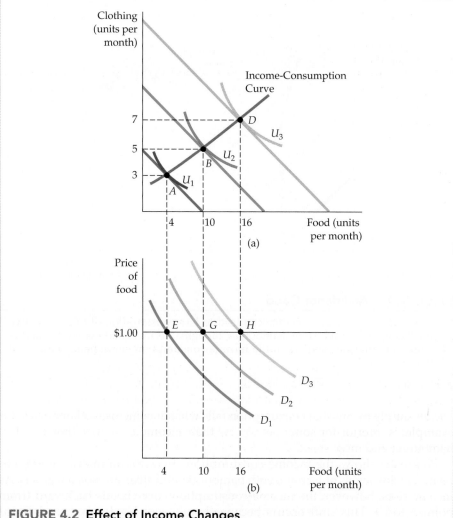

**FIGURE 4.2 Effect of Income Changes**

An increase in income, with the prices of all goods fixed, causes consumers to alter their choice of market baskets. In part **(a)**, the baskets that maximize consumer satisfaction for various incomes (point *A*, $10; *B*, $20; *D*, $30) trace out the income-consumption curve. The shift to the right of the demand curve in response to the increases in income is shown in part **(b)**. (Points *E*, *G*, and *H* correspond to points *A*, *B*, and *D*, respectively.)

increase in income causes a shift to the right in the demand curve—in this case from $D_1$ to $D_2$ to $D_3$.

## Normal versus Inferior Goods

When the income-consumption curve has a positive slope, the quantity demanded increases with income. As a result, the income elasticity of demand is positive. The greater the shifts to the right of the demand curve, the larger the income elasticity. In this case, the goods are described as *normal*: Consumers want to buy more of them as their incomes increase.

In some cases, the quantity demanded *falls* as income increases; the income elasticity of demand is negative. We then describe the good as *inferior*. The term

> In §2.4, we explain that the income elasticity of demand is the percentage change in the quantity demanded resulting from a 1-percent increase in income.

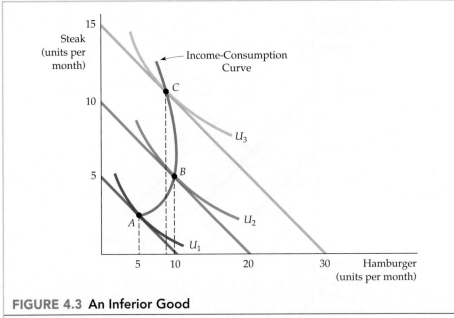

**FIGURE 4.3 An Inferior Good**

An increase in a person's income can lead to less consumption of one of the two goods being purchased. Here, hamburger, though a normal good between *A* and *B*, becomes an inferior good when the income-consumption curve bends backward between *B* and *C*.

*inferior* simply means that consumption falls when income rises. Hamburger, for example, is inferior for some people: As their income increases, they buy less hamburger and more steak.

Figure 4.3 shows the income-consumption curve for an inferior good. For relatively low levels of income, both hamburger and steak are normal goods. As income rises, however, the income-consumption curve bends backward (from point *B* to *C*). This shift occurs because hamburger has become an inferior good—its consumption has fallen as income has increased.

## Engel Curves

• **Engel curve** Curve relating the quantity of a good consumed to income.

Income-consumption curves can be used to construct **Engel curves**, which relate the quantity of a good consumed to an individual's income. Figure 4.4 shows how such curves are constructed for two different goods. Figure 4.4(a), which shows an upward-sloping Engel curve, is derived directly from Figure 4.2(a). In both figures, as the individual's income increases from $10 to $20 to $30, her consumption of food increases from 4 to 10 to 16 units. Recall that in Figure 4.2(a) the vertical axis measured units of clothing consumed per month and the horizontal axis units of food per month; changes in income were reflected as shifts in the budget line. In Figures 4.4(a) and (b), we have replotted the data to put income on the vertical axis, while keeping food and hamburger on the horizontal.

The upward-sloping Engel curve in Figure 4.4(a)—like the upward-sloping income-consumption curve in Figure 4.2(a)—applies to all normal goods. Note that an Engel curve for clothing would have a similar shape (clothing consumption increases from 3 to 5 to 7 units as income increases).

Figure 4.4(b), derived from Figure 4.3, shows the Engel curve for hamburger. We see that hamburger consumption increases from 5 to 10 units as income

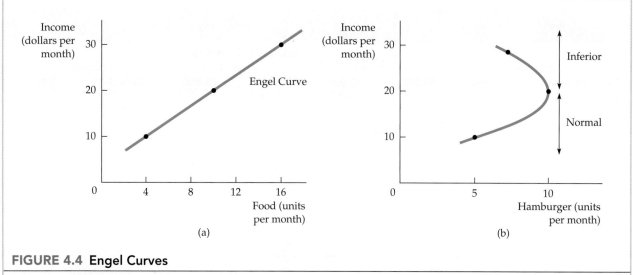

**FIGURE 4.4** **Engel Curves**

Engel curves relate the quantity of a good consumed to income. In **(a)**, food is a normal good and the Engel curve is upward sloping. In **(b)**, however, hamburger is a normal good for income less than $20 per month and an inferior good for income greater than $20 per month.

increases from $10 to $20. As income increases further, from $20 to $30, consumption falls to 8 units. The portion of the Engel curve that slopes downward is the income range within which hamburger is an inferior good.

---

**EXAMPLE 4.1**     ## Consumer Expenditures in the United States

The Engel curves we just examined apply to individual consumers. However, we can also derive Engel curves for groups of consumers. This information is particularly useful if we want to see how consumer spending varies among different income groups. Table 4.1 illustrates spending patterns for several items taken from a survey by the U.S. Bureau of Labor Statistics.

Although the data are averaged over many households, they can be interpreted as describing the expenditures of a typical family.

Note that the data relate *expenditures* on a particular item rather than the *quantity* of the item to income. The first two items, entertainment and owned dwellings, are consumption goods for which the income elasticity of demand is high. Average family expenditures on entertainment increase more than five-fold when we move from the lowest to highest income group. The same pattern applies to the purchase of homes: There is a more than a threefold increase in expenditures from the lowest to the highest category.

In contrast, expenditures on *rental* housing actually *fall* as income rises. This pattern reflects the fact that most higher-income individuals own rather than rent homes. Thus rental housing is an inferior good, at least for incomes above

**TABLE 4.1** Annual U.S. Household Consumer Expenditures

| Expenditures ($) on: | INCOME GROUP (2005$) | | | | | | |
|---|---|---|---|---|---|---|---|
| | Less than $10,000 | 10,000–19,999 | 20,000–29,999 | 30,000–39,999 | 40,000–49,999 | 50,000–69,999 | 70,000 and above |
| Entertainment | 844 | 947 | 1191 | 1677 | 1933 | 2402 | 4542 |
| Owned Dwelling | 4272 | 4716 | 5701 | 6776 | 7771 | 8972 | 14763 |
| Rented Dwelling | 2672 | 2779 | 2980 | 2977 | 2818 | 2255 | 1379 |
| Health Care | 1108 | 1874 | 2241 | 2361 | 2778 | 2746 | 3812 |
| Food | 2901 | 3242 | 3942 | 4552 | 5234 | 6570 | 9247 |
| Clothing | 861 | 884 | 1106 | 1472 | 1450 | 1961 | 3245 |

*Source:* U.S. Department of Labor, Bureau of Labor Statistics, "Consumer Expenditure Survey, Annual Report 2005."

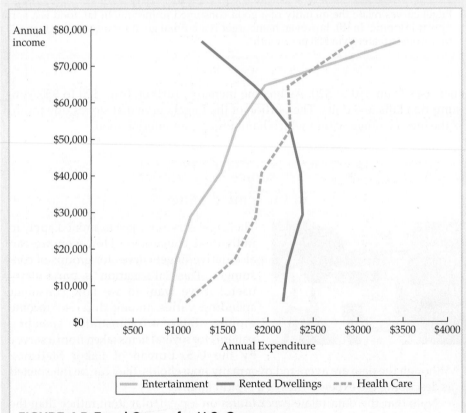

**FIGURE 4.5 Engel Curves for U.S. Consumers**

Average per-household expenditures on rented dwellings, health care, and entertainment are plotted as functions of annual income. Health care and entertainment are normal goods, as expenditures increase with income. Rental housing, however, is an inferior good for incomes above $35,000.

$35,000 per year. Finally, note that health care, food, and clothing are consumption items for which the income elasticities are positive, but not as high as for entertainment or owner-occupied housing.

The data in Table 4.1 for rented dwellings, health care, and entertainment have been plotted in Figure 4.5. Observe in the three Engel curves that as income rises, expenditures on entertainment increase rapidly, while expenditures on rental housing increase when income is low, but decrease once income exceeds $35,000.

## Substitutes and Complements

The demand curves that we graphed in Chapter 2 showed the relationship between the price of a good and the quantity demanded, with preferences, income, and the prices of all other goods held constant. For many goods, demand is related to the consumption and prices of other goods. Baseball bats and baseballs, hot dogs and mustard, and computer hardware and software are all examples of goods that tend to be used together. Other goods, such as cola and diet cola, owner-occupied houses and rental apartments, movie tickets and videocassette rentals, tend to substitute for one another.

Recall from Section 2.1 (page 22) that two goods are *substitutes* if an increase in the price of one leads to an increase in the quantity demanded of the other. If the price of a movie ticket rises, we would expect individuals to rent more videos, because movie tickets and videos are substitutes. Similarly, two goods are *complements* if an increase in the price of one good leads to a decrease in the quantity demanded of the other. If the price of gasoline goes up, causing gasoline consumption to fall, we would expect the consumption of motor oil to fall as well, because gasoline and motor oil are used together. Two goods are *independent* if a change in the price of one good has no effect on the quantity demanded of the other.

One way to see whether two goods are complements or substitutes is to examine the price-consumption curve. Look again at Figure 4.1 (page 112). Note that in the downward-sloping portion of the price-consumption curve, food and clothing are substitutes: The lower price of food leads to a lower consumption of clothing (perhaps because as food expenditures increase, less income is available to spend on clothing). Similarly, food and clothing are complements in the upward-sloping portion of the curve: The lower price of food leads to higher clothing consumption (perhaps because the consumer eats more meals at restaurants and must be suitably dressed).

The fact that goods can be complements or substitutes suggests that when studying the effects of price changes in one market, it may be important to look at the consequences in related markets. (Interrelationships among markets are discussed in more detail in Chapter 16.) Determining whether two goods are complements, substitutes, or independent goods is ultimately an empirical question. To answer the question, we need to look at the ways in which the demand for the first good shifts (if at all) in response to a change in the price of the second. This question is more difficult than it sounds because lots of things are likely to be changing at the same time that the price of the first good changes. In fact, Section 4.6 of this chapter is devoted to examining ways to distinguish empirically among the many possible explanations for a change in the demand for the second good. First, however, it will be useful to undertake a basic theoretical exercise. In the next section, we delve into the ways in which a change in the price of a good can affect consumer demand.

## 4.2 INCOME AND SUBSTITUTION EFFECTS

A fall in the price of a good has two effects:

1. *Consumers will tend to buy more of the good that has become cheaper and less of those goods that are now relatively more expensive.* This response to a change in the relative prices of goods is called the *substitution effect*.

2. *Because one of the goods is now cheaper, consumers enjoy an increase in real purchasing power.* They are better off because they can buy the same amount of the good for less money, and thus have money left over for additional purchases. The change in demand resulting from this change in real purchasing power is called the *income effect*.

Normally, these two effects occur simultaneously, but it will be useful to distinguish between them for purposes of analysis. The specifics are illustrated in Figure 4.6, where the initial budget line is $RS$ and there are two goods, food and clothing. Here, the consumer maximizes utility by choosing the market basket at $A$, thereby obtaining the level of utility associated with the indifference curve $U_1$.

Now let's see what happens if the price of food falls, causing the budget line to rotate outward to line $RT$. The consumer now chooses the market basket at $B$

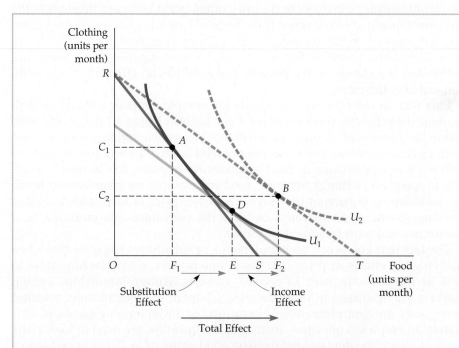

**FIGURE 4.6 Income and Substitution Effects: Normal Good**

A decrease in the price of food has both an income effect and a substitution effect. The consumer is initially at $A$, on budget line $RS$. When the price of food falls, consumption increases by $F_1F_2$ as the consumer moves to $B$. The substitution effect $F_1E$ (associated with a move from $A$ to $D$) changes the relative prices of food and clothing but keeps real income (satisfaction) constant. The income effect $EF_2$ (associated with a move from $D$ to $B$) keeps relative prices constant but increases purchasing power. Food is a normal good because the income effect $EF_2$ is positive.

on indifference curve $U_2$. Because market basket $B$ was chosen even though market basket $A$ was feasible, we know (from our discussion of revealed preference in Section 3.4) that $B$ is preferred to $A$. Thus, the reduction in the price of food allows the consumer to increase her level of satisfaction—her purchasing power has increased. The total change in the consumption of food caused by the lower price is given by $F_1F_2$. Initially, the consumer purchased $OF_1$ units of food, but after the price change, food consumption has increased to $OF_2$. Line segment $F_1F_2$, therefore, represents the increase in desired food purchases.

> In §3.4, we show how information about consumer preferences is revealed by consumption choices made.

## Substitution Effect

The drop in price has both a substitution effect and an income effect. The **substitution effect** is *the change in food consumption associated with a change in the price of food, with the level of utility held constant*. The substitution effect captures the change in food consumption that occurs as a result of the price change that makes food relatively cheaper than clothing. This substitution is marked by a movement along an indifference curve. In Figure 4.6, the substitution effect can be obtained by drawing a budget line which is parallel to the new budget line $RT$ (reflecting the lower relative price of food), but which is just tangent to the original indifference curve $U_1$ (holding the level of satisfaction constant). The new, lower imaginary budget line reflects the fact that nominal income was reduced in order to accomplish our conceptual goal of isolating the substitution effect. Given that budget line, the consumer chooses market basket $D$ and consumes $OE$ units of food. The line segment $F_1E$ thus represents the substitution effect.

• **substitution effect** Change in consumption of a good associated with a change in its price, with the level of utility held constant.

Figure 4.6 makes it clear that when the price of food declines, the substitution effect always leads to an increase in the quantity of food demanded. The explanation lies in the fourth assumption about consumer preferences discussed in Section 3.1—namely, that indifference curves are convex. Thus, with the convex indifference curves shown in the figure, the point that maximizes satisfaction on the new imaginary budget line parallel to $RT$ must lie below and to the right of the original point of tangency.

## Income Effect

Now let's consider the **income effect**: *the change in food consumption brought about by the increase in purchasing power, with relative prices held constant*. In Figure 4.6, we can see the income effect by moving from the imaginary budget line that passes through point $D$ to the parallel budget line, $RT$, which passes through $B$. The consumer chooses market basket $B$ on indifference curve $U_2$ (because the lower price of food has increased her level of utility). The increase in food consumption from $OE$ to $OF_2$ is the measure of the income effect, which is positive, because food is a *normal* good (consumers will buy more of it as their incomes increase). Because it reflects a movement from one indifference curve to another, the income effect measures the change in the consumer's purchasing power.

• **income effect** Change in consumption of a good resulting from an increase in purchasing power, with relative prices held constant.

We have seen in Figure 4.6 that the total effect of a change in price is given theoretically by the sum of the substitution effect and the income effect:

Total Effect $(F_1F_2)$ = Substitution Effect $(F_1E)$ + Income Effect $(EF_2)$

Recall that the direction of the substitution effect is always the same: A decline in price leads to an increase in consumption of the good. However, the income effect can move demand in either direction, depending on whether the good is normal or inferior.

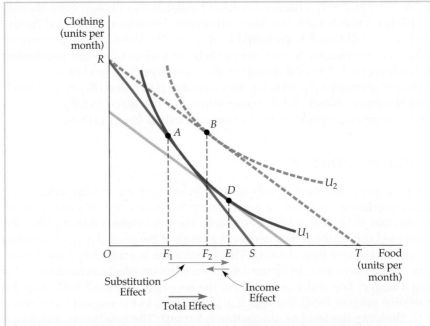

**FIGURE 4.7 Income and Substitution Effects: Inferior Good**

The consumer is initially at $A$ on budget line $RS$. With a decrease in the price of food, the consumer moves to $B$. The resulting change in food purchased can be broken down into a substitution effect, $F_1E$ (associated with a move from $A$ to $D$), and an income effect, $EF_2$ (associated with a move from $D$ to $B$). In this case, food is an inferior good because the income effect is negative. However, because the substitution effect exceeds the income effect, the decrease in the price of food leads to an increase in the quantity of food demanded.

A good is *inferior* when the income effect is negative: As income rises, consumption falls. Figure 4.7 shows income and substitution effects for an inferior good. The negative income effect is measured by line segment $EF_2$. Even with inferior goods, the income effect is rarely large enough to outweigh the substitution effect. As a result, when the price of an inferior good falls, its consumption almost always increases.

## A Special Case: The Giffen Good

• **Giffen good**  Good whose demand curve slopes upward because the (negative) income effect is larger than the substitution effect.

Theoretically, the income effect may be large enough to cause the demand curve for a good to slope upward. We call such a good a **Giffen good**, and Figure 4.8 shows its income and substitution effects. Initially, the consumer is at $A$, consuming relatively little clothing and much food. Now the price of food declines. The decline in the price of food frees enough income so that the consumer desires to buy more clothing and fewer units of food, as illustrated by $B$. Revealed preference tells us that the consumer is better off at $B$ rather than $A$ even though less food is consumed.

Though intriguing, the Giffen good is rarely of practical interest because it requires a large negative income effect. But the income effect is usually small: Individually, most goods account for only a small part of a consumer's budget. Large income effects are often associated with normal rather than inferior goods (e.g., total spending on food or housing).

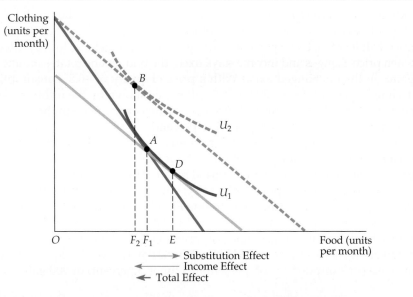

**FIGURE 4.8 Upward-Sloping Demand Curve: The Giffen Good**

When food is an inferior good, and when the income effect is large enough to dominate the substitution effect, the demand curve will be upward-sloping. The consumer is initially at point $A$, but, after the price of food falls, moves to $B$ and consumes less food. Because the income effect $EF_2$ is larger than the substitution effect $F_1E$, the decrease in the price of food leads to a lower quantity of food demanded.

## EXAMPLE 4.2  The Effects of a Gasoline Tax

In part to conserve energy and in part to raise revenues, the U.S. government has often considered increasing the federal gasoline tax. In 1993, for example, a modest 7.5 cent increase was enacted as part of a larger budget-reform package. This increase was much less than the increase that would have been necessary to put U.S. gasoline prices on a par with those in Europe. Because an important goal of higher gasoline taxes is to discourage gasoline consumption, the government has also considered ways of passing the resulting income back to consumers. One popular suggestion is a rebate program in which tax revenues would be returned to households on an equal per-capita basis. What would be the effect of such a program?

Let's begin by focusing on the effect of the program over a period of five years. The relevant price elasticity of demand is about $-0.5$.[1] Suppose that a low-income consumer uses about 1200 gallons of gasoline per year, that gasoline costs \$1 per gallon, and that our consumer's annual income is \$9000.

Figure 4.9 shows the effect of the gasoline tax. (The graph has intentionally been drawn not to scale so that the effects we are discussing can be seen more clearly.) The original budget line is $AB$, and the consumer maximizes utility (on

---

[1]We saw in Chapter 2 that the price elasticity of demand for gasoline varied substantially from the short run to the long run, ranging from $-0.11$ in the short run to $-1.17$ in the long run.

indifference curve $U_2$) by consuming the market basket at $C$, buying 1200 gallons of gasoline and spending $7800 on other goods. If the tax is 50 cents per gallon, price will increase by 50 percent, shifting the new budget line to $AD$.[2] (Recall that when price changes and income stays fixed, the budget line rotates around a pivot point on the unchanged axis.) With a price elasticity of −0.5, consumption will decline 25 percent, from 1200 to 900 gallons, as shown by the utility-maximizing point $E$ on indifference curve $U_1$ (for every 1-percent increase in the price of gasoline, quantity demanded drops by 1/2 percent).

The rebate program, however, partially counters this effect. Suppose that because the tax revenue per person is about $450 (900 gallons times 50 cents per gallon), each consumer receives a $450 rebate. How does this increased income affect gasoline consumption? The effect can be shown graphically by shifting the budget line upward by $450, to line $FJ$, which is parallel to $AD$. How much gasoline does our consumer buy now? In Chapter 2, we saw that the income elasticity of demand for gasoline is approximately 0.3. Because $450 represents a 5-percent increase in income ($450/$9000 = 0.05), we would expect the rebate to increase consumption by 1.5 percent (0.3 times 5 percent) of 900 gallons, or 13.5

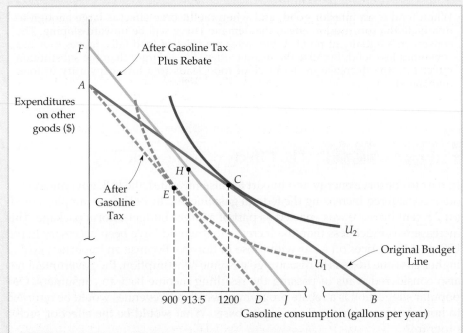

**FIGURE 4.9** **Effect of a Gasoline Tax with a Rebate**

A gasoline tax is imposed when the consumer is initially buying 1200 gallons of gasoline at point $C$. After the tax takes effect, the budget line shifts from $AB$ to $AD$ and the consumer maximizes his preferences by choosing $E$, with a gasoline consumption of 900 gallons. However, when the proceeds of the tax are rebated to the consumer, his consumption increases somewhat, to 913.5 gallons at $H$. Despite the rebate program, the consumer's gasoline consumption has fallen, as has his level of satisfaction.

---

[2]To simplify the example, we have assumed that the entire tax is paid by consumers in the form of a higher price. A broader analysis of tax shifting is presented in Chapter 9.

gallons. The new utility-maximizing consumption choice at $H$ reflects this expectation. (We omitted the indifference curve that is tangent at $H$ to simplify the diagram.) With the rebate program, the tax would reduce gasoline consumption by 286.5 gallons, from 1200 to 913.5. Because the income elasticity of demand for gasoline is relatively low, the income effect of the rebate program is dominated by the substitution effect, and the program with a rebate does indeed reduce consumption.

In order to put a real tax-rebate program into effect, Congress would have to solve a variety of practical problems. First, incoming tax receipts and rebate expenditures would vary from year to year, making it difficult to plan the budgeting process. For example, the tax rebate of $450 in the first year of the program is an increase in income. During the second year, it would lead to some increase in gasoline consumption among the low-income consumers that we are studying. With increased consumption, however, the tax paid and the rebate received by an individual will increase in the second year. As a result, it may be difficult to predict the size of the program budget.

Figure 4.9 reveals that the gasoline tax program makes this particular low-income consumer slightly worse off because $H$ lies just below indifference curve $U_2$. Of course, some low-income consumers might actually benefit from the program (if, for example, they consume less gasoline on average than the group of consumers whose consumption determines the selected rebate). Nevertheless, the substitution effect caused by the tax will make consumers, on average, worse off.

Why, then, introduce such a program? Those who support gasoline taxes argue that they promote national security (by reducing dependence on foreign oil) and encourage conservation, thus helping to slow global warming by reducing the buildup of carbon dioxide in the atmosphere. We will further examine the impact of a gasoline tax in Chapter 9.

## 4.3 MARKET DEMAND

So far, we have discussed the demand curve for an individual consumer. Now we turn to the market demand curve. Recall from Chapter 2 that a market demand curve shows how much of a good consumers overall are willing to buy as its price changes. In this section, we show how **market demand curves** can be derived as the sum of the individual demand curves of all consumers in a particular market.

• **market demand curve** Curve relating the quantity of a good that all consumers in a market will buy to its price.

### From Individual to Market Demand

To keep things simple, let's assume that only three consumers ($A$, $B$, and $C$) are in the market for coffee. Table 4.2 tabulates several points on each consumer's demand curve. The market demand, column (5), is found by adding columns (2), (3), and (4), representing our three consumers, to determine the total quantity demanded at every price. When the price is $3, for example, the total quantity demanded is $2 + 6 + 10$, or 18.

Figure 4.10 shows these same three consumers' demand curves for coffee (labeled $D_A$, $D_B$, and $D_C$). In the graph, the market demand curve is the

| TABLE 4.2 | Determining the Market Demand Curve | | | |
|---|---|---|---|---|
| **(1)**<br>**Price**<br>**($)** | **(2)**<br>**Individual A**<br>**(Units)** | **(3)**<br>**Individual B**<br>**(Units)** | **(4)**<br>**Individual C**<br>**(Units)** | **(5)**<br>**Market**<br>**(Units)** |
| 1 | 6 | 10 | 16 | 32 |
| 2 | 4 | 8 | 13 | 25 |
| 3 | 2 | 6 | 10 | 18 |
| 4 | 0 | 4 | 7 | 11 |
| 5 | 0 | 2 | 4 | 6 |

*horizontal summation* of the demands of each consumer. We sum horizontally to find the total amount that the three consumers will demand at any given price. For example, when the price is $4, the quantity demanded by the market (11 units) is the sum of the quantity demanded by A (no units), by B (4 units), and by C (7 units). Because all of the individual demand curves slope downward, the market demand curve will also slope downward. However, even though each of the individual demand curves is a straight line, the market demand curve need not be. In Figure 4.10, for example, the market demand curve is *kinked* because one consumer makes no purchases at prices that the other consumers find acceptable (those above $4).

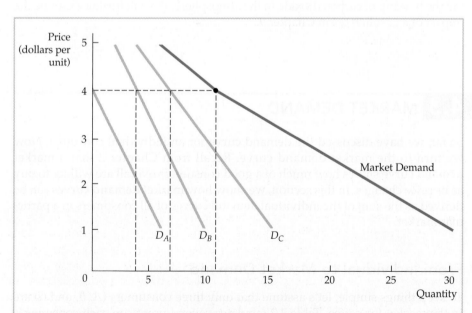

**FIGURE 4.10 Summing to Obtain a Market Demand Curve**

The market demand curve is obtained by summing our three consumers' demand curves $D_A$, $D_B$, and $D_C$. At each price, the quantity of coffee demanded by the market is the sum of the quantities demanded by each consumer. At a price of $4, for example, the quantity demanded by the market (11 units) is the sum of the quantity demanded by A (no units), B (4 units), and C (7 units).

Two points should be noted as a result of this analysis:

1. *The market demand curve will shift to the right as more consumers enter the market.*
2. *Factors that influence the demands of many consumers will also affect market demand.* Suppose, for example, that most consumers in a particular market earn more income and, as a result, increase their demands for coffee. Because each consumer's demand curve shifts to the right, so will the market demand curve.

The aggregation of individual demands into market demands is not just a theoretical exercise. It becomes important in practice when market demands are built up from the demands of different demographic groups or from consumers located in different areas. For example, we might obtain information about the demand for home computers by adding independently obtained information about the demands of the following groups:

- Households with children
- Households without children
- Single individuals

Or, we might determine U.S. wheat demand by aggregating domestic demand (i.e., by U.S. consumers) and export demand (i.e., by foreign consumers), as we will see in Example 4.3.

## Elasticity of Demand

Recall from Section 2.4 (page 34) that the price elasticity of demand measures the percentage change in the quantity demanded resulting from a 1-percent increase in price. Denoting the quantity of a good by $Q$ and its price by $P$, the *price elasticity of demand* is

> In §2.4, we show how the price elasticity of demand describes the responsiveness of consumer demands to changes in price.

$$E_P = \frac{\Delta Q/Q}{\Delta P/P} = \left(\frac{P}{Q}\right)\left(\frac{\Delta Q}{\Delta P}\right) \qquad \text{(4.1)}$$

(Here, because $\Delta$ means "a change in," $\Delta Q/Q$ is the percentage change in $Q$.)

**Inelastic Demand** When demand is inelastic (i.e., $E_P$ is less than 1 in absolute value), the quantity demanded is relatively unresponsive to changes in price. As a result, total expenditure on the product increases when the price increases. Suppose, for example, that a family currently uses 1000 gallons of gasoline a year when the price is $1 per gallon; suppose also that our family's price elasticity of demand for gasoline is –0.5. If the price of gasoline increases to $1.10 (a 10-percent increase), the consumption of gasoline falls to 950 gallons (a 5-percent decrease). Total expenditure on gasoline, however, will increase from $1000 (1000 gallons × $1 per gallon) to $1045 (950 gallons × $1.10 per gallon).

> Recall from §2.4 that because the magnitude of an elasticity refers to its absolute value, an elasticity of –0.5 is less in magnitude than a –1.0 elasticity.

**Elastic Demand** In contrast, when demand is elastic ($E_P$ is greater than 1 in absolute value), total expenditure on the product decreases as the price goes up.

Suppose that a family buys 100 pounds of chicken per year at a price of $2 per pound; the price elasticity of demand for chicken is −1.5. If the price of chicken increases to $2.20 (a 10-percent increase), our family's consumption of chicken falls to 85 pounds a year (a 15-percent decrease). Total expenditure on chicken will also fall, from $200 (100 pounds × $2 per pound) to $187 (85 pounds × $2.20 per pound).

• **isoelastic demand curve**
Demand curve with a constant price elasticity.

In §2.4, we show that when the demand curve is linear, demand becomes more elastic as the price of the product increases.

**Isoelastic Demand** When the price elasticity of demand is constant all along the demand curve, we say that the curve is **isoelastic**. Figure 4.11 shows an isoelastic demand curve. Note how this demand curve is bowed inward. In contrast, recall from Section 2.4 what happens to the price elasticity of demand as we move along a *linear demand curve*. Although the slope of the linear curve is constant, the price elasticity of demand is not. It is zero when the price is zero, and it increases in magnitude until it becomes infinite when the price is sufficiently high for the quantity demanded to become zero.

A special case of the isoelastic curve is the *unit-elastic demand curve*: a demand curve with price elasticity always equal to −1, as is the case for the curve in Figure 4.11. In this case, total expenditure remains the same after a price change. A price increase, for instance, leads to a decrease in the quantity demanded that leaves the total expenditure on the good unchanged. Suppose, for example, that the total expenditure on first-run movies in Berkeley, California, is $5.4 million per year, regardless of the price of a movie ticket. For all points along the demand curve, the price times the quantity will be $5.4 million. If the price is $6, the quantity will be 900,000 tickets; if the price increases to $9, the quantity will drop to 600,000 tickets, as shown in Figure 4.11.

Table 4.3 summarizes the relationship between elasticity and expenditure. It is useful to review this table from the perspective of the seller of the good rather than the buyer. (What the seller perceives as total revenue, the consumer views as total expenditures.) When demand is inelastic, a price increase leads only to a

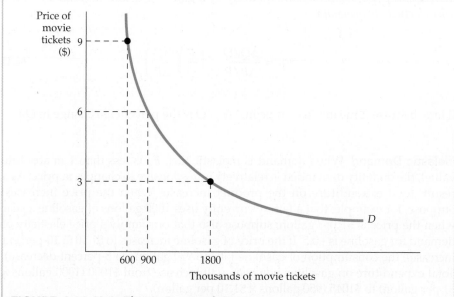

**FIGURE 4.11 Unit-Elastic Demand Curve**

When the price elasticity of demand is −1.0 at every price, the total expenditure is constant along the demand curve *D*.

| TABLE 4.3 Price Elasticity and Consumer Expenditures | | |
|---|---|---|
| **Demand** | **If Price Increases, Expenditures** | **If Price Decreases, Expenditures** |
| Inelastic | Increase | Decrease |
| Unit elastic | Are unchanged | Are unchanged |
| Elastic | Decrease | Increase |

small decrease in quantity demanded; thus, the seller's total revenue increases. But when demand is elastic, a price increase leads to a large decline in quantity demanded and total revenue falls.

**EXAMPLE 4.3**     The Aggregate Demand for Wheat

In Chapter 2 (Example 2.5—page 38), we explained that the demand for U.S. wheat has two components: domestic demand (by U.S. consumers) and export demand (by foreign consumers). Let's see how the total demand for wheat during 2007 can be obtained by aggregating the domestic and foreign demands.

Domestic demand for wheat is given by the equation

$$Q_{DD} = 1430 - 55P$$

where $Q_{DD}$ is the number of bushels (in millions) demanded domestically, and $P$ is the price in dollars per bushel. Export demand is given by

$$Q_{DE} = 1470 - 70P$$

where $Q_{DE}$ is the number of bushels (in millions) demanded from abroad. As shown in Figure 4.12, domestic demand, given by $AB$, is relatively price inelastic. (Statistical studies have shown that price elasticity of domestic demand is about $-0.2$ to $-0.3$.) However, export demand, given by $CD$, is more price elastic, with an elasticity of about $-0.4$. Why? Export demand is more elastic than domestic demand because poorer countries that import U.S. wheat turn to other grains and foodstuffs if wheat prices rise.[3]

To obtain the world demand for wheat, we set the left side of each demand equation equal to the quantity of wheat (the variable on the horizontal axis). We then add the right side of the equations, obtaining

$$Q_{DD} + Q_{DE} = (1430 - 55P) + (1470 - 70P) = 2900 - 125P$$

This generates the line segment $EF$ in Figure 4.12.

At all prices above point $C$, however, there is no export demand, so that world demand and domestic demand are identical. As a result, for all prices above $C$, world demand is given by line segment $AE$. (If we were to add $Q_{DE}$ for prices above $C$, we would be incorrectly adding a negative export demand to a positive domestic demand.) As the figure shows, the resulting total demand for wheat, given by $AEF$, is kinked. The kink occurs at point $E$, the price level above which there is no export demand.

---

[3]For a survey of statistical studies of demand and supply elasticities and an analysis of the U.S. wheat market, see Larry Salathe and Sudchada Langley, "An Empirical Analysis of Alternative Export Subsidy Programs for U.S. Wheat," *Agricultural Economics Research* 38, No. 1 (Winter 1986).

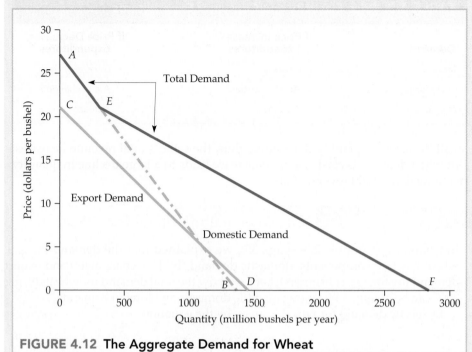

**FIGURE 4.12 The Aggregate Demand for Wheat**

The total world demand for wheat is the horizontal sum of the domestic demand *AB* and the export demand *CD*. Even though each individual demand curve is linear, the market demand curve is kinked, reflecting the fact that there is no export demand when the price of wheat is greater than about $21 per bushel.

---

**EXAMPLE 4.4**　　The Demand for Housing

Housing is typically the most important single expenditure in a household's budget—on average, households spend 25 percent of their income on housing. A family's demand for housing depends on the age and status of the household making the purchasing decision. One approach to the housing demand is to relate the number of rooms per house for each household (the quantity demanded) both to an estimate of the price of an additional room in a house and to the household's family income. (Prices of rooms vary because of differences in construction costs, including the price of land.) Table 4.4 lists price and income elasticities for different demographic groups.

Elasticities show that the size of houses that consumers demand (as measured by the number of rooms) is relatively insensitive to either income or price. However, there are significant differences among subgroups of the population. For example, families with young household heads have a price elasticity of −0.25, which is more price elastic than the demands of families with older household heads. Presumably, families buying houses are more price sensitive when parents and their children are younger and there may be plans for more children. Among married households, the income elasticity of demand for rooms also increases with age, which tells us that older households buy larger houses than younger households.

| TABLE 4.4 Price and Income Elasticities of the Demand for Rooms | | |
|---|:---:|:---:|
| **Group** | **Price Elasticity** | **Income Elasticity** |
| Single individuals | −0.10 | 0.21 |
| Married, head of household age less than 30, 1 child | −0.25 | 0.06 |
| Married, head age 30–39, 2 or more children | −0.15 | 0.12 |
| Married, head age 50 or older, 1 child | −0.08 | 0.19 |

Price and income elasticities of demand for housing also depend on where people live.[4] Demand in central cities is much more price elastic than in suburbs. Income elasticities, however, increase as one moves farther from the central city. Thus poorer (on average) central-city residents (who live where the price of land is relatively high) are more price sensitive in their housing choices than their wealthier suburban counterparts.

For poor families, the fraction of income spent on housing is large. For instance, renters with an income in the bottom 20 percent of the income distribution spend roughly 55 percent of their income on housing.[5] Many government programs, such as subsidies, rent controls, and land-use regulations, have been proposed to shape the housing market in ways that might ease the housing burden on the poor.

How effective are income subsidies? To answer this, we need to know the income elasticity of demand for housing for low-income households. If the subsidy increases the demand for housing substantially, then we can presume that the subsidy will lead to improved housing for the poor.[6] On the other hand, if the extra money were spent on items other than housing, the subsidy, while perhaps still beneficial, will have failed to address policy concerns related to housing.

The evidence indicates that for poor households (with incomes in the bottom tenth percentile of all households), the income elasticity of housing is only about 0.09, which implies that income subsidies would be spent primarily on items other than housing. By comparison, the income elasticity for housing among the wealthiest households (the top 10 percent) is about 0.54.

---

[4]See Allen C. Goodman and Masahiro Kawai, "Functional Form, Sample Selection, and Housing Demand," *Journal of Urban Economics* 2 (September 1986): 155–67. Also see Paul Cheshire and Stephen Sheppard, "Estimating the Demand for Housing, Land, and Neighborhood Characteristics," *Oxford Bulletin of Economics and Statistics*, 60 (1998): 357–82.

[5]This is the starting point of the "affordable" housing debate. For an overview, see John Quigley and Steven Raphael, "Is Housing Unaffordable? Why Isn't It More Affordable," *Journal of Economic Perspectives* 18 (2004): 191–214.

[6]Julia L. Hansen, John P. Formby, and W. James Smith, "Estimating the Income Elasticity of Demand for Housing: A Comparison of Traditional and Lorenz-Concentration Curve Methodologies," *Journal of Housing Economics* 7 (1998): 328–42.

## 4.4 CONSUMER SURPLUS

**• consumer surplus**
Difference between what a consumer is willing to pay for a good and the amount actually paid.

Consumers buy goods because the purchase makes them better off. **Consumer surplus** measures *how much* better off individuals are, in the aggregate, because they can buy goods in the market. Because different consumers place different values on the consumption of particular goods, the maximum amount they are willing to pay for those goods also differs. *Individual consumer surplus is the difference between the maximum amount that a consumer is willing to pay for a good and the amount that the consumer actually pays.* Suppose, for example, that a student would have been willing to pay $13 for a rock concert ticket even though she only had to pay $12. The $1 difference is her consumer surplus.[7] When we add the consumer surpluses of all consumers who buy a good, we obtain a measure of the *aggregate* consumer surplus.

### Consumer Surplus and Demand

Consumer surplus can be calculated easily if we know the demand curve. To see the relationship between demand and consumer surplus, let's examine the individual demand curve for concert tickets shown in Figure 4.13. (Although the following discussion applies to this particular individual demand curve, a similar argument also applies to a market demand curve.) Drawing the demand

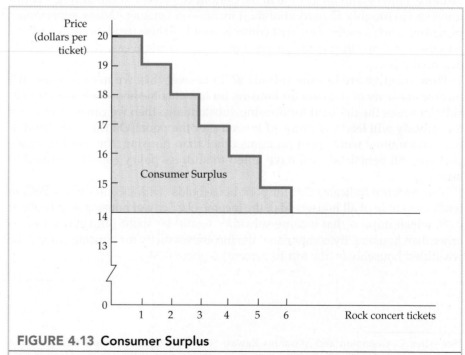

**FIGURE 4.13 Consumer Surplus**

Consumer surplus is the total benefit from the consumption of a product, less the total cost of purchasing it. Here, the consumer surplus associated with six concert tickets (purchased at $14 per ticket) is given by the yellow-shaded area.

---

[7]Measuring consumer surplus in dollars involves an implicit assumption about the shape of consumers' indifference curves: namely, that the marginal utility associated with increases in a consumer's income remains constant within the range of income in question. In many cases, this is a reasonable assumption. It may be suspect, however, when large changes in income are involved.

curve as a staircase rather than a straight line shows us how to measure the value that our consumer obtains from buying different numbers of tickets.

When deciding how many tickets to buy, our student might reason as follows: The first ticket costs $14 but is worth $20. This $20 valuation is obtained by using the demand curve to find the maximum amount that she will pay for each *additional* ticket ($20 being the maximum that she will pay for the *first* ticket). The first ticket is worth purchasing because it generates $6 of surplus value above and beyond its cost. The second ticket is also worth buying because it generates a surplus of $5 ($19 – $14). The third ticket generates a surplus of $4. The fourth, however, generates a surplus of only $3, the fifth a surplus of $2, and the sixth a surplus of just $1. Our student is indifferent about purchasing the seventh ticket (which generates zero surplus) and prefers not to buy any more than that because the value of each additional ticket is less than its cost. In Figure 4.13, consumer surplus is found by *adding the excess values or surpluses for all units purchased.* In this case, then, consumer surplus equals

$$\$6 + \$5 + \$4 + \$3 + \$2 + \$1 = \$21$$

To calculate the aggregate consumer surplus in a market, we simply find the area below the *market* demand curve and above the price line. For our rock concert example, this principle is illustrated in Figure 4.14. Now, because the number of tickets sold is measured in thousands and individuals' demand curves differ, the market demand curve appears as a straight line. Note that the

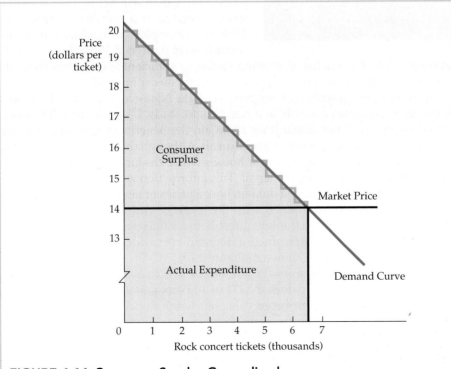

**FIGURE 4.14 Consumer Surplus Generalized**

For the market as a whole, consumer surplus is measured by the area under the demand curve and above the line representing the purchase price of the good. Here, the consumer surplus is given by the yellow-shaded triangle and is equal to 1/2 × ($20 – $14) × 6500 = $19,500.

actual expenditure on tickets is 6500 × $14 = $91,000. Consumer surplus, shown as the yellow-shaded triangle, is

$$1/2 \times (\$20 - \$14) \times 6500 = \$19,500$$

This amount is the total benefit to consumers, less what they paid for the tickets.

Of course, market demand curves are not always straight lines. Nonetheless, we can always measure consumer surplus by finding the area below the demand curve and above the price line.

**Applying Consumer Surplus** Consumer surplus has important applications in economics. When added over many individuals, it measures the aggregate benefit that consumers obtain from buying goods in a market. When we combine consumer surplus with the aggregate profits that producers obtain, we can evaluate both the costs and benefits not only of alternative market structures, but of public policies that alter the behavior of consumers and firms in those markets.

---

**EXAMPLE 4.5** The Value of Clean Air

Air is free in the sense that we don't pay to breathe it. But the absence of a market for air may help explain why the air quality in some cities has been deteriorating for decades. To encourage cleaner air, Congress passed the Clean Air Act in 1977 and has since amended it a number of times. In 1990, for example, automobile emissions controls were tightened. Were these controls worth it? Were the benefits of cleaning up the air sufficient to outweigh the costs imposed directly on car producers and indirectly on car buyers?

To answer these questions, Congress asked the National Academy of Sciences to evaluate emissions controls in a cost-benefit study. Using empirically determined estimates of the demand for clean air, the benefits portion of the study determined how much people value clean air. Although there is no actual market for clean air, people do pay more for houses where the air is clean than for comparable houses in areas with dirtier air. This information was used to estimate the demand for clean air.[8] Detailed data on house prices in neighborhoods of Boston and Los Angeles were compared with the levels of various air pollutants. The effects of other variables that might affect house values were taken into account statistically. The study determined a demand curve for clean air that looked approximately like the one shown in Figure 4.15.

The horizontal axis measures the amount of *air pollution reduction*, as exemplified by a level of nitrogen oxides (NOX) of 10 parts per 100 million (pphm); the vertical axis measures the increased value of a home associated with those reductions. Consider, for example, the demand for cleaner air of a homeowner in a city in which the air is rather dirty. If the family were required to pay $1000 for each 1 pphm reduction in air pollution, it would choose $A$ on the demand curve in order to obtain a pollution reduction of 5 pphm.

---

[8]The results are summarized in Daniel L. Rubinfeld, "Market Approaches to the Measurement of the Benefits of Air Pollution Abatement," in Ann Friedlaender, ed., *The Benefits and Costs of Cleaning the Air* (Cambridge: MIT Press, 1976), 240–73.

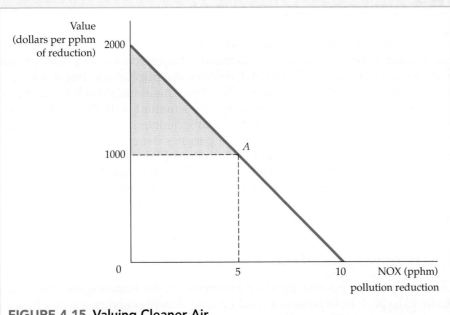

**FIGURE 4.15 Valuing Cleaner Air**

The yellow-shaded triangle gives the consumer surplus generated when air pollution is reduced by 5 parts per 100 million of nitrogen oxide at a cost of $1000 per part reduced. The surplus is created because most consumers are willing to pay more than $1000 for each unit reduction of nitrogen oxide.

How much is a 50-percent, or 5-pphm, reduction in pollution worth to this same family? We can measure this value by calculating the consumer surplus associated with reducing air pollution. Because the price for this reduction is $1000 per unit, the family would pay $5000. However, the family values all but the last unit of reduction by more than $1000. As a result, the yellow-shaded triangle in Figure 4.15 gives the value of the cleanup (above and beyond the payment). Because the demand curve is a straight line, the surplus can be calculated from the area of the triangle whose height is $1000 ($2000 − $1000) and whose base is 5 pphm. Therefore, the value to the household of the nitrogen oxide pollution reduction is $2500.

A more recent study that focused on suspended participates also found that households place substantial value on air pollution reduction.[9] A one-milligram per cubic meter reduction in total suspended particulates (from a mean of about 60 milligrams per cubic meter) was valued at $2,400 per household.

A complete cost-benefit analysis would use a measure of the total benefit of the cleanup—the benefit per household times the number of households. This figure could be compared with the total cost of the cleanup to determine whether such a project was worthwhile. We will discuss clean air further in Chapter 18, when we describe the tradeable emissions permits that were introduced by the Clean Air Act Amendments of 1990.

---

[9]Kenneth Y. Chay and Michael Greenstone, "Does Air Quality Matter? Evidence from the Housing Market," *Journal of Political Economy* 113 (2005): 376–424.

## 4.5 NETWORK EXTERNALITIES

So far, we have assumed that people's demands for a good are independent of one another. In other words, Tom's demand for coffee depends on Tom's tastes and income, the price of coffee, and perhaps the price of tea. But it does not depend on Dick's or Harry's demand for coffee. This assumption has enabled us to obtain the market demand curve simply by summing individuals' demands.

For some goods, however, one person's demand also depends on the demands of *other* people. In particular, a person's demand may be affected by the number of other people who have purchased the good. If this is the case, there exists a **network externality**. Network externalities can be positive or negative. A *positive* network externality exists *if the quantity of a good demanded by a typical consumer increases in response to the growth in purchases of other consumers.* If the quantity demanded decreases, there is a *negative* network externality.

> • **network externality**
> Situation in which each individual's demand depends on the purchases of other individuals.

### The Bandwagon Effect

> • **bandwagon effect**
> Positive network externality in which a consumer wishes to possess a good in part because others do.

One example of a positive network externality is the **bandwagon effect**—the desire to be in style, to possess a good because almost everyone else has it, or to indulge in a fad. The bandwagon effect often arises with children's toys (Nintendo video games, for example). In fact, exploiting this effect is a major objective in marketing and advertising toys. Often it is also the key to success in selling clothing.

The bandwagon effect is illustrated in Figure 4.16, in which the horizontal axis measures the sales of some fashionable good in thousands per month. Suppose consumers think that only 20,000 people have bought a certain good. Because this is a small number relative to the total population, consumers will have little motivation to buy the good in order to be in style. Some consumers may still buy it (depending on price), but only for its intrinsic value. In this case, demand is given by the curve $D_{20}$. (This hypothetical demand curve assumes that there are no externalities.)

Suppose instead that consumers think that 40,000 people have bought the good. Now they find the good more attractive and want to buy more. The demand curve is $D_{40}$, which is to the right of $D_{20}$. Similarly, if consumers think that 60,000 people have bought the good, the demand curve will be $D_{60}$, and so on. The more people consumers believe to have bought the good, the farther to the right the demand curve shifts.

Ultimately, consumers will get a good sense of how many people have in fact purchased a good. This number will depend, of course, on its price. In Figure 4.16, for example, we see that if the price were $30, 40,000 people would buy the good. Thus the relevant demand curve would be $D_{40}$. If the price were $20, 80,000 people would buy the good and the relevant demand curve would be $D_{80}$. *The market demand curve is therefore found by joining the points on the curves $D_{20}$, $D_{40}$, $D_{60}$, $D_{80}$, and $D_{100}$ that correspond to the quantities 20,000, 40,000, 60,000, 80,000 and 100,000.*

Compared with the curves $D_{20}$, etc., the market demand curve is relatively elastic. To see why the bandwagon effect leads to a more elastic demand curve, consider the effect of a drop in price from $30 to $20, with a demand curve of $D_{40}$. If there were no bandwagon effect, quantity demanded would increase from 40,000 to only 48,000. But as more people buy the good and it becomes stylish to own it, the bandwagon effect increases quantity demanded further, to 80,000. Thus, the bandwagon effect increases the response of demand to price

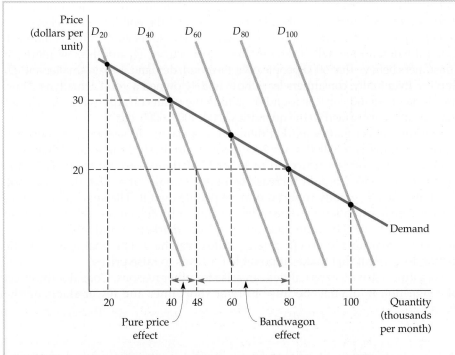

**FIGURE 4.16 Positive Network Externality: Bandwagon Effect**

A bandwagon effect is a positive network externality in which the quantity of a good that an individual demands grows in response to the growth of purchases by other individuals. Here, as the price of the product falls from \$30 to \$20, the bandwagon effect causes the demand for the good to shift to the right, from $D_{40}$ to $D_{80}$.

changes—i.e., it makes demand more elastic. As we'll see later, this result has important implications for producers' pricing strategies.

Although the bandwagon effect is associated with fads and stylishness, positive network externalities can arise for other reasons. The greater the number of people who own a particular good, the greater the intrinsic value of that good to each owner. For example, if I am the only person to own a compact disc player, it will not be economical for companies to manufacture compact discs; without the discs, the CD player will obviously be of little value to me. But the greater the number of people who own players, the more discs will be manufactured and the greater will be the value of the player to me. The same is true for personal computers: The more people who own them, the more software will be written, and thus the more useful computers will be to people who own them.

## The Snob Effect

Network externalities are sometimes negative. Consider the **snob effect**, which refers to the desire to own exclusive or unique goods. The quantity demanded of a "snob good" is higher the *fewer* the people who own it. Rare works of art, specially designed sports cars, and made-to-order clothing are snob goods. The value one gets from a painting or a sports car is partly the prestige, status, and exclusivity resulting from the fact that few other people own one like it.

• **snob effect** Negative network externality in which a consumer wishes to own an exclusive or unique good.

Figure 4.17 illustrates the snob effect. $D_2$ is the demand curve that would apply if consumers believed that only 2000 people owned the good. If they believe that 4000 people own the good, it is less exclusive, and so its snob value is reduced. Quantity demanded will therefore be lower; curve $D_4$ applies. Similarly, if consumers believe that 6000 people own the good, demand is even smaller and $D_6$ applies. Eventually, consumers learn how widely owned a good actually is. Thus, the market demand curve is found by joining the points on curves $D_2$, $D_4$, $D_6$, etc., that actually correspond to the quantities 2000, 4000, 6000, etc.

The snob effect makes market demand less elastic. To see why, suppose the price was initially $30,000, with 2000 people purchasing the good. What happens when the price is lowered to $15,000? If there were no snob effect, the quantity purchased would increase to 14,000 (along curve $D_2$). But as a snob good, its value is greatly reduced if more people own it. The snob effect dampens the increase in quantity demanded, cutting it by 8000 units; the net increase in sales is only to 6000 units. For many goods, marketing and advertising are geared to creating a snob effect (e.g., Rolex watches). The goal is less elastic demand—a result that makes it possible for firms to raise prices.

Negative network externalities can arise for other reasons. Consider the effect of congestion in queues. Because I prefer short lines and fewer skiers on the

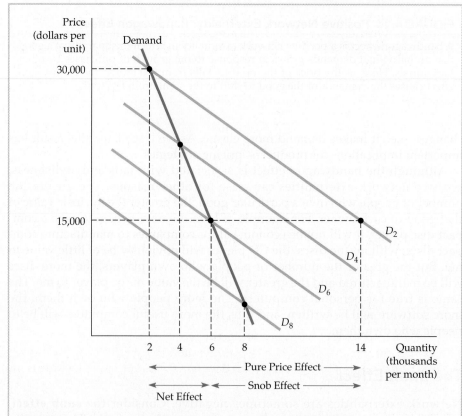

**FIGURE 4.17 Negative Network Externality: Snob Effect**

The snob effect is a negative network externality in which the quantity of a good that an individual demands falls in response to the growth of purchases by other individuals. Here, as the price falls from $30,000 to $15,000 and more people buy the good, the snob effect causes the demand for the good to shift to the left, from $D_2$ to $D_6$.

slopes, the value I obtain from a lift ticket at a ski resort is lower the more people there are who have bought tickets. Likewise for entry to an amusement park, skating rink, or beach.[10]

---

**EXAMPLE 4.6**  Network Externalities and the Demands for Computers and E-Mail

The 1950s and 1960s witnessed phenomenal growth in the demand for mainframe computers. From 1954 to 1965, for example, annual revenues from the leasing of mainframes increased at the extraordinary rate of 78 percent per year, while prices declined by 20 percent per year. Granted, prices were falling and the quality of computers was also increasing dramatically, but to account for this kind of growth, the elasticity of demand would have to be quite large. IBM, among other computer manufacturers, wanted to know what was going on.

An econometric study by Gregory Chow helped provide some answers.[11] Chow found that the demand for computers follows a "saturation curve"—a dynamic process whereby demand, though small at first, grows slowly. Soon, however, it grows rapidly, until finally nearly everyone likely to buy a product has done so, whereby the market becomes saturated. This rapid growth occurs because of a positive network externality: As more and more organizations own computers, as more and better software is written, and as more people are trained to use computers, the value of having a computer increases. Because this process causes demand to increase, still more software and better trained users are needed, and so on.

This network externality was an important part of the demand for computers. Chow found that it could account for nearly half the rapid growth of computer use between 1954 and 1965. Reductions in the inflation-adjusted price (he found a price elasticity of demand for computers of −1.44) and major increases in power and quality, which also made computers much more useful and effective, accounted for the other half. Other studies have shown that this process continued through the following decades.[12] In fact, this same kind of network externality helped to fuel a rapid growth rate in the demand for personal computers.

Today there is little debate about the importance of network externalities as an explanation for the success of Microsoft's Windows PC operating system, which by 2008 was being used in about 90 percent of personal computers worldwide. At least as significant has been the phenomenal success of the Microsoft Office Suite of PC applications (which includes Word and Excel). In 2008, Microsoft Office enjoyed well over 90 percent of the market.

Network externalities are, of course, not limited to computers. Consider the explosive growth in Internet usage, particularly the use of e-mail and instant

---

[10]Tastes, of course, differ. Some people associate a *positive* network externality with skiing or a day on the beach; they enjoy crowds and may even find the slope or beach lonely without them.

[11]See Gregory Chow, "Technological Change and the Demand for Computers," *American Economic Review* 57: 5 (December 1967): 1117–30.

[12]See Robert J. Gordon, "The Postwar Evolution of Computer Prices," in Dale W. Jorgenson and Ralph Landau, eds., *Technology and Capital Formation* (Cambridge: MIT Press, 1989).

messaging. Use of the Internet has grown at 20 percent per year since 1998, and as of 2002, over 55 percent of the U.S. population was connected. Clearly a strong positive network externality is at work. Because e-mail can only be transmitted to another e-mail user, the value of using e-mail depends crucially on how many other people use it. By 2002, nearly 50 percent of the U.S. population claimed to use e-mail, up from 35 percent in 2000.

Like e-mail, instant messaging enables one computer to communicate directly with another. Unlike e-mail, however, instant messaging simulates a real-time conversation. Again, a positive network externality is present because both parties must be using compatible software. Many Internet service providers, such as America Online (AOL) and Microsoft Network (MSN), offer free instant messaging to both their customers and the online public. By offering the service for free, they hope to capitalize on this positive network externality to promote use of other software.

# *4.6 EMPIRICAL ESTIMATION OF DEMAND

Later in this book, we will explain how demand information is used as input into a firm's economic decision-making process. General Motors, for example, must understand automobile demand to decide whether to offer rebates or below-market-rate loans for new cars. Knowledge about demand is also important for public policy decisions. Understanding the demand for oil, for instance, can help Congress decide whether to pass an oil import tax. You may wonder how it is that economists determine the shape of demand curves and how price and income elasticities of demand are actually calculated. In this starred section, we will briefly examine some methods for evaluating and forecasting demand. The section is starred not only because the material is more advanced, but also because it is not essential for much of the later analysis in the book. Nonetheless, this material is instructive and will help you appreciate the empirical foundation of the theory of consumer behavior. The basic statistical tools for estimating demand curves and demand elasticities are described in the appendix to this book, entitled "The Basics of Regression."

## The Statistical Approach to Demand Estimation

Firms often rely on market information based on actual studies of demand. Properly applied, the statistical approach to demand estimation can help researchers sort out the effects of variables, such as income and the prices of other products, on the quantity of a product demanded. Here we outline some of the conceptual issues involved in the statistical approach.

Table 4.5 shows the quantity of raspberries sold in a market each year. Information about the market demand for raspberries would be valuable to an organization representing growers because it would allow them to predict sales on the basis of their own estimates of price and other demand-determining variables. Let's suppose that, focusing on demand, researchers find that the quantity of raspberries produced is sensitive to weather conditions but not to the current market price (because farmers make their planting decisions based on last year's price).

The price and quantity data from Table 4.5 are graphed in Figure 4.18. If we believe that price alone determines demand, it would be plausible to describe

| TABLE 4.5 | Demand Data | | |
|---|---|---|---|
| Year | Quantity (Q) | Price (P) | Income (I) |
| 1995 | 4 | 24 | 10 |
| 1996 | 7 | 20 | 10 |
| 1997 | 8 | 17 | 10 |
| 1998 | 13 | 17 | 17 |
| 1999 | 16 | 10 | 17 |
| 2000 | 15 | 15 | 17 |
| 2001 | 19 | 12 | 20 |
| 2002 | 20 | 9 | 20 |
| 2003 | 22 | 5 | 20 |

the demand for the product by drawing a straight line (or other appropriate curve), $Q = a - bP$, which "fit" the points as shown by demand curve $D$. (The "least-squares" method of curve-fitting is described in the appendix to the book.)

Does curve $D$ (given by the equation $Q = 28.2 - 1.00P$) really represent the demand for the product? The answer is yes—but only if no important factors other than price affect demand. In Table 4.5, however, we have included data for one other variable: the average income of purchasers of the product. Note that income ($I$) has increased twice during the study, suggesting that the demand curve has shifted twice. Thus demand curves $d_1$, $d_2$, and $d_3$ in Figure 4.18 give a

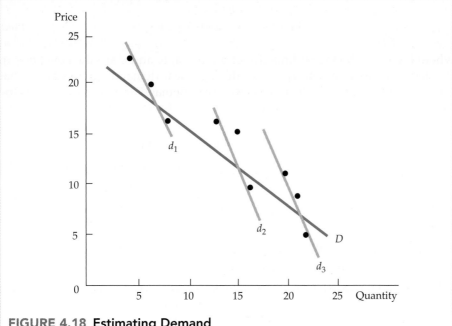

**FIGURE 4.18 Estimating Demand**

Price and quantity data can be used to determine the form of a demand relationship. But the same data could describe a single demand curve $D$ or three demand curves $d_1$, $d_2$, and $d_3$ that shift over time.

more likely description of demand. This *linear demand curve* would be described algebraically as

$$Q = a - bP + cI \qquad (4.2)$$

The income term in the demand equation allows the demand curve to shift in a parallel fashion as income changes. The demand relationship, calculated using the least-squares method, is given by $Q = 8.08 - .49P + .81I$.

## The Form of the Demand Relationship

Because the demand relationships discussed above are straight lines, the effect of a change in price on quantity demanded is constant. However, the price elasticity of demand varies with the price level. For the demand equation $Q = a - bP$, for example, the price elasticity $E_p$ is

$$E_p = (\Delta Q / \Delta P)(P/Q) = -b(P/Q) \qquad (4.3)$$

Thus elasticity increases in magnitude as the price increases (and the quantity demanded falls).

Consider, for example, the linear demand for raspberries, which was estimated to be $Q = 8.08 - .49P + .81I$. The elasticity of demand in 1999 (when $Q = 16$ and $P = 10$) is equal to $-.49 (10/16) = -.31$, whereas the elasticity in 2003 (when $Q = 22$ and $P = 5$) is substantially lower: $-.11$.

There is no reason to expect elasticities of demand to be constant. Nevertheless, we often find it useful to work with the *isoelastic demand curve*, in which the price elasticity and the income elasticity are constant. When written in its *log-linear form*, the isoelastic demand curve appears as follows:

$$\log(Q) = a - b \log(P) + c \log(I) \qquad (4.4)$$

where log ( ) is the logarithmic function and $a$, $b$, and $c$ are the constants in the demand equation. The appeal of the log-linear demand relationship is that the slope of the line $-b$ is the price elasticity of demand and the constant $c$ is the income elasticity.[13] Using the data in Table 4.5, for example, we obtained the regression line

$$\log(Q) = -0.23 - 0.34 \log(P) + 1.33 \log(I)$$

This relationship tells us that the price elasticity of demand for raspberries is $-0.34$ (that is, demand is inelastic), and that the income elasticity is 1.33.

We have seen that it can be useful to distinguish between goods that are complements and goods that are substitutes. Suppose that $P_2$ represents the price of a second good—one which is believed to be related to the product we are studying. We can then write the demand function in the following form:

$$\log(Q) = a - b \log(P) + b_2 \log(P_2) + c \log(I)$$

When $b_2$, the cross-price elasticity, is positive, the two goods are substitutes; when $b_2$ is negative, the two goods are complements.

---

[13]The natural logarithmic function with base $e$ has the property that $\Delta(\log(Q)) = \Delta Q/Q$ for any change in $\log(Q)$. Similarly, $\Delta(\log(P)) = \Delta P/P$ for any change in $\log(P)$. It follows that $\Delta(\log(Q)) = \Delta Q/Q = -b[\Delta(\log(P))] = -b(\Delta P/P)$. Therefore, $(\Delta Q/Q)/(\Delta P/P) = -b$, which is the price elasticity of demand. By a similar argument, the income elasticity of demand $c$ is given by $(\Delta Q/Q)/(\Delta I/I)$.

The specification and estimation of demand curves has been a rapidly growing endeavor, not only in marketing, but also in antitrust analyses. It is now commonplace to use estimated demand relationships to evaluate the likely effects of mergers.[14] What were once prohibitively costly analyses involving mainframe computers can now be carried out in a few seconds on a personal computer. Accordingly, governmental competition authorities and economic and marketing experts in the private sector make frequent use of supermarket scanner data as inputs for estimating demand relationships. Once the price elasticity of demand for a particular product is known, a firm can decide whether it is profitable to raise or lower price. Other things being equal, the lower in magnitude the elasticity, the more likely the profitability of a price increase.

## EXAMPLE 4.7    The Demand for Ready-to-Eat Cereal

The Post Cereals division of Kraft General Foods acquired the Shredded Wheat cereals of Nabisco in 1995. The acquisition raised the legal and economic question of whether Post would raise the price of its best-selling brand, Grape Nuts, or the price of Nabisco's most successful brand, Shredded Wheat Spoon Size.[15] One important issue in a lawsuit brought by the state of New York was whether the two brands were close substitutes for one another. If so, it would be more profitable for Post to increase the price of Grape Nuts (or Shredded Wheat) *after* rather than *before* the acquisition. Why? Because after the acquisition the lost sales from consumers who switched away from Grape Nuts (or Shredded Wheat) would be recovered to the extent that they switched to the substitute product.

The extent to which a price increase will cause consumers to switch is given (in part) by the price elasticity of demand for Grape Nuts. Other things being equal, the higher the demand elasticity, the greater the loss of sales associated with a price increase. The more likely, too, that the price increase will be unprofitable.

The substitutability of Grape Nuts and Shredded Wheat can be measured by the cross-price elasticity of demand for Grape Nuts with respect to the price of Shredded Wheat. The relevant elasticities were calculated using weekly data obtained from supermarket scanning of household purchases for 10 cities over a three-year period. One of the estimated isoelastic demand equations appeared in the following log-linear form:

$$\log(Q_{GN}) = 1.998 - 2.085 \log(P_{GN}) + 0.62 \log(I) + 0.14 \log(P_{SW})$$

where $Q_{GN}$ is the amount (in pounds) of Grape Nuts sold weekly, $P_{GN}$ the price per pound of Grape Nuts, $I$ real personal income, and $P_{SW}$ the price per pound of Shredded Wheat Spoon Size.

The demand for Grape Nuts is elastic (at current prices), with a price elasticity of about –2. The income elasticity is 0.62: In other words, increases in income

[14]See Jonathan B. Baker and Daniel L. Rubinfeld, "Empirical Methods in Antitrust Litigation: Review and Critique," *American Law and Economics Review*, 1(1999): 386–435.

[15]*State of New York v. Kraft General Foods, Inc.*, 926 F. Supp. 321, 356 (S.D.N.Y. 1995).

lead to increases in cereal purchases, but at less than a 1-for-1 rate. Finally, the cross-price elasticity is 0.14. This figure is consistent with the fact that although the two cereals are substitutes (the quantity demanded of Grape Nuts increases in response to an increase in the price of Shredded Wheat), they are not very close substitutes.

## Interview and Experimental Approaches to Demand Determination

Another way to obtain information about demand is through *interviews* in which consumers are asked how much of a product they might be willing to buy at a given price. This approach, however, may not succeed when people lack information or interest or even want to mislead the interviewer. Therefore, market researchers have designed various indirect survey techniques. Consumers might be asked, for example, what their current consumption behavior is and how they would respond if a certain product were available at, say, a 10-percent discount. They might be asked how they would expect others to behave. Although indirect approaches to demand estimation can be fruitful, the difficulties of the interview approach have forced economists and marketing specialists to look to alternative methods.

In *direct marketing experiments*, actual sales offers are posed to potential customers. An airline, for example, might offer a reduced price on certain flights for six months, partly to learn how the price change affects demand for flights and partly to learn how competitors will respond. Alternatively, a cereal company might test market a new brand in Buffalo, New York, and Omaha, Nebraska, with some potential customers being given coupons ranging in value from 25 cents to $1 per box. The response to the coupon offer tells the company the shape of the underlying demand curve, helping the marketers decide whether to market the product nationally and internationally, and at what price.

Direct experiments are real, not hypothetical, but even so, problems remain. The wrong experiment can be costly, and even if profits and sales rise, the firm cannot be entirely sure that these increases resulted from the experimental change; other factors probably changed at the same time. Moreover, the response to experiments—which consumers often recognize as short-lived—may differ from the response to permanent changes. Finally, a firm can afford to try only a limited number of experiments.

# SUMMARY

1. Individual consumers' demand curves for a commodity can be derived from information about their tastes for all goods and services and from their budget constraints.

2. Engel curves, which describe the relationship between the quantity of a good consumed and income, can be useful in showing how consumer expenditures vary with income.

3. Two goods are substitutes if an increase in the price of one leads to an increase in the quantity demanded of the other. In contrast, two goods are complements if an increase in the price of one leads to a decrease in the quantity demanded of the other.

4. The effect of a price change on the quantity demanded of a good can be broken into two parts: a substitution effect, in which the level of utility remains constant while price changes, and an income effect, in which the price remains constant while the level of utility changes. Because the income effect can be positive or negative, a price change can have a small or a large effect on quantity demanded. In the unusual case of a

so-called Giffen good, the quantity demanded may move in the same direction as the price change, thereby generating an upward-sloping individual demand curve.

5. The market demand curve is the horizontal summation of the individual demand curves of all consumers in the market for a good. It can be used to calculate how much people value the consumption of particular goods and services.

6. Demand is price inelastic when a 1-percent increase in price leads to a less than 1-percent decrease in quantity demanded, thereby increasing the consumer's expenditure. Demand is price elastic when a 1-percent increase in price leads to a more than 1-percent decrease in quantity demanded, thereby decreasing the consumer's expenditure. Demand is unit elastic when a 1-percent increase in price leads to a 1-percent decrease in quantity demanded.

7. The concept of consumer surplus can be useful in determining the benefits that people receive from the consumption of a product. Consumer surplus is the difference between the maximum amount a consumer is willing to pay for a good and what he actually pays for it.

8. A network externality occurs when one person's demand is affected directly by the purchasing decisions of other consumers. A positive network externality, the bandwagon effect, occurs when a typical consumer's quantity demanded increases because she considers it stylish to buy a product that others have purchased. Conversely, a negative network externality, the snob effect, occurs when the quantity demanded increases because fewer people own the good.

9. A number of methods can be used to obtain information about consumer demand. These include interview and experimental approaches, direct marketing experiments, and the more indirect statistical approach. The statistical approach can be very powerful in its application, but it is necessary to determine the appropriate variables that affect demand before the statistical work is done.

# QUESTIONS FOR REVIEW

1. Explain the difference between each of the following terms:
   a. a price consumption curve and a demand curve
   b. an individual demand curve and a market demand curve
   c. an Engel curve and a demand curve
   d. an income effect and a substitution effect

2. Suppose that an individual allocates his or her entire budget between two goods, food and clothing. Can both goods be inferior? Explain.

3. Explain whether the following statements are true or false:
   a. The marginal rate of substitution diminishes as an individual moves downward along the demand curve.
   b. The level of utility increases as an individual moves downward along the demand curve.
   c. Engel curves always slope upward.

4. Tickets to a rock concert sell for $10. But at that price, the demand is substantially greater than the available number of tickets. Is the value or marginal benefit of an additional ticket greater than, less than, or equal to $10? How might you determine that value?

5. Which of the following combinations of goods are complements and which are substitutes? Can they be either in different circumstances? Discuss.
   a. a mathematics class and an economics class
   b. tennis balls and a tennis racket
   c. steak and lobster
   d. a plane trip and a train trip to the same destination
   e. bacon and eggs

6. Suppose that a consumer spends a fixed amount of income per month on the following pairs of goods:
   a. tortilla chips and salsa
   b. tortilla chips and potato chips
   c. movie tickets and gourmet coffee
   d. travel by bus and travel by subway
   If the price of one of the goods increases, explain the effect on the quantity demanded of each of the goods. In each pair, which are likely to be complements and which are likely to be substitutes?

7. Which of the following events would cause a movement *along* the demand curve for U.S. produced clothing, and which would cause a *shift* in the demand curve?
   a. the removal of quotas on the importation of foreign clothes
   b. an increase in the income of U.S. citizens
   c. a cut in the industry's costs of producing domestic clothes that is passed on to the market in the form of lower prices

8. For which of the following goods is a price increase likely to lead to a substantial income (as well as substitution) effect?
   a. salt
   b. housing
   c. theater tickets
   d. food

9. Suppose that the average household in a state consumes 800 gallons of gasoline per year. A 20-cent gasoline tax is introduced, coupled with a $160 annual tax rebate per household. Will the household be better or worse off under the new program?

10. Which of the following three groups is likely to have the most, and which the least, price-elastic demand for membership in the Association of Business Economists?
    a. students
    b. junior executives
    c. senior executives

11. Explain which of the following items in each pair is more price elastic.

a. The demand for a specific brand of toothpaste and the demand for toothpaste in general

b. The demand for gasoline in the short run and the demand for gasoline in the long run

12. Explain the difference between a positive and a negative network externality and give an example of each.

# EXERCISES

1. An individual sets aside a certain amount of his income per month to spend on his two hobbies, collecting wine and collecting books. Given the information below, illustrate both the price-consumption curve associated with changes in the price of wine and the demand curve for wine.

| Price Wine | Price Book | Quantity Wine | Quantity Book | Budget |
|---|---|---|---|---|
| $10 | $10 | 7 | 8 | $150 |
| $12 | $10 | 5 | 9 | $150 |
| $15 | $10 | 4 | 9 | $150 |
| $20 | $10 | 2 | 11 | $150 |

2. An individual consumes two goods, clothing and food. Given the information below, illustrate both the income-consumption curve and the Engel curve for clothing and food.

| Price Clothing | Price Food | Quantity Clothing | Quantity Food | Income |
|---|---|---|---|---|
| $10 | $2 | 6 | 20 | $100 |
| $10 | $2 | 8 | 35 | $150 |
| $10 | $2 | 11 | 45 | $200 |
| $10 | $2 | 15 | 50 | $250 |

3. Jane always gets twice as much utility from an extra ballet ticket as she does from an extra basketball ticket, regardless of how many tickets of either type she has. Draw Jane's income-consumption curve and her Engel curve for ballet tickets.

4. a. Orange juice and apple juice are known to be perfect substitutes. Draw the appropriate price-consumption curve (for a variable price of orange juice) and income-consumption curve.

   b. Left shoes and right shoes are perfect complements. Draw the appropriate price-consumption and income-consumption curves.

5. Each week, Bill, Mary, and Jane select the quantity of two goods, $x_1$ and $x_2$, that they will consume in order to maximize their respective utilities. They each spend their entire weekly income on these two goods.

   a. Suppose you are given the following information about the choices that Bill makes over a three-week period:

| | $x_1$ | $x_2$ | $P_1$ | $P_2$ | $I$ |
|---|---|---|---|---|---|
| Week 1 | 10 | 20 | 2 | 1 | 40 |
| Week 2 | 7 | 19 | 3 | 1 | 40 |
| Week 3 | 8 | 31 | 3 | 1 | 55 |

   Did Bill's utility increase or decrease between week 1 and week 2? Between week 1 and week 3? Explain using a graph to support your answer.

   b. Now consider the following information about the choices that Mary makes:

| | $x_1$ | $x_2$ | $P_1$ | $P_2$ | $I$ |
|---|---|---|---|---|---|
| Week 1 | 10 | 20 | 2 | 1 | 40 |
| Week 2 | 6 | 14 | 2 | 2 | 40 |
| Week 3 | 20 | 10 | 2 | 2 | 60 |

   Did Mary's utility increase or decrease between week 1 and week 3? Does Mary consider both goods to be normal goods? Explain.

   *c. Finally, examine the following information about Jane's choices:

| | $x_1$ | $x_2$ | $P_1$ | $P_2$ | $I$ |
|---|---|---|---|---|---|
| Week 1 | 12 | 24 | 2 | 1 | 48 |
| Week 2 | 16 | 32 | 1 | 1 | 48 |
| Week 3 | 12 | 24 | 1 | 1 | 36 |

   Draw a budget line-indifference curve graph that illustrates Jane's three chosen bundles. What can you say about Jane's preferences in this case? Identify the income and substitution effects that result from a change in the price of good $x_1$.

6. Two individuals, Sam and Barb, derive utility from the hours of leisure ($L$) they consume and from the amount of goods ($G$) they consume. In order to maximize utility,

they need to allocate the 24 hours in the day between leisure hours and work hours. Assume that all hours not spent working are leisure hours. The price of a good is equal to $1 and the price of leisure is equal to the hourly wage. We observe the following information about the choices that the two individuals make:

| | | Sam | Barb | Sam | Barb |
|---|---|---|---|---|---|
| Price of G | Price of L | L (hours) | L (hours) | G ($) | G ($) |
| 1 | 8 | 16 | 14 | 64 | 80 |
| 1 | 9 | 15 | 14 | 81 | 90 |
| 1 | 10 | 14 | 15 | 100 | 90 |
| 1 | 11 | 14 | 16 | 110 | 88 |

Graphically illustrate Sam's leisure demand curve and Barb's leisure demand curve. Place price on the vertical axis and leisure on the horizontal axis. Given that they both maximize utility, how can you explain the difference in their leisure demand curves?

7. The director of a theater company in a small college town is considering changing the way he prices tickets. He has hired an economic consulting firm to estimate the demand for tickets. The firm has classified people who go to the theater into two groups and has come up with two demand functions. The demand curves for the general public ($Q_{gp}$) and students ($Q_s$) are given below:

$$Q_{gp} = 500 - 5P$$
$$Q_s = 200 - 4P$$

a. Graph the two demand curves on one graph, with $P$ on the vertical axis and $Q$ on the horizontal axis. If the current price of tickets is $35, identify the quantity demanded by each group.

b. Find the price elasticity of demand for each group at the current price and quantity.

c. Is the director maximizing the revenue he collects from ticket sales by charging $35 for each ticket? Explain.

d. What price should he charge each group if he wants to maximize revenue collected from ticket sales?

8. Judy has decided to allocate exactly $500 to college textbooks every year, even though she knows that the prices are likely to increase by 5 to 10 percent per year and that she will be getting a substantial monetary gift from her grandparents next year. What is Judy's price elasticity of demand for textbooks? Income elasticity?

9. The ACME Corporation determines that at current prices, the demand for its computer chips has a price elasticity of −2 in the short run, while the price elasticity for its disk drives is −1.

a. If the corporation decides to raise the price of both products by 10 percent, what will happen to its sales? To its sales revenue?

b. Can you tell from the available information which product will generate the most revenue? If yes, why? If not, what additional information do you need?

10. By observing an individual's behavior in the situations outlined below, determine the relevant income elasticities of demand for each good (i.e., whether it is normal or inferior). If you cannot determine the income elasticity, what additional information do you need?

a. Bill spends all his income on books and coffee. He finds $20 while rummaging through a used paperback bin at the bookstore. He immediately buys a new hardcover book of poetry.

b. Bill loses $10 he was going to use to buy a double espresso. He decides to sell his new book at a discount to a friend and use the money to buy coffee.

c. Being bohemian becomes the latest teen fad. As a result, coffee and book prices rise by 25 percent. Bill lowers his consumption of both goods by the same percentage.

d. Bill drops out of art school and gets an M.B.A. instead. He stops reading books and drinking coffee. Now he reads the *Wall Street Journal* and drinks bottled mineral water.

11. Suppose the income elasticity of demand for food is 0.5 and the price elasticity of demand is −1.0. Suppose also that Felicia spends $10,000 a year on food, the price of food is $2, and that her income is $25,000.

a. If a sales tax on food caused the price of food to increase to $2.50, what would happen to her consumption of food? (*Hint:* Because a large price change is involved, you should assume that the price elasticity measures an arc elasticity, rather than a point elasticity.)

b. Suppose that Felicia gets a tax rebate of $2500 to ease the effect of the sales tax. What would her consumption of food be now?

c. Is she better or worse off when given a rebate equal to the sales tax payments? Draw a graph and explain.

12. You run a small business and would like to predict what will happen to the quantity demanded for your product if you raise your price. While you do not know the exact demand curve for your product, you do know that in the first year you charged $45 and sold 1200 units and that in the second year you charged $30 and sold 1800 units.

a. If you plan to raise your price by 10 percent, what would be a reasonable estimate of what will happen to quantity demanded in percentage terms?

b. If you raise your price by 10 percent, will revenue increase or decrease?

13. Suppose you are in charge of a toll bridge that costs essentially nothing to operate. The demand for bridge crossings $Q$ is given by $P = 15 - (1/2)Q$.

a. Draw the demand curve for bridge crossings.

b. How many people would cross the bridge if there were no toll?

c. What is the loss of consumer surplus associated with a bridge toll of $5?

d. The toll-bridge operator is considering an increase in the toll to $7. At this higher price, how many people would cross the bridge? Would the toll-bridge revenue increase or decrease? What does your answer tell you about the elasticity of demand?

e. Find the lost consumer surplus associated with the increase in the price of the toll from $5 to $7.

14. Vera has decided to upgrade the operating system on her new PC. She hears that the new Linux operating system is technologically superior to Windows and substantially lower in price. However, when she asks her friends, it turns out they all use PCs with Windows. They agree that Linux is more appealing but add that they see relatively few copies of Linux on sale at local stores. Vera chooses Windows. Can you explain her decision?

15. Suppose that you are the consultant to an agricultural cooperative that is deciding whether members should cut their production of cotton in half next year. The cooperative wants your advice as to whether this action will increase members' revenues. Knowing that cotton (C) and watermelons (W) both compete for agricultural land in the South, you estimate the demand for cotton to be $C = 3.5 - 1.0P_C + 0.25P_W + 0.50I$, where $P_C$ is the price of cotton, $P_W$ the price of watermelon, and $I$ income. Should you support or oppose the plan? Is there any additional information that would help you to provide a definitive answer?

# Appendix to Chapter 4

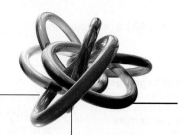

## DEMAND THEORY—A MATHEMATICAL TREATMENT

This appendix presents a mathematical treatment of the basics of demand theory. Our goal is to provide a short overview of the theory of demand for students who have some familiarity with the use of calculus. To do this, we will explain and then apply the concept of constrained optimization.

### Utility Maximization

The theory of consumer behavior is based on the assumption that consumers maximize utility subject to the constraint of a limited budget. We saw in Chapter 3 that for each consumer, we can define a *utility function* that attaches a level of utility to each market basket. We also saw that the *marginal utility* of a good is defined as the change in utility associated with a one-unit increase in the consumption of the good. Using calculus, as we do in this appendix, we measure marginal utility as the utility change that results from a very small increase in consumption.

> In §3.1, we explain that a utility function is a formula that assigns a level of utility to each market basket.

Suppose, for example, that Bob's utility function is given by $U(X, Y) = \log X + \log Y$, where, for the sake of generality, $X$ is now used to represent food and $Y$ represents clothing. In that case, the marginal utility associated with the additional consumption of $X$ is given by *the partial derivative of the utility function with respect to good $X$*. Here, $MU_X$, representing the marginal utility of good $X$, is given by

> In §3.5, marginal utility is described as the additional satisfaction obtained by consuming an additional amount of a good.

$$\frac{\partial U(X, Y)}{\partial X} = \frac{\partial(\log X + \log Y)}{\partial X} = \frac{1}{X}$$

In the following analysis, we will assume, as in Chapter 3, that while the level of utility is an *increasing* function of the quantities of goods consumed, marginal utility *decreases* with consumption. When there are two goods, $X$ and $Y$, the consumer's optimization problem may thus be written as

$$\text{Maximize } U(X, Y) \qquad \textbf{(A4.1)}$$

subject to the constraint that all income is spent on the two goods:

$$P_X X + P_Y Y = I \qquad \textbf{(A4.2)}$$

Here, $U(\ )$ is the utility function, $X$ and $Y$ the quantities of the two goods purchased, $P_X$ and $P_Y$ the prices of the goods, and $I$ income.[1]

To determine the individual consumer's demand for the two goods, we choose those values of $X$ and $Y$ that maximize (A4.1) subject to (A4.2). When we know the particular form of the utility function, we can solve to find the consumer's demand for $X$ and $Y$ directly. However, even if we write the utility function in its general form $U(X, Y)$, the technique of *constrained optimization* can be used to describe the conditions that must hold if the consumer is maximizing utility.

---

[1]To simplify the mathematics, we assume that the utility function is continuous (with continuous derivatives) and that goods are infinitely divisible. The logarithmic function log (.) measures the natural logarithm of a number.

## The Method of Lagrange Multipliers

• **method of Lagrange multipliers** Technique to maximize or minimize a function subject to one or more constraints.

The **method of Lagrange multipliers** is a technique that can be used to maximize or minimize a function subject to one or more constraints. Because we will use this technique to analyze production and cost issues later in the book, we will provide a step-by-step application of the method to the problem of finding the consumer's optimization given by equations (A4.1) and (A4.2).

1. **Stating the Problem** First, we write the Lagrangian for the problem. The **Lagrangian** is the function to be maximized or minimized (here, utility is being maximized), plus a variable which we call $\lambda$ times the constraint (here, the consumer's budget constraint). We will interpret the meaning of $\lambda$ in a moment. The Lagrangian is then

• **Lagrangian** Function to be maximized or minimized, plus a variable (the *Lagrange multiplier*) multiplied by the constraint.

$$\Phi = U(X, Y) - \lambda(P_X X + P_Y Y - I) \tag{A4.3}$$

Note that we have written the budget constraint as

$$P_X X + P_Y Y - I = 0$$

i.e., as a sum of terms that is equal to zero. We then insert this sum into the Lagrangian.

2. **Differentiating the Lagrangian** If we choose values of $X$ and $Y$ that satisfy the budget constraint, then the second term in equation (A4.3) will be zero. Maximizing will therefore be equivalent to maximizing $U(X, Y)$. By differentiating $\Phi$ with respect to $X$, $Y$, and $\lambda$ and then equating the derivatives to zero, we can obtain the necessary conditions for a maximum.[2] The resulting equations are

$$\frac{\partial \Phi}{\partial X} = \text{MU}_X(X, Y) - \lambda P_X = 0$$

$$\frac{\partial \Phi}{\partial Y} = \text{MU}_Y(X, Y) - \lambda P_Y = 0 \tag{A4.4}$$

$$\frac{\partial \Phi}{\partial \lambda} = I - P_X X - P_Y Y = 0$$

Here as before, MU is short for *marginal utility*: In other words, $\text{MU}_X(X, Y) = \partial U(X, Y)/\partial X$, the change in utility from a very small increase in the consumption of good $X$.

3. **Solving the Resulting Equations** The three equations in (A4.4) can be rewritten as

$$\text{MU}_X = \lambda P_X$$

$$\text{MU}_Y = \lambda P_Y$$

$$P_X X + P_Y Y = I$$

---

[2]These conditions are necessary for an "interior" solution in which the consumer consumes positive amounts of both goods. The solution, however, could be a "corner" solution in which all of one good and none of the other is consumed.

Now we can solve these three equations for the three unknowns. The resulting values of $X$ and $Y$ are the solution to the consumer's optimization problem: They are the utility-maximizing quantities.

## The Equal Marginal Principle

The third equation above is the consumer's budget constraint with which we started. The first two equations tell us that each good will be consumed up to the point at which the marginal utility from consumption is a multiple ($\lambda$) of the price of the good. To see the implication of this, we combine the first two conditions to obtain the *equal marginal principle*:

$$\lambda = \frac{MU_X(X,Y)}{P_X} = \frac{MU_Y(X,Y)}{P_Y} \qquad \textbf{(A4.5)}$$

In other words, the marginal utility of each good divided by its price is the same. To optimize, *the consumer must get the same utility from the last dollar spent by consuming either X or Y*. If this were not the case, consuming more of one good and less of the other would increase utility.

To characterize the individual's optimum in more detail, we can rewrite the information in (A4.5) to obtain

$$\frac{MU_X(X,Y)}{MU_Y(X,Y)} = \frac{P_X}{P_Y} \qquad \textbf{(A4.6)}$$

In other words, *the ratio of the marginal utilities is equal to the ratio of the prices*.

## Marginal Rate of Substitution

We can use equation (A4.6) to see the link between utility functions and indifference curves that was spelled out in Chapter 3. An indifference curve represents all market baskets that give the consumer the same level of utility. If $U^*$ is a fixed utility level, the indifference curve that corresponds to that utility level is given by

> In §3.5, we show that the marginal rate of substitution is equal to the ratio of the marginal utilities of the two goods being consumed.

$$U(X, Y) = U^*$$

As the market baskets are changed by adding small amounts of $X$ and subtracting small amounts of $Y$, the total change in utility must equal zero. Therefore,

$$MU_X(X,Y)dX + MU_Y(X,Y)dY = dU^* = 0 \qquad \textbf{(A4.7)}$$

Rearranging,

$$-dY/dX = MU_X(X,Y)/MU_Y(X,Y) = MRS_{XY} \qquad \textbf{(A4.8)}$$

where $MRS_{XY}$ represents the individual's marginal rate of substitution of $X$ for $Y$. Because the left-hand side of (A4.8) represents the negative of the slope of the indifference curve, it follows that at the point of tangency, the individual's marginal rate of substitution (which trades off goods while keeping utility constant) is equal to the individual's ratio of marginal utilities, which in turn is equal to the ratio of the prices of the two goods, from (A4.6).[3]

When the individual indifference curves are convex, the tangency of the indifference curve to the budget line solves the consumer's optimization problem. This principle was illustrated by Figure 3.13 (page 87) in Chapter 3.

### Marginal Utility of Income

Whatever the form of the utility function, the Lagrange multiplier $\lambda$ represents the extra utility generated when the budget constraint is relaxed—in this case by adding one dollar to the budget. To show how the principle works, we differentiate the utility function $U(X, Y)$ totally with respect to $I$:

$$dU/dI = \text{MU}_X (X, Y)(dX/dI) + \text{MU}_Y (X, Y)(dY/dI) \qquad \textbf{(A4.9)}$$

Because any increment in income must be divided between the two goods, it follows that

$$dI = P_X dX + P_Y dY \qquad \textbf{(A4.10)}$$

Substituting from (A4.5) into (A4.9), we get

$$dU/dI = \lambda P_X(dX/dI) + \lambda P_Y(dY/dI) = \lambda(P_X dX + P_Y dY)/dI \quad \textbf{(A4.11)}$$

and substituting (A4.10) into (A4.11), we get

$$dU/dI = \lambda(P_X dX + P_Y dY)/(P_X dX + P_Y dY) = \lambda \qquad \textbf{(A4.12)}$$

Thus the *Lagrange multiplier* is the extra utility that results from an extra dollar of income.

Going back to our original analysis of the conditions for utility maximization, we see from equation (A4.5) that maximization requires the utility obtained from the consumption of every good, per dollar spent on that good, to be equal to the marginal utility of an additional dollar of income. If this were not the case, utility could be increased by spending more on the good with the higher ratio of marginal utility to price and less on the other good.

### An Example

In general, the three equations in (A4.4) can be solved to determine the three unknowns $X$, $Y$, and $\lambda$ as a function of the two prices and income. Substitution for $\lambda$ then allows us to solve for the demand for each of the two goods in terms of income and the prices of the two commodities. This principle can be most easily seen in terms of an example.

A frequently used utility function is the **Cobb-Douglas utility function**, which can be represented in two forms:

$$U(X, Y) = a \log(X) + (1 - a) \log(Y)$$

• **Cobb-Douglas utility function** Utility function $U(X,Y) = X^a Y^{1-a}$, where $X$ and $Y$ are two goods and $a$ is a constant.

---

[3]We implicitly assume that the "second-order conditions" for a utility maximum hold. The consumer, therefore, is maximizing rather than minimizing utility. The convexity condition is sufficient for the second-order conditions to be satisfied. In mathematical terms, the condition is that $d(\text{MRS})/dX < 0$ or that $dY^2/dX^2 > 0$ where $-dY/dX$ is the slope of the indifference curve. Remember: diminishing marginal utility is not sufficient to ensure that indifference curves are convex.

and

$$U(X, Y) = X^a Y^{1-a}$$

For the purposes of demand theory, these two forms are equivalent because they both yield the identical demand functions for goods $X$ and $Y$. We will derive the demand functions for the first form and leave the second as an exercise for the student.

To find the demand functions for $X$ and $Y$, given the usual budget constraint, we first write the Lagrangian:

$$\Phi = a \log(X) + (1 - a)\log(Y) - \lambda(P_X X + P_Y Y - I)$$

Now differentiating with respect to $X$, $Y$, and $\lambda$ and setting the derivatives equal to zero, we obtain

$$\partial\Phi/\partial X = a/X - \lambda P_X = 0$$
$$\partial\Phi/\partial Y = (1 - a)/Y - \lambda P_Y = 0$$
$$\partial\Phi/\partial\lambda = P_X X + P_Y Y - I = 0$$

The first two conditions imply that

$$P_X X = a/\lambda \tag{A4.13}$$

$$P_Y Y = (1 - a)/\lambda \tag{A4.14}$$

Combining these expressions with the last condition (the budget constraint) gives us

$$a/\lambda + (1 - a)/\lambda - I = 0$$

or $\lambda = 1/I$. Now we can substitute this expression for $\lambda$ back into (A4.13) and (A4.14) to obtain the demand functions:

$$X = (a/P_X)I$$
$$Y = [(1 - a)/P_Y]I$$

In this example, the demand for each good depends only on the price of that good and on income, not on the price of the other good. Thus, the cross-price elasticities of demand are 0.

We can also use this example to review the meaning of Lagrange multipliers. To do so, let's substitute specific values for each of the parameters in the problem. Let $a = 1/2$, $P_X = \$1$, $P_Y = \$2$, and $I = \$100$. In this case, the choices that maximize utility are $X = 50$ and $Y = 25$. Also note that $\lambda = 1/100$. The Lagrange multiplier tells us that if an additional dollar of income were available to the consumer, the level of utility achieved would increase by $1/100$. This conclusion is relatively easy to check. With an income of \$101, the maximizing choices of the two goods are $X = 50.5$ and $Y = 25.25$. A bit of arithmetic tells us that the original level of utility is 3.565 and the new level of utility 3.575. As we can see, the additional dollar of income has indeed increased utility by .01, or $1/100$.

> In §2.4, we explain that the cross-price elasticity of demand refers to the percentage change in the quantity demanded of one good that results from a 1-percent increase in the price of another good.

### Duality in Consumer Theory

There are two different ways of looking at the consumer's optimization decision. The optimum choice of $X$ and $Y$ can be analyzed not only as the problem of choosing the highest indifference curve—the maximum value of $U(\ )$—that touches the budget line, but also as the problem of choosing the lowest budget line—the minimum budget expenditure—that touches a given indifference curve. We use the term **duality** to refer to these two perspectives. To see how this principle works, consider the following dual consumer optimization problem: the problem of minimizing the cost of achieving a particular level of utility:

• **duality** Alternative way of looking at the consumer's utility maximization decision: Rather than choosing the highest indifference curve, given a budget constraint, the consumer chooses the lowest budget line that touches a given indifference curve.

$$\text{Minimize } P_X X + P_Y Y$$

subject to the constraint that

$$U(X, Y) = U^*$$

The corresponding Lagrangian is given by

$$\Phi = P_X X + P_Y Y - \mu(U(X, Y) - U^*) \tag{A4.15}$$

where $\mu$ is the Lagrange multiplier. Differentiating $\Phi$ with respect to $X$, $Y$, and $\mu$ and setting the derivatives equal to zero, we find the following necessary conditions for expenditure minimization:

$$P_X - \mu MU_X(X, Y) = 0$$
$$P_Y - \mu MU_Y(X, Y) = 0$$

and

$$U(X, Y) = U^*$$

By solving the first two equations, and recalling (A4.5) we see that

$$\mu = [P_X/MU_X(X, Y)] = [P_Y/MU_Y(X, Y)] = 1/\lambda$$

Because it is also true that

$$MU_X(X, Y)/MU_Y(X, Y) = MRS_{XY} = P_X/P_Y$$

the cost-minimizing choice of $X$ and $Y$ must occur at the point of tangency of the budget line and the indifference curve that generates utility $U^*$. Because this is the same point that maximized utility in our original problem, the dual expenditure-minimization problem yields the same demand functions that are obtained from the direct utility-maximization problem.

To see how the dual approach works, let's reconsider our Cobb-Douglas example. The algebra is somewhat easier to follow if we use the exponential form of the Cobb-Douglas utility function, $U(X, Y) = X^a Y^{1-a}$. In this case, the Lagrangian is given by

$$\Phi = P_X X + P_Y Y - \mu[X^a Y^{1-a} - U^*] \tag{A4.16}$$

Differentiating with respect to $X$, $Y$, and $\mu$ and equating to zero, we obtain

$$P_X = \mu a U^* / X$$
$$P_Y = \mu(1-a)U^*/Y$$

Multiplying the first equation by $X$ and the second by $Y$ and adding, we get

$$P_X X + P_Y Y = \mu U^*$$

First, we let $I$ be the cost-minimizing expenditure (if the individual did not spend all of his income to get utility level $U^*$, $U^*$ would not have maximized utility in the original problem). Then it follows that $\mu = I/U^*$. Substituting in the equations above, we obtain

$$X = aI/P_X \quad \text{and} \quad Y = (1-a)I/P_Y$$

These are the same demand functions that we obtained before.

### Income and Substitution Effects

The demand function tells us how any individual's utility-maximizing choices respond to changes in both income and the prices of goods. It is important, however, to distinguish that portion of any price change that involves *movement along an indifference curve* from that portion which involves *movement to a different indifference curve* (and therefore a change in purchasing power). To make this distinction, we consider what happens to the demand for good $X$ when the price of $X$ changes. As we explained in Section 4.2, the change in demand can be divided into a *substitution effect* (the change in quantity demanded when the level of utility is fixed) and an *income effect* (the change in the quantity demanded with the level of utility changing but the relative price of good $X$ unchanged). We denote the change in $X$ that results from a unit change in the price of $X$, holding utility constant, by

> In §4.2, the effect of a price change is divided into an income effect and a substitution effect.

$$\partial X / \partial P_X \,|_{U=U^*}$$

Thus the total change in the quantity demanded of $X$ resulting from a unit change in $P_X$ is

$$dX/dP_X = \partial X/\partial P_X \,|_{U=U^*} + (\partial X/\partial I)(\partial I/\partial P_X) \qquad \textbf{(A4.17)}$$

The first term on the right side of equation (A4.17) is the substitution effect (because utility is fixed); the second term is the income effect (because income increases).

From the consumer's budget constraint, $I = P_X X + P_Y Y$, we know by differentiation that

$$\partial I / \partial P_X = X \qquad \textbf{(A4.18)}$$

Suppose for the moment that the consumer owned goods $X$ and $Y$. In that case, equation (A4.18) would tell us that when the price of good $X$ increases by \$1, the amount of income that the consumer can obtain by selling the good increases by $X. In our theory of consumer behavior, however, the consumer does not own the good. As a result, equation (A4.18) tells us how much additional income the consumer would need in order to be as well off after the price change as he or she was before. For this reason, it is customary to write the income effect as negative (reflecting a loss of purchasing power) rather than as a positive. Equation (A4.17) then appears as follows:

$$dX/dP_X = \partial X/\partial P_X \,|\, U=U^* - X(\partial X/\partial I) \qquad \textbf{(A4.19)}$$

• **Slutsky equation** Formula for decomposing the effects of a price change into substitution and income effects.

In this new form, called the **Slutsky equation**, the first term represents the *substitution effect*: the change in demand for good $X$ obtained by keeping utility fixed. The second term is the *income effect*: the change in purchasing power resulting from the price change times the change in demand resulting from a change in purchasing power.

An alternative way to decompose a price change into substitution and income effects, which is usually attributed to John Hicks, does not involve indifference curves. In Figure A4.1, the consumer initially chooses market basket $A$ on budget line $RS$. Suppose that after the price of food falls (and the budget line moves to $RT$), we take away enough income so that the individual is no better off (and no worse off) than he was before. To do so, we draw a budget line parallel to $RT$. If the budget line passed through $A$, the consumer would be at

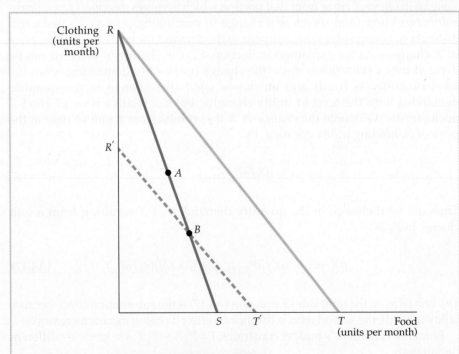

**FIGURE A4.1 Hicksian Substitution Effect**

The individual initially consumes market basket $A$. A decrease in the price of food shifts the budget line from $RS$ to $RT$. If a sufficient amount of income is taken away to make the individual no better off than he or she was at $A$, two conditions must be met: The new market basket chosen must lie on line segment $BT'$ of budget line $R'T'$ (which intersects $RS$ to the right of $A$), and the quantity of food consumed must be greater than at $A$.

least as satisfied as he was before the price change: He still has the option to purchase market basket $A$ if he wishes. According to the **Hicksian substitution effect**, therefore, the budget line that leaves him equally well off must be a line such as $R'T'$, which is parallel to $RT$ and which intersects $RS$ at a point $B$ below and to the right of point $A$.

Revealed preference tells us that the newly chosen market basket must lie on line segment $BT'$. Why? Because all market baskets on line segment $R'B$ could have been chosen but were not when the original budget line was $RS$. (Recall that the consumer preferred basket $A$ to any other feasible market basket.) Now note that all points on line segment $BT'$ involve more food consumption than does basket $A$. It follows that the quantity of food demanded increases whenever there is a decrease in the price of food with utility held constant. This negative substitution effect holds for all price changes and does not rely on the assumption of convexity of indifference curves that we made in Section 3.1 (page 69).

> • **Hicksian substitution effect** Alternative to the Slutsky equation for decomposing price changes without recourse to indifference curves.

> In §3.4, we explain how information about consumer preferences is revealed through the consumption choices that consumers make.

> In §3.1, we explain that an indifference curve is convex if the marginal rate of substitution diminishes as we move down along the curve.

# EXERCISES

1. Which of the following utility functions are consistent with convex indifference curves and which are not?
   a. $U(X, Y) = 2X + 5Y$
   b. $U(X, Y) = (XY)^{.5}$
   c. $U(X, Y) = \text{Min}(X, Y)$, where Min is the minimum of the two values of $X$ and $Y$.
2. Show that the two utility functions given below generate identical demand functions for goods $X$ and $Y$:
   a. $U(X, Y) = \log(X) + \log(Y)$
   b. $U(X, Y) = (XY)^{.5}$
3. Assume that a utility function is given by $\text{Min}(X, Y)$, as in Exercise 1(c). What is the Slutsky equation that decomposes the change in the demand for $X$ in response to a change in its price? What is the income effect? What is the substitution effect?
4. Sharon has the following utility function:

$$U(X, Y) = \sqrt{X} + \sqrt{Y}$$

where $X$ is her consumption of candy bars, with price $P_X = \$1$, and $Y$ is her consumption of espressos, with $P_Y = \$3$.
   a. Derive Sharon's demand for candy bars and espresso.
   b. Assume that her income $I = \$100$. How many candy bars and how many espressos will Sharon consume?
   c. What is the marginal utility of income?
5. Maurice has the following utility function:

$$U(X, Y) = 20X + 80Y - X^2 - 2Y^2$$

where $X$ is his consumption of CDs with a price of $\$1$ and $Y$ is his consumption of movie videos, with a rental price of $\$2$. He plans to spend $\$41$ on both forms of entertainment. Determine the number of CDs and video rentals that will maximize Maurice's utility.

# Uncertainty and Consumer Behavior

5

So far, we have assumed that prices, incomes, and other variables are known with certainty. However, many of the choices that people make involve considerable uncertainty. Most people, for example, borrow to finance large purchases, such as a house or a college education, and plan to pay for them out of future income. But for most of us, future incomes are uncertain. Our earnings can go up or down; we can be promoted or demoted, or even lose our jobs. And if we delay buying a house or investing in a college education, we risk price increases that could make such purchases less affordable. How should we take these uncertainties into account when making major consumption or investment decisions?

Sometimes we must choose how much *risk* to bear. What, for example, should you do with your savings? Should you invest your money in something safe, such as a savings account, or something riskier but potentially more lucrative, such as the stock market? Another example is the choice of a job or career. Is it better to work for a large, stable company with job security but slim chance for advancement, or is it better to join (or form) a new venture that offers less job security but more opportunity for advancement?

To answer such questions, we must examine the ways that people can compare and choose among risky alternatives. We will do this by taking the following steps:

1. In order to compare the riskiness of alternative choices, we need to quantify risk. We therefore begin this chapter by discussing measures of risk.

2. We will examine people's preferences toward risk. Most people find risk undesirable, but some people find it more undesirable than others.

3. We will see how people can sometimes reduce or eliminate risk. Sometimes risk can be reduced by diversification, by buying insurance, or by investing in additional information.

4. In some situations, people must choose the amount of risk they wish to bear. A good example is investing in stocks or bonds. We will see that such investments involve tradeoffs between the monetary gain that one can expect and the riskiness of that gain.

In a world of uncertainty, individual behavior may sometimes seem unpredictable, even irrational, and perhaps contrary to the basic

159

assumptions of consumer theory. In the final section of this chapter, we offer an overview of the flourishing field of behavioral economics, which, by introducing important ideas from psychology, has broadened and enriched the study of microeconomics.

## 5.1 DESCRIBING RISK

To describe risk quantitatively, we begin by listing all the possible outcomes of a particular action or event, as well as the likelihood that each outcome will occur.[1] Suppose, for example, that you are considering investing in a company that explores for offshore oil. If the exploration effort is successful, the company's stock will increase from $30 to $40 per share; if not, the price will fall to $20 per share. Thus there are two possible future outcomes: a $40-per-share price and a $20-per-share price.

### Probability

• **probability** Likelihood that a given outcome will occur.

**Probability** is the likelihood that a given outcome will occur. In our example, the probability that the oil exploration project will be successful might be 1/4 and the probability that it is unsuccessful 3/4. (Note that the probabilities for all possible events must add up to 1.)

Our interpretation of probability can depend on the nature of the uncertain event, on the beliefs of the people involved, or both. One *objective* interpretation of probability relies on the frequency with which certain events tend to occur. Suppose we know that of the last 100 offshore oil explorations, 25 have succeeded and 75 failed. In that case, the probability of success of 1/4 is objective because it is based directly on the frequency of similar experiences.

But what if there are no similar past experiences to help measure probability? In such instances, objective measures of probability cannot be deduced and more subjective measures are needed. *Subjective probability* is the perception that an outcome will occur. This perception may be based on a person's judgment or experience, but not necessarily on the frequency with which a particular outcome has actually occurred in the past. When probabilities are subjectively determined, different people may attach different probabilities to different outcomes and thereby make different choices. For example, if the search for oil were to take place in an area where no previous searches had ever occurred, I might attach a higher subjective probability than you to the chance that the project will succeed: Perhaps I know more about the project or I have a better understanding of the oil business and can therefore make better use of our common information. Either different information or different abilities to process the same information can cause subjective probabilities to vary among individuals.

Regardless of the interpretation of probability, it is used in calculating two important measures that help us describe and compare risky choices. One measure tells us the *expected value* and the other the *variability* of the possible outcomes.

---

[1]Some people distinguish between uncertainty and risk along the lines suggested some 60 years ago by economist Frank Knight. *Uncertainty* can refer to situations in which many outcomes are possible but the likelihood of each is unknown. *Risk* then refers to situations in which we can list all possible outcomes and know the likelihood of each occurring. In this chapter, we will always refer to risky situations, but will simplify the discussion by using *uncertainty* and *risk* interchangeably.

## Expected Value

The **expected value** associated with an uncertain situation is a weighted average of the **payoffs** or values associated with all possible outcomes. The probabilities of each outcome are used as weights. Thus the expected value measures the *central tendency*—the payoff or value that we would expect on average.

Our offshore oil exploration example had two possible outcomes: Success yields a payoff of $40 per share, failure a payoff of $20 per share. Denoting "probability of" by Pr, we express the expected value in this case as

$$\text{Expected value} = \text{Pr(success)}(\$40/\text{share}) + \text{Pr(failure)}(\$20/\text{share})$$
$$= (1/4)(\$40/\text{share}) + (3/4)(\$20/\text{share}) = \$25/\text{share}$$

More generally, if there are two possible outcomes having payoffs $X_1$ and $X_2$ and if the probabilities of each outcome are given by $\text{Pr}_1$ and $\text{Pr}_2$, then the expected value is

$$E(X) = \text{Pr}_1 X_1 + \text{Pr}_2 X_2$$

When there are $n$ possible outcomes, the expected value becomes

$$E(X) = \text{Pr}_1 X_1 + \text{Pr}_2 X_2 + \cdots + \text{Pr}_n X_n$$

> • **expected value** Probability-weighted average of the payoffs associated with all possible outcomes.
>
> • **payoff** Value associated with a possible outcome.

## Variability

**Variability** is the extent to which the possible outcomes of an uncertain situation differ. To see why variability is important, suppose you are choosing between two part-time summer sales jobs that have the same expected income ($1500). The first job is based entirely on commission—the income earned depends on how much you sell. There are two equally likely payoffs for this job: $2000 for a successful sales effort and $1000 for one that is less successful. The second job is salaried. It is very likely (.99 probability) that you will earn $1510, but there is a .01 probability that the company will go out of business, in which case you would earn only $510 in severance pay. Table 5.1 summarizes these possible outcomes, their payoffs, and their probabilities.

Note that these two jobs have the same expected income. For Job 1, expected income is .5($2000) + .5($1000) = $1500; for Job 2, it is .99($1510) + .01($510) = $1500. However, the *variability* of the possible payoffs is different. We measure variability by recognizing that large differences between actual and expected payoffs (whether positive or negative) imply greater risk. We call these differences **deviations**. Table 5.2 shows the deviations of the possible income from the expected income from each job.

By themselves, deviations do not provide a measure of variability. Why? Because they are sometimes positive and sometimes negative, and as you can see

> • **variability** Extent to which possible outcomes of an uncertain event differ.

> • **deviation** Difference between expected payoff and actual payoff.

| TABLE 5.1 | Income from Sales Jobs | | | | |
|---|---|---|---|---|---|
| | **OUTCOME 1** | | **OUTCOME 2** | | **Expected Income ($)** |
| | Probability | Income ($) | Probability | Income ($) | |
| Job 1: Commission | .5 | 2000 | .5 | 1000 | 1500 |
| Job 2: Fixed Salary | .99 | 1510 | .01 | 510 | 1500 |

| TABLE 5.2 | Deviations from Expected Income ($) | | | |
|---|---|---|---|---|
| | Outcome 1 | Deviation | Outcome 2 | Deviation |
| Job 1 | 2000 | 500 | 1000 | −500 |
| Job 2 | 1510 | 10 | 510 | −990 |

• **standard deviation**
Square root of the weighted average of the squares of the deviations of the payoffs associated with each outcome from their expected values.

from Table 5.2, the average of the probability-weighted deviations is always 0.[2] To get around this problem, we square each deviation, yielding numbers that are always positive. We then measure variability by calculating the **standard deviation**: the square root of the average of the *squares* of the deviations of the payoffs associated with each outcome from their expected values.[3]

Table 5.3 shows the calculation of the standard deviation for our example. Note that the average of the squared deviations under Job 1 is given by

$$.5(\$250,000) + .5(\$250,000) = \$250,000$$

The standard deviation is therefore equal to the square root of $250,000, or $500. Likewise, the probability-weighted average of the squared deviations under Job 2 is

$$.99(\$100) + .01(\$980,100) = \$9900$$

The standard deviation is the square root of $9900, or $99.50. Thus the second job is much less risky than the first; the standard deviation of the incomes is much lower.[4]

The concept of standard deviation applies equally well when there are many outcomes rather than just two. Suppose, for example, that the first summer job yields incomes ranging from $1000 to $2000 in increments of $100 that are all equally likely. The second job yields incomes from $1300 to $1700 (again in increments of $100) that are also equally likely. Figure 5.1 shows the alternatives graphically. (If there had been only two equally probable outcomes, then the figure would be drawn as two vertical lines, each with a height of 0.5.)

You can see from Figure 5.1 that the first job is riskier than the second. The "spread" of possible payoffs for the first job is much greater than the spread for the second. As a result, the standard deviation of the payoffs associated with the first job is greater than that associated with the second.

| TABLE 5.3 | Calculating Variance ($) | | | | | |
|---|---|---|---|---|---|---|
| | Outcome 1 | Deviation Squared | Outcome 2 | Deviation Squared | Weighted Average Deviation Squared | Standard Deviation |
| Job 1 | 2000 | 250,000 | 1000 | 250,000 | 250,000 | 500 |
| Job 2 | 1510 | 100 | 510 | 980,100 | 9900 | 99.50 |

---

[2]For Job 1, the average deviation is .5($500) + .5(−$500) = 0; for Job 2 it is .99($10) + .01(−$990) = 0.

[3]Another measure of variability, *variance*, is the square of the standard deviation.

[4]In general, when there are two outcomes with payoffs $X_1$ and $X_2$, occurring with probability $Pr_1$ and $Pr_2$, and $E(X)$ is the expected value of the outcomes, the standard deviation is given by $\sigma$, where

$$\sigma^2 = Pr_1[(X_1 - E(X))^2] + Pr_2[(X_2 - E(X))^2]$$

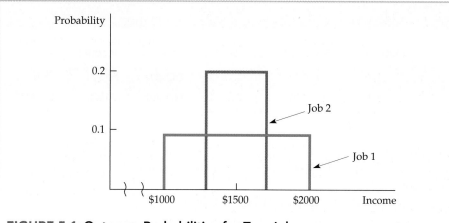

**FIGURE 5.1 Outcome Probabilities for Two Jobs**

The distribution of payoffs associated with Job 1 has a greater spread and a greater standard deviation than the distribution of payoffs associated with Job 2. Both distributions are flat because all outcomes are equally likely.

In this particular example, all payoffs are equally likely. Thus the curves describing the probabilities for each job are flat. In many cases, however, some payoffs are more likely than others. Figure 5.2 shows a situation in which the most extreme payoffs are the least likely. Again, the salary from Job 1 has a greater standard deviation. From this point on, we will use the standard deviation of payoffs to measure the degree of risk.

## Decision Making

Suppose you are choosing between the two sales jobs described in our original example. Which job would you take? If you dislike risk, you will take the second job: It offers the same expected income as the first but with less risk. But suppose

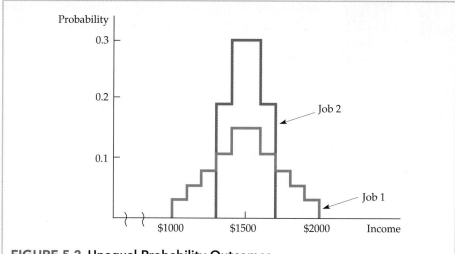

**FIGURE 5.2 Unequal Probability Outcomes**

The distribution of payoffs associated with Job 1 has a greater spread and a greater standard deviation than the distribution of payoffs associated with Job 2. Both distributions are peaked because the extreme payoffs are less likely than those near the middle of the distribution.

| TABLE 5.4 | Incomes from Sales Jobs—Modified ($) | | | | | |
|---|---|---|---|---|---|---|
| | Outcome 1 | Deviation Squared | Outcome 2 | Deviation Squared | Expected Income | Standard Deviation |
| Job 1 | 2100 | 250,000 | 1100 | 250,000 | 1600 | 500 |
| Job 2 | 1510 | 100 | 510 | 980,100 | 1500 | 99.50 |

we add $100 to each of the payoffs in the first job, so that the expected payoff increases from $1500 to $1600. Table 5.4 gives the new earnings and the squared deviations.

The two jobs can now be described as follows:

Job 1:   Expected Income = $1600   Standard Deviation = $500

Job 2:   Expected Income = $1500   Standard Deviation = $99.50

Job 1 offers a higher expected income but is much riskier than Job 2. Which job is preferred depends on the individual. While an aggressive entrepreneur who doesn't mind taking risks might choose Job 1, with the higher expected income and higher standard deviation, a more conservative person might choose the second job.

People's attitudes toward risk affect many of the decisions they make. In Example 5.1 we will see how attitudes toward risk affect people's willingness to break the law, and how this has implications for the fines that should be set for various violations. Then in Section 5.2, we will further develop our theory of consumer choice by examining people's risk preferences in greater detail.

**EXAMPLE 5.1**

### Deterring Crime

Fines may be better than incarceration in deterring certain types of crimes, such as speeding, double-parking, tax evasion, and air polluting.[5] A person choosing to violate the law in these ways has good information and can reasonably be assumed to be behaving rationally.

Other things being equal, the greater the fine, the more a potential criminal will be discouraged from committing the crime. For example, if it cost nothing to catch criminals, and if the crime imposed a calculable cost of $1000 on society, we might choose to catch all violations and impose a fine of $1000 on each. This practice would discourage people whose benefit from engaging in the activity was less than the $1000 fine.

In practice, however, it is very costly to catch lawbreakers. Therefore, we save on administrative costs by imposing relatively high fines (which are no more costly to collect than low fines), while allocating resources so that only a fraction of the violators are apprehended. Thus the size of the fine that must be imposed to

[5]This discussion builds indirectly on Gary S. Becker, "Crime and Punishment: An Economic Approach," *Journal of Political Economy* (March/April 1968): 169–217. See also A. Mitchell Polinsky and Steven Shavell, "The Optimal Tradeoff Between the Probability and the Magnitude of Fines," *American Economic Review* 69 (December 1979): 880–91.

discourage criminal behavior depends on the attitudes toward risk of potential violators.

Suppose that a city wants to deter people from double-parking. By double-parking, a typical resident saves $5 in terms of his own time for engaging in activities that are more pleasant than searching for a parking space. If it costs nothing to catch a double-parker, a fine of just over $5—say, $6—should be assessed every time he double-parks. This policy will ensure that the net benefit of double-parking (the $5 benefit less the $6 fine) would be less than zero. Our citizen will therefore choose to obey the law. In fact, all potential violators whose benefit was less than or equal to $5 would be discouraged, while a few whose benefit was greater than $5 (say, someone who double-parks because of an emergency) would violate the law.

In practice, it is too costly to catch all violators. Fortunately, it's also unnecessary. The same deterrence effect can be obtained by assessing a fine of $50 and catching only one in ten violators (or perhaps a fine of $500 with a one-in-100 chance of being caught). In each case, the expected penalty is $5, i.e., [$50][.1] or [$500][.01]. A policy that combines a high fine and a low probability of apprehension is likely to reduce enforcement costs. This approach is especially effective if drivers don't like to take risks. In our example, a $50 fine with a .1 probability of being caught might discourage most people from violating the law. We will examine attitudes toward risk in the next section.

## 5.2 PREFERENCES TOWARD RISK

We used a job example to show how people might evaluate risky outcomes, but the principles apply equally well to other choices. In this section, we concentrate on consumer choices generally and on the *utility* that consumers obtain from choosing among risky alternatives. To simplify things, we'll consider the utility that a consumer gets from his or her income—or, more appropriately, the market basket that the consumer's income can buy. We now measure payoffs, therefore, in terms of utility rather than dollars.

Figure 5.3(a) shows how we can describe one woman's preferences toward risk. The curve $0E$, which gives her utility function, tells us the level of utility (on the vertical axis) that she can attain for each level of income (measured in thousands of dollars on the horizontal axis). The level of utility increases from 10 to 16 to 18 as income increases from $10,000 to $20,000 to $30,000. But note that *marginal utility* is diminishing, falling from 10 when income increases from 0 to $10,000, to 6 when income increases from $10,000 to $20,000, and to 2 when income increases from $20,000 to $30,000.

> In §3.1, we explained that a utility function assigns a level of utility to each possible market basket.

> In §3.5, marginal utility is described as the additional satisfaction obtained by consuming an additional amount of a good.

Now suppose that our consumer has an income of $15,000 and is considering a new but risky sales job that will either double her income to $30,000 or cause it to fall to $10,000. Each possibility has a probability of .5. As Figure 5.3 (a) shows, the utility level associated with an income of $10,000 is 10 (at point $A$) and the utility level associated with an income of $30,000 is 18 (at $E$). The risky job must be compared with the current $15,000 job, for which the utility is 13.5 (at $B$).

To evaluate the new job, she can calculate the expected value of the resulting income. Because we are measuring value in terms of her utility, we must calculate the **expected utility** $E(u)$ that she can obtain. The expected utility is *the sum of the utilities associated with all possible outcomes, weighted by the probability that each outcome will occur*. In this case expected utility is

• **expected utility** Sum of the utilities associated with all possible outcomes, weighted by the probability that each outcome will occur.

$$E(u) = (1/2)u(\$10,000) + (1/2)u(\$30,000) = 0.5(10) + 0.5(18) = 14$$

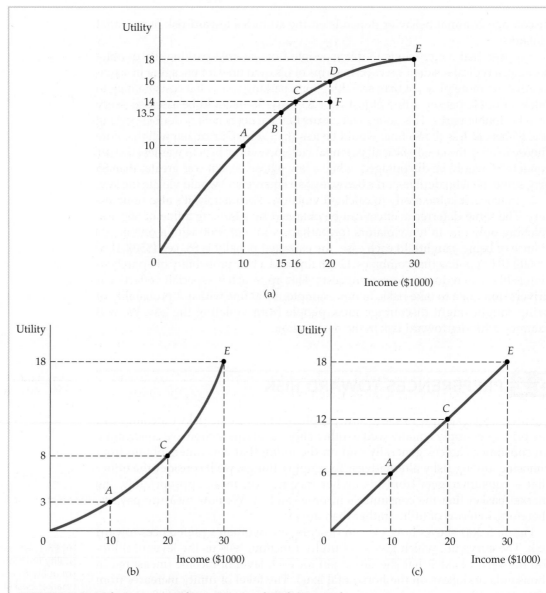

**FIGURE 5.3 Risk Averse, Risk Loving, and Risk Neutral**

People differ in their preferences toward risk. In (a), a consumer's marginal utility diminishes as income increases. The consumer is risk averse because she would prefer a certain income of $20,000 (with a utility of 16) to a gamble with a .5 probability of $10,000 and a .5 probability of $30,000 (and expected utility of 14). In (b), the consumer is risk loving: She would prefer the same gamble (with expected utility of 10.5) to the certain income (with a utility of 8). Finally, the consumer in (c) is risk neutral and indifferent between certain and uncertain events with the same expected income.

The risky new job is thus preferred to the original job because the expected utility of 14 is greater than the original utility of 13.5.

The old job involved no risk—it guaranteed an income of $15,000 and a utility level of 13.5. The new job is risky but offers both a higher expected income ($20,000) and, more importantly, a higher expected utility. If the woman wishes to increase her expected utility, she will take the risky job.

## Different Preferences Toward Risk

People differ in their willingness to bear risk. Some are risk averse, some risk loving, and some risk neutral. An individual who is **risk averse** prefers a certain given income to a risky income with the same expected value. (Such a person has a diminishing marginal utility of income.) Risk aversion is the most common attitude toward risk. To see that most people are risk averse most of the time, note that most people not only buy life insurance, health insurance, and car insurance, but also seek occupations with relatively stable wages.

> • **risk averse** Condition of preferring a certain income to a risky income with the same expected value.

Figure 5.3(a) applies to a woman who is risk averse. Suppose hypothetically that she can have either a certain income of $20,000, or a job yielding an income of $30,000 with probability .5 and an income of $10,000 with probability .5 (so that the expected income is also $20,000). As we saw, the expected utility of the uncertain income is 14—an average of the utility at point *A*(10) and the utility at *E*(18)—and is shown by *F*. Now we can compare the expected utility associated with the risky job to the utility generated if $20,000 were earned without risk. This latter utility level, 16, is given by *D* in Figure 5.3(a). It is clearly greater than the expected utility of 14 associated with the risky job.

For a risk-averse person, losses are more important (in terms of the change in utility) than gains. Again, this can be seen from Figure 5.3(a). A $10,000 increase in income, from $20,000 to $30,000, generates an increase in utility of two units; a $10,000 decrease in income, from $20,000 to $10,000, creates a loss of utility of six units.

A person who is **risk neutral** is indifferent between a certain income and an uncertain income with the same expected value. In Figure 5.3(c) the utility associated with a job generating an income of either $10,000 or $30,000 with equal probability is 12, as is the utility of receiving a certain income of $20,000. As you can see from the figure, the marginal utility of income is constant for a risk-neutral person.[6]

> • **risk neutral** Condition of being indifferent between a certain income and an uncertain income with the same expected value.

Finally, an individual who is **risk loving** prefers an uncertain income to a certain one, even if the expected value of the uncertain income is less than that of the certain income. Figure 5.3(b) shows this third possibility. In this case, the expected utility of an uncertain income, which will be either $10,000 with probability .5 or $30,000 with probability .5, is *higher* than the utility associated with a certain income of $20,000. Numerically,

> • **risk loving** Condition of preferring a risky income to a certain income with the same expected value.

$$E(u) = .5u(\$10,000) + .5u(\$30,000) = .5(3) + .5(18) = 10.5 > u(\$20,000) = 8$$

Of course, some people may be averse to some risks and act like risk lovers with respect to others. For example, many people purchase life insurance and are conservative with respect to their choice of jobs, but still enjoy gambling. Some criminologists might describe criminals as risk lovers, especially if they commit crimes despite a high prospect of apprehension and punishment. Except for such special cases, however, few people are risk loving, at least with respect to major purchases or large amounts of income or wealth.

**Risk Premium** The **risk premium** is the maximum amount of money that a risk-averse person will pay to avoid taking a risk. In general, the magnitude of the

> • **risk premium** Maximum amount of money that a risk-averse person will pay to avoid taking a risk.

---

[6]Thus, when people are risk neutral, the income they earn can be used as an indicator of well-being. A government policy that doubles incomes would then also double their utility. At the same time, government policies that alter the risks that people face, without changing their expected incomes, would not affect their well-being. Risk neutrality allows a person to avoid the complications that might be associated with the effects of governmental actions on the riskiness of outcomes.

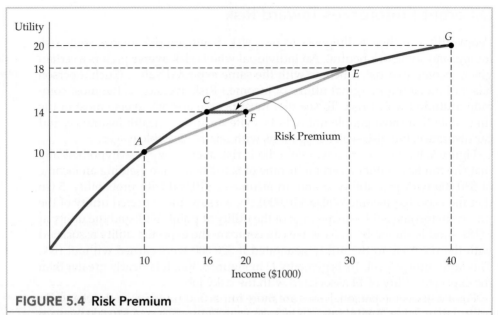

**FIGURE 5.4** **Risk Premium**

The risk premium, *CF*, measures the amount of income that an individual would give up to leave her indifferent between a risky choice and a certain one. Here, the risk premium is $4000 because a certain income of $16,000 (at point *C*) gives her the same expected utility (14) as the uncertain income (a .5 probability of being at point *A* and a .5 probability of being at point *E*) that has an expected value of $20,000.

risk premium depends on the risky alternatives that the person faces. To determine the risk premium, we have reproduced the utility function of Figure 5.3(a) in Figure 5.4 and extended it to an income of $40,000. Recall that an expected utility of 14 is achieved by a woman who is going to take a risky job with an expected income of $20,000. This outcome is shown graphically by drawing a horizontal line to the vertical axis from point *F*, which bisects straight line *AE* (thus representing an average of $10,000 and $30,000). But the utility level of 14 can also be achieved if the woman has a *certain* income of $16,000, as shown by dropping a vertical line from point *C*. Thus, the risk premium of $4000, given by line segment *CF*, is the amount of expected income ($20,000 minus $16,000) that she would give up in order to remain indifferent between the risky job and a hypothetical job that would pay her a certain income of $16,000.

**Risk Aversion and Income** The extent of an individual's risk aversion depends on the nature of the risk and on the person's income. Other things being equal, risk-averse people prefer a smaller variability of outcomes. We saw that when there are two outcomes—an income of $10,000 and an income of $30,000—the risk premium is $4000. Now consider a second risky job, also illustrated in Figure 5.4. With this job, there is a .5 probability of receiving an income of $40,000, with a utility level of 20, and a .5 probability of getting an income of $0, with a utility level of 0. The expected income is again $20,000, but the expected utility is only 10:

$$\text{Expected utility} = .5u(\$0) + .5u(\$40,000) = 0 + .5(20) = 10$$

Compared to a hypothetical job that pays $20,000 with certainty, the person holding this risky job gets 6 fewer units of expected utility: 10 rather than 16 units. At the same time, however, this person could also get 10 units of utility from a job that pays $10,000 with certainty. Thus the risk premium in this case is $10,000,

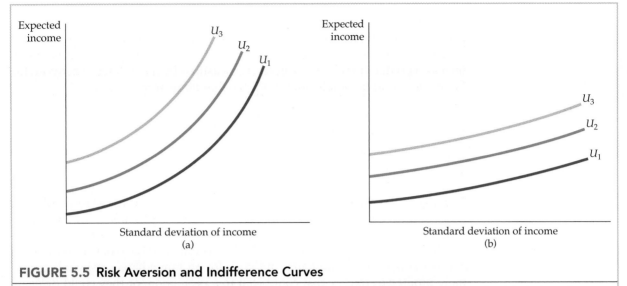

**FIGURE 5.5** **Risk Aversion and Indifference Curves**

Part **(a)** applies to a person who is highly risk averse: An increase in this individual's standard deviation of income requires a large increase in expected income if he or she is to remain equally well off. Part **(b)** applies to a person who is only slightly risk averse: An increase in the standard deviation of income requires only a small increase in expected income if he or she is to remain equally well off.

because this person would be willing to give up $10,000 of her $20,000 expected income to avoid bearing the risk of an uncertain income. The greater the variability of income, the more the person would be willing to pay to avoid the risky situation.

**Risk Aversion and Indifference Curves** We can also describe the extent of a person's risk aversion in terms of indifference curves that relate expected income to the variability of income, where the latter is measured by the standard deviation. Figure 5.5 shows such indifference curves for two individuals, one who is highly risk averse and another who is only slightly risk averse. Each indifference curve shows the combinations of expected income and standard deviation of income that give the individual the same amount of utility. Observe that all of the indifference curves are upward sloping: Because risk is undesirable, the greater the amount of risk, the greater the expected income needed to make the individual equally well off.

> In §3.1, we define an indifference curve as all market baskets that generate the same level of satisfaction for a consumer.

Figure 5.5(a) describes an individual who is highly risk averse. Observe that in order to leave this person equally well off, an increase in the standard deviation of income requires a large increase in expected income. Figure 5.5(b) applies to a slightly risk-averse person. In this case, a large increase in the standard deviation of income requires only a small increase in expected income.

---

**EXAMPLE 5.2**   Business Executives and the Choice
of Risk

Are business executives more risk loving than most people? When they are presented with alternative strategies, some risky, some safe, which do they choose? In one study, 464 executives were asked to respond to a questionnaire describing risky situations that an individual might face as vice president of a hypothetical company.[7] Respondents were presented with four risky events, each of which had a given probability of a favorable and unfavorable outcome. The payoffs and probabilities were chosen so that each event had the same expected value. In increasing order of the risk involved (as measured by the difference between the favorable and unfavorable outcomes), the four items were:

1. A lawsuit involving a patent violation
2. A customer threatening to buy from a competitor
3. A union dispute
4. A joint venture with a competitor

To gauge their willingness to take or avoid risks, researchers asked respondents a series of questions regarding business strategy. In one situation, they could pursue a risky strategy with the possibility of a high return right away or delay making a choice until the outcomes became more certain and the risk was reduced. In another situation, respondents could opt for an immediately risky but potentially profitable strategy that could lead to a promotion, or they could delegate the decision to someone else, which would protect their job but eliminate the promotion possibility.

The study found that executives vary substantially in their preferences toward risk. Roughly 20 percent indicated that they were relatively risk neutral; 40 percent opted for the more risky alternatives; and 20 percent were clearly risk averse (20 percent did not respond). More importantly, executives (including those who chose risky alternatives) typically made efforts to reduce or eliminate risk, usually by delaying decisions and collecting more information.

We will return to the use of indifference curves as a means of describing risk aversion in Section 5.4, where we discuss the demand for risky assets. First, however, we will turn to the ways in which an individual can reduce risk.

## 5.3 REDUCING RISK

As the recent growth in state lotteries shows, people sometimes choose risky alternatives that suggest risk-loving rather than risk-averse behavior. Most people, however, spend relatively small amounts on lottery tickets and casinos. When more important decisions are involved, they are generally risk averse. In this section, we describe three ways by which both consumers and businesses commonly reduce risks: *diversification, insurance,* and *obtaining more information* about choices and payoffs.

### Diversification

Recall the old saying, "Don't put all your eggs in one basket." Ignoring this advice is unnecessarily risky: If your basket turns out to be a bad bet, all will be lost. Instead, you can reduce risk through **diversification**: allocating your resources to a variety of activities whose outcomes are not closely related.

• **diversification** Practice of reducing risk by allocating resources to a variety of activities whose outcomes are not closely related.

[7]This example is based on Kenneth R. MacCrimmon and Donald A. Wehrung, "The Risk In-Basket," *Journal of Business* 57 (1984): 367–87.

| TABLE 5.5 Income from Sales of Appliances ($) | | |
|---|---|---|
| | **Hot Weather** | **Cold Weather** |
| Air conditioner sales | 30,000 | 12,000 |
| Heater sales | 12,000 | 30,000 |

Suppose, for example, that you plan to take a part-time job selling appliances on a commission basis. You can decide to sell only air conditioners or only heaters, or you can spend half your time selling each. Of course, you can't be sure how hot or cold the weather will be next year. How should you apportion your time in order to minimize the risk involved?

Risk can be minimized by *diversification*—by allocating your time so that you sell two or more products (whose sales are not closely related) rather than a single product. Suppose there is a 0.5 probability that it will be a relatively hot year, and a 0.5 probability that it will be cold. Table 5.5 gives the earnings that you can make selling air conditioners and heaters.

If you sell only air conditioners or only heaters, your actual income will be either $12,000 or $30,000, but your expected income will be $21,000 (.5[$30,000] + .5[$12,000]). But suppose you diversify by dividing your time evenly between the two products. In that case, your income will certainly be $21,000, regardless of the weather. If the weather is hot, you will earn $15,000 from air conditioner sales and $6000 from heater sales; if it is cold, you will earn $6000 from air conditioners and $15,000 from heaters. In this instance, diversification eliminates all risk.

Of course, diversification is not always this easy. In our example, heater and air conditioner sales are **negatively correlated variables**—they tend to move in opposite directions; whenever sales of one are strong, sales of the other are weak. But the principle of diversification is a general one: As long as you can allocate your resources toward a variety of activities whose outcomes are *not* closely related, you can eliminate some risk.

**• negatively correlated variables** Variables having a tendency to move in opposite directions.

**The Stock Market** Diversification is especially important for people who invest in the stock market. On any given day, the price of an individual stock can go up or down by a large amount, but some stocks rise in price while others fall. An individual who invests all her money in a single stock (i.e., puts all her eggs in one basket) is therefore taking much more risk than necessary. Risk can be reduced—although not eliminated—by investing in a portfolio of ten or twenty different stocks. Likewise, you can diversify by buying shares in **mutual funds**: organizations that pool funds of individual investors to buy a large number of different stocks. There are thousands of mutual funds available today for both stocks and bonds. These funds are popular because they reduce risk through diversification and because their fees are typically much lower than the cost of assembling one's own portfolio of stocks.

**• mutual fund** Organization that pools funds of individual investors to buy a large number of different stocks or other financial assets.

In the case of the stock market, not all risk is diversifiable. Although some stocks go up in price when others go down, stock prices are to some extent **positively correlated variables**: They tend to move in the same direction in response to changes in economic conditions. For example, the onset of a severe recession, which is likely to reduce the profits of many companies, may be accompanied by a decline in the overall market. Even with a diversified portfolio of stocks, therefore, you still face some risk.

**• positively correlated variables** Variables having a tendency to move in the same direction.

## Insurance

We have seen that risk-averse people are willing to pay to avoid risk. In fact, if the cost of insurance is equal to the expected loss (e.g., a policy with an expected loss of $1000 will cost $1000), risk-averse people will buy enough insurance to recover fully from any financial losses they might suffer.

Why? The answer is implicit in our discussion of risk aversion. Buying insurance assures a person of having the same income whether or not there is a loss. Because the insurance cost is equal to the expected loss, this certain income is equal to the expected income from the risky situation. For a risk-averse consumer, the guarantee of the same income regardless of the outcome generates more utility than would be the case if that person had a high income when there was no loss and a low income when a loss occurred.

To clarify this point, let's suppose a homeowner faces a 10-percent probability that his house will be burglarized and he will suffer a $10,000 loss. Let's assume he has $50,000 worth of property. Table 5.6 shows his wealth in two situations—with insurance costing $1000 and without insurance.

Note that expected wealth is the same ($49,000) in both situations. The variability, however, is quite different. As the table shows, with no insurance the standard deviation of wealth is $3000; with insurance, it is 0. If there is no burglary, the uninsured homeowner gains $1000 relative to the insured homeowner. But with a burglary, the uninsured homeowner loses $9000 relative to the insured homeowner. Remember: for a risk-averse individual, losses count more (in terms of changes in utility) than gains. A risk-averse homeowner, therefore, will enjoy higher utility by purchasing insurance.

**The Law of Large Numbers** Consumers usually buy insurance from companies that specialize in selling it. Insurance companies are firms that offer insurance because they know that when they sell a large number of policies, they face relatively little risk. The ability to avoid risk by operating on a large scale is based on the *law of large numbers*, which tells us that although single events may be random and largely unpredictable, the average outcome of many similar events can be predicted. For example, I may not be able to predict whether a coin toss will come out heads or tails, but I know that when many coins are flipped, approximately half will turn up heads and half tails. Likewise, if I am selling automobile insurance, I cannot predict whether a particular driver will have an accident, but I can be reasonably sure, judging from past experience, what fraction of a large group of drivers will have accidents.

**Actuarial Fairness** By operating on a large scale, insurance companies can be sure that over a sufficiently large number of events, total premiums paid in will be equal to the total amount of money paid out. Let's return to our burglary example. A man knows that there is a 10-percent probability that his house will be burgled; if it is, he will suffer a $10,000 loss. Prior to facing this risk, he calculates the expected loss to be $1000 (.10 × $10,000). The risk involved is considerable,

| **TABLE 5.6** | The Decision to Insure ($) | | | |
|---|---|---|---|---|
| Insurance | Burglary (Pr = .1) | No Burglary (Pr = .9) | Expected Wealth | Standard Deviation |
| No | 40,000 | 50,000 | 49,000 | 3000 |
| Yes | 49,000 | 49,000 | 49,000 | 0 |

however, because there is a 10-percent probability of a large loss. Now suppose that 100 people are similarly situated and that all of them buy burglary insurance from the same company. Because they all face a 10-percent probability of a $10,000 loss, the insurance company might charge each of them a premium of $1000. This $1000 premium generates an insurance fund of $100,000 from which losses can be paid. The insurance company can rely on the law of large numbers, which holds that the expected loss to the 100 individuals as a whole is likely to be very close to $1000 each. The total payout, therefore, will be close to $100,000, and the company need not worry about losing more than that.

When the insurance premium is equal to the expected payout, as in the example above, we say that the insurance is **actuarially fair**. But because they must cover administrative costs and make some profit, insurance companies typically charge premiums *above* expected losses. If there are a sufficient number of insurance companies to make the market competitive, these premiums will be close to actuarially fair levels. In some states, however, insurance premiums are regulated in order to protect consumers from "excessive" premiums. We will examine government regulation of markets in detail in Chapters 9 and 10 of this book.

In recent years, some insurance companies have come to the view that catastrophic disasters such as earthquakes are so unique and unpredictable that they cannot be viewed as diversifiable risks. Indeed, as a result of losses from past disasters, these companies do not feel that they can determine actuarially fair insurance rates. In California, for example, the state itself has had to enter the insurance business to fill the gap created when private companies refused to sell earthquake insurance. The state-run pool offers less insurance coverage at higher rates than was previously offered by private insurers.

• **actuarially fair**
Characterizing a situation in which an insurance premium is equal to the expected payout.

**EXAMPLE 5.3** The Value of Title Insurance When Buying a House

Suppose you are buying your first house. To close the sale, you will need a deed that gives you clear "title." Without such a clear title, there is always a chance that the seller of the house is not its true owner. Of course, the seller could be engaging in fraud, but it is more likely that the seller is unaware of the exact nature of his or her ownership rights. For example, the owner may have borrowed heavily, using the house as "collateral" for a loan. Or the property might carry with it a legal requirement that limits the use to which it may be put.

Suppose you are willing to pay $300,000 for the house, but you believe there is a one-in-twenty chance that careful research will reveal that the seller does not actually own the property. The property would then be worth nothing. If there were no insurance available, a risk-neutral person would bid at most $285,000 for the property (.95[$300,000] + .05[0]). However, if you expect to tie up most of your assets in the house, you would probably be risk averse and, therefore, bid much less—say, $230,000.

In situations such as this, it is clearly in the interest of the buyer to be sure that there is no risk of a lack of full ownership. The buyer does this by purchasing "title insurance." The title insurance company researches the history of the property, checks to see whether any legal liabilities are attached to it, and generally assures itself that there is no ownership problem. The insurance company then agrees to bear any remaining risk that might exist.

Because the title insurance company is a specialist in such insurance and can collect the relevant information relatively easily, the cost of title insurance is often less than the expected value of the loss involved. A fee of $1500 for title insurance is not unusual, even though the expected loss can be much higher. It is also in the interest of sellers to provide title insurance, because all but the most risk-loving buyers will pay much more for a house when it is insured than when it is not. In fact, most states require sellers to provide title insurance before a sale can be completed. In addition, because mortgage lenders are all concerned about such risks, they usually require new buyers to have title insurance before issuing a mortgage.

## The Value of Information

People often make decisions based on limited information. If more information were available, one could make better predictions and reduce risk. Because information is a valuable commodity, people will pay for it. The **value of complete information** is the difference between the expected value of a choice when there is complete information and the expected value when information is incomplete.

• **value of complete information** Difference between the expected value of a choice when there is complete information and the expected value when information is incomplete.

To see how information can be valuable, suppose you manage a clothing store and must decide how many suits to order for the fall season. If you order 100 suits, your cost is $180 per suit. If you order only 50 suits, your cost increases to $200. You know that you will be selling suits for $300 each, but you are not sure how many you can sell. All suits not sold can be returned, but for only half of what you paid for them. Without additional information, you will act on your belief that there is a .5 probability that you will sell 100 suits and a .5 probability that you will sell 50. Table 5.7 gives the profit that you would earn in each of these two cases.

Without additional information, you would choose to buy 100 suits if you were risk neutral, taking the chance that your profit might be either $12,000 or $1500. But if you were risk averse, you might buy 50 suits: In that case, you would know for sure that your profit would be $5000.

With complete information, you can place the correct order regardless of future sales. If sales were going to be 50 and you ordered 50 suits, your profits would be $5000. If, on the other hand, sales were going to be 100 and you ordered 100 suits, your profits would be $12,000. Because both outcomes are equally likely, your expected profit with complete information would be $8500. The value of information is computed as

| | Expected value with complete information: | $8500 |
|---|---|---|
| Less: | Expected value with uncertainty (buy 100 suits): | −6750 |
| | Value of complete information | $1750 |

Thus it is worth paying up to $1750 to obtain an accurate prediction of sales. Even though forecasting is inevitably imperfect, it may be worth investing in a marketing study that provides a reasonable forecast of next year's sales.

| TABLE 5.7 | Profits from Sales of Suits ($) | | |
|---|---|---|---|
| | **Sales of 50** | **Sales of 100** | **Expected Profit** |
| Buy 50 suits | 5000 | 5000 | 5000 |
| Buy 100 suits | 1500 | 12,000 | 6750 |

| EXAMPLE 5.4 | The Value of Information in the Dairy Industry |

Historically, the U.S. dairy industry has allocated its advertising expenditures more or less uniformly throughout the year.[8] But per-capita consumption of milk has declined over the years—a situation that has stirred producers to look for new strategies to encourage milk consumption. One strategy would be to increase advertising expenditures and to continue advertising at a uniform rate throughout the year. A second strategy would be to invest in market research in order to obtain more information about the seasonal demand for milk; marketers could then reallocate expenditures so that advertising was most intense when the demand for milk was greatest.

Research into milk demand shows that sales follow a seasonal pattern, with demand being greatest during the spring and lowest during the summer and early fall. The price elasticity of milk demand is negative but small and the income elasticity positive and large. Most important is the fact that milk advertising has the most effect on sales when consumers have the strongest preference for the product (March, April, and May) and least when preferences are weakest (August, September, and October).

> In §2.4, we define the price elasticity of demand as the percentage change in quantity demanded resulting from a 1-percent change in the price of a good.

In this case, the cost of obtaining seasonal information about milk demand is relatively low and the value of the information substantial. To estimate this value, we can compare the actual sales of milk during a typical year with sales levels that would have been reached had advertising expenditures been made in proportion to the strength of seasonal demand. In the latter case, 30 percent of the advertising budget would be allocated in the first quarter of the year and only 20 percent in the third quarter.

Applying these calculations to the New York metropolitan area, we discover that the value of information—the value of the additional annual milk sales—is about $4 million. This figure corresponds to a 9-percent increase in the profit to producers.

You might think that more information is always a good thing. As the following example shows, however, that is not always the case.

| EXAMPLE 5.5 | Doctors, Patients, and the Value of Information |

Suppose you were seriously ill and required major surgery. Assuming you wanted to get the best care possible, how would you go about choosing a surgeon and a hospital to provide that care? Many people would ask their friends or their primary-care physician for a recommendation. Although this might be helpful, a truly informed decision would probably require more detailed information. For example, how successful has a recommended surgeon and her affiliated hospital been in performing the particular operation that you need? How many of her patients have died or had serious complications from the operation, and how do

---

[8]This example is based on Henry Kinnucan and Olan D. Forker, "Seasonality in the Consumer Response to Milk Advertising with Implications for Milk Promotion Policy," *American Journal of Agricultural Economics* 68 (1986): 562–71.

these numbers compare with those for other surgeons and hospitals? This kind of information is likely to be difficult or impossible for most patients to obtain. Would patients be better off if detailed information about the performance records of doctors and hospitals were readily available?

Not necessarily. More information is often, but not always, better. Interestingly in this case, access to performance information could actually lead to worse health outcomes. Why? Because access to such information would create two different incentives that would affect the behavior of both doctors and patients. First, it would allow patients to choose doctors with better performance records, which creates an incentive for doctors to perform better. That is a good thing. But second, it would encourage doctors to limit their practices to patients who are in relatively good health. The reason is that very old or very sick patients are more likely to have complications or die as a result of treatment; doctors who treat such patients are likely to have worse performance records (other factors being equal). To the extent that doctors would be judged according to performance, they would have an incentive to avoid treating very old or sick patients. As a result, such patients would find it difficult or impossible to obtain treatment.

Whether more information is better depends on which effect dominates—the ability of patients to make more informed choices versus the incentive for doctors to avoid very sick patients. In a recent study, economists examined the impact of the mandatory "report cards" introduced in New York and Pennsylvania in the early 1990s to evaluate outcomes of coronary bypass surgeries.[9] They analyzed hospital choices and outcomes for all elderly heart attack patients and patients receiving coronary bypass surgery in the United States from 1987 through 1994. By comparing trends in New York and Pennsylvania to the trends in other states, they could determine the effect of the increased information made possible by the availability of report cards. They found that although report cards improved matching of patients with hospitals and doctors, they also caused a shift in treatment from sicker patients towards healthier ones. Overall, this led to worse outcomes, especially among sicker patients. Thus the study concluded that report cards reduced welfare.

More information often improves welfare because it allows people to reduce risk and to take actions that might reduce the effect of bad outcomes. However, as this example makes clear, information can cause people to change their behavior in undesirable ways. We will discuss this issue further in Chapter 17.

---

## *5.4 THE DEMAND FOR RISKY ASSETS

Most people are risk averse. Given a choice, they prefer fixed monthly incomes to those which, though equally large on average, fluctuate randomly from month to month. Yet many of these same people will invest all or part of their savings in stocks, bonds, and other assets that carry some risk. Why do risk-averse people invest in the stock market and thereby risk losing part or all of

---

[9]David Dranove, Daniel Kessler, Mark McClennan, and Mark Satterthwaite, "Is More Information Better? The Effects of 'Report Cards' on Health Care Providers," *Journal of Political Economy* 3 (June 2003).

their investments?[10] How do people decide how much risk to bear when making investments and planning for the future? To answer these questions, we must examine the demand for risky assets.

## Assets

An **asset** is *something that provides a flow of money or services to its owner*. A home, an apartment building, a savings account, or shares of General Motors stock are all assets. A home, for example, provides a flow of housing services to its owner, and, if the owner did not wish to live there, could be rented out, thereby providing a monetary flow. Likewise, apartments can be rented out, providing a flow of rental income to the owner of the building. A savings account pays interest (usually every day or every month), which is usually reinvested in the account.

The monetary flow that one receives from asset ownership can take the form of an explicit payment, such as the rental income from an apartment building: Every month, the landlord receives rent checks from the tenants. Another form of explicit payment is the dividend on shares of common stock: Every three months, the owner of a share of General Motors stock receives a quarterly dividend payment.

But sometimes the monetary flow from ownership of an asset is implicit: It takes the form of an increase or decrease in the price or value of the asset. An increase in the value of an asset is a *capital gain*; a decrease is a *capital loss*. For example, as the population of a city grows, the value of an apartment building may increase. The owner of the building will then earn a capital gain beyond the rental income. The capital gain is *unrealized* until the building is sold because no money is actually received until then. There is, however, an implicit monetary flow because the building *could* be sold at any time. The monetary flow from owning General Motors stock is also partly implicit. The price of the stock changes from day to day, and each time it does, owners gain or lose.

> • **asset** Something that provides a flow of money or services to its owner.

## Risky and Riskless Assets

A **risky asset** provides *a monetary flow that is at least in part random*. In other words, the monetary flow is not known with certainty in advance. A share of General Motors stock is an obvious example of a risky asset: You cannot know whether the price of the stock will rise or fall over time, nor can you even be sure that the company will continue to pay the same (or any) dividend per share. Although people often associate risk with the stock market, most other assets are also risky.

An apartment building is one example. You cannot know how much land values will rise or fall, whether the building will be fully rented all the time, or even whether the tenants will pay their rents promptly. Corporate bonds are another example—the issuing corporation could go bankrupt and fail to pay bond owners their interest and principal. Even long-term U.S. government bonds that mature in 10 or 20 years are risky. Although it is highly unlikely that the federal government will go bankrupt, the rate of inflation could unexpectedly increase and make future interest payments and the eventual repayment of principal worth less in real terms, thereby reducing the value of the bonds.

> • **risky asset** Asset that provides an uncertain flow of money or services to its owner.

[10]Most Americans have at least some money invested in stocks or other risky assets, though often indirectly. For example, many people who hold full-time jobs have shares in pension funds underwritten in part by their own salary contributions and in part by employer contributions. Usually such funds are partly invested in the stock market.

• **riskless (or risk-free) asset**
Asset that provides a flow of
money or services that is
known with certainty.

In contrast, a **riskless (or risk-free) asset** pays a monetary flow that is known with certainty. Short-term U.S. government bonds—called Treasury bills—are riskless, or almost riskless. Because they mature in a few months, there is very little risk from an unexpected increase in the rate of inflation. You can also be reasonably confident that the U.S. government will not default on the bond (i.e., refuse to pay back the holder when the bond comes due). Other examples of riskless or almost riskless assets include passbook savings accounts and short-term certificates of deposit.

## Asset Returns

• **return** Total monetary flow
of an asset as a fraction of its
price.

People buy and hold assets because of the monetary flows they provide. To compare assets with each other, it helps to think of this monetary flow relative to an asset's price or value. The **return** on an asset is *the total monetary flow it yields— including capital gains or losses—as a fraction of its price.* For example, a bond worth $1000 today that pays out $100 this year (and every year) has a return of 10 percent.[11] If an apartment building was worth $10 million last year, increased in value to $11 million this year, and also provided rental income (after expenses) of $0.5 million, it would have yielded a return of 15 percent over the past year. If a share of General Motors stock was worth $80 at the beginning of the year, fell to $72 by the end of the year, and paid a dividend of $4, it will have yielded a return of −5 percent (the dividend yield of 5 percent less the capital loss of 10 percent).

When people invest their savings in stocks, bonds, land, or other assets, they usually hope to earn a return that exceeds the rate of inflation. Thus, by delaying consumption, they can buy more in the future than they can by spending all their income now. Consequently, we often express the return on an asset in *real*—i.e., *inflation-adjusted*—terms. The **real return** on an asset is its simple (or nominal) return *less* the rate of inflation. For example, with an annual inflation rate of 5 percent, our bond, apartment building, and share of GM stock have yielded real returns of 5 percent, 10 percent, and −10 percent, respectively.

• **real return** Simple (or
nominal) return on an asset,
less the rate of inflation.

**Expected versus Actual Returns** Because most assets are risky, an investor cannot know in advance what returns they will yield over the coming year. For example, our apartment building might have depreciated in value instead of appreciating, and the price of GM stock might have risen instead of fallen. However, we can still compare assets by looking at their expected returns. The **expected return** on an asset is *the expected value of its return*, i.e., the return that it should earn on average. In some years, an asset's **actual return** may be much higher than its expected return and in some years much lower. Over a long period, however, the average return should be close to the expected return.

• **expected return** Return
that an asset should earn on
average.

• **actual return** Return that
an asset earns.

Different assets have different expected returns. Table 5.8, for example, shows that while the expected real return of a U.S. Treasury bill has been less than 1 percent, the expected real return on a group of representative stocks on the New York Stock Exchange has been more than 9 percent.[12] Why would anyone

---

[11]The price of a bond often changes during the course of a year. If the bond appreciates (or depreciates) in value during the year, its return will be greater (or less) than 10 percent. In addition, the definition of *return* given above should not be confused with the "internal rate of return," which is sometimes used to compare monetary flows occurring over a period of time. We discuss other return measures in Chapter 15, when we deal with present discounted values.

[12]For some stocks, the expected return is higher, and for some it is lower. Stocks of smaller companies (e.g., some of those traded on the NASDAQ) have higher expected rates of return—and higher return standard deviations.

| TABLE 5.8 Investments—Risk and Return (1926–2006*) | | | |
|---|---|---|---|
| | **Average Rate of Return (%)** | **Average Real Rate of Return (%)** | **Risk (Standard Deviation, %)** |
| Common stocks (S&P 500) | 12.3 | 9.2 | 20.1 |
| Long-term corporate bonds | 6.2 | 3.1 | 8.5 |
| U.S. Treasury bills | 3.8 | 0.7 | 3.1 |
| *Source: Stocks, Bonds, Bills, and Inflation: 2007 Yearbook, Morningstar, Inc. | | | |

buy a Treasury bill when the expected return on stocks is so much higher? Because the demand for an asset depends not just on its expected return, but also on its *risk*: Although stocks have a higher expected return than Treasury bills, they also carry much more risk. One measure of risk, the standard deviation of the real annual return, is equal to 20.1 percent for common stocks, 8.5 percent for corporate bonds, and only 3.1 percent for U.S. Treasury bills.

The numbers in Table 5.8 suggest that the higher the expected return on an investment, the greater the risk involved. Assuming that one's investments are well diversified, this is indeed the case.[13] As a result, the risk-averse investor must balance expected return against risk. We examine this trade-off in more detail in the next section.

## The Trade-Off Between Risk and Return

Suppose a woman wants to invest her savings in two assets—Treasury bills, which are almost risk free, and a representative group of stocks. She must decide how much to invest in each asset. She might, for instance, invest only in Treasury bills, only in stocks, or in some combination of the two. As we will see, this problem is analogous to the consumer's problem of allocating a budget between purchases of food and clothing.

Let's denote the risk-free return on the Treasury bill by $R_f$. Because the return is risk free, the expected and actual returns are the same. In addition, let the *expected* return from investing in the stock market be $R_m$ and the actual return be $r_m$. The actual return is risky. At the time of the investment decision, we know the set of possible outcomes and the likelihood of each, but we do not know what particular outcome will occur. The risky asset will have a higher expected return than the risk-free asset ($R_m > R_f$). Otherwise, risk-averse investors would buy only Treasury bills and no stocks would be sold.

**The Investment Portfolio** To determine how much money the investor should put in each asset, let's set $b$ equal to the fraction of her savings placed in the stock market and $(1 - b)$ the fraction used to purchase Treasury bills. The

---

[13]It is *nondiversifiable* risk that matters. An individual stock may be very risky but still have a low expected return because most of the risk could be diversified away by holding a large number of such stocks. *Nondiversifiable risk*, which arises from the fact that individual stock prices are correlated with the overall stock market, is the risk that remains even if one holds a diversified portfolio of stocks. We discuss this point in detail in the context of the *capital asset pricing model* in Chapter 15.

expected return on her total portfolio, $R_p$, is a weighted average of the expected return on the two assets:[14]

$$R_p = bR_m + (1 - b)R_f \tag{5.1}$$

Suppose, for example, that Treasury bills pay 4 percent ($R_f = .04$), the stock market's expected return is 12 percent ($R_m = .12$), and $b = 1/2$. Then $R_p = 8$ percent. How risky is this portfolio? One measure of riskiness is the standard deviation of its return. We will denote the *standard deviation* of the risky stock market investment by $\sigma_m$. With some algebra, we can show that the *standard deviation of the portfolio*, $\sigma_p$ (with one risky and one risk-free asset) is the fraction of the portfolio invested in the risky asset times the standard deviation of that asset:[15]

$$\sigma_p = b\sigma_m \tag{5.2}$$

## The Investor's Choice Problem

In §3.2 we explain how a budget line is determined from an individual's income and the prices of the available goods.

We have still not determined how the investor should choose this fraction $b$. To do so, we must first show that she faces a risk-return trade-off analogous to a consumer's budget line. To identify this trade-off, note that equation (5.1) for the expected return on the portfolio can be rewritten as

$$R_p = R_f + b(R_m - R_f)$$

Now, from equation (5.2) we see that $b = \sigma_p/\sigma_m$, so that

$$R_p = R_f + \frac{(R_m - R_f)}{\sigma_m}\sigma_p \tag{5.3}$$

**Risk and the Budget Line** This equation is a *budget line* because it describes the trade-off between risk ($\sigma_p$) and expected return ($R_p$). Note that it is the equation for a straight line: Because $R_m$, $R_f$, and $\sigma_m$ are constants, the slope $(R_m - R_f)/\sigma_m$ is a constant, as is the intercept, $R_f$. The equation says that *the expected return on the portfolio $R_p$ increases as the standard deviation of that return $\sigma_p$ increases*. We call the slope of this budget line, $(R_m - R_f)/\sigma_m$, the **price of risk,** because it tells us how much extra risk an investor must incur to enjoy a higher expected return.

• **Price of risk** Extra risk that an investor must incur to enjoy a higher expected return.

The budget line is drawn in Figure 5.6. If our investor wants no risk, she can invest all her funds in Treasury bills ($b = 0$) and earn an expected return $R_f$. To receive a higher expected return, she must incur some risk. For example, she could invest all her funds in stocks ($b = 1$), earning an expected return $R_m$ but incurring a standard deviation $\sigma_m$. Or she might invest some fraction of her

---

[14]The expected value of the sum of two variables is the sum of the expected values. Therefore

$$R_p = E[br_m] + E[(1 - b)R_f] = bE[r_m] + (1 - b)R_f = bR_m + (1 - b)R_f$$

[15]To see why, we observe from footnote 4 that we can write the variance of the portfolio return as

$$\sigma_p^2 = E[br_m + (1 - b)R_f - R_p]^2$$

Substituting equation (5.1) for the expected return on the portfolio, $R_p$, we have

$$\sigma_p^2 = E[br_m + (1 - b)R_f - bR_m - (1 - b)R_f]^2 = E[b(r_m - R_m)]^2 = b^2\sigma_m^2$$

Because the standard deviation of a random variable is the square root of its variance, $\sigma_p = b\sigma_m$.

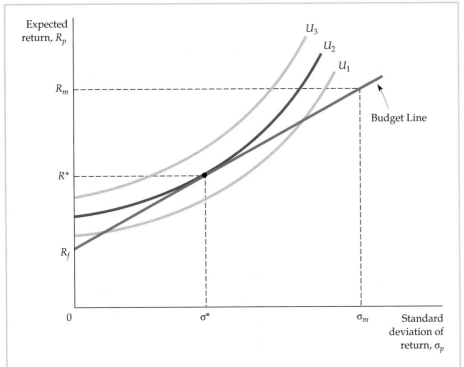

**FIGURE 5.6 Choosing Between Risk and Return**

An investor is dividing her funds between two assets—Treasury bills, which are risk free, and stocks. The budget line describes the trade-off between the expected return and its riskiness, as measured by the standard deviation of the return. The slope of the budget line is $(R_m - R_f)/\sigma_m$, which is the price of risk. Three indifference curves are drawn, each showing combinations of risk and return that leave an investor equally satisfied. The curves are upward-sloping because a risk-averse investor will require a higher expected return if she is to bear a greater amount of risk. The utility-maximizing investment portfolio is at the point where indifference curve $U_2$ is tangent to the budget line.

funds in each type of asset, earning an expected return somewhere between $R_f$ and $R_m$ and facing a standard deviation less than $\sigma_m$ but greater than zero.

**Risk and Indifference Curves** Figure 5.6 also shows the solution to the investor's problem. Three indifference curves are drawn in the figure. Each curve describes combinations of risk and return that leave the investor equally satisfied. The curves are upward-sloping because risk is undesirable. Thus, with a greater amount of risk, it takes a greater expected return to make the investor equally well-off. Curve $U_3$ yields the greatest amount of satisfaction and $U_1$ the least amount: For a given amount of risk, the investor earns a higher expected return on $U_3$ than on $U_2$ and a higher expected return on $U_2$ than on $U_1$.

Of the three indifference curves, the investor would prefer to be on $U_3$. This position, however, is not feasible, because $U_3$ does not touch the budget line. Curve $U_1$ is feasible, but the investor can do better. Like the consumer choosing quantities of food and clothing, our investor does best by choosing a combination of risk and return at the point where an indifference curve (in this case $U_2$) is tangent to the budget line. At that point, the investor's return has an expected value $R^*$ and a standard deviation $\sigma^*$.

Naturally, people differ in their attitudes toward risk. This fact is illustrated in Figure 5.7, which shows how two different investors choose their portfolios.

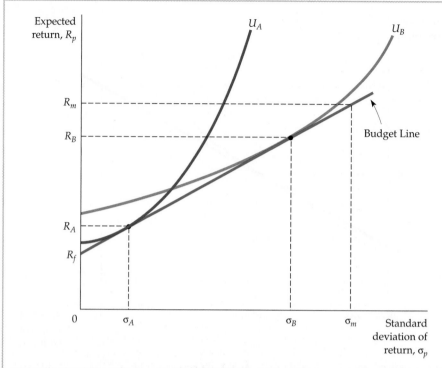

**FIGURE 5.7 The Choices of Two Different Investors**

Investor $A$ is highly risk averse. Because his portfolio will consist mostly of the risk-free asset, his expected return $R_A$ will be only slightly greater than the risk-free return. His risk $\sigma_A$, however, will be small. Investor $B$ is less risk averse. She will invest a large fraction of her funds in stocks. Although the expected return on her portfolio $R_B$ will be larger, it will also be riskier.

Investor $A$ is quite risk averse. Because his indifference curve $U_A$ is tangent to the budget line at a point of low risk, he will invest almost all of his funds in Treasury bills and earn an expected return $R_A$ just slightly larger than the risk-free return $R_f$. Investor $B$ is less risk averse. She will invest most of her funds in stocks, and while the return on her portfolio will have a higher expected value $R_B$, it will also have a higher standard deviation $\sigma_B$.

If Investor $B$ has a sufficiently low level of risk aversion, she might buy stocks on *margin*: that is, she would borrow money from a brokerage firm in order to invest more than she actually owns in the stock market. In effect, a person who buys stocks on margin holds a portfolio with more than 100 percent of the portfolio's value invested in stocks. This situation is illustrated in Figure 5.8, which shows indifference curves for two investors. Investor $A$, who is relatively risk-averse, invests about half of his funds in stocks. Investor $B$, however, has an indifference curve that is relatively flat and tangent with the budget line at a point where the expected return on the portfolio exceeds the expected return on the stock market. In order to hold this portfolio, the investor must borrow money because she wants to invest *more* than 100 percent of her wealth in the stock market. Buying stocks on margin in this way is a form of *leverage*: the investor increases her expected return above that for the overall stock market, but at the cost of increased risk.

In Chapters 3 and 4, we simplified the problem of consumer choice by assuming that the consumer had only two goods from which to choose—food and

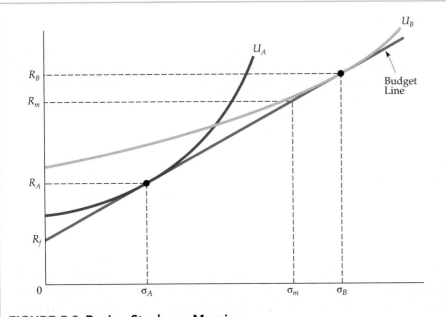

**FIGURE 5.8 Buying Stocks on Margin**

Because Investor *A* is risk averse, his portfolio contains a mixture of stocks and risk-free Treasury bills. Investor *B*, however, has a very low degree of risk aversion. Her indifference curve, $U_B$, is tangent to the budget line at a point where the expected return and standard deviation for her portfolio exceed those for the stock market overall. This implies that she would like to invest *more* than 100 percent of her wealth in the stock market. She does so by buying stocks *on margin*—i.e., by borrowing from a brokerage firm to help finance her investment.

clothing. In the same spirit, we have simplified the investor's choice by limiting it to Treasury bills and stocks. The basic principles, however, would be the same if we had more assets (e.g., corporate bonds, land, and different types of stocks). Every investor faces a trade-off between risk and return.[16] The degree of extra risk that each is willing to bear in order to earn a higher expected return depends on how risk averse he or she is. Less risk-averse investors tend to include a larger fraction of risky assets in their portfolios.

**EXAMPLE 5.6** Investing in the Stock Market

The 1990s witnessed a shift in the investing behavior of Americans. First, many people started investing in the stock market for the first time. In 1989, about 32 percent of families in the United States had part of their wealth invested in the stock market, either directly (by owning individual stocks) or indirectly (through mutual funds or pension

---

[16]As mentioned earlier, what matters is nondiversifiable risk, because investors can eliminate diversifiable risk by holding many different stocks (e.g., via mutual funds). We discuss diversifiable versus nondiversifiable risk in Chapter 15.

plans invested in stocks). By 1998, that fraction had risen to 49 percent. In addition, the share of wealth invested in stocks increased from about 26 percent to about 54 percent during the same period.[17] Much of this shift is attributable to younger investors. For those under the age of 35, participation in the stock market increased from about 22 percent in 1989 to about 41 percent in 1998. For those older than 35, participation also increased, but by much less.

Why have more people started investing in the stock market? One reason is the advent of online trading, which has made investing much easier. Another reason may be the considerable increase in stock prices that occurred during the late 1990s, driven in part by the so-called "dot com euphoria." These increases may have convinced some investors that prices could only continue to rise in the future. As one analyst put it, "The market's relentless seven-year climb, the popularity of mutual funds, the shift by employers to self-directed retirement plans, and the avalanche of do-it-yourself investment publications all have combined to create a nation of financial know-it-alls."[18]

Figure 5.9 shows the dividend yield and price/earnings (P/E) ratio for the S&P 500 (an index of stocks of 500 large corporations) over the period 1980 to 2007. Observe that the dividend yield (the annual dividend divided by the stock price) fell from about 5 percent in 1980 to below 2 percent by 2000. Meanwhile, however, the price/earnings ratio (the share price divided by annual earnings per share)

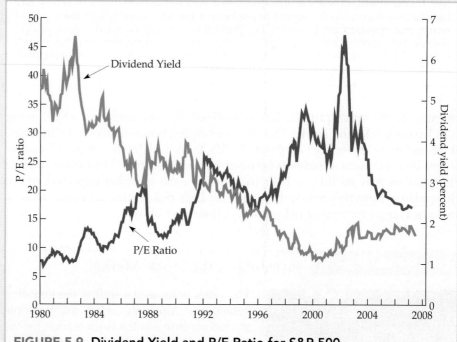

**FIGURE 5.9  Dividend Yield and P/E Ratio for S&P 500**

The dividend yield for the S&P 500 (the annual dividend divided by the stock price) has fallen dramatically, while the price/earnings ratio (the stock price divided by the annual earnings-per-share) rose from 1980 to 2002 and then dropped.

---

[17]Data are from the *Federal Reserve Bulletin*, January 2000.

[18]"We're All Bulls Here: Strong Market Makes Everybody an Expert," *Wall Street Journal*, September 12, 1997.

increased from about 8 in 1980 to over 40 in 2002, before falling to around 20 between 2005 and 2007. In retrospect, the increase in the P/E ratio through 2002 could only have occurred if investors believed that corporate profits would continue to grow rapidly in the coming decade. This suggests that in the late 1990s, many investors had a low degree of risk aversion, were quite optimistic about the economy, or both. Alternatively, some economists have argued that the run-up of stock prices during the 1990s was the result of "herd behavior," in which investors rushed to get into the market after hearing of the successful experiences of others.[19]

The psychological motivations that explain herd behavior can help to explain stock market bubbles. However, they go far beyond the stock market. They also apply to the behavior of consumers and firm managers in a wide variety of settings. Such behavior cannot always be captured by the simplified assumptions that we have made up to this point about consumer choice. In the next section, we will discuss these aspects of behavior in detail, and we will see how the traditional models of Chapters 3 and 4 can be expanded to help us understand this behavior.

## 5.5 BEHAVIORAL ECONOMICS

Recall that the basic theory of consumer demand is based on three assumptions: (1) consumers have clear preferences for some goods over others; (2) consumers face budget constraints; and (3) given their preferences, limited incomes, and the prices of different goods, consumers choose to buy combinations of goods that maximize their satisfaction (or utility). These assumptions, however, are not always realistic: Preferences are not always clear or might vary depending on the context in which choices are made, and consumer choices are not always utility-maximizing.

Perhaps our understanding of consumer demand (as well as the decisions of firms) would be improved if we incorporated more realistic and detailed assumptions regarding human behavior. This has been the objective of the newly flourishing field of *behavioral economics*, which has broadened and enriched the study of microeconomics.[20] We introduce this topic by highlighting some examples of consumer behavior that cannot be easily explained with the basic utility-maximizing assumptions that we have relied on so far:

- There has just been a big snowstorm, so you stop at the hardware store to buy a snow shovel. You had expected to pay $20 for the shovel—the price that the store normally charges. However, you find that the store has suddenly raised the price to $40. Although you would expect a price increase because of the storm, you feel that a doubling of the price is unfair and that the store is trying to take advantage of you. Out of spite, you do not buy the shovel.[21]

- Tired of being snowed in at home you decide to take a vacation in the country. On the way, you stop at a highway restaurant for lunch. Even though you are

[19]See, for example, Robert Shiller, *Irrational Exuberance*, Princeton University Press, 2000.

[20]For more detailed discussion of the material presented in this section, see Stefano DellaVigna, "Psychology and Economics: Evidence from the Field," *Journal of Economic Literature* (forthcoming); Colin Camerer and George Loewenstein, "Behavioral Economics: Past, Present, Future," in Colin Camerer, George Loewenstein, and Matthew Rabin (eds.), *Advances in Behavioral Economics*, Princeton University Press, 2003.

[21]This example is based on Daniel Kahneman, Jack Knetsch, and Richard Thaler, "Fairness as a Constraint on Profit Seeking: Entitlements in the Market," *American Economic Review* 76 (September 1986): 728–741.

unlikely to return to that restaurant, you believe that it is fair and appropriate to leave a 15-percent tip in appreciation of the good service that you received.

• You buy this textbook from an Internet bookseller because the price is lower than the price at your local bookstore. However, you ignore the shipping cost when comparing prices.

Each of these examples illustrates plausible behavior that cannot be explained by a model based solely on the basic assumptions described in Chapters 3 and 4. Instead, we need to draw on insights from psychology and sociology to augment our basic assumptions about consumer behavior. These insights will enable us to account for more complex consumer preferences, for the use of simple rules in decision-making, and for the difficulty that people often have in understanding the laws of probability.

## More Complex Preferences

The standard model of consumer behavior assumes that consumers place unique values on the goods and services that they purchase. However, psychologists have found that perceived value depends on the circumstances. Consider, for example, apartment prices in Pittsburgh and San Francisco. In Pittsburgh, the median monthly rent in 2006 for a two-bedroom apartment was about $650, while in San Francisco the rent for a similar apartment was $2,125. For someone accustomed to San Francisco housing prices, Pittsburgh might seem like a bargain. On the other hand, someone moving from Pittsburgh to San Francisco might feel "gouged"—thinking it unfair for housing to cost that much.[22]

• **reference point** The point from which an individual makes a consumption decision.

In this example, the **reference point**—the point from which the individual makes the consumption decision—is clearly different for long-time residents of San Francisco and Pittsburgh. Reference points can develop for many reasons: our past consumption, our experience in a market, our expectations about how prices should behave, and even the context in which we consume a good. Reference points can strongly affect the way people approach economic decisions.

• **endowment effect** Tendency of individuals to value an item more when they own it than when they do not.

A well-known example of a reference point is the **endowment effect**—the fact that individuals tend to value an item more when they happen to own it than when they do not. One way to think about this effect is to consider the gap between the price that a person is willing to pay for a good and the price at which she is willing to sell the same good to someone else. Our basic theory of consumer behavior says that this price should be the same, but many experiments suggest that is not what happens in practice.[23]

In one classroom experiment, half of the students chosen at random were given a free coffee mug with a market value of $5; the other half got nothing.[24] Students with the mug were asked the price at which they would sell it back to the professor; the second group was asked the minimum amount of money that they would accept in lieu of a mug. The decision faced by both groups is similar but their reference points are different. For the first group, whose reference point was possession of a mug, the average selling price was $7. For the second

---

[22]This example is based on Uri Simonsohn and George Loewenstein, "Mistake #37: The Effects of Previously Encountered Prices on Current Housing Demand," *The Economic Journal* 116 (January 2006): 175–199.

[23]Experimental work such as this has been important to the development of behavioral economics. It is for this reason that the 2002 Nobel Prize in economics was shared by Vernon Smith, who did much of the pioneering work in the use of experiments to test economic theories.

[24]Daniel Kahneman, Jack L. Knetsch, and Richard H. Thaler, "Experimental Tests of the Endowment Effect and the Coase Theorem," *Journal of Political Economy 98*, (December 1990): 1925–48.

group, which did not have a mug, the average amount desired in lieu of a mug was $3.50. This gap in prices shows that giving up the mug was perceived to be a greater "loss" to those who had one than the "gain" from obtaining a mug for those without one. Such a result, aptly called **loss aversion**, has been apparent in many experimental studies.

• **loss aversion** Tendency for individuals to prefer avoiding losses over acquiring gains.

As another example of loss aversion, people are sometimes hesitant to sell stocks at a loss, even if they could invest the proceeds in other stocks that they think are better investments. Why? Because the original price paid for the stock—which turned out to be too high given the realities of the market—acts as a reference point, and people are averse to losses. (A $1000 loss on an investment seems to "hurt" more than the perceived benefit from a $1000 gain.) While there are a variety of circumstances in which endowment effects arise, we now know that these effects tend to disappear as consumers gain relevant experience. We would not expect to see stockbrokers or other investment professionals exhibit the loss aversion described above.[25]

Many people do things because they think it is appropriate to do so, even though there is no financial or other material benefit. Examples include charitable giving, volunteering time, or tipping in a restaurant. And, as in our examples of renting an apartment, buying a snow shovel, and tipping pointed out, there are occasions in which consumers' views about fairness also affect their behavior.

Our basic consumer theory does not appear to account for fairness, at least at first glance. The so-called *ultimatum game* illustrates this supposition. Imagine that, under the following rules, you are offered a chance to divide 100 one-dollar bills with a stranger whom you will never meet again: You first propose a division of the money between you and the stranger. The stranger will respond by either accepting or rejecting your proposal. If he accepts, you each get the share that you proposed. If he rejects, you both get nothing. What should you do?

Because more money means more utility, our basic theory provides a clear answer to this question. You should propose that you get $99 while the other person gets only $1. Moreover, the responder should be happy to accept this proposal, because $1 is more than he had before and more than he would get if he rejected your offer (in both cases zero). This is a beneficial deal for both of you.

Yet most people facing this choice hesitate to make such an offer because they think it unfair, and many "strangers" would reject the offer. Why? The stranger might believe that because you both received the windfall opportunity to divide $100, a simple and fair division would be 50/50 or something close to that. Maybe the stranger will turn down the $1 offer to teach you that greediness is not appropriate behavior. Indeed, if you believe that the stranger will feel this way, it will be rational for you to offer a greater amount. In fact, when this game is played experimentally, typical sharing proposals range between 67/33 and 50/50, and such offers are normally accepted.

The ultimatum game shows how fairness can affect economic decisions. Not surprisingly, fairness concerns can also affect negotiations between firms and their workers. A firm may offer a higher wage to employees because the managers believe that workers deserve a comfortable standard of living or because they want to foster a pleasant working environment. Moreover, workers who do not get a wage that they feel is fair may not put much effort into their work.[26]

[25]John A. List, "Does Market Experience Eliminate Market Anomalies?" *Quarterly Journal of Economics* 118 (January 2003): 41–71.

[26]For a general discussion of behavioral economics and the theory of wages and employment, see George Akerlof, "Behavioral Macroeconomics and Macroeconomic Behavior," *American Economic Review* 92 (June 2002): 411–33.

(In Section 17.6, we will see that paying workers higher-than-market wages can also be explained by the "efficiency wage theory" of labor markets, in which fairness concerns do not apply.) Fairness also affects the ways in which firms set prices and can explain why firms can more easily raise prices in response to higher costs than to increases in demand.[27]

Fortunately, fairness concerns can be taken into account in the basic model of consumer behavior. If individuals moving to San Francisco believe that high apartment rents are unfair, their maximum willingness to pay for rental housing will be reduced. If a sufficient number of individuals feel this way, the resulting reduction in demand will lead to lower rental prices. Similarly, if enough workers do not feel that their wages are fair, there will be a reduction in the supply of labor, and wage rates will increase.

## Rules of Thumb and Biases in Decision Making

Many economic (and everyday) decisions can be quite complex, especially if they involve choices about matters in which we have little experience. In such cases, people often resort to rule of thumb or other mental shortcuts to help them make decisions. In the tipping example, you took a mental shortcut when you decided to offer a 15-percent tip. The use of such rules of thumb, however, can introduce a bias into our economic decision making—something that our basic model does not allow.[28]

The mental rules that we use in making decisions frequently depend on both the context in which the decisions are made and the information available. For example, imagine that you just received a solicitation from a new local charity to make a donation. Rather than asking for a gift of any amount, the charity asks you to choose: $20, $50, $100, $250, or "other." The purpose of these suggestions is to induce you to anchor your final donation. **Anchoring** refers to the impact that a suggested (perhaps unrelated) piece of information may have on your final decision. Rather than trying to decide precisely how much to donate—say $44.52—and not wanting to appear miserly, one might simply write a check for the next higher category—$50. Another individual wishing to make only a token donation of $10 might choose the lowest stated amount, $20. In both cases, anchoring can bias individual choices toward larger donations.

• **anchoring** Tendency to rely heavily on one prior (suggested) piece of information when making a decision.

A common way to economize on the effort involved in making decisions is to ignore seemingly unimportant pieces of information. For example, goods purchased over the Internet often involve shipping costs. Although small, these costs should be included as part of the good's final price when making a consumption decision. However, a recent study has shown that shipping costs are typically ignored by many consumers when deciding to buy things online. Their decisions are biased because they view the price of goods to be lower than they really are.[29]

Whereas depending on rules of thumb can introduce biases in decision making, it is important to understand that they do serve a useful purpose. Frequently, rules of thumb help to save time and effort and result in only small biases. Thus, they should not be dismissed outright.

---

[27]See, for example, Julio J. Rotemberg, "Fair Pricing," NBER Working Paper No. W10915, 2004.

[28]For an introduction to this topic see Amos Tversky and Daniel Kahneman, "Judgment under Uncertainty: Heuristics and Biases," *Science* 185 (September 1974): 1124–31.

[29]Tankim Hossain and John Morgan, ". . . Plus Shipping and Handling: Revenue (Non) Equivalence in Field Experiments on eBay," *Advances in Economic Analysis* & Policy 6: 2 (2006).

## Probabilities and Uncertainty

An important part of decision making under uncertainty is the calculation of expected utility, which requires two pieces of information: a utility value for each outcome (from the utility function) and the probability of each outcome. Although the expected-utility approach may seem simple, in practice we tend to have difficulty making such calculations. In part, this is because many of us lack a basic understanding of probability.

People are sometimes prone to a bias called the *law of small numbers*: They tend to overstate the probability that certain events will occur when faced with relatively little information from recent memory. For example, many people tend to overstate the likelihood that they or someone they know will die in a plane crash or win the lottery. Recall the roulette player who bets on black after seeing red come up three times in a row: He has ignored the laws of probability.

Research has shown that investors in the stock market are often subject to a small-numbers bias, believing that high returns over the past few years are likely to be followed by more high returns over the next few years—thereby contributing to the kind of "herd behavior" that we discussed in the previous section. In this case, investors assess the likely payoff from investing by observing the market over a short period of time. In fact, one would have to study stock market returns for many decades in order to estimate accurately the expected return on equity investments. Similarly when people assess the likelihood that housing prices will rise based on several years of data, the resulting misperceptions can result in housing price bubbles.[30]

Although individuals may have some understanding of true probabilities (as when flipping a coin), complications arise when probabilities are unknown. For instance, few people have an idea about the probability that they or a friend will be in a car or airplane accident. In such cases, we form subjective probability assessments about such events. Our estimation of subjective probabilities may be close to true probabilities, but often they are not.

Forming subjective probabilities is not always an easy task and people are generally prone to several biases in the process. For instance, when evaluating the likelihood of an event, the context in which the evaluation is made can be very important. If a tragedy such as a plane crash has occurred recently, many people will tend to overestimate the probability of it happening to them. Likewise, when a probability for a particular event is very, very small, many people simply ignore that possibility in their decision making.

## Summing Up

Where does this leave us? Should we dispense with the traditional consumer theory discussed in Chapters 3 and 4? Not at all. In fact, the basic theory that we learned up to now works quite well in many situations. It helps us to understand and evaluate the characteristics of consumer demand and to predict the impact on demand of changes in prices or incomes. Although it does not explain all consumer decisions, it sheds light on many of them. The developing field of behavioral economics tries to explain and to elaborate on those situations that are not well explained by the basic consumer model.

---

[30]See Charles Himmelberg, Christopher Mayer, and Todd Sinai, "Assessing High House Prices: Bubbles, Fundamentals and Misperceptions," *Journal of Economic Perspectives* 19 (Fall 2005).

**EXAMPLE 5.7**  New York City Taxicab Drivers

Most cab drivers rent their taxicabs for a fixed daily fee from a company that owns a fleet of cars. They can then choose to drive the cab as little or as much as they want during a 12-hour period. As with many services, business is highly variable from day to day, depending on the weather, subway breakdowns, holidays, and so on. How do cabdrivers respond to these variations, many of which are largely unpredictable?

In many cities, taxicab rates are fixed by regulation and do not change from day to day. However, on busy days drivers can earn a higher income because they do not have to spend as much time searching for riders. Traditional economic theory would predict that drivers will work longer hours on busy days than on slow days; an extra hour on a busy day might bring in $20, whereas an extra hour on a slow day might yield only $10. Does traditional theory explain the actual behavior of taxicab drivers?

A recent study analyzed actual taxicab trip records obtained from the New York Taxi and Limousine Commission for the spring of 1994.[31] The daily fee to rent a taxi was then $76, and gasoline cost about $15 per day. Surprisingly, the researchers found that most drivers drive *more* hours on slow days and *fewer* hours on busy days. In other words, there is a *negative relationship* between the effective hourly wage and the number of hours worked each day; the higher the wage, the sooner the cabdrivers quit for the day. Behavioral economics can explain this result. Suppose that most taxicab drivers have an income target for each day. That target effectively serves as a reference point. Daily income targeting makes sense from a behavioral perspective. An income target provides a simple decision rule for drivers because they need only keep a record of their fares for the day. A daily target also helps drivers with potential self-control problems; without a target, a driver may choose to quit earlier on many days just to avoid the hassles of the job. The target in the 1994 study appeared to be about $150 per day.

Still other studies challenge this "behavioral" explanation of behavior. A different study, also of New York City cab drivers who rented their taxis, concluded that the traditional economic model does indeed offer important insights into drivers' behavior.[32] The study concluded that daily income had only a small effect on a driver's decision as to when to quit for the day. Rather, the decision to stop appears to be based on the cumulative number of hours already worked that day and not on hitting a specific income target.

What can account for these two seemingly contradictory results? The two studies used different techniques in analyzing and interpreting the taxicab trip records. Although behavioral models, such as those with reference points or targeted goals, often lead to interesting implications for economic theory, the traditional model can indeed go a long way in explaining what we frequently observe.

---

[31]Colin Camerer, Linda Babcock, George Loewenstein, and Richard Thaler, "Labor Supply of New York City Cabdrivers: One Day at a Time," *Quarterly Journal of Economics* (May 1997): 404–41.

[32]Henry S. Farber, "Is Tomorrow Another Day? The Labor Supply of New York City Cabdrivers," *Journal of Political Economy* 113 (2005): 46–82.

# SUMMARY

1. Consumers and managers frequently make decisions in which there is uncertainty about the future. This uncertainty is characterized by the term *risk*, which applies when each of the possible outcomes and its probability of occurrence is known.

2. Consumers and investors are concerned about the expected value and the variability of uncertain outcomes. The expected value is a measure of the central tendency of the values of risky outcomes. Variability is frequently measured by the standard deviation of outcomes, which is the square root of the probability-weighted average of the squares of the deviation from the expected value of each possible outcome.

3. Facing uncertain choices, consumers maximize their expected utility—an average of the utility associated with each outcome—with the associated probabilities serving as weights.

4. A person who would prefer a certain return of a given amount to a risky investment with the same expected return is risk averse. The maximum amount of money that a risk-averse person would pay to avoid taking a risk is called the *risk premium*. A person who is indifferent between a risky investment and the certain receipt of the expected return on that investment is risk neutral. A risk-loving consumer would prefer a risky investment with a given expected return to the certain receipt of that expected return.

5. Risk can be reduced by (a) diversification, (b) insurance, and (c) additional information.

6. The *law of large numbers* enables insurance companies to provide insurance for which the premiums paid equal the expected value of the losses being insured against. We call such insurance *actuarially fair*.

7. Consumer theory can be applied to decisions to invest in risky assets. The budget line reflects the price of risk, and consumers' indifference curves reflect their attitudes toward risk.

8. Individual behavior sometimes seems unpredictable, even irrational, and contrary to the assumptions that underlie the basic model of consumer choice. The study of behavioral economics enriches consumer theory by accounting for *reference points, endowment effects, anchoring,* fairness considerations, and deviations from the laws of probability.

# QUESTIONS FOR REVIEW

1. What does it mean to say that a person is *risk averse*? Why are some people likely to be risk averse while others are risk lovers?

2. Why is the variance a better measure of variability than the range?

3. George has $5000 to invest in a mutual fund. The expected return on mutual fund *A* is 15 percent and the expected return on mutual fund B is 10 percent. Should George pick mutual fund *A* or fund *B*?

4. What does it mean for consumers to maximize expected utility? Can you think of a case in which a person might *not* maximize expected utility?

5. Why do people often want to insure fully against uncertain situations even when the premium paid exceeds the expected value of the loss being insured against?

6. Why is an insurance company likely to behave as if it were risk neutral even if its managers are risk-averse individuals?

7. When is it worth paying to obtain more information to reduce uncertainty?

8. How does the diversification of an investor's portfolio avoid risk?

9. Why do some investors put a large portion of their portfolios into risky assets while others invest largely in risk-free alternatives? (*Hint*: Do the two investors receive exactly the same return on average? If so, why?)

10. What is an endowment effect? Give an example of such an effect.

11. Jennifer is shopping and sees an attractive shirt. However, the price of $50 is more than she is willing to pay. A few weeks later, she finds the same shirt on sale for $25 and buys it. When a friend offers her $50 for the shirt, she refuses to sell it. Explain Jennifer's behavior.

# EXERCISES

1. Consider a lottery with three possible outcomes:

   - $125 will be received with probability .2
   - $100 will be received with probability .3
   - $50 will be received with probability .5

   a. What is the expected value of the lottery?

   b. What is the variance of the outcomes?

   c. What would a risk-neutral person pay to play the lottery?

2. Suppose you have invested in a new computer company whose profitability depends on two factors: (1) whether the U.S. Congress passes a tariff raising the

cost of Japanese computers and (2) whether the U.S. economy grows slowly or quickly. What are the four mutually exclusive states of the world that you should be concerned about?

3. Richard is deciding whether to buy a state lottery ticket. Each ticket costs $1, and the probability of winning payoffs is given as follows:

| Probability | Return |
|:---:|:---:|
| .5 | $0.00 |
| .25 | $1.00 |
| .2 | $2.00 |
| .05 | $7.50 |

a. What is the expected value of Richard's payoff if he buys a lottery ticket? What is the variance?
b. Richard's nickname is "No-Risk Rick" because he is an extremely risk-averse individual. Would he buy the ticket?
c. Richard has been given 1000 lottery tickets. Discuss how you would determine the smallest amount for which he would be willing to sell all 1000 tickets.
d. In the long run, given the price of the lottery tickets and the probability/return table, what do you think the state would do about the lottery?

4. Suppose an investor is concerned about a business choice in which there are three prospects—the probability and returns are given below:

| Probability | Return |
|:---:|:---:|
| .4 | $100 |
| .3 | 30 |
| .3 | −30 |

What is the expected value of the uncertain investment? What is the variance?

5. You are an insurance agent who must write a policy for a new client named Sam. His company, Society for Creative Alternatives to Mayonnaise (SCAM), is working on a low-fat, low-cholesterol mayonnaise substitute for the sandwich-condiment industry. The sandwich industry will pay top dollar to the first inventor to patent such a mayonnaise substitute. Sam's SCAM seems like a very risky proposition to you. You have calculated his possible returns table as follows:

| Probability | Return | Outcome |
|:---:|:---:|:---:|
| .999 | −$1,000,000 | (he fails) |
| .001 | $1,000,000,000 | (he succeeds and sells his formula) |

a. What is the expected return of Sam's project? What is the variance?
b. What is the most that Sam is willing to pay for insurance? Assume Sam is risk neutral.
c. Suppose you found out that the Japanese are on the verge of introducing their own mayonnaise substitute next month. Sam does not know this and has just turned down your final offer of $1000 for the insurance. Assume that Sam tells you SCAM is only six months away from perfecting its mayonnaise substitute *and* that you know what you know about the Japanese. Would you raise or lower your policy premium on any subsequent proposal to Sam? Based on his information, would Sam accept?

6. Suppose that Natasha's utility function is given by $u(I) = \sqrt{10I}$, where $I$ represents annual income in thousands of dollars.
a. Is Natasha risk loving, risk neutral, or risk averse? Explain.
b. Suppose that Natasha is currently earning an income of $40,000 ($I = 40$) and can earn that income next year with certainty. She is offered a chance to take a new job that offers a .6 probability of earning $44,000 and a .4 probability of earning $33,000. Should she take the new job?
c. In (b), would Natasha be willing to buy insurance to protect against the variable income associated with the new job? If so, how much would she be willing to pay for that insurance? (*Hint*: What is the risk premium?)

7. Suppose that two investments have the same three payoffs, but the probability associated with each payoff differs, as illustrated in the table below:

| Payoff | Probability (Investment A) | Probability (Investment B) |
|:---:|:---:|:---:|
| $300 | 0.10 | 0.30 |
| $250 | 0.80 | 0.40 |
| $200 | 0.10 | 0.30 |

a. Find the expected return and standard deviation of each investment.
b. Jill has the utility function $U = 5I$, where $I$ denotes the payoff. Which investment will she choose?
c. Ken has the utility function $U = 5\sqrt{I}$. Which investment will he choose?
d. Laura has the utility function $U = 5I^2$. Which investment will she choose?

8. As the owner of a family farm whose wealth is $250,000, you must choose between sitting this season out and investing last year's earnings ($200,000) in a safe money market fund paying 5.0 percent or planting summer corn. Planting costs $200,000, with a six-month time to harvest. If there is rain, planting summer corn will yield $500,000 in revenues at harvest. If there is a drought, planting will yield $50,000 in revenues.

As a third choice, you can purchase AgriCorp drought-resistant summer corn at a cost of $250,000 that will yield $500,000 in revenues at harvest if there is rain, and $350,000 in revenues if there is a drought. You are risk averse, and your preference for family wealth ($W$) is specified by the relationship $U(W) = \sqrt{W}$. The probability of a summer drought is 0.30, while the probability of summer rain is 0.70.

Which of the three options should you choose? Explain.

9. Draw a utility function over income $u(I)$ that describes a man who is a risk lover when his income is low but risk averse when his income is high. Can you explain why such a utility function might reasonably describe a person's preferences?

10. A city is considering how much to spend to hire people to monitor its parking meters. The following information is available to the city manager:

- Hiring each meter monitor costs $10,000 per year.
- With one monitoring person hired, the probability of a driver getting a ticket each time he or she parks illegally is equal to .25.
- With two monitors, the probability of getting a ticket is .5; with three monitors, the probability is .75; and with four, it's equal to 1.
- With two monitors hired, the current fine for overtime parking is $20.

a. Assume first that all drivers are risk neutral. What parking fine would you levy, and how many meter monitors would you hire (1, 2, 3, or 4) to achieve the current level of deterrence against illegal parking at the minimum cost?

b. Now assume that drivers are highly risk averse. How would your answer to (a) change?

c. (For discussion) What if drivers could insure themselves against the risk of parking fines? Would it make good public policy to permit such insurance?

11. A moderately risk-averse investor has 50 percent of her portfolio invested in stocks and 50 percent in risk-free Treasury bills. Show how each of the following events will affect the investor's budget line and the proportion of stocks in her portfolio:

a. The standard deviation of the return on the stock market increases, but the expected return on the stock market remains the same.

b. The expected return on the stock market increases, but the standard deviation of the stock market remains the same.

c. The return on risk-free Treasury bills increases.

# Production  6

In the last three chapters, we focused on the *demand side* of the market—the preferences and behavior of consumers. Now we turn to the *supply side* and examine the behavior of producers. We will see how firms can produce efficiently and how their costs of production change with changes in both input prices and the level of output. We will also see that there are strong similarities between the optimizing decisions made by firms and those made by consumers. In other words, understanding consumer behavior will help us understand producer behavior.

In this chapter and the next we discuss the **theory of the firm**, which describes how a firm makes cost-minimizing production decisions and how the firm's resulting cost varies with its output. Our knowledge of production and cost will help us understand the characteristics of market supply. It will also prove useful for dealing with problems that arise regularly in business. To see this, just consider some of the problems often faced by a company like General Motors. How much assembly-line machinery and how much labor should it use in its new automobile plants? If it wants to increase production, should it hire more workers, construct new plants, or both? Does it make more sense for one automobile plant to produce different models, or should each model be manufactured in a separate plant? What should GM expect its costs to be during the coming year? How are these costs likely to change over time and be affected by the level of production? These questions apply not only to business firms but also to other producers of goods and services, such as governments and nonprofit agencies.

## The Production Decisions of a Firm

In Chapters 3 and 4, we studied consumer behavior by breaking it down into three steps. First, we explained how to describe consumer preferences. Second, we accounted for the fact that consumers face budget constraints. Third, we saw how, given their preferences and budget constraints, consumers can choose combinations of goods to maximize their satisfaction. The production decisions of firms are analogous to the purchasing decisions of consumers, and can likewise be understood in three steps:

1. **Production Technology:** We need a practical way of describing how *inputs* (such as labor, capital, and raw materials) can be transformed into *outputs* (such as cars and televisions). Just as a consumer can reach a level of satisfaction from buying different combinations of goods, the firm can produce a particular level of output by using different combinations of inputs. For example, an electronics firm

195

might produce 10,000 televisions per month by using a substantial amount of labor (e.g., workers assembling the televisions by hand) and very little capital, or by building a highly automated capital-intensive factory and using very little labor.

2. **Cost Constraints:** Firms must take into account the *prices* of labor, capital, and other inputs. Just as a consumer is constrained by a limited budget, the firm will be concerned about its cost of production. For example, the firm that produces 10,000 televisions per month will want to do so in a way that minimizes its total production cost, which is determined in part by the prices of the inputs it uses.

3. **Input Choices:** Given its production technology and the prices of labor, capital, and other inputs, the firm must choose *how much of each input* to use in producing its output. Just as a consumer takes account of the prices of different goods when deciding how much of each good to buy, the firm must take into account the prices of different inputs when deciding how much of each input to use. If our electronics firm operates in a country with low wage rates, it may decide to produce televisions by using a large amount of labor, thereby using very little capital.

• **theory of the firm**
Explanation of how a firm makes cost-minimizing production decisions and how its cost varies with its output.

These three steps are the building blocks of the theory of the firm, and we will discuss them in detail in this chapter and the next. We will also address other important aspects of firm behavior. For example, assuming that the firm is always using a cost-minimizing combination of inputs, we will see how its total cost of production varies with the quantity it produces and how it can choose that quantity to maximize its profit.

We begin this chapter by showing how the firm's production technology can be represented in the form of a *production function*—a compact description of how inputs are turned into output. We then use the production function to show how the firm's output changes when just one of its inputs (labor) is varied, holding the other inputs fixed. Next, we turn to the more general case in which the firm can vary all of its inputs, and we show how the firm chooses a cost-minimizing combination of inputs to produce its output. We will be particularly concerned with the *scale* of the firm's operation. Are there, for example, any technological advantages that make the firm more productive as its scale increases?

## 6.1 THE TECHNOLOGY OF PRODUCTION

• **factors of production**
Inputs into the production process (e.g., labor, capital, and materials).

In the production process, firms turn *inputs* into *outputs* (or products). Inputs, which are also called **factors of production**, include anything that the firm must use as part of the production process. In a bakery, for example, inputs include the labor of its workers; raw materials, such as flour and sugar; and the capital invested in its ovens, mixers, and other equipment needed to produce such outputs as bread, cakes, and pastries.

As you can see, we can divide inputs into the broad categories of *labor*, *materials*, and *capital*, each of which might include more narrow subdivisions. Labor inputs include skilled workers (carpenters, engineers) and unskilled workers (agricultural workers), as well as the entrepreneurial efforts of the firm's managers. Materials include steel, plastics, electricity, water, and any other goods that the firm buys and transforms into final products. Capital includes land, buildings, machinery and other equipment, as well as inventories.

## The Production Function

Firms can turn inputs into outputs in a variety of ways, using various combinations of labor, materials, and capital. We can describe the relationship between the inputs into the production process and the resulting output by a *production function*. A **production function** indicates the highest output $q$ that a firm can produce for every specified combination of inputs.[1] Although in practice firms use a wide variety of inputs, we will keep our analysis simple by focusing on only two, labor $L$ and capital $K$. We can then write the production function as

$$q = F(K, L) \qquad\qquad (6.1)$$

• **production function**
Function showing the highest output that a firm can produce for every specified combination of inputs.

This equation relates the quantity of output to the quantities of the two inputs, capital and labor. For example, the production function might describe the number of personal computers that can be produced each year with a 10,000-square-foot plant and a specific amount of assembly-line labor. Or it might describe the crop that a farmer can obtain using specific amounts of machinery and workers.

It is important to keep in mind that inputs and outputs are *flows*. For example, our PC manufacturer uses a certain amount of labor *each year* to produce some number of computers over that year. Although it might own its plant and machinery, we can think of the firm as paying a cost for the use of that plant and machinery over the year. To simplify things, we will frequently ignore the reference to time and refer only to amounts of labor, capital, and output. Unless otherwise indicated, however, we mean the amount of labor and capital used each year and the amount of output produced each year.

Because the production function allows inputs to be combined in varying proportions, output can be produced in many ways. For the production function in equation (6.1), this could mean using more capital and less labor, or vice versa. For example, wine can be produced in a labor-intensive way using many workers, or in a capital-intensive way using machines and only a few workers.

Note that equation (6.1) applies to a *given technology*—that is, to a given state of knowledge about the various methods that might be used to transform inputs into outputs. As the technology becomes more advanced and the production function changes, a firm can obtain more output for a given set of inputs. For example, a new, faster assembly line may allow a hardware manufacturer to produce more high-speed computers in a given period of time.

Production functions describe what is *technically feasible* when the firm operates *efficiently*—that is, when the firm uses each combination of inputs as effectively as possible. The presumption that production is always technically efficient need not always hold, but it is reasonable to expect that profit-seeking firms will not waste resources.

## The Short Run versus the Long Run

It takes time for a firm to adjust its inputs to produce its product with differing amounts of labor and capital. A new factory must be planned and built, and machinery and other capital equipment must be ordered and delivered. Such activities can easily take a year or more to complete. As a result, if we

---

[1] In this chapter and those that follow, we will use the variable $q$ for the output of the firm, and $Q$ for the output of the industry.

are looking at production decisions over a short period of time, such as a month or two, the firm is unlikely to be able to substitute very much capital for labor.

Because firms must consider whether or not inputs can be varied, and if they can, over what period of time, it is important to distinguish between the short and long run when analyzing production. The **short run** refers to a period of time in which the quantities of one or more factors of production cannot be changed. In other words, in the short run there is at least one factor that cannot be varied; such a factor is called a **fixed input**. The **long run** is the amount of time needed to make *all* inputs variable.

As you might expect, the kinds of decisions that firms can make are very different in the short run than *those made* in the long run. In the short run, firms vary the intensity with which they utilize a given plant and machinery; in the long run, they vary the size of the plant. All fixed inputs in the short run represent the outcomes of previous long-run decisions based on estimates of what a firm could profitably produce and sell.

There is no specific time period, such as one year, that separates the short run from the long run. Rather, one must distinguish them on a case-by-case basis. For example, the long run can be as brief as a day or two for a child's lemonade stand or as long as five or ten years for a petrochemical producer or an automobile manufacturer.

We will see that in the long run firms can vary the amounts of all their inputs to minimize the cost of production. Before treating this general case, however, we begin with an analysis of the short run, in which only one input to the production process can be varied. We assume that capital is the fixed input, and labor is variable.

- **short run** Period of time in which quantities of one or more production factors cannot be changed.

- **fixed input** Production factor that cannot be varied.

- **long run** Amount of time needed to make all production inputs variable.

## 6.2 PRODUCTION WITH ONE VARIABLE INPUT (LABOR)

When deciding how much of a particular input to buy, a firm has to compare the benefit that will result with the cost. Sometimes it is useful to look at the benefit and the cost on an *incremental* basis by focusing on the additional output that results from an incremental addition to an input. In other situations, it is useful to make the comparison on an *average* basis by considering the result of substantially increasing an input. We will look at benefits and costs in both ways.

When capital is fixed but labor is variable, the only way the firm can produce more output is by increasing its labor input. Imagine, for example, that you are managing a clothing factory. Although you have a fixed amount of equipment, you can hire more or less labor to sew and to run the machines. You must decide how much labor to hire and how much clothing to produce. To make the decision, you will need to know how the amount of output $q$ increases (if at all) as the input of labor $L$ increases.

Table 6.1 gives this information. The first three columns show the amount of output that can be produced in one month with different amounts of labor and capital fixed at 10 units. The first column shows the amount of labor, the second the fixed amount of capital, and the third total output. When labor input is zero, output is also zero. Output then increases as labor is increased up to an input of 8 units. Beyond that point, total output declines: Although initially each unit of labor can take greater and greater advantage of the existing machinery and plant, after a certain point, additional labor is no longer useful and indeed can

| TABLE 6.1 | Production with One Variable Input | | | |
|---|---|---|---|---|
| Amount of Labor (L) | Amount of Capital (K) | Total Output (q) | Average Product (q/L) | Marginal Product (Δq/ΔL) |
| 0 | 10 | 0 | — | — |
| 1 | 10 | 10 | 10 | 10 |
| 2 | 10 | 30 | 15 | 20 |
| 3 | 10 | 60 | 20 | 30 |
| 4 | 10 | 80 | 20 | 20 |
| 5 | 10 | 95 | 19 | 15 |
| 6 | 10 | 108 | 18 | 13 |
| 7 | 10 | 112 | 16 | 4 |
| 8 | 10 | 112 | 14 | 0 |
| 9 | 10 | 108 | 12 | −4 |
| 10 | 10 | 100 | 10 | −8 |

be counterproductive. Five people can run an assembly line better than two, but ten people may get in one another's way.

## Average and Marginal Products

The contribution that labor makes to the production process can be described on both an *average* and a *marginal* (i.e., incremental) basis. The fourth column in Table 6.1 shows the **average product** of labor ($AP_L$), which is the output per unit of labor input. The average product is calculated by dividing the total output $q$ by the total input of labor $L$. The average product of labor measures the productivity of the firm's workforce in terms of how much output each worker produces on average. In our example, the average product increases initially but falls when the labor input becomes greater than four.

• **average product** Output per unit of a particular input.

The fifth column of Table 6.1 shows the **marginal product** of labor ($MP_L$). This is the *additional* output produced as the labor input is increased by 1 unit. For example, with capital fixed at 10 units, when the labor input increases from 2 to 3, total output increases from 30 to 60, creating an additional output of 30 (i.e., 60 − 30) units. The marginal product of labor can be written as $\Delta q/\Delta L$—in other words, the change in output $\Delta q$ resulting from a 1-unit increase in labor input $\Delta L$.

• **marginal product** Additional output produced as an input is increased by one unit.

Remember that the marginal product of labor depends on the amount of capital used. If the capital input increased from 10 to 20, the marginal product of labor most likely would increase. Why? Because additional workers are likely to be more productive if they have more capital to use. Like the average product, the marginal product first increases then falls—in this case, after the third unit of labor.

To summarize:

Average product of labor = Output/labor input = $q/L$

Marginal product of labor = Change in output/change in labor input

= $\Delta q/\Delta L$

## The Slopes of the Product Curve

Figure 6.1 plots the information contained in Table 6.1. (We have connected all the points in the figure with solid lines.) Figure 6.1(a) shows that as labor is increased, output increases until it reaches the maximum output of 112; thereafter, it falls. The portion of the total output curve that is declining is drawn with a dashed line to denote that producing with more than eight workers is not

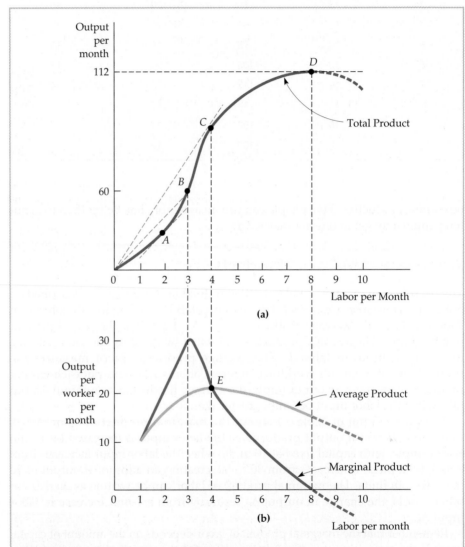

**FIGURE 6.1 Production with One Variable Input**

The total product curve in **(a)** shows the output produced for different amounts of labor input. The average and marginal products in **(b)** can be obtained (using the data in Table 6.1) from the total product curve. At point $A$ in **(a)**, the marginal product is 20 because the tangent to the total product curve has a slope of 20. At point $B$ in **(a)** the average product of labor is 20, which is the slope of the line from the origin to $B$. The average product of labor at point $C$ in **(a)** is given by the slope of the line $0C$. To the left of point $E$ in **(b)**, the marginal product is above the average product and the average is increasing; to the right of $E$, the marginal product is below the average product and the average is decreasing. As a result, $E$ represents the point at which the average and marginal products are equal, when the average product reaches its maximum.

economically rational; it can never be profitable to use additional amounts of a costly input to produce *less* output.

Figure 6.1(b) shows the average and marginal product curves. (The units on the vertical axis have changed from output per month to output per worker per month.) Note that the marginal product is positive as long as output is increasing, but becomes negative when output is decreasing.

It is no coincidence that the marginal product curve crosses the horizontal axis of the graph at the point of maximum total product. This happens because adding a worker in a manner that slows production and decreases total output implies a negative marginal product for that worker.

The average product and marginal product curves are closely related. *When the marginal product is greater than the average product, the average product is increasing.* This is the case for labor inputs up to 4 in Figure 6.1(b). If the output of an additional worker is greater than the average output of each existing worker (i.e., the marginal product is greater than the average product), then adding the worker causes average output to rise. In Table 6.1, two workers produce 30 units of output, for an average product of 15 units per worker. Adding a third worker increases output by 30 units (to 60), which raises the average product from 15 to 20.

Similarly, *when the marginal product is less than the average product, the average product is decreasing.* This is the case when the labor input is greater than 4 in Figure 6.1(b). In Table 6.1, six workers produce 108 units of output, for an average product of 18. Adding a seventh worker contributes a marginal product of only 4 units (less than the average product), reducing the average product to 16.

We have seen that the marginal product is above the average product when the average product is increasing and below the average product when the average product is decreasing. It follows, therefore, that the marginal product must equal the average product when the average product reaches its maximum. This happens at point *E* in Figure 6.1(b).

Why, in practice, should we expect the marginal product curve to rise and then fall? Think of a television assembly plant. Fewer than ten workers might be insufficient to operate the assembly line at all. Ten to fifteen workers might be able to run the assembly line, but not very efficiently. If adding a few more workers allowed the assembly line to operate much more efficiently, the marginal product of those workers would be very high. This added efficiency, however, might start to diminish once there were more than 20 workers. The marginal product of the twenty-second worker, for example, might still be very high (and above the average product), but not as high as the marginal product of the nineteenth or twentieth worker. The marginal product of the twenty-fifth worker might be lower still, perhaps equal to the average product. With 30 workers, adding one more worker would yield more output, but not very much more (so that the marginal product, while positive, would be below the average product). Once there were more than 40 workers, additional workers would simply get in each other's way and actually reduce output (so that the marginal product would be negative).

## The Average Product of Labor Curve

The geometric relationship between the total product and the average and marginal product curves is shown in Figure 6.1(a). The average product of labor is the total product divided by the quantity of labor input. At *B*, for example, the average product is equal to the output of 60 divided by the input of 3, or 20 units of output per unit of labor input. This ratio, however, is exactly the slope of the line running from the origin to $B$ in Figure 6.1(a). In general, *the average product of labor is given by the slope of the line drawn from the origin to the corresponding point on the total product curve.*

## The Marginal Product of Labor Curve

As we have seen, the marginal product of labor is the change in the total product resulting from an increase of one unit of labor. At $A$, for example, the marginal product is 20 because the tangent to the total product curve has a slope of 20. In general, *the marginal product of labor at a point is given by the slope of the total product at that point.* We can see in Figure 6.1(b) that the marginal product of labor increases initially, peaks at an input of 3, and then declines as we move up the total product curve to $C$ and $D$. At $D$, when total output is maximized, the slope of the tangent to the total product curve is 0, as is the marginal product. Beyond that point, the marginal product becomes negative.

**The Relationship between the Average and Marginal Products**  Note the graphical relationship between average and marginal products in Figure 6.1(a). At $B$, the marginal product of labor (the slope of the tangent to the total product curve at $B$—not shown explicitly) is greater than the average product (dashed line $0B$). As a result, the average product of labor increases as we move from $B$ to $C$. At $C$, the average and marginal products of labor are equal: While the average product is the slope of the line from the origin, $0C$, the marginal product is the tangent to the total product curve at $C$ (note the equality of the average and marginal products at point $E$ in Figure 6.1(b)). Finally, as we move beyond $C$ toward $D$, the marginal product falls below the average product; you can check that the slope of the tangent to the total product curve at any point between $C$ and $D$ is lower than the slope of the line from the origin.

## The Law of Diminishing Marginal Returns

• **law of diminishing marginal returns**  Principle that as the use of an input increases with other inputs fixed, the resulting additions to output will eventually decrease.

A diminishing marginal product of labor (as well as a diminishing marginal product of other inputs) holds for most production processes. The **law of diminishing marginal returns** states that as the use of an input increases in equal increments (with other inputs fixed), a point will eventually be reached at which the resulting additions to output decrease. When the labor input is small (and capital is fixed), extra labor adds considerably to output, often because workers are allowed to devote themselves to specialized tasks. Eventually, however, the law of diminishing marginal returns applies: When there are too many workers, some workers become ineffective and the marginal product of labor falls.

The law of diminishing marginal returns usually applies to the short run when at least one input is fixed. However, it can also apply to the long run. Even though inputs are variable in the long run, a manager may still want to analyze production choices for which one or more inputs are unchanged. Suppose, for example, that only two plant sizes are feasible and that management must decide which to build. In that case, management would want to know when diminishing marginal returns will set in for each of the two options.

Do not confuse the law of diminishing marginal returns with possible changes in the *quality* of labor as labor inputs are increased (as would likely occur, for example, if the most highly qualified laborers are hired first and the least qualified last). In our analysis of production, we have assumed that all labor inputs are of equal quality; diminishing marginal returns results from limitations on the use of other fixed inputs (e.g., machinery), not from declines in worker quality. In addition, do not confuse diminishing marginal returns with *negative* returns. The law of diminishing marginal returns describes a *declining* marginal product but not necessarily a negative one.

The law of diminishing marginal returns applies to a given production technology. Over time, however, inventions and other improvements in technology may allow the entire total product curve in Figure 6.1(a) to shift upward, so that more output can be produced with the same inputs. Figure 6.2 illustrates this principle. Initially the output curve is given by $O_1$, but improvements in technology may allow the curve to shift upward, first to $O_2$, and later to $O_3$.

Suppose, for example, that over time, as labor is increased in agricultural production, technological improvements are being made. These improvements might include genetically engineered pest-resistant seeds, more powerful and effective fertilizers, and better farm equipment. As a result, output changes from $A$ (with an input of 6 on curve $O_1$) to $B$ (with an input of 7 on curve $O_2$) to $C$ (with an input of 8 on curve $O_3$).

The move from $A$ to $B$ to $C$ relates an increase in labor input to an increase in output and makes it appear that there are no diminishing marginal returns when in fact there are. Indeed, the shifting of the total product curve suggests that there may be no negative long-run implications for economic growth. In fact, as we can see in Example 6.1, the failure to account for long-run improvements in technology led British economist Thomas Malthus wrongly to predict dire consequences from continued population growth.

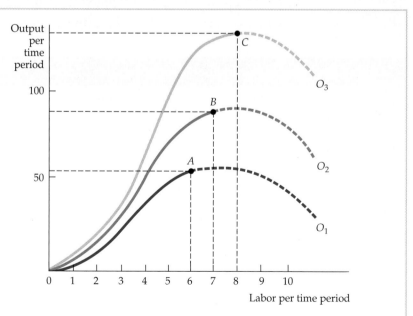

**FIGURE 6.2 The Effect of Technological Improvement**

Labor productivity (output per unit of labor) can increase if there are improvements in technology, even though any given production process exhibits diminishing returns to labor. As we move from point $A$ on curve $O_1$ to $B$ on curve $O_2$ to $C$ on curve $O_3$ over time, labor productivity increases.

**EXAMPLE 6.1** Malthus and the Food Crisis

The law of diminishing marginal returns was central to the thinking of political economist Thomas Malthus (1766–1834).[2] Malthus believed that the world's limited amount of land would not be able to supply enough food as the population grew. He predicted that as both the marginal and average productivity of labor fell and there were more mouths to feed, mass hunger and starvation would result. Fortunately, Malthus was wrong (although he was right about the diminishing marginal returns to labor).

Over the past century, technological improvements have dramatically altered food production in most countries (including developing countries, such as India). As a result, the average product of labor and total food output have increased. These improvements include new high-yielding, disease-resistant strains of seeds, better fertilizers, and better harvesting equipment. As the food production index in Table 6.2 shows, overall food production throughout the world has outpaced population growth continually since 1960.[3] This increase in world agricultural productivity is also illustrated in Figure 6.3, which shows average cereal yields from 1970 through 2005, along with a world price index for food.[4] Note that cereal yields have increased steadily over the period. Because growth in agricultural productivity led to increases in food supplies that outstripped the growth in demand, prices, apart from a temporary increase in the early 1970s, have been declining.

Hunger remains a severe problem in some areas, such as the Sahel region of Africa, in part because of the low productivity of labor there. Although other countries produce an agricultural surplus, mass hunger still occurs because of the difficulty of redistributing food from more to less productive regions of the world and because of the low incomes of those less productive regions.

| TABLE 6.2 | Index of World Food Production per Capita |
|---|---|
| **Year** | **Index** |
| 1948–1952 | 100 |
| 1960 | 115 |
| 1970 | 123 |
| 1980 | 128 |
| 1990 | 138 |
| 2000 | 150 |
| 2005 | 156 |

---

[2]Thomas Malthus, *Essay on the Principle of Population*, 1798.

[3]World per capita food production data are from the United Nations Food and Agriculture Organization (FAO). See also **http://faostat.fao.org**.

[4]Data are from the United Nations Food and Agriculture Organization and the World Bank. See also **http://faostat.fao.org**.

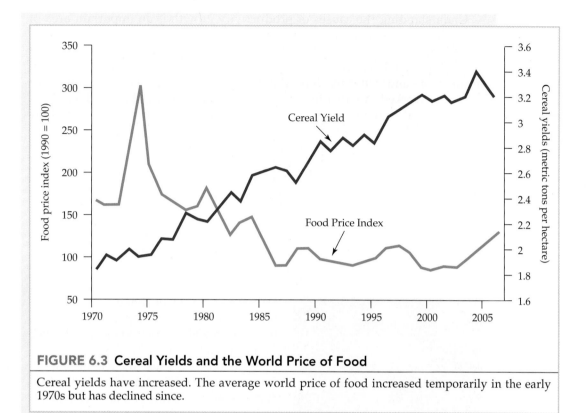

**FIGURE 6.3** **Cereal Yields and the World Price of Food**

Cereal yields have increased. The average world price of food increased temporarily in the early 1970s but has declined since.

## Labor Productivity

Although this is a textbook in microeconomics, many of the concepts developed here provide a foundation for macroeconomic analysis. Macroeconomists are particularly concerned with **labor productivity**—the average product of labor for an entire industry or for the economy as a whole. In this subsection we discuss labor productivity in the United States and a number of foreign countries. This topic is interesting in its own right, but will also help to illustrate one of the links between micro- and macroeconomics.

Because the average product measures output per unit of labor input, it is relatively easy to measure (total labor input and total output are the only pieces of information you need). Labor productivity can provide useful comparisons across industries and for one industry over a long period. But labor productivity is especially important because it determines the real *standard of living* that a country can achieve for its citizens.

**Productivity and the Standard of Living** There is a simple link between labor productivity and the standard of living. In any particular year, the aggregate value of goods and services produced by an economy is equal to the payments made to all factors of production, including wages, rental payments to capital, and profit to firms. Consumers ultimately receive these factor payments in the form of wages, salaries, dividends, or interest payments. As a result, consumers in the aggregate can increase their rate of consumption in the long run only by increasing the total amount they produce.

**• labor productivity**
Average product of labor for an entire industry or for the economy as a whole.

• **stock of capital** Total amount of capital available for use in production.

• **technological change** Development of new technologies allowing factors of production to be used more effectively.

Understanding the causes of productivity growth is an important area of research in economics. We do know that one of the most important sources of growth in labor productivity is growth in the **stock of capital**—i.e., the total amount of capital available for use in production. Because an increase in capital means more and better machinery, each worker can produce more output for each hour worked. Another important source of growth in labor productivity is **technological change**—i.e., the development of new technologies that allow labor (and other factors of production) to be used more effectively and to produce new and higher-quality goods.

As Example 6.2 shows, levels of labor productivity have differed considerably across countries, as have rates of growth of productivity. Given the central role that productivity has in affecting our standards of living, understanding these differences is important.

---

**EXAMPLE 6.2**  **Labor Productivity and the Standard of Living**

Will the standard of living in the United States, Europe, and Japan continue to improve, or will these economies barely keep future generations from being worse off than they are today? Because the real incomes of consumers in these countries increase only as fast as productivity does, the answer depends on the labor productivity of workers.

As Table 6.3 shows, the level of output per employed person in the United States in 2006 was higher than in other industrial countries. But two patterns over the post–World War II period have been disturbing. First, until the 1990s, productivity in the United States grew on average less rapidly than productivity in most other developed nations. Second, productivity growth during 1974–2006 was much lower in all developed countries than it had been in the past.[5]

| TABLE 6.3 | Labor Productivity in Developed Countries | | | | |
|---|---|---|---|---|---|
| | **UNITED STATES** | **JAPAN** | **FRANCE** | **GERMANY** | **UNITED KINGDOM** |
| | **Real Output per Employed Person (2006)** | | | | |
| | $82,158 | $57,721 | $72,949 | $60,692 | $65,224 |
| Years | *Annual Rate of Growth of Labor Productivity (%)* | | | | |
| 1960–1973 | 2.29 | 7.86 | 4.70 | 3.98 | 2.84 |
| 1974–1982 | 0.22 | 2.29 | 1.73 | 2.28 | 1.53 |
| 1983–1991 | 1.54 | 2.64 | 1.50 | 2.07 | 1.57 |
| 1992–2000 | 1.94 | 1.08 | 1.40 | 1.64 | 2.22 |
| 2001–2006 | 1.78 | 1.73 | 1.02 | 1.10 | 1.47 |

---

[5]Recent growth numbers on GDP, employment, and PPP data are from the OECD. For more information, visit **http://www.oecd.org**: select Frequently Requested Statistics within the Statistics directory.

Throughout most of the 1960–1991 period, Japan had the highest rate of productivity growth, followed by Germany and France. U.S. productivity growth was the lowest, even somewhat lower than that of the United Kingdom. This is partly due to differences in rates of investment and growth in the stock of capital in each country. The greatest capital growth during the postwar period was in Japan, France, and Germany, which were rebuilt substantially after World War II. To some extent, therefore, the lower rate of growth of productivity in the United States, when compared to that of Japan, France, and Germany, is the result of these countries catching up after the war.

Productivity growth is also tied to the natural resource sector of the economy. As oil and other resources began to be depleted, output per worker fell. Environmental regulations (e.g., the need to restore land to its original condition after strip-mining for coal) magnified this effect as the public became more concerned with the importance of cleaner air and water.

Observe from Table 6.3 that productivity growth in the United States accelerated in the 1990s. Some economists believe that information and communication technology (ICT) has been the key impetus for this growth. However, sluggish growth in more recent years suggests that ICT's contribution may have already peaked.

## 6.3 PRODUCTION WITH TWO VARIABLE INPUTS

We have completed our analysis of the short-run production function in which one input, labor, is variable, and the other, capital, is fixed. Now we turn to the long run, for which both labor and capital are variable. The firm can now produce its output in a variety of ways by combining different amounts of labor and capital. In this section, we will see how a firm can choose among combinations of labor and capital that generate the same output. In the first subsection, we will examine the scale of the production process, analyzing how output changes as input combinations are doubled, tripled, and so on.

### Isoquants

Let's begin by examining the production technology of a firm that uses two inputs and can vary both of them. Suppose that the inputs are labor and capital and that they are used to produce food. Table 6.4 tabulates the output achievable for various combinations of inputs.

| TABLE 6.4 Production with Two Variable Inputs | | | | | |
|---|---|---|---|---|---|
| | **LABOR INPUT** | | | | |
| Capital Input | 1 | 2 | 3 | 4 | 5 |
| 1 | 20 | 40 | 55 | 65 | ⑦⑤ |
| 2 | 40 | 60 | ⑦⑤ | 85 | 90 |
| 3 | 55 | ⑦⑤ | 90 | 100 | 105 |
| 4 | 65 | 85 | 100 | 110 | 115 |
| 5 | ⑦⑤ | 90 | 105 | 115 | 120 |

Labor inputs are listed across the top row, capital inputs down the column on the left. Each entry in the table is the maximum (technically efficient) output that can be produced each year with each combination of labor and capital used over that year. For example, 4 units of labor per year and 2 units of capital per year yield 85 units of food per year. Reading along each row, we see that output increases as labor inputs are increased, while capital inputs remain fixed. Reading down each column, we see that output also increases as capital inputs are increased, while labor inputs remain fixed.

The information in Table 6.4 can also be represented graphically using isoquants. An **isoquant** is a *curve that shows all the possible combinations of inputs that yield the same output*. Figure 6.4 shows three isoquants. (Each axis in the figure measures the quantity of inputs.) These isoquants are based on the data in Table 6.4, but are drawn as smooth curves to allow for the use of fractional amounts of inputs.

For example, isoquant $q_1$ shows all combinations of labor and capital per year that together yield 55 units of output per year. Two of these points, $A$ and $D$, correspond to Table 6.4. At $A$, 1 unit of labor and 3 units of capital yield 55 units of output; at $D$, the same output is produced from 3 units of labor and 1 unit of capital. Isoquant $q_2$ shows all combinations of inputs that yield 75 units of output and corresponds to the four combinations of labor and capital circled in the table (e.g., at $B$, where 2 units of labor and 3 units of capital are combined). Isoquant $q_2$ lies above and to the right of $q_1$ because obtaining a higher level of output requires more labor and capital. Finally, isoquant $q_3$ shows labor-capital combinations that yield 90 units of output. Point $C$, for example, involves 3 units

• **isoquant** Curve showing all possible combinations of inputs that yield the same output.

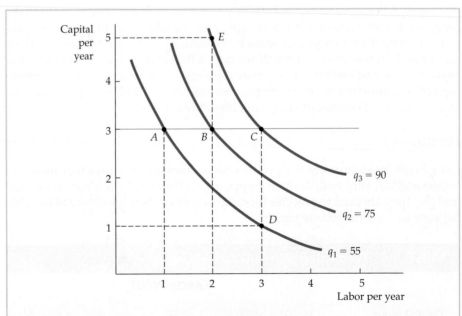

**FIGURE 6.4 Production with Two Variable Inputs**

Production isoquants show the various combinations of inputs necessary for the firm to produce a given output. A set of isoquants, or *isoquant map*, describes the firm's production function. Output increases as we move from isoquant $q_1$ (at which 55 units per year are produced at points such as $A$ and $D$), to isoquant $q_2$ (75 units per year at points such as $B$) and to isoquant $q_3$ (90 units per year at points such as $C$ and $E$).

of labor and 3 units of capital, whereas Point *E* involves 2 units of labor and 5 units of capital.

**Isoquant Maps** When a number of isoquants are combined in a single graph, we call the graph an **isoquant map**. Figure 6.4 shows three of the many isoquants that make up an isoquant map. An isoquant map is another way of describing a production function, just as an indifference map is a way of describing a utility function. Each isoquant corresponds to a different level of output, and the level of output increases as we move up and to the right in the figure.

• **isoquant map** Graph combining a number of isoquants, used to describe a production function.

## Input Flexibility

Isoquants show the flexibility that firms have when making production decisions: They can usually obtain a particular output by substituting one input for another. It is important for managers to understand the nature of this flexibility. For example, fast-food restaurants have recently faced shortages of young, low-wage employees. Companies have responded by automating—adding self-service salad bars and introducing more sophisticated cooking equipment. They have also recruited older people to fill positions. As we will see in Chapters 7 and 8, by taking into account this flexibility in the production process, managers can choose input combinations that minimize cost and maximize profit.

## Diminishing Marginal Returns

Even though both labor and capital are variable in the long run, it is useful for a firm that is choosing the optimal mix of inputs to ask what happens to output as each input is increased, with the other input held fixed. The outcome of this exercise is described in Figure 6.4, which reflects diminishing marginal returns to both labor and capital. We can see why there is diminishing marginal returns to labor by drawing a horizontal line at a particular level of capital—say, 3. Reading the levels of output from each isoquant as labor is increased, we note that each additional unit of labor generates less and less additional output. For example, when labor is increased from 1 unit to 2 (from *A* to *B*), output increases by 20 (from 55 to 75). However, when labor is increased by an additional unit (from *B* to *C*), output increases by only 15 (from 75 to 90). Thus there are diminishing marginal returns to labor both in the long and short run. Because adding one factor while holding the other factor constant eventually leads to lower and lower incremental output, the isoquant must become steeper as more capital is added in place of labor and flatter when labor is added in place of capital.

There are also diminishing marginal returns to capital. With labor fixed, the marginal product of capital decreases as capital is increased. For example, when capital is increased from 1 to 2 and labor is held constant at 3, the marginal product of capital is initially 20 (75 − 55) but falls to 15 (90 − 75) when capital is increased from 2 to 3.

## Substitution Among Inputs

With two inputs that can be varied, a manager will want to consider substituting one input for another. The slope of each isoquant indicates how the quantity of one input can be traded off against the quantity of the other, while output

• **marginal rate of technical substitution (MRTS)**
Amount by which the quantity of one input can be reduced when one extra unit of another input is used, so that output remains constant.

---

In §3.1, we explain that the marginal rate of substitution is the maximum amount of one good that the consumer is willing to give up to obtain one unit of another good.

---

is held constant. When the negative sign is removed, we call the slope the **marginal rate of technical substitution (MRTS)**. The *marginal rate of technical substitution of labor for capital* is the amount by which the input of capital can be reduced when one extra unit of labor is used, so that output remains constant. This is analogous to the marginal rate of substitution (MRS) in consumer theory. Recall from Section 3.1 that the MRS describes how consumers substitute among two goods while holding the level of satisfaction constant. Like the MRS, the MRTS is always measured as a positive quantity:

$$\text{MRTS} = -\text{ Change in capital input/change in labor input}$$
$$= -\Delta K/\Delta L \text{ (for a fixed level of } q\text{)}$$

where $\Delta K$ and $\Delta L$ are small changes in capital and labor along an isoquant.

In Figure 6.5 the MRTS is equal to 2 when labor increases from 1 unit to 2 and output is fixed at 75. However, the MRTS falls to 1 when labor is increased from 2 units to 3, and then declines to 2/3 and to 1/3. Clearly, as more and more labor replaces capital, labor becomes less productive and capital becomes relatively more productive. Therefore, we need less capital to keep output constant, and the isoquant becomes flatter.

**Diminishing MRTS** We assume that there is a *diminishing MRTS*. In other words, the MRTS falls as we move down along an isoquant. The mathematical implication is that isoquants, like indifference curves, are *convex*, or bowed inward. This is indeed the case for most production technologies. The diminishing MRTS tells us that the productivity of any one input is limited. As more

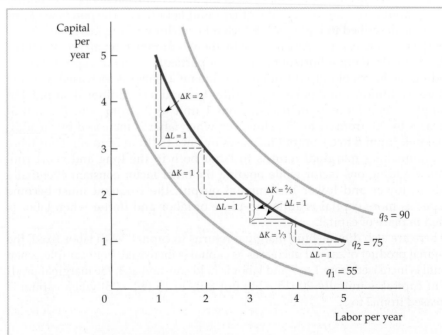

**FIGURE 6.5 Marginal Rate of Technical Substitution**

Like indifference curves, isoquants are downward sloping and convex. The slope of the isoquant at any point measures the marginal rate of technical substitution—the ability of the firm to replace capital with labor while maintaining the same level of output. On isoquant $q_2$, the MRTS falls from 2 to 1 to 2/3 to 1/3.

and more labor is added to the production process in place of capital, the productivity of labor falls. Similarly, when more capital is added in place of labor, the productivity of capital falls. Production needs a balanced mix of both inputs.

As our discussion has just suggested, the MRTS is closely related to the marginal products of labor $MP_L$ and capital $MP_K$. To see how, imagine adding some labor and reducing the amount of capital sufficient to keep output constant. The additional output resulting from the increased labor input is equal to the additional output per unit of additional labor (the marginal product of labor) times the number of units of additional labor:

Additional output from increased use of labor $= (MP_L)(\Delta L)$

Similarly, the decrease in output resulting from the reduction in capital is the loss of output per unit reduction in capital (the marginal product of capital) times the number of units of capital reduction:

Reduction in output from decreased use of capital $= (MP_K)(\Delta K)$

Because we are keeping output constant by moving along an isoquant, the total change in output must be zero. Thus,

$$(MP_L)(\Delta L) + (MP_K)(\Delta K) = 0$$

Now, by rearranging terms we see that

$$(MP_L)/(MP_K) = -(\Delta K/\Delta L) = MRTS \qquad \textbf{(6.2)}$$

Equation (6.2) tells us that *the marginal rate of technical substitution between two inputs is equal to the ratio of the marginal products of the inputs.* This formula will be useful when we look at the firm's cost-minimizing choice of inputs in Chapter 7.

## Production Functions—Two Special Cases

Two extreme cases of production functions show the possible range of input substitution in the production process. In the first case, shown in Figure 6.6, inputs to production are *perfect substitutes* for one another. Here the MRTS is constant at all points on an isoquant. As a result, the same output (say $q_3$) can be produced with mostly capital (at $A$), with mostly labor (at $C$), or with a balanced combination of both (at $B$). For example, musical instruments can be manufactured almost entirely with machine tools or with very few tools and highly skilled labor.

Figure 6.7 illustrates the opposite extreme, the **fixed-proportions production function**, sometimes called a *Leonitief production function*. In this case, it is impossible to make any substitution among inputs. Each level of output requires a specific combination of labor and capital: Additional output cannot be obtained unless more capital and labor are added in specific proportions. As a result, the isoquants are L-shaped, just as indifference curves are L-shaped when two goods are perfect complements. An example is the reconstruction of concrete sidewalks using jackhammers. It takes one person to use a jackhammer—neither two people and one jackhammer nor one person and two jackhammers will increase production. As another example, suppose that a cereal company offers a new breakfast cereal, Nutty Oat Crunch, whose two inputs, not surprisingly, are oats and nuts. The secret formula for the cereal requires exactly one ounce of nuts for every four ounces of oats in every serving. If the company were to purchase additional nuts but not additional oats, the output of cereal would remain unchanged, since the

*In §3.1, we explain that an indifference curve is convex if the marginal rate of substitution diminishes as we move down along the curve.*

*In §3.1, we explain that two goods are perfect substitutes if the marginal rate of substitution of one for the other is a constant.*

• **fixed-proportions production function** Production function with L-shaped isoquants, so that only one combination of labor and capital can be used to produce each level of output.

*In §3.1, we explain that two goods are perfect complements when the indifference curves for the goods are shaped as right angles.*

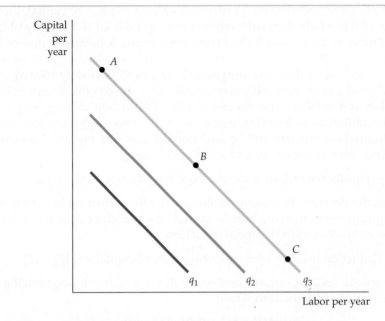

**FIGURE 6.6 Isoquants When Inputs Are Perfect Substitutes**

When the isoquants are straight lines, the MRTS is constant. Thus the rate at which capital and labor can be substituted for each other is the same no matter what level of inputs is being used. Points $A$, $B$, and $C$ represent three different capital-labor combinations that generate the same output $q_3$.

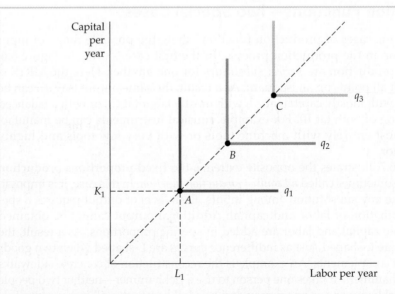

**FIGURE 6.7 Fixed-Proportions Production Function**

When the isoquants are L-shaped, only one combination of labor and capital can be used to produce a given output (as at point $A$ on isoquant $q_1$, point $B$ on isoquant $q_2$, and point $C$ on isoquant $q_3$). Adding more labor alone does not increase output, nor does adding more capital alone.

nuts must be combined with the oats in a fixed proportion. Similarly, purchasing additional oats without additional nuts would also be unproductive.

In Figure 6.7 points $A$, $B$, and $C$ represent technically efficient combinations of inputs. For example, to produce output $q_1$, a quantity of labor $L_1$ and capital $K_1$ can be used, as at $A$. If capital stays fixed at $K_1$, adding more labor does not change output. Nor does adding capital with labor fixed at $L_1$. Thus, on the vertical and the horizontal segments of the L-shaped isoquants, either the marginal product of capital or the marginal product of labor is zero. Higher output results only when both labor and capital are added, as in the move from input combination $A$ to input combination $B$.

The fixed-proportions production function describes situations in which methods of production are limited. For example, the production of a television show might involve a certain mix of capital (camera and sound equipment, etc.) and labor (producer, director, actors, etc.). To make more television shows, all inputs to production must be increased proportionally. In particular, it would be difficult to increase capital inputs at the expense of labor, because actors are necessary inputs to production (except perhaps for animated films). Likewise, it would be difficult to substitute labor for capital, because filmmaking today requires sophisticated film equipment.

**EXAMPLE 6.3** A Production Function for Wheat

Crops can be produced using different methods. Food grown on large farms in the United States is usually produced with a *capital-intensive technology*, which involves substantial investments in capital, such as buildings and equipment, and relatively little input of labor. However, food can also be produced using very little capital (a hoe) and a lot of labor (several people with the patience and stamina to work the soil). One way to describe the agricultural production process is to show one isoquant (or more) that describes the combination of inputs which generates a given level of output (or several output levels). The description that follows comes from a production function for wheat that was estimated statistically.[6]

Figure 6.8 shows one isoquant, associated with the production function, corresponding to an output of 13,800 bushels of wheat per year. The manager of the farm can use this isoquant to decide whether it is profitable to hire more labor or use more machinery. Assume the farm is currently operating at $A$, with a labor input $L$ of 500 hours and a capital input $K$ of 100 machine hours. The manager decides to experiment by using only 90 hours of machine time. To produce the same crop per year, he finds that he needs to replace this machine time by adding 260 hours of labor.

The results of this experiment tell the manager about the shape of the wheat production isoquant. When he compares points $A$ (where $L = 500$ and $K = 100$) and $B$ (where $L = 760$ and $K = 90$) in Figure 6.8, both of which are on the same isoquant, the manager finds that the marginal rate of technical substitution is equal to 0.04 ($-\Delta K/\Delta L = -(-10)/260 = .04$).

---

[6]The food production function on which this example is based is given by the equation $q = 100(K^{.8}L^{.2})$, where $q$ is the rate of output in bushels of wheat per year, $K$ is the quantity of machines in use per year, and $L$ is the number of hours of labor per year.

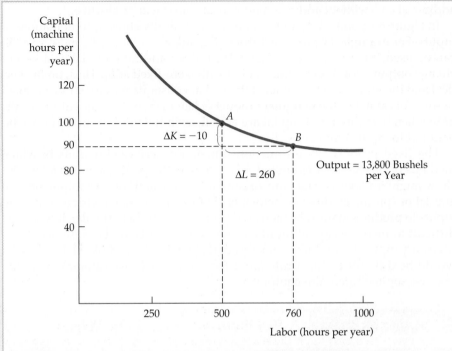

**FIGURE 6.8 Isoquant Describing the Production of Wheat**

A wheat output of 13,800 bushels per year can be produced with different combinations of labor and capital. The more capital-intensive production process is shown as point *A*, the more labor-intensive process as point *B*. The marginal rate of technical substitution between *A* and *B* is 10/260 = 0.04.

The MRTS reveals the nature of the trade-off involved in adding labor and reducing the use of farm machinery. Because the MRTS is substantially less than 1 in value, the manager knows that when the wage of a laborer is equal to the cost of running a machine, he ought to use more capital. (At his current level of production, he needs 260 units of labor to substitute for 10 units of capital.) In fact, he knows that unless labor is much less expensive than the use of a machine, his production process ought to become more capital-intensive.

The decision about how many laborers to hire and machines to use cannot be fully resolved until we discuss the costs of production in the next chapter. However, this example illustrates how knowledge about production isoquants and the marginal rate of technical substitution can help a manager. It also suggests why most farms in the United States and Canada, where labor is relatively expensive, operate in the range of production in which the MRTS is relatively high (with a high capital-to-labor ratio), whereas farms in developing countries, in which labor is cheap, operate with a lower MRTS (and a lower capital-to-labor ratio).[7] The exact labor/capital combination to use depends on input prices, a subject that we discuss in Chapter 7.

---

[7]With the production function given in footnote 6, it is not difficult (using calculus) to show that the marginal rate of technical substitution is given by MRTS = $(MP_L/MP_K) = (1/4)(K/L)$. Thus, the MRTS decreases as the capital-to-labor ratio falls. For an interesting study of agricultural production in Israel, see Richard E. Just, David Zilberman, and Eithan Hochman, "Estimation of Multicrop Production Functions," *American Journal of Agricultural Economics* 65 (1983): 770–80.

## 6.4 RETURNS TO SCALE

Our analysis of input substitution in the production process has shown us what happens when a firm substitutes one input for another while keeping output constant. However, in the long run, with all inputs variable, the firm must also consider the best way to increase output. One way to do so is to change the *scale* of the operation by increasing *all of the inputs to production in proportion*. If it takes one farmer working with one harvesting machine on one acre of land to produce 100 bushels of wheat, what will happen to output if we put two farmers to work with two machines on two acres of land? Output will almost certainly increase, but will it double, more than double, or less than double? **Returns to scale** is the rate at which output increases as inputs are increased proportionately. We will examine three different cases: increasing, constant, and decreasing returns to scale.

**Increasing Returns to Scale** If output more than doubles when inputs are doubled, there are **increasing returns to scale**. This might arise because the larger scale of operation allows managers and workers to specialize in their tasks and to make use of more sophisticated, large-scale factories and equipment. The automobile assembly line is a famous example of increasing returns.

The prospect of increasing returns to scale is an important issue from a public-policy perspective. If there are increasing returns, then it is economically advantageous to have one large firm producing (at relatively low cost) rather than to have many small firms (at relatively high cost). Because this large firm can control the price that it sets, it may need to be regulated. For example, increasing returns in the provision of electricity is one reason why we have large, regulated power companies.

**Constant Returns to Scale** A second possibility with respect to the scale of production is that output may double when inputs are doubled. In this case, we say there are **constant returns to scale**. With constant returns to scale, the size of the firm's operation does not affect the productivity of its factors: Because one plant using a particular production process can easily be replicated, two plants produce twice as much output. For example, a large travel agency might provide the same service per client and use the same ratio of capital (office space) and labor (travel agents) as a small agency that services fewer clients.

**Decreasing Returns to Scale** Finally, output may less than double when all inputs double. This case of **decreasing returns to scale** applies to some firms with large-scale operations. Eventually, difficulties in organizing and running a large-scale operation may lead to decreased productivity of both labor and capital. Communication between workers and managers can become difficult to monitor as the workplace becomes more impersonal. Thus, the decreasing-returns case is likely to be associated with the problems of coordinating tasks and maintaining a useful line of communication between management and workers.

### Describing Returns to Scale

Returns to scale need not be uniform across all possible levels of output. For example, at lower levels of output, the firm could have increasing

---

**• returns to scale** Rate at which output increases as inputs are increased proportionately.

**• increasing returns to scale** Situation in which output more than doubles when all inputs are doubled.

**• constant returns to scale** Situation in which output doubles when all inputs are doubled.

**• decreasing returns to scale** Situation in which output less than doubles when all inputs are doubled.

returns to scale, but constant and eventually decreasing returns at higher levels of output.

The presence or absence of returns to scale is seen graphically in the two parts of Figure 6.9. The line 0*A* from the origin in each panel describes a production process in which labor and capital are used as inputs to produce various levels of output in the ratio of 5 hours of labor to 2 hours of machine time. In Figure 6.9(a), the firm's production function exhibits constant returns to scale. When 5 hours of labor and 2 hours of machine time are used, an output of 10 units is produced. When both inputs double, output doubles from 10 to 20 units; when both inputs triple, output triples, from 10 to 30 units. Put differently, twice as much of both inputs is needed to produce 20 units, and three times as much is needed to produce 30 units.

In Figure 6.9(b), the firm's production function exhibits increasing returns to scale. Now the isoquants come closer together as we move away from the origin along 0*A*. As a result, *less* than twice the amount of both inputs is needed to increase production from 10 units to 20; substantially less than three times the inputs are needed to produce 30 units. The reverse would be true if the production function exhibited decreasing returns to scale (not shown here). With decreasing returns, the isoquants are increasingly distant from one another as output levels increase proportionally.

Returns to scale vary considerably across firms and industries. Other things being equal, the greater the returns to scale, the larger the firms in an industry are likely to be. Because manufacturing involves large investments in capital equipment, manufacturing industries are more likely to have increasing returns to scale than service-oriented industries. Services are more labor-intensive and can usually be provided as efficiently in small quantities as they can on a large scale.

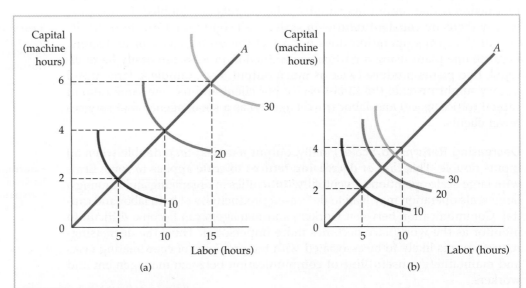

**FIGURE 6.9 Returns to Scale**

When a firm's production process exhibits constant returns to scale as shown by a movement along line 0*A* in part **(a)**, the isoquants are equally spaced as output increases proportionally. However, when there are increasing returns to scale as shown in **(b)**, the isoquants move closer together as inputs are increased along the line.

## EXAMPLE 6.4   Returns to Scale in the Carpet Industry

The carpet industry in the United States centers around the town of Dalton in northern Georgia. From a relatively small industry with many small firms in the first half of the twentieth century, it grew rapidly and became a major industry with a large number of firms of all sizes. For example, the top five carpet manufacturers, ranked by shipments in millions of dollars in 2005, are shown in Table 6.5.[8]

Currently, there are three relatively large manufacturers (Shaw, Mohawk, and Beaulieu), along with a number of smaller producers. There are also many retailers, wholesale distributors, buying groups, and national retail chains. The carpet industry has grown rapidly for several reasons. Consumer demand for wool, nylon, and polypropylene carpets in commercial and residential uses has skyrocketed. In addition, innovations such as the introduction of larger, faster, and more efficient carpet-tufting machines have reduced costs and greatly increased carpet production. Along with the increase in production, innovation and competition have worked together to reduce real carpet prices.

To what extent, if any, can the growth of the carpet industry be explained by the presence of returns to scale? There have certainly been substantial improvements in the processing of key production inputs (such as stain-resistant yarn) and in the distribution of carpets to retailers and consumers. But what about the production of carpets? Carpet production is capital intensive—manufacturing plants require heavy investments in high-speed tufting machines that turn various types of yarn into carpet, as well as machines that put the backings onto the carpets, cut the carpets into appropriate sizes, and package, label, and distribute them.

Overall, physical capital (including plant and equipment) accounts for about 77 percent of a typical carpet manufacturer's costs, while labor accounts for the remaining 23 percent. Over time, the major carpet manufacturers have increased the scale of their operations by putting larger and more efficient tufting machines into larger plants. At the same time, the use of labor in these plants has also increased significantly. The result? Proportional increases in inputs have

| TABLE 6.5   The U.S. Carpet Industry |  |
| --- | --- |
| **Carpet Sales, 2005 (Millions of Dollars per Year)** | |
| 1. Shaw | 4346 |
| 2. Mohawk | 3779 |
| 3. Beaulieu | 1115 |
| 4. Interface | 421 |
| 5. Royalty | 298 |

[8]*Floor Focus*, May 2005.

resulted in a more than proportional increase in output for these larger plants. For example, a doubling of capital and labor inputs might lead to a 110-percent increase in output. This pattern has not, however, been uniform across the industry. Most smaller carpet manufacturers have found that small changes in scale have little or no effect on output; i.e., small proportional increases in inputs have only increased output proportionally.

We can therefore characterize the carpet industry as one in which there are constant returns to scale for relatively small plants but increasing returns to scale for larger plants. These increasing returns, however, are limited, and we can expect that if plant size were increased further, there would eventually be decreasing returns to scale.

# SUMMARY

1. A *production function* describes the maximum output that a firm can produce for each specified combination of inputs.
2. In the short run, one or more inputs to the production process are fixed. In the long run, all inputs are potentially variable.
3. Production with one variable input, labor, can be usefully described in terms of the *average product of labor* (which measures output per unit of labor input) and the *marginal product of labor* (which measures the additional output as labor is increased by 1 unit).
4. According to the *law of diminishing marginal returns,* when one or more inputs are fixed, a variable input (usually labor) is likely to have a marginal product that eventually diminishes as the level of input increases.
5. An *isoquant* is a curve that shows all combinations of inputs that yield a given level of output. A firm's production function can be represented by a series of isoquants associated with different levels of output.
6. Isoquants always slope downward because the marginal product of all inputs is positive. The shape of

each isoquant can be described by the marginal rate of technical substitution at each point on the isoquant. The *marginal rate of technical substitution of labor for capital* (MRTS) is the amount by which the input of capital can be reduced when one extra unit of labor is used so that output remains constant.
7. The standard of living that a country can attain for its citizens is closely related to its level of labor productivity. Decreases in the rate of productivity growth in developed countries are due in part to the lack of growth of capital investment.
8. The possibilities for substitution among inputs in the production process range from a production function in which inputs are *perfect substitutes* to one in which the proportions of inputs to be used are fixed (a *fixed-proportions production function*).
9. In long-run analysis, we tend to focus on the firm's choice of its scale or size of operation. *Constant returns to scale* means that doubling all inputs leads to doubling output. *Increasing returns to scale* occurs when output more than doubles when inputs are doubled; *decreasing returns to scale* applies when output less than doubles.

# QUESTIONS FOR REVIEW

1. What is a production function? How does a long-run production function differ from a short-run production function?
2. Why is the marginal product of labor likely to increase initially in the short run as more of the variable input is hired?
3. Why does production eventually experience diminishing marginal returns to labor in the short run?
4. You are an employer seeking to fill a vacant position on an assembly line. Are you more concerned with the average product of labor or the marginal product of labor for the last person hired? If you observe that your average product is just beginning to decline, should you hire any more workers? What does this situation imply about the marginal product of your last worker hired?

5. What is the difference between a production function and an isoquant?

6. Faced with constantly changing conditions, why would a firm ever keep *any* factors fixed? What criteria determine whether a factor is fixed or variable?

7. Isoquants can be convex, linear, or L-shaped. What does each of these shapes tell you about the nature of the production function? What does each of these shapes tell you about the MRTS?

8. Can an isoquant ever slope upward? Explain.

9. Explain the term "marginal rate of technical substitution." What does a MRTS = 4 mean?

10. Explain why the marginal rate of technical substitution is likely to diminish as more and more labor is substituted for capital.

11. It is possible to have diminishing returns to a single factor of production and constant returns to scale at the same time. Discuss.

12. Can a firm have a production function that exhibits increasing returns to scale, constant returns to scale, and decreasing returns to scale as output increases? Discuss.

13. Give an example of a production process in which the short run involves a day or a week and the long run any period longer than a week.

# EXERCISES

1. The menu at Joe's coffee shop consists of a variety of coffee drinks, pastries, and sandwiches. The marginal product of an additional worker can be defined as the number of customers that can be served by that worker in a given time period. Joe has been employing one worker, but is considering hiring a second and a third. Explain why the marginal product of the second and third workers might be higher than the first. Why might you expect the marginal product of additional workers to diminish eventually?

2. Suppose a chair manufacturer is producing in the short run (with its existing plant and equipment). The manufacturer has observed the following levels of production corresponding to different numbers of workers:

| Number of Workers | Number of Chairs |
|---|---|
| 1 | 10 |
| 2 | 18 |
| 3 | 24 |
| 4 | 28 |
| 5 | 30 |
| 6 | 28 |
| 7 | 25 |

a. Calculate the marginal and average product of labor for this production function.

b. Does this production function exhibit diminishing returns to labor? Explain.

c. Explain intuitively what might cause the marginal product of labor to become negative.

3. Fill in the gaps in the table below.

| Quantity of Variable Input | Total Output | Marginal Product of Variable Input | Average Product of Variable Input |
|---|---|---|---|
| 0 | 0 | — | — |
| 1 | 225 | | |
| 2 | | | 300 |
| 3 | | 300 | |
| 4 | 1140 | | |
| 5 | | 225 | |
| 6 | | | 225 |

4. A political campaign manager must decide whether to emphasize television advertisements or letters to potential voters in a reelection campaign. Describe the production function for campaign votes. How might information about this function (such as the shape of the isoquants) help the campaign manager to plan strategy?

5. For each of the following examples, draw a representative isoquant. What can you say about the marginal rate of technical substitution in each case?

a. A firm can hire only full-time employees to produce its output, or it can hire some combination of full-time and part-time employees. For each full-time worker let go, the firm must hire an increasing number of temporary employees to maintain the same level of output.

b. A firm finds that it can always trade two units of labor for one unit of capital and still keep output constant.

c. A firm requires exactly two full-time workers to operate each piece of machinery in the factory.

6. A firm has a production process in which the inputs to production are perfectly substitutable in the long run. Can you tell whether the marginal rate of technical substitution is high or low, or is further information necessary? Discuss.

7. The marginal product of labor in the production of computer chips is 50 chips per hour. The marginal rate of technical substitution of hours of labor for hours of machine capital is 1/4. What is the marginal product of capital?

8. Do the following functions exhibit increasing, constant, or decreasing returns to scale? What happens to the marginal product of each individual factor as that factor is increased and the other factor held constant?
   a. $q = 3L + 2K$
   b. $q = (2L + 2K)^{1/2}$
   c. $q = 3LK^2$
   d. $q = L^{1/2}K^{1/2}$
   e. $q = 4L^{1/2} + 4K$

9. The production function for the personal computers of DISK, Inc., is given by
$$q = 10K^{0.5}L^{0.5}$$

where $q$ is the number of computers produced per day, $K$ is hours of machine time, and $L$ is hours of labor input. DISK's competitor, FLOPPY, Inc., is using the production function
$$q = 10K^{0.6}L^{0.4}$$

a. If both companies use the same amounts of capital and labor, which will generate more output?
b. Assume that capital is limited to 9 machine hours, but labor is unlimited in supply. In which company is the marginal product of labor greater? Explain.

10. In Example 6.3, wheat is produced according to the production function
$$q = 100(K^{0.8}L^{0.2})$$

a. Beginning with a capital input of 4 and a labor input of 49, show that the marginal product of labor and the marginal product of capital are both decreasing.
b. Does this production function exhibit increasing, decreasing, or constant returns to scale?

# The Cost of Production

7

In the last chapter, we examined the firm's production technology—the relationship that shows how factor inputs can be transformed into outputs. Now we will see how the production technology, together with the prices of factor inputs, determines the firm's cost of production.

Given a firm's production technology, managers must decide *how* to produce. As we saw, inputs can be combined in different ways to yield the same amount of output. For example, one can produce a certain output with a lot of labor and very little capital, with very little labor and a lot of capital, or with some other combination of the two. In this chapter we see how the *optimal*—i.e., cost-minimizing—combination of inputs is chosen. We will also see how a firm's costs depend on its rate of output and show how these costs are likely to change over time.

We begin by explaining how *cost* is defined and measured, distinguishing between the concept of cost used by economists, who are concerned about the firm's future performance, and by accountants, who focus on the firm's financial statements. We then examine how the characteristics of the firm's production technology affect costs, both in the short run, when the firm can do little to change its capital stock, and in the long run, when the firm can change all its factor inputs.

We then show how the concept of returns to scale can be generalized to allow for both changes in the mix of inputs and the production of many different outputs. We also show how cost sometimes falls over time as managers and workers learn from experience and make production processes more efficient. Finally, we show how empirical information can be used to estimate cost functions and predict future costs.

4

## 7.1 MEASURING COST: WHICH COSTS MATTER?

Before we can analyze how firms minimize costs, we must clarify what we mean by *cost* in the first place and how we should measure it. What items, for example, should be included as part of a firm's cost? Cost obviously includes the wages that a firm pays its workers and the rent that it pays for office space. But what if the firm already owns an office building and doesn't have to pay rent? How should we treat money that the firm spent two or three years ago (and can't recover) for equipment or for research and development? We'll answer questions such as these in the context of the economic decisions that managers make.

5

1

## Economic Cost versus Accounting Cost

• **accounting cost**  Actual expenses plus depreciation charges for capital equipment.

Economists think of cost differently from financial accountants, who are usually concerned with keeping track of assets and liabilities and reporting past performance for external use, as in annual reports. Financial accountants tend to take a retrospective view of the firm's finances and operations. As a result **accounting cost**—the cost that financial accountants measure—can include items that an economist would not include and may not include items that economists usually do include. For example, accounting cost includes actual expenses plus depreciation expenses for capital equipment, which are determined on the basis of the allowable tax treatment by the Internal Revenue Service.

• **economic cost**  Cost to a firm of utilizing economic resources in production, including opportunity cost.

Economists—and we hope managers—take a forward-looking view. They are concerned with the allocation of scarce resources. Therefore, they care about what cost is likely to be in the future and about ways in which the firm might be able to rearrange its resources to lower its costs and improve its profitability. As we will see, economists are therefore concerned with **economic cost**, which is the cost of utilizing resources in production. The word *economic* tells us to distinguish between costs that the firm can control and those it cannot. Here the concept of opportunity cost plays an important role.

## Opportunity Cost

• **opportunity cost**  Cost associated with opportunities that are forgone when a firm's resources are not put to their best alternative use.

**Opportunity cost** is the cost associated with opportunities that are forgone by not putting the firm's resources to their best alternative use. For example, consider a firm that owns a building and therefore pays no rent for office space. Does this mean that the cost of office space is zero? While the firm's accountant might say yes, an economist would note that the firm could have earned rent on the office space by leasing it to another company. This forgone rent is the opportunity cost of utilizing the office space and should be included as part of the economic cost of doing business.

Let's take a look at how opportunity cost can make economic cost differ from accounting cost in the treatment of wages and economic depreciation. Consider an owner who manages her own retail store but chooses not to pay herself a salary. Although no monetary transaction has occurred (and thus no accounting cost is recorded), the business nonetheless incurs an opportunity cost because the owner could have earned a competitive salary by working elsewhere.

Likewise, accountants and economists often treat depreciation differently. When estimating the future profitability of a business, economists and managers are concerned with the capital cost of plant and machinery. This cost involves not only the monetary outlay for buying and then running the machinery, but also the cost associated with wear and tear. When evaluating past performance, cost accountants use tax rules that apply to broadly defined types of assets to determine allowable depreciation in their cost and profit calculations. But these depreciation allowances need not reflect the actual wear and tear on the equipment, which is likely to vary asset by asset.

## Sunk Costs

• **sunk cost**  Expenditure that has been made and cannot be recovered.

Although an opportunity cost is often hidden, it should be taken into account when making economic decisions. Just the opposite is true of a **sunk cost**: an expenditure that has been made and cannot be recovered. A sunk cost is usually visible, but after it has been incurred it should always be ignored when making future economic decisions.

Because a sunk cost cannot be recovered, it should not influence the firm's decisions. For example, consider the purchase of specialized equipment for a plant. Suppose the equipment can be used to do only what it was originally designed for and cannot be converted for alternative use. The expenditure on this equipment is a sunk cost. *Because it has no alternative use, its opportunity cost is zero.* Thus it should not be included as part of the firm's economic costs. The decision to buy this equipment may have been good or bad. It doesn't matter. It's water under the bridge and shouldn't affect current decisions.

What if, instead, the equipment could be put to other use or could be sold or rented to another firm? In that case, its use would involve an economic cost—namely, the opportunity cost of using it rather than selling or renting it to another firm.

Now consider a *prospective* sunk cost. Suppose, for example, that the firm has not yet bought the specialized equipment but is merely considering whether to do so. A prospective sunk cost is an *investment*. Here the firm must decide whether that investment in specialized equipment is *economical*—i.e., whether it will lead to a flow of revenues large enough to justify its cost. In Chapter 15, we explain in detail how to make investment decisions of this kind.

As an example, suppose a firm is considering moving its headquarters to a new city. Last year it paid $500,000 for an option to buy a building in the city. The option gives the firm the right to buy the building at a cost of $5,000,000, so that if it ultimately makes the purchase its total expenditure will be $5,500,000. Now it finds that a comparable building has become available in the same city at a price of $5,250,000. Which building should it buy? The answer is the original building. The $500,000 option is a cost that has been sunk and thus should not affect the firm's current decision. What's at issue is spending an additional $5,000,000 or an additional $5,250,000. Because the economic analysis removes the sunk cost of the option from the analysis, the economic cost of the original property is $5,000,000. The newer property, meanwhile, has an economic cost of $5,250,000. Of course, if the new building costs $4,900,000, the firm should buy it and forgo its option.

---

**EXAMPLE 7.1**  Choosing the Location for a New Law School Building

The Northwestern University Law School has long been located in Chicago, along the shores of Lake Michigan. However, the main campus of the university is located in the suburb of Evanston. In the mid-1970s, the law school began planning the construction of a new building and needed to decide on an appropriate location. Should it be built on the current site, where it would remain near downtown Chicago law firms? Or should it be moved to Evanston, where it would be physically integrated with the rest of the university?

The downtown location had many prominent supporters. They argued in part that it was cost-effective to locate the new building in the city because the university already owned the land. A large parcel of land would have to be purchased in Evanston if the building were to be built there. Does this argument make economic sense?

No. It makes the common mistake of failing to appreciate opportunity costs. From an economic point of view, it is very expensive to locate downtown because the opportunity cost of the valuable lakeshore location is high: That property could have been sold for enough money to buy the Evanston land with substantial funds left over.

In the end, Northwestern decided to keep the law school in Chicago. This was a costly decision. It may have been appropriate if the Chicago location was particularly valuable to the law school, but it was inappropriate if it was made on the presumption that the downtown land had no cost.

## Fixed Costs and Variable Costs

Some costs vary with output, while others remain unchanged as long as the firm is producing any output at all. This distinction will be important when we examine the firm's profit-maximizing choice of output in the next chapter. We therefore divide **total cost (TC or C)**—the total economic cost of production—into two components.

- **Fixed cost (FC):** A cost that does not vary with the level of output and that can be eliminated only by going out of business.
- **Variable cost (VC):** A cost that varies as output varies.

Depending on circumstances, fixed costs may include expenditures for plant maintenance, insurance, heat and electricity, and perhaps a minimal number of employees. They remain the same no matter how much output the firm produces. Variable costs, which include expenditures for wages, salaries, and raw materials used for production, increase as output increases.

Fixed cost does not vary with the level of output—it must be paid even if there is no output. *The only way that a firm can eliminate its fixed costs is by shutting down.*

**Shutting Down** Shutting down doesn't necessarily mean going out of business. Suppose a clothing company owns several factories, is experiencing declining demand, and wants to reduce output and costs as much as possible at one factory. By reducing the output of that factory to zero, the company could eliminate the costs of raw materials and much of the labor, but it would still incur the fixed costs of paying the factory's managers, security guards, and ongoing maintenance. The only way to eliminate those fixed costs would be to close the doors, turn off the electricity, and perhaps even sell off or scrap the machinery. The company would still remain in business and could operate its remaining factories. It might even be able to re-open the factory it had closed, although doing so could be costly if it involved buying new machinery or refurbishing the old machinery.

**Fixed or Variable?** How do we know which costs are fixed and which are variable? The answer depends on the time horizon that we are considering. Over a very short time horizon—say, a few months—most costs are fixed. Over such a short period, a firm is usually obligated to pay for contracted shipments of materials and cannot easily lay off workers, no matter how much or how little the firm produces.

On the other hand, over a longer time period—say, two or three years—many costs become variable. Over this time horizon, if the firm wants to reduce its output, it can reduce its workforce, purchase fewer raw materials, and perhaps

---

• **total cost (TC or C)** Total economic cost of production, consisting of fixed and variable costs.

• **fixed cost (FC)** Cost that does not vary with the level of output and that can be eliminated only by shutting down.

• **variable cost (VC)** Cost that varies as output varies.

even sell off some of its machinery. Over a very long time horizon—say, ten years—nearly all costs are variable. Workers and managers can be laid off (or employment can be reduced by attrition), and much of the machinery can be sold off or not replaced as it becomes obsolete and is scrapped.

Knowing which costs are fixed and which are variable is important for the management of a firm. When a firm plans to increase or decrease its production, it will want to know how that change will affect its costs. Consider, for example, a problem that Delta Air Lines faced. Delta wanted to know how its costs would change if it reduced the number of its scheduled flights by 10 percent. The answer depends on whether we are considering the short run or the long run. Over the short run—say six months—schedules are fixed and it is difficult to lay off or discharge workers. As a result, most of Delta's short-run costs are fixed and won't be reduced significantly with the flight reduction. In the long run— say two years or more—the situation is quite different. Delta has sufficient time to sell or lease planes that are not needed and to discharge unneeded workers. In this case, most of Delta's costs are variable and thus can be reduced significantly if a 10-percent flight reduction is put in place.

## Fixed versus Sunk Costs

People often confuse fixed and sunk costs. As we just explained, fixed costs are costs that are paid by a firm that is operating, regardless of the level of output it produces. Such costs can include, for example, the salaries of the key executives and expenses for their office space and support staff, as well as insurance and the costs of plant maintenance. Fixed costs can be avoided if the firm shuts down a plant or goes out of business—the key executives and their support staff, for example, will no longer be needed.

Sunk costs, on the other hand, are costs that have been incurred and *cannot be recovered*. An example is the cost of R&D to a pharmaceutical company to develop and test a new drug and then, if the drug has been proven to be safe and effective, the cost of marketing it. Whether the drug is a success or a failure, these costs cannot be recovered and thus are sunk. Another example is the cost of a chip-fabrication plant to produce microprocessors for use in computers. Because the plant's equipment is too specialized to be of use in any other industry, most if not all of this expenditure is sunk, i.e., cannot be recovered. (Some small part of the cost might be recovered if the equipment is sold for scrap.)

Suppose, on the other hand, that a firm had agreed to make annual payments into an employee retirement plan as long as the firm was in operation, regardless of its output or its profitability. These payments could cease only if the firm went out of business. In this case, the payments should be viewed as a fixed cost.

Why distinguish between fixed and sunk costs? Because fixed costs affect the firm's decisions looking forward, whereas sunk costs do not. Fixed costs that are high relative to revenue and cannot be reduced might lead a firm to shut down—eliminating those fixed costs and earning zero profit might be better than incurring ongoing losses. Incurring a high sunk cost might later turn out to be a bad decision (for example, the unsuccessful development of a new product), but the expenditure is gone and cannot be recovered by shutting down. Of course a *prospective* sunk cost is different and, as we mentioned earlier, would certainly affect the firm's decisions looking forward. (Should the firm, for example, undertake the development of that new product?)

**Amortizing Sunk Costs** In practice, many firms don't always distinguish between sunk and fixed costs. For example, the semiconductor company that spent $600 million for a chip-fabrication plant (clearly a sunk cost) might **amortize** the expenditure over six years and treat it as a fixed cost of $100 million per year. This is fine as long as the firm's managers understand that shutting down will not make the $100 million annual cost go away. In fact, amortizing capital expenditures this way—spreading them out over many years and treating them as fixed costs—can be a useful way of evaluating the firm's long-term profitability.

Amortizing large capital expenditures and treating them as ongoing fixed costs can also simplify the economic analysis of a firm's operation. As we will see, for example, treating capital expenditures this way can make it easier to understand the tradeoff that a firm faces in its use of labor versus capital. For simplicity, we will usually treat sunk costs in this way as we examine the firm's production decisions. When distinguishing sunk from fixed costs does become essential to the economic analysis, we will let you know.

• **amortization** Policy of treating a one-time expenditure as an annual cost spread out over some number of years.

---

### EXAMPLE 7.2    Sunk, Fixed, and Variable Costs: Computers, Software, and Pizzas

As you progress through this book, you will see that a firm's pricing and production decisions—and its profitability—depend strongly on the structure of its costs. It is therefore important for managers to understand the characteristics of production costs and to be able to identify which costs are fixed, which are variable, and which are sunk. The relative sizes of these different cost components can vary considerably across industries. Good examples include the personal computer industry (where most costs are variable), the computer software industry (where most costs are sunk), and the pizzeria business (where most costs are fixed). Let's look at each of these in turn.

Companies like Dell, Gateway, Hewlett-Packard, and IBM produce millions of personal computers every year. Because computers are very similar, competition is intense, and profitability depends critically on the ability to keep costs down. Most of these costs are variable—they increase in proportion to the number of computers produced each year. Most important is the cost of components: the microprocessor that does much of the actual computation, memory chips, hard disk drives and other storage devices, video and sound cards, etc. Typically, the majority of these components are purchased from outside suppliers in quantities that depend on the number of computers to be produced.

Another important variable cost is labor: Workers are needed to assemble computers and then package and ship them. There is little in the way of sunk costs because factories cost little relative to the value of the company's annual output. Likewise, there is little in the way of fixed costs—perhaps the salaries of the top executives, some security guards, and electricity. Thus, when Dell and Hewlett-Packard think about ways of reducing cost, they focus largely on getting better prices for components or reducing labor requirements—both of which are ways of reducing variable cost.

What about the software programs that run on these personal computers? Microsoft produces the Windows operating system as well as a variety of applications such as Word, Excel, and PowerPoint. But many other firms—some large and some small—also produce software programs that run on personal computers. For such firms, production costs are quite different from those facing hardware manufacturers. In software production, most costs are *sunk*. Typically, a software firm will spend a large amount of money to develop a new application program. These expenditures cannot be recovered.

Once the program is completed, the company can try to recoup its investment (and make a profit as well) by selling as many copies of the program as possible. The variable cost of producing copies of the program is very small—largely the cost of copying the program to CDs and then packaging and shipping the product. Likewise, the fixed cost of production is small. Because most costs are sunk, entering the software business can involve considerable risk. Until the development money has been spent and the product has been released for sale, an entrepreneur is unlikely to know how many copies can be sold and whether or not he will be able to make money.

Finally, let's turn to your neighborhood pizzeria. For the pizzeria, the largest component of cost is fixed. Sunk costs are fairly low because pizza ovens, chairs, tables, and dishes can be resold if the pizzeria goes out of business. Variable costs are also fairly low—mainly the ingredients for pizza (flour, tomato sauce, cheese, and pepperoni for a typical large pizza might cost $1 or $2) and perhaps wages for a couple of workers to help produce, serve, and deliver pizzas. Most of the cost is fixed—the opportunity cost of the owner's time (he might typically work a 60- or 70-hour week), rent, and utilities. Because of these high fixed costs, most pizzerias (which might charge $12 for a large pizza costing about $3 in variable cost to produce) don't make very high profits.

## Marginal and Average Cost

To complete our discussion of costs, we now turn to the distinction between marginal and average cost. In explaining this distinction, we use a specific numerical example of a cost function (the relationship between cost and output) that typifies the cost situation of many firms. The example in shown in Table 7.1. After we explain the concepts of marginal and average cost, we will consider how the analysis of costs differs between the short run and the long run.

**Marginal Cost (MC)** **Marginal cost**—sometimes called *incremental cost*—is the increase in cost that results from producing one extra unit of output. Because fixed cost does not change as the firm's level of output changes, marginal cost is equal to the increase in variable cost or the increase in total cost that results from an extra unit of output. We can therefore write marginal cost as

$$MC = \Delta VC/\Delta q = \Delta TC/\Delta q$$

> • **marginal cost (MC)**
> Increase in cost resulting from the production of one extra unit of output.

Marginal cost tells us how much it will cost to expand output by one unit. In Table 7.1, marginal cost is calculated from either the variable cost (column 2) or the total cost (column 3). For example, the marginal cost of increasing output from 2 to 3 units is $20 because the variable cost of the firm increases from $78 to $98. (The total cost of production also increases by $20, from $128 to $148. Total cost differs from variable cost only by the fixed cost, which by definition does not change as output changes.)

**Average Total Cost (ATC)** **Average total cost**, used interchangeably with AC and *average economic cost*, is the firm's total cost divided by its level of output, $TC/q$. Thus the average total cost of producing at a rate of five units is $36—that is, $180/5. Basically, average total cost tells us the per-unit cost of production.

> • **average total cost (ATC)**
> Firm's total cost divided by its level of output.

| TABLE 7.1 | A Firm's Costs | | | | | | |
|---|---|---|---|---|---|---|---|
| Rate of Output (Units per Year) | Fixed Cost (Dollars per Year) | Variable Cost (Dollars per Year) | Total Cost (Dollars per Year) | Marginal Cost (Dollars per Unit) | Average Fixed Cost (Dollars per Unit) | Average Variable Cost (Dollars per Unit) | Average Total Cost (Dollars per Unit) |
| | (FC) (1) | (VC) (2) | (TC) (3) | (MC) (4) | (AFC) (5) | (AVC) (6) | (ATC) (7) |
| 0 | 50 | 0 | 50 | — | — | — | — |
| 1 | 50 | 50 | 100 | 50 | 50 | 50 | 100 |
| 2 | 50 | 78 | 128 | 28 | 25 | 39 | 64 |
| 3 | 50 | 98 | 148 | 20 | 16.7 | 32.7 | 49.3 |
| 4 | 50 | 112 | 162 | 14 | 12.5 | 28 | 40.5 |
| 5 | 50 | 130 | 180 | 18 | 10 | 26 | 36 |
| 6 | 50 | 150 | 200 | 20 | 8.3 | 25 | 33.3 |
| 7 | 50 | 175 | 225 | 25 | 7.1 | 25 | 32.1 |
| 8 | 50 | 204 | 254 | 29 | 6.3 | 25.5 | 31.8 |
| 9 | 50 | 242 | 292 | 38 | 5.6 | 26.9 | 32.4 |
| 10 | 50 | 300 | 350 | 58 | 5 | 30 | 35 |
| 11 | 50 | 385 | 435 | 85 | 4.5 | 35 | 39.5 |

• **average fixed cost (AFC)** Fixed cost divided by the level of output.

• **average variable cost (AVC)** Variable cost divided by the level of output.

ATC has two components. **Average fixed cost (AFC)** is the fixed cost (column 1 of Table 7.1) divided by the level of output, FC/$q$. For example, the average fixed cost of producing 4 units of output is $12.50 ($50/4). Because fixed cost is constant, average fixed cost declines as the rate of output increases. **Average variable cost (AVC)** is variable cost divided by the level of output, VC/$q$. The average variable cost of producing 5 units of output is $26—that is, $130/5.

We have now discussed all of the different types of costs that are relevant to production decisions in both competitive and non-competitive markets. Now we turn to how costs differ in the short run versus the long run. This is particularly important for fixed costs. Costs that are fixed in the very short run, e.g., the wages of employees under fixed-term contracts—may not be fixed over a longer time horizon. Similarly, the fixed capital costs of plant and equipment become variable if the time horizon is sufficiently long to allow the firm to purchase new equipment and build a new plant. Fixed costs, however, need not disappear, even in the long run. Suppose, for example, that a firm has been contributing to an employee retirement program. Its obligations, which are fixed in part, may remain even in the long run; they might only disappear if the firm were to declare bankruptcy.

## 7.2 COST IN THE SHORT RUN

In this section we focus our attention on short-run costs. We turn to long-run costs in Section 7.3.

### The Determinants of Short-Run Cost

The data in Table 7.1 show how variable and total costs increase with output in the short run. The rate at which these costs increase depends on the nature of the production process and, in particular, on the extent to which production involves diminishing marginal returns to variable factors. Recall from Chapter 6 that diminishing marginal returns to labor occur when the marginal product of labor is decreasing. If labor is the only input, what happens as we increase the firm's output? To produce more output, the firm must hire more labor. Then, if the marginal product of labor decreases as the amount of labor hired is increased (owing to diminishing returns), successively greater expenditures must be made to produce output at the higher rate. As a result, variable and total costs increase as the rate of output is increased. On the other hand, if the marginal product of labor decreases only slightly as the amount of labor is increased, costs will not rise so quickly when the rate of output is increased.[1]

> In §6.2, we explain that diminishing marginal returns occurs when additional inputs result in decreasing additions to output.

Let's look at the relationship between production and cost in more detail by concentrating on the costs of a firm that can hire as much labor as it wishes at a fixed wage $w$. Recall that marginal cost MC is the change in variable cost for a 1-unit change in output (i.e., $\Delta VC/\Delta q$). But the change in variable cost is the per-unit cost of the extra labor $w$ times the amount of extra labor needed to produce the extra output $\Delta L$. Because $\Delta VC = w\Delta L$, it follows that

$$MC = \Delta VC/\Delta q = w\Delta L/\Delta q$$

Recall from Chapter 6 that the marginal product of labor $MP_L$ is the change in output resulting from a 1-unit change in labor input, or $\Delta q/\Delta L$. Therefore, the extra labor needed to obtain an extra unit of output is $\Delta L/\Delta q = 1/MP_L$. As a result,

> The marginal product of labor is discussed in §6.2.

$$MC = w/MP_L \qquad\qquad (7.1)$$

Equation (7.1) states that when there is only one variable input, the marginal cost is equal to the price of the input divided by its marginal product. Suppose, for example, that the marginal product of labor is 3 and the wage rate is $30 per hour. In that case, 1 hour of labor will increase output by 3 units, so that 1 unit of output will require 1/3 additional hour of labor and will cost $10. The marginal cost of producing that unit of output is $10, which is equal to the wage, $30, divided by the marginal product of labor, 3. A low marginal product of labor means that a large amount of additional labor is needed to produce more output—a fact that leads, in turn, to a high marginal cost. Conversely, a high marginal product means that the labor requirement is low, as is the marginal cost. More generally, whenever the marginal product of labor decreases, the marginal cost of production increases, and vice versa.[2]

**Diminishing Marginal Returns and Marginal Cost** Diminishing marginal returns means that the marginal product of labor declines as the quantity of labor employed increases. As a result, when there are diminishing marginal returns, marginal cost will increase as output increases. This can be seen by looking at the numbers for marginal cost in Table 7.1. For output levels from 0 through 4, marginal cost is declining; for output levels from 4 through 11, however, marginal cost is increasing—a reflection of the presence of diminishing marginal returns.

---

[1]We are implicitly assuming that because labor is hired in competitive markets, the payment per unit of labor used is the same regardless of the firm's output.

[2]With two or more variable inputs, the relationship is more complex. The basic principle, however, still holds: The greater the productivity of factors, the less the variable cost that the firm must incur to produce any given level of output.

## The Shapes of the Cost Curves

Figure 7.1 illustrates how various cost measures change as output changes. The top part of the figure shows total cost and its two components, variable cost and fixed cost; the bottom part shows marginal cost and average costs. These cost curves, which are based on the information in Table 7.1, provide different kinds of information.

Observe in Figure 7.1(a) that fixed cost FC does not vary with output—it is shown as a horizontal line at $50. Variable cost VC is zero when output is zero and then increases continuously as output increases. The total cost curve TC is determined by vertically adding the fixed cost curve to the variable cost curve. Because fixed cost is constant, the vertical distance between the two curves is always $50.

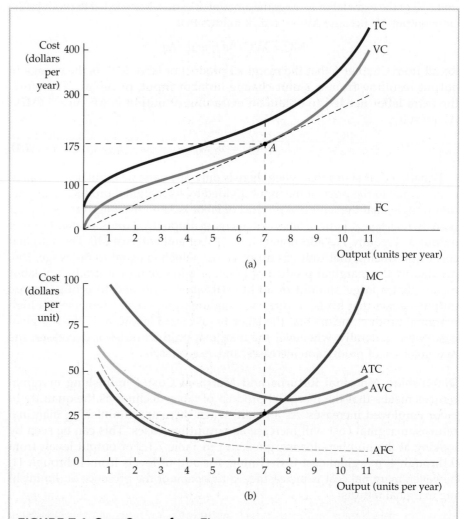

**FIGURE 7.1 Cost Curves for a Firm**

In **(a)** total cost TC is the vertical sum of fixed cost FC and variable cost VC. In **(b)** average total cost ATC is the sum of average variable cost AVC and average fixed cost AFC. Marginal cost MC crosses the average variable cost and average total cost curves at their minimum points.

Figure 7.1(b) shows the corresponding set of marginal and average variable cost curves.[3] Because total fixed cost is $50, the average fixed cost curve AFC falls continuously from $50 when output is 1, toward zero for large output. The shapes of the remaining curves are determined by the relationship between the marginal and average cost curves. Whenever marginal cost lies below average cost, the average cost curve falls. Whenever marginal cost lies above average cost, the average cost curve rises. When average cost is at a minimum, marginal cost equals average cost.

**The Average-Marginal Relationship** Marginal and average costs are another example of the average-marginal relationship described in Chapter 6 (with respect to marginal and average product). At an output of 5 in Table 7.1, for example, the marginal cost of $18 is below the average variable cost of $26; thus the average is lowered in response to increases in output. But when marginal cost is $29, which is greater than average variable cost ($25.5), the average increases as output increases. Finally, when marginal cost ($25) and average variable cost ($25) are nearly the same, average variable cost increases only slightly.

The ATC curve shows the average total cost of production. Because average total cost is the sum of average variable cost and average fixed cost and the AFC curve declines everywhere, the vertical distance between the ATC and AVC curves decreases as output increases. The AVC cost curve reaches its minimum point at a lower output than the ATC curve. This follows because MC = AVC at its minimum point and MC = ATC at its minimum point. Because ATC is always greater than AVC and the marginal cost curve MC is rising, the minimum point of the ATC curve must lie above and to the right of the minimum point of the AVC curve.

Another way to see the relationship between the total cost curves and the average and marginal cost curves is to consider the line drawn from origin to point A in Figure 7.1(a). In that figure, the slope of the line measures average variable cost (a total cost of $175 divided by an output of 7, or a cost per unit of $25). Because the slope of the VC curve is the marginal cost (it measures the change in variable cost as output increases by 1 unit), the tangent to the VC curve at A is the marginal cost of production when output is 7. At A, this marginal cost of $25 is equal to the average variable cost of $25 because average variable cost is minimized at this output.

**Total Cost as a Flow** Note that the firm's output is measured as a flow: The firm produces a certain number of units *per year*. Thus its total cost is a flow—for example, some number of dollars per year. (Average and marginal costs, however, are measured in dollars *per unit*.) For simplicity, we will often drop the time reference, and refer to total cost in dollars and output in units. But you should remember that a firm's production of output and expenditure of cost occur over some time period. In addition, we will often use *cost* (C) to refer to total cost. Likewise, unless noted otherwise, we will use *average cost* (AC) to refer to average total cost.

Marginal and average cost are very important concepts. As we will see in Chapter 8, they enter critically into the firm's choice of output level. Knowledge of short-run costs is particularly important for firms that operate in an environment

---

[3]The curves do not exactly match the numbers in Table 7.1. Because marginal cost represents the change in cost associated with a change in output, we have plotted the MC curve for the first unit of output by setting output equal to $\frac{1}{2}$, for the second unit by setting output equal to $1\frac{1}{2}$, and so on.

in which demand conditions fluctuate considerably. If the firm is currently producing at a level of output at which marginal cost is sharply increasing, and if demand may increase in the future, management might want to expand production capacity to avoid higher costs.

| EXAMPLE 7.3 | The Short-Run Cost of Aluminum Smelting |
|---|---|

Aluminum is a lightweight versatile metal used in a wide variety of applications, including airplanes, automobiles, packaging, and building materials. The production of aluminum begins with the mining of bauxite in such countries as Australia, Brazil, Guinea, Jamaica, and Suriname. Bauxite is an ore that contains a relatively high concentration of alumina (aluminum oxide), which is separated from the bauxite through a chemical refining process. The alumina is then converted to aluminum through a smelting process in which an electric current is used to separate the oxygen atoms from the aluminum oxide molecules. It is this smelting process—which is the most costly step in producing aluminum—that we focus on here.

All of the major aluminum producers, including Alcoa, Alcan, Reynolds, Alumax, and Kaiser, operate smelting plants. A typical smelting plant will have two production lines, each of which produces approximately 300 to 400 tons of aluminum per day. We will examine the short-run cost of production. Thus we consider the cost of operating an existing plant because there is insufficient time in the short run to build additional plants. (It takes about four years to plan, build, and fully equip an aluminum smelting plant.)

Although the cost of a smelting plant is substantial (over $1 billion), we will assume that the plant cannot be sold; the expenditure is therefore sunk and can be ignored. Furthermore, because fixed costs, which are largely for administrative expenses, are relatively small, we will ignore them also. Thus we can focus entirely on short-run variable costs. Table 7.2 shows the average (per-ton) production costs for a typical aluminum smelter.[4] The cost numbers apply to a plant that runs two shifts per day to produce 600 tons of aluminum per day. If prices were sufficiently high, the firm could choose to operate the plant on a three-shifts-per-day basis by asking workers to work overtime. However, wage and maintenance costs would likely increase about 50 percent for this third shift because of the need to pay higher overtime wages. We have divided the cost components in Table 7.2 into two groups. The first group includes those costs that would remain the same at any output level; the second includes costs that would increase if output exceeded 600 tons per day.

Note that the largest cost components for an aluminum smelter are electricity and the cost of alumina; together, they represent about 60 percent of total production costs. Because electricity, alumina, and other raw materials are used in direct proportion to the amount of aluminum produced, they represent per-ton production costs that are constant with respect to the level of output. The costs of labor, maintenance, and freight are also proportional to the level of output, but only when the plant operates two shifts per day. To increase output above 600 tons per day, a third shift would be necessary and would result in a 50-percent increase in the per-ton costs of labor, maintenance, and freight.

The short-run marginal cost and average variable cost curves for the smelting plant are shown in Figure 7.2. For an output $q$ up to 600 tons per day, total

<hr>

[4]This example is based on Kenneth S. Corts, "The Aluminum Industry in 1994," Harvard Business School Case N9-799-129, April 1999.

| TABLE 7.2 Production Costs for Aluminum Smelting ($/ton) (based on an output of 600 tons/day) | | |
|---|---|---|
| **Per-ton costs that are constant for all output levels** | **Output ≤ 600 tons/day** | **Output > 600 tons/day** |
| Electricity | $316 | $316 |
| Alumina | 369 | 369 |
| Other raw materials | 125 | 125 |
| Plant power and fuel | 10 | 10 |
| Subtotal | $820 | $820 |
| **Per-ton costs that increase when output exceeds 600 tons/day** | | |
| Labor | $150 | $225 |
| Maintenance | 120 | 180 |
| Freight | 50 | 75 |
| Subtotal | $320 | $480 |
| **Total per-ton production costs** | **$1140** | **$1300** |

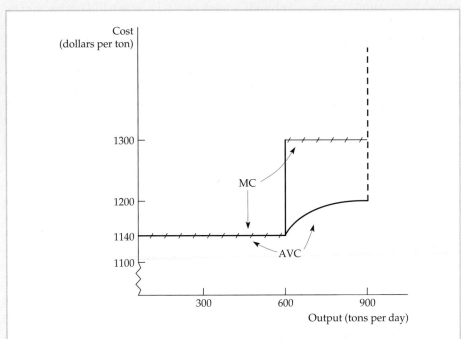

**FIGURE 7.2  The Short-Run Variable Costs of Aluminum Smelting**

The short-run average variable cost of smelting is constant for output levels using up to two labor shifts. When a third shift is added, marginal cost and average variable cost increase until maximum capacity is reached.

variable cost is $1140q$, so marginal cost and average variable cost are constant at $1140 per ton. If we increase production beyond 600 tons per day by means of a third shift, the marginal cost of labor, maintenance, and freight increases from $320 per ton to $480 per ton, which causes marginal cost as a whole to increase from $1140 per ton to $1300 per ton.

What happens to average variable cost when output is greater than 600 tons per day? When $q > 600$, total variable cost is given by:

$$TVC = (1140)(600) + 1300(q - 600) = 1300q - 96{,}000$$

Therefore average variable cost is

$$AVC = 1300 - \frac{96{,}000}{q}$$

As Figure 7.2 shows, when output reaches 900 tons per day, an absolute capacity constraint is reached, at which point the marginal and average costs of production become infinite.

## 7.3 COST IN THE LONG RUN

In the long run, a firm has much more flexibility. It can expand its capacity by expanding existing factories or building new ones; it can expand or contract its labor force, and in some cases, it can change the design of its products or introduce new products. In this section, we show how a firm can choose its combination of inputs to minimize its cost of producing a given output. We will also examine the relationship between long-run cost and the level of output. We begin by taking a careful look at the cost of using capital equipment. We then show how this cost, along with the cost of labor, enters into the production decision.

### The User Cost of Capital

Firms often rent or lease equipment, buildings, and other capital used in the production process. On other occasions, the capital is purchased. In our analysis, however, it will be useful to treat capital as though it were rented even if it was purchased. An illustration will help to explain how and why we do this. Let's suppose that Delta Airlines is thinking about purchasing a new Boeing 777 airplane for $150 million. Even though Delta would pay a large sum for the airplane now, for economic purposes the purchase price can be allocated or *amortized* across the life of the airplane. This will allow Delta to compare its revenues and costs on an *annual flow basis*. We will assume that the life of the airplane is 30 years; the amortized cost is therefore $5 million per year. The $5 million can be viewed as the *annual economic depreciation* for the airplane.

So far, we have ignored the fact that had the firm not purchased the airplane, it could have earned interest on its $150 million. This forgone interest is an *opportunity cost* that must be accounted for. Therefore, the **user cost of capital**—the annual cost of owning and using the airplane instead of selling it or never buying it in the first place—is given by the *sum of the economic depreciation and the*

**• user cost of capital** Annual cost of owning and using a capital asset, equal to economic depreciation plus forgone interest.

*interest (i.e., the financial return) that could have been earned had the money been invested elsewhere.*[5] Formally,

**User Cost of Capital = Economic Depreciation + (Interest Rate)(Value of Capital)**

In our example, economic depreciation on the airplane is $5 million per year. Suppose Delta could have earned a return of 10 percent had it invested its money elsewhere. In that case, the user cost of capital is $5 million + (.10) ($150 million – depreciation). As the plane depreciates over time, its value declines, as does the opportunity cost of the financial capital that is invested in it. For example, at the time of purchase, looking forward for the first year, the user cost of capital is $5 million + (.10)($150 million) = $20 million. In the tenth year of ownership, the airplane, which will have depreciated by $50 million, will be worth $100 million. At that point, the user cost of capital will be $5 million + (.10)($100 million) = $15 million per year.

We can also express the user cost of capital as a *rate* per dollar of capital:

$$r = \text{Depreciation rate} + \text{Interest rate}$$

For our airplane example, the depreciation rate is $1/30 = 3.33$ percent per year. If Delta could have earned a rate of return of 10 percent per year, its user cost of capital would be $r = 3.33 + 10 = 13.33$ percent per year.

As we've already pointed out, in the long run the firm can change all of its inputs. We will now show how the firm chooses the combination of inputs that minimizes the cost of producing a certain output, given information about wages and the user cost of capital. We will then examine the relationship between long-run cost and the level of output.

## The Cost-Minimizing Input Choice

We now turn to a fundamental problem that all firms face: *how to select inputs to produce a given output at minimum cost.* For simplicity, we will work with two variable inputs: labor (measured in hours of work per year) and capital (measured in hours of use of machinery per year).

The amount of labor and capital that the firm uses will depend, of course, on the prices of these inputs. We will assume that because there are competitive markets for both inputs, their prices are unaffected by what the firm does. (In Chapter 14 we will examine labor markets that are not competitive.) In this case, the price of labor is simply the *wage rate, w.* But what about the price of capital?

**The Price of Capital** In the long run, the firm can adjust the amount of capital it uses. Even if the capital includes specialized machinery that has no alternative use, expenditures on this machinery are not yet sunk and must be taken into account; the firm is deciding *prospectively* how much capital to obtain. Unlike labor expenditures, however, large initial expenditures on capital are necessary. In order to compare the firm's expenditure on capital with its ongoing cost of labor, we want to express this capital expenditure as a *flow*—e.g., in dollars per year. To do this, we must amortize the expenditure by spreading it over the lifetime of the capital, and we must also account for the forgone interest that the firm could have earned by investing the money elsewhere. As we have just seen,

---

[5]More precisely, the financial return should reflect an investment with similar risk. The interest rate, therefore, should include a risk premium. We discuss this point in Chapter 15. Note also that the user cost of capital is not adjusted for taxes; when taxes are taken into account, revenues and costs should be measured on an after-tax basis.

this is exactly what we do when we calculate the *user cost of capital*. As above, the price of capital is its *user cost*, given by r = Depreciation rate + Interest rate.

**The Rental Rate of Capital** As we noted, capital is often rented rather than purchased. An example is office space in a large office building. In this case, the price of capital is its **rental rate**—i.e., the cost per year for renting a unit of capital.

• **rental rate** Cost per year of renting one unit of capital.

Does this mean that we must distinguish between capital that is rented and capital that is purchased when we determine the price of capital? No. If the capital market is competitive (as we have assumed it is), *the rental rate should be equal to the user cost, r*. Why? Because in a competitive market, firms that own capital (e.g., the owner of the large office building) expect to earn a competitive return when they rent it—namely, the rate of return that they could have earned by investing their money elsewhere, plus an amount to compensate for the depreciation of the capital. *This competitive return is the user cost of capital.*

Many textbooks simply assume that all capital is rented at a rental rate r. As we have just seen, this assumption is reasonable. However, you should now understand *why* it is reasonable: *Capital that is purchased can be treated as though it were rented at a rental rate equal to the user cost of capital.*

For the remainder of this chapter, we will therefore assume that a firm rents all of its capital at a rental rate, or "price," r, just as it hires labor at a wage rate, or "price," w. We will also assume that firms treat any sunk cost of capital as a fixed cost that is spread out over time. We need not, therefore, concern ourselves with sunk costs. Rather, we can now focus on how a firm takes these prices into account when determining how much capital and labor to utilize.[6]

## The Isocost Line

• **isocost line** Graph showing all possible combinations of labor and capital that can be purchased for a given total cost.

We begin by looking at the cost of hiring factor inputs, which can be represented by a firm's isocost lines. An **isocost line** shows all possible combinations of labor and capital that can be purchased for a given total cost. To see what an isocost line looks like, recall that the total cost C of producing any particular output is given by the sum of the firm's labor cost wL and its capital cost rK:

$$C = wL + rK \qquad \textbf{(7.2)}$$

For each different level of total cost, equation (7.2) describes a different isocost line. In Figure 7.3, for example, the isocost line $C_0$ describes all possible combinations of labor and capital that cost a total of $C_0$ to hire.

If we rewrite the total cost equation as an equation for a straight line, we get

$$K = C/r - (w/r)L$$

It follows that the isocost line has a slope of $\Delta K/\Delta L = -(w/r)$, which is the ratio of the wage rate to the rental cost of capital. Note that this slope is similar to the slope of the budget line that the consumer faces (because it is determined solely by the prices of the goods in question, whether inputs or outputs). It tells us that if the firm gave up a unit of labor (and recovered w dollars in cost) to buy w/r units of capital at a cost of r dollars per unit, its total cost of production would remain the same. For example, if the wage rate were $10 and the rental cost of capital $5, the firm could replace one unit of labor with two units of capital with no change in total cost.

---

[6]It is possible, of course, that input prices might increase with demand because of overtime or a relative shortage of capital equipment. We discuss the possibility of a relationship between the price of factor inputs and the quantities demanded by a firm in Chapter 14.

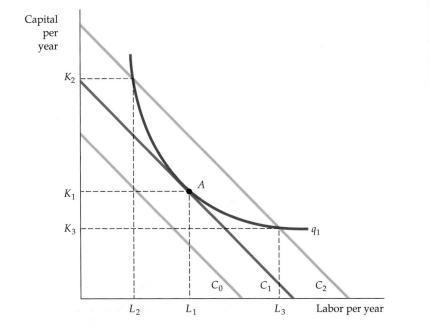

**FIGURE 7.3 Producing a Given Output at Minimum Cost**

Isocost curves describe the combination of inputs to production that cost the same amount to the firm. Isocost curve $C_1$ is tangent to isoquant $q_1$ at $A$ and shows that output $q_1$ can be produced at minimum cost with labor input $L_1$ and capital input $K_1$. Other input combinations—$L_2$, $K_2$ and $L_3$, $K_3$—yield the same output but at higher cost.

## Choosing Inputs

Suppose we wish to produce at an output level $q_1$. How can we do so at minimum cost? Look at the firm's production isoquant, labeled $q_1$, in Figure 7.3. The problem is to choose the point on this isoquant that minimizes total cost.

Figure 7.3 illustrates the solution to this problem. Suppose the firm were to spend $C_0$ on inputs. Unfortunately, no combination of inputs can be purchased for expenditure $C_0$ that will allow the firm to achieve output $q_1$. However, output $q_1$ can be achieved with the expenditure of $C_2$, either by using $K_2$ units of capital and $L_2$ units of labor, or by using $K_3$ units of capital and $L_3$ units of labor. But $C_2$ is not the minimum cost. The same output $q_1$ can be produced more cheaply, at a cost of $C_1$, by using $K_1$ units of capital and $L_1$ units of labor. In fact, isocost line $C_1$ is the lowest isocost line that allows output $q_1$ to be produced. The point of tangency of the isoquant $q_1$ and the isocost line $C_1$ at point $A$ gives us the cost-minimizing choice of inputs, $L_1$ and $K_1$, which can be read directly from the diagram. At this point, the slopes of the isoquant and the isocost line are just equal.

When the expenditure on all inputs increases, the slope of the isocost line does not change because the prices of the inputs have not changed. The intercept, however, increases. Suppose that the price of one of the inputs, such as labor, were to increase. In that case, the slope of the isocost line $-(w/r)$ would increase in magnitude and the isocost line would become steeper. Figure 7.4 shows this. Initially, the isocost line is $C_1$, and the firm minimizes its costs of producing output $q_1$ at $A$ by using $L_1$ units of labor and $K_1$ units of capital. When the price of labor increases, the isocost line becomes steeper. The isocost line $C_2$

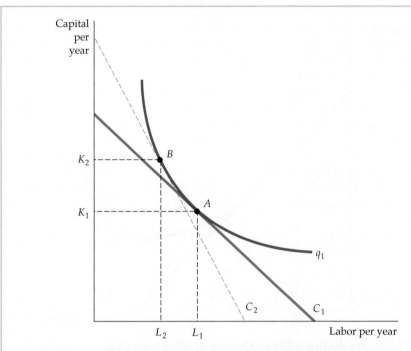

**FIGURE 7.4  Input Substitution When an Input Price Changes**

Facing an isocost curve $C_1$, the firm produces output $q_1$ at point $A$ using $L_1$ units of labor and $K_1$ units of capital. When the price of labor increases, the isocost curves become steeper. Output $q_1$ is now produced at point $B$ on isocost curve $C_2$ by using $L_2$ units of labor and $K_2$ units of capital.

reflects the higher price of labor. Facing this higher price of labor, the firm minimizes its cost of producing output $q_1$ by producing at $B$, using $L_2$ units of labor and $K_2$ units of capital. The firm has responded to the higher price of labor by substituting capital for labor in the production process.

How does the isocost line relate to the firm's production process? Recall that in our analysis of production technology, we showed that the marginal rate of technical substitution of labor for capital (MRTS) is the negative of the slope of the isoquant and is equal to the ratio of the marginal products of labor and capital:

> In §6.3, we explain that the MRTS is the amount by which the input of capital can be reduced when one extra unit of labor is used, so that output remains constant.

$$\text{MRTS} = -\Delta K/\Delta L = \text{MP}_L/\text{MP}_K \tag{7.3}$$

Above, we noted that the isocost line has a slope of $\Delta K/\Delta L = -w/r$. It follows that when a firm minimizes the cost of producing a particular output, the following condition holds:

$$\text{MP}_L/\text{MP}_K = w/r$$

We can rewrite this condition slightly as follows:

$$\text{MP}_L/w = \text{MP}_K/r \tag{7.4}$$

$\text{MP}_L/w$ is the additional output that results from spending an additional dollar for labor. Suppose that the wage rate is $10 and that adding a worker to the production process will increase output by 20 units. The additional output per dollar spent on an additional worker will be $20/10 = 2$ units of output per dollar. Similarly, $MP_K/r$ is the additional output that results from spending an additional dollar for capital. Therefore, equation (7.4) tells us that a cost-minimizing firm should choose its quantities of inputs so that the last dollar's worth of any input added to the production process yields the same amount of extra output.

Why must this condition hold for cost minimization? Suppose that in addition to the $10 wage rate, the rental rate on capital is $2. Suppose also that adding a unit of capital will increase output by 20 units. In that case, the additional output per dollar of capital input would be $20/\$2 = 10$ units of output per dollar. Because a dollar spent for capital is five times more productive than a dollar spent for labor, the firm will want to use more capital and less labor. If the firm reduces labor and increases capital, its marginal product of labor will rise and its marginal product of capital will fall. Eventually, the point will be reached at which the production of an additional unit of output costs the same regardless of which additional input is used. At that point, the firm is minimizing its cost.

---

**EXAMPLE 7.4**  The Effect of Effluent Fees on Input Choices

Steel plants are often built on or near rivers. Rivers offer readily available, inexpensive transportation for both the iron ore that goes into the production process and the finished steel itself. Unfortunately, rivers also provide cheap disposal methods for by-products of the production process, called *effluent*. For example, a steel plant processes iron ore for use in blast furnaces by grinding taconite deposits into a fine consistency. During this process, the ore is extracted by a magnetic field as a flow of water and fine ore passes through the plant. One by-product of this process—fine taconite particles—can be dumped in the river at relatively little cost to the firm. Alternative removal methods or private treatment plants are relatively expensive.

Because taconite particles are a nondegradable waste that can harm vegetation and fish, the Environmental Protection Agency (EPA) has imposed an effluent fee—a per-unit fee that the steel firm must pay for the effluent that goes into the river. How should the manager of a steel plant deal with the imposition of this fee to minimize production costs?

Suppose that without regulation the plant is producing 2000 tons of steel per month, using 2000 machine-hours of capital and 10,000 gallons of water (which contains taconite particles when returned to the river). The manager estimates that a machine-hour costs $40 and that dumping each gallon of wastewater in the river costs $10. The total cost of production is therefore $180,000: $80,000 for capital and $100,000 for wastewater. How should the manager respond to an EPA-imposed effluent fee of $10 per gallon of wastewater dumped? The manager knows that there is some flexibility in the production process. If the firm puts into place more expensive effluent treatment equipment, it can achieve the same output with less wastewater.

Figure 7.5 shows the cost-minimizing response. The vertical axis measures the firm's input of capital in machine-hours per month—the horizontal axis measures

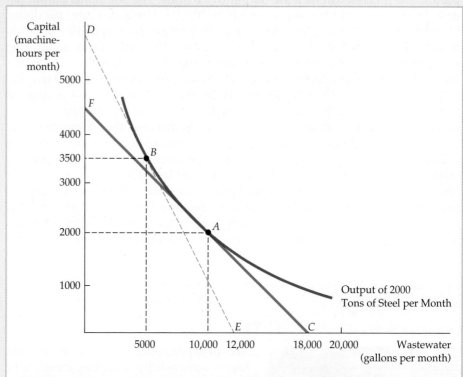

**FIGURE 7.5 The Cost-Minimizing Response to an Effluent Fee**

When the firm is not charged for dumping its wastewater in a river, it chooses to produce a given output using 10,000 gallons of wastewater and 2000 machine-hours of capital at *A*. However, an effluent fee raises the cost of wastewater, shifts the isocost curve from *FC* to *DE*, and causes the firm to produce at *B*—a process that results in much less effluent.

the quantity of wastewater in gallons per month. First, consider the level at which the firm produces when there is no effluent fee. Point *A* represents the input of capital and the level of wastewater that allows the firm to produce its quota of steel at minimum cost. Because the firm is minimizing cost, *A* lies on the isocost line *FC*, which is tangent to the isoquant. The slope of the isocost line is equal to –$10/$40 = –0.25 because a unit of capital costs four times more than a unit of wastewater.

When the effluent fee is imposed, the cost of wastewater increases from $10 per gallon to $20: For every gallon of wastewater (which costs $10), the firm has to pay the government an additional $10. The effluent fee therefore increases the cost of wastewater relative to capital. To produce the same output at the lowest possible cost, the manager must choose the isocost line with a slope of –$20/$40 = –0.5 that is tangent to the isoquant. In Figure 7.5, *DE* is the appropriate isocost line, and *B* gives the appropriate combination of capital and wastewater. The move from *A* to *B* shows that with an effluent fee the use of an alternative production technology that emphasizes the greater use of capital (3500 machine-hours) and less production of wastewater (5000 gallons) is cheaper than the original process which did not emphasize recycling. Note that the total cost of production has increased to $240,000: $140,000 for capital, $50,000 for wastewater, and $50,000 for the effluent fee.

We can learn two lessons from this decision. First, the more easily factors can be substituted in the production process—that is, the more easily the firm can deal with its taconite particles without using the river for waste treatment—the more effective the fee will be in reducing effluent. Second, the greater the degree of substitution, the less the firm will have to pay. In our example, the fee would have been $100,000 had the firm not changed its inputs. By moving production from $A$ to $B$, however, the steel company pays only a $50,000 fee.

## Cost Minimization with Varying Output Levels

In the previous section we saw how a cost-minimizing firm selects a combination of inputs to produce a given level of output. Now we extend this analysis to see how the firm's costs depend on its output level. To do this, we determine the firm's cost-minimizing input quantities for each output level and then calculate the resulting cost.

The cost-minimization exercise yields the result illustrated by Figure 7.6. We have assumed that the firm can hire labor $L$ at $w = $10$/hour and rent a unit of capital $K$ for $r = $20$/hour. Given these input costs, we have drawn three of the firm's isocost lines. Each isocost line is given by the following equation:

$$C = (\$10/\text{hour})(L) + (\$20/\text{hour})(K)$$

In Figure 7.6(a), the lowest (unlabeled) line represents a cost of $1000, the middle line $2000, and the highest line $3000.

You can see that each of the points $A$, $B$, and $C$ in Figure 7.6(a) is a point of tangency between an isocost curve and an isoquant. Point $B$, for example, shows us that the lowest-cost way to produce 200 units of output is to use 100 units of labor and 50 units of capital; this combination lies on the $2000 isocost line. Similarly, the lowest-cost way to produce 100 units of output (the lowest unlabeled isoquant) is $1000 (at point $A$, $L = 50$, $K = 25$); the least-cost means of getting 300 units of output is $3000 (at point $C$, $L = 150$, $K = 75$).

The curve passing through the points of tangency between the firm's isocost lines and its isoquants is its *expansion path*. The **expansion path** describes the combinations of labor and capital that the firm will choose to minimize costs at each output level. As long as the use of both labor and capital increases with output, the curve will be upward sloping. In this particular case we can easily calculate the slope of the line. As output increases from 100 to 200 units, capital increases from 25 to 50 units, while labor increases from 50 to 100 units. For each level of output, the firm uses half as much capital as labor. Therefore, the expansion path is a straight line with a slope equal to

$$\Delta K / \Delta L = (50 - 25)/(100 - 50) = \tfrac{1}{2}$$

* **expansion path** Curve passing through points of tangency between a firm's isocost lines and its isoquants.

## The Expansion Path and Long-Run Costs

The firm's expansion path contains the same information as its long-run total cost curve, $C(q)$. This can be seen in Figure 7.6(b). To move from the expansion path to the cost curve, we follow three steps:

**1.** Choose an output level represented by an isoquant in Figure 7.6(a). Then find the point of tangency of that isoquant with an isocost line.

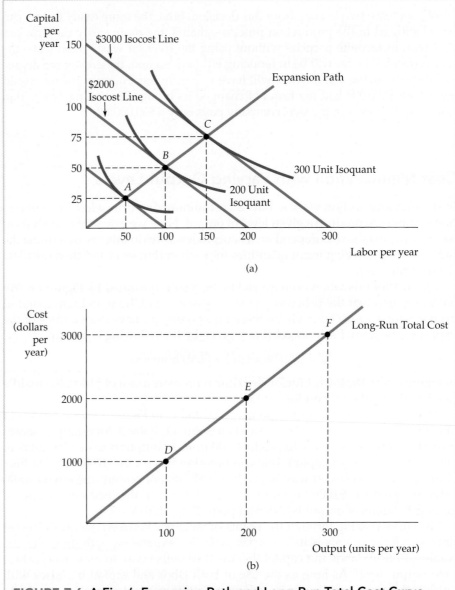

**FIGURE 7.6 A Firm's Expansion Path and Long-Run Total Cost Curve**

In **(a)**, the expansion path (from the origin through points *A*, *B*, and *C*) illustrates the lowest-cost combinations of labor and capital that can be used to produce each level of output in the long run—i.e., when both inputs to production can be varied. In **(b)**, the corresponding long-run total cost curve (from the origin through points *D*, *E*, and *F*) measures the least cost of producing each level of output.

**2.** From the chosen isocost line determine the minimum cost of producing the output level that has been selected.

**3.** Graph the output-cost combination in Figure 7.6(b).

Suppose we begin with an output of 100 units. The point of tangency of the 100-unit isoquant with an isocost line is given by point *A* in Figure 7.6(a). Because *A* lies on the $1000 isocost line, we know that the minimum cost of producing an output of 100 units in the long run is $1000. We graph this combination of 100 units of output and $1000 cost as point *D* in Figure 7.6(b). Point *D* thus represents the $1000 cost of producing 100 units of output. Similarly, point *E* represents the $2000 cost of producing 200 units which corresponds to point *B* on the expansion path. Finally, point *F* represents the $3000 cost of 300 units corresponding to point *C*. Repeating these steps for every level of output gives the *long-run total cost curve* in Figure 7.6(b)—i.e., the minimum long-run cost of producing each level of output.

In this particular example, the long-run total cost curve is a straight line. Why? Because there are constant returns to scale in production: As inputs increase proportionately, so do outputs. As we will see in the next section, the shape of the expansion path provides information about how costs change with the scale of the firm's operation.

## 7.4 LONG-RUN VERSUS SHORT-RUN COST CURVES

We saw earlier (see Figure 7.1—page 230) that short-run average cost curves are U-shaped. We will see that long-run average cost curves can also be U-shaped, but different economic factors explain the shapes of these curves. In this section, we discuss long-run average and marginal cost curves and highlight the differences between these curves and their short-run counterparts.

### The Inflexibility of Short-Run Production

Recall that we defined the long run as occurring when all inputs to the firm are variable. In the long run, the firm's planning horizon is long enough to allow for a change in plant size. This added flexibility allows the firm to produce at a lower average cost than in the short run. To see why, we might compare the situation in which capital and labor are both flexible to the case in which capital is fixed in the short run.

Figure 7.7 shows the firm's production isoquants. The firm's *long-run expansion path* is the straight line from the origin that corresponds to the expansion path in Figure 7.6. Now, suppose capital is fixed at a level $K_1$ in the short run. To produce output $q_1$, the firm would minimize costs by choosing labor equal to $L_1$, corresponding to the point of tangency with the isocost line *AB*. The inflexibility appears when the firm decides to increase its output to $q_2$ without increasing its use of capital. If capital were not fixed, it would produce this output with capital $K_2$ and labor $L_2$. Its cost of production would be reflected by isocost line *CD*.

However, the fact that capital is fixed forces the firm to increase its output by using capital $K_1$ and labor $L_3$ at point *P*. Point *P* lies on the isocost line *EF*, which represents a higher cost than isocost line *CD*. Why is the cost of production higher when capital is fixed? Because the firm is unable to substitute relatively inexpensive capital for more costly labor when it expands production. This inflexibility is reflected in the *short-run expansion path*, which begins as a line from the origin and then becomes a horizontal line when the capital input reaches $K_1$.

### Long-Run Average Cost

In the long run, the ability to change the amount of capital allows the firm to reduce costs. To see how costs vary as the firm moves along its expansion path in the long run, we can look at the long-run average and marginal cost

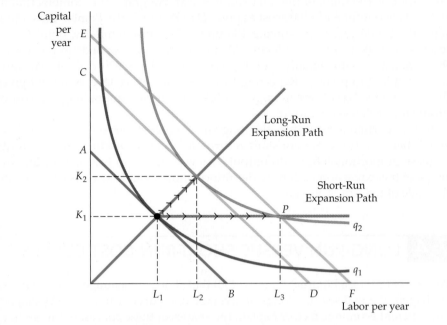

#### FIGURE 7.7 The Inflexibility of Short-Run Production

When a firm operates in the short run, its cost of production may not be minimized because of inflexibility in the use of capital inputs. Output is initially at level $q_1$. In the short run, output $q_2$ can be produced only by increasing labor from $L_1$ to $L_3$ because capital is fixed at $K_1$. In the long run, the same output can be produced more cheaply by increasing labor from $L_1$ to $L_2$ and capital from $K_1$ to $K_2$.

curves.[7] The most important determinant of the shape of the long-run average and marginal cost curves is the relationship between the scale of the firm's operation and the inputs that are required to minimize its costs. Suppose, for example, that the firm's production process exhibits constant returns to scale at all input levels. In this case, a doubling of inputs leads to a doubling of output. Because input prices remain unchanged as output increases, the average cost of production must be the same for all levels of output.

Suppose instead that the firm's production process is subject to increasing returns to scale: A doubling of inputs leads to more than a doubling of output. In that case, the average cost of production falls with output because a doubling of costs is associated with a more than twofold increase in output. By the same logic, when there are decreasing returns to scale, the average cost of production must be increasing with output.

We saw that the long-run total cost curve associated with the expansion path in Figure 7.6(a) was a straight line from the origin. In this constant-returns-to-scale case, the long-run average cost of production is constant: It is unchanged as output increases. For an output of 100, long-run average cost is $1000/100 = \$10$ per unit. For an output of 200, long-run average cost is $2000/200 = \$10$ per unit;

---

[7]In the short run, the shapes of the average and marginal cost curves were determined primarily by diminishing returns. As we showed in Chapter 6, diminishing returns to each factor is consistent with constant (or even increasing) returns to scale.

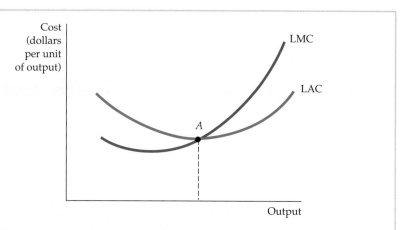

**FIGURE 7.8 Long-Run Average and Marginal Cost**

When a firm is producing at an output at which the long-run average cost LAC is falling, the long-run marginal cost LMC is less than LAC. Conversely, when LAC is increasing, LMC is greater than LAC. The two curves intersect at *A*, where the LAC curve achieves its minimum.

for an output of 300, average cost is also $10 per unit. Because a constant average cost means a constant marginal cost, the long-run average and marginal cost curves are given by a horizontal line at a $10/unit cost.

Recall that in the last chapter we examined a firm's production technology that exhibits first increasing returns to scale, then constant returns to scale, and eventually decreasing returns to scale. Figure 7.8 shows a typical **long-run average cost curve (LAC)** consistent with this description of the production process. Like the **short-run average cost curve (SAC)**, the long-run average cost curve is U-shaped, but the source of the U-shape is increasing and decreasing returns to scale, rather than diminishing returns to a factor of production.

The **long-run marginal cost curve (LMC)** can be determined from the long-run average cost curve; it measures the change in long-run total costs as output is increased incrementally. LMC lies below the long-run average cost curve when LAC is falling and above it when LAC is rising.[8] The two curves intersect at *A*, where the long-run average cost curve achieves its minimum. In the special case in which LAC is constant, LAC and LMC are equal.

- **long-run average cost curve (LAC)** Curve relating average cost of production to output when all inputs, including capital, are variable.

- **short-run average cost curve (SAC)** Curve relating average cost of production to output when level of capital is fixed.

- **long-run marginal cost curve (LMC)** Curve showing the change in long-run total cost as output is increased incrementally by 1 unit.

## Economies and Diseconomies of Scale

As output increases, the firm's average cost of producing that output is likely to decline, at least to a point. This can happen for the following reasons:

1. If the firm operates on a larger scale, workers can specialize in the activities at which they are most productive.

2. Scale can provide flexibility. By varying the combination of inputs utilized to produce the firm's output, managers can organize the production process more effectively.

---

[8]Recall that AC = TC/$q$. It follows that, $\Delta$AC/$\Delta q$ = [$q(\Delta$TC/$\Delta q)$ − TC]/$q^2$ = (MC − AC)/$q$. Clearly, when AC is increasing, $\Delta$AC/$\Delta q$ is positive and MC > AC. Correspondingly, when AC is decreasing, $\Delta$AC/$\Delta q$ is negative and MC < AC.

3. The firm may be able to acquire some production inputs at lower cost because it is buying them in large quantities and can therefore negotiate better prices. The mix of inputs might change with the scale of the firm's operation if managers take advantage of lower-cost inputs.

At some point, however, it is likely that the average cost of production will begin to increase with output. There are three reasons for this shift:

1. At least in the short run, factory space and machinery may make it more difficult for workers to do their jobs effectively.
2. Managing a larger firm may become more complex and inefficient as the number of tasks increases.
3. The advantages of buying in bulk may have disappeared once certain quantities are reached. At some point, available supplies of key inputs may be limited, pushing their costs up.

• **economies of scale** Situation in which output can be doubled for less than a doubling of cost.

• **diseconomies of scale** Situation in which a doubling of output requires more than a doubling of cost.

In §6.4, we explain that increasing returns to scale occurs when output more than doubles as inputs are doubled proportionately.

To analyze the relationship between the scale of the firm's operation and the firm's costs, we need to recognize that when input proportions do change, the firm's expansion path is no longer a straight line, and the concept of returns to scale no longer applies. Rather, we say that a firm enjoys **economies of scale** when it can double its output for less than twice the cost. Correspondingly, there are **diseconomies of scale** when a doubling of output requires more than twice the cost. The term *economies of scale* includes increasing returns to scale as a special case, but it is more general because it reflects input proportions that change as the firm changes its level of production. In this more general setting, a U-shaped long-run average cost curve characterizes the firm facing economies of scale for relatively low output levels and diseconomies of scale for higher levels.

To see the difference between returns to scale (in which inputs are used in constant proportions as output is increased) and economies of scale (in which input proportions are variable), consider a dairy farm. Milk production is a function of land, equipment, cows, and feed. A dairy farm with 50 cows will use an input mix weighted toward labor and not equipment (i.e., cows are milked by hand). If all inputs were doubled, a farm with 100 cows could double its milk production. The same will be true for the farm with 200 cows, and so forth. In this case, there are constant returns to scale.

Large dairy farms, however, have the option of using milking machines. If a large farm continues milking cows by hand, regardless of the size of the farm, constant returns would continue to apply. However, when the farm moves from 50 to 100 cows, it switches its technology toward the use of machines, and, in the process, is able to reduce its average cost of milk production from 20 cents per gallon to 15 cents per gallon. In this case, there are economies of scale.

This example illustrates the fact that a firm's production process can exhibit constant returns to scale, but still have economies of scale as well. Of course, firms can enjoy both increasing returns to scale and economies of scale. It is helpful to compare the two:

| | |
|---|---|
| *Increasing Returns to Scale*: | Output more than doubles when the quantities of all inputs are doubled. |
| *Economies of Scale*: | A doubling of output requires less than a doubling of cost. |

Economies of scale are often measured in terms of a cost-output elasticity, $E_C$. $E_C$ is the percentage change in the cost of production resulting from a 1-percent increase in output:

$$E_C = (\Delta C / C) / (\Delta q / q) \tag{7.5}$$

To see how $E_C$ relates to our traditional measures of cost, rewrite equation (7.5) as follows:

$$E_C = (\Delta C / \Delta q) / (C / q) = MC / AC \tag{7.6}$$

Clearly, $E_C$ is equal to 1 when marginal and average costs are equal. In that case, costs increase proportionately with output, and there are neither economies nor diseconomies of scale (constant returns to scale would apply if input proportions were fixed). When there are economies of scale (when costs increase less than proportionately with output), marginal cost is less than average cost (both are declining) and $E_C$ is less than 1. Finally, when there are diseconomies of scale, marginal cost is greater than average cost and $E_C$ is greater than 1.

## The Relationship between Short-Run and Long-Run Cost

Figure 7.9 shows the relationship between short-run and long-run cost. Assume that a firm is uncertain about the future demand for its product and is considering three alternative plant sizes. The short-run average cost curves for the three plants are given by $SAC_1$, $SAC_2$, and $SAC_3$. The decision is important because, once built, the firm may not be able to change the plant size for some time.

Figure 7.9 illustrates the case in which there are three possible plant sizes. If the firm expects to produce $q_0$ units of output, then it should build the smallest plant. Its average cost of production would be $8. (If it then decided to produce

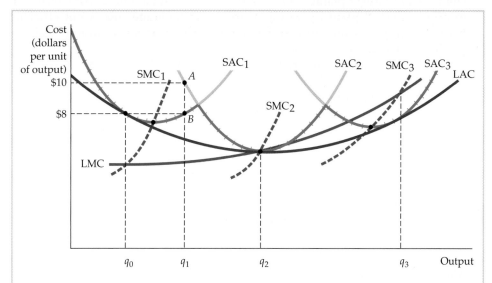

**FIGURE 7.9 Long-Run Cost with Economies and Diseconomies of Scale**

The long-run average cost curve LAC is the envelope of the short-run average cost curves $SAC_1$, $SAC_2$, and $SAC_3$. With economies and diseconomies of scale, the minimum points of the short-run average cost curves do not lie on the long-run average cost curve.

an output of $q_1$, its short run average cost would still be \$8.) However, if it expects to produce $q_2$, the middle-size plant is best. Similarly, with an output of $q_3$, the largest of the three plants would be the most efficient choice.

What is the firm's long-run average cost curve? In the long run, the firm can change the size of its plant. In doing so, it will always choose the plant that minimizes the average cost of production.

The long-run average cost curve is given by the crosshatched portions of the short-run average cost curves because these show the minimum cost of production for any output level. The long-run average cost curve is the *envelope* of the short-run average cost curves—it envelops or surrounds the short-run curves.

Now suppose that there are many choices of plant size, each having a different short-run average cost curve. Again, the long-run average cost curve is the envelope of the short-run curves. In Figure 7.9 it is the curve LAC. Whatever the firm wants to produce, it can choose the plant size (and the mix of capital and labor) that allows it to produce that output at the minimum average cost. The long-run average cost curve exhibits economies of scale initially but exhibits diseconomies at higher output levels.

To clarify the relationship between short-run and long-run cost curves, consider a firm that wants to produce output $q_1$. If it builds a small plant, the short-run average cost curve $SAC_1$ is relevant. The average cost of production (at $B$ on $SAC_1$) is \$8. A small plant is a better choice than a medium-sized plant with an average cost of production of \$10 ($A$ on curve $SAC_2$). Point $B$ would therefore become one point on the long-run cost function when only three plant sizes are possible. If plants of other sizes could be built, and if at least one size allowed the firm to produce $q_1$ at less than \$8 per unit, then $B$ would no longer be on the long-run cost curve.

In Figure 7.9, the envelope that would arise if plants of any size could be built is U-shaped. Note, once again, that the LAC curve never lies above any of the short-run average cost curves. Also note that because there are economies and diseconomies of scale in the long run, the points of minimum average cost of the smallest and largest plants do *not* lie on the long-run average cost curve. For example, a small plant operating at minimum average cost is not efficient because a larger plant can take advantage of increasing returns to scale to produce at a lower average cost.

Finally, note that the long-run marginal cost curve LMC is not the envelope of the short-run marginal cost curves. Short-run marginal costs apply to a particular plant; long-run marginal costs apply to all possible plant sizes. Each point on the long-run marginal cost curve is the short-run marginal cost associated with the most cost-efficient plant. Consistent with this relationship, $SMC_1$ intersects LMC in Figure 7.9 at the output level $q_0$ at which $SAC_1$ is tangent to LAC.

## 7.5 PRODUCTION WITH TWO OUTPUTS— ECONOMIES OF SCOPE

Many firms produce more than one product. Sometimes a firm's products are closely linked to one another: A chicken farm, for instance, produces poultry and eggs, an automobile company produces automobiles and trucks, and a university produces teaching and research. At other times, firms produce physically unrelated products. In both cases, however, a firm is likely to enjoy production or cost advantages when it produces two or more products.

These advantages could result from the joint use of inputs or production facilities, joint marketing programs, or possibly the cost savings of a common administration. In some cases, the production of one product yields an automatic and unavoidable by-product that is valuable to the firm. For example, sheet metal manufacturers produce scrap metal and shavings that they can sell.

## Product Transformation Curves

To study the economic advantages of joint production, let's consider an automobile company that produces two products, cars and tractors. Both products use capital (factories and machinery) and labor as inputs. Cars and tractors are not typically produced at the same plant, but they do share management resources, and both rely on similar machinery and skilled labor. The managers of the company must choose how much of each product to produce. Figure 7.10 shows two **product transformation curves**, each showing the various combinations of cars and tractors that can be produced with a given input of labor and machinery. Curve $O_1$ describes all combinations of the two outputs that can be produced with a relatively low level of inputs, and curve $O_2$ describes the output combinations associated with twice the inputs.

Why does the product transformation curve have a negative slope? Because in order to get more of one output, the firm must give up some of the other output. For example, a firm that emphasizes car production will devote less of its resources to producing tractors. In Figure 7.10, curve $O_2$ lies twice as far from the origin as curve $O_1$, signifying that this firm's production process exhibits constant returns to scale in the production of both commodities.

If curve $O_1$ were a straight line, joint production would entail no gains (or losses). One smaller company specializing in cars and another in tractors

> • **product transformation curve** Curve showing the various combinations of two different outputs (products) that can be produced with a given set of inputs.

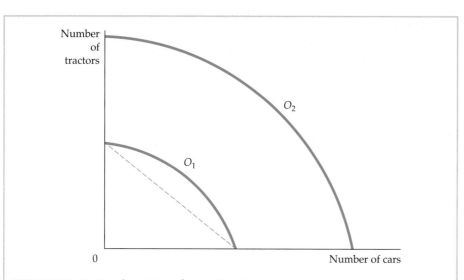

**FIGURE 7.10  Product Transformation Curve**

The product transformation curve describes the different combinations of two outputs that can be produced with a fixed amount of production inputs. The product transformation curves $O_1$ and $O_2$ are bowed out (or concave) because there are economies of scope in production.

would generate the same output as a single company producing both. However, the product transformation curve is bowed outward (or *concave*) because joint production usually has advantages that enable a single company to produce more cars and tractors with the same resources than would two companies producing each product separately. These production advantages involve the joint sharing of inputs. A single management, for example, is often able to schedule and organize production and to handle accounting and financial activities more effectively than separate managements.

## Economies and Diseconomies of Scope

• **economies of scope**
Situation in which joint output of a single firm is greater than output that could be achieved by two different firms when each produces a single product.

• **diseconomies of scope**
Situation in which joint output of a single firm is less than could be achieved by separate firms when each produces a single product.

In general, **economies of scope** are present when the joint output of a single firm is greater than the output that could be achieved by two different firms each producing a single product (with equivalent production inputs allocated between them). If a firm's joint output is *less* than that which could be achieved by separate firms, then its production process involves **diseconomies of scope**. This possibility could occur if the production of one product somehow conflicted with the production of the second.

There is no direct relationship between economies of scale and economies of scope. A two-output firm can enjoy economies of scope even if its production process involves diseconomies of scale. Suppose, for example, that manufacturing flutes and piccolos jointly is cheaper than producing both separately. Yet the production process involves highly skilled labor and is most effective if undertaken on a small scale. Likewise, a joint-product firm can have economies of scale for each individual product yet not enjoy economies of scope. Imagine, for example, a large conglomerate that owns several firms that produce efficiently on a large scale but that do not take advantage of economies of scope because they are administered separately.

## The Degree of Economies of Scope

• **degree of economies of scope (SC)** Percentage of cost savings resulting when two or more products are produced jointly rather than individually.

The extent to which there are economies of scope can also be determined by studying a firm's costs. If a combination of inputs used by one firm generates more output than two independent firms would produce, then it costs less for a single firm to produce both products than it would cost the independent firms. To measure the *degree* to which there are economies of scope, we should ask what percentage of the cost of production is saved when two (or more) products are produced jointly rather than individually. Equation (7.7) gives the **degree of economies of scope (SC)** that measures this savings in cost:

$$SC = \frac{C(q_1) + C(q_2) - C(q_1, q_2)}{C(q_1, q_2)} \tag{7.7}$$

$C(q_1)$ represents the cost of producing only output $q_1$, $C(q_2)$ represents the cost of producing only output $q_2$, and $C(q_1, q_2)$ the joint cost of producing both outputs. When the physical units of output can be added, as in the car–tractor example, the expression becomes $C(q_1 + q_2)$. With economies of scope, the joint cost is less than the sum of the individual costs. Thus, SC is greater than 0. With diseconomies of scope, SC is negative. In general, the larger the value of SC, the greater the economies of scope.

**EXAMPLE 7.5** Economies of Scope in the Trucking Industry

Suppose that you are managing a trucking firm that hauls loads of different sizes between cities.[9] In the trucking business, several related but distinct products can be offered, depending on the size of the load and the length of the haul. First, any load, small or large, can be taken directly from one location to another without intermediate stops. Second, a load can be combined with other loads (which may go between different locations) and eventually be shipped indirectly from its origin to the appropriate destination. Each type of load, partial or full, may involve different lengths of haul.

This range of possibilities raises questions about both economies of scale and economies of scope. The scale question asks whether large-scale, direct hauls are cheaper and more profitable than individual hauls by small truckers. The scope question asks whether a large trucking firm enjoys cost advantages in operating both direct quick hauls and indirect, slower (but less expensive) hauls. Central planning and organization of routes could provide for economies of scope. The key to the presence of economies of scale is the fact that the organization of routes and the types of hauls we have described can be accomplished more efficiently when many hauls are involved. In such cases, a firm is more likely to be able to schedule hauls in which most truckloads are full rather than half-full.

Studies of the trucking industry show that economies of scope are present. For example, one analysis of 105 trucking firms looked at four distinct outputs: (1) short hauls with partial loads, (2) intermediate hauls with partial loads, (3) long hauls with partial loads, and (4) hauls with total loads. The results indicate that the degree of economies of scope SC was 1.576 for a reasonably large firm. However, the degree of economies of scope falls to 0.104 when the firm becomes very large. Because large firms carry sufficiently large truckloads, there is usually no advantage to stopping at an intermediate terminal to fill a partial load. A direct trip from the origin to the destination is sufficient. Apparently, however, because other disadvantages are associated with the management of very large firms, the economies of scope get smaller as the firm gets bigger. In any event, the ability to combine partial loads at an intermediate location lowers the firm's costs and increases its profitability.

The study suggests, therefore, that to compete in the trucking industry, a firm must be large enough to be able to combine loads at intermediate stopping points.

## *7.6 DYNAMIC CHANGES IN COSTS—THE LEARNING CURVE

Our discussion thus far has suggested one reason why a large firm may have a lower long-run average cost than a small firm: increasing returns to scale in production. It is tempting to conclude that firms that enjoy lower average cost over

---

[9]This example is based on Judy S. Wang Chiang and Ann F. Friedlaender, "Truck Technology and Efficient Market Structure," *Review of Economics and Statistics* 67 (1985): 250–58.

time are growing firms with increasing returns to scale. But this need not be true. In some firms, long-run average cost may decline over time because workers and managers absorb new technological information as they become more experienced at their jobs.

As management and labor gain experience with production, the firm's marginal and average costs of producing a given level of output fall for four reasons:

1. Workers often take longer to accomplish a given task the first few times they do it. As they become more adept, their speed increases.

2. Managers learn to schedule the production process more effectively, from the flow of materials to the organization of the manufacturing itself.

3. Engineers who are initially cautious in their product designs may gain enough experience to be able to allow for tolerances in design that save costs without increasing defects. Better and more specialized tools and plant organization may also lower cost.

4. Suppliers may learn how to process required materials more effectively and pass on some of this advantage in the form of lower costs.

As a consequence, a firm "learns" over time as cumulative output increases. Managers can use this learning process to help plan production and forecast future costs. Figure 7.11 illustrates this process in the form of a **learning curve**—a curve that describes the relationship between a firm's cumulative output and the amount of inputs needed to produce each unit of output.

• **learning curve** Graph relating amount of inputs needed by a firm to produce each unit of output to its cumulative output.

## Graphing the Learning Curve

Figure 7.11 shows a learning curve for the production of machine tools. The horizontal axis measures the *cumulative* number of lots of machine tools (groups of approximately 40) that the firm has produced. The vertical axis shows the

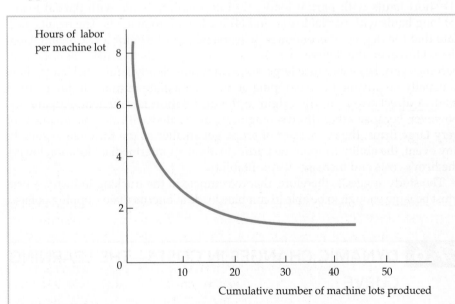

**FIGURE 7.11 The Learning Curve**

A firm's production cost may fall over time as managers and workers become more experienced and more effective at using the available plant and equipment. The learning curve shows the extent to which hours of labor needed per unit of output fall as the cumulative output increases.

number of hours of labor needed to produce each lot. Labor input per unit of output directly affects the production cost because the fewer the hours of labor needed, the lower the marginal and average cost of production.

The learning curve in Figure 7.11 is based on the relationship

$$L = A + BN^{-\beta} \tag{7.8}$$

where $N$ is the cumulative units of output produced and $L$ the labor input per unit of output. $A$, $B$, and $\beta$ are constants, with $A$ and $B$ positive, and $\beta$ between 0 and 1. When $N$ is equal to 1, $L$ is equal to $A + B$, so that $A + B$ measures the labor input required to produce the first unit of output. When $\beta$ equals 0, labor input per unit of output remains the same as the cumulative level of output increases; there is no learning. When $\beta$ is positive and $N$ gets larger and larger, $L$ becomes arbitrarily close to $A$. $A$, therefore, represents the minimum labor input per unit of output after all learning has taken place.

The larger $\beta$ is, the more important the learning effect. With $\beta$ equal to 0.5, for example, the labor input per unit of output falls proportionately to the square root of the cumulative output. This degree of learning can substantially reduce production costs as a firm becomes more experienced.

In this machine tool example, the value of $\beta$ is 0.31. For this particular learning curve, every doubling in cumulative output causes the input requirement (less the minimum attainable input requirement) to fall by about 20 percent.[10] As Figure 7.11 shows, the learning curve drops sharply as the cumulative number of lots increases to about 20. Beyond an output of 20 lots, the cost savings are relatively small.

## Learning versus Economies of Scale

Once the firm has produced 20 or more machine lots, the entire effect of the learning curve would be complete, and we could use the usual analysis of cost. If, however, the production process were relatively new, relatively high cost at low levels of output (and relatively low cost at higher levels) would indicate learning effects, not economies of scale. With learning, the cost of production for a mature firm is relatively low regardless of the scale of the firm's operation. If a firm that produces machine tools in lots knows that it enjoys economies of scale, it should produce its machines in very large lots to take advantage of the lower cost associated with size. If there is a learning curve, the firm can lower its cost by scheduling the production of many lots regardless of individual lot size.

Figure 7.12 shows this phenomenon. $AC_1$ represents the long-run average cost of production of a firm that enjoys economies of scale in production. Thus the increase in the rate of output from $A$ to $B$ along $AC_1$ leads to lower cost due to economies of scale. However, the move from $A$ on $AC_1$ to $C$ on $AC_2$ leads to lower cost due to learning, which shifts the average cost curve downward.

The learning curve is crucial for a firm that wants to predict the cost of producing a new product. Suppose, for example, that a firm producing machine tools knows that its labor requirement per machine for the first 10 machines is 1.0, the minimum labor requirement $A$ is equal to zero, and $\beta$ is approximately equal to 0.32. Table 7.3 calculates the total labor requirement for producing 80 machines.

Because there is a learning curve, the per-unit labor requirement falls with increased production. As a result, the total labor requirement for producing more and more output increases in smaller and smaller increments.

---

[10]Because $(L - A) = BN^{-.31}$, we can check that $0.8(L - A)$ is approximately equal to $B(2N)^{-.31}$.

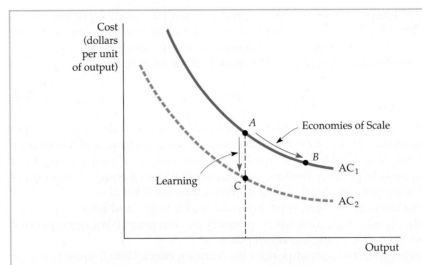

**FIGURE 7.12 Economies of Scale versus Learning**

A firm's average cost of production can decline over time because of growth of sales when increasing returns are present (a move from $A$ to $B$ on curve $AC_1$), or it can decline because there is a learning curve (a move from $A$ on curve $AC_1$ to $C$ on curve $AC_2$).

Therefore, a firm looking only at the high initial labor requirement will obtain an overly pessimistic view of the business. Suppose the firm plans to be in business for a long time, producing 10 units per year. Suppose the total labor requirement for the first year's production is 10. In the first year of production, the firm's cost will be high as it learns the business. But once the learning effect has taken place, production costs will fall. After 8 years, the labor required to produce 10 units will be only 5.1, and per-unit cost will be roughly half what it was in the first year of production. Thus, the learning curve can be important for a firm deciding whether it is profitable to enter an industry.

**TABLE 7.3 Predicting the Labor Requirements of Producing a Given Output**

| Cumulative Output (N) | Per-Unit Labor Requirement for Each 10 Units of Output (L)* | Total Labor Requirement |
|:---:|:---:|:---:|
| 10 | 1.00 | 10.0 |
| 20 | .80 | 18.0 = (10.0 + 8.0) |
| 30 | .70 | 25.0 = (18.0 + 7.0) |
| 40 | .64 | 31.4 = (25.0 + 6.4) |
| 50 | .60 | 37.4 = (31.4 + 6.0) |
| 60 | .56 | 43.0 = (37.4 + 5.6) |
| 70 | .53 | 48.3 = (43.0 + 5.3) |
| 80 | .51 | 53.4 = (48.3 + 5.1) |

*The numbers in this column were calculated from the equation $\log(L) = -0.322 \log(N/10)$, where $L$ is the unit labor input and $N$ is cumulative output.

## EXAMPLE 7.6  The Learning Curve in Practice

Suppose that as the manager of a firm that has just entered the chemical processing industry, you face the following problem: Should you produce a relatively low level of output and sell at a high price, or should you price your product lower and increase your rate of sales? The second alternative is appealing if there is a learning curve in the industry: The increased volume will lower your average production costs over time and increase profitability.

To decide what to do, you can examine the available statistical evidence that distinguishes the components of the learning curve (learning new processes by labor, engineering improvements, etc.) from increasing returns to scale. For example, a study of 37 chemical products reveals that cost reductions in the chemical processing industry are directly tied to the growth of cumulative industry output, to investment in improved capital equipment, and, to a lesser extent, to economies of scale.[11] In fact, for the entire sample of chemical products, average costs of production fall at 5.5 percent per year. The study reveals that for each doubling of plant scale, the average cost of production falls by 11 percent. For each doubling of cumulative output, however, the average cost of production falls by 27 percent. The evidence shows clearly that learning effects are more important than economies of scale in the chemical processing industry.[12]

The learning curve has also been shown to be important in the semiconductor industry. A study of seven generations of dynamic random-access memory (DRAM) semiconductors from 1974 to 1992 found that the learning rates averaged about 20 percent; thus a 10-percent increase in cumulative production would lead to a 2-percent decrease in cost.[13] The study also compared learning by firms in Japan to firms in the United States and found that there was no distinguishable difference in the speed of learning.

Another example is the aircraft industry, where studies have found learning rates that are as high as 40 percent. This is illustrated in Figure 7.13, which shows the labor requirements for producing aircraft by Airbus Industrie. Observe that the first 10 or 20 airplanes require far more labor to produce than the hundredth or two hundredth airplane. Also note how the learning curve flattens out after a certain point; in this case nearly all learning is complete after 200 airplanes have been built.

---

[11]The study was conducted by Marvin Lieberman, "The Learning Curve and Pricing in the Chemical Processing Industries," *RAND Journal of Economics* 15 (1984): 213–28.

[12]The author used the average cost AC of the chemical products, the cumulative industry output $X$, and the average scale of a production plant $Z$. He then estimated the relationship log (AC) = $-0.387$ log $(X)$ $-0.173$ log $(Z)$. The $-0.387$ coefficient on cumulative output tells us that for every 1-percent increase in cumulative output, average cost decreases 0.387 percent. The $-0.173$ coefficient on plant size tells us that for every 1-percent increase in plant size, average cost decreases 0.173 percent.

By interpreting the two coefficients in light of the output and plant-size variables, we can allocate about 15 percent of the cost reduction to increases in the average scale of plants and 85 percent to increases in cumulative industry output. Suppose plant scale doubled while cumulative output increased by a factor of 5 during the study. In that case, costs would fall by 11 percent from the increased scale and by 62 percent from the increase in cumulative output.

[13]The study was conducted by D. A. Irwin and P. J. Klenow, "Learning-by-Doing Spillovers in the Semiconductor Industry," *Journal of Political Economy* 102 (December 1994): 1200–27.

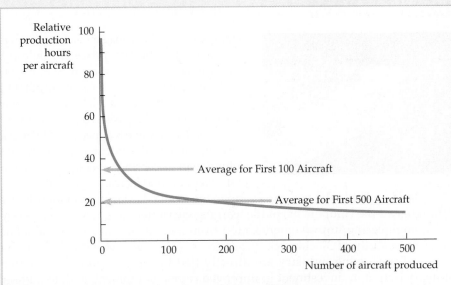

**FIGURE 7.13 Learning Curve for Airbus Industrie**

The learning curve relates the labor requirement per aircraft to the cumulative number of aircraft produced. As the production process becomes better organized and workers gain familiarity with their jobs, labor requirements fall dramatically.

Learning-curve effects can be important in determining the shape of long-run cost curves and can thus help guide management decisions. Managers can use learning-curve information to decide whether a production operation is profitable and, if so, how to plan how large the plant operation and the volume of cumulative output need be to generate a positive cash flow.

## *7.7 ESTIMATING AND PREDICTING COST

• **cost function** Function relating cost of production to level of output and other variables that the firm can control.

A business that is expanding or contracting its operation must predict how costs will change as output changes. Estimates of future costs can be obtained from a **cost function**, which relates the cost of production to the level of output and other variables that the firm can control.

Suppose we wanted to characterize the short-run cost of production in the automobile industry. We could obtain data on the number of automobiles $Q$ produced by each car company and relate this information to the company's variable cost of production VC. The use of variable cost, rather than total cost, avoids the problem of trying to allocate the fixed cost of a multiproduct firm's production process to the particular product being studied.[14]

Figure 7.14 shows a typical pattern of cost and output data. Each point on the graph relates the output of an auto company to that company's variable cost of production. To predict cost accurately, we must determine the underlying relationship between variable cost and output. Then, if a company expands its

---

[14]If an additional piece of equipment is needed as output increases, then the annual rental cost of the equipment should be counted as a variable cost. If, however, the same machine can be used at all output levels, its cost is fixed and should not be included.

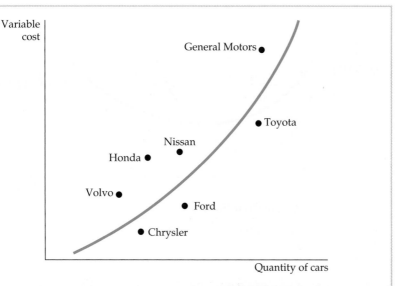

**FIGURE 7.14 Variable Cost Curve for the Automobile Industry**

An empirical estimate of the variable cost curve can be obtained by using data for individual firms in an industry. The variable cost curve for automobile production is obtained by determining statistically the curve that best fits the points that relate the output of each firm to the firm's variable cost of production.

production, we can calculate what the associated cost is likely to be. The curve in the figure is drawn with this in mind—it provides a reasonably close fit to the cost data. (Typically, least-squares regression analysis would be used to fit the curve to the data.) But what shape is the most appropriate, and how do we represent that shape algebraically?

Least-squares regression is explained in the appendix to this book.

Here is one cost function that we might choose:

$$VC = \beta q \qquad (7.9)$$

Although easy to use, this *linear* relationship between cost and output is applicable only if marginal cost is constant.[15] For every unit increase in output, variable cost increases by $\beta$; marginal cost is thus constant and equal to $\beta$.

If we wish to allow for a U-shaped average cost curve and a marginal cost that is not constant, we must use a more complex cost function. One possibility is the *quadratic* cost function, which relates variable cost to output and output squared:

$$VC = \beta q + \gamma q^2 \qquad (7.10)$$

This function implies a straight-line marginal cost curve of the form MC = $\beta + 2\gamma q$.[16] Marginal cost increases with output if $\gamma$ is positive and decreases with output if $\gamma$ is negative.

If the marginal cost curve is not linear, we might use a *cubic* cost function:

$$VC = \beta q + \gamma q^2 + \delta q^3 \qquad (7.11)$$

---

[15]In statistical cost analyses, other variables might be added to the cost function to account for differences in input costs, production processes, production mix, etc., among firms.

[16]Short-run marginal cost is given by $\Delta VC/\Delta q = \beta + \gamma\Delta(q^2)$. But $\Delta(q^2)/\Delta q = 2q$. (Check this by using calculus or by numerical example.) Therefore, MC = $\beta + 2\gamma q$.

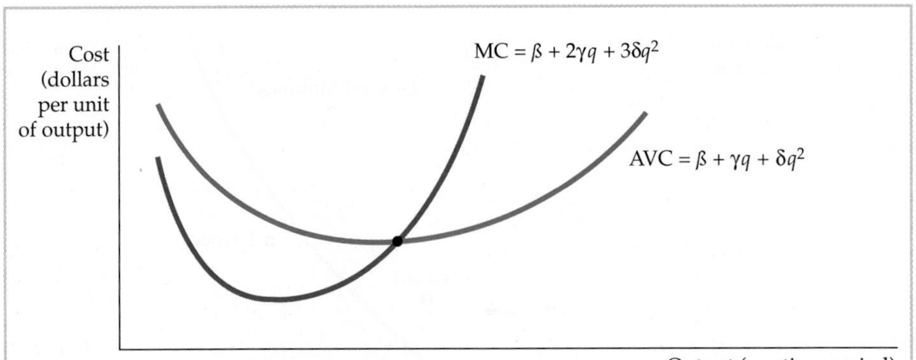


**FIGURE 7.15 Cubic Cost Function**

A cubic cost function implies that the average and the marginal cost curves are U-shaped.

Figure 7.15 shows this cubic cost function. It implies U-shaped marginal as well as average cost curves.

Cost functions can be difficult to measure for several reasons. First, output data often represent an aggregate of different types of products. The automobiles produced by General Motors, for example, involve different models of cars. Second, cost data are often obtained directly from accounting information that fails to reflect opportunity costs. Third, allocating maintenance and other plant costs to a particular product is difficult when the firm is a conglomerate that produces more than one product line.

## Cost Functions and the Measurement of Scale Economies

Recall that the cost-output elasticity $E_C$ is less than one when there are economies of scale and greater than one when there are diseconomies of scale. The *scale economies index (SCI)* provides an index of whether or not there are scale economies. SCI is defined as follows:

$$\text{SCI} = 1 - E_C \qquad \textbf{(7.12)}$$

When $E_C = 1$, SCI = 0 and there are no economies or diseconomies of scale. When $E_C$ is greater than one, SCI is negative and there are diseconomies of scale. Finally, when $E_C$ is less than 1, SCI is positive and there are economies of scale.

### EXAMPLE 7.7 Cost Functions for Electric Power

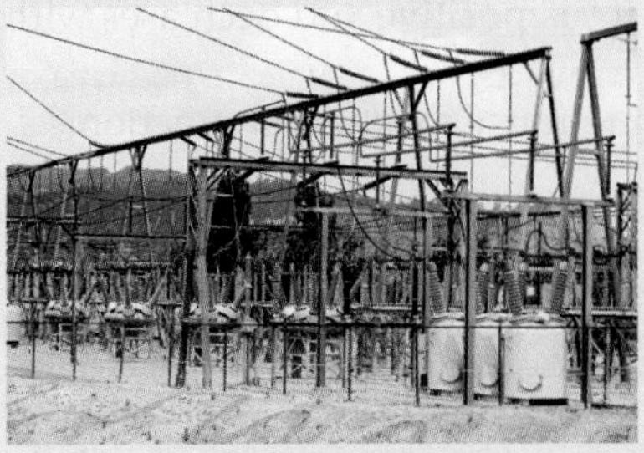

In 1955, consumers bought 369 billion kilowatt-hours (kwh) of electricity; in 1970 they bought 1083 billion. Because there were fewer electric utilities in 1970, the output per firm had increased substantially. Was this increase due to economies of scale or to other factors? If it was the result of economies of scale, it would be economically inefficient for regulators to "break up" electric utility monopolies.

| TABLE 7.4 Scale Economies in the Electric Power Industry | | | | | |
|---|---|---|---|---|---|
| Output (million kwh) | 43 | 338 | 1109 | 2226 | 5819 |
| Value of SCI, 1955 | .41 | .26 | .16 | .10 | .04 |

An interesting study of scale economies was based on the years 1955 and 1970 for investor-owned utilities with more than $1 million in revenues.[17] The cost of electric power was estimated by using a cost function that is somewhat more sophisticated than the quadratic and cubic functions discussed earlier.[18] Table 7.4 shows the resulting estimates of the scale economies index. The results are based on a classification of all utilities into five size categories, with the median output (measured in kilowatt-hours) in each category listed.

The positive values of SCI tell us that all sizes of firms had some economies of scale in 1955. However, the magnitude of the economies of scale diminishes as firm size increases. The average cost curve associated with the 1955 study is drawn in Figure 7.16 and labeled 1955. The point of minimum average cost occurs at point $A$, at an output of approximately 20 billion kilowatts. Because there were no firms of this size in 1955, no firm had exhausted the opportunity for returns to scale in production. Note, however, that the average cost curve is relatively flat from an output of 9 billion kilowatts and higher, a range in which 7 of 124 firms produced.

When the same cost functions were estimated with 1970 data, the cost curve labeled 1970 in Figure 7.16 was the result. The graph shows clearly that the

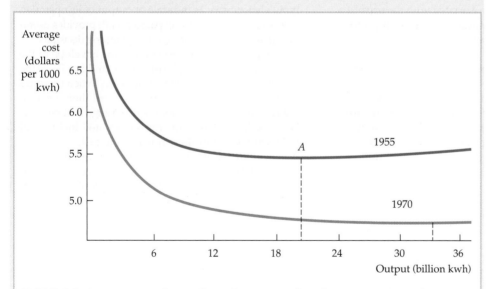

**FIGURE 7.16 Average Cost of Production in the Electric Power Industry**

The average cost of electric power in 1955 achieved a minimum at approximately 20 billion kilowatt-hours. By 1970 the average cost of production had fallen sharply and achieved a minimum at an output of more than 33 billion kilowatt-hours.

---

[17]This example is based on Laurits Christensen and William H. Greene, "Economies of Scale in U.S. Electric Power Generation," *Journal of Political Economy* 84 (1976): 655–76.

[18]The translog cost function used in this study provides a more general functional relationship than any of those we have discussed.

average costs of production fell from 1955 to 1970. (The data are in real 1970 dollars.) But the flat part of the curve now begins at about 15 billion kwh. By 1970, 24 of 80 firms were producing in this range. Thus, many more firms were operating in the flat portion of the average cost curve in which economies of scale are not an important phenomenon. More important, most of the firms were producing in a portion of the 1970 cost curve that was flatter than their point of operation on the 1955 curve. (Five firms were at points of diseconomies of scale: Consolidated Edison [SCI = −0.003], Detroit Edison [SCI = −0.004], Duke Power [SCI = −0.012], Commonwealth Edison [SCI = −0.014], and Southern [SCI = −0.028].) Thus, unexploited scale economies were much smaller in 1970 than in 1955.

This cost function analysis makes it clear that the decline in the cost of producing electric power cannot be explained by the ability of larger firms to take advantage of economies of scale. Rather, improvements in technology unrelated to the scale of the firms' operation and the decline in the real cost of energy inputs, such as coal and oil, are important reasons for the lower costs. The tendency toward lower average cost reflecting a movement to the right along an average cost curve is minimal compared with the effect of technological improvement.

# SUMMARY

1. Managers, investors, and economists must take into account the *opportunity cost* associated with the use of a firm's resources: the cost associated with the opportunities forgone when the firm uses its resources in its next best alternative.

2. A *sunk cost* is an expenditure that has been made and cannot be recovered. After it has been incurred, it should be ignored when making future economic decisions.

3. In the short run, one or more of a firm's inputs are fixed. Total cost can be divided into fixed cost and variable cost. A firm's *marginal cost* is the additional variable cost associated with each additional unit of output. The *average variable cost* is the total variable cost divided by the number of units of output.

4. In the short run, when not all inputs are variable, the presence of diminishing returns determines the shape of the cost curves. In particular, there is an inverse relationship between the marginal product of a single variable input and the marginal cost of production. The average variable cost and average total cost curves are U-shaped. The short-run marginal cost curve increases beyond a certain point, and cuts both average cost curves from below at their minimum points.

5. In the long run, all inputs to the production process are variable. As a result, the choice of inputs depends both on the relative costs of the factors of production and on the extent to which the firm can substitute among inputs in its production process. The cost-minimizing input choice is made by finding the point of tangency between the isoquant representing the level of desired output and an isocost line.

6. The firm's *expansion path* shows how its cost-minimizing input choices vary as the scale or output of its operation increases. As a result, the expansion path provides useful information relevant for long-run planning decisions.

7. The long-run average cost curve is the envelope of the firm's short-run average cost curves, and it reflects the presence or absence of returns to scale. When there are increasing returns to scale initially and then decreasing returns to scale, the long-run average cost curve is U-shaped, and the envelope does not include all points of minimum short-run average cost.

8. A firm enjoys *economies of scale* when it can double its output at less than twice the cost. Correspondingly, there are diseconomies of scale when a doubling of output requires more than twice the cost. Scale economies and diseconomies apply even when input proportions are variable; returns to scale apply only when input proportions are fixed.

9. When a firm produces two (or more) outputs, it is important to note whether there are *economies of scope* in production. Economies of scope arise when the firm can produce any combination of the two outputs more cheaply than could two independent firms that each produced a single output. The degree of economies of scope is measured by the percentage reduction in cost when one firm produces two products relative to the cost of producing them individually.

10. A firm's average cost of production can fall over time if the firm "learns" how to produce more effectively. The *learning curve* shows how much the input needed to produce a given output falls as the cumulative output of the firm increases.

11. Cost functions relate the cost of production to the firm's level of output. The functions can be measured in both the short run and the long run by using either data for firms in an industry at a given time or data for an industry over time. A number of functional relationships, including linear, quadratic, and cubic, can be used to represent cost functions.

# QUESTIONS FOR REVIEW

1. A firm pays its accountant an annual retainer of $10,000. Is this an economic cost?

2. The owner of a small retail store does her own accounting work. How would you measure the opportunity cost of her work?

3. Please explain whether the following statements are true or false.
   a. If the owner of a business pays himself no salary, then the accounting cost is zero, but the economic cost is positive.
   b. A firm that has positive accounting profit does not necessarily have positive economic profit.
   c. If a firm hires a currently unemployed worker, the opportunity cost of utilizing the worker's services is zero.

4. Suppose that labor is the only variable input to the production process. If the marginal cost of production is diminishing as more units of output are produced, what can you say about the marginal product of labor?

5. Suppose a chair manufacturer finds that the marginal rate of technical substitution of capital for labor in her production process is substantially greater than the ratio of the rental rate on machinery to the wage rate for assembly-line labor. How should she alter her use of capital and labor to minimize the cost of production?

6. Why are isocost lines straight lines?

7. Assume that the marginal cost of production is increasing. Can you determine whether the average variable cost is increasing or decreasing? Explain.

8. Assume that the marginal cost of production is greater than the average variable cost. Can you determine whether the average variable cost is increasing or decreasing? Explain.

9. If the firm's average cost curves are U-shaped, why does its average variable cost curve achieve its minimum at a lower level of output than the average total cost curve?

10. If a firm enjoys economies of scale up to a certain output level, and cost then increases proportionately with output, what can you say about the shape of the long-run average cost curve?

11. How does a change in the price of one input change the firm's long-run expansion path?

12. Distinguish between economies of scale and economies of scope. Why can one be present without the other?

13. Is the firm's expansion path always a straight line?

14. What is the difference between economies of scale and returns to scale?

# EXERCISES

1. Joe quits his computer programming job, where he was earning a salary of $50,000 per year, to start his own computer software business in a building that he owns and was previously renting out for $24,000 per year. In his first year of business he has the following expenses: salary paid to himself, $40,000; rent, $0; other expenses, $25,000. Find the accounting cost and the economic cost associated with Joe's computer software business.

2. a. Fill in the blanks in the table on page 262.
   b. Draw a graph that shows marginal cost, average variable cost, and average total cost, with cost on the vertical axis and quantity on the horizontal axis.

3. A firm has a fixed production cost of $5000 and a constant marginal cost of production of $500 per unit produced.
   a. What is the firm's total cost function? Average cost?
   b. If the firm wanted to minimize the average total cost, would it choose to be very large or very small? Explain.

4. Suppose a firm must pay an annual tax, which is a fixed sum, independent of whether it produces any output.
   a. How does this tax affect the firm's fixed, marginal, and average costs?
   b. Now suppose the firm is charged a tax that is proportional to the number of items it produces. Again, how does this tax affect the firm's fixed, marginal, and average costs?

5. A recent issue of *Business Week* reported the following:

   During the recent auto sales slump, GM, Ford, and Chrysler decided it was cheaper to sell cars to rental companies at a loss than to lay off workers. That's because closing and reopening plants is expensive, partly because the auto makers' current union contracts obligate them to pay many workers even if they're not working.

   When the article discusses selling cars "at a loss," is it referring to accounting profit or economic profit? How will the two differ in this case? Explain briefly.

| Units of Output | Fixed Cost | Variable Cost | Total Cost | Marginal Cost | Average Fixed Cost | Average Variable Cost | Average Total Cost |
|---|---|---|---|---|---|---|---|
| 0 | | | 100 | | | | |
| 1 | | | 125 | | | | |
| 2 | | | 145 | | | | |
| 3 | | | 157 | | | | |
| 4 | | | 177 | | | | |
| 5 | | | 202 | | | | |
| 6 | | | 236 | | | | |
| 7 | | | 270 | | | | |
| 8 | | | 326 | | | | |
| 9 | | | 398 | | | | |
| 10 | | | 490 | | | | |

6. Suppose the economy takes a downturn, and that labor costs fall by 50 percent and are expected to stay at that level for a long time. Show graphically how this change in the relative price of labor and capital affects the firm's expansion path.

7. The cost of flying a passenger plane from point A to point B is $50,000. The airline flies this route four times per day at 7 AM, 10 AM, 1 PM, and 4 PM. The first and last flights are filled to capacity with 240 people. The second and third flights are only half full. Find the average cost per passenger for each flight. Suppose the airline hires you as a marketing consultant and wants to know which type of customer it should try to attract—the off-peak customer (the middle two flights) or the rush-hour customer (the first and last flights). What advice would you offer?

8. You manage a plant that mass-produces engines by teams of workers using assembly machines. The technology is summarized by the production function

$$q = 5\,KL$$

where $q$ is the number of engines per week, $K$ is the number of assembly machines, and $L$ is the number of labor teams. Each assembly machine rents for $r = \$10,000$ per week, and each team costs $w = \$5000$ per week. Engine costs are given by the cost of labor teams and machines, plus $2000 per engine for raw materials. Your plant has a fixed installation of 5 assembly machines as part of its design.

a. What is the cost function for your plant—namely, how much would it cost to produce $q$ engines? What are average and marginal costs for producing $q$ engines? How do average costs vary with output?

b. How many teams are required to produce 250 engines? What is the average cost per engine?

c. You are asked to make recommendations for the design of a new production facility. What capital/labor $(K/L)$ ratio should the new plant accommodate if it wants to minimize the total cost of producing at any level of output $q$?

9. The short-run cost function of a company is given by the equation TC = 200 + 55$q$, where TC is the total cost and $q$ is the total quantity of output, both measured in thousands.

a. What is the company's fixed cost?

b. If the company produced 100,000 units of goods, what would be its average variable cost?

c. What would be its marginal cost of production?

d. What would be its average fixed cost?

e. Suppose the company borrows money and expands its factory. Its fixed cost rises by $50,000, but its variable cost falls to $45,000 per 1000 units. The cost of interest ($i$) also enters into the equation. Each 1-point increase in the interest rate raises costs by $3000. Write the new cost equation.

*10. A chair manufacturer hires its assembly-line labor for $30 an hour and calculates that the rental cost of its machinery is $15 per hour. Suppose that a chair can be produced using 4 hours of labor or machinery in any combination. If the firm is currently using 3 hours of labor for each hour of machine time, is it minimizing its costs of production? If so, why? If not, how can it improve the situation? Graphically illustrate the isoquant and the two isocost lines for the current combination of labor and capital and for the optimal combination of labor and capital.

*11. Suppose that a firm's production function is $q = 10L^{\frac{1}{2}}K^{\frac{1}{2}}$. The cost of a unit of labor is $20 and the cost of a unit of capital is $80.

a. The firm is currently producing 100 units of output and has determined that the cost-minimizing quantities of labor and capital are 20 and 5, respectively. Graphically illustrate this using isoquants and isocost lines.

**b.** The firm now wants to increase output to 140 units. If capital is fixed in the short run, how much labor will the firm require? Illustrate this graphically and find the firm's new total cost.

**c.** Graphically identify the cost-minimizing level of capital and labor in the long run if the firm wants to produce 140 units.

**d.** If the marginal rate of technical substitution is $K/L$, find the optimal level of capital and labor required to produce the 140 units of output.

**\*12.** A computer company's cost function, which relates its average cost of production AC to its cumulative output in thousands of computers $Q$ and its plant size in terms of thousands of computers produced per year $q$ (within the production range of 10,000 to 50,000 computers), is given by

$$AC = 10 - 0.1Q + 0.3q$$

**a.** Is there a learning-curve effect?

**b.** Are there economies or diseconomies of scale?

**c.** During its existence, the firm has produced a total of 40,000 computers and is producing 10,000 computers this year. Next year it plans to increase production to 12,000 computers. Will its average cost of production increase or decrease? Explain.

**\*13.** Suppose the long-run total cost function for an industry is given by the cubic equation $TC = a + bq + cq^2 + dq^3$. Show (using calculus) that this total cost function is consistent with a U-shaped average cost curve for at least some values of a, b, c, and d.

**\*14.** A computer company produces hardware and software using the same plant and labor. The total cost of producing computer processing units $H$ and software programs $S$ is given by

$$TC = aH + bS - cHS$$

where $a$, $b$, and $c$ are positive. Is this total cost function consistent with the presence of economies or diseconomies of scale? With economies or diseconomies of scope?

# Appendix to Chapter 7

## PRODUCTION AND COST THEORY—A MATHEMATICAL TREATMENT

This appendix presents a mathematical treatment of the basics of production and cost theory. As in the appendix to Chapter 4, we use the method of Lagrange multipliers to solve the firm's cost-minimizing problem.

### Cost Minimization

The theory of the firm relies on the assumption that firms choose inputs to the production process that minimize the cost of producing output. If there are two inputs, capital $K$ and labor $L$, the production function $F(K, L)$ describes the maximum output that can be produced for every possible combination of inputs. We assume that each factor in the production process has positive but decreasing marginal products. Therefore, writing the marginal product of capital and labor as $MP_K(K, L)$ and $MP_L(K, L)$, respectively, it follows that

$$MP_K(K, L) = \frac{\partial F(K, L)}{\partial K} > 0, \quad \frac{\partial^2 F(K, L)}{\partial K^2} < 0$$

$$MP_L(K, L) = \frac{\partial F(K, L)}{\partial L} > 0, \quad \frac{\partial^2 F(K, L)}{\partial L^2} < 0$$

A competitive firm takes the prices of both labor $w$ and capital $r$ as given. Then the cost-minimization problem can be written as

$$\text{Minimize } C = wL + rK \tag{A7.1}$$

subject to the constraint that a fixed output $q_0$ be produced:

$$F(K, L) = q_0 \tag{A7.2}$$

$C$ represents the cost of producing the fixed level of output $q_0$.

To determine the firm's demand for capital and labor inputs, we choose the values of $K$ and $L$ that minimize (A7.1) subject to (A7.2). We can solve this constrained optimization problem in three steps using the method discussed in the appendix to Chapter 4:

• **Step 1:** Set up the Lagrangian, which is the sum of two components: the cost of production (to be minimized) and the Lagrange multiplier $\lambda$ times the output constraint faced by the firm:

$$\Phi = wL + rK - \lambda[F(K, L) - q_0] \tag{A7.3}$$

- **Step 2:** Differentiate the Lagrangian with respect to $K$, $L$, and $\lambda$. Then equate the resulting derivatives to zero to obtain the necessary conditions for a minimum.[1]

$$\partial \Phi / \partial K = r - \lambda \mathrm{MP}_K(K, L) = 0$$

$$\partial \Phi / \partial L = w - \lambda \mathrm{MP}_L(K, L) = 0 \qquad \textbf{(A7.4)}$$

$$\partial \Phi / \partial \lambda = q_0 - F(K, L) = 0$$

- **Step 3:** In general, these equations can be solved to obtain the optimizing values of $L$, $K$, and $\lambda$. It is particularly instructive to combine the first two conditions in (A7.4) to obtain

$$\mathrm{MP}_K(K, L)/r = \mathrm{MP}_L(K, L)/w \qquad \textbf{(A7.5)}$$

Equation (A7.5) tells us that if the firm is minimizing costs, it will choose its factor inputs to equate the ratio of the marginal product of each factor divided by its price. This is exactly the same condition that we derived as Equation 7.4 (page 238) in the text.

Finally, we can rewrite the first two conditions of (A7.4) to evaluate the Lagrange multiplier:

$$r - \lambda \mathrm{MP}_K(K, L) = 0 \Rightarrow \lambda = \frac{r}{\mathrm{MP}_K(K, L)}$$

$$w - \lambda \mathrm{MP}_L(K, L) = 0 \Rightarrow \lambda = \frac{w}{\mathrm{MP}_L(K, L)} \qquad \textbf{(A7.6)}$$

Suppose output increases by one unit. Because the marginal product of capital measures the extra output associated with an additional input of capital, $1/\mathrm{MP}_K(K, L)$ measures the extra capital needed to produce one unit of output. Therefore, $r/\mathrm{MP}_K(K, L)$ measures the additional input cost of producing an additional unit of output by increasing capital. Likewise, $w/\mathrm{MP}_L(K, L)$ measures the additional cost of producing a unit of output using additional labor as an input. In both cases, the Lagrange multiplier is equal to the marginal cost of production because it tells us how much the cost increases if the amount produced is increased by one unit.

## Marginal Rate of Technical Substitution

Recall that an *isoquant* is a curve that représents the set of all input combinations that give the firm the same level of output—say, $q_0$. Thus, the condition that $F(K, L) = q_0$ represents a production isoquant. As input combinations are changed along an isoquant, the change in output, given by the total derivative of $F(K, L)$ equals zero (i.e., $dq = 0$). Thus

$$\mathrm{MP}_K(K, L)dK + \mathrm{MP}_L(K, L)dL = dq = 0 \qquad \textbf{(A7.7)}$$

It follows by rearrangement that

$$-dK/dL = \mathrm{MRTS}_{LK} = \mathrm{MP}_L(K, L)/\mathrm{MP}_K(K, L) \qquad \textbf{(A7.8)}$$

where $\mathrm{MRTS}_{LK}$ is the firm's marginal rate of technical substitution between labor and capital.

---

[1]These conditions are necessary for a solution involving positive amounts of both inputs.

Now, rewrite the condition given by (A7.5) to get

$$\mathrm{MP}_L(K, L)/\mathrm{MP}_K(K, L) = w/r \qquad \textbf{(A7.9)}$$

Because the left side of (A7.8) represents the negative of the slope of the isoquant, it follows that at the point of tangency of the isoquant and the isocost line, the firm's marginal rate of technical substitution (which trades off inputs while keeping output constant) is equal to the ratio of the input prices (which represents the slope of the firm's isocost line).

We can look at this result another way by rewriting (A7.9) again:

$$\mathrm{MP}_L/w = \mathrm{MP}_K/r \qquad \textbf{(A7.10)}$$

Equation (A7.10) is the same as (A7.5) and tells us that the marginal products of all production inputs must be equal when these marginal products are adjusted by the unit cost of each input.

## Duality in Production and Cost Theory

As in consumer theory, the firm's input decision has a dual nature. The optimum choice of $K$ and $L$ can be analyzed not only as the problem of choosing the lowest isocost line tangent to the production isoquant, but also as the problem of choosing the highest production isoquant tangent to a given isocost line. Suppose we wish to spend $C_0$ on production. The dual problem asks what combination of $K$ and $L$ will let us produce the most output at a cost of $C_0$. We can see the equivalence of the two approaches by solving the following problem:

$$\text{Maximize } F(K, L) \text{ subject to } wL + rL = C_0$$

We can solve this problem using the Lagrangian method:

- **Step 1:** We set up the Lagrangian

$$\Phi = F(K, L) - \mu(wL + rK - C_0) \qquad \textbf{(A7.12)}$$

  where $\mu$ is the Lagrange multiplier.

- **Step 2:** We differentiate the Lagrangian with respect to $K$, $L$, and $\mu$ and set the resulting equation equal to zero to find the necessary conditions for a maximum:

$$\frac{\partial \Phi}{\partial K} = \mathrm{MP}_K(K, L) - \mu r = 0$$

$$\frac{\partial \Phi}{\partial K} = \mathrm{MP}_L(K, L) - \mu w = 0 \qquad \textbf{(A7.13)}$$

$$\frac{\partial \Phi}{\partial K} = wL - rK + C_0 = 0$$

- **Step 3:** Normally, we can use the equations of A7.13 to solve for $K$ and $L$. In particular, we combine the first two equations to see that

$$\mu = \frac{\mathrm{MP}_K(K, L)}{r}$$

$$\mu = \frac{\mathrm{MP}_L(K, L)}{w}$$

$$\Rightarrow \frac{\mathrm{MP}_K(K, L)}{r} = \frac{\mathrm{MP}_L(K, L)}{w} \qquad \textbf{(A7.14)}$$

This is the same result as A7.5—that is, the necessary condition for cost minimization.

## The Cobb-Douglas Cost and Production Functions

Given a specific production function $F(K, L)$, conditions (A7.13) and (A7.14) can be used to derive the *cost function* $C(q)$. To understand this principle, let's work through the example of a **Cobb-Douglas production function**. This production function is

$$F(K, L) = AK^\alpha L^\beta$$

where $A$, $\alpha$, and $\beta$ are positive constants.

> • **Cobb-Douglas production function**  Production function of the form $q = AK^\alpha L^\beta$, where $q$ is the rate of output, $K$ is the quantity of capital, and $L$ is the quantity of labor, and where $A$, $\alpha$, and $\beta$ are positive constants.

We assume that $\alpha < 1$ and $\beta < 1$, so that the firm has decreasing marginal products of labor and capital.[2] If $\alpha + \beta = 1$, the firm has *constant returns to scale*, because doubling $K$ and $L$ doubles $F$. If $\alpha + \beta > 1$, the firm has *increasing returns to scale*, and if $\alpha + \beta < 1$, it has *decreasing returns to scale*.

As an application, consider the carpet industry described in Example 6.4 (page 217). The production of both small and large firms can be described by Cobb-Douglas production functions. For small firms, $\alpha = .77$ and $\beta = .23$. Because $\alpha + \beta = 1$, there are constant returns to scale. For larger firms, however, $\alpha = .83$ and $\beta = .22$. Thus $\alpha + \beta = 1.05$, and there are increasing returns to scale. The Cobb-Douglas production function is frequently encountered in economics and can be used to model many kinds of production. We have already seen how it can accommodate differences in returns to scale. It can also account for changes in technology or productivity through changes in the value of $A$: The larger the value of $A$, more can be produced for a given level of $K$ and $L$.

To find the amounts of capital and labor that the firm should utilize to minimize the cost of producing an output $q_0$, we first write the Lagrangian

$$\Phi = wL + rK - \lambda(AK^\alpha L^\beta - q_0) \qquad \textbf{(A7.15)}$$

Differentiating with respect to $L$, $K$, and $\lambda$, and setting those derivatives equal to 0, we obtain

$$\partial\Phi/\partial L = w - \lambda(\beta AK^\alpha L^{\beta-1}) = 0 \qquad \textbf{(A7.16)}$$

$$\partial\Phi/\partial K = r - \lambda(\alpha AK^{\alpha-1}L^\beta) = 0 \qquad \textbf{(A7.17)}$$

$$\partial\Phi/\partial\lambda = AK^\alpha L^\beta - q_0 = 0 \qquad \textbf{(A7.18)}$$

From equation (A7.16) we have

$$\lambda = w/A\beta K^\alpha L^{\beta-1} \qquad \textbf{(A7.19)}$$

Substituting this formula into equation (A7.17) gives us

$$r\beta AK^\alpha L^{\beta-1} = w\alpha AK^{\alpha-1}L^\beta \qquad \textbf{(A7.20)}$$

---

[2]For example, the marginal product of labor is given by $MP_L = \partial[F(K, L)]/\partial L = \beta AK^\alpha L^{\beta-1}$. Thus, $MP_L$ falls as $L$ increases.

or

$$L = \frac{\beta r}{\alpha w} K \qquad \text{(A7.21)}$$

A7.21 is the expansion path. Now use Equation (A7.21) to substitute for $L$ in equation (A7.18):

$$AK^{\alpha}\left(\frac{\beta r}{\alpha w} K\right)^{\beta} - q_0 = 0 \qquad \text{(A7.22)}$$

We can rewrite the new equation as:

$$K^{\alpha+\beta} = \left(\frac{\alpha w}{\beta r}\right)^{\beta} \frac{q_0}{A} \qquad \text{(A7.23)}$$

or

$$K = \left(\frac{\alpha w}{\beta r}\right)^{\frac{\beta}{\alpha+\beta}} \left(\frac{q_0}{A}\right)^{\frac{1}{\alpha+\beta}} \qquad \text{(A7.24)}$$

A7.24 is the factor demand for capital. We have now determined the cost-minimizing quantity of capital: Thus, if we wish to produce $q_0$ units of output at least cost, (A7.24) tells us how much capital we should employ as part of our production plan. To determine the cost-minimizing quantity of labor, we simply substitute equation (A7.24) into equation (A7.21):

$$L = \frac{\beta r}{\alpha w} K = \frac{\beta r}{\alpha w}\left[\left(\frac{\alpha w}{\beta r}\right)^{\frac{\beta}{\alpha+\beta}} \left(\frac{q_0}{A}\right)^{\frac{1}{\alpha+\beta}}\right] \qquad \text{(A7.25)}$$

$$L = \left(\frac{\beta r}{\alpha w}\right)^{\frac{\alpha}{\alpha+\beta}} \left(\frac{q_0}{A}\right)^{\frac{1}{\alpha+\beta}}$$

A7.25 is the constrained factor demand for labor. Note that if the wage rate $w$ rises relative to the price of capital $r$, the firm will use more capital and less labor. Suppose that, because of technological change, $A$ increases (so the firm can produce more output with the same inputs); in that case, both $K$ and $L$ will fall.

We have shown how cost-minimization subject to an output constraint can be used to determine the firm's optimal mix of capital and labor. Now we will determine the firm's cost function. The total cost of producing *any output q* can be obtained by substituting equations (A7.24) for $K$ and (A7.25) for $L$ into the equation $C = wL + rK$. After some algebraic manipulation we find that

$$C = w^{\beta/(\alpha+\beta)} r^{\alpha/(\alpha+\beta)}\left[\left(\frac{\alpha}{\beta}\right)^{\beta/(\alpha+\beta)} + \left(\frac{\alpha}{\beta}\right)^{-\alpha/(\alpha+\beta)}\right]\left(\frac{q}{A}\right)^{1/(\alpha+\beta)} \qquad \text{(A7.26)}$$

This *cost function* tells us (1) how the total cost of production increases as the level of output $q$ increases, and (2) how cost changes as input prices change. When $\alpha + \beta$ equals 1, equation (A7.26) simplifies to

$$C = w^\beta r^\alpha [(\alpha/\beta)^\beta + (\alpha/\beta)^{-\alpha}](1/A)q \qquad \textbf{(A7.27)}$$

In this case, therefore, cost will increase proportionately with output. As a result, the production process exhibits constant returns to scale. Likewise, if $\alpha + \beta$ is greater than 1, there are increasing returns to scale; if $\alpha + \beta$ is less than 1, there are decreasing returns to scale.

The firm's cost function contains many desirable features. To appreciate this fact, consider the special constant returns to scale cost function (A7.27). Suppose that we wish to produce $q_0$ in output but are faced with a doubling of the wage. How should we expect our costs to change? New costs are given by

$$C_1 = (2w)^\beta r^\alpha \left[ \left(\frac{\alpha}{\beta}\right)^\beta + \left(\frac{\alpha}{\beta}\right)^{-\alpha} \right] \left(\frac{1}{A}\right) q_0 = 2^\beta \underbrace{ w^\beta r^\alpha \left[ \left(\frac{\alpha}{\beta}\right)^\beta + \left(\frac{\alpha}{\beta}\right)^{-\alpha} \right] \left(\frac{1}{A}\right) q_0 }_{C_0} = 2^\beta C_0$$

Recall that at the beginning of this section, we assumed that $\alpha < 1$ and $\beta < 1$. Therefore, $C_1 < 2C_0$. Even though wages doubled, the cost of producing $q_0$ less than doubled. This is the expected result. If a firm suddenly had to pay more for labor, it would substitute away from labor and employ more of the relatively cheaper capital, thereby keeping the increase in total cost in check.

Now consider the dual problem of maximizing the output that can be produced with the expenditure of $C_0$ dollars. We leave it to you to work through this problem for the Cobb-Douglas production function. You should be able to show that equations (A7.24) and (A7.25) describe the cost-minimizing input choices. To get you started, note that the Lagrangian for this dual problem is $\Phi = AK^\alpha L^\beta - \mu(wL + rK - C_0)$.

# EXERCISES

1. Of the following production functions, which exhibit increasing, constant, or decreasing returns to scale?
   a. $F(K, L) = K^2 L$
   b. $F(K, L) = 10K + 5L$
   c. $F(K, L) = (KL)^{.5}$

2. The production function for a product is given by $q = 100KL$. If the price of capital is $120 per day and the price of labor $30 per day, what is the minimum cost of producing 1000 units of output?

3. Suppose a production function is given by $F(K, L) = KL^2$; the price of capital is $10 and the price of labor $15. What combination of labor and capital minimizes the cost of producing any given output?

4. Suppose the process of producing lightweight parkas by Polly's Parkas is described by the function

   $$q = 10K^{.8}(L - 40)^{.2}$$

   where $q$ is the number of parkas produced, $K$ the number of computerized stitching-machine hours, and $L$ the number of person-hours of labor. In addition to capital and labor, $10 worth of raw materials is used in the production of each parka.

   a. By minimizing cost subject to the production function, derive the cost-minimizing demands for $K$ and $L$ as a function of output ($q$), wage rates ($w$), and rental rates on machines ($r$). Use these results to derive the total cost function: that is, costs as a function of $q, r, w$, and the constant $10 per unit materials cost.

   b. This process requires skilled workers, who earn $32 per hour. The rental rate on the machines used in the process is $64 per hour. At these factor prices, what are total costs as a function of $q$? Does this technology exhibit decreasing, constant, or increasing returns to scale?

   c. Polly's Parkas plans to produce 2000 parkas per week. At the factor prices given above, how many workers should the firm hire (at 40 hours per week) and how many machines should it rent (at 40 machine-hours per week)? What are the marginal and average costs at this level of production?

# Profit Maximization and Competitive Supply

8

A cost curve describes the minimum cost at which a firm can produce various amounts of output. Once we know its cost curve, we can turn to a fundamental problem faced by every firm: *How much should be produced*? In this chapter, we will see how a firm chooses the level of output that maximizes its profit. We will also see how the output choices of individual firms lead to a supply curve for an entire industry.

Because our discussion of production and cost in Chapters 6 and 7 applies to firms in all kinds of markets, we will begin by explaining the profit-maximizing output decision in a general setting. However, we will then turn to the focus of this chapter—*perfectly competitive markets*, in which all firms produce an identical product and each is so small in relation to the industry that its production decisions have no effect on market price. New firms can easily enter the industry if they perceive a potential for profit, and existing firms can exit if they start losing money.

We begin by explaining exactly what is meant by a *competitive market*. We then explain why it makes sense to assume that firms (in any market) have the objective of maximizing profit. We provide a rule for choosing the profit-maximizing output for firms in all markets, competitive or otherwise. Following this we show how a competitive firm chooses its output in the short and long run.

We next examine how the firm's output choice changes as the cost of production or the prices of inputs change. In this way, we show how to derive the *firm's supply curve*. We then aggregate the supply curves of individual firms to obtain the *industry supply curve*. In the short run, firms in an industry choose which level of output to produce in order to maximize profit. In the long run, they not only make output choices, but also decide whether to be in a market at all. We will see that while the prospect of high profits encourages firms to enter an industry, losses encourage them to leave.

## 8.1 PERFECTLY COMPETITIVE MARKETS

In Chapter 2, we used supply–demand analysis to explain how changing market conditions affect the market price of such products as wheat and gasoline. We saw that the equilibrium price and quantity of each product was determined by the intersection of the market demand and market supply curves. Underlying this analysis is the model of a *perfectly competitive market*. The model of perfect competition is very useful for studying a variety of markets, including agriculture, fuels and other commodities, housing, services, and financial markets. Because this model is so important, we will spend some time laying out the basic assumptions that underlie it.

The model of perfect competition rests on three basic assumptions: (1) price taking, (2) product homogeneity, and (3) free entry and exit. You have encountered these assumptions earlier in the book; here we summarize and elaborate on them.

**Price Taking** Because many firms compete in the market, each firm faces a significant number of direct competitors for its products. Because *each individual firm sells a sufficiently small proportion of total market output, its decisions have no impact on market price*. Thus, each firm *takes the market price as given*. In short, firms in perfectly competitive markets are **price takers**.

• **price taker** Firm that has no influence over market price and thus takes the price as given.

Suppose, for example, that you are the owner of a small electric lightbulb distribution business. You buy your lightbulbs from the manufacturer and resell them at wholesale to small businesses and retail outlets. Unfortunately, you are only one of many competing distributors. As a result, you find that there is little room to negotiate with your customers. If you do not offer a competitive price—one that is determined in the marketplace—your customers will take their business elsewhere. In addition, you know that the number of lightbulbs that you sell will have little or no effect on the wholesale price of bulbs. You are a price taker.

The assumption of price taking applies to *consumers* as well as firms. In a perfectly competitive market, each consumer buys such a small proportion of total industry output that he or she has no impact on the market price, and therefore takes the price as given.

Another way of stating the price-taking assumption is that there are many independent firms and independent consumers in the market, all of whom believe—correctly—that their decisions will not affect prices.

**Product Homogeneity** Price-taking behavior typically occurs in markets where firms produce identical, or nearly identical, products. When *the products of all of the firms in a market are perfectly substitutable with one another*—that is, when they are *homogeneous*—no firm can raise the price of its product above the price of other firms without losing most or all of its business. Most agricultural products are homogeneous: Because product quality is relatively similar among farms in a given region, for example, buyers of corn do not ask which individual farm grew the product. Oil, gasoline, and raw materials such as copper, iron, lumber, cotton, and sheet steel are also fairly homogeneous. Economists refer to such homogeneous products as *commodities*.

In contrast, when products are heterogeneous, each firm has the opportunity to raise its price above that of its competitors without losing all of its sales. Premium ice creams such as Häagen-Dazs, for example, can be sold at higher prices because Häagen-Dazs has different ingredients and is perceived by many consumers to be a higher-quality product.

The assumption of product homogeneity is important because it ensures that there is a *single market price*, consistent with supply-demand analysis.

• **free entry** (or **exit**) Condition under which there are no special costs that make it difficult for a firm to enter (or exit) an industry.

**Free Entry and Exit** This third assumption, **free entry** (or **exit**), means that there are no special costs that make it difficult for a new firm either to enter an industry and produce, or to exit if it cannot make a profit. *As a result,* *buyers can easily switch from one supplier to another, and suppliers can easily enter or exit a market.*

The special costs that could restrict entry are costs which an entrant to a market would have to bear, but which a firm that is already producing would not. The pharmaceutical industry, for example, is not perfectly competitive because Merck, Pfizer, and other firms hold patents that give them unique rights to produce drugs. Any new entrant would either have to invest in research and development to obtain its own competing drugs or pay substantial license fees to one or more firms already in the market. R&D expenditures or license fees could limit a firm's ability to enter the market. Likewise, the aircraft industry is not perfectly competitive because entry requires an immense investment in plant and equipment that has little or no resale value.

The assumption of free entry and exit is important for competition to be effective. It means that consumers can easily switch to a rival firm if a current supplier raises its price. For businesses, it means that a firm can freely enter an industry if it sees a profit opportunity and exit if it is losing money. Thus a firm can hire labor and purchase capital and raw materials as needed, and it can release or move these factors of production if it wants to shut down or relocate.

If these three assumptions of perfect competition hold, market demand and supply curves can be used to analyze the behavior of market prices. In most markets, of course, these assumptions are unlikely to hold exactly. This does not mean, however, that the model of perfect competition is not useful. Some markets do indeed come close to satisfying our assumptions. But even when one or more of these three assumptions fails to hold, so that a market is not perfectly competitive, much can be learned by making comparisons with the perfectly competitive ideal.

## When Is a Market Highly Competitive?

Apart from agriculture, few real-world markets are *perfectly* competitive in the sense that each firm faces a perfectly horizontal demand curve for a homogeneous product in an industry that it can freely enter or exit. Nevertheless, many markets are *highly* competitive in the sense that firms face highly elastic demand curves and relatively easy entry and exit.

A simple rule of thumb to describe whether a market is close to being perfectly competitive would be appealing. Unfortunately, we have no such rule, and it is important to understand why. Consider the most obvious candidate: an industry with many firms (say, at least 10 to 20). Because firms can implicitly or explicitly collude in setting prices, the presence of many firms is not sufficient for an industry to approximate perfect competition. Conversely, the presence of only a few firms in a market does not rule out competitive behavior. Suppose that only three firms are in the market but that market demand for the product is very elastic. In this case, the demand curve facing each firm is likely to be nearly horizontal and the firms will behave *as if* they were operating in a perfectly competitive market. Even if market demand is not very elastic, these three firms might compete very aggressively (as we will see in Chapter 13). The important point to remember is that although firms may behave competitively in many situations, there is no simple indicator to tell us when a market is highly competitive. Often it is necessary to analyze both the firms themselves and their strategic interactions, as we do in Chapters 12 and 13.

> In §2.4, we explain that demand is price elastic when the percentage decline in quantity demanded is greater than the percentage increase in price.

## 8.2 PROFIT MAXIMIZATION

We now turn to the analysis of profit maximization. In this section, we ask whether firms do indeed seek to maximize profit. Then in Section 8.3, we will describe a rule that any firm—whether in a competitive market or not—can use to find its profit-maximizing output level. Finally, we will consider the special case of a firm in a competitive market. We distinguish the demand curve facing a competitive firm from the market demand curve, and use this information to describe the competitive firm's profit-maximization rule.

### Do Firms Maximize Profit?

The assumption of *profit maximization* is frequently used in microeconomics because it predicts business behavior reasonably accurately and avoids unnecessary analytical complications. But the question of whether firms actually do seek to maximize profit has been controversial.

For smaller firms managed by their owners, profit is likely to dominate almost all decisions. In larger firms, however, managers who make day-to-day decisions usually have little contact with the owners (i.e., the stockholders). As a result, owners cannot monitor the managers' behavior on a regular basis. Managers then have some leeway in how they run the firm and can deviate from profit-maximizing behavior.

Managers may be more concerned with such goals as revenue maximization, revenue growth, or the payment of dividends to satisfy shareholders. They might also be overly concerned with the firm's short-run profit (perhaps to earn a promotion or a large bonus) at the expense of its longer-run profit, even though long-run profit maximization better serves the interests of the stockholders.[1] Because technical and marketing information is costly to obtain, managers may sometimes operate using rules of thumb that require less-than-ideal information. On some occasions they may engage in acquisition and/or growth strategies that are substantially more risky than the owners of the firm might wish.

The recent rise in the number of corporate bankruptcies, especially those in the dot-com, telecom, and energy areas, along with the rapid increase in CEO salaries, has raised questions about the motivations of managers of large corporations. These are important questions, which we will address in Chapter 17, when we discuss the incentives of managers and owners in detail. For now, it is important to realize that a manager's freedom to pursue goals other than long-run profit maximization is limited. If they do pursue such goals, shareholders or boards of directors can replace them, or the firm can be taken over by new management. In any case, firms that do not come close to maximizing profit are not likely to survive. Firms that do survive in competitive industries make long-run profit maximization one of their highest priorities.

Thus our working assumption of profit maximization is reasonable. Firms that have been in business for a long time are likely to care a lot about profit, whatever else their managers may appear to be doing. For example, a firm that subsidizes public television may seem public-spirited and altruistic. Yet this beneficence is likely to be in the long-run financial interest of the firm because it generates goodwill.

---

[1]To be more exact, *maximizing the market value of the firm* is a more appropriate goal than profit maximization because market value includes the stream of profits that the firm earns over time. It is the stream of current and future profits that is of direct interest to the stockholders.

## Alternative Forms of Organization

Now that we've underscored the fact that profit maximization is a fundamental assumption in most economic analyses of firm behavior, let's pause to consider an important qualifier to this assumption: Some forms of organizations have objectives that are quite different from profit maximization. An important such organization is the **cooperative**—an association of businesses or people jointly owned and operated by members for mutual benefit. For example, several farms might decide to enter into a cooperative agreement by which they pool their resources in order to distribute and market milk to consumers. Because each participating member of the milk cooperative is an autonomous economic unit, each farm will act to maximize its own profits (rather than the profits of the cooperative as a whole), taking the common marketing and distribution agreement as given. Such cooperative agreements are common in agricultural markets.

> **• cooperative** Association of businesses or people jointly owned and operated by members for mutual benefit.

In many towns or cities, one can join a food cooperative, the objective of which is to provide its members with food and other groceries at the lowest possible cost. Usually, a food cooperative looks like a store or small supermarket. Shopping is either restricted to members or else unrestricted with members receiving discounts. Prices are set so that the cooperative avoids losing money, but any profits are incidental and are returned to the members (usually in proportion to their purchases).

Housing cooperatives, or *co-ops*, are another example of this form of organization. A co-op might be an apartment building for which the title to the land and the building is owned by a corporation. The member residents of the co-op own shares in the corporation, accompanied by a right to occupy a unit—an arrangement much like a long-term lease. The members of the co-op can participate in the management of their building in a variety of ways: organizing social events, handling finances, or even deciding who their neighbors will be. As with other types of cooperatives, the objective is not to maximize profits, but rather to provide members with high-quality housing at the lowest possible cost.

A related type of housing organization is the *condominium*. A condominium is not a cooperative because housing units (or "condos") are individually owned. This has the important advantage of simplifying governance, as discussed in Example 8.1.

---

**EXAMPLE 8.1**   Condominiums versus Cooperatives in New York City

While owners of condominiums must join with fellow condo owners to manage common spaces (e.g., entry areas), they can make their own decisions as to how to manage their individual units so as to achieve the greatest value possible. In contrast, co-ops share joint liability on any outstanding mortgage on the co-op building and are subject to more complex governance rules. Although much of the governance is usually delegated to a board that represents all co-op members, members must often spend substantial time in the governance of the association. In addition, condo members can sell their units whenever and to whomever they choose, whereas co-op members must get permission from the co-op board before a sale can be made.

Nationwide, condos are a far more common than co-ops, outnumbering them by a factor of nearly 10 to 1. In this regard, New York City is very different from the rest of the nation—co-ops are more popular, and outnumber condos by a factor of about 4 to 1. What accounts for the relative popularity of housing cooperatives in New York City? Part of the answer is historical. Housing cooperatives are a much older form of organization in the U.S., dating back to the mid-nineteenth century, whereas the development of condominiums began only in the 1960s, at which point a large number of buildings in New York were already co-ops. In addition, while condominiums were becoming increasingly popular in other parts of the country, building regulations in New York made the co-op the required governance structure.

But that's history. The building restrictions in New York have long disappeared, and yet the conversion of apartments from co-ops to condos has been relatively slow. Why? A recent study provides some interesting answers.[2] The authors find that the typical condominium apartment is worth about 15.5 percent more than an equivalent apartment held in the form of a co-op. Clearly, holding an apartment in the form of a co-op is not the best way to maximize the apartment's value. On the other hand, co-op owners can be more selective in choosing their neighbors when sales are made—something that New Yorkers seem to care a great deal about. It appears that in New York, many owners have been willing to forgo substantial amounts of money in order to achieve non-monetary benefits.

## 8.3 MARGINAL REVENUE, MARGINAL COST, AND PROFIT MAXIMIZATION

We now return to our working assumption of profit maximization and examine the implications of this objective for the operation of a firm. We will begin by looking at the profit-maximizing output decision for *any* firm, whether it operates in a perfectly competitive market or is one that can influence price. Because **profit** is the difference between (total) revenue and (total) cost, finding the firm's profit-maximizing output level means analyzing its revenue. Suppose that the firm's output is $q$, and that it obtains revenue $R$. This revenue is equal to the price of the product $P$ times the number of units sold: $R = Pq$. The cost of production $C$ also depends on the level of output. The firm's profit, $\pi$, is the difference between revenue and cost:

$$\pi(q) = R(q) - C(q)$$

(Here we show explicitly that $\pi$, $R$, and $C$ depend on output. Usually we will omit this reminder.)

To maximize profit, the firm selects the output for which the difference between revenue and cost is the greatest. This principle is illustrated in Figure 8.1. Revenue $R(q)$ is a curved line, which reflects the fact that the firm can sell a greater level of output only by lowering its price. The slope of this revenue curve is **marginal revenue**: the change in revenue resulting from a one-unit increase in output.

Also shown is the total cost curve $C(q)$. The slope of this curve, which measures the additional cost of producing one additional unit of output, is the firm's *marginal cost*. Note that total cost $C(q)$ is positive when output is zero because there is a fixed cost in the short run.

• **profit**  Difference between total revenue and total cost.

• **marginal revenue**  Change in revenue resulting from a one-unit increase in output.

---

[2]Michael H. Schill, Ioan Voicu, and Jonathan Miller, "The Condominium v. Cooperative Puzzle: An Empirical Analysis of Housing in New York City," NYU, Law & Economics Research Paper No. 04-003, Feb. 10, 2004.

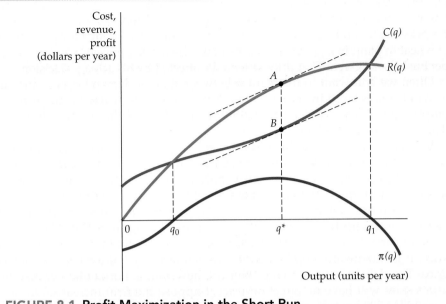

**FIGURE 8.1 Profit Maximization in the Short Run**

A firm chooses output $q^*$, so that profit, the difference $AB$ between revenue $R$ and cost $C$, is maximized. At that output, marginal revenue (the slope of the revenue curve) is equal to marginal cost (the slope of the cost curve).

For the firm illustrated in Figure 8.1, profit is negative at low levels of output because revenue is insufficient to cover fixed and variable costs. As output increases, revenue rises more rapidly than cost, so that profit eventually becomes positive. Profit continues to increase until output reaches the level $q^*$. At this point, marginal revenue and marginal cost are equal, and the vertical distance between revenue and cost, $AB$, is greatest. $q^*$ is the profit-maximizing output level. Note that at output levels above $q^*$, cost rises more rapidly than revenue—i.e., marginal revenue is less than marginal cost. Thus, profit declines from its maximum when output increases above $q^*$.

The rule that profit is maximized when marginal revenue is equal to marginal cost holds for all firms, whether competitive or not. This important rule can also be derived algebraically. Profit, $\pi = R - C$, is maximized at the point at which an additional increment to output leaves profit unchanged (i.e., $\Delta\pi/\Delta q = 0$):

$$\Delta\pi/\Delta q = \Delta R/\Delta q - \Delta C/\Delta q = 0$$

$\Delta R/\Delta q$ is marginal revenue MR and $\Delta C/\Delta q$ is marginal cost MC. Thus we conclude that profit is maximized when MR − MC = 0, so that

$$MR(q) = MC(q)$$

## Demand and Marginal Revenue for a Competitive Firm

Because each firm in a competitive industry sells only a small fraction of the entire industry output, *how much output the firm decides to sell will have no effect on the market price of the product*. The market price is determined by the industry demand and supply curves. Therefore, the competitive firm is a *price taker*. Recall that price taking is one of the fundamental assumptions of perfect competition. The price-taking firm knows that its production decision will have no effect on the price of the product. For example, when a farmer is deciding how many acres of wheat to plant in a given year, he can take the market price of wheat—say, $4 per bushel—as given. That price will not be affected by his acreage decision.

Often we will want to distinguish between market demand curves and the demand curves faced by individual firms. In this chapter we will denote *market* output and demand by capital letters ($Q$ and $D$) and the *firm's* output and demand by lowercase letters ($q$ and $d$).

> In §4.1, we explain how the demand curve relates the quantity of a good that a consumer will buy to the price of that good.

Because it is a price taker, *the demand curve d facing an individual competitive firm is given by a horizontal line*. In Figure 8.2(a), the farmer's demand curve corresponds to a price of $4 per bushel of wheat. The horizontal axis measures the amount of wheat that the farmer can sell, and the vertical axis measures the price.

Compare the demand curve facing the firm (in this case, the farmer) in Figure 8.2(a) with the market demand curve $D$ in Figure 8.2(b). The market demand curve shows how much wheat *all consumers* will buy at each possible price. It is downward sloping because consumers buy more wheat at a lower price. The demand curve facing the firm, however, is horizontal because the firm's sales will have no effect on price. Suppose the firm increased its sales from 100 to 200 bushels of wheat. This would have almost no effect on the market because industry output is 100 million bushels. Price is determined by the interaction of all firms and consumers in the market, not by the output decision of a single firm.

By the same token, when an individual firm faces a horizontal demand curve, it can sell an additional unit of output without lowering price. As a result, when it sells an additional unit, the firm's *total revenue* increases by an amount equal to the price: one bushel of wheat sold for $4 yields additional revenue of $4. Thus,

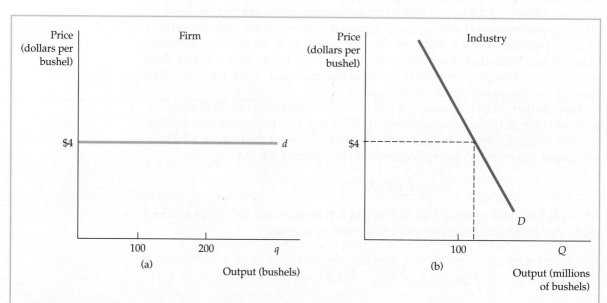

**FIGURE 8.2 Demand Curve Faced by a Competitive Firm**

A competitive firm supplies only a small portion of the total output of all the firms in an industry. Therefore, the firm takes the market price of the product as given, choosing its output on the assumption that the price will be unaffected by the output choice. In **(a)** the demand curve facing the firm is perfectly elastic, even though the market demand curve in **(b)** is downward sloping.

marginal revenue is constant at $4. At the same time, *average revenue* received by the firm is also $4 because every bushel of wheat produced will be sold at $4. Therefore:

> The demand curve *d* facing an individual firm in a competitive market is both its average revenue curve and its marginal revenue curve. Along this demand curve, marginal revenue, average revenue, and price are all equal.

## Profit Maximization by a Competitive Firm

Because the demand curve facing a competitive firm is horizontal, so that MR = P, the general rule for profit maximization that applies to any firm can be simplified. A perfectly competitive firm should choose its output so that *marginal cost equals price*:

$$MC(q) = MR = P$$

Note that because competitive firms take price as fixed, this is a rule for setting output, not price.

   The choice of the profit-maximizing output by a competitive firm is so important that we will devote most of the rest of this chapter to analyzing it. We begin with the short-run output decision and then move to the long run.

## 8.4 CHOOSING OUTPUT IN THE SHORT RUN

How much output should a firm produce over the short run, when its plant size is fixed? In this section we show how a firm can use information about revenue and cost to make a profit-maximizing output decision.

### Short-Run Profit Maximization by a Competitive Firm

In the short run, a firm operates with a fixed amount of capital and must choose the levels of its variable inputs (labor and materials) to maximize profit. Figure 8.3 shows the firm's short-run decision. The average and marginal revenue curves are drawn as a horizontal line at a price equal to $40. In this figure, we have drawn the average total cost curve ATC, the average variable cost curve AVC, and the marginal cost curve MC so that we can see the firm's profit more easily.

| Marginal, average, and total cost are discussed in §7.1. |
| --- |

   Profit is maximized at point $A$, where output is $q^* = 8$ and the price is $40, because marginal revenue is equal to marginal cost at this point. To see that $q^* = 8$ is indeed the profit-maximizing output, note that at a lower output, say $q_1 = 7$, marginal revenue is greater than marginal cost; profit could thus be increased by increasing output. The shaded area between $q_1 = 7$ and $q^*$ shows the lost profit associated with producing at $q_1$. At a higher output, say $q_2$, marginal cost is greater than marginal revenue; thus, reducing output saves a cost that exceeds the reduction in revenue. The shaded area between $q^*$ and $q_2 = 9$ shows the lost profit associated with producing at $q_2$. When output is $q^* = 8$, profit is given by the area of rectangle ABCD.

   The MR and MC curves cross at an output of $q_0$ as well as $q^*$. At $q_0$, however, profit is clearly not maximized. An increase in output beyond $q_0$ increases profit because marginal cost is well below marginal revenue. We can thus state the condition for profit maximization as follows: *Marginal revenue equals marginal*

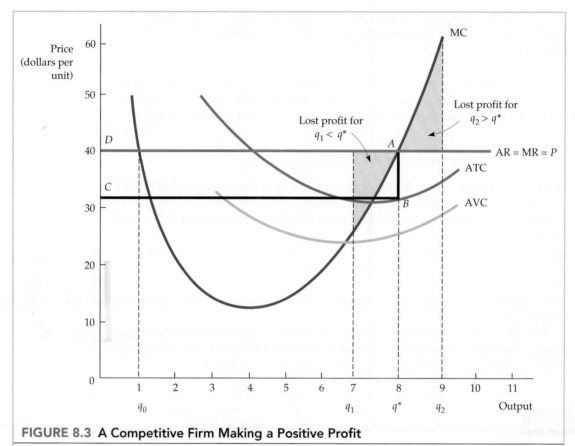

**FIGURE 8.3 A Competitive Firm Making a Positive Profit**

In the short run, the competitive firm maximizes its profit by choosing an output $q^*$ at which its marginal cost MC is equal to the price $P$ (or marginal revenue MR) of its product. The profit of the firm is measured by the rectangle $ABCD$. Any change in output, whether lower at $q_1$ or higher at $q_2$, will lead to lower profit.

*cost at a point at which the marginal cost curve is rising.* This conclusion is very important because it applies to the output decisions of firms in markets that may or may not be perfectly competitive. We can restate it as follows:

**Output Rule:** If a firm is producing any output, it should produce at the level at which marginal revenue equals marginal cost.

## The Short-Run Profit of a Competitive Firm

Figure 8.3 also shows the competitive firm's short-run profit. The distance $AB$ is the difference between price and average cost at the output level $q^*$, which is the average profit per unit of output. Segment $BC$ measures the total number of units produced. Rectangle $ABCD$, therefore, is the firm's profit.

A firm need not always earn a profit in the short run, as Figure 8.4 shows. The major difference from Figure 8.3 is a higher fixed cost of production. This higher fixed cost raises average total cost but does not change the average variable cost and marginal cost curves. At the profit-maximizing output $q^*$, the price $P$ is less than average cost. Line segment $AB$, therefore, measures the

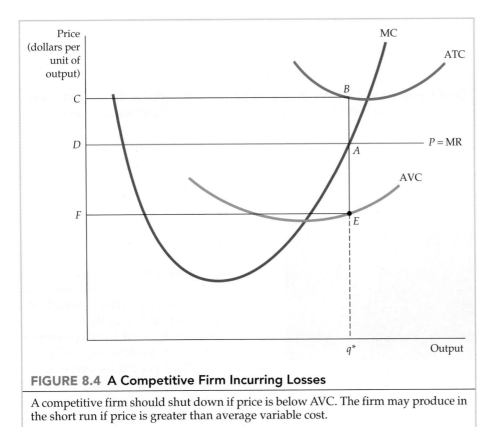

**FIGURE 8.4 A Competitive Firm Incurring Losses**

A competitive firm should shut down if price is below AVC. The firm may produce in the short run if price is greater than average variable cost.

average *loss* from production. Likewise, the rectangle *ABCD* now measures the firm's total loss.

Why doesn't a firm that is losing money leave an industry entirely? A firm might operate at a loss *in the short run* because it expects to earn a profit in the future, when the price of its product increases or the cost of production falls, and because stopping production and later starting up again would be costly. In fact, a firm has two choices in the short run: It can produce some output, or it can stop producing temporarily. It will compare the profitability of producing with the profitability of not producing and choose the preferred outcome.

If the price of the product is greater than average total cost, this decision is easy because the firm will earn profits if it continues to produce but nothing if it stops producing. But suppose the price is *less* than average total cost but greater than average variable cost, as shown in Figure 8.4. If it continues to produce, the firm minimizes its losses at output $q^*$. Note that in Figure 8.4, because of the presence of fixed costs, average variable cost is less than average total cost and the firm is indeed losing money. Should the firm shut down and thereby eliminate its fixed costs? If it does shut down—closes its factories, fires its managers, and turns off the lights—it will avoid losses. But should the price increase in the future, re-opening the factories and hiring and training new managers could be quite costly, and the firm would regret its decision to shut down. Furthermore, if it stays in business over the long run, the firm would retain the flexibility to change the amount of capital that it uses and thereby reduce its average total cost. Thus, the firm is unlikely to shut down if it can at least cover its average variable cost.

What if the price of the product is below average variable cost? In this case, the firm should certainly stop producing, because it is losing money on every

> Remember from §7.1 that a fixed cost is an ongoing cost that does not change with the level of output but is eliminated if the firm shuts down.

unit it produces. Thus, the firm is likely to shut down and thereby eliminate its fixed as well as its variable costs, because its factories are idle anyway. In general, the following shut-down rule will apply:

> **Shut-Down Rule:** The firm should shut down if the price of the product is less than the average variable cost of production at the profit-maximizing output.

---

**EXAMPLE 8.2** The Short-Run Output Decision of an Aluminum Smelting Plant

How should the manager of an aluminum smelting plant determine the plant's profit-maximizing output? Recall from Example 7.3 (page 232) that the smelting plant's short-run marginal cost of production depends on whether it is running two or three shifts per day. As shown in Figure 8.5, marginal cost is $1140 per ton for output levels up to 600 tons per day and $1300 per ton for output levels between 600 and 900 tons per day.

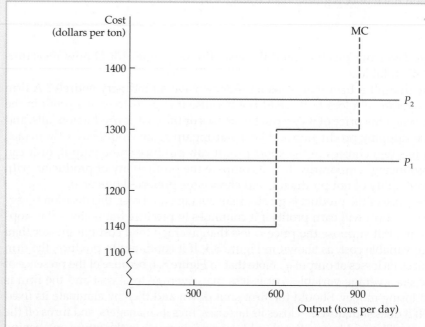

**FIGURE 8.5 The Short-Run Output of an Aluminum Smelting Plant**

In the short run, the plant should produce 600 tons per day if price is above $1140 per ton but less than $1300 per ton. If price is greater than $1300 per ton, it should run an overtime shift and produce 900 tons per day. If price drops below $1140 per ton, the firm should stop producing, but it should probably stay in business because the price may rise in the future.

Suppose that the price of aluminum is initially $P_1 = \$1250$ per ton. In that case, the profit-maximizing output is 600 tons; the firm can make a profit above its variable cost of $110 per ton by employing workers for two shifts a day. Running a third shift would involve overtime, and the price of the aluminum is insufficient to make the added production profitable. Suppose, however, that the price of aluminum were to increase to $P_2 = \$1360$ per ton. This price is greater than the $1300 marginal cost of the third shift, making it profitable to increase output to 900 tons per day.

Finally, suppose the price drops to only $1100 per ton. In this case, the firm should stop producing, but it should probably stay in business. By taking this step, it could resume producing in the future should the price increase.

---

**EXAMPLE 8.3**  **Some Cost Considerations for Managers**

The application of the rule that marginal revenue should equal marginal cost depends on a manager's ability to estimate marginal cost.[3] To obtain useful measures of cost, managers should keep three guidelines in mind.

First, except under limited circumstances, *average variable cost should not be used as a substitute for marginal cost*. When marginal and average variable cost are nearly constant, there is little difference between them. However, if both marginal and average cost are increasing sharply, the use of average variable cost can be misleading in deciding how much to produce. Suppose for example, that a company has the following cost information:

| | |
|---|---|
| Current output | 100 units per day, 80 of which are produced during the regular shift and 20 of which are produced during overtime |
| Materials cost | $8 per unit for all output |
| Labor cost | $30 per unit for the regular shift; $50 per unit for the overtime shift |

Let's calculate average variable cost and marginal cost for the first 80 units of output and then see how both cost measures change when we include the additional 20 units produced with overtime labor. For the first 80 units, average variable cost is simply the labor cost ($2400 = $30 per unit × 80 units) plus the materials cost ($640 = $8 per unit × 80 units) divided by the 80 units—($2400 + $640)/80 = $38 per unit. Because average variable cost is the same for each unit of output, marginal cost is also equal to $38 per unit.

When output increases to 100 units per day, both average variable cost and marginal cost change. The variable cost has now increased; it includes the additional materials cost of $160 (20 units × $8 per unit) and the additional labor cost of $1000 (20 units × $50 per unit). Average variable cost is therefore the total labor cost plus the materials cost ($2400 + $1000 + $640 + $160) divided by the 100 units of output, or $42 per unit.

What about marginal cost? While the materials cost per unit has remained unchanged at $8 per unit, the marginal cost of labor has now increased to $50 per unit, so that the marginal cost of each unit of overtime output is $58 per day.

---

[3]This example draws on the discussion of costs and managerial decision-making in Thomas Nagle and Reed Holden, *The Strategy and Tactics of Pricing*, 3rd ed. (Upper Saddle River, NJ: Prentice Hall, 2002), ch. 2.

Because marginal cost is higher than average variable cost, a manager who relies on average variable cost will produce too much.

Second, *a single item on a firm's accounting ledger may have two components, only one of which involves marginal cost.* Suppose that a manager is trying to cut back production. She reduces the number of hours that some employees work and lays off others. But the salary of an employee who is laid off may not be an accurate measure of the marginal cost of production when cuts are made. Union contracts, for example, often require the firm to pay laid-off employees part of their salaries. In this case, the marginal cost of increasing production is not the same as the savings in marginal cost when production is decreased. The savings is the labor cost after the required layoff salary has been subtracted.

Third, *all opportunity costs should be included in determining marginal cost.* Suppose a department store wants to sell children's furniture. Instead of building a new selling area, the manager decides to use part of the third floor, which had been used for appliances, for the furniture. The marginal cost of this space is the $90 per square foot per day in profit that would have been earned had the store continued to sell appliances there. This opportunity cost measure may be much greater than what the store actually paid for that part of the building.

These three guidelines can help a manager to measure marginal cost correctly. Failure to do so can cause production to be too high or too low and thereby reduce profit.

## 8.5 THE COMPETITIVE FIRM'S SHORT-RUN SUPPLY CURVE

A *supply curve* for a firm tells us how much output it will produce at every possible price. We have seen that competitive firms will increase output to the point at which price is equal to marginal cost, but will shut down if price is below average variable cost. Therefore, the firm's supply curve is *the portion of the marginal cost curve for which marginal cost is greater than average variable cost.*

Figure 8.6 illustrates the short-run supply curve. Note that for any $P$ greater than minimum AVC, the profit-maximizing output can be read directly from the graph. At a price $P_1$, for example, the quantity supplied will be $q_1$; and at $P_2$, it will be $q_2$. For $P$ less than (or equal to) minimum AVC, the profit-maximizing output is equal to zero. In Figure 8.6 the entire short-run supply curve consists of the crosshatched portion of the vertical axis plus the marginal cost curve above the point of minimum average variable cost.

Short-run supply curves for competitive firms slope upward for the same reason that marginal cost increases—the presence of diminishing marginal returns to one or more factors of production. As a result, an increase in the market price will induce those firms already in the market to increase the quantities they produce. The higher price not only makes the additional production profitable, but also increases the firm's *total* profit because it applies to all units that the firm produces.

> In §6.2, we explain that diminishing marginal returns occurs when each additional increase in an input results in a smaller and smaller increase in output.

### The Firm's Response to an Input Price Change

When the price of its product changes, the firm changes its output level to ensure that marginal cost of production remains equal to price. Often, however, the product price changes at the same time that the prices of *inputs* change.

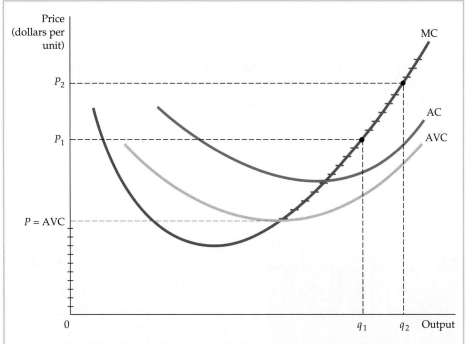

**FIGURE 8.6 The Short-Run Supply Curve for a Competitive Firm**

In the short run, the firm chooses its output so that marginal cost MC is equal to price as long as the firm covers its average variable cost. The short-run supply curve is given by the crosshatched portion of the marginal cost curve.

In this section we show how the firm's output decision changes in response to a change in the price of one of its inputs.

Figure 8.7 shows a firm's marginal cost curve that is initially given by $MC_1$ when the firm faces a price of $5 for its product. The firm maximizes profit by producing an output of $q_1$. Now suppose the price of one input increases.

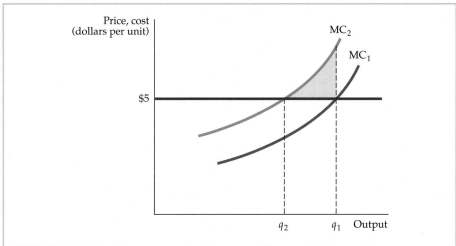

**FIGURE 8.7 The Response of a Firm to a Change in Input Price**

When the marginal cost of production for a firm increases (from $MC_1$ to $MC_2$), the level of output that maximizes profit falls (from $q_1$ to $q_2$).

Because it now costs more to produce each unit of output, this increase causes the marginal cost curve to shift upward from $MC_1$ to $MC_2$. The new profit-maximizing output is $q_2$, at which $P = MC_2$. Thus, the higher input price causes the firm to reduce its output.

If the firm had continued to produce $q_1$, it would have incurred a loss on the last unit of production. In fact, all production beyond $q_2$ would reduce profit. The shaded area in the figure gives the total savings to the firm (or equivalently, the reduction in lost profit) associated with the reduction in output from $q_1$ to $q_2$.

---

| EXAMPLE 8.4 | The Short-Run Production of Petroleum Products |
|---|---|

Suppose you are managing an oil refinery that converts crude oil into a particular mix of products, including gasoline, jet fuel, and residual fuel oil for home heating. Although plenty of crude oil is available, the amount that you refine depends on the capacity of the refinery and the cost of production. How much should you produce each day?[4]

Information about the refinery's marginal cost of production is essential for this decision. Figure 8.8 shows the short-run marginal cost curve (SMC). Marginal cost increases with output, but in a series of uneven segments rather than as a smooth curve. The increase occurs in segments because the refinery uses different processing units to turn crude oil into finished products. When a particular processing unit reaches capacity, output can be increased only by substituting a more expensive process. For example, gasoline can be produced from light crude oils rather inexpensively in a processing unit called a "thermal cracker." When this unit becomes full, additional gasoline can still be produced (from heavy as well as light crude oil), but only at a higher cost. In the case illustrated by Figure 8.8, the first capacity constraint comes into effect when production reaches about 9700 barrels a day. A second capacity constraint becomes important when production increases beyond 10,700 barrels a day.

Deciding how much output to produce now becomes relatively easy. Suppose that refined products can be sold for $23 per barrel. Because the marginal cost of production is close to $24 for the first unit of output, no crude oil should be run through the refinery when the price is $23. If, however, price is between $24 and $25, the refinery should produce 9700 barrels a day (filling the thermal cracker). Finally, if the price is above $25, the more expensive refining unit should be used and production expanded toward 10,700 barrels a day.

Because the cost function rises in steps, you know that your production decisions need not change much in response to *small* changes in price. You will typically use sufficient crude oil to fill the appropriate processing unit until price increases (or decreases) substantially. In that case, you need simply calculate whether the increased price warrants using an additional, more expensive processing unit.

---

[4]This example is based on James M. Griffin, "The Process Analysis Alternative to Statistical Cost Functions: An Application to Petroleum Refining," *American Economic Review* 62 (1972): 46–56. The numbers have been updated and applied to a particular refinery.

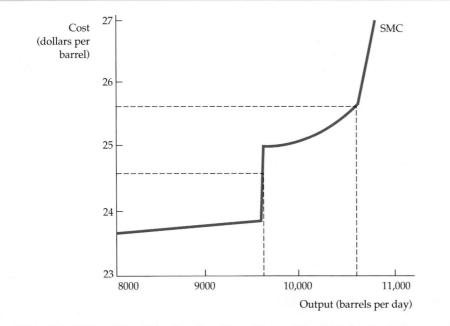

**FIGURE 8.8 The Short-Run Production of Petroleum Products**

As the refinery shifts from one processing unit to another, the marginal cost of producing petroleum products from crude oil increases sharply at several levels of output. As a result, the output level can be insensitive to some changes in price but very sensitive to others.

## 8.6 THE SHORT-RUN MARKET SUPPLY CURVE

The *short-run market supply curve* shows the amount of output that the industry will produce in the short run for every possible price. The industry's output is the sum of the quantities supplied by all of its individual firms. Therefore, the market supply curve can be obtained by adding the supply curves of each of these firms. Figure 8.9 shows how this is done when there are only three firms, all of which have different short-run production costs. Each firm's marginal cost curve is drawn only for the portion that lies above its average variable cost curve. (We have shown only three firms to keep the graph simple, but the same analysis applies when there are many firms.)

At any price below $P_1$, the industry will produce no output because $P_1$ is the minimum average variable cost of the lowest-cost firm. Between $P_1$ and $P_2$, only firm 3 will produce. The industry supply curve, therefore, will be identical to that portion of firm 3's marginal cost curve $MC_3$. At price $P_2$, the industry supply will be the sum of the quantity supplied by all three firms. Firm 1 supplies 2 units, firm 2 supplies 5 units, and firm 3 supplies 8 units. Industry supply is thus 15 units. At price $P_3$, firm 1 supplies 4 units, firm 2 supplies 7 units, and firm 3 supplies 10 units; the industry supplies 21 units. Note that the industry supply curve is upward sloping but has a kink at price $P_2$, the lowest price at which all three firms produce. With many firms in the market, however, the kink becomes unimportant. Thus we usually draw industry supply as a smooth, upward-sloping curve.

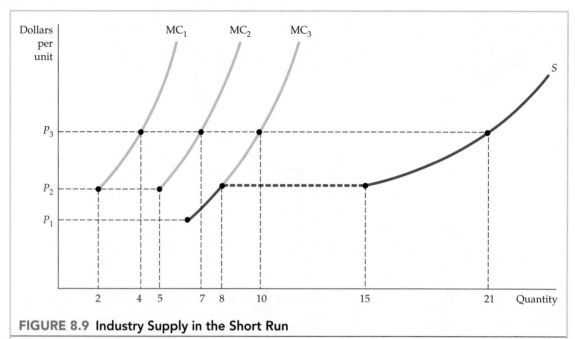

**FIGURE 8.9 Industry Supply in the Short Run**

The short-run industry supply curve is the summation of the supply curves of the individual firms. Because the third firm has a lower average variable cost curve than the first two firms, the market supply curve $S$ begins at price $P_1$ and follows the marginal cost curve of the third firm $MC_3$ until price equals $P_2$, when there is a kink. For $P_2$ and all prices above it, the industry quantity supplied is the sum of the quantities supplied by each of the three firms.

## Elasticity of Market Supply

Unfortunately, finding the industry supply curve is not always as simple as adding up a set of individual supply curves. As price rises, all firms in the industry expand their output. This additional output increases the demand for inputs to production and may lead to higher input prices. As we saw in Figure 8.7, increasing input prices shifts a firm's marginal cost curve upward. For example, an increased demand for beef could also increase demand for corn and soybeans (which are used to feed cattle) and thereby cause the prices of these crops to rise. In turn, higher input prices will cause firms' marginal cost curves to shift upward. This increase lowers each firm's output choice (for any given market price) and causes the industry supply curve to be less responsive to changes in output price than it would otherwise be.

The price elasticity of market supply measures the sensitivity of industry output to market price. The elasticity of supply $E_s$ is the percentage change in quantity supplied $Q$ in response to a 1-percent change in price $P$:

> In §2.4, we define the elasticity of supply as the percentage change in quantity supplied resulting from a 1-percent increase in price.

$$E_s = (\Delta Q/Q)/(\Delta P/P)$$

Because marginal cost curves are upward sloping, the short-run elasticity of supply is always positive. When marginal cost increases rapidly in response to increases in output, the elasticity of supply is low. In the short run, firms are capacity-constrained and find it costly to increase output. But when marginal cost increases slowly in response to increases in output, supply is relatively elastic; in this case, a small price increase induces firms to produce much more.

At one extreme is the case of *perfectly inelastic supply*, which arises when the industry's plant and equipment are so fully utilized that greater output can be achieved only if new plants are built (as they will be in the long run). At the other extreme is the case of *perfectly elastic supply*, which arises when marginal cost is constant.

### EXAMPLE 8.5    The Short-Run World Supply of Copper

In the short run, the shape of the market supply curve for a mineral such as copper depends on how the cost of mining varies within and among the world's major producers. Costs of mining, smelting, and refining copper differ because of differences in labor and transportation costs and because of differences in the copper content of the ore. Table 8.1 summarizes some of the relevant cost and production data for the nine largest copper-producing nations.[5] Remember that in, the short run, because the costs of building mines, smelters, and refineries are taken as sunk, the marginal cost numbers in Table 8.1 reflect the costs of operating (but not building) these facilities.

These data can be used to plot the short-run world supply curve for copper. It is a short-run curve because it takes the existing mines and refineries as fixed. Figure 8.10 shows how the curve is constructed for the nine countries listed in the table. (The curve is incomplete because there are a few smaller and higher-cost producers that we have not included.) Note that the curve in Figure 8.10 is an approximation. The marginal cost number for each country

| TABLE 8.1 | The World Copper Industry (2006) | |
|---|---|---|
| **Country** | **Annual Production (Thousand Metric Tons)** | **Marginal Cost (Dollars Per Pound)** |
| Australia | 950 | 1.15 |
| Canada | 600 | 1.30 |
| Chile | 5,400 | 0.80 |
| Indonesia | 800 | 0.90 |
| Peru | 1050 | 0.85 |
| Poland | 530 | 1.20 |
| Russia | 720 | 0.65 |
| US | 1220 | 0.85 |
| Zambia | 540 | 0.75 |

*Source for Annual Production Data:* U.S. Geological Survey, Mineral Commodity Summaries, January 2007.
**http://minerals.usgs.gov/minerals/pubs/mcs/2007/mcs2007.pdf.**
*Source for Marginal Cost Data:* Charles River Associates' Estimates.

---

[5]Our thanks to James Burrows of Charles River Associates, Inc., who was kind enough to provide data on marginal production cost. Updated data and related information are available on the Web at: **http://minerals.usgs.gov/minerals**.

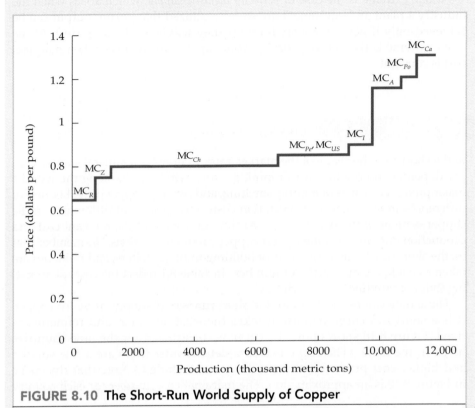

**FIGURE 8.10 The Short-Run World Supply of Copper**

The supply curve for world copper is obtained by summing the marginal cost curves for each of the major copper-producing countries. The supply curve slopes upward because the marginal cost of production ranges from a low of 65 cents in Russia to a high of $1.30 in Canada.

is an average for all copper producers in that country, and we are assuming that marginal cost and average cost are approximately the same. In the United States, for example, some producers have a marginal cost greater than 85 cents and some less.

The lowest-cost copper is mined in Russia, where the marginal cost of refined copper is roughly 65 cents per pound. The line segment labeled $MC_R$ represents the marginal cost curve for Russia. The curve is horizontal until the total capacity for mining and refining copper in Russia is reached. (That point is reached at a production level of 720 thousand metric tons per year.) Line segment $MC_Z$ represents the marginal cost curve for Zambia, segment $MC_{Ch}$ the marginal cost curve for Chile, and so on.

The world supply curve is obtained by summing each nation's supply curve horizontally. As can be seen from the figure, the elasticity of supply depends on the price of copper. At relatively low prices, such as 65 to 90 cents per pound, the curve is quite elastic because small price increases lead to large increases in the quantity of copper supplied. At higher prices—say, above $1.20 per pound— the curve becomes more inelastic because, at those prices, most producers would be operating close to or at capacity.

## Producer Surplus in the Short Run

In Chapter 4, we measured *consumer surplus* as the difference between the maximum that a person would pay for an item and its market price. An analogous concept applies to firms. If marginal cost is rising, the price of the product is greater than marginal cost for every unit produced except the last one. As a result, firms earn a surplus on all but the last unit of output. The **producer surplus** of a firm is the sum over all units produced of the differences between the market price of the good and the marginal cost of production. Just as consumer surplus measures the area below an individual's demand curve and above the market price of the product, producer surplus measures the area above a producer's supply curve and below the market price.

Figure 8.11 illustrates short-run producer surplus for a firm. The profit-maximizing output is $q^*$, where $P = MC$. The surplus that the producer obtains from selling each unit is the difference between the price and the marginal cost of producing the unit. The producer surplus is then the sum of these "unit surpluses" over all units that the firm produces. It is given by the yellow area under the firm's horizontal demand curve and above its marginal cost curve, from zero output to the profit-maximizing output $q^*$.

When we add the marginal cost of producing each level of output from 0 to $q^*$, we find that the sum is the total variable cost of producing $q^*$. Marginal cost reflects increments to cost associated with increases in output; because fixed cost does not vary with output, the sum of all marginal costs must equal the sum of the firm's variable costs.[6] Thus producer surplus can alternatively be defined as *the difference between the firm's revenue and its total variable cost.*

> For a review of consumer surplus, see §4.4, where it is defined as the difference between what a consumer is willing to pay for a good and what the consumer actually pays when buying it.

• **producer surplus** Sum over all units produced by a firm of differences between the market price of a good and the marginal cost of production.

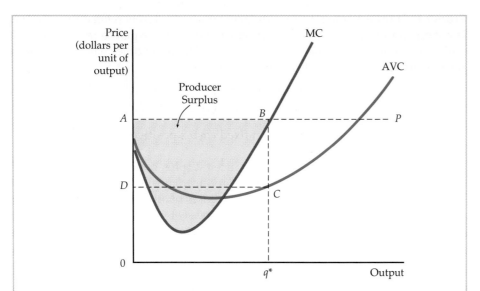

**FIGURE 8.11 Producer Surplus for a Firm**

The producer surplus for a firm is measured by the yellow area below the market price and above the marginal cost curve, between outputs 0 and $q^*$, the profit-maximizing output. Alternatively, it is equal to rectangle $ABCD$ because the sum of all marginal costs up to $q^*$ is equal to the variable costs of producing $q^*$.

---

[6]The area under the marginal cost curve from 0 to $q^*$ is $TC(q^*) - TC(0) = TC - FC = VC$.

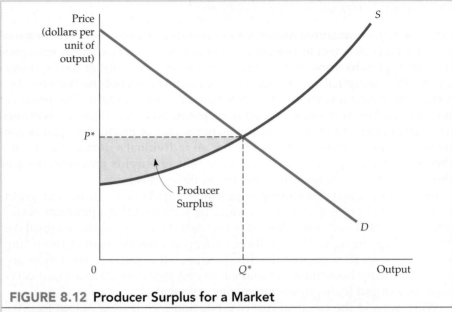

**FIGURE 8.12 Producer Surplus for a Market**

The producer surplus for a market is the area below the market price and above the market supply curve, between 0 and output $Q^*$.

In Figure 8.11, producer surplus is also given by the rectangle *ABCD*, which equals revenue ($0ABq^*$) minus variable cost ($0DCq^*$).

**Producer Surplus versus Profit** Producer surplus is closely related to profit but is not equal to it. In the short run, producer surplus is equal to revenue minus variable cost, which is *variable profit*. Total profit, on the other hand, is equal to revenue minus *all* costs, both variable and fixed:

$$\text{Producer surplus} = PS = R - VC$$
$$\text{Profit} = \pi = R - VC - FC$$

It follows that in the short run, when fixed cost is positive, producer surplus is greater than profit.

The extent to which firms enjoy producer surplus depends on their costs of production. Higher-cost firms have less producer surplus and lower-cost firms have more. By adding up the producer surpluses of all firms, we can determine the producer surplus for a market. This can be seen in Figure 8.12. The market supply curve begins at the vertical axis at a point representing the average variable cost of the lowest-cost firm in the market. Producer surplus is the area that lies below the market price of the product and above the supply curve between the output levels 0 and $Q^*$.

## 8.7 CHOOSING OUTPUT IN THE LONG RUN

In the short run, one or more of the firm's inputs are fixed. Depending on the time available, this may limit the flexibility of the firm to adapt its production process to new technological developments, or to increase or decrease its scale of operation as economic conditions change. In contrast, in the long run, a firm can alter all its inputs, including plant size. It can decide to shut down (i.e., to *exit* the industry) or to begin producing a product for the first time (i.e., to *enter* an industry). Because we are concerned here with competitive markets, we allow for *free entry* and *free exit*. In other words, we are assuming that firms may enter or exit without legal restriction or any special costs associated with entry. (Recall from Section 8.1 that this is one of the key assumptions underlying perfect competition.) After analyzing the long-run output decision of a profit-maximizing firm in a competitive market, we discuss the nature of competitive equilibrium in the long run. We also discuss the relationship between entry and exit, and economic and accounting profits.

## Long-Run Profit Maximization

Figure 8.13 shows how a competitive firm makes its long-run, profit-maximizing output decision. As in the short run, the firm faces a horizontal demand curve. (In Figure 8.13 the firm takes the market price of $40 as given.) Its short-run average (total) cost curve SAC and short-run marginal cost curve SMC are low enough for the firm to make a positive profit, given by rectangle $ABCD$, by producing an output of $q_1$, where SMC = $P$ = MR. The long-run average cost curve LAC reflects the presence of economies of scale up to output level $q_2$ and diseconomies of scale at higher output levels. The long-run marginal cost curve LMC cuts the long-run average cost from below at $q_2$, the point of minimum long-run average cost.

> In §7.4, we explain that economies of scale arise when a firm can double its output for less than twice the cost.

If the firm believes that the market price will remain at $40, it will want to increase the size of its plant to produce at output $q_3$, at which its *long-run* marginal cost equals the $40 price. When this expansion is complete, the profit margin will increase from $AB$ to $EF$, and total profit will increase from $ABCD$ to $EFGD$.

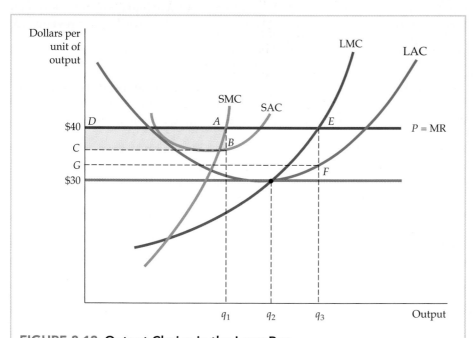

**FIGURE 8.13 Output Choice in the Long Run**

The firm maximizes its profit by choosing the output at which price equals long-run marginal cost LMC. In the diagram, the firm increases its profit from $ABCD$ to $EFGD$ by increasing its output in the long run.

Output $q_3$ is profit-maximizing because at any lower output (say, $q_2$), the marginal revenue from additional production is greater than the marginal cost. Expansion is, therefore, desirable. But at any output greater than $q_3$, marginal cost is greater than marginal revenue. Additional production would therefore reduce profit. In summary, *the long-run output of a profit-maximizing competitive firm is the point at which long-run marginal cost equals the price.*

Note that the higher the market price, the higher the profit that the firm can earn. Correspondingly, as the price of the product falls from $40 to $30, the profit also falls. At a price of $30, the firm's profit-maximizing output is $q_2$, the point of long-run minimum average cost. In this case, because $P = $ ATC, the firm earns zero economic profit.

## Long-Run Competitive Equilibrium

For an equilibrium to arise in the long run, certain economic conditions must prevail. Firms in the market must have no desire to withdraw at the same time that no firms outside the market wish to enter. But what is the exact relationship between profitability, entry, and long-run competitive equilibrium? We can see the answer by relating economic profit to the incentive to enter and exit a market.

**Accounting Profit and Economic Profit** As we saw in Chapter 7, it is important to distinguish between accounting profit and economic profit. Accounting profit is measured by the difference between the firm's revenues and its cash flows for labor, raw materials, and interest plus depreciation expenses. Economic profit takes into account opportunity costs. One such opportunity cost is the return to the firm's owners if their capital were used elsewhere. Suppose, for example, that the firm uses labor and capital inputs; its capital equipment has been purchased. Accounting profit will equal revenues $R$ minus labor cost $wL$, which is positive. Economic profit $\pi$, however, equals revenues $R$ minus labor cost $wL$ minus the capital cost, $rK$:

$$\pi = R - wL - rK$$

As we explained in Chapter 7, the correct measure of capital cost is the user cost of capital, which is the annual return that the firm could earn by investing its money elsewhere instead of purchasing capital, plus the annual depreciation on the capital.

**Zero Economic Profit** When a firm goes into a business, it does so in the expectation that it will earn a return on its investment. A **zero economic profit** means that the firm is earning a *normal*—i.e., competitive—return on that investment. This normal return, which is part of the user cost of capital, is the firm's opportunity cost of using its money to buy capital rather than investing it elsewhere. Thus, *a firm earning zero economic profit is doing as well by investing its money in capital as it could by investing elsewhere*—it is earning a competitive return on its money. Such a firm, therefore, is performing adequately and should stay in business. (A firm earning a *negative* economic profit, however, should consider going out of business if it does not expect to improve its financial picture.)

As we will see, in competitive markets economic profit becomes zero in the long run. Zero economic profit signifies not that firms are performing poorly, but rather that the industry is competitive.

**Entry and Exit** Figure 8.13 shows how a $40 price induces a firm to increase output and realize a positive profit. Because profit is calculated after subtracting the opportunity cost of capital, a positive profit means an unusually high return

> • **zero economic profit** A firm is earning a normal return on its investment—i.e., it is doing as well as it could by investing its money elsewhere.

on a financial investment, which can be earned by entering a profitable industry. This high return causes investors to direct resources away from other industries and into this one—there will be *entry* into the market. Eventually the increased production associated with new entry causes the market supply curve to shift to the right. As a result, market output increases and the market price of the product falls.[7] Figure 8.14 illustrates this. In part (b) of the figure, the supply curve has shifted from $S_1$ to $S_2$, causing the price to fall from $P_1$ ($40) to $P_2$ ($30). In part (a), which applies to a single firm, the long-run average cost curve is tangent to the horizontal price line at output $q_2$.

A similar story would apply to exit. Suppose that each firm's minimum long-run average cost remains $30 but the market price falls to $20. Firms will lose money, causing *exit* from the market. Eventually the decreased production will cause the market supply curve to shift to the left. Market output will decrease and the price of the product will rise until an equilibrium is reached at a break-even price of $30. To summarize:

> In a market with entry and exit, a firm enters when it can earn a positive long-run profit and exits when it faces the prospect of a long-run loss.

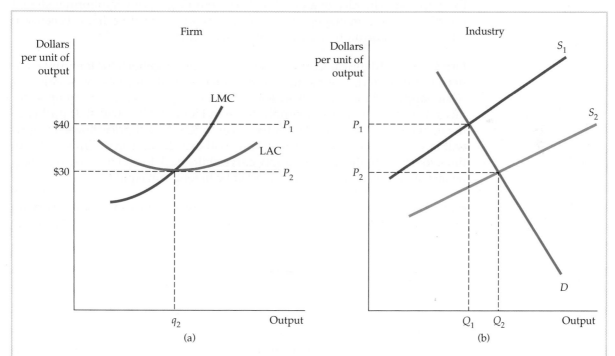

**FIGURE 8.14 Long-Run Competitive Equilibrium**

Initially the long-run equilibrium price of a product is $40 per unit, shown in (b) as the intersection of demand curve $D$ and supply curve $S_1$. In (a) we see that firms earn positive profits because long-run average cost reaches a minimum of $30 (at $q_2$). Positive profit encourages entry of new firms and causes a shift to the right in the supply curve to $S_2$, as shown in **(b)**. The long-run equilibrium occurs at a price of $30, as shown in **(a)**, where each firm earns zero profit and there is no incentive to enter or exit the industry.

---

[7]We discuss why the long-run supply curve might be upward sloping in the next section.

• **long-run competitive equilibrium** All firms in an industry are maximizing profit, no firm has an incentive to enter or exit, and price is such that quantity supplied equals quantity demanded.

When a firm earns zero economic profit, it has no incentive to exit the industry. Likewise, other firms have no special incentive to enter. A **long-run competitive equilibrium** occurs when three conditions hold:

1. All firms in the industry are maximizing profit.

2. No firm has an incentive either to enter or exit the industry because all firms are earning zero economic profit.

3. The price of the product is such that the quantity supplied by the industry is equal to the quantity demanded by consumers.

The dynamic process that leads to long-run equilibrium may seem puzzling. Firms enter the market because they hope to earn a profit, and likewise they exit because of economic losses. In long-run equilibrium, however, firms earn zero economic profit. Why does a firm enter a market knowing that it will eventually earn zero profit? The answer is that zero economic profit represents a competitive return for the firm's investment of financial capital. With zero economic profit, the firm has no incentive to go elsewhere because it cannot do better financially by doing so. If the firm happens to enter a market sufficiently early to enjoy an economic profit in the short run, so much the better. Similarly, if a firm exits an unprofitable market quickly, it can save its investors money. Thus the concept of long-run equilibrium tells us the direction that a firm's behavior is likely to take. The idea of an eventual zero-profit, long-run equilibrium should not discourage a manager—it should be seen in a positive light, because it reflects the opportunity to earn a competitive return.

**Firms Having Identical Costs** To see why all the conditions for long-run equilibrium must hold, assume that all firms have identical costs. Now consider what happens if too many firms enter the industry in response to an opportunity for profit. The industry supply curve in Figure 8.14(b) will shift further to the right, and price will fall below $30—say, to $25. At that price, however, firms will lose money. As a result, some firms will exit the industry. Firms will continue to exit until the market supply curve shifts back to $S_2$. Only when there is no incentive to exit or enter can a market be in long-run equilibrium.

**Firms Having Different Costs** Now suppose that all firms in the industry do not have identical cost curves. Perhaps one firm has a patent that lets it produce at a lower average cost than all the others. In that case, it is consistent with long-run equilibrium for that firm to earn a greater *accounting* profit and to enjoy a higher producer surplus than other firms. As long as other investors and firms cannot acquire the patent that lowers costs, they have no incentive to enter the industry. Conversely, as long as the process is particular to this product and this industry, the fortunate firm has no incentive to exit the industry.

The distinction between accounting profit and economic profit is important here. If the patent is profitable, other firms in the industry will pay to use it (or attempt to buy the entire firm to acquire it). The increased value of the patent thus represents an opportunity cost to the firm that holds it. It could sell the rights to the patent rather than use it. If all firms are equally efficient otherwise, the *economic* profit of the firm falls to zero. However, if the firm with the patent is more efficient than other firms, then it will be earning a positive profit. But if the patent holder is otherwise less efficient, it should sell off the patent and exit the industry.

**The Opportunity Cost of Land** There are other instances in which firms earning positive accounting profit may be earning zero economic profit. Suppose, for example, that a clothing store happens to be located near a large shopping center. The additional flow of customers can substantially increase the store's accounting profit because the cost of the land is based on its historical cost. However, as far as economic profit is concerned, the cost of the land should reflect its opportunity cost, which in this case is the current market value of the land. When the opportunity cost of land is included, the profitability of the clothing store is no higher than that of its competitors.

Thus the condition that economic profit be zero is essential for the market to be in long-run equilibrium. By definition, positive economic profit represents an opportunity for investors and an incentive to enter an industry. Positive accounting profit, however, may signal that firms already in the industry possess valuable assets, skills, or ideas, which will not necessarily encourage entry.

## Economic Rent

We have seen that some firms earn higher accounting profit than others because they have access to factors of production that are in limited supply; these might include land and natural resources, entrepreneurial skill, or other creative talent. In these situations, what makes economic profit zero in the long run is the willingness of other firms to use the factors of production that are in limited supply. The positive accounting profits are therefore translated into *economic rent* that is earned by the scarce factors. **Economic rent** is what firms are willing to pay for an input less the minimum amount necessary to buy it. In competitive markets, in both the short and the long run, economic rent is often positive even though profit is zero.

● **economic rent** Amount that firms are willing to pay for an input less the minimum amount necessary to obtain it.

For example, suppose that two firms in an industry own their land outright; thus the minimum cost of obtaining the land is zero. One firm, however, is located on a river and can ship its products for $10,000 a year less than the other firm, which is inland. In this case, the $10,000 higher profit of the first firm is due to the $10,000 per year economic rent associated with its river location. The rent is created because the land along the river is valuable and other firms would be willing to pay for it. Eventually, the competition for this specialized factor of production will increase the value of that factor to $10,000. Land rent—the difference between $10,000 and the zero cost of obtaining the land—is also $10,000. Note that while the economic rent has increased, the economic profit of the firm on the river has become zero.

The presence of economic rent explains why there are some markets in which firms cannot enter in response to profit opportunities. In those markets, the supply of one or more inputs is fixed, one or more firms earn economic rents, and all firms enjoy zero economic profit. Zero economic profit tells a firm that it should remain in a market only if it is at least as efficient in production as other firms. It also tells possible entrants to the market that entry will be profitable only if they can produce more efficiently than firms already in the market.

## Producer Surplus in the Long Run

Suppose that a firm is earning a positive accounting profit but that there is no incentive for other firms to enter or exit the industry. This profit must reflect economic rent. How then does rent relate to producer surplus? To begin with, note that while economic rent applies to factor inputs, producer surplus applies to outputs. Note also that producer surplus measures the difference between the market price that a producer receives and the marginal cost of production.

Thus, in the long run, in a competitive market, *the producer surplus that a firm earns on the output that it sells consists of the economic rent that it enjoys from all its scarce inputs.*[8]

Let's say, for example, that a baseball team has a franchise allowing it to operate in a particular city. Suppose also that the only alternative location for the team is a city in which it will generate substantially lower revenues. The team will therefore earn an economic rent associated with its current location. This rent will reflect the difference between what the firm would be willing to pay for its current location and the amount needed to locate in the alternative city. The firm will also be earning a producer surplus associated with the sale of baseball tickets and other franchise items at its current location. This surplus will reflect all economic rents, including those rents associated with the firm's other factor inputs (the stadium and the players).

Figure 8.15 shows that firms earning economic rent earn the same economic profit as firms that do not earn rent. Part (a) shows the economic profit of a baseball team located in a moderate-sized city. The average price of a ticket is $7, and costs are such that the team earns zero economic profit. Part (b) shows the profit of a team that has the same cost curves even though it is located in a larger city. Because more people want to see baseball games, the latter team can sell tickets for $10 apiece and thereby earn an accounting profit of $2.80 above its average cost of $7.20 on each ticket. However, the rent associated with the more desirable location represents a cost to the firm—an opportunity cost—because it could sell its franchise to another team. As a result, the economic profit in the larger city is also zero.

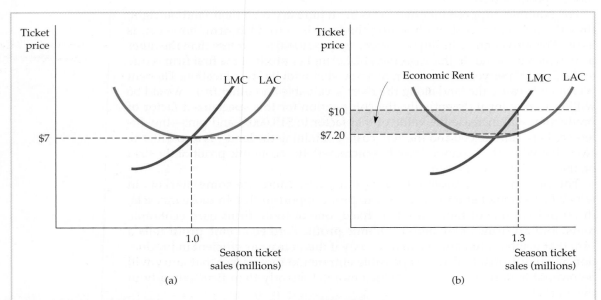

(a)  (b)

**FIGURE 8.15 Firms Earn Zero Profit in Long-Run Equilibrium**

In long-run equilibrium, all firms earn zero economic profit. In **(a)**, a baseball team in a moderate-sized city sells enough tickets so that price ($7) is equal to marginal and average cost. In **(b)**, the demand is greater, so a $10 price can be charged. The team increases sales to the point at which the average cost of production plus the average economic rent is equal to the ticket price. When the opportunity cost associated with owning the franchise is taken into account, the team earns zero economic profit.

---

[8]In a noncompetitive market, producer surplus will reflect economic profit as well as economic rent.

## 8.8 THE INDUSTRY'S LONG-RUN SUPPLY CURVE

In our analysis of short-run supply, we first derived the firm's supply curve and then showed how the summation of individual firms' supply curves generated a market supply curve. We cannot, however, analyze long-run supply in the same way: In the long run, firms enter and exit markets as the market price changes. This makes it impossible to sum up supply curves—we do not know which firms' supplies to add up in order to get market totals.

The shape of the long-run supply curve depends on the extent to which increases and decreases in industry output affect the prices that firms must pay for inputs into the production process. In cases in which there are economies of scale in production or cost savings associated with the purchase of large volumes of inputs, input prices will decline as output increases. In cases where diseconomies of scale are present, input prices may increase with output. The third possibility is that input costs may not change with output. In any of these cases, to determine long-run supply, we assume that all firms have access to the available production technology. Output is increased by using more inputs, not by invention. We also assume that the conditions underlying the market for inputs to production do not change when the industry expands or contracts. For example, an increased demand for labor does not increase a union's ability to negotiate a better wage contract for its workers.

In our analysis of long-run supply, it will be useful to distinguish among three types of industries: *constant cost, increasing cost,* and *decreasing cost.*

### Constant-Cost Industry

Figure 8.16 shows the derivation of the long-run supply curve for a **constant-cost industry**. A firm's output choice is given in (a), while industry output is shown in (b). Assume that the industry is initially in equilibrium at the intersection of market demand curve $D_1$ and short-run market supply curve $S_1$. Point $A$ at the intersection of demand and supply is on the long-run supply curve $S_L$ because it tells us that the industry will produce $Q_1$ units of output when the long-run equilibrium price is $P_1$.

To obtain other points on the long-run supply curve, suppose the market demand for the product unexpectedly increases (say, because of a reduction in personal income taxes). A typical firm is initially producing at an output of $q_1$, where $P_1$ is equal to long-run marginal cost and long-run average cost. But because the firm is also in short-run equilibrium, price also equals short-run marginal cost. Suppose that the tax cut shifts the market demand curve from $D_1$ to $D_2$. Demand curve $D_2$ intersects supply curve $S_1$ at $C$. As a result, price increases from $P_1$ to $P_2$.

Part (a) of Figure 8.16 shows how this price increase affects a typical firm in the industry. When the price increases to $P_2$, the firm follows its short-run marginal cost curve and increases output to $q_2$. This output choice maximizes profit because it satisfies the condition that price equal short-run marginal cost. If every firm responds this way, each will be earning a positive profit in short-run equilibrium. This profit will be attractive to investors and will cause existing firms to expand operations and new firms to enter the market.

As a result, in Figure 8.16(b) the short-run supply curve shifts to the right from $S_1$ to $S_2$. This shift causes the market to move to a new long-run equilibrium at the intersection of $D_2$ and $S_2$. For this intersection to be a long-run equilibrium, output must expand enough so that firms are earning zero profit and the incentive to enter or exit the industry disappears.

• **constant-cost industry** Industry whose long-run supply curve is horizontal.

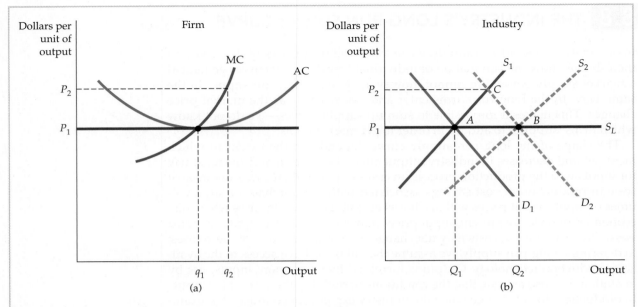

**FIGURE 8.16** **Long-Run Supply in a Constant-Cost Industry**

In **(b)**, the long-run supply curve in a constant-cost industry is a horizontal line $S_L$. When demand increases, initially causing a price rise (represented by a move from point $A$ to point $C$), the firm initially increases its output from $q_1$ to $q_2$, as shown in **(a)**. But the entry of new firms causes a shift to the right in industry supply. Because input prices are unaffected by the increased output of the industry, entry occurs until the original price is obtained (at point $B$ in **(b)**).

In a constant-cost industry, the additional inputs necessary to produce higher output can be purchased without an increase in per-unit price. This might happen, for example, if unskilled labor is a major input in production, and the market wage of unskilled labor is unaffected by the increase in the demand for labor. Because the prices of inputs have not changed, firms' cost curves are also unchanged; the new equilibrium must be at a point such as $B$ in Figure 8.16(b), at which price is equal to $P_1$, the original price before the unexpected increase in demand occurred.

*The long-run supply curve for a constant-cost industry is, therefore, a horizontal line at a price that is equal to the long-run minimum average cost of production.* At any higher price, there would be positive profit, increased entry, increased short-run supply, and thus downward pressure on price. Remember that in a constant-cost industry, input prices do not change when conditions change in the output market. Constant-cost industries can have horizontal long-run average cost curves.

## Increasing-Cost Industry

• **increasing-cost industry**
Industry whose long-run supply curve is upward sloping.

In an **increasing-cost industry** the prices of some or all inputs to production increase as the industry expands and the demand for the inputs grows. Diseconomies of scale in the production of one or more inputs may be the explanation. Suppose, for example, that the industry uses skilled labor, which becomes in short supply as the demand for it increases. Or, if a firm requires mineral resources that are available only on certain types of land, the cost of land as an input increases with output. Figure 8.17 shows the derivation of

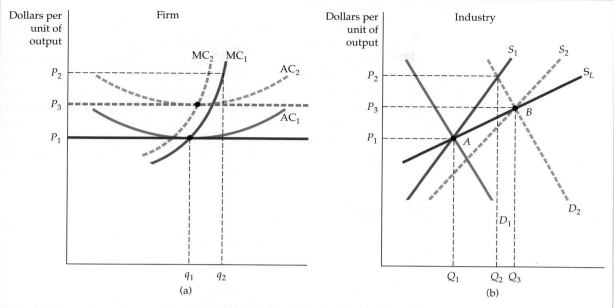

**FIGURE 8.17 Long-Run Supply in an Increasing-Cost Industry**

In **(b)**, the long-run supply curve in an increasing-cost industry is an upward-sloping curve $S_L$. When demand increases, initially causing a price rise, the firms increase their output from $q_1$ to $q_2$ in **(a)**. In that case, the entry of new firms causes a shift to the right in supply from $S_1$ to $S_2$. Because input prices increase as a result, the new long-run equilibrium occurs at a higher price than the initial equilibrium.

long-run supply, which is similar to the previous constant-cost derivation. The industry is initially in equilibrium at $A$ in part (b). When the demand curve unexpectedly shifts from $D_1$ to $D_2$, the price of the product increases in the short run to $P_2$, and industry output increases from $Q_1$ to $Q_2$. A typical firm, as shown in part (a), increases its output from $q_1$ to $q_2$ in response to the higher price by moving along its short-run marginal cost curve. The higher profit earned by this and other firms induces new firms to enter the industry.

As new firms enter and output expands, increased demand for inputs causes some or all input prices to increase. The short-run market supply curve shifts to the right as before, though not as much, and the new equilibrium at $B$ results in a price $P_3$ that is higher than the initial price $P_1$. Because the higher input prices raise the firms' short-run and long-run cost curves, the higher market price is needed to ensure that firms earn zero profit in long-run equilibrium. Figure 8.17(a) illustrates this. The average cost curve shifts up from $AC_1$ to $AC_2$, while the marginal cost curve shifts to the left, from $MC_1$ to $MC_2$. The new long-run equilibrium price $P_3$ is equal to the new minimum average cost. As in the constant-cost case, the higher short-run profit caused by the initial increase in demand disappears in the long run as firms increase output and input costs rise.

The new equilibrium at $B$ in Figure 8.17(b) is, therefore, on the long-run supply curve for the industry. *In an increasing-cost industry, the long-run industry supply curve is upward sloping.* The industry produces more output, but only at the higher price needed to compensate for the increase in input costs. The term "increasing cost" refers to the upward shift in the firms' long-run average cost curves, not to the positive slope of the cost curve itself.

## Decreasing-Cost Industry

The industry supply curve can also be downward sloping. In this case, the unexpected increase in demand causes industry output to expand as before. But as the industry grows larger, it can take advantage of its size to obtain some of its inputs more cheaply. For example, a larger industry may allow for an improved transportation system or for a better, less expensive financial network. In this case, firms' average cost curves shift downward (even if they do not enjoy economies of scale), and the market price of the product falls. The lower market price and lower average cost of production induce a new long-run equilibrium with more firms, more output, and a lower price. Therefore, in a **decreasing-cost industry**, the long-run supply curve for the industry is downward sloping.

> • **decreasing-cost industry**
> Industry whose long-run
> supply curve is downward
> sloping.

---

| **EXAMPLE 8.6** | Constant-, Increasing-, and Decreasing-Cost Industries: Coffee, Oil, and Automobiles |
|---|---|

As you have progressed through this book, you have been introduced to industries that have constant, increasing, and decreasing long-run costs. Let's look back at some of these industries, beginning with one that has constant long-run costs. In Example 2.7 (page 46), we saw that the supply of coffee is extremely elastic in the long run (see Figure 2.18c—page 48). The reason is that land for growing coffee is widely available and the costs of planting and caring for trees remains constant as the volume of coffee produced grows. Thus, coffee is a constant-cost industry.

Now consider the case of an increasing-cost industry. We explained in Example 2.9 (page 54) that the oil industry is an increasing cost industry with an upward-sloping long-run supply curve (see Figure 2.23b page 57). Why are costs increasing? Because there is a limited availability of easily accessible, large-volume oil fields. Consequently, as oil companies increase output, they are forced to obtain oil from increasingly expensive fields.

Finally, a decreasing-cost industry. We discussed the demand for automobiles in Examples 3.1 (page 77) and 3.3 (page 89), but what about supply? In the automobile industry, certain cost advantages arise because inputs can be acquired more cheaply as the volume of production increases. Indeed, the major automobile manufacturers—such as General Motors, Toyota, Ford, and DaimlerChrysler—acquire batteries, engines, brake systems, and other key inputs from firms that specialize in producing those inputs efficiently. As a result, the average cost of automobile production decreases as the volume of production increases.

---

## The Effects of a Tax

In Chapter 7, we saw that a tax on one of a firm's inputs (in the form of an effluent fee) creates an incentive for the firm to change the way it uses inputs in its production process. Now we consider ways in which a firm responds to a tax on its output. To simplify the analysis, assume that the firm uses a fixed-proportions production technology. If it's a polluter, the output tax might encourage the firm to reduce its output, and therefore its effluent, or it might be imposed merely to raise revenue.

First, suppose the output tax is imposed only on this firm and thus does not affect the market price of the product. We will see that the tax on output encourages the firm to reduce its output. Figure 8.18 shows the relevant short-run cost

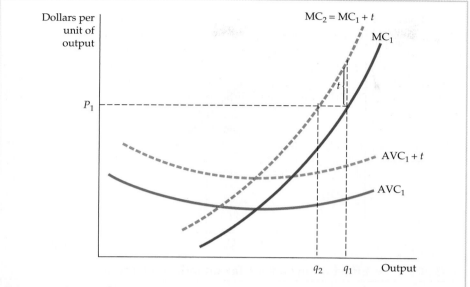

**FIGURE 8.18 Effect of an Output Tax on a Competitive Firm's Output**

An output tax raises the firm's marginal cost curve by the amount of the tax. The firm will reduce its output to the point at which the marginal cost plus the tax is equal to the price of the product.

curves for a firm enjoying positive economic profit by producing an output of $q_1$ and selling its product at the market price $P_1$. Because the tax is assessed for every unit of output, it raises the firm's marginal cost curve from $MC_1$ to $MC_2 = MC_1 + t$, where $t$ is the tax per unit of the firm's output. The tax also raises the average variable cost curve by the amount $t$.

The output tax can have two possible effects. If the firm can still earn a positive or zero economic profit after the imposition of the tax, it will maximize its profit by choosing an output level at which marginal cost plus the tax is equal to the price of the product. Its output falls from $q_1$ to $q_2$, and the *implicit* effect of the tax is to shift its supply curve upward (by the amount of the tax). If the firm can no longer earn an economic profit after the tax has been imposed, it will choose to exit the market.

Now suppose that every firm in the industry is taxed and so has increasing marginal costs. Because each firm reduces its output at the current market price, the total output supplied by the industry will also fall, causing the price of the product to increase. Figure 8.19 illustrates this. An upward shift in the supply curve, from $S_1$ to $S_2 = S_1 + t$, causes the market price of the product to increase (by less than the amount of the tax) from $P_1$ to $P_2$. This increase in price diminishes some of the effects that we described previously. Firms will reduce their output less than they would without a price increase.

Finally, output taxes may also encourage some firms (those whose costs are somewhat higher than others) to exit the industry. In the process, the tax raises the long-run average cost curve for each firm.

## Long-Run Elasticity of Supply

The long-run elasticity of industry supply is defined in the same way as the short-run elasticity: It is the percentage change in output ($\Delta Q/Q$) that results from a percentage change in price ($\Delta P/P$). In a constant-cost industry, the

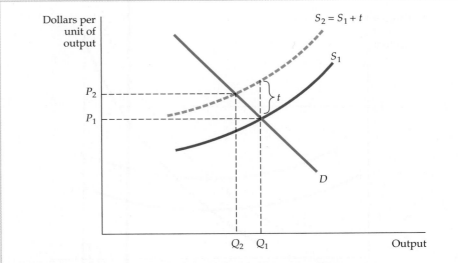

**FIGURE 8.19 Effect of an Output Tax on Industry Output**

An output tax placed on all firms in a competitive market shifts the supply curve for the industry upward by the amount of the tax. This shift raises the market price of the product and lowers the total output of the industry.

long-run supply curve is horizontal, and the long-run supply elasticity is infinitely large. (A small increase in price will induce an extremely large increase in output.) In an increasing-cost industry, however, the long-run supply elasticity will be positive but finite. Because industries can adjust and expand in the long run, we would generally expect long-run elasticities of supply to be larger than short-run elasticities.[9] The magnitude of the elasticity will depend on the extent to which input costs increase as the market expands. For example, an industry that depends on inputs that are widely available will have a more elastic long-run supply than will an industry that uses inputs in short supply.

**EXAMPLE 8.7**   The Long-Run Supply of Housing

Owner-occupied and rental housing provide interesting examples of the range of possible supply elasticities. People buy or rent housing to obtain the services that a house provides—a place to eat and sleep, comfort, and so on. If the price of housing services were to rise in one area of the country, the quantity of services provided could increase substantially.

---

[9]In some cases the opposite is true. Consider the elasticity of supply of scrap metal from a durable good like copper. Recall from Chapter 2 that because there is an existing stock of scrap, the long-run elasticity of supply will be *smaller* than the short-run elasticity.

To begin, consider the supply of owner-occupied housing in suburban or rural areas where land is not scarce. In this case, the price of land does not increase substantially as the quantity of housing supplied increases. Likewise, costs associated with construction are not likely to increase because there is a national market for lumber and other materials. Therefore, the long-run elasticity of the housing supply is likely to be very large, approximating that of a constant-cost industry. In fact, many studies find the long-run supply curve to be nearly horizontal.[10]

Even when elasticity of supply is measured within urban areas, where land costs rise as the demand for housing services increases, the long-run elasticity of supply is still likely to be large because land costs make up only about one-quarter of total housing costs. In one study of urban housing supply, the price elasticity was found to be 5.3.[11]

The market for rental housing is different, however. The construction of rental housing is often restricted by local zoning laws. Many communities outlaw it entirely, while others limit it to certain areas. Because urban land on which most rental housing is located is restricted and valuable, the long-run elasticity of supply of rental housing is much lower than the elasticity of supply of owner-occupied housing. As the price of rental-housing services rises, new high-rise rental units are built and older units are renovated—a practice that increases the quantity of rental services. With urban land becoming more valuable as housing density increases, and with the cost of construction soaring with the height of buildings, increased demand causes the input costs of rental housing to rise. In this increasing-cost case, the elasticity of supply can be much less than 1; in one study, the authors found it to be between 0.3 and 0.7.[12]

# SUMMARY

1. Managers can operate in accordance with a complex set of objectives and under various constraints. However, we can assume that firms act as if they are maximizing long-run profit.

2. Many markets may approximate perfect competition in that one or more firms act as if they face a nearly horizontal demand curve. In general, the number of firms in an industry is not always a good indicator of the extent to which that industry is competitive.

3. Because a firm in a competitive market accounts for a small share of total industry output, it makes its

output choice under the assumption that its production decision will have no effect on the price of the product. In this case, the demand curve and the marginal revenue curve are identical.

4. In the short run, a competitive firm maximizes its profit by choosing an output at which price is equal to (short-run) marginal cost. Price must, however, be greater than or equal to the firm's minimum average variable cost of production.

5. The short-run market supply curve is the horizontal summation of the supply curves of the firms in an

[10]For a review of the relevant literature, see Dixie M. Blackley, "The Long-Run Elasticity of New Housing Supply in the United States: Empirical Evidence for 1950 to 1994," *Journal of Real Estate Finance and Economics* 18 (1999): 25–42.

[11]See Barton A. Smith, "The Supply of Urban Housing," *Journal of Political Economy* 40 (August 1976): 389–405.

[12]See Frank deLeeuw and Nkanta Ekanem, "The Supply of Rental Housing," *American Economic Review* 61 (December 1971): 806–17, Table 5.2.

industry. It can be characterized by the elasticity of supply: the percentage change in quantity supplied in response to a percentage change in price.

6. The producer surplus for a firm is the difference between its revenue and the minimum cost that would be necessary to produce the profit-maximizing output. In both the short run and the long run, producer surplus is the area under the horizontal price line and above the marginal cost of production.

7. Economic rent is the payment for a scarce factor of production less the minimum amount necessary to hire that factor. In the long run in a competitive market, producer surplus is equal to the economic rent generated by all scarce factors of production.

8. In the long run, profit-maximizing competitive firms choose the output at which price is equal to long-run marginal cost.

9. A long-run competitive equilibrium occurs under these conditions: (a) when firms maximize profit; (b) when all firms earn zero economic profit, so that there is no incentive to enter or exit the industry; and (c) when the quantity of the product demanded is equal to the quantity supplied.

10. The long-run supply curve for a firm is horizontal when the industry is a constant-cost industry in which the increased demand for inputs to production (associated with an increased demand for the product) has no effect on the market price of the inputs. But the long-run supply curve for a firm is upward sloping in an increasing-cost industry, where the increased demand for inputs causes the market price of some or all inputs to rise.

# QUESTIONS FOR REVIEW

1. Why would a firm that incurs losses choose to produce rather than shut down?

2. Explain why the industry supply curve is not the long-run industry marginal cost curve.

3. In long-run equilibrium, all firms in the industry earn zero economic profit. Why is this true?

4. What is the difference between economic profit and producer surplus?

5. Why do firms enter an industry when they know that in the long run economic profit will be zero?

6. At the beginning of the twentieth century, there were many small American automobile manufacturers. At the end of the century, there were only three large ones. Suppose that this situation is not the result of lax federal enforcement of antimonopoly laws. How do you explain the decrease in the number of manufacturers? (*Hint*: What is the inherent cost structure of the automobile industry?)

7. Because industry *X* is characterized by perfect competition, every firm in the industry is earning zero economic profit. If the product price falls, no firm can survive. Do you agree or disagree? Discuss.

8. An increase in the demand for video films also increases the salaries of actors and actresses. Is the long-run supply curve for films likely to be horizontal or upward sloping? Explain.

9. True or false: A firm should always produce at an output at which long-run average cost is minimized. Explain.

10. Can there be constant returns to scale in an industry with an upward-sloping supply curve? Explain.

11. What assumptions are necessary for a market to be perfectly competitive? In light of what you have learned in this chapter, why is each of these assumptions important?

12. Suppose a competitive industry faces an increase in demand (i.e., the demand curve shifts upward). What are the steps by which a competitive market insures increased output? Will your answer change if the government imposes a price ceiling?

13. The government passes a law that allows a substantial subsidy for every acre of land used to grow tobacco. How does this program affect the long-run supply curve for tobacco?

14. A certain brand of vacuum cleaners can be purchased from several local stores as well as from several catalogue or website sources.
   a. If all sellers charge the same price for the vacuum cleaner, will they all earn zero economic profit in the long run?
   b. If all sellers charge the same price and one local seller owns the building in which he does business, paying no rent, is this seller earning a positive economic profit?
   c. Does the seller who pays no rent have an incentive to lower the price that he charges for the vacuum cleaner?

# EXERCISES

1. The data in the table on page 307 give information about the price (in dollars) for which a firm can sell a unit of output and the total cost of production.

   a. Fill in the blanks in the table.
   b. Show what happens to the firm's output choice and profit if the price of the product falls from $60 to $50.

| | R | | π | MC | MR | R | MR | π |
|---|---|---|---|---|---|---|---|---|
| q | P | P = 60 C | P = 60 | P = 60 | P = 60 | P = 50 | P = 50 | P = 50 |
| 0 | 60 | 100 | | | | | | |
| 1 | 60 | 150 | | | | | | |
| 2 | 60 | 178 | | | | | | |
| 3 | 60 | 198 | | | | | | |
| 4 | 60 | 212 | | | | | | |
| 5 | 60 | 230 | | | | | | |
| 6 | 60 | 250 | | | | | | |
| 7 | 60 | 272 | | | | | | |
| 8 | 60 | 310 | | | | | | |
| 9 | 60 | 355 | | | | | | |
| 10 | 60 | 410 | | | | | | |
| 11 | 60 | 475 | | | | | | |

2. Using the data in the table, show what happens to the firm's output choice and profit if the fixed cost of production increases from $100 to $150 and then to $200. Assume that the price of the output remains at $60 per unit. What general conclusion can you reach about the effects of fixed costs on the firm's output choice?

3. Use the same information as in Exercise 1.
   a. Derive the firm's short-run supply curve. (*Hint*: You may want to plot the appropriate cost curves.)
   b. If 100 identical firms are in the market, what is the industry supply curve?

4. Suppose you are the manager of a watchmaking firm operating in a competitive market. Your cost of production is given by $C = 200 + 2q^2$, where $q$ is the level of output and $C$ is total cost. (The marginal cost of production is $4q$; the fixed cost is $200$.)
   a. If the price of watches is $100, how many watches should you produce to maximize profit?
   b. What will the profit level be?
   c. At what minimum price will the firm produce a positive output?

5. Suppose that a competitive firm's marginal cost of producing output $q$ is given by $MC(q) = 3 + 2q$. Assume that the market price of the firm's product is $9.
   a. What level of output will the firm produce?
   b. What is the firm's producer surplus?
   c. Suppose that the average variable cost of the firm is given by $AVC(q) = 3 + q$. Suppose that the firm's fixed costs are known to be $3. Will the firm be earning a positive, negative, or zero profit in the short run?

6. A firm produces a product in a competitive industry and has a total cost function $C = 50 + 4q + 2q^2$ and a marginal cost function $MC = 4 + 4q$. At the given market price of $20, the firm is producing 5 units of output. Is the firm maximizing its profit? What quantity of output should the firm produce in the long run?

7. Suppose the same firm's cost function is $C(q) = 4q^2 + 16$.
   a. Find variable cost, fixed cost, average cost, average variable cost, and average fixed cost. (*Hint*: Marginal cost is given by $MC = 8q$.)
   b. Show the average cost, marginal cost, and average variable cost curves on a graph.
   c. Find the output that minimizes average cost.
   d. At what range of prices will the firm produce a positive output?
   e. At what range of prices will the firm earn a negative profit?
   f. At what range of prices will the firm earn a positive profit?

*8. A competitive firm has the following short-run cost function: $C(q) = q^3 - 8q^2 + 30q + 5$.
   a. Find MC, AC, and AVC and sketch them on a graph.
   b. At what range of prices will the firm supply zero output?
   c. Identify the firm's supply curve on your graph.
   d. At what price would the firm supply exactly 6 units of output?

*9. a. Suppose that a firm's production function is $q = 9x^{1/2}$ in the short run, where there are fixed costs of $1000, and $x$ is the variable input whose cost is $4000 per unit. What is the total cost of producing a level of output $q$? In other words, identify the total cost function $C(q)$.
   b. Write down the equation for the supply curve.
   c. If price is $1000, how many units will the firm produce? What is the level of profit? Illustrate your answer on a cost-curve graph.

*10. Suppose you are given the following information about a particular industry:

$$Q^D = 6500 - 100P \qquad \text{Market demand}$$
$$Q^S = 1200P \qquad \text{Market supply}$$
$$C(q) = 722 + \frac{q^2}{200} \qquad \text{Firm total cost function}$$
$$MC(q) = \frac{2q}{200} \qquad \text{Firm marginal cost function}$$

Assume that all firms are identical and that the market is characterized by perfect competition.
   a. Find the equilibrium price, the equilibrium quantity, the output supplied by the firm, and the profit of each firm.
   b. Would you expect to see entry into or exit from the industry in the long run? Explain. What effect will entry or exit have on market equilibrium?
   c. What is the lowest price at which each firm would sell its output in the long run? Is profit positive, negative, or zero at this price? Explain.
   d. What is the lowest price at which each firm would sell its output in the short run? Is profit positive, negative, or zero at this price? Explain.

*11. Suppose that a competitive firm has a total cost function $C(q) = 450 + 15q + 2q^2$ and a marginal cost function

$MC(q) = 15 + 4q$. If the market price is $P = \$115$ per unit, find the level of output produced by the firm. Find the level of profit and the level of producer surplus.

**\*12.** A number of stores offer film developing as a service to their customers. Suppose that each store offering this service has a cost function $C(q) = 50 + 0.5q + 0.08q^2$ and a marginal cost $MC = 0.5 + 0.16q$.

   **a.** If the going rate for developing a roll of film is $8.50, is the industry in long-run equilibrium? If not, find the price associated with long-run equilibrium.

   **b.** Suppose now that a new technology is developed which will reduce the cost of film developing by 25 percent. Assuming that the industry is in long-run equilibrium, how much would any one store be willing to pay to purchase this new technology?

**\*13.** Consider a city that has a number of hot dog stands operating throughout the downtown area. Suppose that each vendor has a marginal cost of $1.50 per hot dog sold and no fixed cost. Suppose the maximum number of hot dogs that any one vendor can sell is 100 per day.

   **a.** If the price of a hot dog is $2, how many hot dogs does each vendor want to sell?

   **b.** If the industry is perfectly competitive, will the price remain at $2 for a hot dog? If not, what will the price be?

   **c.** If each vendor sells exactly 100 hot dogs a day and the demand for hot dogs from vendors in the city is $Q = 4400 - 1200P$, how many vendors are there?

   **d.** Suppose the city decides to regulate hot dog vendors by issuing permits. If the city issues only 20 permits and if each vendor continues to sell 100 hot dogs a day, what price will a hot dog sell for?

   **e.** Suppose the city decides to sell the permits. What is the highest price that a vendor would pay for a permit?

**\*14.** A sales tax of $1 per unit of output is placed on a particular firm whose product sells for $5 in a competitive industry with many firms.

   **a.** How will this tax affect the cost curves for the firm?

   **b.** What will happen to the firm's price, output, and profit?

   **c.** Will there be entry or exit in the industry?

**\*15.** A sales tax of 10 percent is placed on half the firms (the polluters) in a competitive industry. The revenue is paid to the remaining firms (the nonpolluters) as a 10 percent subsidy on the value of output sold.

   **a.** Assuming that all firms have identical constant long-run average costs before the sales tax-subsidy policy, what do you expect to happen (in both the short run and the long run), to the price of the product, the output of firms, and industry output? (*Hint*: How does price relate to industry input?)

   **b.** Can such a policy *always* be achieved with a balanced budget in which tax revenues are equal to subsidy payments? Why or why not? Explain.

# The Analysis of Competitive Markets

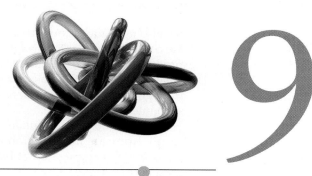

# 9

In Chapter 2, we saw how supply and demand curves can help us describe and understand the behavior of competitive markets. In Chapters 3 to 8, we saw how these curves are derived and what determines their shapes. Building on this foundation, we return to supply–demand analysis and show how it can be applied to a wide variety of economic problems—problems that might concern a consumer faced with a purchasing decision, a firm faced with a long-range planning problem, or a government agency that has to design a policy and evaluate its likely impact.

We begin by showing how consumer and producer surplus can be used to study the *welfare effects* of a government policy—in other words, who gains and who loses from the policy, and by how much. We also use consumer and producer surplus to demonstrate the *efficiency* of a competitive market—why the equilibrium price and quantity in a competitive market maximizes the aggregate economic welfare of producers and consumers.

Then we apply supply–demand analysis to a variety of problems. Because very few markets in the United States have been untouched by government interventions of one kind or another, most of the problems that we will study deal with the effects of such interventions. Our objective is not simply to solve these problems, but to show you how to use the tools of economic analysis to deal with them and others like them on your own. We hope that by working through the examples we provide, you will see how to calculate the response of markets to changing economic conditions or government policies and to evaluate the resulting gains and losses to consumers and producers.

## 9.1 EVALUATING THE GAINS AND LOSSES FROM GOVERNMENT POLICIES— CONSUMER AND PRODUCER SURPLUS

We saw at the end of Chapter 2 that a government-imposed price ceiling causes the quantity of a good demanded to rise (at the lower price, consumers want to buy more) and the quantity supplied to fall (producers are not willing to supply as much at the lower price). The result is a shortage—i.e., excess demand. Of course, those consumers who can still buy the good will be better off because they will now pay less. (Presumably, this was the objective of the policy in the first place.) But if

In §2.7, we explain that under price controls, the price of a product can be no higher than a maximum allowable ceiling price.

we also take into account those who cannot obtain the good, how much better off are consumers *as a whole?* Might they be worse off? And if we lump consumers and producers together, will their *total welfare* be greater or lower, and by how much? To answer questions such as these, we need a way to measure the gains and losses from government interventions and the changes in market price and quantity that such interventions cause.

Our method is to calculate the changes in *consumer and producer surplus* that result from an intervention. In Chapter 4, we saw that *consumer surplus* measures the aggregate net benefit that consumers obtain from a competitive market. In Chapter 8, we saw how *producer surplus* measures the aggregate net benefit to producers. Here we will see how consumer and producer surplus can be applied in practice.

## Review of Consumer and Producer Surplus

For a review of consumer surplus, see §4.4, where it is defined as the difference between what a consumer is willing to pay for a good and what the consumer actually pays when buying it.

In an unregulated, competitive market, consumers and producers buy and sell at the prevailing market price. But remember, for some consumers the value of the good *exceeds* this market price; they would pay more for the good if they had to. *Consumer surplus* is the total benefit or value that consumers receive beyond what they pay for the good.

For example, suppose the market price is $5 per unit, as in Figure 9.1. Some consumers probably value this good very highly and would pay much more

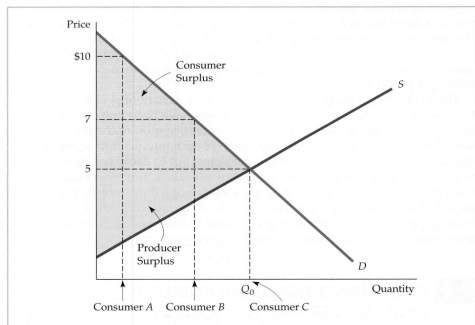

**FIGURE 9.1 Consumer and Producer Surplus**

Consumer *A* would pay $10 for a good whose market price is $5 and therefore enjoys a benefit of $5. Consumer *B* enjoys a benefit of $2, and Consumer *C*, who values the good at exactly the market price, enjoys no benefit. Consumer surplus, which measures the total benefit to all consumers, is the yellow-shaded area between the demand curve and the market price. Producer surplus measures the total profits of producers, plus rents to factor inputs. It is the green-shaded area between the supply curve and the market price. Together, consumer and producer surplus measure the welfare benefit of a competitive market.

than \$5 for it. Consumer *A*, for example, would pay up to \$10 for the good. However, because the market price is only \$5, he enjoys a net benefit of \$5—the \$10 value he places on the good, less the \$5 he must pay to obtain it. Consumer *B* values the good somewhat less highly. She would be willing to pay \$7, and thus enjoys a \$2 net benefit. Finally, Consumer *C* values the good at exactly the market price, \$5. He is indifferent between buying or not buying the good, and if the market price were one cent higher, he would forgo the purchase. Consumer *C*, therefore, obtains no net benefit.[1]

For consumers in the aggregate, consumer surplus is the area between the demand curve and the market price (i.e., the yellow-shaded area in Figure 9.1). Because *consumer surplus measures the total net benefit to consumers*, we can measure the gain or loss to consumers from a government intervention by measuring the resulting change in consumer surplus.

*Producer surplus* is the analogous measure for producers. Some producers are producing units at a cost just equal to the market price. Other units, however, could be produced for less than the market price and would still be produced and sold even if the market price were lower. Producers, therefore, enjoy a benefit—a surplus—from selling those units. For each unit, this surplus is the difference between the market price the producer receives and the marginal cost of producing this unit.

For the market as a whole, producer surplus is the area above the supply curve up to the market price; this is *the benefit that lower-cost producers enjoy by selling at the market price*. In Figure 9.1, it is the green triangle. And because producer surplus measures the total net benefit to producers, we can measure the gain or loss to producers from a government intervention by measuring the resulting change in producer surplus.

> For a review of producer surplus, see §8.6, where it is defined as the sum over all units produced of the difference between the market price of the good and the marginal cost of its production.

## Application of Consumer and Producer Surplus

With consumer and producer surplus, we can evaluate the **welfare effects** of a government intervention in the market. We can determine who gains and who loses from the intervention, and by how much. To see how this is done, let's return to the example of *price controls* that we first encountered toward the end of Chapter 2. The government makes it illegal for producers to charge more than a *ceiling price* set below the market-clearing level. Recall that by decreasing production and increasing the quantity demanded, such a price ceiling creates a shortage (excess demand).

> • **welfare effects** Gains and losses to consumers and producers.

Figure 9.2 replicates Figure 2.23 (page 57), except that it also shows the changes in consumer and producer surplus that result from the government price-control policy. Let's go through these changes step by step.

1. **Change in Consumer Surplus:** Some consumers are worse off as a result of the policy, and others are better off. The ones who are worse off are those who have been rationed out of the market because of the reduction in production and sales from $Q_0$ to $Q_1$. Other consumers, however, can still purchase the good (perhaps because they are in the right place at the right time or are willing to wait in line). These consumers are better off because they can buy the good at a lower price ($P_{max}$ rather than $P_0$).

   *How much* better off or worse off is each group? The consumers who can still buy the good enjoy an *increase* in consumer surplus, which is given by

---

[1]Of course, some consumers value the good at *less* than \$5. These consumers make up the part of the demand curve to the right of the equilibrium quantity $Q_0$ and will not purchase the good.

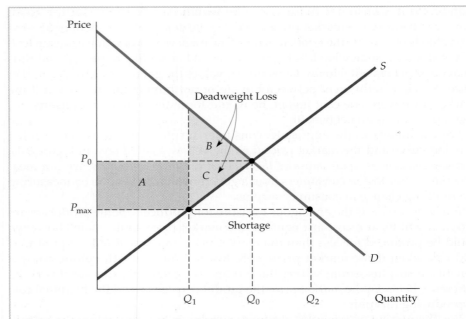

**FIGURE 9.2 Change in Consumer and Producer Surplus from Price Controls**

The price of a good has been regulated to be no higher than $P_{max}$, which is below the market-clearing price $P_0$. The gain to consumers is the difference between rectangle $A$ and triangle $B$. The loss to producers is the sum of rectangle $A$ and triangle $C$. Triangles $B$ and $C$ together measure the deadweight loss from price controls.

the blue-shaded rectangle $A$. This rectangle measures the reduction of price in each unit times the number of units consumers are able to buy at the lower price. On the other hand, those consumers who can no longer buy the good lose surplus; their *loss* is given by the green-shaded triangle $B$. This triangle measures the value to consumers, less what they would have had to pay, that is lost because of the reduction in output from $Q_0$ to $Q_1$. The net change in consumer surplus is therefore $A - B$. In Figure 9.2, because rectangle $A$ is larger than triangle $B$, we know that the net change in consumer surplus is positive.

It is important to stress that we have assumed that those consumers who are able to buy the good are the ones who value it most highly. If that were not the case—e.g., if the output $Q_1$ were rationed randomly—the amount of lost consumer surplus would be larger than triangle $B$. In addition, we have ignored the opportunity costs of rationing. For example, those people who want the good might have to wait in line to obtain it. In that case, the opportunity cost of their time should be included as part of lost consumer surplus.

2. **Change in Producer Surplus:** With price controls, some producers (those with relatively lower costs) will stay in the market but will receive a lower price for their output, while other producers will leave the market. Both groups will lose producer surplus. Those who remain in the market and produce quantity $Q_1$ are now receiving a lower price. They have lost the producer surplus given by rectangle $A$. However, *total* production has also dropped. The purple-shaded triangle $C$ measures the additional loss of

producer surplus for those producers who have left the market and those who have stayed in the market but are producing less. Therefore, the total change in producer surplus is $-A - C$. Producers clearly lose as a result of price controls.

3. **Deadweight Loss:** Is the loss to producers from price controls offset by the gain to consumers? No. As Figure 9.2 shows, price controls result in a net loss of total surplus, which we call a **deadweight loss**. Recall that the change in consumer surplus is $A - B$ and that the change in producer surplus is $- A - C$. The *total* change in surplus is therefore $(A - B) + (- A - C) = -B - C$. We thus have a deadweight loss, which is given by the two triangles $B$ and $C$ in Figure 9.2. This deadweight loss is an inefficiency caused by price controls; the loss in producer surplus exceeds the gain in consumer surplus.

> • **deadweight loss** Net loss of total (consumer plus producer) surplus.

If politicians value consumer surplus more than producer surplus, this deadweight loss from price controls may not carry much political weight. However, if the demand curve is very inelastic, price controls can result in a *net loss of consumer surplus*, as Figure 9.3 shows. In that figure, triangle $B$, which measures the loss to consumers who have been rationed out of the market, is larger than rectangle $A$, which measures the gain to consumers able to buy the good. Here, because consumers value the good highly, those who are rationed out suffer a large loss.

The demand for gasoline is very inelastic in the short run (but much more elastic in the long run). During the summer of 1979, gasoline shortages resulted

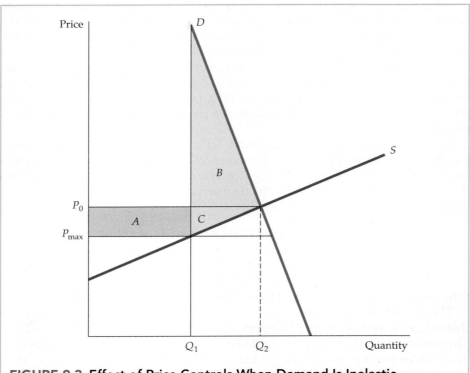

**FIGURE 9.3 Effect of Price Controls When Demand Is Inelastic**

If demand is sufficiently inelastic, triangle $B$ can be larger than rectangle $A$. In this case, consumers suffer a net loss from price controls.

from oil price controls that prevented domestic gasoline prices from increasing to rising world levels. Consumers spent hours waiting in line to buy gasoline. This was a good example of price controls making consumers—the group whom the policy was presumably intended to protect—worse off.

---

**EXAMPLE 9.1**  Price Controls and Natural Gas Shortages

In Example 2.10 (page 59), we discussed the price controls that were imposed on natural gas markets during the 1970s, and we analyzed what would happen if the government were once again to regulate the wholesale price of natural gas. Specifically, we saw that, in 2007, the free-market wholesale price of natural gas was about $6.40 per thousand cubic feet (mcf), and we calculated the quantities that would be supplied and demanded if the price were regulated to be no higher than $3.00 per mcf. Now, equipped with the concepts of *consumer surplus*, *producer surplus*, and *deadweight loss*, we can calculate the welfare impact of this ceiling price.

Recall from Example 2.10 that we found that the supply and demand curves for natural gas could be approximated as follows:

$$Supply: \quad Q^S = 15.90 + 0.72P_G + 0.05P_O$$
$$Demand: \quad Q^D = 0.02 - 1.8P_G + 0.69P_O$$

where $Q^S$ and $Q^D$ are the quantities supplied and demanded, each measured in trillion cubic feet (Tcf), $P_G$ is the price of natural gas in dollars per thousand cubic feet ($/mcf), and $P_O$ is the price of oil in dollars per barrel ($/b). As you can verify by setting $Q^S$ equal to $Q^D$ and using a price of oil of $50 per barrel, the equilibrium free market price and quantity are $6.40 per mcf and 23 Tcf, respectively. Under the hypothetical regulations, however, the maximum allowable price was $3.00 per mcf, which implies a supply of 20.6 Tcf and a demand of 29.1 Tcf.

Figure 9.4 shows these supply and demand curves and compares the free market and regulated prices. Rectangle $A$ and triangles $B$ and $C$ measure the changes in consumer and producer surplus resulting from price controls. By calculating the areas of the rectangle and triangles, we can determine the gains and losses from controls.

To do the calculations, first note that 1 Tcf is equal to 1 billion mcf. (We must put the quantities and prices in common units.) Also, by substituting the quantity 20.6 Tcf into the equation for the demand curve, we can determine that the vertical line at 20.6 Tcf intersects the demand curve at a price of $7.73 per mcf. Then we can calculate the areas as follows:

$$A = (20.6 \text{ billion mcf}) \times (\$3.40/\text{mcf}) = \$70.04 \text{ billion}$$
$$B = (1/2) \times (2.4 \text{ billion mcf}) \times (\$1.33/\text{mcf}) = \$1.60 \text{ billion}$$
$$C = (1/2) \times (2.4 \text{ billion mcf}) \times (\$3.40/\text{mcf}) = \$4.08 \text{ billion}$$

(The area of a triangle is one-half the product of its altitude and its base.)

The annual change in consumer surplus that would result from these hypothetical price controls would therefore be $A - B = 70.04 - 1.60 = \$68.44$ billion. The change in producer surplus would be $-A - C = -70.04 - 4.08 = -\$74.12$ billion. And finally, the annual deadweight loss would be $-B - C = -1.60 - 4.08 = -\$5.68$ billion. Note that most of this deadweight loss is from triangle $C$, i.e., the loss to those consumers who are unable to obtain natural gas as a result of the price controls.

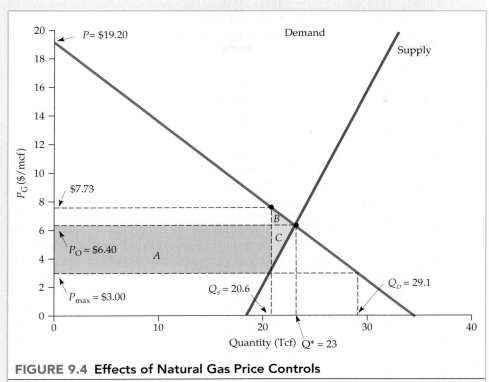

**FIGURE 9.4** **Effects of Natural Gas Price Controls**

The market-clearing price of natural gas is $6.40 per mcf, and the (hypothetical) maximum allowable price is $3.00. A shortage of $29.1 - 20.6 = 8.5$ Tcf results. The gain to consumers is rectangle $A$ minus triangle $B$, and the loss to producers is rectangle $A$ plus triangle $C$. The deadweight loss is the sum of triangles $B$ plus $C$.

## 9.2 THE EFFICIENCY OF A COMPETITIVE MARKET

To evaluate a market outcome, we often ask whether it achieves **economic efficiency**—the maximization of aggregate consumer and producer surplus. We just saw how price controls create a deadweight loss. The policy therefore imposes an *efficiency cost* on the economy: Taken together, producer and consumer surplus are reduced by the amount of the deadweight loss. (Of course, this does not mean that such a policy is bad; it may achieve other objectives that policymakers and the public deem important.)

**Market Failure** One might think that if the only objective is to achieve economic efficiency, a competitive market is better left alone. This is sometimes, but not always, the case. In some situations, a **market failure** occurs: Because prices fail to provide the proper signals to consumers and producers, the unregulated competitive market is inefficient—i.e., does not maximize aggregate consumer and producer surplus. There are two important instances in which market failure can occur:

1. **Externalities:** Sometimes the actions of either consumers or producers result in either costs or benefits that do not show up as part of the market price. Such costs or benefits are called **externalities** because they are "external" to the market. One example is the cost to society of environmental pollution by

• **economic efficiency** Maximization of aggregate consumer and producer surplus.

• **market failure** Situation in which an unregulated competitive market is inefficient because prices fail to provide proper signals to consumers and producers.

• **externality** Action taken by either a producer or a consumer which affects other producers or consumers but is not accounted for by the market price.

a producer of industrial chemicals. Without government intervention, such a producer will have no incentive to consider the social cost of pollution. We examine externalities and the proper government response to them in Chapter 18.

2. **Lack of Information:** Market failure can also occur when consumers lack information about the quality or nature of a product and so cannot make utility-maximizing purchasing decisions. Government intervention (e.g., requiring "truth in labeling") may then be desirable. The role of information is discussed in detail in Chapter 17.

In the absence of externalities or a lack of information, an unregulated competitive market does lead to the economically efficient output level. To see this, let's consider what happens if price is constrained to be something other than the equilibrium market-clearing price.

We have already examined the effects of a *price ceiling* (a price held below the market-clearing price). As you can see in Figure 9.2 (page 312), production falls (from $Q_0$ to $Q_1$), and there is a corresponding loss of total surplus (the deadweight-loss triangles $B$ and $C$). Too little is produced, and consumers and producers in the aggregate are worse off.

Now suppose instead that the government required the price to be *above* the market-clearing price—say, $P_2$ instead of $P_0$. As Figure 9.5 shows, although producers would like to produce more at this higher price ($Q_2$ instead of $Q_0$), consumers will now buy less ($Q_3$ instead of $Q_0$). If we assume that producers produce only what can be sold, the market output level will be $Q_3$, and again, there is a net loss of total surplus. In Figure 9.5, rectangle $A$ now represents a transfer from consumers to producers (who now receive a higher price), but triangles $B$ and $C$ again represent a deadweight loss. Because of the higher price, some consumers are no longer buying the good (a loss of consumer surplus given by triangle $B$), and some producers are no longer producing it (a loss of producer surplus given by triangle $C$).

In fact, the deadweight loss triangles $B$ and $C$ in Figure 9.5 give an optimistic assessment of the efficiency cost of policies that force price above market-clearing

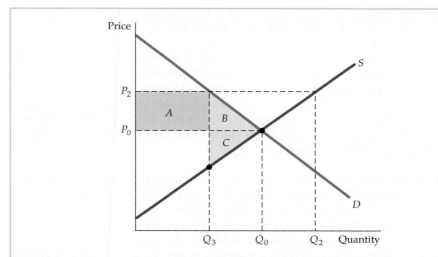

**FIGURE 9.5 Welfare Loss When Price is Held Above Market-Clearing Level**

When price is regulated to be no lower than $P_2$, only $Q_3$ will be demanded. If $Q_3$ is produced, the deadweight loss is given by triangles $B$ and $C$. At price $P_2$, producers would like to produce more than $Q_3$. If they do, the deadweight loss will be even larger.

levels. Some producers, enticed by the high price $P_2$, might increase their capacity and output levels, which would result in unsold output. (This happened in the airline industry when, prior to 1980, fares were regulated above market-clearing levels by the Civil Aeronautics Board.) Or to satisfy producers, the government might buy up unsold output to maintain production at $Q_2$ or close to it. (This is what happens in U.S. agriculture.) In both cases, the total welfare loss will exceed the areas of triangles $B$ and $C$.

We will examine minimum prices, price supports, and related policies in some detail in the next few sections. Besides showing how supply–demand analysis can be used to understand and assess these policies, we will see how deviations from the competitive market equilibrium lead to efficiency costs.

---

**EXAMPLE 9.2**  The Market for Human Kidneys

Should people have the right to sell parts of their bodies? Congress believes the answer is no. In 1984, it passed the National Organ Transplantation Act, which prohibits the sale of organs for transplantation. Organs may only be donated.

Although the law prohibits their sale, it does not make organs valueless. Instead, it prevents those who supply organs (living persons or the families of the deceased) from reaping their economic value. It also creates a shortage of organs. Each year, about 16,000 kidneys, 44,000 corneas, and 2200 hearts are transplanted in the United States.[2] But there is considerable excess demand for these organs, so that many potential recipients must do without them, some of whom die as a result. For example, as of July 2007, there were about 97,000 patients on the national Organ Procurement and Transplantation Network (OPTN) waiting list. However, only 29,000 transplant surgeries were performed in the United States in 2006. Although the number of transplant surgeries has increased by approximately 93 percent since 1990, the number of patients waiting for organs has increased by about 340 percent.[3]

To understand the effects of this law, let's consider the supply and demand for kidneys. First the supply curve. Even at a price of zero (the effective price under the law), donors supply about 16,000 kidneys per year. But many other people who need kidney transplants cannot obtain them because of a lack of donors. It has been estimated that 8000 more kidneys would be supplied if the price were $20,000. We can fit a linear supply curve to this data—i.e., a supply curve of the form $Q = a + bP$. When $P = 0$, $Q = 16,000$, so $a = 16,000$. If $P = \$20,000$, $Q = 24,000$, so $b = (24,000 - 16,000)/20,000 = 0.4$. Thus the supply curve is

$$Supply: \quad Q^S = 16,000 + 0.4P$$

Note that at a price of $20,000, the elasticity of supply is 0.33.

---

[2]These numbers are for 2006. Source: Table 171 of the 2007 *Statistical Abstract of the U.S.*

[3]Source: Organ Procurement and Transplantation Network, **http://www.optn.org.**

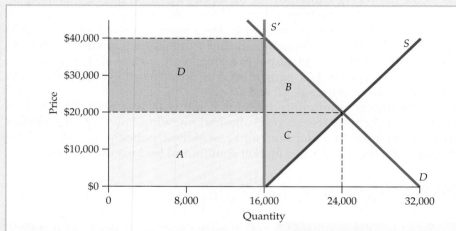

**FIGURE 9.6** **The Market for Kidneys and the Effect of the National Organ Transplantation Act**

The market-clearing price is $20,000; at this price, about 24,000 kidneys per year would be supplied. The law effectively makes the price zero. About 16,000 kidneys per year are still donated; this constrained supply is shown as $S'$. The loss to suppliers is given by rectangle $A$ and triangle $C$. If consumers received kidneys at no cost, their gain would be given by rectangle $A$ less triangle $B$. In practice, kidneys are often rationed on the basis of willingness to pay, and many recipients pay most or all of the $40,000 price that clears the market when supply is constrained. Rectangles $A$ and $D$ measure the total value of kidneys when supply is constrained.

It is expected that at a price of $20,000, the number of kidneys demanded would be 24,000 per year. Like supply, demand is relatively price inelastic; a reasonable estimate for the price elasticity of demand at the $20,000 price is –0.33. This implies the following linear demand curve:

*Demand:* $Q^D = 32,000 - 0.4P$

These supply and demand curves are plotted in Figure 9.6, which shows the market-clearing price and quantity of $20,000 and 24,000, respectively.

Because the sale of kidneys is prohibited, supply is limited to 16,000 (the number of kidneys that people donate). This constrained supply is shown as the vertical line $S'$. How does this affect the welfare of kidney suppliers and recipients?

First consider suppliers. Those who provide kidneys fail to receive the $20,000 that each kidney is worth—a loss of surplus represented by rectangle $A$ and equal to (16,000)($20,000) = $320 million. Moreover, some people who would supply kidneys if they were paid do not. These people lose an amount of surplus represented by triangle $C$, which is equal to (1/2)(8000)($20,000) = $80 million. Therefore, the total loss to suppliers is $400 million.

What about recipients? Presumably the law intended to treat the kidney as a gift to the recipient. In this case, those recipients who obtain kidneys *gain* rectangle $A$ ($320 million) because they (or their insurance companies) do not have to pay the $20,000 price. Those who cannot obtain kidneys lose surplus of an amount given by triangle $B$ and equal to $80 million. This implies a net increase in the surplus of recipients of $320 million – $80 million = $240 million. It also implies a deadweight loss equal to the areas of triangles $B$ and $C$ (i.e., $160 million).

In §2.6, we explain how to fit linear demand and supply curves from information about the equilibrium price and quantity and the price elasticities of demand and supply.

These estimates of the welfare effects of the policy may need adjustment for two reasons. First, kidneys will not necessarily be allocated to those who value them most highly. If the limited supply of kidneys is partly allocated to people with valuations below $40,000, the true deadweight loss will be higher than our estimate. Second, with excess demand, there is no way to ensure that recipients will receive their kidneys as gifts. In practice, kidneys are often rationed on the basis of willingness to pay, and many recipients end up paying all or most of the $40,000 price that is needed to clear the market when supply is constrained to 16,000. A good part of the value of the kidneys—rectangles *A* and *D* in the figure—is then captured by hospitals and middlemen. As a result, the law reduces the surplus of recipients as well as of suppliers.[4]

There are, of course, arguments in favor of prohibiting the sale of organs.[5] One argument stems from the problem of imperfect information; if people receive payment for organs, they may hide adverse information about their health histories. This argument is probably most applicable to the sale of blood, where there is a possibility of transmitting hepatitis, AIDS, or other viruses. But even in such cases, screening (at a cost that would be included in the market price) may be more efficient than prohibiting sales. This issue has been central to the debate in the United States over blood policy.

A second argument holds that it is simply unfair to allocate a basic necessity of life on the basis of ability to pay. This argument transcends economics. However, two points should be kept in mind. First, when the price of a good that has a significant opportunity cost is forced to zero, there is bound to be reduced supply and excess demand. Second, it is not clear why live organs should be treated differently from close substitutes; artificial limbs, joints, and heart valves, for example, are sold even though real kidneys are not.

Many complex ethical and economic issues are involved in the sale of organs. These issues are important, and this example is not intended to sweep them away. Economics, the dismal science, simply shows us that human organs have economic value that cannot be ignored, and that prohibiting their sale imposes a cost on society that must be weighed against the benefits.

## 9.3 MINIMUM PRICES

As we have seen, government policy sometimes seeks to *raise* prices above market-clearing levels, rather than lower them. Examples include the former regulation of the airlines by the Civil Aeronautics Board, the minimum wage law, and a variety of agricultural policies. (Most import quotas and tariffs also have this intent, as we

---

[4]For further analyses of these efficiency costs, see Dwane L. Barney and R. Larry Reynolds, "An Economic Analysis of Transplant Organs," *Atlantic Economic Journal* 17 (September 1989): 12–20; David L. Kaserman and A. H. Barnett, "An Economic Analysis of Transplant Organs: A Comment and Extension," *Atlantic Economic Journal* 19 (June 1991): 57–64; and A. Frank Adams III, A. H. Barnett, and David L. Kaserman, "Markets for Organs: The Question of Supply," *Contemporary Economic Policy* 17 (April 1999); 147–55. Kidney exchange is also complicated by the need to match blood type; for a recent analysis, see Alvin E. Roth, Tayfun Sönmez, and M. Utku Ünver, "Efficient Kidney Exchange: Coincidence of Wants in Markets with Compatibility-Based Preferences," *American Economic Review* 97 (June 2007).

[5]For discussions of the strengths and weaknesses of these arguments, see Susan Rose-Ackerman, "Inalienability and the Theory of Property Rights," *Columbia Law Review* 85 (June 1985): 931–69, and Roger D. Blair and David L. Kaserman, "The Economics and Ethics of Alternative Cadaveric Organ Procurement Policies," *Yale Journal on Regulation* 8 (Summer 1991): 403–52.

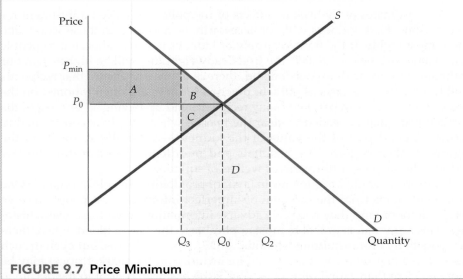

**FIGURE 9.7 Price Minimum**

Price is regulated to be no lower than $P_{min}$. Producers would like to supply $Q_2$, but consumers will buy only $Q_3$. If producers indeed produce $Q_2$, the amount $Q_2 - Q_3$ will go unsold and the change in producer surplus will be $A - C - D$. In this case, producers as a group may be worse off.

will see in Section 9.5.) One way to raise prices above market-clearing levels is by direct regulation—simply make it illegal to charge a price lower than a specific minimum level.

Look again at Figure 9.5 (page 316). If producers correctly anticipate that they can sell only the lower quantity $Q_3$, the net welfare loss will be given by triangles $B$ and $C$. But as we explained, producers might not limit their output to $Q_3$. What happens if producers think they can sell all they want at the higher price and produce accordingly? That situation is illustrated in Figure 9.7, where $P_{min}$ denotes a minimum price set by the government. The quantity supplied is now $Q_2$ and the quantity demanded is $Q_3$, the difference representing excess, unsold supply. Now let's determine the resulting changes in consumer and producer surplus.

Those consumers who still purchase the good must now pay a higher price and so suffer a loss of surplus, which is given by rectangle $A$ in Figure 9.7. Some consumers have also dropped out of the market because of the higher price, with a corresponding loss of surplus given by triangle $B$. The total change in consumer surplus is therefore

$$\Delta CS = -A - B$$

Consumers clearly are worse off as a result of this policy.

What about producers? They receive a higher price for the units they sell, which results in an increase of surplus, given by rectangle $A$. (Rectangle $A$ represents a transfer of money from consumers to producers.) But the drop in sales from $Q_0$ to $Q_3$ results in a loss of surplus, which is given by triangle $C$. Finally, consider the cost to producers of expanding production from $Q_0$ to $Q_2$. Because they sell only $Q_3$, there is no revenue to cover the cost of producing $Q_2 - Q_3$. How can we measure this cost? Remember that the supply curve is the aggregate marginal cost curve for the industry. The supply curve therefore gives us the additional cost of producing each incremental unit. Thus the area under the

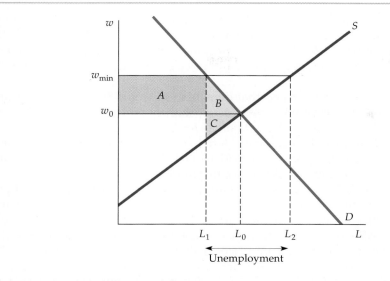

**FIGURE 9.8 The Minimum Wage**

Although the market-clearing wage is $w_0$, firms are not allowed to pay less than $w_{min}$. This results in unemployment of an amount $L_2 - L_1$ and a deadweight loss given by triangles $B$ and $C$.

supply curve from $Q_3$ to $Q_2$ is the cost of producing the quantity $Q_2 - Q_3$. This cost is represented by the shaded trapezoid $D$. So unless producers respond to unsold output by cutting production, the total change in producer surplus is

$$\Delta PS = A - C - D$$

Given that trapezoid $D$ can be large, a minimum price can even result in a net loss of surplus to producers alone! As a result, this form of government intervention can reduce producers' profits because of the cost of excess production.

Another example of a government-imposed price minimum is a minimum wage law. The effect of this policy is illustrated in Figure 9.8, which shows the supply and demand for labor. The wage is set at $w_{min}$, a level higher than the market-clearing wage $w_0$. As a result, those workers who can find jobs obtain a higher wage. However, some people who want to work will be unable to. The policy results in unemployment, which in the figure is $L_2 - L_1$. We will examine the minimum wage in more detail in Chapter 14.

**EXAMPLE 9.3** **Airline Regulation**

Before 1980, the airline industry in the United States looked very different than it does today. Fares and routes were tightly regulated by the Civil Aeronautics Board (CAB). The CAB set most fares well above what would have prevailed in a free market. It also restricted entry, so that many routes were served by only one or two airlines. By the late 1970s, however, the CAB liberalized fare regulation and allowed airlines to serve any routes they wished. By 1981, the industry had been completely deregulated, and the CAB itself was dissolved in 1982. Since that time, many new airlines have begun service, others have gone out of business, and price competition has become much more intense.

Many airline executives feared that deregulation would lead to chaos in the industry, with competitive pressure causing sharply reduced profits and even bankruptcies. After all, the original rationale for CAB regulation was to provide "stability" in an industry that was considered vital to the U.S. economy. And one might think that as long as price was held above its market-clearing level, profits would be higher than they would be in a free market.

Deregulation did lead to major changes in the industry. Some airlines merged or went out of business as new ones entered. Although prices fell considerably (to the benefit of consumers), profits overall did not fall much because the CAB's minimum prices had caused inefficiencies and artificially high costs. The effect of minimum prices is illustrated in Figure 9.9, where $P_0$ and $Q_0$ are the market-clearing price and quantity, $P_{min}$ is the minimum price, and $Q_1$ is the amount demanded at this higher price. The problem was that at price $P_{min}$, airlines wanted to supply a quantity $Q_2$, much larger than $Q_1$. Although they did not expand output to $Q_2$, they did expand it well beyond $Q_1$—to $Q_3$ in the figure—hoping to sell this quantity at the expense of competitors. As a result, load factors (the percentage of seats filled) were relatively low, and so were profits. (Trapezoid $D$ measures the cost of unsold output.)

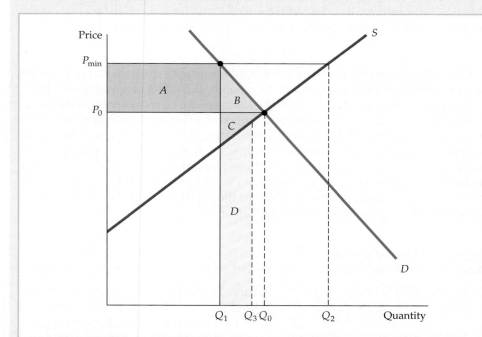

**FIGURE 9.9 Effect of Airline Regulation by the Civil Aeronautics Board**

At price $P_{min}$, airlines would like to supply $Q_2$, well above the quantity $Q_1$ that consumers will buy. Here they supply $Q_3$. Trapezoid $D$ is the cost of unsold output. Airline profits may have been lower as a result of regulation because triangle $C$ and trapezoid $D$ can together exceed rectangle $A$. In addition, consumers lose $A + B$.

| TABLE 9.1   Airline Industry Data | | | | | | | |
|---|---|---|---|---|---|---|---|
| | **1975** | **1980** | **1985** | **1990** | **1995** | **2000** | **2005** |
| Number of Carriers | 36 | 63 | 102 | 70 | 96 | 94 | 80 |
| Passenger Load Factor (%) | 54 | 58 | 61 | 62 | 67 | 72 | 78 |
| Passenger Mile Rate (Constant 1995 dollars) | .218 | .210 | .165 | .150 | .129 | .118 | .092 |
| Real Cost Index (1995 = 100) | 101 | 122 | 111 | 109 | 100 | 101 | 93 |
| Real Fuel Cost Index (1995 = 100) | 249 | 300 | 204 | 163 | 100 | 125 | 237 |
| Real Cost Index Corrected for Fuel Cost Changes | 71 | 73 | 88 | 95 | 100 | 96 | 67 |

Table 9.1 gives some key numbers that illustrate the evolution of the industry.[6] The number of carriers increased dramatically after deregulation, as did passenger load factors. The passenger-mile rate (the revenue per passenger-mile flown) fell sharply in real (inflation-adjusted) terms from 1980 to 1985, and then continued to drop from 1985 through 2005. This decline was the result of increased competition and reductions in fares. And what about costs? The real cost index indicates that even after adjusting for inflation, costs increased by about 20 percent from 1975 to 1980, and then fell gradually over the next 15 years. Changes in cost, however, are driven to a great extent by changes in the cost of fuel, which is driven in turn by changes in the price of oil. (For most airlines, fuel accounts for over 20 percent of total operating costs.) As Table 9.1 shows, the real cost of fuel has fluctuated dramatically, and this had nothing to do with deregulation. Because airlines have no control over oil prices, it is more informative to examine a "corrected" real cost index which removes the effects of changing fuel costs. Real fuel costs increased considerably from 1975 to 1980, which accounts for most of the increase in the real cost index. (Had fuel costs not increased, the real cost index would have increased by only about 3 percent.)

From 1980 to 1995, airlines benefited from the fact that the cost of fuel declined by about 65 percent in real terms. As shown in Table 9.1, had the cost of fuel remained fixed, the real cost index would have increased by about 35 percent, due largely to increases in labor costs. Airline bankruptcies and renegotiated labor contracts pushed labor costs down during 2000–2005, so that, even though fuel costs rose sharply again, the real cost index fell.

What, then, did airline deregulation do for consumers and producers? As new airlines entered the industry and fares went down, consumers benefited. This fact is borne out by the increase in consumer surplus given by rectangle *A* and triangle *B* in Figure 9.9. (The actual benefit to consumers was somewhat smaller because *quality* declined as planes became more crowded and delays and cancellations multiplied.) As for the airlines, they had to learn to live in a more competitive—and therefore more turbulent—environment, and some firms did not survive. But overall, airlines became so much more efficient that producer surplus may have increased. The total welfare gain from deregulation was positive and quite large.[7]

---

[6]Department of Commerce, *U.S. Statistical Abstract*, 1986, 1989, 1992, 1995, 2002.

[7]Studies of the effects of deregulation include John M. Trapani and C. Vincent Olson, "An Analysis of the Impact of Open Entry on Price and the Quality of Service in the Airline Industry," *Review of Economics and Statistics* 64 (February 1982): 118–38; David R. Graham, Daniel P. Kaplan, and David S. Sibley, "Efficiency and Competition in the Airline Industry," *Bell Journal of Economics* (Spring 1983): 118–38; S. Morrison and Clifford Whinston, *The Economic Effects of Airline Deregulation* (Washington: Brookings Institution, 1986); and Nancy L. Rose, "Profitability and Product Quality: Economic Determinants of Airline Safety Performance," *Journal of Political Economy* 98 (October 1990): 944–64.

## 9.4 PRICE SUPPORTS AND PRODUCTION QUOTAS

Besides imposing a minimum price, the government can increase the price of a good in other ways. Much of American agricultural policy is based on a system of **price supports**, whereby the government sets the market price of a good above the free-market level and buys up whatever output is needed to maintain that price. The government can also increase prices by *restricting production*, either directly or through incentives to producers. In this section, we show how these policies work and examine their impact on consumers, producers, and the federal budget.

• **price support**  Price set by government above free-market level and maintained by governmental purchases of excess supply.

### Price Supports

In the United States, price supports aim to increase the prices of dairy products, tobacco, corn, peanuts, and so on, so that the producers of those goods can receive higher incomes. Under a price support program, the government sets a support price $P_s$ and then buys up whatever output is needed to keep the market price at this level. Figure 9.10 illustrates this. Let's examine the resulting gains and losses to consumers, producers, and the government.

**Consumers**  At price $P_s$, the quantity that consumers demand falls to $Q_1$, but the quantity supplied increases to $Q_2$. To maintain this price and avoid having inventories pile up in producer warehouses, the government must buy the quantity $Q_g = Q_2 - Q_1$. In effect, because the government adds its demand $Q_g$ to the demand of consumers, producers can sell all they want at price $P_s$.

Because those consumers who purchase the good must pay the higher price $P_s$ instead of $P_0$, they suffer a loss of consumer surplus given by rectangle $A$. Because of the higher price, other consumers no longer buy the good or buy less of it, and their loss of surplus is given by triangle $B$. So, as with the minimum price that we examined above, consumers lose, in this case by an amount

$$\Delta CS = -A - B$$

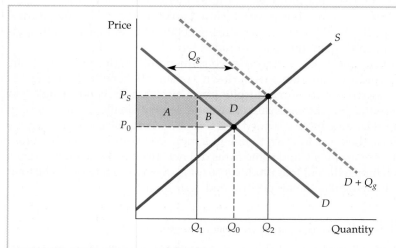

**FIGURE 9.10  Price Supports**

To maintain a price $P_s$ above the market-clearing price $P_0$, the government buys a quantity $Q_g$. The gain to producers is $A + B + D$. The loss to consumers is $A + B$. The cost to the government is the speckled rectangle, the area of which is $P_s(Q_2 - Q_1)$.

**Producers** On the other hand, producers gain (which is why such a policy is implemented). Producers are now selling a larger quantity $Q_2$ instead of $Q_0$, and at a higher price $P_s$. Observe from Figure 9.10 that producer surplus increases by the amount

$$\Delta PS = A + B + D$$

**The Government** But there is also a cost to the government (which must be paid for by taxes, and so is ultimately a cost to consumers). That cost is $(Q_2 - Q_1)P_s$, which is what the government must pay for the output it purchases. In Figure 9.10, this amount is represented by the large speckled rectangle. This cost may be reduced if the government can "dump" some of its purchases—i.e., sell them abroad at a low price. Doing so, however, hurts the ability of domestic producers to sell in foreign markets, and it is domestic producers that the government is trying to please in the first place.

What is the total welfare cost of this policy? To find out, we add the change in consumer surplus to the change in producer surplus and then subtract the cost to the government. Thus the total change in welfare is

$$\Delta CS + \Delta PS - \text{Cost to Govt.} = D - (Q_2 - Q_1)P_s$$

In terms of Figure 9.10, society as a whole is worse off by an amount given by the large speckled rectangle, less triangle $D$.

As we will see in Example 9.4, this welfare loss can be very large. But the most unfortunate part of this policy is the fact that there is a much more efficient way to help farmers. If the objective is to give farmers an additional income equal to $A + B + D$, it is far less costly to society to give them this money directly rather than via price supports. Because price supports are costing consumers $A + B$ anyway, by paying farmers directly, society saves the large speckled rectangle, less triangle $D$. So why doesn't the government simply give farmers money? Perhaps because price supports are a less obvious giveaway and, therefore, politically more attractive.[8]

## Production Quotas

Besides entering the market and buying up output—thereby increasing total demand—the government can also cause the price of a good to rise by *reducing supply*. It can do this by decree—that is, by simply setting quotas on how much each firm can produce. With appropriate quotas, the price can then be forced up to any arbitrary level.

This is exactly how many city governments maintain high taxi fares. They limit total supply by requiring each taxicab to have a medallion, and then limit the total number of medallions.[9] Another example is the control of liquor

---

[8]In practice, price supports for many agricultural commodities are effected through loans. The loan rate is in effect a price floor. If during the loan period market prices are not sufficiently high, farmers can forfeit their grain to the government (specifically to the Commodity Credit Corporation) as *full payment for the loan*. Farmers have the incentive to do this unless the market price rises above the support price.

[9]For example, as of 1995 New York City had not issued any new taxi medallions for half a century. Only 11,800 taxis were permitted to cruise the city's streets, the same number as in 1937! As a result, in 1995 a medallion could be sold for about $120,000. It shouldn't be a surprise, then, that the city's taxicab companies have vigorously opposed phasing out medallions in favor of an open system. Washington, D.C., has such an open system: An average taxi ride there costs about half of what it does in New York, and taxis are more available.

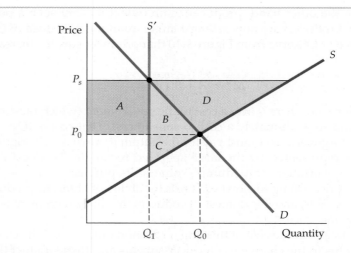

**FIGURE 9.11 Supply Restrictions**

To maintain a price $P_s$ above the market-clearing price $P_0$, the government can restrict supply to $Q_1$, either by imposing production quotas (as with taxicab medallions) or by giving producers a financial incentive to reduce output (as with acreage limitations in agriculture). For an incentive to work, it must be at least as large as $B + C + D$, which would be the additional profit earned by planting, given the higher price $P_s$. The cost to the government is therefore at least $B + C + D$.

licenses by state governments. By requiring any bar or restaurant that serves alcohol to have a liquor license and then limiting the number of licenses, entry by new restaurateurs is limited, which allows those who have licenses to earn higher prices and profit margins.

The welfare effects of production quotas are shown in Figure 9.11. The government restricts the quantity supplied to $Q_1$, rather than the market-clearing level $Q_0$. Thus the supply curve becomes the vertical line $S'$ at $Q_1$. Consumer surplus is reduced by rectangle $A$ (those consumers who buy the good pay a higher price) plus triangle $B$ (at this higher price, some consumers no longer purchase the good). Producers gain rectangle $A$ (by selling at a higher price) but lose triangle $C$ (because they now produce and sell $Q_1$ rather than $Q_0$). Once again, there is a deadweight loss, given by triangles $B$ and $C$.

**Incentive Programs** In U.S. agricultural policy, output is reduced by incentives rather than by outright quotas. *Acreage limitation programs* give farmers financial incentives to leave some of their acreage idle. Figure 9.11 also shows the welfare effects of reducing supply in this way. Note that because farmers agree to limit planted acreage, the supply curve again becomes completely inelastic at the quantity $Q_1$, and the market price is increased from $P_0$ to $P_s$.

As with direct production quotas, the change in consumer surplus is

$$\Delta CS = -A - B$$

Farmers now receive a higher price for the production $Q_1$, which corresponds to a gain in surplus of rectangle $A$. But because production is reduced from $Q_0$ to $Q_1$, there is a loss of producer surplus corresponding to triangle $C$. Finally, farmers receive money from the government as an incentive to reduce production. Thus the total change in producer surplus is now

$$\Delta PS = A - C + \text{Payments for not producing}$$

The cost to the government is a payment sufficient to give farmers an incentive to reduce output to $Q_1$. That incentive must be at least as large as $B + C + D$ because that area represents the additional profit that could be made by planting, *given the higher price* $P_s$. (Remember that the higher price $P_s$ gives farmers an incentive to produce *more* even though the government is trying to get them to produce *less*.) Thus the cost to the government is at least $B + C + D$, and the total change in producer surplus is

$$\Delta PS = A - C + B + C + D = A + B + D$$

This is the same change in producer surplus as with price supports maintained by government purchases of output. (Refer to Figure 9.10.) Farmers, then, should be indifferent between the two policies because they end up gaining the same amount of money from each. Likewise, consumers lose the same amount of money.

Which policy costs the government more? The answer depends on whether the sum of triangles $B + C + D$ in Figure 9.11 is larger or smaller than $(Q_2 - Q_1)P_s$ (the large speckled rectangle) in Figure 9.10. Usually it will be smaller, so that an acreage-limitation program costs the government (and society) less than price supports maintained by government purchases.

Still, even an acreage-limitation program is more costly to society than simply handing the farmers money. The total change in welfare ($\Delta CS + \Delta PS -$ Cost to Govt.) under the acreage-limitation program is

$$\Delta \text{Welfare} = -A - B + A + B + D - B - C - D = -B - C$$

Society would clearly be better off in efficiency terms if the government simply gave the farmers $A + B + D$, leaving price and output alone. Farmers would then gain $A + B + D$ and the government would lose $A + B + D$, for a total welfare change of zero, instead of a loss of $B + C$. However, economic efficiency is not always the objective of government policy.

**EXAMPLE 9.4**

## Supporting the Price of Wheat

In Examples 2.5 (page 38) and 4.3 (page 129), we began to examine the market for wheat in the United States. Using linear demand and supply curves, we found that the market-clearing price of wheat was about $3.46 in 1981, but it fell to about $2.78 by 2002 because of a drop in export demand. In fact, government programs kept the actual price of wheat higher and provided direct subsidies to farmers. How did these programs work, how much did they end up costing consumers, and how much did they add to the federal deficit?

First, let's examine the market in 1981. In that year, although there were no effective limitations on the production of wheat, the price was increased to $3.70 by government purchases. How much would the government have had to buy to get the price from $3.46 to $3.70? To answer this question, first write the equations for supply and for total private (domestic plus export) demand:

$$1981 \text{ Supply:} \quad Q_S = 1800 + 240P$$

$$1981 \text{ Demand:} \quad Q_D = 3550 - 266P$$

By equating supply and demand, you can check that the market-clearing price is $3.46, and that the quantity produced is 2630 million bushels. Figure 9.12 illustrates this.

To increase the price to $3.70, the government must buy a quantity of wheat $Q_g$. *Total* demand (private plus government) will then be

$$1981 \text{ Total demand:} \quad Q_{DT} = 3550 - 266P + Q_g$$

Now equate supply with this total demand:

$$1800 + 240P = 3550 - 266P + Q_g$$

or

$$Q_g = 506P - 1750$$

This equation can be used to determine the required quantity of government wheat purchases $Q_g$ as a function of the desired support price $P$. To achieve a price of $3.70, the government must buy

$$Q_g = (506)(3.70) - 1750 = 122 \text{ million bushels}$$

Note in Figure 9.12 that these 122 million bushels are the difference between the quantity supplied at the $3.70 price (2688 million bushels) and the quantity of private demand (2566 million bushels). The figure also shows the gains and losses to consumers and producers. Recall that consumers lose rectangle $A$ and triangle $B$. You can verify that rectangle $A$ is $(3.70 - 3.46)(2566) = \$616$ million, and triangle $B$ is $(1/2)(3.70 - 3.46)(2630 - 2566) = \$8$ million, so that the total cost to consumers is $624 million.

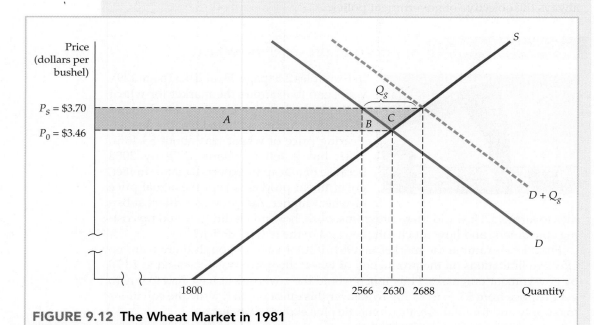

**FIGURE 9.12 The Wheat Market in 1981**

By buying 122 million bushels of wheat, the government increased the market-clearing price from $3.46 per bushel to $3.70.

The cost to the government is the $3.70 it pays for the wheat times the 122 million bushels it buys, or $451.4 million. The total cost of the program is then $624 million + $451.4 million = $1075 million. Compare this with the gain to producers, which is rectangle $A$ plus triangles $B$ and $C$. You can verify that this gain is $638 million.

Price supports for wheat were expensive in 1981. To increase the surplus of farmers by $638 million, consumers and taxpayers had to pay $1076 million. In fact, taxpayers paid even more than that. Wheat producers were also given subsidies of about 30 cents per bushel, which adds up to another $806 million.

In 1985, the situation became even worse because of the drop in export demand. In that year, the supply and demand curves were as follows:

$$1985\ Supply:\quad Q_S = 1800 + 240P$$

$$1985\ Demand:\quad Q_D = 2580 - 194P$$

You can verify that the market-clearing price and quantity were $1.80 and 2232 million bushels, respectively. The actual price, however, was $3.20.

To increase the price to $3.20, the government bought wheat and imposed a production quota of about 2425 million bushels. (Farmers who wanted to take part in the subsidy program—and most did—had to agree to limit their acreage.) Figure 9.13 illustrates this situation. At the quantity 2425 million bushels, the supply curve becomes vertical. Now, to determine how much wheat $Q_g$ the government had to buy, set this quantity of 2425 equal to total demand:

$$2425 = 2580 - 194P + Q_g$$

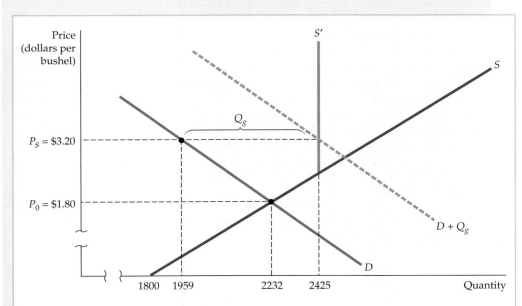

**FIGURE 9.13 The Wheat Market in 1985**

In 1985, the demand for wheat was much lower than in 1981, because the market-clearing price was only $1.80. To increase the price to $3.20, the government bought 466 million bushels and also imposed a production quota of 2425 million bushels.

or

$$Q_g = -155 + 194P$$

Substituting \$3.20 for $P$, we see that $Q_g$ must be 466 million bushels. This program cost the government (\$3.20)(466) = \$1491 million.

Again, this is not the whole story. The government also provided a subsidy of 80 cents per bushel, so that producers again received about \$4.00 for their wheat. Because 2425 million bushels were produced, that subsidy cost an additional \$1940 million. In all, U.S. wheat programs cost taxpayers nearly \$3.5 billion in 1985. Of course, there was also a loss of consumer surplus and a gain of producer surplus; you can calculate what they were.

In 1996, the U.S. Congress passed a new farm bill, nicknamed the "Freedom to Farm" law. It was designed to reduce the role of government and to make agriculture more market oriented. The law eliminated production quotas (for wheat, corn, rice, and other products) and gradually reduced government purchases and subsidies through 2003. However, the law did not completely deregulate U.S. agriculture. For example, price support programs for peanuts and sugar remained in place. Furthermore, pre-1996 price supports and production quotas would be reinstated unless Congress renewed the law in 2003. (Congress did not renew it—more on this below.) Even under the 1996 law, agricultural subsidies remained substantial.

In Example 2.5, we saw that the market-clearing price of wheat in 2007 had increased to about \$6.00 per bushel. The supply and demand curves in 2007 were as follows:

$$\textit{Demand}: \quad Q_D = 2900 - 125P$$

$$\textit{Supply}: \quad Q_S = 1460 + 115P$$

You can check to see that the market-clearing quantity is 2150 million bushels.

Congress did not renew the 1996 Freedom to Farm Act. Instead, in 2002, Congress and the Bush administration essentially reversed the effects of the 1996 bill through passage of the Farm Security and Rural Investment Act, which reinstates subsidies for most crops, in particular grain and cotton.[10] Although the bill does not explicitly restore price supports, it calls for the government to issue "fixed direct payments" to producers based on a fixed payment rate and the base acreage for a particular crop. Using U.S. wheat acreage and production levels in 2001, we can calculate that this bill cost taxpayers nearly \$1.1 billion in annual payments to wheat producers alone.[11] The 2002 farm bill was projected to cost taxpayers \$190 billion over 10 years.

Congress revisited agricultural subsidies in 2007. For most crops, previous subsidy rates were either maintained or increased, thus making the burden on U.S. taxpayers even higher.

---

[10]See Mike Allen, "Bush Signs Bill Providing Big Farm Subsidy Increases," *The Washington Post*, May 14, 2002; see David E. Sanger, "Reversing Course, Bush Signs Bill Raising Farm Subsidies," *The New York Times*, May 14, 2002.

[11]Estimated 2001 Wheat direct payments = (payment rate)*(payment yield)*(base acres)* 0.85 = (\$0.52)*(40.2)*(59,617,000)*0.85 = \$1.06 billion.

## 9.5 IMPORT QUOTAS AND TARIFFS

Many countries use **import quotas** and **tariffs** to keep the domestic price of a product above world levels and thereby enable the domestic industry to enjoy higher profits than it would under free trade. As we will see, the cost to taxpayers from this protection can be high, with the loss to consumers exceeding the gain to domestic producers.

Without a quota or tariff, a country will import a good when its world price is below the price that would prevail domestically were there no imports. Figure 9.14 illustrates this principle. $S$ and $D$ are the domestic supply and demand curves. If there were no imports, the domestic price and quantity would be $P_0$ and $Q_0$, which equate supply and demand. But because the world price $P_w$ is below $P_0$, domestic consumers have an incentive to purchase from abroad and will do so if imports are not restricted. How much will be imported? The domestic price will fall to the world price $P_w$; at this lower price, domestic production will fall to $Q_s$, and domestic consumption will rise to $Q_d$. Imports are then the difference between domestic consumption and domestic production, $Q_d - Q_s$.

Now suppose the government, bowing to pressure from the domestic industry, eliminates imports by imposing a quota of zero—that is, forbidding any importation of the good. What are the gains and losses from such a policy?

• **import quota** Limit on the quantity of a good that can be imported.

• **tariff** Tax on an imported good.

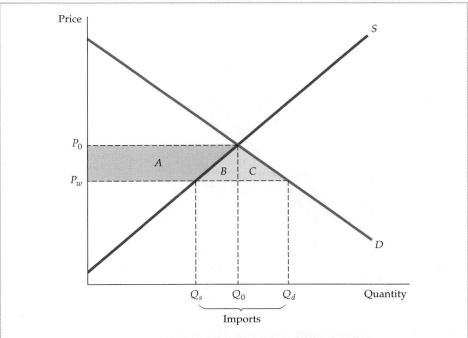

**FIGURE 9.14 Import Tariff or Quota That Eliminates Imports**

In a free market, the domestic price equals the world price $P_w$. A total $Q_d$ is consumed, of which $Q_s$ is supplied domestically and the rest imported. When imports are eliminated, the price is increased to $P_0$. The gain to producers is trapezoid $A$. The loss to consumers is $A + B + C$, so the deadweight loss is $B + C$.

With no imports allowed, the domestic price will rise to $P_0$. Consumers who still purchase the good (in quantity $Q_0$) will pay more and will lose an amount of surplus given by trapezoid $A$ and triangle $B$. In addition, given this higher price, some consumers will no longer buy the good, so there is an additional loss of consumer surplus, given by triangle $C$. The total change in consumer surplus is therefore

$$\Delta CS = -A - B - C$$

What about producers? Output is now higher ($Q_0$ instead of $Q_s$) and is sold at a higher price ($P_0$ instead of $P_w$). Producer surplus therefore increases by the amount of trapezoid $A$:

$$\Delta PS = A$$

The change in total surplus, $\Delta CS + \Delta PS$, is therefore $-B - C$. Again, there is a deadweight loss—consumers lose more than producers gain.

Imports could also be reduced to zero by imposing a sufficiently large tariff. The tariff would have to be equal to or greater than the difference between $P_0$ and $P_w$. With a tariff of this size, there will be no imports and, therefore, no government revenue from tariff collections, so the effect on consumers and producers would be the same as with a quota.

More often, government policy is designed to reduce but not eliminate imports. Again, this can be done with either a tariff or a quota, as Figure 9.15 shows. Under free trade, the domestic price will equal the world price $P_w$, and imports will be $Q_d - Q_s$. Now suppose that a tariff of $T$ dollars per unit is imposed on imports. Then the domestic price will rise to $P^*$ (the world price plus the tariff); domestic production will rise and domestic consumption will fall.

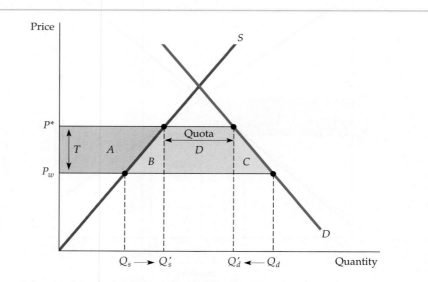

**FIGURE 9.15 Import Tariff or Quota (General Case)**

When imports are reduced, the domestic price is increased from $P_w$ to $P^*$. This can be achieved by a quota, or by a tariff $T = P^* - P_w$. Trapezoid $A$ is again the gain to domestic producers. The loss to consumers is $A + B + C + D$. If a tariff is used, the government gains $D$, the revenue from the tariff, so the net domestic loss is $B + C$. If a quota is used instead, rectangle $D$ becomes part of the profits of foreign producers, and the net domestic loss is $B + C + D$.

In Figure 9.15, this tariff leads to a change of consumer surplus given by

$$\Delta CS = -A - B - C - D$$

The change in producer surplus is again

$$\Delta PS = A$$

Finally, the government will collect revenue in the amount of the tariff times the quantity of imports, which is rectangle $D$. The total change in welfare, $\Delta CS$ plus $\Delta PS$ plus the revenue to the government, is therefore $-A - B - C - D + A + D = -B - C$. Triangles $B$ and $C$ again represent the deadweight loss from restricting imports. ($B$ represents the loss from domestic overproduction and $C$ the loss from too little consumption.)

Suppose the government uses a quota instead of a tariff to restrict imports: Foreign producers can only ship a specific quantity ($Q'_d - Q'_s$ in Figure 9.15) to the United States and can then charge the higher price $P^*$ for their U.S. sales. The changes in U.S. consumer and producer surplus will be the same as with the tariff, but instead of the U.S. government collecting the revenue given by rectangle $D$, this money will go to the foreign producers in the form of higher profits. The United States as a whole will be even worse off than it was under the tariff, losing $D$ as well as the deadweight loss $B$ and $C$.[12]

This situation is exactly what transpired with automobile imports from Japan in the 1980s. Under pressure from domestic automobile producers, the Reagan administration negotiated "voluntary" import restraints, under which the Japanese agreed to restrict shipments of cars to the United States. The Japanese could therefore sell those cars that were shipped at a price higher than the world level and capture a higher profit margin on each one. The United States would have been better off by simply imposing a tariff on these imports.

**EXAMPLE 9.5** The Sugar Quota

In recent years, the world price of sugar has been as low as 4 cents per pound, while the U.S. price has been 20 to 30 cents per pound. Why? By restricting imports, the U.S. government protects the $3 billion domestic sugar industry, which would virtually be put out of business if it had to compete with low-cost foreign producers. This policy has been good for U.S. sugar producers. It has even been good for some foreign sugar producers—in particular, those whose successful lobbying efforts have given them big shares of the quota. But like most policies of this sort, it has been bad for consumers.

---

[12]Alternatively, an import quota can be maintained by rationing imports to U.S. importing firms or trading companies. These middlemen would have the rights to import a fixed amount of the good each year. These rights are valuable because the middleman can buy the product on the world market at price $P_w$ and then sell it at price $P^*$. The aggregate value of these rights is, therefore, given by rectangle $D$. If the government *sells* the rights for this amount of money, it can capture the same revenue it would receive with a tariff. But if these rights are given away, as sometimes happens, the money becomes a windfall to middlemen.

To see just how bad, let's look at the sugar market in 2005. Here are the relevant data for that year:

| | |
|---|---|
| U.S. production: | 15.2 billion pounds |
| U.S. consumption: | 20.5 billion pounds |
| U.S. price: | 27 cents per pound |
| World price: | 12 cents per pound |

At these prices and quantities, the price elasticity of U.S. supply is 1.5, and the price elasticity of U.S. demand is -0.3.[13]

In §2.6, we explain how to fit linear supply and demand functions to data of this kind.

We will fit linear supply and demand curves to these data, and then use them to calculate the effects of the quotas. You can verify that the following U.S. supply curve is consistent with a production level of 15.2 billion pounds, a price of 27 cents per pound, and a supply elasticity of 1.5:

$$U.S.\ supply: \qquad Q_S = -7.48 + 0.84P$$

where quantity is measured in billions of pounds and price in cents per pound. Similarly, the −0.3 demand elasticity, together with the data for U.S. consumption and U.S. price, give the following linear demand curve:

$$U.S.\ demand: \qquad Q_D = 26.7 - 0.23P$$

These supply and demand curves are plotted in Figure 9.16. At the 12-cent world price, U.S. production would have been only about 2.6 billion pounds and U.S. consumption about 23.95 billion pounds, most of this imports. But fortunately for U.S. producers, imports were limited to only 5.3 billion pounds, which pushed the U.S. price up to 27 cents.

What did this policy cost U.S. consumers? The lost consumer surplus is given by the sum of trapezoid $A$, triangles $B$ and $C$, and rectangle $D$. You should go through the calculations to verify that trapezoid $A$ is equal to $1335 million, triangle $B$ to $945 million, triangle $C$ to $255 million, and rectangle $D$ to $795 million. The total cost to consumers in 2005 was about $3.3 billion.

How much did producers gain from this policy? Their increase in surplus is given by trapezoid $A$ (i.e., about $1.3 billion). The $795 million of rectangle $D$ was a gain for those foreign producers who succeeded in obtaining large allotments of the quota because they received a higher price for their sugar. Triangles $B$ and $C$ represent a deadweight loss of about $1.2 billion.

---

[13]Prices and quantities are from Won W. Koo and Richard D. Taylor, "2006 Outlook of the U.S. and World Sugar Markets, 2005–2015," Agribusiness & Applied Economics Report No. 589, *Center for Agricultural Policy and Trade Studies*, North Dakota State University, 2006. The elasticity estimates are based on Morris E. Morkre and David G. Tarr, *Effects of Restrictions on United States Imports: Five Case Studies and Theory*, U.S. Federal Trade Commission Staff Report, June 1981; and F. M. Scherer, "The United States Sugar Program," Kennedy School of Government Case Study, Harvard University, 1992. For a general discussion of sugar quotas and other aspects of U.S. agricultural policy, see D. Gale Johnson, *Agricultural Policy and Trade* (New York: New York University Press, 1985); and Gail L. Cramer and Clarence W. Jensen, *Agricultural Economics and Agribusiness* (New York: Wiley, 1985).

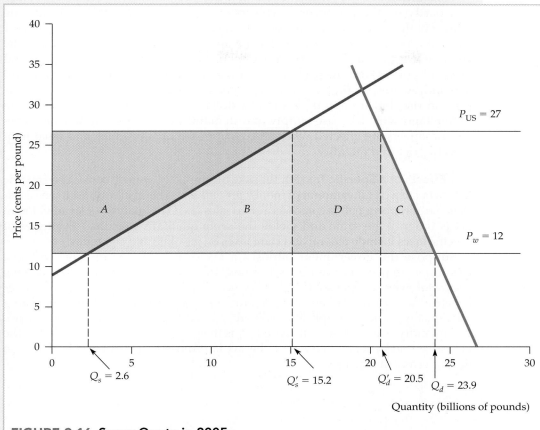

**FIGURE 9.16 Sugar Quota in 2005**

At the world price of 12 cents per pound, about 23.9 billion pounds of sugar would have been consumed in the United States in 2005, of which all but 2.6 billion pounds would have been imported. Restricting imports to 5.3 billion pounds caused the U.S. price to go up by 15 cents. The cost to consumers, $A + B + C + D$, was about $3.3 billion. The gain to domestic producers was trapezoid $A$, about $1.3 billion. Rectangle $D$, $795 million, was a gain to those foreign producers who obtained quota allotments. Triangles $B$ and $C$ represent the deadweight loss of about $1.2 billion.

## 9.6 THE IMPACT OF A TAX OR SUBSIDY

What would happen to the price of widgets if the government imposed a $1 tax on every widget sold? Many people would answer that the price would increase by a dollar, with consumers now paying a dollar more per widget than they would have paid without the tax. But this answer is wrong.

Or consider the following question. The government wants to impose a 50-cent-per-gallon tax on gasoline and is considering two methods of collecting it. Under Method 1, the owner of each gas station would deposit the tax money (50 cents times the number of gallons sold) in a locked box, to be collected by a government agent. Under Method 2, the buyer would pay the tax (50 cents times the number of gallons purchased) directly to the government. Which method costs the buyer more? Many people would say Method 2, but this answer is also wrong.

The burden of a tax (or the benefit of a subsidy) falls partly on the consumer and partly on the producer. Furthermore, it does not matter who puts the money in the collection box (or sends the check to the government)—Methods 1 and 2 both cost the consumer the same amount of money. As we will see, the share of a tax borne by consumers depends on the shapes of the supply and demand curves and, in particular, on the relative elasticities of supply and demand. As for our first question, a $1 tax on widgets would indeed cause the price to rise, but usually by *less* than a dollar and sometimes by *much* less. To understand why, let's use supply and demand curves to see how consumers and producers are affected when a tax is imposed on a product, and what happens to price and quantity.

• **specific tax**  Tax of a certain amount of money per unit sold.

**The Effects of a Specific Tax**  For the sake of simplicity, we will consider a **specific tax**—a tax of a certain amount of money *per unit sold*. This is in contrast to an *ad valorem* (i.e., proportional) *tax*, such as a state sales tax. (The analysis of an ad valorem tax is roughly the same and yields the same qualitative results.) Examples of specific taxes include federal and state taxes on gasoline and cigarettes.

Suppose the government imposes a tax of $t$ cents per unit on widgets. Assuming that everyone obeys the law, the government must then receive $t$ cents for every widget sold. *This means that the price the buyer pays must exceed the net price the seller receives by t cents.* Figure 9.17 illustrates this simple accounting relationship—and its implications. Here, $P_0$ and $Q_0$ represent the market price and quantity *before* the tax is imposed. $P_b$ is the price that buyers pay, and $P_s$ is the net price that sellers receive *after* the tax is imposed. Note that $P_b - P_s = t$, so the government is happy.

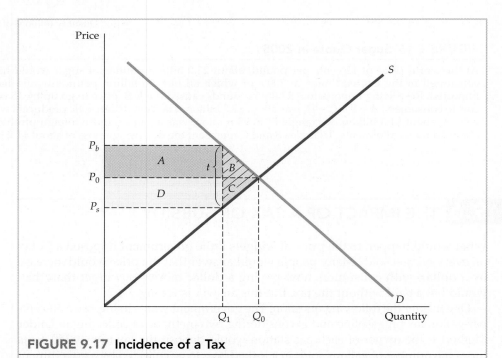

**FIGURE 9.17  Incidence of a Tax**

$P_b$ is the price (including the tax) paid by buyers. $P_s$ is the price that sellers receive, less the tax. Here the burden of the tax is split evenly between buyers and sellers. Buyers lose $A + B$, sellers lose $D + C$, and the government earns $A + D$ in revenue. The deadweight loss is $B + C$.

How do we determine what the market quantity will be after the tax is imposed, and how much of the tax is borne by buyers and how much by sellers? First, remember that what buyers care about is the price that they must pay: $P_b$. The amount that they will buy is given by the demand curve; it is the quantity that we read off of the demand curve given a price $P_b$. Similarly, sellers care about the net price they receive, $P_s$. Given $P_s$, the quantity that they will produce and sell is read off the supply curve. Finally, we know that the quantity sold must equal the quantity bought. The solution, then, is to find the quantity that corresponds to a price of $P_b$ on the demand curve, and a price of $P_s$ on the supply curve, such that the difference $P_b - P_s$ is equal to the tax $t$. In Figure 9.17, this quantity is shown as $Q_1$.

Who bears the burden of the tax? In Figure 9.17, this burden is shared roughly equally by buyers and sellers. The market price (the price buyers pay) rises by half of the tax, and the price that sellers receive falls by roughly half of the tax.

As Figure 9.17 shows, market clearing requires *four conditions* to be satisfied after the tax is in place:

1. The quantity sold and the buyer's price $P_b$ must lie on the demand curve (because buyers are interested only in the price they must pay).

2. The quantity sold and the seller's price $P_s$ must lie on the supply curve (because sellers are concerned only with the amount of money they receive net of the tax).

3. The quantity demanded must equal the quantity supplied ($Q_1$ in the figure).

4. The difference between the price the buyer pays and the price the seller receives must equal the tax $t$.

These conditions can be summarized by the following four equations:

$$Q^D = Q^D(P_b) \qquad \textbf{(9.1a)}$$

$$Q^S = Q^S(P_s) \qquad \textbf{(9.1b)}$$

$$Q^D = Q^S \qquad \textbf{(9.1c)}$$

$$P_b - P_s = t \qquad \textbf{(9.1d)}$$

If we know the demand curve $Q^D(P_b)$, the supply curve $Q^S(P_s)$, and the size of the tax $t$, we can solve these equations for the buyers' price $P_b$, the sellers' price $P_s$, and the total quantity demanded and supplied. This task is not as difficult as it may seem, as we will demonstrate in Example 9.6.

Figure 9.17 also shows that a tax results in a *deadweight loss*. Because buyers pay a higher price, there is a change in consumer surplus given by

$$\Delta CS = -A - B$$

Because sellers now receive a lower price, there is also a change in producer surplus given by

$$\Delta PS = -C - D$$

Government tax revenue is $tQ_1$, the sum of rectangles $A$ and $D$. The total change in welfare, $\Delta CS$ plus $\Delta PS$ plus the revenue to the government, is therefore $-A - B - C - D + A + D = -B - C$. Triangles $B$ and $C$ represent the deadweight loss from the tax.

In Figure 9.17, the burden of the tax is shared almost evenly between buyers and sellers, but this is not always the case. If demand is relatively inelastic and supply is relatively elastic, the burden of the tax will fall mostly on buyers. Figure 9.18(a) shows why: It takes a relatively large increase in price to reduce the quantity demanded by even a small amount, whereas only a small price decrease is needed to reduce the quantity supplied. For example, because cigarettes are addictive, the elasticity of demand is small (about −0.4); thus federal and state cigarette taxes are borne largely by cigarette buyers.[14] Figure 9.18(b) shows the opposite case: If demand is relatively elastic and supply is relatively inelastic, the burden of the tax will fall mostly on sellers.

So even if we have only estimates of the elasticities of demand and supply at a point or for a small range of prices and quantities, instead of the entire demand and supply curves, we can still roughly determine who will bear the greatest burden of a tax (whether the tax is actually in effect or is only under discussion as a policy option). In general, *a tax falls mostly on the buyer if $E_d/E_s$ is small, and mostly on the seller if $E_d/E_s$ is large.*

In fact, by using the following "pass-through" formula, we can calculate the percentage of the tax borne by buyers:

$$\text{Pass-through fraction} = E_s/(E_s - E_d)$$

This formula tells us what fraction of the tax is "passed through" to consumers in the form of higher prices. For example, when demand is totally inelastic, so

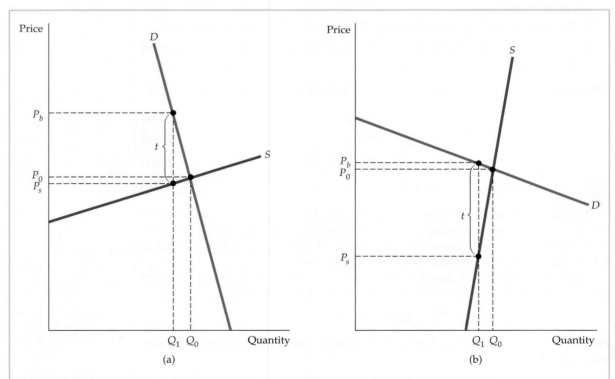

**FIGURE 9.18 Impact of a Tax Depends on Elasticities of Supply and Demand**

**(a)** If demand is very inelastic relative to supply, the burden of the tax falls mostly on buyers. **(b)** If demand is very elastic relative to supply, it falls mostly on sellers.

[14]See Daniel A. Sumner and Michael K. Wohlgenant, "Effects of an Increase in the Federal Excise Tax on Cigarettes," *American Journal of Agricultural Economics* 67 (May 1985): 235–42.

that $E_d$ is zero, the pass-through fraction is 1 and all the tax is borne by consumers. When demand is totally elastic, the pass-through fraction is zero and producers bear all the tax. (The fraction of the tax that producers bear is given by $-E_d/(E_s - E_d)$.)

## The Effects of a Subsidy

A **subsidy** can be analyzed in much the same way as a tax—in fact, you can think of a subsidy as a *negative tax*. With a subsidy, the sellers' price *exceeds* the buyers' price, and the difference between the two is the amount of the subsidy. As you would expect, the effect of a subsidy on the quantity produced and consumed is just the opposite of the effect of a tax—the quantity will increase.

Figure 9.19 illustrates this. At the presubsidy market price $P_0$, the elasticities of supply and demand are roughly equal. As a result, the benefit of the subsidy is shared roughly equally between buyers and sellers. As with a tax, this is not always the case. In general, *the benefit of a subsidy accrues mostly to buyers if $E_d/E_s$ is small and mostly to sellers if $E_d/E_s$ is large.*

As with a tax, given the supply curve, the demand curve, and the size of the subsidy $s$, we can solve for the resulting prices and quantity. The same four conditions needed for the market to clear apply for a subsidy as for a tax, but now the difference between the sellers' price and the buyers' price is equal to the subsidy. Again, we can write these conditions algebraically:

> **subsidy** Payment reducing the buyer's price below the seller's price; i.e., a negative tax.

$$Q^D = Q^D(P_b) \tag{9.2a}$$

$$Q^S = Q^S(P_s) \tag{9.2b}$$

$$Q^D = Q^S \tag{9.2c}$$

$$P_s - P_b = s \tag{9.2d}$$

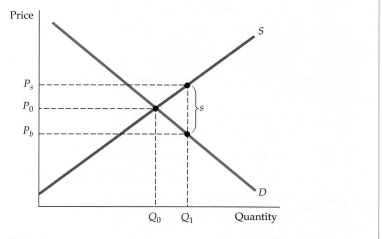

**FIGURE 9.19 Subsidy**

A subsidy can be thought of as a negative tax. Like a tax, the benefit of a subsidy is split between buyers and sellers, depending on the relative elasticities of supply and demand.

To make sure you understand how to analyze the impact of a tax or subsidy, you might find it helpful to work through one or two examples, such as Exercises 2 and 14 at the end of this chapter.

---

**EXAMPLE 9.6**  A Tax on Gasoline

The idea of a large tax on gasoline, both to raise government revenue and to reduce oil consumption and U.S. dependence on oil imports, has been discussed for many years. Let's see how a $1.00-per-gallon tax would affect the price and consumption of gasoline.

We will do this analysis in the setting of market conditions during 2005–2007—when gasoline was selling for about $2 per gallon and total consumption was about 100 billion gallons per year (bg/yr).[15] We will also use intermediate-run elasticities: elasticities that would apply to a period of about three to six years after a price change.

A reasonable number for the intermediate-run elasticity of gasoline demand is −0.5 (see Example 2.6 in Chapter 2—page 44). We can use this figure, together with the $2 and 100 bg/yr price and quantity numbers, to calculate a linear demand curve for gasoline. You can verify that the following demand curve fits these data:

> In §2.5, we explain that demand is often more price elastic in the long run than in the short run because it takes time for people to change their consumption habits and/or because the demand for a good might be linked to the stock of another good that changes slowly.

*Gasoline demand:*     $Q^D = 150 - 25P$

Gasoline is refined from crude oil, some of which is produced domestically and some imported. (Some gasoline is also imported directly.) The supply curve for gasoline will therefore depend on the world price of oil, on domestic oil supply, and on the cost of refining. The details are beyond the scope of this example, but a reasonable number for the elasticity of supply is 0.4. You should verify that this elasticity, together with the $2 and 100 bg/yr price and quantity, gives the following linear supply curve:

*Gasoline supply:*     $Q^S = 60 + 20P$

You should also verify that these demand and supply curves imply a market price of $2 and quantity of 100 bg/yr.

> For a review of the procedure for calculating linear curves, see §2.6. Given data for price and quantity, as well as estimates of demand and supply elasticities, we can use a two-step procedure to solve for quantity demanded and supplied.

We can use these linear demand and supply curves to calculate the effect of a $1-per-gallon tax. First, we write the four conditions that must hold, as given by equations (9.1a–d):

$$Q^D = 150 - 25P_b \qquad \text{(Demand)}$$
$$Q^S = 60 + 20P_s \qquad \text{(Supply)}$$
$$Q^D = Q^S \qquad \text{(Supply must equal demand)}$$
$$P_b - P_s = 1.00 \qquad \text{(Government must receive \$1.00/gallon)}$$

Now combine the first three equations to equate supply and demand:

$$150 - 25P_b = 60 + 20P_s$$

---

[15]Of course, this price varied across regions and grades of gasoline, but we can ignore this here. Quantities of oil and oil products are often measured in barrels; there are 42 gallons in a barrel, so the quantity figure could also be written as 2.4 billion barrels per year.

We can rewrite the last of the four equations as $P_b = P_s + 1.00$ and substitute this for $P_b$ in the above equation:

$$150 - 25(P_s + 1.00) = 60 + 20P_s$$

Now we can rearrange this equation and solve for $P_s$:

$$20P_s + 25P_s = 150 - 25 - 60$$

$$45P_s = 65, \text{ or } P_s = 1.44$$

Remember that $P_b = P_s + 1.00$, so $P_b = 2.44$. Finally, we can determine the total quantity from either the demand or supply curve. Using the demand curve (and the price $P_b = 2.44$), we find that $Q = 150 - (25)(2.44) = 150 - 61$, or $Q = 89$ bg/yr. This represents an 11-percent decline in gasoline consumption. Figure 9.20 illustrates these calculations and the effect of the tax.

The burden of this tax would be split roughly evenly between consumers and producers. Consumers would pay about 44 cents per gallon more for gasoline, and producers would receive about 56 cents per gallon less. It should not be surprising, then, that both consumers and producers opposed such a tax, and politicians representing both groups fought the proposal every time it came up. But note that the tax would raise significant revenue for the government. The annual revenue would be $tQ = (1.00)(89) = \$89$ billion per year.

The cost to consumers and producers, however, will be more than the $89 billion in tax revenue. Figure 9.20 shows the deadweight loss from this tax as the two

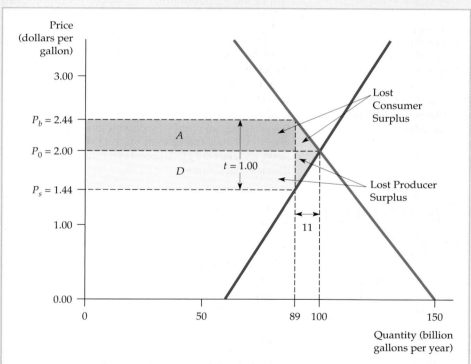

**FIGURE 9.20  Impact of $1 Gasoline Tax**

The price of gasoline at the pump increases from $2.00 per gallon to $2.44, and the quantity sold falls from 100 to 89 bg/yr. Annual revenue from the tax is $(1.00)(89) = \$89$ billion. The two triangles show the deadweight loss of $5.5 billion per year.

shaded triangles. The two rectangles $A$ and $D$ represent the total tax collected by the government, but the total loss of consumer and producer surplus is larger.

Before deciding whether a gasoline tax is desirable, it is important to know how large the resulting deadweight loss is likely to be. We can easily calculate this from Figure 9.20. Combining the two small triangles into one large one, we see that the area is

$$(1/2) \times (\$1.00/\text{gallon}) \times (11 \text{ billion gallons/year})$$

$$= \$5.5 \text{ billion per year}$$

This deadweight loss is about 6 percent of the government revenue resulting from the tax, and must be balanced against any additional benefits that the tax might bring.

# SUMMARY

1. Simple models of supply and demand can be used to analyze a wide variety of government policies, including price controls, minimum prices, price support programs, production quotas or incentive programs to limit output, import tariffs and quotas, and taxes and subsidies.

2. In each case, consumer and producer surplus are used to evaluate the gains and losses to consumers and producers. Applying the methodology to natural gas price controls, airline regulation, price supports for wheat, and the sugar quota shows that these gains and losses can be quite large.

3. When government imposes a tax or subsidy, price usually does not rise or fall by the full amount of the tax or subsidy. Also, the incidence of a tax or subsidy is usually split between producers and consumers. The fraction that each group ends up paying or receiving depends on the relative elasticities of supply and demand.

4. Government intervention generally leads to a deadweight loss; even if consumer surplus and producer surplus are weighted equally, there will be a net loss from government policies that shifts surplus from one group to the other. In some cases, this deadweight loss will be small, but in other cases—price supports and import quotas are examples—it is large. This deadweight loss is a form of economic inefficiency that must be taken into account when policies are designed and implemented.

5. Government intervention in a competitive market is not always bad. Government—and the society it represents—might have objectives other than economic efficiency. There are also situations in which government intervention can improve economic efficiency. Examples are externalities and cases of market failure. These situations, and the way government can respond to them, are discussed in Chapters 17 and 18.

# QUESTIONS FOR REVIEW

1. What is meant by *deadweight loss*? Why does a price ceiling usually result in a deadweight loss?

2. Suppose the supply curve for a good is completely inelastic. If the government imposed a price ceiling below the market-clearing level, would a deadweight loss result? Explain.

3. How can a price ceiling make consumers better off? Under what conditions might it make them worse off?

4. Suppose the government regulates the price of a good to be no lower than some minimum level. Can such a minimum price make producers as a whole worse off? Explain.

5. How are production limits used in practice to raise the prices of the following goods or services: (a) taxi rides, (b) drinks in a restaurant or bar, (c) wheat or corn?

6. Suppose the government wants to increase farmers' incomes. Why do price supports or acreage-limitation programs cost society more than simply giving farmers money?

7. Suppose the government wants to limit imports of a certain good. Is it preferable to use an import quota or a tariff? Why?

8. The burden of a tax is shared by producers and consumers. Under what conditions will consumers pay most of the tax? Under what conditions will producers pay most of it? What determines the share of a subsidy that benefits consumers?

9. Why does a tax create a deadweight loss? What determines the size of this loss?

# EXERCISES

1. In 1996, Congress raised the minimum wage from $4.25 per hour to $5.15 per hour, and then raised it again in 2007. (See Example 1.3 [page 13].) Some people suggested that a government subsidy could help employers finance the higher wage. This exercise examines the economics of a minimum wage and wage subsidies. Suppose the supply of low-skilled labor is given by

$$L^S = 10w$$

where $L^S$ is the quantity of low-skilled labor (in millions of persons employed each year), and $w$ is the wage rate (in dollars per hour). The demand for labor is given by

$$L^D = 80 - 10w$$

   a. What will be the free-market wage rate and employment level? Suppose the government sets a minimum wage of $5 per hour. How many people would then be employed?
   b. Suppose that instead of a minimum wage, the government pays a subsidy of $1 per hour for each employee. What will the total level of employment be now? What will the equilibrium wage rate be?

2. Suppose the market for widgets can be described by the following equations:

$$\text{Demand:} \quad P = 10 - Q$$
$$\text{Supply:} \quad P = Q - 4$$

   where $P$ is the price in dollars per unit and $Q$ is the quantity in thousands of units. Then:
   a. What is the equilibrium price and quantity?
   b. Suppose the government imposes a tax of $1 per unit to reduce widget consumption and raise government revenues. What will the new equilibrium quantity be? What price will the buyer pay? What amount per unit will the seller receive?
   c. Suppose the government has a change of heart about the importance of widgets to the happiness of the American public. The tax is removed and a subsidy of $1 per unit granted to widget producers. What will the equilibrium quantity be? What price will the buyer pay? What amount per unit (including the subsidy) will the seller receive? What will be the total cost to the government?

3. Japanese rice producers have extremely high production costs, due in part to the high opportunity cost of land and to their inability to take advantage of economies of large-scale production. Analyze two policies intended to maintain Japanese rice production: (1) a per-pound subsidy to farmers for each pound of rice produced, or (2) a per-pound tariff on imported rice. Illustrate with supply-and-demand diagrams the equilibrium price and quantity, domestic rice production, government revenue or deficit, and deadweight loss from each policy. Which policy is the Japanese government likely to prefer? Which policy are Japanese farmers likely to prefer?

4. In 1983, the Reagan administration introduced a new agricultural program called the Payment-in-Kind Program. To see how the program worked, let's consider the wheat market:
   a. Suppose the demand function is $Q^D = 28 - 2P$ and the supply function is $Q^S = 4 + 4P$, where $P$ is the price of wheat in dollars per bushel, and $Q$ is the quantity in billions of bushels. Find the free-market equilibrium price and quantity.
   b. Now suppose the government wants to lower the supply of wheat by 25 percent from the free-market equilibrium by paying farmers to withdraw land from production. However, the payment is made in wheat rather than in dollars—hence the name of the program. The wheat comes from vast government reserves accumulated from previous price support programs. The amount of wheat paid is equal to the amount that could have been harvested on the land withdrawn from production. Farmers are free to sell this wheat on the market. How much is now produced by farmers? How much is indirectly supplied to the market by the government? What is the new market price? How much do farmers gain? Do consumers gain or lose?
   c. Had the government not given the wheat back to the farmers, it would have stored or destroyed it. Do taxpayers gain from the program? What potential problems does the program create?

5. About 100 million pounds of jelly beans are consumed in the United States each year, and the price has been about 50 cents per pound. However, jelly bean producers feel that their incomes are too low and have convinced the government that price supports are in order. The government will therefore buy up as many jelly beans as necessary to keep the price at $1 per pound. However, government economists are worried about the impact of this program because they have no estimates of the elasticities of jelly bean demand or supply.
   a. Could this program cost the government *more* than $50 million per year? Under what conditions? Could it cost *less* than $50 million per year? Under what conditions? Illustrate with a diagram.
   b. Could this program cost consumers (in terms of lost consumer surplus) *more* than $50 million per year? Under what conditions? Could it cost consumers *less* than $50 million per year? Under what conditions? Again, use a diagram to illustrate.

6. In Exercise 4 in Chapter 2 (page 62), we examined a vegetable fiber traded in a competitive world market and imported into the United States at a world price of

$9 per pound. U.S. domestic supply and demand for various price levels are shown in the following table.

| Price | U.S. Supply (million pounds) | U.S. Demand (million pounds) |
|---|---|---|
| 3 | 2 | 34 |
| 6 | 4 | 28 |
| 9 | 6 | 22 |
| 12 | 8 | 16 |
| 15 | 10 | 10 |
| 18 | 12 | 4 |

Answer the following questions about the U.S. market:

**a.** Confirm that the demand curve is given by $Q_D = 40 - 2P$, and that the supply curve is given by $Q_S = 2/3P$.

**b.** Confirm that if there were no restrictions on trade, the United States would import 16 million pounds.

**c.** If the United States imposes a tariff of $3 per pound, what will be the U.S. price and level of imports? How much revenue will the government earn from the tariff? How large is the deadweight loss?

**d.** If the United States has no tariff but imposes an import quota of 8 million pounds, what will be the U.S. domestic price? What is the cost of this quota for U.S. consumers of the fiber? What is the gain for U.S. producers?

**7.** The United States currently imports all of its coffee. The annual demand for coffee by U.S. consumers is given by the demand curve $Q = 250 - 10P$, where $Q$ is quantity (in millions of pounds) and $P$ is the market price per pound of coffee. World producers can harvest and ship coffee to U.S. distributors at a constant marginal (= average) cost of $8 per pound. U.S. distributors can in turn distribute coffee for a constant $2 per pound. The U.S. coffee market is competitive. Congress is considering a tariff on coffee imports of $2 per pound.

**a.** If there is no tariff, how much do consumers pay for a pound of coffee? What is the quantity demanded?

**b.** If the tariff is imposed, how much will consumers pay for a pound of coffee? What is the quantity demanded?

**c.** Calculate the lost consumer surplus.

**d.** Calculate the tax revenue collected by the government.

**e.** Does the tariff result in a net gain or a net loss to society as a whole?

**8.** A particular metal is traded in a highly competitive world market at a world price of $9 per ounce. Unlimited quantities are available for import into the United States at this price. The supply of this metal from domestic U.S. mines and mills can be represented by the equation $Q^S = 2/3P$, where $Q^S$ is U.S. output in million ounces and $P$ is the domestic price. The demand for the metal in the United States is $Q^D = 40 - 2P$, where $Q^D$ is the domestic demand in million ounces.

In recent years the U.S. industry has been protected by a tariff of $9 per ounce. Under pressure from other foreign governments, the United States plans to reduce this tariff to zero. Threatened by this change, the U.S. industry is seeking a voluntary restraint agreement that would limit imports into the United States to 8 million ounces per year.

**a.** Under the $9 tariff, what was the U.S. domestic price of the metal?

**b.** If the United States eliminates the tariff and the voluntary restraint agreement is approved, what will be the U.S. domestic price of the metal?

**9.** Among the tax proposals regularly considered by Congress is an additional tax on distilled liquors. The tax would not apply to beer. The price elasticity of supply of liquor is 4.0, and the price elasticity of demand is −0.2. The cross-elasticity of demand for beer with respect to the price of liquor is 0.1.

**a.** If the new tax is imposed, who will bear the greater burden—liquor suppliers or liquor consumers? Why?

**b.** Assuming that beer supply is infinitely elastic, how will the new tax affect the beer market?

**10.** In Example 9.1 (page 314), we calculated the gains and losses from price controls on natural gas and found that there was a deadweight loss of $5.68 billion. This calculation was based on a price of oil of $50 per barrel.

**a.** If the price of oil were $60 per barrel, what would be the free-market price of gas? How large a deadweight loss would result if the maximum allowable price of natural gas were $3.00 per thousand cubic feet?

**b.** What price of oil would yield a free-market price of natural gas of $3?

**11.** Example 9.5 (page 333) describes the effects of the sugar quota. In 2005, imports were limited to 5.3 billion pounds, which pushed the domestic price to 27 cents per pound. Suppose imports were expanded to 10 billion pounds.

**a.** What would be the new U.S. domestic price?

**b.** How much would consumers gain and domestic producers lose?

**c.** What would be the effect on deadweight loss and foreign producers?

**12.** The domestic supply and demand curves for hula beans are as follows:

Supply:  $P = 50 + Q$
Demand:  $P = 200 - 2Q$

where $P$ is the price in cents per pound and $Q$ is the quantity in millions of pounds. The U.S. is a small producer in the world hula bean market, where the current price (which will not be affected by anything we do) is 60 cents per pound. Congress is considering a tariff of 40 cents per pound. Find the domestic price of hula beans that will result if the tariff is imposed. Also compute the dollar gain or loss to domestic consumers, domestic producers, and government revenue from the tariff.

13. Currently, the social security payroll tax in the United States is evenly divided between employers and employees. Employers must pay the government a tax of 6.2 percent of the wages they pay, and employees must pay 6.2 percent of the wages they receive. Suppose the tax were changed so that employers paid the full 12.4 percent and employees paid nothing. Would employees be better off?

*14. You know that if a tax is imposed on a particular product, the burden of the tax is shared by producers and consumers. You also know that the demand for automobiles is characterized by a stock adjustment process. Suppose a special 20-percent sales tax is suddenly imposed on automobiles. Will the share of the tax paid by consumers rise, fall, or stay the same over time? Explain briefly. Repeat for a 50-cents-per-gallon gasoline tax.

*15. In 2007, Americans smoked 19.2 billion packs of cigarettes. They paid an average retail price of $4.50 per pack.

    a. Given that the elasticity of supply is 0.5 and the elasticity of demand is −0.4, derive linear demand and supply curves for cigarettes.

    b. Cigarettes are subject to a federal tax, which was about 40 cents per pack in 2007. What does this tax do to the market-clearing price and quantity?

    c. How much of the federal tax will consumers pay? What part will producers pay?

# PART·THREE

# Market Structure and Competitive Strategy

Part 3 examines a broad range of markets and explains how the pricing, investment, and output decisions of firms depend on market structure and the behavior of competitors.

Chapters 10 and 11 examine *market power*: the ability to affect price, either by a seller or a buyer. We will see how market power arises, how it differs across firms, how it affects the welfare of consumers and producers, and how it can be limited by government. We will also see how firms can design pricing and advertising strategies to take maximum advantage of their market power.

Chapters 12 and 13 deal with markets in which the number of firms is limited. We will examine a variety of such markets, ranging from *monopolistic competition*, in which many firms sell differentiated products, to a *cartel*, in which a group of firms coordinates decisions and acts as a monopolist. We are particularly concerned with markets in which there are only a few firms. In these cases, each firm must design its pricing, output, and investment strategies, while keeping in mind how competitors are likely to react. We will develop and apply principles from game theory to analyze such strategies.

Chapter 14 shows how markets for factor inputs, such as labor and raw materials, operate. We will examine the firm's input decisions and show how those decisions depend on the structure of the input market. Chapter 15 then focuses on capital investment decisions. We will see how a firm can value the future profits that it expects an investment to yield and then compare this value with the cost of the investment to determine whether the investment is worthwhile. We will also apply this idea to the decisions of individuals to purchase a car or household appliance, or to invest in education.

# Market Power: Monopoly and Monopsony

10

In a perfectly competitive market, the large number of sellers and buyers of a good ensures that no single seller or buyer can affect its price. The market forces of supply and demand determine price. Individual firms take the market price as a given in deciding how much to produce and sell, and consumers take it as a given in deciding how much to buy.

*Monopoly* and *monopsony*, the subjects of this chapter, are the polar opposites of perfect competition. A **monopoly** is a market that has only one seller but many buyers. A **monopsony** is just the opposite: a market with many sellers but only one buyer. Monopoly and monopsony are closely related, which is why we cover them in the same chapter.

First we discuss the behavior of a monopolist. Because a monopolist is the sole producer of a product, the demand curve that it faces is the market demand curve. This market demand curve relates the price that the monopolist receives to the quantity it offers for sale. We will see how a monopolist can take advantage of its control over price and how the profit-maximizing price and quantity differ from what would prevail in a competitive market.

In general, the monopolist's quantity will be lower and its price higher than the competitive quantity and price. This imposes a cost on society because fewer consumers buy the product, and those who do pay more for it. This is why antitrust laws exist which forbid firms from monopolizing most markets. When economies of scale make monopoly desirable—for example, with local electric power companies—we will see how the government can increase efficiency by regulating the monopolist's price.

*Pure monopoly* is rare, but in many markets only a few firms compete with each other. The interactions of firms in such markets can be complicated and often involve aspects of *strategic gaming*, a topic covered in Chapters 12 and 13. In any case, the firms may be able to affect price and may find it profitable to charge a price higher than marginal cost. These firms have *monopoly power*. We will discuss the determinants of monopoly power, its measurement, and its implications for pricing.

Next we will turn to *monopsony*. Unlike a competitive buyer, a monopsonist pays a price that depends on the quantity that it purchases. The monopsonist's problem is to choose the quantity that maximizes its net benefit from the purchase—the value derived from the good less the money paid for it. By showing how the choice is made, we will demonstrate the close parallel between monopsony and monopoly.

- **monopoly**   Market with only one seller.

- **monopsony**   Market with only one buyer.

- **market power**   Ability of a seller or buyer to affect the price of a good.

Although pure monopsony is also unusual, many markets have only a few buyers who can purchase the good for less than they would pay in a competitive market. These buyers have *monopsony power*. Typically, this situation occurs in markets for inputs to production. For example, General Motors, the largest U.S. car manufacturer, has monopsony power in the markets for tires, car batteries, and other parts. We will discuss the determinants of monopsony power, its measurement, and its implications for pricing.

Monopoly and monopsony power are two forms of **market power**: the ability—of either a seller or a buyer—to affect the price of a good.[1] Because sellers or buyers often have at least some market power (in most real-world markets), we need to understand how market power works and how it affects producers and consumers.

## 10.1 MONOPOLY

As the sole producer of a product, a monopolist is in a unique position. If the monopolist decides to raise the price of the product, it need not worry about competitors who, by charging lower prices, would capture a larger share of the market at the monopolist's expense. The monopolist *is* the market and completely controls the amount of output offered for sale.

But this does not mean that the monopolist can charge any price it wants—at least not if its objective is to maximize profit. This textbook is a case in point. Pearson Prentice Hall owns the copyright and is therefore a monopoly producer of this book. So why doesn't it sell the book for $500 a copy? Because few people would buy it, and Prentice Hall would earn a much lower profit.

To maximize profit, the monopolist must first determine its costs and the characteristics of market demand. Knowledge of demand and cost is crucial for a firm's economic decision making. Given this knowledge, the monopolist must then decide how much to produce and sell. The price per unit that the monopolist receives then follows directly from the market demand curve. Equivalently, the monopolist can determine price, and the quantity it will sell at that price follows from the market demand curve.

### Average Revenue and Marginal Revenue

- **marginal revenue**   Change in revenue resulting from a one-unit increase in output.

In §8.3, we explain that marginal revenue is a measure of how much revenue increases when output increases by one unit.

The monopolist's *average revenue*—the price it receives per unit sold—is precisely the market demand curve. To choose its profit-maximizing output level, the monopolist also needs to know its **marginal revenue**: the change in revenue that results from a unit change in output. To see the relationship among total, average, and marginal revenue, consider a firm facing the following demand curve:

$$P = 6 - Q$$

Table 10.1 shows the behavior of total, average, and marginal revenue for this demand curve. Note that revenue is zero when the price is $6: At that price, nothing is sold. At a price of $5, however, one unit is sold, so total (and marginal) revenue is $5. An increase in quantity sold from 1 to 2 increases revenue from $5 to $8; marginal revenue is thus $3. As quantity sold increases from 2 to 3, marginal revenue falls to $1, and when quantity increases from 3 to 4, marginal revenue

---

[1]The courts use the term "monopoly power" to mean significant and sustainable market power, sufficient to warrant particular scrutiny under the antitrust laws. In this book, however, for pedagogic reasons we use "monopoly power" differently, to mean market power on the part of sellers, whether substantial or not.

| TABLE 10.1 | Total, Marginal, and Average Revenue | | | |
| --- | --- | --- | --- | --- |
| Price (P) | Quantity (Q) | Total Revenue (R) | Marginal Revenue (MR) | Average Revenue (AR) |
| $6 | 0 | $0 | — | — |
| 5 | 1 | 5 | $5 | $5 |
| 4 | 2 | 8 | 3 | 4 |
| 3 | 3 | 9 | 1 | 3 |
| 2 | 4 | 8 | −1 | 2 |
| 1 | 5 | 5 | −3 | 1 |

becomes negative. When marginal revenue is positive, revenue is increasing with quantity, but when marginal revenue is negative, revenue is decreasing.

When the demand curve is downward sloping, the price (average revenue) is greater than marginal revenue because all units are sold at the same price. If sales are to increase by 1 unit, the price must fall. In that case, all units sold, not just the additional unit, will earn less revenue. Note, for example, what happens in Table 10.1 when output is increased from 1 to 2 units and price is reduced to $4. Marginal revenue is $3: $4 (the revenue from the sale of the additional unit of output) less $1 (the loss of revenue from selling the first unit for $4 instead of $5). Thus, marginal revenue ($3) is less than price ($4).

Figure 10.1 plots average and marginal revenue for the data in Table 10.1. Our demand curve is a straight line and, in this case, the marginal revenue curve has twice the slope of the demand curve (and the same intercept).[2]

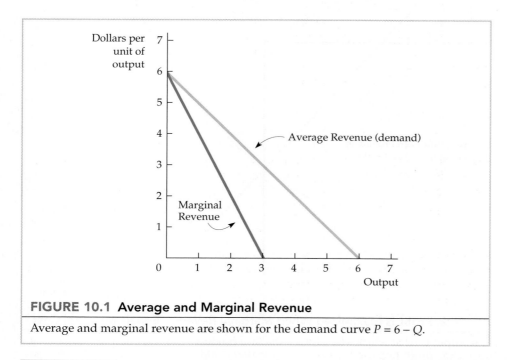

**FIGURE 10.1  Average and Marginal Revenue**

Average and marginal revenue are shown for the demand curve $P = 6 - Q$.

---

[2]If the demand curve is written so that price is a function of quantity, $P = a - bQ$, total revenue is given by $PQ = aQ - bQ^2$. Marginal revenue (using calculus) is $d(PQ)/dQ = a - 2bQ$. In this example, demand is $P = 6 - Q$ and marginal revenue is $MR = 6 - 2Q$. (This holds only for small changes in $Q$ and therefore does not exactly match the data in Table 10.1.)

## The Monopolist's Output Decision

In §7.1, we explain that marginal cost is the change in variable cost associated with a one-unit increase in output.

What quantity should the monopolist produce? In Chapter 8, we saw that to maximize profit, a firm must set output so that marginal revenue is equal to marginal cost. This is the solution to the monopolist's problem. In Figure 10.2, the market demand curve $D$ is the monopolist's average revenue curve. It specifies the price per unit that the monopolist receives as a function of its output level. Also shown are the corresponding marginal revenue curve MR and the average and marginal cost curves, AC and MC. Marginal revenue and marginal cost are equal at quantity $Q^*$. Then from the demand curve, we find the price $P^*$ that corresponds to this quantity $Q^*$.

How can we be sure that $Q^*$ is the profit-maximizing quantity? Suppose the monopolist produces a smaller quantity $Q_1$ and receives the corresponding higher price $P_1$. As Figure 10.2 shows, marginal revenue would then exceed marginal cost. In that case, if the monopolist produced a little more than $Q_1$, it would receive extra profit (MR − MC) and thereby increase its total profit. In fact, the monopolist could keep increasing output, adding more to its total profit until output $Q^*$, at which point the incremental profit earned from producing one more

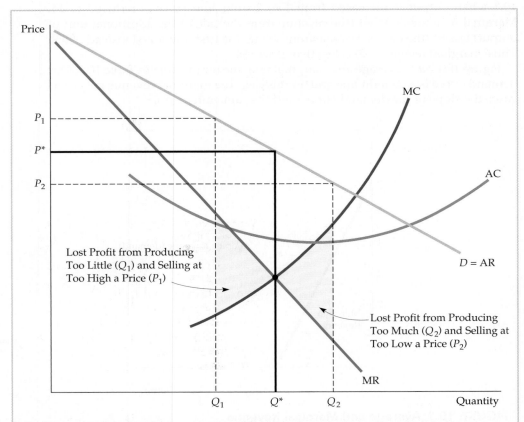

**FIGURE 10.2 Profit Is Maximized When Marginal Revenue Equals Marginal Cost**

$Q^*$ is the output level at which MR = MC. If the firm produces a smaller output—say, $Q_1$—it sacrifices some profit because the extra revenue that could be earned from producing and selling the units between $Q_1$ and $Q^*$ exceeds the cost of producing them. Similarly, expanding output from $Q^*$ to $Q_2$ would reduce profit because the additional cost would exceed the additional revenue.

unit is zero. So the smaller quantity $Q_1$ is not profit maximizing, even though it allows the monopolist to charge a higher price. If the monopolist produced $Q_1$ instead of $Q^*$, its total profit would be smaller by an amount equal to the shaded area below the MR curve and above the MC curve, between $Q_1$ and $Q^*$.

In Figure 10.2, the larger quantity $Q_2$ is likewise not profit maximizing. At this quantity, marginal cost exceeds marginal revenue. Therefore, if the monopolist produced a little less than $Q_2$, it would increase its total profit (by MC − MR). It could increase its profit even more by reducing output all the way to $Q^*$. The increased profit achieved by producing $Q^*$ instead of $Q_2$ is given by the area below the MC curve and above the MR curve, between $Q^*$ and $Q_2$.

We can also see algebraically that $Q^*$ maximizes profit. Profit $\pi$ is the difference between revenue and cost, both of which depend on $Q$:

$$\pi(Q) = R(Q) - C(Q)$$

As $Q$ is increased from zero, profit will increase until it reaches a maximum and then begin to decrease. Thus the profit-maximizing $Q$ is such that the incremental profit resulting from a small increase in $Q$ is just zero (i.e., $\Delta\pi/\Delta Q = 0$). Then

$$\Delta\pi/\Delta Q = \Delta R/\Delta Q - \Delta C/\Delta Q = 0$$

But $\Delta R/\Delta Q$ is marginal revenue and $\Delta C/\Delta Q$ is marginal cost. Thus the profit-maximizing condition is that MR − MC = 0, or MR = MC.

## An Example

To grasp this result more clearly, let's look at an example. Suppose the cost of production is

$$C(Q) = 50 + Q^2$$

In other words, there is a fixed cost of $50, and variable cost is $Q^2$. Suppose demand is given by

$$P(Q) = 40 - Q$$

By setting marginal revenue equal to marginal cost, you can verify that profit is maximized when $Q = 10$, an output level that corresponds to a price of $30.[3]

Cost, revenue, and profit are plotted in Figure 10.3(a). When the firm produces little or no output, profit is negative because of the fixed cost. Profit increases as $Q$ increases, reaching a maximum of $150 at $Q^* = 10$, and then decreases as $Q$ is increased further. At the point of maximum profit, the slopes of the revenue and cost curves are the same. (Note that the tangent lines $rr'$ and $cc'$ are parallel.) The slope of the revenue curve is $\Delta R/\Delta Q$, or marginal revenue, and the slope of the cost curve is $\Delta C/\Delta Q$, or marginal cost. Because profit is maximized when marginal revenue equals marginal cost, the slopes are equal.

Figure 10.3(b) shows both the corresponding average and marginal revenue curves and average and marginal cost curves. Marginal revenue and marginal cost intersect at $Q^* = 10$. At this quantity, average cost is $15 per unit and price is $30 per unit. Thus average profit is $30 − $15 = $15 per unit. Because 10 units are sold, profit is (10)($15) = $150, the area of the shaded rectangle.

---

[3]Note that average cost is $C(Q)/Q = 50/Q + Q$ and marginal cost is $\Delta C/\Delta Q = 2Q$. Revenue is $R(Q) = P(Q)Q = 40Q − Q^2$, so marginal revenue is MR $= \Delta R/\Delta Q = 40 − 2Q$. Setting marginal revenue equal to marginal cost gives $40 − 2Q = 2Q$, or $Q = 10$.

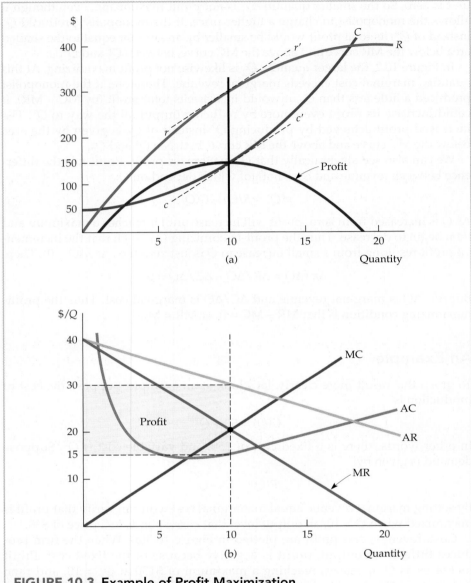

**FIGURE 10.3 Example of Profit Maximization**

Part **(a)** shows total revenue $R$, total cost $C$, and profit, the difference between the two. Part **(b)** shows average and marginal revenue and average and marginal cost. Marginal revenue is the slope of the total revenue curve, and marginal cost is the slope of the total cost curve. The profit-maximizing output is $Q^* = 10$, the point where marginal revenue equals marginal cost. At this output level, the slope of the profit curve is zero, and the slopes of the total revenue and total cost curves are equal. The profit per unit is $15, the difference between average revenue and average cost. Because 10 units are produced, total profit is $150.

## A Rule of Thumb for Pricing

We know that price and output should be chosen so that marginal revenue equals marginal cost, but how can the manager of a firm find the correct price and output level in practice? Most managers have only limited knowledge of the average and marginal revenue curves that their firms face. Similarly, they might know the firm's marginal cost only over a limited output range. We therefore want to translate the condition that marginal revenue should equal marginal cost into a rule of thumb that can be more easily applied in practice.

To do this, we first write the expression for marginal revenue:

$$MR = \frac{\Delta R}{\Delta Q} = \frac{\Delta(PQ)}{\Delta Q}$$

Note that the extra revenue from an incremental unit of quantity, $\Delta(PQ)/\Delta Q$, has two components:

1. Producing one extra unit and selling it at price $P$ brings in revenue $(1)(P) = P$.
2. But because the firm faces a downward-sloping demand curve, producing and selling this extra unit also results in a small drop in price $\Delta P/\Delta Q$, which reduces the revenue from all units sold (i.e., a change in revenue $Q[\Delta P/\Delta Q]$).

Thus,

$$MR = P + Q\frac{\Delta P}{\Delta Q} = P + P\left(\frac{Q}{P}\right)\left(\frac{\Delta P}{\Delta Q}\right)$$

We obtained the expression on the right by taking the term $Q(\Delta P/\Delta Q)$ and multiplying and dividing it by $P$. Recall that the elasticity of demand is defined as $E_d = (P/Q)(\Delta Q/\Delta P)$. Thus $(Q/P)(\Delta P/\Delta Q)$ is the reciprocal of the elasticity of demand, $1/E_d$, measured at the profit-maximizing output, and

> The elasticity of demand is discussed in §§2.4 and 4.3.

$$MR = P + P(1/E_d)$$

Now, because the firm's objective is to maximize profit, we can set marginal revenue equal to marginal cost:

$$P + P(1/E_d) = MC$$

which can be rearranged to give us

$$\frac{P - MC}{P} = -\frac{1}{E_d} \qquad \textbf{(10.1)}$$

This relationship provides a rule of thumb for pricing. The left-hand side, $(P - MC)/P$, is the markup over marginal cost as a percentage of price. The relationship says that this markup should equal minus the inverse of the elasticity of demand.[4] (This figure will be a *positive* number because the elasticity of demand is *negative*.) Equivalently, we can rearrange this equation to express price directly as a markup over marginal cost:

$$P = \frac{MC}{1 + \left(1/E_d\right)} \qquad \textbf{(10.2)}$$

---

[4]Remember that this markup equation applies at the point of a profit maximum. If both the elasticity of demand and marginal cost vary considerably over the range of outputs under consideration, you may have to know the entire demand and marginal cost curves to determine the optimum output level. On the other hand, you can use this equation to check whether a particular output level and price are optimal.

For example, if the elasticity of demand is − 4 and marginal cost is $9 per unit, price should be $9/(1 − 1/4) = $9/.75 = $12 per unit.

How does the price set by a monopolist compare with the price under competition? In Chapter 8, we saw that in a perfectly competitive market, price equals marginal cost. A monopolist charges a price that exceeds marginal cost, *but by an amount that depends inversely on the elasticity of demand.* As the markup equation (10.1) shows, if demand is extremely elastic, $E_d$ is a large negative number, and price will be very close to marginal cost. In that case, a monopolized market will look much like a competitive one. In fact, when demand is very elastic, there is little benefit to being a monopolist.

> In §8.1, we explain that a perfectly competitive firm will choose its output so that marginal cost equals price.

Also note that a monopolist will never produce a quantity of output that is on the inelastic portion of the demand curve—i.e., where the elasticity of demand is less than 1 in absolute value. To see why, suppose that the monopolist is producing at a point on the demand curve where the elasticity is −0.5. In that case, the monopolist could make a greater profit by producing less and selling at a higher price. (A 10-percent reduction in output, for example, would allow for a 20-percent increase in price and thus a 10-percent increase in revenue. If marginal cost were greater than zero, the increase in profit would be even more than 10 percent because the lower output would reduce the firm's costs.) As the monopolist reduces output and raises price, it will move up the demand curve to a point where the elasticity is greater than 1 in absolute value and the markup rule of equation (10.2) will be satisfied.

> In §4.3 and Table 4.3, we explain that when price is increased, expenditure—and thus revenue—increases if demand is inelastic, decreases if demand is elastic, and is unchanged if demand has unit elasticity.

Suppose, however, that marginal cost is zero. In that case, we cannot use equation (10.2) directly to determine the profit-maximizing price. However, we can see from equation (10.1) that in order to maximize profit, the firm will produce at the point where the elasticity of demand is exactly −1. If marginal cost is zero, maximizing profit is equivalent to maximizing revenue, and revenue is maximized when $E_d = -1$.

---

**EXAMPLE 10.1**  Astra-Merck Prices Prilosec

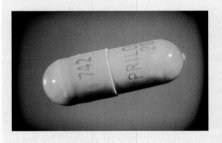

In 1995, a new drug developed by Astra-Merck became available for the long-term treatment of ulcers. The drug, Prilosec, represented a new generation of antiulcer medication. Other drugs to treat ulcer conditions were already on the market: Tagamet had been introduced in 1977, Zantac in 1983, Pepcid in 1986, and Axid in 1988. As we explained in Example 1.1 (page 10), these four drugs worked in much the same way to reduce the stomach's secretion of acid. Prilosec, however, was based on a very different biochemical mechanism and was much more effective than these earlier drugs. By 1996, it had become the best-selling drug in the world and faced no major competitor.[5]

---

[5]Prilosec, developed through a joint venture of the Swedish firm Astra and the U.S. firm Merck, was introduced in 1989, but only for the treatment of gastroesophageal reflux disease, and was approved for short-term ulcer treatment in 1991. It was the approval for long-term ulcer treatment in 1995, however, that created a very large market for the drug. In 1998, Astra bought Merck's share of the rights to Prilosec. In 1999, Astra acquired the firm Zeneca and is now called AstraZeneca. In 2001, AstraZeneca earned over $4.9 billion in sales of Prilosec, which remained the world's best-selling prescription drug. As AstraZeneca's patent on Prilosec neared expiration, the company introduced Nexium, a new (and, according to the company, better) antiulcer drug. In 2006, Nexium was the third-biggest-selling pharmaceutical drug in the world, with sales of about $5.7 billion.

In 1995, Astra-Merck was pricing Prilosec at about $3.50 per daily dose. (By contrast, the prices for Tagamet and Zantac were about $1.50 to $2.25 per daily dose.) Is this pricing consistent with the markup formula (10.1)? The marginal cost of producing and packaging Prilosec is only about 30 to 40 cents per daily dose. This low marginal cost implies that the price elasticity of demand, $E_D$, should be in the range of roughly −1.0 to −1.2. Based on statistical studies of pharmaceutical demand, this is indeed a reasonable estimate for the demand elasticity. Thus, setting the price of Prilosec at a markup exceeding 400 percent over marginal cost is consistent with our rule of thumb for pricing.

## Shifts in Demand

In a competitive market, there is a clear relationship between price and the quantity supplied. That relationship is the supply curve, which, as we saw in Chapter 8, represents the marginal cost of production for the industry as a whole. The supply curve tells us how much will be produced at every price.

*A monopolistic market has no supply curve.* In other words, there is no one-to-one relationship between price and the quantity produced. The reason is that the monopolist's output decision depends not only on marginal cost but also on the shape of the demand curve. As a result, shifts in demand do not trace out the series of prices and quantities that correspond to a competitive supply curve. Instead, shifts in demand can lead to changes in price with no change in output, changes in output with no change in price, or changes in both price and output.

This principle is illustrated in Figure 10.4(a) and (b). In both parts of the figure, the demand curve is initially $D_1$, the corresponding marginal revenue curve is $MR_1$, and the monopolist's initial price and quantity are $P_1$ and $Q_1$. In Figure 10.4(a), the demand curve is shifted down and rotated. The new demand and marginal revenue curves are shown as $D_2$ and $MR_2$. Note that $MR_2$ intersects the marginal cost curve at the same point that $MR_1$ does. As a result, the quantity produced stays the same. Price, however, falls to $P_2$.

In Figure 10.4(b), the demand curve is shifted up and rotated. The new marginal revenue curve $MR_2$ intersects the marginal cost curve at a larger quantity, $Q_2$ instead of $Q_1$. But the shift in the demand curve is such that the price charged is exactly the same.

Shifts in demand usually cause changes in both price and quantity. But the special cases shown in Figure 10.4 illustrate an important distinction between monopoly and competitive supply. A competitive industry supplies a specific quantity at every price. No such relationship exists for a monopolist, which, depending on how demand shifts, might supply several different quantities at the same price, or the same quantity at different prices.

## The Effect of a Tax

A tax on output can also have a different effect on a monopolist than on a competitive industry. In Chapter 9, we saw that when a specific (i.e., per-unit) tax is imposed on a competitive industry, the market price rises by an amount that is less than the tax, and that the burden of the tax is shared by producers and consumers. Under monopoly, however, price can sometimes rise by *more* than the amount of the tax.

In §9.6, we explain that a specific tax is a tax of a certain amount of money per unit sold, and we show how the tax affects price and quantity.

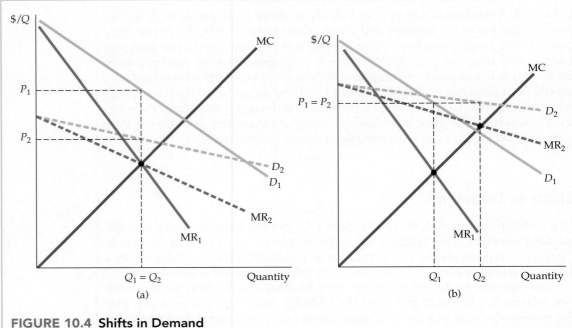

**FIGURE 10.4 Shifts in Demand**

Shifting the demand curve shows that a monopolistic market has no supply curve—i.e., there is no one-to-one relationship between price and quantity produced. In **(a)**, the demand curve $D_1$ shifts to new demand curve $D_2$. But the new marginal revenue curve $MR_2$ intersects marginal cost at the same point as the old marginal revenue curve $MR_1$. The profit-maximizing output therefore remains the same, although price falls from $P_1$ to $P_2$. In **(b)**, the new marginal revenue curve $MR_2$ intersects marginal cost at a higher output level $Q_2$. But because demand is now more elastic, price remains the same.

Analyzing the effect of a tax on a monopolist is straightforward. Suppose a specific tax of $t$ dollars per unit is levied, so that the monopolist must remit $t$ dollars to the government for every unit it sells. Therefore, the firm's marginal (and average) cost is increased by the amount of the tax $t$. If MC was the firm's original marginal cost, its optimal production decision is now given by

$$MR = MC + t$$

Graphically, we shift the marginal cost curve upward by an amount $t$, and find the new intersection with marginal revenue. Figure 10.5 shows this. Here $Q_0$ and $P_0$ are the quantity and price before the tax is imposed, and $Q_1$ and $P_1$ are the quantity and price after the tax.

Shifting the marginal cost curve upward results in a smaller quantity and higher price. Sometimes price increases by less than the tax, but not always—in Figure 10.5, price increases by *more* than the tax. This would be impossible in a competitive market, but it can happen with a monopolist because the relationship between price and marginal cost depends on the elasticity of demand. Suppose, for example, that a monopolist faces a constant elasticity demand curve, with elasticity −2, and has constant marginal cost MC. Equation (10.2) then tells us that price will equal twice marginal cost. With a tax $t$, marginal cost increases to $MC + t$, so price increases to $2(MC + t) = 2MC + 2t$; that is, it rises by twice the amount of the tax. (However, the monopolist's profit nonetheless falls with the tax.)

> In §8.2, we explain that a firm maximizes its profit by choosing the output at which marginal revenue is equal to marginal cost.

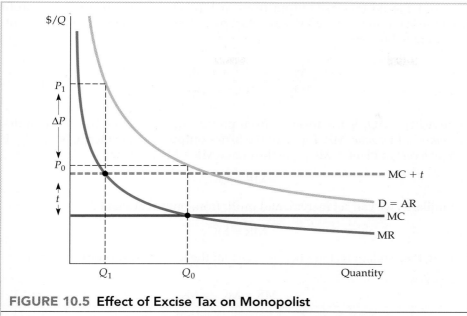

**FIGURE 10.5 Effect of Excise Tax on Monopolist**

With a tax $t$ per unit, the firm's effective marginal cost is increased by the amount $t$ to $MC + t$. In this example, the increase in price $\Delta P$ is larger than the tax $t$.

## *The Multiplant Firm

We have seen that a firm maximizes profit by setting output at a level where marginal revenue equals marginal cost. For many firms, production takes place in two or more different plants whose operating costs can differ. However, the logic used in choosing output levels is very similar to that for the single-plant firm.

Suppose a firm has two plants. What should its total output be, and how much of that output should each plant produce? We can find the answer intuitively in two steps.

- **Step 1.** Whatever the total output, it should be divided between the two plants so that *marginal cost is the same in each plant*. Otherwise, the firm could reduce its costs and increase its profit by reallocating production. For example, if marginal cost at Plant 1 were higher than at Plant 2, the firm could produce the same output at a lower total cost by producing less at Plant 1 and more at Plant 2.

- **Step 2.** We know that total output must be such that *marginal revenue equals marginal cost*. Otherwise, the firm could increase its profit by raising or lowering total output. For example, suppose marginal costs were the same at each plant, but marginal revenue exceeded marginal cost. In that case, the firm would do better by producing more at both plants because the revenue earned from the additional units would exceed the cost. Because marginal costs must be the same at each plant, and because marginal revenue must equal marginal cost, we see that profit is maximized when *marginal revenue equals marginal cost at each plant*.

We can also derive this result algebraically. Let $Q_1$ and $C_1$ be the output and cost of production for Plant 1, $Q_2$ and $C_2$ be the output and cost of production for Plant 2, and $Q_T = Q_1 + Q_2$ be total output. Then profit is

$$\pi = PQ_T - C_1(Q_1) - C_2(Q_2)$$

The firm should increase output from each plant until the incremental profit from the last unit produced is zero. Start by setting incremental profit from output at Plant 1 to zero:

$$\frac{\Delta\pi}{\Delta Q_1} = \frac{\Delta(PQ_T)}{\Delta Q_1} - \frac{\Delta C_1}{\Delta Q_1} = 0$$

Here $\Delta(PQ_T)/\Delta Q_1$ is the revenue from producing and selling one more unit—i.e., *marginal revenue*, MR, for all of the firm's output. The next term, $\Delta C_1/\Delta Q_1$, is *marginal cost* at Plant 1, $MC_1$. We thus have $MR - MC_1 = 0$, or

$$MR = MC_1$$

Similarly, we can set incremental profit from output at Plant 2 to zero,

$$MR = MC_2$$

Putting these relations together, we see that the firm should produce so that

$$MR = MC_1 = MC_2 \qquad \textbf{(10.3)}$$

Figure 10.6 illustrates this principle for a firm with two plants. $MC_1$ and $MC_2$ are the marginal cost curves for the two plants. (Note that Plant 1 has higher marginal costs than Plant 2.) Also shown is a curve labeled $MC_T$. This is the firm's total marginal cost and is obtained by horizontally summing $MC_1$ and

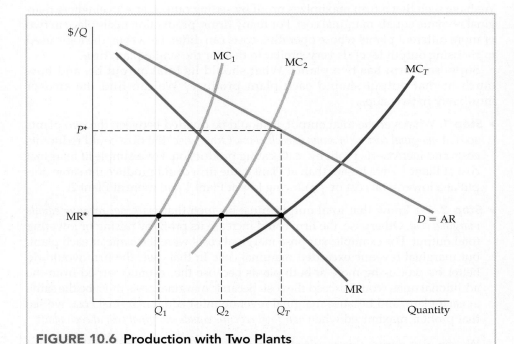

**FIGURE 10.6 Production with Two Plants**

A firm with two plants maximizes profits by choosing output levels $Q_1$ and $Q_2$ so that marginal revenue MR (which depends on *total* output) equals marginal costs for each plant, $MC_1$ and $MC_2$.

$MC_2$. Now we can find the profit-maximizing output levels $Q_1$, $Q_2$, and $Q_T$. First, find the intersection of $MC_T$ with MR; that point determines total output $Q_T$. Next, draw a horizontal line from that point on the marginal revenue curve to the vertical axis; point MR* determines the firm's marginal revenue. The intersections of the marginal revenue line with $MC_1$ and $MC_2$ give the outputs $Q_1$ and $Q_2$ for the two plants, as in equation (10.3).

> Note the similarity to the way we obtained a competitive industry's supply curve in §8.5 by horizontally summing the marginal cost curves of the individual firms.

Note that total output $Q_T$ determines the firm's marginal revenue (and hence its price $P^*$). $Q_1$ and $Q_2$, however, determine marginal costs at each of the two plants. Because $MC_T$ was found by horizontally summing $MC_1$ and $MC_2$, we know that $Q_1 + Q_2 = Q_T$. Thus these output levels satisfy the condition that $MR = MC_1 = MC_2$.

## 10.2 MONOPOLY POWER

Pure monopoly is rare. Markets in which several firms compete with one another are much more common. We say more about the forms that this competition can take in Chapters 12 and 13. But we should explain here why each firm in a market with several firms is likely to face a downward-sloping demand curve and, as a result, to produce so that price exceeds marginal cost.

Suppose, for example, that four firms produce toothbrushes and have the market demand curve $Q = 50,000 - 20,000P$, as shown in Figure 10.7(a). Let's assume that these four firms are producing an aggregate of 20,000 toothbrushes per day (5000 each per day) and selling them at $1.50 each. Note that market demand is relatively inelastic; you can verify that at this $1.50 price, the elasticity of demand is −1.5.

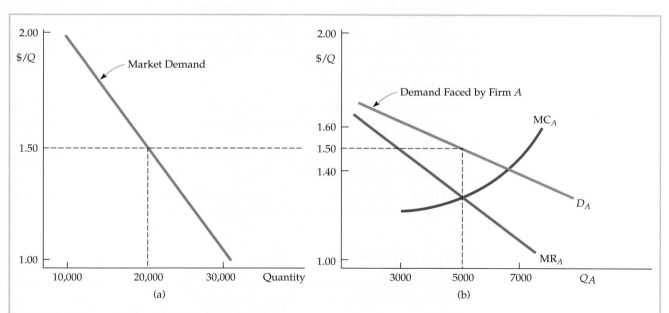

**FIGURE 10.7 The Demand for Toothbrushes**

Part **(a)** shows the market demand for toothbrushes. Part **(b)** shows the demand for toothbrushes as seen by Firm $A$. At a market price of $1.50, elasticity of market demand is −1.5. Firm $A$, however, sees a much more elastic demand curve $D_A$ because of competition from other firms. At a price of $1.50, Firm $A$'s demand elasticity is −6. Still, Firm $A$ has some monopoly power: Its profit-maximizing price is $1.50, which exceeds marginal cost.

Now suppose that Firm *A* is deciding whether to lower its price to increase sales. To make this decision, it needs to know how its sales would respond to a change in its price. In other words, it needs some idea of the demand curve *it* faces, as opposed to the *market* demand curve. A reasonable possibility is shown in Figure 10.7(b), where the firm's demand curve $D_A$ is much more elastic than the market demand curve. (At the $1.50 price the elasticity is −6.0.) The firm might predict that by raising the price from $1.50 to $1.60, its sales will drop— say, from 5000 units to 3000—as consumers buy more toothbrushes from other firms. (If *all* firms raised their prices to $1.60, sales for Firm *A* would fall only to 4500.) For several reasons, sales won't drop to zero as they would in a perfectly competitive market. First, if Firm *A*'s toothbrushes are a little different from those of its competitors, some consumers will pay a bit more for them. Second, other firms might also raise their prices. Similarly, Firm *A* might anticipate that by lowering its price from $1.50 to $1.40, it can sell more toothbrushes—perhaps 7000 instead of 5000. But it will not capture the entire market: Some consumers might still prefer the competitors' toothbrushes, and competitors might also lower their prices.

Thus, Firm *A*'s demand curve depends both on how much its product differs from its competitors' products and on how the four firms compete with one another. We will discuss product differentiation and interfirm competition in Chapters 12 and 13. But one important point should be clear: *Firm A is likely to face a demand curve which is more elastic than the market demand curve, but which is not infinitely elastic like the demand curve facing a perfectly competitive firm.*

Given knowledge of its demand curve, how much should Firm *A* produce? The same principle applies: The profit-maximizing quantity equates marginal revenue and marginal cost. In Figure 10.7(b), that quantity is 5000 units. The corresponding price is $1.50, which exceeds marginal cost. Thus, although Firm *A* is not a pure monopolist, *it does have monopoly power*—it can profitably charge a price greater than marginal cost. Of course, its monopoly power is less than it would be if it had driven away the competition and monopolized the market, but it might still be substantial.

This raises two questions.

1. How can we *measure* monopoly power in order to compare one firm with another? (So far we have been talking about monopoly power only in *qualitative* terms.)

2. What are the *sources* of monopoly power, and why do some firms have more monopoly power than others?

We address both these questions below, although a more complete answer to the second question will be provided in Chapters 12 and 13.

## Measuring Monopoly Power

Remember the important distinction between a perfectly competitive firm and a firm with monopoly power: *For the competitive firm, price equals marginal cost; for the firm with monopoly power, price exceeds marginal cost.* Therefore, a natural way to measure monopoly power is to examine the extent to which the profit-maximizing price exceeds marginal cost. In particular, we can use the markup ratio of price minus marginal cost to price that we introduced earlier as part of a rule of thumb for pricing. This measure of monopoly power, introduced by economist Abba

Lerner in 1934, is called the **Lerner Index of Monopoly Power**. It is the difference between price and marginal cost, divided by price. Mathematically:

$$L = (P - MC)/P$$

The Lerner index always has a value between zero and one. For a perfectly competitive firm, $P = MC$, so that $L = 0$. The larger is $L$, the greater is the degree of monopoly power.

This index of monopoly power can also be expressed in terms of the elasticity of demand facing the firm. Using equation (10.1), we know that

$$L = (P - MC)/P = -1/E_d \qquad \textbf{(10.4)}$$

Remember, however, that $E_d$ is now the elasticity of the *firm's* demand curve, not the market demand curve. In the toothbrush example discussed previously, the elasticity of demand for Firm $A$ is $-6.0$, and the degree of monopoly power is $1/6 = 0.167$.[6]

Note that considerable monopoly power does not necessarily imply high profits. Profit depends on *average* cost relative to price. Firm $A$ might have more monopoly power than Firm $B$ but earn a lower profit because of higher average costs.

## The Rule of Thumb for Pricing

In the previous section, we used equation (10.2) to compute price as a simple markup over marginal cost:

$$P = \frac{MC}{1 + \left(1/E_d\right)}$$

This relationship provides a rule of thumb for *any* firm with monopoly power. We must remember, however, that $E_d$ is the elasticity of demand for the *firm*, not the elasticity of *market* demand.

It is harder to determine the elasticity of demand for the firm than for the market because the firm must consider how its competitors will react to price changes. Essentially, the manager must estimate the percentage change in the firm's unit sales that is likely to result from a 1-percent change in the firm's price. This estimate might be based on a formal model or on the manager's intuition and experience.

Given an estimate of the firm's elasticity of demand, the manager can calculate the proper markup. If the firm's elasticity of demand is large, this markup will be small (and we can say that the firm has very little monopoly power). If the firm's elasticity of demand is small, this markup will be large (and the firm will have considerable monopoly power). Figures 10.8(a) and 10.8(b) illustrate these two extremes.

**• Lerner Index of Monopoly Power** Measure of monopoly power calculated as excess of price over marginal cost as a fraction of price.

---

[6]There are three problems with applying the Lerner index to the analysis of public policy toward firms. First, because marginal cost is difficult to measure, average variable cost is often used in Lerner index calculations. Second, if the firm prices below its optimal price (possibly to avoid legal scrutiny), its potential monopoly power will not be noted by the index. Third, the index ignores dynamic aspects of pricing such as effects of the learning curve and shifts in demand. See Robert S. Pindyck, "The Measurement of Monopoly Power in Dynamic Markets," *Journal of Law and Economics* 28 (April 1985): 193–222.

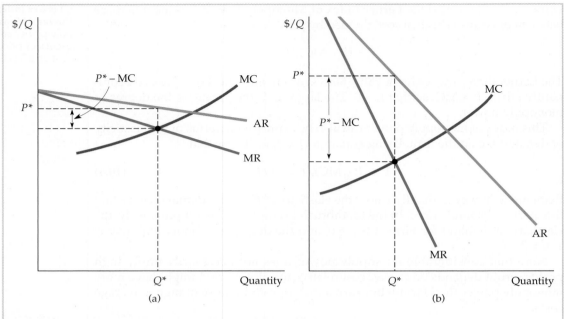

**FIGURE 10.8** **Elasticity of Demand and Price Markup**

The markup $(P - MC)/P$ is equal to minus the inverse of the elasticity of demand facing the firm. If the firm's demand is elastic, as in **(a)**, the markup is small and the firm has little monopoly power. The opposite is true if demand is relatively inelastic, as in **(b)**.

---

**EXAMPLE 10.2**  **Markup Pricing: Supermarkets to Designer Jeans**

Three examples should help clarify the use of markup pricing. Consider a supermarket chain. Although the elasticity of market demand for food is small (about −1), several supermarkets usually serve most areas. Thus no single supermarket can raise its prices very much without losing customers to other stores. As a result, the elasticity of demand for any one supermarket is often as large as −10. Substituting this number for $E_d$ in equation (10.2), we find $P = MC/(1 - 0.1) = MC/(0.9) = (1.11)MC$. In other words, the manager of a typical supermarket should set prices about 11 percent above marginal cost. For a reasonably wide range of output levels (over which the size of the store and the number of its employees will remain fixed), marginal cost includes the cost of purchasing the food at wholesale, plus the costs of storing the food, arranging it on the shelves, etc. For most supermarkets, the markup is indeed about 10 or 11 percent.

Small convenience stores, which are often open 7 days a week and even 24 hours a day, typically charge higher prices than supermarkets. Why? Because a convenience store faces a less elastic demand curve. Its customers are generally less price sensitive. They might need a quart of milk or a loaf of bread late at night or may find it inconvenient to drive to the supermarket. Because the elasticity of demand for a convenience store is about −5, the markup equation implies that its prices should be about 25 percent above marginal cost, as indeed they typically are.

The Lerner index, $(P - MC)/P$, tells us that the convenience store has more monopoly power, but does it make larger profits? No. Because its volume is far smaller and its average fixed costs are larger, it usually earns a much smaller profit than a large supermarket despite its higher markup.

Finally, consider a producer of designer jeans. Many companies produce jeans, but some consumers will pay much more for jeans with a designer label. Just how much more they will pay—or more exactly, how much sales will drop in response to higher prices—is a question that the producer must carefully consider because it is critical in determining the price at which the clothing will be sold (at wholesale to retail stores, which then mark up the price further). With designer jeans, demand elasticities in the range of −2 to −3 are typical for the major labels. This means that price should be 50 to 100 percent higher than marginal cost. Marginal cost is typically $15 to $20 per pair, and depending on the brand, the wholesale price is in the $20 to $40 range. In contrast, "mass-market" jeans will typically wholesale for $18 to $25 per pair. Why? Because without the designer label, they are far more price elastic.

---

**EXAMPLE 10.3**  The Pricing of Videos

During the mid-1980s, the number of households owning videocassette recorders (VCRs) grew rapidly, as did the markets for rentals and sales of prerecorded cassettes. Although at that time many more videocassettes were rented through small retail outlets than sold outright, the market for sales was large and growing. Producers, however, found it difficult to decide what price to charge for cassettes. As a result, in 1985 popular movies were selling for vastly different prices, as you can see from the data in Table 10.2.

Note that while *The Empire Strikes Back* was selling for nearly $80, *Star Trek*, a film that appealed to the same audience and was about as popular, sold for only about $25. These price differences reflected uncertainty and a wide divergence of

**TABLE 10.2** Retail Prices of VHS and DVDs

| 1985 | | 2007 | |
|------|------|------|------|
| **Title** | **Retail Price VHS** | **Title** | **Retail Price DVD** |
| Purple Rain | $29.98 | Pirates of the Caribbean | $19.99 |
| Raiders of the Lost Ark | $24.95 | The Da Vinci Code | $19.99 |
| Jane Fonda Workout | $59.95 | Mission: Impossible III | $17.99 |
| The Empire Strikes Back | $79.98 | King Kong | $19.98 |
| An Officer and a Gentleman | $24.95 | Harry Potter and the Goblet of Fire | $17.49 |
| Star Trek: The Motion Picture | $24.95 | Ice Age | $19.99 |
| Star Wars | $39.98 | The Devil Wears Prada | $17.99 |

*Source (2007): Based on* http://www.amazon.com. *Suggested retail price.*

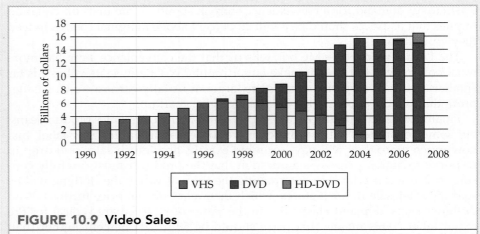

**FIGURE 10.9 Video Sales**

Between 1990 and 1998, lower prices induced consumers to buy many more videos. By 2001, sales of DVDs overtook sales of VHS videocassettes. High-definition DVDs were introduced in 2006, and are expected to displace sales of conventional DVDs.

views on pricing by producers. The issue was whether lower prices would induce consumers to buy videocassettes rather than rent them. Because producers do not share in the retailers' revenues from rentals, they should charge a low price for cassettes only if that will induce enough consumers to buy them. Because the market was young, producers had no good estimates of the elasticity of demand, so they based prices on hunches or trial and error.[7]

As the market matured, however, sales data and market research studies put pricing decisions on firmer ground. Those studies strongly indicated that demand was price elastic and that the profit-maximizing price was in the range of $15 to $30. By the 1990s, most producers had lowered prices across the board. When DVDs were first introduced in 1997, the prices of top-selling DVDs were much more uniform. Since that time, prices of popular DVDs have remained fairly uniform and continued to fall. As Table 10.2 shows, by 2007, prices were typically $20 or less. As a result, video sales have steadily increased, as shown in Figure 10.9. With the introduction of high-definition (HD) DVDs in 2006, sales of conventional DVDs are expected to fall as consumers gradually switch to the new format.

## 10.3 SOURCES OF MONOPOLY POWER

Why do some firms have considerable monopoly power while other firms have little or none? Remember that monopoly power is the ability to set price above marginal cost and that the amount by which price exceeds marginal cost depends inversely on the elasticity of demand facing the firm. As equation (10.4) shows, *the less elastic its demand curve, the more monopoly power a firm has*. The ultimate determinant of monopoly power is therefore the firm's elasticity of demand. Thus we should rephrase our question: Why do some firms (e.g., a

---

[7]"Video Producers Debate the Value of Price Cuts," *New York Times*, February 19, 1985. For a study of videocassette pricing, see Carl E. Enomoto and Soumendra N. Ghosh, "Pricing in the Home-Video Market" (working paper, New Mexico State University, 1992).

supermarket chain) face demand curves that are more elastic than those faced by others (e.g., a producer of designer clothing)?

Three factors determine a firm's elasticity of demand.

1. *The elasticity of market demand.* Because the firm's own demand will be at least as elastic as market demand, the elasticity of market demand limits the potential for monopoly power.

2. *The number of firms in the market.* If there are many firms, it is unlikely that any one firm will be able to affect price significantly.

3. *The interaction among firms.* Even if only two or three firms are in the market, each firm will be unable to profitably raise price very much if the rivalry among them is aggressive, with each firm trying to capture as much of the market as it can.

Let's examine each of these three determinants of monopoly power.

## The Elasticity of Market Demand

If there is only one firm—a pure monopolist—its demand curve is the market demand curve. In this case, the firm's degree of monopoly power depends completely on the elasticity of market demand. More often, however, several firms compete with one another; then the elasticity of market demand sets a lower limit on the magnitude of the elasticity of demand for each firm. Recall our example of the toothbrush producers illustrated in Figure 10.7 (page 361). The market demand for toothbrushes might not be very elastic, but each firm's demand will be more elastic. (In Figure 10.7, the elasticity of market demand is −1.5, and the elasticity of demand for each firm is −6.) A particular firm's elasticity depends on how the firms compete with one another. But no matter how they compete, the elasticity of demand for each firm could never become smaller in magnitude than −1.5.

Because the demand for oil is fairly inelastic (at least in the short run), OPEC could raise oil prices far above marginal production cost during the 1970s and early 1980s. Because the demands for such commodities as coffee, cocoa, tin, and copper are much more elastic, attempts by producers to cartelize these markets and raise prices have largely failed. In each case, the elasticity of market demand limits the potential monopoly power of individual producers.

## The Number of Firms

The second determinant of a firm's demand curve—and thus of its monopoly power—is the number of firms in its market. Other things being equal, the monopoly power of each firm will fall as the number of firms increases: As more and more firms compete, each firm will find it harder to raise prices and avoid losing sales to other firms.

What matters, of course, is not just the total number of firms, but the number of "major players"—firms with significant market share. For example, if only two large firms account for 90 percent of sales in a market, with another 20 firms accounting for the remaining 10 percent, the two large firms might have considerable monopoly power. When only a few firms account for most of the sales in a market, we say that the market is highly *concentrated*.[8]

---

[8]A statistic called the *concentration ratio*, which measures the percentage of sales accounted for by, say, the four largest firms, is often used to describe the concentration of a market. Concentration is one, but not the only, determinant of market power.

It is sometimes said (not always jokingly) that the greatest fear of American business is competition. That may or may not be true. But we would certainly expect that when only a few firms are in a market, their managers will prefer that no new firms enter. An increase in the number of firms can only reduce the monopoly power of each incumbent firm. An important aspect of competitive strategy (discussed in detail in Chapter 13) is finding ways to create **barriers to entry**—conditions that deter entry by new competitors.

Sometimes there are natural barriers to entry. For example, one firm may have a *patent* on the technology needed to produce a particular product. This makes it impossible for other firms to enter the market, at least until the patent expires. Other legally created rights work in the same way—a *copyright* can limit the sale of a book, music, or a computer software program to a single company, and the need for a government *license* can prevent new firms from entering the markets for telephone service, television broadcasting, or interstate trucking. Finally, *economies of scale* may make it too costly for more than a few firms to supply the entire market. In some cases, economies of scale may be so large that it is most efficient for a single firm—*a natural monopoly*—to supply the entire market. We will discuss scale economies and natural monopoly in more detail shortly.

## The Interaction Among Firms

The ways in which competing firms interact is also an important—and sometimes the most important—determinant of monopoly power. Suppose there are four firms in a market. They might compete aggressively, undercutting one another's prices to capture more market share. This could drive prices down to nearly competitive levels. Each firm will fear that if it raises its price it will be undercut and lose market share. As a result, it will have little monopoly power.

On the other hand, the firms might not compete much. They might even collude (in violation of the antitrust laws), agreeing to limit output and raise prices. Because raising prices in concert rather than individually is more likely to be profitable, collusion can generate substantial monopoly power.

We will discuss the interaction among firms in detail in Chapters 12 and 13. Now we simply want to point out that, other things being equal, monopoly power is smaller when firms compete aggressively and is larger when they cooperate.

Remember that a firm's monopoly power often changes over time, as its operating conditions (market demand and cost), its behavior, and the behavior of its competitors change. Monopoly power must therefore be thought of in a dynamic context. For example, the market demand curve might be very inelastic in the short run but much more elastic in the long run. (Because this is the case with oil, the OPEC cartel enjoyed considerable short-run but much less long-run monopoly power.) Furthermore, real or potential monopoly power in the short run can make an industry more competitive in the long run: Large short-run profits can induce new firms to enter an industry, thereby reducing monopoly power over the longer term.

• **barrier to entry** Condition that impedes entry by new competitors.

In §7.4, we explain that a firm enjoys economies of scale when it can double its output with less than a doubling of cost.

## 10.4 THE SOCIAL COSTS OF MONOPOLY POWER

In a competitive market, price equals marginal cost. Monopoly power, on the other hand, implies that price exceeds marginal cost. Because monopoly power results in higher prices and lower quantities produced, we would expect it to make consumers worse off and the firm better off. But suppose we value the welfare of consumers the same as that of producers. In the aggregate, does monopoly power make consumers and producers better or worse off?

We can answer this question by comparing the consumer and producer surplus that results when a competitive industry produces a good with the surplus that results when a monopolist supplies the entire market.[9] (We assume that the competitive market and the monopolist have the same cost curves.) Figure 10.10 shows the average and marginal revenue curves and marginal cost curve for the monopolist. To maximize profit, the firm produces at the point where marginal revenue equals marginal cost, so that the price and quantity are $P_m$ and $Q_m$. In a competitive market, price must equal marginal cost, so the competitive price and quantity, $P_c$ and $Q_c$ are found at the intersection of the average revenue (demand) curve and the marginal cost curve. Now let's examine how surplus changes if we move from the competitive price and quantity, $P_c$ and $Q_c$ to the monopoly price and quantity, $P_m$ and $Q_m$.

Under monopoly, the price is higher and consumers buy less. Because of the higher price, those consumers who buy the good lose surplus of an amount given by rectangle $A$. Those consumers who do not buy the good at price $P_m$ but who would buy at price $P_c$ also lose surplus—namely, an amount given by triangle $B$. The total loss of consumer surplus is therefore $A + B$. The producer, however, gains rectangle $A$ by selling at the higher price but loses triangle $C$, the additional profit it would have earned by selling $Q_c - Q_m$ at price $P_c$. The total gain in producer surplus is therefore $A - C$. Subtracting the loss of consumer surplus from the gain in producer surplus, we see a net loss of surplus given by

> In §9.1, we explain that consumer surplus is the total benefit or value that consumers receive beyond what they pay for a good; producer surplus is the analogous measure for producers.

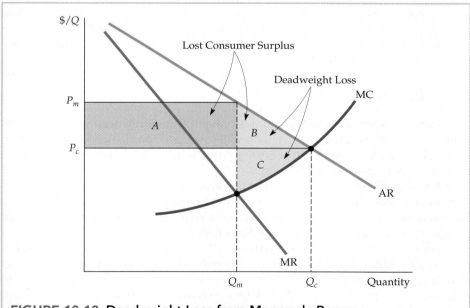

**FIGURE 10.10  Deadweight Loss from Monopoly Power**

The shaded rectangle and triangles show changes in consumer and producer surplus when moving from competitive price and quantity, $P_c$ and $Q_c$, to a monopolist's price and quantity, $P_m$ and $Q_m$. Because of the higher price, consumers lose $A + B$ and producer gains $A - C$. The deadweight loss is $B + C$.

---

[9]If there were two or more firms, each with some monopoly power, the analysis would be more complex. However, the basic results would be the same.

$B + C$. This is the *deadweight loss from monopoly power*. Even if the monopolist's profits were taxed away and redistributed to the consumers of its products, there would be an inefficiency because output would be lower than under conditions of competition. The deadweight loss is the social cost of this inefficiency.

## Rent Seeking

• **rent seeking** Spending money in socially unproductive efforts to acquire, maintain, or exercise monopoly.

In practice, the social cost of monopoly power is likely to exceed the deadweight loss in triangles $B$ and $C$ of Figure 10.10. The reason is that the firm may engage in **rent seeking**: spending large amounts of money in socially unproductive efforts to acquire, maintain, or exercise its monopoly power. Rent seeking might involve lobbying activities (and perhaps campaign contributions) to obtain government regulations that make entry by potential competitors more difficult. Rent-seeking activity could also involve advertising and legal efforts to avoid antitrust scrutiny. It might also mean installing but not utilizing extra production capacity to convince potential competitors that they cannot sell enough to make entry worthwhile. We would expect the economic incentive to incur rent-seeking costs to bear a direct relation to the gains from monopoly power (i.e., rectangle $A$ minus triangle $C$.) Therefore, the larger the transfer from consumers to the firm (rectangle $A$), the larger the social cost of monopoly.[10]

Here's an example. In 1996, the Archer Daniels Midland Company (ADM) successfully lobbied the Clinton administration for regulations requiring that the ethanol (ethyl alcohol) used in motor vehicle fuel be produced from corn. (The government had already planned to add ethanol to gasoline in order to reduce the country's dependence on imported oil.) Ethanol is chemically the same whether it is produced from corn, potatoes, grain, or anything else. Then why require that it be produced only from corn? Because ADM had a near monopoly on corn-based ethanol production, so the regulation would increase its gains from monopoly power.

## Price Regulation

Because of its social cost, antitrust laws prevent firms from accumulating excessive amounts of monopoly power. We will say more about such laws at the end of the chapter. Here, we examine another means by which government can limit monopoly power—price regulation.

We saw in Chapter 9 that in a competitive market, price regulation always results in a deadweight loss. This need not be the case, however, when a firm has monopoly power. On the contrary, price regulation can eliminate the deadweight loss that results from monopoly power.

Figure 10.11 illustrates price regulation. $P_m$ and $Q_m$ are the price and quantity that result without regulation—i.e., at the point where marginal revenue equals marginal cost. Now suppose the price is regulated to be no higher than $P_1$. To find the firm's profit-maximizing output, we must determine how its average and marginal revenue curves are affected by the regulation.

Because the firm can charge no more than $P_1$ for output levels up to $Q_1$, its new average revenue curve is a horizontal line at $P_1$. For output levels greater than $Q_1$, the new average revenue curve is identical to the old average revenue

---

[10]The concept of rent seeking was first developed by Gordon Tullock. For more detailed discussions, see Gordon Tullock, *Rent Seeking* (Brookfield, VT: Edward Elgar, 1993), or Robert D. Tollison and Roger D. Congleton, *The Economic Analysis of Rent Seeking* (Brookfield, VT: Edward Elgar, 1995).

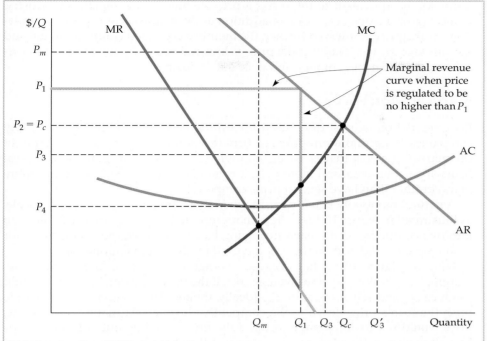

**FIGURE 10.11 Price Regulation**

If left alone, a monopolist produces $Q_m$ and charges $P_m$. When the government imposes a price ceiling of $P_1$ the firm's average and marginal revenue are constant and equal to $P_1$ for output levels up to $Q_1$. For larger output levels, the original average and marginal revenue curves apply. The new marginal revenue curve is, therefore, the dark purple line, which intersects the marginal cost curve at $Q_1$. When price is lowered to $P_c$, at the point where marginal cost intersects average revenue, output increases to its maximum $Q_c$. This is the output that would be produced by a competitive industry. Lowering price further, to $P_3$ reduces output to $Q_3$ and causes a shortage, $Q_3' - Q_3$.

curve: At these output levels, the firm will charge less than $P_1$ and so will be unaffected by the regulation.

The firm's new marginal revenue curve corresponds to its new average revenue curve and is shown by the purple line in Figure 10.11. For output levels up to $Q_1$, marginal revenue equals average revenue. (Recall that, as with a competitive firm, if average revenue is constant, average revenue and marginal revenue are equal.) For output levels greater than $Q_1$, the new marginal revenue curve is identical to the original curve. Thus the complete marginal revenue curve now has three pieces: (1) the horizontal line at $P_1$ for quantities up to $Q_1$; (2) a vertical line at the quantity $Q_1$ connecting the original average and marginal revenue curves; and (3) the original marginal revenue curve for quantities greater than $Q_1$.

To maximize its profit, the firm should produce the quantity $Q_1$ because that is the point at which its marginal revenue curve intersects its marginal cost curve. You can verify that at price $P_1$ and quantity $Q_1$, the deadweight loss from monopoly power is reduced.

As the price is lowered further, the quantity produced continues to increase and the deadweight loss to decline. At price $P_c$ where average revenue and marginal cost intersect, the quantity produced has increased to the competitive level; the deadweight loss from monopoly power has been eliminated. Reducing the price even more—say, to $P_3$—results in a *reduction* in quantity. This reduction is equivalent to imposing a price ceiling on a competitive industry. A shortage develops, $(Q'_3 - Q_3)$, in addition to the deadweight loss from regulation. As the price is lowered further, the quantity produced continues to fall and the shortage grows. Finally, if the price is lowered below $P_4$, the minimum average cost, the firm loses money and goes out of business.

## Natural Monopoly

• **natural monopoly** Firm that can produce the entire output of the market at a cost lower than what it would be if there were several firms.

Price regulation is most often used for *natural monopolies*, such as local utility companies. A **natural monopoly** is a firm that can produce the entire output of the market at a cost that is lower than what it would be if there were several firms. If a firm is a natural monopoly, it is more efficient to let it serve the entire market rather than have several firms compete.

A natural monopoly usually arises when there are strong economies of scale, as illustrated in Figure 10.12. If the firm represented by the figure was broken up into two competing firms, each supplying half the market, the average cost for each would be higher than the cost incurred by the original monopoly.

Note in Figure 10.12 that because average cost is declining everywhere, marginal cost is always below average cost. If the firm were unregulated, it would produce $Q_m$ and sell at the price $P_m$. Ideally, the regulatory agency would like to push the firm's price down to the competitive level $P_c$. At that level, however, price would not cover average cost and the firm would go out of business. The best alternative is therefore to set the price at $P_r$, where average cost and average revenue intersect. In that case, the firm earns no monopoly profit, while output remains as large as possible without driving the firm out of business.

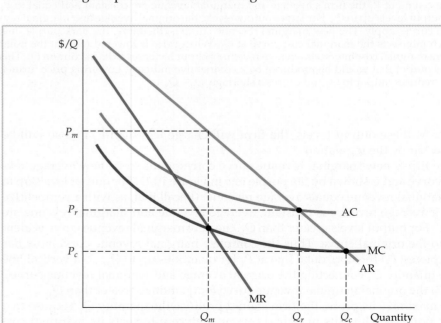

**FIGURE 10.12 Regulating the Price of a Natural Monopoly**

A firm is a natural monopoly because it has economies of scale (declining average and marginal costs) over its entire output range. If price were regulated to be $P_c$ the firm would lose money and go out of business. Setting the price at $P_r$ yields the largest possible output consistent with the firm's remaining in business; excess profit is zero.

## Regulation in Practice

Recall that the competitive price ($P_c$ in Figure 10.11) is found at the point at which the firm's marginal cost and average revenue (demand) curves intersect. Likewise for a natural monopoly: The minimum feasible price ($P_r$ in Figure 10.12) is found at the point at which average cost and demand intersect. Unfortunately, it is often difficult to determine these prices accurately in practice because the firm's demand and cost curves may shift as market conditions evolve.

As a result, the regulation of a monopoly is sometimes based on the rate of return that it earns on its capital. The regulatory agency determines an allowed price, so that this rate of return is in some sense "competitive" or "fair." This practice is called **rate-of-return regulation**: The maximum price allowed is based on the (expected) rate of return that the firm will earn.[11]

> **• rate-of-return regulation**
> Maximum price allowed by a regulatory agency is based on the (expected) rate of return that a firm will earn.

Unfortunately, difficult problems arise when implementing rate-of-return regulation. First, although it is a key element in determining the firm's rate of return, a firm's capital stock is difficult to value. Second, while a "fair" rate of return must be based on the firm's actual cost of capital, that cost depends in turn on the behavior of the regulatory agency (and on investors' perceptions of what allowed rates of return will be in the future).

The difficulty of agreeing on a set of numbers to be used in rate-of-return calculations often leads to delays in the regulatory response to changes in cost and other market conditions (not to mention long and expensive regulatory hearings). The major beneficiaries are usually lawyers, accountants, and, occasionally, economic consultants. The net result is *regulatory lag*—the delays of a year or more usually entailed in changing regulated prices.

Another approach to regulation is setting price caps based on the firm's variable costs, past prices, and possibly inflation and productivity growth. A price cap can allow for more flexibility than rate-of-return regulation. Under price cap regulation, for example, a firm would typically be allowed to raise its prices each year (without having to get approval from the regulatory agency) by an amount equal to the actual rate of inflation, minus expected productivity growth. Price cap regulation of this sort has been used to control prices of long distance and local telephone service.

By the 1990s, the regulatory environment in the United States had changed dramatically. Many parts of the telecommunications industry had been deregulated, as had electric utilities in many states. Because scale economies had been largely exhausted, there was no reason to regard these firms as natural monopolies. In addition, technological change made entry by new firms relatively easy.

## 10.5 MONOPSONY

So far, our discussion of market power has focused entirely on the seller side of the market. Now we turn to the *buyer* side. We will see that if there are not too many buyers, they can also have market power and use it profitably to affect the price they pay for a product.

---

[11]Regulatory agencies often use a formula like the following to determine price:

$$P = \text{AVC} + (D + T + sK)/Q$$

where AVC is average variable cost, $Q$ is output, $s$ is the allowed "fair" rate of return, $D$ is depreciation, $T$ is taxes, and $K$ is the firm's current capital stock.

First, a few terms.

- **Monopsony** refers to a market in which there is a single buyer.
- An **oligopsony** is a market with only a few buyers.
- With one or only a few buyers, some buyers may have **monopsony power**: a buyer's ability to affect the price of a good. Monopsony power enables the buyer to purchase a good for less than the price that would prevail in a competitive market.

Suppose you are trying to decide how much of a good to purchase. You could apply the basic marginal principle—keep purchasing units of the good until the last unit purchased gives additional value, or utility, just equal to the cost of that last unit. In other words, on the margin, additional benefit should just be offset by additional cost.

Let's look at this additional benefit and additional cost in more detail. We use the term **marginal value** to refer to the additional benefit from purchasing one more unit of a good. How do we determine marginal value? Recall from Chapter 4 that an individual demand curve determines marginal value, or marginal utility, as a function of the quantity purchased. Therefore, your *marginal value schedule* is your *demand* curve for the good. An individual's demand curve slopes downward because the marginal value obtained from buying one more unit of a good declines as the total quantity purchased increases.

The additional cost of buying one more unit of a good is called the **marginal expenditure**. What that marginal expenditure is depends on whether you are a competitive buyer or a buyer with monopsony power. Suppose you are a competitive buyer—in other words, you have no influence over the price of the good. In that case, the cost of each unit you buy is the same no matter how many units you purchase; it is the market price of the good. Figure 10.13(a) illustrates this principle. The price you pay per unit is your **average expenditure** per unit, and it is the same for all units. But what is your *marginal expenditure* per unit? As a competitive buyer, your marginal expenditure is equal to your average expenditure, which in turn is equal to the market price of the good.

Figure 10.13(a) also shows your marginal value schedule (i.e., your demand curve). How much of the good should you buy? You should buy until the marginal value of the last unit is just equal to the marginal expenditure on that unit. Thus you should purchase quantity $Q^*$ at the intersection of the marginal expenditure and demand curves.

We introduced the concepts of marginal and average expenditure because they will make it easier to understand what happens when buyers have monopsony power. But before considering that situation, let's look at the analogy between competitive buyer conditions and competitive seller conditions. Figure 10.13(b) shows how a perfectly competitive seller decides how much to produce and sell. Because the seller takes the market price as given, both average and marginal revenue are equal to the price. The profit-maximizing quantity is at the intersection of the marginal revenue and marginal cost curves.

Now suppose that you are the *only* buyer of the good. Again you face a market supply curve, which tells you how much producers are willing to sell as a function of the price you pay. Should the quantity you purchase be at the point where your marginal value curve intersects the market supply curve? No. If you want to maximize your net benefit from purchasing the good, you should purchase a smaller quantity, which you will obtain at a lower price.

**• oligopsony** Market with only a few buyers.

**• monopsony power** Buyer's ability to affect the price of a good.

**• marginal value** Additional benefit derived from purchasing one more unit of a good.

In §4.1, we explain that as we move down along a demand curve, the value the consumer places on an additional unit of the good falls.

**• marginal expenditure** Additional cost of buying one more unit of a good.

**• average expenditure** Price paid per unit of a good.

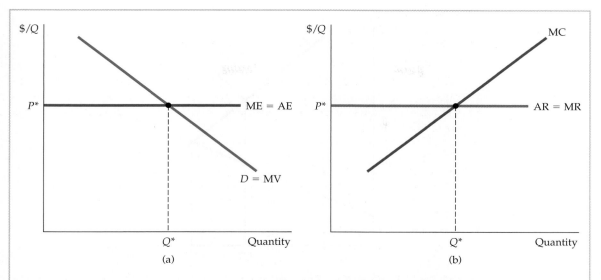

**FIGURE 10.13 Competitive Buyer Compared to Competitive Seller**

In **(a)**, the competitive buyer takes market price $P^*$ as given. Therefore, marginal expenditure and average expenditure are constant and equal; quantity purchased is found by equating price to marginal value (demand). In **(b)**, the competitive seller also takes price as given. Marginal revenue and average revenue are constant and equal; quantity sold is found by equating price to marginal cost.

To determine how much to buy, set the marginal value from the last unit purchased equal to the marginal expenditure on that unit.[12] Note, however, that the market supply curve is not the marginal expenditure curve. The market supply curve shows how much you must pay *per unit*, as a function of the total number of units you buy. In other words, the supply curve is the *average expenditure* curve. And because this average expenditure curve is upward sloping, the marginal expenditure curve must lie above it. The decision to buy an extra unit raises the price that must be paid for *all* units, not just the extra one.[13]

Figure 10.14 illustrates this principle. The optimal quantity for the monopsonist to buy, $Q_m^*$, is found at the intersection of the demand and marginal expenditure curves. The price that the monopsonist pays is found from the supply curve: It is the price $P_m^*$ that brings forth the supply $Q_m^*$. Finally, note that this quantity $Q_m^*$ is less, and the price $P_m^*$ is lower, than the quantity and price that would prevail in a competitive market, $Q_c$ and $P_c$.

---

[12]Mathematically, we can write the net benefit NB from the purchase as NB = $V - E$, where $V$ is the value to the buyer of the purchase and $E$ is the expenditure. Net benefit is maximized when $\Delta NB/\Delta Q = 0$. Then

$$\Delta NB/\Delta Q = \Delta V/\Delta Q - \Delta E/\Delta Q = MV - ME = 0$$

so that MV = ME.

[13]To obtain the marginal expenditure curve algebraically, write the supply curve with price on the left-hand side: $P = P(Q)$. Then total expenditure $E$ is price times quantity, or $E = P(Q)Q$, and marginal expenditure is

$$ME = \Delta E/\Delta Q = P(Q) + Q(\Delta P/\Delta Q)$$

Because the supply curve is upward sloping, $\Delta P/\Delta Q$ is positive, and marginal expenditure is greater than average expenditure.

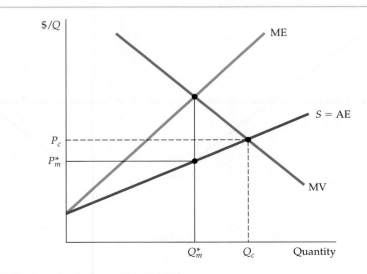

**FIGURE 10.14 Monopsonist Buyer**

The market supply curve is monopsonist's average expenditure curve AE. Because average expenditure is rising, marginal expenditure lies above it. The monopsonist purchases quantity $Q_m^*$, where marginal expenditure and marginal value (demand) intersect. The price paid per unit $P_m^*$ is then found from the average expenditure (supply) curve. In a competitive market, price and quantity, $P_c$ and $Q_c$, are both higher. They are found at the point where average expenditure (supply) and marginal value (demand) intersect.

## Monopsony and Monopoly Compared

Monopsony is easier to understand if you compare it with monopoly. Figures 10.15(a) and 10.15(b) illustrate this comparison. Recall that a monopolist can charge a price above marginal cost because it faces a downward-sloping demand, or average revenue curve, so that marginal revenue is less than average revenue. Equating marginal cost with marginal revenue leads to a quantity $Q^*$ that is less than what would be produced in a competitive market, and to a price $P^*$ that is higher than the competitive price $P_c$.

The monopsony situation is exactly analogous. As Figure 10.15(b) illustrates, the monopsonist can purchase a good *at a price below its marginal value* because it faces an upward-sloping supply, or average expenditure, curve. Thus for a monopsonist, marginal expenditure is greater than average expenditure. Equating marginal value with marginal expenditure leads to a quantity $Q^*$ that is less than what would be bought in a competitive market, and to a price $P^*$ that is lower than the competitive price $P_c$.

## 10.6 MONOPSONY POWER

Much more common than pure monopsony are markets with only a few firms competing among themselves as buyers, so that each firm has some monopsony power. For example, the major U.S. automobile manufacturers compete with one another as buyers of tires. Because each of them accounts for a large share of the tire market, each has some monopsony power in that market. General

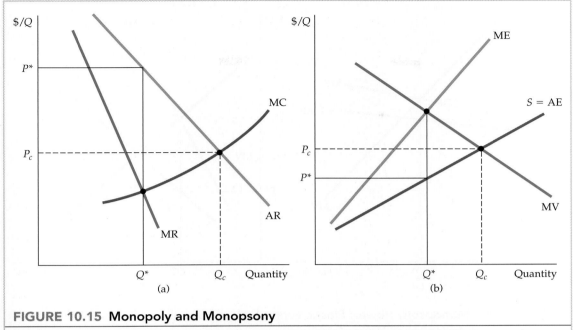

**FIGURE 10.15 Monopoly and Monopsony**

These diagrams show the close analogy between monopoly and monopsony. **(a)** The monopolist produces where marginal revenue intersects marginal cost. Average revenue exceeds marginal revenue, so that price exceeds marginal cost. **(b)** The monopsonist purchases up to the point where marginal expenditure intersects marginal value. Marginal expenditure exceeds average expenditure, so that marginal value exceeds price.

Motors, the largest, might be able to exert considerable monopsony power when contracting for supplies of tires (and other automotive parts).

In a competitive market, price and marginal value are equal. A buyer with monopsony power, however, can purchase a good at a price below marginal value. The extent to which price is marked down below marginal value depends on the elasticity of supply facing the buyer.[14] If supply is very elastic ($E_S$ is large), the markdown will be small and the buyer will have little monopsony power. Conversely, if supply is very inelastic, the markdown will be large and the buyer will have considerable monopsony power. Figures 10.16(a) and 10.16(b) illustrate these two cases.

## Sources of Monopsony Power

What determines the degree of monopsony power in a market? Again, we can draw analogies with monopoly and monopoly power. We saw that monopoly power depends on three things: the elasticity of market demand, the number of sellers in the market, and the way those sellers interact. Monopsony power depends on three similar things: The elasticity of market supply, the number of buyers in the market, and the way those buyers interact.

**Elasticity of Market Supply** A monopsonist benefits because it faces an upward-sloping supply curve, so that marginal expenditure exceeds average

---

[14]The exact relationship (analogous to equation (10.1)) is given by $(MV - P)/P = 1/E_s$. This equation follows because $MV = ME$ and $ME = \Delta(PQ)/\Delta Q = P + Q(\Delta P/\Delta Q)$.

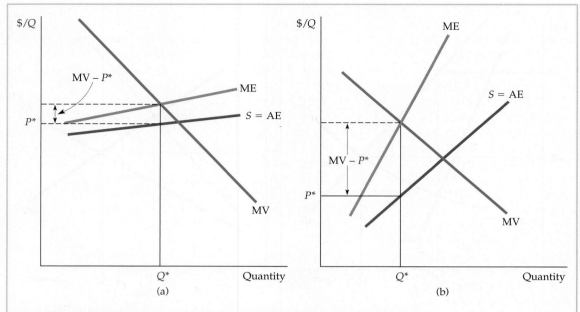

**FIGURE 10.16 Monopsony Power: Elastic versus Inelastic Supply**

Monopsony power depends on the elasticity of supply. When supply is elastic, as in **(a)**, marginal expenditure and average expenditure do not differ by much, so price is close to what it would be in a competitive market. The opposite is true when supply is inelastic, as in **(b)**.

expenditure. The less elastic the supply curve, the greater the difference between marginal expenditure and average expenditure and the more monopsony power the buyer enjoys. If only one buyer is in the market—a pure monopsonist—its monopsony power is completely determined by the elasticity of market supply. If supply is highly elastic, monopsony power is small and there is little gain in being the only buyer.

**Number of Buyers** Most markets have more than one buyer, and the number of buyers is an important determinant of monopsony power. When the number of buyers is very large, no single buyer can have much influence over price. Thus each buyer faces an extremely elastic supply curve, so that the market is almost completely competitive. The potential for monopsony power arises when the number of buyers is limited.

**Interaction Among Buyers** Finally, suppose three or four buyers are in the market. If those buyers compete aggressively, they will bid up the price close to their marginal value of the product, and will thus have little monopsony power. On the other hand, if those buyers compete less aggressively, or even collude, prices will not be bid up very much, and the buyers' degree of monopsony power might be nearly as high as if there were only one buyer.

So, as with monopoly power, there is no simple way to predict how much monopsony power buyers will have in a market. We can count the number of buyers, and we can often estimate the elasticity of supply, but that is not enough. Monopsony power also depends on the interaction among buyers, which can be more difficult to ascertain.

## The Social Costs of Monopsony Power

Because monopsony power results in lower prices and lower quantities purchased, we would expect it to make the buyer better off and sellers worse off. But suppose we value the welfare of buyers and sellers equally. How is aggregate welfare affected by monopsony power?

We can find out by comparing the buyer and seller surplus that results from a competitive market to the surplus that results when a monopsonist is the sole buyer. Figure 10.17 shows the average and marginal expenditure curves and marginal value curve for the monopsonist. The monopsonist's net benefit is maximized by purchasing a quantity $Q_m$ at a price $P_m$ such that marginal value equals marginal expenditure. In a competitive market, price equals marginal value. Thus the competitive price and quantity, $P_c$ and $Q_c$, are found where the average expenditure and marginal value curves intersect. Now let's see how surplus changes if we move from the competitive price and quantity, $P_c$ and $Q_c$, to the monopsony price and quantity, $P_m$ and $Q_m$.

With monopsony, the price is lower and less is sold. Because of the lower price, sellers lose an amount of surplus given by rectangle $A$. In addition, sellers lose the surplus given by triangle $C$ because of the reduced sales. The total loss of producer (seller) surplus is therefore $A + C$. By buying at a lower price, the buyer gains the surplus given by rectangle $A$. However, the buyer buys less, $Q_m$ instead of $Q_c$, and so loses the surplus given by triangle $B$. The total gain in surplus to the buyer is therefore $A - B$. Altogether, there is a net loss of surplus given by $B + C$. This is the *deadweight loss from monopsony power*. Even if the monopsonist's gains were taxed away and redistributed to the producers, there would be an inefficiency because output would be lower than under competition. The deadweight loss is the social cost of this inefficiency.

> Note the similarity with the deadweight loss from monopoly power discussed in §10.4.

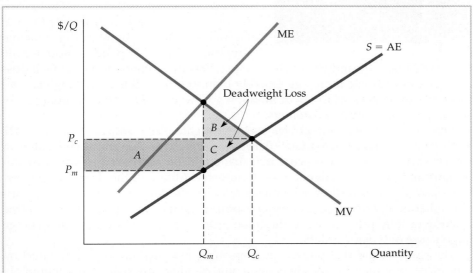

**FIGURE 10.17  Deadweight Loss from Monopsony Power**

The shaded rectangle and triangles show changes in buyer and seller surplus when moving from competitive price and quantity, $P_c$ and $Q_c$, to the monopsonist's price and quantity, $P_m$ and $Q_m$. Because both price and quantity are lower, there is an increase in buyer (consumer) surplus given by $A - B$. Producer surplus falls by $A + C$, so there is a deadweight loss given by triangles $B$ and $C$.

## Bilateral Monopoly

● **bilateral monopoly**
Market with only one seller
and one buyer.

What happens when a monopolist meets a monopsonist? It's hard to say. We call a market with only one seller and only one buyer a **bilateral monopoly**. If you think about such a market, you'll see why it is difficult to predict the price and quantity. Both the buyer and the seller are in a bargaining situation. Unfortunately, no simple rule determines which, if either, will get the better part of the bargain. One party might have more time and patience, or might be able to convince the other party that it will walk away if the price is too low or too high.

Bilateral monopoly is rare. Markets in which a few producers have some monopoly power and sell to a few buyers who have some monopsony power are more common. Although bargaining may still be involved, we can apply a rough principle here: *Monopsony power and monopoly power will tend to counteract each other.* In other words, the monopsony power of buyers will reduce the effective monopoly power of sellers, and vice versa. This tendency does not mean that the market will end up looking perfectly competitive; if, for example, monopoly power is large and monopsony power small, the residual monopoly power would still be significant. But in general, monopsony power will push price closer to marginal cost, and monopoly power will push price closer to marginal value.

**EXAMPLE 10.4** Monopsony Power in U.S. Manufacturing

Monopoly power, as measured by the price-cost margin $(P - MC)/P$, varies considerably across manufacturing industries in the United States. Some industries have price-cost margins close to zero, while in others margins are as high as 0.4 or 0.5. These variations are due in part to differences in the determinants of monopoly power: In some industries, market demand is more elastic than in others; some industries have more sellers than others; and in some industries, sellers compete more aggressively than in others. But something else can help explain these variations in monopoly power—differences in monopsony power among the firms' customers.

The role of monopsony power was investigated in a statistical study of 327 U.S. manufacturing industries.[15] The study sought to determine the extent to which variations in price—cost margins could be attributed to variations in monopsony power by buyers in each industry. Although the degree of buyers' monopsony power could not be measured directly, data were available for variables that help determine monopsony power, such as buyer concentration (the fraction of total sales going to the three or four largest firms) and the average annual size of buyers' orders.

The study found that buyers' monopsony power had an important effect on the price—cost margins of sellers and could significantly reduce any monopoly power that sellers might otherwise have. Take, for example, the concentration of buyers, an important determinant of monopsony power. In industries where

---

[15]The study was by Steven H. Lustgarten, "The Impact of Buyer Concentration in Manufacturing Industries," *Review of Economics and Statistics* 57 (May 1975): 125—32.

only four or five buyers account for all or nearly all sales, the price-cost margins of sellers would on average be as much as 10 percentage points lower than in comparable industries with hundreds of buyers accounting for sales.

A good example of monopsony power in manufacturing is the market for automobile parts and components, such as brakes and radiators. Each major car producer in the United States typically buys an individual part from at least three, and often as many as a dozen, suppliers. In addition, for a standardized product, such as brakes, each automobile company usually produces part of its needs itself, so that it is not totally reliant on outside firms. This puts companies like General Motors and Ford in an excellent bargaining position with respect to their suppliers. Each supplier must compete for sales against five or 10 other suppliers, but each can sell to only a few buyers. For a specialized part, a single auto company may be the *only* buyer. As a result, the automobile companies have considerable monopsony power.

This monopsony power becomes evident from the conditions under which suppliers must operate. To obtain a sales contract, a supplier must have a track record of reliability, in terms of both product quality and ability to meet tight delivery schedules. Suppliers are also often required to respond to changes in volume as auto sales and production levels fluctuate. Finally, pricing negotiations are notoriously difficult; a potential supplier will sometimes lose a contract because its bid is a penny per item higher than those of its competitors. Not surprisingly, producers of parts and components usually have little or no monopoly power.

# 10.7 LIMITING MARKET POWER: THE ANTITRUST LAWS

We have seen that market power—whether wielded by sellers or buyers—harms potential purchasers who could have bought at competitive prices. In addition, market power reduces output, which leads to a deadweight loss. Excessive market power also raises problems of equity and fairness: If a firm has significant monopoly power, it will profit at the expense of consumers. In theory, a firm's excess profits could be taxed away and redistributed to the buyers of its products, but such a redistribution is often impractical. It is difficult to determine what portion of a firm's profit is attributable to monopoly power, and it is even more difficult to locate all the buyers and reimburse them in proportion to their purchases.

How, then, can society limit market power and prevent it from being used anticompetitively? For a natural monopoly, such as an electric utility company, direct price regulation is the answer. But more generally, the answer is to prevent firms from acquiring excessive market power in the first place, and to limit the use of that power if it is acquired. In the United States, this is done via the **antitrust laws:** a set of rules and regulations designed to promote a competitive economy by prohibiting actions that restrain, or are likely to restrain, competition, and by restricting the forms of allowable market structure.

Monopoly power can arise in a number of ways, each of which is covered by the antitrust laws. Section 1 of the Sherman Act (which was passed in 1890) prohibits contracts, combinations, or conspiracies in restraint of trade. One obvious example of an illegal combination is an explicit agreement among producers

• **antitrust laws** Rules and regulations prohibiting actions that restrain, or are likely to restrain, competition.

to restrict their outputs and/or "fix" price above the competitive level. There have been numerous instances of such illegal combinations. For example:

- In 1996, Archer Daniels Midland Company (ADM) and two other major producers of lysine (an animal feed additive) pleaded guilty to criminal charges of price fixing. In 1999, three ADM executives were sentenced to prison terms ranging from two to three years for their roles in the price-fixing scheme.[16]

- In 1999, four of the world's largest drug and chemical companies—Roche A.G. of Switzerland, BASF A.G. of Germany, Rhone-Poulenc of France, and Takeda Chemical Industries of Japan—were charged by the U.S. Department of Justice with taking part in a global conspiracy to fix the prices of vitamins sold in the United States. The companies pleaded guilty to price fixing and agreed to pay fines totaling more than $1 billion.[17]

- In 2002, the U.S. Department of Justice began an investigation of price fixing by DRAM (dynamic access random memory) producers. By 2006, five manufacturers—Hynix, Infineon, Micron Technology, Samsung, and Elpida—had pled guilty for participating in an international price-fixing scheme. As part of these pleas, the companies agreed to pay fines totaling close to $1 billion to the DOJ, and several executives received prison sentences.

**• parallel conduct** Form of implicit collusion in which one firm consistently follows actions of another.

Two firms need not meet or talk on the telephone to violate Section 1 of the Sherman Act; *implicit* collusion in the form of **parallel conduct** can also be construed as violating the law. For example, if Firm *B* consistently follows Firm *A*'s pricing (parallel pricing), and if the firm's conduct is contrary to what one would expect companies to do in the absence of collusion (such as raising prices in the face of decreased demand and over-supply), an implicit understanding may be inferred.[18]

Section 2 of the Sherman Act makes it illegal to monopolize or to attempt to monopolize a market and prohibits conspiracies that result in monopolization. The Clayton Act (1914) did much to pinpoint the kinds of practices that are likely to be anticompetitive. For example, the act makes it unlawful for a firm with a large market share to require the buyer or lessor of a good not to buy from a competitor. It also makes it illegal to engage in **predatory pricing**—pricing designed to drive current competitors out of business and to discourage new entrants (so that the predatory firm can enjoy higher prices in the future).

**• predatory pricing** Practice of pricing to drive current competitors out of business and to discourage new entrants in a market so that a firm can enjoy higher future profits.

Monopoly power can also be achieved by a merger of firms into a larger and more dominant firm, or by one firm acquiring or taking control of another firm by purchasing its stock. The Clayton Act prohibits mergers and acquisitions if they "substantially lessen competition" or "tend to create a monopoly."

---

[16]In the lysine case, proof of the conspiracy came in part from tapes of meetings at which prices were set and market shares divided up. At one meeting with executives from Ajinimoto Company of Japan, another lysine producer, James Randall, then the president of ADM, said, "We have a saying at this company. Our competitors are our friends and our customers are our enemies." See "Video Tapes Take Star Role at Archer Daniels Trial," *New York Times*, August 4, 1998; "Three Sentenced in Archer Daniels Midland Case," *New York Times*, July 10, 1999. In 1993, ADM and three other firms were also charged with fixing carbon dioxide prices.

[17]"Tearing Down the Facades of 'Vitamins Inc.'," *New York Times*, October 10, 1999.

[18]The Sherman Act applies to all firms that do business in the United States (to the extent that a conspiracy to restrain trade could affect U.S. markets). However, foreign governments (or firms operating under their government's control) are not subject to the act, so OPEC need not fear the wrath of the Justice Department. Also, firms *can* collude with respect to *exports*. The Webb-Pomerene Act (1918) allows price fixing and related collusion with respect to export markets, *as long as domestic markets are unaffected by such collusion.* Firms operating in this manner must form a "Webb-Pomerene Association" and register it with the government.

The antitrust laws also limit possible anticompetitive conduct by firms in other ways. For example, the Clayton Act, as amended by the Robinson-Patman Act (1936), makes it illegal to discriminate by charging buyers of essentially the same product different prices if those price differences are likely to injure competition. Even then, firms are not liable if they can show that the price differences were necessary to meet competition. (As we will see in the next chapter, price discrimination is a common practice. It becomes the target of antitrust action only when buyers suffer economic damages and competition is reduced.)

Another important component of the antitrust laws is the Federal Trade Commission Act (1914, amended in 1938, 1973, 1975), which created the Federal Trade Commission (FTC). This act supplements the Sherman and Clayton acts by fostering competition through a whole set of prohibitions against unfair and anticompetitive practices, such as deceptive advertising and labeling, agreements with retailers to exclude competing brands, and so on. Because these prohibitions are interpreted and enforced in administrative proceedings before the FTC, the act provides broad powers that reach further than those of other antitrust laws.

The antitrust laws are actually phrased vaguely in terms of what is and what is not allowed. They are intended to provide a general statutory framework to give the Justice Department, the FTC, and the courts wide discretion in interpreting and applying them. This approach is important because it is difficult to know in advance what might be an impediment to competition. Such ambiguity creates a need for common law (i.e., the practice whereby courts interpret statutes) and supplemental provisions and rulings (e.g., by the FTC or the Justice Department).

## Enforcement of the Antitrust Laws

The antitrust laws are enforced in three ways:

1. *Through the Antitrust Division of the Department of Justice.* As an arm of the executive branch, its enforcement policies closely reflect the view of the administration in power. Responding to an external complaint or an internal study, the department can institute a criminal proceeding, bring a civil suit, or both. The result of a criminal action can be fines for the corporation and fines or jail sentences for individuals. For example, individuals who conspire to fix prices or rig bids can be charged with a felony and, if found guilty, may be sentenced to jail—something to remember if you are planning to parlay your knowledge of microeconomics into a successful business career! Losing a civil action forces a corporation to cease its anticompetitive practices and often to pay damages.

2. *Through the administrative procedures of the Federal Trade Commission.* Again, action can result from an external complaint or from the FTC's own initiative. Should the FTC decide that action is required, it can either request a voluntary understanding to comply with the law or seek a formal commission order requiring compliance.

3. *Through private proceedings.* Individuals or companies can sue for *treble (three-fold) damages* inflicted on their businesses or property. The prospect of treble damages can be a strong deterrent to would-be violators. Individuals or companies can also ask the courts for injunctions to force wrongdoers to cease anticompetitive actions.

U.S. antitrust laws are more stringent and far-reaching than those of most other countries. In fact, some people have argued that they have prevented American industry from competing effectively in international markets. The laws certainly constrain American business and may at times have put American firms at a disadvantage in world markets. But this criticism must be weighed against their benefits: Antitrust laws have been crucial for maintaining competition, and competition is essential for economic efficiency, innovation, and growth.

## Antitrust in Europe

As the European Union has grown, its methods of antitrust enforcement have evolved. The responsibility for the enforcement of antitrust concerns that involve two or more member states resides in a single entity, the Competition Directorate, located in Brussels. Separate and distinct antitrust authorities within individual member states are responsible for those issues whose effects are felt largely or entirely within particular countries.

At first glance, the antitrust laws of the European Union are quite similar to those of the United States. Article 81 of the Treaty of the European Community concerns restraints of trade, much like Section 1 of the Sherman Act. Article 82, which focuses on abuses of market power by *dominant* firms, is similar in many ways to Section 2 of the Sherman Act. Finally, with respect to mergers, the European Merger Control Act is similar in spirit to Section 7 of the Clayton Act.

Nevertheless, there remain a number of procedural and substantive differences between antitrust laws in Europe and the United States. Merger evaluations typically are conducted more quickly in Europe, and it is easier in practice to prove that a European firm is dominant than it is to show that a U.S. firm has monopoly power. Both the European Union and the U.S. have been actively enforcing laws against price fixing, but Europe imposes only civil penalties, whereas the U.S. can impose prison sentences as well as fines.

---

**EXAMPLE 10.5**    **A Phone Call About Prices**

In 1981 and early 1982, American Airlines and Braniff Airways were competing fiercely with each other for passengers. A fare war broke out as the firms undercut each other's prices to capture market share. On February 21, 1982, Robert Crandall, president and CEO of American, made a phone call to Howard Putnam, president and chief executive of Braniff. To Crandall's later surprise, the call had been taped. It went like this:[19]

> *Crandall:* I think it's dumb as hell for Christ's sake, all right, to sit here and pound the @!#$%&! out of each other and neither one of us making a @!#$%&! dime.
>
> *Putnam:* Well . . .
>
> *Crandall:* I mean, you know, @!#$%&!, what the hell is the point of it?
>
> *Putnam:* But if you're going to overlay every route of American's on top of every route that Braniff has—I just can't sit here and allow you to bury us without giving our best effort.
>
> *Crandall:* Oh sure, but Eastern and Delta do the same thing in Atlanta and have for years.
>
> *Putnam:* Do you have a suggestion for me?

---

[19]According to the *New York Times*, February 24, 1983.

*Crandall:* Yes, I have a suggestion for you. Raise your @!#$%&! fares 20 percent. I'll raise mine the next morning.

*Putnam:* Robert, we...

*Crandall:* You'll make more money and I will, too.

*Putnam:* We can't talk about pricing!

*Crandall:* Oh @!#$%&!, Howard. We can talk about any @!#$%&! thing we want to talk about.

Crandall was wrong. Corporate executives cannot talk about anything they want. Talking about prices and agreeing to fix them is a clear violation of Section 1 of the Sherman Act. Putnam must have known this because he promptly rejected Crandall's suggestion. After learning about the call, the Justice Department filed a suit accusing Crandall of violating the antitrust laws by proposing to fix prices.

However, *proposing* to fix prices is not enough to violate Section 1 of the Sherman Act: For the law to be violated, the two parties must *agree* to collude. Therefore, because Putnam had rejected Crandall's proposal, Section 1 was not violated. The court later ruled, however, that a proposal to fix prices could be an attempt to monopolize part of the airline industry and, if so, would violate Section 2 of the Sherman Act. American Airlines promised the Justice Department never again to engage in such activity.

**EXAMPLE 10.6** **The United States versus Microsoft**

Over the past decade, Microsoft Corporation has grown to become the largest computer software company in the world. Its Windows operating system has over 94 percent of the worldwide market for personal computer operating systems. Microsoft also dominates the office productivity market: Its Office Suite, which includes Word (word processing), Excel (spreadsheets), and Powerpoint (presentations), held over a 95-percent worldwide market share in 2006.

Microsoft's incredible success has been due in good part to the creative technological and marketing decisions of the company and its CEO, Bill Gates. Is there anything wrong as a matter of either economics or law with being so successful and dominant? It all depends. Under the antitrust laws, efforts by firms to restrain trade or to engage in activities that inappropriately maintain monopolies are illegal. Did Microsoft engage in anticompetitive, illegal practices?

The U.S. Government said yes; Microsoft disagreed. In October 1998, the Antitrust Division of the U.S. Department of Justice (DOJ) put Microsoft's behavior to the test: It filed suit, raising a broad set of issues that created the most significant antitrust law suit of the past two decades. The ensuing trial ended in June 1999, but it wasn't until early in 2003 that a settlement between the government and Microsoft was finalized. Here is a brief road map of some of the DOJ's major claims and Microsoft's responses.

- **DOJ claim:** Microsoft has a great deal of market power in the market for PC operating systems—enough to meet the legal definition of monopoly power.

  **MS response:** Microsoft does not meet the legal test for monopoly power because it faces significant threats from potential competitors that offer or will offer platforms to compete with Windows.

- **DOJ claim:** Microsoft viewed Netscape's Internet browser (Netscape Navigator) as a threat to its monopoly over the PC operating system market. The threat existed because Netscape's browser includes Sun's Java software, which can run programs that have been written for *any* operating system, including those that compete with Windows, such as Apple, Unix, and Linux. In violation of Section 1 of the Sherman Act, Microsoft entered into exclusionary agreements with computer manufacturers and Internet service providers with the objective of raising the cost to Netscape of making its browser available to consumers. This action impaired Netscape's ability to compete fairly with Microsoft's Internet Explorer for the browser business.

  **MS response:** The contracts were not unduly restrictive. In any case, Microsoft unilaterally agreed to stop most of them.

- **DOJ claim:** In violation of Section 2 of the Sherman Act, Microsoft engaged in practices designed to maintain its monopoly in the market for desktop PC operating systems. Most importantly, it tied its browser to the Windows 98 operating system, even though doing so was technically unnecessary and provides little or no benefit to consumers. This action was predatory because it made it difficult or impossible for Netscape and other firms to successfully offer competing products.

  **MS response:** There are benefits to incorporating the browser functionality into the operating system. Not being allowed to integrate new functionality into an operating system will discourage innovation. Offering consumers a choice between separate or integrated browsers would cause confusion in the marketplace.

- **DOJ claim:** In violation of Section 2 of the Sherman Act, Microsoft attempted to divide the browser business with Netscape and engaged in similar conduct with both Apple Computer and Intel.

  **MS response:** Microsoft's meetings with Netscape, Apple, and Intel were for valid business reasons. Indeed, it is useful for consumers and firms to agree on common standards and protocols in developing computer software.

These are some of the highlights of an eight-month trial that was hard-fought on a range of economic issues. The District Court reached its findings regarding the facts of the case in November 1999 and the legal conclusions in April 2000. It found that Microsoft did have monopoly power in the market for PC operating systems. The Court concluded further that Microsoft had viewed Netscape as a threat and that in responding to that threat, it had engaged in a series of anticompetitive acts to protect and extend its operating system monopoly. The court deemed these actions to violate Section 2 of the Sherman Act. However, the Court also found that the exclusionary agreements with computer manufacturers and Internet service providers had not foreclosed competition sufficiently to violate Section 1 of the Sherman Act. Microsoft's appeal to the Circuit Court of

Appeals for the District of Columbia was decided in June 2001. The Appellate Court supported the District Court's conclusions that Microsoft was a monopoly and had engaged in anticompetitive practices to protect that monopoly. However, the Court left undecided whether including Internet Explorer in the operating system was itself illegal.

Since this decision, the DOJ and Microsoft agreed to settle the case. Among other things, the agreement required Microsoft (1) to give computer manufacturers the ability to offer its operating system without Internet Explorer and (2) to include competing browser programs when loading the Windows operating system onto the machines they sell. Microsoft also agreed to a program that would monitor its compliance with the terms of the settlement. Despite opposition from critics who believed the remedy insufficient, the settlement was approved by the Appellate Court in 2004, putting an end to this landmark antitrust case in the United States.

Microsoft's problems did not end with the U.S. settlement, however. In 2004, the European Commission ordered Microsoft to pay $610 million in fines for its anticompetitive practices and to produce a version of Windows without the Windows Media Player to be sold alongside its standard editions. In addition, numerous private lawsuits were brought in the United States, with most settling for substantial sums of money.

## SUMMARY

1. Market power is the ability of sellers or buyers to affect the price of a good.
2. Market power comes in two forms. When sellers charge a price that is above marginal cost, we say that they have monopoly power, which we measure by the extent to which price exceeds marginal cost. When buyers can obtain a price below their marginal value of the good, we say they have monopsony power, which we measure by the extent to which marginal value exceeds price.
3. Monopoly power is determined in part by the number of firms competing in a market. If there is only one firm—a pure monopoly—monopoly power depends entirely on the elasticity of market demand. The less elastic the demand, the more monopoly power the firm will have. When there are several firms, monopoly power also depends on how the firms interact. The more aggressively they compete, the less monopoly power each firm will have.

4. Monopsony power is determined in part by the number of buyers in a market. If there is only one buyer— a pure monopsony—monopsony power depends on the elasticity of market supply. The less elastic the supply, the more monopsony power the buyer will have. When there are several buyers, monopsony power also depends on how aggressively they compete for supplies.
5. Market power can impose costs on society. Because monopoly and monopsony power both cause production to fall below the competitive level, there is a deadweight loss of consumer and producer surplus. There can be additional social costs from rent seeking.
6. Sometimes, scale economies make pure monopoly desirable. But the government will still want to regulate price to maximize social welfare.
7. More generally, we rely on the antitrust laws to prevent firms from obtaining excessive market power.

## QUESTIONS FOR REVIEW

1. A monopolist is producing at a point at which marginal cost exceeds marginal revenue. How should it adjust its output to increase profit?
2. We write the percentage markup of price over marginal cost as $(P - MC)/P$. For a profit-maximizing monopolist, how does this markup depend on the elasticity of demand? Why can this markup be viewed as a measure of monopoly power?
3. Why is there no market supply curve under conditions of monopoly?
4. Why might a firm have monopoly power even if it is not the only producer in the market?

5. What are some of the different types of barriers to entry that give rise to monopoly power? Give an example of each.

6. What factors determine the amount of monopoly power an individual firm is likely to have? Explain each one briefly.

7. Why is there a social cost to monopoly power? If the gains to producers from monopoly power could be redistributed to consumers, would the social cost of monopoly power be eliminated? Explain briefly.

8. Why will a monopolist's output increase if the government forces it to lower its price? If the government wants to set a price ceiling that maximizes the monopolist's output, what price should it set?

9. How should a monopsonist decide how much of a product to buy? Will it buy more or less than a competitive buyer? Explain briefly.

10. What is meant by the term "monopsony power"? Why might a firm have monopsony power even if it is not the only buyer in the market?

11. What are some sources of monopsony power? What determines the amount of monopsony power an individual firm is likely to have?

12. Why is there a social cost to monopsony power? If the gains to buyers from monopsony power could be redistributed to sellers, would the social cost of monopsony power be eliminated? Explain briefly.

13. How do the antitrust laws limit market power in the United States? Give examples of major provisions of these laws.

14. Explain briefly how the U.S. antitrust laws are actually enforced.

# EXERCISES

1. Will an increase in the demand for a monopolist's product always result in a higher price? Explain. Will an increase in the supply facing a monopsonist buyer always result in a lower price? Explain.

2. Caterpillar Tractor, one of the largest producers of farm machinery in the world, has hired you to advise it on pricing policy. One of the things the company would like to know is how much a 5-percent increase in price is likely to reduce sales. What would you need to know to help the company with this problem? Explain why these facts are important.

3. A monopolist firm faces a demand with constant elasticity of −2.0. It has a constant marginal cost of $20 per unit and sets a price to maximize profit. If marginal cost should increase by 25 percent, would the price charged also rise by 25 percent?

4. A firm faces the following average revenue (demand) curve:

$$P = 120 - 0.02Q$$

where $Q$ is weekly production and $P$ is price, measured in cents per unit. The firm's cost function is given by $C = 60Q + 25,000$. Assume that the firm maximizes profits.

a. What is the level of production, price, and total profit per week?

b. If the government decides to levy a tax of 14 cents per unit on this product, what will be the new level of production, price, and profit?

5. The following table shows the demand curve facing a monopolist who produces at a constant marginal cost of $10:

| Price | Quantity |
|-------|----------|
| 18 | 0 |
| 16 | 4 |
| 14 | 8 |
| 12 | 12 |
| 10 | 16 |
| 8 | 20 |
| 6 | 24 |
| 4 | 28 |
| 2 | 32 |
| 0 | 36 |

a. Calculate the firm's marginal revenue curve.

b. What are the firm's profit-maximizing output and price? What is its profit?

c. What would the equilibrium price and quantity be in a competitive industry?

d. What would the social gain be if this monopolist were forced to produce and price at the competitive equilibrium? Who would gain and lose as a result?

6. Suppose that an industry is characterized as follows:

| | |
|---|---|
| $C = 100 + 2q^2$ | each firm's total cost function |
| $MC = 4q$ | firm's marginal cost function |
| $P = 90 - 2Q$ | industry demand curve |
| $MR = 90 - 4Q$ | industry marginal revenue curve |

**a.** If there is *only one firm* in the industry, find the monopoly price, quantity, and level of profit.

**b.** Find the price, quantity, and level of profit if the industry is competitive.

**c.** Graphically illustrate the demand curve, marginal revenue curve, marginal cost curve, and average cost curve. Identify the difference between the profit level of the monopoly and the profit level of the competitive industry in two different ways. Verify that the two are numerically equivalent.

7. Suppose a profit-maximizing monopolist is producing 800 units of output and is charging a price of $40 per unit.

   **a.** If the elasticity of demand for the product is –2, find the marginal cost of the last unit produced.

   **b.** What is the firm's percentage markup of price over marginal cost?

   **c.** Suppose that the average cost of the last unit produced is $15 and the firm's fixed cost is $2000. Find the firm's profit.

8. A firm has two factories, for which costs are given by:

$$\text{Factory \#1: } C_1(Q_1) = 10Q_1^2$$
$$\text{Factory \#2: } C_2(Q_2) = 20Q_2^2$$

The firm faces the following demand curve:

$$P = 700 - 5Q$$

where $Q$ is total output—i.e., $Q = Q_1 + Q_2$.

   **a.** On a diagram, draw the marginal cost curves for the two factories, the average and marginal revenue curves, and the total marginal cost curve (i.e., the marginal cost of producing $Q = Q_1 + Q_2$). Indicate the profit-maximizing output for each factory, total output, and price.

   **b.** Calculate the values of $Q_1$, $Q_2$, $Q$, and $P$ that maximize profit.

   **c.** Suppose that labor costs increase in Factory 1 but not in Factory 2. How should the firm adjust (i.e., raise, lower, or leave unchanged) the following: Output in Factory 1? Output in Factory 2? Total output? Price?

9. A drug company has a monopoly on a new patented medicine. The product can be made in either of two plants. The costs of production for the two plants are $MC_1 = 20 + 2Q_1$ and $MC_2 = 10 + 5Q_2$. The firm's estimate of demand for the product is $P = 20 - 3(Q_1 + Q_2)$. How much should the firm plan to produce in each plant? At what price should it plan to sell the product?

10. One of the more important antitrust cases of the 20th century involved the Aluminum Company of America (Alcoa) in 1945. At that time, Alcoa controlled about 90 percent of primary aluminum production in the United States, and the company had been accused of monopolizing the aluminum market. In its defense,

Alcoa argued that although it indeed controlled a large fraction of the primary market, secondary aluminum (i.e., aluminum produced from the recycling of scrap) accounted for roughly 30 percent of the total supply of aluminum and that many competitive firms were engaged in recycling. Therefore, Alcoa argued, it did not have much monopoly power.

   **a.** Provide a clear argument *in favor* of Alcoa's position.

   **b.** Provide a clear argument *against* Alcoa's position.

   **c.** The 1945 decision by Judge Learned Hand has been called "one of the most celebrated judicial opinions of our time." Do you know what Judge Hand's ruling was?

11. A monopolist faces the demand curve $P = 11 - Q$, where $P$ is measured in dollars per unit and $Q$ in thousands of units. The monopolist has a constant average cost of $6 per unit.

   **a.** Draw the average and marginal revenue curves and the average and marginal cost curves. What are the monopolist's profit-maximizing price and quantity? What is the resulting profit? Calculate the firm's degree of monopoly power using the Lerner index.

   **b.** A government regulatory agency sets a price ceiling of $7 per unit. What quantity will be produced, and what will the firm's profit be? What happens to the degree of monopoly power?

   **c.** What price ceiling yields the largest level of output? What is that level of output? What is the firm's degree of monopoly power at this price?

12. Michelle's Monopoly Mutant Turtles (MMMT) has the exclusive right to sell Mutant Turtle t-shirts in the United States. The demand for these t-shirts is $Q = 10,000/P^2$. The firm's short-run cost is $SRTC = 2000 + 5Q$, and its long-run cost is $LRTC = 6Q$.

   **a.** What price should MMMT charge to maximize profit in the short run? What quantity does it sell, and how much profit does it make? Would it be better off shutting down in the short run?

   **b.** What price should MMMT charge in the long run? What quantity does it sell and how much profit does it make? Would it be better off shutting down in the long run?

   **c.** Can we expect MMMT to have lower marginal cost in the short run than in the long run? Explain why.

13. You produce widgets for sale in a perfectly competitive market at a market price of $10 per widget. Your widgets are manufactured in two plants, one in Massachusetts and the other in Connecticut. Because of labor problems in Connecticut, you are forced to raise wages there, so that marginal costs in that plant increase. In response to this, should you shift production and produce more in your Massachusetts plant?

14. The employment of teaching assistants (TAs) by major universities can be characterized as a monopsony. Suppose the demand for TAs is $W = 30,000 - 125n$,

where $W$ is the wage (as an annual salary) and $n$ is the number of TAs hired. The supply of TAs is given by $W = 1000 + 75n$.

a. If the university takes advantage of its monopsonist position, how many TAs will it hire? What wage will it pay?

b. If, instead, the university faced an infinite supply of TAs at the annual wage level of $10,000, how many TAs would it hire?

*15. Dayna's Doorstops, Inc. (DD) is a monopolist in the doorstop industry. Its cost is $C = 100 - 5Q + Q^2$, and demand is $P = 55 - 2Q$.

a. What price should DD set to maximize profit? What output does the firm produce? How much profit and consumer surplus does DD generate?

b. What would output be if DD acted like a perfect competitor and set $MC = P$? What profit and consumer surplus would then be generated?

c. What is the deadweight loss from monopoly power in part (a)?

d. Suppose the government, concerned about the high price of doorstops, sets a maximum price at $27. How does this affect price, quantity, consumer surplus, and DD's profit? What is the resulting deadweight loss?

e. Now suppose the government sets the maximum price at $23. How does this decision affect price, quantity, consumer surplus, DD's profit, and deadweight loss?

f. Finally, consider a maximum price of $12. What will this do to quantity, consumer surplus, profit, and deadweight loss?

*16. There are 10 households in Lake Wobegon, Minnesota, each with a demand for electricity of $Q = 50 - P$. Lake Wobegon Electric's (LWE) cost of producing electricity is $TC = 500 + Q$.

a. If the regulators of LWE want to make sure that there is no deadweight loss in this market, what price will they force LWE to charge? What will output be in that case? Calculate consumer surplus and LWE's profit with that price.

b. If regulators want to ensure that LWE doesn't lose money, what is the lowest price they can impose? Calculate output, consumer surplus, and profit. Is there any deadweight loss?

c. Kristina knows that deadweight loss is something that this small town can do without. She suggests that each household be required to pay a fixed amount just to receive any electricity at all, and then a per-unit charge for electricity. Then LWE can break even while charging the price calculated in part (a). What fixed amount would each household have to pay for Kristina's plan to work? Why can you be sure that no household will choose instead to refuse the payment and go without electricity?

17. A certain town in the Midwest obtains all of its electricity from one company, Northstar Electric. Although the company is a monopoly, it is owned by the citizens of the town, all of whom split the profits equally at the end of each year. The CEO of the company claims that because all of the profits will be given back to the citizens, it makes economic sense to charge a monopoly price for electricity. True or false? Explain.

18. A monopolist faces the following demand curve:

$$Q = 144/P^2$$

where $Q$ is the quantity demanded and $P$ is price. Its *average variable* cost is

$$AVC = Q^{1/2}$$

and its *fixed cost* is 5.

a. What are its profit-maximizing price and quantity? What is the resulting profit?

b. Suppose the government regulates the price to be no greater than $4 per unit. How much will the monopolist produce? What will its profit be?

c. Suppose the government wants to set a ceiling price that induces the monopolist to produce the largest possible output. What price will accomplish this goal?

# Pricing with Market Power

As we explained in Chapter 10, market power is quite common. Many industries have only a few producers, so that each producer has some monopoly power. And many firms, as buyers of raw materials, labor, or specialized capital goods, have some monopsony power in the markets for these factor inputs. The problem faced by the managers of these firms is *how to use their market power most effectively*. They must decide how to set prices, choose quantities of factor inputs, and determine output in both the short and long run to maximize profit.

Managers of firms with market power have a harder job than those who manage perfectly competitive firms. A firm that is perfectly competitive in output markets has no influence over market price. As a result, its managers need worry only about the cost side of the firm's operations, choosing output so that price is equal to marginal cost. But the managers of a firm with monopoly power must also worry about the characteristics of demand. Even if they set a single price for the firm's output, they must obtain at least a rough estimate of the elasticity of demand to determine what that price (and corresponding output level) should be. Furthermore, firms can often do much better by using a more complicated pricing strategy—for example, charging different prices to different customers. To design such pricing strategies, managers need ingenuity and even more information about demand.

This chapter explains how firms with market power set prices. We begin with the basic objective of every pricing strategy: capturing consumer surplus and converting it into additional profit for the firm. Then we discuss how this goal can be achieved using *price discrimination*—charging different prices to different customers, sometimes for the same product and sometimes for small variations in the product. Because price discrimination is widely practiced in one form or another, it is important to understand how it works.

Next, we discuss the *two-part tariff*—requiring customers to pay in advance for the right to purchase units of a good at a later time (and at additional cost). The classic example of this is an amusement park, where customers pay a fee to enter and then additional fees for each ride. Although amusement parks may seem like a rather specialized market, there are many other examples of two-part tariffs: the price of a Gillette razor, which gives the owner the opportunity to purchase Gillette razor blades; a tennis club, where members pay an annual fee and then an hourly rate for court time; or the monthly subscription cost of long-distance telephone service, which gives users the opportunity to make long-distance calls, paying by the minute as they do so.

We will also discuss *bundling*, a pricing strategy that involves tying products together and selling them as a package. For example: a personal computer that comes bundled with several software packages; a one-week vacation in which the airfare, rental car, and hotel are bundled and sold at a single package price; or a luxury car, in which the sun roof, power windows, and leather seats are "standard" features.

Finally, we will examine the use of *advertising* by firms with market power. As we will see, deciding how much money to spend on advertising requires information about demand and is closely related to the firm's pricing decision. We will derive a simple rule of thumb for determining the profit-maximizing advertising-to-sales ratio.

## 11.1 CAPTURING CONSUMER SURPLUS

> Consumer surplus is explained in §4.4 and reviewed in §9.1.

All the pricing strategies that we will examine have one thing in common: *They are means of capturing consumer surplus and transferring it to the producer*. You can see this more clearly in Figure 11.1. Suppose the firm sold all its output at a single price. To maximize profit, it would pick a price $P^*$ and corresponding output $Q^*$ at the intersection of its marginal cost and marginal revenue curves. Although the firm would then be profitable, its managers might still wonder if they could make it even more profitable.

They know that some customers (in region $A$ of the demand curve) would pay more than $P^*$. But raising the price would mean losing some customers, selling less, and earning smaller profits. Similarly, other potential customers are not buying the firm's product because they will not pay a price as high as $P^*$. Many

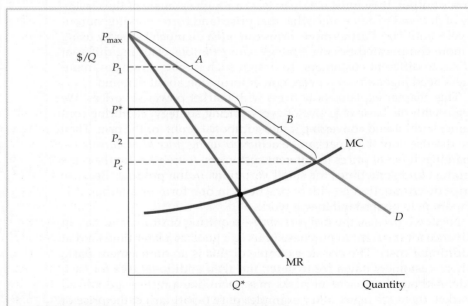

**FIGURE 11.1 Capturing Consumer Surplus**

If a firm can charge only one price for all its customers, that price will be $P^*$ and the quantity produced will be $Q^*$. Ideally, the firm would like to charge a higher price to consumers willing to pay more than $P^*$, thereby capturing some of the consumer surplus under region $A$ of the demand curve. The firm would also like to sell to consumers willing to pay prices lower than $P^*$, but only if doing so does not entail lowering the price to other consumers. In that way, the firm could also capture some of the surplus under region $B$ of the demand curve.

of them, however, would pay prices higher than the firm's marginal cost. (These customers are in region *B* of the demand curve.) By lowering its price, the firm could sell to some of these customers. Unfortunately, it would then earn less revenue from its existing customers, and again profits would shrink.

How can the firm capture the consumer surplus (or at least part of it) from its customers in region *A*, and perhaps also sell profitably to some of its potential customers in region *B*? Charging a single price clearly will not do the trick. However, the firm might charge different prices to different customers, according to where the customers are along the demand curve. For example, some customers in the upper end of region *A* would be charged the higher price $P_1$, some in region *B* would be charged the lower price $P_2$, and some in between would be charged $P^*$. This is the basis of **price discrimination**: charging different prices to different customers. The problem, of course, is to identify the different customers, and to get them to pay different prices. We will see how this can be done in the next section.

The other pricing techniques that we will discuss in this chapter—two-part tariffs and bundling—also expand the range of a firm's market to include more customers and to capture more consumer surplus. In each case, we will examine both the amount by which the firm's profit can be increased and the effect on consumer welfare. (As we will see, when there is a high degree of monopoly power, these pricing techniques can sometimes make both consumers and the producer better off.) We turn first to price discrimination.

* **price discrimination**
Practice of charging different prices to different consumers for similar goods.

## 11.2 PRICE DISCRIMINATION

Price discrimination can take three broad forms, which we call first-, second-, and third-degree price discrimination. We will examine them in turn.

### First-Degree Price Discrimination

Ideally, a firm would like to charge a different price to each of its customers. If it could, it would charge each customer the maximum price that the customer is willing to pay for each unit bought. We call this maximum price the customer's **reservation price**. The practice of charging each customer his or her reservation price is called perfect **first-degree price discrimination**.[1] Let's see how it affects the firm's profit.

First, we need to know the profit that the firm earns when it charges only the single price $P^*$ in Figure 11.2. To find out, we can add the profit on each incremental unit produced and sold, up to the total quantity $Q^*$. This incremental profit is the marginal revenue less the marginal cost for each unit. In Figure 11.2, this marginal revenue is highest and marginal cost lowest for the first unit. For each additional unit, marginal revenue falls and marginal cost rises. Thus the firm produces the total output $Q^*$, at which point marginal revenue and marginal cost are equal.

If we add up the profits on each incremental unit produced, we obtain the firm's **variable profit**; the firm's profit, ignoring its fixed costs. In Figure 11.2, variable profit is given by the *yellow-shaded* area between the marginal revenue and

* **reservation price**  Maximum price that a customer is willing to pay for a good.

* **first-degree price discrimination**  Practice of charging each customer her reservation price.

In §8.3, we explain that a firm's profit-maximizing output is the output at which marginal revenue is equal to marginal cost.

* **variable profit**  Sum of profits on each incremental unit produced by a firm; i.e., profit ignoring fixed costs.

---

[1]We are assuming that each customer buys one unit of the good. If a customer buys more than one unit, the firm will have to charge different prices for each of the units.

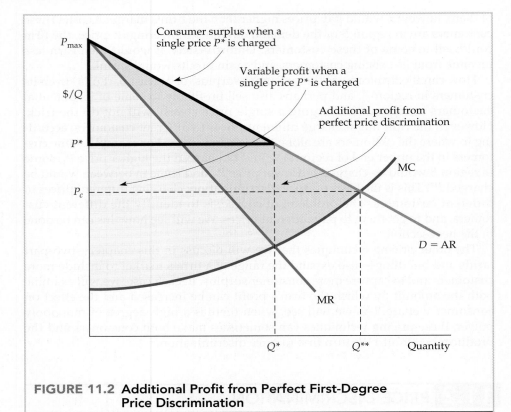

**FIGURE 11.2 Additional Profit from Perfect First-Degree
Price Discrimination**

Because the firm charges each consumer her reservation price, it is profitable to
expand output to $Q^{**}$. When only a single price, $P^*$, is charged, the firm's variable
profit is the area between the marginal revenue and marginal cost curves. With perfect
price discrimination, this profit expands to the area between the demand curve and
the marginal cost curve.

marginal cost curves.[2] Consumer surplus, which is the area between the average
revenue curve and the price $P^*$ that customers pay, is outlined as a black triangle.

**Perfect Price Discrimination** What happens if the firm can perfectly price
discriminate? Because each consumer is charged exactly what he or she is willing
to pay, the marginal revenue curve is no longer relevant to the firm's output decision. Instead, the incremental revenue earned from each additional unit sold is
simply the price paid for that unit; it is therefore given by the demand curve.

Since price discrimination does not affect the firm's cost structure, the cost of
each additional unit is again given by the firm's marginal cost curve. Therefore,
*the additional profit from producing and selling an incremental unit is now the difference
between demand and marginal cost.* As long as demand exceeds marginal cost, the
firm can increase its profit by expanding production. It will do so until it produces a total output $Q^{**}$. At $Q^{**}$, demand is equal to marginal cost, and producing any more reduces profit.

---

[2]Recall from Chapter 10 that because total profit $\pi$ is the difference between total revenue $R$ and total
cost $C$, incremental profit is just $\Delta\pi = \Delta R - \Delta C = MR - MC$. Variable profit is found by summing all the
$\Delta\pi$s, and thus it is the area between the MR and MC curves. This ignores fixed costs, which are independent of the firm's output and pricing decisions. Thus, total profit equals variable profit minus fixed cost.

Variable profit is now given by the area between the demand and marginal cost curves.[3] Observe from Figure 11.2 how the firm's profit has increased. (The additional profit resulting from price discrimination is shown by the purple-shaded area.) Note also that because every customer is being charged the maximum amount that he or she is willing to pay, all consumer surplus has been captured by the firm.

**Imperfect Price Discrimination** In practice, perfect first-degree price discrimination is almost never possible. First, it is usually impractical to charge each and every customer a different price (unless there are only a few customers). Second, a firm usually does not know the reservation price of each customer. Even if it could ask how much each customer would be willing to pay, it probably would not receive honest answers. After all, it is in the customers' interest to claim that they would pay very little.

Sometimes, however, firms can discriminate imperfectly by charging a few different prices based on estimates of customers' reservation prices. This practice is often used by professionals, such as doctors, lawyers, accountants, or architects, who know their clients reasonably well. In such cases, the client's willingness to pay can be assessed and fees set accordingly. For example, a doctor may offer a reduced fee to a low-income patient whose willingness to pay or insurance coverage is low but charge higher fees to upper-income or better-insured patients. And an accountant, having just completed a client's tax returns, is in an excellent position to estimate how much the client is willing to pay for the service.

Another example is a car salesperson, who typically works with a 15-percent profit margin. The salesperson can give part of this margin away to the customer by making a "deal," or can insist that the customer pay the full sticker price. A good salesperson knows how to size up customers: A customer who is likely to look elsewhere for a car is given a large discount (from the salesperson's point of view, a small profit is better than no sale and no profit), but the customer in a hurry is offered little or no discount. In other words, *a successful car salesperson knows how to price discriminate!*

Still another example is college and university tuition. Colleges don't charge different tuition rates to different students in the same degree programs. Instead, they offer financial aid, in the form of scholarships or subsidized loans, which reduces the *net* tuition that the student must pay. By requiring those who seek aid to disclose information about family income and wealth, colleges can link the amount of aid to ability (and hence willingness) to pay. Thus students who are financially well off pay more for their education, while students who are less well off pay less.

Figure 11.3 illustrates imperfect first-degree price discrimination. If only a single price were charged, it would be $P_4^*$. Instead, six different prices are charged, the lowest of which, $P_6$, is set at about the point where marginal cost intersects the demand curve. Note that those customers who would not have been willing to pay a price of $P_4^*$ or greater are actually better off in this situation—they are now in the market and may be enjoying at least some consumer surplus. In fact, if price discrimination brings enough new customers into the market, consumer welfare can increase to the point that both the producer and consumers are better off.

---

[3]Incremental profit is again $\Delta \pi = \Delta R - \Delta C$, but $\Delta R$ is given by the price to each customer (i.e., the average revenue curve), so $\Delta \pi = AR - MC$. Variable profit is the sum of these $\Delta \pi$s and is given by the area between the AR and MC curves.

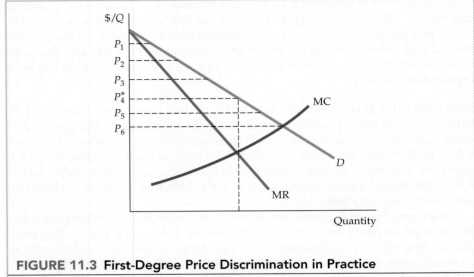

**FIGURE 11.3 First-Degree Price Discrimination in Practice**

Firms usually don't know the reservation price of every consumer, but sometimes reservation prices can be roughly identified. Here, six different prices are charged. The firm earns higher profits, but some consumers may also benefit. With a single price $P_4^*$, there are fewer consumers. The consumers who now pay $P_5$ or $P_6$ enjoy a surplus.

## Second-Degree Price Discrimination

In some markets, as each consumer purchases many units of a good over any given period, his reservation price declines with the number of units purchased. Examples include water, heating fuel, and electricity. Consumers may each purchase a few hundred kilowatt-hours of electricity a month, but their willingness to pay declines with increasing consumption. The first 100 kilowatt-hours may be worth a lot to the consumer—operating a refrigerator and providing for minimal lighting. Conservation becomes easier with the additional units and may be worthwhile if the price is high. In this situation, a firm can discriminate according to the quantity consumed. This is called **second-degree price discrimination**, and it works by charging different prices for different quantities of the same good or service.

• **second-degree price discrimination** Practice of charging different prices per unit for different quantities of the same good or service.

Quantity discounts are an example of second-degree price discrimination. A single roll of Kodak film might be priced at $5, while a box containing four rolls of the same film might be priced at $14, making the average price per roll $3.50. Similarly, the price per ounce for breakfast cereal is likely to be smaller for the 24-ounce box than for the 16-ounce box.

• **block pricing** Practice of charging different prices for different quantities or "blocks" of a good.

Another example of second-degree price discrimination is *block pricing* by electric power companies, natural gas utilities, and municipal water companies. With **block pricing**, the consumer is charged different prices for different quantities or "blocks" of a good. If scale economies cause average and marginal costs to decline, the government agency that controls rates may encourage block pricing. Because it leads to expanded output and greater scale economies, this policy can increase consumer welfare while allowing for greater profit to the company: While prices are reduced overall, the savings from the lower unit cost still permits the company to increase its profit.

Figure 11.4 illustrates second-degree price discrimination for a firm with declining average and marginal costs. If a single price were charged, it would be $P_0$, and the quantity produced would be $Q_0$. Instead, three different prices are

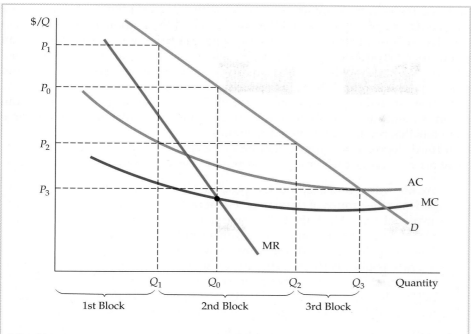

**FIGURE 11.4 Second-Degree Price Discrimination**

Different prices are charged for different quantities, or "blocks," of the same good. Here, there are three blocks, with corresponding prices $P_1$, $P_2$, and $P_3$. There are also economies of scale, and average and marginal costs are declining. Second-degree price discrimination can then make consumers better off by expanding output and lowering cost.

charged, based on the quantities purchased. The first block of sales is priced at $P_1$, the second at $P_2$, and the third at $P_3$.

## Third-Degree Price Discrimination

A well-known liquor company has what seems to be a strange pricing practice. The company produces a vodka that it advertises as one of the smoothest and best-tasting available. This vodka is called "Three Star Golden Crown" and sells for about $16 a bottle.[4] However, the company also takes some of this same vodka and bottles it under the name "Old Sloshbucket," which is sold for about $8 a bottle. Why does it do this? Has the president of the company been spending too much time near the vats?

Perhaps, but this company is also practicing **third-degree price discrimination**, and it does so because the practice is profitable. This form of price discrimination divides consumers into two or more groups with separate demand curves for each group. It is the most prevalent form of price discrimination, and examples abound: regular versus "special" airline fares; premium versus nonpremium brands of liquor, canned food or frozen vegetables; discounts to students and senior citizens; and so on.

**Creating Consumer Groups** In each case, some characteristic is used to divide consumers into distinct groups. For many goods, for example, students and senior citizens are usually willing to pay less on average than the rest of the population

• **third-degree price discrimination** Practice of dividing consumers into two or more groups with separate demand curves and charging different prices to each group.

---

[4]We have changed the names to protect the innocent.

(because their incomes are lower), and identity can be readily established (via a college ID or driver's license). Likewise, to separate vacationers from business travelers (whose companies are usually willing to pay higher fares), airlines can put restrictions on special low-fare tickets, such as requiring advance purchase or a Saturday night stay. With the liquor company, or the premium versus nonpremium (e.g., supermarket label) brand of food, the label itself divides consumers; many consumers are willing to pay more for a name brand even though the nonpremium brand is identical or nearly identical (and might be manufactured by the same company that produced the premium brand).

If third-degree price discrimination is feasible, how should the firm decide what price to charge each group of consumers? Let's think about this in two steps.

1. We know that however much is produced, total output should be divided between the groups of customers so that marginal revenues for each group are equal. Otherwise, the firm would not be maximizing profit. For example, if there are two groups of customers and the marginal revenue for the first group, $MR_1$, exceeds the marginal revenue for the second group, $MR_2$, the firm could clearly do better by shifting output from the second group to the first. It would do this by lowering the price to the first group and raising the price to the second group. Thus, whatever the two prices, they must be such that the marginal revenues for the different groups are equal.

2. We know that *total* output must be such that the marginal revenue for each group of consumers is equal to the marginal cost of production. Again, if this were not the case, the firm could increase its profit by raising or lowering total output (and lowering or raising its prices to both groups). For example, suppose that marginal revenues were the same for each group of consumers but that marginal revenue exceeded marginal cost. The firm could then make a greater profit by increasing its total output. It would lower its prices to both groups of consumers, so that marginal revenues for each group would fall (but would still be equal to each other) and would approach marginal cost.

Let's look at this problem algebraically. Let $P_1$ be the price charged to the first group of consumers, $P_2$ the price charged to the second group, and $C(Q_T)$ the total cost of producing output $Q_T = Q_1 + Q_2$. Total profit is then

$$\pi = P_1Q_1 + P_2Q_2 - C(Q_T)$$

The firm should increase its sales to each group of consumers, $Q_1$ and $Q_2$, until the incremental profit from the last unit sold is zero. First, we set incremental profit for sales to the first group of consumers equal to zero:

$$\frac{\Delta\pi}{\Delta Q_1} = \frac{\Delta(P_1Q_1)}{\Delta Q_1} - \frac{\Delta C}{\Delta Q_1} = 0$$

Here, $\Delta(P_1Q_1)/\Delta Q_1$ is the incremental revenue from an extra unit of sales to the first group of consumers (i.e., $MR_1$). The next term, $\Delta C/\Delta Q_1$, is the incremental cost of producing this extra unit—i.e., marginal cost, MC. We thus have

$$MR_1 = MC$$

Similarly, for the second group of consumers, we must have

$$MR_2 = MC$$

Putting these relations together, we see that prices and output must be set so that

$$MR_1 = MR_2 = MC \qquad \textbf{(11.1)}$$

Again, marginal revenue must be equal across groups of consumers and must equal marginal cost.

**Determining Relative Prices** Managers may find it easier to think in terms of the relative prices that should be charged to each group of consumers and to relate these prices to the elasticities of demand. Recall from Section 10.1 that we can write marginal revenue in terms of the elasticity of demand:

$$MR = P(1 + 1/E_d)$$

Thus $MR_1 = P_1(1 + 1/E_1)$ and $MR_2 = P_2(1 + 1/E_2)$, where $E_1$ and $E_2$ are the elasticities of demand for the firm's sales in the first and second markets, respectively. Now equating $MR_1$ and $MR_2$ as in equation (11.1) gives the following relationship that must hold for the prices:

> In our discussion of a rule of thumb for pricing in §10.1, we explained that a profit-maximizing firm chooses an output at which its marginal revenue is equal to the price of the product plus the ratio of the price to the price elasticity of demand.

$$\frac{P_1}{P_2} = \frac{(1+1/E_2)}{(1+1/E_1)} \qquad \textbf{(11.2)}$$

As you would expect, the higher price will be charged to consumers with the lower demand elasticity. For example, if the elasticity of demand for consumers in group 1 is –2 and the elasticity for consumers in group 2 is –4, we will have $P_1/P_2 = (1 - 1/4)/(1 - 1/2) = (3/4)/(1/2) = 1.5$. In other words, the price charged to the first group of consumers should be 1.5 times as high as the price charged to the second group.

Figure 11.5 illustrates third-degree price discrimination. Note that the demand curve $D_1$ for the first group of consumers is less elastic than the curve for the second

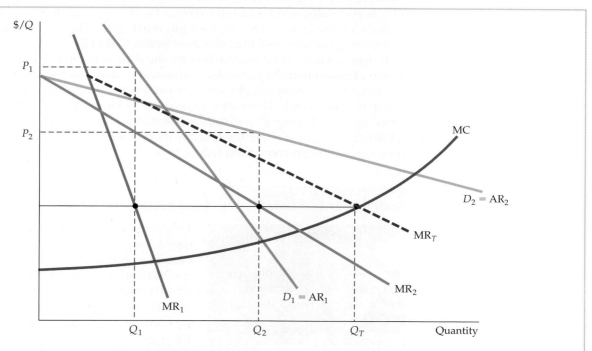

**FIGURE 11.5 Third-Degree Price Discrimination**

Consumers are divided into two groups, with separate demand curves for each group. The optimal prices and quantities are such that the marginal revenue from each group is the same and equal to marginal cost. Here group 1, with demand curve $D_1$, is charged $P_1$, and group 2, with the more elastic demand curve $D_2$, is charged the lower price $P_2$. Marginal cost depends on the total quantity produced $Q_T$. Note that $Q_1$ and $Q_2$ are chosen so that $MR_1 = MR_2 = MC$.

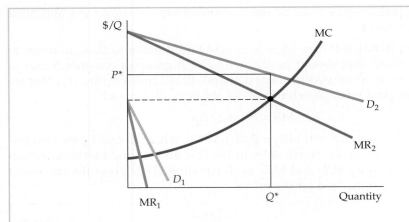

**FIGURE 11.6 No Sales to Smaller Market**

Even if third-degree price discrimination is feasible, it may not pay to sell to both groups of consumers if marginal cost is rising. Here the first group of consumers, with demand $D_1$, are not willing to pay much for the product. It is unprofitable to sell to them because the price would have to be too low to compensate for the resulting increase in marginal cost.

group; thus the price charged to the first group is higher. The total quantity produced, $Q_T = Q_1 + Q_2$, is found by summing the marginal revenue curves $MR_1$ and $MR_2$ horizontally, which yields the dashed curve $MR_T$, and finding its intersection with the marginal cost curve. Because MC must equal $MR_1$ and $MR_2$, we can draw a horizontal line leftward from this intersection to find the quantities $Q_1$ and $Q_2$.

It may not always be worthwhile for the firm to try to sell to more than one group of consumers. In particular, if demand is small for the second group and marginal cost is rising steeply, the increased cost of producing and selling to this group may outweigh the increase in revenue. In Figure 11.6, the firm is better off charging a single price $P^*$ and selling only to the larger group of consumers: The additional cost of serving the smaller market would outweigh the additional revenue that might come from selling to it.

| EXAMPLE 11.1 | The Economics of Coupons and Rebates |

Producers of processed foods and related consumer goods often issue coupons that let customers buy products at discounts. These coupons are usually distributed as part of an advertisement for the product. They may appear in newspapers or magazines or in promotional mailings. For example, a coupon for a particular breakfast cereal might be worth 50 cents toward the purchase of a box of the cereal. Why do firms issue these coupons? Why not just lower the price of the product and thereby save the costs of printing and collecting the coupons?

Coupons provide a means of price discrimination. Studies show that only about 20 to 30 percent of all consumers regularly bother to clip, save, and use coupons. These consumers tend to be more sensitive to price than those who ignore coupons. They generally have more price-elastic demands and lower reservation prices. By issuing coupons, therefore, a cereal company can separate its customers into two groups and, in effect, charge the more price-sensitive customers a lower price than the other customers.

Rebate programs work the same way. For example, Kodak ran a program in which a consumer could mail in a form together with the proof of purchase of three rolls of film and receive a rebate of $1.50. Why not just lower the price of film by 50 cents a roll? Because only those consumers with relatively price-sensitive demands bother to send in the materials and request rebates. Again, the program is a means of price discrimination.

Can consumers really be divided into distinct groups in this way? Table 11.1 shows the results of a statistical study in which, for a variety of products, price elasticities of demand were estimated for users and nonusers of coupons.[5] This study confirms that users of coupons tend to have more price-sensitive demands. It also shows the extent to which the elasticities differ for the two groups of consumers and how the difference varies from one product to another.

By themselves, these elasticity estimates do not tell a firm what price to set and how large a discount to offer because they pertain to *market demand*, not to the demand for the firm's particular brand. For example, Table 11.1 indicates that the elasticity of demand for cake mix is −0.21 for nonusers of coupons and −0.43

| TABLE 11.1 | Price Elasticities of Demand for Users versus Nonusers of Coupons | |
|---|---|---|
| | **PRICE ELASTICITY** | |
| **Product** | **Nonusers** | **Users** |
| Toilet tissue | −0.60 | −0.66 |
| Stuffing/dressing | −0.71 | −0.96 |
| Shampoo | −0.84 | −1.04 |
| Cooking/salad oil | −1.22 | −1.32 |
| Dry mix dinners | −0.88 | −1.09 |
| Cake mix | −0.21 | −0.43 |
| Cat food | −0.49 | −1.13 |
| Frozen entrees | −0.60 | −0.95 |
| Gelatin | −0.97 | −1.25 |
| Spaghetti sauce | −1.65 | −1.81 |
| Creme rinse/conditioner | −0.82 | −1.12 |
| Soups | −1.05 | −1.22 |
| Hot dogs | −0.59 | −0.77 |

---

[5]The study is by Chakravarthi Narasimhan, "A Price Discrimination Theory of Coupons," *Marketing Science* (Spring 1984). A recent study of coupons for breakfast cereals finds that contrary to the predictions of the price-discrimination model, shelf prices for cereals tend to be lower during periods when coupons are more widely available. This might occur because couponing spurs more price competition among cereal manufacturers. See Aviv Nevo and Catherine Wolfram, "Prices and Coupons for Breakfast Cereals," *RAND Journal of Economics* 33 (2002): 319–39.

for users. But the elasticity of demand for any of the five or six major brands of cake mix on the market will be much larger than either of these numbers—about five or six times as large, as a rule of thumb.[6] So for any one brand of cake mix—say, Pillsbury—the elasticity of demand for users of coupons might be about −2.4, versus about −1.2 for nonusers. From equation (11.2), therefore, we can determine that the price to nonusers of coupons should be about 1.5 times the price to users. In other words, if a box of cake mix sells for $3.00, the company should offer coupons that give a $1.00 discount.

---

**EXAMPLE 11.2**   Airline Fares

Travelers are often amazed at the variety of fares available for round-trip flights from New York to Los Angeles. Recently, for example, the first-class fare was above $2000; the regular (unrestricted) economy fare was about $1700, and special discount fares (often requiring the purchase of a ticket two weeks in advance and/or a Saturday night stayover) could be bought for as little as $400. Although first-class service is not the same as economy service with a minimum stay requirement, the difference would not seem to warrant a price that is seven times as high. Why do airlines set such fares?

These fares provide a profitable form of price discrimination. The gains from discriminating are large because different types of customers, with very different elasticities of demand, purchase these different types of tickets. Table 11.2 shows price (and income) elasticities of demand for three categories of service within the United States: first class, unrestricted coach, and discounted tickets (which often have restrictions and may be partly nonrefundable).

Note that the demand for discounted fares is about two or three times as price elastic as first-class or unrestricted coach service. Why the difference? While discounted tickets are usually used by families and other leisure travelers, first-class and unrestricted coach tickets are more often bought by business travelers, who have little choice about when they travel and whose companies pick up the tab. Of course, these elasticities pertain to market demand, and with several airlines competing for customers, the elasticities of demand for each airline will be larger. But the *relative* sizes of elasticities across the three categories of service should be about the same. When elasticities of demand differ so widely, it should not be surprising that airlines set such different fares for different categories of service.

| TABLE 11.2  Elasticities of Demand for Air Travel | | | |
|---|---|---|---|
| | **FARE CATEGORY** | | |
| **Elasticity** | **First Class** | **Unrestricted Coach** | **Discounted** |
| Price | −0.3 | −0.4 | −0.9 |
| Income | 1.2 | 1.2 | 1.8 |

---

[6]This rule of thumb applies if interfirm competition can be described by the Cournot model, which we will discuss in Chapter 12.

Airline price discrimination has become increasingly sophisticated. A wide variety of fares is available, depending on how far in advance the ticket is bought, the percentage of the fare that is refundable if the trip is changed or cancelled, and whether the trip includes a weekend stay.[7] The objective of the airlines has been to discriminate more finely among travelers with different reservation prices. As one industry executive puts it, "You don't want to sell a seat to a guy for $69 when he is willing to pay $400."[8] At the same time, an airline would rather sell a seat for $69 than leave it empty.

## 11.3 INTERTEMPORAL PRICE DISCRIMINATION AND PEAK-LOAD PRICING

Two other closely related forms of price discrimination are important and widely practiced. The first of these is **intertemporal price discrimination**: separating consumers with different demand functions into different groups by charging different prices at different points in time. The second is **peak-load pricing**: charging higher prices during peak periods when capacity constraints cause marginal costs to be high. Both of these strategies involve charging different prices at different times, but the reasons for doing so are somewhat different in each case. We will take each in turn.

### Intertemporal Price Discrimination

The objective of intertemporal price discrimination is to divide consumers into high-demand and low-demand groups by charging a price that is high at first but falls later. To see how this strategy works, think about how an electronics company might price new, technologically advanced equipment, such as high-performance digital cameras or LCD television monitors. In Figure 11.7, $D_1$ is the (inelastic) demand curve for a small group of consumers who value the product highly and do not want to wait to buy it (e.g., photography buffs who want the latest camera). $D_2$ is the demand curve for the broader group of consumers who are more willing to forgo the product if the price is too high. The strategy, then, is to offer the product initially at the high price $P_1$, selling mostly to consumers on demand curve $D_1$. Later, after this first group of consumers has bought the product, the price is lowered to $P_2$, and sales are made to the larger group of consumers on demand curve $D_2$.[9]

There are other examples of intertemporal price discrimination. One involves charging a high price for a first-run movie and then lowering the price after the movie has been out a year. Another, practiced almost universally by publishers, is to charge a high price for the hardcover edition of a book and then to release the paperback version at a much lower price about a year later. Many people

• **intertemporal price discrimination** Practice of separating consumers with different demand functions into different groups by charging different prices at different points in time.

• **peak-load pricing** Practice of charging higher prices during peak periods when capacity constraints cause marginal costs to be high.

---

[7]Airlines also allocate the number of seats on each flight that will be available for each fare category. The allocation is based on the total demand and mix of passengers expected for each flight, and can change as the departure of the flight nears and estimates of demand and passenger mix change.

[8]"The Art of Devising Air Fares," *New York Times*, March 4, 1987.

[9]The prices of new electronic products also come down over time because costs fall as producers start to achieve greater scale economies and move down the learning curve. But even if costs did not fall, producers can make more money by first setting high prices and then reducing them over time, thereby discriminating and capturing consumer surplus.

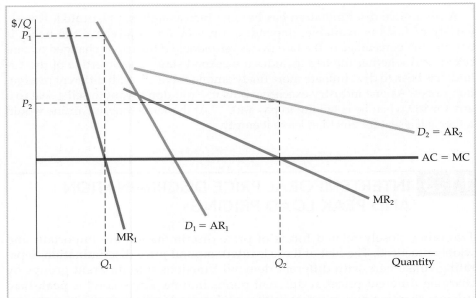

**FIGURE 11.7 Intertemporal Price Discrimination**

Consumers are divided into groups by changing the price over time. Initially, the price is high. The firm captures surplus from consumers who have a high demand for the good and who are unwilling to wait to buy it. Later the price is reduced to appeal to the mass market.

think that the lower price of the paperback is due to a much lower cost of production, but this is not true. Once a book has been edited and typeset, the marginal cost of printing an additional copy, whether hardcover or paperback, is quite low, perhaps a dollar or so. The paperback version is sold for much less not because it is much cheaper to print but because high-demand consumers have already purchased the hardbound edition. The remaining consumers—paperback buyers—generally have more elastic demands.

## Peak-Load Pricing

Peak-load pricing also involves charging different prices at different points in time. Rather than capturing consumer surplus, however, the objective is to increase economic efficiency by charging consumers prices that are close to marginal cost.

For some goods and services, demand peaks at particular times—for roads and tunnels during commuter rush hours, for electricity during late summer afternoons, and for ski resorts and amusement parks on weekends. Marginal cost is also high during these peak periods because of capacity constraints. Prices should thus be higher during peak periods.

This is illustrated in Figure 11.8, where $D_1$ is the demand curve for the peak period and $D_2$ the demand curve for the nonpeak period. The firm sets marginal revenue equal to marginal cost for each period, obtaining the high price $P_1$ for the peak period and the lower price $P_2$ for the nonpeak period, selling corresponding quantities $Q_1$ and $Q_2$. This strategy increases the firm's profit above what it would be if it charged one price for all periods. It is also more efficient: The sum of producer and consumer surplus is greater because prices are closer to marginal cost.

In §9.2, we explain that economic efficiency means that aggregate consumer and producer surplus is maximized.

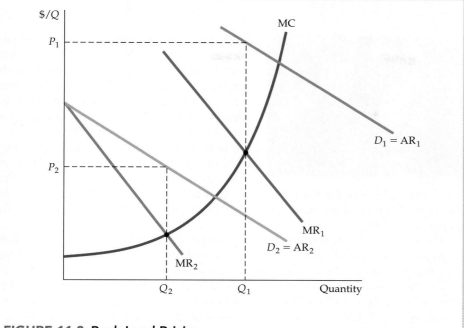

**FIGURE 11.8 Peak-Load Pricing**

Demands for some goods and services increase sharply during particular times of the day or year. Charging a higher price $P_1$ during the peak periods is more profitable for the firm than charging a single price at all times. It is also more efficient because marginal cost is higher during peak periods.

The efficiency gain from peak-load pricing is important. If the firm were a regulated monopolist (e.g., an electric utility), the regulatory agency should set the prices $P_1$ and $P_2$ at the points where the *demand* curves, $D_1$ and $D_2$, intersect the marginal cost curve, rather than where the marginal revenue curves intersect marginal cost. In that case, consumers realize the entire efficiency gain.

Note that peak-load pricing is different from third-degree price discrimination. With third-degree price discrimination, marginal revenue must be equal for each group of consumers and equal to marginal cost. Why? Because the costs of serving the different groups are not independent. For example, with unrestricted versus discounted air fares, increasing the number of seats sold at discounted fares affects the cost of selling unrestricted tickets—marginal cost rises rapidly as the airplane fills up. But this is not so with peak-load pricing (or for that matter, with most instances of intertemporal price discrimination). Selling more tickets for ski lifts or amusement parks on a weekday does not significantly raise the cost of selling tickets on the weekend. Similarly, selling more electricity during off-peak periods will not significantly increase the cost of selling electricity during peak periods. As a result, price and sales in each period can be determined independently by setting marginal cost equal to marginal revenue for each period.

Movie theaters, which charge more for evening shows than for matinees, are another example. For most movie theaters, the marginal cost of serving customers during the matinee is independent of marginal cost during the evening. The owner of a movie theater can determine the optimal prices for the evening and matinee shows independently, using estimates of demand and marginal cost in each period.

**EXAMPLE 11.3** How to Price a Best-Selling Novel

Publishing both hardbound and paperback editions of a book allows publishers to price discriminate. As they do with most goods, consumers differ considerably in their willingness to pay for books. For example, some consumers want to buy a new bestseller as soon as it is released, even if the price is $25. Other consumers, however, will wait a year until the book is available in paperback for $10. But how does a publisher decide that $25 is the right price for the new hardbound edition and $10 is the right price for the paperback edition? And how long should it wait before bringing out the paperback edition?

The key is to divide consumers into two groups, so that those who are willing to pay a high price do so and *only* those unwilling to pay a high price wait and buy the paperback. This means that significant time must be allowed to pass before the paperback is released. If consumers know that the paperback will be available within a few months, they will have little incentive to buy the hardbound edition.[10] On the other hand, if the publisher waits too long to bring out the paperback edition, interest will wane and the market will dry up. As a result, publishers typically wait 12 to 18 months before releasing paperback editions.

What about price? Setting the price of the hardbound edition is difficult: Except for a few authors whose books always seem to sell, publishers have little data with which to estimate demand for a book that is about to be published. Often, they can judge only from the past sales of similar books. But usually only aggregate data are available for each category of book. Most new novels, therefore, are released at similar prices. It is clear, however, that those consumers willing to wait for the paperback edition have demands that are far more elastic than those of bibliophiles. It is not surprising, then, that paperback editions sell for so much less than hardbacks.[11]

# 11.4 THE TWO-PART TARIFF

• **two-part tariff** Form of pricing in which consumers are charged both an entry and a usage fee.

The **two-part tariff** is related to price discrimination and provides another means of extracting consumer surplus. It requires consumers to pay a fee up front for the right to buy a product. Consumers then pay an additional fee for each unit of the product they wish to consume. The classic example of this strategy is an amusement park.[12] You pay an admission fee to enter, and you also

---

[10]Some consumers will buy the hardbound edition even if the paperback is already available because it is more durable and more attractive on a bookshelf. This must be taken into account when setting prices, but it is of secondary importance compared with intertemporal price discrimination.

[11]Hardbound and paperback editions are often published by different companies. The author's agent auctions the rights to the two editions, but the contract for the paperback specifies a delay to protect the sales of the hardbound edition. The principle still applies, however. The length of the delay and the prices of the two editions are chosen to price discriminate intertemporally.

[12]This pricing strategy was first analyzed by Walter Oi, "A Disneyland Dilemma: Two-Part Tariffs for a Mickey Mouse Monopoly," *Quarterly Journal of Economics* (February 1971): 77–96.

pay a certain amount for each ride. The owner of the park must decide whether to charge a high entrance fee and a low price for the rides or, alternatively, to admit people for free but charge high prices for the rides.

The two-part tariff has been applied in many settings: tennis and golf clubs (you pay an annual membership fee plus a fee for each use of a court or round of golf); the rental of large mainframe computers (a flat monthly fee plus a fee for each unit of processing time consumed); telephone service (a monthly hook-up fee plus a fee for minutes of usage). The strategy also applies to the sale of products like safety razors (you pay for the razor, which lets you consume the blades that fit that brand of razor).

The problem for the firm is how to set the *entry fee* (which we denote by $T$) versus the *usage fee* (which we denote by $P$). Assuming that the firm has some market power, should it set a high entry fee and low usage fee, or vice versa? To solve this problem, we need to understand the basic principles involved.

**Single Consumer** Let's begin with the artificial but simple case illustrated in Figure 11.9. Suppose there is only one consumer in the market (or many consumers with identical demand curves). Suppose also that the firm knows this consumer's demand curve. Now, remember that the firm wants to capture as much consumer surplus as possible. In this case, the solution is straightforward: Set the usage fee $P$ equal to marginal cost and the entry fee $T$ equal to the total consumer surplus for each consumer. Thus, the consumer pays $T^*$ (or a bit less) to use the product, and $P^* = MC$ per unit consumed. With the fees set in this way, the firm captures *all* the consumer surplus as its profit.

**Two Consumers** Now suppose that there are two different consumers (or two groups of identical consumers). The firm, however, can set only *one* entry fee and one usage fee. It would thus no longer want to set the usage fee equal to marginal cost. If it did, it could make the entry fee no larger than the consumer surplus of the consumer with the smaller demand (or else it would lose that consumer), and this would not yield a maximum profit. Instead, the firm should set the usage fee *above* marginal cost and then set the entry fee equal to the remaining consumer surplus of the consumer with the smaller demand.

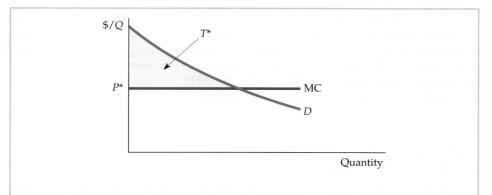

**FIGURE 11.9 Two-Part Tariff with a Single Consumer**

The consumer has demand curve $D$. The firm maximizes profit by setting usage fee $P$ equal to marginal cost and entry fee $T^*$ equal to the entire surplus of the consumer.

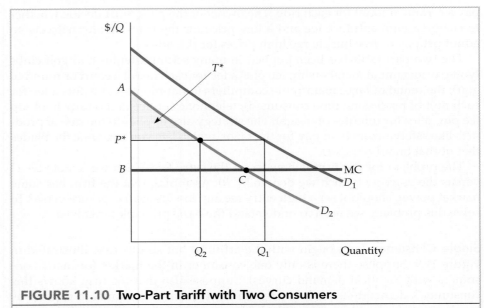

**FIGURE 11.10 Two-Part Tariff with Two Consumers**

The profit-maximizing usage fee $P^*$ will exceed marginal cost. The entry fee $T^*$ is equal to the surplus of the consumer with the smaller demand. The resulting profit is $2T^* + (P^* - MC)(Q_1 + Q_2)$. Note that this profit is larger than twice the area of triangle $ABC$.

Figure 11.10 illustrates this. With the optimal usage fee at $P^*$ greater than MC, the firm's profit is $2T^* + (P^* - MC)(Q_1 + Q_2)$. (There are two consumers, and each pays $T^*$.) You can verify that this profit is more than twice the area of triangle $ABC$, the consumer surplus of the consumer with the smaller demand when $P =$ MC. To determine the exact values of $P^*$ and $T^*$, the firm would need to know (in addition to its marginal cost) the demand curves $D_1$ and $D_2$. It would then write down its profit as a function of $P$ and $T$ and choose the two prices that maximize this function. (See Exercise 10 for an example of how to do this.)

**Many Consumers** Most firms, however, face a variety of consumers with different demands. Unfortunately, there is no simple formula to calculate the optimal two-part tariff in this case, and some trial-and-error experiments might be required. But there is always a trade-off: A lower entry fee means more entrants and thus more profit from sales of the item. On the other hand, as the entry fee becomes smaller and the number of entrants larger, the profit derived from the entry fee will fall. The problem, then, is to pick an entry fee that results in the optimum number of entrants—that is, the fee that allows for maximum profit. In principle, we can do this by starting with a price for sales of the item $P$, finding the optimum entry fee $T$, and then estimating the resulting profit. The price $P$ is then changed, and the corresponding entry fee calculated, along with the new profit level. By iterating this way, we can approach the optimal two-part tariff.

Figure 11.11 illustrates this principle. The firm's profit $\pi$ is divided into two components, each of which is plotted as a function of the entry fee $T$, assuming a fixed sales price $P$. The first component, $\pi_a$, is the profit from the entry fee and is equal to the revenue $n(T)T$, where $n(T)$ is the number of entrants. (Note that a high $T$ implies a small $n$.) Initially, as $T$ is increased from zero, revenue $n(T)T$

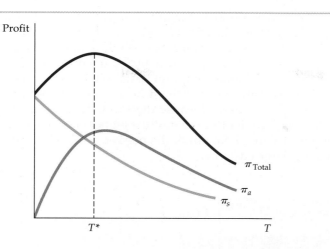

**FIGURE 11.11 Two-Part Tariff with Many Different Consumers**

Total profit $\pi$ is the sum of the profit from the entry fee $\pi_a$ and the profit from sales $\pi_s$. Both $\pi_a$ and $\pi_s$ depend on $T$, the entry fee. Therefore

$$\pi = \pi_a + \pi_s = n(T)T + (P - MC)Q(n)$$

where $n$ is the number of entrants, which depends on the entry fee $T$, and $Q$ is the rate of sales, which is greater the larger is $n$. Here $T^*$ is the profit-maximizing entry fee, given $P$. To calculate optimum values for $P$ and $T$, we can start with a number for $P$, find the optimum $T$, and then estimate the resulting profit. $P$ is then changed and the corresponding $T$ recalculated, along with the new profit level.

rises. Eventually, however, further increases in $T$ will make $n$ so small that $n(T)T$ falls. The second component, $\pi_s$, is the profit from sales of the item itself at price $P$ and is equal to $(P - MC)Q$, where $Q$ is the rate at which entrants purchase the item. The larger the number of entrants $n$, the larger $Q$ will be. Thus $\pi_s$ falls when $T$ is increased because a higher $T$ reduces $n$.

Starting with a number for $P$, we determine the optimal (profit-maximizing) $T^*$. We then change $P$, find a new $T^*$, and determine whether profit is now higher or lower. This procedure is repeated until profit has been maximized.

Obviously, more data are needed to design an optimal two-part tariff than to choose a single price. Knowing marginal cost and the aggregate demand curve is not enough. It is impossible (in most cases) to determine the demand curve of every consumer, but one would at least like to know by how much individual demands differ from one another. If consumers' demands for your product are fairly similar, you would want to charge a price $P$ that is close to marginal cost and make the entry fee $T$ large. This is the ideal situation from the firm's point of view because most of the consumer surplus could then be captured. On the other hand, if consumers have different demands for your product, you would probably want to set $P$ well above marginal cost and charge a lower entry fee $T$. In that case, however, the two-part tariff is a less effective means of capturing consumer surplus; setting a single price may do almost as well.

At Disneyland in California and Walt Disney World in Florida, the strategy is to charge a high entry fee and charge nothing for the rides. This policy makes sense because consumers have reasonably similar demands for Disney vacations. Most people visiting the parks plan daily budgets (including expenditures for food and beverages) that, for most consumers, do not differ very much.

Firms are perpetually searching for innovative pricing strategies, and a few have devised and introduced a two-part tariff with a "twist"—the entry fee $T$ entitles the customer to a certain number of free units. For example, if you buy a Gillette razor, several blades are usually included in the package. The monthly lease fee for a mainframe computer usually includes some free usage before usage is charged. This twist lets the firm set a higher entry fee $T$ without losing as many small customers. Because these small customers might pay little or nothing for usage under this scheme, the higher entry fee will capture their surplus without driving them out of the market, while also capturing more of the surplus of the large customers.

**EXAMPLE 11.4** Polaroid Cameras

In 1971, Polaroid introduced its SX-70 camera. This camera was sold, not leased, to consumers. Nevertheless, because film was sold separately, Polaroid could apply a two-part tariff to the pricing of the SX-70. Let's see how this pricing strategy gave Polaroid greater profits than would have been possible if its camera had used ordinary roll film, and how Polaroid might have determined the optimal prices for each part of its two-part tariff.

Why did the pricing of Polaroid's cameras and film involve a two-part tariff? Because Polaroid had a monopoly on both its camera and the film, only Polaroid film could be used in the camera. Consumers bought the camera and film to take instant pictures: The camera was the "entry fee" that provided access to the consumption of instant pictures, which was what consumers ultimately demanded.[13] In this sense, the price of the camera was like the entry fee at an amusement park. However, while the marginal cost of allowing someone entry into the park is close to zero, the marginal cost of producing a camera is significantly above zero, and thus had to be taken into account when designing the two-part tariff.

It was important that Polaroid have a monopoly on the film as well as the camera. If the camera had used ordinary roll film, competitive forces would have pushed the price of film close to its marginal cost. If all consumers had identical demands, Polaroid could still have captured all the consumer surplus by setting a high price for the camera (equal to the surplus of each consumer). But in practice, consumers were heterogeneous, and the optimal two-part tariff required a price for the film well above marginal cost.

How should Polaroid have selected its prices for the camera and film? It could have begun with some analytical spadework. Its profit is given by

$$\pi = PQ + nT - C_1(Q) - C_2(n)$$

where $P$ is the price of the film, $T$ the price of the camera, $Q$ the quantity of film sold, $n$ the number of cameras sold, and $C_1(Q)$ and $C_2(n)$ the costs of producing film and cameras, respectively.

---

[13]We are simplifying here. In fact, some consumers obtain utility just from owning the camera, even if they take few or no pictures. Adults, like children, enjoy new toys and can obtain pleasure from the mere possession of a technologically innovative good.

Polaroid wanted to maximize its profit $\pi$, taking into account that $Q$ and $n$ depend on $P$ and $T$. Given a heterogeneous base of potential consumers, managers might initially have guessed at this dependence on $P$ and $T$, drawing on knowledge of related products. Later, they may have gotten a better understanding of demand and of how $Q$ and $n$ depend on $P$ and $T$ as they accumulated data from the firm's sales experience. They may have found knowledge of $C_1$ and $C_2$ easier to come by, perhaps from engineering and statistical studies (as discussed in Chapter 7).

Given some initial guesses or estimates for $Q(P)$, $n(T)$, $C_1(Q)$, and $C_2(n)$, Polaroid could have calculated the profit-maximizing prices $P$ and $T$. It could also have determined how sensitive these prices were to uncertainty over demand and cost. This knowledge could have provided a guideline for trial-and-error pricing experiments. Over time these experiments would also have told Polaroid more about demand and cost, so that it could refine its two-part tariff accordingly.[14]

In 1999, Polaroid introduced its I-Zone camera and film, which takes matchbook-size pictures. The camera was priced at $25 and the film at $7 per pack. In 2003, Polaroid's One Step cameras sold for $30 to $50 and used Polaroid 600 film, which was priced at about $14 per pack of 10 pictures. Polaroid's higher-end Spectra cameras sold for $60 to over $100 and used Spectra film, priced at about $13 per pack. These film prices were well above marginal cost, reflecting the considerable heterogeneity of consumer demands.

**EXAMPLE 11.5** **Pricing Cellular Phone Service**

Most telephone service is priced using a two-part tariff: a monthly access fee, which may include some free minutes, plus a per-minute charge for additional minutes. This is also true for cellular phone service, which has grown explosively, both in the United States and around the world. In the case of cellular service, providers have taken the two-part tariff and turned it into an art form.

In most parts of the United States, consumers can choose among four national network providers—Verizon, T-Mobile, AT&T, and Sprint. These providers compete among themselves for customers, but each has some market power. This market power arises in part from oligopolistic pricing and output decisions, as we will explain in Chapters 12 and 13. Market power also arises because consumers face *switching costs*: When they sign up for a cellular plan, they must typically make a commitment to stay for at least one year, and breaking the contract is quite expensive. Most service providers impose a penalty upwards of $200 for early termination.

Because providers have market power, they must think carefully about profit-maximizing pricing strategies. The two-part tariff provides an ideal means by which cellular providers can capture consumer surplus and turn it into profit.

Table 11.3 shows cellular rate plans (for 2007) offered by Verizon Wireless, T-Mobile, and AT&T. The plans are structured in similar ways, so let's focus on

[14]Setting prices for a product such as a Polaroid camera is clearly not a simple matter. We have ignored the *dynamic* behavior of cost and demand: namely, how production costs fall as the firm moves down its learning curve and how demand changes over time as the market becomes saturated.

| TABLE 11.3 Cellular Rate Plans (2007) | | | |
| --- | --- | --- | --- |
| Anytime Minutes | Monthly Access Fee | Unlimited Nights/ Weekends | Per-Minute Rate After Allowance |
| **A. Verizon: America's Choice Basic** | | | |
| 450 | $39.99 | Included | $0.45 |
| 900 | $59.99 | Included | $0.40 |
| 1350 | $79.99 | Included | $0.35 |
| 2000 | $99.99 | Included | $0.25 |
| 4000 | $149.99 | Included | $0.25 |
| 6000 | $199.99 | Included | $0.20 |
| **B. T-Mobile Individual Plans** | | | |
| 300 | $29.99 | Unlimited weekends, not weeknights | $0.40 |
| 1000 | $39.99 | Included | $0.40 |
| 1500 | $59.99 | Included | $0.40 |
| 2500 | $99.99 | Included | $0.30 |
| 5000 | $129.99 | Included | $0.30 |
| **C. AT&T Individual Plans** | | | |
| 450 | $39.99 | Includes 5000 minutes | $0.45 |
| 900 | $59.99 | Included | $0.40 |
| 1350 | $79.99 | Included | $0.35 |
| 2000 | $99.99 | Included | $0.25 |
| 4000 | $149.99 | Included | $0.25 |
| 6000 | $199.99 | Included | $0.20 |

*Note:* T-Mobile plans do not include any mobile-to-mobile minutes; for T-Mobile these calls are charged from the Anytime Minutes. All other plans include unlimited mobile to mobile minutes.

the Verizon plan. The least expensive Verizon plan has a monthly access charge of $39.99 and includes 450 "anytime" minutes (i.e., 450 minutes of talk time per month that can be used at any hour of the day). The plan also includes an unlimited amount of talk time during nights and weekends (periods when demand is generally much lower). A subscriber who uses more than the 450 "anytime" minutes is charged $0.45 for each additional minute. A customer who uses her cell phone more frequently could sign up for a more expensive plan, e.g., one that costs $59.99 per month but includes 900 "anytime" minutes and a charge of $0.40 for additional minutes. And if you, the reader, use your cell phone constantly (and thus have time for little else), you could sign up for a plan that includes 6000 "anytime" minutes, at a monthly cost of $199.99.

Why do cellular phone providers offer several different types of plans and options within each? Why don't they simply offer a single two-part tariff with a monthly access charge and a per-minute usage charge? Offering several different plans and options allows companies to combine third-degree price discrimination with the two-part tariff. The plans are structured so that consumers sort themselves into groups based on their plan choices. A different two-part tariff is then applied to each group.

To see how this sorting works, consider the plan choices of different types of consumers. People who use a cell phone only occasionally will want to spend as little as possible on the service and will choose the least expensive plan (with the fewest "anytime" minutes). The most expensive plans are best suited to very heavy users (perhaps a salesperson who travels extensively and makes call throughout the day), who will want to minimize their per-minute cost. Other plans are better suited to consumers with moderate calling needs.

Consumers will choose a plan that best matches their needs. Thus they will sort themselves into groups, and the consumers in each group will be relatively homogeneous in terms of demands for cellular service. Remember that the two-part tariff works best when consumers have identical or very similar demands. (Recall from Figure 11.9 that with identical consumers, the two-part tariff can be used to capture *all* consumer surplus.) Creating a situation in which consumers sort themselves into groups in this way makes best use of the two-part tariff.

## *11.5 BUNDLING

You have probably seen the 1939 film *Gone with the Wind*. It is a classic that is nearly as popular now as it was then.[15] Yet we would guess that you have not seen *Getting Gertie's Garter*, a flop that the same company (MGM, a division of Loews) also distributed. And we would also guess that you did not know that these two films were priced in what was then an unusual and innovative way.[16]

Movie theaters that leased *Gone with the Wind* also had to lease *Getting Gertie's Garter*. (Movie theaters pay the film companies or their distributors a daily or weekly fee for the films they lease.) In other words, these two films were **bundled**—i.e., sold as a package. Why would the film company do this?

> • **bundling** Practice of selling two or more products as a package.

You might think that the answer is obvious: *Gone with the Wind* was a great film and *Gertie* was a lousy film, so bundling the two forced movie theaters to lease *Gertie*. But this answer doesn't make economic sense. Suppose a theater's reservation price (the maximum price it will pay) for *Gone with the Wind* is $12,000 per week, and its reservation price for *Gertie* is $3000 per week. Then the most it would pay for *both* films is $15,000, whether it takes the films individually or as a package.

Bundling makes sense when *customers have heterogeneous demands* and when the firm cannot price discriminate. With films, different movie theaters serve different groups of patrons and therefore different theaters may face different demands for films. For example, different theaters might appeal to different age groups, who in turn have different relative film preferences.

---

[15]Adjusted for inflation, *Gone with the Wind* was also the largest grossing film of all time. *Titanic*, released in 1997, made $601 million. *Gone with the Wind* grossed $81.5 million in 1939 dollars, which is equivalent to $941 million in 1997 dollars.

[16]For those readers who claim to know all this, our final trivia question is: Who played the role of Gertie in *Getting Gertie's Garter*?

To see how a film company can use customer heterogeneity to its advantage, suppose that there are *two* movie theaters and that their reservation prices for our two films are as follows:

|  | Gone with the Wind | Getting Gertie's Garter |
|---|---|---|
| Theater A | $12,000 | $3000 |
| Theater B | $10,000 | $4000 |

If the films are rented separately, the maximum price that could be charged for *Wind* is $10,000 because charging more would exclude Theater *B*. Similarly, the maximum price that could be charged for *Gertie* is $3000. Charging these two prices would yield $13,000 from each theater, for a total of $26,000 in revenue. But suppose the films are *bundled*. Theater *A* values the *pair* of films at $15,000 ($12,000 + $3000), and Theater *B* values the pair at $14,000 ($10,000 + $4000). Therefore, we can charge each theater $14,000 for the pair of films and earn a total revenue of $28,000. Clearly, we can earn more revenue ($2000 more) by bundling the films.

## Relative Valuations

Why is bundling more profitable than selling the films separately? Because (in this example) the *relative valuations* of the two films are reversed. In other words, although both theaters would pay much more for *Wind* than for *Gertie*, Theater *A* would pay more than Theater *B* for *Wind* ($12,000 vs. $10,000), while Theater *B* would pay more than Theater *A* for *Gertie* ($4000 vs. $3000). In technical terms, we say that the demands are *negatively correlated*—the customer willing to pay the most for *Wind* is willing to pay the least for *Gertie*. To see why this is critical, suppose demands were *positively correlated*—that is, Theater *A* would pay more for *both* films:

|  | Gone with the Wind | Getting Gertie's Garter |
|---|---|---|
| Theater A | $12,000 | $4000 |
| Theater B | $10,000 | $3000 |

The most that Theater *A* would pay for the pair of films is now $16,000, but the most that Theater *B* would pay is only $13,000. Thus if we bundled the films, the maximum price that could be charged for the package is $13,000, yielding a total revenue of $26,000, the same as by renting the films separately.

Now, suppose a firm is selling two different goods to many consumers. To analyze the possible advantages of bundling, we will use a simple diagram to describe the preferences of the consumers in terms of their reservation prices and their consumption decisions given the prices charged. In Figure 11.12 the horizontal axis is $r_1$, which is the reservation price of a consumer for good 1, and the vertical axis is $r_2$, which is the reservation price for good 2. The figure shows the reservation prices for three consumers. Consumer *A* is willing to pay up to $3.25 for good 1 and up to $6 for good 2; consumer *B* is willing to pay up to $8.25 for good 1 and up to $3.25 for good 2; and consumer *C* is willing to pay up to $10 for each of the goods. In general, the reservation prices for any number of consumers can be plotted this way.

Suppose that there are many consumers and that the products are sold separately, at prices $P_1$ and $P_2$, respectively. Figure 11.13 shows how consumers can

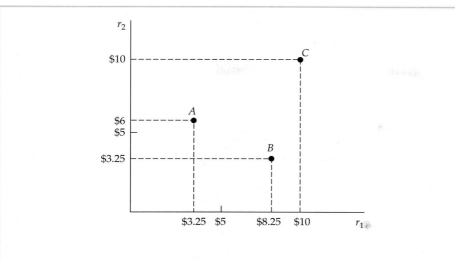

**FIGURE 11.12 Reservation Prices**

Reservation prices $r_1$ and $r_2$ for two goods are shown for three consumers, labeled $A$, $B$, and $C$. Consumer $A$ is willing to pay up to $3.25 for good 1 and up to $6 for good 2.

be divided into groups. Consumers in region I of the graph have reservation prices that are above the prices being charged for each of the goods, so they will buy both goods. Consumers in region II have a reservation price for good 2 that is above $P_2$, but a reservation price for good 1 that is below $P_1$; they will buy

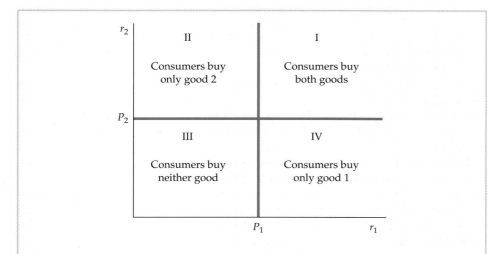

**FIGURE 11.13 Consumption Decisions When Products Are Sold Separately**

The reservation prices of consumers in region I exceed the prices $P_1$ and $P_2$ for the two goods, so these consumers buy both goods. Consumers in regions II and IV buy only one of the goods, and consumers in region III buy neither good.

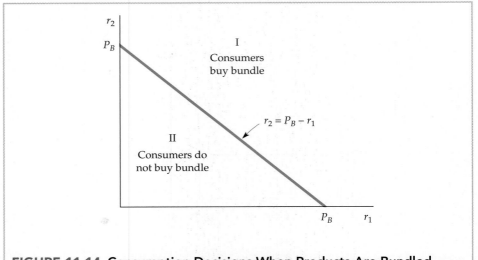

**FIGURE 11.14 Consumption Decisions When Products Are Bundled**

Consumers compare the *sum* of their reservation prices $r_1 + r_2$, with the price of the bundle $P_B$. They buy the bundle only if $r_1 + r_2$ is at least as large as $P_B$.

only good 2. Similarly, consumers in region IV will buy only good 1. Finally, consumers in region III have reservation prices below the prices charged for each of the goods, and so will buy neither.

Now suppose the goods are sold only as a bundle, for a total price of $P_B$. We can then divide the graph into two regions, as in Figure 11.14. Any given consumer will buy the bundle only if its price is less than or equal to the sum of that consumer's reservation prices for the two goods. The dividing line is therefore the equation $P_B = r_1 + r_2$ or, equivalently, $r_2 = P_B - r_1$. Consumers in region I have reservation prices that add up to more than $P_B$, so they will buy the bundle. Consumers in region II, who have reservation prices that add up to less than $P_B$, will not buy the bundle.

Depending on the prices, some of the consumers in region II of Figure 11.14 might have bought one of the goods if they had been sold separately. These consumers are lost to the firm, however, when it sells the goods only as a bundle. The firm, then, must determine whether it can do better by bundling.

In general, the effectiveness of bundling depends on the extent to which demands are negatively correlated. In other words, it works best when consumers who have a high reservation price for good 1 have a low reservation price for good 2, and vice versa. Figure 11.15 shows two extremes. In part (a), each point represents the two reservation prices of a consumer. Note that the demands for the two goods are perfectly positively correlated—consumers with a high reservation price for good 1 also have a high reservation price for good 2. If the firm bundles and charges a price $P_B = P_1 + P_2$, it will make the same profit that it would make by selling the goods separately at prices $P_1$ and $P_2$. In part (b), on the other hand, demands are perfectly negatively correlated—a higher reservation price for good 2 implies a proportionately lower one for good 1. In this case, bundling is the ideal strategy. By charging the price $P_B$ the firm can capture *all* the consumer surplus.

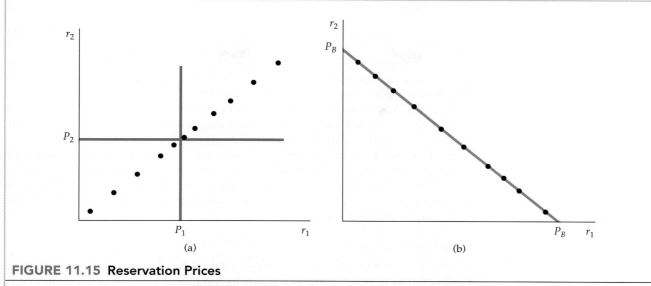

**FIGURE 11.15 Reservation Prices**

In (a), because demands are perfectly positively correlated, the firm does not gain by bundling: It would earn the same profit by selling the goods separately. In (b), demands are perfectly negatively correlated. Bundling is the ideal strategy— all the consumer surplus can be extracted.

Figure 11.16, which shows the movie example that we introduced at the beginning of this section, illustrates how the demands of the two movie theaters are negatively correlated. (Theater *A* will pay relatively more for *Gone with the Wind*, but Theater *B* will pay relatively more for *Getting Gertie's Garter*.) This makes it more profitable to rent the films as a bundle priced at $14,000.

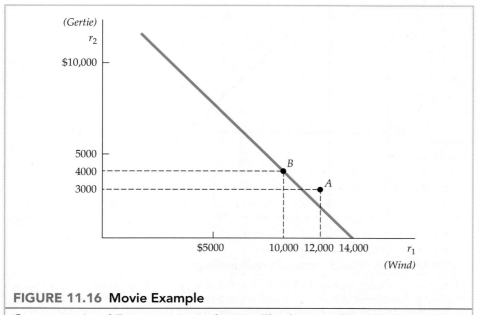

**FIGURE 11.16 Movie Example**

Consumers *A* and *B* are two movie theaters. The diagram shows their reservation prices for the films *Gone with the Wind* and *Getting Gertie's Garter*. Because the demands are negatively correlated, bundling pays.

## Mixed Bundling

• **mixed bundling** Selling
two or more goods both as
a package and individually.

• **pure bundling** Selling
products only as a package.

So far, we have assumed that the firm has two options: to sell the goods either separately or as a bundle. But there is a third option, called **mixed bundling**. As the name suggests, the firm offers its products *both* separately and as a bundle, with a package price below the sum of the individual prices. (We use the term **pure bundling** to refer to the strategy of selling the products *only* as a bundle.) Mixed bundling is often the ideal strategy when demands are only somewhat negatively correlated and/or when marginal production costs are significant. (Thus far, we have assumed that marginal production costs are zero.)

In Figure 11.17, mixed bundling is the most profitable strategy. Although demands are perfectly negatively correlated, there are significant marginal costs. (The marginal cost of producing good 1 is $20, and the marginal cost of producing good 2 is $30.) We have four consumers, labeled $A$ through $D$. Now, let's compare three strategies:

1.  Selling the goods separately at prices $P_1 = \$50$ and $P_2 = \$90$
2.  Selling the goods only as a bundle at a price of $100
3.  Mixed bundling, whereby the goods are offered separately at prices $P_1 = P_2 = \$89.95$, or as a bundle at a price of $100.

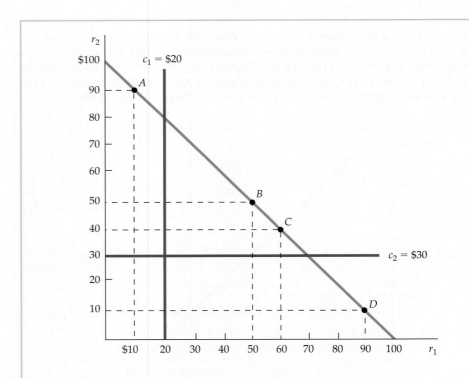

**FIGURE 11.17 Mixed versus Pure Bundling**

With positive marginal costs, mixed bundling may be more profitable than pure bundling. Consumer $A$ has a reservation price for good 1 that is below marginal cost $c_1$, and consumer $D$ has a reservation price for good 2 that is below marginal cost $c_2$. With mixed bundling, consumer $A$ is induced to buy only good 2, and consumer $D$ is induced to buy only good 1, thus reducing the firm's cost.

| TABLE 11.4 | Bundling Example | | | |
|---|---|---|---|---|
| | $P_1$ | $P_2$ | $P_B$ | Profit |
| Sold separately | $50 | $90 | — | $150 |
| Pure bundling | — | — | $100 | $200 |
| Mixed bundling | $89.95 | $89.95 | $100 | $229.90 |

Table 11.4 shows these three strategies and the resulting profits. (You can try other prices for $P_1$, $P_2$, and $P_B$ to verify that those given in the table maximize profit for each strategy.) When the goods are sold separately, only consumers $B$, $C$, and $D$ buy good 1, and only consumer $A$ buys good 2; total profit is 3($50 − $20) + 1($90 − $30) = $150. With pure bundling, all four consumers buy the bundle for $100, so that total profit is 4($100 − $20 − $30) = $200. As we should expect, pure bundling is better than selling the goods separately because consumers' demands are negatively correlated. But what about mixed bundling? Consumer $D$ buys only good 1 for $89.95, consumer $A$ buys only good 2 for $89.95, and consumers $B$ and $C$ buy the bundle for $100. Total profit is now ($89.95 − $20) + ($89.95 − $30) + 2($100 − $20 − $30) = $229.90.[17]

In this case, mixed bundling is the most profitable strategy, even though demands are perfectly negatively correlated (i.e., all four consumers have reservation prices on the line $r_2 = 100 − r_1$). Why? For each good, marginal production cost exceeds the reservation price of one consumer. For example, consumer $A$ has a reservation price of $90 for good 2 but a reservation price of only $10 for good 1. Because the cost of producing a unit of good 1 is $20, the firm would prefer that consumer $A$ buy only good 2, not the bundle. It can achieve this goal by offering good 2 separately for a price just below consumer $A$'s reservation price, while also offering the bundle at a price acceptable to consumers $B$ and $C$.

Mixed bundling would *not* be the preferred strategy in this example if marginal costs were zero: In that case, there would be no benefit in excluding consumer $A$ from buying good 1 and consumer $D$ from buying good 2. We leave it to you to demonstrate this (see Exercise 12).[18]

If marginal costs are zero, mixed bundling can still be more profitable than pure bundling if consumers' demands are not perfectly negatively correlated. (Recall that in Figure 11.17, the reservation prices of the four consumers are perfectly negatively correlated.) This is illustrated by Figure 11.18, in which we have modified the example of Figure 11.17. In Figure 11.18, marginal costs are zero, but the reservation prices for consumers $B$ and $C$ are now higher. Once again, let's compare three strategies: selling the two goods separately, pure bundling, and mixed bundling.

Table 11.5 shows the optimal prices and the resulting profits for each strategy. (Once again, you should try other prices for $P_1$, $P_2$, and $P_B$ to verify that those given in the table maximize profit for each strategy.) When the goods are sold

---

[17]Note that in the mixed bundling strategy, goods 1 and 2 are priced at $89.95 rather than at $90. If they were priced at $90, consumers $A$ and $D$ would be indifferent between buying a single good and buying the bundle, and if they buy the bundle, total profit will be lower.

[18]Sometimes a firm with monopoly power will find it profitable to bundle its product with the product of another firm; see Richard L. Schmalensee, "Commodity Bundling by Single-Product Monopolies," *Journal of Law and Economics* 25 (April 1982): 67–71. Bundling can also be profitable when the products are substitutes or complements. See Arthur Lewbel, "Bundling of Substitutes or Complements," *International Journal of Industrial Organization* 3 (1985): 101–7.

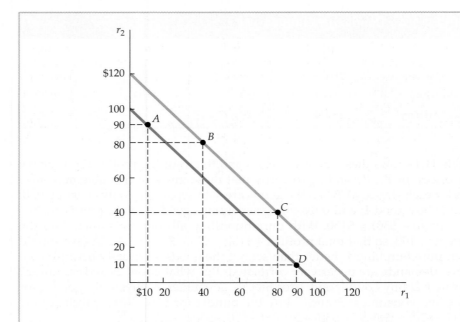

**FIGURE 11.18 Mixed Bundling with Zero Marginal Costs**

If marginal costs are zero, and if consumers' demands are not perfectly negatively correlated, mixed bundling is still more profitable than pure bundling. In this example, consumers $B$ and $C$ are willing to pay $20 more for the bundle than are consumers $A$ and $D$. With pure bundling, the price of the bundle is $100. With mixed bundling, the price of the bundle can be increased to $120 and consumers $A$ and $D$ can still be charged $90 for a single good.

separately, only consumers $C$ and $D$ buy good 1, and only consumers $A$ and $B$ buy good 2; total profit is thus $320. With pure bundling, all four consumers buy the bundle for $100, so that total profit is $400. As expected, pure bundling is better than selling the goods separately because consumers' demands are negatively correlated. But mixed bundling is better still. With mixed bundling, consumer $A$ buys only good 2, consumer $D$ buys only good 1, and consumers $B$ and $C$ buy the bundle at a price of $120. Total profit is now $420.

Why does mixed bundling give higher profits than pure bundling even though marginal costs are zero? The reason is that demands are not perfectly negatively correlated: The two consumers who have high demands for both goods ($B$ and $C$) are willing to pay more for the bundle than are consumers $A$ and $D$. With mixed bundling, therefore, we can increase the price of the bundle (from $100 to $120), sell this bundle to two consumers, and charge the remaining consumers $90 for a single good.

| TABLE 11.5 Mixed Bundling with Zero Marginal Costs | | | | |
|---|---|---|---|---|
| | $P_1$ | $P_2$ | $P_B$ | Profit |
| Sell separately | $80 | $80 | — | $320 |
| Pure bundling | — | — | $100 | $400 |
| Mixed bundling | $90 | $90 | $120 | $420 |

## Bundling in Practice

Bundling is a widely used pricing strategy. When you buy a new car, for example, you can purchase such options as power windows, power seats, or a sunroof separately, or you can purchase a "luxury package" in which these options are bundled. Manufacturers of luxury cars (such as Lexus, BMW, or Infiniti) tend to include such "options" as standard equipment; this practice is pure bundling. For more moderately priced cars, however, these items are optional, but are usually offered as part of a bundle. Automobile companies must decide which items to include in such bundles and how to price them.

Another example is vacation travel. If you plan a vacation to Europe, you might make your own hotel reservations, buy an airplane ticket, and order a rental car. Alternatively, you might buy a vacation package in which airfare, land arrangements, hotels, and even meals are all bundled together.

Still another example is cable television. Cable operators typically offer a basic service for a low monthly fee, plus individual "premium" channels, such as Cinemax, Home Box Office, and the Disney Channel, on an individual basis for additional monthly fees. However, they also offer packages in which two or more premium channels are sold as a bundle. Bundling cable channels is profitable because demands are negatively correlated. How do we know that? Given that there are only 24 hours in a day, the time that a consumer spends watching HBO is time that cannot be spent watching the Disney Channel. Thus consumers with high reservation prices for some channels will have relatively low reservation prices for others.

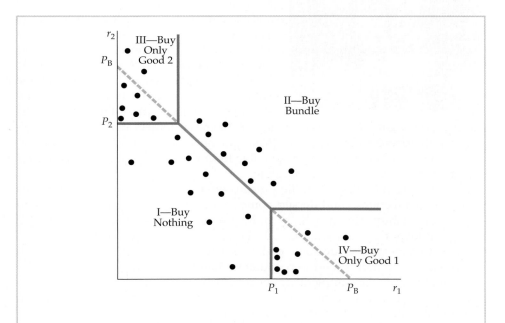

### FIGURE 11.19 **Mixed Bundling in Practice**

The dots in this figure are estimates of reservation prices for a representative sample of consumers. A company could first choose a price for the bundle, $P_B$, such that a diagonal line connecting these prices passes roughly midway through the dots. The company could then try individual prices $P_1$ and $P_2$. Given $P_1$, $P_2$, and $P_B$, profits can be calculated for this sample of consumers. Managers can then raise or lower $P_1$, $P_2$, and $P_B$ and see whether the new pricing leads to higher profits. This procedure is repeated until total profit is roughly maximized.

How can a company decide whether to bundle its products, and determine the profit-maximizing prices? Most companies do not know their customers' reservation prices. However, by conducting market surveys, they may be able to estimate the distribution of reservation prices, and then use this information to design a pricing strategy.

This is illustrated in Figure 11.19. The dots are estimates of reservation prices or a representative sample of consumers (obtained, say, from a market survey). The company might first choose a price for the bundle, $P_B$, such that a diagonal line connecting these prices passes roughly midway through the dots in the figure. It could then try individual prices $P_1$ and $P_2$. Given $P_1$, $P_2$, and $P_B$, we can separate consumers into four regions, as shown in the figure. Consumers in Region I buy nothing (because $r_1 < P_1$, $r_2 < P_2$, and $r_1 + r_2 < P_B$). Consumers in Region II buy the bundle (because $r_1 + r_2 > P_B$). Consumers in Region III buy only good 2 (because $r_2 > P_2$ but $r_1 < P_B - P_2$). Likewise, consumers in Region IV buy only good 1. Given this distribution, we can calculate the resulting profits. We can then raise or lower $P_1$, $P_2$, and $P_B$ and see whether doing so leads to higher profits. This can be done repeatedly (on a computer) until prices are found that roughly maximize total profit.

---

### EXAMPLE 11.6   The Complete Dinner versus à la Carte: A Restaurant's Pricing Problem

Many restaurants offer both complete dinners and à la carte menus. Why? Most customers go out to eat knowing roughly how much they are willing to spend for dinner (and choose the restaurant accordingly). Diners, however, have different preferences. For example, some value appetizers highly but could happily skip dessert. Others attach little value to the appetizer but regard dessert as essential. And some customers attach moderate values to both appetizers and desserts. What pricing strategy lets the restaurant capture as much consumer surplus as possible from these heterogeneous customers? The answer, of course, is mixed bundling.

For a restaurant, mixed bundling means offering both complete dinners (the appetizer, main course, and dessert come as a package) and an à la carte menu (the customer buys the appetizer, main course, and dessert separately). This strategy allows the à la carte menu to be priced to capture consumer surplus from customers who value some dishes much more highly than others. (Such customers would correspond to consumers A and D in Figure 11.17 (page 418).) At the same time, the complete dinner retains those customers who have lower variations in their reservation prices for different dishes (e.g., customers who attach moderate values to both appetizers and desserts).

For example, if the restaurant expects to attract customers willing to spend about $20 for dinner, it might charge about $5 for appetizers, $14 for a typical main dish, and $4 for dessert. It could also offer a complete dinner, which includes an appetizer, main course, and dessert, for $20. Then, the customer who loves dessert but couldn't care less about an appetizer will order only the main dish and dessert, and spend $18 (saving the restaurant the cost of preparing an appetizer). At the same time, another customer who attaches a moderate value (say, $3 or $3.50) to both the appetizer and dessert will buy the complete dinner.

| Individual Item | Price | Meal (Includes Soda and Fries) | Unbundled Price | Price of Bundle | Savings |
|---|---|---|---|---|---|
| Chicken Sandwich | $3.49 | Chicken Sandwich | $7.77 | $5.89 | $1.88 |
| Filet-O-Fish | $2.59 | Filet-O-Fish | $6.87 | $4.89 | $1.98 |
| Big Mac | $2.99 | Big Mac | $7.27 | $5.29 | $1.98 |
| Quarter Pounder | $3.09 | Quarter Pounder | $7.37 | $5.39 | $1.98 |
| Double Quarter Pounder | $3.69 | Double Quarter Pounder | $7.97 | $5.99 | $1.98 |
| 10-piece Chicken McNuggets | $3.89 | 10-piece Chicken McNuggets | $8.17 | $6.19 | $1.98 |
| Large French Fries | $2.29 | | | | |
| Large Soda | $1.99 | | | | |

**TABLE 11.6** Mixed Bundling at McDonald's (2007)

You don't have to go to an expensive French restaurant to experience mixed bundling. Table 11.6 shows the prices of some individual items at a Boston-area McDonald's, as well as the prices of "super meals" that include meat or fish items along with a large order of French fries and a large soda. Note that you can buy a Big Mac, a large fries, and a large soda separately for a total of $7.27, or you can buy them as a bundle for $5.29. You say you don't care for fries? Then just buy the Big Mac and large soda separately, for a total of $4.98, which is $0.31 less than the price of the bundle.

Unfortunately for consumers, perhaps, creative pricing is sometimes more important than creative cooking for the financial success of a restaurant. Successful restaurateurs know their customers' demand characteristics and use that knowledge to design a pricing strategy that extracts as much consumer surplus as possible.

## Tying

**Tying** is a general term that refers to any requirement that products be bought or sold in some combination. Pure bundling is a common form of tying, but tying can also take other forms. For example, suppose a firm sells a product (such as a copying machine) that requires the consumption of a secondary product (such as paper). The consumer who buys the first product is also required to buy the secondary product from the same company. This requirement is usually imposed through a contract. Note that this is different from the examples of bundling discussed earlier. In those examples, the consumer might have been happy to buy just one of the products. In this case, however, the first product is useless without access to the secondary product.

Why might firms use this kind of pricing practice? One of the main benefits of tying is that it often allows a firm to *meter demand* and thereby practice price discrimination more effectively. During the 1950s, for example, when Xerox had a monopoly on copying machines but not on paper, customers who leased Xerox copiers also had to buy Xerox paper. This allowed Xerox to meter consumption (customers who used a machine intensively bought more paper), and thereby apply a two-part tariff to the pricing of its machines. Also during the 1950s, IBM required customers who leased its mainframe computers to use paper computer cards made only by IBM. By pricing cards well above marginal

• **tying** Practice of requiring a customer to purchase one good in order to purchase another.

cost, IBM was effectively charging higher prices for computer usage to customers with larger demands.[19]

Tying can also be used to extend a firm's market power. As we discussed in Example 10.6 (page 385), in 1998 the Department of Justice brought suit against Microsoft, claiming that the company had tied its Internet Explorer Web browser to its Windows 98 operating system in order to maintain its monopoly power in the market for PC operating systems.

Tying can have other uses. An important one is to protect customer goodwill connected with a brand name. This is why franchises are often required to purchase inputs from the franchiser. For example, Mobil Oil requires its service stations to sell only Mobil motor oil, Mobil batteries, and so on. Similarly, until recently, a McDonald's franchisee had to purchase all materials and supplies—from the hamburgers to the paper cups—from McDonald's, thus ensuring product uniformity and protecting the brand name.[20]

## *11.6 ADVERTISING

We have seen how firms can utilize their market power when making pricing decisions. Pricing is important for a firm, but most firms with market power have another important decision to make: how much to advertise. In this section, we will see how firms with market power can make profit-maximizing advertising decisions, and how those decisions depend on the characteristics of demand for the firm's product.[21]

For simplicity, we will assume that the firm sets only one price for its product. We will also assume that having done sufficient market research, it knows how its quantity demanded depends on both its price $P$ *and* its advertising expenditures in dollars $A$; that is, it knows $Q(P,A)$. Figure 11.20 shows the firm's demand and cost curves with and without advertising. AR and MR are the firm's average and marginal revenue curves when it does not advertise, and AC and MC are its average and marginal cost curves. It produces a quantity $Q_0$, where MR = MC, and receives a price $P_0$. Its profit per unit is the difference between $P_0$ and average cost, so its total profit $\pi_0$ is given by the gray-shaded rectangle.

Now suppose the firm advertises. This causes its demand curve to shift out and to the right; the new average and marginal revenue curves are given by AR' and MR'. Advertising is a fixed cost, so the firm's average cost curve rises (to AC'). Marginal cost, however, remains the same. With advertising, the firm produces $Q_1$ (where MR' = MC) and receives a price $P_1$. Its total profit $\pi_1$, given by the purple-shaded rectangle, is now much larger.

Although the firm in Figure 11.20 is clearly better off when it advertises, the figure does not help us determine *how much* advertising it should do. It must choose its price $P$ and advertising expenditure $A$ to maximize profit, which is now given by:

$$\pi = PQ(P, A) - C(Q) - A$$

> In §7.1, marginal cost—the increase in cost that results from producing one extra unit of output—is distinguished from average cost—the cost per unit of output.

---

[19]Antitrust actions ultimately forced IBM to discontinue this pricing practice.

[20]In some cases, the courts have ruled that tying is not necessary to protect customer goodwill and is anticompetitive. Today, a McDonald's franchisee can buy supplies from any McDonald's-approved source. For a discussion of some of the antitrust issues involved in franchise tying, see Benjamin Klein and Lester F. Saft, "The Law and Economics of Franchise Tying Contracts," *Journal of Law and Economics* 28 (May 1985): 345–61.

[21]A perfectly competitive firm has little reason to advertise: By definition it can sell as much as it produces at a market price that it takes as given. That is why it would be unusual to see a producer of corn or soybeans advertise.

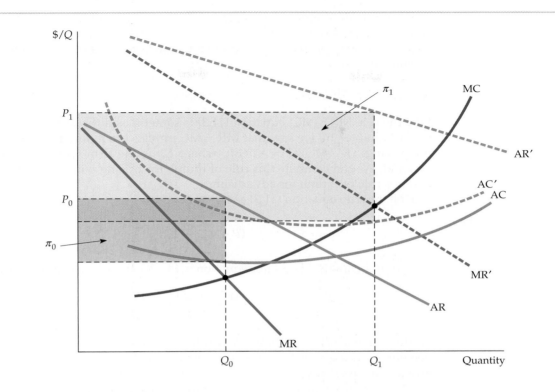

**FIGURE 11.20 Effects of Advertising**

AR and MR are average and marginal revenue when the firm doesn't advertise, and AC and MC are average and marginal cost. The firm produces $Q_0$ and receives a price $P_0$. Its total profit $\pi_0$ is given by the gray-shaded rectangle. If the firm advertises, its average and marginal revenue curves shift to the right. Average cost rises (to AC') but marginal cost remains the same. The firm now produces $Q_1$ (where MR' = MC), and receives a price $P_1$. Its total profit, $\pi_1$, is now larger.

Given a price, more advertising will result in more sales and thus more revenue. But what is the firm's profit-maximizing advertising expenditure? You might be tempted to say that the firm should increase its advertising expenditures until the last dollar of advertising just brings forth an additional dollar of revenue—that is, until the marginal revenue from advertising, $\Delta(P, Q)/\Delta A$, is just equal to 1. But as Figure 11.20 shows, this reasoning omits an important element. Remember that *advertising leads to increased output* (in the figure, output increased from $Q_0$ to $Q_1$). But increased output in turn means increased production costs, and this must be taken into account when comparing the costs and benefits of an extra dollar of advertising.

The correct decision is to increase advertising until the marginal revenue from an additional dollar of advertising, $MR_{Ads}$, just equals the *full* marginal cost of that advertising. That full marginal cost is the sum of the dollar spent directly on the advertising and the marginal production cost resulting from the increased sales that advertising brings about. Thus the firm should advertise up to the point that

$$MR_{Ads} = P\frac{\Delta Q}{\Delta A} = 1 + MC\frac{\Delta Q}{\Delta A} \tag{11.3}$$

$$= \textit{full marginal cost of advertising}$$

This rule is often ignored by managers, who justify advertising budgets by comparing the expected benefits (i.e., added sales) only with the cost of the advertising. But additional sales mean increased production costs that must also be taken into account.[22]

## A Rule of Thumb for Advertising

Like the rule MR = MC, equation (11.3) is sometimes difficult to apply in practice. In Chapter 10, we saw that MR = MC implies the following rule of thumb for pricing: $(P - MC)/P = -1/E_D$, where $E_D$ is the firm's price elasticity of demand. We can combine this rule of thumb for pricing with equation (11.3) to obtain a rule of thumb for advertising.

First, rewrite equation (11.3) as follows:

$$(P - MC)\frac{\Delta Q}{\Delta A} = 1$$

> In equation (10.1), we offer a rule of thumb for pricing for a profit-maximizing firm—the markup over marginal cost as a percentage of price should equal minus the inverse of the price elasticity of demand.

Now multiply both sides of this equation by $A/PQ$, the **advertising-to-sales ratio**:

$$\frac{P - MC}{P}\left[\frac{A}{Q}\frac{\Delta Q}{\Delta A}\right] = \frac{A}{PQ}$$

• **advertising-to-sales ratio** Ratio of a firm's advertising expenditures to its sales.

The term in brackets, $(A/Q)(\Delta Q/\Delta A)$, is the **advertising elasticity of demand**, the percentage change in the quantity demanded that results from a 1-percent increase in advertising expenditures. We will denote this elasticity by $E_A$. Because $(P - MC)/P$ must equal $-1/E_P$, we can rewrite this equation as follows:

• **advertising elasticity of demand** Percentage change in quantity demanded resulting from a 1-percent increase in advertising expenditures.

$$A/PQ = -(E_A/E_P) \tag{11.4}$$

Equation (11.4) is a rule of thumb for advertising. It says that to maximize profit, the firm's advertising-to-sales ratio should be equal to minus the ratio of the advertising and price elasticities of demand. Given information (from, say, market research studies) on these two elasticities, the firm can use this rule to check that its advertising budget is not too small or too large.

To put this rule into perspective, assume that a firm is generating sales revenue of $1 million per year while allocating only $10,000 (1 percent of its revenues) to advertising. The firm knows that its advertising elasticity of demand is .2, so that a doubling of its advertising budget from $10,000 to $20,000 should increase sales by 20 percent. The firm also knows that the price elasticity of demand for its product is −4. Should it increase its advertising budget, knowing that with a price elasticity of demand of −4, its markup of price over marginal cost is substantial? The answer is yes; equation (11.4) tells us that the firm's advertising-to-sales ratio should be −(.2/−4) = 5 percent, so the firm should increase its advertising budget from $10,000 to $50,000.

This rule makes intuitive sense. It says firms should advertise a lot if (i) demand is very sensitive to advertising ($E_A$ is large), or if (ii) demand is not very price elastic ($E_P$ is small). Although (i) is obvious, why should firms advertise more when the price elasticity of demand is small? A small elasticity of demand

---

[22]To derive this result using calculus, differentiate $\pi(Q,A)$ with respect to $A$, and set the derivative equal to zero:

$$\partial\pi/\partial A = P(\partial Q/\partial A) - MC(\partial Q/\partial A) - 1 = 0$$

Rearranging gives equation (11.3).

implies a large markup of price over marginal cost. Therefore, the marginal profit from each extra unit sold is high. In this case, if advertising can help sell a few more units, it will be worth its cost.[23]

| EXAMPLE 11.7 | Advertising in Practice |

In Example 10.2 (page 364), we looked at the use of markup pricing by supermarkets, convenience stores, and makers of designer jeans. We saw in each case how the markup of price over marginal cost depended on the firm's price elasticity of demand. Now let's see why these firms, as well as producers of other goods, advertise as much (or as little) as they do.

First, supermarkets. We said that the price elasticity of demand for a typical supermarket is around −10. To determine the advertising-to-sales ratio, we also need to know the advertising elasticity of demand. This number can vary considerably depending on what part of the country the supermarket is located in and whether it is in a city, suburb, or rural area. A reasonable range, however, would be 0.1 to 0.3. Substituting these numbers into equation (11.4), we find that the manager of a typical supermarket should have an advertising budget of around 1 to 3 percent of sales—which is indeed what many supermarkets spend on advertising.

Convenience stores have lower price elasticities of demand (around −5), but their advertising-to-sales ratios are usually less than those for supermarkets (and are often zero). Why? Because convenience stores mostly serve customers who live nearby; they may need a few items late at night or may simply not want to drive to the supermarket. These customers already know about the convenience store and are unlikely to change their buying habits if the store advertises. Thus $E_A$ is very small, and advertising is not worthwhile.

Advertising is quite important for makers of designer jeans, who will have advertising-to-sales ratios as high as 10 or 20 percent. Advertising helps to make consumers aware of the label and gives it an aura and image. We said that price elasticities of demand in the range of −3 to −4 are typical for the major labels, and advertising elasticities of demand can range from .3 to as high as 1. So, these levels of advertising would seem to make sense.

Laundry detergents have among the highest advertising-to-sales ratios of all products, sometimes exceeding 30 percent, even though demand for any one brand is at least as price elastic as it is for designer jeans. What justifies all the advertising? A very large advertising elasticity. The demand for any one brand of laundry detergent depends crucially on advertising; without it, consumers would have little basis for selecting that particular brand.[24]

---

[23]Advertising often affects the price elasticity of demand, and this fact must be taken into account. For some products, advertising broadens the market by attracting a large range of customers, or by creating a bandwagon effect. This is likely to make demand more price elastic than it would have been otherwise. (But $E_A$ is likely to be large, so that advertising will still be worthwhile.) Sometimes advertising is used to differentiate a product from others (by creating an image, allure, or brand identification), making the product's demand less price elastic than it would otherwise be.

[24]For an overview of statistical approaches to estimating the advertising elasticity of demand, see Ernst R. Berndt, *The Practice of Econometrics* (Reading, MA: Addison-Wesley, 1991), ch. 8.

| TABLE 11.7 | Sales and Advertising Expenditures for Leading Brands of Over-the-Counter Drugs (in millions of dollars) | | |
|---|---|---|---|
| | **Sales** | **Advertising** | **Ratio (%)** |
| **Pain Medications** | | | |
| Tylenol | 855 | 143.8 | 17 |
| Advil | 360 | 91.7 | 26 |
| Bayer | 170 | 43.8 | 26 |
| Excedrin | 130 | 26.7 | 21 |
| **Antacids** | | | |
| Alka-Seltzer | 160 | 52.2 | 33 |
| Mylanta | 135 | 32.8 | 24 |
| Tums | 135 | 27.6 | 20 |
| **Cold Remedies (decongestants)** | | | |
| Benadryl | 130 | 30.9 | 24 |
| Sudafed | 115 | 28.6 | 25 |
| **Cough Medicine** | | | |
| Vicks | 350 | 26.6 | 8 |
| Robitussin | 205 | 37.7 | 19 |
| Halls | 130 | 17.4 | 13 |

*Source: New York Times, September 27, 1994.*

Finally, Table 11.7 shows sales, advertising expenditures, and the ratio of the two for leading brands of over-the-counter drugs. Observe that overall, the ratios are quite high. As with laundry detergents, the advertising elasticity for name-brand drugs is very high. Alka-Seltzer, Mylanta, and Tums, for instance, are all antacids that do much the same thing. Sales depend on consumer identification with a particular brand, which requires advertising.

# SUMMARY

1. Firms with market power are in an enviable position because they have the potential to earn large profits. Realizing that potential, however, may depend critically on pricing strategy. Even if the firm sets a single price, it needs an estimate of the elasticity of demand for its output. More complicated strategies, which can involve setting several different prices, require even more information about demand.

2. A pricing strategy aims to enlarge the customer base that the firm can sell to and capture as much consumer surplus as possible. There are a number of ways to do this, and they usually involve setting more than a single price.

3. Ideally, the firm would like to price discriminate perfectly—i.e., to charge each customer his or her reservation price. In practice, this is almost always impossible. On the other hand, various forms of imperfect price discrimination are often used to increase profits.

4. The two-part tariff is another means of capturing consumer surplus. Customers must pay an "entry" fee that allows them to buy the good at a per-unit price. The two-part tariff is most effective when customer demands are relatively homogeneous.

5. When demands are heterogeneous and negatively correlated, bundling can increase profits. With pure bundling, two or more different goods are sold only as

a package. With mixed bundling, the customer can buy the goods individually or as a package. Mixed bundling can be more profitable than pure bundling if marginal costs are significant or if demands are not perfectly negatively correlated.

6. Bundling is a special case of tying, a requirement that products be bought or sold in some combination.

Tying can be used to meter demand or to protect customer goodwill associated with a brand name.

7. Advertising can further increase profits. The profit-maximizing advertising-to-sales ratio is equal in magnitude to the ratio of the advertising and price elasticities of demand.

# QUESTIONS FOR REVIEW

1. Suppose a firm can practice perfect, first-degree price discrimination. What is the lowest price it will charge, and what will its total output be?

2. How does a car salesperson practice price discrimination? How does the ability to discriminate correctly affect his or her earnings?

3. Electric utilities often practice second-degree price discrimination. Why might this improve consumer welfare?

4. Give some examples of third-degree price discrimination. Can third-degree price discrimination be effective if the different groups of consumers have different levels of demand but the same price elasticities?

5. Show why optimal, third-degree price discrimination requires that marginal revenue for each group of consumers equals marginal cost. Use this condition to explain how a firm should change its prices and total output if the demand curve for one group of consumers shifts outward, causing marginal revenue for that group to increase.

6. When pricing automobiles, American car companies typically charge a much higher percentage markup over cost for "luxury option" items (such as leather trim, etc.) than for the car itself or for more "basic" options such as power steering and automatic transmission. Explain why.

7. How is peak-load pricing a form of price discrimination? Can it make consumers better off? Give an example.

8. How can a firm determine an optimal two-part tariff if it has two customers with different demand curves? (Assume that it knows the demand curves.)

9. Why is the pricing of a Gillette safety razor a form of two-part tariff? Must Gillette be a monopoly producer of its blades as well as its razors? Suppose you were advising Gillette on how to determine the two parts of the tariff. What procedure would you suggest?

10. In the town of Woodland, California, there are many dentists but only one eye doctor. Are senior citizens more likely to be offered discount prices for dental exams or for eye exams? Why?

11. Why did MGM bundle *Gone with the Wind* and *Getting Gertie's Garter*? What characteristic of demands is needed for bundling to increase profits?

12. How does mixed bundling differ from pure bundling? Under what conditions is mixed bundling preferable to pure bundling? Why do many restaurants practice mixed bundling (by offering a complete dinner as well as an à la carte menu) instead of pure bundling?

13. How does tying differ from bundling? Why might a firm want to practice tying?

14. Why is it incorrect to advertise up to the point that the last dollar of advertising expenditures generates another dollar of sales? What is the correct rule for the marginal advertising dollar?

15. How can a firm check that its advertising-to-sales ratio is not too high or too low? What information does it need?

# EXERCISES

1. Price discrimination requires the ability to sort customers and the ability to prevent arbitrage. Explain how the following can function as price discrimination schemes and discuss both sorting and arbitrage:
   a. Requiring airline travelers to spend at least one Saturday night away from home to qualify for a low fare.
   b. Insisting on delivering cement to buyers and basing prices on buyers' locations.
   c. Selling food processors along with coupons that can be sent to the manufacturer for a $10 rebate.
   d. Offering temporary price cuts on bathroom tissue.
   e. Charging high-income patients more than low-income patients for plastic surgery.

2. If the demand for drive-in movies is more elastic for couples than for single individuals, it will be optimal for theaters to charge one admission fee for the driver of the car and an extra fee for passengers. True or false? Explain.

3. In Example 11.1 (page 400), we saw how producers of processed foods and related consumer goods use coupons as a means of price discrimination. Although coupons are widely used in the United States, that is not the case in other countries. In Germany, coupons are illegal.
   a. Does prohibiting the use of coupons in Germany make German *consumers* better off or worse off?

**b.** Does prohibiting the use of coupons make German *producers* better off or worse off?

**4.** Suppose that BMW can produce any quantity of cars at a constant marginal cost equal to $20,000 and a fixed cost of $10 billion. You are asked to advise the CEO as to what prices and quantities BMW should set for sales in Europe and in the United States. The demand for BMWs in each market is given by

$$Q_E = 4{,}000{,}000 - 100P_E$$

and

$$Q_U = 1{,}000{,}000 - 20P_U$$

where the subscript $E$ denotes Europe, the subscript $U$ denotes the United States. Assume that BMW can restrict U.S. sales to authorized BMW dealers only.

**a.** What quantity of BMWs should the firm sell in each market, and what should the price be in each market? What should the total profit be?

**b.** If BMW were forced to charge the same price in each market, what would be the quantity sold in each market, the equilibrium price, and the company's profit?

**5.** A monopolist is deciding how to allocate output between two geographically separated markets (East Coast and Midwest). Demand and marginal revenue for the two markets are

$$P_1 = 15 - Q_1 \qquad MR_1 = 15 - 2Q_1$$
$$P_2 = 25 - 2Q_2 \qquad MR_2 = 25 - 4Q_2$$

The monopolist's total cost is $C = 5 + 3(Q_1 + Q_2)$. What are price, output, profits, marginal revenues, and deadweight loss (i) if the monopolist can price discriminate? (ii) if the law prohibits charging different prices in the two regions?

**\*6.** Elizabeth Airlines (EA) flies only one route: Chicago–Honolulu. The demand for each flight is $Q = 500 - P$. EA's cost of running each flight is $30,000 plus $100 per passenger.

**a.** What is the profit-maximizing price that EA will charge? How many people will be on each flight? What is EA's profit for each flight?

**b.** EA learns that the fixed costs per flight are in fact $41,000 instead of $30,000. Will the airline stay in business for long? Illustrate your answer using a graph of the demand curve that EA faces, EA's average cost curve when fixed costs are $30,000, and EA's average cost curve when fixed costs are $41,000.

**c.** Wait! EA finds out that two different types of people fly to Honolulu. Type $A$ consists of business people with a demand of $Q_A = 260 - 0.4P$. Type $B$ consists of students whose total demand is $Q_B = 240 - 0.6P$. Because the students are easy to spot, EA decides to charge them different prices. Graph each of these demand curves and their horizontal sum. What price does EA charge the students? What

price does it charge other customers? How many of each type are on each flight?

**d.** What would EA's profit be for each flight? Would the airline stay in business? Calculate the consumer surplus of each consumer group. What is the total consumer surplus?

**e.** Before EA started price discriminating, how much consumer surplus was the Type $A$ demand getting from air travel to Honolulu? Type $B$? Why did total consumer surplus decline with price discrimination, even though total quantity sold remained unchanged?

**7.** Many retail video stores offer two alternative plans for renting films:

• **A two-part tariff:** Pay an annual membership fee (e.g., $40) and then pay a small fee for the daily rental of each film (e.g., $2 per film per day).

• **A straight rental fee:** Pay no membership fee, but pay a higher daily rental fee (e.g., $4 per film per day).

What is the logic behind the two-part tariff in this case? Why offer the customer a choice of two plans rather than simply a two-part tariff?

**8.** Sal's satellite company broadcasts TV to subscribers in Los Angeles and New York. The demand functions for each of these two groups are

$$Q_{NY} = 60 - 0.25P_{NY}$$
$$Q_{LA} = 100 - 0.50P_{LA}$$

where $Q$ is in thousands of subscriptions per year and $P$ is the subscription price per year. The cost of providing $Q$ units of service is given by

$$C = 1000 + 40Q$$

where $Q = Q_{NY} + Q_{LA}$.

**a.** What are the profit-maximizing prices and quantities for the New York and Los Angeles markets?

**b.** As a consequence of a new satellite that the Pentagon recently deployed, people in Los Angeles receive Sal's New York broadcasts and people in New York receive Sal's Los Angeles broadcasts. As a result, anyone in New York or Los Angeles can receive Sal's broadcasts by subscribing in either city. Thus Sal can charge only a single price. What price should he charge, and what quantities will he sell in New York and Los Angeles?

**c.** In which of the above situations, (a) or (b), is Sal better off? In terms of consumer surplus, which situation do people in New York prefer and which do people in Los Angeles prefer? Why?

**\*9.** You are an executive for Super Computer, Inc. (SC), which rents out super computers. SC receives a fixed rental payment per time period in exchange for the right to unlimited computing at a rate of $P$ cents per second. SC has two types of potential customers of equal number—10 businesses and 10 academic institutions. Each business customer has the demand function $Q = 10 - P$, where $Q$ is in millions of seconds per month; each academic institution has the demand $Q = 8 - P$. The marginal cost to SC of additional computing is 2 cents per second, regardless of volume.

a. Suppose that you could separate business and academic customers. What rental fee and usage fee would you charge each group? What would be your profits?

b. Suppose you were unable to keep the two types of customers separate and charged a zero rental fee. What usage fee would maximize your profits? What would be your profits?

c. Suppose you set up one two-part tariff—that is, you set one rental and one usage fee that both business and academic customers pay. What usage and rental fees would you set? What would be your profits? Explain why price would not be equal to marginal cost.

10. As the owner of the only tennis club in an isolated wealthy community, you must decide on membership dues and fees for court time. There are two types of tennis players. "Serious" players have demand

$$Q_1 = 10 - P$$

where $Q_1$ is court hours per week and $P$ is the fee per hour for each individual player. There are also "occasional" players with demand

$$Q_2 = 4 - 0.25P$$

Assume that there are 1000 players of each type. Because you have plenty of courts, the marginal cost of court time is zero. You have fixed costs of $10,000 per week. Serious and occasional players look alike, so you must charge them the same prices.

a. Suppose that to maintain a "professional" atmosphere, you want to limit membership to serious players. How should you set the *annual* membership dues and court fees (assume 52 weeks per year) to maximize profits, keeping in mind the constraint that only serious players choose to join? What would profits be (per week)?

b. A friend tells you that you could make greater profits by encouraging both types of players to join. Is your friend right? What annual dues and court fees would maximize weekly profits? What would these profits be?

c. Suppose that over the years, young, upwardly mobile professionals move to your community, all of whom are serious players. You believe there are now 3000 serious players and 1000 occasional players. Would it still be profitable to cater to the occasional player? What would be the profit-maximizing annual dues and court fees? What would profits be per week?

11. Look again at Figure 11.12 (p. 415), which shows the reservation prices of three consumers for two goods. Assuming that marginal production cost is zero for both goods, can the producer make the most money by selling

the goods separately, by using pure bundling, or by using mixed bundling? What prices should be charged?

12. Look again at Figure 11.17 (p. 418). Suppose that the marginal costs $c_1$ and $c_2$ were zero. Show that in this case, pure bundling, not mixed bundling, is the most profitable pricing strategy. What price should be charged for the bundle? What will the firm's profit be?

13. Some years ago, an article appeared in the *New York Times* about IBM's pricing policy. The previous day, IBM had announced major price cuts on most of its small and medium-sized computers. The article said:

> IBM probably has no choice but to cut prices periodically to get its customers to purchase more and lease less. If they succeed, this could make life more difficult for IBM's major competitors. Outright purchases of computers are needed for ever larger IBM revenues and profits, says Morgan Stanley's Ulric Weil in his new book, *Information Systems in the '80's*. Mr. Weil declares that IBM cannot revert to an emphasis on leasing.

a. Provide a brief but clear argument in *support* of the claim that IBM should try "to get its customers to purchase more and lease less."

b. Provide a brief but clear argument *against* this claim.

c. What factors determine whether leasing or selling is preferable for a company like IBM? Explain briefly.

14. You are selling two goods, 1 and 2, to a market consisting of three consumers with reservation prices as follows:

| | Reservation Price ($) | |
|---|---|---|
| Consumer | For 1 | For 2 |
| A | 20 | 100 |
| B | 60 | 60 |
| C | 100 | 20 |

The unit cost of each product is $30.

a. Compute the optimal prices and profits for (i) selling the goods separately, (ii) pure bundling, and (iii) mixed bundling.

b. Which strategy would be most profitable? Why?

15. Your firm produces two products, the demands for which are independent. Both products are produced at zero marginal cost. You face four consumers (or groups of consumers) with the following reservation prices:

| Consumer | Good 1($) | Good 2($) |
|---|---|---|
| A | 25 | 100 |
| B | 40 | 80 |
| C | 80 | 40 |
| D | 100 | 25 |

a. Consider three alternative pricing strategies: (i) selling the goods separately; (ii) pure bundling;

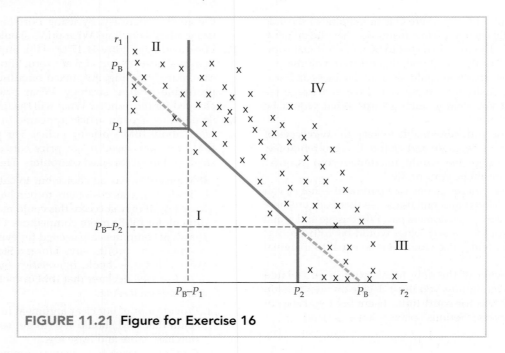

**FIGURE 11.21 Figure for Exercise 16**

(iii) mixed bundling. For *each strategy*, determine the optimal prices to be charged and the resulting profits. Which strategy would be best?

**b.** Now suppose that the production of each good entails a marginal cost of $30. How does this information change your answers to (a)? Why is the optimal strategy now different?

**16.** A cable TV company offers, in addition to its basic service, two products: a Sports Channel (Product 1) and a Movie Channel (Product 2). Subscribers to the basic service can subscribe to these additional services individually at the monthly prices $P_1$ and $P_2$, respectively, or they can buy the two as a bundle for the price $P_B$, where $P_B < P_1 + P_2$. They can also forgo the additional services and simply buy the basic service. The company's marginal cost for these additional services is *zero*. Through market research, the cable company has estimated the reservation prices for these two services for a representative group of consumers in the company's service area. These reservation prices are plotted (as x's) in Figure 11.21, as are the prices $P_1$, $P_2$, and $P_B$ that the cable company is currently charging. The graph is divided into regions I, II, III, and IV.

**a.** Which products, if any, will be purchased by the consumers in region I? In region II? In region III? In region IV? Explain briefly.

**b.** Note that as drawn in the figure, the reservation prices for the Sports Channel and the Movie Channel

are negatively correlated. Why would you, or why would you not, expect consumers' reservation prices for cable TV channels to be negatively correlated?

**c.** The company's vice president has said: "Because the marginal cost of providing an additional channel is zero, mixed bundling offers no advantage over pure bundling. Our profits would be just as high if we offered the Sports Channel and the Movie Channel together as a bundle, and only as a bundle." Do you agree or disagree? Explain why.

**d.** Suppose the cable company continues to use mixed bundling to sell these two services. Based on the distribution of reservation prices shown in Figure 11.21, do you think the cable company should alter any of the prices that it is now charging? If so, how?

**\*17.** Consider a firm with monopoly power that faces the demand curve

$$P = 100 - 3Q + 4A^{1/2}$$

and has the total cost function

$$C = 4Q^2 + 10Q + A$$

where $A$ is the level of advertising expenditures, and $P$ and $Q$ are price and output.

**a.** Find the values of $A$, $Q$, and $P$ that maximize the firm's profit.

**b.** Calculate the Lerner index, $L = (P - MC)/P$, for this firm at its profit-maximizing levels of $A$, $Q$, and $P$.

# Appendix to Chapter 11

## TRANSFER PRICING IN THE INTEGRATED FIRM

So far, we have studied the firm's pricing decision assuming that it sells its output in an *outside market*, i.e., to consumers or to other firms. Many firms, however, are *vertically integrated*—they contain several divisions, with some divisions producing parts and components that other divisions use to produce the finished product.[1] For example, automobile companies have "upstream" divisions that produce engines, brakes, radiators, and other components that the "downstream" divisions use to produce the finished cars. *Transfer pricing* refers to the valuation of these parts and components within the firm. **Transfer prices** are internal prices at which the parts and components from upstream divisions are "sold" to downstream divisions. Transfer prices must be chosen correctly because they are the signals that divisional managers use to determine output levels.

> **• transfer prices** Internal prices at which parts and components from upstream divisions are "sold" to downstream divisions within a firm.

This appendix shows how a profit-maximizing firm chooses its transfer prices and divisional output levels. We will also examine other issues raised by vertical integration. For example, suppose a computer firm's upstream division produces memory chips used by a downstream division to produce the final product. If other firms also produce these chips, should our firm obtain all its chips from the upstream division, or should it also buy some on the outside market? Should the upstream division produce more chips than the downstream division needs and sell the excess in the market? How should the firm coordinate its upstream and downstream divisions? In particular, can we design incentives for the divisions that help the firm to maximize its profits?

We begin with the simplest case: There is no outside market for the output of the upstream division—i.e., the upstream division produces a good that is neither produced nor used by any other firm. Next we consider what happens when there is an outside market for the upstream division's output.

### Transfer Pricing When There Is No Outside Market

Consider a firm with three divisions: Two upstream divisions produce inputs to a downstream processing division. The two upstream divisions produce quantities $Q_1$ and $Q_2$ and have total costs $C_1(Q_1)$ and $C_2(Q_2)$. The downstream division produces a quantity $Q$ using the production function

$$Q = f(K, L, Q_1, Q_2)$$

where $K$ and $L$ are capital and labor inputs, and $Q_1$ and $Q_2$ are the intermediate inputs from the upstream divisions. Excluding the costs of the inputs $Q_1$ and $Q_2$, the downstream division has a total production cost $C_d(Q)$. Total revenue from sales of the final product is $R(Q)$.

We assume there are *no outside markets* for the intermediate inputs $Q_1$ and $Q_2$; they can be used only by the downstream division. Then the firm has two problems:

1. What quantities $Q_1$, $Q_2$, and $Q$ will maximize its profit?

2. Is there an incentive scheme that will decentralize the firm's management? In particular, is there a set of transfer prices $P_1$ and $P_2$, so that *if each division*

---

[1] A firm is *horizontally integrated* when it has several divisions that produce the same or closely related products. Many firms are both vertically and horizontally integrated.

*maximizes its own divisional profit, the profit of the overall firm will also be maximized?*

To solve these problems, we note that the firm's total profit is

$$\pi(Q) = R(Q) - C_d(Q) - C_1(Q_1) - C_2(Q_2) \tag{A11.1}$$

What is the level of $Q_1$ that maximizes this profit? It is the level at which *the cost of the last unit of $Q_1$ is just equal to the additional revenue it brings to the firm.* The cost of producing one extra unit of $Q_1$ is the marginal cost $\Delta C_1/\Delta Q_1 = MC_1$. How much extra revenue results from that one extra unit? An extra unit of $Q_1$ allows the firm to produce more final output $Q$ of an amount $\Delta Q/\Delta Q_1 = MP_1$, the marginal product of $Q_1$. An extra unit of final output results in additional revenue $\Delta R/\Delta Q = MR$, but it also results in additional cost to the downstream division of an amount $\Delta C_d/\Delta Q = MC_d$. Thus the *net marginal revenue* $NMR_1$ that the firm earns from an extra unit of $Q_1$ is $(MR - MC_d)MP_1$. Setting this equal to the marginal cost of the unit, we obtain the following rule for profit maximization[2]:

> In §10.1, we explain that a firm maximizes its profit at the output at which marginal revenue is equal to marginal cost.

$$NMR_1 = (MR - MC_d)MP_1 = MC_1 \tag{A11.2}$$

Going through the same steps for the second intermediate input gives

$$NMR_2 = (MR - MC_d)MP_2 = MC_2 \tag{A11.3}$$

Note from equations (A11.2) and (A11.3) that it is *incorrect* to determine the firm's final output level $Q$ by setting marginal revenue equal to marginal cost for the downstream division—i.e., by setting $MR = MC_d$. Doing so ignores the cost of producing the intermediate input. ($MR$ exceeds $MC_d$ because this cost is positive.) Also, note that equations (A11.2) and (A11.3) are standard conditions of marginal analysis: The output of each upstream division should be such that its marginal cost is equal to its marginal contribution to the profit of the overall firm.

Now, what transfer prices $P_1$ and $P_2$ should be "charged" to the downstream division for its use of the intermediate inputs? Remember that if each of the three divisions uses these transfer prices to maximize its own divisional profit, the profit of the overall firm should be maximized. The two upstream divisions will maximize their divisional profits, $\pi_1$ and $\pi_2$, which are given by

$$\pi_1 = P_1Q_1 - C_1(Q_1)$$

and

$$\pi_2 = P_2Q_2 - C_2(Q_2)$$

Because the upstream divisions take $P_1$ and $P_2$ as given, they will choose $Q_1$ and $Q_2$ so that $P_1 = MC_1$ and $P_2 = MC_2$. Similarly, the downstream division will maximize

$$\pi(Q) = R(Q) - C_d(Q) - P_1Q_1 - P_2Q_2$$

Because the downstream division also takes $P_1$ and $P_2$ as given, it will choose $Q_1$ and $Q_2$ so that

$$(MR - MC_d)MP_1 = NMR_1 = P_1 \tag{A11.4}$$

---

[2]Using calculus, we can obtain this rule by differentiating equation (A11.1) with respect to $Q_1$:

$$d\pi/dQ_1 = (dR/dQ)(\partial Q/\partial Q_1) - (dC_d/dQ)(\partial Q/\partial Q_1) - dC_1/dQ_1$$
$$= (MR - MC_d)MP_1 - MC_1$$

Setting $d\pi/dQ = 0$ to maximize profit gives equation (A11.2).

and

$$(MR - MC_d)MP_2 = NMR_2 = P_2 \qquad \textbf{(A11.5)}$$

Note that by setting the transfer prices equal to the respective marginal costs ($P_1 = MC_1$ and $P_2 = MC_2$), the profit-maximizing conditions given by equations (A11.2) and (A11.3) will be satisfied. We therefore have a simple solution to the transfer pricing problem: *Set each transfer price equal to the marginal cost of the respective upstream division.* Then when each division is required to maximize its own profit, the quantities $Q_1$ and $Q_2$ that the upstream divisions will want to produce will be the same quantities that the downstream division will want to "buy," and they will maximize the firm's total profit.

To illustrate this graphically, suppose Race Car Motors, Inc., has two divisions. The upstream Engine Division produces engines, and the downstream Assembly Division puts together automobiles, using one engine (and a few other parts) in each car. In Figure A11.1, the average revenue curve AR is Race Car Motors' demand curve for cars. (Note that the firm has monopoly power in the automobile market.) $MC_A$ is the marginal cost of assembling automobiles, *given the engines* (i.e., it does not include the cost of the engines). Because the car requires one engine, the marginal product of the engines is one. Thus the curve labeled $MR - MC_A$ is also the net marginal revenue curve for engines:

$$NMR_E = (MR - MC_A)MP_E = MR - MC_A$$

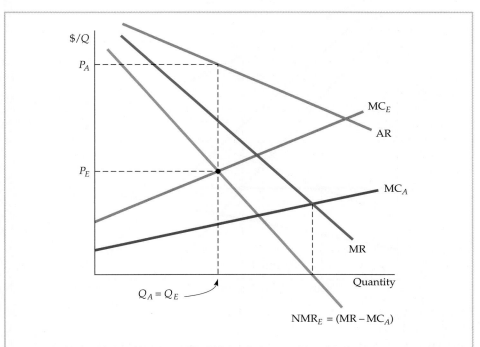

**FIGURE A11.1  Race Car Motors, Inc.**

The firm's upstream division should produce a quantity of engines $Q_E$ that equates its marginal cost of engine production $MC_E$ with the downstream division's net marginal revenue of engines $NMR_E$. Because the firm uses one engine in every car, $NMR_E$ is the difference between the marginal revenue from selling cars and the marginal cost of assembling them, i.e., $MR - MC_A$. The optimal transfer price for engines $P_E$ equals the marginal cost of producing them. Finished cars are sold at price $P_A$.

The profit-maximizing number of engines (and number of cars) is given by the intersection of the net marginal revenue curve $NMR_E$ with the marginal cost curve for engines $MC_E$. Having determined the number of cars that it will produce, and knowing its divisional cost functions, the management of Race Car Motors can now set the transfer price $P_E$ that correctly values the engines used to produce its cars. This is the transfer price that should be used to calculate divisional profit (and year-end bonuses for divisional managers).

## Transfer Pricing with a Competitive Outside Market

Now suppose there is a *competitive* outside market for the intermediate good produced by an upstream division. Because the outside market is competitive, there is a single market price at which one can buy or sell the good. Therefore, *the marginal cost of the intermediate good is simply the market price.* Because the optimal transfer price must equal marginal cost, it must also equal the competitive market price.

To see this, suppose there is a competitive market for the engines that Race Car Motors produces. If the market price is low, Race Car Motors may want to buy some or all of its engines in the market; if it is high, it may want to sell engines in the market. Figure A11.2 illustrates the first case. For quantities below $Q_{E,1}$, the upstream division's marginal cost of producing engines $MC_E$ is below the market price $P_{E,M}$; for quantities above $Q_{E,1}$, it is above the market price. The

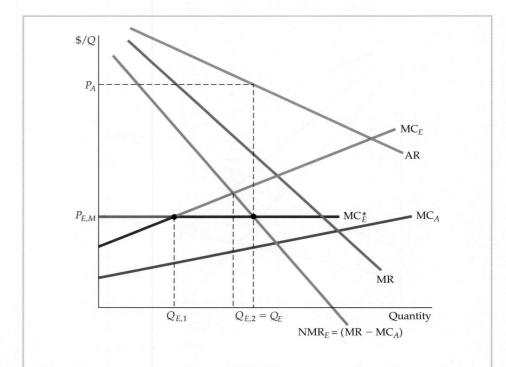

**FIGURE A11.2 Buying Engines in a Competitive Outside Market**

Race Car Motors' marginal cost of engines $MC_E^*$ is the upstream division's marginal cost for quantities up to $Q_{E,1}$ and the market price $P_{E,M}$ for quantities above $Q_{E,1}$. The downstream division should use a total of $Q_{E,2}$ engines to produce an equal number of cars; in that case, the marginal cost of engines equals net marginal revenue. $Q_{E,2} - Q_{E,1}$ of these engines are bought in the outside market. The downstream division "pays" the upstream division the transfer price $P_{E,M}$ for the remaining $Q_{E,1}$ engines.

firm should obtain engines at the least cost, so the marginal cost of engines $MC^*_E$ will be the upstream division's marginal cost for quantities up to $Q_{E,1}$ and the market price for quantities above $Q_{E,1}$. Note that Race Car Motors uses more engines and produces more cars than it would have had there been no outside engine market. The downstream division now buys $Q_{E,2}$ engines and produces an equal number of automobiles. However, it "buys" only $Q_{E,1}$ of these engines from the upstream division and the rest on the open market.

It might seem strange that Race Car Motors must go into the open market to buy engines that it can make itself. If it made all of its own engines, however, its marginal cost of producing them would exceed the competitive market price. Although the profit of the upstream division would be higher, *the total profit of the firm would be lower*.

Figure A11.3 shows the case where Race Car Motors *sells* engines in the outside market. Now the competitive market price $P_{E,M}$ is above the transfer price that the firm would have set had there been no outside market. In this case, although the upstream Engine Division produces $Q_{E,1}$ engines, only $Q_{E,2}$ engines are used by the downstream division to produce automobiles. The rest are sold in the outside market at the price $P_{E,M}$.

Note that compared with a situation in which there is no outside engine market, Race Car Motors is producing more engines but fewer cars. Why not produce this larger number of engines but use all of them to produce more cars?

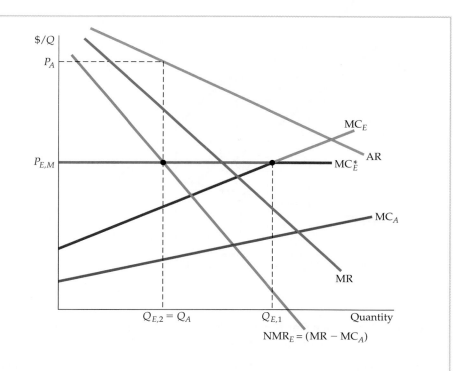

**FIGURE A11.3  Selling Engines in a Competitive Outside Market**

The optimal transfer price for Race Car Motors is again the market price $P_{E,M}$. This price is above the point at which $MC_E$ intersects $NMR_E$, so the upstream division sells some of its engines in the outside market. The upstream division produces $Q_{E,1}$ engines, the quantity at which $MC_E$ equals $P_{E,M}$. The downstream division uses only $Q_{E,2}$ of these engines, the quantity at which $NMR_E$ equals $P_{E,M}$. Compared with Figure A11.1, in which there is no outside market, more engines but fewer cars are produced.

Because the engines are too valuable. On the margin, the net revenue that can be earned from selling them in the outside market is higher than the net revenue from using them to build additional cars.

### Transfer Pricing with a Noncompetitive Outside Market

Now suppose there is an outside market for the output of the upstream division, but that market is not competitive—the firm has monopoly power. The same principles apply, but we must be careful when measuring net marginal revenue.

Suppose the engine produced by the upstream Engine Division is a special one that only Race Car Motors can make. There is, however, an outside market for this engine. Race Car Motors, therefore, can be a monopoly supplier to that market while also producing engines for its own use. What is the optimal transfer price for use of the engines by the downstream division, and at what price (if any) should engines be sold in the outside market?

We must find the firm's net marginal revenue from the sale of engines. In Figure A11.4, $D_{E,M}$ is the outside market demand curve for engines and $MR_{E,M}$

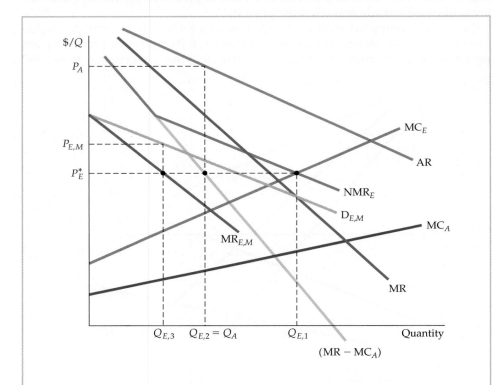

**FIGURE A11.4  Race Car Motors—A Monopoly Supplier of Engines to an Outside Market**

$D_{E,M}$ is the outside market demand curve for engines; $MR_{E,M}$ is the corresponding marginal revenue curve; $(MR - MC_A)$ is the net marginal revenue from the use of engines by the downstream division. The *total net marginal revenue curve for engines* $NMR_E$ is the horizontal sum of these two marginal revenues. The optimal transfer price $P_E^*$ and the quantity of engines that the upstream division produces, $Q_{E,1}$, are found where $MC_E = NMR_E$. $Q_{E,2}$ of these engines are used by the downstream division, the quantity at which the downstream division's net marginal revenue, $MR - MC_A$, is equal to the transfer price $P_E^*$. The remaining engines, $Q_{E,3}$, are sold in the outside market at the price $P_{E,M}$.

is the corresponding marginal revenue curve. Race Car Motors thus has two sources of marginal revenue from the production and sale of an additional engine: marginal revenue $MR_{E,M}$ from sales in the outside market and net marginal revenue $(MR - MC_A)$ from the use of the engines by the downstream division. By summing these two curves horizontally, we obtain the *total net marginal revenue curve for engines*; it is the green line labeled $NMR_E$.

The intersection of the marginal cost and total net marginal revenue curves gives the quantity of engines $Q_{E,1}$ that the upstream division should produce and the optimal transfer price $P_E^*$. Again, the optimal transfer price is equal to marginal cost. But note that only $Q_{E,2}$ of these engines are used by the downstream division to make cars. This is the quantity at which the downstream division's net marginal revenue, $MR - MC_A$, is equal to the transfer price $P_E^*$. The remaining engines $Q_{E,3}$ are sold in the outside market. However, they are not sold at the transfer price $P_E^*$. Instead the firm exercises its monopoly power and sells them at the higher price $P_{E,M}$.

Why pay the upstream division only $P_E^*$ per engine when the firm is selling engines in the outside market at the higher price $P_{E,M}$? Because if the upstream division is paid more than $P_E^*$ (and thereby encouraged to produce more engines), the marginal cost of engines will rise and exceed the net marginal revenue from their use by the downstream division. And if the price charged in the outside market were lowered, the marginal revenue from sales in that market would fall below marginal cost. At the prices $P_E^*$ and $P_{E,M}$, marginal revenues and marginal cost are equal:

$$MR_{E,M} = (MR - MC_A) = MC_E$$

Sometimes a vertically integrated firm can buy components in an outside market in which it has *monopsony* power. Suppose, for example, that Race Car Motors can obtain engines from its upstream Engine Division, or can purchase them *as a monopsonist* in an outside market. Although we have not illustrated this case graphically, you should be able to see that in this case, the transfer price paid to the Engine Division will be *above* the price at which engines are bought in the outside market. Why "pay" the upstream division a price that is higher than that paid in the outside market? With monopsony power, purchasing one additional engine in the outside market incurs a *marginal expenditure* that is greater than the actual price per engine paid in that market. The marginal expenditure is higher because purchasing an additional unit raises the average expenditure paid *for all* units bought in the outside market.

> In §10.5, we explain that when a buyer has monopsony power, its marginal expenditure curve lies above its average expenditure curve because the decision to buy an extra unit of the good raises the price that must be paid on all units.

## A Numerical Example

Suppose Race Car Motors has the following demand for its automobiles:

$$P = 20,000 - Q$$

Its marginal revenue is thus

$$MR = 20,000 - 2Q$$

The downstream division's cost of assembling cars is

$$C_A(Q) = 8000Q$$

so that the division's marginal cost is $MC_A = 8000$. The upstream division's cost of producing engines is

$$C_E(Q_E) = 2Q_E^2$$

The division's marginal cost is thus $MC_E(Q_E) = 4Q_E$.

First, suppose there is *no outside market* for the engines. How many engines and cars should the firm produce? What should be the transfer price for engines? To solve this problem, we set the net marginal revenue for engines equal to the marginal cost of producing engines. Because each car has one engine, $Q_E = Q$. The net marginal revenue of engines is thus

$$\mathrm{NMR}_E = \mathrm{MR} - \mathrm{MC}_A = 12{,}000 - 2Q_E$$

Now set $\mathrm{NMR}_E$ equal to $\mathrm{MC}_E$:

$$12{,}000 - 2Q_E = 4Q_E$$

Thus $6Q_E = 12{,}000$ and $Q_E = 2000$. The firm should therefore produce 2000 engines and 2000 cars. The optimal transfer price is the marginal cost of these 2000 engines:

$$P_E = 4Q_E = \$8000$$

Second, suppose that engines can be bought or sold for $6000 in an *outside competitive market*. This is below the $8000 transfer price that is optimal when there is no outside market, so the firm should buy some engines outside. Its marginal cost of engines, and the optimal transfer price, is now $6000. Set this $6000 marginal cost equal to the net marginal revenue of engines:

$$6000 = \mathrm{NMR}_E = 12{,}000 - 2Q_E$$

Thus the total quantity of engines and cars is now 3000. The company now produces more cars (and sells them at a lower price) because its cost of engines is lower. Also, since the transfer price for the engines is now $6000, the upstream Engine Division supplies only 1500 engines (because $\mathrm{MC}_E(1500) = \$6000$). The remaining 1500 engines are bought in the outside market.

Finally, suppose Race Car Motors is the only producer of these engines but can sell them in an outside market. Demand in the outside market is

$$P_{E,M} = 10{,}000 - Q_E$$

The marginal revenue from sales in the market is therefore

$$\mathrm{MR}_{E,M} = 10{,}000 - 2Q_E$$

To determine the optimal transfer price, we find the *total* net marginal revenue by horizontally summing $\mathrm{MR}_{E,M}$ with the net marginal revenue from "sales" to the downstream division, $12{,}000 - 2Q_E$, as in Figure A11.4. For outputs $Q_E$ greater than 1000, this is

$$\mathrm{NMR}_{E,Total} = 11{,}000 - Q_E$$

Now set this equal to the marginal cost of producing engines:

$$11{,}000 - Q_E = 4Q_E$$

The total quantity of engines produced should therefore be $Q_E = 2200$.

How many of these engines should go to the downstream division and how many to the outside market? Note that the marginal cost of producing these 2200 engines—and therefore the optimal transfer price—is $4Q_E = \$8800$. Set this price equal to the marginal revenue from sales in the outside market:

$$8800 = 10{,}000 - 2Q_E$$

or $Q_E = 600$. Therefore, 600 engines should be sold in the outside market. Finally, set this $8800 transfer price equal to the net marginal revenue from "sales" to the downstream division:

$$8800 = 12{,}000 - 2Q_E$$

or $Q_E = 1600$. Thus 1600 engines should be supplied to the downstream division for use in the production of 1600 cars.

# EXERCISES

1. Review the numerical example about Race Car Motors. Calculate the profit earned by the upstream division, the downstream division, and the firm as a whole in each of the three cases examined: (a) there is no outside market for engines; (b) there is a competitive market for engines in which the market price is $6000; and (c) the firm is a monopoly supplier of engines to an outside market. In which case does Race Car Motors earn the most profit? In which case does the upstream division earn the most? The downstream division?

2. Ajax Computer makes a computer for climate control in office buildings. The company uses a microprocessor produced by its upstream division, along with other parts bought in outside competitive markets. The microprocessor is produced at a constant marginal cost of $500, and the marginal cost of assembling the computer (including the cost of the other parts) by the downstream division is a constant $700. The firm has been selling the computer for $2000, and until now there has been no outside market for the microprocessor.

    a. Suppose an outside market for the microprocessor develops and that Ajax has monopoly power in that market, selling microprocessors for $1000 each. Assuming that demand for the microprocessor is unrelated to the demand for the Ajax computer, what transfer price should Ajax apply to the microprocessor for its use by the downstream computer division? Should production of computers be increased, decreased, or left unchanged? Explain briefly.

    b. How would your answer to (a) change if the demands for the computer and the microprocessors were competitive; i.e., if some of the people who buy the microprocessors use them to make climate control systems of their own?

3. Reebok produces and sells running shoes. It faces a market demand schedule $P = 11 - 1.5Q_s$, where $Q_s$ is the number of pairs of shoes sold and $P$ is the price in dollars per pair of shoes. Production of each pair of shoes requires 1 square yard of leather. The leather is shaped and cut by the Form Division of Reebok. The cost function for leather is

$$TC_L = 1 + Q_L + 0.5Q_L^2$$

where $Q_L$ is the quantity of leather (in square yards) produced. Excluding leather, the cost function for running shoes is

$$TC_s = 2Q_s$$

    a. What is the optimal transfer price?

    b. Leather can be bought and sold in a competitive market at the price of $P_F = 1.5$. In this case, how much leather should the Form Division supply internally? How much should it supply to the outside market? Will Reebok buy any leather in the outside market? Find the optimal transfer price.

    c. Now suppose the leather is unique and of extremely high quality. Therefore, the Form Division may act as a monopoly supplier to the outside market as well as a supplier to the downstream division. Suppose the outside demand for leather is given by $P = 32 - Q_L$. What is the optimal transfer price for the use of leather by the downstream division? At what price, if any, should leather be sold to the outside market? What quantity, if any, will be sold to the outside market?

4. The House Products Division of Acme Corporation manufactures and sells digital clock radios. A major component is supplied by the electronics division of Acme. The cost functions for the radio and the electronic component divisions are, respectively,

$$TC_r = 30 + 2Q_r$$
$$TC_c = 70 + 6Q_c + Q_c^2$$

Note that $TC_r$ does not include the cost of the component. Manufacture of one radio set requires the use of one electronic component. Market studies show that the firm's demand curve for the digital clock radio is given by

$$P_r = 108 - Q_r$$

    a. If there is no outside market for the components, how many of them should be produced to maximize profits for Acme as a whole? What is the optimal transfer price?

    b. If other firms are willing to purchase in the outside market the component manufactured by the electronics division (which is the only supplier of this product), what is the optimal transfer price? Why? What price should be charged in the outside market? Why? How many units will the electronics division supply internally and to the outside market? Why? (*Note:* The demand for components in the outside market is $P_c = 72 - 1.5Q_c$.)

# Monopolistic Competition and Oligopoly

In the last two chapters, we saw how firms with monopoly power can choose prices and output levels to maximize profit. We also saw that monopoly power does not require a firm to be a pure monopolist. In many industries, even though several firms compete with each other, each firm has at least some monopoly power: It has control over price and can profitably charge a price that exceeds marginal cost.

In this chapter, we examine market structures other than pure monopoly that can give rise to monopoly power. We begin with what might seem like an oxymoron: **monopolistic competition**. A monopolistically competitive market is similar to a perfectly competitive market in two key respects: There are many firms and entry by new firms is not restricted. But it differs from perfect competition in that the product is *differentiated*: Each firm sells a brand or version of the product that differs in quality, appearance, or reputation, and each firm is the sole producer of its own brand. The amount of monopoly power wielded by a firm depends on its success in differentiating its product from those of other firms. Examples of monopolistically competitive industries abound: Toothpaste, laundry detergent, and packaged coffee are a few.

The second form of market structure we will examine is **oligopoly**: a market in which only a few firms compete with one another, and entry by new firms is impeded. The product that the firms produce might be differentiated, as with automobiles, or it might not be, as with steel. Monopoly power and profitability in oligopolistic industries depend in part on how the firms interact. For example, if the interaction is more cooperative than competitive, firms could charge prices well above marginal cost and earn large profits.

In some oligopolistic industries, firms do cooperate, but in others, they compete aggressively, even though this means lower profits. To see why, we need to consider how oligopolistic firms decide on output and prices. These decisions are complicated because each firm must operate *strategically*—when making a decision, it must weigh the probable reactions of its competitors. To understand oligopolistic markets, we must therefore introduce some basic concepts of gaming and strategy. We develop these concepts more fully in Chapter 13.

The third form of market structure that we examine is a **cartel**. In a cartelized market, some or all firms explicitly *collude*: They coordinate prices and output levels to maximize *joint* profits. Cartels can arise in markets that would otherwise be competitive, as with the OPEC oil cartel, or oligopolistic, as with the international bauxite cartel.

- **monopolistic competition** Market in which firms can enter freely, each producing its own brand or version of a differentiated product.

- **oligopoly** Market in which only a few firms compete with one another, and entry by new firms is impeded.

- **cartel** Market in which some or all firms explicitly collude, coordinating prices and output levels to maximize joint profits.

At first glance, a cartel may seem like a pure monopoly. After all, the firms in a cartel appear to operate as though they were parts of one big company. But a cartel differs from a monopoly in two important respects. First, because cartels rarely control the entire market, they must consider how their pricing decisions will affect noncartel production levels. Second, because the members of a cartel are *not* part of one big company, they may be tempted to "cheat" their partners by undercutting prices and grabbing bigger shares of the market. As a result, many cartels tend to be unstable and short-lived.

## 12.1 MONOPOLISTIC COMPETITION

In many industries, the products are differentiated. For one reason or another, consumers view each firm's brand as different from other brands. Crest toothpaste, for example, is perceived to be different from Colgate, Aim, and other toothpastes. The difference is partly flavor, partly consistency, and partly reputation—the consumer's image (correct or incorrect) of the relative decay-preventing efficacy of Crest. As a result, some consumers (but not all) will pay more for Crest.

Because Procter & Gamble is the sole producer of Crest, it has monopoly power. But its monopoly power is limited because consumers can easily substitute other brands if the price of Crest rises. Although consumers who prefer Crest will pay more for it, most of them will not pay much more. The typical Crest user might pay 25 or 50 cents a tube more, but probably not one or two dollars more. For most consumers, toothpaste is toothpaste, and the differences among brands are small. Therefore, the demand curve for Crest toothpaste, though downward sloping, is fairly elastic. (A reasonable estimate of the elasticity of demand for Crest is −5.) Because of its limited monopoly power, Procter & Gamble will charge a price that is higher, but not much higher, than marginal cost. The situation is similar for Tide detergent or Scott paper towels.

### The Makings of Monopolistic Competition

A monopolistically competitive market has two key characteristics:

In §10.2, we explain that a seller of a product has some monopoly power if it can profitably charge a price greater than marginal cost.

1. Firms compete by selling differentiated products that are highly substitutable for one another but not perfect substitutes. In other words, the cross-price elasticities of demand are large but not infinite.

2. There is *free entry and exit:* it is relatively easy for new firms to enter the market with their own brands and for existing firms to leave if their products become unprofitable.

To see why free entry is an important requirement, let's compare the markets for toothpaste and automobiles. The toothpaste market is monopolistically competitive, but the automobile market is better characterized as an oligopoly. It is relatively easy for other firms to introduce new brands of toothpaste, and this limits the profitability of producing Crest or Colgate. If the profits were large, other firms would spend the necessary money (for development, production, advertising, and promotion) to introduce new brands of their own, which would reduce the market shares and profitability of Crest and Colgate.

The automobile market is also characterized by product differentiation. However, the large scale economies involved in production make entry by new firms difficult. Thus, until the mid-1970s, when Japanese producers became important competitors, the three major U.S. automakers had the market largely to themselves.

There are many other examples of monopolistic competition besides tooth-paste. Soap, shampoo, deodorants, shaving cream, cold remedies, and many other items found in a drugstore are sold in monopolistically competitive markets. The markets for bicycles and other sporting goods are likewise monopolistically competitive. So is most retail trade, because goods are sold in many different stores that compete with one another by differentiating their services according to location, availability and expertise of salespeople, credit terms, etc. Entry is relatively easy, so if profits are high in a neighborhood because there are only a few stores, new stores will enter.

## Equilibrium in the Short Run and the Long Run

As with monopoly, in monopolistic competition firms face downward-sloping demand curves. Therefore, they have some monopoly power. But this does not mean that monopolistically competitive firms are likely to earn large profits. Monopolistic competition is also similar to perfect competition: Because there is free entry, the potential to earn profits will attract new firms with competing brands, driving economic profits down to zero.

To make this clear, let's examine the equilibrium price and output level for a monopolistically competitive firm in the short and long run. Figure 12.1(a) shows the short-run equilibrium. Because the firm's product differs from its competitors', its demand curve $D_{SR}$ is downward sloping. (This is the *firm's* demand curve, not the market demand curve, which is more steeply sloped.) The profit-maximizing

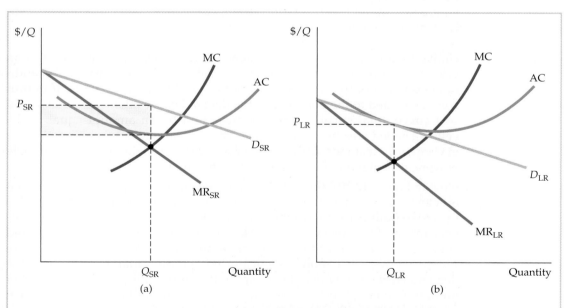

**FIGURE 12.1 A Monopolistically Competitive Firm in the Short and Long Run**

Because the firm is the only producer of its brand, it faces a downward-sloping demand curve. Price exceeds marginal cost and the firm has monopoly power. In the short run, described in part **(a)**, price also exceeds average cost, and the firm earns profits shown by the yellow-shaded rectangle. In the long run, these profits attract new firms with competing brands. The firm's market share falls, and its demand curve shifts downward. In long-run equilibrium, described in part **(b)**, price equals average cost, so the firm earns zero profit even though it has monopoly power.

In §10.1, we explain that a monopolist maximizes profit by choosing an output at which marginal revenue is equal to marginal cost.

Recall from §8.7 that with the possibility of entry and exit, firms will earn zero economic profit in long-run equilibrium.

In §9.2, we explain that competitive markets are efficient because they maximize the sum of consumers' and producers' surplus.

In §10.4, we discuss the deadweight loss from monopoly power.

quantity $Q_{SR}$ is found at the intersection of the marginal revenue and marginal cost curves. Because the corresponding price $P_{SR}$ exceeds average cost, the firm earns a profit, as shown by the shaded rectangle in the figure.

In the long run, this profit will induce entry by other firms. As they introduce competing brands, our firm will lose market share and sales; its demand curve will shift down, as in Figure 12.1(b). (In the long run, the average and marginal cost curves may also shift. We have assumed for simplicity that costs do not change.) The long-run demand curve $D_{LR}$ will be just tangent to the firm's average cost curve. Here, profit maximization implies the quantity $Q_{LR}$ and the price $P_{LR}$. It also implies *zero profit* because price is equal to average cost. Our firm still has monopoly power: Its long-run demand curve is downward sloping because its particular brand is still unique. But the entry and competition of other firms have driven its profit to zero.

More generally, firms may have different costs, and some brands will be more distinctive than others. In this case, firms may charge slightly different prices, and some will earn small profits.

## Monopolistic Competition and Economic Efficiency

Perfectly competitive markets are desirable because they are economically efficient: As long as there are no externalities and nothing impedes the workings of the market, the total surplus of consumers and producers is as large as possible. Monopolistic competition is similar to competition in some respects, but is it an efficient market structure? To answer this question, let's compare the long-run equilibrium of a monopolistically competitive industry to the long-run equilibrium of a perfectly competitive industry.

Figure 12.2 shows that there are two sources of inefficiency in a monopolistically competitive industry:

1. Unlike perfect competition, with monopolistic competition the equilibrium price exceeds marginal cost. This means that the value to consumers of additional units of output exceeds the cost of producing those units. If output were expanded to the point where the demand curve intersects the marginal cost curve, total surplus could be increased by an amount equal to the yellow-shaded area in Figure 12.2(b). This should not be surprising. We saw in Chapter 10 that monopoly power creates a deadweight loss, and monopoly power exists in monopolistically competitive markets.

2. Note in Figure 12.2(b) that for the monopolistically competitive firm, output is below that which minimizes average cost. Entry of new firms drives profits to zero in both perfectly competitive and monopolistically competitive markets. In a perfectly competitive market, each firm faces a horizontal demand curve, so the zero-profit point occurs at minimum average cost, as Figure 12.2(a) shows. In a monopolistically competitive market, however, the demand curve is downward sloping, so the zero-profit point is to the left of minimum average cost. Excess capacity is inefficient because average cost would be lower with fewer firms.

These inefficiencies make consumers worse off. Is monopolistic competition then a socially undesirable market structure that should be regulated? The answer—for two reasons—is probably no:

1. In most monopolistically competitive markets, monopoly power is small. Usually enough firms compete, with brands that are sufficiently substitutable,

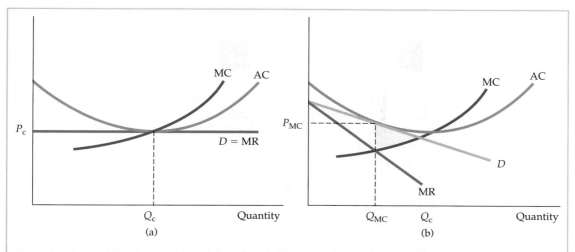

**FIGURE 12.2** **Comparison of Monopolistically Competitive Equilibrium and Perfectly Competitive Equilibrium**

Under perfect competition, as in **(a)**, price equals marginal cost, but under monopolistic competition, price exceeds marginal cost. Thus there is a deadweight loss, as shown by the yellow-shaded area in **(b)**. In both types of markets, entry occurs until profits are driven to zero. Under perfect competition, the demand curve facing the firm is horizontal, so the zero-profit point occurs at the point of minimum average cost. Under monopolistic competition the demand curve is downward-sloping, so the zero-profit point is to the left of the point of minimum average cost. In evaluating monopolistic competition, these inefficiencies must be balanced against the gains to consumers from product diversity.

so that no single firm has much monopoly power. Any resulting deadweight loss will therefore be small. And because firms' demand curves will be fairly elastic, average cost will be close to the minimum.

2. Any inefficiency must be balanced against an important benefit from monopolistic competition: *product diversity*. Most consumers value the ability to choose among a wide variety of competing products and brands that differ in various ways. The gains from product diversity can be large and may easily outweigh the inefficiency costs resulting from downward-sloping demand curves.

**EXAMPLE 12.1** Monopolistic Competition in the Markets for Colas and Coffee

The markets for soft drinks and coffee illustrate the characteristics of monopolistic competition. Each market has a variety of brands that differ slightly but are close substitutes for one another. Each brand of cola, for example, tastes a little different from the next. (Can you tell the difference between Coke and Pepsi? Between Coke and Royal Crown Cola?) And each brand of ground coffee has a slightly different flavor, fragrance, and caffeine content. Most consumers develop their own preferences; you might prefer Maxwell House coffee to other brands and buy it regularly. Brand loyalties, however, are usually limited. If the price of Maxwell House were to rise substantially above those of other brands, you and most other consumers who had been buying it would probably switch brands.

Just how much monopoly power does General Foods, the producer of Maxwell House, have with this brand? In other words, how elastic is the demand for Maxwell House? Most large companies carefully study product demands as part of their market research. Company estimates are usually proprietary, but two published studies of the demands for various brands of colas and ground coffees used simulated shopping experiments to determine how market shares for each brand would change in response to specific changes in price. Table 12.1 summarizes the results by showing the elasticities of demand for several brands.[1]

First, note that among colas, Royal Crown is much less price elastic than Coke. Although it has a small share of the cola market, its taste is more distinctive than that of Coke, Pepsi, and other brands, so consumers who buy it have stronger brand loyalty. But even though Royal Crown has more monopoly power than Coke, it is not necessarily more profitable. Profits depend on fixed costs and volume, as well as price. Even if its average profit is smaller, Coke will generate more profit because it has a much larger share of the market.

| TABLE 12.1 | Elasticities of Demand for Brands of Colas and Coffee | |
|---|---|---|
| | **Brand** | **Elasticity of Demand** |
| Colas | Royal Crown | −2.4 |
| | Coke | −5.2 to −5.7 |
| Ground coffee | Folgers | −6.4 |
| | Maxwell House | −8.2 |
| | Chock Full o'Nuts | −3.6 |

Second, note that coffees as a group are more price elastic than colas. There is less brand loyalty among coffee buyers than among cola buyers because the differences among coffees are less perceptible than the differences among colas. Note that the demand for Chock Full o' Nuts is less price elastic than its competitors. Why? Because Chock Full o' Nuts, like Royal Crown Cola, has a more distinctive taste than Folgers or Maxwell House, and so consumers who buy it tend to remain loyal. Fewer consumers notice or care about the taste differences between Folgers and Maxwell House.

With the exception of Royal Crown and Chock Full o' Nuts, all the colas and coffees are quite price elastic. With elasticities on the order of −4 to −8, each brand has only limited monopoly power. This is typical of monopolistic competition.

---

[1]The elasticity estimates in Table 12.1 are from John R. Nevin, "Laboratory Experiments for Estimating Consumer Demand: A Validation Study," *Journal of Marketing Research* 11 (August 1974): 261–68; and Lakshman Krishnamurthi and S. P. Raj, "A Model of Brand Choice and Purchase Quantity Price Sensitivities," *Marketing Science* (1991). In typical simulated shopping experiments, consumers are asked to choose the brands that they prefer from a variety of prepriced brands. This trial is repeated several times, with different prices each time.

# 12.2 OLIGOPOLY

In oligopolistic markets, the products may or may not be differentiated. What matters is that only a few firms account for most or all of total production. In some oligopolistic markets, some or all firms earn substantial profits over the long run because *barriers to entry* make it difficult or impossible for new firms to enter. Oligopoly is a prevalent form of market structure. Examples of oligopolistic industries include automobiles, steel, aluminum, petrochemicals, electrical equipment, and computers.

Why might barriers to entry arise? We discussed some of the reasons in Chapter 10. Scale economies may make it unprofitable for more than a few firms to coexist in the market; patents or access to a technology may exclude potential competitors; and the need to spend money for name recognition and market reputation may discourage entry by new firms. These are "natural" entry barriers—they are basic to the structure of the particular market. In addition, incumbent firms may take *strategic actions* to deter entry. For example, they might threaten to flood the market and drive prices down if entry occurs, and to make the threat credible, they can construct excess production capacity.

Managing an oligopolistic firm is complicated because pricing, output, advertising, and investment decisions involve important strategic considerations. Because only a few firms are competing, each firm must carefully consider how its actions will affect its rivals, and how its rivals are likely to react.

Suppose that because of sluggish car sales, Ford is considering a 10-percent price cut to stimulate demand. It must think carefully about how competing auto companies will react. They might not react at all, or they might cut their prices only slightly, in which case Ford could enjoy a substantial increase in sales, largely at the expense of its competitors. Or they might match Ford's price cut, in which case all of the firms will sell more cars, but might make much lower profits because of the lower prices. Another possibility is that some firms will cut their prices by *even more* than Ford to punish Ford for rocking the boat, and this in turn might lead to a price war and to a drastic fall in profits for the entire industry. Ford must carefully weigh all these possibilities. In fact, for almost any major economic decision that a firm makes—setting price, determining production levels, undertaking a major promotion campaign, or investing in new production capacity—it must try to determine the most likely response of its competitors.

These strategic considerations can be complex. When making decisions, each firm must weigh its competitors' reactions, knowing that these competitors will also weigh *its* reactions to *their* decisions. Furthermore, decisions, reactions, reactions to reactions, and so forth are dynamic, evolving over time. When the managers of a firm evaluate the potential consequences of their decisions, they must assume that their competitors are as rational and intelligent as they are. Then, they must put themselves in their competitors' place and consider how they would react.

## Equilibrium in an Oligopolistic Market

When we study a market, we usually want to determine the price and quantity that will prevail in equilibrium. For example, we saw that in a perfectly competitive market, the equilibrium price equates the quantity supplied with the quantity demanded. Then we saw that for a monopoly, an equilibrium occurs when marginal revenue equals marginal cost. Finally, when we studied monopolistic competition, we saw how a long-run equilibrium results as the entry of new firms drives profits to zero.

In these markets, each firm could take price or market demand as given and largely ignore its competitors. In an oligopolistic market, however, a firm sets price or output based partly on strategic considerations regarding the behavior of its competitors. At the same time, competitors' decisions depend on the first firm's decision. How, then, can we figure out what the market price and output will be in equilibrium—or whether there will even be an equilibrium? To answer these questions, we need an underlying principle to describe an equilibrium when firms make decisions that explicitly take each other's behavior into account.

Remember how we described an equilibrium in competitive and monopolistic markets: *When a market is in equilibrium, firms are doing the best they can and have no reason to change their price or output.* Thus a competitive market is in equilibrium when the quantity supplied equals the quantity demanded: Each firm is doing the best it can—it is selling all that it produces and is maximizing its profit. Likewise, a monopolist is in equilibrium when marginal revenue equals marginal cost because it, too, is doing the best it can and is maximizing its profit.

**Nash Equilibrium** With some modification, we can apply this same principle to an oligopolistic market. Now, however, each firm will want to do the best it can *given what its competitors are doing.* And what should the firm assume that its competitors are doing? Because the firm will do the best it can given what its competitors are doing, *it is natural to assume that these competitors will do the best they can given what that firm is doing.* Each firm, then, takes its competitors into account, and assumes that its competitors are doing likewise.

This may seem a bit abstract at first, but it is logical, and as we will see, it gives us a basis for determining an equilibrium in an oligopolistic market. The concept was first explained clearly by the mathematician John Nash in 1951, so we call the equilibrium it describes a **Nash equilibrium**. It is an important concept that we will use repeatedly:

> *Nash Equilibrium:* Each firm is doing the best it can given what its competitors are doing.

We discuss this equilibrium concept in more detail in Chapter 13, where we show how it can be applied to a broad range of strategic problems. In this chapter, we will apply it to the analysis of oligopolistic markets.

To keep things as uncomplicated as possible, this chapter will focus largely on markets in which two firms are competing with each other. We call such a market a **duopoly**. Thus each firm has just one competitor to take into account in making its decisions. Although we focus on duopolies, our basic results will also apply to markets with more than two firms.

## The Cournot Model

We will begin with a simple model of duopoly first introduced by the French economist Augustin Cournot in 1838. Suppose the firms produce a homogeneous good and know the market demand curve. *Each firm must decide how much to produce, and the two firms make their decisions at the same time.* When making its production decision, each firm takes its competitor into account. It knows that its competitor is *also* deciding how much to produce, and the market price will depend on the *total output* of both firms.

---

In §8.7, we explain that in a competitive market, long-run equilibrium occurs when no firm has an incentive to enter or exit because firms are earning zero economic profit and the quantity demanded is equal to the quantity supplied.

• **Nash equilibrium** Set of strategies or actions in which each firm does the best it can given its competitors' actions.

• **duopoly** Market in which two firms compete with each other.

Recall from §8.8 that when firms produce homogeneous or identical goods, consumers consider only price when making their purchasing decisions.

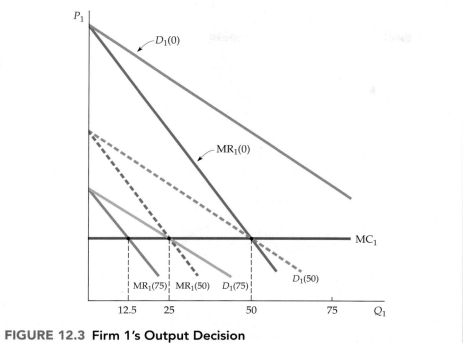

**FIGURE 12.3 Firm 1's Output Decision**

Firm 1's profit-maximizing output depends on how much it thinks that Firm 2 will produce. If it thinks Firm 2 will produce nothing, its demand curve, labeled $D_1(0)$, is the market demand curve. The corresponding marginal revenue curve, labeled $MR_1(0)$, intersects Firm 1's marginal cost curve $MC_1$ at an output of 50 units. If Firm 1 thinks that Firm 2 will produce 50 units, its demand curve, $D_1(50)$, is shifted to the left by this amount. Profit maximization now implies an output of 25 units. Finally, if Firm 1 thinks that Firm 2 will produce 75 units, Firm 1 will produce only 12.5 units.

The essence of the **Cournot model** is that *each firm treats the output level of its competitor as fixed when deciding how much to produce.* To see how this works, let's consider the output decision of Firm 1. Suppose Firm 1 thinks that Firm 2 will produce nothing. In that case, Firm 1's demand curve is the market demand curve. In Figure 12.3 this is shown as $D_1(0)$, which means the demand curve for Firm 1, assuming Firm 2 produces zero. Figure 12.3 also shows the corresponding marginal revenue curve $MR_1(0)$. We have assumed that Firm 1's marginal cost $MC_1$ is constant. As shown in the figure, Firm 1's profit-maximizing output is 50 units, the point where $MR_1(0)$ intersects $MC_1$. So if Firm 2 produces zero, Firm 1 should produce 50.

Suppose, instead, that Firm 1 thinks Firm 2 will produce 50 units. Then Firm 1's demand curve is the market demand curve shifted to the left by 50. In Figure 12.3, this curve is labeled $D_1(50)$, and the corresponding marginal revenue curve is labeled $MR_1(50)$. Firm 1's profit-maximizing output is now 25 units, the point where $MR_1(50) = MC_1$. Now, suppose Firm 1 thinks that Firm 2 will produce 75 units. Then Firm 1's demand curve is the market demand curve shifted to the left by 75. It is labeled $D_1(75)$ in Figure 12.3, and the corresponding marginal revenue curve is labeled $MR_1(75)$. Firm 1's profit-maximizing output is now 12.5 units, the point where $MR_1(75) = MC_1$. Finally, suppose Firm 1 thinks that Firm 2 will produce 100 units. Then Firm 1's demand and marginal revenue curves (which are not shown in the figure) would intersect its marginal cost

• **Cournot model** Oligopoly model in which firms produce a homogeneous good, each firm treats the output of its competitors as fixed, and all firms decide simultaneously how much to produce.

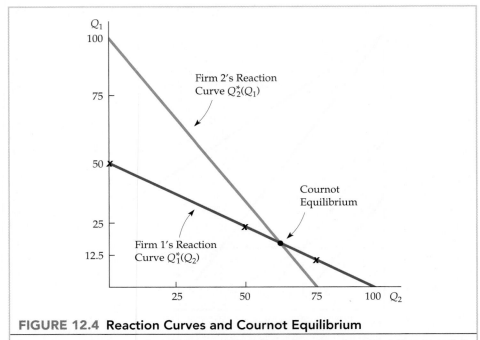

**FIGURE 12.4 Reaction Curves and Cournot Equilibrium**

Firm 1's reaction curve shows how much it will produce as a function of how much it thinks Firm 2 will produce. (The xs at $Q_2 = 0$, 50, and 75 correspond to the examples shown in Figure 12.3.) Firm 2's reaction curve shows its output as a function of how much it thinks Firm 1 will produce. In Cournot equilibrium, each firm correctly assumes the amount that its competitor will produce and thereby maximizes its own profits. Therefore, neither firm will move from this equilibrium.

curve on the vertical axis; if Firm 1 thinks that Firm 2 will produce 100 units or more, it should produce nothing.

**Reaction Curves** To summarize: If Firm 1 thinks that Firm 2 will produce nothing, it will produce 50; if it thinks Firm 2 will produce 50, it will produce 25; if it thinks Firm 2 will produce 75, it will produce 12.5; and if it thinks Firm 2 will produce 100, then it will produce nothing. *Firm 1's profit-maximizing output is thus a decreasing schedule of how much it thinks Firm 2 will produce.* We call this schedule Firm 1's **reaction curve** and denote it by $Q_1^*(Q_2)$. This curve is plotted in Figure 12.4, where each of the four output combinations that we found above is shown as an x.

We can go through the same kind of analysis for Firm 2; that is, we can determine Firm 2's profit-maximizing quantity given various assumptions about how much Firm 1 will produce. The result will be a reaction curve for Firm 2—i.e., a schedule $Q_2^*(Q_1)$ that relates its output to the output that it thinks Firm 1 will produce. If Firm 2's marginal revenue or marginal cost curve is different from that of Firm 1, its reaction curve will also differ in form. For example, Firm 2's reaction curve might look like the one drawn in Figure 12.4.

**Cournot Equilibrium** How much will each firm produce? Each firm's reaction curve tells it how much to produce, given the output of its competitor. In equilibrium, each firm sets output according to its own reaction curve; the equilibrium output levels are therefore found at the *intersection* of the two reaction curves. We call the resulting set of output levels a **Cournot equilibrium**. In this

• **reaction curve** Relationship between a firm's profit-maximizing output and the amount it thinks its competitor will produce.

• **Cournot equilibrium** Equilibrium in the Cournot model in which each firm correctly assumes how much its competitor will produce and sets its own production level accordingly.

equilibrium, each firm correctly assumes how much its competitor will produce, and it maximizes its profit accordingly.

Note that this Cournot equilibrium is an example of a Nash equilibrium (and thus it is sometimes called a *Cournot-Nash equilibrium*). Remember that in a Nash equilibrium, each firm is doing the best it can given what its competitors are doing. As a result, no firm would individually want to change its behavior. In the Cournot equilibrium, each firm is producing an amount that maximizes its profit *given what its competitor is producing*, so neither would want to change its output.

Suppose the two firms are initially producing output levels that differ from the Cournot equilibrium. Will they adjust their outputs until the Cournot equilibrium is reached? Unfortunately, the Cournot model says nothing about the dynamics of the adjustment process. In fact, during any adjustment process, the model's central assumption that each firm can assume that its competitor's output is fixed will not hold. Because both firms would be adjusting their outputs, neither output would be fixed. We need different models to understand dynamic adjustment, and we will examine some in Chapter 13.

When is it rational for each firm to assume that its competitor's output is fixed? It is rational if the two firms are choosing their outputs only once because then their outputs cannot change. It is also rational once they are in Cournot equilibrium because then neither firm will have any incentive to change its output. When using the Cournot model, we must therefore confine ourselves to the behavior of firms in equilibrium.

## The Linear Demand Curve—An Example

Let's work through an example—two identical firms facing a linear market demand curve. This will help clarify the meaning of a Cournot equilibrium and let us compare it with the competitive equilibrium and the equilibrium that results if the firms collude and choose their output levels cooperatively.

Suppose our duopolists face the following market demand curve:

$$P = 30 - Q$$

where $Q$ is the *total* production of both firms (i.e., $Q = Q_1 + Q_2$). Also, suppose that both firms have zero marginal cost:

$$MC_1 = MC_2 = 0$$

We can determine the reaction curve for Firm 1 as follows. To maximize profit, it sets marginal revenue equal to marginal cost. Its total revenue $R_1$ is given by

$$R_1 = PQ_1 = (30 - Q)Q_1$$
$$= 30Q_1 - (Q_1 + Q_2)Q_1$$
$$= 30Q_1 - Q_1^2 - Q_2Q_1$$

Its marginal revenue $MR_1$ is just the incremental revenue $\Delta R_1$ resulting from an incremental change in output $\Delta Q_1$:

$$MR_1 = \Delta R_1 / \Delta Q_1 = 30 - 2Q_1 - Q_2$$

Now, setting $MR_1$ equal to zero (the firm's marginal cost) and solving for $Q_1$, we find

$$\textit{Firm 1's reaction curve:} \quad Q_1 = 15 - \frac{1}{2}Q_2 \qquad \textbf{(12.1)}$$

The same calculation applies to Firm 2:

$$\text{Firm 2's reaction curve:} \quad Q_2 = 15 - \frac{1}{2}Q_1 \tag{12.2}$$

The equilibrium output levels are the values for $Q_1$ and $Q_2$ at the intersection of the two reaction curves—i.e., the levels that solve equations (12.1) and (12.2). By replacing $Q_2$ in equation (12.1) with the expression on the righthand side of (12.2), you can verify that the equilibrium output levels are

$$\text{Cournot equilibrium:} \quad Q_1 = Q_2 = 10$$

The total quantity produced is therefore $Q = Q_1 + Q_2 = 20$, so the equilibrium market price is $P = 30 - Q = 10$, and each firm earns a profit of 100.

Figure 12.5 shows the firms' reaction curves and this Cournot equilibrium. Note that Firm 1's reaction curve shows its output $Q_1$ in terms of Firm 2's output $Q_2$. Likewise, Firm 2's reaction curve shows $Q_2$ in terms of $Q_1$. (Because the firms are identical, the two reaction curves have the same form. They look different because one gives $Q_1$ in terms of $Q_2$ and the other gives $Q_2$ in terms of $Q_1$.)

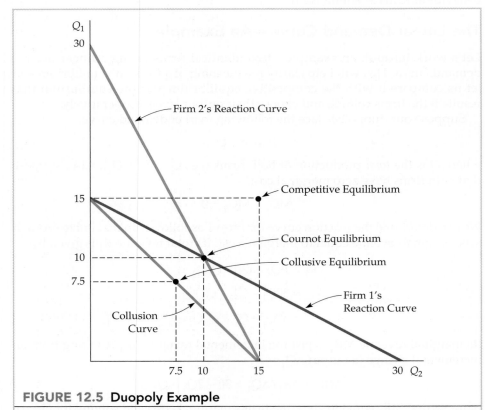

**FIGURE 12.5 Duopoly Example**

The demand curve is $P = 30 - Q$, and both firms have zero marginal cost. In Cournot equilibrium, each firm produces 10. The collusion curve shows combinations of $Q_1$ and $Q_2$ that maximize *total* profits. If the firms collude and share profits equally, each will produce 7.5. Also shown is the competitive equilibrium, in which price equals marginal cost and profit is zero.

The Cournot equilibrium is at the intersection of the two curves. At this point, each firm is maximizing its own profit, given its competitor's output.

We have assumed that the two firms compete with each other. Suppose, instead, that the antitrust laws were relaxed and the two firms could collude. They would set their outputs to maximize *total profit*, and presumably they would split that profit evenly. Total profit is maximized by choosing total output $Q$ so that marginal revenue equals marginal cost, which in this example is zero. Total revenue for the two firms is

$$R = PQ = (30 - Q)Q = 30Q - Q^2$$

Marginal revenue is therefore

$$MR = \Delta R / \Delta Q = 30 - 2Q$$

Setting MR equal to zero, we see that total profit is maximized when $Q = 15$.

Any combination of outputs $Q_1$ and $Q_2$ that add up to 15 maximizes total profit. The curve $Q_1 + Q_2 = 15$, called the *collusion curve*, therefore gives all pairs of outputs $Q_1$ and $Q_2$ that maximize total profit. This curve is also shown in Figure 12.5. If the firms agree to share profits equally, each will produce half of the total output:

$$Q_1 = Q_2 = 7.5$$

As you would expect, both firms now produce less—and earn higher profits (112.50)—than in the Cournot equilibrium. Figure 12.5 shows this collusive equilibrium and the *competitive* output levels found by setting price equal to marginal cost. (You can verify that they are $Q_1 = Q_2 = 15$, which implies that each firm makes zero profit.) Note that the Cournot outcome is much better (for the firms) than perfect competition, but not as good as the outcome from collusion.

## First Mover Advantage—The Stackelberg Model

We have assumed that our two duopolists make their output decisions at the same time. Now let's see what happens if one of the firms can set its output first. There are two questions of interest. First, is it advantageous to go first? Second, how much will each firm produce?

Continuing with our example, we assume that both firms have zero marginal cost, and that market demand is given by $P = 30 - Q$, where $Q$ is total output. *Suppose Firm 1 sets its output first and then Firm 2, after observing Firm 1's output, makes its output decision.* In setting output, *Firm 1 must therefore consider how Firm 2 will react*. This **Stackelberg model** of duopoly is different from the Cournot model, in which neither firm has any opportunity to react.

* **Stackelberg model** Oligopoly model in which one firm sets its output before other firms do.

Let's begin with Firm 2. Because it makes its output decision *after* Firm 1, it takes Firm 1's output as fixed. Therefore, Firm 2's profit-maximizing output is given by its Cournot reaction curve, which we derived above as equation (12.2):

*Firm 2's reaction curve:* $\quad Q_2 = 15 - \dfrac{1}{2}Q_1$ **(12.2)**

What about Firm 1? To maximize profit, it chooses $Q_1$ so that its marginal revenue equals its marginal cost of zero. Recall that Firm 1's revenue is

$$R_1 = PQ_1 = 30Q_1 - Q_1^2 - Q_2Q_1$$ **(12.3)**

Because $R_1$ depends on $Q_2$, Firm 1 must anticipate how much Firm 2 will produce. Firm 1 knows, however, that Firm 2 will choose $Q_2$ according to the reaction curve (12.2). Substituting equation (12.2) for $Q_2$ into equation (12.3), we find that Firm 1's revenue is

$$R_1 = 30Q_1 - Q_1^2 - Q_1\left(15 - \frac{1}{2}Q_1\right)$$

$$= 15Q_1 - \frac{1}{2}Q_1^2$$

Its marginal revenue is therefore

$$\text{MR}_1 = \Delta R_1/\Delta Q_1 = 15 - Q_1 \qquad\qquad \textbf{(12.4)}$$

Setting $\text{MR}_1 = 0$ gives $Q_1 = 15$. And from Firm 2's reaction curve (12.2), we find that $Q_2 = 7.5$. Firm 1 produces twice as much as Firm 2 and makes twice as much profit. *Going first gives Firm 1 an advantage.* This may appear counterintuitive: It seems disadvantageous to announce your output first. Why, then, is going first a strategic advantage?

The reason is that announcing first creates a *fait accompli*: No matter what your competitor does, your output will be large. To maximize profit, your competitor must take your large output level as given and set a low level of output for itself. If your competitor produced a large level of output, it would drive price down and you would both lose money. So unless your competitor views "getting even" as more important than making money, it would be irrational for it to produce a large amount. As we will see in Chapter 13, this kind of "first-mover advantage" occurs in many strategic situations.

The Cournot and Stackelberg models are alternative representations of oligopolistic behavior. Which model is the more appropriate depends on the industry. For an industry composed of roughly similar firms, none of which has a strong operating advantage or leadership position, the Cournot model is probably the more appropriate. On the other hand, some industries are dominated by a large firm that usually takes the lead in introducing new products or setting price; the mainframe computer market is an example, with IBM the leader. Then the Stackelberg model may be more realistic.

## 12.3 PRICE COMPETITION

We have assumed that our oligopolistic firms compete by setting quantities. In many oligopolistic industries, however, competition occurs along price dimensions. For example, automobile companies view price as a key strategic variable, and each one chooses its price with its competitors in mind. In this section, we use the Nash equilibrium concept to study price competition, first in an industry that produces a homogeneous good and then in an industry with some degree of product differentiation.

### Price Competition with Homogeneous Products—The Bertrand Model

• **Bertrand model** Oligopoly model in which firms produce a homogeneous good, each firm treats the price of its competitors as fixed, and all firms decide simultaneously what price to charge.

The **Bertrand model** was developed in 1883 by another French economist, Joseph Bertrand. Like the Cournot model, it applies to firms that produce the same homogeneous good and make their decisions at the same time. In this case, however, the firms choose *prices* instead of quantities. As we will see, this change can dramatically affect the market outcome.

Let's return to the duopoly example of the last section, in which the market demand curve is

$$P = 30 - Q$$

where $Q = Q_1 + Q_2$ is again total production of a homogeneous good. This time, however, we will assume that both firms have a marginal cost of $3:

$$MC_1 = MC_2 = \$3$$

As an exercise, you can show that the Cournot equilibrium for this duopoly, which results when both firms choose *output* simultaneously, is $Q_1 = Q_2 = 9$. You can also check that in this Cournot equilibrium, the market price is $12, so that each firm makes a profit of $81.

Now suppose that these two duopolists compete by simultaneously choosing a *price* instead of a quantity. What price will each firm choose, and how much profit will each earn? To answer these questions, note that because the good is homogeneous, consumers will purchase only from the lowest-price seller. Thus, if the two firms charge different prices, the lower-price firm will supply the entire market and the higher-price firm will sell nothing. If both firms charge the same price, consumers will be indifferent as to which firm they buy from and each firm will supply half the market.

What is the Nash equilibrium in this case? If you think about this problem a little, you will see that because of the incentive to cut prices, the Nash equilibrium is the competitive outcome—i.e., both firms set price equal to marginal cost: $P_1 = P_2 = \$3$. Then industry output is 27 units, of which each firm produces 13.5 units. And because price equals marginal cost, both firms earn zero profit. To check that this outcome is a Nash equilibrium, ask whether either firm would have any incentive to change its price. Suppose Firm 1 raised its price. It would then lose all of its sales to Firm 2 and therefore be no better off. If, instead, it lowered its price, it would capture the entire market but would lose money on every unit it produced; again, it would be worse off. Therefore, Firm 1 (and likewise Firm 2) has no incentive to deviate: It is doing the best it can to maximize profit, given what its competitor is doing.

Why couldn't there be a Nash equilibrium in which the firms charged the same price, but a higher one (say, $5), so that each made some profit? Because if either firm lowered its price just a little, it could capture the entire market and nearly double its profit. Thus each firm would want to undercut its competitor. Such undercutting would continue until the price dropped to $3.

By changing the strategic choice variable from output to price, we get a dramatically different outcome. In the Cournot model, because each firm produces only 9 units, the market price is $12. Now the market price is $3. In the Cournot model, each firm made a profit; in the Bertrand model, the firms price at marginal cost and make no profit.

The Bertrand model has been criticized on several counts. First, when firms produce a homogeneous good, it is more natural to compete by setting quantities rather than prices. Second, even if firms do set prices *and* choose the same price (as the model predicts), what share of total sales will go to each one? We *assumed* that sales would be divided equally among the firms, but there is no reason why this must be the case. Despite these shortcomings, the Bertrand model is useful because it shows how the equilibrium outcome in an oligopoly can depend crucially on the firms' choice of strategic variable.[2]

## Price Competition with Differentiated Products

Oligopolistic markets often have at least some degree of product differentiation.[3] Market shares are determined not just by prices, but also by differences in the design, performance, and durability of each firm's product. In such cases, it is natural for firms to compete by choosing prices rather than quantities.

To see how price competition with differentiated products can work, let's go through the following simple example. Suppose each of two duopolists has fixed costs of $20 but zero variable costs, and that they face the same demand curves:

$$\text{Firm 1's demand:} \quad Q_1 = 12 - 2P_1 + P_2 \qquad \textbf{(12.5a)}$$

$$\text{Firm 2's demand:} \quad Q_2 = 12 - 2P_2 + P_1 \qquad \textbf{(12.5b)}$$

where $P_1$ and $P_2$ are the prices that Firms 1 and 2 charge, respectively, and $Q_1$ and $Q_2$ are the resulting quantities that they sell. Note that the quantity that each firm can sell decreases when it raises its own price but increases when its competitor charges a higher price.

**Choosing Prices** We will assume that both firms set their prices at the same time and that each firm takes its competitor's price as fixed. We can therefore use the Nash equilibrium concept to determine the resulting prices. Let's begin with Firm 1. Its profit $\pi_1$ is its revenue $P_1 Q_1$ less its fixed cost of $20. Substituting for $Q_1$ from the demand curve of equation (12.5a), we have

$$\pi_1 = P_1 Q_1 - 20 = 12P_1 - 2P_1^2 + P_1 P_2 - 20$$

At what price $P_1$ is this profit maximized? The answer depends on $P_2$, which Firm 1 assumes to be fixed. However, whatever price Firm 2 is charging, Firm 1's profit is maximized when the incremental profit from a very small increase in its own price is just zero. Taking $P_2$ as fixed, Firm 1's profit-maximizing price is therefore given by

$$\Delta\pi_1 / \Delta P_1 = 12 - 4P_1 + P_2 = 0$$

This equation can be rewritten to give the following pricing rule, or *reaction curve*, for Firm 1:

$$\text{Firm 1's reaction curve:} \quad P_1 = 3 + \frac{1}{4}P_2$$

This equation tells Firm 1 what price to set, given the price $P_2$ that Firm 2 is setting. We can similarly find the following pricing rule for Firm 2:

$$\text{Firm 2's reaction curve:} \quad P_2 = 3 + \frac{1}{4}P_1$$

---

[2]Also, it has been shown that if firms produce a homogeneous good and compete by first setting output *capacities* and then setting price, the Cournot equilibrium in quantities again results. See David Kreps and Jose Scheinkman, "Quantity Precommitment and Bertrand Competition Yield Cournot Outcomes," *Bell Journal of Economics* 14 (1983): 326–38.

[3]Product differentiation can exist even for a seemingly homogeneous product. Consider gasoline, for example. Although gasoline itself is a homogeneous good, service stations differ in terms of location and services provided. As a result, gasoline prices may differ from one service station to another.

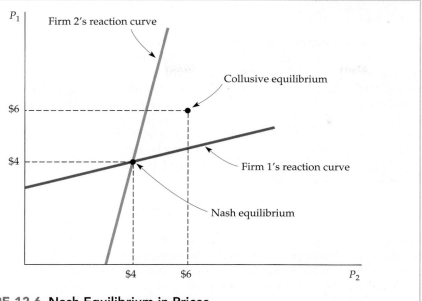

**FIGURE 12.6 Nash Equilibrium in Prices**

Here two firms sell a differentiated product, and each firm's demand depends both on its own price and on its competitor's price. The two firms choose their prices at the same time, each taking its competitor's price as given. Firm 1's reaction curve gives its profit-maximizing price as a function of the price that Firm 2 sets, and similarly for Firm 2. The Nash equilibrium is at the intersection of the two reaction curves: When each firm charges a price of $4, it is doing the best it can given its competitor's price and has no incentive to change price. Also shown is the collusive equilibrium: If the firms cooperatively set price, they will choose $6.

These reaction curves are drawn in Figure 12.6. The Nash equilibrium is at the point where the two reaction curves cross; you can verify that each firm is then charging a price of $4 and earning a profit of $12. *At this point, because each firm is doing the best it can given the price its competitor has set, neither firm has an incentive to change its price.*

Now suppose the two firms collude: Instead of choosing their prices independently, they both decide to charge the same price—namely, the price that maximizes both of their profits. You can verify that the firms would then charge $6, and that they would be better off colluding because each would now earn a profit of $16.[4] Figure 12.6 shows this collusive equilibrium.

Finally, suppose Firm 1 sets its price first and that, after observing Firm 1's decision, Firm 2 makes its pricing decision. Unlike the Stackelberg model in which the firms set their quantities, in this case Firm 1 would be at a distinct *disadvantage* by moving first. (To see this, calculate Firm 1's profit-maximizing price, *taking Firm 2's reaction curve into account*.) Why is moving first now a disadvantage? Because it gives the firm that moves second an opportunity to undercut slightly and thereby capture a larger market share. (See Exercise 11 at the end of the chapter.)

---

[4]The firms have the same costs, so they will charge the same price $P$. Total profit is given by

$$\pi_T = \pi_1 + \pi_2 = 24P - 4P^2 + 2P^2 - 40 = 24P - 2P^2 - 40.$$

This is maximized when $\Delta\pi_T/\Delta P = 0$. $\Delta\pi_T/\Delta P = 24 - 4P$, so the joint profit-maximizing price is $P = \$6$. Each firm's profit is therefore

$$\pi_1 = \pi_2 = 12P - P^2 - 20 = 72 - 36 - 20 = \$16$$

---

**EXAMPLE 12.2**     A Pricing Problem for Procter & Gamble

When Procter & Gamble (P&G) planned to enter the Japanese market for Gypsy Moth Tape, it knew its production costs and understood the market demand curve but found it hard to determine the right price to charge because two other firms—Kao Soap, Ltd., and Unilever, Ltd.—were also planning to enter the market. All three firms would be choosing their prices at about the same time, and P&G had to take this into account when setting its own price.[5]

Because all three firms were using the same technology for producing Gypsy Moth Tape, they had the same production costs. Each firm faced a fixed cost of $480,000 per month and a variable cost of $1 per unit. From market research, P&G ascertained that its demand curve for monthly sales was

$$Q = 3375P^{-3.5}(P_U)^{.25}(P_K)^{.25}$$

where $Q$ is monthly sales in thousands of units, and $P$, $P_U$, and $P_K$ are P&G's, Unilever's, and Kao's prices, respectively. Now, put yourself in P&G's position. Assuming that Unilever and Kao face the same demand conditions, *with what price should you enter the market, and how much profit should you expect to earn?*

You might begin by calculating the profit you would earn as a function of the price you charge, under alternative assumptions about the prices that Unilever and Kao will charge. Using the demand curve and cost numbers given above, we have done these calculations and tabulated the results in Table 12.2. Each entry shows your profit, in thousands of dollars per month, for a particular combination of prices (while assuming in each case that Unilever and Kao set the same price). For example, if you charge $1.30 and Unilever and Kao both charge $1.50, you will earn a profit of $15,000 per month.

But remember that in all likelihood, the managers of Unilever and Kao are making the same calculations that you are and probably have their own versions of Table 12.2. Now suppose your competitors charge $1.50 or more. As the table

**TABLE 12.2**   P&G's Profit (in thousands of dollars per month)

| P&G's Price ($) | Competitor's (Equal) Prices ($) | | | | | | | |
|---|---|---|---|---|---|---|---|---|
| | 1.10 | 1.20 | 1.30 | 1.40 | 1.50 | 1.60 | 1.70 | 1.80 |
| 1.10 | −226 | −215 | −204 | −194 | −183 | −174 | −165 | −155 |
| 1.20 | −106 | −89 | −73 | −58 | −43 | −28 | −15 | −2 |
| 1.30 | −56 | −37 | −19 | 2 | 15 | 31 | 47 | 62 |
| 1.40 | −44 | −25 | −6 | 12 | 29 | 46 | 62 | 78 |
| 1.50 | −52 | −32 | −15 | 3 | 20 | 36 | 52 | 68 |
| 1.60 | −70 | −51 | −34 | −18 | −1 | 14 | 30 | 44 |
| 1.70 | −93 | −76 | −59 | −44 | −28 | −13 | 1 | 15 |
| 1.80 | −118 | −102 | −87 | −72 | −57 | −44 | −30 | −17 |

---

[5]This example is based on classroom material developed by Professor John Hauser of MIT. To protect P&G's proprietary interests, some of the facts about the product and the market have been altered. The fundamental description of P&G's problem, however, is accurate.

shows, you would want to charge only $1.40, because that price gives you the highest profit. (For example, if they charged $1.50, you would make $29,000 per month by charging $1.40 but only $20,000 by charging $1.50, and $15,000 by charging $1.30.) Consequently, you would not want to charge $1.50 (or more). Assuming that your competitors have followed the same reasoning, you should not expect them to charge $1.50 (or more) either.

What if your competitors charge $1.30? In that case, you will lose money, but you will lose the least amount of money ($6000 per month) by charging $1.40. Your competitors would therefore not expect you to charge $1.30, and by the same reasoning, you should not expect them to charge a price this low. What price lets you do the best you can, given your competitors' prices? It is $1.40. This is also the price at which your competitors are doing the best *they* can, so it is a Nash equilibrium.[6] As the table shows, in this equilibrium you and your competitors each make a profit of $12,000 per month.

If you could *collude* with your competitors, you could make a larger profit. You would all agree to charge $1.50, and each of you would earn $20,000. But this collusive agreement might be hard to enforce: You could increase your profit further at your competitor's expense by dropping your price below theirs, and of course your competitors could do the same thing to you.

## 12.4 COMPETITION VERSUS COLLUSION: THE PRISONERS' DILEMMA

A Nash equilibrium is a *noncooperative* equilibrium: Each firm makes the decisions that give it the highest possible profit, given the actions of its competitors. As we have seen, the resulting profit earned by each firm is higher than it would be under perfect competition but lower than if the firms colluded.

Collusion, however, is illegal, and most managers prefer to stay out of jail. But if cooperation can lead to higher profits, why don't firms cooperate *without* explicitly colluding? In particular, if you and your competitor can both figure out the profit-maximizing price you would agree to charge *if* you were to collude, *why not just set that price and hope your competitor will do the same*? If your competitor *does* do the same, you will both make more money.

The problem is that your competitor *probably won't* choose to set price at the collusive level. Why not? *Because your competitor would do better by choosing a lower price, even if it knew that you were going to set price at the collusive level.*

To understand this, let's go back to our example of price competition from the last section. The firms in that example each have a fixed cost of $20, have zero variable cost, and face the following demand curves:

$$Firm\ 1's\ demand: \quad Q_1 = 12 - 2P_1 + P_2$$
$$Firm\ 2's\ demand: \quad Q_2 = 12 - 2P_2 + P_1$$

We found that in the Nash equilibrium each firm will charge a price of $4 and earn a profit of $12, whereas if the firms collude, they will charge a price of $6 and earn a profit of $16. Now suppose that the firms do not collude, but that

---

[6]This Nash equilibrium can also be derived algebraically from the demand curve and cost data above. We leave this to you as an exercise.

Firm 1 charges the $6 collusive price, hoping that Firm 2 will do the same. If Firm 2 *does* do the same, it will earn a profit of $16. But what if it charges the $4 price instead? In that case, Firm 2 would earn a profit of

$$\pi_2 = P_2Q_2 - 20 = (4)[12 - (2)(4) + 6] - 20 = \$20$$

Firm 1, on the other hand, will earn a profit of only

$$\pi_1 = P_1Q_1 - 20 = (6)[12 - (2)(6) + 4] - 20 = \$4$$

So if Firm 1 charges $6 but Firm 2 charges only $4, Firm 2's profit will increase to $20. And it will do so at the expense of Firm 1's profit, which will fall to $4. Clearly, Firm 2 does best by charging only $4. Similarly, Firm 1 does best by charging only $4. If Firm 2 charges $6 and Firm 1 charges $4, Firm 1 will earn a $20 profit and Firm 2 only $4.

**Payoff Matrix**  Table 12.3 summarizes the results of these different possibilities. In deciding what price to set, the two firms are playing a **noncooperative game**: Each firm independently does the best it can, taking its competitor into account. Table 12.3 is called the **payoff matrix** for this game because it shows the profit (or payoff) to each firm given its decision and the decision of its competitor. For example, the upper left-hand corner of the payoff matrix tells us that if both firms charge $4, each will make a $12 profit. The upper right-hand corner tells us that if Firm 1 charges $4 and Firm 2 charges $6, Firm 1 will make $20 and Firm 2 $4.

This payoff matrix can clarify the answer to our original question: Why don't firms behave cooperatively, and thereby earn higher profits, even if they can't collude? In this case, cooperating means *both* firms charging $6 instead of $4 and thereby earning $16 instead of $12. The problem is that each firm always makes more money by charging $4, *no matter what its competitor does*. As the payoff matrix shows, if Firm 2 charges $4, Firm 1 does best by charging $4. And if Firm 2 charges $6, Firm 1 still does best by charging $4. Similarly, Firm 2 always does best by charging $4, no matter what Firm 1 does. As a result, unless the two firms can sign an enforceable agreement to charge $6, neither firm can expect its competitor to charge $6, and both will charge $4.

**The Prisoners' Dilemma**  A classic example in game theory, called the **prisoners' dilemma**, illustrates the problem faced by oligopolistic firms. It goes as follows: Two prisoners have been accused of collaborating in a crime. They are in separate jail cells and cannot communicate with each other. Each has been asked to confess. If both prisoners confess, each will receive a prison term of five years. If neither confesses, the prosecution's case will be difficult to make, so the prisoners can expect to plea bargain and receive terms of two years. On the other hand, if one prisoner confesses and the other does not, the one who confesses will receive a term of only one year, while the other will go to prison for 10 years. If you were one of these prisoners, what would you do—confess or not confess?

**• noncooperative game**  Game in which negotiation and enforcement of binding contracts are not possible.

**• payoff matrix**  Table showing profit (or payoff) to each firm given its decision and the decision of its competitor.

**• prisoners' dilemma**  Game theory example in which two prisoners must decide separately whether to confess to a crime; if a prisoner confesses, he will receive a lighter sentence and his accomplice will receive a heavier one, but if neither confesses, sentences will be lighter than if both confess.

| TABLE 12.3  Payoff Matrix for Pricing Game | | |
|---|---|---|
| | **Firm 2** | |
| | **Charge $4** | **Charge $6** |
| **Firm 1**  Charge $4 | $12, $12 | $20, $4 |
| Charge $6 | $4, $20 | $16, $16 |

| TABLE 12.4 | Payoff Matrix for Prisoners' Dilemma | | |
|---|---|---|---|
| | | **Prisoner B** | |
| | | **Confess** | **Don't confess** |
| **Prisoner A** | Confess | −5, −5 | −1, −10 |
| | Don't confess | −10, −1 | −2, −2 |

The payoff matrix in Table 12.4 summarizes the possible outcomes. (Note that the "payoffs" are negative; the entry in the lower right-hand corner means a two-year sentence for each prisoner.) As the table shows, our prisoners face a dilemma. If they could both agree not to confess (in a way that would be binding), then each would go to jail for only two years. But they can't talk to each other, and even if they could, can they trust each other? If Prisoner *A* does not confess, he risks being taken advantage of by his former accomplice. After all, *no matter what Prisoner* A *does, Prisoner* B *comes out ahead by confessing*. Likewise, Prisoner *A* always comes out ahead by confessing, so Prisoner *B* must worry that by not confessing, she will be taken advantage of. Therefore, both prisoners will probably confess and go to jail for five years.

Oligopolistic firms often find themselves in a prisoners' dilemma. They must decide whether to compete aggressively, attempting to capture a larger share of the market at their competitor's expense, or to "cooperate" and compete more passively, coexisting with their competitors and settling for their current market share, and perhaps even implicitly colluding. If the firms compete passively, setting high prices and limiting output, they will make higher profits than if they compete aggressively.

Like our prisoners, however, each firm has an incentive to "fink" and undercut its competitors, and each knows that its competitors have the same incentive. As desirable as cooperation is, each firm worries—with good reason—that if it competes passively, its competitor might decide to compete aggressively and seize the lion's share of the market. In the pricing problem illustrated in Table 12.3, both firms do better by "cooperating" and charging a high price. But the firms are in a prisoners' dilemma, where neither can trust its competitor to set a high price.

**EXAMPLE 12.3**   Procter & Gamble in a Prisoners' Dilemma

In Example 12.2, we examined the problem that arose when P&G, Unilever, and Kao Soap all planned to enter the Japanese market for Gypsy Moth Tape at the same time. They all faced the same cost and demand conditions, and each firm had to decide on a price that took its competitors into account. In Table 12.2, (page 460) we tabulated the profits to P&G corresponding to alternative prices that the firm and its competitors might charge. We argued that P&G should expect its competitors to charge a price of $1.40 and should do the same.[7]

---

[7]As in Example 12.2, some of the facts about the product and the market have been altered to protect P&G's proprietary interests.

P&G would be better off if it *and its competitors* all charged a price of $1.50. This is clear from the payoff matrix in Table 12.5. This payoff matrix is the portion of Table 12.2 corresponding to prices of $1.40 and $1.50, with the payoffs to P&G's competitors also tabulated.[8] If all the firms charge $1.50, each will make a profit of $20,000 per month, instead of the $12,000 per month they make by charging $1.40. So why don't they charge $1.50?

Because these firms are in a prisoners' dilemma. No matter what Unilever and Kao do, P&G makes more money by charging $1.40. For example, if Unilever and Kao charge $1.50, P&G can make $29,000 per month by charging $1.40, versus $20,000 by charging $1.50. Unilever and Kao are in the same boat. For example, if P&G charges $1.50 and Unilever and Kao both charge $1.40, P&G's competitors will each make $21,000, instead of $20,000.[9] As a result, P&G knows that if it sets a price of $1.50, its competitors will have a strong incentive to undercut and charge $1.40. P&G will then have only a small share of the market and make only $3000 per month profit. Should P&G make a leap of faith and charge $1.50? If you were faced with this dilemma, what would you do?

**TABLE 12.5** Payoff Matrix for Pricing Problem

|  |  | Unilever and KAO | |
| --- | --- | --- | --- |
|  |  | Charge $1.40 | Charge $1.50 |
| **P&G** | Charge $1.40 | $12, $12 | $29, $11 |
|  | Charge $1.50 | $3, $21 | $20, $20 |

## 12.5 IMPLICATIONS OF THE PRISONERS' DILEMMA FOR OLIGOPOLISTIC PRICING

Does the prisoners' dilemma doom oligopolistic firms to aggressive competition and low profits? Not necessarily. Although our imaginary prisoners have only one opportunity to confess, most firms set output and price over and over again, continually observing their competitors' behavior and adjusting their own accordingly. This allows firms to develop reputations from which trust can arise. As a result, oligopolistic coordination and cooperation can sometimes prevail.

Take, for example, an industry made up of three or four firms that have coexisted for a long time. Over the years, the managers of those firms might grow tired of losing money because of price wars, and an implicit understanding might arise by which all the firms maintain high prices and no firm tries to take market share from its competitors. Although each firm might be tempted to undercut its competitors, its managers know that the resulting gains will be short lived: Competitors will retaliate, and the result will be renewed warfare and lower profits over the long run.

---

[8]This payoff matrix assumes that Unilever and Kao both charge the same price. Entries represent profits in thousands of dollars per month.

[9]If P&G and Kao both charged $1.50 and *only* Unilever undercut and charged $1.40, Unilever would make $29,000 per month. It is especially profitable to be the only firm charging the low price.

This resolution of the prisoners' dilemma occurs in some industries, but not in others. Sometimes managers are not content with the moderately high profits resulting from implicit collusion and prefer to compete aggressively in order to increase market share. Sometimes implicit understandings are difficult to reach. For example, firms with different costs and different assessments of market demand might disagree about the "correct" collusive price. Firm *A* might think the "correct" price is $10, while Firm *B* thinks it is $9. When it sets a $9 price, Firm *A* might view this as an attempt to undercut and retaliate by lowering its price to $8. The result is a price war.

In many industries, therefore, implicit collusion is short lived. There is often a fundamental layer of mistrust, so warfare erupts as soon as one firm is perceived by its competitors to be "rocking the boat" by changing its price or increasing advertising.

## Price Rigidity

Because implicit collusion tends to be fragile, oligopolistic firms often have a strong desire for price stability. This is why **price rigidity** can be a characteristic of oligopolistic industries. Even if costs or demand change, firms are reluctant to change price. If costs fall or market demand declines, they fear that lower prices might send the wrong message to their competitors and set off a price war. And if costs or demand rises, they are reluctant to raise prices because they are afraid that their competitors may not raise theirs.

Price rigidity is the basis of the **kinked demand curve model** of oligopoly. According to this model, each firm faces a demand curve kinked at the currently prevailing price $P^*$. (See Figure 12.7.) At prices above $P^*$, the demand curve is very elastic. The reason is that the firm believes that if it raises its price above $P^*$, other firms will not follow suit, and it will therefore lose sales and much of its market share. On the other hand, the firm believes that if it lowers its price below $P^*$, other firms will follow suit because they will not want to lose *their* shares of the market. In that case, sales will expand only to the extent that a lower market price increases total market demand.

Because the firm's demand curve is kinked, its marginal revenue curve is discontinuous. (The bottom part of the marginal revenue curve corresponds to the less elastic part of the demand curve, as shown by the solid portions of each curve.) As a result, the firm's costs can change without resulting in a change in price. As shown in Figure 12.7, marginal cost could increase but still equal marginal revenue at the same output level, so that price stays the same.

Although the kinked demand curve model is attractively simple, it does not really explain oligopolistic pricing. It says nothing about how firms arrived at price $P^*$ in the first place, and why they didn't arrive at some different price. It is useful mainly as a *description* of price rigidity rather than as an *explanation* of it. The explanation for price rigidity comes from the prisoners' dilemma and from firms' desires to avoid mutually destructive price competition.

## Price Signaling and Price Leadership

A big impediment to implicitly collusive pricing is the fact that it is difficult for firms to agree (without talking to each other) on what the price should be. Coordination is particularly difficult when cost and demand conditions—and thus the "correct" price—are changing. **Price signaling** is a form of implicit collusion that sometimes gets around this problem. For example, a firm might announce that it has raised its price (perhaps through a press release) and hope

* **price rigidity** Characteristic of oligopolistic markets by which firms are reluctant to change prices even if costs or demands change.

* **kinked demand curve model** Oligopoly model in which each firm faces a demand curve kinked at the currently prevailing price: at higher prices demand is very elastic, whereas at lower prices it is inelastic.

* **price signaling** Form of implicit collusion in which a firm announces a price increase in the hope that other firms will follow suit.

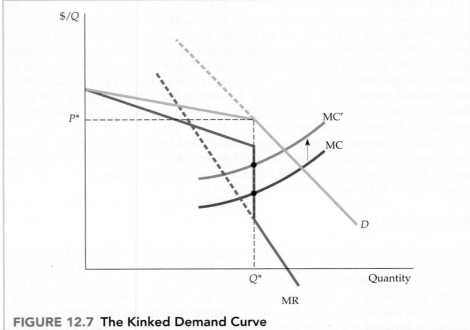

**FIGURE 12.7 The Kinked Demand Curve**

Each firm believes that if it raises its price above the current price P*, none of its competitors will follow suit, so it will lose most of its sales. Each firm also believes that if it lowers price, everyone will follow suit, and its sales will increase only to the extent that market demand increases. As a result, the firm's demand curve D is kinked at price P*, and its marginal revenue curve MR is discontinuous at that point. If marginal cost increases from MC to MC', the firm will still produce the same output level Q* and charge the same price P*.

that its competitors will take this announcement as a signal that they should also raise prices. If competitors follow suit, all of the firms will earn higher profits.

Sometimes a pattern is established whereby one firm regularly announces price changes and other firms in the industry follow suit. This pattern is called **price leadership**: One firm is implicitly recognized as the "leader," while the other firms, the "price followers," match its prices. This behavior solves the problem of coordinating price: Everyone charges what the leader is charging.

Suppose, for example, that three oligopolistic firms are currently charging $10 for their product. (If they all know the market demand curve, this might be the Nash equilibrium price.) Suppose that by colluding, they could all set a price of $20 and greatly increase their profits. Meeting and agreeing to set a price of $20 is illegal. But suppose instead that Firm A raises its price to $15, and announces to the business press that it is doing so because higher prices are needed to restore economic vitality to the industry. Firms B and C might view this as a clear message—namely, that Firm A is seeking their cooperation in raising prices. They might then raise their own prices to $15. Firm A might then increase price further—say, to $18—and Firms B and C might raise their prices as well. Whether or not the profit-maximizing price of $20 is reached (or surpassed), a pattern of

• **price leadership** Pattern of pricing in which one firm regularly announces price changes that other firms then match.

coordination has been established that, from the firm's point of view, may be nearly as effective as meeting and formally agreeing on a price.[10]

This example of signaling and price leadership is extreme and might lead to an antitrust lawsuit. But in some industries, a large firm might naturally emerge as a leader, with the other firms deciding that they are best off just matching the leader's prices, rather than trying to undercut the leader or each other. An example is the U.S. automobile industry, where General Motors has traditionally been the price leader.

Price leadership can also serve as a way for oligopolistic firms to deal with the reluctance to change prices, a reluctance that arises out of the fear of being undercut or "rocking the boat." As cost and demand conditions change, firms may find it increasingly necessary to change prices that have remained rigid for some time. In that case, they might look to a price leader to signal when and by how much price should change. Sometimes a large firm will naturally act as leader; sometimes different firms will act as leader from time to time. The example that follows illustrates this.

---

**EXAMPLE 12.4** Price Leadership and Price Rigidity in Commercial Banking

Commercial banks borrow money from individuals and companies who deposit funds in checking accounts, savings accounts, and certificates of deposit. They then use this money to make loans to household and corporate borrowers. By lending at an interest rate higher than the rate that they pay on their deposits, they earn a profit.

The largest commercial banks in the United States compete with each other to make loans to large corporate clients. The main form of competition is over price—in this case, the interest rates they charge. If competition becomes aggressive, the interest rates fall, and so do profits. The incentive to avoid aggressive competition leads to price rigidity, and to a form of price leadership.

The interest rate that banks charge large corporate clients is called the *prime rate*. Because it is widely known, it is a convenient focal point for price leadership. Most large banks charge the same or nearly the same prime rate; they avoid making frequent changes in the rate that might be destabilizing and lead to competitive warfare. The prime rate changes only when money market conditions cause other interest rates to rise or fall substantially. When that happens, one of the major banks announces a change in its rate and other banks quickly follow suit. Different banks act as leader from time to time, but when one bank announces a change, the others follow within two or three days.

Figure 12.8 compares the prime rate with the interest rate on high-grade (AAA) corporate bonds. Observe that although the corporate bond rate fluctuated continuously, there were extended periods during which the prime rate did the change. This is an example of price rigidity—banks are reluctant to change their lending rate for fear of being undercut and losing business to their competitors.

---

[10]For a formal model of how such price leadership can facilitate collusion, see Julio J. Rotemberg and Garth Saloner, "Collusive Price Leadership," *Journal of Industrial Economics*, 1990.

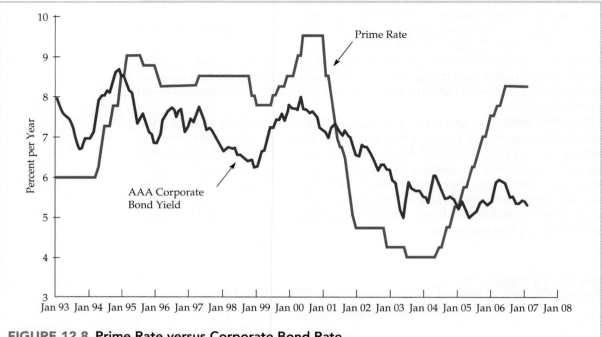

**FIGURE 12.8 Prime Rate versus Corporate Bond Rate**

The prime rate is the rate that major banks charge large corporate customers for short-term loans. It changes only infrequently because banks are reluctant to undercut one another. When a change does occur, it begins with one bank, and other banks quickly follow suit. The corporate bond rate is the return on long-term corporate bonds. Because these bonds are widely traded, this rate fluctuates with market conditions.

## The Dominant Firm Model

• **dominant firm** Firm with a large share of total sales that sets price to maximize profits, taking into account the supply response of smaller firms.

In some oligopolistic markets, one large firm has a major share of total sales while a group of smaller firms supplies the remainder of the market. The large firm might then act as a **dominant firm**, setting a price that maximizes its own profits. The other firms, which individually could have little influence over price, would then act as perfect competitors: They take the price set by the dominant firm as given and produce accordingly. But what price should the dominant firm set? To maximize profit, it must take into account how the output of the other firms depends on the price it sets.

Figure 12.9 shows how a dominant firm sets its price. Here, $D$ is the market demand curve, and $S_F$ is the supply curve (i.e., the aggregate marginal cost curve) of the smaller fringe firms. The dominant firm must determine *its* demand curve $D_D$. As the figure shows, this curve is just the difference between market demand and the supply of fringe firms. For example, at price $P_1$, the supply of fringe firms is just equal to market demand; thus the dominant firm can sell nothing at this price. At a price $P_2$ or less, fringe firms will not supply any of the good, so the dominant firm faces the market demand curve. At prices between $P_1$ and $P_2$, the dominant firm faces the demand curve $D_D$.

Corresponding to $D_D$ is the dominant firm's marginal revenue curve $MR_D$. $MC_D$ is the dominant firm's marginal cost curve. To maximize its profit, the

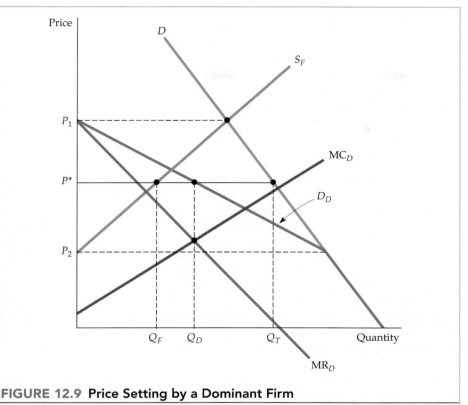

**FIGURE 12.9 Price Setting by a Dominant Firm**

The dominant firm sets price, and the other firms sell all they want at that price. The dominant firm's demand curve, $D_D$, is the difference between market demand $D$ and the supply of fringe firms $S_F$. The dominant firm produces a quantity $Q_D$ at the point where its marginal revenue $MR_D$ is equal to its marginal cost $MC_D$. The corresponding price is $P^*$. At this price, fringe firms sell $Q_F$, so that total sales equal $Q_T$.

dominant firm produces quantity $Q_D$ at the intersection of $MR_D$ and $MC_D$. From the demand curve $D_D$, we find price $P^*$. At this price, fringe firms sell a quantity $Q_F$; thus the total quantity sold is $Q_T = Q_D + Q_F$.

## 12.6 CARTELS

Producers in a *cartel* explicitly agree to cooperate in setting prices and output levels. Not all the producers in an industry need to join the cartel, and most cartels involve only a subset of producers. But if enough producers adhere to the cartel's agreements, and if market demand is sufficiently inelastic, the cartel may drive prices well above competitive levels.

Cartels are often international. While U.S. antitrust laws prohibit American companies from colluding, those of other countries are much weaker and are sometimes poorly enforced. Furthermore, nothing prevents countries, or companies owned or controlled by foreign governments, from forming cartels. For example, the OPEC cartel is an international agreement among oil-producing countries which has succeeded in raising world oil prices above competitive levels.

Other international cartels have also succeeded in raising prices. During the mid-1970s, for example, the International Bauxite Association (IBA) quadrupled bauxite prices, and a secretive international uranium cartel pushed up uranium prices. Some cartels had longer successes: From 1928 through the early 1970s, a cartel called Mercurio Europeo kept the price of mercury close to monopoly levels, and an international cartel monopolized the iodine market from 1878 through 1939. However, most cartels have failed to raise prices. An international copper cartel operates to this day, but it has never had a significant impact on copper prices. Cartel attempts to drive up the prices of tin, coffee, tea, and cocoa have also failed.[11]

**Conditions for Cartel Success** Why do some cartels succeed while others fail? There are two conditions for cartel success. First, a stable cartel organization must be formed whose members agree on price and production levels and then adhere to that agreement. Unlike our prisoners in the prisoners' dilemma, cartel members can talk to each other to formalize an agreement. This does not mean, however, that agreeing is easy. Different members may have different costs, different assessments of market demand, and even different objectives, and they may therefore want to set price at different levels. Furthermore, each member of the cartel will be tempted to "cheat" by lowering its price slightly to capture a larger market share than it was allotted. Most often, only the threat of a long-term return to competitive prices deters cheating of this sort. But if the profits from cartelization are large enough, that threat may be sufficient.

The second condition is the potential for monopoly power. Even if a cartel can solve its organizational problems, there will be little room to raise price if it faces a highly elastic demand curve. Potential monopoly power may be the most important condition for success; if the potential gains from cooperation are large, cartel members will have more incentive to solve their organizational problems.

> Recall from §10.2 that monopoly power refers to market power on the part of a seller—the ability of a firm to price its product above its marginal cost of production.

## Analysis of Cartel Pricing

Only rarely do *all* the producers of a good combine to form a cartel. A cartel usually accounts for only a portion of total production and must take into account the supply response of competitive (noncartel) producers when it sets price. Cartel pricing can thus be analyzed by using the dominant firm model discussed earlier. We will apply this model to two cartels, the OPEC oil cartel and the CIPEC copper cartel.[12] This will help us understand why OPEC was successful in raising price while CIPEC was not.

**Analyzing OPEC** Figure 12.10 illustrates the case of OPEC. Total demand TD is the total world demand curve for crude oil, and $S_c$ is the competitive (non-OPEC) supply curve. The demand for OPEC oil $D_{OPEC}$ is the difference between total demand and competitive supply, and $MR_{OPEC}$ is the corresponding marginal revenue curve. $MC_{OPEC}$ is OPEC's marginal cost curve; as you can see, OPEC has

---

[11]See Jeffrey K. MacKie-Mason and Robert S. Pindyck, "Cartel Theory and Cartel Experience in International Minerals Markets," in *Energy: Markets and Regulation* (Cambridge, MA: MIT Press, 1986).

[12]CIPEC is the French acronym for International Council of Copper Exporting Countries.

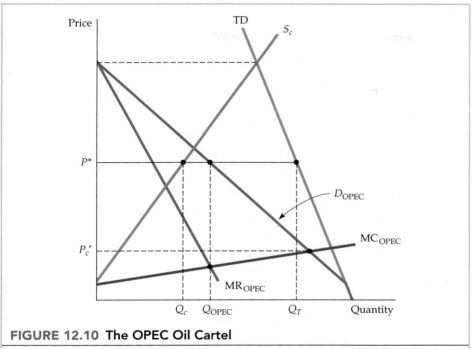

**FIGURE 12.10 The OPEC Oil Cartel**

TD is the total world demand curve for oil, and $S_c$ is the competitive (non-OPEC) supply curve. OPEC's demand $D_{OPEC}$ is the difference between the two. Because both total demand and competitive supply are inelastic, OPEC's demand is inelastic. OPEC's profit-maximizing quantity $Q_{OPEC}$ is found at the intersection of its marginal revenue and marginal cost curves; at this quantity, OPEC charges price $P^*$. If OPEC producers had not cartelized, price would be $P_c$, where OPEC's demand and marginal cost curves intersect.

much lower production costs than do non-OPEC producers. OPEC's marginal revenue and marginal cost are equal at quantity $Q_{OPEC}$, which is the quantity that OPEC will produce. We see from OPEC's demand curve that the price will be $P^*$, at which competitive supply is $Q_c$.

Suppose petroleum-exporting countries had not formed a cartel but had instead produced competitively. Price would then have equaled marginal cost. We can therefore determine the competitive price from the point where OPEC's demand curve intersects its marginal cost curve. That price, labeled $P_c$, is much lower than the cartel price $P^*$. Because both total demand and non-OPEC supply are inelastic, the demand for OPEC oil is also fairly inelastic. Thus the cartel has substantial monopoly power, and it has used that power to drive prices well above competitive levels.

In Chapter 2, we stressed the importance of distinguishing between short-run and long-run supply and demand. That distinction is important here. The total demand and non-OPEC supply curves in Figure 12.10 apply to a short- or intermediate-run analysis. In the long run, both demand and supply will be much more elastic, which means that OPEC's demand curve will also be much more elastic. We would thus expect that in the long run OPEC would be unable to maintain a price that is so much above the competitive level. Indeed, during 1982–1989, oil prices fell in real terms, largely because of the long-run adjustment of demand and non-OPEC supply.

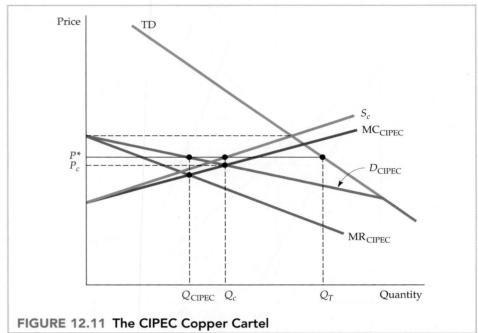

**FIGURE 12.11 The CIPEC Copper Cartel**

TD is the total demand for copper and $S_c$ is the competitive (non-CIPEC) supply. CIPEC's demand $D_{CIPEC}$ is the difference between the two. Both total demand and competitive supply are relatively elastic, so CIPEC's demand curve is elastic, and CIPEC has very little monopoly power. Note that CIPEC's optimal price $P^*$ is close to the competitive price $P_c$.

**Analyzing CIPEC** Figure 12.11 provides a similar analysis of CIPEC, which consists of four copper-producing countries: Chile, Peru, Zambia, and Congo (formerly Zaire), that collectively account for less than half of world copper production. In these countries, production costs are lower than those of non-CIPEC producers, but except for Chile, not much lower. In Figure 12.11, CIPEC's marginal cost curve is therefore drawn only a little below the non-CIPEC supply curve. CIPEC's demand curve $D_{CIPEC}$ is the difference between total demand TD and non-CIPEC supply $S_c$. CIPEC's marginal cost and marginal revenue curves intersect at quantity $Q_{CIPEC}$, with the corresponding price $P^*$. Again, the competitive price $P_c$ is found at the point where CIPEC's demand curve intersects its marginal cost curve. Note that this price is very close to the cartel price $P^*$.

Why can't CIPEC increase copper prices much? As Figure 12.11 shows, the total demand for copper is more elastic than that for oil. (Other materials, such as aluminum, can easily be substituted for copper.) Also, competitive supply is much more elastic. Even in the short run, non-CIPEC producers can easily expand supply if prices should rise (in part because of the availability of supply from scrap metal). Thus CIPEC's potential monopoly power is small.

As the examples of OPEC and CIPEC illustrate, successful cartelization requires two things. First, the total demand for the good must not be very price elastic. Second, either the cartel must control nearly all the world's supply or, if it does not, the supply of noncartel producers must not be price elastic. Most international commodity cartels have failed because few world markets meet both conditions.

**EXAMPLE 12.5**    The Cartelization of Intercollegiate Athletics

Many people think of intercollegiate athletics as an extracurricular activity for college students and a diversion for fans. They assume that universities support athletics because it not only gives amateur athletes a chance to develop their skills and play football or basketball before large audiences but also provides entertainment and promotes school spirit and alumni support. Although it does these things, intercollegiate athletics is also a big—and an extremely profitable—industry.

Like any industry, intercollegiate athletics has firms and consumers. The "firms" are the universities that support and finance teams. The inputs to production are the coaches, student athletes, and capital in the form of stadiums and playing fields. The consumers, many of whom are current or former college students, are the fans who buy tickets to games and the TV and radio networks that pay to broadcast them. There are many firms and consumers, which suggests that the industry is competitive. But the persistently high level of profits in this industry is inconsistent with competition—a large state university can regularly earn more than $6 million a year in profits from football games alone.[13] This profitability is the result of monopoly power, obtained via cartelization.

The cartel organization is the National Collegiate Athletic Association (NCAA). The NCAA restricts competition in a number of important ways. To reduce bargaining power by student athletes, the NCAA creates and enforces rules regarding eligibility and terms of compensation. To reduce competition by universities, it limits the number of games that can be played each season and the number of teams that can participate in each division. And to limit price competition, the NCAA has, until 1984, been the sole negotiator for all football television contracts, thereby monopolizing one of the main sources of industry revenues.

Has the NCAA been a successful cartel? Like most cartels, its members have occasionally broken its rules and regulations. But until 1984, it had increased the monopoly power of this industry well above what it would have been otherwise. In 1984, however, the Supreme Court ruled that the NCAA's monopolization of football television contracts was illegal and that individual universities could negotiate their own contracts. The ensuing competition led to a drop in contract fees. As a result, more college football is shown on television but, because of the lower fees, the revenues to the schools have dropped somewhat. All in all, although the Supreme Court's ruling reduced the NCAA's monopoly power, it did not eliminate it. Despite no longer retaining exclusive rights to negotiate college football television contracts, the NCAA still negotiates fees for other televised collegiate sports. In 2001, CBS signed a $6 billion deal with the NCAA to cover the men's Division I basketball tournament for 11 years, and ESPN agreed

---

[13]See "In Big-Time College Athletics, the Real Score Is in Dollars," *New York Times*, March 1, 1987.

to pay the NCAA $200 million over 11 years for coverage of 11 nonrevenue sports (such as soccer, men's ice hockey, and the College World Series).[14]

Since then, the NCAA's anticompetitive practices have come under numerous attacks. In 2005, the National Invitation Tournament (NIT), a college basketball tournament operated by the Metropolitan Intercollegiate Basketball Committee, challenged the NCAA's rule that effectively forced schools invited to its tournament to boycott the NIT. The NIT claimed that this practice was anticompetitive and an illegal use of the NCAA's powers. The parties ultimately settled the lawsuit for nearly $60 million. In 2007, the NCAA was sued by 11,500 Division I football and basketball players claiming that it illegally fixed the price of an athletic scholarship below the cost of a college education. According to the players, the NCAA shortchanged them, on average, $2,500 a year because of its arbitrary limit on scholarships.

---

**EXAMPLE 12.6**  The Milk Cartel

The U.S. government has supported the price of milk since the Great Depression and continues to do so today. The government, however, scaled back price supports during the 1990s, and as a result, wholesale prices of milk have fluctuated more widely. Not surprisingly, farmers have been complaining.

In response to these complaints, in 1996 the federal government allowed milk producers in the six New England states to cartelize. The cartel—called the Northeast Interstate Dairy Compact—set minimum wholesale prices for milk, and was exempt from the antitrust laws. The result was that consumers in New England paid more for a gallon of milk than consumers elsewhere in the nation.

In 1999, Congress responded to the lobbying efforts of farmers in other states by attempting to expand the milk cartel. Legislation was introduced that would have allowed dairy farmers in New York, New Jersey, Maryland, Delaware, and Pennsylvania to join the New England states and thereby form a cartel covering most of the northeast United States.[15] Not wanting to be left out, dairy farmers in the South also lobbied Congress for higher milk prices. As a result, the 1999 legislation also authorized 16 southern states, including Texas, Florida, and Georgia, to create their own regional cartel.

Studies have suggested that the original cartel (covering only the New England states) has caused retail prices of milk to rise by only a few cents a gallon. Why so little? The reason is that the New England cartel is surrounded by a fringe of noncartel producers—namely, dairy farmers in New York, New Jersey, and other states. Expanding the cartel, however, would have shrunk the competitive fringe, thereby giving the cartel a greater influence over milk prices.

---

[14]"Sweeping Changes Suggested for NCAA; Graduation Rates, Commercialism Cited," *The Washington Post*, June 27, 2001; "NCAA Panel Trying to Turn Back Clock; Big Bucks Make the Knight Commission's Recent Call for Academic Integrity Obsolete," *San Antonio Express-News*, July 20, 2001.

[15]"Congress Weighs an Expanded Milk Cartel That Would Aid Farmers by Raising Prices," *New York Times*, May 2, 1999. For an update, go to the following Web site: **www.dairycompact.org**.

Recognizing the political headaches and regional conflict caused by these attempts at cartelization, Congress ended the Northeast Interstate Dairy Compact in October 2001. Although proponents of the Compact attempted to revive the cartel, opposition in Congress has been strong and, as of 2007, has not been re-authorized. Nonetheless, milk production continues to benefit from federal price supports.

# SUMMARY

1. In a monopolistically competitive market, firms compete by selling differentiated products, which are highly substitutable. New firms can enter or exit easily. Firms have only a small amount of monopoly power. In the long run, entry will occur until profits are driven to zero. Firms then produce with excess capacity (i.e., at output levels below those that minimize average cost).

2. In an oligopolistic market, only a few firms account for most or all of production. Barriers to entry allow some firms to earn substantial profits, even over the long run. Economic decisions involve strategic considerations—each firm must consider how its actions will affect its rivals, and how they are likely to react.

3. In the Cournot model of oligopoly, firms make their output decisions at the same time, each taking the other's output as fixed. In equilibrium, each firm is maximizing its profit, given the output of its competitor, so no firm has an incentive to change its output. The firms are therefore in a Nash equilibrium. Each firm's profit is higher than it would be under perfect competition but less than what it would earn by colluding.

4. In the Stackelberg model, one firm sets its output first. That firm has a strategic advantage and earns a higher profit. It knows that it can choose a large output and

that its competitors will have to choose smaller outputs if they want to maximize profits.

5. The Nash equilibrium concept can also be applied to markets in which firms produce substitute goods and compete by setting price. In equilibrium, each firm maximizes its profit, given the prices of its competitors, and so has no incentive to change price.

6. Firms would earn higher profits by collusively agreeing to raise prices, but the antitrust laws usually prohibit this. They might all set high prices without colluding, each hoping its competitors will do the same, but they are in a prisoners' dilemma, which makes this unlikely. Each firm has an incentive to cheat by lowering its price and capturing sales from competitors.

7. The prisoners' dilemma creates price rigidity in oligopolistic markets. Firms are reluctant to change prices for fear of setting off price warfare.

8. Price leadership is a form of implicit collusion that sometimes gets around the prisoners' dilemma. One firm sets price and other firms follow suit.

9. In a cartel, producers explicitly collude in setting prices and output levels. Successful cartelization requires that the total demand not be very price elastic, and that either the cartel control most supply or else the supply of noncartel producers be inelastic.

# QUESTIONS FOR REVIEW

1. What are the characteristics of a monopolistically competitive market? What happens to the equilibrium price and quantity in such a market if one firm introduces a new, improved product?

2. Why is the firm's demand curve flatter than the total market demand curve in monopolistic competition? Suppose a monopolistically competitive firm is making a profit in the short run. What will happen to its demand curve in the long run?

3. Some experts have argued that too many brands of breakfast cereal are on the market. Give an argument to support this view. Give an argument against it.

4. Why is the Cournot equilibrium stable? (i.e., Why don't firms have any incentive to change their output levels once in equilibrium?) Even if they can't collude,

why don't firms set their outputs at the joint profit-maximizing levels (i.e., the levels they would have chosen had they colluded)?

5. In the Stackelberg model, the firm that sets output first has an advantage. Explain why.

6. What do the Cournot and Bertrand models have in common? What is different about the two models?

7. Explain the meaning of a Nash equilibrium when firms are competing with respect to price. Why is the equilibrium stable? Why don't the firms raise prices to the level that maximizes joint profits?

8. The kinked demand curve describes price rigidity. Explain how the model works. What are its limitations? Why does price rigidity occur in oligopolistic markets?

9. Why does price leadership sometimes evolve in oligopolistic markets? Explain how the price leader determines a profit-maximizing price.

10. Why has the OPEC oil cartel succeeded in raising prices substantially while the CIPEC copper cartel has not? What conditions are necessary for successful cartelization? What organizational problems must a cartel overcome?

# EXERCISES

1. Suppose all firms in a monopolistically competitive industry were merged into one large firm. Would that new firm produce as many different brands? Would it produce only a single brand? Explain.

2. Consider two firms facing the demand curve $P = 50 - 5Q$, where $Q = Q_1 + Q_2$. The firms' cost functions are $C_1(Q_1) = 20 + 10Q_1$ and $C_2(Q_2) = 10 + 12Q_2$.
   a. Suppose both firms have entered the industry. What is the joint profit-maximizing level of output? How much will each firm produce? How would your answer change if the firms have not yet entered the industry?
   b. What is each firm's equilibrium output and profit if they behave noncooperatively? Use the Cournot model. Draw the firms' reaction curves and show the equilibrium.
   c. How much should Firm 1 be willing to pay to purchase Firm 2 if collusion is illegal but a takeover is not?

3. A monopolist can produce at a constant average (and marginal) cost of AC = MC = $5. It faces a market demand curve given by $Q = 53 - P$.
   a. Calculate the profit-maximizing price and quantity for this monopolist. Also calculate its profits.
   b. Suppose a second firm enters the market. Let $Q_1$ be the output of the first firm and $Q_2$ be the output of the second. Market demand is now given by
   $$Q_1 + Q_2 = 53 - P$$
   Assuming that this second firm has the same costs as the first, write the profits of each firm as functions of $Q_1$ and $Q_2$.
   c. Suppose (as in the Cournot model) that each firm chooses its profit-maximizing level of output on the assumption that its competitor's output is fixed. Find each firm's "reaction curve" (i.e., the rule that gives its desired output in terms of its competitor's output).
   d. Calculate the Cournot equilibrium (i.e., the values of $Q_1$ and $Q_2$ for which each firm is doing as well as it can given its competitor's output). What are the resulting market price and profits of each firm?
   *e. Suppose there are N firms in the industry, all with the same constant marginal cost, MC = $5. Find the Cournot equilibrium. How much will each firm produce, what will be the market price, and how much profit will each firm earn? Also, show that as N becomes large, the market price approaches the price that would prevail under perfect competition.

4. This exercise is a continuation of Exercise 3. We return to two firms with the same constant average and marginal cost, AC = MC = 5, facing the market demand curve $Q_1 + Q_2 = 53 - P$. Now we will use the Stackelberg model to analyze what will happen if one of the firms makes its output decision before the other.
   a. Suppose Firm 1 is the Stackelberg leader (i.e., makes its output decisions before Firm 2). Find the reaction curves that tell each firm how much to produce in terms of the output of its competitor.
   b. How much will each firm produce, and what will its profit be?

5. Two firms compete in selling identical widgets. They choose their output levels $Q_1$ and $Q_2$ simultaneously and face the demand curve
   $$P = 30 - Q$$
   where $Q = Q_1 + Q_2$. Until recently, both firms had zero marginal costs. Recent environmental regulations have increased Firm 2's marginal cost to $15. Firm 1's marginal cost remains constant at zero. True or false: As a result, the market price will rise to the monopoly level.

6. Suppose that two identical firms produce widgets and that they are the only firms in the market. Their costs are given by $C_1 = 60Q_1$ and $C_2 = 60Q_2$, where $Q_1$ is the output of Firm 1 and $Q_2$ the output of Firm 2. Price is determined by the following demand curve:
   $$P = 300 - Q$$
   where $Q = Q_1 + Q_2$.
   a. Find the Cournot-Nash equilibrium. Calculate the profit of each firm at this equilibrium.
   b. Suppose the two firms form a cartel to maximize joint profits. How many widgets will be produced? Calculate each firm's profit.
   c. Suppose Firm 1 were the only firm in the industry. How would market output and Firm 1's profit differ from that found in part (b) above?
   d. Returning to the duopoly of part (b), suppose Firm 1 abides by the agreement but Firm 2 cheats by increasing production. How many widgets will Firm 2 produce? What will be each firm's profits?

7. Suppose that two competing firms, A and B, produce a homogeneous good. Both firms have a marginal cost of MC = $50. Describe what would happen to output and price in each of the following situations if the firms are at (i) Cournot equilibrium, (ii) collusive equilibrium, and (iii) Bertrand equilibrium.

a. Because Firm *A* must increase wages, its MC increases to $80.

b. The marginal cost of both firms increases.

c. The demand curve shifts to the right.

8. Suppose the airline industry consisted of only two firms: American and Texas Air Corp. Let the two firms have identical cost functions, $C(q) = 40q$. Assume that the demand curve for the industry is given by $P = 100 - Q$ and that each firm expects the other to behave as a Cournot competitor.

   a. Calculate the Cournot-Nash equilibrium for each firm, assuming that each chooses the output level that maximizes its profits when taking its rival's output as given. What are the profits of each firm?

   b. What would be the equilibrium quantity if Texas Air had constant marginal and average costs of $25 and American had constant marginal and average costs of $40?

   c. Assuming that both firms have the original cost function, $C(q) = 40q$, how much should Texas Air be willing to invest to lower its marginal cost from 40 to 25, assuming that American will not follow suit? How much should American be willing to spend to reduce its marginal cost to 25, assuming that Texas Air will have marginal costs of 25 regardless of American's actions?

*9. Demand for light bulbs can be characterized by $Q = 100 - P$, where $Q$ is in millions of boxes of lights sold and $P$ is the price per box. There are two producers of lights, Everglow and Dimlit. They have identical cost functions:

$$C_i = 10Q_i + \tfrac{1}{2}Q_i^2 \,(i = E, D)$$
$$Q = Q_E + Q_D$$

   a. Unable to recognize the potential for collusion, the two firms act as short-run perfect competitors. What are the equilibrium values of $Q_E$, $Q_D$, and $P$? What are each firm's profits?

   b. Top management in both firms is replaced. Each new manager independently recognizes the oligopolistic nature of the light bulb industry and plays Cournot. What are the equilibrium values of $Q_E$, $Q_D$, and $P$? What are each firm's profits?

   c. Suppose the Everglow manager guesses correctly that Dimlit is playing Cournot, so Everglow plays Stackelberg. What are the equilibrium values of $Q_E$, $Q_D$, and $P$? What are each firm's profits?

   d. If the managers of the two companies collude, what are the equilibrium values of $Q_E$, $Q_D$, and $P$? What are each firm's profits?

10. Two firms produce luxury sheepskin auto seat covers: Western Where (WW) and B.B.B. Sheep (BBBS). Each firm has a cost function given by

$$C(q) = 30q + 1.5q^2$$

The market demand for these seat covers is represented by the inverse demand equation

$$P = 300 - 3Q$$

where $Q = q_1 + q_2$, total output.

   a. If each firm acts to maximize its profits, taking its rival's output as given (i.e., the firms behave as Cournot oligopolists), what will be the equilibrium quantities selected by each firm? What is total output, and what is the market price? What are the profits for each firm?

   b. It occurs to the managers of WW and BBBS that they could do a lot better by colluding. If the two firms collude, what will be the profit-maximizing choice of output? The industry price? The output and the profit for each firm in this case?

   c. The managers of these firms realize that explicit agreements to collude are illegal. Each firm must decide on its own whether to produce the Cournot quantity or the cartel quantity. To aid in making the decision, the manager of WW constructs a payoff matrix like the one below. Fill in each box with the profit of WW and the profit of BBBS. Given this payoff matrix, what output strategy is each firm likely to pursue?

| Profit Payoff Matrix | | BBBS | |
|---|---|---|---|
| (WW Profit, BBBS Profit) | | Produce Cournot *q* | Produce Cartel *q* |
| WW | Produce Cournot *q* | | |
| | Produce Cartel *q* | | |

   d. Suppose WW can set its output level *before* BBBS does. How much will WW choose to produce in this case? How much will BBBS produce? What is the market price, and what is the profit for each firm? Is WW better off by choosing its output first? Explain why or why not.

*11. Two firms compete by choosing price. Their demand functions are

$$Q_1 = 20 - P_1 + P_2$$

and

$$Q_2 = 20 + P_1 - P_2$$

where $P_1$ and $P_2$ are the prices charged by each firm, respectively, and $Q_1$ and $Q_2$ are the resulting demands. Note that the demand for each good depends only on the difference in prices; if the two firms colluded and set the same price, they could make that price as high as they wanted, and earn infinite profits. Marginal costs are zero.

   a. Suppose the two firms set their prices at the *same time*. Find the resulting Nash equilibrium. What price will each firm charge, how much will it sell, and what will its profit be? (*Hint:* Maximize the profit of each firm with respect to its price.)

**b.** Suppose Firm 1 sets its price *first* and then Firm 2 sets its price. What price will each firm charge, how much will it sell, and what will its profit be?

**c.** Suppose you are one of these firms and that there are three ways you could play the game: (i) Both firms set price at the same time; (ii) You set price first; or (iii) Your competitor sets price first. If you could choose among these options, which would you prefer? Explain why.

**\*12.** The dominant firm model can help us understand the behavior of some cartels. Let's apply this model to the OPEC oil cartel. We will use isoelastic curves to describe world demand $W$ and noncartel (competitive) supply $S$. Reasonable numbers for the price elasticities of world demand and noncartel supply are $-1/2$ and $1/2$, respectively. Then, expressing $W$ and $S$ in millions of barrels per day (mb/d), we could write

$$W = 160P^{-1/2}$$

and

$$S = (3\tfrac{1}{3})P^{1/2}$$

Note that OPEC's net demand is $D = W - S$.

**a.** Draw the world demand curve $W$, the non-OPEC supply curve $S$, OPEC's net demand curve $D$, and OPEC's marginal revenue curve. For purposes of approximation, assume OPEC's production cost is zero. Indicate OPEC's optimal price, OPEC's optimal production, and non-OPEC production on the diagram. Now, show on the diagram how the various curves will shift and how OPEC's optimal price will change if non-OPEC supply becomes more expensive because reserves of oil start running out.

**b.** Calculate OPEC's optimal (profit-maximizing) price. (*Hint*: Because OPEC's cost is zero, just write the expression for OPEC revenue and find the price that maximizes it.)

**c.** Suppose the oil-consuming countries were to unite and form a "buyers' cartel" to gain monopsony power. What can we say, and what can't we say, about the impact this action would have on price?

**13.** Suppose the market for tennis shoes has one dominant firm and five fringe firms. The market demand is $Q = 400 - 2P$. The dominant firm has a constant marginal cost of 20. The fringe firms each have a marginal cost of $MC = 20 + 5q$.

**a.** Verify that the total supply curve for the five fringe firms is $Q_f = P - 20$.

**b.** Find the dominant firm's demand curve.

**c.** Find the profit-maximizing quantity produced and price charged by the dominant firm, and the quantity produced and price charged by each of the fringe firms.

**d.** Suppose there are 10 fringe firms instead of five. How does this change your results?

**e.** Suppose there continue to be five fringe firms but that each manages to reduce its marginal cost to $MC = 20 + 2q$. How does this change your results?

**\*14.** A lemon-growing cartel consists of four orchards. Their total cost functions are

$$TC_1 = 20 + 5Q_1^2$$
$$TC_2 = 25 + 3Q_2^2$$
$$TC_3 = 15 + 4Q_3^2$$
$$TC_4 = 20 + 6Q_4^2$$

TC is in hundreds of dollars, and Q is in cartons per month picked and shipped.

**a.** Tabulate total, average, and marginal costs for each firm for output levels between 1 and 5 cartons per month (i.e., for 1, 2, 3, 4, and 5 cartons).

**b.** If the cartel decided to ship 10 cartons per month and set a price of $25 per carton, how should output be allocated among the firms?

**c.** At this shipping level, which firm has the most incentive to cheat? Does any firm *not* have an incentive to cheat?

# Game Theory and Competitive Strategy

In Chapter 12, we began to explore some of the strategic output and pricing decisions that firms must often make. We saw how a firm can take into account the likely responses of its competitors when it makes these decisions. However, there are many questions about market structure and firm behavior that we have not yet addressed. For example, why do firms tend to collude in some markets and to compete aggressively in others? How do some firms manage to deter entry by potential competitors? And how should firms make pricing decisions when demand or cost conditions are changing or new competitors are entering the market?

To answer these questions, we will use game theory to extend our analysis of strategic decision making. The application of game theory has been an important development in microeconomics. This chapter explains some key aspects of this theory and shows how it can be used to understand how markets evolve and operate, and how managers should think about the strategic decisions they continually face. We will see, for example, what happens when oligopolistic firms must set and adjust prices strategically over time, so that the prisoners' dilemma, which we discussed in Chapter 12, is repeated over and over. We will show how firms can make strategic moves that give them advantages over competitors or an edge in bargaining situations, and how they can use threats, promises, or more concrete actions to deter entry. Finally, we will turn to auctions and see how game theory can be applied to auction design and bidding strategies.

## 13.1 GAMING AND STRATEGIC DECISIONS

First, we should clarify what gaming and strategic decision making are all about. A **game** is any situation in which *players* (the participants) make *strategic decisions*—i.e., decisions that take into account each other's actions and responses. Examples of games include firms competing with each other by setting prices, or a group of consumers bidding against each other at an auction for a work of art. Strategic decisions result in **payoffs** to the players: outcomes that generate rewards or benefits. For the price-setting firms, the payoffs are profits; for the bidders at the auction, the winner's payoff is her consumer surplus—i.e., the value she places on the artwork less the amount she must pay.

A key objective of game theory is to determine the optimal strategy for each player. A **strategy** is a rule or plan of action for playing the

- **game** Situation in which players (participants) make strategic decisions that take into account each other's actions and responses.

- **payoff** Value associated with a possible outcome.

- **strategy** Rule or plan of action for playing a game.

- **optimal strategy** Strategy that maximizes a player's expected payoff.

game. For our price-setting firms, a strategy might be: "I'll keep my price high as long as my competitors do the same, but once a competitor lowers his price, I'll lower mine even more." For a bidder at an auction, a strategy might be: "I'll make a first bid of $2000 to convince the other bidders that I'm serious about winning, but I'll drop out if other bidders push the price above $5000." The **optimal strategy** for a player is the one that maximizes her expected payoff.

We will focus on games involving players who are *rational*, in the sense that they think through the consequences of their actions. In essence, we are concerned with the following question: *If I believe that my competitors are rational and act to maximize their own payoffs, how should I take their behavior into account when making my decisions?* In real life, of course, you may encounter competitors who are irrational, or are less capable than you of thinking through the consequences of their actions. Nonetheless, a good place to start is by assuming that your competitors are just as rational and just as smart as you are.[1] As we will see, taking competitors' behavior into account is not as simple as it might seem. Determining optimal strategies can be difficult, even under conditions of complete symmetry and perfect information (i.e., my competitors and I have the same cost structure and are fully informed about each others' costs, about demand, etc.). Moreover, we will be concerned with more complex situations in which firms face different costs, different types of information, and various degrees and forms of competitive "advantage" and "disadvantage."

## Noncooperative versus Cooperative Games

- **cooperative game** Game in which participants can negotiate binding contracts that allow them to plan joint strategies.

- **noncooperative game** Game in which negotiation and enforcement of binding contracts are not possible.

The economic games that firms play can be either *cooperative* or *noncooperative*. In a **cooperative game**, players can negotiate binding contracts that allow them to plan joint strategies. In a **noncooperative game**, negotiation and enforcement of binding contracts are not possible.

An example of a cooperative game is the bargaining between a buyer and a seller over the price of a rug. If the rug costs $100 to produce and the buyer values the rug at $200, a cooperative solution to the game is possible: An agreement to sell the rug at any price between $101 and $199 will maximize the sum of the buyer's consumer surplus and the seller's profit, while making both parties better off. Another cooperative game would involve two firms negotiating a joint investment to develop a new technology (assuming that neither firm would have enough know-how to succeed on its own). If the firms can sign a binding contract to divide the profits from their joint investment, a cooperative outcome that makes both parties better off is possible.[2]

An example of a noncooperative game is a situation in which two competing firms take each other's likely behavior into account when independently setting their prices. Each firm knows that by undercutting its competitor, it can capture more market share. But it also knows that in doing so, it risks setting off a price war. Another noncooperative game is the auction mentioned above: Each bidder must take the likely behavior of the other bidders into account when determining an optimal bidding strategy.

---

[1]When we asked, 80 percent of our students told us that they were smarter and more capable than most of their classmates. We hope that you don't find it too much of a strain to imagine competing against people who are as smart and capable as you are.

[2]Bargaining over a rug is called a *constant sum* game because no matter what the selling price, the sum of consumer surplus and profit will be the same. Negotiating over a joint venture is a *nonconstant sum* game: The total profit that results from the venture will depend on the outcome of the negotiations (e.g., the resources that each firm devotes to the venture).

Note that the fundamental difference between cooperative and noncooperative games lies in the *contracting possibilities*. In cooperative games, binding contracts are possible; in noncooperative games, they are not.

We will be concerned mostly with noncooperative games. Whatever the game, however, keep in mind the following key point about strategic decision making:

> *It is essential to understand your opponent's point of view and to deduce his or her likely responses to your actions.*

This point may seem obvious—of course, one must understand an opponent's point of view. Yet even in simple gaming situations, people often ignore or misjudge opponents' positions and the rational responses that those positions imply.

**How to Buy a Dollar Bill** Consider the following game devised by Martin Shubik.[3] A dollar bill is auctioned, but in an unusual way. The highest bidder receives the dollar in return for the amount bid. However, the second-highest bidder must also hand over the amount that he or she bid—and get nothing in return. *If you were playing this game, how much would you bid for the dollar bill?*

Classroom experience shows that students often end up bidding more than a dollar for the dollar. In a typical scenario, one player bids 20 cents and another 30 cents. The lower bidder now stands to lose 20 cents but figures he can earn a dollar by raising his bid, and so bids 40 cents. The escalation continues until two players carry the bidding to a dollar against 90 cents. Now the 90-cent bidder has to choose between bidding $1.10 for the dollar or paying 90 cents to get nothing. Most often, he raises his bid, and the bidding escalates further. In some experiments, the "winning" bidder has ended up paying more than $3 for the dollar!

How could intelligent students put themselves in this position? By failing to think through the likely response of the other players and the sequence of events it implies.

In the rest of this chapter, we will examine simple games that involve pricing, advertising, and investment decisions. The games are simple in that, *given some behavioral assumptions*, we can determine the best strategy for each firm. But even for these simple games, we will find that the correct behavioral assumptions are not always easy to make. Often they will depend on how the game is played (e.g., how long the firms stay in business, their reputations, etc.). Therefore, when reading this chapter, you should try to understand the basic issues involved in making strategic decisions. You should also keep in mind the importance of carefully assessing your opponent's position and rational response to your actions, as Example 13.1 illustrates.

| EXAMPLE 13.1 | Acquiring a Company |

You represent Company *A* (the acquirer), which is considering acquiring Company *T* (the target).[4] You plan to offer cash for all of Company *T*'s shares, but you are unsure what price to offer. The complication is this: The value of Company *T*—indeed, its viability—depends on the outcome of a major oil exploration project. If the project fails, Company *T* under current management will be worth nothing. But if it succeeds, Company *T*'s value under current management

---

[3]Martin Shubik, *Game Theory in the Social Sciences* (Cambridge, MA: MIT Press, 1982).

[4]This is a revised version of an example designed by Max Bazerman for a course at MIT.

could be as high as $100/share. All share values between $0 and $100 are considered equally likely.

It is well known, however, that Company *T* will be worth much more under the progressive management of Company *A* than under current management. In fact, whatever the ultimate value under current management, *Company T will be worth 50 percent more under the management of Company A*. If the project fails, Company *T* is worth $0/share under either management. If the exploration project generates a $50/share value under current management, the value under Company *A* will be $75/share. Similarly, a $100/share value under Company *T* implies a $150/share value under Company *A*, and so on.

You must determine what price Company *A* should offer for Company *T*'s shares. This offer must be made *now—before* the outcome of the exploration project is known. From all indications, Company *T* would be happy to be acquired by Company *A—for the right price*. You expect Company *T* to delay a decision on your bid until the exploration results are in and then accept or reject your offer before news of the drilling results reaches the press.

Thus, *you (Company A) will not know the results of the exploration project when submitting your price offer, but Company T will know the results when deciding whether to accept your offer. Also, Company T will accept any offer by Company A that is greater than the (per share) value of the company under current management*. As the representative of Company *A*, you are considering price offers in the range $0/share (i.e., making no offer at all) to $150/share. *What price per share should you offer for Company T's stock?*

*Note:* The typical response—to offer between $50 and $75 per share—is wrong. The correct answer to this problem appears at the end of this chapter, but we urge you to try to answer it on your own.

## 13.2 DOMINANT STRATEGIES

How can we decide on the best strategy for playing a game? How can we determine a game's likely outcome? We need something to help us determine how the rational behavior of each player will lead to an equilibrium solution. Some strategies may be successful if competitors make certain choices but fail if they make other choices. Other strategies, however, may be successful regardless of what competitors do. We begin with the concept of a **dominant strategy**—*one that is optimal no matter what an opponent does*.

* **dominant strategy**
Strategy that is optimal no matter what an opponent does.

> In §12.4, we explain that a payoff matrix is a table showing the payoffs to each player given her decision and the decision of her competitor.

The following example illustrates this in a duopoly setting. Suppose Firms *A* and *B* sell competing products and are deciding whether to undertake advertising campaigns. Each firm will be affected by its competitor's decision. The possible outcomes of the game are illustrated by the payoff matrix in Table 13.1. (Recall that the payoff matrix summarizes the possible outcomes of the game; the first number in each cell is the payoff to *A* and the second is the payoff to *B*.) Observe that if both firms advertise, Firm *A* will earn a profit of 10 and Firm *B* a profit of 5. If Firm *A* advertises and Firm *B* does not, Firm *A* will earn 15 and Firm *B* zero. The table also shows the outcomes for the other two possibilities.

What strategy should each firm choose? First consider Firm *A*. It should clearly advertise because no matter what firm *B* does, Firm *A* does best by advertising. If Firm *B* advertises, *A* earns a profit of 10 if it advertises but only 6 if it doesn't. If *B* does not advertise, *A* earns 15 if it advertises but only 10 if it

| TABLE 13.1 | Payoff Matrix for Advertising Game | | |
|---|---|---|---|
| | | **Firm B** | |
| | | Advertise | Don't advertise |
| **Firm A** | Advertise | 10, 5 | 15, 0 |
| | Don't advertise | 6, 8 | 10, 2 |

doesn't. Thus advertising is a dominant strategy for Firm *A*. The same is true for Firm *B*: No matter what firm *A* does, Firm *B* does best by advertising. Therefore, assuming that both firms are rational, we know that the outcome for this game is that both *firms will advertise*. This outcome is easy to determine because both firms have dominant strategies.

When every player has a dominant strategy, we call the outcome of the game an **equilibrium in dominant strategies**. Such games are straightforward to ana-lyze because each player's optimal strategy can be determined without worry-ing about the actions of the other players.

Unfortunately, not every game has a dominant strategy for each player. To see this, let's change our advertising example slightly. The payoff matrix in Table 13.2 is the same as in Table 13.1 except for the bottom right-hand corner—if neither firm advertises, Firm *B* will again earn a profit of 2, but Firm *A* will earn a profit of 20. (Perhaps Firm *A*'s ads are expensive and largely designed to refute Firm *B*'s claims, so by not advertising, Firm *A* can reduce its expenses considerably.)

Now Firm *A* has no dominant strategy. *Its optimal decision depends on what Firm B does.* If Firm *B* advertises, Firm *A* does best by advertising; but if Firm *B* does not advertise, Firm *A* also does best by not advertising. Now suppose both firms must make their decisions at the same time. What should Firm *A* do?

To answer this, Firm *A* must put itself in Firm *B*'s shoes. What decision is best from Firm *B*'s point of view, and what is Firm *B* likely to do? The answer is clear: Firm *B* has a dominant strategy—advertise, no matter what Firm *A* does. (If Firm *A* advertises, *B* earns 5 by advertising and 0 by not advertising; if *A* doesn't advertise, *B* earns 8 if it advertises and 2 if it doesn't.) Therefore, Firm *A* can con-clude that Firm *B* will advertise. This means that Firm *A* should advertise (and thereby earn 10 instead of 6). The logical outcome of the game is that both firms will advertise because Firm *A* is doing the best it can given Firm *B*'s decision; and Firm *B* is doing the best it can given Firm *A*'s decision.

• **equilibrium in dominant strategies** Outcome of a game in which each firm is doing the best it can regard-less of what its competitors are doing.

| TABLE 13.2 | Modified Advertising Game | | |
|---|---|---|---|
| | | **Firm B** | |
| | | Advertise | Don't advertise |
| **Firm A** | Advertise | 10, 5 | 15, 0 |
| | Don't advertise | 6, 8 | 20, 2 |

# 13.3 THE NASH EQUILIBRIUM REVISITED

To determine the likely outcome of a game, we have been seeking "self-enforcing," or "stable" strategies. Dominant strategies are stable, but in many games, one or more players do not have a dominant strategy. We therefore need a more general equilibrium concept. In Chapter 12, we introduced the concept of a *Nash equilibrium* and saw that it is widely applicable and intuitively appealing.[5]

Recall that a Nash equilibrium is a set of strategies (or actions) such that *each player is doing the best it can given the actions of its opponents*. Because each player has no incentive to deviate from its Nash strategy, the strategies are stable. In the example shown in Table 13.2, the Nash equilibrium is that both firms advertise: Given the decision of its competitor, each firm is satisfied that it has made the best decision possible, and so has no incentive to change its decision.

In Chapter 12, we used the Nash equilibrium to study output and pricing by oligopolistic firms. In the Cournot model, for example, each firm sets its own output while taking the outputs of its competitors as fixed. We saw that in a Cournot equilibrium, no firm has an incentive to change its output unilaterally because each firm is doing the best it can given the decisions of its competitors. Thus a Cournot equilibrium is a Nash equilibrium.[6] We also examined models in which firms choose price, taking the prices of their competitors as fixed. Again, in the Nash equilibrium, each firm is earning the largest profit it can given the prices of its competitors, and thus has no incentive to change its price.

> In §12.2, we explain that the Cournot equilibrium is a Nash equilibrium in which each firm correctly assumes how much its competitor will produce.

It is helpful to compare the concept of a Nash equilibrium with that of an equilibrium in dominant strategies:

| *Dominant Strategies*: | I'm doing the best I can *no matter what you do.* |
| | You're doing the best you can *no matter what I do.* |
| *Nash Equilibrium*: | I'm doing the best I can *given what you are doing.* |
| | You're doing the best you can *given what I am doing.* |

Note that a dominant strategy equilibrium is a special case of a Nash equilibrium.

In the advertising game of Table 13.2, there is a single Nash equilibrium—both firms advertise. In general, a game need not have a single Nash equilibrium. Sometimes there is no Nash equilibrium, and sometimes there are several (i.e., several sets of strategies are stable and self-enforcing). A few more examples will help to clarify this.

**The Product Choice Problem** Consider the following "product choice" problem. Two breakfast cereal companies face a market in which two new variations of cereal can be successfully introduced—provided that each variation is introduced by only one firm. There is a market for a new "crispy" cereal and a market for a new "sweet" cereal, but each firm has the resources to introduce only one new product. The payoff matrix for the two firms might look like the one in Table 13.3.

---

[5]Our discussion of the Nash equilibrium, and of game theory in general, is at an introductory level. For a more in-depth discussion of game theory and its applications, see James W. Friedman, *Game Theory with Applications to Economics* (New York: Oxford University Press, 1990); Drew Fudenberg and Jean Tirole, *Game Theory* (Cambridge, MA: MIT Press, 1991); and Avinash Dixit and Susan Skeath, *Games of Strategy*, 2nd ed. (New York: Norton, 2004).

[6]A *Stackelberg equilibrium* is also a Nash equilibrium. In the Stackelberg model, however, the rules of the game are different: One firm makes its output decision before its competitor does. Under these rules, each firm is doing the best it can given the decision of its competitor.

| TABLE 13.3 | Product Choice Problem | | |
|---|---|---|---|
| | | Firm 2 | |
| | | Crispy | Sweet |
| Firm 1 | Crispy | −5, −5 | 10, 10 |
| | Sweet | 10, 10 | −5, −5 |

In this game, each firm is indifferent about which product it produces—so long as it does not introduce the same product as its competitor. If coordination were possible, the firms would probably agree to divide the market. But what if the firms must behave *noncooperatively*? Suppose that somehow—perhaps through a news release—Firm 1 indicates that it is about to introduce the sweet cereal, and that Firm 2 (after hearing this) announces its plan to introduce the crispy one. Given the action that it believes its opponent to be taking, neither firm has an incentive to deviate from its proposed action. If it takes the proposed action, its payoff is 10, but if it deviates—and its opponent's action remains unchanged—its payoff will be −5. Therefore, the strategy set given by the bottom left-hand corner of the payoff matrix is stable and constitutes a Nash equilibrium: Given the strategy of its opponent, each firm is doing the best it can and has no incentive to deviate.

Note that the upper right-hand corner of the payoff matrix is also a Nash equilibrium, which might occur if Firm 1 indicated that it was about to produce the crispy cereal. Each Nash equilibrium is stable because *once the strategies are chosen*, no player will unilaterally deviate from them. However, without more information, we have no way of knowing *which* equilibrium (crispy/sweet vs. sweet/crispy) is likely to result—or if *either* will result. Of course, both firms have a strong incentive to reach *one* of the two Nash equilibria—if they both introduce the same type of cereal, they will both lose money. The fact that the two firms are not allowed to collude does not mean that they will not reach a Nash equilibrium. As an industry develops, understandings often evolve as firms "signal" each other about the paths the industry is to take.

**The Beach Location Game** Suppose that you (*Y*) and a competitor (*C*) plan to sell soft drinks on a beach this summer. The beach is 200 yards long, and sunbathers are spread evenly across its length. You and your competitor sell the same soft drinks at the same prices, so customers will walk to the closest vendor. Where on the beach will you locate, and where do you think your competitor will locate?

If you think about this for a minute, you will see that the only Nash equilibrium calls for both you and your competitor to locate at the same spot in the center of the beach (see Figure 13.1). To see why, suppose your competitor located at some other point (*A*), which is three quarters of the way to the end of the beach. In that case, you would no longer want to locate in the center; you would locate near your competitor, just to the left. You would thus capture nearly three-fourths of all sales, while your competitor got only the remaining fourth. This outcome is not an equilibrium because your competitor would then want to move to the center of the beach, and you would do the same.

The "beach location game" can help us understand a variety of phenomena. Have you ever noticed how, along a two- or three-mile stretch of road, two or three gas stations or several car dealerships will be located close to each other?

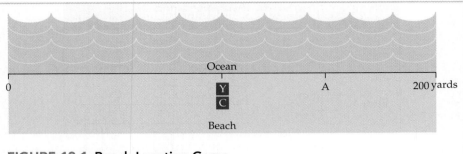

**FIGURE 13.1 Beach Location Game**

You (*Y*) and a competitor (*C*) plan to sell soft drinks on a beach. If sunbathers are spread evenly across the beach and will walk to the closest vendor, the two of you will locate next to each other at the center of the beach. This is the only Nash equilibrium. If your competitor located at point *A*, you would want to move until you were just to the left, where you could capture three-fourths of all sales. But your competitor would then want to move back to the center, and you would do the same.

Likewise, as a U.S. presidential election approaches, the Democratic and Republican candidates typically move close to the center as they define their political positions.

## Maximin Strategies

The concept of a Nash equilibrium relies heavily on individual rationality. Each player's choice of strategy depends not only on its own rationality, but also on the rationality of its opponent. This can be a limitation, as the example in Table 13.4 shows.

In this game, two firms compete in selling file-encryption software. Because both firms use the same encryption standard, files encrypted by one firm's software can be read by the other's—an advantage for consumers. Nonetheless, Firm 1 has a much larger market share. (It entered the market earlier and its software has a better user interface.) Both firms are now considering an investment in a new encryption standard.

Note that investing is a dominant strategy for Firm 2 because by doing so it will do better regardless of what Firm 1 does. Thus Firm 1 should expect Firm 2 to invest. In this case, Firm 1 would also do better by investing (and earning $20 million) than by not investing (and losing $10 million). Clearly the outcome (invest, invest) is a Nash equilibrium for this game, and you can verify that it is the only Nash equilibrium. But note that Firm 1's managers had better be sure that Firm 2's managers understand the game and are rational. If Firm 2 should happen to make a mistake and fail to invest, it would be extremely costly to

| **TABLE 13.4** | **Maximin Strategy** | | |
|---|---|---|---|
| | | **Firm 2** | |
| | | **Don't invest** | **Invest** |
| **Firm 1** | Don't invest | 0, 0 | −10, 10 |
| | Invest | −100, 0 | 20, 10 |

Firm 1. (Consumer confusion over incompatible standards would arise, and Firm 1, with its dominant market share, would lose $100 million.)

If you were Firm 1, what would you do? If you tend to be cautious—and if you are concerned that the managers of Firm 2 might not be fully informed or rational—you might choose to play "don't invest." In that case, the worst that can happen is that you will lose $10 million; you no longer have a chance of losing $100 million. This strategy is called a **maximin strategy** because it *maximizes the minimum gain that can be earned*. If both firms used maximin strategies, the outcome would be that Firm 1 does not invest and Firm 2 does. A maximin strategy is conservative, but it is not profit-maximizing. (Firm 1, for example, loses $10 million rather than earning $20 million.) Note that if Firm 1 *knew for certain* that Firm 2 was using a maximin strategy, it would prefer to invest (and earn $20 million) instead of following its own maximin strategy of not investing.

> • **maximin strategy**
> Strategy that maximizes the minimum gain that can be earned.

**Maximizing the Expected Payoff** If Firm 1 is unsure about what Firm 2 will do but can assign probabilities to each feasible action for Firm 2, it could instead use a strategy that *maximizes its expected payoff*. Suppose, for example, that Firm 1 thinks that there is only a 10-percent chance that Firm 2 will not invest. In that case, Firm 1's expected payoff from investing is $(.1)(-100) + (.9)(20) = \$8$ million. Its expected payoff if it doesn't invest is $(.1)(0) + (.9)(-10) = -\$9$ million. In this case, Firm 1 should invest.

On the other hand, suppose Firm 1 thinks that the probability that Firm 2 will not invest is 30 percent. Then Firm 1's expected payoff from investing is $(.3)(-100) + (.7)(20) = -\$16$ million, while its expected payoff from not investing is $(.3)(0) + (.7)(-10) = -\$7$ million. Thus Firm 1 will choose not to invest.

You can see that Firm 1's strategy depends critically on its assessment of the probabilities of different actions by Firm 2. Determining these probabilities may seem like a tall order. However, firms often face uncertainty (over market conditions, future costs, and the behavior of competitors), and must make the best decisions they can based on probability assessments and expected values.

> For a review of expected value, see §5.1, where it is defined as a weighted average of the payoffs associated with all possible outcomes, with the probabilities of each outcome used as weights.

**The Prisoners' Dilemma** What is the Nash equilibrium for the prisoners' dilemma discussed in Chapter 12? Table 13.5 shows the payoff matrix for the prisoners' dilemma. Recall that the ideal outcome is one in which neither prisoner confesses, so that both get two years in prison. Confessing, however, is a *dominant strategy* for each prisoner—it yields a higher payoff regardless of the strategy of the other prisoner. Dominant strategies are also maximin strategies. Therefore, the outcome in which both prisoners confess is both a Nash equilibrium and a maximin solution. Thus, in a very strong sense, it is rational for each prisoner to confess.

| TABLE 13.5 | Prisoners' Dilemma | | |
|---|---|---|---|
| | | **Prisoner B** | |
| | | **Confess** | **Don't confess** |
| **Prisoner A** | Confess | −5, −5 | −1, −10 |
| | Don't confess | −10, −1 | −2, −2 |

## *Mixed Strategies

In all of the games that we have examined so far, we have considered strategies in which players make a specific choice or take a specific action: advertise or don't advertise, set a price of $4 or a price of $6, and so on. Strategies of this kind are called **pure strategies**. There are games, however, in which a pure strategy is not the best way to play.

• **pure strategy** Strategy in which a player makes a specific choice or takes a specific action.

**Matching Pennies** An example is the game of "Matching Pennies." In this game, each player chooses heads or tails and the two players reveal their coins at the same time. If the coins match (i.e., both are heads or both are tails), Player *A* wins and receives a dollar from Player *B*. If the coins do not match, Player *B* wins and receives a dollar from Player *A*. The payoff matrix is shown in Table 13.6.

Note that there is no Nash equilibrium in pure strategies for this game. Suppose, for example, that Player *A* chose the strategy of playing heads. Then Player *B* would want to play tails. But if Player *B* plays tails, Player *A* would also want to play tails. No combination of heads or tails leaves both players satisfied—one player or the other will always want to change strategies.

• **mixed strategy** Strategy in which a player makes a random choice among two or more possible actions, based on a set of chosen probabilities.

Although there is no Nash equilibrium in pure strategies, there is a Nash equilibrium in **mixed strategies**: *strategies in which players make random choices among two or more possible actions, based on sets of chosen probabilities*. In this game, for example, Player *A* might simply flip the coin, thereby playing heads with probability 1/2 and playing tails with probability 1/2. In fact, if Player *A* follows this strategy and Player *B* does the same, we will have a Nash equilibrium: Both players will be doing the best they can given what the opponent is doing. Note that although the outcome is random, the *expected payoff* is 0 for each player.

It may seem strange to play a game by choosing actions randomly. But put yourself in the position of Player *A* and think what would happen if you followed a strategy *other* than just flipping the coin. Suppose you decided to play heads. If Player *B* knows this, she would play tails and you would lose. Even if Player *B* didn't know your strategy, if the game were played repeatedly, she could eventually discern your pattern of play and choose a strategy that countered it. Of course, you would then want to change your strategy—which is why this would not be a Nash equilibrium. Only if you and your opponent both choose heads or tails randomly with probability 1/2 would neither of you have any incentive to change strategies. (You can check that the use of different probabilities, say 3/4 for heads and 1/4 for tails, does not generate a Nash equilibrium.)

One reason to consider mixed strategies is that some games (such as "Matching Pennies") do not have any Nash equilibria in pure strategies. It can be shown, however, that once we allow for mixed strategies, *every* game has

| TABLE 13.6 | Matching Pennies | | |
|---|---|---|---|
| | | **Player B** | |
| | | **Heads** | **Tails** |
| **Player A** | Heads | 1, −1 | −1, 1 |
| | Tails | −1, 1 | 1, −1 |

at least one Nash equilibrium.[7] Mixed strategies, therefore, provide solutions to games when pure strategies fail. Of course, whether solutions involving mixed strategies are reasonable will depend on the particular game and players. Mixed strategies are likely to be very reasonable for "Matching Pennies," poker, and other such games. A firm, on the other hand, might not find it reasonable to believe that its competitor will set its price randomly.

**The Battle of the Sexes** Some games have Nash equilibria both in pure strategies and in mixed strategies. An example is "The Battle of the Sexes," a game that you might find familiar. It goes like this. Jim and Joan would like to spend Saturday night together but have different tastes in entertainment. Jim would like to go to the opera, but Joan prefers mud wrestling. As the payoff matrix in Table 13.7 shows, Jim would most prefer to go to the opera with Joan, but prefers watching mud wrestling with Joan to going to the opera alone, and similarly for Joan.

First, note that there are two Nash equilibria in pure strategies for this game—the one in which Jim and Joan both watch mud wrestling, and the one in which they both go to the opera. Joan, of course, would prefer the first of these outcomes and Jim the second, but both outcomes are equilibria—neither Jim nor Joan would want to change his or her decision, given the decision of the other.

This game also has an equilibrium in mixed strategies: Joan chooses wrestling with probability 2/3 and opera with probability 1/3, and Jim chooses wrestling with probability 1/3 and opera with probability 2/3. You can check that if Joan uses this strategy, Joan cannot do better with any other strategy, and vice versa.[8] The outcome is random, and Jim and Joan will each have an expected payoff of 2/3.

Should we expect Jim and Joan to use these mixed strategies? Unless they're very risk loving or in some other way a strange couple, probably not. By agreeing to either form of entertainment, each will have a payoff of at least 1, which exceeds the expected payoff of 2/3 from randomizing. In this game as in many others, mixed strategies provide another solution, but not a very realistic one. Hence, for the remainder of this chapter we will focus on pure strategies.

| TABLE 13.7 | The Battle of the Sexes | | |
|---|---|---|---|
| | | **Jim** | |
| | | **Wrestling** | **Opera** |
| **Joan** | Wrestling | 2, 1 | 0, 0 |
| | Opera | 0, 0 | 1, 2 |

---

[7]More precisely, every game with a finite number of players and a finite number of actions has at least one Nash equilibrium. For a proof, see David M. Kreps, *A Course in Microeconomic Theory* (Princeton, NJ: Princeton University Press, 1990), p. 409.

[8]Suppose Joan randomizes, letting $p$ be the probability of wrestling and $(1 - p)$ the probability of opera. Because Jim is using probabilities of 1/3 for wrestling and 2/3 for opera, the probability that both will choose wrestling is $(1/3)p$, and the probability that both will choose opera is $(2/3)(1 - p)$. Thus, Joan's expected payoff is $2(1/3)p + 1(2/3)(1 - p) = (2/3)p + 2/3 - (2/3)p = 2/3$. This payoff is independent of $p$, so Joan cannot do better in terms of expected payoff no matter what she chooses.

# 13.4 REPEATED GAMES

We saw in Chapter 12 that in oligopolistic markets, firms often find themselves in a prisoners' dilemma when making output or pricing decisions. Can firms find a way out of this dilemma, so that oligopolistic coordination and cooperation (whether explicit or implicit) could prevail?

To answer this question, we must recognize that the prisoners' dilemma, as we have described it so far, is limited: Although some prisoners may have only one opportunity in life to confess or not, most firms set output and price over and over again. In real life, firms play **repeated games**: Actions are taken and payoffs received over and over again. In repeated games, strategies can become more complex. For example, with each repetition of the prisoners' dilemma, each firm can develop a reputation about its own behavior and can study the behavior of its competitors.

How does repetition change the likely outcome of the game? Suppose you are Firm 1 in the prisoners' dilemma illustrated by the payoff matrix in Table 13.8. If you and your competitor both charge a high price, you will both make a higher profit than if you both charged a low price. However, you are afraid to charge a high price because if your competitor charges a low price, you will lose money and, to add insult to injury, your competitor will get rich. But suppose this game is repeated over and over again—for example, you and your competitor simultaneously announce your prices on the first day of every month. Should you then play the game differently, perhaps changing your price over time in response to your competitor's behavior?

In an interesting study, Robert Axelrod asked game theorists to come up with the best strategy they could think of to play this game in a repeated manner.[9] (A possible strategy might be: "I'll start off with a high price, then lower my price. But then if my competitor lowers his price, I'll raise mine for a while before lowering it again, etc.") Then, in a computer simulation, Axelrod played these strategies off against one another to see which worked best.

**Tit-for-Tat Strategy** As you would expect, any given strategy would work better against some strategies than it would against others. The objective, however, was to find the strategy that was most robust—that would work best on average against *all*, or almost all, other strategies. The result was surprising. The strategy that worked best was an extremely simple **tit-for-tat strategy**: I start out with a high price, which I maintain so long as you continue to "cooperate" and also charge a high price. As soon as you lower your price, however, I follow suit and lower mine. If you later decide to cooperate and raise your price again, I'll immediately raise my price as well.

• **repeated game**   Game in which actions are taken and payoffs received over and over again.

• **tit-for-tat strategy**  Repeated-game strategy in which a player responds in kind to an opponent's previous play, cooperating with cooperative opponents and retaliating against uncooperative ones.

| TABLE 13.8 | Pricing Problem | | |
|---|---|---|---|
| | | **Firm 2** | |
| | | Low price | High price |
| **Firm 1** | Low price | 10, 10 | 100, −50 |
| | High price | −50, 100 | 50, 50 |

[9]See Robert Axelrod, *The Evolution of Cooperation* (New York: Basic Books, 1984).

Why does this tit-for-tat strategy work best? In particular, can I expect that using the tit-for-tat strategy will induce my competitor to behave cooperatively (and charge a high price)?

**Infinitely Repeated Game** Suppose the game is *infinitely repeated*. In other words, my competitor and I repeatedly set prices month after month, *forever*. Cooperative behavior (i.e., charging a high price) is then the rational response to a tit-for-tat strategy. (This assumes that my competitor knows, or can figure out, that I am using a tit-for-tat strategy.) To see why, suppose that in one month my competitor sets a low price and undercuts me. In that month he will make a large profit. But my competitor knows that the following month I will set a low price, so that his profit will fall and will remain low as long as we both continue to charge a low price. Because the game is infinitely repeated, the cumulative loss of profits that results must outweigh any short-term gain that accrued during the first month of undercutting. Thus, it is not rational to undercut.

In fact, with an infinitely repeated game, my competitor need not even be sure that I am playing tit-for-tat to make cooperation its own rational strategy. Even if my competitor believes there is only *some* chance that I am playing tit-for-tat, he will still find it rational to start by charging a high price and maintain it as long as I do. Why? With infinite repetition of the game, the *expected* gains from cooperation will outweigh those from undercutting. This will be true even if the probability that I am playing tit-for-tat (and so will continue cooperating) is small.

**Finite Number of Repetitions** Now suppose the game is repeated a *finite* number of times—say, N months. (N can be large as long as it is finite.) If my competitor (Firm 2) is rational *and believes that I am rational*, he will reason as follows: "Because Firm 1 is playing tit-for-tat, I (Firm 2) cannot undercut—that is, *until the last month*. I *should* undercut the last month because then I can make a large profit that month, and afterward the game is over, so Firm 1 cannot retaliate. Therefore, I will charge a high price until the last month, and then I will charge a low price."

However, since I (Firm 1) have also figured this out, I also plan to charge a low price in the last month. Of course, Firm 2 can figure this out as well, and therefore *knows* that I will charge a low price in the last month. But then what about the next-to-last month? Because there will be no cooperation in the last month, anyway, Firm 2 figures that it should undercut and charge a low price in the next-to-last month. But, of course, I have figured this out too, so I *also* plan to charge a low price in the next-to-last month. And because the same reasoning applies to each preceding month, the game *unravels*: The only rational outcome is for both of us to charge a low price every month.

**Tit-for-Tat in Practice** Since most of us do not expect to live forever, the unravelling argument would seem to make the tit-for-tat strategy of little value, leaving us stuck in the prisoners' dilemma. In practice, however, tit-for-tat can sometimes work and cooperation can prevail. There are two primary reasons.

First, most managers don't know how long they will be competing with their rivals, and this also serves to make cooperative behavior a good strategy. If the end point of the repeated game is unknown, the unravelling argument that begins with a clear expectation of undercutting in the last month no longer applies. As with an infinitely repeated game, it will be rational to play tit-for-tat.

Second, my competitor might have some doubt about the extent of my rationality. Suppose my competitor *thinks* (and he need not be certain) that I am playing tit-for-tat. He also thinks that *perhaps* I am playing tit-for-tat "blindly," or with limited rationality, in the sense that I have failed to work out the logical implications of a finite time horizon as discussed above. My competitor thinks, for example, that perhaps I have not figured out that he will undercut me in the last month, so that I should also charge a low price in the last month, and so on. *"Perhaps,"* thinks my competitor, "Firm 1 will play tit-for-tat blindly, charging a high price as long as I charge a high price." Then (if the time horizon is long enough), it is rational for my competitor to maintain a high price until the last month (when he will undercut me).

Note that we have stressed the word *perhaps*. My competitor need not be sure that I am playing tit-for-tat "blindly," or even that I am playing tit-for-tat at all. Just the *possibility* can make cooperative behavior a good strategy (until near the end) if the time horizon is long enough. Although my competitor's conjecture about how I am playing the game might be wrong, cooperative behavior is profitable *in expected value terms*. With a long time horizon, the sum of current and future profits, weighted by the probability that the conjecture is correct, can exceed the sum of profits from price competition, even if my competitor is the first to undercut. After all, if I am wrong and my competitor charges a low price, I can shift my strategy at the cost of only one period's profit—a minor cost in light of the substantial profit that I can make if we both choose to set a high price.

Thus, in a repeated game, the prisoners' dilemma can have a cooperative outcome. In most markets, the game is in fact repeated over a long and uncertain length of time, and managers have doubts about how "perfectly rationally" they and their competitors operate. As a result, in some industries, particularly those in which only a few firms compete over a long period under stable demand and cost conditions, cooperation prevails, even though no contractual arrangements are made. (The water meter industry, discussed below, is an example.) In many other industries, however, there is little or no cooperative behavior.

Sometimes cooperation breaks down or never begins because there are too many firms. More often, failure to cooperate is the result of rapidly shifting demand or cost conditions. Uncertainties about demand or costs make it difficult for the firms to reach an implicit understanding of what cooperation should entail. (Remember that an *explicit* understanding, arrived at through meetings and discussions, could lead to an antitrust violation.) Suppose, for example, that cost differences or different beliefs about demand lead one firm to conclude that cooperation means charging $50 while a second firm thinks it means $40. If the second firm charges $40, the first firm might view that as a grab for market share and respond in tit-for-tat fashion with a $35 price. A price war could then develop.

**EXAMPLE 13.2** — Oligopolistic Cooperation in the Water Meter Industry

For some four decades, almost all the water meters sold in the United States have been produced by four American companies: Rockwell International, Badger Meter, Neptune Water Meter Company, and Hersey Products. Rockwell has had about a 35-percent share of the market, and the other three firms have together had about a 50- to 55-percent share.[10]

---

[10]This example is based in part on Nancy Taubenslag, "Rockwell International," Harvard Business School Case No. 9-383-019, July 1983. In 1979, Neptune Water Meter Company was acquired by Wheelabrator-Frye. Hersey Products is a small privately held company.

Most buyers of water meters are municipal water utilities, who install the meters in residential and commercial establishments in order to measure water consumption and bill consumers accordingly. Because the cost of meters is a small part of the total cost of providing water, utilities are concerned mainly that the meters be accurate and reliable. Price is not a primary issue, and demand is very inelastic. Demand is also very stable; because every residence or business must have a water meter, demand grows slowly along with the population.

In addition, utilities tend to have long-standing relationships with suppliers and are reluctant to shift from one to another. Because any new entrant will find it difficult to lure customers from existing firms, this creates a barrier to entry. Substantial economies of scale create a second barrier to entry: To capture a significant share of the market, a new entrant must invest in a large factory. This requirement virtually precludes entry by new firms.

With inelastic and stable demand and little threat of entry by new firms, the existing four firms could earn substantial monopoly profits if they set prices cooperatively. If, on the other hand, they compete aggressively, with each firm cutting price to increase its own share of the market, profits would fall to nearly competitive levels. The firms thus face a prisoners' dilemma. Can cooperation prevail?

It can and *has* prevailed. Remember that the same four firms have been playing a *repeated game* for decades. Demand has been stable and predictable, and over the years, the firms have been able to assess their own and each other's costs. In this situation, tit-for-tat strategies work well: It pays each firm to cooperate as long as its competitors are cooperating.

As a result, the four firms operate as though they were members of a country club. There is rarely an attempt to undercut price, and each firm appears satisfied with its share of the market. While the business may appear dull, it is certainly profitable. All four firms have been earning returns on their investments that far exceed those in more competitive industries.

---

**EXAMPLE 13.3**   ## Competition and Collusion in the Airline Industry

In March 1983, American Airlines, whose president, Robert Crandall, had become notable for his use of the telephone (see Example 10.5—page 384), proposed that all airlines adopt a uniform fare schedule based on mileage. The rate per mile would depend on the length of the trip, with the lowest rate of 15 cents per mile for trips over 2500 miles, higher rates for shorter trips, and the highest rate, 53 cents per mile, for trips under 250 miles. For example, a one-way coach ticket from Boston to Chicago, a distance of 932 miles, would cost $233 (based on a rate of 25 cents per mile for trips between 751 and 1000 miles).

This proposal would have done away with the many different fares (some heavily discounted) then available. The cost of a ticket from one city to another would depend only on the number of miles between those cities. As a senior vice-president of American Airlines said, "The new streamlined fare structure will help reduce fare confusion." Most other major airlines reacted favorably to the plan and began to adopt it. A vice-president of TWA said, "It's a good move. It's very businesslike." United Airlines quickly announced that it would adopt the plan on routes where it competes with American, which included most of its system, and TWA and Continental said that they would adopt it for all their routes.[11]

Why did American propose this plan, and what made it so attractive to the other airlines? Was it really to "help reduce fare confusion"? No, the aim was to reduce price competition and achieve a collusive pricing arrangement. Prices had been driven down by competitive undercutting, as airlines competed for market share. And as Robert Crandall had learned less than a year earlier, fixing prices over the telephone is illegal. Instead, the companies would implicitly fix prices by agreeing to use the same fare-setting formula.

The plan failed, a victim of the prisoners' dilemma. Only two weeks after the plan was announced and adopted by most airlines, Pan Am, which was dissatisfied with its small share of the U.S. market, dropped its fares. American, United, and TWA, afraid of losing their own shares of the market, quickly dropped their fares to match Pan Am. The price-cutting continued, and fortunately for consumers, the plan was soon dead.

American Airlines introduced another simplified, four-tier fare structure in April 1992, which was quickly adopted by most major carriers. But it, too, soon fell victim to competitive discounts. In May 1992, Northwest Airlines announced a "kids fly free" program, and American responded with a summer half-price sale, which other carriers matched. As a result, the airline industry lost billions.

Why is airline pricing so intensively competitive? Airlines plan route capacities two or more years into the future, but they make pricing decisions over short horizons—month by month or even week by week. In the short run, the marginal cost of adding passengers to a flight is very low—essentially the cost of a soft drink and a bag of peanuts. Each airline, therefore, has an incentive to lower fares in order to capture passengers from its competitors. In addition, the demand for air travel often fluctuates unpredictably. Such factors as these stand in the way of implicit price cooperation.

Thus, aggressive competition has continued to be the rule in the airline industry. In 2002, for example, both American Airlines and US Airways introduced price increases, only to abandon them when other carriers refused to cooperate. In fact, for several reasons, pricing has become even more competitive in recent years. First, discount airlines—such as Southwest and JetBlue—have attracted millions of price-conscious consumers and forced the major carriers to cut fares. Second, during periods of sluggish demand, airlines are compelled to reduce prices in order to attract consumers. Finally, Internet services such as Expedia, Orbitz, and Travelocity have promoted "fare shopping" by online consumers and encouraged more competitive pricing. These developments have forced several major airlines into bankruptcy and resulted in record losses for the industry.

## 13.5 SEQUENTIAL GAMES

In most of the games we have discussed so far, both players move at the same time. In the Cournot model of duopoly, for example, both firms set output at the same time. In **sequential games**, players move in turn. The Stackelberg model

• **sequential game** Game in which players move in turn, responding to each other's actions and reactions.

---

[11]"American to Base Fares on Mileage," *New York Times*, March 15, 1983; "Most Big Airlines Back American's Fare Plan," *New York Times*, March 17, 1983.

| TABLE 13.9 | Modified Product Choice Problem | | | |
|---|---|---|---|---|
| | | | **Firm 2** | |
| | | | **Crispy** | **Sweet** |
| **Firm 1** | Crispy | | –5, –5 | 10, 20 |
| | Sweet | | 20, 10 | –5, –5 |

discussed in Chapter 12 is an example of a sequential game; one firm sets output before the other does. There are many other examples: an advertising decision by one firm and the response by its competitor; entry-deterring investment by an incumbent firm and the decision whether to enter the market by a potential competitor; or a new government regulatory policy and the investment and output response of the regulated firms.

We will look at a variety of sequential games in the remainder of this chapter. As we will see, they are often easier to analyze than games in which the players move at the same time. In a sequential game, the key is to think through the possible actions and rational reactions of each player.

As a simple example, let's return to the product choice problem first discussed in Section 13.3. This problem involves two companies facing a market in which two new variations of breakfast cereal can be successfully introduced as long as each firm introduces only one variation. This time, let's change the payoff matrix slightly. As Table 13.9 shows, the new sweet cereal will inevitably be a better seller than the new crispy cereal, earning a profit of 20 rather than 10 (perhaps because consumers prefer sweet things to crispy things). Both new cereals will still be profitable, however, as long as each is introduced by only one firm. (Compare Table 13.9 with Table 13.3—page 485.)

Suppose that both firms, in ignorance of each other's intentions, must announce their decisions independently and simultaneously. In that case, both will probably introduce the sweet cereal—and both will lose money.

Now suppose that Firm 1 can gear up its production faster and introduce its new cereal first. We now have a sequential game: Firm 1 introduces a new cereal, and *then* Firm 2 introduces one. What will be the outcome of this game? When making its decision, Firm 1 must consider the rational response of its competitor. It knows that whichever cereal it introduces, Firm 2 will introduce the other kind. Thus it will introduce the sweet cereal, knowing that Firm 2 will respond by introducing the crispy one.

## The Extensive Form of a Game

Although this outcome can be deduced from the payoff matrix in Table 13.9, sequential games are sometimes easier to visualize if we represent the possible moves in the form of a decision tree. This representation is called the **extensive form of a game** and is shown in Figure 13.2. The figure shows the possible choices of Firm 1 (introduce a crispy or a sweet cereal) and the possible responses of Firm 2 to each of those choices. The resulting payoffs are given at the end of each branch. For example, if Firm 1 produces a crispy cereal and Firm 2 responds by also producing a crispy cereal, each firm will have a payoff of –5.

To find the solution to the extensive form game, work backward from the end. For Firm 1, the best sequence of moves is the one in which it earns 20 and

• **extensive form of a game** Representation of possible moves in a game in the form of a decision tree.

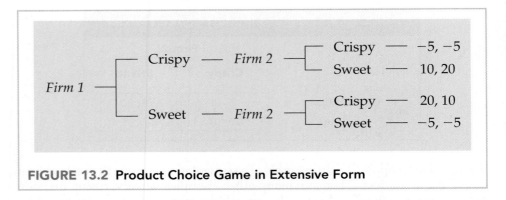

**FIGURE 13.2 Product Choice Game in Extensive Form**

Firm 2 earns 10. Thus it can deduce that it should produce the sweet cereal because Firm 2's best response is then to produce the crispy cereal.

## The Advantage of Moving First

In this product-choice game, there is a clear advantage to moving first: By introducing the sweet cereal, Firm 1 leaves Firm 2 little choice but to introduce the crispy one. This is much like the first-mover advantage that we saw in the Stackelberg model in Chapter 12. In that model, the firm that moves first can choose a large level of output, thereby giving its competitor little choice but to choose a small level.

> In §12.2, we explain that the Stackelberg model is an oligopoly model in which one firm sets its output before other firms do.

> Recall that in §12.2, we explain that in the Cournot model each firm treats the output of its competitors as fixed, and that all firms simultaneously decide how much to produce.

To clarify the nature of this first-mover advantage, it will be useful to review the Stackelberg model and compare it to the Cournot model in which both firms choose their outputs simultaneously. As in Chapter 12, we will use the example in which two duopolists face the market demand curve

$$P = 30 - Q$$

where $Q$ is the total production, i.e., $Q = Q_1 + Q_2$. As before, we will also assume that both firms have zero marginal cost. Recall that the Cournot equilibrium is then $Q_1 = Q_2 = 10$, so that $P = 10$ and each firm earns a profit of 100. Recall also that if the two firms colluded, they would set $Q_1 = Q_2 = 7.5$, so that $P = 15$ and each firm earns a profit of 112.50. Finally, recall from Section 12.3 that in the Stackelberg model, in which Firm 1 moves first, the outcome is $Q_1 = 15$ and $Q_2 = 7.5$, so that $P = 7.50$ and the firms' profits are 112.50 and 56.25, respectively.

These and a few other possible outcomes are summarized in the payoff matrix in Table 13.10. If both firms move simultaneously, the only solution to the

| TABLE 13.10 | Choosing Output | | |
|---|---|---|---|
| | | **Firm 2** | |
| | **7.5** | **10** | **15** |
| Firm 1   7.5 | 112.50, 112.50 | 93.75, 125 | 56.25, 112.50 |
| **Firm 1**   10 | 125, 93.75 | 100, 100 | 50, 75 |
|   15 | 112.50, 56.25 | 75, 50 | 0, 0 |

game is that both produce 10 and earn 100. In this Cournot equilibrium each firm is doing the best it can given what its competitor is doing. If Firm 1 moves first, however, it knows that its decision will constrain Firm 2's choice. Observe from the payoff matrix that if Firm 1 sets $Q_1 = 7.5$, Firm 2's best response will be to set $Q_2 = 10$. This will give Firm 1 a profit of 93.75 and Firm 2 a profit of 125. If Firm 1 sets $Q_1 = 10$, Firm 2 will set $Q_2 = 10$, and both firms will earn 100. But if Firm 1 sets $Q_1 = 15$, Firm 2 will set $Q_2 = 7.5$, so that Firm 1 earns 112.50, and Firm 2 earns 56.25. Therefore, the most that Firm 1 can earn is 112.50, and it does so by setting $Q_1 = 15$. Compared to the Cournot outcome, when Firm 1 moves first, it does better—and Firm 2 does much worse.

## 13.6 THREATS, COMMITMENTS, AND CREDIBILITY

The product choice problem and the Stackelberg model are two examples of how a firm that moves first can create a *fait accompli* that gives it an advantage over its competitor. In this section, we'll take a broader look at the advantage that a firm can have by moving first. We'll also consider what determines *which* firm goes first. We will focus on the following question: *What actions can a firm take to gain advantage in the marketplace?* For example, how might a firm deter entry by potential competitors, or induce existing competitors to raise prices, reduce output, or leave the market altogether?

Recall that in the Stackelberg model, the firm that moved first gained an advantage by *committing itself to a large output*. Making a commitment—constraining its future behavior—is crucial. To see why, suppose that the first mover (Firm 1) could later change its mind in response to what Firm 2 does. What would happen? Clearly, Firm 2 would produce a large output. Why? Because it knows that Firm 1 will respond by reducing the output that it first announced. The only way that Firm 1 can gain a first-mover advantage is by committing itself. In effect, *Firm 1 constrains Firm 2's behavior by constraining its own behavior.*

The idea of constraining your own behavior to gain an advantage may seem paradoxical, but we'll soon see that it is not. Let's consider a few examples.

First, let's return once more to the product-choice problem shown in Table 13.9. The firm that introduces its new breakfast cereal first will do best. *But which firm will introduce its cereal first?* Even if both firms require the same amount of time to gear up production, each has an incentive to *commit itself first to the sweet cereal.* The key word is *commit.* If Firm 1 simply announces it will produce the sweet cereal, Firm 2 will have little reason to believe it. After all, Firm 2, knowing the incentives, can make the same announcement louder and more vociferously. Firm 1 must constrain its own behavior in some way that convinces Firm 2 that Firm 1 has *no choice* but to produce the sweet cereal. Firm 1 might launch an expensive advertising campaign describing the new sweet cereal well before its introduction, thereby putting its reputation on the line. Firm 1 might also sign a contract for the forward delivery of a large quantity of sugar (and make the contract public, or at least send a copy to Firm 2). The idea is for Firm 1 to *commit itself* to produce the sweet cereal. Commitment is a strategic move that will induce Firm 2 to make the decision that Firm 1 wants it to make—namely, to produce the crispy cereal.

Why can't Firm 1 simply *threaten* Firm 2, vowing to produce the sweet cereal even if Firm 2 does the same? Because Firm 2 has little reason to believe the threat—and can make the same threat itself. A threat is useful only if it is credible. The following example should help make this clear.

**TABLE 13.11** Pricing of Computers and Word Processors

| | | Firm 2 | |
|---|---|---|---|
| | | **High price** | **Low price** |
| **Firm 1** | High price | 100, 80 | 80, 100 |
| | Low price | 20, 0 | 10, 20 |

## Empty Threats

Suppose Firm 1 produces personal computers that can be used both as word processors and to do other tasks. Firm 2 produces only dedicated word processors. As the payoff matrix in Table 13.11 shows, as long as Firm 1 charges a high price for its computers, both firms can make a good deal of money. Even if Firm 2 charges a low price for its word processors, many people will still buy Firm 1's computers (because they can do so many other things), although some buyers will be induced by the price differential to buy the dedicated word processor instead. However, if Firm 1 charges a low price, Firm 2 will also have to charge a low price (or else make zero profit), and the profit of both firms will be significantly reduced.

Firm 1 would prefer the outcome in the upper left-hand corner of the matrix. For Firm 2, however, charging a low price is clearly a dominant strategy. Thus the outcome in the upper right-hand corner will prevail (no matter which firm sets its price first).

Firm 1 would probably be viewed as the "dominant" firm in this industry because its pricing actions will have the greatest impact on overall industry profits. Can Firm 1 induce Firm 2 to charge a high price by *threatening* to charge a low price if Firm 2 charges a low price? No, as the payoff matrix in Table 13.11 makes clear: *Whatever* Firm 2 does, Firm 1 will be much worse off if it charges a low price. As a result, its threat is not credible.

## Commitment and Credibility

Sometimes firms can make threats credible. To see how, consider the following example. Race Car Motors, Inc., produces cars, and Far Out Engines, Ltd., produces specialty car engines. Far Out Engines sells most of its engines to Race Car Motors, and a few to a limited outside market. Nonetheless, it depends heavily on Race Car Motors and makes its production decisions in response to Race Car's production plans.

We thus have a sequential game in which Race Car is the "leader." It will decide what kind of cars to build, and Far Out Engines will then decide what kind of engines to produce. The payoff matrix in Table 13.12(a) shows the possible outcomes of this game. (Profits are in millions of dollars.) Observe that Race Car will do best by deciding to produce small cars. It knows that in response to this decision, Far Out will produce small engines, most of which Race Car will then buy. As a result, Far Out will make $3 million and Race Car $6 million.

Far Out, however, would much prefer the outcome in the lower right-hand corner of the payoff matrix. If it could produce big engines, *and* if Race Car produced big cars and thus bought the big engines, it would make $8 million. (Race Car,

| TABLE 13.12(a) Production Choice Problem | | | |
|---|---|---|---|
| | | **Race Car Motors** | |
| | | **Small cars** | **Big cars** |
| **Far Out Engines** | Small engines | 3, 6 | 3, 0 |
| | Big engines | 1, 1 | 8, 3 |

however, would make only $3 million.) Can Far Out induce Race Car to produce big cars instead of small ones?

Suppose Far Out *threatens* to produce big engines no matter what Race Car does; suppose, too, that no other engine producer can easily satisfy the needs of Race Car. If Race Car believed Far Out's threat, it would produce big cars: Otherwise, it would have trouble finding engines for its small cars and would earn only $1 million instead of $3 million. But the threat is not credible: Once Race Car responded by announcing its intentions to produce small cars, Far Out would have no incentive to carry out its threat.

Far Out can make its threat credible by visibly and irreversibly reducing some of its own payoffs in the matrix, thereby constraining its own choices. In particular, Far Out must reduce its profits from small engines (the payoffs in the top row of the matrix). It might do this by *shutting down or destroying some of its small engine production capacity*. This would result in the payoff matrix shown in Table 13.12(b). Now Race Car *knows* that whatever kind of car it produces, Far Out will produce big engines. If Race Car produces the small cars, Far Out will sell the big engines as best it can to other car producers and settle for making only $1 million. But this is better than making no profits by producing small engines. Because Race Car will have to look elsewhere for engines, its profit will also be lower ($1 million). Now it is clearly in Race Car's interest to produce large cars. By taking an action that *seemingly puts itself at a disadvantage*, Far Out has improved its outcome in the game.

Although strategic commitments of this kind can be effective, they are risky and depend heavily on having accurate knowledge of the payoff matrix and the industry. Suppose, for example, that Far Out commits itself to producing big engines but is surprised to find that another firm can produce small engines at a low cost. The commitment may then lead Far Out to bankruptcy rather than continued high profits.

**The Role of Reputation** Developing the right kind of *reputation* can also give one a strategic advantage. Again, consider Far Out Engines' desire to produce big engines for Race Car Motors' big cars. Suppose that the managers of Far Out

| TABLE 13.12(b) Modified Production Choice Problem | | | |
|---|---|---|---|
| | | **Race Car Motors** | |
| | | **Small cars** | **Big cars** |
| **Far Out Engines** | Small engines | 0, 6 | 0, 0 |
| | Big engines | 1, 1 | 8, 3 |

Engines develop a reputation for being irrational—perhaps downright crazy. They threaten to produce big engines no matter what Race Car Motors does (refer to Table 13.12a). Now the threat might be credible without any further action; after all, you can't be sure that an irrational manager will always make a profit-maximizing decision. In gaming situations, the party that is known (or thought) to be a little crazy can have a significant advantage.

Developing a reputation can be an especially important strategy in a repeated game. A firm might find it advantageous to behave irrationally for several plays of the game. This might give it a reputation that will allow it to increase its long-run profits substantially.

## Bargaining Strategy

Our discussion of commitment and credibility also applies to bargaining problems. The outcome of a bargaining situation can depend on the ability of either side to take an action that alters its relative bargaining position.

For example, consider two firms that are each planning to introduce one of two products which are complementary goods. As the payoff matrix in Table 13.13 shows, Firm 1 has a cost advantage over Firm 2 in producing A. Therefore, if both firms produce A, Firm 1 can maintain a lower price and earn a higher profit. Similarly, Firm 2 has a cost advantage over Firm 1 in producing product B. If the two firms could agree about who will produce what, the rational outcome would be the one in the upper right-hand corner: Firm 1 produces A, Firm 2 produces B, and both firms make profits of 50. Indeed, *even without cooperation*, this outcome will result whether Firm 1 or Firm 2 moves first or both firms move simultaneously. Why? Because producing B is a dominant strategy for Firm 2, so (A, B) is the only Nash equilibrium.

Firm 1, of course, would prefer the outcome in the lower left-hand corner of the payoff matrix. But in the context of this limited set of decisions, it cannot achieve that outcome. Suppose, however, that Firms 1 and 2 are also bargaining over a second issue—whether to join a research consortium that a third firm is trying to form. Table 13.14 shows the payoff matrix for this decision problem. Clearly, the dominant strategy is for both firms to enter the consortium, thereby increasing profits to 40.

Now suppose that Firm 1 *links the two bargaining problems* by announcing that it will join the consortium *only* if Firm 2 agrees to produce product A. In this case, it is indeed in Firm 2's interest to produce A (with Firm 1 producing B) in return for Firm 1's participation in the consortium. This example illustrates how combining issues in a bargaining agenda can sometimes benefit one side at the other's expense.

As another example, consider bargaining over the price of a house. Suppose I, as a potential buyer, do not want to pay more than $200,000 for a house that is actually worth $250,000 to me. The seller is willing to part with the house at any

| TABLE 13.13 | Production Decision | | |
|---|---|---|---|
| | | **Firm 2** | |
| | | **Produce A** | **Produce B** |
| **Firm 1** | Produce A | 40, 5 | 50, 50 |
| | Produce B | 60, 40 | 5, 45 |

**TABLE 13.14** Decision to Join Consortium

|  |  | Firm 2 | |
|---|---|---|---|
|  |  | Work alone | Enter consortium |
| **Firm 1** | Work alone | 10, 10 | 10, 20 |
|  | Enter consortium | 20, 10 | 40, 40 |

price above $180,000 but would like to receive the highest price she can. If I am the only bidder for the house, how can I make the seller think that I will walk away rather than pay more than $200,000?

I might declare that I will never, ever pay more than $200,000 for the house. But is such a promise credible? It may be if the seller knows that I have a reputation for toughness and that I have never reneged on a promise of this sort. But suppose I have no such reputation. Then the seller knows that I have every incentive to make the promise (making it costs nothing) but little incentive to keep it. (This will probably be our only business transaction together.) As a result, this promise by itself is not likely to improve my bargaining position.

The promise can work, however, if it is combined with an action that gives it credibility. Such an action must reduce my flexibility—limit my options—so that I have no choice but to keep the promise. One possibility would be to make an enforceable bet with a third party—for example, "If I pay more than $200,000 for that house, I'll pay you $60,000." Alternatively, if I am buying the house on behalf of my company, the company might insist on authorization by the Board of Directors for a price above $200,000, and announce that the board will not meet again for several months. In both cases, my promise becomes credible because I have destroyed my ability to break it. The result is less flexibility—and more bargaining power.

**EXAMPLE 13.4** **Wal-Mart Stores' Preemptive Investment Strategy**

Wal-Mart Stores, Inc., is an enormously successful chain of discount retail stores started by Sam Walton in 1969.[12] Its success was unusual in the industry. During the 1960s and 1970s, rapid expansion by existing firms and the entry and expansion of new firms made discount retailing increasingly competitive. During the 1970s and 1980s, industry-wide profits fell, and large discount chains—including such giants as King's, Korvette's, Mammoth Mart, W. T. Grant, and Woolco—went bankrupt. Wal-Mart Stores, however, kept on growing and became even more profitable. By the end of 1985, Sam Walton was one of the richest people in the United States.

[12]This example is based in part on information in Pankaj Ghemawat, "Wal-Mart Stores' Discount Operations," Harvard Business School, 1986.

How did Wal-Mart Stores succeed where others failed? The key was Wal-Mart's expansion strategy. To charge less than ordinary department stores and small retail stores, discount stores rely on size, no frills, and high inventory turnover. Through the 1960s, the conventional wisdom held that a discount store could succeed only in a city with a population of 100,000 or more. Sam Walton disagreed and decided to open his stores in small Southwestern towns; by 1970, there were 30 Wal-Mart stores in small towns in Arkansas, Missouri, and Oklahoma. The stores succeeded because Wal-Mart had created 30 "local monopolies." Discount stores that had opened in larger towns and cities were competing with other discount stores, which drove down prices and profit margins. These small towns, however, had room for only one discount operation. Wal-Mart could undercut the nondiscount retailers and never had to worry that another discount store would open and compete with it.

By the mid-1970s, other discount chains realized that Wal-Mart had a profitable strategy: Open a store in a small town that could support only one discount store and enjoy a local monopoly. There are a lot of small towns in the United States, so the issue became who would get to each town first. Wal-Mart now found itself in a *preemption game* of the sort illustrated by the payoff matrix in Table 13.15. As the matrix shows, if Wal-Mart enters a town but Company *X* does not, Wal-Mart will make 20 and Company *X* will make 0. Similarly, if Wal-Mart doesn't enter but Company *X* does, Wal-Mart makes 0 and Company *X* makes 20. But if Wal-Mart and Company *X* *both* enter, *they both lose 10*.

This game has two Nash equilibria—the lower left-hand corner and the upper right-hand corner. Which equilibrium results depends on *who moves first*. If Wal-Mart moves first, it can enter, knowing that the rational response of Company *X* will be not to enter, so that Wal-Mart will be assured of earning 20. *The trick, therefore, is to preempt*—to set up stores in other small towns quickly, before Company *X* (or Company *Y* or *Z*) can do so. That is exactly what Wal-Mart did. By 1986, it had 1009 stores in operation and was earning an annual profit of $450 million. And while other discount chains were going under, Wal-Mart continued to grow. By 1999, Wal-Mart had become the world's largest retailer, with 2454 stores in the United States and another 729 stores in the rest of the world, and had annual sales of $138 billion.

In recent years, Wal-Mart has continued to preempt other retailers by opening new discount stores, warehouse stores (such as Sam's Club), and combination discount and grocery stores (Wal-Mart Supercenters) all over the world. Wal-Mart has been especially aggressive in applying its preemption strategy in other countries. As of 2007, Wal-Mart had about 3800 stores in the United States and about 2800 stores throughout Europe, Latin America, and Asia. Wal-Mart had also become the world's largest private employer, employing more than 1.6 million people worldwide.

**TABLE 13.15** **The Discount Store Preemption Game**

|  |  | Company X | |
|---|---|---|---|
|  |  | **Enter** | **Don't enter** |
| **Wal-Mart** | Enter | −10, −10 | 20, 0 |
|  | Don't enter | 0, 20 | 0, 0 |

## 13.7 ENTRY DETERRENCE

Barriers to entry, which are an important source of monopoly power and profits, sometimes arise naturally. For example, economies of scale, patents and licenses, or access to critical inputs can create entry barriers. However, firms themselves can sometimes deter entry by potential competitors.

To deter entry, *the incumbent firm must convince any potential competitor that entry will be unprofitable.* To see how this might be done, put yourself in the position of an incumbent monopolist facing a prospective entrant, Firm X. Suppose that to enter the industry, Firm X will have to pay a (sunk) cost of $80 million to build a plant. You, of course, would like to induce Firm X to stay out of the industry. If X stays out, you can continue to charge a high price and enjoy monopoly profits. As shown in the upper right-hand corner of the payoff matrix in Table 13.16 (a), you would earn $200 million in profits.

If Firm X does enter the market, you must make a decision. You can be "accommodating," maintaining a high price in the hope that X will do the same. In that case, you will earn only $100 million in profit because you will have to share the market. New entrant X will earn a *net* profit of $20 million: $100 million minus the $80 million cost of constructing a plant. (This outcome is shown in the upper left-hand corner of the payoff matrix.) Alternatively, you can increase your production capacity, produce more, and lower your price. The lower price will give you a greater market share and a $20 million increase in revenues. Increasing production capacity, however, will cost $50 million, reducing your net profit to $70 million. Because warfare will also reduce the entrant's revenue by $30 million, it will have a net loss of $10 million. (This outcome is shown in the lower left-hand corner of the payoff matrix.) Finally, if Firm X stays out but you expand capacity and lower price nonetheless, your net profit will fall by $70 million (from $200 million to $130 million): the $50 million cost of the extra capacity and a $20 million reduction in revenue from the lower price with no gain in market share. Clearly this choice, shown in the lower right-hand corner of the matrix, would make no sense.

If Firm X thinks you will be accommodating and maintain a high price after it has entered, it will find it profitable to enter and will do so. Suppose you threaten to expand output and wage a price war in order to keep X out. If X takes the threat seriously, it will not enter the market because it can expect to lose $10 million. The threat, however, is not credible. As Table 13.16(a) shows (and as the potential competitor knows), *once entry has occurred, it will be in your best interest to accommodate and maintain a high price.* Firm X's rational move is to enter the market; the outcome will be the upper left-hand corner of the matrix.

> In §7.1, we explain that a sunk cost is an expenditure that has been made and cannot be recovered.

| TABLE 13.16(a) | Entry Possibilities | | |
|---|---|---|---|
| | | **Potential Entrant** | |
| | | **Enter** | **Stay out** |
| **Incumbent** | High price (accommodation) | 100, 20 | 200, 0 |
| | Low price (warfare) | 70, –10 | 130, 0 |

| TABLE 13.16(b)  Entry Deterrence | | Potential Entrant | |
| --- | --- | --- | --- |
| | | **Enter** | **Stay out** |
| **Incumbent** | High price (accommodation) | 50, 20 | 150, 0 |
| | Low price (warfare) | 70, −10 | 130, 0 |

But what if you can make an irrevocable commitment that will alter your incentives once entry occurs—a commitment that will give you little choice but to charge a low price if entry occurs? In particular, suppose you invest the $50 million *now*, rather than later, in the extra capacity needed to increase output and engage in competitive warfare should entry occur. Of course, if you later maintain a high price (whether or not *X* enters), this added cost will reduce your payoff.

We now have a new payoff matrix, as shown in Table 13.16 (b). As a result of your decision to invest in additional capacity, your threat to engage in competitive warfare is *completely credible*. Because you already have the additional capacity with which to wage war, you will do better in competitive warfare than you would by maintaining a high price. Because the potential competitor now knows that entry will result in warfare, it is rational for it to stay out of the market. Meanwhile, having deterred entry, you can maintain a high price and earn a profit of $150 million.

Can an incumbent monopolist deter entry without making the costly move of installing additional production capacity? Earlier we saw that a reputation for irrationality can bestow a strategic advantage. Suppose the incumbent firm has such a reputation. Suppose also that by means of vicious price-cutting, this firm has eventually driven out every entrant in the past, even though it incurred losses in doing so. Its threat might then be credible: The incumbent's irrationality suggests to the potential competitor that it might be better off staying away.

Of course, if the game described above were to be *indefinitely repeated*, then the incumbent might have a *rational* incentive to engage in warfare whenever entry actually occurs. Why? Because short-term losses from warfare might be outweighed by longer-term gains from preventing entry. Understanding this, the potential competitor might find the incumbent's threat of warfare credible and decide to stay out. Now the incumbent relies on its reputation for being rational—and far-sighted—to provide the credibility needed to deter entry. The success of this strategy depends on the time horizon and the relative gains and losses associated with accommodation and warfare.

We have seen that the attractiveness of entry depends largely on the way incumbents can be expected to react. In general, once entry has occurred, incumbents cannot be expected to maintain output at their pre-entry levels. Eventually, they may back off and reduce output, raising price to a new joint profit-maximizing level. Because potential entrants know this, incumbent firms must create a credible threat of warfare to deter entry. A reputation for irrationality can help. Indeed, this seems to be the basis for much of the entry-preventing behavior that goes on in actual markets. The potential entrant must consider that *rational* industry discipline can break down after entry occurs. By fostering an image of irrationality and belligerence, an incumbent firm might convince potential entrants that the risk of warfare is too high.[13]

## Strategic Trade Policy and International Competition

We have seen how a preemptive investment can give a firm an advantage by creating a credible threat to potential competitors. In some situations, a preemptive investment—subsidized or otherwise encouraged by the government—can give a *country* an advantage in international markets and so be an important instrument of trade policy.

Does this conflict with what you have learned about the benefits of free trade? In Chapter 9, for example, we saw how trade restrictions such as tariffs or quotas lead to deadweight losses. In Chapter 16 we go further and show how, in a general way, free trade between people (or between countries) is mutually beneficial. Given the virtues of free trade, how can government intervention in an international market ever be warranted? In certain situations, a country can benefit by adopting policies that give its domestic industries a competitive advantage.

To see how this might occur, consider an industry with substantial economies of scale—one in which a few large firms can produce much more efficiently than many small ones. Suppose that by granting subsidies or tax breaks, the government can encourage domestic firms to expand faster than they would otherwise. This might prevent firms in other countries from entering the world market, so that the domestic industry can enjoy higher prices and greater sales. Such a policy works by creating a credible threat to potential entrants. Large domestic firms, taking advantage of scale economies, would be able to satisfy world demand at a low price; if other firms entered, price would be driven below the point at which they could make a profit.

**The Commercial Aircraft Market** As an example, consider the international market for commercial aircraft. The development and production of a new line of aircraft are subject to substantial economies of scale; it would not pay to develop a new aircraft unless a firm expected to sell many of them. Suppose that Boeing and Airbus (a European consortium that includes France, Germany, Britain, and Spain) are each considering developing a new aircraft. The ultimate payoff to each firm depends in part on what the other firm does. Suppose it is only economical for one firm to produce the new aircraft. Then the payoffs might look like those in Table 13.17(a).[14]

If Boeing has a head start in the development process, the outcome of the game is the upper right-hand corner of the payoff matrix. Boeing will produce a

---

[13]There is an analogy here to *nuclear deterrence*. Consider the use of a nuclear threat to deter the former Soviet Union from invading Western Europe during the Cold War. If it invaded, would the United States actually react with nuclear weapons, knowing that the Soviets would then respond in kind? Because it is not rational for the United States to react this way, a nuclear threat might not seem credible. But this assumes that everyone is rational; there is a reason to fear an *irrational* response by the United States. Even if an irrational response is viewed as very improbable, it can be a deterrent, given the costliness of an error. The United States can thus gain by promoting the idea that it might act irrationally, or that events might get out of control once an invasion occurs. This is the "rationality of irrationality." See Thomas Schelling, *The Strategy of Conflict* (Harvard Univ. Press, 1980).

[14]This example is drawn from Paul R. Krugman, "Is Free Trade Passé?" *Journal of Economic Perspectives* 1 (Fall 1987): 131–44.

### TABLE 13.17(a)   Development of a New Aircraft

|  |  | Airbus | |
|---|---|---|---|
|  |  | **Produce** | **Don't produce** |
| **Boeing** | Produce | −10, −10 | 100, 0 |
|  | Don't produce | 0, 100 | 0, 0 |

new aircraft, and Airbus, realizing that it will lose money if it does the same, will not. Boeing will then earn a profit of 100.

European governments, of course, would prefer that Airbus produce the new aircraft. Can they change the outcome of this game? Suppose they commit to subsidizing Airbus and make this commitment before Boeing has committed itself to produce. If the European governments commit to a subsidy of 20 to Airbus if it produces the plane *regardless of what Boeing does*, the payoff matrix would change to the one in Table 13.17 (b).

Now Airbus will make money from a new aircraft whether or not Boeing produces one. Boeing knows that even if it commits to producing, Airbus will produce as well, and Boeing will lose money. Thus Boeing will decide not to produce, and the outcome will be the one in the lower left-hand corner of Table 13.17(b). A subsidy of 20, then, changes the outcome from one in which Airbus does not produce and earns 0, to one in which it does produce and earns 120. Of this, 100 is a transfer of profit from the United States to Europe. From the European point of view, subsidizing Airbus yields a high return.

European governments *did* commit to subsidizing Airbus, and during the 1980s, Airbus successfully introduced several new airplanes. The result, however, was not quite the one reflected in our simplified example. Boeing also introduced new airplanes (the 757 and 767 models) that were quite profitable. As commercial air travel grew, it became clear that both companies could profitably develop and sell new airplanes. Nonetheless, Boeing's market share would have been much larger without the European subsidies to Airbus. One study estimated that those subsidies totalled $25.9 billion during the 1980s and found that Airbus would not have entered the market without them.[15]

### TABLE 13.17(b)   Development of Aircraft after European Subsidy

|  |  | Airbus | |
|---|---|---|---|
|  |  | **Produce** | **Don't produce** |
| **Boeing** | Produce | −10, 10 | 100, 0 |
|  | Don't produce | 0, 120 | 0, 0 |

---

[15]"Aid to Airbus Called Unfair in U.S. Study," *New York Times*, September 8, 1990.

This example shows how strategic trade policy can transfer profits from one country to another. Bear in mind, however, that a country that uses such a policy may provoke retaliation from its trading partners. If a trade war results, all countries can end up much worse off. The possibility of such an outcome must be considered before a nation adopts a strategic trade policy.

---

**EXAMPLE 13.5**     DuPont Deters Entry in the Titanium Dioxide Industry

Titanium dioxide is a whitener used in paints, paper, and other products. In the early 1970s, DuPont and National Lead each accounted for about a third of U.S. titanium dioxide sales; another seven firms produced the remainder. In 1972, DuPont was considering whether to expand capacity. The industry was changing, and with the right strategy, those changes might enable DuPont to capture more of the market and dominate the industry.[16]

Three factors had to be considered. First, although future demand for titanium dioxide was uncertain, it was expected to grow substantially. Second, the government had announced that new environmental regulations would be imposed. Third, the prices of raw materials used to make titanium dioxide were rising. The new regulations and the higher input prices would have a major effect on production cost and give DuPont a cost advantage, both because its production technology was less sensitive to the change in input prices and because its plants were in areas that made disposal of corrosive wastes much less difficult than for other producers. Because of these cost changes, DuPont anticipated that National Lead and some other producers would have to shut down part of their capacity. DuPont's competitors would in effect have to "re-enter" the market by building new plants. Could DuPont deter them from taking this step?

DuPont considered the following strategy: invest nearly $400 million in increased production capacity to try to capture 64 percent of the market by 1985. The production capacity that would be put on line would be much more than what was actually needed. The idea was to *deter competitors from investing*. Scale economies and movement down the learning curve would give DuPont a cost advantage. This would not only make it hard for other firms to compete, but would make credible the implicit threat that in the future, DuPont would fight rather than accommodate.

The strategy was sensible and seemed to work for a few years. By 1975, however, things began to go awry. First, because demand grew by much less than expected, there was excess capacity industrywide. Second, because the environmental regulations were only weakly enforced, competitors did not have to shut down capacity as expected. Finally, DuPont's strategy led to antitrust action by the Federal Trade Commission in 1978. The FTC claimed that DuPont was attempting to monopolize the market. DuPont won the case, but the decline in demand made its victory moot.

---

[16]This example is based on Pankaj Ghemawat, "Capacity Expansion in the Titanium Dioxide Industry," *Journal of Industrial Economics* 33 (December 1984): 145–63; and P. Ghemawat, "DuPont in Titanium Dioxide," Harvard Business School, Case No. 9–385–140, June 1986.

---

**EXAMPLE 13.6** Diaper Wars

For more than two decades, the disposable diaper industry in the United States has been dominated by two firms: Procter & Gamble, with an approximately 50-percent market share, and Kimberly-Clark, with another 30–40 percent.[17] How do these firms compete? And why haven't other firms been able to enter and take a significant share of this $5-billion-per-year market?

Even though there are only two major firms, competition is intense. The competition occurs mostly in the form of *cost-reducing innovation*. The key to success is to perfect the manufacturing process so that a plant can manufacture diapers in high volume and at low cost. This is not as simple as it might seem. Packing cellulose fluff for absorbency, adding an elastic gatherer, and binding, folding, and packaging the diapers—at a rate of about 3000 diapers per minute and at a cost of about 10 cents per diaper—requires an innovative, carefully designed, and finely tuned process. Furthermore, small technological improvements in the manufacturing process can result in a significant competitive advantage. If a firm can shave its production cost even slightly, it can reduce price and capture market share. As a result, both firms are forced to spend heavily on research and development (R&D) in a race to reduce cost.

The payoff matrix in Table 13.18 illustrates this. If both firms spend aggressively on R&D, they can expect to maintain their current market shares. P&G will earn a profit of 40, and Kimberly-Clark (with a smaller market share) will earn 20. If neither firm spends money on R&D, their costs and prices will remain constant and the money saved will become part of profits. P&G's profit will increase to 60 and Kimberly-Clark's to 40. However, if one firm continues to do R&D and the other doesn't, the innovating firm will eventually capture most of its competitor's market share. For example, if Kimberly-Clark does R&D and P&G does not, P&G can expect to lose 20 while Kimberly-Clark's profit increases to 60. The two firms are therefore in a prisoners' dilemma: Spending money on R&D is a dominant strategy for each firm.

Why hasn't cooperative behavior evolved? After all, the two firms have been competing in this market for years, and the demand for diapers is fairly stable. For several reasons, a prisoners' dilemma involving R&D is particularly hard to resolve. First, it is difficult for a firm to monitor its competitor's R&D activities

| TABLE 13.18 | | Competing through R&D | |
|---|---|---|---|
| | | **Kimberly-Clark** | |
| | | **R&D** | **No R&D** |
| **P&G** | R&D | 40, 20 | 80, −20 |
| | No R&D | −20, 60 | 60, 40 |

---

[17]Procter & Gamble makes Pampers, Ultra Pampers, and Luvs. Kimberly-Clark has only one major brand, Huggies.

the way it can monitor price. Second, it can take several years to complete an R&D program that leads to a major product improvement. As a result, tit-for-tat strategies, in which both firms cooperate until one of them "cheats," are less likely to work. A firm may not find out that its competitor has been secretly doing R&D until the competitor announces a new and improved product. By then it may be too late to gear up an R&D program of its own.

The ongoing R&D expenditures by P&G and Kimberly-Clark also serve to deter entry. In addition to brand name recognition, these two firms have accumulated so much technological know-how and manufacturing proficiency that they would have a considerable cost advantage over any firm just entering the market. Besides building new factories, an entrant would have to make a large investment in R&D to capture even a small share of the market. After it began producing, a new firm would have to continue to spend heavily on R&D to reduce its costs over time. Entry would be profitable only if P&G and Kimberly-Clark stop doing R&D, so that the entrant could catch up and eventually gain a cost advantage. But as we have seen, no rational firm would expect this to happen.[18]

## *13.8 AUCTIONS

In this section, we examine **auction markets**—markets in which products are bought and sold through formal bidding processes.[19] Auctions come in all sizes and shapes. They are often used for differentiated products, especially unique items such as art, antiques, and the rights to extract oil from a piece of land. In recent years, for example, the U.S. Treasury has relied on auctions to sell Treasury bills, the Federal Communications Commission has used auctions for the sale of portions of the electromagnetic spectrum for cellular telephone services, the International Olympic Committee has auctioned television rights, and the Department of Defense has used auctions to procure military equipment. Auctions like these have important advantages: They are likely to be less time-consuming than one-on-one bargaining, and they encourage competition among buyers in a way that increases the seller's revenue.

Why have auctions become so popular and so successful? The low cost of transacting is only part of the answer. Unlike sales in retail stores, auctions are inherently interactive, with many buyers competing to obtain an item of interest. This interaction can be particularly valuable for the sale of items such as artwork or sports memorabilia that are unique, and therefore do not have established market values. It can also be helpful for the sale of items that are not unique but whose value fluctuates over time.

An example is the daily auctioning of fresh tuna at a Tokyo fish market.[20] Each tuna is unique in size, shape, and quality, and consequently in value. If each transaction were carried out through rounds of bargaining and negotiation with potential buyers, it would be extremely time-consuming. Instead, sales

• **auction market** Market in which products are bought and sold through formal bidding processes.

---

[18]Example 15.3 in Chapter 15 examines in more detail the profitability of capital investment by a new entrant in the diaper market.

[19]There is a vast literature on auctions; for example, see Paul Milgrom, "Auctions and Bidding: A Primer," *Journal of Economic Perspectives* (Summer 1989): 3–22; Avinash Dixit and Susan Skeath, *Games of Strategy*, 2nd ed. (New York: Norton, 2004); and Preston McAfee, *Competitive Solutions: The Strategist's Toolkit*, Princeton University Press (2002): ch. 12.

[20]John McMillan, *Reinventing the Bazaar: A Natural History of Markets* (New York, Norton, 2002).

occur every morning by means of an auction in which each tuna is sold to the highest bidder. This format creates large savings in transaction costs and thereby increases the efficiency of the market.

The design of an auction, which involves choosing the rules under which it operates, greatly affects its outcome. A seller will usually want an auction format that maximizes the revenue from the sale of the product. On the other hand, a buyer collecting bids from a group of potential sellers will want an auction that minimizes the expected cost of the product.

## Auction Formats

We will see that the choice of auction format can affect the seller's auction revenue. Several different kinds of auction formats are widely used:

- **English (or oral) auction** Auction in which a seller actively solicits progressively higher bids from a group of potential buyers.

- **Dutch auction** Auction in which a seller begins by offering an item at a relatively high price, then reduces it by fixed amounts until the item is sold.

- **sealed-bid auction** Auction in which all bids are made simultaneously in sealed envelopes, the winning bidder being the individual who has submitted the highest bid.

- **first-price auction** Auction in which the sales price is equal to the highest bid.

- **second-price auction** Auction in which the sales price is equal to the second-highest bid.

- **private-value auction** Auction in which each bidder knows his or her individual valuation of the object up for bid, with valuations differing from bidder to bidder.

> Recall from §11.2 that the reservation price is the maximum amount of money that an individual will pay for a product.

- **common-value auction** Auction in which the item has the same value to all bidders, but bidders do not know that value precisely and their estimates of it vary.

1. **English (or oral) auction:** The seller actively solicits progressively higher bids from a group of potential buyers. At each point, all participants are aware of the current high bid. The auction stops when no bidder is willing to surpass the current high bid; the item is then sold to the highest bidder at a price equal to the amount of the high bid.

2. **Dutch auction:** The seller begins by offering the item at a relatively high price. If no potential buyer agrees to that price, the seller reduces the price by fixed amounts. The first buyer who accepts an offered price can buy the item at that price.

3. **Sealed-bid auction:** All bids are made simultaneously in sealed envelopes, and the winning bidder is the individual who has submitted the highest bid. The price paid by the winning bidder will vary, however, depending on the rules of the auction. In a **first-price auction**, the sales price is equal to the highest bid. In a **second-price auction**, the sales price is equal to the second-highest bid.

## Valuation and Information

Suppose you want to sell a distinctive and valuable product such as a painting or a rare coin. Which type of auction is best for you? The answer depends on the preferences of the bidders and the information available to them. We consider two cases:

1. In **private-value auctions,** each bidder knows his or her individual valuation or *reservation price*, and valuations differ from bidder to bidder. In addition, each bidder is uncertain about the value that other bidders place on the product. For example, I might value a signed Barry Bonds home run baseball very highly but not know that you value it less highly.

2. In **common-value auctions**, the item to be auctioned has approximately the same value to all bidders. Bidders, however, do not know precisely what that value is—they can only estimate it, and bidders' estimates will vary. For example, in an auction of an offshore oil reserve, the value of the reserve is the price of oil minus the extraction cost, times the amount of oil in the reserve. As a result, the value should be about the same for all bidders. However, bidders will not know the amount of oil or the extraction cost—they can only estimate these numbers. Because their estimates will differ, they might bid very different amounts to get the reserve.

In reality, auctions can have both private-value and common-value elements. In the oil reserve auction, for example, there may be some private-value elements because different oil reserves may entail different extraction costs. However, to simplify matters we will separate the two. We begin our discussion with private-value auctions and then move on to common-value auctions.

## Private-Value Auctions

In private-value auctions, bidders have different reservation prices for the offered item. We might suppose, for example, that in an auction for a signed Barry Bonds baseball, individuals' reservation prices range from $1 (someone who doesn't like baseball but is bidding just for fun) to $600 (a San Francisco Giants fan). Of course, if you are bidding for the baseball, you don't know how many people will bid against you or what their bids will be.

Whatever the auction format, each bidder must choose his or her bidding strategy. For an open English auction, this strategy is a choice of a price at which to stop bidding. For a Dutch auction, the strategy is the price at which the individual expects to make his or her only bid. For a sealed-bid auction, the strategy is the choice of bid to place in a sealed envelope.

What are the payoffs in this bidding game? The payoff for winning is the difference between the winner's reservation price and the price paid; the payoff for losing is zero. Given these payoffs, let's examine bidding strategies and outcomes for different auction formats.

We will begin by showing that English oral auctions and second-price sealed-bid auctions generate nearly identical outcomes. Let's begin with the second-price sealed-bid auction. In this auction, bidding truthfully is a *dominant strategy*—there is no advantage to bidding below your reservation price. Why? Because the price you pay is based on the valuation of the *second highest bidder*, not on your own valuation. Suppose that your reservation price is $100. If you bid below your reservation price—say, $80—you risk losing to the second-highest bidder, who bids $85, when winning (at, say, $87) would have given you a positive payoff. If you bid above your reservation price—say $105—you risk winning but receiving a negative payoff.

Similarly, in an English auction the dominant strategy is to continue bidding until the second person is unwilling to make a bid. Then the winning bid will be approximately equal to the reservation price of the second person. In any case, you should stop bidding *when the bidding reaches your reservation price*. Why? Because if you stop bidding at a point below your reservation price, you risk losing a positive payoff; if you continue beyond your reservation price, you will be guaranteed a negative payoff. How high will the bidding go? It will continue until the winning bid is approximately equal to the reservation price of the second-highest bidder. Likewise, in the sealed-bid auction the winning bid will equal the reservation price of the second-highest bidder. Thus, both auction formats generate nearly identical outcomes. (The outcomes should differ in theory only by a dollar or two.) To illustrate, suppose that there are three bidders whose valuations are $50, $40, and $30, respectively, and furthermore the auctioneer and the bidders have complete information about these valuations. In an English auction, if your valuation was $50 you would offer a winning bid of $40.01 in order to win the bidding from the individual whose reservation price was $40.00. You would make the identical bid in a sealed-bid auction.

Even in a world of incomplete information, we would expect similar results. Indeed, you know that as a seller, you should be indifferent between an oral English auction and a second-price sealed-bid auction, because bidders in each case have private values. Suppose that you plan to sell an item using a sealed-bid auction. Which should you choose, a first-price or a second-price auction? You might think that the first-price auction is better because the payment is given by the highest rather than the second-highest bid. Bidders, however, are aware of this reasoning and will alter their bidding strategies accordingly: They will bid less in anticipation of paying the winning bid if they are successful.

The second-price sealed-bid auction generates revenue equal to the second-highest reservation price. However, the revenue implications of a first-price sealed-bid auction for the seller are more complicated because the optimal strategy of bidders is more complex. The best strategy is to choose a bid that you believe will be equal to or slightly above the reservation price of the individual with the second-highest reservation price.[21] Why? Because the winner must pay his or her bid, and it is never worth paying more than the second-highest reservation price. Thus, we see that the first-price and second-price sealed-bid auctions generate the same expected revenue.

## Common-Value Auctions

Suppose that you and four other people participate in an oral auction to purchase a large jar of pennies, which will go to the winning bidder at a price equal to the highest bid. Each bidder can examine the jar but cannot open it and count the pennies. Once you have estimated the number of pennies in the jar, what is your optimal bidding strategy? This is a classic common-value auction, because the jar of pennies has the same value for all bidders. The problem for you and other bidders is the fact that the value is unknown.

You might be tempted to do what many novices would do in this situation—bid up to your own estimate of the number of pennies in the jar, and no higher. This, however, is not the best way to bid. Remember that neither you nor the other bidders knows the number of pennies for certain. All of you have independently made estimates of the number, and those estimates are subject to error—some will be too high and some too low. Who, then, will be the winning bidder? If each bidder bids up to his or her estimate, *the winning bidder is likely to be the person with the largest positive error*—i.e., the person with the largest overestimate of the number of pennies.

**The Winner's Curse** To appreciate this possibility, suppose that there are actually 620 pennies in the jar. Let's say the bidders' estimates are 540, 590, 615, 650, and 690. Finally, suppose that you are the bidder whose estimate is 690 and that you win the auction with a bid of $6.80. Should you be happy about winning? No—you will have paid $6.80 for $6.20 worth of pennies. You will have fallen prey to the **winner's curse**: The winner of a common-value auction is often worse off than those who did not win because the winner was overly optimistic and, as a consequence, bid more for the item than it was actually worth.

The winner's curse can arise in any common-value auction, and bidders often fail to take it into account. Suppose, for example, that your house needs to be painted. You ask five companies to give you cost estimates for the job, telling each that you will accept the lowest estimate. Who will win the job? It will probably be the painter who has most seriously underestimated the amount of work

• **winner's curse** Situation in which the winner of a common-value auction is worse off as a consequence of overestimating the value of the item and thereby overbidding.

---

[21]To be more exact, the best strategy is to choose a bid that you believe will be equal to or slightly above the second-highest expected reservation price *conditional on your value being the highest.*

involved. At first, that painter might be happy to have won the job, only later to realize that much more work is required than was anticipated. The same problem can arise for oil companies bidding for offshore oil reserves when the size of the reserve and cost of extraction are uncertain (so that the value of the reserve is uncertain). Unless the companies take the winner's curse into account, the winning bidder is likely to win by overestimating the value of the reserve and will thus pay more than the reserve is worth.

How should you take the winner's curse into account when bidding for an item in a common-value auction? You must not only estimate the value of the item that you are bidding for, but also account for the fact that your estimate—and the estimates of the other bidders—are subject to error. To avoid the winner's curse, you must reduce your maximum bid below your value estimate by an amount equal to the expected error of the winning bidder. The more precise your estimate, the less you need to reduce your bid. If you can't assess the precision of your estimate directly, you can estimate the variation in the estimates of the other bidders. If there is a lot of disagreement among these bidders, it is likely that your estimate will be similarly imprecise. To measure the variation in bids, you can use the standard deviation of the estimates, which can be calculated using statistical methods.

Oil companies have been bidding for oil reserves for years, and thus are able to estimate this standard deviation quite well. They can thereby take the winner's curse into account by reducing their maximum bids below their value estimates by an amount equal to the expected error of the winning bidder. As a result, oil companies rarely feel they have made a mistake after winning an auction. House painters, on the other hand, are often less sophisticated in their bidding decisions and suffer from the winner's curse.

The winner's curse is more likely to be a problem in a sealed-bid auction than in a traditional English auction. In a traditional auction, if you are the only bidder who is overly optimistic, you can still win the bidding by offering only slightly more than the second-highest bidder. Therefore, for the winner's curse to be a problem, at least two bidders must be overly optimistic. By contrast, in a sealed-bid auction, your optimism could encourage you to outbid everyone else by a substantial margin.

## Maximizing Auction Revenue

Now let's return to the question of auction design from the viewpoint of the seller. Here are some useful tips for choosing the best auction format.

1. In a private-value auction, you should encourage as many bidders as possible: Additional bidders increase the expected bid of the winner and the expected valuation of the second-highest bidder as well.

2. In a common-value auction, you should (a) use an open rather than a sealed-bid auction because, as a general rule, an English (open) common-value auction will generate greater expected revenue than a sealed-bid auction; and (b) reveal information about the true value of the object being auctioned, thereby reducing concern about the winner's curse and, consequently, encouraging more bidding.

3. In a private-value auction, set a minimum bid equal to or even somewhat higher than the value to you of keeping the good for future sale. This will protect against a loss if there are relatively few bidders who do not value the good very highly. Moreover, it could increase the size of the bids by signaling to buyers that the object is valuable. Having the opportunity to

try again to sell the good if there is no minimum bid is obviously an advantage; however, it can be a disadvantage if failure to sell the good the first time is seen as a signal of low quality to bidders in future auctions.

Why use an open auction? Recall that in order to avoid the winner's curse, each bidder in a common value auction will bid below his individual valuation. The greater the uncertainty about the true value of the object, the greater the likelihood of an overbid, and therefore the greater the incentive for the bidder to reduce his bid. (If the bidder is risk-averse, this effect will be magnified.) However, the bidder faces less uncertainty in an English auction than in a sealed-bid auction because he can observe the prices at which other bidders drop out of the competition—an advantage that provides information about their valuations. In short, when you provide more information to bidders, risk-averse bidders will be encouraged to bid more because they will be more confident that they can account for the possibility of a winner's curse.

## Bidding and Collusion

We have seen that sellers at auctions can obtain a significant share of the gains from trade by encouraging competition among buyers. It follows, therefore, that buyers can increase their bargaining power by reducing the number of bidders or the frequency of bidding. In some cases this can be accomplished legally through the formation of buying groups, but it may also be accomplished illegally through collusive agreements that violate the antitrust laws. Collusion among buyers is not easy, because even if an "agreement" is reached, individual buyers will have an incentive to cheat by increasing their bids at the last minute in order to obtain the desired item. However, repeated auctions allow for participants to penalize those that break from the agreement by outbidding the "cheater" again and again. Buyer collusion is more of a problem in open-bid auctions than in the case of sealed bids because open auctions offer the best opportunity for colluding bidders to detect and punish cheating.

A well-known case of buyer collusion was the agreement in the mid-1980s among baseball owners to limit their bidding for free-agent players. The fact that such bidding was repeated and open made it possible for owners to retaliate against those that bid too often and too aggressively. Collusion, however, is not limited to buyers. In 2001, two of the world's most successful auction houses, Sotheby's and Christie's, were found guilty of agreeing to fix the price of commissions offered to sellers of auctioned items. Former Sotheby's chairman Alfred Taubman was sentenced to a year in jail for his involvement in the scheme.

---

| EXAMPLE 13.7 | Auctioning Legal Services |
| --- | --- |

After Sotheby's and Christie's auction houses were found guilty in 2001 of fixing commission prices, a federal class-action lawsuit followed, on behalf of those who paid too much in commissions. The lawsuit was administrated by Judge Kaplan of the Southern District of New York. When federal courts manage class-action suits, they are responsible for awarding attorney's fees. In this case, Judge Kaplan decided to hold an auction to select the law firm that would represent the plaintiff class.

Judge Kaplan entertained secret sealed bids from 20 law firms. Each firm was told to offer a fee arrangement consisting of a base and a percentage. A settlement or trial award at or below the base would be given entirely to the plaintiffs, with the law firm receiving nothing. If the settlement or award was higher than the base, the law firm would receive the stated percentage of the amount over the base. Many attorneys operate under a contingent fee system in which they offer a base of zero and expect to receive one-third of the award.

The winning bidder was the law firm of Boies, Schiller, & Flexner, which bid a base of $405 million and a percentage of 25 percent to be earned on any award above $405 million. Some of the losing bidders were outraged that Boies had bid so high to get the business. Indeed, some suggested that the firm might not work hard in the plaintiffs' interest because the minimum might be unachievable. Prior to the bidding, observers expected the case to generate a settlement of $130 million. In the end, it appears that Judge Kaplan, the plaintiffs' class, and the Boies law firm were all winners. Months after taking on the case, Boies settled with defendants for $512 million, earning the attorneys a $26.75 million fee (25 percent of the $107 excess over the base guarantee of $405 million) and generating just over $475 million for the class members.[22]

**EXAMPLE 13.8** **Internet Auctions**

The popularity of auctions has skyrocketed in recent years with the growth of the Internet. Indeed, the Internet has lowered transaction costs by so much that individuals anywhere in the world can now trade relatively low-value items without leaving the comfort of home. Many Internet sites are now devoted to auctions at which participants can buy and sell a wide variety of items. Let's see how these Internet auctions work.[23]

The most popular Internet auction site is **www.ebay.com**. It conducts auctions each day for items ranging from antiques and automobiles to Beanie Babies and Pokémon cards. Founded in 1995 by Pierre Omidyar in an effort to sell a broken laser pointer, eBay dominates the online person-to-person auction industry. It recently listed millions of products for sale, including such unusual items as a Caribbean island, 154 acres in the Catskills, and a ghost town in Nevada. In 2005, eBay accounted for about 85 percent of all online auction sales, totalling over $50 billion. On average, over 14 million items are listed for sale at any given time.

---

[22]Some experts have speculated that Boies was successful in obtaining a higher settlement because the defendant was aware that any settlement less than $405 million would generate no legal fees.

[23]For more information on Internet auctions, see Patrick Bajari and Ali Hortaçsu, "Economic Insights from Internet Auctions," *Journal of Economic Literature* 42 (June 2004): 457–86.

In §4.5 we explain how network externalities affect sales of a product.

How has eBay come to dominate the Internet auction market? Why haven't other Internet auction sites (such as Yahoo and Amazon) succeeded in taking market share from eBay? The answer is that Internet auctions are subject to very strong *network externalities*. If you wanted to auction off some rare coins or Pokémon cards, which auction site would you choose? The one that had the largest number of potential bidders. Likewise, if you wanted to bid for rare coins or Pokémon cards, you would choose the auction site with the largest number of sellers. Thus, both sellers and buyers gravitate to the auction site with the largest market share. Because eBay was the first major Internet auction site, it began with a large market share, and its share grew thanks to the network externality.

Two auction formats are used on eBay: (1) an increasing-bid auction for a single item, in which the highest bidder at the close of the auction wins and pays the seller a price equal to the second-highest bid; and (2) an increasing-bid auction for several identical items, in which the highest $n$ bidders win the $n$ items sold. In both auctions, ties are broken by awarding the item to the buyer who bid first. Notice that neither of these auctions corresponds precisely to any of the four auction formats discussed previously. The first approximates the standard English auction, but the existence of a fixed and known stopping time can cause bidders to place bids strategically at the end of the auction. The second format differs from a conventional Dutch auction in two respects: Bids are increasing rather than decreasing and the auction has a fixed and known stopping time. In both auction formats, sellers can impose a minimum acceptable bid—called a *reserve price*—and although buyers know that a reserve price exists, they are generally not told what it is.

Many Internet auctions are dominated by private-value items. (However, because anyone can put an item up for sale, there are common-value issues—how reliable is the seller, and are there possibilities for resale?) The private-value emphasis of these auctions is especially true of unique antiques that may have considerable value to particular bidders. With private-value auctions, you needn't worry so much about the prior history of bidding: The bids of others tell you about their preferences, but the value that you place on the object is personal to you. Although you want to win the bidding at a price as far below your valuation as possible, the winner's curse needn't be a concern: You can't be disappointed if your value for the object is more than what you paid for it.

Finally, a few caveats are in order when buying items via Internet auctions. Unlike traditional auction houses, low-end auction sites like eBay provide only a forum for buyers and sellers to interact; they provide no quality-control functions. Although many sites, including eBay, make available feedback from buyers for each seller, this is usually the only evidence of a seller's reliability that buyers receive. Furthermore, there is obviously no feedback available for first-time sellers (or for sellers who have recently changed their eBay user names). In addition, the possibility of bid manipulation looms large in Internet auctions. At eBay, for example, a valid e-mail address is the only thing you need to bid on an item. Given the relative ease of obtaining e-mail addresses, sellers may file spurious bids in order to manipulate the bidding process. Thus, caveat emptor is a sound philosophy when buying items on the Internet.

# SUMMARY

1. A game is cooperative if the players can communicate and arrange binding contracts; otherwise, it is noncooperative. In either kind of game, the most important aspect of strategy design is understanding your opponent's position, and (if your opponent is rational) correctly deducing the likely response to your actions. Misjudging an opponent's position is a common mistake, as Example 13.1 "Acquiring a Company" (page 481) illustrates.[24]

2. A Nash equilibrium is a set of strategies such that all players are doing their best given the strategies of the other players. An equilibrium in dominant strategies is a special case of a Nash equilibrium; a dominant strategy is optimal no matter what the other players do. A Nash equilibrium relies on the rationality of each player. A maximin strategy is more conservative because it maximizes the minimum possible outcome.

3. Some games have no Nash equilibria in pure strategies but have one or more equilibria in mixed strategies. A mixed strategy is one in which the player makes a random choice among two or more possible actions, based on a set of chosen probabilities.

4. Strategies that are not optimal for a one-shot game may be optimal for a repeated game. Depending on the number of repetitions, a "tit-for-tat" strategy, in which you play cooperatively as long as your competitor does the same, may be optimal for the repeated prisoners' dilemma.

5. In a sequential game, the players move in turn. In some cases, the player who moves first has an advantage.

6. An empty threat is a threat that one has no incentive to carry out. If one's competitors are rational, empty threats are of no value. To make a threat credible, it is sometimes necessary to make a strategic move to constrain one's later behavior, thereby creating an incentive to carry out the threat.

7. Bargaining situations are examples of cooperative games. As in noncooperative games, in bargaining, players can sometimes gain a strategic advantage by limiting their own flexibility.

8. To deter entry, an incumbent firm must convince any potential competitor that entry will be unprofitable. This may be done by investing, and thereby giving credibility to the threat that entry will be met by price warfare. Strategic trade policies by governments sometimes have this objective.

9. Auctions can be conducted in a number of formats, including English (oral with increasing bids), Dutch (oral with decreasing bids), and sealed bid. The opportunity for a seller to raise revenue and for a buyer to obtain an object at a reasonable price depends on the auction format, and on whether the items being auctioned have the same value to all bidders (as in a common-value auction) or different values to different bidders (as in a private-value auction).

# QUESTIONS FOR REVIEW

1. What is the difference between a cooperative and a noncooperative game? Give an example of each.

2. What is a dominant strategy? Why is an equilibrium stable in dominant strategies?

3. Explain the meaning of a Nash equilibrium. How does it differ from an equilibrium in dominant strategies?

4. How does a Nash equilibrium differ from a game's maximin solution? When is a maximin solution a more likely outcome than a Nash equilibrium?

5. What is a "tit-for-tat" strategy? Why is it a rational strategy for the infinitely repeated prisoners' dilemma?

6. Consider a game in which the prisoners' dilemma is repeated 10 times and both players are rational and fully informed. Is a tit-for-tat strategy optimal in this case? Under what conditions would such a strategy be optimal?

7. Suppose you and your competitor are playing the pricing game shown in Table 13.8 (page 490). Both of you must announce your prices at the same time. Can you improve your outcome by promising your competitor that you will announce a high price?

8. What is meant by "first-mover advantage"? Give an example of a gaming situation with a first-mover advantage.

---

[24]Here is the solution to Company A's problem: *It should offer nothing for Company T's stock.* Remember that Company T will accept an offer only if it is greater than the per-share value under current management. Suppose you offer $50. Thus Company T will accept this offer only if the outcome of the exploration project results in a per-share value under current management of $50 or less. Any values between $0 and $100 are equally likely. Therefore, the *expected value* of Company T's stock, *given that it accepts the offer*—i.e., given that the outcome of the exploration project leads to a value less than $50—is $25. Under the management of Company A, therefore, the value would be (1.5)($25) = $37.5, which is less than $50. In fact, for any price P, if the offer is accepted, Company A can expect a value of only (3/4)P.

9. What is a "strategic move"? How can the development of a certain kind of reputation be a strategic move?

10. Can the threat of a price war deter entry by potential competitors? What actions might a firm take to make this threat credible?

11. A strategic move limits one's flexibility and yet gives one an advantage. Why? How might a strategic move give one an advantage in bargaining?

12. Why is the winner's curse potentially a problem for a bidder in a common-value auction but not in a private-value auction?

# EXERCISES

1. In many oligopolistic industries, the same firms compete over a long period of time, setting prices and observing each other's behavior repeatedly. Given the large number of repetitions, why don't collusive outcomes typically result?

2. Many industries are often plagued by overcapacity: Firms simultaneously invest in capacity expansion, so that total capacity far exceeds demand. This happens not only in industries in which demand is highly volatile and unpredictable, but also in industries in which demand is fairly stable. What factors lead to overcapacity? Explain each briefly.

3. Two computer firms, A and B, are planning to market network systems for office information management. Each firm can develop either a fast, high-quality system (High), or a slower, low-quality system (Low). Market research indicates that the resulting profits to each firm for the alternative strategies are given by the following payoff matrix:

|  |  | Firm B | |
|---|---|---|---|
|  |  | High | Low |
| **Firm A** | High | 50, 40 | 60, 45 |
|  | Low | 55, 55 | 15, 20 |

a. If both firms make their decisions at the same time and follow *maximin* (low-risk) strategies, what will the outcome be?

b. Suppose that both firms try to maximize profits, but that Firm A has a head start in planning and can commit first. Now what will be the outcome? What will be the outcome if Firm B has the head start in planning and can commit first?

c. Getting a head start costs money. (You have to gear up a large engineering team.) Now consider the *two-stage* game in which, *first*, each firm decides how much money to spend to speed up its planning, and, *second*, it announces which product (H or L) it will produce. Which firm will spend more to speed up its planning? How much will it spend?

Should the other firm spend *anything* to speed up its planning? Explain.

4. Two firms are in the chocolate market. Each can choose to go for the high end of the market (high quality) or the low end (low quality). Resulting profits are given by the following payoff matrix:

|  |  | Firm 2 | |
|---|---|---|---|
|  |  | Low | High |
| **Firm 1** | Low | −20, −30 | 900, 600 |
|  | High | 100, 800 | 50, 50 |

a. What outcomes, if any, are Nash equilibria?

b. If the managers of both firms are conservative and each follows a maximin strategy, what will be the outcome?

c. What is the cooperative outcome?

d. Which firm benefits most from the cooperative outcome? How much would that firm need to offer the other to persuade it to collude?

5. Two major networks are competing for viewer ratings in the 8:00–9:00 P.M. and 9:00–10:00 P.M. slots on a given weeknight. Each has two shows to fill these time periods and is juggling its lineup. Each can choose to put its "bigger" show first or to place it second in the 9:00–10:00 P.M. slot. The combination of decisions leads to the following "ratings points" results:

|  |  | Network 2 | |
|---|---|---|---|
|  |  | First | Second |
| **Network 1** | First | 20, 30 | 18, 18 |
|  | Second | 15, 15 | 30, 10 |

a. Find the Nash equilibria for this game, assuming that both networks make their decisions at the same time.

b. If each network is risk-averse and uses a maximin strategy, what will be the resulting equilibrium?

c. What will be the equilibrium if Network 1 makes its selection first? If Network 2 goes first?

**d.** Suppose the network managers meet to coordinate schedules and Network 1 promises to schedule its big show first. Is this promise credible? What would be the likely outcome?

**6.** Two competing firms are each planning to introduce a new product. Each will decide whether to produce Product A, Product B, or Product C. They will make their choices at the same time. The resulting payoffs are shown below.

|  |  | **Firm 2** | | |
|---|---|---|---|---|
|  |  | A | B | C |
| **Firm 1** | A | −10, −10 | 0, 10 | 10, 20 |
|  | B | 10, 0 | −20, −20 | −5, 15 |
|  | C | 20, 10 | 15, −5 | −30, −30 |

**a.** Are there any Nash equilibria in pure strategies? If so, what are they?

**b.** If both firms use maximin strategies, what outcome will result?

**c.** If Firm 1 uses a maximin strategy and Firm 2 knows this, what will Firm 2 do?

**7.** We can think of U.S. and Japanese trade policies as a prisoners' dilemma. The two countries are considering policies to open or close their import markets. The payoff matrix is shown below.

|  |  | **Japan** | |
|---|---|---|---|
|  |  | Open | Close |
| **U.S.** | Open | 10, 10 | 5, 5 |
|  | Close | −100, 5 | 1, 1 |

**a.** Assume that each country knows the payoff matrix and believes that the other country will act in its own interest. Does either country have a dominant strategy? What will be the equilibrium policies if each country acts rationally to maximize its welfare?

**b.** Now assume that Japan is not certain that the United States will behave rationally. In particular, Japan is concerned that U.S. politicians may want to penalize Japan even if that does not maximize U.S. welfare. How might this concern affect Japan's choice of strategy? How might this change the equilibrium?

**8.** You are a duopolist producer of a homogeneous good. Both you and your competitor have zero marginal costs. The market demand curve is

$$P = 30 - Q$$

where $Q = Q_1 + Q_2$. $Q_1$ is your output and $Q_2$ your competitor's output. Your competitor has also read this book.

**a.** Suppose you will play this game only once. If you and your competitor must announce your outputs at the same time, how much will you choose to produce? What do you expect your profit to be? Explain.

**b.** Suppose you are told that you must announce your output *before* your competitor does. How much will you produce in this case, and how much do you think your competitor will produce? What do you expect your profit to be? Is announcing first an advantage or a disadvantage? Explain briefly. How much would you pay for the option of announcing either first or second?

**c.** Suppose instead that you are to play the first round of a series of 10 rounds (with the same competitor). In each round, you and your competitor announce your outputs at the same time. You want to maximize the sum of your profits over the 10 rounds. How much will you produce in the first round? How much do you expect to produce in the tenth round? In the ninth round? Explain briefly.

**d.** Once again you will play a series of 10 rounds. This time, however, in each round your competitor will announce its output before you announce yours. How will your answers to (c) change in this case?

**9.** You play the following bargaining game. Player A moves first and makes Player B an offer for the division of $100. (For example, Player A could suggest that she take $60 and Player B take $40.) Player B can accept or reject the offer. If he rejects it, the amount of money available drops to $90, and he then makes an offer for the division of this amount. If Player A rejects this offer, the amount of money drops to $80 and Player A makes an offer for its division. If Player B rejects this offer, the amount of money drops to 0. Both players are rational, fully informed, and want to maximize their payoffs. Which player will do best in this game?

**\*10.** Defendo has decided to introduce a revolutionary video game. As the first firm in the market, it will have a monopoly position for at least some time. In deciding what type of manufacturing plant to build, it has the choice of two technologies. Technology A is publicly available and will result in annual costs of

$$C^A(q) = 10 + 8q$$

Technology B is a proprietary technology developed in Defendo's research labs. It involves a higher fixed cost of production but lower marginal costs:

$$C^B(q) = 60 + 2q$$

Defendo must decide which technology to adopt. Market demand for the new product is $P = 20 - Q$, where $Q$ is total industry output.

**a.** Suppose Defendo were certain that it would maintain its monopoly position in the market for the entire product lifespan (about five years) without threat of entry. Which technology would you advise Defendo to adopt? What would be Defendo's profit given this choice?

**b.** Suppose Defendo expects its archrival, Offendo, to consider entering the market shortly after Defendo introduces its new product. Offendo will have access only to Technology $A$. If Offendo does enter the market, the two firms will play a Cournot game (in quantities) and arrive at the Cournot-Nash equilibrium.

    **i.** If Defendo adopts Technology $A$ and Offendo enters the market, what will be the profit of each firm? Would Offendo choose to enter the market given these profits?

    **ii.** If Defendo adopts Technology $B$ and Offendo enters the market, what will be the profit of each firm? Would Offendo choose to enter the market given these profits?

    **iii.** Which technology would you advise Defendo to adopt given the threat of possible entry? What will be Defendo's profit given this choice? What will be consumer surplus given this choice?

**c.** What happens to social welfare (the sum of consumer surplus and producer profit) as a result of the threat of entry in this market? What happens to equilibrium price? What might this imply about the role of *potential* competition in limiting market power?

**11.** Three contestants, $A$, $B$, and $C$, each have a balloon and a pistol. From fixed positions, they fire at each other's balloons. When a balloon is hit, its owner is out. When only one balloon remains, its owner gets a $1000 prize. At the outset, the players decide by lot the order in which they will fire, and each player can choose any remaining balloon as his target. Everyone knows that $A$ is the best shot and always hits the target, that $B$ hits the target with probability .9, and that $C$ hits the target with probability .8. Which contestant has the highest probability of winning the $1000? Explain why.

**12.** An antique dealer regularly buys objects at hometown auctions whose bidders are limited to other dealers. Most of her successful bids turn out to be financially worthwhile because she is able to resell the antiques for a profit. On occasion, however, she travels to a nearby town to bid in an auction that is open to the public. She often finds that on the rare occasions in which she does bid successfully, she is disappointed—the antique cannot be sold at a profit. Can you explain the difference in her success between the two sets of circumstances?

**13.** You are in the market for a new house and have decided to bid for a house at auction. You believe that the value of the house is between $125,000 and $150,000, but you are uncertain as to where in the range it might be. You do know, however, that the seller has reserved the right to withdraw the house from the market if the winning bid is not satisfactory.

**a.** Should you bid in this auction? Why or why not?

**b.** Suppose you are a building contractor. You plan to improve the house and then to resell it at a profit. How does this situation affect your answer to (a)? Does it depend on the extent to which your skills are uniquely suitable to improving this particular house?

# Markets for Factor Inputs

# 14

So far we have concentrated on *output markets*: markets for goods and services that firms sell and consumers purchase. In this chapter, we discuss *factor markets*: markets for labor, raw materials, and other inputs to production. Much of our material will be familiar because the same forces that shape supply and demand in output markets also affect factor markets.

We have seen that some output markets are perfectly or almost perfectly competitive, while producers in others have market power. The same is true for factor markets. We will examine three different factor market structures:

1. Perfectly competitive factor markets;
2. Markets in which buyers of factors have monopsony power;
3. Markets in which sellers of factors have monopoly power.

We will also point out instances in which equilibrium in the factor market depends on the extent of market power in *output* markets.

## 14.1 COMPETITIVE FACTOR MARKETS

A competitive *factor market* is one in which there are a large number of sellers and buyers of a factor of production, such as labor or raw materials. Because no single seller or buyer can affect the price of a given factor, each is a price taker. For example, if individual firms that buy lumber to construct homes purchase a small share of the total volume of lumber available, their purchasing decision will have no effect on price. Likewise, if each supplier of lumber controls only a small share of the market, no individual supplier's decision will affect the price of the lumber that he sells. Instead, the price of lumber (and the total quantity produced) will be determined by the aggregate supply and demand for lumber.

We begin by analyzing the demands for a factor by individual firms. These demands are added to get market demand. We then shift to the supply side of the market and show how market price and input levels are determined.

## Demand for a Factor Input When Only One Input Is Variable

• **derived demand** Demand for an input that depends on, and is derived from, both the firm's level of output and the cost of inputs.

Like demand curves for the final goods that result from the production process, demand curves for factors of production are downward sloping. Unlike consumers' demands for goods and services, however, factor demands are **derived demands**: they depend on, and are derived from, the firm's level of output and the costs of inputs. For example, the demand of the Microsoft Corporation for computer programmers is a derived demand that depends not only on the current salaries of programmers, but also on how much software Microsoft expects to sell.

To analyze factor demands, we will use the material from Chapter 7 that shows how a firm chooses its production inputs. We will assume that the firm produces its output using two inputs, capital $K$ and labor $L$, that can be hired at the prices $r$ (the rental cost of capital) and $w$ (the wage rate), respectively.[1] We will also assume that the firm has its plant and equipment in place (as in a short-run analysis) and must only decide how much labor to hire.

Suppose that the firm has hired a certain number of workers and wants to know whether it is profitable to hire one additional worker. This will be profitable if the additional revenue from the output of the worker's labor is greater than its cost. The additional revenue from an incremental unit of labor, the **marginal revenue product of labor**, is denoted $\text{MRP}_L$. The cost of an incremental unit of labor is the wage rate, $w$. Thus, it is profitable to hire more labor if the $\text{MRP}_L$ is at least as large as the wage rate $w$.

• **marginal revenue product** Additional revenue resulting from the sale of output created by the use of one additional unit of an input.

How do we measure the $\text{MRP}_L$? It's *the additional output obtained from the additional unit of this labor, multiplied by the additional revenue from an extra unit of output*. The additional output is given by the marginal product of labor $\text{MP}_L$ and the additional revenue by the marginal revenue MR.

Recall that in §8.3, marginal revenue is defined to be the increase in revenue resulting from a one-unit increase in output.

Formally, the marginal revenue product is $\Delta R/\Delta L$, where $L$ is the number of units of labor input and $R$ is revenue. The additional output per unit of labor, the $\text{MP}_L$, is given by $\Delta Q/\Delta L$, and marginal revenue, MR, is equal to $\Delta R/\Delta Q$. Because $\Delta R/\Delta L = (\Delta R)/(\Delta Q)(\Delta Q/\Delta L)$, it follows that

$$\text{MRP}_L = (\text{MR})(\text{MP}_L) \tag{14.1}$$

In §8.2, we explain that because the demand facing each firm in a competitive market is perfectly elastic, each firm will sell its output at a price equal to its average revenue and to its marginal revenue.

This important result holds for any competitive factor market, whether or not the output market is competitive. However, to examine the characteristics of the $\text{MRP}_L$, let's begin with the case of a perfectly competitive output (and input) market. In a competitive output market, a firm will sell all its output at the market price $P$. The marginal revenue from the sale of an additional unit of output is then equal to $P$. In this case, the marginal revenue product of labor is equal to the marginal product of labor times the price of the product:

$$\text{MRP}_L = (\text{MP}_L)(P) \tag{14.2}$$

In §6.2, we explain the law of diminishing marginal returns—as the use of an input increases with other inputs fixed, the resulting additions to output will eventually decrease.

The higher of the two curves in Figure 14.1 represents the $\text{MRP}_L$ curve for a firm in a competitive output market. Note that because there are diminishing marginal returns to labor, the marginal product of labor falls as the amount of labor increases. The marginal revenue product curve thus slopes downward, even though the price of the output is constant.

---

[1]We implicitly assume that all inputs to production are identical in quality. Differences in workers' skills and abilities are discussed in Chapter 17.

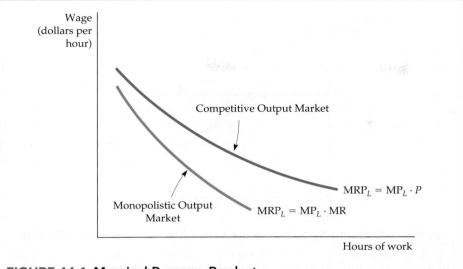

**FIGURE 14.1 Marginal Revenue Product**

In a competitive factor market in which the producer is a price taker, the buyer's demand for an input is given by the marginal revenue product curve. The MRP curve falls because the marginal product of labor falls as hours of work increase. When the producer of the product has monopoly power, the demand for the input is also given by the MRP curve. In this case, however, the MRP curve falls because both the marginal product of labor and marginal revenue fall.

The lower curve in Figure 14.1 is the $MRP_L$ curve when the firm has monopoly power in the output market. When firms have monopoly power, they face a downward-sloping demand curve and must therefore lower the price of all units of the product in order to sell more of it. As a result, marginal revenue is always less than price (MR < P). This explains why the monopolistic curve lies below the competitive curve and why marginal revenue falls as output increases. Thus the marginal revenue product curve slopes downward in this case because the marginal revenue curve *and* the marginal product curve slope downward.

Note that the marginal revenue product tells us how much the firm should be willing to pay to hire an additional unit of labor. As long as the $MRP_L$ is greater than the wage rate, the firm should hire more labor. If the marginal revenue product is less than the wage rate, the firm should lay off workers. Only when the marginal revenue product is equal to the wage rate will the firm have hired the profit-maximizing amount of labor. The profit-maximizing condition is therefore

$$MRP_L = w \tag{14.3}$$

Figure 14.2 illustrates this condition. The demand for labor curve $D_L$ is the $MRP_L$. Note that the quantity of labor demanded increases as the wage rate falls. Because the labor market is perfectly competitive, the firm can hire as many workers as it wants at the market wage $w^*$ and is not able to affect the market wage. The supply of labor curve facing the firm $S_L$ is thus a horizontal line. The profit-maximizing amount of labor that the firm hires, $L^*$, is at the intersection of the supply and demand curves.

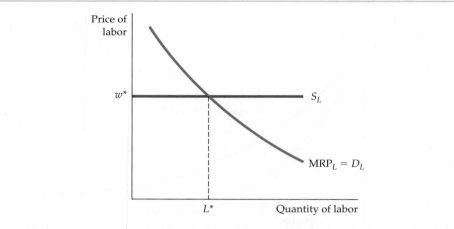

**FIGURE 14.2 Hiring by a Firm in the Labor Market (with Fixed Capital)**

In a competitive labor market, a firm faces a perfectly elastic supply of labor $S_L$ and can hire as many workers as it wants at a wage rate $w^*$. The firm's demand for labor $D_L$ is given by its marginal revenue product of labor $MRP_L$. The profit-maximizing firm will hire $L^*$ units of labor at the point where the marginal revenue product of labor is equal to the wage rate.

Figure 14.3 shows how the quantity of labor demanded changes in response to a drop in the market wage rate from $w_1$ to $w_2$. The wage rate might decrease if more people entering the labor force are looking for jobs for the first time (as happened, for example, when the baby boomers came of age). The quantity of labor demanded by the firm is initially $L_1$, at the intersection of $MRP_L$ and $S_1$. However, when the supply of labor curve shifts from $S_1$ to $S_2$, the wage falls from $w_1$ to $w_2$ and the quantity of labor demanded increases from $L_1$ to $L_2$.

> In §8.3, we explain that a firm maximizes its profit by choosing an output at which marginal revenue equals marginal cost.

Factor markets are similar to output markets in many ways. For example, the factor market profit-maximizing condition that the marginal revenue product of labor be equal to the wage rate is analogous to the output market condition that marginal revenue be equal to marginal cost. To see why this is true, recall that $MRP_L = (MP_L)(MR)$ and divide both sides of equation (14.3) by the marginal product of labor. Then,

$$MR = w/MP_L \qquad (14.4)$$

Because $MP_L$ measures additional output per unit of input, the right-hand side of equation (14.4) measures the marginal cost of an additional unit of output (the wage rate multiplied by the labor needed to produce one unit of output). Equation (14.4) shows that *both the hiring and output choices of the firm follow the same rule: Inputs or outputs are chosen so that marginal revenue (from the sale of output) is equal to marginal cost (from the purchase of inputs)*. This principle holds in both competitive and noncompetitive markets.

## Demand for a Factor Input When Several Inputs Are Variable

When the firm simultaneously chooses quantities of two or more variable inputs, the hiring problem becomes more difficult because a change in the price of one input will change the demand for others. Suppose, for example, that both

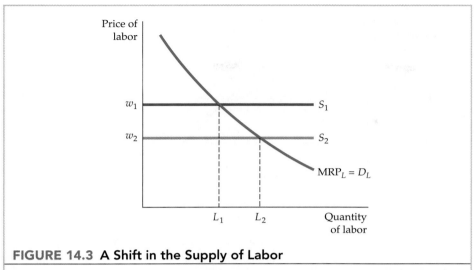

**FIGURE 14.3 A Shift in the Supply of Labor**

When the supply of labor facing the firms is $S_1$, the firm hires $L_1$ units of labor at wage $w_1$. But when the market wage rate decreases and the supply of labor shifts to $S_2$, the firm maximizes its profit by moving along the demand for labor curve until the new wage rate $w_2$ is equal to the marginal revenue product of labor. As a result, $L_2$ units of labor are hired.

labor and assembly-line machinery are variable inputs for producing farm equipment. Let's say that we wish to determine the firm's demand for labor curve. As the wage rate falls, more labor will be demanded even if the firm's investment in machinery is unchanged. But as labor becomes less expensive, the marginal cost of producing the farm equipment falls. Consequently, it is profitable for the firm to increase its output. In that case, the firm is likely to invest in additional machinery to expand production capacity. Expanding the use of machinery causes the marginal revenue product of labor curve to shift to the right; in turn, the quantity of labor demanded increases.

Figure 14.4 illustrates this. Suppose that when the wage rate is $20 per hour, the firm hires 100 worker-hours, as shown by point $A$ on the $MRP_{L1}$ curve. Now consider what happens when the wage rate falls to $15 per hour. Because the marginal revenue product of labor is now greater than the wage rate, the firm will demand more labor. But the $MRP_{L1}$ curve describes the demand for labor when the use of machinery is fixed. In fact, a greater amount of labor causes the marginal product of *capital* to rise, which encourages the firm to rent more machinery as well as hire more labor. Because there is more machinery, the marginal product of labor will increase. (With more machinery, workers can be more productive.) The marginal revenue product curve will therefore shift to the right (to $MRP_{L2}$). Thus, when the wage rate falls, the firm will use 140 hours of labor. This is shown by a new point on the demand curve, $C$, rather than 120 hours as given by $B$. $A$ and $C$ are both on the firm's demand for labor curve (with machinery variable) $D_L$; $B$ is not.

Note that as constructed, the demand for labor curve is more elastic than either of the two marginal product of labor curves (which presume no change in the amount of machinery). Thus, when capital inputs are variable in the long run, there is a greater elasticity of demand because firms can substitute capital for labor in the production process.

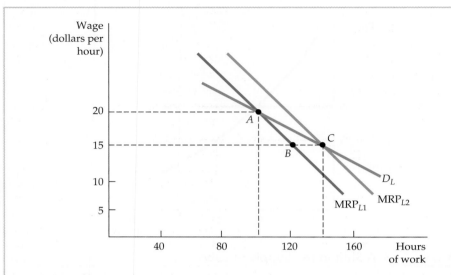

**FIGURE 14.4 Firm's Demand Curve for Labor (with Variable Capital)**

When two or more inputs are variable, a firm's demand for one input depends on the marginal revenue product of both inputs. When the wage rate is $20, $A$ represents one point on the firm's demand for labor curve. When the wage rate falls to $15, the marginal product of capital rises, encouraging the firm to rent more machinery and hire more labor. As a result, the MRP curve shifts from $MRP_{L1}$ to $MRP_{L2}$, generating a new point $C$ on the firm's demand for labor curve. Thus $A$ and $C$ are on the demand for labor curve, but $B$ is not.

## The Market Demand Curve

> Recall from §4.3 that the market demand curve for a product shows how much of the product consumers are willing to buy as the price of the product changes.

When we aggregated the individual demand curves of consumers to obtain the market demand curve for a product, we were concerned with a single industry. However, a factor input such as skilled labor is demanded by firms in many different industries. Moreover, as we move from industry to industry, we are likely to find that firms' demands for labor (which are derived in part from the demands for the firms' output) vary substantially. Therefore, to obtain the total market demand for labor curve, we must first determine each industry's demand for labor, and then add the industry demand curves horizontally. The second step is straightforward. Adding industry demand curves for labor to obtain a market demand curve for labor is just like adding individual product demand curves to obtain the market demand curve for that product. So let's concentrate our attention on the more difficult first step.

**Determining Industry Demand** The first step—determining industry demand—takes into account the fact that both the level of output produced by the firm and its product price change as the prices of the inputs to production change. It is easiest to determine market demand when there is a single producer. In that case, the marginal revenue product curve is the industry demand curve for the input. When there are many firms, however, the analysis is more complex because of the possible interaction among the firms. Consider, for instance, the demand for labor when output markets are perfectly competitive. Then, the marginal revenue product of labor is the product of the price of the good and the marginal product of labor (see equation 14.2), as shown by the curve $MRP_{L1}$ in Figure 14.5(a).

Suppose initially that the wage rate for labor is $15 per hour and that the firm demands 100 worker-hours of labor. Now the wage rate for this firm falls to $10 per hour. If no other firms could hire workers at the lower wage, then our firm would hire 150 worker-hours of labor (by finding the point on the $MRP_{L1}$ curve that corresponds to the $10-per-hour wage rate). But if the wage rate falls for all firms in an industry, the industry as a whole will hire more labor. This will lead to more output from the industry, a shift to the right of the industry supply curve, and a lower market price for its product.

In Figure 14.5(a), when the product price falls, the original marginal revenue product curve shifts downward, from $MRP_{L1}$ to $MRP_{L2}$. This shift results in a lower quantity of labor demanded by the firm—120 worker-hours rather than 150. Consequently, industry demand for labor will be lower than it would be if only one firm were able to hire workers at the lower wage. Figure 14.5(b) illustrates this. The lighter line shows the horizontal sum of the individual firms' demands for labor that would result if product price did not change as the wage falls. The darker line shows the industry demand curve for labor, which takes into account the fact that product price will fall as all firms expand their output in response to the lower wage rate. When the wage rate is $15 per hour, industry demand for labor is $L_0$ worker-hours. When it falls to $10 per hour, industry demand increases to $L_1$. Note that this is a smaller increase than $L_2$, which would occur if the product price were fixed. The aggregation of industry demand curves into the market demand curve for labor is the final step: To complete it, we simply add the labor demanded in all industries.

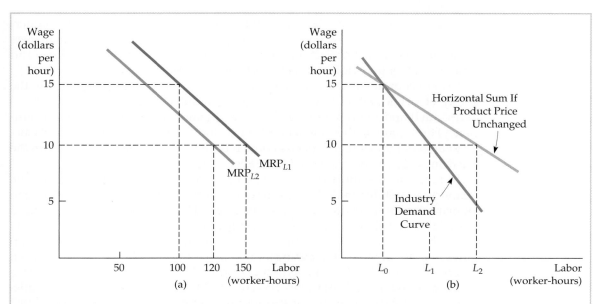

**FIGURE 14.5 The Industry Demand for Labor**

The demand curve for labor of a competitive firm, $MRP_{L1}$ in (a), takes the product price as given. But as the wage rate falls from $15 to $10 per hour, the product price also falls. Thus the firm's demand curve shifts downward to $MRP_{L2}$. As a result, the industry demand curve, shown in (b), is more inelastic than the demand curve that would be obtained if the product price were assumed to be unchanged.

The derivation of the market demand curve for labor (or for any other input) is essentially the same when the output market is noncompetitive. The only difference is that it is more difficult to predict the change in product price in response to a change in the wage rate because each firm in the market is likely to be pricing strategically rather than taking price as given.

---

**EXAMPLE 14.1**    The Demand for Jet Fuel

As discussed in Example 9.3 on the airline industry (page 321), there have been several periods during the past few decades when fuel costs for U.S. airlines increased rapidly, in tandem with rising world oil prices. For example, whereas fuel costs made up 12.4 percent of total operating costs in 1971, that number rose to about 30 percent in 1980. As we would expect, the amount of jet fuel used by airlines during this period fell as its price rose. Thus the output of the airline industry, as measured by the number of ton-miles, rose by 29.6 percent, while the amount of jet fuel consumed increased by only 8.8 percent. (One ton-mile is short for one ton of passengers, baggage, or freight transported one mile.) Fuel prices fell substantially during the mid-1980s and, relative to 1980 levels, remained low (in real terms) until about 2005, at which point they again increased dramatically. Overall, the cost of jet fuel, as a share of operating costs, remains the second-highest expense for airlines (after labor), averaging about 20 percent of total operating costs while fluctuating between 10 and 30 percent.

Understanding the demand for jet fuel is important to managers of oil refineries, who must decide how much jet fuel to produce. It is also crucial to managers of airlines, who must project fuel purchases and costs when fuel prices rise and decide whether to invest in more fuel-efficient planes.[2]

The effect of the increase in fuel costs on the airline industry depends on the ability of airlines either to cut fuel usage by reducing weight (by carrying less excess fuel) and flying more slowly (reducing drag and increasing engine efficiency) or to pass on their higher costs in customer prices. Thus the price elasticity of demand for jet fuel depends both on the ability to conserve fuel and on the elasticities of demand and supply of travel.

To measure the short-run elasticity of demand for jet fuel, we use as the quantity of fuel demanded the number of gallons of fuel used by an airline in all markets within its domestic route network. The price of jet fuel is measured in dollars per gallon. A statistical analysis of demand must control for factors other than price that can explain why some firms demand more fuel than others. Some airlines, for example, use more fuel-efficient jet aircraft than others. A second factor is the length of flights: The shorter the flight, the more fuel consumed per mile of travel. Both of these factors were included in a statistical analysis that relates the quantity of fuel demanded to its price. Table 14.1 shows some short-run price elasticities. (They do not account for the introduction of new types of aircraft.)

---

In §2.4, we define the price elasticity of demand as the percentage change in quantity demanded resulting from a 1-percent change in the price of a good.

---

[2]This example is drawn in part from Joseph M. Cigliano, "The Demand for Jet Fuel by the U.S. Domestic Trunk Airlines," *Business Economics* (September 1982): 32–36.

| TABLE 14.1 Short-Run Price Elasticity of Demand for Jet Fuel | | | |
|---|---|---|---|
| **Airline** | **Elasticity** | **Airline** | **Elasticity** |
| American | −.06 | Delta | −.15 |
| Continental | −.09 | United | −.10 |
| Northwest | −.07 | | |

The jet fuel price elasticities for the airlines range in value from −.06 (for American) to −.15 (for Delta). Overall, the results show that the demand for jet fuel as an input to the production of airline flight-miles is very inelastic. This finding is not surprising: In the short run, there is no good substitute for jet fuel. The long-run elasticity of demand is higher, however, because airlines can eventually introduce more energy-efficient airplanes.

Figure 14.6 shows the short- and long-run demands for jet fuel. The short-run demand curve, $MRP_{SR}$, is much less elastic than the long-run demand curve because it takes time to substitute newer, more fuel-efficient airplanes when the price of fuel goes up.

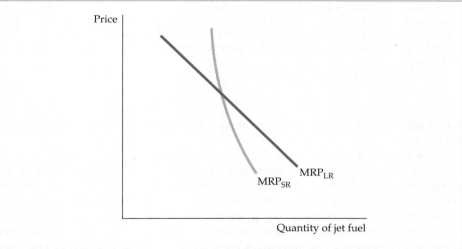

**FIGURE 14.6 The Short- and Long-Run Demand for Jet Fuel**

The short-run demand for jet fuel $MRP_{SR}$ is more inelastic than the long-run demand $MRP_{LR}$. In the short run, airlines cannot reduce fuel consumption much when fuel prices increase. In the long run, however, they can switch to longer, more fuel-efficient routes and put more fuel-efficient planes into service.

## The Supply of Inputs to a Firm

When the market for a factor input is perfectly competitive, a firm can purchase as much of that input as it wants at a fixed market price, which is determined by the intersection of the market demand and supply curves, as shown in Figure 14.7(a). The input supply curve facing a firm is then perfectly elastic. Thus, in Figure 14.7(b), a firm is buying fabric at $10 per yard to sew into clothing. Because the

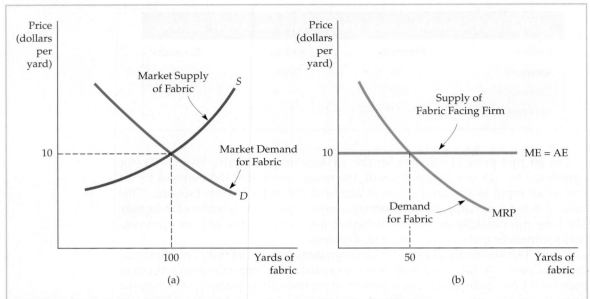

**FIGURE 14.7 A Firm's Input Supply in a Competitive Factor Market**

In a competitive factor market, a firm can buy any amount of the input it wants without affecting the price. Therefore, the firm faces a perfectly elastic supply curve for that input. As a result, the quantity of the input purchased by the producer of the product is determined by the intersection of the input demand and supply curves. In (a), the industry quantity demanded and quantity supplied of fabric are equated at a price of $10 per yard. In (b), the firm faces a horizontal marginal expenditure curve at a price of $10 per yard of fabric and chooses to buy 50 yards.

• **average expenditure curve**
Supply curve representing the price per unit that a firm pays for a good.

• **marginal expenditure curve**
Curve describing the additional cost of purchasing one additional unit of a good.

firm is only a small part of the fabric market, it can buy all it wants without affecting the price.

In Section 10.5 we explained that the supply curve AE facing the firm in Figure 14.7(b) is its **average expenditure curve** (just as the demand curve facing a firm is its *average revenue curve*), because it represents the price per unit that the firm pays for the good. On the other hand, the **marginal expenditure curve** represents the firm's expenditure on an *additional unit* that it buys. (The marginal expenditure curve in a factor market is analogous to the marginal revenue curve in the output market.) The marginal expenditure depends on whether you are a competitive buyer or a buyer with monopsony power. If you are a competitive buyer, the cost of each unit is the same no matter how many units you purchase; it is the market price of the good. The price paid is the average expenditure per unit, and the marginal expenditure is equal to the average. Consequently, when the factor market is competitive, the average expenditure and marginal expenditure curves are identical horizontal lines, just as the marginal and average revenue curves are identical (and horizontal) for a competitive firm in the output market.

How much of the input should a firm facing a competitive factor market purchase? As long as the marginal revenue product curve lies above the marginal expenditure curve, profit can be increased by purchasing more of the input because the benefit of an additional unit (MRP) exceeds the cost (ME). However, when the marginal revenue product curve lies below the marginal expenditure curve, some units yield benefits that are less than cost. Therefore, profit maximization requires that *marginal revenue product be equal to marginal expenditure*:

$$ME = MRP \qquad (14.5)$$

When we considered the special case of a competitive output market, we saw that the firm bought inputs, such as labor, up to the point at which the marginal revenue product was equal to the price of the input $\omega$, as in equation (14.3). In the competitive case, therefore, the condition for profit maximization is that the price of the input be equal to marginal expenditure:

$$ME = w \qquad (14.6)$$

In our example, the price of the fabric ($10 per yard) is determined in the competitive fabric market shown in Figure 14.7(a) at the intersection of the demand and supply curves. Figure 14.7(b) shows the amount of fabric purchased by a firm at the intersection of the marginal expenditure and marginal revenue product curves. When 50 yards of fabric are purchased, the marginal expenditure of $10 is equal to the marginal revenue from the sale of clothing made possible by the increased use of fabric in the production process. If less than 50 yards of fabric were purchased, the firm would be forgoing an opportunity to make additional profit from clothing sales. If more than 50 yards were purchased, the cost of the fabric would be greater than the additional revenue from the sale of the extra clothing.

## The Market Supply of Inputs

The market supply curve for a factor input is usually upward sloping. We saw in Chapter 8 that the market supply for a good sold in a competitive market is usually upward sloping because the marginal cost of producing the good is typically increasing. This is also the case for fabric and other raw material inputs.

When the input is labor, however, people rather than firms are making supply decisions. In this case, utility maximization by workers rather than profit maximization by firms determines supply. In the discussion that follows, we use the analysis of income and substitution effects from Chapter 4 to show that although the market supply curve for labor can be upward sloping, it may also, as in Figure 14.8, be *backward bending*. In other words, a higher wage rate can lead to less labor being supplied.

To see why a labor supply curve may be backward bending, divide the day into hours of work and hours of leisure. *Leisure* is a term that describes enjoyable non-work activities, including sleeping and eating. *Work* benefits the worker only through the income that it generates. We also assume that a worker has the flexibility to choose how many hours per day to work.

The wage rate measures the price that the worker places on leisure time, because his or her wage measures the amount of money that the worker gives up to enjoy leisure. As the wage rate increases, therefore, the price of leisure also increases. This price change brings about both a substitution effect (a change in relative price with utility held constant) and an income effect (a change in utility with relative prices unchanged). There is a substitution effect because the higher price of leisure encourages workers to substitute work for leisure. An income effect occurs because the higher wage rate increases the worker's purchasing

In §8.6, we explain that the short-run market supply curve shows the amount of output that will be produced by firms in the market for every possible price.

In §4.2, we explain that an increase in the price of a good has two effects: The real purchasing power of each consumer decreases (the income effect) and the good becomes relatively expensive (the substitution effect).

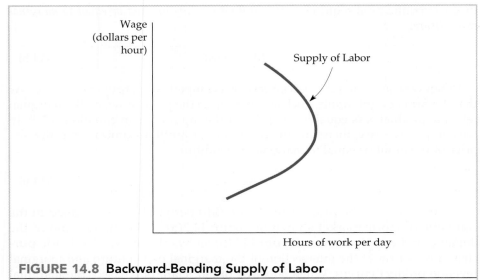

**FIGURE 14.8 Backward-Bending Supply of Labor**

When the wage rate increases, the hours of work supplied increase initially but can eventually decrease as individuals choose to enjoy more leisure and to work less. The backward-bending portion of the labor supply curve arises when the income effect of the higher wage (which encourages more leisure) is greater than the substitution effect (which encourages more work).

power. With higher income, the worker can buy more of many goods, one of which is leisure. If more leisure was chosen, it is because the income effect has encouraged the worker to work fewer hours. Income effects can be large because wages are the primary component of most people's income. When the income effect outweighs the substitution effect, the result is a backward-bending supply curve.

Figure 14.9 illustrates how a backward-bending supply curve for labor can result from the work-leisure decision for a typical weekday. The horizontal axis shows hours of leisure per day, the vertical axis income generated by work. (We assume there are no other sources of income.) Initially the wage rate is $10 per hour, and the budget line is given by *PQ*. Point *P*, for example, shows that if an individual worked a 24-hour day he would earn an income of $240.

The worker maximizes utility by choosing point *A*, thus enjoying 16 hours of leisure per day (with 8 hours of work) and earning $80. When the wage rate increases to $30 per hour, the budget line rotates about the horizontal intercept to line *RQ*. (Only 24 hours of leisure are possible.) Now the worker maximizes utility at *B* by choosing 19 hours of leisure per day (with 5 hours of work), while earning $150. If only the substitution effect came into play, the higher wage rate would encourage the worker to work 12 hours (at *C*) instead of 8. However, the income effect works in the opposite direction. It overcomes the substitution effect and lowers the work day from 8 hours to 5.

In real life, a backward-bending labor supply curve might apply to a college student working during the summer to earn living expenses for the school year. As soon as a target level of earnings is reached, the student stops working and allocates more time to leisure. An increase in the wage rate will then lead to fewer hours worked because it enables the student to reach the target level of earnings more quickly.

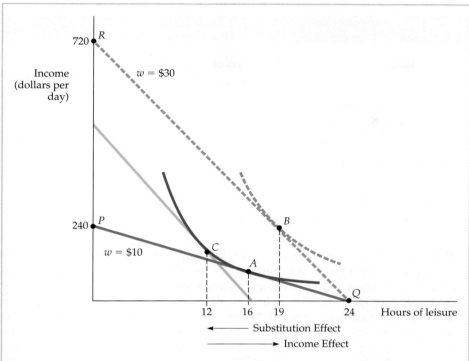

**FIGURE 14.9  Substitution and Income Effects of a Wage Increase**

When the wage rate increases from \$10 to \$30 per hour, the worker's budget line shifts from $PQ$ to $RQ$. In response, the worker moves from $A$ to $B$ while decreasing work hours from 8 to 5. The reduction in hours worked arises because the income effect outweighs the substitution effect. In this case, the supply of labor curve is backward bending.

---

**EXAMPLE 14.2**  Labor Supply for One- and Two-Earner Households

One of the most dramatic changes in the labor market in the twentieth century has been the increase in women's participation in the labor force. Whereas only 34 percent of women had entered the labor force in 1950, the number had risen to well over 60 percent by 2007. Married women account for a substantial portion of this increase. The increased role of women in the labor market has also had a major impact on housing markets: Where to live and work has increasingly become a joint husband-and-wife decision.

The complex nature of the work choice was analyzed in a study that compared the work decisions of 94 unmarried females with the work decisions of heads of households and spouses in 397 families.[3] One way to describe the work decisions of the various family groups is to calculate labor supply elasticities. Each elasticity relates the numbers of hours worked not only to the wage earned by the head of the household, but also to the wage of the other member of two-earner households. Table 14.2 summarizes the results.

---

[3]See Janet E. Kohlhase, "Labor Supply and Housing Demand for One- and Two-Earner Households," *Review of Economics and Statistics* 68 (1986): 48–56; and Ray C. Fair and Diane J. Macunovich, "Explaining the Labor Force Participation of Women 20–24" (unpublished, February 1997).

| TABLE 14.2  Elasticities of Labor Supply (Hours Worked) | | | |
|---|---|---|---|
| **Group** | **Head's Hours with Respect to Head's Wage** | **Spouse's Hours with Respect to Spouse's Wage** | **Head's Hours with Respect to Spouse's Wage** |
| Unmarried males, no children | .026 | | |
| Unmarried females, children | .106 | | |
| Unmarried females, no children | .011 | | |
| One-earner family, children | −.078 | | |
| One-earner family, no children | .007 | | |
| Two-earner family, children | −.002 | −.086 | −.004 |
| Two-earner family, no children | −.107 | −.028 | −.059 |

When a higher wage rate leads to fewer hours worked, the labor supply curve is backward bending: The income effect, which encourages more leisure, outweighs the substitution effect, which encourages more work. The elasticity of labor supply is then negative. Table 14.2 shows that heads of one-earner families with children and two-earner families (with or without children) all have backward-bending labor supply curves, with elasticities ranging from −.002 to −.078. Most single-earner heads of households are on the upward-sloping portion of the labor supply curve, with the largest elasticity of .106 associated with single women with children. Married women (listed as spouses of heads of households) are also on the backward-bending portion of the labor supply curve, with elasticities of −.028 and −.086.

# 14.2 EQUILIBRIUM IN A COMPETITIVE FACTOR MARKET

A competitive factor market is in equilibrium when the price of the input equates the quantity demanded to the quantity supplied. Figure 14.10(a) shows such an equilibrium for a labor market. At point $A$, the equilibrium wage rate is $w_C$ and the equilibrium quantity supplied is $L_C$. Because they are well informed, all workers receive the identical wage and generate the identical marginal revenue product of labor wherever they are employed. If any worker had a wage lower than her marginal product, a firm would find it profitable to offer that worker a higher wage.

If the output market is also perfectly competitive, the demand curve for an input measures the benefit that consumers of the product place on the additional use of the input in the production process. The wage rate also reflects the cost to the firm and to society of using an additional unit of the input. Thus, at $A$ in Figure 14.10(a), the marginal benefit of an hour of labor (its marginal revenue product $MRP_L$) is equal to its marginal cost (the wage rate $w$).

When output and input markets are both perfectly competitive, resources are used efficiently because the difference between total benefits and total costs is maximized. Efficiency requires that the additional revenue generated by employing an additional unit of labor (the marginal revenue product of labor, $MRP_L$) equal the benefit to consumers of the additional output,

In §9.2, we explain that in a perfectly competitive market, efficiency is achieved because the sum of aggregate consumer and producer surplus is maximized.

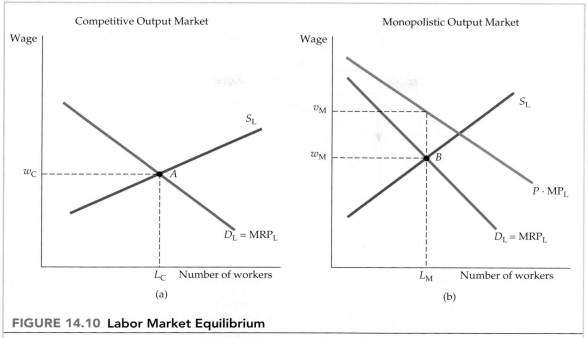

**FIGURE 14.10 Labor Market Equilibrium**

In a competitive labor market in which the output market is competitive, the equilibrium wage $w_c$ is given by the intersection of the demand for labor (marginal revenue product) curve and the supply of labor curve. This is point $A$ in part (a) of the figure. Part (b) shows that when the producer has monopoly power, the marginal value of a worker $v_M$ is greater than the wage $w_M$. Thus too few workers are employed. (Point $B$ determines the quantity of labor that the firm hires and the wage rate paid.)

which is given by the price of the product times the marginal product of labor, $(P)(MP_L)$.

When the output market is not perfectly competitive, the condition $MRP_L = (P)(MP_L)$ no longer holds. Note in Figure 14.10(b) that the curve representing the product price multiplied by the marginal product of labor $[(P)(MP_L)]$ lies above the marginal revenue product curve $[(MR)(MP_L)]$. Point $B$ is the equilibrium wage $w_M$ and the equilibrium labor supply $L_M$. But because the price of the product is a measure of the value to consumers of each additional unit of output that they buy, $(P)(MP_L)$ is the value that consumers place on additional units of labor. Therefore, when $L_M$ laborers are employed, the marginal cost to the firm $w_M$ is less than the marginal benefit to consumers $v_M$. Although the firm is maximizing its profit, its output is below the efficient level and it uses less than the efficient level of the input. Economic efficiency would be increased if more laborers were hired and, consequently, more output produced. (The gains to consumers would outweigh the firm's lost profit.)

## Economic Rent

The concept of economic rent helps explain how factor markets work. When discussing output markets in the long run in Chapter 8, we defined economic rent as the payments received by a firm over and above the minimum cost of producing its output. For a factor market, *economic rent is the difference between the payments made to a factor of production and the minimum amount that must be*

> In §8.7, we explain that economic rent is the amount that firms are willing to pay for an input less the minimum amount necessary to buy it.

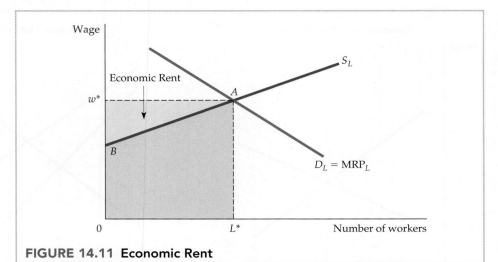

**FIGURE 14.11 Economic Rent**

The economic rent associated with the employment of labor is the excess of wages paid above the minimum amount needed to hire workers. The equilibrium wage is given by $A$, at the intersection of the labor supply and labor demand curves. Because the supply curve is upward sloping, some workers would have accepted jobs for a wage less than $w^*$. The green-shaded area $ABw^*$ is the economic rent received by all workers.

*spent to obtain the use of that factor.* Figure 14.11 illustrates the concept of economic rent as applied to a competitive labor market. The equilibrium price of labor is $w^*$, and the quantity of labor supplied is $L^*$. The supply of labor curve is the upward-sloping curve, and the demand for labor is the downward-sloping marginal revenue product curve. Because the supply curve tells us how much labor will be supplied at each wage rate, the minimum expenditure needed to employ $L^*$ units of labor is given by the tan-shaded area $AL^*0B$, below the supply curve to the left of the equilibrium labor supply $L^*$.

In perfectly competitive markets, all workers are paid the wage $w^*$. This wage is required to get the last "marginal" worker to supply his or her labor, but all other workers earn rents because their wage is greater than the wage that would be needed to get them to work. Because total wage payments are equal to the rectangle $0w^*AL^*$, the economic rent earned by labor is given by the area $ABw^*$.

Note that if the supply curve were perfectly elastic, economic rent would be zero. There are rents only when supply is somewhat inelastic. And when supply is perfectly inelastic, all payments to a factor of production are economic rents because the factor will be supplied no matter what price is paid.

As Figure 14.12 shows, one example of an inelastically supplied factor is land. The supply curve is perfectly inelastic because land for housing (or for agriculture) is fixed, at least in the short run. With land inelastically supplied, its price is determined entirely by demand. The demand for land is given by $D_1$, and its price per unit is $s_1$. Total land rent is given by the green-shaded rectangle. But when the demand for land increases to $D_2$, the rental value per unit of land increases to $s_2$; in this case, total land rent includes the blue-shaded area as well. Thus, an increase in the demand for land (a shift to the right in the demand curve) leads both to a higher price per acre and to a higher economic rent.

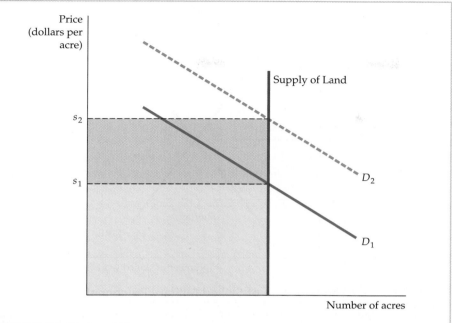

**FIGURE 14.12 Land Rent**

When the supply of land is perfectly inelastic, the market price of land is determined at the point of intersection with the demand curve. The entire value of the land is then an economic rent. When demand is given by $D_1$, the economic rent per acre is given by $s_1$, and when demand increases to $D_2$, rent per acre increases to $s_2$.

---

**EXAMPLE 14.3**   Pay in the Military

The U.S. Army has had a personnel problem for many years. During the Civil War, roughly 90 percent of the armed forces were unskilled workers involved in ground combat. Since then, however, the nature of warfare has evolved. Ground combat forces now make up only 16 percent of the armed forces. Meanwhile, changes in technology have led to a severe shortage in skilled technicians, trained pilots, computer analysts, mechanics, and others needed to operate sophisticated military equipment. Why has such a shortage developed? Why has the military been unable to keep skilled personnel? An economic study provides some answers.[4]

The rank structure of the army has remained essentially unchanged over the years. Among the officer ranks, pay increases are determined primarily by the number of years of service. Consequently, officers with differing skill levels and abilities are usually paid similar salaries. Moreover, some skilled workers are underpaid relative to salaries that they could receive in the private sector. As a

---

[4]Walter Y. Oi, "Paying Soldiers: On a Wage Structure for a Large Internal Labor Market" (unpublished, undated paper).

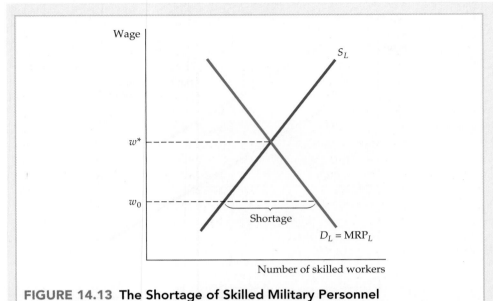

**FIGURE 14.13 The Shortage of Skilled Military Personnel**

When the wage $w^*$ is paid to military personnel, the labor market is in equilibrium. When the wage is kept below $w^*$, at $w_0$, there is a shortage of personnel because the quantity of labor demanded is greater than the quantity supplied.

result, skilled workers who join the army because of attractive salaries find that their marginal revenue products are eventually higher than their wages. Thus, a married Air Force pilot with eight years of training would have earned an annual salary of $45,000 in 1989. This salary would increase gradually to $61,000 in 2009, but is substantially less than a commercial airline pilot would make with only 10 years of service.[5] Some officers remain in the army, but many leave.

This study of army pay applies to all of the armed forces. Figure 14.13 shows the inefficiency that can result from the military pay policy. The equilibrium wage rate $w^*$ is the wage that equates the demand for labor to the supply. Because of inflexibility in its pay structure, however, the military pays the wage $w_0$, which is below the equilibrium wage. At $w_0$, demand is greater than supply, and there is a shortage of skilled labor. By contrast, competitive labor markets pay more productive workers higher wages than their less productive counterparts.

So how can the military attract and keep a skilled labor force?

The military's choice of wage structure affects the nation's ability to maintain an effective fighting force, and a 7.2-percent military pay raise went into effect in 2007. Even so, military pay remains low: A first-class private earns $18,400, a sergeant $22,250, a captain $39,500, and a major $44,950. In response to its personnel problems, the military has begun to change its salary structure by expanding the number and size of its reenlistment bonuses. Selective reenlistment bonuses targeted at skilled jobs for which there are shortages can be an effective recruiting device. The immediate bonuses create more of an incentive than the uncertain promise of higher wages in the future. As the demand for skilled military jobs increases, we can expect the armed forces to make greater use of reenlistment bonuses and other market-based incentives.

[5]Department of Defense, Department of Defense Aviator Retention Study—1988, Table 2–4. (Washington: GPO, November 28, 1988).

## 14.3 FACTOR MARKETS WITH MONOPSONY POWER

In some factor markets, individual buyers have *buyer power* that allows them to affect the prices they pay. Often this happens either when one firm is a monopsony buyer or there are only a few buyers, in which case each firm has some monopsony power. For example, we saw in Chapter 10 that automobile companies have monopsony power as buyers of parts and components. GM and Toyota, for example, buy large quantities of brakes, radiators, and other parts and can negotiate lower prices than those charged smaller purchasers. In other cases, there might be only two or three sellers of a factor and a dozen or more buyers, but each buyer nonetheless has *bargaining power*—it can negotiate low prices because it makes large and infrequent purchases and can play the sellers off against each other when bargaining over price.

> In §10.5, we explain that a buyer has monopsony power when his purchasing decision can affect the price of the product.

Throughout this section, we will assume that the output market is perfectly competitive. In addition, because a single buyer is easier to visualize than several buyers who all have some monopsony power, we will restrict our attention at first to pure monopsony.

### Monopsony Power: Marginal and Average Expenditure

When you are deciding how much of a good to purchase, you keep increasing the number of units purchased until the additional value from the last unit purchased— the *marginal value*—is just equal to the cost of that unit—the *marginal expenditure*. In perfect competition, the price that you pay for the good—the *average expenditure*—is equal to the marginal expenditure. However, when you have monopsony power, the marginal expenditure is greater than the average expenditure, as Figure 14.14 shows.

> In §10.5, we explain that marginal expenditure is the cost of one more unit, and average expenditure is the average price paid per unit.

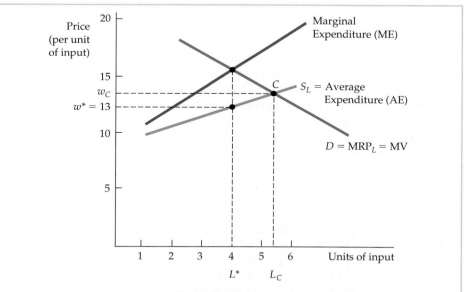

**FIGURE 14.14 Marginal and Average Expenditure**

When the buyer of an input has monopsony power, the marginal expenditure curve lies above the average expenditure curve because the decision to buy an extra unit raises the price that must be paid for all units, not just for the last one. The number of units of input purchased is given by $L^*$, at the intersection of the marginal revenue product and marginal expenditure curves. The corresponding wage rate $w^*$ is lower than the competitive wage $w_c$.

The factor supply curve facing the monopsonist is the market supply curve, which shows how much of the factor suppliers are willing to sell as its price increases. Because the monopsonist pays the same price for each unit, the supply curve is its *average expenditure curve*. The average expenditure curve is upward sloping because the decision to buy an extra unit raises the price that must be paid for all units, not just the last one. For a profit-maximizing firm, however, the *marginal expenditure curve* is relevant in deciding how much to buy. The marginal expenditure curve lies above the average expenditure curve: When the firm increases the price of the factor to hire more units, it must pay *all* units that higher price, not just the last unit hired.

## Purchasing Decisions with Monopsony Power

How much of the input should the firm buy? As we saw earlier, it should buy up to the point where marginal expenditure equals marginal revenue product. Here the benefit from the last unit bought (MRP) is just equal to the cost (ME). Figure 14.14 illustrates this principle for a labor market. Note that the monopsonist hires $L^*$ units of labor; at that point, $ME = MRP_L$. The wage rate $w^*$ that workers are paid is given by finding the point on the average expenditure or supply curve with $L^*$ units of labor.

As we showed in Chapter 10, a buyer with monopsony power maximizes net benefit (utility less expenditure) from a purchase by buying up to the point where marginal value (MV) is equal to marginal expenditure:

$$MV = ME$$

For a firm buying a factor input, MV is just the marginal revenue product of the factor MRP. Thus, we have (as in the case of a competitive factor market)

$$ME = MRP \qquad (14.7)$$

Note from Figure 14.14 that the monopsonist hires less labor than a firm or group of firms with no monopsony power. In a competitive labor market, $L_C$ workers would be hired: At that level, the quantity of labor demanded (given by the marginal revenue product curve) is equal to the quantity of labor supplied (given by the average expenditure curve). Note also that the monopsonistic firm will be paying its workers a wage $w^*$ that is less than the wage $w_C$ that would be paid in a competitive market.

Monopsony power can arise in different ways. One source can be the specialized nature of a firm's business. If the firm buys a component that no one else buys, it is likely to be a monopsonist in the market for that component. Another source can be a business's location—it may be the only major employer within an area. Monopsony power can also arise when the buyers of a factor form a cartel to limit purchases of the factor, in order to buy it at less than the competitive price. (But as we explained in Chapter 10, this is a violation of the antitrust laws.)

Few firms in our economy are pure monopsonists. But many firms (or individuals) have some monopsony power because their purchases account for a large portion of the market. The government is a monopsonist when it hires volunteer soldiers or buys missiles, aircraft, and other specialized military equipment. A mining firm or other company that is the only major employer in a community also has monopsony power in the local labor market. Even in these cases, however, monopsony power may be limited because the government competes to some extent with other firms that offer similar jobs. Likewise, the mining firm competes to some extent with companies in nearby communities.

## Bargaining Power

In some factor markets, there are a small number of sellers and a small number of buyers. In such cases, an individual buyer and an individual seller will negotiate with each other to determine a price. The resulting price might be high or low, depending on which side has more bargaining power.

The amount of bargaining power that a buyer or seller has is determined in part by the number of competing buyers and competing sellers. But it is also determined by the nature of the purchase itself. If each buyer makes large and infrequent purchases, it can sometimes play the sellers off against each other when negotiating a price and thereby amass considerable bargaining power.

An example of this kind of bargaining power occurs in the market for commercial aircraft. Airplanes are clearly key factor inputs for airlines, and airlines want to buy planes at the lowest possible prices. There are dozens of airlines, however, and only two major producers of commercial aircraft—Boeing and Airbus. One might think that as a result, Boeing and Airbus would have a considerable advantage when negotiating prices. The opposite is true. It is important to understand why.

Airlines do not buy planes every day, and they do not usually buy one plane at a time. A company like American Airlines will typically order new planes only every three or four years, and each order might be for 20 or 30 planes, at a cost of several billion dollars. As big as Boeing and Airbus are, this is no small purchase, and each seller will do all it can to win the order. American Airlines knows this and can use it to its advantage. If, for example, American is choosing between 20 new Boeing 777s or 20 new Airbus A340s (which are similar airplanes), it can play the two companies off against each other when negotiating a price. Thus if Boeing offers a price of, say, $150 million per plane, American might go to Airbus and ask it to do better. Whatever Airbus offers, American will then go back to Boeing and demand a bigger discount, claiming (truthfully or otherwise) that Airbus is offering large discounts. Then back to Airbus, back to Boeing, and so on, until American has succeeded in obtaining a large discount from one of the two companies.

---

**EXAMPLE 14.4**   Monopsony Power in the Market for Baseball Players

In the United States, major league baseball is exempt from the antitrust laws, the result of a Supreme Court decision and the policy of Congress not to apply those laws to labor markets.[6] This exemption allowed baseball team owners (before 1975) to operate a monopsonistic cartel. Like all cartels, this one depended on an agreement among owners. The agreement involved an annual draft of players and a *reserve clause* that effectively tied each player to one team for life, thereby eliminating most interteam competition for players. Once a player was drafted by a team, he could not play for another team unless rights

---

[6]This example builds on an analysis of the structure of baseball players' salaries by Roger Noll, who has kindly supplied us with the relevant data.

were sold to that team. As a result, baseball owners had monopsony power in negotiating new contracts with their players: The only alternative to signing an agreement was to give up the game or play it outside the United States.

During the 1960s and early 1970s, baseball players' salaries were far below the market value of their marginal products (determined in part by the incremental attention that better hitting or pitching might achieve). For example, if the players' market had been perfectly competitive, those players receiving a salary of about $42,000 in 1969 would have instead received a salary of $300,000 in 1969 dollars (which is $1.7 million in year 2007 dollars).

Fortunately for the players, and unfortunately for the owners, there was a strike in 1972 followed by a lawsuit by one player (Curt Flood of the St. Louis Cardinals) and an arbitrated labor-management agreement. This process eventually led in 1975 to an agreement by which players could become free agents after playing for a team for six years. The reserve clause was no longer in effect, and a highly monopsonistic labor market became much more competitive.

The result was an interesting experiment in labor market economics. Between 1975 and 1980, the market for baseball players adjusted to a new post-reserve clause equilibrium. Before 1975, expenditures on players' contracts made up approximately 25 percent of all team expenditures. By 1980, those expenditures had increased to 40 percent. Moreover, the average player's salary doubled in real terms. By 1992, the average baseball player was earning $1,014,942—a very large increase from the monopsonistic wages of the 1960s. In 1969, for example, the average baseball salary was approximately $42,000 adjusted for inflation, about $236,000 in year 2007 dollars.

Salaries for baseball players continued to grow. Whereas the average salary was just less than $600,000 in 1990, it had risen to $1,998,000 by 2000 and $2,950,000 by 2007, and many players earned much more. The New York Yankees as a team averaged over $8,010,000 in 2005.

---

**EXAMPLE 14.5**  Teenage Labor Markets and the Minimum Wage

Increases in the national minimum wage rate (which was $4.50 in early 1996 and $5.15 in 1999) were controversial, raising the question of whether the cost of any unemployment that might be generated would be outweighed by the benefit of higher incomes to those whose wages have been increased.[7] A study of the effects of the minimum wage on employment in fast-food restaurants in New Jersey added to that controversy.[8]

---

[7]See Example 1.4 (page 14) for an initial discussion of the minimum wage, and Section 9.3 (page 319) for an analysis of its effects on employment.

[8]David Card and Alan Krueger, "Minimum Wages and Employment: A Case Study of the Fast-Food Industry in New Jersey and Pennsylvania," *American Economic Review* 84 (September 1994). See also David Card and Alan B. Krueger, "A Reanalysis of the Effect of the New Jersey Minimum Wage on the Fast-Food Industry with Representative Payroll Data," Working Paper No. 6386, Cambridge, MA: National Bureau of Economic Research, 1998; and Madeline Zavodny, "Why Minimum Wage Hikes May Not Reduce Employment," Federal Reserve Bank of Atlanta, Economic Review, Second Quarter, 1998.

Some states have minimum wages above the Federal level. In April 1992 the New Jersey minimum wage was increased from $4.25 to $5.05 per hour. Using a survey of 410 fast-food restaurants, David Card and Alan Krueger found that employment had actually *increased* by 13 percent after the minimum wage went up. What is the explanation for this surprising result? One possibility is that restaurants responded to the higher minimum wage by reducing fringe benefits, which usually take the form of free and reduced-price meals for employees. A related explanation is that employers responded by providing less on-the-job training and by lowering the wages for those with experience who had previously been paid more than the new minimum wage.

An alternative explanation for the increased New Jersey employment holds that the labor market for teenage (and other) unskilled workers is not highly competitive. If so, the analysis of Chapter 9 does not apply. If the unskilled fast-food labor market were monopsonistic, for example, we would expect a different effect from the increased minimum wage. Suppose that the wage of $4.25 was the wage that fast-food employers with monopsony power in the labor market would offer their workers even if there were no minimum wage. Suppose also that $5.10 would be the wage enjoyed by workers if the labor market were fully competitive. As Figure 14.14 shows, the increase in the minimum wage would not only raise the wage, but would also increase the employment level (from $L^*$ to $L_C$).

Does the fast-food study show that employers have monopsony power in this labor market? The evidence suggests no. If firms do have monopsony power but the fast-food market is competitive, then the increase in the minimum wage should have no effect on the price of fast food. Because the market for fast food is so competitive, firms paying the higher minimum wage would be forced to absorb the higher wage cost themselves. The study suggests, however, that prices did increase after the introduction of the higher minimum wage.

The Card-Krueger analysis of the minimum wage remains hotly debated. A number of critics argued that the New Jersey study was atypical. Others questioned the reliability of the data, arguing that a higher minimum wage reduces employment (see our discussion in Chapter 9).[9] In response, Card and Krueger repeated their study, using a more comprehensive and accurate data set. They obtained the same results. Where does this leave us? Perhaps a better characterization of low-wage labor markets requires a more sophisticated theory (e.g., the efficiency wage theory discussed in Chapter 17). In any case, new empirical analyses should shed more light on the effects of the minimum wage.

> In §9.3, we explain that setting a minimum wage in a perfectly competitive market can create unemployment and a deadweight loss.

## 14.4 FACTOR MARKETS WITH MONOPOLY POWER

Just as buyers of inputs can have monopsony power, sellers of inputs can have monopoly power. In the extreme, the seller of an input may be a monopolist, as when a firm has a patent to produce a computer chip that no other firm can duplicate. Because the most important example of monopoly power in factor

---

[9]For example, see Donald Deere, Kevin M. Murply, and Finis Welch, "Employment and the 1990–1991 Minimum Wage Hike," *American Economic Review, Papers and Proceedings* 85 (May 1995): 232–37; and David Neumark and William Wascher, "Minimum Wages and Employment: A Case Study of the Fast-Food Industry in New Jersey and Pennsylvania: Comment," *American Economic Review* 90 (2000): 1362–96.

In §10.2, we explain that a seller of a product has some monopoly power if it can profitably charge a price greater than marginal cost.

markets involves labor unions, we will concentrate most of our attention there. In the subsections that follow, we show how a labor union, which is a monopolist in the sale of labor services, might increase the well-being of its members and substantially affect nonunionized workers.

## Monopoly Power over the Wage Rate

Figure 14.15 shows a demand for labor curve in a market with no monopsony power: It aggregates the marginal revenue products of firms that compete to buy labor. The labor supply curve describes how union members would supply labor *if* the union exerted no monopoly power. In that case, the labor market would be competitive, and $L^*$ workers would be hired at a wage of $w^*$, where demand $D_L$ equals supply $S_L$.

Because of its monopoly power, however, the union can choose any wage rate and the corresponding quantity of labor supplied, just as a monopolist seller of output chooses price and the corresponding quantity of output. If the union wanted to maximize the number of workers hired, it would choose the competitive outcome at $A$. However, if the union wished to obtain a higher-than-competitive wage, it could restrict its membership to $L_1$ workers. As a result, the firm would pay a wage rate of $w_1$. Although union members who work would be better off, those who cannot find jobs would be worse off.

Is a policy of restrictive union membership worthwhile? If the union wishes to maximize the economic rent that its workers receive, the answer is yes. By

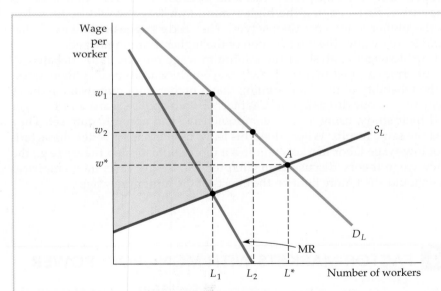

**FIGURE 14.15 Monopoly Power of Sellers of Labor**

When a labor union is a monopolist, it chooses among points on the buyer's demand for labor curve $D_L$. The seller can maximize the number of workers hired, at $L^*$, by agreeing that workers will work at wage $w^*$. The quantity of labor $L_1$ that maximizes the rent earned by employees is determined by the intersection of the marginal revenue and supply of labor curves; union members will receive a wage rate of $w_1$. Finally, if the union wishes to maximize total wages paid to workers, it should allow $L_2$ union members to be employed at a wage rate of $w_2$. At that point, the marginal revenue to the union will be zero.

restricting membership, the union would be acting like a monopolist, which restricts output in order to maximize profit. To a firm, profit is the revenue that it receives less its opportunity costs. To a union, rent represents the wages that its members earn as a group in excess of their opportunity cost. To maximize rent, the union must choose the number of workers hired so that the marginal revenue to the union (the additional wages earned) is equal to the extra cost of inducing workers to work. This cost is a *marginal* opportunity cost because it is a measure of what an employer has to offer an additional worker to get him or her to work for the firm. However, the wage that is necessary to encourage additional workers to take jobs is given by the supply of labor curve $S_L$.

> In §7.1, we explain that opportunity cost is the cost associated with opportunities that are foregone by not putting a firm's resources to their best alternative use.

The rent-maximizing combination of wage rate and number of workers is given by the intersection of the MR and $S_L$ curves. We have chosen the wage-employment combination of $w_1$ and $L_1$ with the rent-maximization premise in mind. The shaded area below the demand for labor curve, above the supply of labor curve and to the left of $L_1$, represents the economic rent that all workers receive.

A rent-maximizing policy might benefit nonunion workers if they can find nonunion jobs. However, if these jobs are not available, rent maximization could create too sharp a distinction between winners and losers. An alternative objective is to maximize the aggregate wages that all union members receive. Look again at the example in Figure 14.15. To achieve this goal, the number of workers hired is increased from $L_1$ until the marginal revenue to the union is equal to zero. Because any further employment decreases total wage payments, aggregate wages are maximized when the wage is equal to $w_2$ and the number of workers is equal to $L_2$.

## Unionized and Nonunionized Workers

When the union uses its monopoly power to increase members' wages, fewer unionized workers are hired. Because these workers either move to the nonunion sector or choose initially not to join the union, it is important to understand what happens in the nonunionized part of the economy.

Assume that the total supply of unionized and nonunionized workers is fixed. In Figure 14.16, the market supply of labor in both sectors is given by $S_L$. The demand for labor by firms in the unionized sector is given by $D_U$, the demand in the nonunionized sector by $D_{NU}$. Total market demand is the horizontal sum of the demands in the two sectors and is given by $D_L$.

Suppose the union chooses to increase the wage rate of its workers above the competitive wage $w^*$, to $w_U$. At that wage rate, the number of workers hired in the unionized sector falls by an amount $\Delta L_U$, as shown on the horizontal axis. As these workers find employment in the nonunionized sector, the wage rate in that sector adjusts until the labor market is in equilibrium. At the new wage rate in the nonunionized sector, $w_{NU}$, the additional number of workers hired in that sector, $\Delta L_{NU}$, is equal to the number of workers who left the unionized sector.

Figure 14.16 shows an adverse consequence of a union strategy directed toward raising union wages: Nonunionized wages fall. Unionization can improve working conditions and provide useful information to workers and management. But when the demand for labor is not perfectly inelastic, union workers are helped at the expense of nonunion workers.

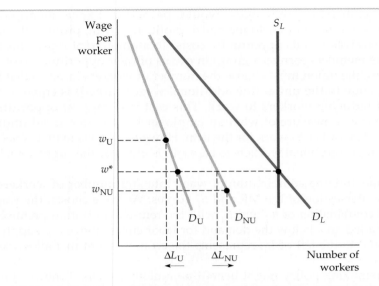

**FIGURE 14.16 Wage Discrimination in Unionized and Nonunionized Sectors**

When a monopolistic union raises the wage in the unionized sector of the economy from $w^*$ to $w_U$, employment in that sector falls, as shown by the movement along the demand curve $D_U$. For the total supply of labor, given by $S_L$, to remain unchanged, the wage in the nonunionized sector must fall from $w^*$ to $w_{NU}$, as shown by the movement along the demand curve $D_{NU}$.

**EXAMPLE 14.6** The Decline of Private-Sector Unionism

For several decades, both the membership and bargaining power of labor unions have been declining.[10] A decline in union monopoly power can lead to different responses by union negotiators and can also affect the wage rate and level of employment. During the 1970s, most of the impact was on union wages: Although levels of employment did not change much, the differential between union and nonunion wages decreased substantially. We would have expected the same pattern to occur in the 1980s because of heavily publicized wage freezes and the rapid growth of two-tier wage provisions in which newer union members are paid less than more experienced counterparts.

Surprisingly, however, the union-management bargaining process changed during this period. From 1980 to 1984, the level of unionized employment fell from 23 percent to 19 percent. Yet the union-nonunion wage differential remained stable—and in fact grew wider in some industries. For example, the union wage rate in mining, forestry, and fisheries declined only slightly, from 25 percent higher than the nonunion wage in 1980 to 24 percent higher in 1984. On the other hand, the union wage rate in manufacturing increased slightly—from approximately 14 percent higher than the nonunion wage in 1980 to 16 percent in 1984. This same pattern has continued over the years. As Figure 14.17 shows, by 2006, unionized employment had fallen to below 12 percent of total employment. The union-nonunion wage differential remained essentially unchanged. In recent years, nonunion wages have increased faster than union wages.

---

[10]This example is based on Richard Edwards and Paul Swaim, "Union-Nonunion Earnings Differentials and the Decline of Private-Sector Unionism," *American Economic Review* 76 (May 1986): 97–102.

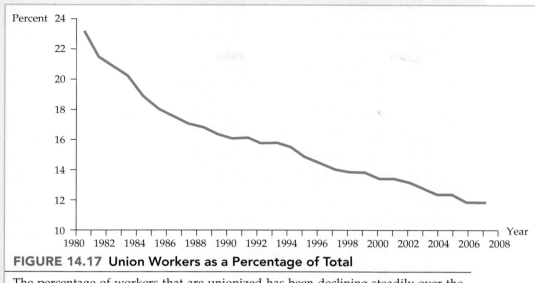

**FIGURE 14.17 Union Workers as a Percentage of Total**

The percentage of workers that are unionized has been declining steadily over the past 25 years.

*Source:* Bureau of Labor Statistics.

Nevertheless, the union-nonunion wage differential remains significant. For example, data from the Employer Costs for Employee Compensation Survey show that in 2006, wages and salaries for private-industry union workers averaged $21.65 per hour, compared with $17.59 for nonunion workers.

One explanation for this pattern of wage-employment responses is a change in union strategy—a move to maximize the wage rate for its members rather than the total wages paid to all union members. However, the demand for unionized employees has probably become increasingly elastic over time as firms find it easier to substitute capital for skilled labor in the production process. Faced with an elastic demand for its services, the union would have little choice but to maintain the wage rate of its members and allow employment levels to fall. Of course, the substitution of nonunion for union workers may cause further losses in the bargaining power of labor unions. How this will affect the differential between union and nonunion wages remains to be seen.

**EXAMPLE 14.7**  Wage Inequality—Have Computers Changed the Labor Market?

In Example 2.2 (page 29), we explained how the rapid growth in the demand for skilled relative to unskilled labor has been partly responsible for the growing inequality in the distribution of income in the United States. What is the underlying source of that change in relative demand? Is it the decline in private-sector unionism and the failure of the minimum wage to keep up with inflation? Or is it the increasing role that computers now play in the labor market? A recent study, which focuses on the wages of college relative to high school graduates, provides some answers.[11]

From 1950 to 1980, the relative wages of college graduates (the ratio of their average wages to those of high school graduates) hardly changed. In contrast, college graduates' (relative) wages grew rapidly from 1980 to 1995. This pattern is not consistent with what one would expect if the decline of unionism (and/or changes in the minimum wage) was the primary reason for the growing inequality. A clue to what happened is given by the dramatic increase in the use of computers by workers. In 1984, 25.1 percent of all workers used computers; that figure increased to 45.8 percent by 1993 and 56.1 percent in 2003. For managers and professionals, the figure was over 80 percent.

While computer use increased for all workers, the largest increases were registered by workers with college degrees—from 42 to 82 percent. For those without a high school degree, the increase was only 11 percentage points (from 5 to 16 percent); for those with high school degrees, the increase was 21 percentage points (from 19 to 40 percent).

Further analysis of data on jobs and wages confirms the importance of computers. Education and computer use have gone hand-in-hand to increase the demand for skilled workers. The wages of college graduates who use computers (relative to high school graduates) grew by about 11 percent from 1983 to 1993; for noncomputer users, wages grew by less than 4 percent. A statistical analysis shows that, overall, the spread of computer technology is responsible for nearly half the increase in relative wages during this period. Furthermore, the growth in the demand for skilled workers has occurred primarily within industries where computers have become increasingly useful.

Is this increase in the relative wages of skilled workers necessarily a bad thing? At least one economist suggests that the answer is no.[12] It is true that the growing inequality can disadvantage low-wage workers, whose limited opportunities might lead them to drop out of the labor force; in the extreme, they might even turn to crime. However, it can also motivate workers, whose opportunities for upward mobility through high-wage jobs have never been better.

Consider the circumstances facing men and women who are deciding whether to complete high school or college. We'll take the median wage of someone who completed high school as the norm. In 2005, college graduates age 25 and over earned on average $500 more per week than workers who stopped with a high school diploma. This figure translates into a real-wage increase for college graduates and a real-wage decrease for high school dropouts in comparison to 1979. Furthermore, the unemployment rate among college graduates is only one-third that among high school dropouts. The college wage premium has more than doubled over the past 30 years and provides strong motivation for college students to finish their studies.

---

[11]David H. Autor, Lawrence Katz, and Alan B. Krueger, "Computing Inequality: Have Computers Changed the Labor Market?" *Quarterly Journal of Economics* 113 (November 1998): 1169–1213.

[12]Finis Welch, "In Defense of Inequality," *American Economic Association, Papers and Proceedings* 89 (May 1999): 1–17.

# SUMMARY

1. In a competitive input market, the demand for an input is given by the marginal revenue product, the product of the firm's marginal revenue, and the marginal product of the input.

2. A firm in a competitive labor market will hire workers to the point at which the marginal revenue product of labor is equal to the wage rate. This principle is analogous to the profit-maximizing output condition that production be increased to the point at which marginal revenue is equal to marginal cost.

3. The market demand for an input is the horizontal sum of industry demands for the input. But industry demand is not the horizontal sum of the demands of all the firms in the industry. To determine industry demand, one must remember that the market price of the product will change in response to changes in the price of an input.

4. When factor markets are competitive, the buyer of an input assumes that its purchases will have no effect on its price. As a result, the firm's marginal expenditure and average expenditure curves are both perfectly elastic.

5. The market supply of a factor such as labor need not be upward sloping. A backward-bending labor supply curve can result if the income effect associated with a higher wage rate (more leisure is demanded because it is a normal good) is greater than the substitution effect (less leisure is demanded because its price has gone up).

6. Economic rent is the difference between the payments to factors of production and the minimum payment that would be needed to employ them. In a labor market, rent is measured by the area below the wage level and above the marginal expenditure curve.

7. When a buyer of an input has monopsony power, the marginal expenditure curve lies above the average expenditure curve, which reflects the fact that the monopsonist must pay a higher price to attract more of the input into employment.

8. When the input seller is a monopolist, such as a labor union, the seller chooses the point on the marginal revenue product curve that best suits its objective. Maximization of employment, economic rent, and wages are three plausible objectives for labor unions.

# QUESTIONS FOR REVIEW

1. Why is a firm's demand for labor curve more inelastic when the firm has monopoly power in the output market than when the firm is producing competitively?

2. Why might a labor supply curve be backward bending?

3. How is a computer company's demand for computer programmers a derived demand?

4. Compare the hiring choices of a monopsonistic and a competitive employer of workers. Which will hire more workers, and which will pay the higher wage? Explain.

5. Rock musicians sometimes earn several million dollars per year. Can you explain such large incomes in terms of economic rent?

6. What happens to the demand for one input when the use of a complementary input increases?

7. For a monopsonist, what is the relationship between the supply of an input and the marginal expenditure on it?

8. Currently the National Football League has a system for drafting college players by which each player is picked by only one team. The player must sign with that team or not play in the league. What would happen to the wages of both newly drafted and more experienced football players if the draft system were repealed and all teams could compete for college players?

9. The government wants to encourage individuals on welfare to become employed. It is considering two possible incentive programs:
   a. Give firms $2 per hour for every individual on welfare who is hired.
   b. Give each firm that hires one or more welfare workers a payment of $1000 per year, irrespective of the number of hires.
   To what extent is each of these programs likely to be effective at increasing the employment opportunities for welfare workers?

10. A small specialty cookie company, whose only variable input is labor, finds that the average worker can produce 50 cookies per day, the cost of the average worker is $64 per day, and the price of a cookie is $1. Is the company maximizing its profit? Explain.

11. A firm uses both labor and machines in production. Explain why an increase in the average wage rate causes both a movement along the labor demand curve and a shift of the curve.

# EXERCISES

1. Suppose that the wage rate is $16 per hour and the price of the product is $2. Values for output and labor are in units per hour.

| q | L |
|---|---|
| 0 | 0 |
| 20 | 1 |
| 35 | 2 |
| 47 | 3 |
| 57 | 4 |
| 65 | 5 |
| 70 | 6 |

   a. Find the profit-maximizing quantity of labor.
   b. Suppose that the price of the product remains at $2 but that the wage rate increases to $21. Find the new profit-maximizing level of $L$.
   c. Suppose that the price of the product increases to $3 and the wage remains at $16 per hour. Find the new profit-maximizing $L$.
   d. Suppose that the price of the product remains at $2 and the wage at $16, but that there is a technological breakthrough that increases output by 25 percent for any given level of labor. Find the new profit-maximizing $L$.

2. Assume that workers whose incomes are less than $10,000 currently pay no federal income taxes. Suppose a new government program guarantees each worker $5000, whether or not he or she earns any income. For all earned income up to $10,000, the worker must pay a 50-percent tax. Draw the budget line facing the worker under this new program. How is the program likely to affect the labor supply curve of workers?

3. Using your knowledge of marginal revenue product, explain the following:
   a. A famous tennis star is paid $200,000 for appearing in a 30-second television commercial. The actor who plays his doubles partner is paid $500.
   b. The president of an ailing savings and loan is paid *not* to stay in his job for the last two years of his contract.
   c. A jumbo jet carrying 400 passengers is priced higher than a 250-passenger model even though both aircraft cost the same to manufacture.

4. The demands for the factors of production listed below have increased. What can you conclude about changes in the demands for the related consumer goods? If demands for the consumer goods remain unchanged, what other explanation is there for an increase in derived demands for these items?

   a. Computer memory chips
   b. Jet fuel for passenger planes
   c. Paper used for newsprint
   d. Aluminum used for beverage cans

5. Suppose there are two groups of workers, unionized and nonunionized. Congress passes a law that requires all workers to join the union. What do you expect to happen to the wage rates of formerly nonunionized workers? Of those workers who were originally unionized? What have you assumed about the union's behavior?

6. Suppose that a firm's production function is given by $Q = 12L - L^2$, for $L = 0$ to 6, where $L$ is labor input per day and $Q$ is output per day. Derive and draw the firm's demand for labor curve if the firm's output sells for $10 in a competitive market. How many workers will the firm hire when the wage rate is $30 per day? $60 per day? (*Hint:* The marginal product of labor is $12 - 2L$.)

7. The only legal employer of military soldiers in the United States is the federal government. If the government uses its knowledge of its monopsonistic position, what criteria will it employ when determining how many soldiers to recruit? What happens if a mandatory draft is implemented?

8. The demand for labor by an industry is given by the curve $L = 1200 - 10w$, where $L$ is the labor demanded per day and $w$ is the wage rate. The supply curve is given by $L = 20w$. What is the equilibrium wage rate and quantity of labor hired? What is the economic rent earned by workers?

9. Using the same information as in Exercise 8, suppose now that the only labor available is controlled by a monopolistic labor union that wishes to maximize the rent earned by union members. What will be the quantity of labor employed and the wage rate? How does your answer compare with your answer to Exercise 8? Discuss. (*Hint:* The union's marginal revenue curve is given by $MR = 120 - 0.2L$.)

*10. A firm uses a single input, labor, to produce output $q$ according to the production function $q = 8\sqrt{L}$. The commodity sells for $150 per unit and the wage rate is $75 per hour.
   a. Find the profit-maximizing quantity of $L$.
   b. Find the profit-maximizing quantity of $q$.
   c. What is the maximum profit?
   d. Suppose now that the firm is taxed $30 per unit of output and that the wage rate is subsidized at a rate of $15 per hour. Assume that the firm is a price taker, so the price of the product remains at $150. Find the new profit-maximizing levels of $L$, $q$, and profit.
   e. Now suppose that the firm is required to pay a 20 percent tax on its profits. Find the new profit-maximizing levels of $L$, $q$, and profit.

# Investment, Time, and Capital Markets

In Chapter 14, we saw that in competitive markets, firms decide how much to purchase each month by comparing the marginal revenue product of each factor to its cost. The decisions of all firms determine the market demand for each factor, and the market price is the price that equates the quantity demanded with the quantity supplied. For factor inputs such as labor and raw materials, this picture is reasonably complete, but not so for capital. The reason is that capital is *durable*: It can last and contribute to production for years after it is purchased.

Firms sometimes rent capital in much the same way that they hire workers. For example, a firm might rent office space for a monthly fee, just as it hires a worker for a monthly wage. But more often, capital expenditures involve the purchases of factories and equipment that are expected to last for years. This introduces the element of *time*. When a firm decides whether to build a factory or purchase machines, it must compare the outlays it would have to make *now* with the additional profit that the new capital will generate *in the future*. To make this comparison, it must address the following question: *How much are future profits worth today?* This problem does not arise when hiring labor or purchasing raw materials. To make those choices, the firm need only compare its *current* expenditure on the factor—e.g., the wage or the price of steel—with the factor's *current* marginal revenue product.

In this chapter, we will learn how to calculate the current value of future flows of money. This is the basis for our study of the firm's investment decisions. Most of these decisions involve comparing an outlay today with profits that will be received in the future; we will see how firms can make this comparison and determine whether the outlay is warranted. Often, the future profits resulting from a capital investment are higher or lower than anticipated. We will see how firms can take this kind of uncertainty into account.

We will also see how individuals can make decisions involving costs and benefits occurring at different points in time. For example, we will see how a consumer choosing a new air conditioner can determine whether it makes economic sense to buy a more energy-efficient model that costs more but will result in lower electricity bills in the future. We will also discuss investments in *human capital*. Does it make economic sense, for example, to go to college or graduate school rather than take a job and start earning an income?

We will examine other intertemporal decisions that firms sometimes face. For example, producing a depletable resource, such as natural gas or oil, in the present means that less will be available to produce in the future. How should a producer take this into account? How long should a timber company let trees grow before harvesting them for lumber?

The answers to these investment and production decisions depend in part on the *interest rate* that one pays or receives when borrowing or lending money. We will discuss the factors that determine interest rates and explain why interest rates on government bonds, corporate bonds, and savings accounts differ.

> In §14.1, we explain that in a competitive factor market, the demand for each factor is given by its marginal revenue product—i.e., the additional revenue earned from an incremental unit of the factor.

## 15.1 STOCKS VERSUS FLOWS

Before proceeding, we must be clear about how to measure capital and other factor inputs that firms purchase. Capital is measured as a *stock*, i.e., as a quantity of plant and equipment that the firm owns. For example, if a firm owns an electric motor factory worth $10 million, we say that it has a *capital stock* worth $10 million. Inputs of labor and raw materials, on the other hand, are measured as *flows*, as is the output of the firm. For example, this same firm might use 20,000 worker-hours of labor and 50,000 pounds of copper *per month* to produce 8000 electric motors *per month*. (The choice of monthly units is arbitrary; we could just as well have expressed these quantities in weekly or annual terms—for example, 240,000 worker-hours of labor per year, 600,000 pounds of copper per year, and 96,000 motors per year.)

> Recall from §6.1 that a firm's production function involves flows of inputs and outputs: It turns certain amounts of labor and capital each year into an amount of output that same year.

Let's look at this producer of electric motors in more detail. Both variable cost and the rate of output are flows. Suppose the wage rate is $15 per hour and the price of copper is 80 cents per pound. Thus the variable cost is (20,000)($15) + (50,000)($0.80) = $340,000 *per month*. Average variable cost, on the other hand, is a cost *per unit*:

$$\frac{\$340,000 \text{ per month}}{8000 \text{ units per month}} = \$42.50 \text{ per unit}$$

Suppose the firm sells its motors for $52.50 each. Then its average profit is $52.50 − $42.50 = $10.00 per unit, and its total profit is $80,000 *per month*. (Note that total profit is also a flow.) To make and sell these motors, however, the firm needs capital—namely, the factory that it built for $10 million. *Thus the firm's $10 million capital stock allows it to earn a flow of profit of $80,000 per month.*

Was the $10 million investment in this factory a sound decision? To answer this question, we must translate the $80,000 per month profit flow into a number that we can compare with the factory's $10 million cost. Suppose the factory is expected to last for 20 years. In that case the problem, simply put, is: What is the value today of $80,000 per month for the next 20 years? If that value is greater than $10 million, the investment was a good one.

A profit of $80,000 per month for 20 years comes to ($80,000)(20)(12) = $19.2 million. That would make the factory seem like an excellent investment. But is $80,000 five years—or 20 years—from now worth $80,000 today? No, because money today can be invested—in a bank account, a bond, or other interest-bearing assets—to yield more money in the future. As a result, $19.2 million received over the next 20 years is worth *less* than $19.2 million today.

## 15.2 PRESENT DISCOUNTED VALUE

We will return to our $10 million electric motor factory in Section 15.4, but first we must address a basic problem: *How much is $1 paid in the future worth today?* The answer depends on the **interest rate**: the rate at which one can borrow or lend money.

• **interest rate**   Rate at which one can borrow or lend money.

Suppose the annual interest rate is $R$. (Don't worry about which interest rate this actually is; later, we'll discuss the various types of interest rates.) Then $1 today can be invested to yield $(1 + R)$ dollars a year from now. Therefore, $1 + R$ dollars is the *future value* of $1 today. Now, what is the value *today*, i.e., **the present discounted value (PDV)**, of $1 paid one year from now? The answer is easy: because $1 + R$ dollars one year from now is worth $(1 + R)/(1 + R) = \$1$ today, $1 *a year from now is worth* $\$1/(1 + R)$ *today*. This is the amount of money that will yield $1 after one year if invested at the rate $R$.

• **present discounted value (PDV)**   The current value of an expected future cash flow.

What is the value today of $1 paid *two* years from now? If $1 were invested today at the interest rate $R$, it would be worth $1 + R$ dollars after one year, and $(1 + R)(1 + R) = (1 + R)^2$ dollars at the end of two years. Because $(1 + R)^2$ dollars two years from now is worth $1 today, $1 two years from now is worth $\$1/(1 + R)^2$ today. Similarly, $1 paid three years from now is worth $\$1/(1 + R)^3$ today, and $1 paid $n$ years from now is worth $\$1/(1 + R)^n$ today.[1]

We can summarize this as follows:

$$\text{PDV of \$1 paid after 1 year } = \frac{\$1}{(1+R)}$$

$$\text{PDV of \$1 paid after 2 years} = \frac{\$1}{(1+R)^2}$$

$$\text{PDV of \$1 paid after 3 years} = \frac{\$1}{(1+R)^3}$$

$$\vdots$$

$$\text{PDV of \$1 paid after } n \text{ years} = \frac{\$1}{(1+R)^n}$$

Table 15.1 shows, for different interest rates, the present value of $1 paid after 1, 2, 5, 10, 20, and 30 years. Note that for interest rates above 6 or 7 percent, $1 paid 20 or 30 years from now is worth very little today. But this is not the case for low interest rates. For example, if $R$ is 3 percent, the PDV of $1 paid 20 years from now is about 55 cents. In other words, if 55 cents were invested now at the rate of 3 percent, it would yield about $1 after 20 years.

### Valuing Payment Streams

We can now determine the present value of a stream of payments over time. For example, consider the two payment streams in Table 15.2. Stream *A* comes to $200: $100 paid now and $100 a year from now. Stream *B* comes to $220: $20 paid

---

[1]We are assuming that the annual rate of interest $R$ is constant from year to year. Suppose the annual interest rate were expected to change, so that $R_1$ is the rate in year 1, $R_2$ is the rate in year 2, and so forth. After two years, $1 invested today would be worth $(1 + R_1)(1 + R_2)$, so that the PDV of $1 received two years from now is $\$1/(1 + R_1)(1 + R_2)$. Similarly, the PDV of $1 paid $n$ years from now is $\$1/(1 + R_1)(1 + R_2)(1 + R_3) \ldots (1 + R_n)$.

### TABLE 15.1 PDV of $1 Paid in the Future

| Interest Rate | 1 Year | 2 Years | 5 Years | 10 Years | 20 Years | 30 Years |
|---|---|---|---|---|---|---|
| 0.01 | $0.990 | $0.980 | $0.951 | $0.905 | $0.820 | $0.742 |
| 0.02 | 0.980 | 0.961 | 0.906 | 0.820 | 0.673 | 0.552 |
| 0.03 | 0.971 | 0.943 | 0.863 | 0.744 | 0.554 | 0.412 |
| 0.04 | 0.962 | 0.925 | 0.822 | 0.676 | 0.456 | 0.308 |
| 0.05 | 0.952 | 0.907 | 0.784 | 0.614 | 0.377 | 0.231 |
| 0.06 | 0.943 | 0.890 | 0.747 | 0.558 | 0.312 | 0.174 |
| 0.07 | 0.935 | 0.873 | 0.713 | 0.508 | 0.258 | 0.131 |
| 0.08 | 0.926 | 0.857 | 0.681 | 0.463 | 0.215 | 0.099 |
| 0.09 | 0.917 | 0.842 | 0.650 | 0.422 | 0.178 | 0.075 |
| 0.10 | 0.909 | 0.826 | 0.621 | 0.386 | 0.149 | 0.057 |
| 0.15 | 0.870 | 0.756 | 0.497 | 0.247 | 0.061 | 0.015 |
| 0.20 | 0.833 | 0.694 | 0.402 | 0.162 | 0.026 | 0.004 |

### TABLE 15.2 Two Payment Streams

| | Today | 1 Year | 2 Years |
|---|---|---|---|
| Payment Stream A: | $100 | $100 | $ 0 |
| Payment Stream B: | $ 20 | $100 | $100 |

now, $100 a year from now, and $100 two years from now. Which payment stream would you prefer to receive? The answer depends on the interest rate.

To calculate the present discounted value of these two streams, we compute and add the present values of each year's payment:

$$\text{PDV of Stream } A = \$100 + \frac{\$100}{(1 + R)}$$

$$\text{PDV of Stream } B = \$20 + \frac{\$100}{(1 + R)} + \frac{\$100}{(1 + R)^2}$$

Table 15.3 shows the present values of the two streams for interest rates of 5, 10, 15, and 20 percent. As the table shows, the preferred stream depends on the interest rate. For interest rates of 10 percent or less, Stream $B$ is worth more; for interest rates of 15 percent or more, Stream $A$ is worth more. Why? Because even though less is paid out in Stream $A$, it is paid out sooner.

### TABLE 15.3 PDV of Payment Streams

| | $R = .05$ | $R = .10$ | $R = .15$ | $R = .20$ |
|---|---|---|---|---|
| PDV of Stream A: | $195.24 | $190.91 | $186.96 | $183.33 |
| PDV of Stream B: | 205.94 | 193.55 | 182.57 | 172.78 |

**EXAMPLE 15.1**    The Value of Lost Earnings

In legal cases involving accidents, victims or their heirs (if the victim is killed) sue the injuring party (or an insurance company) to recover damages. In addition to compensating for pain and suffering, those damages include the future income that the injured or deceased person would have earned had the accident not occurred. To see how the present value of lost earnings can be calculated, let's examine an actual 1996 accident case. (The names and some of the data have been changed to preserve anonymity.)

Harold Jennings died in an automobile accident on January 1, 1996, at the age of 53. His family sued the driver of the other car for negligence. A major part of the damages they asked to be awarded was the present value of the earnings that Jennings would have received from his job as an airline pilot had he not been killed. The calculation of present value is typical of cases like this.

Had he worked in 1996, Jennings' salary would have been $85,000. The normal age of retirement for an airline pilot is 60. To calculate the present value of Jennings' lost earnings, we must take several things into account. First, Jennings' salary would probably have increased over the years. Second, we cannot be sure that he would have lived to retirement had the accident not occurred; he might have died from some other cause. Therefore, the PDV of his lost earnings until retirement at the end of 2003 is

$$PDV = W_0 + \frac{W_0(1 + g)(1 - m_1)}{(1 + R)} + \frac{W_0(1 + g)^2(1 - m_2)}{(1 + R)^2}$$
$$+ \cdots + \frac{W_0(1 + g)^7(1 - m_7)}{(1 + R)^7}$$

where $W_0$ is his salary in 1996, $g$ is the annual percentage rate at which his salary is likely to have grown (so that $W_0(1 + g)$ would be his salary in 1997, $W_0(1 + g)^2$ his salary in 1998, etc.), and $m_1, m_2, \ldots, m_7$ are *mortality rates*, i.e., the probabilities that he would have died from some other cause by 1997, 1998, ..., 2003.

To calculate this PDV, we need to know the mortality rates $m_1, \ldots, m_7$, the expected rate of growth of Jennings' salary $g$, and the interest rate $R$. Mortality data are available from insurance tables that provide death rates for men of similar age and race.[2] As a value for $g$, we can use 8 percent, the average rate of growth of wages for airline pilots over the period 1985–1995. Finally, for the interest rate we can use the rate on government bonds, which at the time was about 9 percent. (We will say more about how one chooses the correct interest rate to discount future cash flows in Sections 15.4 and 15.5.) Table 15.4 shows the details of the present value calculation.

By summing the last column, we obtain a PDV of $650,254. If Jennings' family was successful in proving that the defendant was at fault, and if there were no other damage issues involved in the case, they could recover this amount as compensation.[3]

---

[2]See, for example, the *Statistical Abstract of the United States*, 2007, Table 100.

[3]Actually, this sum should be reduced by the amount of Jennings' wages which would have been spent on his own consumption and which would not therefore have benefited his wife or children.

**TABLE 15.4    Calculating Lost Wages**

| Year | $W_0(1 + g)^t$ | $(1 - m_t)$ | $1/(1 + R)^t$ | $W_0(1 + g)^t (1 - m_t)/(1 + R)^t$ |
|------|------|------|------|------|
| 1996 | $ 85,000 | .991 | 1.000 | $84,235 |
| 1997 | 91,800 | .990 | .917 | 83,339 |
| 1998 | 99,144 | .989 | .842 | 82,561 |
| 1999 | 107,076 | .988 | .772 | 81,671 |
| 2000 | 115,642 | .987 | .708 | 80,810 |
| 2001 | 124,893 | .986 | .650 | 80,044 |
| 2002 | 134,884 | .985 | .596 | 79,185 |
| 2003 | 145,675 | .984 | .547 | 78,409 |

## 15.3 THE VALUE OF A BOND

• **bond** Contract in which a borrower agrees to pay the bondholder (the lender) a stream of money.

A **bond** is a contract in which a borrower agrees to pay the bondholder (the lender) a stream of money. For example, a corporate bond (a bond issued by a corporation) might make "coupon" payments of $100 per year for the next ten years, and then a principal payment of $1000 at the end of the ten-year period.[4] How much would you pay for such a bond? To find out how much the bond is worth, we simply compute the present value of the payment stream:

$$PDV = \frac{\$100}{(1 + R)} + \frac{\$100}{(1 + R)^2} + \cdots + \frac{\$100}{(1 + R)^{10}} + \frac{\$1000}{(1 + R)^{10}} \quad \textbf{(15.1)}$$

Again, the present value depends on the interest rate. Figure 15.1 shows the value of the bond—the present value of its payment stream—for interest rates up to 20 percent. Note that the higher the interest rate, the lower the value of the bond. At an interest rate of 5 percent, the bond is worth about $1386, but at an interest rate of 15 percent, its value is only $749.

### Perpetuities

• **perpetuity** Bond paying out a fixed amount of money each year, forever.

A **perpetuity** is a bond that pays out a fixed amount of money each year, *forever*. How much is a perpetuity that pays $100 per year worth? The present value of the payment stream is given by the infinite summation:

$$PDV = \frac{\$100}{(1 + R)} + \frac{\$100}{(1 + R)^2} + \frac{\$100}{(1 + R)^3} + \frac{\$100}{(1 + R)^4} + \cdots$$

---

[4]In the United States, the coupon payments on most corporate bonds are made in semiannual installments. To keep the arithmetic simple, we will assume that they are made annually.

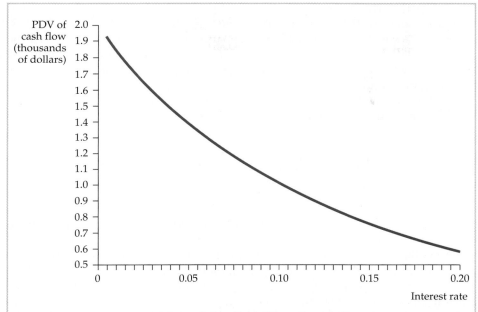

**FIGURE 15.1 Present Value of the Cash Flow from a Bond**

Because most of the bond's payments occur in the future, the present discounted value declines as the interest rate increases. For example, if the interest rate is 5 percent, the PDV of a 10-year bond paying $100 per year on a principal of $1000 is $1386. At an interest rate of 15 percent, the PDV is $749.

Fortunately, it isn't necessary to calculate and add up all these terms to find the value of this perpetuity; the summation can be expressed in terms of a simple formula.[5]

$$PDV = \$100/R \qquad \textbf{(15.2)}$$

So if the interest rate is 5 percent, the perpetuity is worth $100/(.05) = $2000, but if the interest rate is 20 percent, the perpetuity is worth only $500.

## The Effective Yield on a Bond

Many corporate and most government bonds are traded on the *bond market*. The value of a traded bond can be determined directly by looking at its market price—the value placed on it by buyers and sellers.[6] Thus we usually know the value of a bond, but to compare the bond with other investment opportunities, we would like to determine the interest rate consistent with that value.

**Effective Yield** Equations (15.1) and (15.2) show how the values of two different bonds depend on the interest rate used to discount future payments. These equations can be "turned around" to relate the interest rate to the bond's value.

---

[5]Let $x$ be the PDV of $1 per year in perpetuity, so $x = 1/(1 + R) + 1/(1 + R)^2 + \ldots$. Then $x(1 + R) = 1 + 1/(1 + R) + 1/(1 + R)^2 + \ldots$, so $x(1 + R) = 1 + x$, $xR = 1$, and $x = 1/R$.

[6]The prices of actively traded corporate and U.S. government bonds are shown on financial market Web sites such as **www.yahoo.com**, **www.bloomberg.com**, and **www.schwab.com**.

• **effective yield (or rate of return)** Percentage return that one receives by investing in a bond.

This is particularly easy to do for the perpetuity. Suppose the market price—and thus the value—of the perpetuity is $P$. Then from equation (15.2), $P = \$100/R$, and $R = \$100/P$. Thus, if the price of the perpetuity is $1000, we know that the interest rate is $R = \$100/\$1000 = 0.10$, or 10 percent. This interest rate is called the **effective yield**, or **rate of return**: the percentage return that one receives by investing in a bond.

For the ten-year coupon bond in equation (15.1), calculating the effective yield is a bit more complicated. If the price of the bond is $P$, we write equation (15.1) as

$$P = \frac{\$100}{(1 + R)} + \frac{\$100}{(1 + R)^2} + \frac{\$100}{(1 + R)^3} + \cdots + \frac{\$100}{(1 + R)^{10}} + \frac{\$1000}{(1 + R)^{10}}$$

Given the price $P$, this equation must be solved for $R$. Although there is no simple formula to express $R$ in terms of $P$ in this case, there are methods (sometimes available on calculators and spreadsheet programs such as Excel) for calculating $R$ numerically. Figure 15.2, which plots the same curve as that in Figure 15.1, shows how $R$ depends on $P$ for this ten-year coupon bond. Note that if the price of the bond is $1000, the effective yield is 10 percent. If the price rises to $1300, the effective yield drops to about 6 percent. If the price falls to $700, the effective yield rises to over 16 percent.

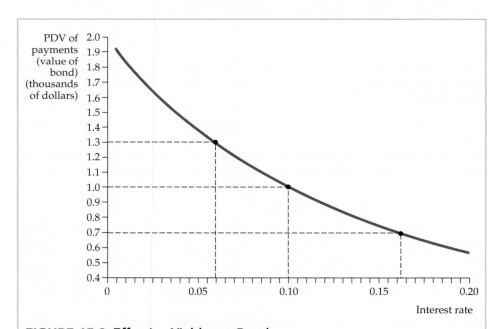

**FIGURE 15.2 Effective Yield on a Bond**

The effective yield is the interest rate that equates the present value of the bond's payment stream with the bond's market price. The figure shows the present value of the payment stream as a function of the interest rate. The effective yield is found by drawing a horizontal line at the level of the bond's price. For example, if the price of this bond were $1000, its effective yield would be 10 percent. If the price were $1300, the effective yield would be about 6 percent; if the price were $700, it would be 16.2 percent.

Yields can differ considerably among different bonds. Corporate bonds generally yield more than government bonds, and as Example 15.2 shows, the bonds of some corporations yield much more than the bonds of others. One of the most important reasons for this is that different bonds carry different degrees of risk. The U.S. government is less likely to *default* (fail to make interest or principal payments) on its bonds than is a private corporation. And some corporations are financially stronger and therefore less likely to default than others. As we saw in Chapter 5, the more risky an investment, the greater the return that an investor demands. As a result, riskier bonds have higher yields.

---

**EXAMPLE 15.2** **The Yields on Corporate Bonds**

To see how corporate bond yields are calculated—and how they can differ from one corporation to another—let's examine the yields for two coupon bonds: one issued by General Electric and the other by Ford Motor Co. Each has a *face value* of $100, which means that when the bond matures, the holder receives a principal payment of that amount. Each bond makes a "coupon" (i.e., interest) payment every six months.[7]

We calculate the bond yields using the closing prices on August 24, 2007. The following information was downloaded from the Yahoo! Finance Web site:

|  | General Electric | Ford |
|---|---|---|
| Price: | 98.77 | 92.00 |
| Coupon: | 5.00 | 8.875 |
| Maturity Date: | Feb. 1, 2013 | Jan. 15, 2022 |
| Yield to Maturity: | 5.256 | 9.925 |
| Current Yield: | 5.062 | 9.647 |
| Rating: | AAA | CCC |

What do these numbers mean? For General Electric, the price of $98.77 was the closing price on August 24, 2007, based on a face value for the bond of $100. The coupon of $5.00 means that $2.50 is paid to the owner of the bond every six months. The maturity date is the date at which the bond comes due and the owner receives the $100 face value. The 5.256-percent yield to maturity, discussed further below, is the effective yield (i.e., rate of return) on the bond. The current yield is simply the coupon divided by the price, i.e., $5.00/98.77 = 5.062$ percent. (The current yield is of limited relevance because it doesn't tell us the actual rate of return on the bond.) Finally, the GE bond is rated AAA, which is the highest rating possible for a corporate bond, indicating that the likelihood of default is very low.

---

[7]These bonds actually have a face value of $1000, not $100. The prices and coupon payments are listed as though the face value were $100; to get the actual prices and payments, just multiply by 10 the numbers that appear on financial Web sites or in the newspaper.

How does one determine the effective yield (i.e., rate of return, or yield to maturity) on this bond? For simplicity, we'll assume that the coupon payments are made annually instead of every six months. (The error that this introduces is small.) Because the bond matures in 2013, coupon payments will be made for 2013 – 2007 = 6 years. Thus the yield is given by the following equation:

$$98.77 = \frac{5.0}{(1+R)} + \frac{5.0}{(1+R)^2} + \frac{5.0}{(1+R)^3} + \cdots + \frac{5.0}{(1+R)^6} + \frac{100}{(1+R)^6}$$

To find the effective yield, we must solve this equation for $R$. You can check (by substituting and checking whether the equation is satisfied) that the solution is approximatly $R^* = 5.256$ percent.

The effective yield on the Ford bond is found in the same way. The bond had a price of $92.00, made coupon payments of $8.875 per year, and had 2022 – 2007 = 15 years to mature. Thus the equation for its yield is:

$$92.00 = \frac{8.875}{(1+R)} + \frac{8.875}{(1+R)^2} + \frac{8.875}{(1+R)^3} + \cdots + \frac{8.875}{(1+R)^{15}} + \frac{100}{(1+R)^{15}}$$

You can check that the solution to this equation is approximatly $R^* = 9.925$ percent.

Why was the yield on the Ford bond so much higher than on the GE bond? Because the Ford bond was much riskier. By 2007, Ford had been experiencing billions of dollars in losses as a result of steady declines in sales of its cars and trucks, and many analysts questioned the likelihood that Ford could recover and avoid bankruptcy. Consistent with this, Ford's bond was rated CCC. Because investors knew that there was a significant possibility that Ford would default on its bond payments, they were prepared to buy the bond only if the expected return was high enough to compensate them for the risk.

## 15.4 THE NET PRESENT VALUE CRITERION FOR CAPITAL INVESTMENT DECISIONS

One of the most common and important decisions that firms make is to invest in new capital. Millions of dollars may be invested in a factory or machines that will last—and affect profits—for many years. The future cash flows that the investment will generate are often uncertain. And once the factory has been built, the firm usually cannot disassemble and resell it to recoup its investment—it becomes a sunk cost.

> In §7.1, we explain that a sunk cost is an expenditure that has been made and cannot be recovered.

How should a firm decide whether a particular capital investment is worthwhile? It should calculate the present value of the future cash flows that it expects to receive from the investment and compare it with the cost of the investment. This method is known as the **net present value (NPV) criterion**:

> **• net present value (NPV) criterion** Rule holding that one should invest if the present value of the expected future cash flow from an investment is larger than the cost of the investment.

> NPV criterion: Invest if the present value of the expected future cash flows from an investment is larger than the cost of the investment.

Suppose a capital investment costs $C$ and is expected to generate profits over the next 10 years of amounts $\pi_1, \pi_2, \ldots, \pi_{10}$. We then write the net present value as

$$NPV = -C + \frac{\pi_1}{(1 + R)} + \frac{\pi_2}{(1 + R)^2} + \cdots + \frac{\pi_{10}}{(1 + R)^{10}} \qquad \textbf{(15.3)}$$

where $R$ is the **discount rate** that we use to discount the future stream of profits. ($R$ might be a market interest rate or some other rate; we will discuss how to choose it shortly.) Equation (15.3) describes the net benefit to the firm from the investment. The firm should make the investment only if that net benefit is positive—i.e., *only if NPV > 0.*

> • **discount rate** Rate used to determine the value today of a dollar received in the future.

**Determining the Discount Rate** What discount rate should the firm use? The answer depends on the alternative ways that the firm could use its money. For example, instead of this investment, the firm might invest in another piece of capital that generates a different stream of profits. Or it might invest in a bond that yields a different return. As a result, we can think of $R$ as the firm's **opportunity cost of capital**. Had the firm not invested in this project, it could have earned a return by investing in something else. *The correct value for R is therefore the return that the firm could earn on a "similar" investment.*

> • **opportunity cost of capital** Rate of return that one could earn by investing in an alternate project with similar risk.

By "similar" investment, we mean one with the same *risk.* As we saw in Chapter 5, the more risky an investment, the greater the return one expects to receive from it. Therefore, the opportunity cost of investing in this project is the return that one could earn from another project or asset of similar riskiness.

We'll see how to evaluate the riskiness of an investment in the next section. For now, let's assume that this project has *no risk* (i.e., the firm is sure that the future profit flows will be $\pi_1, \pi_2$, etc.). In that case, the opportunity cost of the investment is the *risk-free* return—e.g., the return one could earn on a government bond. If the project is expected to last for 10 years, the firm could use the annual interest rate on a 10-year government bond to compute the NPV of the project, as in equation (15.3).[8] If the NPV is zero, the benefit from the investment would just equal the opportunity cost, so the firm should be indifferent between investing and not investing. If the NPV is greater than zero the benefit exceeds the opportunity cost, so the investment should be made.[9]

## The Electric Motor Factory

In Section 15.1, we discussed a decision to invest $10 million in a factory to produce electric motors. This factory would enable the firm to use labor and copper to produce 8000 motors per month for 20 years at a cost of $42.50 each. The motors could be sold for $52.50 each, for a profit of $10 per unit, or $80,000 per month. We will assume that after 20 years, the factory will be obsolete but can be sold for scrap for $1 million. Is this a good investment? To find out, we must calculate its net present value.

We will assume for now that the $42.50 production cost and the $52.50 price at which the motors can be sold are certain, so that the firm is sure that it will receive $80,000 per month, or $960,000 per year, in profit. We also assume that

---

[8]This is an approximation. To be precise, the firm should use the rate on a one-year bond to discount $\pi_1$, the rate on a two-year bond to discount $\pi_2$, etc.

[9]This NPV rule is incorrect when the investment is irreversible, subject to uncertainty, and can be delayed. For a treatment of irreversible investment, see Avinash Dixit and Robert Pindyck, *Investment under Uncertainty* (Princeton, NJ: Princeton University Press, 1994).

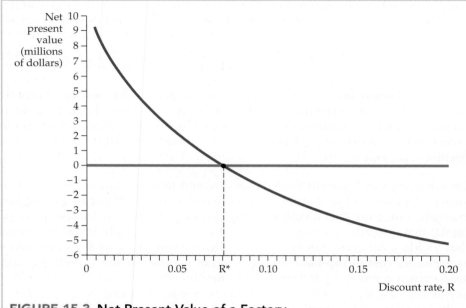

**FIGURE 15.3 Net Present Value of a Factory**

The NPV of a factory is the present discounted value of all the cash flows involved in building and operating it. Here it is the PDV of the flow of future profits less the current cost of construction. The NPV declines as the discount rate increases. At discount rate $R^*$, the NPV is zero.

the $1 million scrap value of the factory is certain. The firm should therefore use a risk-free interest rate to discount future profits. Writing the cash flows in millions of dollars, the NPV is

$$\text{NPV} = -10 + \frac{.96}{(1 + R)} + \frac{.96}{(1 + R)^2} + \frac{.96}{(1 + R)^3}$$
$$+ \cdots + \frac{.96}{(1 + R)^{20}} + \frac{1}{(1 + R)^{20}} \tag{15.4}$$

Figure 15.3 shows the NPV as a function of the discount rate $R$. Note that at the rate $R^*$, which is about 7.5 percent, the NPV is equal to zero. (The rate $R^*$ is sometimes referred to as the *internal rate of return* on the investment.) For discount rates below 7.5 percent, the NPV is positive, so the firm should invest in the factory. For discount rates above 7.5 percent, the NPV is negative, and the firm should not invest.

## Real versus Nominal Discount Rates

In the example above, we assumed that future cash flows are certain, so that the discount rate $R$ should be a risk-free interest rate, such as the rate on U.S. government bonds. Suppose that rate happened to be 9 percent. Does that mean the NPV is negative and the firm should not invest?

To answer this question, we must distinguish between real and nominal discount rates, and between real and nominal cash flows. Let's begin with the cash flows. In Chapter 1, we discussed real versus nominal prices. We explained that whereas the real price is *net of inflation*, the nominal price includes inflation.

In our example, we assumed that the electric motors coming out of our factory could be sold for $52.50 each over the next 20 years. We said nothing, however, about the effect of inflation. Is the $52.50 a real price, i.e., net of inflation, or does it include inflation? As we will see, the answer to this question can be critical.

Let's assume that the $52.50 price—and the $42.50 production cost—are in real terms. This means that if we expect a 5-percent annual rate of inflation, the nominal price of the motors will increase from $52.50 in the first year to (1.05)(52.50) = $55.13 in the second year, to (1.05)(55.13) = $57.88 in the third year, and so on. Therefore, our profit of $960,000 per year is also in real terms.

Now let's turn to the discount rate. *If the cash flows are in real terms, the discount rate must also be in real terms.* Why? Because the discount rate is the opportunity cost of the investment. If inflation is not included in the cash flows, it should not be included in the opportunity cost either.

In our example, the discount rate should therefore be the real interest rate on government bonds. The nominal interest rate (9 percent) is the rate that we see in the newspapers; it includes inflation. *The real interest rate is the nominal rate minus the expected rate of inflation.*[10] If we expect inflation to be 5 percent per year on average, the real interest rate would be 9 − 5 = 4 percent. This is the discount rate that should be used to calculate the NPV of the investment in the electric motor factory. Note from Figure 15.3 that at this rate the NPV is clearly positive, so the investment should be undertaken.

When the NPV rule is used to evaluate investments, the numbers in the calculations may be in real or in nominal terms, as long as they are consistent. If cash flows are in real terms, the discount rate should also be in real terms. If a nominal discount rate is used, the effect of future inflation must also be included in the cash flows.

> Opportunity cost is discussed in §7.1.

## Negative Future Cash Flows

Factories and other production facilities can take several years to build and equip. The cost of the investment will also be spread out over several years, instead of occurring only at the outset. In addition, some investments are expected to result in *losses*, rather than profits, for the first few years. (For example, demand may be low until consumers learn about the product, or costs may start high and fall only when managers and workers have moved down the learning curve.) Negative future cash flows create no problem for the NPV rule; they are simply discounted, just like positive cash flows.

For example, suppose that our electric motor factory will take a year to build: $5 million is spent right away, and another $5 million is spent next year. Also, suppose the factory is expected to *lose* $1 million in its first year of operation and $0.5 million in its second year. Afterward, it will earn $0.96 million a year until year 20, when it will be scrapped for $1 million, as before. (All these cash flows are in real terms.) Now the net present value is

$$\text{NPV} = -5 - \frac{5}{(1+R)} - \frac{1}{(1+R)^2} - \frac{.5}{(1+R)^3} + \frac{.96}{(1+R)^4} + \frac{.96}{(1+R)^5}$$
$$+ \cdots + \frac{.96}{(1+R)^{20}} + \frac{1}{(1+R)^{20}} \tag{15.5}$$

Suppose the real interest rate is 4 percent. Should the firm build this factory? You can confirm that the NPV is negative, so this project is not a good investment.

---

[10]People may have different views about future inflation and may therefore have different estimates of the real interest rate.

# 15.5 ADJUSTMENTS FOR RISK

We have seen that a risk-free interest rate is an appropriate discount rate for future cash flows that are certain. For most projects, however, future cash flows are far from certain. At our electric motor factory, for example, we would expect uncertainty over future copper prices, over the future demand and the price of motors, and even over future wage rates. Thus the firm cannot know what its profits from the factory will be over the next 20 years. Its best estimate of profits might be $960,000 per year, but actual profits may turn out to be higher or lower. How should the firm take this uncertainty into account when calculating the net present value of the project?

• **risk premium** Amount of money that a risk-averse individual will pay to avoid taking a risk.

A common practice is to increase the discount rate by adding a **risk premium** to the risk-free rate. The idea is that the owners of the firm are risk averse, which makes future cash flows that are risky worth less than those that are certain. Increasing the discount rate takes this into account by reducing the present value of those future cash flows. But how large should the risk premium be? As we will see, the answer depends on the nature of the risk.

## Diversifiable versus Nondiversifiable Risk

• **diversifiable risk** Risk that can be eliminated either by investing in many projects or by holding the stocks of many companies.

Adding a risk premium to the discount rate must be done with care. If the firm's managers are operating in the stockholders' interests, they must distinguish between two kinds of risk—*diversifiable* and *nondiversifiable*.[11] **Diversifiable risk** can be eliminated by investing in many projects or by holding the stocks of many companies. **Nondiversifiable risk** cannot be eliminated in this way. *Only nondiversifiable risk affects the opportunity cost of capital and should enter into the risk premium.*

• **nondiversifiable risk** Risk that cannot be eliminated by investing in many projects or by holding the stocks of many companies.

**Diversifiable Risk** To understand this, recall from Chapter 5 that diversifying can eliminate many risks. For example, I cannot know whether the result of a coin flip will be heads or tails. But I can be reasonably sure that out of a thousand coin flips, roughly half will be heads. Similarly, an insurance company that sells me life insurance cannot know how long I will live. But by selling life insurance to thousands of people, it can be reasonably sure about the percentage of those who will die each year.

Much the same is true about capital investment decisions. Although the profit flow from a single investment may be very risky, overall risk will be much less if the firm invests in dozens of projects (as most large firms do). Furthermore, even if the company invests in only one project, stockholders can easily diversify by holding the stocks of a dozen or more different companies, or by holding a mutual fund that invests in many stocks. Thus, stockholders—the owners of the firm—can eliminate diversifiable risk.

Because investors can eliminate diversifiable risk, they cannot expect to earn a return higher than the risk-free rate by bearing it: No one will pay you for bearing a risk that there is no need to bear. And indeed, assets that have only diversifiable risk tend on average to earn a return close to the risk-free rate. Now, remember that the discount rate for a project is the opportunity cost of *investing in that project rather than in some other project or asset with similar risk*

[11]Diversifiable risk is also called *nonsystematic* risk and nondiversifiable risk is called *systematic* risk. Adding a simple risk premium to the discount rate may not always be the correct way of dealing with risk. See, for example, Richard Brealey and Stewart Myers, *Principles of Corporate Finance* (New York: McGraw-Hill, 2007).

*characteristics*. Therefore, if the project's only risk is diversifiable, the opportunity cost is the risk-free rate. *No risk premium should be added to the discount rate.*

**Nondiversifiable Risk** What about nondiversifiable risk? First, let's be clear about how such risk can arise. For a life insurance company, the possibility of a major war poses nondiversifiable risk. Because a war may increase mortality rates sharply, the company cannot expect that an "average" number of its customers will die each year, no matter how many customers it has. As a result, most insurance policies, whether for life, health, or property, do not cover losses resulting from acts of war.

For capital investments, nondiversifiable risk arises because a firm's profits tend to depend on the overall economy. When economic growth is strong, corporate profits tend to be higher. (For our electric motor factory, the demand for motors is likely to be strong, so profits increase.) On the other hand, profits tend to fall in a recession. Because future economic growth is uncertain, diversification cannot eliminate all risk. Investors should (and indeed can) earn higher returns by bearing this risk.

To the extent that a project has nondiversifiable risk, the opportunity cost of investing in that project is higher than the risk-free rate. Thus a risk premium must be included in the discount rate. Let's see how the size of that risk premium can be determined.

## The Capital Asset Pricing Model

The **Capital Asset Pricing Model (CAPM)** measures the risk premium for a capital investment by comparing the expected return on that investment with the expected return on the entire stock market. To understand the model, suppose, first, that you invest in the entire stock market (say, through a mutual fund). In that case, your investment would be completely diversified and you would bear no diversifiable risk. You would, however, bear nondiversifiable risk because the stock market tends to move with the overall economy. (The stock market reflects expected future profits, which depend in part on the economy.) As a result, the expected return on the stock market is higher than the risk-free rate. Denoting the expected return on the stock market by $r_m$ and the risk-free rate by $r_f$, the risk premium on the market is $r_m - r_f$. This is the additional expected return you get for bearing the nondiversifiable risk associated with the stock market.

Now consider the nondiversifiable risk associated with one asset, such as a company's stock. We can measure that risk in terms of the extent to which the return on the asset tends to be *correlated* with (i.e., move in the same direction as) the return on the stock market as a whole. For example, one company's stock might have almost no correlation with the market as a whole. On average, the price of that stock would move independently of changes in the market, so it would have little or no nondiversifiable risk. The return on that stock should therefore be about the same as the risk-free rate. Another stock, however, might be highly correlated with the market. Its price changes might even amplify changes in the market as a whole. That stock would have substantial nondiversifiable risk, perhaps more than the stock market as a whole. If so, its return on average will exceed the market return $r_m$.

The CAPM summarizes this relationship between expected returns and the risk premium by the following equation:

• **Capital Asset Pricing Model (CAPM)** Model in which the risk premium for a capital investment depends on the correlation of the investment's return with the return on the entire stock market.

$$r_i - r_f = \beta \ (r_m - r_f) \qquad \text{(15.6)}$$

• **asset beta** A constant that measures the sensitivity of an asset's return to market movements and, therefore, the asset's nondiversifiable risk.

where $r_i$ is the expected return on an asset. The equation says that the risk premium on the asset (its expected return less the risk-free rate) is proportional to the risk premium on the market. The constant of proportionality, $\beta$, is called the **asset beta**. It measures the sensitivity of the asset's return to market movements and, therefore, the asset's nondiversifiable risk. If a 1-percent rise in the market tends to result in a 2-percent rise in the asset price, the beta is 2. If a 1-percent rise in the market tends to result in a 1-percent rise in the asset price, the beta is 1. And if a 1-percent rise in the market tends to result in no change in the price of the asset, the beta is zero. As equation (15.6) shows, the larger the beta, the greater the expected return on the asset. Why? Because the asset's nondiversifiable risk is greater.

**The Risk-Adjusted Discount Rate** Given beta, we can determine the correct discount rate to use in computing an asset's net present value. That discount rate is the expected return on the asset or on another asset with the same risk. It is therefore the risk-free rate plus a risk premium to reflect nondiversifiable risk:

$$\text{Discount rate} = r_f + \beta\, (r_m - r_f) \tag{15.7}$$

Over the past 60 years, the risk premium on the stock market, $(r_m - r_f)$, has been about 8 percent on average. If the real risk-free rate were 4 percent and beta were 0.6, the correct discount rate would be $0.04 + 0.6(0.08) = 0.09$, or 9 percent.

If the asset is a stock, its beta can usually be estimated statistically.[12] When the asset is a new factory, however, determining its beta is more difficult. Many firms therefore use the company cost of capital as a (nominal) discount rate. The **company cost of capital** is a weighted average of the expected return on the company's stock (which depends on the beta of the stock) and the interest rate that it pays for debt. This approach is correct as long as the capital investment in question is typical for the company as a whole. It can be misleading, however, if the capital investment has much more or much less nondiversifiable risk than the company as a whole. In that case, it may be better to make a reasoned guess as to how much the revenues from the investment are likely to depend on the overall economy.

• **company cost of capital** Weighted average of the expected return on a company's stock and the interest rate that it pays for debt.

---

**EXAMPLE 15.3**   Capital Investment in the Disposable Diaper Industry

In Example 13.6 (page 508), we discussed the disposable diaper industry, which has been dominated by Procter & Gamble, with about a 50-percent market share, and Kimberly-Clark, with another 30–40 percent. We explained that their continuing R&D (research and development) expenditures have given these firms a cost advantage that deters entry. Now we'll examine the capital investment decision of a potential entrant.

---

[12]You can estimate beta by running a linear regression of the return on the stock against the excess return on the market, $r_m - r_f$. You would find, for example, that the beta for Intel Corporation is about 1.4, the beta for Eastman Kodak is about 0.8, and the beta for General Motors is about 0.5.

Suppose you are considering entering this industry. To take advantage of scale economies in production, advertising, and distribution, you would need to build three plants at a cost of $60 million each, with the cost spread over three years. When operating at capacity, the plants would produce a total of 2.5 billion diapers per year. These would be sold at wholesale for about 16 cents per diaper, yielding revenues of about $400 million per year. You can expect your variable production costs to be about $290 million per year, for a net revenue of $110 million per year.

You will, however, have other expenses. Using the experience of P&G and Kimberly-Clark as a guide, you can expect to spend about $60 million in R&D before start-up to design an efficient manufacturing process, and another $20 million in R&D during each year of production to maintain and improve that process. Finally, once you are operating at full capacity, you can expect to spend another $50 million per year for a sales force, advertising, and marketing. Your net operating profit will be $40 million per year. The plants will last for 15 years and will then be obsolete.

Is the investment a good idea? To find out, let's calculate its net present value. Table 15.5 shows the relevant numbers. We assume that production begins at 33 percent of capacity when the plant is completed in 2010, takes two years to reach full capacity, and continues through the year 2025. Given the net cash flows, the NPV is calculated as

$$NPV = -120 - \frac{93.4}{(1+R)} - \frac{56.6}{(1+R)^2} + \frac{40}{(1+R)^3}$$
$$+ \frac{40}{(1+R)^4} + \cdots + \frac{40}{(1+R)^{15}}$$

Table 15.5 shows the NPV for discount rates of 5, 10, and 15 percent.

Note that the NPV is positive for a discount rate of 5 percent, but it is negative for discount rates of 10 or 15 percent. What is the correct discount rate? First, we have ignored inflation, so the discount rate should be in *real* terms. Second, the cash flows are risky—we don't know how efficient our plants will be, how effective our advertising and promotion will be, or even what the future demand for

## TABLE 15.5 Data for NPV Calculation ($ millions)

|  | Pre-2010 | 2010 | 2011 | 2012 | . . . | 2025 |
|---|---|---|---|---|---|---|
| Sales |  | 133.3 | 266.7 | 400.0 | . . . | 400.0 |
| LESS |  |  |  |  |  |  |
| Variable cost |  | 96.7 | 193.3 | 290.0 | . . . | 290.0 |
| Ongoing R&D |  | 20.0 | 20.0 | 20.0 | . . . | 20.0 |
| Sales force, ads, and marketing |  | 50.0 | 50.0 | 50.0 | . . . | 50.0 |
| Operating profit |  | −33.4 | 3.4 | 40.0 | . . . | 40.0 |
| LESS |  |  |  |  |  |  |
| Construction cost | 60.0 | 60.0 | 60.0 |  |  |  |
| Initial R&D | 60.0 |  |  |  |  |  |
| NET CASH FLOW | −120.0 | −93.4 | −56.6 | 40.0 | . . . | 40.0 |
| Discount Rate: |  | 0.05 | 0.10 | 0.15 |  |  |
| NPV: |  | 80.5 | −16.9 | −75.1 |  |  |

disposable diapers will be. Some of this risk is nondiversifiable. To calculate the risk premium, we will use a beta of 1, which is typical for a producer of consumer products of this sort. Using 4 percent for the real risk-free interest rate and 8 percent for the risk premium on the stock market, our discount rate should be

$$R = 0.04 + 1(0.08) = 0.12$$

At this discount rate, the NPV is clearly negative, so the investment does not make sense. You will not enter the industry, and P&G and Kimberly-Clark can breathe a sigh of relief. Don't be surprised, however, that these firms can make money in this market while you cannot. Their experience, years of earlier R&D (they need not spend $60 million on R&D before building new plants), and brand name recognition give them a competitive advantage that a new entrant will find hard to overcome.

## 15.6 INVESTMENT DECISIONS BY CONSUMERS

We have seen how firms value future cash flows and thereby decide whether to invest in long-lived capital. Consumers face similar decisions when they purchase durable goods, such as cars or major appliances. Unlike the decision to purchase food, entertainment, or clothing, the decision to buy a durable good involves comparing a flow of *future* benefits with the *current* purchase cost.

Suppose that you are deciding whether to buy a new car. If you keep the car for six or seven years, most of the benefits (and costs of operation) will occur in the future. You must therefore compare the future flow of net benefits from owning the car (the benefit of having transportation less the cost of insurance, maintenance, and gasoline) with the purchase price. Likewise, when deciding whether to buy a new air conditioner, you must compare its price with the present value of the flow of net benefits (the benefit of a cool room less the cost of electricity to operate the unit).

These problems are analogous to the problem of a firm that must compare a future flow of profits with the current cost of plant and equipment when making a capital investment decision. We can therefore analyze these problems just as we analyzed the firm's investment problem. Let's do this for a consumer's decision to buy a car.

The main benefit from owning a car is the flow of transportation services it provides. The value of those services differs from consumer to consumer. Let's assume our consumer values the service at $S$ dollars per year. Let's also assume that the total operating expense (insurance, maintenance, and gasoline) is $E$ dollars per year, that the car costs $20,000, and that after six years, its resale value will be $4000. The decision to buy the car can then be framed in terms of net present value:

$$NPV = -20,000 + (S - E) + \frac{(S - E)}{(1 + R)} + \frac{(S - E)}{(1 + R)^2}$$
$$+ \cdots + \frac{(S - E)}{(1 + R)^6} + \frac{4000}{(1 + R)^6} \tag{15.8}$$

What discount rate $R$ should the consumer use? The consumer should apply the same principle that a firm does: The discount rate is the opportunity cost of money. If the consumer already has $20,000 and does not need a loan, the correct discount rate is the return that could be earned by investing the money in another asset—say, a savings account or a government bond. On the other hand, if the consumer is in debt, the discount rate would be the borrowing rate that he or she is already paying. Because this rate is likely to be much higher than the interest rate on a bond or savings account, the NPV of the investment will be smaller.

Consumers must often make trade-offs between up-front versus future payments. An example is the decision of whether to buy or lease a new car. Suppose you can buy a new Toyota Corolla for $15,000 and, after six years, sell it for $6000. Alternatively, you could lease the car for $300 per month for three years, and at the end of the three years, return the car. Which is better—buying or leasing? The answer depends on the interest rate. If the interest rate is very low, buying the car is preferable because the present value of the future lease payments is high. If the interest rate is high, leasing is preferable because the present value of the future lease payments is low.

---

**EXAMPLE 15.4** Choosing an Air Conditioner and a New Car

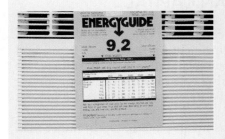

Buying a new air conditioner involves making a trade-off. Some air conditioners cost less but are less efficient—they consume a lot of electricity relative to their cooling power. Others cost more but are more efficient. Should you buy an inefficient air conditioner that costs less now but will cost more to operate in the future, or an efficient one that costs more now but will cost less to operate?

Let's assume that you are comparing air conditioners of equivalent cooling power, so that they yield the same flow of benefits. We can then compare the present discounted values of their costs. Assuming an eight-year lifetime and no resale, the PDV of the cost of buying and operating air conditioner $i$ is

$$\text{PDV} = C_i + OC_i + \frac{OC_i}{(1 + R)} + \frac{OC_i}{(1 + R)^2} + \cdots + \frac{OC_i}{(1 + R)^8}$$

where $C_i$ is the purchase price of air conditioner $i$ and $OC_i$ is its average annual operating cost.

The preferred air conditioner depends on your discount rate. If you have little free cash and must borrow, you should use a high discount rate. Because this would make the present value of the future operating costs smaller, you would probably choose a less expensive but relatively inefficient unit. If you have plenty of free cash, so that your opportunity cost of money (and thus your discount rate) is low, you would probably buy the more expensive unit.

An econometric study of household purchases of air conditioners shows that consumers tend to trade off capital costs and expected future operating costs in just this way, although the discount rates that people use are high—about

20 percent for the population as a whole.[13] (American consumers seem to behave myopically by overdiscounting future savings.) The study also shows that consumers' discount rates vary inversely with their incomes. For example, people with above-average incomes used discount rates of about 9 percent, while those in the bottom quarter of the income distribution used discount rates of 39 percent or more. We would expect this result because higher-income people are likely to have more free cash available and therefore have a lower opportunity cost of money.

Buying a new car involves a similar trade-off. One car might cost less than another but offer lower fuel efficiency and require more maintenance and repairs, so that expected future operating costs are higher. As with air conditioners, a consumer can compare two or more cars by calculating and comparing the PDV of the purchase price and expected average annual operating cost for each. An econometric study of automobile purchases found that consumers indeed trade off the purchase price and expected operating costs in this way.[14] It found the average discount rate for all consumers to be in the range of 11 to 17 percent. These discount rate estimates are somewhat lower than those for air conditioners, and probably reflect the widespread availability of auto loans.

## 15.7 INVESTMENTS IN HUMAN CAPITAL

So far, we have discussed how firms and consumers can decide whether to invest in *physical capital*—buildings and equipment, in the case of firms, and durable goods such as cars and major appliances, in the case of consumers. We have seen how to apply the net present value rule to these decisions: Invest when the present value of the gains from the investment exceeds the present value of the costs.

Some very important investment decisions involve *human capital* rather than physical capital. Given that you are now reading this book, you are probably making an investment in your own human capital at this very moment.[15] By studying microeconomics, perhaps as part of an undergraduate or graduate degree program, you are obtaining valuable knowledge and skills that will make you more productive in the future.

• **human capital**
Knowledge, skills, and experience that make an individual more productive and thereby able to earn a higher income over a lifetime.

**Human capital** is *the knowledge, skills, and experience that make an individual more productive and thereby able to earn a higher income over a lifetime.* If you go to college or graduate school, take postgraduate courses, or enroll in a specialized job training program, you are investing in human capital. Most likely, the money, time, and effort that you invest to build up your human capital will pay off in the form of more rewarding or high-paying job opportunities.

How should an individual decide whether to invest in human capital? To answer this question, we can use the same net present value rule that we have applied to investments in physical capital.

---

[13]See Jerry A. Hausman, "Individual Discount Rates and the Purchase and Utilization of Energy-Using Durables," *Bell Journal of Economics* 10 (Spring 1979): 33–54.

[14]See Mark K. Dreyfus and W. Kip Viscusi, "Rates of Time Preference and Consumer Valuations of Automobile Safety and Fuel Efficiency," *Journal of Law and Economics* 38 (April 1995): 79–105.

[15]On the other hand, finding this book more entertaining than a good novel, you might be reading it purely for pleasure.

Suppose, for example, that upon completing high school you are deciding whether to go to college for four years or skip college and go to work instead. To keep things as simple as possible, let's analyze this decision on a purely financial basis and ignore any pleasure (in the form of parties and football games) or pain (in the form of exams and papers) that college might entail. We will calculate the NPV of the costs and benefits of getting a college degree.

**The NPV of a College Education** There are two major costs associated with college. First, because you will be studying rather than working, you will incur the opportunity cost of the lost wages that you could have earned had you taken a job. For a typical high school graduate in the United States, a reasonable estimate of those lost wages would be about $20,000 per year. The second major cost is for tuition, room and board, and related expenses (such as the cost of this book). Tuition and room and board can vary widely, depending on whether one is attending a public or private college, whether one is living at home or on campus, and whether one is receiving a scholarship. Let's use $20,000 per year as a rough average number. (Most public universities are less expensive, but many private colleges and universities cost more.) Thus we will take the total economic cost of attending college to be $40,000 per year for each of four years.

An important benefit of college is the ability to earn a higher salary throughout your working life. In the United States, a college graduate will on average earn about $20,000 per year more than a high school graduate. In practice, the salary differential is largest during the first 5 to 10 years following college graduation, and then becomes smaller. For simplicity, however, we will assume that this $20,000 salary differential persists for 20 years. In that case, the NPV (in $1000's) of investing in a college education is

$$NPV = -40 - \frac{40}{(1+R)} - \frac{40}{(1+R)^2} - \frac{40}{(1+R)^3} + \frac{20}{(1+R)^4} + \cdots + \frac{20}{(1+R)^{23}}$$

What discount rate, $R$, should one use to calculate this NPV? Because we have kept the costs and benefits fixed over time, we are implicitly ignoring inflation. Thus we should use a *real* discount rate. In this case, a reasonable real discount rate would be about 5 percent. This rate would reflect the opportunity cost of money for many households—the return that could be made by investing in assets other than human capital. You can check that the NPV is then about $66,000. With a 5-percent discount rate, investing in a college education is a good idea, at least as a purely financial matter.

Although the NPV of a college education is a positive number, it is not very large. Why isn't the financial return from going to college higher? Because in the United States, entry into college has become attainable for the majority of graduating high school seniors.[16] In other words, a college education is an investment with close to free entry. As we saw in Chapter 8, in markets with free entry, we should expect to see zero economic profits, which implies that investments will earn a competitive return. Of course, a low economic return doesn't mean that you shouldn't complete your college degree—there are many benefits to a college education that go beyond increases in future earnings.

In §15.4, we discuss real versus nominal discount rates, and explain that the real discount rate is the nominal rate minus the expected rate of inflation.

In §8.7 we explain that zero economic profit means that a firm is earning a competitive return on its investment.

---

[16]This is not to say that all high school graduates can go to the college of their choice. Some colleges are selective and require high grades and test scores for admission. But the large number of colleges and universities in the United States makes an undergraduate education an option for the majority of high school graduates.

**EXAMPLE 15.5** Should You Go to Business School?

Many readers of this book are contemplating attending business school and earning an MBA degree or are already enrolled in an MBA program. Those of you thinking about business school (or already attending) might be wondering whether an MBA is worth the investment. Let's see if we can help you with your concern.

For most people, getting an MBA means an increase—very often a big increase—in salary. Table 15.6 shows estimates of average pre-MBA and post-MBA salaries for 25 business schools.[17] As you can see, the increases in salaries are dramatic. Bear

**TABLE 15.6** Salaries Before and After Business School

| University | Pre-MBA Salary | Median Base Salary after MBA |
|---|---|---|
| Stanford | $65,000 | $165,500 |
| Harvard | $65,000 | $160,000 |
| U. of Pennsylvania (Wharton) | $60,000 | $156,000 |
| Dartmouth (Tuck) | $50,000 | $149,500 |
| MIT (Sloan) | $55,000 | $149,000 |
| Columbia | $50,000 | $142,500 |
| Northwestern (Kellogg) | $56,000 | $142,000 |
| U. of Chicago | $55,000 | $140,000 |
| NYU (Stern) | $45,000 | $140,000 |
| UCLA (Anderson) | $55,000 | $136,500 |
| Cornell (Johnson) | $50,000 | $135,000 |
| UC—Berkeley (Haas) | $50,000 | $135,000 |
| U. of Virginia (Darden) | $50,000 | $135,000 |
| U. of Michigan | $50,000 | $131,000 |
| Yale | $45,000 | $130,000 |
| Duke (Fuqua) | $49,000 | $128,500 |
| Carnegie Mellon | $45,000 | $125,000 |
| UNC—Chapel Hill | $48,000 | $125,000 |
| Georgetown (McDonough) | $45,000 | $116,000 |
| U. of Indiana (Kelley) | $42,000 | $114,000 |
| USC (Marshall) | $45,000 | $112,000 |
| U. of Rochester (Simon) | $40,000 | $110,000 |
| Washington U. (Olin) | $42,000 | $109,000 |
| U. of Texas—Austin (McCombs) | $45,000 | $107,000 |
| Purdue (Krannert) | $35,000 | $101,500 |

---

[17]The data are for students receiving their MBAs in 2005 and are from **http://www.business schooladmission.com/mbasalaries/asp**.

in mind, however, that not all MBA programs are included in Table 15.6. Indeed, because the list includes many of the top MBA programs—and because the salaries are self-reported—they probably overstate average MBA salaries for all graduates. For the United States as a whole, a rough estimate of the average salary of students about to enter business school is around $45,000 per year and the average *increase* in salary upon obtaining the MBA degree is about $30,000 per year. For our simple analysis, we will assume that this $30,000 per year gain in salary persists for 20 years.

The typical MBA program in the United States takes two years and involves tuition and expenses of $45,000 per year. (Very few MBA students obtain scholarships.) In addition to tuition and expenses, it is important to include the opportunity cost of the foregone pre-MBA salary, i.e., another $45,000 per year. Thus, the total economic cost of getting an MBA is $90,000 per year for each of two years. The NPV of this investment is therefore

$$\text{NPV} = -90 - \frac{90}{(1+R)} + \frac{30}{(1+R)^2} + \cdots + \frac{30}{(1+R)^{21}}$$

You can check that using a real discount rate of 5 percent, the NPV comes out to about $180,000.

Why is the payoff from an MBA at schools like those listed in Table 15.6 so much higher than the payoff from a four-year undergraduate degree? Because entry into many MBA programs (and especially the programs listed in Table 15.6) is selective and difficult. (The same is true for other professional degree programs, such as law and medicine.) Because many more people apply to MBA programs than there are spaces, the return on the degree remains high.

Should you go to business school? As we have just seen, the financial part of this decision is easy: Though costly, the return on this investment is very high. Of course, there are other factors that might influence your decision. Some students, for example, find the courses they take in business school (especially economics) to be very interesting. Others find the experience to be about as much fun as having a root canal. And then there is the question of whether your undergraduate grades and test scores are sufficiently high to make this particular investment in human capital an option for you. Finally, and most importantly, you might find another career choice more rewarding, whether or not it turns out to be more profitable. We leave it to you to calculate the returns to educational investments in the arts, law, or education itself (teaching).

## *15.8 INTERTEMPORAL PRODUCTION DECISIONS— DEPLETABLE RESOURCES

Production decisions often have *intertemporal* aspects—production today affects sales or costs in the future. The learning curve, which we discussed in Chapter 7, is an example of this. By producing today, the firm gains experience that lowers future costs. In this case, production today is partly an investment in future cost reduction, and the value of this investment must be taken into account when comparing costs and benefits. Another example is the production of a depletable resource. When the owner of an oil well pumps oil today, less oil is available for future production. This must be taken into account when deciding how much to produce.

> Recall from §7.6 that with a learning curve, the firm's cost of production falls over time as managers and workers become more experienced and more effective at using available plant and equipment.

Production decisions in cases like these involve comparisons between costs and benefits today with costs and benefits in the future. We can make those comparisons using the concept of present discounted value. We'll look in detail at the case of a depletable resource, although the same principles apply to other intertemporal production decisions.

## The Production Decision of an Individual Resource Producer

Suppose your rich uncle gives you an oil well. The well contains 1000 barrels of oil that can be produced at a constant average and marginal cost of $10 per barrel. Should you produce all the oil today, or should you save it for the future?[18]

You might think that the answer depends on the profit you can earn if you remove the oil from the ground. After all, why not remove the oil if its price is greater than the cost of extraction? However, this ignores the opportunity cost of using up the oil today so that it is not available for the future.

The correct answer, then, depends not on the current profit level but on how fast you expect the price of oil to rise. Oil in the ground is like money in the bank: You should keep it in the ground only if it earns a return at least as high as the market interest rate. If you expect the price of oil to remain constant or rise very slowly, you would be better off extracting and selling all of it now and investing the proceeds. But if you expect the price of oil to rise rapidly, you should leave it in the ground.

How fast must the price rise for you to keep the oil in the ground? The value of each barrel of oil in your well is equal to the price of oil less the $10 cost of extracting it. (This is the profit you can obtain by extracting and selling each barrel.) This value must rise at least as fast as the rate of interest for you to keep the oil. Your production decision rule is therefore: *Keep all your oil if you expect its price less its extraction cost to rise faster than the rate of interest. Extract and sell all of it if you expect price less cost to rise at less than the rate of interest.* What if you expect price less cost to rise at exactly the rate of interest? Then you would be indifferent between extracting the oil and leaving it in the ground. Letting $P_t$ be the price of oil this year, $P_{t+1}$ the price next year, and $c$ the cost of extraction, we can write this production rule as follows:

If $(P_{t+1} - c) > (1 + R)(P_t - c)$, keep the oil in the ground.

If $(P_{t+1} - c) < (1 + R)(P_t - c)$, sell all the oil now.

If $(P_{t+1} - c) = (1 + R)(P_t - c)$, makes no difference.

Given our expectation about the growth rate of oil prices, we can use this rule to determine production. But how fast should we expect the market price of oil to rise?

## The Behavior of Market Price

Suppose there were no OPEC cartel and the oil market consisted of many competitive producers with oil wells like our own. We could then determine how quickly oil prices are likely to rise by considering the production decisions of other producers. If other producers want to earn the highest possible return, they

---

[18]For most real oil wells, marginal and average cost are not constant, and it would be extremely costly to extract all the oil in a short time. We will ignore this complication.

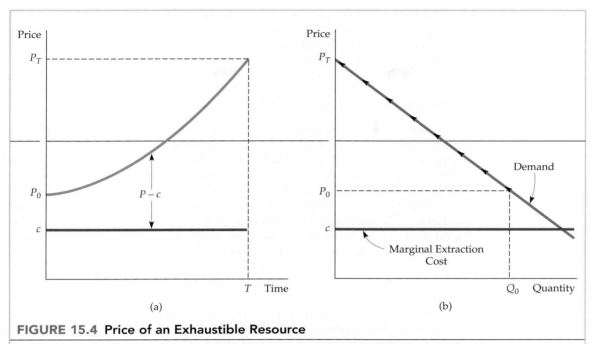

**FIGURE 15.4 Price of an Exhaustible Resource**

In **(a)**, the price is shown rising over time. Units of a resource in the ground must earn a return commensurate with that on other assets. Therefore, in a competitive market, price less marginal production cost will rise at the rate of interest. Part **(b)** shows the movement up the demand curve as price rises.

will follow the production rule we stated above. This means that *price less marginal cost must rise at exactly the rate of interest.*[19] To see why, suppose price less cost were to rise faster than the rate of interest. In that case, no one would sell any oil. Inevitably, this would drive up the current price. If, on the other hand, price less cost were to rise at a rate less than the rate of interest, everyone would try to sell all of their oil immediately, which would drive the current price down.

Figure 15.4 illustrates how the market price must rise. The marginal cost of extraction is $c$, and the price and total quantity produced are initially $P_0$ and $Q_0$. Part (a) shows the net price, $P - c$, rising at the rate of interest. Part (b) shows that as price rises, the quantity demanded falls. This continues until time $T$, when all the oil has been used up and the price $P_T$ is such that demand is just zero.

## User Cost

We saw in Chapter 8 that a competitive firm always produces up to the point at which price is equal to marginal cost. However, in a competitive market for an exhaustible resource, price *exceeds* marginal cost (and the difference between price and marginal cost rises over time). Does this conflict with what we learned in Chapter 8?

No, once we recognize that the *total* marginal cost of producing an exhaustible resource is greater than the marginal cost of extracting it from the ground. There is an additional opportunity cost because producing and selling a unit today makes it unavailable for production and sale in the future. We call

---

[19]This result is called the *Hotelling rule* because it was first demonstrated by Harold Hotelling in "The Economics of Exhaustible Resources," *Journal of Political Economy* 39 (April 1931): 137–75.

• **user cost of production**
Opportunity cost of producing and selling a unit today and so making it unavailable for production and sale in the future.

this opportunity cost the **user cost of production**. In Figure 15.4, user cost is the difference between price and marginal production cost. It rises over time because as the resource remaining in the ground becomes scarcer, the opportunity cost of depleting another unit becomes higher.

## Resource Production by a Monopolist

What if the resource is produced by a *monopolist* rather than by a competitive industry? Should price less marginal cost still rise at the rate of interest?

Suppose a monopolist is deciding between keeping an incremental unit of a resource in the ground, or producing and selling it. The value of that unit is the *marginal revenue* less the marginal cost. The unit should be left in the ground if its value is expected to rise faster than the rate of interest; it should be produced and sold if its value is expected to rise at *less* than the rate of interest. Since the monopolist controls total output, it will produce so that marginal revenue less marginal cost—i.e., the value of an incremental unit of resource—rises at exactly the rate of interest:

> In §10.1, we explain that a monopolist maximizes its profit by choosing an output at which marginal revenue is equal to marginal cost.

$$(MR_{t+1} - c) = (1 + R)(MR_t - c)$$

Note that this rule also holds for a competitive firm. For a competitive firm, however, marginal revenue equals the market price $p$.

For a monopolist facing a downward-sloping demand curve, price is greater than marginal revenue. Therefore, if marginal revenue less marginal cost rises at the rate of interest, *price* less marginal cost will rise at less than the rate of interest. We thus have the interesting result that a monopolist is *more conservationist* than a competitive industry. In exercising monopoly power, the monopolist starts out charging a higher price and depletes the resource more slowly.

**EXAMPLE 15.6**  How Depletable Are Depletable Resources?

Resources such as oil, natural gas, coal, uranium, copper, iron, lead, zinc, nickel, and helium are all depletable: Because there is a finite amount of each in the earth's crust, the production and consumption of each will ultimately cease. Nonetheless, some resources are more depletable than others.

For oil, natural gas, and helium, known and potentially discoverable in-ground reserves are equal to only 50 to 100 years of current consumption. For these resources, the user cost of production can be a significant component of the market price. Other resources, such as coal and iron, have a proven and potential reserve base equal to several hundred or even thousands of years of current consumption. For these resources, the user cost is very small.

The user cost for a resource can be estimated from geological information about existing and potentially discoverable reserves, and from knowledge of the demand curve and the rate at which that curve is likely to shift out over time in response to economic growth. If the market is competitive, user cost can be determined from the economic rent earned by the owners of resource-bearing lands.

| TABLE 15.7 | User Cost as a Fraction of Competitive Price |
|---|---|
| **Resource** | **User Cost/Competitive Price** |
| Crude oil | .4 to .5 |
| Natural gas | .4 to .5 |
| Uranium | .1 to .2 |
| Copper | .2 to .3 |
| Bauxite | .05 to .2 |
| Nickel | .1 to .3 |
| Iron ore | .1 to .2 |
| Gold | .05 to .1 |

Table 15.7 shows estimates of user cost as a fraction of the competitive price for crude oil, natural gas, uranium, copper, bauxite, nickel, iron ore, and gold.[20] Note that only for crude oil and natural gas is user cost a substantial component of price. For the other resources, it is small and in some cases almost negligible. Moreover, although most of these resources have experienced sharp price fluctuations, user cost had almost nothing to do with those fluctuations. For example, oil prices changed because of OPEC and political turmoil in the Persian Gulf, natural gas prices because of changes in energy demand, uranium and bauxite prices because of cartelization during the 1970s, and copper prices because of strikes and changes in demand.

Resource depletion, then, has not been very important as a determinant of resource prices over the past few decades. Much more important have been market structure and changes in market demand. But the role of depletion should not be ignored. Over the long term, it will be the ultimate determinant of resource prices.

## 15.9 HOW ARE INTEREST RATES DETERMINED?

We have seen how market interest rates are used to help make capital investment and intertemporal production decisions. But what determines interest rate levels? Why do they fluctuate over time? To answer these questions, remember that an interest rate is the price that borrowers pay lenders to use their funds. Like any market price, interest rates are determined by supply and demand—in this case, the supply and demand for loanable funds.

The *supply of loanable funds* comes from households that wish to save part of their incomes in order to consume more in the future (or make bequests to their heirs).

---

[20]These numbers are based on Michael J. Mueller, "Scarcity and Ricardian Rents for Crude Oil," *Economic Inquiry* 23 (1985): 703–24; Kenneth R. Stollery, "Mineral Depletion with Cost as the Extraction Limit: A Model Applied to the Behavior of Prices in the Nickel Industry," *Journal of Environmental Economics and Management* 10 (1983): 151–65; Robert S. Pindyck, "On Monopoly Power in Extractive Resource Markets," *Journal of Environmental Economics and Management* 14 (1987): 128–42; Martin L. Weitzman, "Pricing the Limits to Growth from Mineral Depletion," *Quarterly Journal of Economics* 114 (May 1999): 691–706; and Gregory M. Ellis and Robert Halvorsen, "Estimation of Market Power in a Nonrenewable Resource Industry," *Journal of Political Economy* 110 (2002): 883–99.

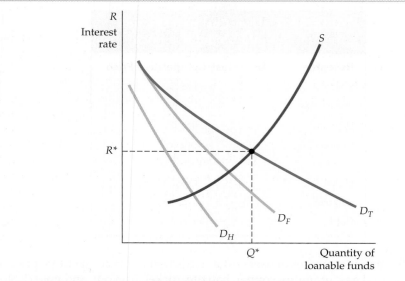

**FIGURE 15.5 Supply and Demand for Loanable Funds**

Market interest rates are determined by the demand and supply of loanable funds. Households supply funds in order to consume more in the future; the higher the interest rate, the more they supply. Households and firms both demand funds, but the higher the interest rate, the less they demand. Shifts in demand or supply cause changes in interest rates.

For example, some households have high incomes now but expect to earn less after retirement. Saving lets them spread their consumption more evenly over time. In addition, because they receive interest on the money they lend, they can consume more in the future in return for consuming less now. As a result, the higher the interest rate, the greater the incentive to save. The supply of loanable funds is therefore an upward-sloping curve, labeled $S$ in Figure 15.5.

The *demand for loanable funds* has two components. First, some households want to consume more than their current incomes, either because their incomes are low now but are expected to grow, or because they want to make a large purchase (e.g., a house) that must be paid for out of future income. These households are willing to pay interest in return for not having to wait to consume. However, the higher the interest rate, the greater the cost of consuming rather than waiting, so the less willing these households will be to borrow. The household demand for loanable funds is therefore a declining function of the interest rate. In Figure 15.5, it is the curve labeled $D_H$.

The second source of demand for loanable funds is firms that want to make capital investments. Remember that firms will invest in projects with NPVs that are positive because a positive NPV means that the expected return on the project exceeds the opportunity cost of funds. That opportunity cost—the discount rate used to calculate the NPV—is the interest rate, perhaps adjusted for risk. Often firms borrow to invest because the flow of profits from an investment comes in the future while the cost of an investment must usually be paid now. The desire of firms to invest is thus an important source of demand for loanable funds.

As we saw earlier, however, the higher the interest rate, the lower the NPV of a project. If interest rates rise, some investment projects that had positive NPVs will now have negative NPVs and will therefore be cancelled. Overall, because firms' willingness to invest falls when interest rates rise, their demand for loanable funds also falls. The demand for loanable funds by firms is thus a downward-sloping curve; in Figure 15.5, it is labeled $D_F$.

The total demand for loanable funds is the sum of household demand and firm demand; in Figure 15.5, it is the curve $D_T$. This total demand curve, together with the supply curve, determines the equilibrium interest rate. In Figure 15.5, that rate is $R^*$.

Figure 15.5 can also help us understand why interest rates change. Suppose the economy goes into a recession. Firms will expect lower sales and lower future profits from new capital investments. The NPVs of projects will fall, and firms' willingness to invest will decline, as will their demand for loanable funds. $D_F$, and therefore $D_T$, will shift to the left, and the equilibrium interest rate will fall. Or suppose the federal government spends much more money than it collects through taxes—i.e., that it runs a large deficit. It will have to borrow to finance the deficit, shifting the total demand for loanable funds $D_T$ to the right, so that $R$ increases. The monetary policies of the Federal Reserve are another important determinant of interest rates. The Federal Reserve can create money, shifting the supply of loanable funds to the right and reducing $R$.

## A Variety of Interest Rates

Figure 15.5 aggregates individual demands and supplies as though there were a single market interest rate. In fact, households, firms, and the government lend and borrow under a variety of terms and conditions. As a result, there is a wide range of "market" interest rates. Here we briefly describe some of the more important rates that are quoted in the newspapers and sometimes used for capital investment decisions.

- **Treasury Bill Rate** A Treasury bill is a short-term (one year or less) bond issued by the U.S. government. It is a pure *discount bond*—i.e., it makes no coupon payments but instead is sold at a price less than its redemption value at maturity. For example, a three-month Treasury bill might be sold for $98. In three months, it can be redeemed for $100; it thus has an effective three-month yield of about 2 percent and an effective annual yield of about 8 percent.[21] The Treasury bill rate can be viewed as a short-term, risk-free rate.

- **Treasury Bond Rate** A Treasury bond is a longer-term bond issued by the U.S. government for more than one year and typically for 10 to 30 years. Rates vary, depending on the maturity of the bond.

- **Discount Rate** Commercial banks sometimes borrow for short periods from the Federal Reserve. These loans are called *discounts*, and the rate that the Federal Reserve charges on them is the discount rate.

- **Federal Funds Rate** This is the interest rate that banks charge one another for overnight loans of federal funds. Federal funds consist of currency in circulation plus deposits held at Federal Reserve Banks. Banks keep funds at Federal Reserve Banks in order to meet reserve requirements. Banks with excess reserves may lend these funds to banks with reserve deficiencies at the federal funds rate. The federal funds rate is a key instrument of monetary policy used by the Federal Reserve.

- **Commercial Paper Rate** Commercial paper refers to short-term (six months or less) discount bonds issued by high-quality corporate borrowers. Because

---

[21]To be exact, the three-month yield is $(100/98) - 1 = 0.0204$, and the annual yield is $(100/98)^4 - 1 = 0.0842$, or 8.42 percent.

commercial paper is only slightly riskier than Treasury bills, the commercial paper rate is usually less than 1 percent higher than the Treasury bill rate.

- **Prime Rate** This is the rate (sometimes called the *reference rate*) that large banks post as a reference point for short-term loans to their biggest corporate borrowers. As we saw in Example 12.4 (page 467), this rate does not fluctuate from day to day as other rates do.

- **Corporate Bond Rate** Newspapers and government publications report the average annual yields on long-term (typically 20-year) corporate bonds in different risk categories (e.g., high-grade, medium-grade, etc.). These average yields indicate how much corporations are paying for long-term debt. However, as we saw in Example 15.2, the yields on corporate bonds can vary considerably, depending on the financial strength of the corporation and the time to maturity for the bond.

# SUMMARY

1. A firm's holding of capital is measured as a stock, but inputs of labor and raw materials are flows. Its stock of capital enables a firm to earn a flow of profits over time.

2. When a firm makes a capital investment, it spends money now in order to earn profits in the future. To decide whether the investment is worthwhile, the firm must determine the present value of future profits by discounting them.

3. The present discounted value (PDV) of $1 paid one year from now is $1/(1 + R)$, where $R$ is the interest rate. The PDV of $1 paid $n$ years from now is $1/(1 + R)^n$.

4. A bond is a contract in which a lender agrees to pay the bondholder a stream of money. The value of the bond is the PDV of that stream. The effective yield on a bond is the interest rate that equates that value with the bond's market price. Bond yields differ because of differences in riskiness and time to maturity.

5. Firms can decide whether to undertake a capital investment by applying the net present value (NPV) criterion: Invest if the present value of the expected future cash flows is larger than the cost of the investment.

6. The discount rate that a firm uses to calculate the NPV for an investment should be the opportunity cost of capital—i.e., the return the firm could earn on a similar investment.

7. When calculating NPVs, if cash flows are in nominal terms (i.e., include inflation), the discount rate should also be nominal; if cash flows are in real terms (i.e., are net of inflation), a real discount rate should be used.

8. An adjustment for risk can be made by adding a risk premium to the discount rate. However, the risk pre-

mium should reflect only nondiversifiable risk. Using the Capital Asset Pricing Model (CAPM), the risk premium is the "asset beta" for the project multiplied by the risk premium on the stock market as a whole. The "asset beta" measures the sensitivity of the project's return to movements in the market.

9. Consumers are faced with investment decisions that require the same kind of analysis as those of firms. When deciding whether to buy a durable good like a car or a major appliance, the consumer must consider the present value of future operating costs.

10. Investments in human capital—the knowledge, skills, and experience that make an individual more productive and thereby able to earn a higher income in the future—can be evaluated in much the same way as other investments. Investing in further education, for example, makes economic sense if the present value of the expected future increases in income exceeds the present value of the costs.

11. An exhaustible resource in the ground is like money in the bank and must earn a comparable return. Therefore, if the market is competitive, price less marginal extraction cost will grow at the rate of interest. The difference between price and marginal cost is called *user cost*—the opportunity cost of depleting a unit of the resource.

12. Market interest rates are determined by the demand and supply of loanable funds. Households supply funds so that they can consume more in the future. Households, firms, and the government demand funds. Changes in demand or supply cause changes in interest rates.

# QUESTIONS FOR REVIEW

1. A firm uses cloth and labor to produce shirts in a factory that it bought for $10 million. Which of its factor inputs are measured as flows and which as stocks?

How would your answer change if the firm had leased a factory instead of buying one? Is its output measured as a flow or a stock? What about its profit?

2. How do investors calculate the net present value of a bond? If the interest rate is 5 percent, what is the present value of a perpetuity that pays $1000 per year forever?

3. What is the *effective yield* on a bond? How does one calculate it? Why do some corporate bonds have higher effective yields than others?

4. What is the net present value (NPV) criterion for investment decisions? How does one calculate the NPV of an investment project? If all the cash flows for a project are certain, what discount rate should be used to calculate NPV?

5. You are retiring from your job and are given two options: You can accept a lump sum payment from the company, or you can accept a smaller annual payment that will continue for as long as you live. How would you decide which option is best? What information do you need?

6. You have noticed that bond prices have been rising over the past few months. All else equal, what does this suggest has been happening to interest rates? Explain.

7. What is the difference between a real discount rate and a nominal discount rate? When should a real discount rate be used in an NPV calculation and when should a nominal rate be used?

8. How is risk premium used to account for risk in NPV calculations? What is the difference between diversifiable and nondiversifiable risk? Why should only nondiversifiable risk enter into the risk premium?

9. What is meant by the "market return" in the Capital Asset Pricing Model (CAPM)? Why is the market return greater than the risk-free interest rate? What does an asset's "beta" measure in the CAPM? Why should high-beta assets have a higher expected return than low-beta assets?

10. Suppose you are deciding whether to invest $100 million in a steel mill. You know the expected cash flows for the project, but they are risky—steel prices could rise or fall in the future. How would the CAPM help you select a discount rate for an NPV calculation?

11. How does a consumer trade off current and future costs when selecting an air conditioner or other major appliance? How could this selection be aided by an NPV calculation?

12. What is meant by the "user cost" of producing an exhaustible resource? Why does price minus extraction cost rise at the rate of interest in a competitive market for an exhaustible resource?

13. What determines the supply of loanable funds? The demand for loanable funds? What might cause the supply or demand for loanable funds to shift? How would such a shift affect interest rates?

# EXERCISES

1. Suppose the interest rate is 10 percent. If $100 is invested at this rate today, how much will it be worth after one year? After two years? After five years? What is the value today of $100 paid one year from now? Paid two years from now? Paid five years from now?

2. You are offered the choice of two payment streams: (a) $150 paid one year from now and $150 paid two years from now; (b) $130 paid one year from now and $160 paid two years from now. Which payment stream would you prefer if the interest rate is 5 percent? If it is 15 percent?

3. Suppose the interest rate is 10 percent. What is the value of a coupon bond that pays $80 per year for each of the next five years and then makes a principal repayment of $1000 in the sixth year? Repeat for an interest rate of 15 percent.

4. A bond has two years to mature. It makes a coupon payment of $100 after one year and both a coupon payment of $100 and a principal repayment of $1000 after two years. The bond is selling for $966. What is its effective yield?

5. Equation (15.5) (page 563) shows the net present value of an investment in an electric motor factory. Half of the $10 million cost is paid initially and the other half after a year. The factory is expected to lose money during its first two years of operation. If the discount rate is 4 percent, what is the NPV? Is the investment worthwhile?

6. The market interest rate is 5 percent and is expected to stay at that level. Consumers can borrow and lend all they want at this rate. Explain your choice in each of the following situations:

   a. Would you prefer a $500 gift today or a $540 gift next year?

   b. Would you prefer a $100 gift now or a $500 loan without interest for four years?

   c. Would you prefer a $350 rebate on an $8000 car or one year of financing for the full price of the car at 0 percent interest?

   d. You have just won a million-dollar lottery and will receive $50,000 a year for the next 20 years. How much is this worth to you today?

   e. You win the "honest million" jackpot. You can have $1 million today or $60,000 per year for eternity (a right that can be passed on to your heirs). Which do you prefer?

   f. In the past, adult children had to pay taxes on gifts of over $10,000 from their parents, but parents could make interest-free loans to their children. Why did some people call this policy unfair? To whom were the rules unfair?

7. Ralph is trying to decide whether to go to graduate school. If he spends two years in graduate school, paying $15,000 tuition each year, he will get a job that will pay $60,000 per year for the rest of his working life. If

he does not go to school, he will go into the workforce immediately. He will then make $30,000 per year for the next three years, $45,000 for the following three years, and $60,000 per year every year after that. If the interest rate is 10 percent, is graduate school a good financial investment?

8. Suppose your uncle gave you an oil well like the one described in Section 15.8. (Marginal production cost is constant at $10.) The price of oil is currently $20 but is controlled by a cartel that accounts for a large fraction of total production. Should you produce and sell all your oil now or wait to produce? Explain your answer.

9. You are planning to invest in fine wine. Each case costs $100, and you know from experience that the value of a case of wine held for $t$ years is $100t^{1/2}$. One hundred cases of wine are available for sale, and the interest rate is 10 percent.

   a. How many cases should you buy, how long should you wait to sell them, and how much money will you receive at the time of their sale?

   b. Suppose that at the time of purchase, someone offers you $130 per case immediately. Should you take the offer?

   c. How would your answers change if the interest rate were only 5 percent?

10. Reexamine the capital investment decision in the disposable diaper industry (Example 15.3) from the point of view of an incumbent firm. If P&G or Kimberly-Clark were to expand capacity by building three new plants, they would not need to spend $60 million on R&D before start-up. How does this advantage affect the NPV calculations in Table 15.5 (page 567)? Is the investment profitable at a discount rate of 12 percent?

11. Suppose you can buy a new Toyota Corolla for $20,000 and sell it for $12,000 after six years. Alternatively, you can lease the car for $300 per month for three years and return it at the end of the three years. For simplification, assume that lease payments are made yearly instead of monthly—i.e., that they are $3600 per year for each of three years.

   a. If the interest rate, $r$, is 4 percent, is it better to lease or buy the car?

   b. Which is better if the interest rate is 12 percent?

   c. At what interest rate would you be indifferent between buying and leasing the car?

12. A consumer faces the following decision: She can buy a computer for $1000 and $10 per month for Internet access for three years, or she can receive a $400 rebate on the computer (so that its cost is $600) but agree to pay $25 per month for three years for Internet access. For simplification, assume that the consumer pays the access fees yearly (i.e., $10 per month = $120 per year).

   a. What should the consumer do if the interest rate is 3 percent?

   b. What if the interest rate is 17 percent?

   c. At what interest rate will the consumer be indifferent between the two options?

# PART FOUR

# Information, Market Failure, and the Role of Government

Much of the analysis in the first three parts of this book has focused on positive questions—how consumers and firms behave and how that behavior affects different market structures. Part IV takes a more normative approach. Here we will describe the goal of economic efficiency, show when markets generate efficient outcomes, and explain when they fail and thus require government intervention.

Chapter 16 discusses general equilibrium analysis, in which the interactions among related markets are taken into account. This chapter also analyzes the conditions that are required for an economy to be efficient and shows when and why a perfectly competitive market is efficient. Chapter 17 examines an important source of market failure—incomplete information. We show that when some economic participants have better information than others, markets may fail to allocate goods efficiently or may not even exist. We also show how sellers can avoid problems of asymmetric information by giving potential buyers signals about product quality. Finally, Chapter 18 discusses two additional sources of market failure: externalities and public goods. We show that although these failures can sometimes be resolved through private bargaining, at other times they require government intervention. We also discuss a number of remedies for market failures, such as pollution taxes and tradeable emission permits.

# General Equilibrium and Economic Efficiency

## 16

For the most part, we have studied individual markets in isolation. But markets are often interdependent: Conditions in one can affect prices and outputs in others either because one good is an input to the production of another good or because two goods are substitutes or complements. In this chapter, we see how a *general equilibrium analysis* can be used to take these interrelationships into account.

We also expand the concept of economic efficiency that we introduced in Chapter 9, and we discuss the benefits of a competitive market economy. To do this, we first analyze economic efficiency, beginning with the exchange of goods among people or countries. We then use this analysis of exchange to discuss whether the outcomes generated by an economy are equitable. To the extent that these outcomes are deemed inequitable, government can help redistribute income.

We then go on to describe the conditions that an economy must satisfy if it is to produce and distribute goods efficiently. We explain why a perfectly competitive market system satisfies those conditions. We also show why free international trade can expand the production possibilities of a country and make its consumers better off. Most markets, however, are not perfectly competitive, and many deviate substantially from that ideal. In the final section of the chapter (as a preview to our detailed discussion of market failure in Chapters 17 and 18), we discuss some key reasons why markets may fail to work efficiently.

## 16.1 GENERAL EQUILIBRIUM ANALYSIS

So far, our discussions of market behavior have been largely based on **partial equilibrium analysis**. When determining the equilibrium prices and quantities in a market using partial equilibrium analysis, we presume that activity in one market has little or no effect on other markets. For example, in Chapters 2 and 9, we presumed that the wheat market was largely independent of the markets for related products, such as corn and soybeans.

Often a partial equilibrium analysis is sufficient to understand market behavior. However, market interrelationships can be important. In Chapter 2, for example, we saw how a change in the price of one good can affect the demand for another if they are complements or substitutes. In Chapter 8, we saw that an increase in a firm's input demand can cause both the market price of the input and the product price to rise.

• **partial equilibrium analysis** Determination of equilibrium prices and quantities in a market independent of effects from other markets.

• **general equilibrium analysis** Simultaneous determination of the prices and quantities in all relevant markets, taking feedback effects into account.

Unlike partial equilibrium analysis, **general equilibrium analysis** *determines the prices and quantities in all markets simultaneously,* and it explicitly takes feedback effects into account. A *feedback effect* is a price or quantity adjustment in one market caused by price and quantity adjustments in related markets. Suppose, for example, that the U.S. government taxes oil imports. This policy would immediately shift the supply curve for oil to the left (by making foreign oil more expensive) and raise the price of oil. But the effect of the tax would not end there. The higher price of oil would increase the demand for and then the price of natural gas. The higher natural gas price would in turn cause oil demand to rise (shift to the right) and increase the oil price even more. The oil and natural gas markets will continue to interact until eventually an equilibrium is reached in which the quantity demanded and quantity supplied are equated in both markets.

In practice, a complete general equilibrium analysis, which evaluates the effects of a change in one market on *all* other markets, is not feasible. Instead, we confine ourselves to two or three markets that are closely related. For example, when looking at a tax on oil, we might also look at markets for natural gas, coal, and electricity.

## Two Interdependent Markets—Moving to General Equilibrium

To study the interdependence of markets, let's examine the competitive markets for DVD rentals and movie theater tickets. The two markets are closely related because DVD players give most consumers the option of watching movies at home as well as at the theater. Changes in pricing policies that affect one market are likely to affect the other, which in turn causes feedback effects in the first market.

Figure 16.1 shows the supply and demand curves for DVDs and movies. In part (a), the price of movie tickets is initially \$6.00; the market is in equilibrium at the intersection of $D_M$ and $S_M$. In part (b), the DVD market is also in equilibrium with a price of \$3.00.

Now suppose that the government places a tax of \$1 on each movie ticket purchased. The effect of this tax is determined on a partial equilibrium basis by shifting the supply curve for movies upward by \$1, from $S_M$ to $S_M^*$ in Figure 16.1(a). Initially, this shift causes the prices of movies to increase to \$6.35 and the quantity of movie tickets sold to fall from $Q_M$ to $Q_M'$. This is as far as a partial equilibrium analysis takes us. But we can go further with a general equilibrium analysis by doing two things: (1) looking at the effects of the movie tax on the market for DVDs, and (2) seeing whether there are any feedback effects from the DVD market to the movie market.

The movie tax affects the market for DVDs because movies and DVDs are *substitutes.* A higher movie price shifts the demand for DVDs from $D_V$ to $D_V'$ in Figure 16.1(b). In turn, this shift causes the rental price of DVDs to increase from \$3.00 to \$3.50. Note that a tax on one product can affect the prices and sales of other products—something that policymakers should remember when designing tax policies.

What about the market for movies? The original demand curve for movies presumed that the price of DVDs was unchanged at \$3.00. But because that price is now \$3.50, the demand for movies will shift upward, from $D_M$ to $D_M'$ in Figure 16.1(a). The new equilibrium price of movies (at the intersection of $S_M^*$ and $D_M'$) is \$6.75, instead of \$6.35, and the quantity of movie tickets purchased has increased from $Q_M'$ to $Q_M''$. Thus a partial equilibrium analysis would have underestimated the effect of the tax on the price of movies. The DVD market is

In §2.1, we explain that two goods are substitutes if an increase in the price of one leads to an increase in the quantity demanded of the other.

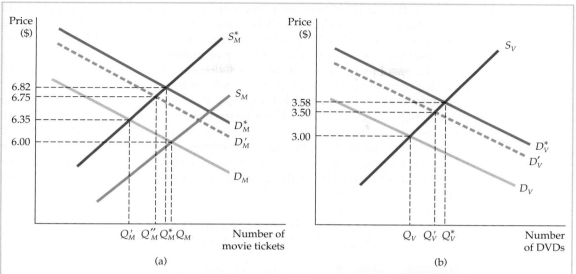

**FIGURE 16.1** **Two Interdependent Markets: (a) Movie Tickets and (b) DVD Rentals**

When markets are interdependent, the prices of all products must be simultaneously determined. Here a tax on movie tickets shifts the supply of movies upward from $S_M$ to $S_M^*$, as shown in **(a)**. The higher price of movie tickets ($6.35 rather than $6.00) initially shifts the demand for DVDs upward (from $D_V$ to $D_V'$), causing the price of DVDs to rise (from $3.00 to $3.50), as shown in **(b)**. The higher video price feeds back into the movie ticket market, causing demand to shift from $D_M$ to $D_M'$ and the price of movies to increase from $6.35 to $6.75. This continues until a general equilibrium is reached, as shown at the intersection of $D_M^*$ and $S_M^*$ in **(a)**, with a movie ticket of $6.82, and the intersection of $D_V^*$ and $S_V$ in **(b)**, with a DVD price of $3.58.

so closely related to the market for movies that to determine the tax's full effect, we need a general equilibrium analysis.

## Reaching General Equilibrium

Our analysis is not yet complete. The change in the market price of movies will generate a feedback effect on the price of DVDs that, in turn, will affect the price of movies, and so on. In the end, we must determine the equilibrium prices and quantities of *both* movies and DVDs *simultaneously*. The equilibrium movie price of $6.82 is given in Figure 16.1(a) by the intersection of the equilibrium supply and demand curves for movie tickets ($S_M^*$ and $D_M^*$). The equilibrium DVD price of $3.58 is given in Figure 16.1(b) by the intersection of the equilibrium supply and demand curves for DVDs ($S_V$ and $D_V^*$). These are the correct general equilibrium prices because the DVD market supply and demand curves have been drawn *on the assumption that the price of movie tickets is $6.82*. Likewise, the movie ticket curves have been drawn *on the assumption that the price of DVDs is $3.58*. In other words, both sets of curves are consistent with the prices in related markets, and we have no reason to expect that the supply and demand curves in either market will shift further. To find the general equilibrium prices (and quantities) in practice, we must simultaneously find two prices that equate quantity demanded and quantity supplied in all related markets. For our two markets, we need to find the solution to four equations (supply of movie tickets, demand for movie tickets, supply of DVDs, and demand for DVDs).

Note that even if we were only interested in the market for movies, it would be important to account for the DVD market when determining the impact of a movie tax. In this example, partial equilibrium analysis would lead us to conclude that the tax will increase the price of movie tickets from $6.00 to $6.35. A general equilibrium analysis, however, shows us that the impact of the tax on the price of movie tickets is greater: It would in fact increase to $6.82.

Movies and DVDs are substitute goods. By drawing diagrams analogous to those in Figure 16.1, you should be able to convince yourself that if the goods in question are *complements*, a partial equilibrium analysis will *overstate* the impact of a tax. Think about gasoline and automobiles, for example. A tax on gasoline will cause its price to go up, but this increase will reduce demand for automobiles, which in turn reduces the demand for gasoline, causing its price to fall somewhat.

> Recall from §2.1 that two goods are complements if an increase in the price of one leads to a decrease in the quantity demanded of the other.

---

**EXAMPLE 16.1** — The Global Market for Ethanol

High crude oil prices, harmful emissions, and growing dependency on volatile foreign oil supplies have led to a growing interest in alternative fuel sources such as ethanol. Ethanol is a clean-burning, high-octane fuel produced from renewable resources such as sugar cane and corn. It is highly touted as a means of reducing automobile emissions and of responding to concerns about global warming. There is a high degree of interdependence between the production and sale of Brazilian ethanol (from sugar cane) and ethanol produced in the United States (from corn). We will see that U.S. regulation of its ethanol market has had significant effects on the Brazilian market, which in turn has had a feedback effect on the market in the United States. Although this interdependence has in all likelihood benefited U.S. producers, it has also had adverse consequences for U.S. consumers, Brazilian producers, and, probably, Brazilian consumers.

The world ethanol market is dominated by Brazil and the United States, which accounted for over 90 percent of world production in 2005.[1] Ethanol is not new; the Brazilian government started promoting ethanol in the mid-1970s as a response to rising oil prices and declining sugar prices, and the program has flourished. In 2007, about 40 percent of all Brazilian automobile fuel was ethanol, a response to the skyrocketing growth in the demand for flex-fuel cars, which can run on any mixture of ethanol and gasoline. U.S. ethanol production was first encouraged by the Energy Tax Act of 1978, which provided for tax exemptions for ethanol-gasoline blends. More recently, the Energy Policy Act of 2005 required that U.S. fuel production include a minimum amount of renewable fuel each year—a stipulation which essentially mandated a baseline level of ethanol production.

The U.S. and Brazilian ethanol markets are closely tied to each other. As a consequence, the U.S. regulation of its own ethanol market can significantly affect Brazil's market. This global interdependence was made evident by the Energy Security Act of 1979, by which the U.S. offered a tax credit of $0.51 per gallon of

---

[1]This example is based on Amani Elobeid and Simla Tokgoz, "Removal of U.S. Ethanol Domestic and Trade Distortions: Impact on U.S. and Brazilian Ethanol Markets," Working paper, 2006.

ethanol to spur alternatives to gasoline. Moreover, to prevent foreign ethanol producers from reaping the benefits of this tax credit, the U.S. government imposed a $0.54 per gallon tax on imported ethanol. The policy has been highly effective: The U.S. has devoted more and more of its corn harvest to ethanol production, while Brazilian imports (which are made from sugar cane) have declined. While this policy has benefited corn producers, it is not in the interests of U.S. ethanol consumers. It is estimated that whereas Brazil can export ethanol for less than $0.90 per gallon, it costs $1.10 to produce a gallon of ethanol from Iowa corn. Thus American consumers would benefit if the tax and subsidy were removed—a move that would increase the imports of the cheaper sugar cane-based ethanol from Brazil.

Figure 16.2 shows the predicted changes in the ethanol market if the U.S. tariffs were completely removed in 2006. The top green line in Figure 16.2(a) estimates Brazil's ethanol exports without U.S. tariffs in place, and the blue line represents Brazil's exports with U.S. tariffs in place. Figure 16.2(b) shows the price of ethanol in the United States with and without the tariff. As you can see, Brazilian ethanol exports would increase dramatically if the tariffs were removed and U.S. consumers will benefit. This would also be advantageous to Brazilian producers and consumers.

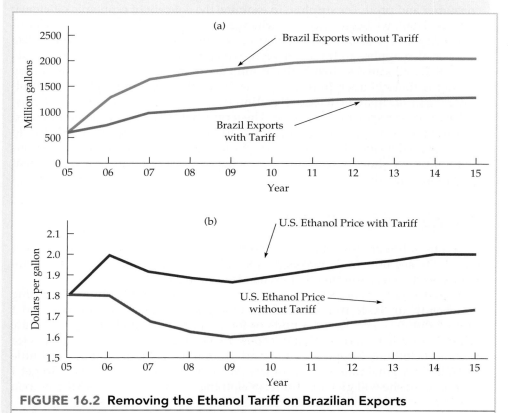

**FIGURE 16.2  Removing the Ethanol Tariff on Brazilian Exports**

If U.S. tariffs on ethanol produced abroad were to be removed, Brazil would export much more ethanol to the United States, displacing much of the more expensive corn-based ethanol produced domestically. As a result, the price of ethanol in the U.S. would fall, benefiting U.S. consumers.

The adverse incentive created by U.S. tariffs does not tell the entire story about ethanol and interdependent markets. In 1984, Congress passed the Caribbean Basin Initiative (CBI)—tax legislation designed to foster economic development in Caribbean countries. Under the CBI, ethanol processed in those countries, up to 60 million gallons a year, receives duty-free status. In response, Brazil has invested in several ethanol dehydration plants in the Caribbean in order to export their sugar-based ethanol to the United States without paying the 54-cent per gallon tariff.

The policy of imposing tariffs on foreign ethanol has remained in force despite the economic inefficiencies that tariffs create. One important reason is the support given by U.S. corn farmers, who devote more than 20 percent of their corn crop to supply the lucrative ethanol market. As of 2007, Congress has approved continuation of the tariffs through 2010.

## 16.2 EFFICIENCY IN EXCHANGE

• **exchange economy** Market in which two or more consumers trade two goods among themselves.

In Chapter 9 we saw that a competitive market is efficient because it maximizes consumer and producer surplus. To examine the concept of economic efficiency in more detail, we begin with an **exchange economy**, analyzing the behavior of two consumers who can trade either of two goods between themselves. (The analysis also applies to trade between two countries.) Suppose the two goods are initially allocated so that both consumers can make themselves better off by trading with each other. In this case, the initial allocation of goods is economically *inefficient*. In an **efficient allocation** of goods, *no one can be made better off without making someone else worse off*. The term *Pareto efficiency* is sometimes used synonymously with *efficient allocation*, to credit Italian economist Vilfredo Pareto, who developed the concept of efficiency in exchange. In the subsections that follow, we show why mutually beneficial trades result in a Pareto efficient allocation of goods.

• **efficient (or Pareto efficient) allocation** Allocation of goods in which no one can be made better off unless someone else is made worse off.

### The Advantages of Trade

In §3.1, we explain that the marginal rate of substitution is the maximum amount of one good that the consumer is willing to give up to obtain one unit of another good.

As a rule, voluntary trade between two people or two countries is mutually beneficial.[2] To see how trade makes people better off, let's look in detail at a two-person exchange, assuming that exchange itself is costless.

Suppose James and Karen have 10 units of food and 6 units of clothing between them. Table 16.1 shows that initially James has 7 units of food and 1 unit of clothing, and Karen 3 units of food and 5 units of clothing. To decide whether a trade would be advantageous, we need to know their preferences for food and clothing. Suppose that because Karen has a lot of clothing and little food, her marginal rate of substitution (MRS) of food for clothing is 3: To get 1 unit of food, she will give up 3 units of clothing. However, James's MRS of food

---

[2]There are several situations in which trade may not be advantageous. First, limited information may lead people to believe that trade will make them better off when in fact it will not. Second, people may be coerced into making trades, either by physical threats or by the threat of future economic reprisals. Third, as we saw in Chapter 13, barriers to free trade can sometimes provide a strategic advantage to a country.

| TABLE 16.1 | The Advantage of Trade | | |
|---|---|---|---|
| **Individual** | **Initial Allocation** | **Trade** | **Final Allocation** |
| James | 7F, 1C | − 1F, + 1C | 6F, 2C |
| Karen | 3F, 5C | + 1F, − 1C | 4F, 4C |

for clothing is only 1/2: He will give up only 1/2 a unit of clothing to get 1 unit of food.

There is thus room for mutually advantageous trade because James values clothing more highly than Karen does, whereas Karen values food more highly than James does. To get another unit of food, Karen would be willing to trade up to 3 units of clothing. But James will give up 1 unit of food for 1/2 unit of clothing. The actual terms of the trade depend on the bargaining process. Among the possible outcomes are a trade of 1 unit of food by James for anywhere between 1/2 and 3 units of clothing from Karen.

Suppose Karen offers James 1 unit of clothing for 1 unit of food, and James agrees. Both will be better off. James will have more clothing, which he values more than food, and Karen will have more food, which she values more than clothing. Whenever two consumers' MRSs are different, there is room for mutually beneficial trade because the allocation of resources is inefficient: trading will make both consumers better off. Conversely, to achieve economic efficiency, the two consumers' MRSs must be equal.

This important result also holds when there are many goods and consumers: *An allocation of goods is efficient only if the goods are distributed so that the marginal rate of substitution between any pair of goods is the same for all consumers.*

## The Edgeworth Box Diagram

If trade is beneficial, which trades can occur? Which of those trades will allocate goods efficiently among customers? How much better off will consumers then be? We can answer these questions for any two-person, two-good example by using a diagram called an **Edgeworth box**.

Figure 16.3 shows an Edgeworth box in which the horizontal axis describes the number of units of food and the vertical axis the units of clothing. The length of the box is 10 units of food, the total quantity of food available; its height is 6 units of clothing, the total quantity of clothing available.

In the Edgeworth box, each point describes the market baskets of *both* consumers. James's holdings are read from the origin at $O_J$ and Karen's holdings in the reverse direction from the origin at $O_K$. For example, point A represents the initial allocation of food and clothing. Reading on the horizontal axis from left to right at the bottom of the box, we see that James has 7 units of food; reading upward along the vertical axis on the left of the diagram, we see that he has 1 unit of clothing. For James, therefore, A represents 7F and 1C. This leaves 3F and 5C for Karen. Karen's allocation of food (3F) is read from right to left at the top of the box diagram beginning at $O_K$; we read her allocation of clothing (5C) from top to bottom at the right of the box diagram.

We can also see the effect of trade between Karen and James. James gives up 1F in exchange for 1C, moving from A to B. Karen gives up 1C and obtains 1F, also moving from A to B. Point B thus represents the market baskets of both James and Karen after the mutually beneficial trade.

• **Edgeworth box** Diagram showing all possible allocations of either two goods between two people or of two inputs between two production processes.

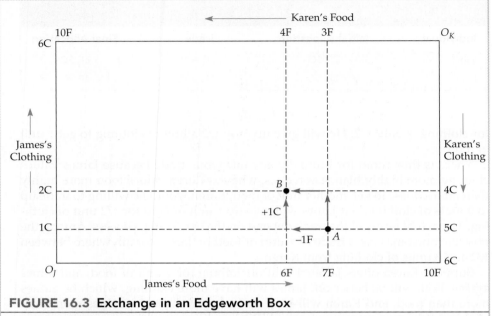

**FIGURE 16.3 Exchange in an Edgeworth Box**

Each point in the Edgeworth box simultaneously represents James's and Karen's market baskets of food and clothing. At *A*, for example, James has 7 units of food and 1 unit of clothing, and Karen 3 units of food and 5 units of clothing.

## Efficient Allocations

A trade from *A* to *B* thus made both Karen and James better off. But is *B* an *efficient* allocation? The answer depends on whether James's and Karen's MRSs are the same at *B*, which depends in turn on the shape of their indifference curves. Figure 16.4 shows several indifference curves for both James and Karen. Because his allocations are measured from the origin $O_J$, James's indifference curves are drawn in the usual way. But for Karen, we have rotated the indifference curves 180 degrees, so that the origin is at the upper right-hand corner of the box. Karen's indifference curves are convex, just like James's; we simply see them from a different perspective.

Now that we are familiar with the two sets of indifference curves, let's examine the curves labeled $U_J^1$ and $U_K^1$ that pass through the initial allocation at *A*. Both James's and Karen's MRSs give the slope of their indifference curves at *A*. James's MRS of clothing for food is equal to 1/2, while Karen's is 3. The shaded area between these two indifference curves represents all possible allocations of food and clothing that would make both James and Karen better off than at *A*. In other words, it describes all possible mutually beneficial trades.

Starting at *A*, any trade that moved the allocation of goods outside the shaded area would make one of the two consumers worse off and should not occur. The move from *A* to *B* was mutually beneficial. But in Figure 16.4, *B* is not an efficient point because indifference curves $U_J^2$ and $U_K^2$ intersect. In this case, James's and Karen's MRSs are not the same and the allocation is not efficient. This situation illustrates an important point: *Even if a trade from an inefficient allocation makes both people better off, the new allocation is not necessarily efficient.*

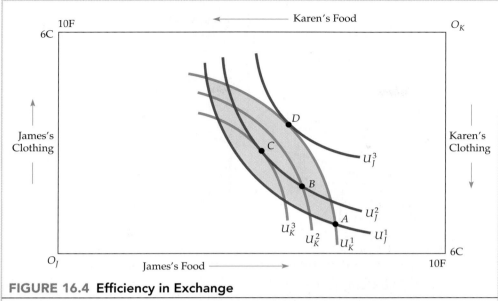

**FIGURE 16.4 Efficiency in Exchange**

The Edgeworth box illustrates the possibilities for both consumers to increase their satisfaction by trading goods. If *A* gives the initial allocation of resources, the shaded area describes all mutually beneficial trades.

Suppose that from *B* an additional trade is made, with James giving up another unit of food to obtain another unit of clothing and Karen giving up a unit of clothing for a unit of food. Point *C* in Figure 16.4 gives the new allocation. At *C*, the MRSs of both people are identical, because at point *C* the indifference curves are tangent. When the indifference curves are tangent, one person cannot be made better off without making the other person worse off. Therefore, *C* represents an efficient allocation.

Of course, *C* is not the only possible efficient outcome of a bargain between James and Karen. For example, if James is an effective bargainer, a trade might change the allocation of goods from *A* to *D*, where indifference curve $U_J^3$ is tangent to indifference curve $U_K^1$. This allocation would leave Karen no worse off than she was at *A* and James much better off. And because no further trade is possible, *D* is an efficient allocation. Thus *C* and *D* are both efficient allocations, although James prefers *D* to *C* and Karen *C* to *D*. In general, it is difficult to predict the allocation that will be reached in a bargain because the end result depends on the bargaining abilities of the people involved.

## The Contract Curve

We have seen that from an initial allocation many possible efficient allocations can be reached through mutually beneficial trade. To find *all possible efficient allocations of food and clothing* between Karen and James, we look for *all points of tangency between each of their indifference curves*. Figure 16.5 shows the **contract curve**: the curve drawn through all such efficient allocations.

The contract curve shows all allocations from which no mutually beneficial trade can be made. *These allocations are efficient because there is no way to reallocate goods to make someone better off without making someone else worse off.* In Figure 16.5 three allocations labeled *E*, *F*, and *G* are Pareto efficient, although each involves

• **contract curve** Curve showing all efficient allocations of goods between two consumers, or of two inputs between two production functions.

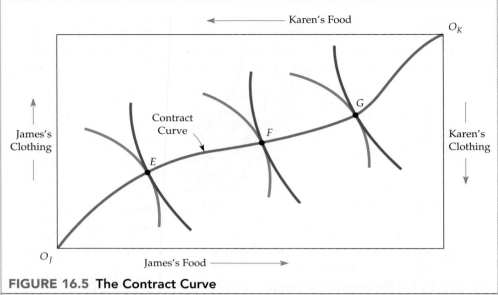

**FIGURE 16.5 The Contract Curve**

The contract curve contains all allocations for which consumers' indifference curves are tangent. Every point on the curve is efficient because one person cannot be made better off without making the other person worse off.

a different distribution of food and clothing, because one person could not be made better off without making someone else worse off.

Several properties of the contract curve may help us understand the concept of efficiency in exchange. Once a point on a contract curve, such as *E*, has been chosen, there is no way to move to another point on the contract curve, say *F*, without making one person worse off (in this case, Karen). Without making further comparison between James's and Karen's preferences, we cannot compare allocations *E* and *F*. We simply know that both are efficient. In this sense, Pareto efficiency is a modest goal: It says that we should make all mutually beneficial exchanges, but it does not say which exchanges are best. Pareto efficiency can be a powerful concept, however. If a change will improve efficiency, it is in *everyone's* self-interest to support it.

We can frequently improve efficiency even when one aspect of a proposed change makes someone worse off. We need only include a second change, such that the *combined* set of changes leaves someone better off and no one worse off. Suppose, for example, that we eliminate the quota on steel imports into the United States. Although U.S. consumers would then enjoy lower prices and a greater selection of cars, some U.S. workers would lose their jobs. But what if eliminating the quota were combined with federal tax breaks and job relocation subsidies for steelworkers? In that case, U.S. consumers would be better off (after accounting for the cost of the job subsidies) and the workers no worse off. This would increase efficiency.

## Consumer Equilibrium in a Competitive Market

In a two-person exchange, the outcome can depend on the bargaining power of the two parties. Competitive markets, however, have many actual or potential buyers and sellers. As a result, each buyer and seller takes the price of the goods as fixed and decides how much to buy and sell at those prices. We can show how competitive markets lead to efficient exchange by using the Edgeworth box to mimic a competitive market. Suppose, for example, that there are many Jameses and many Karens. This allows us to think of each individual James and Karen as a price taker, even though we are working with only a two-person box diagram.

Figure 16.6 shows the opportunities for trade when we start at the allocation given by point $A$ and when the prices of both food and clothing are equal to 1. (The actual prices do not matter; what matters is the price of food relative to the price of clothing.) When the prices of food and clothing are equal, each unit of food can be exchanged for 1 unit of clothing. As a result, the price line $PP'$ in the diagram, which has a slope of $-1$, describes all possible allocations that exchange can achieve.

Suppose each James decides to buy 2 units of clothing and sell 2 units of food in exchange. This would move each James from $A$ to $C$ and increase satisfaction from indifference curve $U_J^1$ to $U_J^2$. Meanwhile, each Karen buys 2 units of food and sells 2 units of clothing. This would move each Karen from $A$ to $C$ as well, increasing satisfaction from indifference curve $U_K^1$ to $U_K^2$.

We choose prices for the two goods so that the quantity of food demanded by each Karen is equal to the quantity of food that each James wishes to sell; likewise, the quantity of clothing demanded by each James is equal to the quantity of clothing that each Karen wishes to sell. As a result, the markets for food and clothing are in equilibrium. An *equilibrium is a set of prices at which the quantity demanded equals the quantity supplied in every market.* This is also a *competitive equilibrium* because all suppliers and demanders are price takers.

Not all prices are consistent with equilibrium. For example, if the price of food is 3 and the price of clothing is 1, any exchange of clothing for food must be

> In §8.7, we explain that in a competitive equilibrium, price-taking firms maximize profit, and the price of the product is such that the quantity demanded is equal to the quantity supplied.

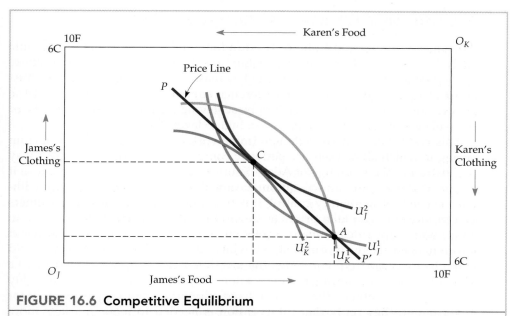

**FIGURE 16.6 Competitive Equilibrium**

In a competitive market the prices of the two goods determine the terms of exchange among consumers. If $A$ is the initial allocation of goods and the price line $PP'$ represents the ratio of prices, the competitive market will lead to an equilibrium at $C$, the point of tangency of both indifference curves. As a result, the competitive equilibrium is efficient.

done on a 3-to-1 basis, i.e., 3 units of clothing must be given up to obtain 1 unit of food. But then each James will be unwilling to trade any clothing to get additional food because his MRS of clothing for food is only 1/2, i.e., he would only be willing to give up 2 units of clothing for 1 unit of food. Each Karen, on the other hand, would be happy to sell clothing to get more food but has no one to trade with. The market is therefore in *disequilibrium* because the quantities of food and clothing demanded are not equal to the quantities supplied.

This disequilibrium should be only temporary. In a competitive market, prices will adjust if there is **excess demand** in some markets (the quantity demanded of one good is greater than the quantity supplied) and **excess supply** in others (the quantity supplied is greater than the quantity demanded). In our example, each Karen's quantity demanded for food is greater than each James's willingness to sell it, whereas each Karen's willingness to trade clothing is greater than each James's quantity demanded. As a result of this excess quantity demanded for food and excess quantity supplied of clothing, we can expect the price of food to increase relative to the price of clothing. As the price changes, so will the quantities demanded by all those in the market. Eventually, the prices will adjust until an equilibrium is reached. In our example, the price of both food and clothing might be 2; we know from the previous analysis that when the price of clothing is equal to the price of food, the market will be in competitive equilibrium. (Recall that only relative prices matter; prices of 2 for clothing and food are equivalent to prices of 1 for each.)

Note the important difference between exchange with two people and an economy with many people. When only two people are involved, bargaining leaves the outcome indeterminate. However, when many people are involved, the prices of the goods are determined by the combined choices of demanders and suppliers of goods.

> • **excess demand** When the quantity demanded of a good exceeds the quantity supplied.
>
> • **excess supply** When the quantity supplied of a good exceeds the quantity demanded.

## The Economic Efficiency of Competitive Markets

We can now understand one of the fundamental results of microeconomic analysis. We can see from point C in Figure 16.6 that *the allocation in a competitive equilibrium is economically efficient*. The key reason why this is so is that C must occur at the tangency of two indifference curves. If it does not, one of the Jameses or one of the Karens will not be achieving maximum satisfaction; he or she will be willing to trade to achieve a higher level of utility.

This result holds in an exchange framework and in a general equilibrium setting in which all markets are perfectly competitive. It is the most direct way of illustrating the workings of Adam Smith's famous *invisible hand*, because it tells us that the economy will automatically allocate resources efficiently without the need for regulatory control. It is the independent actions of consumers and producers, who take prices as given, that allows markets to function in an economically efficient manner. Not surprisingly, the invisible-hand result is often used as the norm against which the workings of all real-world markets are compared. For some, the invisible hand supports the normative argument for less government intervention; they argue that markets are highly competitive. For others, the invisible hand supports a more expansive role for government; they reply that intervention is needed to make markets more competitive.

Whatever one's view of government intervention, most economists consider the invisible-hand result important. In fact, the result that a competitive equilibrium is economically efficient is often described as the first theorem of **welfare economics**, which involves the normative evaluation of markets and economic policy. Formally, the first theorem states the following:

• **welfare economics**
Normative evaluation of markets and economic policy.

> If everyone trades in the competitive marketplace, all mutually beneficial trades will be completed and the resulting equilibrium allocation of resources will be economically efficient.

Let's summarize what we know about a competitive equilibrium from the consumer's perspective:

1. Because the indifference curves are tangent, all marginal rates of substitution between consumers are equal.

2. Because each indifference curve is tangent to the price line, each person's MRS of clothing for food is equal to the ratio of the prices of the two goods.

To be as clear as possible, we will use the notation $\mathrm{MRS_{FC}}$ to denote the MRS *of food for clothing*. Then, if $P_C$ and $P_F$ are the two prices,

$$\mathrm{MRS}^{J}_{FC} = P_F/P_C = \mathrm{MRS}^{K}_{FC} \qquad (16.1)$$

To achieve an efficient allocation when there are many consumers (and many producers) is not easy. It can be done if all markets are perfectly competitive. But efficient outcomes can also be achieved by other means—for example, through a centralized system in which the government allocates all goods and services. The competitive solution is often preferred because it allocates  resources with a minimum of information. All consumers must know their own preferences and the prices they face, but they need not know what is being produced or the demands of other consumers. Other allocation methods need more information, and as a result, they become difficult and cumbersome to manage.

## 16.3 EQUITY AND EFFICIENCY

We have shown that different efficient allocations of goods are possible, and we have seen how a perfectly competitive economy generates an efficient allocation. But some allocations are likely to be more fair than others. How do we decide what is the most *equitable* allocation? That is a difficult question—economists and others disagree both about how to define *equity* and how to quantify it. Any such view would involve subjective comparisons of utility, and reasonable people could disagree about how to make these comparisons. In this section, we discuss this general point and then illustrate it in a particular case by showing that there is no reason to believe that the allocation associated with a competitive equilibrium will be equitable.

### The Utility Possibilities Frontier

Recall that every point on the contract curve in our two-person exchange economy shows the levels of utility that James and Karen can achieve. In Figure 16.7 we put the information from the Edgeworth box in a different form. James's utility is measured on the horizontal axis and Karen's on the vertical axis. Every point in the Edgeworth box corresponds to a point in Figure 16.7 because every allocation generates utility for both people. Every movement to the right in

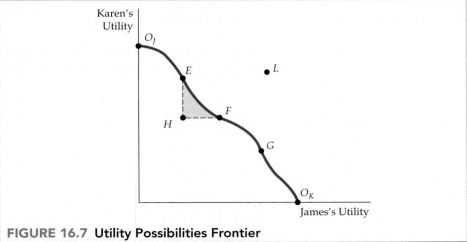

**FIGURE 16.7 Utility Possibilities Frontier**

The utility possibilities frontier shows the levels of satisfaction that each of two people achieve when they have traded to an efficient outcome on the contract curve. Points *E*, *F*, and *G* correspond to points on the contract curve and are efficient. Point *H* is inefficient because any trade within the shaded area will make one or both people better off.

Figure 16.7 represents an increase in James's utility, and every upward movement an increase in Karen's.

• **utility possibilities frontier**
Curve showing all efficient allocations of resources measured in terms of the utility levels of two individuals.

The **utility possibilities frontier** *represents all allocations that are efficient*. It shows the levels of satisfaction that are achieved when the two individuals have reached the contract curve. Point $O_J$ is one extreme at which James has no goods and therefore zero utility, while point $O_K$ is the opposite extreme at which Karen has no goods. Because all other points on the frontier, such as *E*, *F*, and *G*, correspond to points on the contract curve, one person cannot be made better off without making the other worse off. Point *H*, however, represents an inefficient allocation because any trade within the shaded area makes one or both parties better off. At *L*, both people would be better off, but *L* is not attainable because there is not enough of both goods to generate the levels of utility that the point represents.

It might seem reasonable to conclude that an allocation must be Pareto efficient to be equitable. Compare point *H* with *F* and *E*. Both *F* and *E* are efficient, and (relative to *H*) each makes one person better off without making the other worse off. We might agree, therefore, that it is inequitable to James or Karen or both for an economy to yield allocation *H* as opposed to *F* or *E*.

But suppose *H* and *G* are the only possible allocations. Is *G* more equitable than *H*? Not necessarily. Compared with *H*, *G* yields more utility for James and less for Karen. Some people may feel that *G* is more equitable than *H*; others may feel the opposite. We can conclude, therefore, that *one inefficient allocation of resources may be more equitable than another efficient allocation*.

The problem is how to define an equitable allocation. Even if we restrict ourselves to all points on the utility possibilities frontier, we can still ask which of these points is the most equitable. *The answer depends on what one thinks equity entails* and, therefore, on the interpersonal comparisons of utility that one is willing to make.

• **social welfare function**
Measure describing the well-being of society as a whole in terms of the utilities of individual members.

**Social Welfare Functions** In economics, we often use a **social welfare function** to describe the well-being of society as a whole in terms of utilities of individual members. A social welfare function is useful when we want to evaluate policies that affect some members of society differently than others.

One such function, the *utilitarian*, weights everyone's utility equally and consequently maximizes the total utility of all members of society. Each social welfare function can be associated with a particular view about equity. But some views do not explicitly weight individual utilities and cannot therefore be represented by a social welfare function. For example, a market-oriented view argues that the outcome of the competitive market process is equitable because it rewards those who are most able and who work the hardest. If *E* is the competitive equilibrium allocation, for example, *E* would be deemed to be more equitable than *F*, even though goods are less equally allocated.

When more than two people are involved, the meaning of the word *equity* becomes even more complex. The *Rawlsian* view[3] considers a world in which individuals do not know what their individual endowments will be. Rawls argues that, faced with a world in which you do not know your own "fate," you would opt for a system assuring that the least well-off person in society will be treated reasonably well. Specifically, according to Rawls, *the most equitable allocation maximizes the utility of the least-well-off person in society*. The Rawlsian perspective could be *egalitarian*—involving an equal allocation of goods among all members of society. But it need not be. Suppose that by rewarding more productive people more highly than less productive people, we can get the most productive people to work harder. This policy could produce more goods and services, some of which could then be reallocated to make the poorest members of society better off.

The four views of equity in Table 16.2 move roughly from most to least egalitarian. While the egalitarian view explicitly requires equal allocations, the Rawlsian puts a heavy weight on equality (otherwise, some people would be much worse off than others). The utilitarian is likely to require some difference between the best- and worst-off members of society. Finally, the market-oriented view may lead to substantial inequality in the allocations of goods and services.

## Equity and Perfect Competition

A competitive equilibrium leads to a Pareto efficient outcome that may or may not be equitable. In fact, a competitive equilibrium could occur at any point on the contract curve, depending on the initial allocation. Imagine, for example, that the initial allocation gave all food and clothing to Karen. This would be at $O_J$ in Figure 16.7, and Karen would have no reason to trade. Point $O_J$ would then be a competitive equilibrium, as would point $O_K$ and all intermediate points on the contract curve.

Because efficient allocations are not necessarily equitable, society must rely to some extent on government to achieve equity goals by redistributing income or goods among households. These goals can be reached through the tax system. For example, a progressive income tax whose funds are used for programs that benefit households proportionally to income will redistribute income from the wealthy to the poor. The government can also provide public services, such as

| TABLE 16.2   Four Views of Equity |
| --- |
| 1. Egalitarian—all members of society receive equal amounts of goods |
| 2. Rawlsian—maximize the utility of the least-well-off person |
| 3. Utilitarian—maximize the total utility of all members of society |
| 4. Market-oriented—the market outcome is the most equitable |

[3]See John Rawls, *A Theory of Justice* (New York: Oxford University Press, 1971).

medical aid to the poor (Medicaid), or it can transfer funds through such programs as Food Stamps.

The result that a competitive equilibrium can sustain every point on the contract curve is a fundamental result in microeconomics. It is important because it suggests an answer to a basic normative question: Is there a trade-off between equity and efficiency? In other words, must a society that wishes to achieve a more equitable allocation of resources necessarily operate in an economically inefficient manner? The answer, which is given by the *second theorem of welfare economics*, tells us that redistribution need not conflict with economic efficiency. Formally, the second theorem states the following:

> If individual preferences are convex, then every efficient allocation (every point on the contract curve) is a competitive equilibrium for some initial allocation of goods.

> Recall from § 3.1 that an indifference curve is convex if the MRS diminishes as one moves down along the curve.

Literally, this theorem tells us that any equilibrium deemed to be equitable can be achieved by a suitable distribution of resources among individuals and that such a distribution need not in itself generate inefficiencies. Unfortunately, all programs that redistribute income in our society are economically costly. Taxes may encourage individuals to work less or cause firms to devote resources to avoiding taxes rather than to producing output. So, in effect, there is a trade-off between the goals of equity and efficiency, and hard choices must be made. Welfare economics, which builds on the first and second theorems, provides a useful framework for debating the normative issues that surround the equity–efficiency issue in public policy.

## 16.4 EFFICIENCY IN PRODUCTION

Having described the conditions required to achieve an efficient allocation in the exchange of two goods, we now consider the efficient use of inputs in the production process. We assume that there are fixed total supplies of two inputs, labor and capital, which are needed to produce the same two products, food and clothing. Instead of only two people, however, we now assume that many consumers own the inputs to production (including labor) and earn income by selling them. This income, in turn, is allocated between the two goods.

This framework links the various supply and demand elements of the economy. People supply inputs to production and then use the income they earn to demand and consume goods and services. When the price of one input increases, the individuals who supply a lot of that input earn more income and consume more of one of the two goods. In turn, this increases the demand for the inputs needed to produce the good and has a feedback effect on the price of those inputs. Only a general equilibrium analysis can find the prices that equate supply and demand in every market.

### Input Efficiency

To see how inputs can be combined efficiently, we must find the various combinations of inputs that can be used to produce each of the two outputs. A particular allocation of inputs into the production process is **technically efficient** if the output of one good cannot be increased without decreasing the output of another good. Efficiency in production is not a new concept; in Chapter 6 we saw that a production function represents the maximum output that can be

• **technical efficiency**
Condition under which firms combine inputs to produce a given output as inexpensively as possible.

achieved with a given set of inputs. Here we extend the concept to the production of two goods rather than one.

If input markets are competitive, a point of efficient production will be achieved. Let's see why. If the labor and capital markets are perfectly competitive, then the wage rate $w$ will be the same in all industries. Likewise, the rental rate of capital $r$ will be the same whether capital is used in the food or clothing industry. We know from Chapter 7 that if producers of food and clothing minimize production costs, they will use combinations of labor and capital so that the ratio of the marginal products of the two inputs is equal to the ratio of the input prices:

$$\mathrm{MP}_L/\mathrm{MP}_K = w/r$$

> In §7.3, we explain that the rental rate is the cost per year for renting a unit of capital.

But we also showed that the ratio of the marginal products of the two inputs is equal to the marginal rate of technical substitution of labor for capital $\mathrm{MRTS}_{LK}$. As a result,

$$\mathrm{MRTS}_{LK} = w/r \qquad \textbf{(16.2)}$$

> In §6.3, we explain that the marginal rate of technical substitution of labor for capital is the amount by which the input of capital can be reduced when one extra unit of labor is used, so that output remains constant.

Because the MRTS is the slope of the firm's isoquant, a competitive equilibrium can occur in the input market only if each producer uses labor and capital so that the slopes of the isoquants are equal to one another and to the ratio of the prices of the two inputs. As a result, *the competitive equilibrium is efficient in production.*

## The Production Possibilities Frontier

The **production possibilities frontier** shows the various combinations of food and clothing that can be produced with fixed inputs of labor and capital, holding technology constant. The frontier in Figure 16.8 is derived from the production contract curve. Each point on both the contract curve and the

> • **production possibilities frontier** Curve showing the combinations of two goods that can be produced with fixed quantities of inputs.

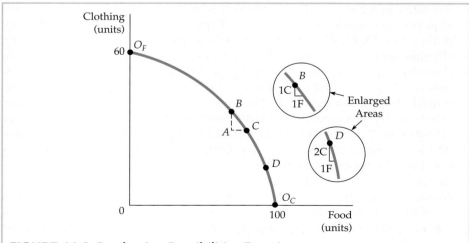

**FIGURE 16.8 Production Possibilities Frontier**

The production possibilities frontier shows all efficient combinations of outputs. The production possibilities frontier is concave because its slope (the marginal rate of transformation) increases as the level of production of food increases.

production possibilities frontier describes an efficiently produced level of both food and clothing.

Point $O_F$ represents one extreme, in which only clothing is produced, and $O_C$ represents the other extreme, in which only food is produced. Points B, C, and D correspond to points at which both food and clothing are efficiently produced.

Point A, representing an inefficient allocation, lies inside the production possibilities frontier. All points within the triangle ABC involve the complete utilization of labor and capital in the production process. However, a distortion in the labor market, perhaps due to a rent-maximizing union, has caused the economy as a whole to be productively inefficient.

Where we end up on the production possibilities frontier depends on consumer demand for the two goods. For example, suppose consumers tend to prefer food rather than clothing. A possible competitive equilibrium occurs at D in Figure 16.8. On the other hand, if consumers prefer clothing to food, the competitive equilibrium will occur on a point on the production possibilities frontier closer to $O_F$.

Why is the production possibilities frontier downward sloping? In order to produce more food efficiently, one must switch inputs from the production of clothing, which in turn lowers the clothing production level. Because all points lying within the frontier are inefficient, they are off the production contract curve.

**Marginal Rate of Transformation** The production possibilities frontier is concave (bowed out)—i.e., its slope increases in magnitude as more food is produced. To describe this, we define the **marginal rate of transformation** of food for clothing (MRT) as the magnitude of the slope of the frontier at each point. *The MRT measures how much clothing must be given up to produce one additional unit of food.* For example, the enlarged areas of Figure 16.8 show that at B on the frontier, the MRT is 1 because 1 unit of clothing must be given up to obtain 1 additional unit of food. At D, however, the MRT is 2 because 2 units of clothing must be given up to obtain 1 more unit of food.

Note that as we increase the production of food by moving along the production possibilities frontier, the MRT increases.[4] This increase occurs because the productivity of labor and capital differs depending on whether the inputs are used to produce more food or clothing. Suppose we begin at $O_F$, where only clothing is produced. Now we remove some labor and capital from clothing production, where their marginal products are relatively low, and put them into food production, where their marginal products are high. Under these circumstances, to obtain the first unit of food, very little clothing production is lost. (The MRT is much less than 1.) But as we move along the frontier and produce less clothing, the productivities of labor and capital in clothing production rise and the productivities of labor and capital in food production fall. At B, the productivities are equal and the MRT is 1. Continuing along the frontier, we note that because the input productivities in clothing rise more and the productivities in food decrease, the MRT becomes greater than 1.

We can also describe the shape of the production possibilities frontier in terms of the costs of production. At $O_F$, where very little clothing output is lost to produce additional food, the marginal cost of producing food is very low: A lot

---

Recall from §14.4 that a rent-maximizing union attempts to maximize the wages that members earn in excess of their opportunity cost.

• **marginal rate of transformation** Amount of one good that must be given up to produce one additional unit of a second good.

---

[4]The production possibilities frontier need not have a continually increasing MRT. Suppose, for example, that there are strongly decreasing returns to scale in the production of food. In that case, as inputs are moved from clothing to food production, the amount of clothing that must be given up to obtain one more unit of food will decline.

of output is produced with very little input. Conversely, the marginal cost of producing clothing is very high: It takes a lot of both inputs to produce another unit of clothing. Thus, when the MRT is low, so is the ratio of the marginal cost of producing food $MC_F$ to the marginal cost of producing clothing $MC_C$. In fact, *the slope of the production possibilities frontier measures the marginal cost of producing one good relative to the marginal cost of producing the other*. The curvature of the production possibilities frontier follows directly from the fact that the marginal cost of producing food relative to the marginal cost of producing clothing is increasing. At every point along the frontier, the following condition holds:

$$\text{MRT} = MC_F/MC_C \qquad (16.3)$$

At *B*, for example, the MRT is equal to 1. Here, when inputs are switched from clothing to food production, 1 unit of output is lost and 1 is gained. If the input cost of producing 1 unit of either good is $100, the ratio of the marginal costs would be $100/$100, or 1. Equation (16.3) also holds at *D* (and at every other point on the frontier). Suppose the inputs needed to produce 1 unit of food cost $160. The marginal cost of food would be $160, but the marginal cost of clothing would be only $80 ($160/2 units of clothing). As a result, the ratio of the marginal costs, 2, is equal to the MRT.

## Output Efficiency

For an economy to be efficient, goods must not only be produced at minimum cost; *goods must also be produced in combinations that match people's willingness to pay for them*. To understand this principle, recall from Chapter 3 that the marginal rate of substitution of clothing for food (MRS) measures the consumer's willingness to pay for an additional unit of food by consuming less clothing. The marginal rate of transformation measures the cost of an additional unit of food in terms of producing less clothing. An economy produces output efficiently only if, for each consumer,

$$\text{MRS} = \text{MRT} \qquad (16.4)$$

To see why this condition is necessary for efficiency, suppose the MRT equals 1, while the MRS equals 2. In that case, consumers are willing to give up 2 units of clothing to get 1 unit of food, but the cost of getting the additional food is only 1 unit of lost clothing. Clearly, too little food is being produced. To achieve efficiency, food production must be increased until the MRS falls and the MRT increases and the two are equal. The outcome is efficient only when MRS = MRT for all pairs of goods.

Figure 16.9 shows this important efficiency condition graphically. Here, we have superimposed one consumer's indifference curve on the production possibilities frontier from Figure 16.8. Note that *C* is the only point on the production possibilities frontier that maximizes the consumer's satisfaction. Although all points on the production frontier are technically efficient, not all involve the most efficient production of goods from the consumer's perspective. At the point of tangency of the indifference curve and the production frontier, the MRS (the slope of the indifference curve) and the MRT (the slope of the production frontier) are equal.

If you were a planner in charge of managing an economy, you would face a difficult problem. To achieve efficiency, you must equate the marginal rate of transformation with the consumer's marginal rate of substitution. But if

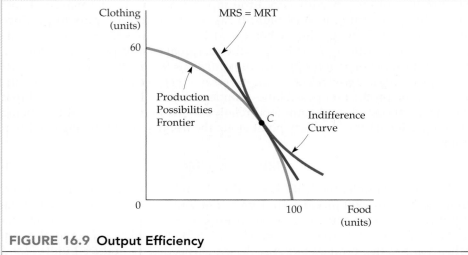

**FIGURE 16.9 Output Efficiency**

The efficient combination of outputs is produced when the marginal rate of transformation between the two goods (which measures the cost of producing one good relative to the other) is equal to the consumer's marginal rate of substitution (which measures the marginal benefit of consuming one good relative to the other).

different consumers have different preferences for food and clothing, how can you decide what levels of food and clothing to produce and what amount of each to give to every consumer, so that all consumers have the same MRS? The informational and logistical costs are enormous. That is one reason why centrally planned economies, like that of the former Soviet Union, performed so poorly. Fortunately, a well-functioning competitive market system can achieve the same efficient outcome as an ideal managed economy.

## Efficiency in Output Markets

When output markets are perfectly competitive, all consumers allocate their budgets so that their marginal rates of substitution between two goods are equal to the price ratio. For our two goods, food and clothing,

$$MRS = P_F/P_C$$

At the same time, each profit-maximizing firm will produce its output up to the point at which price is equal to marginal cost. Again, for our two goods,

$$P_F = MC_F \quad \text{and} \quad P_C = MC_C$$

Because the marginal rate of transformation is equal to the ratio of the marginal costs of production, it follows that

$$MRT = MC_F/MC_C = P_F/P_C = MRS \tag{16.5}$$

When output and input markets are competitive, production will be efficient in that the MRT is equal to the MRS. This condition is just another version of the marginal benefit–marginal cost rule discussed in Chapter 4. There we saw that consumers buy additional units of a good up to the point at which the marginal benefit of consumption is equal to the marginal cost. Here we see that the production of food and clothing is chosen so that the marginal benefit of consuming

---

*In §3.3, we explain that utility maximization is generally achieved when the marginal rate of substitution of one good for another is equal to the ratio of their two prices.*

*In §3.3, we explain that utility maximization is achieved when the marginal benefit of consuming an additional unit of each product is equal to its marginal cost.*

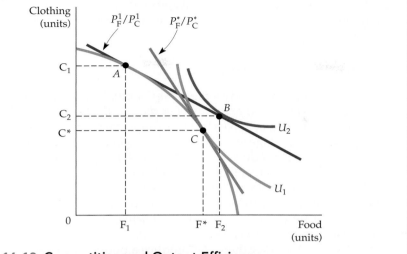

**FIGURE 16.10 Competition and Output Efficiency**

In a competitive output market, people consume to the point where their marginal rate of substitution is equal to the price ratio. Producers choose outputs so that the marginal rate of transformation is equal to the price ratio. Because the MRS equals the MRT, the competitive output market is efficient. Any other price ratio will lead to an excess demand for one good and an excess supply of the other.

another unit of food is equal to the marginal cost of producing another unit of food; the same is true for the consumption and production of clothing.

Figure 16.10 shows that efficient competitive output markets are achieved when production and consumption choices are separated. Suppose the market generates a price ratio of $P_F^1/P_C^1$. If producers are using inputs efficiently, they will produce food and clothing at $A$, where the price ratio is equal to the MRT, the slope of the production possibilities frontier. When faced with this budget constraint, however, consumers would like to consume at $B$, where they maximize their satisfaction at the higher indifference curve $U_2$. However, at the price ratio $P_F^1/P_C^1$, producers will not produce the combination of food and clothing at $B$. Because the producer wants to produce $F_1$ units of food, while consumers want to buy $F_2$, there will be an excess demand for food. Correspondingly, because consumers wish to buy $C_2$ units of clothing while producers wish to sell $C_1$, there will be an excess supply of clothing. Prices in the market will then adjust: The price of food will rise and that of clothing will fall. As price ratio $P_F/P_C$ increases, the price line will move along the production frontier.

An equilibrium results when the price ratio is $P_F^*/P_C^*$ at $C$. Here, producers want to sell $F^*$ units of food and $C^*$ units of clothing; consumers want to buy the same amounts. At this equilibrium, the MRT and the MRS are equal again; therefore, the competitive equilibrium is efficient.

# 16.5 THE GAINS FROM FREE TRADE

Clearly there are gains from international trade in an exchange economy. We have seen that two persons or two countries can benefit by trading to reach a point on the contract curve. However, there are additional gains from trade when the economies of two countries differ so that one country has a *comparative advantage* in producing one good while the other has a comparative advantage in producing another.

## Comparative Advantage

• **comparative advantage**
Situation in which Country 1 has an advantage over Country 2 in producing a good because the cost of producing the good in 1, relative to the cost of producing other goods in 1, is lower than the cost of producing the good in 2, relative to the cost of producing other goods in 2.

*Country 1 has a* **comparative advantage** *over Country 2 in producing a good if the cost of producing that good, relative to the cost of producing other goods in 1, is lower than the cost of producing the good in 2, relative to the cost of producing other goods in 2.*[5] Note that comparative advantage is not the same as *absolute* advantage. A country has an **absolute advantage** in producing a good if its cost is lower than the cost in another country. A comparative advantage, on the other hand, implies that a country's cost, *relative to the costs of other goods it produces*, is lower than the other country's.

• **absolute advantage**
Situation in which Country 1 has an advantage over Country 2 in producing a good because the cost of producing the good in 1 is lower than the cost of producing it in 2.

When each of two countries has a comparative advantage, they are better off producing what they are best at and purchasing the rest. To see this, suppose that the first country, Holland, has an *absolute* advantage in producing both cheese and wine. A worker there can produce a pound of cheese in 1 hour and a gallon of wine in 2 hours. In Italy, on the other hand, it takes a worker 6 hours to produce a pound of cheese and 3 hours to produce a gallon of wine. The production relationships are summarized in Table 16.3.[6]

Holland has a *comparative* advantage over Italy in producing cheese. Holland's cost of cheese production (in terms of hours of labor used) is half its cost of producing wine, whereas Italy's cost of producing cheese is twice its cost of producing wine. Likewise, Italy has a comparative advantage in producing wine, which it can produce at half the cost at which it can produce cheese.

**What Happens when Nations Trade** The comparative advantage of each country determines what happens when they trade. The outcome will depend on the price of each good relative to the other when trade occurs. To see how this might work, suppose that with trade, one gallon of wine sells for the same price as one pound of cheese in both Holland and Italy. Suppose also that because there is full employment in both countries, the only way to increase production of wine is to take labor out of the production of cheese, and vice versa.

Without trade, Holland could, with 24 hours of labor input, produce 24 pounds of cheese, 12 gallons of wine, or a combination of the two, such as 18 pounds of cheese and 3 gallons of wine. But Holland can do better. For every hour of labor Holland can produce 1 pound of cheese, which it can trade for 1

| TABLE 16.3 | Hours of Labor Required to Produce Cheese and Wine | |
| --- | --- | --- |
| | **Cheese (1 *LB*)** | **Wine (1 *GAL*)** |
| Holland | 1 | 2 |
| Italy | 6 | 3 |

---

[5]Formally, if there are 2 goods, $x$ and $y$, and 2 countries, $i$ and $j$, we say that country $i$ has a comparative advantage in the production of good $x$ if $\dfrac{a_x^i}{a_y^i} < \dfrac{a_x^j}{a_y^j}$ where $a_x^i$ is the cost of producing good $x$ in county $i$.

[6]This example is based on "World Trade: Jousting for Advantage," *The Economist* (September 22, 1990): 5–40.

gallon of wine; if the wine were produced at home, 2 hours of labor would be required. It is, therefore, in Holland's interest to specialize in the production of cheese, which it will export to Italy in exchange for wine. If, for example, Holland produced 24 pounds of cheese and traded 6, it would be able to consume 18 pounds of cheese and 6 gallons of wine—a definite improvement over the 18 pounds of cheese and 3 gallons of wine available in the absence of trade.

Italy is also better off with trade. Note that without trade, Italy can, with the same 24 hours of labor input, produce 4 pounds of cheese, 8 gallons of wine, or a combination of the two, such as 3 pounds of cheese and 2 gallons of wine. On the other hand, with every hour of labor, Italy can produce one-third of a gallon of wine, which it can trade for one-third of a pound of cheese. If it produced cheese at home, twice as much time would be involved. Specialization in wine production, therefore, is advantageous for Italy. Suppose that Italy produced 8 gallons of wine and traded 6; in that case, it would be able to consume 6 pounds of cheese and 2 gallons of wine—likewise an improvement over the 3 pounds of cheese and 2 gallons of wine available without trade.

## An Expanded Production Possibilities Frontier

When there is comparative advantage, international trade has the effect of allowing a country to consume outside its production possibilities frontier. This can be seen graphically in Figure 16.11, which shows a production possibilities frontier for Holland. Suppose initially that Holland has been prevented from

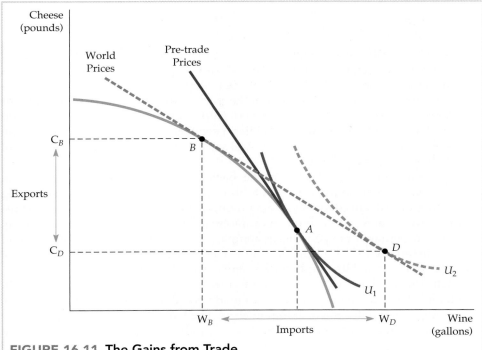

**FIGURE 16.11 The Gains from Trade**

Without trade, production and consumption are at point $A$, where the price of wine is twice the price of cheese. With trade at a relative price of 1 cheese to 1 wine, domestic production is now at $B$, while domestic consumption is at $D$. Free trade has allowed utility to increase from $U_1$ to $U_2$.

trading with Italy because of a protectionist trade barrier. What is the outcome of the competitive process in Holland? Production is at point $A$, on indifference curve $U_1$, where the MRT and the pre-trade price of wine is twice the price of cheese. If Holland were able to trade, it would want to export 2 pounds of cheese in exchange for 1 gallon of wine.

Suppose now that the trade barrier is dropped and Holland and Italy are both open to trade. Suppose also that, as a result of differences in demand and costs in the two countries, trade occurs on a one-to-one basis. Holland will find it advantageous to produce at point $B$, the point of tangency of the 1/1 price line and Holland's production possibilities frontier.

That is not the end of the story, however. Point $B$ represents the production decision in Holland. (Once the trade barrier has been removed, Holland will produce less wine and more cheese domestically.) With trade, however, consumption will occur at point $D$, at which the higher indifference curve $U_2$ is tangent to the trade price line. Thus trade has the effect of expanding Holland's consumption choices beyond its production possibilities frontier. Holland will import $W_D - W_B$ units of wine and export $C_B - C_D$ units of cheese.

With trade, each country will undergo a number of important adjustments. As Holland imports wine, the production of domestic wine will fall, as will employment in the wine industry. Cheese production will increase, however, as will the number of jobs in that industry. Workers with job-specific skills may find it difficult to change employment. Not everyone will, therefore, gain as the result of free trade. Although consumers will clearly be better off, producers of wine and workers in the wine industry are likely to be worse off, at least temporarily.

---

**EXAMPLE 16.2**   Trading Tasks and iPod Production

Most people think of foreign trade as importing or exporting manufactured products. However, trade often involves many steps that transform raw materials into finished products. At each of these steps, intermediate goods are combined with labor or machines to make part or all of finished products. For instance, workers might assemble a set of chips and other components for a computer. Thus, a typical product embodies a sequence of tasks, each of which can also be traded. Where and how those tasks are performed is an important part of efficient production and trade.[7]

Consider an Apple iPod. On the back, it says "Designed by Apple in California. Assembled in China." But this is only the beginning and end of a long sequence of tasks needed to make an iPod, as can be seen in Table 16.4.[8] Three things are of note. First, iPod manufacturing is a truly global undertaking. Product design occurs in one place, company management somewhere else, and actual assembly in yet a third location. This is true not only for the iPod as a whole, but also for its major components. This "unbundling" of production, which allows firms to use different countries' comparative advantages in different steps of production, has been made possible by better communications technology and a decline in shipping costs. The United States, for instance, may have a comparative advantage in the task of product design. The designs are sent

---

[7]Gene M. Grossman and Esteban Rossi-Hansberg, "The Rise of Offshoring: It's Not Wine for Cloth Anymore," Working Paper, Princeton University, 2006.

[8]This example is based on Greg Linden, Kenneth L. Kraemer, and Jason Dedrick, "Who Captures Value in a Global Innovation System? The case of Apple's iPod," PCIC UC-Irvine, June 2007.

| Component | Company | Manufacturing Location | Price ($) | % of Retail Price |
|---|---|---|---|---|
| Product Design / Concept | Apple (U.S.) | U.S. | 79.85 | 26.7 |
| Hard Drive (30GB) | Toshiba (Japan) | China | 73.39 | 24.6 |
| Display | Matsushita & Toshiba | Japan | 20.39 | 6.8 |
| Video Processor | Broadcom (U.S.) | Taiwan or Singapore | 8.36 | 2.8 |
| Central Processor | PortalPlayer (U.S.) | U.S. or Taiwan | 4.94 | 1.7 |
| Unit Assembly | Inventec (Taiwan) | China | 3.70 | 1.2 |
| All other parts (about 450) | - | - | 33.62 | 11.2 |
| Total Parts | - | - | 144.40 | 48.3 |
| Distribution and Retail | - | U.S. | 74.75 | 25.0 |
| Final Retail Price (2005) | | | 299.00 | 100.0 |

**TABLE 16.4  Different Tasks in iPod Production**

to China, which has a comparative advantage in the task of assembly. The assembled product is then shipped back to the United States, where U.S. companies perform distribution and retail tasks.

Second, note that most of an iPod's components are semi-finished products, such as hard drives or displays, rather than raw materials, such as plastic or silicon. To make production more efficient, specialized firms design and manufacture most parts. Certainly, Apple could have set up its own factories to make processors, hard drives, or displays, but it is more efficient to trade and make use of the production skills of other firms in other countries. For instance, Toshiba may have a comparative advantage in making hard drives because of the sheer scale of its production capacity.

Finally, observe that physical parts account for just under half of the iPod's retail price. As with most products, a bundle of different services is needed to design, develop, and distribute the iPod. The firms that perform those services—Apple included—also end up with a sizable share of the final selling price.

## EXAMPLE 16.3  The Costs and Benefits of Special Protection

The demands for protectionist policies increased steadily during the 1980s and into the 1990s. They remain a subject of debate today, whether out of concern for trade with various Asian countries or in relation to the North American Free Trade Agreement (NAFTA). Protectionism can take many forms, including tariffs and quotas of the kind that we analyzed in Chapter 9, regulatory hurdles, subsidies to domestic producers, and controls on the use of

### TABLE 16.5 Quantifying the Costs of Protection

| Industry | Producer Gains[a] ($ Millions) | Consumer Losses[b] ($ Millions) | Efficiency Losses[c] ($ Millions) |
|---|---|---|---|
| Book manufacturing | 305 | 500 | 29 |
| Orange juice | 390 | 525 | 130 |
| Textiles and apparel | 22,000 | 27,000 | 4850 |
| Carbon steel | 3800 | 6800 | 330 |
| Color televisions | 190 | 420 | 7 |
| Sugar | 550 | 930 | 130 |
| Dairy products | 5000 | 5500 | 1370 |
| Meat | 1600 | 1800 | 145 |

[a]Producer gains in the tariff case are defined as the area of trapezoid *A* in Figure 9.15.
[b]Consumer losses are the sum of areas *A*, *B*, *C*, and *D* in Figure 9.15.
[c]These are given by triangles *B* and *C* in Figure 9.15.

foreign exchange. Table 16.5 highlights the findings of one study of U.S.-imposed trade restrictions.[9]

Because one of the major purposes of protectionism is to protect jobs in particular industries, it is not surprising that these policies create gains to producers. The costs, however, involve losses to consumers and a substantial reduction in economic efficiency. These efficiency losses are the sum of the loss of producer surplus resulting from inefficient excess domestic production and the loss of consumer surplus resulting from higher domestic prices and lower consumption.

As Table 16.5 shows, the textiles and apparel industry is the largest source of efficiency losses. Although there were substantial gains to producers, consumer losses are larger in each case. In addition, efficiency losses from excess (inefficient) domestic production of textiles and reduced domestic consumption of imported textile products were also large—an estimated $4.85 billion. The second largest source of inefficiency was the dairy industry, where losses amounted to $1.37 billion.

Finally, note that the efficiency cost of helping domestic producers varies considerably across industries. In textiles the ratio of efficiency costs to producer gains is 22 percent and in dairy products 27 percent; only orange juice is higher (33.3 percent). However, much lower ratios apply to color televisions (3.7 percent), carbon steel (8.7 percent), and book manufacturing (9.5 percent).

> In §9.1, we explain that consumer surplus is the total benefit or value that consumers receive beyond what they pay for a good; producer surplus is the analogous measure for producers.

## 16.6 AN OVERVIEW—THE EFFICIENCY OF COMPETITIVE MARKETS

Our analysis of general equilibrium and economic efficiency is now complete. In the process, we have obtained two remarkable results. First, we have shown that for any initial allocation of resources, a competitive process of exchange

---

[9]This example is based on Cletus Coughlin, K. Alec Chrystal, and Geoffrey E. Wood, "Protectionist Trade Policies: A Survey of Theory, Evidence, and Rationale," *Federal Reserve Bank of St. Louis* (January/February 1988): 12–30. The data in the table are taken from Gary Clyde Hufbauer, Diane T. Berliner, and Kimberly Ann Elliott, "Trade Protection in the United States: 31 Case Studies," *Institute for International Economics* (1986).

among individuals, whether through exchange, input markets, or output markets, will lead to an economically efficient outcome. The first theorem of welfare economics tells us that a competitive system, building on the self-interested goals of consumers and producers and on the ability of market prices to convey information to both parties, will achieve an efficient allocation of resources.

Second, we have shown that with indifference curves that are convex, any efficient allocation of resources can be achieved by a competitive process with a suitable redistribution of those resources. The second theorem of welfare economics tells us that under certain (admittedly ideal) conditions, issues of equity and efficiency can be treated distinctly from one another.

Both theorems of welfare economics depend crucially on the assumption that markets are competitive. Unfortunately, neither of these results necessarily holds when, for some reason, markets are no longer competitive. In the next two chapters, we will discuss ways in which markets fail and what government can do about it. Before proceeding, however, it is essential to review our understanding of the workings of the competitive process. We thus list the conditions required for economic efficiency in exchange, in input markets, and in output markets. These conditions are important; in each of these three cases, you should review the explanation of the conditions in this chapter and the underlying building blocks in prior chapters.

1. *Efficiency in exchange:* All allocations must lie on the exchange contract curve so that every consumer's marginal rate of substitution of food for clothing is the same:

$$MRS^J_{FC} = MRS^K_{FC}$$

A competitive market achieves this efficient outcome because, for consumers, the tangency of the budget line and the highest attainable indifference curve assure that:

$$MRS^J_{FC} = P_F/P_C = MRS^K_{FC}$$

> Recall from §3.3 that consumer satisfaction is maximized when the marginal rate of substitution of food for clothing is equal to the ratio of the price of food to that of clothing.

2. *Efficiency in the use of inputs in production:* Every producer's marginal rate of technical substitution of labor for capital is equal in the production of both goods:

$$MRTS^F_{LK} = MRTS^C_{LK}$$

A competitive market achieves this efficient outcome because each producer maximizes profit by choosing labor and capital inputs so that the ratio of the input prices is equal to the marginal rate of technical substitution:

$$MRTS^F_{LK} = w/r = MRTS^C_{LK}$$

> Recall from §7.3 that profit maximization requires that the marginal rate of technical substitution of labor for capital be equal to the ratio of the wage rate to the cost of capital.

3. *Efficiency in the output market:* The mix of outputs must be chosen so that the marginal rate of transformation between outputs is equal to consumers' marginal rates of substitution:

$$MRT_{FC} = MRS_{FC} \text{ (for all consumers)}$$

A competitive market achieves this efficient outcome because profit-maximizing producers increase their output to the point at which marginal cost equals price:

$$P_F = MC_F, \qquad P_C = MC_C$$

> In §8.3, we explain that because a competitive firm faces a horizontal demand curve, choosing its output so that marginal cost is equal to price is profit-maximizing.

As a result,

$$MRT_{FC} = MC_F/MC_C = P_F/P_C$$

But consumers maximize their satisfaction in competitive markets only if

$$P_F/P_C = MRS_{FC} \text{ (for all consumers)}$$

Therefore,

$$MRS_{FC} = MRT_{FC}$$

and the output efficiency conditions are satisfied. Thus efficiency requires that goods be produced in combinations and at costs that match people's willingness to pay for them.

## 16.7 WHY MARKETS FAIL

We can give two different interpretations of the conditions required for efficiency. The first stresses that competitive markets work. It also tells us that we ought to ensure that the prerequisites for competition hold, so that resources can be efficiently allocated. The second stresses that the prerequisites for competition are unlikely to hold. It tells us that we ought to concentrate on ways of dealing with market failures. Thus far we have focused on the first interpretation. For the remainder of the book, we concentrate on the second.

Competitive markets fail for four basic reasons: *market power, incomplete information, externalities,* and *public goods.* We will discuss each in turn.

### Market Power

We have seen that inefficiency arises when a producer or supplier of a factor input has market power. Suppose, for example, that the producer of food in our Edgeworth box diagram has monopoly power. It therefore chooses the output quantity at which marginal revenue (rather than price) is equal to marginal cost and sells less output at a price higher than it would charge in a competitive market. The lower output will mean a lower marginal cost of food production. Meanwhile, the freed-up production inputs will be allocated to produce clothing, whose marginal cost will increase. As a result, the marginal rate of transformation will decrease because $MRT_{FC} = MC_F/MC_C$. We might end up, for example, at $A$ on the production possibilities frontier in Figure 16.8. Producing too little food and too much clothing is an output inefficiency because firms with market power use different prices in their output decisions than consumers use in their consumption decisions.

> In §10.2, we explain that a seller of a product has monopoly power if it can profitably charge a price greater than marginal cost; similarly, §10.5 explains that a buyer has monopsony power when its purchasing decision can affect the price of a good.

A similar argument would apply to market power in an input market. Suppose that unions gave workers market power over the supply of their labor in the production of food. Too little labor would then be supplied to the food industry at too high a wage ($w_F$) and too much labor to the clothing industry at too low a wage ($w_C$). In the clothing industry, the input efficiency conditions would be satisfied because $MRTS_{LK}^C = w_C/r$. But in the food industry, the wage paid would be greater than the wage paid in the clothing industry. Therefore, $MRTS_{LK}^F = w_F/r > w_C/r = MRTS_{LK}^C$. The result is input inefficiency because efficiency requires that the marginal rates of technical substitution be equal in the production of all goods.

## Incomplete Information

If consumers do not have accurate information about market prices or product quality, the market system will not operate efficiently. This lack of information may give producers an incentive to supply too much of some products and too little of others. In other cases, while some consumers may not buy a product even though they would benefit from doing so, others buy products that leave them worse off. For example, consumers may buy pills that guarantee weight loss, only to find that they have no medical value. Finally, a lack of information may prevent some markets from ever developing. It may, for example, be impossible to purchase certain kinds of insurance because suppliers of insurance lack adequate information about consumers likely to be at risk.

Each of these informational problems can lead to competitive market inefficiency. We will describe informational inefficiencies in detail in Chapter 17 and see whether government intervention might help to reduce them.

## Externalities

The price system works efficiently because market prices convey information to both producers and consumers. Sometimes, however, market prices do not reflect the activities of either producers or consumers. There is an *externality* when a consumption or production activity has an indirect effect on other consumption or production activities that is not reflected directly in market prices. As we explained in Section 9.2 (page 315), the word *externality* is used because the effects on others (whether benefits or costs) are external to the market.

Suppose, for example, that a steel plant dumps effluent in a river, thus making a recreation site downstream unsuitable for swimming or fishing. There is an externality because the steel producer does not bear the true cost of wastewater and so uses too much wastewater to produce its steel. This externality causes an input inefficiency. If this externality prevails throughout the industry, the price of steel (which is equal to the marginal cost of production) will be lower than if the cost of production reflected the effluent cost. As a result, too much steel will be produced, and there will be an output inefficiency.

We will discuss externalities and ways to deal with them in Chapter 18.

## Public Goods

The last source of market failure arises when the market fails to supply goods that many consumers value. A **public good** can be made available cheaply to many consumers, but once it is provided to some consumers, it is very difficult to prevent others from consuming it. For example, suppose a firm is considering whether to undertake research on a new technology for which it cannot obtain a patent. Once the invention is made public, others can duplicate it. As long as it is difficult to exclude other firms from selling the product, the research will be unprofitable.

Markets therefore undersupply public goods. We will see in Chapter 18 that government can sometimes resolve this problem either by supplying a good itself or by altering the incentives for private firms to produce it.

• **public good**
Nonexclusive, nonrival good that can be made available cheaply but which, once available, is difficult to prevent others from consuming.

## SUMMARY

1. Partial equilibrium analyses of markets assume that related markets are unaffected. General equilibrium analyses examine all markets simultaneously, taking into account feedback effects of other markets on the market being studied.

2. An allocation is efficient when no consumer can be made better off by trade without making someone else worse off. When consumers make all mutually advantageous trades, the outcome is Pareto efficient and lies on the contract curve.

3. A competitive equilibrium describes a set of prices and quantities. When each consumer chooses her most preferred allocation, the quantity demanded is equal to the quantity supplied in every market. All competitive equilibrium allocations lie on the exchange contract curve and are Pareto efficient.

4. The utility possibilities frontier measures all efficient allocations in terms of the levels of utility that each of two people achieves. Although both individuals prefer some allocations to an inefficient allocation, not *every* efficient allocation must be so preferred. Thus an inefficient allocation can be more equitable than an efficient one.

5. Because a competitive equilibrium need not be equitable, the government may wish to help redistribute wealth from rich to poor. Because such redistribution is costly, there is some conflict between equity and efficiency.

6. An allocation of production inputs is technically efficient if the output of one good cannot be increased without decreasing the output of another.

7. A competitive equilibrium in input markets occurs when the marginal rate of technical substitution between pairs of inputs is equal to the ratio of the prices of the inputs.

8. The production possibilities frontier measures all efficient allocations in terms of the levels of output that can be produced with a given combination of inputs. The marginal rate of transformation of good 1 for good 2 increases as more of good 1 and less of good 2 are produced. The marginal rate of transformation is equal to the ratio of the marginal cost of producing good 1 to the marginal cost of producing good 2.

9. Efficiency in the allocation of goods to consumers is achieved only when the marginal rate of substitution of one good for another in consumption (which is the same for all consumers) is equal to the marginal rate of transformation of one good for another in production.

10. When input and output markets are perfectly competitive, the marginal rate of substitution (which equals the ratio of the prices of the goods) will equal the marginal rate of transformation (which equals the ratio of the marginal costs of producing the goods).

11. Free international trade expands a country's production possibilities frontier. As a result, consumers are better off.

12. Competitive markets may be inefficient for four reasons. First, firms or consumers may have market power in input or output markets. Second, consumers or producers may have incomplete information and may therefore err in their consumption and production decisions. Third, externalities may be present. Fourth, some socially desirable public goods may not be produced.

## QUESTIONS FOR REVIEW

1. Why can feedback effects make a general equilibrium analysis substantially different from a partial equilibrium analysis?

2. In the Edgeworth box diagram, explain how one point can simultaneously represent the market baskets owned by two consumers.

3. In the analysis of exchange using the Edgeworth box diagram, explain why both consumers' marginal rates of substitution are equal at every point on the contract curve.

4. "Because all points on a contract curve are efficient, they are all equally desirable from a social point of view." Do you agree with this statement? Explain.

5. How does the utility possibilities frontier relate to the contract curve?

6. In the Edgeworth production box diagram, what conditions must hold for an allocation to be on the production contract curve? Why is a competitive equilibrium on the contract curve?

7. How is the production possibilities frontier related to the production contract curve?

8. What is the marginal rate of transformation (MRT)? Explain why the MRT of one good for another is equal to the ratio of the marginal costs of producing the two goods.

9. Explain why goods will not be distributed efficiently among consumers if the MRT is not equal to the consumers' marginal rate of substitution.

10. Why can free trade between two countries make consumers of both countries better off?

11. If Country A has an absolute advantage in the production of two goods compared to Country B, then it is not in Country A's best interest to trade with Country B. True or false? Explain.

12. Do you agree or disagree with each of the following statements? Explain.
    a. If it is possible to exchange 3 pounds of cheese for 2 bottles of wine, then the price of cheese is 2/3 the price of wine.

b. A country can only gain from trade if it can produce a good at a lower absolute cost than its trading partner.

c. If there are constant marginal and average costs of production, then it is in a country's best interest to specialize completely in the production of some goods but to import others.

d. Assuming that labor is the only input, if the opportunity cost of producing a yard of cloth is 3 bushels of wheat per yard, then wheat must require 3 times as much labor per unit produced as cloth.

13. What are the four major sources of market failure? Explain briefly why each prevents the competitive market from operating efficiently.

# EXERCISES

1. Suppose gold (G) and silver (S) are substitutes for each other because both serve as hedges against inflation. Suppose also that the supplies of both are fixed in the short run ($Q_G = 75$ and $Q_S = 300$) and that the demands for gold and silver are given by the following equations:

$$P_G = 975 - Q_G + 0.5P_S \text{ and } P_S = 600 - Q_S + 0.5P_G.$$

a. What are the equilibrium prices of gold and silver?

b. What if a new discovery of gold doubles the quantity supplied to 150? How will this discovery affect the prices of both gold and silver?

2. Using general equilibrium analysis, and taking into account feedback effects, analyze the following:

a. The likely effects of outbreaks of disease on chicken farms on the markets for chicken and pork.

b. The effects of increased taxes on airline tickets on travel to major tourist destinations such as Florida and California and on the hotel rooms in those destinations.

3. Jane has 3 liters of soft drinks and 9 sandwiches. Bob, on the other hand, has 8 liters of soft drinks and 4 sandwiches. With these endowments, Jane's marginal rate of substitution (MRS) of soft drinks for sandwiches is 4 and Bob's MRS is equal to 2. Draw an Edgeworth box diagram to show whether this allocation of resources is efficient. If it is, explain why. If it is not, what exchanges will make both parties better off?

4. Jennifer and Drew consume orange juice and coffee. Jennifer's MRS of orange juice for coffee is 1 and Drew's MRS of orange juice for coffee is 3. If the price of orange juice is $2 and the price of coffee is $3, which market is in excess demand? What do you expect to happen to the prices of the two goods?

5. Fill in the missing information in the following tables. For each table, use the information provided to identify a possible trade. Then identify the final allocation and a possible value for the MRS at the efficient solution. (*Note:* There is more than one correct answer.) Illustrate your results using Edgeworth box diagrams.

a. Norman's MRS of food for clothing is 1 and Gina's MRS of food for clothing is 4:

| Individual | Initial Allocation | Trade | Final Allocation |
|---|---|---|---|
| Norman | 6F, 2C | | |
| Gina | 1F, 8C | | |

b. Michael's MRS of food for clothing is 1/2 and Kelly's MRS of food for clothing is 3.

| Individual | Initial Allocation | Trade | Final Allocation |
|---|---|---|---|
| Michael | 10F, 3C | | |
| Kelly | 5F, 15C | | |

6. In the analysis of an exchange between two people, suppose both people have identical preferences. Will the contract curve be a straight line? Explain. Can you think of a counterexample?

7. Give an example of conditions when the production possibilities frontier might not be concave.

8. A monopsonist buys labor for less than the competitive wage. What type of inefficiency will this use of monopsony power cause? How would your answer change if the monopsonist in the labor market were also a monopolist in the output market?

9. The Acme Corporation produces $x$ and $y$ units of goods Alpha and Beta, respectively.

a. Use a production possibility frontier to explain how the willingness to produce more or less Alpha depends on the marginal rate of transformation of Alpha or Beta.

b. Consider two cases of production extremes: (i) Acme produces zero units of Alpha initially, or (ii) Acme produces zero units of Beta initially. If Acme always tries to stay on its production possibility frontier, describe the initial positions of cases (i) and (ii). What happens as the Acme Corporation begins to produce *both* goods?

10. In the context of our analysis of the Edgeworth production box, suppose that a new invention changes a constant-returns-to-scale food production process into one that exhibits sharply increasing returns. How does this change affect the production contract curve?

**11.** Suppose that country *A* and country *B* both produce wine and cheese. Country *A* has 800 units of available labor, while country *B* has 600 units. Prior to trade, country *A* consumes 40 pounds of cheese and 8 bottles of wine, and country *B* consumes 30 pounds of cheese and 10 bottles of wine.

|  | Country A | Country B |
|---|---|---|
| Labor per pound cheese | 10 | 10 |
| Labor per bottle wine | 50 | 30 |

**a.** Which country has a comparative advantage in the production of each good? Explain.

**b.** Determine the production possibilities curve for each country, both graphically and algebraically. (Label the pretrade production point *PT* and the post-trade point *P*.)

**c.** Given that 36 pounds of cheese and 9 bottles of wine are traded, label the post-trade consumption point *C*.

**d.** Prove that both countries have gained from trade.

**e.** What is the slope of the price line at which trade occurs?

# Markets with Asymmetric Information

For most of this book, we have assumed that consumers and producers have complete information about the economic variables that are relevant for the choices they face. Now we will see what happens when some parties know more than others—i.e., when there is **asymmetric information**.

Asymmetric information is quite common. Frequently, a seller of a product knows more about its quality than the buyer does. Workers usually know their own skills and abilities better than employers. And business managers know more about their firms' costs, competitive positions, and investment opportunities than do the firms' owners.

Asymmetric information also explains many institutional arrangements in our society. It is one reason why automobile companies offer warranties on parts and service for new cars; why firms and employees sign contracts that include incentives and rewards; and why the shareholders of corporations must monitor the behavior of managers.

We begin by examining a situation in which the sellers of a product have better information about its quality than buyers have. We will see how this kind of asymmetric information can lead to market failure. In the second section, we see how sellers can avoid some of the problems associated with asymmetric information by giving potential buyers signals about the quality of their product. Product warranties provide a type of insurance that can be helpful when buyers have less information than sellers. But as the third section shows, the purchase of insurance entails difficulties of its own when buyers have better information than sellers.

In the fourth section, we show that managers may pursue goals other than profit maximization when it is costly for owners of private corporations to monitor their behavior. In other words, managers have better information than owners. We also show how firms can give managers an incentive to maximize profits even when monitoring their behavior is costly. Finally, we show that labor markets may operate inefficiently when employees have better information about their productivity than employers have.

## 17.1 QUALITY UNCERTAINTY AND THE MARKET FOR LEMONS

Suppose you bought a new car for $20,000, drove it 100 miles, and then decided you really didn't want it. There was nothing wrong with the car—it performed beautifully and met all your expectations. You

• **asymmetric information**
Situation in which a buyer and a seller possess different information about a transaction.

simply felt that you could do just as well without it and would be better off saving the money for other things. So you decide to sell the car. How much should you expect to get for it? Probably not more than $16,000—even though the car is brand new, has been driven only 100 miles, and has a warranty that is transferable to a new owner. And if you were a prospective buyer, you probably wouldn't pay much more than $16,000 yourself.

Why does the mere fact that the car is second-hand reduce its value so much? To answer this question, think about your own concerns as a prospective buyer. Why, you would wonder, is this car for sale? Did the owner really change his or her mind about the car just like that, or is there something wrong with it? Is this car a "lemon"?

Used cars sell for much less than new cars because *there is asymmetric information about their quality*: The seller of a used car knows much more about the car than the prospective buyer does. The buyer can hire a mechanic to check the car, but the seller has had experience with it and will know more about it. Furthermore, the very fact that the car is for sale indicates that it may be a "lemon"—why sell a reliable car? As a result, the prospective buyer of a used car will always be suspicious of its quality—and with good reason.

The implications of asymmetric information about product quality were first analyzed by *George Akerlof* and go far beyond the market for used cars.[1] The markets for insurance, financial credit, and even employment are also characterized by asymmetric information about product quality. To understand the implications of asymmetric information, we will start with the market for used cars and then see how the same principles apply to other markets.

## The Market for Used Cars

Suppose two kinds of used cars are available—high-quality cars and low-quality cars. Also *suppose that both sellers and buyers can tell which kind of car is which*. There will then be two markets, as illustrated in Figure 17.1. In part (a), $S_H$ is the supply curve for high-quality cars, and $D_H$ is the demand curve. Similarly, $S_L$ and $D_L$ in part (b) are the supply and demand curves for low-quality cars. For any given price, $S_H$ lies to the left of $S_L$ because owners of high-quality cars are more reluctant to part with them and must receive a higher price to do so. Similarly, $D_H$ is higher than $D_L$ because buyers are willing to pay more to get a high-quality car. As the figure shows, the market price for high-quality cars is $10,000, for low-quality cars $5000, and 50,000 cars of each type are sold.

In reality, the seller of a used car knows much more about its quality than a buyer does. (Buyers discover the quality only after they buy a car and drive it for a while.) Consider what happens, then, if sellers know the quality of cars, but buyers do not. Initially, buyers might think that the odds are 50-50 that a car will be high quality. Why? Because when both sellers *and* buyers know the quality, 50,000 cars of each type are sold. When making a purchase, buyers therefore view all cars as "medium quality," in the sense that there is an equal chance of getting a high-quality or a low-quality car. (Of course, after buying the car and driving it for a while, they will learn its true quality.) The demand for cars perceived to be medium quality, denoted by $D_M$ in Figure 17.1, is below $D_H$ but above $D_L$. As the figure shows, these medium-quality cars will sell for about $7500 each. However, *fewer high-quality cars (25,000) and more low-quality cars (75,000) will now be sold*.

---

[1]George A. Akerlof, "The Market for 'Lemons': Quality Uncertainty and the Market Mechanism," *Quarterly Journal of Economics* (August 1970): 488–500.

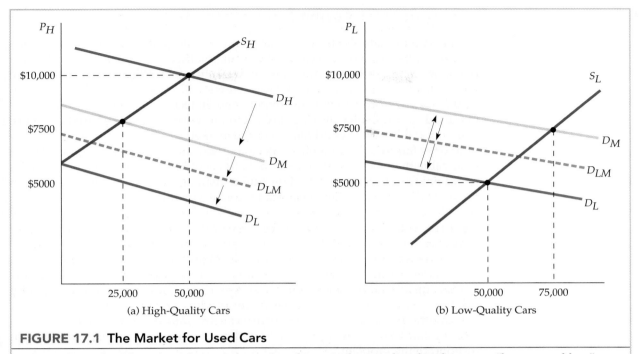

**FIGURE 17.1 The Market for Used Cars**

When sellers of products have better information about product quality than buyers, a "lemons problem" may arise in which low-quality goods drive out high quality goods. In **(a)** the demand curve for high-quality cars is $D_H$. However, as buyers lower their expectations about the average quality of cars on the market, their perceived demand shifts to $D_M$. Likewise, in **(b)** the perceived demand curve for low-quality cars shifts from $D_L$ to $D_M$. As a result, the quantity of high-quality cars sold falls from 50,000 to 25,000, and the quantity of low-quality cars sold increases from 50,000 to 75,000. Eventually, only low quality cars are sold.

As consumers begin to realize that most cars sold (about three-fourths of the total) are low quality, their perceived demand shifts. As Figure 17.1 shows, the new perceived demand curve might be $D_{LM}$, which means that, on average, cars are thought to be of low to medium quality. However, the mix of cars then shifts even more heavily to low quality. As a result, the perceived demand curve shifts further to the left, pushing the mix of cars even further toward low quality. *This shifting continues until only low-quality cars are sold.* At that point, the market price would be too low to bring forth any high-quality cars for sale, so consumers correctly assume that any car they buy will be low quality. As a result, the only relevant demand curve will be $D_L$.

The situation in Figure 17.1 is extreme. The market may come into equilibrium at a price that brings forth at least some high-quality cars. *But the fraction of high-quality cars will be smaller than it would be if consumers could identify quality before making the purchase.* That is why you should expect to sell your brand new car, which *you know* is in perfect condition, for much less than you paid for it. Because of asymmetric information, low-quality goods drive high-quality goods out of the market. This phenomenon, which is sometimes referred to as the *lemons problem*, is an important source of market failure. It is worth emphasizing:

The lemons problem: With asymmetric information, low-quality goods can drive high-quality goods out of the market.

## Implications of Asymmetric Information

Our used cars example shows how asymmetric information can result in market failure. In an ideal world of fully functioning markets, consumers would be able to choose between low-quality and high-quality cars. While some will choose low-quality cars because they cost less, others will prefer to pay more for high-quality cars. Unfortunately, consumers cannot in fact easily determine the quality of a used car until after they purchase it. As a result, the price of used cars falls, and high-quality cars are driven out of the market.

Market failure arises, therefore, because there are owners of high-quality cars who value their cars less than potential buyers of high-quality cars. Both parties could enjoy gains from trade, but, unfortunately, buyers' lack of information prevents this mutually beneficial trade from occurring.

**Adverse Selection** Our used car scenario is a simplified illustration of an important problem that affects many markets—the problem of adverse selection. **Adverse selection** arises when products of different qualities are sold at a single price because buyers or sellers are not sufficiently informed to determine the true quality at the time of purchase. As a result, too much of the low-quality product and too little of the high-quality product are sold in the marketplace. Let's look at some other examples of asymmetric information and adverse selection. In doing so, we will also see how the government or private firms might respond to the problem.

• **adverse selection** Form of market failure resulting when products of different qualities are sold at a single price because of asymmetric information, so that too much of the low-quality product and too little of the high-quality product are sold.

**The Market for Insurance** Why do people over age 65 have difficulty buying medical insurance at almost any price? Older people do have a much higher risk of serious illness, but why doesn't the price of insurance rise to reflect that higher risk? Again, the reason is asymmetric information. People who buy insurance know much more about their general health than any insurance company can hope to know, even if it insists on a medical examination. As a result, adverse selection arises, much as it does in the market for used cars. Because unhealthy people are more likely to want insurance, the proportion of unhealthy people in the pool of insured people increases. This forces the price of insurance to rise, so that more healthy people, aware of their low risks, elect not to be insured. This further increases the proportion of unhealthy people among the insured, thus forcing the price of insurance up more. The process continues until most people who want to buy insurance are unhealthy. At that point, insurance becomes very expensive, or—in the extreme—insurance companies stop selling the insurance.

Adverse selection can make the operation of insurance markets problematic in other ways. Suppose an insurance company wants to offer a policy for a particular event, such as an auto accident that results in property damage. It selects a target population—say, men under age 25—to whom it plans to market this policy, and it estimates that the probability of an accident for people in this group is .01. However, for some of these people, the probability of having an accident is much less than .01; for others, it is much higher than .01. If the insurance company cannot distinguish between high- and low-risk men, it will base the premium on the average accident probability of .01. What will happen? Those people with low probabilities of having an accident will choose not to insure, while those with high probabilities of an accident will purchase the insurance. This in turn raises the accident probability among those who choose to be insured above .01, forcing the insurance company to raise its premium. In the extreme, only those who are likely to be in an accident will choose to insure, making it impractical to sell insurance.

One solution to the problem of adverse selection is to *pool risks*. For health insurance, the government might take on this role, as it does with the Medicare program. By providing insurance for *all* people over age 65, the government eliminates the problem of adverse selection. Likewise, insurance companies will try to avoid or at least reduce the adverse selection problem by offering group health insurance policies at places of employment. By covering all workers in a firm, whether healthy or sick, the insurance company spreads risks and thereby reduces the likelihood that large numbers of high-risk individuals will purchase insurance.[2]

**The Market for Credit**  By using a credit card, many of us borrow money without providing any collateral. Most credit cards allow the holder to run a debt of several thousand dollars, and many people hold several credit cards. Credit card companies earn money by charging interest on the debit balance. But how can a credit card company or bank distinguish high-quality borrowers (who pay their debts) from low-quality borrowers (who don't)? Clearly, borrowers have better information—i.e., they know more about whether they will pay than the lender does. Again, the lemons problem arises. Low-quality borrowers are more likely than high-quality borrowers to want credit, which forces the interest rate up, which increases the number of low-quality borrowers, which forces the interest rate up further, and so on.

In fact, credit card companies and banks *can*, to some extent, use computerized credit histories, which they often share with one another, to distinguish low-quality from high-quality borrowers. Many people, however, think that computerized credit histories invade their privacy. Should companies be allowed to keep these credit histories and share them with other lenders? We can't answer this question for you, but we can point out that credit histories perform an important function: They eliminate, or at least greatly reduce, the problem of asymmetric information and adverse selection—a problem that might otherwise prevent credit markets from operating. Without these histories, even the creditworthy would find it extremely costly to borrow money.

## The Importance of Reputation and Standardization

Asymmetric information is also present in many other markets. Here are just a few examples:

- **Retail stores:** Will the store repair or allow you to return a defective product? The store knows more about its policy than you do.

- **Dealers of rare stamps, coins, books, and paintings:** Are the items real or counterfeit? The dealer knows much more about their authenticity than you do.

- **Roofers, plumbers, and electricians:** When a roofer repairs or renovates the roof of your house, do you climb up to check the quality of the work?

- **Restaurants:** How often do you go into the kitchen to check if the chef is using fresh ingredients and obeying health laws?

---

[2]Some people argue that pooling risks is not the main justification for Medicare, because most people's medical histories are well established by age 65, making it feasible for insurance companies to distinguish among high-risk and low-risk individuals. Another justification for Medicare is a distributional one. After age 65, even relatively healthy people are likely to need more medical care, making insurance expensive even without asymmetric information, and many older people would not have sufficient income to purchase the insurance.

In all these cases, the seller knows much more about the quality of the product than the buyer does. Unless sellers can provide information about quality to buyers, low-quality goods and services will drive out high-quality ones, and there will be market failure. Sellers of high-quality goods and services, therefore, have a big incentive to convince consumers that their quality is indeed high. In the examples cited above, this task is performed largely by *reputation*. You shop at a particular store because it has a reputation for servicing its products; you hire particular roofers or plumbers because they have reputations for doing good work; you go to a particular restaurant because it has a reputation for using fresh ingredients and nobody you know has become sick after eating there.

Sometimes, however, it is impossible for a business to develop a reputation. For example, because most of the customers of highway diners or motels go there only once or infrequently, the businesses have no opportunity to develop reputations. How, then, can they deal with the lemons problem? One way is *standardization*. In your hometown, you may not prefer to eat regularly at McDonald's. But a McDonald's may look more attractive when you are driving along a highway and want to stop for lunch. Why? Because McDonald's provides a standardized product: The same ingredients are used and the same food is served in every McDonald's anywhere in the country. Who knows? Joe's Diner might serve better food, but at least you *know* exactly what you will be buying at McDonald's.

---

**EXAMPLE 17.1**   Lemons in Major League Baseball

How can we test for the presence of a lemons market? One way is to compare the performance of products that are resold with similar products that are seldom put up for resale. In a lemons market, because purchasers of second-hand products will have limited information, resold products should be lower in quality than products that rarely appear on the market. One such "second-hand" market was created some time ago by a change in the rules governing contracts in major league baseball.[3]

Before 1976, major league baseball teams had the exclusive right to renew a player's contract. After a 1976 ruling declared this system illegal, a new contracting arrangement was created. After six years of major league service, players can now sign new contracts with their original teams or become free agents and sign with new teams. The availability of many free agents creates a second-hand market in baseball players.

Asymmetric information is prominent in the free-agent market. One potential purchaser, the player's original team, has better information about the player's abilities than other teams have. If we were looking at used cars, we could test for the existence of asymmetric information by comparing their repair records. In baseball, we can compare player disability records. If players are working hard and following rigorous conditioning programs, we would expect a low probability of

---

[3]This example is based on Kenneth Lehn's study of the free-agent market. See "Information Asymmetries in Baseball's Free-Agent Market," *Economic Inquiry* (1984): 37–44.

injury and a high probability that they will be able to perform if injured. In other words, more motivated players will spend less time on the bench owing to disabilities. If a lemons market exists, we would expect free agents to have higher disability rates than players who are renewed. Players may also have preexisting physical conditions which their original teams know about and which make them less desirable candidates for contract renewal. Because more such players would become free agents, free agents would experience higher disability rates for health reasons.

Table 17.1, which lists the post-contract performance of all players who have signed multiyear contracts, makes two points. First, both free agents and renewed players have increased disability rates after signing new contracts. The disabled days per season increase from an average of 4.73 to an average of 12.55. Second, the postcontract disability rates of renewed and non-renewed players are significantly different. On average, renewed players are disabled for 9.68 days, free agents for 17.23 days.

These two findings suggest that there is a lemons market in free agents that exists because baseball teams know their own players better than the teams with which they compete.

| TABLE 17.1 Player Disability | | | |
| --- | --- | --- | --- |
| | **Days Spent on Disabled List per Season** | | |
| | **Precontract** | **Postcontract** | **Percentage Change** |
| All players | 4.73 | 12.55 | 165.4 |
| Renewed players | 4.76 | 9.68 | 103.4 |
| Free agents | 4.67 | 17.23 | 268.9 |

## 17.2 MARKET SIGNALING

We have seen that asymmetric information can sometimes lead to a lemons problem: Because sellers know more about the quality of a good than buyers do, buyers may assume that quality is low, causing price to fall and only low-quality goods to be sold. We also saw how government intervention (in the market for health insurance, for example) or the development of a reputation (in service industries, for example) can alleviate this problem. Now we will examine another important mechanism through which sellers and buyers deal with the problem of asymmetric information: **market signaling**. The concept of market signaling was first developed by Michael Spence, who showed that in some markets, sellers send buyers *signals* that convey information about a product's quality.[4]

• **market signaling** Process by which sellers send signals to buyers conveying information about product quality.

To see how market signaling works, let's look at a *labor market*, which is a good example of a market with asymmetric information. Suppose a firm is thinking about hiring some new people. The new workers (the "sellers" of labor) know much more about the quality of the labor they can provide than does the firm (the buyer of labor). For example, they know how hard they tend to work, how

---

[4]Michael Spence, *Market Signaling* (Cambridge, MA: Harvard University Press, 1974).

responsible they are, what their skills are, and so forth. The firm will learn these things only after workers have been hired and have been working for some time.

Why don't firms simply hire workers, see how well they work, and then fire those with low productivity? Because this policy is often very costly. In many countries, and in many firms in the United States, it is difficult to fire someone who has been working more than a few months. (The firm may have to show just cause or provide severance pay.) Moreover, in many jobs, workers do not become fully productive for at least six months. Before that time, considerable on-the-job training may be required, for which the firm must invest substantial resources. Thus the firm might not learn how good workers are for six months to a year. Clearly, firms would be much better off if they knew how productive potential employees were *before* they hired them.

What characteristics can a firm examine to obtain information about people's productivity before it hires them? Can potential employees convey information about their productivity? Dressing well for the job interview might convey some information, but even unproductive people can dress well. Dressing well is thus a *weak signal*—it doesn't do much to distinguish high-productivity from low-productivity people. *To be strong, a signal must be easier for high-productivity people to give than for low-productivity people to give, so that high-productivity people are more likely to give it.*

For example, *education* is a strong signal in labor markets. A person's educational level can be measured by several things—the number of years of schooling, degrees obtained, the reputation of the university or college that granted the degrees, the person's grade-point average, and so on. Of course, education can directly and indirectly improve a person's productivity by providing information, skills, and general knowledge that are helpful in work. But even if education did *not* improve productivity, it would still be a useful *signal* of productivity because more productive people find it easier to attain high levels of education. Not surprisingly, productive people tend to be more intelligent, more motivated, more disciplined, and more energetic and hard-working—characteristics that are also helpful in school. More productive people are therefore more likely to attain high levels of education *in order to signal their productivity to firms and thereby obtain better-paying jobs*. Thus, firms are correct in considering education a signal of productivity.

## A Simple Model of Job Market Signaling

To understand how signaling works, we will discuss a simple model.[5] Let's assume that there are only low-productivity workers (Group I), whose average and marginal product is 1, and high-productivity workers (Group II), whose average and marginal product is 2. Workers will be employed by competitive firms whose products sell for $10,000, and who expect an average of 10 years' work from each employee. We also assume that half the workers in the population are in Group I and the other half in Group II, so that the *average* productivity of all workers is 1.5. Note that the revenue expected to be generated from Group I workers is $100,000 ($10,000/year × 10 years) and from Group II workers is $200,000 ($20,000/year × 10 years).

If firms could identify people by their productivity, they would offer them a wage equal to their marginal revenue product. Group I people would be paid $10,000 per year, Group II people $20,000. On the other hand, if firms could not identify productivity before they hired people, they would pay all workers an

---

[5]This is essentially the model developed in Spence, *Market Signaling*.

annual wage equal to the average productivity—$15,000. Group I people would then earn more ($15,000 instead of $10,000), at the expense of Group II people (who would earn $15,000 instead of $20,000).

Now let's consider what can happen with signaling via education. Suppose all the attributes of an education (degrees earned, grade-point average, etc.) can be summarized by a single index $y$ that represents years of higher education. All education involves a cost, and the higher the educational level $y$, the higher the cost. This cost includes tuition and books, the opportunity cost of foregone wages, and the psychic cost of having to work hard to obtain high grades. What is important is that *the cost of education is greater for the low-productivity group than for the high-productivity group.* We might expect this to be the case for two reasons. First, low-productivity workers may simply be less studious. Second, low-productivity workers may progress more slowly through degree programs. In particular, suppose that for Group I people, the cost of attaining educational level $y$ is given by

$$C_I(y) = \$40,000y$$

and that for Group II people, it is

$$C_{II}(y) = \$20,000y$$

Now suppose (to keep things simple and to dramatize the importance of signaling) that *education does nothing to increase one's productivity; its only value is as a signal.* Let's see if we can find a market equilibrium in which different people obtain different levels of education, and in which firms look at education as a signal of productivity.

**Equilibrium** Consider the following possible equilibrium. Suppose firms use this decision rule: *Anyone with an education level of $y^*$ or more is a Group II person and is offered a wage of $20,000, while anyone with an education level below $y^*$ is a Group I person and is offered a wage of $10,000.* The particular level $y^*$ that the firms choose is arbitrary, but for this decision rule to be part of an equilibrium, firms must have identified people correctly. Otherwise, the firms will want to change the rule. Will it work?

To answer this question, we must determine how much education the people in each group will obtain, *given that firms are using this decision rule.* To do this, remember that education allows one to get a better-paying job. The benefit of education $B(y)$ is the *increase* in the wage associated with each level of education, as shown in Figure 17.2. Observe that $B(y)$ is 0 initially, which represents the $100,000 base 10-year earnings that are earned without any college education. For an education level less than $y^*$, $B(y)$ remains 0, because 10-year earnings remain at the $100,000 base level. But when the education level reaches $y^*$ or greater, 10-year earnings increase to $200,000, increasing $B(y)$ to $100,000.

How much education should a person obtain? Clearly the choice is between *no* education (i.e., $y = 0$) and an education level of $y^*$. Why? Any level of education less than $y^*$ results in the same base earnings of $100,000. Thus there is no benefit from obtaining an education at a level above 0 but below $y^*$. Similarly, there is no benefit from obtaining an educational level above $y^*$ because $y^*$ is sufficient to allow one to enjoy the higher total earnings of $200,000.

**Cost–Benefit Comparison** In deciding how much education to obtain, people compare the benefit of education with the cost. People in each group make the following cost-benefit calculation: *Obtain the education level $y^*$ if the benefit (i.e., the increase in earnings) is at least as large as the cost of this education.* For both groups,

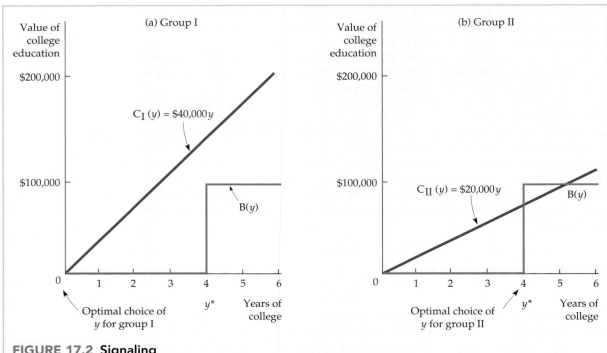

**FIGURE 17.2 Signaling**

Education can be a useful signal of the high productivity of a group of workers if education is easier to obtain for this group than for a low-productivity group. In **(a)**, the low-productivity group will choose an education level of $y = 0$ because the cost of education is greater than the increased earnings resulting from education. However, in **(b)**, the high-productivity group will choose an education level of $y^* = 4$ because the gain in earnings is greater than the cost.

the benefit (the increase in earnings) is $100,000. The costs, however, differ. For Group I, the cost is $40,000y$, but for Group II it is only $20,000y$. Therefore, Group I will obtain *no* education as long as

$$\$100{,}000 < \$40{,}000y^* \text{ or } y^* > 2.5$$

and Group II will obtain an education level $y^*$ as long as

$$\$100{,}000 > \$20{,}000y^* \text{ or } y^* < 5$$

These results give us an equilibrium *as long as $y^*$ is between 2.5 and 5*. Suppose, for example, that $y^*$ is 4.0, as in Figure 17.2. In that case, people in Group I will find that education does not pay and will not obtain any, whereas people in Group II will find that education does pay and will obtain the level $y = 4.0$. Now, when a firm interviews job candidates who have no college education, it correctly assumes they have low productivity and offers them a wage of $10,000. Similarly, when the firm interviews people who have four years of college, it correctly assumes their productivity is high, warranting a wage of $20,000. We therefore have an equilibrium. High-productivity people will obtain a college education to signal their productivity; firms will read this signal and offer them a high wage.

This is a highly simplified model, but it illustrates a significant point: Education can be an important signal that allows firms to sort workers according to productivity. Some workers (those with high productivity) will want to obtain a college education *even if that education does nothing to increase their productivity*. These workers simply want to identify themselves as highly productive, so they obtain the education needed to send a signal.

In the real world, of course, education *does* provide useful knowledge and *does* increase one's ultimate productivity. (We wouldn't have written this book if we didn't believe that.) But education also serves a signaling function. For example, many firms insist that a prospective manager have an MBA. One reason is that MBAs learn economics, finance, and other useful subjects. But there is a second reason: To complete an MBA program takes intelligence, discipline, and hard work, and people with those qualities tend to be very productive.

## Guarantees and Warranties

We have stressed the role of signaling in labor markets, but it can also play an important role in many other markets in which there is asymmetric information. Consider the markets for such durable goods as televisions, stereos, cameras, and refrigerators. Many firms produce these items, but some brands are more dependable than others. If consumers could not tell which brands tend to be more dependable, the better brands could not be sold for higher prices. Firms that produce a higher-quality, more dependable product must therefore make consumers aware of this difference. But how can they do it in a convincing way? The answer is *guarantees and warranties*.

Guarantees and warranties effectively signal product quality because an extensive warranty is more costly for the producer of a low-quality item than for the producer of a high-quality item. The low-quality item is more likely to require servicing under the warranty, for which the producer will have to pay. In their own self-interest, therefore, producers of low-quality items will not offer extensive warranties. Thus consumers can correctly view extensive warranties as signals of high quality and will pay more for products that offer them.

---

**EXAMPLE 17.2**  Working into the Night

Job market signaling does not end when one is hired. Even after a few years of employment, a worker will still know more about his abilities than will the employer. This is especially true for workers in knowledge-based fields such as engineering, computer programming, finance, law, management, and consulting. Although an unusually talented computer programmer, for example, will be more skilled than his co-workers at writing programs that are efficient and bug-free, it may take several years before the firm fully recognizes this talent. Given this asymmetric information, what policy should employers use to determine promotions and salary increases? Can workers who are unusually talented and productive signal this fact and thereby receive earlier promotions and larger salary increases?

Workers can often signal talent and productivity *by working harder and longer hours*. Because more talented and productive workers tend to get more enjoyment and satisfaction from their jobs, it is less costly for them to send this signal than it is for other workers. The signal is therefore strong: It conveys information. As a result, employers can—and do—rely on this signal when making promotion and salary decisions.

This signalling process has affected the way many people work. Rather than an hourly wage, knowledge-based workers are typically paid a fixed salary for a 35- or 40-hour week and do not receive overtime pay if they work additional hours. Yet such workers increasingly work well beyond their weekly schedules. Surveys by the U.S. Labor Department, for example, found that the percentage of all workers who toil 49 hours or more a week rose from 13 percent in 1976 to over 18 percent in 2006.[6] Many young lawyers, accountants, consultants, investment bankers, and computer programmers regularly work into the night and on weekends, putting in 60- or 70-hour weeks. Is it surprising that these people are working so hard? Not at all. They are trying to send signals that can greatly affect their careers.

Employers rely increasingly on the signaling value of long hours as rapid technological change makes it harder for them to find other ways of assessing workers' skills and productivity. A study of software engineers at the Xerox Corporation, for example, found that many people work into the night because they fear that otherwise their bosses will conclude that they are shirkers who choose the easiest assignments. As the bosses make clear, this fear is warranted: "We don't know how to assess the value of a knowledge worker in these new technologies," says one Xerox manager, "so we value those who work into the night."

As corporations become more reluctant to offer lifetime job security, and as competition for promotion intensifies, salaried workers feel more and more pressure to work long hours. If you find yourself working 60- or 70-hour weeks, look at the bright side—the signal you're sending is a strong one.[7]

## 17.3 MORAL HAZARD

When one party is fully insured and cannot be accurately monitored by an insurance company with limited information, the insured party may take an action that increases the likelihood that an accident or an injury will occur. For example, if my home is fully insured against theft, I may be less diligent about locking doors when I leave, and I may choose not to install an alarm system. The possibility that an individual's behavior may change because she has insurance is an example of a problem known as *moral hazard*.

The concept of moral hazard applies not only to problems of insurance, but also to problems of workers who perform below their capabilities when employers cannot monitor their behavior ("job shirking"). In general, **moral hazard** occurs when a party whose actions are unobserved affects the probability or magnitude of a payment. For example, if I have complete medical insurance coverage, I may visit the doctor more often than I would if my coverage were limited. If the insurance provider can monitor its insurees' behavior, it can charge higher fees for those who make more claims. But if the company cannot monitor behavior, it may find its payments to be larger than expected. Under conditions of moral hazard, insurance companies may be forced to increase premiums for everyone or even to refuse to sell insurance at all.

• **moral hazard** When a party whose actions are unobserved can affect the probability or magnitude of a payment associated with an event.

---

[6]"At the Desk, Off the Clock and Below Statistical Radar," *New York Times*, July 18, 1999. Data on hours worked are available from the Current Population Survey (CPS), Bureau of Labor Statistics (BLS), at **http://www.bls.gov/cps/#charemp**; *Persons at Work in Agriculture and Nonagricultural Industries by Hours of Work.*

[7]For an interesting study of "time stress," see Daniel Hamermesh and Jungmin Lee, "Stressed Out on Four Continents: Time Crunch or Yuppie Kvetch?" *Review of Econ. and Stat.*, May 2007, 89, 374–383.

Consider, for example, the decisions faced by the owners of a warehouse valued at $100,000 by their insurance company. Suppose that if they run a $50 fire-prevention program for their employees, the probability of a fire is .005. Without this program, the probability increases to .01. Knowing this, the insurance company faces a dilemma if it cannot monitor the company's decision to conduct a fire-prevention program. The policy that the insurance company offers cannot include a clause stating that payments will be made only if there is a fire-prevention program. If the program were in place, the company could insure the warehouse for a premium equal to the expected loss from a fire—an expected loss equal to .005 × $100,000 = $500. Once the insurance policy is purchased, however, the owners no longer have an incentive to run the program. If there is a fire, they will be fully compensated for their financial loss. Thus, if the insurance company sells a policy for $500, it will incur losses because the expected loss from the fire will be $1000 (.01 × $100,000).

   Moral hazard is a problem not only for insurance companies. It also alters the ability of markets to allocate resources efficiently. In Figure 17.3, for example, D gives the demand for automobile driving in miles per week. The demand curve, which measures the marginal benefits of driving, is downward sloping because some people switch to alternative transportation as the cost of driving increases. Suppose that initially, the cost of driving includes the insurance cost and that insurance companies can accurately measure miles driven. In this case, there is no moral hazard and the marginal cost of driving is given by MC. Drivers know that more driving will increase their insurance premiums and so increase their total cost of driving (the cost per mile is assumed to be constant). For example, if the cost of driving is $1.50 per mile (50 cents of which is insurance cost), drivers will go 100 miles per week.

   A moral hazard problem arises when insurance companies cannot monitor individual driving habits, so that insurance premiums do not depend on miles driven. In that case, drivers assume that any additional accident costs that they incur will be spread over a large group, with only a negligible portion accruing to

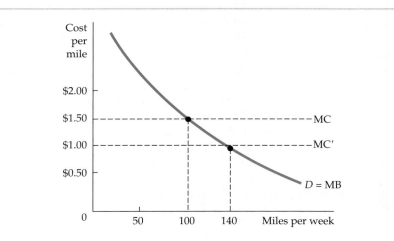

**FIGURE 17.3 The Effects of Moral Hazard**

Moral hazard alters the ability of markets to allocate resources efficiently. D gives the demand for automobile driving. With no moral hazard, the marginal cost of transportation MC is $1.50 per mile; the driver drives 100 miles, which is the efficient amount. With moral hazard, the driver perceives the cost per mile to be MC = $1.00 and drives 140 miles.

each of them individually. Because their insurance premiums do not vary with the number of miles that they drive, an additional mile of transportation will cost $1.00, as shown by the marginal cost curve MC', rather than $1.50. The number of miles driven will increase from 100 to the socially inefficient level of 140.

Moral hazard not only alters behavior; it also creates economic inefficiency. The inefficiency arises because the insured individual perceives either the cost or the benefit of the activity differently from the true social cost or benefit. In the driving example of Figure 17.3, the efficient level of driving is given by the intersection of the marginal benefit (MB) and marginal cost (MC) curves. With moral hazard, however, the individual's perceived marginal cost (MC') is less than actual cost, and the number of miles driven per week (140) is higher than the efficient level at which marginal benefit is equal to marginal cost (100).

**EXAMPLE 17.3** Reducing Moral Hazard: Warranties of Animal Health

For buyers of livestock, information about the animals' health is very important.[8] Unhealthy animals gain weight more slowly and are less likely to reproduce. Because of asymmetric information in the livestock market (sellers know the health of an animal better than buyers do), most states require warranties on the sale of livestock. Under these laws, sellers not only promise (warrant) that animals are free from hidden diseases, but are responsible for all costs arising from any diseased animals.

Although warranties solve the problem of the seller having better information than the buyer, they also create a form of moral hazard. Guaranteeing reimbursement to the buyer for all costs associated with diseased animals means that insurance rates are not tied to the level of care that buyers or their agents take to protect their livestock against disease. As a result of these warranties, livestock buyers avoid paying for early diagnoses of diseased livestock, and losses increase.

In response to the moral hazard problem, many states have modified their animal warranty laws by requiring sellers to tell buyers whether livestock are diseased at the time of sale. Some states also require sellers to comply with state and federal animal health regulations, thereby reducing disease. Beyond these measures, however, warranties that animals are free from hidden disease must be in the form of explicit written or oral guarantees to buyers.

# 17.4 THE PRINCIPAL–AGENT PROBLEM

If monitoring the productivity of workers were costless, the owners of a business would ensure that their managers and workers were working effectively. In most firms, however, owners can't monitor everything that employees

---

[8]This example is based on Terence J. Centner and Michael E. Wetzstein, "Reducing Moral Hazard Associated with Implied Warranties of Animal Health," *American Journal of Agricultural Economics* 69 (1987): 143–50.

do—employees are better informed than owners. This information asymmetry creates a **principal–agent problem**.

An *agency relationship* exists whenever there is an arrangement in which one person's welfare depends on what another person does. The **agent** is the person who acts, and the **principal** is the party whom the action affects. *A principal–agent problem arises when agents pursue their own goals rather than the goals of the principal.* In our example, the manager and the workers are the agents, and the owners of the firm are the principals. In this case, the principal–agent problem results from the fact that managers may pursue their own goals, even at the cost of lower profits for the owners.

Agency relationships are widespread in our society. For example, doctors serve as agents for hospitals and, as such, may select patients and do procedures which, though consistent with their personal preferences, are not necessarily consistent with the objectives of the hospital. Similarly, managers of housing properties may not maintain the property the way that the owners would like. And sometimes insured parties may be seen as agents and insurance companies as principals.

How does incomplete information and costly monitoring affect the way agents act? And what mechanisms can give managers the incentives to operate in the owner's interest? These questions are central to any principal–agent analysis. In this section, we study the principal–agent problem from several perspectives. First, we look at the owner–manager problem within private and public enterprises. Second, we discuss ways in which owners can use contractual relationships with their employees to deal with principal–agent problems.

## The Principal–Agent Problem in Private Enterprises

Most large firms are controlled by management. Indeed, an individual family or financial institution owns more than 10 percent of the shares of only 16 of the 100 largest U.S. industrial corporations.[9] The fact that most individual stockholders have only a small percentage of a firm's total equity makes it difficult for them to obtain information about how well the firm's managers are performing. One function of owners (or their representatives) is to monitor the behavior of managers. But monitoring is costly, and information is expensive to gather and use, especially for an individual.

Managers of private enterprises can thus pursue their own objectives. But what are these objectives? One view is that managers are more concerned with growth than with profit per se: More rapid growth and larger market share provide more cash flow, which in turn allows managers to enjoy more perks. Another view emphasizes the utility that managers get from their jobs, not only from profit but also from the respect of their peers, the power to control the corporation, the fringe benefits and other perks, and long job tenure.

However, there are limitations to managers' ability to deviate from the objectives of owners. First, stockholders can complain loudly when they feel that managers are behaving improperly. In exceptional cases, they can oust the current management (perhaps with the help of the board of directors, whose job it is to monitor managerial behavior). Second, a vigorous market for corporate control can develop. If a takeover bid becomes more likely when the firm is poorly managed, managers will have a strong incentive to pursue the goal of profit maximization. Third, there can be a highly developed market for managers.

---

[9]See Merritt B. Fox, *Finance and Industrial Performance in a Dynamic Economy* (New York: Columbia University Press, 1987).

**• principal–agent problem**
Problem arising when agents (e.g., a firm's managers) pursue their own goals rather than the goals of principals (e.g., the firm's owners).

**• agent** Individual employed by a principal to achieve the principal's objective.

**• principal** Individual who employs one or more agents to achieve an objective.

If managers who maximize profit are in great demand, they will earn high wages and so give other managers an incentive to pursue the same goal.

Unfortunately, the means by which stockholders control managers' behavior are limited and imperfect. Corporate takeovers may be motivated by personal and economic power, for example, instead of economic efficiency. The managerial labor market may also work imperfectly because top managers are frequently near retirement and have long-term contracts. The problem of limited stockholder control shows up most dramatically in executive compensation, which has grown very rapidly over the past several decades. In 2002, a *Business Week* survey of the 365 largest U.S. companies showed that the average CEO earned $13.1 million in 2000, and executive pay has continued to increase at a double-digit rate. Even more disturbing is the fact that for the 10 public companies led by the highest-paid CEOs, there was a *negative* correlation between CEO pay and company performance.

It is clear that shareholders have been unable to adequately control managers' behavior. What can be done to address this problem? In theory, the answer is simple: One must find mechanisms that more closely align the interests of managers and shareholders. In practice, however, this is likely to prove difficult. Among those suggestions put into effect recently by the Securities and Exchange Commission, which regulates public companies, are reforms that grant more authority to independent outside directors. Other possible reforms would tie executive pay more closely to the long-term performance of the company. Reward structures that focus on profitability over a 5- to 10-year period are more likely to generate efficient incentives than more shortsighted reward structures. We will consider some additional solutions to this important principal–agent problem in the next section.

**EXAMPLE 17.4** CEO Salaries

When Jack Welch retired as CEO of General Electric in 2001, his salary was $16.7 million, and his benefits from stock options and other perks were worth millions more. In addition, his post-retirement benefits included a monthly income of $2.1 million, the use of a company-owned Manhattan apartment, and unlimited use of the company's Boeing 737 business jet. In 2005, AT&T CEO Edward Whitacre was paid $17.1 million, bringing his total pay to more than $85 million over the previous five years—even though shareholder return during the period was negative 40 percent.[10] Other CEOs have also received extremely generous compensation packages, even when their companies were performing poorly.

CEO compensation has increased sharply over time. The average annual salary for production workers in the U.S. went from $27,632 in 1990 to $28,315 in 2005. Over the same period, the average annual compensation for CEOs grew from $2.9 million to $11 million. In other words, CEO compensation has gone from 107 times the pay of an average production worker to over 411 times as much.[11] Why? Have top managers become more productive, or are CEOs simply becoming more effective at extracting economic rents from their companies? The answer lies in the principal-agent problem, which is at the heart of CEO salary determination.

For years, many economists believed that executive compensation reflected an appropriate reward for talent. Recent evidence, however, suggests that managers

---

[10]Adam Geller, "Rise in Pay for CEOs Slows but Doesn't Stop," *International Herald Tribune*, April 20, 2006.

[11]Source: Institute for Policy Studies—United for a Fair Economy (2006).

have been able to increase their power over boards of directors and have used that power to extract compensation packages that are out of line with their economic contributions. In essence, managers have steadily increased their ability to extract economic rents. How has this happened?

First, most board of directors do not have the necessary information or independence to negotiate effectively with managers. Directors often cannot properly monitor executives' activities and therefore cannot effectively negotiate compensation packages that are tightly linked to their performance. Furthermore, boards consist of a mix of inside members, who either are or represent top executives, and outside members, who are chosen by and are often on close terms with top executives. Therefore, directors have a strong incentive to support executives in order to be re-nominated to the board or otherwise rewarded. Only if a compensation package is seen as outrageous from the point of view of outsiders do board members appear to bargain aggressively in shareholders' interests.

Second, managers have introduced forms of compensation that camouflage the extraction of rents from shareholders. For example, stock options, post-retirement perks, and pension plans can give executives substantial payoffs that appear costless because companies do not have to count them as expenses on their books.

Why has the amount of rent extraction grown so much over time? One reason is that boards of directors frequently use compensation consultants to advise them on comparable salaries paid to CEOs of other companies. Because a firm usually wants its CEO to be paid at least the average salary of other CEOs, the net result has been a gradual upward trend.

With the wave of corporate scandals that began in late 2001, the picture of rent extraction created by the principal-agent problem changed in 2002 and 2003. The median total executive pay package for 209 companies rose 11.8 percent, well above the rate of inflation, but a much smaller increase than in previous years. However, recent trends suggest that executive compensation may be heading back to its pre-2001 levels.

## The Principal–Agent Problem in Public Enterprises

The principal–agent framework can also help us understand the behavior of the managers of public organizations. These managers may also be interested in power and perks, both of which can be obtained by expanding their organization beyond its "efficient" level. Because it is also costly to monitor the behavior of public managers, there are no guarantees that they will produce the efficient output. Legislative checks on a government agency are not likely to be effective as long as the agency has better information about its costs than the legislature has.

Although the public sector lacks some of the market forces that keep private managers in line, government agencies can still be effectively monitored. First, managers of government agencies care about more than just the size of their agencies. Indeed, many choose lower-paying public jobs because they are concerned about the "public interest." Second, much like private managers, public managers are subject to the rigors of the managerial job market. If public managers are perceived to be pursuing improper objectives, their ability to obtain high salaries in the future might be impaired. Third, legislatures and other government agencies perform an oversight function. For example, the

Government Accounting Office and the Office of Management and Budget spend much of their energy monitoring other agencies.

At the local rather than the federal level, public managers are subject to even more checks. Suppose, for example, that a city transit agency has expanded bus service beyond the efficient level. Citizens can vote the transit managers out of office, or, if all else fails, use alternative transportation (or even move). Competition among agencies can be as effective as competition among private firms in constraining the behavior of managers.

---

**EXAMPLE 17.5** — Managers of Nonprofit Hospitals as Agents

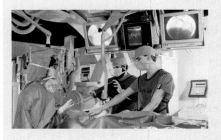

Do the managers of nonprofit organizations have the same goals as those of for-profit organizations? Are nonprofit organizations more or less efficient than for-profit firms? We can get some insight into these issues by looking at the provision of health care. In a study of 725 hospitals, from 14 major hospital chains, researchers compared the return on investment and average costs of nonprofit and for-profit hospitals to determine if they performed differently.[12]

The study found that for 1977 and 1981, the rate of returns did indeed differ. In 1977, for example, for-profits earned an 11.6-percent return, while nonprofits earned 8.8 percent. In 1981, for-profits earned 12.7 percent and nonprofits only 7.4 percent. A straight comparison of returns and costs is not appropriate, however, because the hospitals perform different functions. For example, 24 percent of the nonprofit hospitals provide medical residency programs, as compared with only 6 percent of the for-profit hospitals. Similar differences can be found in the provision of specialty care, with 10 percent of the nonprofits having open-heart units, as compared to only 5 percent of the for-profits. In addition, while 43 percent of nonprofits have premature infant units, only 29 percent of the for-profits have equivalent units.

Using a statistical regression analysis, which controls for differences in the services performed, one can determine whether differences in services account for the higher costs. The study found that after adjusting for services performed, the average cost of a patient day in nonprofit hospitals was 8 percent higher than in for-profit hospitals. This difference implies that the profit status of the hospital affects its performance in the way principal–agent theory predicts: Without the competitive forces faced by for-profit hospitals, nonprofit hospitals may be less cost-conscious and therefore less likely to serve appropriately as agents for their principals—namely, society at large.

Of course, nonprofit hospitals provide services that society may well wish to subsidize. But the added cost of running a nonprofit hospital should be considered when determining whether it should be granted tax-exempt status.

---

[12]Regina E. Herzlinger and William S. Krasker, "Who Profits from Nonprofits?" *Harvard Business Review* 65 (January–February 1987): 93–106.

## Incentives in the Principal–Agent Framework

We have seen why managers' and owners' objectives are likely to differ within the principal–agent framework. How, therefore, can owners design reward systems so that managers and workers come as close as possible to meeting owners' goals? To answer this question, let's study a specific problem.

A small manufacturer uses labor and machinery to produce watches. The owners want to maximize profit. They must rely on a machine repairperson whose effort will influence the likelihood that machines break down and thus affect the firm's profit level. Revenue also depends on other random factors, such as the quality of parts and the reliability of other labor. As a result of high monitoring costs, the owners can neither measure the effort of the repairperson directly nor be sure that the same effort will always generate the same profit level. Table 17.2 describes these circumstances.

The table shows that the repairperson can work with either a low or high amount of effort. Low effort ($a = 0$) generates either $10,000 or $20,000 in revenue (with equal probability), depending on the random factors that we mentioned. We've labeled the lower of the two revenue levels "bad luck" and the higher level "good luck." When the repairperson makes a high effort ($a = 1$), revenue will be either $20,000 (bad luck) or $40,000 (good luck). These numbers highlight the problem of incomplete information: When the firm's revenue is $20,000, the owners cannot know whether the repairperson has made a low or high effort.

Suppose the repairperson's goal is to maximize his wage payment less the cost (in terms of lost leisure and unpleasant work time) of the effort that he makes. To simplify, we'll suppose that the cost of effort is 0 for low effort and $10,000 for high effort. (Formally, $c = \$10,000a$.)

Now we can state the principal–agent problem from the owners' perspective. The owners' goal is to maximize expected profit, given the uncertainty of outcomes and given the fact that the repairperson's behavior cannot be monitored. The owners can contract to pay the repairperson for his work, but the payment scheme must be based entirely on the measurable output of the manufacturing process, not on the repairperson's effort. To signify this link, we describe the payment scheme as $w(R)$, stressing that payments can depend only on measured revenue.

What is the best payment scheme? And can that scheme be as effective as one based on effort rather than output? The best payment scheme depends on the nature of production, the degree of uncertainty, and the objectives of both owners and managers. The arrangement will not always be as effective as an ideal scheme directly tied to effort. A lack of information can lower economic efficiency because both the owners' revenue and the repairperson's payment may fall at the same time.

Let's see how to design a payment scheme when the repairperson wishes to maximize his payment received net of the cost of effort made.[13] Suppose first

| TABLE 17.2 Revenue from Making Watches | | |
|---|---|---|
| | **Bad Luck** | **Good Luck** |
| Low effort ($a = 0$) | $10,000 | $20,000 |
| High effort ($a = 1$) | $20,000 | $40,000 |

---

[13]We assume that because the repairperson is risk neutral, no efficiency is lost. If, however, the repairperson were risk averse, there would be an efficiency loss.

that the owners offer a fixed wage payment. Any wage will do, but we can see things most clearly if we assume that the wage is 0. (Here, 0 could represent a wage equal to the wage paid in other comparable jobs.) Facing a wage of 0, the repairperson has no incentive to make a high level of effort. The reason is that the repairperson does not share in any of the gains that the owners enjoy from the increased effort. It follows, therefore, that a fixed payment will lead to an inefficient outcome. When $a = 0$ and $w = 0$, the owner will earn an expected revenue of $15,000 and the repairperson a net wage of 0.

Both the owners and the repairperson will be better off if the repairperson is rewarded for his productive effort. Suppose, for example, that the owners offer the repairperson the following payment scheme:

$$\text{If } R = \$10,000 \text{ or } \$20,000, w = 0 \qquad \qquad \textbf{(17.1)}$$
$$\text{If } R = \$40,000, w = \$24,000$$

Under this bonus arrangement, a low effort generates no payment. A high effort, however, generates an expected payment of $12,000, and an expected payment less the cost of effort of $12,000 – $10,000 = $2000. Under this system, the repairperson will choose to make a high level of effort. This arrangement makes the owners better off than before because they get an expected revenue of $30,000 and an expected profit of $18,000.

This is not the only payment scheme that will work for the owners, however. Suppose they contract to have the worker participate in the following revenue-sharing arrangement. When revenues are greater than $18,000,

$$w = R - \$18,000 \qquad \qquad \textbf{(17.2)}$$

(Otherwise the wage is zero.) In this case, if the repairperson makes a low effort, he receives an expected payment of $1000. But if he makes a high level of effort, his expected payment is $12,000, and his expected payment less the $10,000 cost of effort is $2000. (The owners' profit is $18,000, as before.)

Thus, in our example, a revenue-sharing arrangement achieves the same outcome as a bonus-payment system. In more complex situations, the incentive effects of the two types of arrangements will differ. However, the basic idea illustrated here applies to all principal–agent problems: When it is impossible to measure effort directly, an incentive structure that rewards the outcome of high levels of effort can induce agents to aim for the goals that the owners set.

## *17.5 MANAGERIAL INCENTIVES IN AN INTEGRATED FIRM

- **horizontal integration**
Organizational form in which several plants produce the same or related products for a firm.

- **vertical integration**
Organizational form in which a firm contains several divisions, with some producing parts and components that others use to produce finished products.

We have seen that owners and managers of firms can have asymmetric information about demand, cost, and other variables. We've also seen how owners can design reward structures to encourage managers to make appropriate efforts. Now we focus our attention on firms that are *integrated*—that consist of several divisions, each with its own managers. Some firms are **horizontally integrated**: Several plants produce the same or related products. Others are also **vertically integrated**: Upstream divisions produce materials, parts, and components that downstream divisions use to produce final products. Integration creates organizational problems. We addressed some of these problems in the appendix to Chapter 11, where we discussed *transfer pricing* in the vertically integrated firm—that is, how the firm sets prices for parts and components that upstream divisions supply to downstream divisions. Here we will examine problems that stem from asymmetric information.

## Asymmetric Information and Incentive Design in the Integrated Firm

In an integrated firm, division managers are likely to have better information about their different operating costs and production potential than central management has. This asymmetric information causes two problems.

1. How can central management elicit accurate information about divisional operating costs and production potential from divisional managers? This information is important because the inputs into some divisions may be the outputs of other divisions, because deliveries must be scheduled to customers, and because prices cannot be set without knowing overall production capacity and costs.

2. What reward or incentive structure should central management use to encourage divisional managers to produce as efficiently as possible? Should they be given bonuses based on how much they produce? If so, how should they be structured?

To understand these problems, consider a firm with several plants that all produce the same product. Each plant's manager has much better information about its production capacity than central management has. In order to avoid bottlenecks and to schedule deliveries reliably, central management wants to learn more about how much each plant can produce. It also wants each plant to produce as much as possible. Let's examine ways in which central management can obtain the information it wants while also encouraging plant managers to run the plants as efficiently as possible.

One way is to give plant managers bonuses based on either the total output of their plant or its operating profit. Although this approach would encourage managers to maximize output, it would penalize managers whose plants have higher costs and lower capacity. Even if these plants produced efficiently, their output and operating profit—and thus their bonuses—would be lower than those of plants with lower costs and higher capacities. Plant managers would also have no incentive to obtain and reveal accurate information about cost and capacity.

A second way is to ask managers about their costs and capacities and *then* base bonuses on how well they do relative to their answers. For example, each manager might be asked how much his or her plant can produce each year. Then at the end of the year, the manager receives a bonus based on how close the plant's output was to this target. For example, if the manager's estimate of the feasible production level is $Q_f$, the annual bonus in dollars, $B$, might be

$$B = 10{,}000 - .5(Q_f - Q) \tag{17.3}$$

where $Q$ is the plant's actual output, 10,000 is the bonus when output is at capacity, and .5 is a factor chosen to reduce the bonus if $Q$ is below $Q_f$.

Under this scheme, however, managers would have an incentive to *underestimate* capacity. By claiming capacities below what they know to be true, they can more easily earn large bonuses even if they do not operate efficiently. For example, if a manager estimates capacity to be 18,000 rather than 20,000, and the plant actually produces only 16,000, her bonus increases from $8000 to

$9000. Thus this scheme fails to elicit accurate information about capacity and does not ensure that plants will be run as efficiently as possible.

Now let's modify this scheme. We will still ask managers how much their plants can feasibly produce and tie their bonuses to this estimate. However, we will use a slightly more complicated formula than the one in (17.3) to calculate the bonus:

$$\text{If } Q > Q_f, \quad B = .3Q_f + .2(Q - Q_f)$$
$$\text{If } Q \leq Q_f, \quad B = .3Q_f - .5(Q_f - Q)$$

**(17.4)**

The parameters (.3, .2, and .5) have been chosen so that each manager has the incentive to reveal the *true* feasible production level *and* to make $Q$, the actual output of the plant, as large as possible.

To see that this scheme does the job, look at Figure 17.4. Assume that the true production limit is $Q^* = 20{,}000$ units per year. The bonus that the manager will receive if she states feasible capacity to be the true production limit is given by the line labeled $Q_f = 20{,}000$. This line is continued for outputs beyond 20,000 to illustrate the bonus scheme but dashed to signify the infeasibility of such production. Note that the manager's bonus is maximized when the firm produces at its limits of 20,000 units; the bonus is then $6000.

Suppose, however, that the manager reports a feasible capacity of only 10,000. Then the bonus is given by the line labeled $Q_f = 10{,}000$. The maximum bonus is now $5000, which is obtained by producing an output of 20,000. But note that this is less than the bonus that the manager would receive if she correctly stated the feasible capacity to be 20,000.

The same line of argument applies when the manager exaggerates available capacity. If the manager states feasible capacity to be 30,000 units per year, the

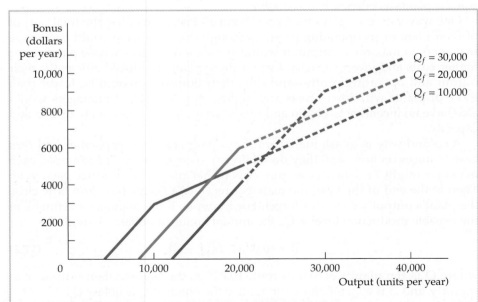

**FIGURE 17.4 Incentive Design in an Integrated Firm**

A bonus scheme can be designed that gives a manager the incentive to estimate accurately the size of the plant. If the manager reports a feasible capacity of 20,000 units per year, equal to the actual capacity, then the bonus will be maximized (at $6000).

bonus is given by the line $Q_f = 30{,}000$. The maximum bonus of \$4000, which is achieved at an output of 20,000, is less than the bonus that she could have received by reporting feasible capacity correctly.[14]

## Applications

Because the problem of asymmetric information and incentive design comes up often in managerial settings, incentive schemes like the one described above arise in many contexts. How, for example, can managers encourage salespeople to set and reveal realistic sales targets and then work as hard as possible to meet them?

Most salespeople cover specific territories. A salesperson assigned to a densely populated urban territory can usually sell more product than a salesperson assigned to a sparsely populated area. The company, however, wants to reward all salespeople equitably. It also wants to give them the incentive to work as hard as possible and to report realistic sales targets, so that it can plan production and delivery schedules. Companies have always used bonuses and commissions to reward salespeople, but incentive schemes have often been poorly designed. Typically, salespeople's commissions were proportional to their sales. This approach elicited neither accurate information about feasible sales targets nor maximum performance.

Today, companies are learning that bonus schemes like the one given by equation (17.4) provide better results. The salesperson can be given an array of numbers showing the bonus as a function of both the sales target (chosen by the salesperson) and the actual level of sales. (The numbers would be calculated from equation (17.4) or some similar formula.) Salespeople will quickly figure out that they do best by reporting feasible sales targets and then working as hard as possible to meet them.[15]

---

## 17.6 ASYMMETRIC INFORMATION IN LABOR MARKETS: EFFICIENCY WAGE THEORY

When the labor market is competitive, all who wish to work will find jobs for wages equal to their marginal products. Yet most countries have substantial unemployment even though many people are aggressively seeking work. Many of the unemployed would presumably work for an even lower wage rate than that being received by employed people. Why don't we see firms cutting wage rates, increasing employment levels, and thereby increasing profit? Can our models of competitive equilibrium explain persistent unemployment?

In this section, we show how the **efficiency wage theory** can explain the presence of unemployment and wage discrimination.[16] We have thus far determined

> Recall from §14.1 that in a perfectly competitive labor market, firms hire labor to the point at which the real wage (the wage divided by the price of the product) is equal to the marginal product of labor.

• **efficiency wage theory** Explanation for the presence of unemployment and wage discrimination which recognizes that labor productivity may be affected by the wage rate.

---

[14]Any bonus of the form $B = \beta Q_f + \alpha(Q = Q_f)$ for $Q > Q_f$, and $B = \beta Q_f - \gamma(Q_f - Q)$ for $Q \le Q_f$, with $\gamma > \beta > \alpha > 0$ will work. See Martin L. Weitzman, "The New Soviet Incentive Model," *Bell Journal of Economics* 7 (Spring 1976): 251–6. There is a dynamic problem with this scheme that we have ignored: Managers must weigh a large bonus for good performance this year against being assigned more ambitious targets in the future. This is discussed in Martin Weitzman, "The 'Ratchet Principle' and Performance Incentives," *Bell Journal of Economics* 11 (Spring 1980): 302–8.

[15]See Jacob Gonik, "Tie Salesmen's Bonuses to Their Forecasts," *Harvard Business Review* (May–June 1978): 116–23.

[16]See Janet L. Yellen, "Efficiency Wage Models of Unemployment," *American Economic Review* 74 (May 1984): 200–5. The analysis relies on Joseph E. Stiglitz, "The Causes and Consequences of the Dependence of Quality on Price," *Journal of Economic Literature* 25 (March 1987): 1–48.

labor productivity according to workers' abilities and firms' investment in capital. Efficiency wage models recognize that labor productivity also depends on the wage rate. There are various explanations for this relationship. Economists have suggested that the productivity of workers in developing countries depends on the wage rate for nutritional reasons: Better-paid workers can afford to buy more and better food and are therefore healthier and can work more productively.

A better explanation for the United States is found in the **shirking model**. Because monitoring workers is costly or impossible, firms have imperfect information about worker productivity, and there is a principal–agent problem. In its simplest form, the shirking model assumes perfectly competitive markets in which all workers are equally productive and earn the same wage. Once hired, workers can either work productively or slack off (shirk). But because information about their performance is limited, workers may not get fired for shirking.

The model works as follows. If a firm pays its workers the market-clearing wage $w^*$, they have an incentive to shirk. Even if they get caught and are fired (and they might not be), they can immediately get hired somewhere else for the same wage. Because the threat of being fired does not impose a cost on workers, they have no incentive to be productive. As an incentive not to shirk, a firm must offer workers a higher wage. At this higher wage, workers who are fired for shirking will face a decrease in wages when hired by another firm at $w^*$. If the difference in wages is large enough, workers will be induced to be productive, and the employer will not have a problem with shirking. The wage at which no shirking occurs is the **efficiency wage**.

Up to this point, we have looked at only one firm. But all firms face the problem of shirking. All firms, therefore, will offer wages greater than the market-clearing wage $w^*$—say, $w_e$ (efficiency wage). Does this remove the incentive for workers not to shirk because they will be hired at the higher wage by other firms if they get fired? No. Because all firms are offering wages greater than $w^*$, the demand for labor is less than the market-clearing quantity, and there is unemployment. Consequently, workers fired for shirking will face spells of unemployment before earning $w_e$ at another firm.

Figure 17.5 shows shirking in the labor market. The demand for labor $D_L$ is downward-sloping for the traditional reasons. If there were no shirking, the intersection of $D_L$ with the supply of labor ($S_L$) would set the market wage at $w^*$, and full employment would result ($L^*$). With shirking, however, individual firms are unwilling to pay $w^*$. Rather, for every level of unemployment in the labor market, firms must pay some wage greater than $w^*$ to induce workers to be productive. This wage is shown as the *no-shirking constraint (NSC) curve*. This curve shows the minimum wage, for each level of unemployment, that workers must earn in order not to shirk. Note that the greater the level of unemployment, the smaller the difference between the efficiency wage and $w^*$. Why is this so? Because with high levels of unemployment, people who shirk risk long periods of unemployment and therefore don't need much inducement to be productive.

In Figure 17.5, the equilibrium wage will be at the intersection of the NSC curve and $D_L$ curves, with $L_e$ workers earning $w_e$. This equilibrium occurs because the NSC curve gives the lowest wage that firms can pay and still discourage shirking. Firms need not pay more than this wage to get the number of workers they need, and they will not pay less because a lower wage will encourage shirking. Note that the NSC curve never crosses the labor supply curve. This means that there will always be some unemployment in equilibrium.

**• shirking model** Principle that workers still have an incentive to shirk if a firm pays them a market-clearing wage, because fired workers can be hired somewhere else for the same wage.

**• efficiency wage** Wage that a firm will pay to an employee as an incentive not to shirk.

In §14.2, we explain that the equilibrium wage is given by the intersection of the demand for labor curve and the supply of labor curve.

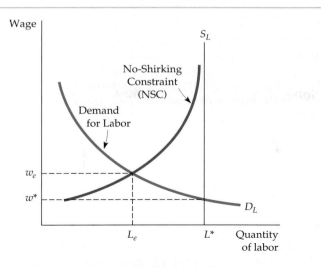

**FIGURE 17.5 Unemployment in a Shirking Model**

Unemployment can arise in otherwise competitive labor markets when employers cannot accurately monitor workers. Here, the "no shirking constraint" (NSC) gives the wage necessary to keep workers from shirking. The firm hires $L_e$ workers (at a higher than competitive efficiency wage $w_e$), creating $L^* - L_e$ of unemployment.

**EXAMPLE 17.6** Efficiency Wages at Ford Motor Company

One of the early examples of the payment of efficiency wages can be found in the history of Ford Motor Company. Before 1913, automobile production depended heavily on skilled workers. But the introduction of the assembly line drastically changed the workplace. Now jobs demanded much less skill, and production depended on maintaining assembly-line equipment. But as automobile plants changed, workers became increasingly disenchanted. In 1913, turnover at Ford was 380 percent. The following year, it rose to 1000 percent, and profit margins fell sharply.

Ford needed to maintain a stable workforce, and Henry Ford (and his business partner James Couzens) provided it. In 1914, when the going wage for a day's work in industry averaged between $2 and $3, Ford introduced a pay policy of $5 a day. The policy was prompted by improved labor efficiency, not generosity. The goal was to attract better workers who would stay with their jobs—and eventually to increase profits.

Although Henry Ford was attacked for it, his policy succeeded. His workforce did become more stable, and the publicity helped Ford's sales. In addition, because Ford had his pick of workers, he could hire a group that was on average more productive. Ford stated that the wage increase did in fact increase the loyalty and personal efficiency of his workers, and quantitative estimates support his statements. According to calculations by Ford's chief of labor relations, productivity increased by 51 percent. Another study found that absenteeism had been cut in half and discharges for cause had declined sharply. Thus the productivity increase more than offset the increase in wages. As a result, Ford's profitability rose from $30 million in 1914 to $60 million in 1916.

## SUMMARY

1. The seller of a product often has better information about its quality than the buyer. Asymmetric information of this type creates a market failure in which bad products tend to drive good products out of the market. Market failure can be eliminated if sellers offer standardized products, provide guarantees or warranties, or find other ways to maintain good reputations for their products.

2. Insurance markets frequently involve asymmetric information because the party buying insurance has better information about the risk involved than the insurance company. This can lead to adverse selection, in which poor risks choose to insure and good risks do not. Another problem for insurance markets is moral hazard, in which the insured takes less care to avoid losses after being insured.

3. Sellers can deal with the problem of asymmetric information by sending buyers signals about the quality of their products. For example, workers can signal high productivity by obtaining high levels of education.

4. Asymmetric information may make it costly for the owners of firms (principals) to monitor accurately the behavior of their managers (agents). Managers may seek higher fringe benefits for themselves or a goal of sales maximization, even though shareholders would prefer to maximize profit.

5. Owners can avoid some principal–agent problems by designing contracts that give their agents the incentive to perform productively.

6. Asymmetric information can explain why labor markets have unemployment even though some workers are actively seeking work. According to efficiency wage theory, a wage higher than the competitive wage (the efficiency wage) increases worker productivity by discouraging workers from shirking on the job.

## QUESTIONS FOR REVIEW

1. Why can asymmetric information between buyers and sellers lead to market failure when a market is otherwise perfectly competitive?

2. If the used car market is a "lemons" market, how would you expect the repair record of used cars that are sold to compare with the repair record of those not sold?

3. Explain the difference between adverse selection and moral hazard in insurance markets. Can one exist without the other?

4. Describe several ways in which sellers can convince buyers that their products are of high quality. Which methods apply to the following products: Maytag washing machines, Burger King hamburgers, large diamonds?

5. Why might a seller find it advantageous to signal the quality of a product? How are guarantees and warranties a form of market signaling?

6. Joe earned a high grade-point average during his four years of college. Is this achievement a strong signal to Joe's future employer that he will be a highly productive worker? Why or why not?

7. Why might managers be able to achieve objectives other than profit maximization, which is the goal of the firm's shareholders?

8. How can the principal–agent model be used to explain why public enterprises, such as post offices, might pursue goals other than profit maximization?

9. Why are bonus and profit-sharing payment schemes likely to resolve principal–agent problems, whereas a fixed-wage payment will not?

10. What is an efficiency wage? Why is it profitable for the firm to pay it when workers have better information about their productivity than firms do?

# EXERCISES

1. Many consumers view a well-known brand name as a signal of quality and will pay more for a brand-name product (e.g., Bayer aspirin instead of generic aspirin, or Birds Eye frozen vegetables instead of the supermarket's own brand). Can a brand name provide a useful signal of quality? Why or why not?

2. Gary is a recent college graduate. After six months at his new job, he has finally saved enough to buy his first car.
   a. Gary knows very little about the difference between makes and models. How could he use market signals, reputation, or standardization to make comparisons?
   b. You are a loan officer in a bank. After selecting a car, Gary comes to you seeking a loan. Because he has only recently graduated, he does not have a long credit history. Nonetheless, the bank has a long history of financing cars for recent college graduates. Is this information useful in Gary's case? If so, how?

3. A major university bans the assignment of D or F grades. It defends its action by claiming that students tend to perform above average when they are free from the pressures of flunking out. The university states that it wants all its students to get As and Bs. If the goal is to raise overall grades to the B level or above, is this a good policy? Discuss this policy with respect to the problem of moral hazard.

4. Professor Jones has just been hired by the economics department at a major university. The president of the board of regents has stated that the university is committed to providing top-quality education for undergraduates. Two months into the semester, Jones fails to show up for his classes. It seems he is devoting all his time to research rather than to teaching. Jones argues that his research will bring prestige to the department and the university. Should he be allowed to continue exclusively with research? Discuss with reference to the principal–agent problem.

5. Faced with a reputation for producing automobiles with poor repair records, a number of American companies have offered extensive guarantees to car purchasers (e.g., a seven-year warranty on all parts and labor associated with mechanical problems).
   a. In light of your knowledge of the lemons market, why is this a reasonable policy?
   b. Is the policy likely to create a moral hazard problem? Explain.

6. To promote competition and consumer welfare, the Federal Trade Commission requires firms to advertise truthfully. How does truth in advertising promote competition? Why would a market be less competitive if firms advertised deceptively?

7. An insurance company is considering issuing three types of fire insurance policies: (i) complete insurance coverage, (ii) complete coverage above and beyond a $10,000 deductible, and (iii) 90 percent coverage of all losses. Which policy is more likely to create moral hazard problems?

8. You have seen how asymmetric information can reduce the average quality of products sold in a market, as low-quality products drive out high-quality products. For those markets in which asymmetric information is prevalent, would you agree or disagree with each of the following? Explain briefly:
   a. The government should subsidize *Consumer Reports*.
   b. The government should impose quality standards—e.g., firms should not be allowed to sell low-quality items.
   c. The producer of a high-quality good will probably want to offer an extensive warranty.
   d. The government should require *all* firms to offer extensive warranties.

9. Two used car dealerships compete side by side on a main road. The first, Harry's Cars, always sells high-quality cars that it carefully inspects and, if necessary, services. On average, it costs Harry's $8000 to buy and service each car that it sells. The second dealership, Lew's Motors, always sells lower-quality cars. On average, it costs Lew's only $5000 for each car that it sells. If consumers knew the quality of the used cars they were buying, they would pay $10,000 on average for Harry's cars and only $7000 on average for Lew's cars.

   Without more information, consumers do not know the quality of each dealership's cars. In this case, they would figure that they have a 50–50 chance of ending up with a high-quality car and are thus willing to pay $8500 for a car.

   Harry has an idea: He will offer a bumper-to-bumper warranty for all cars that he sells. He knows that a warranty lasting $Y$ years will cost $500Y$ on average, and he also knows that if Lew tries to offer the same warranty, it will cost Lew $1000Y$ on average.
   a. Suppose Harry offers a one-year warranty on all of the cars he sells.
      i. What is Lew's profit if he *does not* offer a one-year warranty? If he *does* offer a one-year warranty?
      ii. What is Harry's profit if Lew does *not* offer a one-year warranty? If he *does* offer a one-year warranty?
      iii. Will Lew's match Harry's one-year warranty?
      iv. Is it a good idea for Harry to offer a one-year warranty?
   b. What if Harry offers a two-year warranty? Will this offer generate a credible signal of quality? What about a three-year warranty?
   c. If you were advising Harry, how long a warranty would you urge him to offer? Explain why.

*10. As chairman of the board of ASP Industries, you estimate that your annual profit is given by the table below. Profit (Π) is conditional upon market demand and the effort of your new CEO. The probabilities of each demand condition occurring are also shown in the table.

| Market Demand | Low Demand | Medium Demand | High Demand |
|---|---|---|---|
| Market Probabilities | .30 | .40 | .30 |
| Low Effort | Π=$5 million | Π=$10 million | Π=$15 million |
| High Effort | Π=$10 million | Π=$15 million | Π=$17 million |

You must design a compensation package for the CEO that will maximize the firm's expected profit. While the firm is risk neutral, the CEO is risk averse. The CEO's utility function is

Utility = $W^{.5}$ when making low effort

Utility = $W^{.5} - 100$ when making high effort

where $W$ is the CEO's income. (The −100 is the "utility cost" to the CEO of making a high effort.) You know the CEO's utility function, and both you and the CEO know all of the information in the preceding table. You do *not* know the level of the CEO's effort at time of compensation or the exact state of demand. You do see the firm's profit, however.

Of the three alternative compensation packages below, which do you as chairman of ASP Industries prefer? Why?

Package 1: Pay the CEO a flat salary of $575,000 per year

Package 2: Pay the CEO a fixed 6 percent of yearly firm profits

Package 3: Pay the CEO a flat salary of $500,000 per year and then 50 percent of any firm profits *above* $15 million

11. A firm's short-run revenue is given by $R = 10e - e^2$, where $e$ is the level of effort by a typical worker (all workers are assumed to be identical). A worker chooses his level of effort to maximize wage less effort $w - e$ (the per-unit cost of effort is assumed to be 1). Determine the level of effort and the level of profit (revenue less wage paid) for each of the following wage arrangements. Explain why these different principal–agent relationships generate different outcomes.
   **a.** $w = 2$ for $e \geq 1$; otherwise $w = 0$.
   **b.** $w = R/2$.
   **c.** $w = R - 12.5$.

# Externalities and Public Goods

In this chapter we study *externalities*—the effects of production and consumption activities not directly reflected in the market—and *public goods*—goods that benefit all consumers but that the market either undersupplies or does not supply at all. Externalities and public goods are important sources of market failure and thus raise serious public policy questions. For example, how much waste, if any, should firms be allowed to dump into rivers and streams? How strict should automobile emission standards be? How much money should the government spend on national defense? Education? Basic research? Public television?

When externalities are present, the price of a good need not reflect its social value. As a result, firms may produce too much or too little, so that the market outcome is inefficient. We begin by describing externalities and showing exactly how they create market inefficiencies. We then evaluate remedies. While some remedies involve government regulation, others rely primarily on bargaining among individuals or on the legal right of those adversely affected to sue those who create an externality.

Next, we analyze public goods. The marginal cost of providing a public good to an additional consumer is zero, and people cannot be prevented from consuming it. We distinguish between those goods that are difficult to provide privately and those that could have been provided by the market. We conclude by describing the problem that policymakers face when trying to decide how much of a public good to provide.

## 18.1 EXTERNALITIES

**Externalities** can arise between producers, between customers, or between consumers and producers. They can be *negative*—when the action of one party imposes costs on another party—or *positive*—when the action of one party benefits another party.

A *negative externality* occurs, for example, when a steel plant dumps its waste in a river that fishermen downstream depend on for their daily catch. The more waste the steel plant dumps in the river, the fewer fish will be supported. The firm, however, has no incentive to account for the external costs that it imposes on fishermen when making its production decision. Furthermore, there is no market in which

• **externality** Action by either a producer or a consumer which affects other producers or consumers, but is not accounted for in the market price.

these external costs can be reflected in the price of steel. A *positive externality* occurs when a home owner repaints her house and plants an attractive garden. All the neighbors benefit from this activity, even though the home owner's decision to repaint and landscape probably did not take these benefits into account.

## Negative Externalities and Inefficiency

Because externalities are not reflected in market prices, they can be a source of economic inefficiency. When firms do not take into account the harms associated with negative externalities, the result is excess production and unnecessary social costs. To see why, let's take our example of a steel plant dumping waste in a river. Figure 18.1(a) shows the production decision of a steel plant in a competitive market. Figure 18.1(b) shows the market demand and supply curves, assuming that all steel plants generate similar externalities. We assume that because the firm has a fixed-proportions production function, it cannot alter its input combinations; waste and other effluent can be reduced only by lowering output. (Without this assumption, firms would be jointly choosing among a variety of combinations of output and pollution abatement.) We will analyze the nature of the externality under two circumstances: first when only one steel plant pollutes and, second, when all steel plants pollute in the same way.

> In §6.3, we explain that with a fixed-proportions production function, it is impossible to substitute among inputs because each level of output requires a specific combination of labor and capital.

> In §8.3, we explain that because a competitive firm faces a horizontal demand curve, choosing its output so that marginal cost is equal to price is profit-maximizing.

The price of steel is $P_1$ at the intersection of the demand and supply curves in Figure 18.1(b). The MC curve in (a) gives a typical steel firm's marginal cost of production. The firm maximizes profit by producing output $q_1$, at which marginal cost is equal to price (which equals marginal revenue because the firm takes price as given). As the firm's output changes, however, the external cost

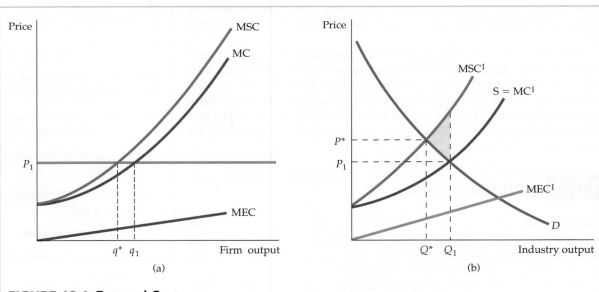

**FIGURE 18.1 External Cost**

When there are negative externalities, the marginal social cost MSC is higher than the marginal cost MC. The difference is the marginal external cost MEC. In **(a)**, a profit-maximizing firm produces at $q_1$, where price is equal to MC. The efficient output is $q^*$, at which price equals MSC. In **(b)**, the industry's competitive output is $Q_1$, at the intersection of industry supply $MC^I$ and demand $D$. However, the efficient output $Q^*$ is lower, at the intersection of demand and marginal social cost $MSC^I$.

imposed on fishermen downstream also changes. This external cost is given by the **marginal external cost** (MEC) curve in Figure 18.1(a). It is intuitively clear why total external cost increases with output—there is more pollution. However, our analysis focuses on the *marginal* external cost, which measures the added cost of the externality associated with each *additional* unit of output produced. In practice, the MEC curve is upward sloping for most forms of pollution: As the firm produces additional output and dumps additional effluent, the incremental harm to the fish industry increases.

> • **marginal external cost** Increase in cost imposed externally as one or more firms increase output by one unit.

From a social point of view, the firm produces too much output. The efficient level of output is the level at which the price of the product is equal to the **marginal social cost** (MSC) of production: the marginal cost of production *plus* the marginal external cost of dumping effluent. In Figure 18.1(a), the marginal social cost curve is obtained by adding marginal cost and marginal external cost for each level of output (i.e., MSC = MC + MEC). The marginal social cost curve MSC intersects the price line at output $q^*$. Because only one plant is dumping effluent into the river, the market price of the product is unchanged. However, the firm is producing too much output ($q_1$ instead of $q^*$) and generating too much effluent.

> • **marginal social cost** Sum of the marginal cost of production and the marginal external cost.

Now consider what happens when all steel plants dump their effluent into rivers. In Figure 18.1(b), the $MC^I$ curve is the industry supply curve. The marginal external cost associated with the industry output, $MEC^I$, is obtained by summing the marginal cost of every person harmed at each level of output. The $MSC^I$ curve represents the sum of the marginal cost of production and the marginal external cost *for all steel firms*. As a result, $MSC^I = MC^I + MEC^I$.

Is industry output efficient when there are externalities? As Figure 18.1(b) shows, the efficient industry output level is the level at which the marginal benefit of an additional unit of output is equal to the marginal social cost. Because the demand curve measures the marginal benefit to consumers, the efficient output is $Q^*$, at the intersection of the marginal social cost $MSC^I$ and demand $D$ curves. The competitive industry output, however, is at $Q_1$, the intersection of the demand curve and the supply curve, $MC^I$. Clearly, industry output is too high.

> In §9.2, we explain that, absent market failure, a competitive market leads to the economically efficient output level.

In our example, each unit of output results in some effluent being dumped. Therefore, whether we are looking at one firm's pollution or the entire industry's, the economic inefficiency is the excess production that results in too much effluent being dumped in the river. The source of the inefficiency is the incorrect pricing of the product. The market price $P_1$ in Figure 18.1(b) is too low—it reflects the firms' marginal private cost of production, but not the marginal *social* cost. Only at the higher price $P^*$ will steel firms produce the efficient level of output.

What is the cost to society of this inefficiency? For each unit produced above $Q^*$, the social cost is given by the difference between the marginal social cost and the marginal benefit (the demand curve). As a result, the aggregate social cost is shown in Figure 18.1(b) as the shaded triangle between $MSC^I$, $D$, and output $Q_1$. When we move from the profit-maximizing to the socially efficient output, firms are worse off because their profits are reduced, and purchasers of steel are worse off because the price of steel has increased. However, these losses are less than the gain to those who were harmed by the adverse effect of the dumping of effluent in the river.

Externalities generate both long-run and short-run inefficiencies. In Chapter 8, we saw that firms enter a competitive industry whenever the price of the product is above the *average cost* of production and exit whenever price is below average cost. In long-run equilibrium, price is equal to (long-run) average cost. When there are negative externalities, the average private cost of production is less than the average social cost. As a result, some firms remain in the industry even when it would be efficient for them to leave. Thus, negative externalities encourage too many firms to remain in the industry.

## Positive Externalities and Inefficiency

Externalities can also result in too little production, as the example of home repair and landscaping shows. In Figure 18.2, the horizontal axis measures the home owner's investment (in dollars) in repairs and landscaping. The marginal cost curve for home repair shows the cost of repairs as more work is done on the house; it is horizontal because this cost is unaffected by the amount of repairs. The demand curve $D$ measures the marginal private benefit of the repairs to the home owner. The home owner will choose to invest $q_1$ in repairs, at the intersection of her demand and marginal cost curves. But repairs generate external benefits to the neighbors, as the **marginal external benefit** curve, MEB, shows. This curve is downward sloping in this example because the marginal benefit is large for a small amount of repair but falls as the repair work becomes extensive.

• **marginal external benefit**
Increased benefit that accrues to other parties as a firm increases output by one unit.

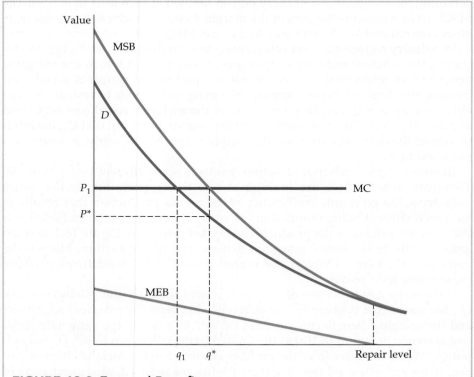

**FIGURE 18.2 External Benefits**

When there are positive externalities, marginal social benefits MSB are higher than marginal benefits $D$. The difference is the marginal external benefit MEB. A self-interested homeowner invests $q_1$ in repairs, determined by the intersection of the marginal benefit curve $D$ and the marginal cost curve MC. The efficient level of repair $q^*$ is higher and is given by the intersection of the marginal social benefit and marginal cost curves.

The **marginal social benefit** curve, MSB, is calculated by adding the marginal private benefit and the marginal external benefit at every level of output. In short, MSB = $D$ + MEB. The efficient level of output $q^*$, at which the marginal social benefit of additional repairs is equal to the marginal cost of those repairs, is found at the intersection of the MSB and MC curves. The inefficiency arises because the homeowner doesn't receive all the benefits of her investment in repairs and landscaping. As a result, the price $P_1$ is too high to encourage her to invest in the socially desirable level of house repair. A lower price, $P^*$, is required to encourage the efficient level of supply, $q^*$.

> **marginal social benefit**
> Sum of the marginal private benefit plus the marginal external benefit.

Another example of a positive externality is the money that firms spend on research and development (R&D). Often the innovations resulting from research cannot be protected from other firms. Suppose, for example, that a firm designs a new product. If that design can be patented, the firm might earn a large profit by manufacturing and marketing the product. But if the new design can be closely imitated by other firms, those firms can appropriate some of the developing firm's profit. Because there is then little reward for doing R&D, the market is likely to underfund it.

The externality concept is not new: In discussing demand in Chapter 4, we explained that positive and negative network externalities can arise if the quantity of a good demanded by a consumer increases or decreases in response to an increase in purchases by other consumers. Network externalities can also lead to market failures. Suppose, for example, that some individuals enjoy socializing at busy ski resorts when many other skiers are present. The resulting congestion could make the skiing experience unpleasant for those skiers who preferred short lift lines to pleasant social occasions.

> In §4.5, we explain that when there is a network externality, each individual's demand depends on the purchases of other individuals.

---

| EXAMPLE 18.1 | The Costs and Benefits of Sulfur Dioxide Emissions |
|---|---|

Although sulfur dioxide gas can be produced naturally by volcanoes, almost two-thirds of all sulfur dioxide emissions in the United States come from electric power generation that depends on burning fossil fuels such as coal and petroleum. The effect of sulfur dioxide pollution on the environment has concerned policymakers for years, but these concerns reached new heights in the 1990s (with a series of amendments to the Clean Air Act) because of the potential adverse effects of acid rain. Acid rain—formed when sulfur dioxide and nitrogen oxides react with the atmosphere to form various acidic compounds—threatens property and health throughout the midwestern and northwestern United States.[1]

Acid rain can adversely affect human health either directly, from the atmosphere, or from the soil in which our food is grown. Acid rain has been shown to increase risk of heart and lung disorders such as asthma and bronchitis and has been linked to premature death in both adults and children. According to one estimate, if sulfur dioxide emissions had been reduced by 50 percent of 1980s levels—a time when emissions were at a historic high in the United States—over 17,000 deaths per year would have been prevented.

In addition to human health, acid rain causes damage to water and forests as well as to man-made structures. According to one study, a 50-percent reduction

---

[1]Further information on sulfur dioxide and acid rain can be found at **http://www.epa.gov**.

in sulfur dioxide levels in the 1980s would have translated into a $24 million annual value in improvements in recreational fishing, an $800 million annual value to the commercial timber sector, and a $700 million annual value to grain crop producers.[2] Furthermore, sulfur dioxide emissions have been shown to cause damage to paint, steel, limestone, and marble through increased surface erosion. While the cost of acid rain to man-made materials is difficult to quantify, automobile manufacturers are now offering acid-resistant paint on new automobiles at an average cost of $5 per car, or $61 million for all new cars and trucks sold in the United States.

What about the costs of achieving reductions in sulfur dioxide emissions? To achieve these reductions, firms need to put emissions-control equipment into use. The incremental cost of achieving some emissions reduction is likely to be small, but that cost increases as greater and greater investments in capital equipment are needed to achieve further reductions.

An example of the costs and benefits of reducing sulfur dioxide emissions is given in Figure 18.3, which is based on a study of pollution abatement in Philadelphia.[3] It is easiest to read the graph from right to left, since we are looking to see how much of a reduction in sulfur dioxide concentrations from the existing level of .08 parts per million is socially desirable. The marginal abatement cost curve is increasing (from right to left); it jumps whenever new capital-intensive pollution-control equipment is needed to improve fuel efficiency.

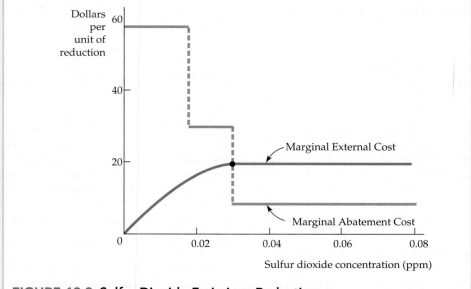

**FIGURE 18.3 Sulfur Dioxide Emissions Reductions**

The efficient sulfur dioxide concentration equates the marginal abatement cost to the marginal external cost. Here the marginal abatement cost curve is a series of steps, each representing the use of a different abatement technology.

---

[2]Spencer Banzhaf et al., "Valuation of Natural Resource Improvements in the Adirondacks" (Washington: Resources for the Future, September 2004).

[3]Thomas R. Irvin, "A Cost Benefit Analysis of Sulfur Dioxide Abatement Regulations in Philadelphia," *Business Economics*, September 1977, pp. 12–20.

The marginal external cost curve reflects (again reading from right to left) the incremental reduction in the harms caused by acid rain. For moderate concentrations, studies of respiratory diseases, corrosion of materials, and lost visibility suggest that marginal social costs are high and relatively constant. However, for very low concentrations, the marginal external cost declines, and eventually there are relatively little adverse health, material, or aesthetic effects.

The efficient level of reduced sulfur dioxide emissions is given by the number of ppm at which the marginal cost of reduced emissions is equal to the marginal external cost. We can see from Figure 18.3 that this level is approximately .0275 ppm.

To sum up, there are clearly substantial benefits to reducing sulfur dioxide emissions. What if any policies are best utilized to achieve those reductions efficiently? We will return to these questions after we consider a variety of policy options for the treatment of externalities in Section 18.2.

## 18.2 WAYS OF CORRECTING MARKET FAILURE

How can the inefficiency resulting from an externality be remedied? If the firm that generates the externality has a fixed-proportions production technology, the externality can be reduced only by encouraging the firm to produce less. As we saw in Chapter 8, this goal can be achieved through an output tax. Fortunately, most firms can substitute among inputs in the production process by altering their choices of technology. For example, a manufacturer can add a scrubber to its smokestack to reduce emissions.

Consider a firm that sells its output in a competitive market. The firm emits pollutants that damage air quality in a neighborhood. The firm can reduce its emissions, but only at a cost. Figure 18.4 illustrates this trade-off. The horizontal axis represents the level of factory emissions and the vertical axis the cost per unit of emissions. To simplify, we assume that the firm's output decision and its emissions decision are independent and that the firm has already chosen its profit-maximizing output level. The firm is therefore ready to choose its preferred level of emissions. The curve labeled MEC represents the *marginal external cost of emissions*. This social cost curve represents the increased harm associated with the emissions. We will use the terms *marginal external cost* and *marginal social cost* interchangeably in the discussion that follows. (Recall that we have assumed that the firm's output is fixed, so that the private costs of production—as opposed to pollution abatement—are unchanged.) The MEC curve slopes upward because the *marginal* cost of the externality gets higher as the externality becomes more extensive. (Evidence from studies of the effects of air and water pollution suggests that small levels of pollutants generate little harm. However, the harm increases substantially as the level of pollutants increases.)

Because our emphasis will be on reducing emissions from existing levels, we will find it useful to read the MEC graph from right to left. From this perspective, we see that the MEC associated with a small reduction in emissions from a level of 26 units, which reflects the incremental benefit of reduced emissions, is greater than $6 per unit. However, as emissions are reduced further and further, the marginal social cost falls (eventually) to below $2 per unit. At some point, the incremental benefit of reducing emissions becomes less than $2.

The curve labeled MCA is the *marginal cost of abating emissions*. It measures the additional cost to the firm of installing pollution-control equipment. The

Recall from §7.3 that a firm can substitute among inputs by changing technologies in response to an effluent fee.

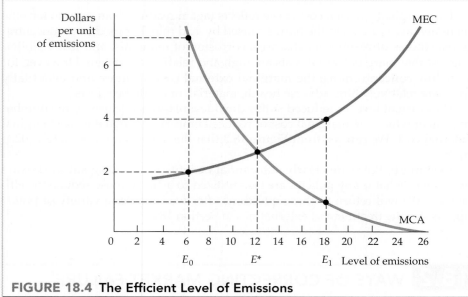

**FIGURE 18.4 The Efficient Level of Emissions**

The efficient level of factory emissions is the level that equates the marginal external cost of emissions MEC to the benefit associated with lower abatement costs MCA. The efficient level of 12 units is $E^*$.

MCA curve is downward sloping because the marginal cost of reducing emissions is low when the reduction has been slight and high when it has been substantial. (A slight reduction is inexpensive—the firm can reschedule production to generate the greatest emissions at night, when few people are outside. Large reductions require costly changes in the production process.) As with the MEC curve, reading the MCA curve from right to left will help with our intuition. From this perspective, the marginal cost of abatement increases as we seek to achieve greater and greater reductions in emissions.

With *no* effort at abatement, the firm's profit-maximizing level of emissions is 26, the level at which the marginal cost of abatement is zero. The efficient level of emissions, 12 units, is at point $E^*$, where the marginal external cost of emissions, $3, is equal to the marginal cost of abating emissions. Note that if emissions are lower than $E^*$—say, $E_0$—the marginal cost of abating emissions, $7, is greater than the marginal external cost of emissions, $2. Emissions, therefore, are too low relative to the social optimum. However, if the level of emissions is $E_1$, the marginal external cost of emissions, $4, is greater than the marginal cost of abatement, $1. Emissions are then too high.

We can encourage the firm to reduce emissions to $E^*$ in three ways: (1) emissions standards; (2) emissions fees; and (3) transferable emissions permits. We will begin by discussing standards and fees and comparing relative advantages and disadvantages. Then we will examine transferable emissions permits.

## An Emissions Standard

• **emissions standard** Legal limit on the amount of pollutants that a firm can emit.

An **emissions standard** is a legal limit on how much pollutant a firm can emit. If the firm exceeds the limit, it can face monetary and even criminal penalties. In Figure 18.5, the efficient emissions standard is 12 units, at point $E^*$. The firm will be heavily penalized for emissions greater than this level.

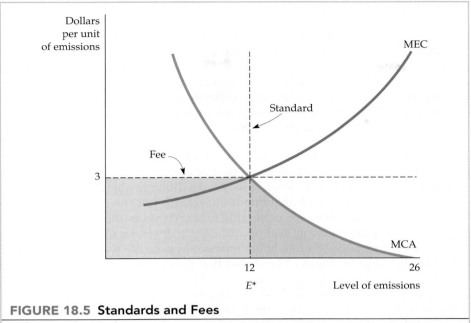

**FIGURE 18.5 Standards and Fees**

The efficient level of emissions at E* can be achieved through either an emissions fee or an emissions standard. Facing a fee of $3 per unit of emissions, a firm reduces emissions to the point at which the fee is equal to the marginal cost of abatement. The same level of emissions reduction can be achieved with a standard that limits emissions to 12 units.

The standard ensures that the firm produces efficiently. The firm meets the standard by installing pollution-abatement equipment. The increased abatement expenditure will cause the firm's average cost curve to rise (by the average cost of abatement). Firms will find it profitable to enter the industry only if the price of the product is greater than the average cost of production plus abatement—the efficient condition for the industry.[4]

## An Emissions Fee

An **emissions fee** is a charge levied on each unit of a firm's emissions. As Figure 18.5 shows, a $3 emissions fee will generate efficient behavior by our factory. Faced with this fee, the firm minimizes costs by reducing emissions from 26 to 12 units. To see why, note that the first unit of emissions can be reduced (from 26 to 25 units of emissions) at very little cost (the marginal cost of additional abatement is close to zero). For very little cost, therefore, the firm can avoid paying the $3 per-unit fee. In fact, for all levels of emissions above 12 units, the marginal cost of abatement is less than the emissions fee. Thus it pays to reduce emissions. Below 12 units, however, the marginal cost of abatement is greater than the fee. In that case, the firm will prefer to pay the fee rather than further reduce emissions. It will therefore pay a total fee given by the gray-shaded rectangle and incur a total abatement cost given by the blue-shaded triangle under the MCA curve to the right of E = 12. This cost is less than the fee that the firm would pay if it did not reduce emissions at all.

• **emissions fee** Charge levied on each unit of a firm's emissions.

---

[4]This analysis assumes that the social costs of emissions do not change over time. If they do, the efficient standard will also change.

## Standards versus Fees

The United States has historically relied on standards to regulate emissions. However, other countries, such as Germany, have used fees successfully. Which method is better? The relative advantages of standards and fees depend on the amount of information available to policymakers and on the actual cost of controlling emissions. To understand these differences, let's suppose that because of administrative costs, the agency that regulates emissions must charge the same fee or set the same standard for all firms.

**The Case for Fees**  First, let's examine the case for fees. Consider two firms that are located so that the marginal social cost of emissions is the same no matter which reduces its emissions. Because they have different abatement costs, however, their marginal cost of abatement curves are not the same. Figure 18.6 shows why emissions fees are preferable to standards in this case. $MCA_1$ and $MCA_2$ represent the marginal cost of abatement curves for the two firms. Each firm initially generates 14 units of emissions. Suppose we want to reduce total emissions by 14 units. Figure 18.6 shows that the cheapest way to do this is to have Firm 1 reduce emissions by 6 units and Firm 2 by 8. With these reductions, both firms have marginal costs of abatement of $3. But consider what happens if the regulatory agency asks both firms to reduce emissions by 7 units. In that case Firm 1's marginal cost of abatement increases from $3 to $3.75, while Firm 2's marginal cost of abatement decreases from $3 to $2.50. This cannot be cost-minimizing because the second firm can reduce emissions more cheaply than the first. Only when the marginal cost of abatement is equal for both firms will emissions be reduced by 14 units at minimum cost.

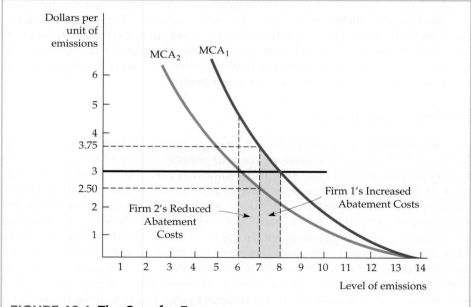

**FIGURE 18.6  The Case for Fees**

With limited information, a policymaker may be faced with the choice of either a single emissions fee or a single emissions standard for all firms. The fee of $3 achieves a total emissions level of 14 units more cheaply than a 7-unit-per-firm emissions standard. With the fee, the firm with a lower abatement cost curve (Firm 2) reduces emissions more than the firm with a higher cost curve (Firm 1).

Now we can see why a fee ($3) might be preferable to a standard (7 units). Faced with a $3 fee, Firm 1 will reduce emissions by 6 units and Firm 2 by 8 units—the efficient outcome. By contrast, under an emissions standard, Firm 1 incurs additional abatement costs given by the green-shaded area between 7 and 8 units of emissions. But Firm 2 enjoys reduced abatement costs given by the purple-shaded area between 6 and 7 units. Clearly, Firm 1's added abatement costs are larger than Firm 2's reduced costs. The emissions fee thus achieves the same level of emissions at a lower cost than the equal per-firm emissions standard.

In general, fees can be preferable to standards for several reasons. First, when standards must be applied equally to all firms, fees achieve the same emissions reduction at a lower cost. Second, fees give a firm a strong incentive to install new equipment that would allow it to reduce emissions *even further*. Suppose the standard requires that each firm reduce its emission by 6 units, from 14 to 8. Firm 1 is considering installing new emissions devices that would lower its marginal cost of abatement from $MCA_1$ to $MCA_2$. If the equipment is relatively inexpensive, the firm will install it because it will lower the cost of meeting the standard. However, a $3 emissions fee would provide a greater incentive for the firm to reduce emissions. With the fee, not only will the firm's cost of abatement be lower on the first 6 units of reduction, but it will also be cheaper to reduce emissions by 2 more units: The emissions fee is greater than the marginal abatement cost for emissions levels between 6 and 8.

**The Case for Standards** Now let's examine the case for standards by looking at Figure 18.7. While the marginal external cost curve is very steep, the marginal cost of abatement is relatively flat. The efficient emissions fee is $8. But suppose

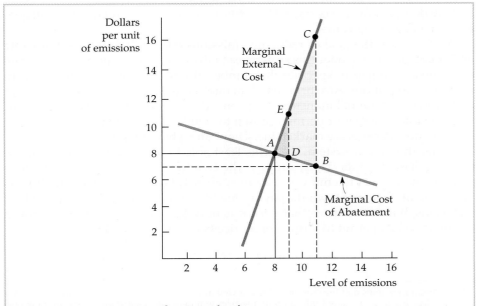

**FIGURE 18.7 The Case for Standards**

When the government has limited information about the costs and benefits of pollution abatement, either a standard or a fee may be preferable. The standard is preferable when the marginal external cost curve is steep and the marginal abatement cost curve is relatively flat. Here a 12.5 percent error in setting the standard leads to extra social costs of triangle *ADE*. The same percentage error in setting a fee would result in excess costs of *ABC*.

that because of limited information, a lower fee of $7 is charged (this fee amounts to a 1/8 or 12.5 percent reduction). Because the MCA curve is flat, the firm's emissions will be increased from 8 to 11 units. This increase lowers the firm's abatement costs somewhat, but because the MEC curve is steep, there will be substantial additional social costs. The increase in social costs, less the savings in abatement costs, is given by the entire shaded (light and dark) triangle *ABC*.

What happens if a comparable error is made in setting the standard? The efficient standard is 8 units of emissions. But suppose the standard is relaxed by 12.5 percent, from 8 to 9 units. As before, this change will lead to an increase in social costs and a decrease in abatement costs. But the net increase in social costs, given by the small triangle *ADE*, is much smaller than before.

This example illustrates the difference between standards and fees. When the marginal external cost curve is relatively steep and the marginal cost of abatement curve relatively flat, the cost of not reducing emissions is high. In such cases, a standard is preferable to a fee. With incomplete information, standards offer more certainty about emissions levels but leave the costs of abatement uncertain. Fees, on the other hand, offer certainty about the costs of abatement but leave the reduction of emissions levels uncertain. The preferable policy depends, therefore, on the nature of uncertainty and on the shapes of the cost curves.[5]

## Tradeable Emissions Permits

If we knew the costs and benefits of abatement and if all firms' costs were identical, we could apply a standard. Alternatively, if the costs of abatement varied among firms, an emissions fee would work. However, when firms' costs vary and we do not know the costs and benefits, neither a standard nor a fee will generate an efficient outcome.

• **tradeable emissions permits** System of marketable permits, allocated among firms, specifying the maximum level of emissions that can be generated.

We can reach the goal of reducing emissions efficiently by using **tradeable emissions permits**. Under this system, each firm must have permits to generate emissions. Each permit specifies the number of units of emissions that the firm is allowed to put out. Any firm that generates emissions not allowed by permit is subject to substantial monetary sanctions. Permits are allocated among firms, with the total number of permits chosen to achieve the desired maximum level of emissions. Permits are marketable: They can be bought and sold.

Under the permit system, the firms least able to reduce emissions are those that purchase permits. Thus, suppose the two firms in Figure 18.6 (page 654) were given permits to emit up to 7 units. Firm 1, facing a relatively high marginal cost of abatement, would pay up to $3.75 to buy a permit for one unit of emissions, but the value of that permit is only $2.50 to Firm 2. Firm 2 should therefore sell its permit to Firm 1 for a price between $2.50 and $3.75.

---

[5]Our analysis presumes that the emissions fee is levied as a fixed fee per unit of emissions. If the fee is set too low because of limited information, the firm will generate a substantial amount of excess emissions. Suppose, however, that a fixed fee were replaced with a fee schedule designed so that the higher the level of emissions the higher the per-unit fee. In this case, if the fee schedule is set too low, the increasing fee will discourage the firm from generating substantial excess emissions. In general, a variable fee is preferable to a standard if the fee schedule can be designed to match the environmental harm caused by the emissions. In this case, firms know that the payment they make will be approximately equal to the harm that they cause and will *internalize* that harm in making their production decisions. See Louis Kaplow and Steven Shavell, "On the Superiority of Corrective Taxes to Quantity Regulation," *American Law and Economics Review* 4 (Spring 2002): 1–17.

If there are enough firms and permits, a competitive market for permits will develop. In market equilibrium, the price of a permit equals the marginal cost of abatement for all firms; otherwise, a firm will find it advantageous to buy more permits. The level of emissions chosen by the government will be achieved at minimum cost. Those firms with relatively low marginal cost of abatement curves will be reducing emissions the most, and those with relatively high marginal cost of abatement curves will be buying more permits and reducing emissions the least.

Marketable emissions permits create a market for externalities. This market approach is appealing because it combines some of the advantageous features of a system of standards with the cost advantages of a fee system. The agency that administers the system determines the total number of permits and, therefore, the total amount of emissions, just as a system of standards would do. But the marketability of the permits allows pollution abatement to be achieved at minimum cost.[6]

**EXAMPLE 18.2**   Reducing Sulfur Dioxide Emissions in Beijing

Taken together, sulfur dioxide emissions produced through the burning of coal for use in electric power generation and the wide use of coal-based home furnaces have caused a huge problem in Beijing as well as other cities in China. Not only have emissions created an acid rain problem, but they have combined with emissions from the growing number of automobiles to make Beijing one of the most polluted cities not only in China, but in the world. In 1995, for example, the level of sulfur dioxide in Beijing was 90 milligrams per cubic meter, which compares unfavorably to Berlin (18 mg/m$^3$), Copenhagen (7), London (25), New York (26), Tokyo (18), and Mexico City (74). Of the major cities in the world, only Moscow had higher sulfur dioxide levels (109 mg/m$^3$).

Over the long term, the key to solving Beijing's problem is to replace coal with cleaner fuels, to encourage the use of public transportation, and, when necessary, to introduce fuel-efficient hybrid vehicles. But prior to its hosting of the Olympics in 2008, Beijing had a problem. What could it do to reduce sulfur dioxide emissions so as to offer a cleaner environment to the Olympic athletes and to the visiting public?

Beijing's choice was to shut down a large number of coal-fired plants. This strategic choice can obviously accomplish the stated goal of reducing emissions. But is it the most efficient policy choice? Our study of pollution-abatement strategies suggests not. For one thing, we have experience with the use of standards for regulating sulfur dioxide emissions in Philadelphia (recall Example 18.1). In 1968, Philadelphia imposed air-quality regulations that limited the maximum allowable sulfur content in fuel oil to 1.0 percent or less. This regulation decreased sulfur dioxide levels in the air substantially—from 0.10 parts per million (ppm) in 1968 to below 0.030 ppm in 1973. Improved air quality led to better human health,

---

[6]With limited information and costly monitoring, a marketable permit system is not always ideal. For example, if the total number of permits is chosen incorrectly and the marginal cost of abatement rises sharply for some firms, a permit system could drive those firms out of business by imposing high abatement costs. (This would also be a problem for fees.)

less damage to materials, and higher property values. Example 18.1 shows that the imposed standards made sense on cost-benefit grounds.

Would the imposition of a system of emissions fees—or better yet a regime of tradeable emissions permits—do even better in Beijing? A study of the regulation of electric-utility sulfur dioxide tradeable emissions shows that marketable permits in the United States can cut in half the cost of complying with a regulatory-based standard.[7] Can similar gains be achieved in Beijing? The answer lies in part on whether the market for tradeable emissions will itself work efficiently. But it also depends on the shape of the marginal abatement cost and marginal external cost curves. As our prior discussion has shown, the case for emissions fees (and for tradeable permits) is strongest (1) when firms vary substantially in their marginal abatement costs; and (2) when the marginal external cost of emissions curve is relatively steep and the marginal cost of abatement curve relatively flat.

| EXAMPLE 18.3 | Emissions Trading and Clean Air |

Controlling emissions cost companies approximately $18 billion during the 1980s, and it cost even more during the first half of the 1990s.[8] An effective emissions trading system could reduce those costs substantially in the decades to come. The Environmental Protection Agency's "bubble" and "offset" programs were modest attempts to use a trading system to lower cleanup costs.

A bubble allows an individual firm to adjust its pollution controls for individual sources of pollutants as long as a *total pollutant limit* for the firm is not exceeded. In theory, a bubble could be used to set pollutant limits for many firms or for an entire geographic region; in practice, however, it has been applied to individual firms. As a result "permits" are, in effect, traded within the firm: If one part of the firm can reduce its emissions, another part will be allowed to emit more. Abatement cost savings associated with the EPA's program of 42 bubbles have been approximately $300 million per year since 1979.

Under the offset program, new sources of emissions may be located in geographic regions in which air-quality standards have not been met, but only if they offset their new emissions by reducing emissions from existing sources by at least as much. Offsets can be obtained by internal trading, but external trading among firms is also allowed. A total of more than 2000 offset transactions have occurred since 1976.

Because of their limited natures, bubble and offset programs substantially understate the potential gain from a broad-based emissions trading program. In one study, the cost of achieving an 85-percent reduction in hydrocarbon emissions in all U.S. DuPont plants was estimated under three alternative policies: (1) each source at each plant must reduce emissions by 85 percent; (2) each plant must reduce its overall emissions by 85 percent with only internal trading possible; and (3) total emissions at all plants must be reduced by 85 percent, with both internal and external trading possible.[9] When no trading was allowed, the

[7]Don Fullerton, Shaun P. McDermott, and Jonathan P. Caulkins, "Sulfur Dioxide Compliance of a Regulated Utility," NBER Working Paper No. 5542, April 1996.

[8]See Robert W. Hahn and Gordon L. Hester, "The Market for Bads: EPA's Experience with Emissions Trading," *Regulation* (1987): 48–53; Brian J. McKean, "Evolution of Marketable Permits: The U.S. Experience with Sulfur-Dioxide Allowance Trading," Environmental Protection Agency, December, 1996.

[9]M. T. Maloney and Bruce Yandle, "Bubbles and Efficiency: Cleaner Air at Lower Cost," *Regulation* (May/June 1980): 49–52.

cost of emissions reduction was $105.7 million. Internal trading reduced the cost to $42.6 million. Allowing for both external and internal trading reduced the cost even further, to $14.6 million.

Clearly, the potential cost savings from an effective tradeable emissions program can be substantial. This may explain why Congress focused on transferable permits as a way of dealing with "acid rain" in the 1990 Clean Air Act. Acid rain can be extremely harmful to people, animals, vegetation, and buildings. The government initially authorized a permit system to reduce annual sulfur dioxide emissions by 10 million tons and nitrogen oxide emissions by 2.5 million tons by the year 2000. That program remains in place today.

Under the plan, each tradeable permit allows a maximum of one ton of sulfur dioxide to be released into the air. Electric utilities and other polluting entities are allocated permits in proportion to their current level of emissions. Companies can make the capital investments necessary to reduce emissions, perhaps selling excess permits, or they can buy permits and avoid having to make costly emissions-reducing investments.

In the early 1990s, economists expected these permits to trade for around $300. In fact, as Figure 18.8 shows, between 1993 and 2003, prices fluctuated between $100 and $200. Why? It turned out that reducing sulfur dioxide emissions was less costly than anticipated (it had become cheaper to mine low-sulfur coal), and many electric utilities took advantage of this development to reduce emissions. During 2005 to 2006, however, the price of permits rose sharply, hitting a high of nearly $1600 in December 2005. This was the result of an increase in the price of low-sulfur coal and, more importantly, the increased

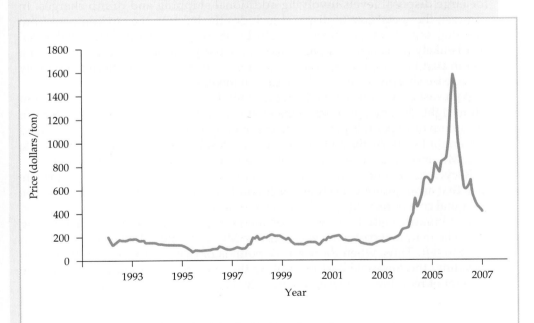

**FIGURE 18.8 Price of Tradeable Emissions Permits**

The price of tradeable permits for sulfur dioxide emissions fluctuated between $100 and $200 in the period 1993 to 2003, but then increased sharply during 2005 and 2006 in response to an increased demand for permits. Since then, the price has fluctuated around $400 to $500 per ton.

demand for permits that resulted as more electric power plants were required to meet tight emissions standards. By 2007, prices had stabilized at around $400 to $500. But the lesson for electric utilities is not only that the cost of abatement had become higher than anticipated, but that it is volatile and difficult to predict.[10]

## Recycling

To the extent that the disposal of waste products involves little or no private cost to either consumers or producers, society will dispose of too much waste material. The overutilization of virgin materials and the underutilization of recycled materials will result in a market failure that may require government intervention. Fortunately, given the appropriate incentive to recycle products, this market failure can be corrected.[11]

To see how recycling incentives can work, consider a typical household's decision with respect to the disposal of glass containers. In many communities, households are charged a fixed annual fee for trash disposal. As a result, these households can dispose of glass and other garbage at very low cost—only the time and effort to put the materials in a trash receptacle.

The low cost of disposal creates a divergence between the private and the social cost of disposal. The marginal private cost, which is the cost to the household of throwing out the glass, is likely to be constant (independent of the amount of disposal) for low to moderate levels of disposal. It will then increase for large disposal levels involving additional shipping and dump charges. In contrast, the social cost of disposal includes the harm to the environment from littering, as well as the injuries caused by sharp glass objects. Marginal social cost is likely to increase, in part because the marginal private cost is increasing and in part because the environmental and aesthetic costs of littering are likely to increase sharply as the level of disposal increases.

Both cost curves are shown in Figure 18.9. The horizontal axis measures, from left to right, the amount of scrap material $m$ that the household disposes, up to a maximum of 12 pounds per week. Consequently, the amount recycled can be read from right to left. As the amount of scrap disposal increases, the marginal private cost, MC, increases, but at a much lower rate than the marginal social cost MSC.

Recycling of containers can be accomplished by a municipality or a private firm that arranges for collection, consolidation, and processing of materials. The marginal cost of recycling is likely to increase as the amount of recycling grows, in part because collection, separation, and cleaning costs grow at an increasing rate. The marginal cost of recycling curve, MCR, in Figure 18.9 is best read from right to left. Thus, when there are 12 pounds of disposed material, there is no recycling; the marginal cost is zero. As the amount of disposal decreases, the amount of recycling increases; the marginal cost of recycling increases.

---

[10]Our thanks to Elizabeth Bailey, Denny Ellerman and Paul Joskow for providing the emissions permit price data and for helpful comments. For a more detailed explanation of permit prices, see A. D. Ellerman, P. L. Joskow, R. Schmalensee, J. P. Montero, and E. M. Bailey, *Markets for Clean Air: The U.S. Acid Rain Program* (Boston: MIT Center for Energy and Environmental Policy Research, 1999). For more information on tradeable permits generally, go to the EPA Web site at **www.epa.gov**.

[11]Even without market intervention, some recycling will occur if the price of virgin material is sufficiently high. For example, recall from Chapter 2 that when the price of copper is high, there is more recycling of scrap copper.

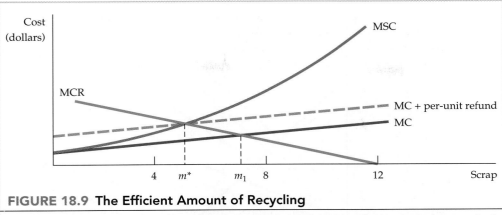

**FIGURE 18.9 The Efficient Amount of Recycling**

The efficient amount of recycling of scrap material is the amount that equates the marginal social cost of scrap disposal, MSC, to the marginal cost of recycling, MCR. The efficient amount of scrap for disposal $m^*$ is less than the amount that will arise in a private market, $m_1$.

The efficient amount of recycling occurs at the point at which the marginal cost of recycling, MCR, is equal to the marginal *social* cost of disposal, MSC. As Figure 18.9 shows, the efficient amount of scrap for disposal $m^*$ is less than the amount that will arise in a private market, $m_1$.

Why not utilize a disposal fee, a disposal standard, or even transferable disposal permits to resolve this externality? Any of these policies can help in theory, but they are not easy to put into practice and are rarely used. For example, a disposal fee is difficult to implement because it would be very costly for a community to sort through trash to separate and then to collect glass materials. Pricing and billing for scrap disposal would also be expensive, because the weight and composition of materials would affect the social cost of the scrap and, therefore, the appropriate price to be charged.

**Refundable Deposits** One policy solution that has been used with some success to encourage recycling is the *refundable deposit*.[12] Under a refundable deposit system, an initial deposit is paid to the store owner when the glass container product is purchased. The deposit is refunded if and when the container is returned to the store or to a recycling center. Refundable deposits create a desirable incentive: The per-unit refund can be chosen so that households (or firms) recycle more material.

From an individual's point of view, the refundable deposit creates an additional private cost of disposal: the opportunity cost of failing to obtain a refund. As shown in Figure 18.9, with the higher cost of disposal, the individual will reduce disposal and increase recycling to the optimal social level $m^*$.

A similar analysis applies at the industry level. Figure 18.10 shows a downward-sloping market demand for glass containers, $D$. The supply of virgin glass containers is given by $S_v$ and the supply of recycled glass by $S_r$. The market supply $S$ is the horizontal sum of these two curves. As a result, the market price of glass is $P$ and the equilibrium supply of recycled glass is $M_1$.

By raising the relative cost of disposal and encouraging recycling, the refundable deposit increases the supply of recycled glass from $S_r$ to $S'_r$, the aggregate

[12]See Frank Ackerman, *Why Do We Recycle: Markets, Values, and Public Policy* (Washington: Island Press, 1997), for a general discussion of recycling.

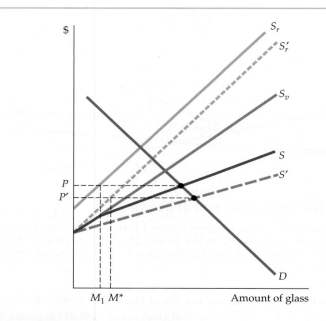

**FIGURE 18.10 Refundable Deposits**

Initially, equilibrium in the market for glass containers involves a price $P$ and a supply of recycled glass $M_1$. By raising the relative cost of disposal and encouraging recycling, the refundable deposit increases the supply of recycled glass from $S_r$ to $S_r'$ and the aggregate supply of glass from $S$ to $S'$. The price of glass then falls to $P'$, the quantity of recycled glass increases to $M^*$, and the amount of disposed glass decreases.

supply increases from $S$ to $S'$, and the price of glass falls to $P'$. As a result, the quantity of recycled glass increases to $M^*$, resulting in a decrease in the amount of disposed glass.

The refundable deposit scheme has another advantage: A market for recycled products is created. In many communities, public or private firms as well as private individuals specialize in collecting and returning recyclable materials. As this market becomes larger and more efficient, the demand for recycled rather than virgin materials increases, therefore increasing the benefit to the environment.

**EXAMPLE 18.4**   Regulating Municipal Solid Wastes

By 1990, the average resident of Los Angeles was generating about 6.4 pounds of solid waste per day, and residents of other large American cities were not far behind. By contrast, residents of Tokyo, Paris, Hong Kong, and Rome generated 3 pounds, 2.4 pounds, 1.9 pounds, and 1.5 pounds, respectively.[13] Some of these

---

[13]This example is based on Peter S. Menell, "Beyond the Throwaway Society: An Incentive Approach to Regulating Municipal Solid Waste," *Ecology Law Quarterly* (1990): 655–739. See also Marie Lynn Miranda et al., "Unit Pricing for Residential Municipal Solid Waste: An Assessment of the Literature," U.S. Environmental Protection Agency, March 1996.

differences are due to variations in consumption levels, but most are due to the efforts that many other countries have made to encourage recycling. In the United States, only about 25 percent of aluminum, 23 percent of paper, and 8.5 percent of glass scrap are recycled.

A number of policy proposals have been introduced to encourage recycling in the United States. The first is the refundable deposit described above. A second is a *curbside charge*, in which communities charge individuals a fee for refuse disposal that is proportional to the weight (or the volume) of the refuse. To encourage separation of recyclable materials, all separable glass materials are collected for free. Curbside charges encourage recycling, but they fail to discourage consumption of products that might require recycling.

A third alternative is to require the *mandatory separation* of recyclable materials such as glass. Random spot checks with substantial penalties for violations are required to make the system effective. Mandatory separation is perhaps the least desirable of the three alternatives, not only because it is difficult to implement, but also because individuals, if the cost of separation is sufficiently high, may be encouraged to shift to alternative containers such as plastic, which are environmentally damaging and cannot readily be recycled.

The potential effectiveness of each of these three policies is illustrated by a study that focused on the mix between glass and plastic. Consumers were assumed to have varying preferences, with half preferring glass and half preferring plastic, for products that are otherwise identical in price, quantity, and quality. Without any incentive to recycle, a 50–50 division between glass and plastic would result. From a social perspective, however, greater use of recyclable glass would be preferred.

Mandatory separation fails as a policy in this case: The cost of separation is so high that the percentage of glass container materials purchased actually falls to 40 percent. A curbside charge, however, does much better: It leads to a 72.5 percent use of recyclable glass. Finally, a refundable deposit system does best, with 78.9 percent of consumers purchasing recyclable glass containers.

A recent case in Perkasie, Pennsylvania, shows that recycling programs can indeed be effective. Prior to implementation of a program combining all three economic incentives just described, the total amount of unseparated solid waste was 2573 tons per year. When the program was implemented, this amount fell to 1038 tons—a 59-percent reduction. As a result, the town saved $90,000 per year in disposal costs.

# 18.3 STOCK EXTERNALITIES

We have studied the negative externalities that result directly from *flows* of harmful pollution. For example, we saw how sulfur dioxide emissions from power plants can adversely affect the air that people breathe, so that government intervention in the form of emissions fees or standards might be warranted. Recall that we compared the marginal cost of reducing the *flow* of emissions to the marginal benefit in order to determine the socially optimal level of emissions.

Sometimes, however, the damage to society comes not directly from the emissions flow, but rather from the *accumulated stock* of the pollutant. A good example is global warming. Global warming is thought to result from the accumulation of carbon dioxide and other greenhouse gasses (GHGs) in the atmosphere. (As the GHG concentration grows, more sunlight is absorbed into the atmosphere rather than being reflected away, causing an increase in average temperatures.) GHG emissions do not cause the kind of immediate harm that sulfur dioxide emissions cause. Rather, it is the *stock of accumulated GHGs in the atmosphere* that ultimately causes harm. Furthermore, the *dissipation rate* for accumulated GHGs is very low: Once the GHG concentration in the atmosphere has increased substantially, it will remain high for many years, even if further GHG emissions were reduced to zero. That is why there is concern about reducing GHG emissions now rather than waiting for concentrations to build up (and temperatures to start rising) fifty or more years from now.

Stock externalities (like flow externalities) can also be positive. An example is the stock of "knowledge" that accumulates as a result of investments in R&D. Over time, R&D leads to new ideas, new products, more efficient production techniques, and other innovations that benefit society as a whole, and not just those who undertake the R&D. Because of this positive externality, there is a strong argument for the government to subsidize R&D. Keep in mind, however, that it is the *stock* of knowledge and innovations that benefits society, and not the flow of R&D that creates the stock.

We examined the distinction between a stock and a flow in Chapter 15. As we explained in Section 15.1 (page 552), the capital that a firm owns is measured as a *stock*, i.e., as a quantity of plant and equipment that the firm owns. The firm can increase its stock of capital by purchasing additional plant and equipment, i.e., by generating a *flow* of investment expenditures. (Recall that inputs of labor and raw materials are also measured as *flows*, as is the firm's output.) We saw that this distinction is important, because it helps the firm decide whether to invest in a new factory, equipment, or other capital. By comparing the *present discounted value (PDV)* of the additional profits likely to result from the investment to the cost of the investment, i.e., by calculating the investment's *net present value (NPV)*, the firm can decide whether or not the investment is economically justified.

The same net present value concept applies when we want to analyze how the government should respond to a stock externality—though with an additional complication. For the case of pollution, we must determine how any ongoing level of emissions leads to a buildup of the stock of pollutant, and we must then determine the economic damage likely to result from that higher stock. We will then be able to compare the present value of the ongoing costs of reducing emissions each year to the present value of the economic benefits resulting from a reduced future stock of the pollutant.

**• stock externality**
Accumulated result of action by a producer or consumer which, though not accounted for in the market price, affects other producers or consumers.

Recall from §15.1 that a firm's capital is measured as a stock, while the investment that creates the capital is a flow. The firm's output is also measured as a flow.

Recall from §15.2 that the present discounted value (PDV) of a series of expected future cash flows is the sum of those cash flows discounted by the appropriate interest rate. Moreover, we observe in §15.4 that, according to the net present value (NPV) rule, a firm should invest if the PDV of the expected future cash flow from an investment is greater than the cost.

## Stock Buildup and Its Impact

Let's focus on pollution to see how the stock of a pollutant changes over time. With ongoing emissions, the stock will accumulate, but some fraction of the stock, $\delta$, will dissipate each year. Thus, assuming the stock starts at zero, in the first year, the stock of pollutant (S) will be just the amount of that year's emissions (E):

$$S_1 = E_1$$

In the second year, the stock of pollutant will equal the emissions that year plus the nondissipated stock from the first year—

$$S_2 = E_2 + (1 - \delta)S_1$$

—and so on. In general, the stock in any year $t$ is given by the emissions generated that year plus the nondissipated stock from the previous year:

$$S_t = E_t + (1 - \delta)S_{t-1}$$

If emissions are at a constant annual rate $E$, then after $N$ years, the stock of pollutant will be[14]:

$$S_N = E[1 + (1 - \delta) + (1 - \delta)^2 + \cdots + (1 - \delta)^{N-1}]$$

As $N$ becomes infinitely large, the stock will approach the long-run equilibrium level $E/\delta$.

The impact of pollution results from the accumulating stock. Initially, when the stock is small, the economic impact is small; but the impact grows as the stock grows. With global warming, for example, higher temperatures result from higher concentrations of GHGs: Thus the concern that if GHG emissions continue at current rates, the atmospheric stock of GHGs will eventually become large enough to cause substantial temperature increases—which, in turn, could have adverse effects on weather patterns, agriculture, and living conditions. Depending on the cost of reducing GHG emissions and the future benefits of averting these temperature increases, it may make sense for governments to adopt policies that would reduce emissions now, rather than waiting for the atmospheric stock of GHGs to become much larger.

**Numerical Example** We can make this concept more concrete with a simple example. Suppose that, absent government intervention, 100 units of a pollutant will be emitted into the atmosphere every year for the next 100 years; the rate at which the stock dissipates, $\delta$, is 2 percent per year, and the stock of pollutant is initially zero. Table 18.1 shows how the stock builds up over time. Note that after 100 years, the stock will reach a level of 4,337 units. (If this level of emissions continued forever, the stock will eventually approach $E/\delta = 100/.02 = 5,000$ units.)

Suppose that the stock of pollutant creates economic damage (in terms of health costs, reduced productivity, etc.) equal to $1 million per unit. Thus, if

| Year | $E$ | $S_t$ | Damage ($ Billion) | Cost of $E = 0$ ($ Billion) | Net Benefit ($ Billion) |
|------|-----|-------|--------------------|-----------------------------|--------------------------|
| 2010 | 100 | 100 | 0.100 | 1.5 | −1.400 |
| 2011 | 100 | 198 | 0.198 | 1.5 | −1.302 |
| 2012 | 100 | 296 | 0.296 | 1.5 | −1.204 |
| . . . | . . . | . . . | . . . | . . . | . . . |
| 2110 | 100 | 4,337 | 4.337 | 1.5 | 2.837 |
| . . . | . . . | . . . | . . . | . . . | . . . |
| ∞ | 100 | 5,000 | 5.000 | 1.5 | 3.500 |

**TABLE 18.1    Buildup in the Stock of Pollutant**

---

[14]To see this, note that after 1 year, the stock of pollutant is $S_1 = E$, in the second year the stock is $S_2 = E + (1 - \delta) S_1 = E + (1 - \delta) E$, in the third year, the stock is $S_3 = E + (1 - \delta) S_2 = E + (1 - \delta) E + (1 - \delta)^2 E$, and so on. As $N$ becomes infinitely large, the stock approaches $E/\delta$.

the total stock of pollutant were, say, 1000 units, the resulting economic damage for that year would be $1 billion. And suppose that the annual cost of reducing emissions is $15 million per unit of reduction. Thus, to reduce emissions from 100 units per year to zero would cost $100 \times \$15$ million = $1.5 billion per year. Would it make sense, in this case, to reduce emissions to zero starting immediately?

To answer this question, we must compare the present value of the annual cost of $1.5 billion with the present value of the annual benefit resulting from a reduced stock of pollutant. Of course, if emissions were reduced to zero starting immediately, the stock of pollutant would likewise be equal to zero over the entire 100 years. Thus, the benefit of the policy would be the savings of social cost associated with a growing stock of pollutant. Table 18.1 shows the annual cost of reducing emissions from 100 units to zero, the annual benefit from averting damage, and the annual *net* benefit (the annual benefit net of the cost of eliminating emissions). As you would expect, the annual net benefit is negative in the early years because the stock of pollutant is low; the net benefit becomes positive only later, after the stock of pollutant has grown.

To determine whether a policy of zero emissions makes sense, we must calculate the NPV of the policy, which in this case is the present discounted value of the annual net benefits shown in Table 18.1. Denoting the discount rate by $R$, the NPV is:

$$\text{NPV} = (-1.5 + .1) + \frac{(-1.5 + .198)}{1 + R} + \frac{(-1.5 + .296)}{(1 + R)^2} + \cdots + \frac{(-1.5 + 4.337)}{(1 + R)^{99}}$$

> Recall from §15.1 that the NPV of an investment declines as the discount rate becomes larger. Figure 15.3 shows the *NPV* for an electric motor factory; note the similarity to our environmental policy problem.

Is this NPV positive or negative? The answer depends on the discount rate, $R$. Table 18.2 shows the NPV as a function of the discount rate. (The middle row of Table 18.2, in which the dissipation rate $\delta$ is 2 percent, corresponds to Table 18.1. Table 18.2 also shows NPVs for dissipation rates of 1 percent and 4 percent.) For discount rates of 4 percent or less, the NPV is clearly positive, but if the discount rate is large, the NPV will be negative.

Table 18.2 also shows how the NPV of a "zero emissions" policy depends on the dissipation rate, $\delta$. If $\delta$ is lower, the accumulated stock of pollutant will reach higher levels and cause more economic damage, so the future benefits of reducing emissions will be greater. Note from Table 18.2 that for any given discount rate, the NPV of eliminating emissions is much larger if $\delta = .01$ and much smaller if $\delta = .04$. As we will see, one of the reasons why there is so much concern over global warming is the fact that the stock of GHGs dissipates very slowly; $\delta$ is only about .005.

**TABLE 18.2 NPV of "Zero Emissions" Policy**

| | | Discount Rate, $R$ | | | | |
|---|---|---|---|---|---|---|
| | | .01 | .02 | .04 | .06 | .08 |
| **Dissipation Rate, $\delta$** | .01 | 108.81 | 54.07 | 12.20 | −0.03 | −4.08 |
| | .02 | 65.93 | 31.20 | 4.49 | −3.25 | −5.69 |
| | .04 | 15.48 | 3.26 | −5.70 | −7.82 | −8.11 |

*Note:* Entries in table are NPVs in $billions. Entries for $\delta = .02$ correspond to net benefit numbers in Table 18.1.

Formulating environmental policy in the presence of stock externalities therefore introduces an additional complicating factor: What discount rate should be used? Because the costs and benefits of a policy apply to society as a whole, the discount rate should likewise reflect the opportunity cost to society of receiving an economic benefit in the future rather than today. This opportunity cost, which should be used to calculate NPVs for government projects, is called the **social rate of discount**. But as we will see in Example 18.5, there is little agreement among economists as to the appropriate number to use for the social rate of discount.

In principle, the social rate of discount depends on three factors: (1) the expected rate of real economic growth; (2) the extent of risk aversion for society as a whole; and (3) the "rate of pure time preference" for society as a whole. With rapid economic growth, future generations will have higher incomes than current generations, and if their marginal utility of income is decreasing (i.e., they are risk-averse), their utility from an extra dollar of income will be lower than the utility to someone living today; that's why future benefits provide less utility and should thus be discounted. In addition, even if we expected no economic growth, people may simply prefer to receive a benefit today than in the future (the rate of pure time preference). Depending on one's beliefs about future real economic growth, the extent of risk aversion for society as a whole, and the rate of pure time preference, one could conclude that the social rate of discount should be as high as 6 percent—or as low as 1 percent. And herein lies the difficulty. With a discount rate of 6 percent, it is hard to justify almost any government policy that imposes costs today but yields benefits only 50 or 100 years in the future (e.g., a policy to deal with global warming). Not so, however, if the discount rate is only 1 or 2 percent.[15] Thus for problems involving long time horizons, the policy debate often boils down to a debate over the correct discount rate.

> • **social rate of discount** Opportunity cost to society as a whole of receiving an economic benefit in the future rather than the present.

## EXAMPLE 18.5   Global Warming

Emissions of carbon dioxide and other greenhouse gases have increased dramatically over the past century as economic growth has been accompanied by the greater use of fossil fuels, which has in turn led to an increase in atmospheric concentrations of GHGs. Even if worldwide GHG emissions were to be stabilized at current levels, atmospheric GHG concentrations would continue to grow throughout the next century. By trapping sunlight, these higher GHG concentrations are likely to cause a significant increase in global mean temperatures in 50 years or so and could have severe environmental consequences—flooding of low-lying areas as the polar ice caps melt and sea levels rise, more extreme weather patterns, disruption of ecosystems, and reduced agricultural output. GHG emissions could be reduced from their current levels—governments, for example, could impose stiff taxes on the use of gasoline and other fossil fuels—but this solution would be costly. The problem is that the costs

---

[15]For example, with a discount rate of 6 percent, $100 received 100 years from now is worth only $0.29 today. With a discount rate of 1 percent, that same $100 is worth $36.97 today, i.e., 127 times as much.

of reducing GHG emissions would occur today but the benefits from reduced emissions would be realized only in some 50 or more years. Should the world's industrialized countries agree to adopt policies to dramatically reduce GHG emissions, or is the present discounted value of the likely benefits of such policies simply too small?

There have been many studies by physical scientists and economists of the buildup of GHG concentrations and the resulting increases in global temperatures if no steps are taken to reduce emissions. Although there is considerable disagreement over the exact economic impact of higher temperatures, there is at least a consensus view that the impact would be significant; thus there would be a future benefit from reducing emissions today.[16] The cost of reducing emissions (or preventing them from growing above current levels) can be assessed as well, although, again, there is disagreement over the specific numbers.

Table 18.3 shows GHG emissions and average global temperature change for two scenarios. The first is a "business as usual" scenario in which GHG emissions more than double over the next century, the average GHG concentration rises, and by 2110 the average temperature increases by 4 degrees Celsius over its current level. The resulting damage from this temperature increase is estimated at 1.3 percent of world GDP per year. World GDP is in turn assumed to grow at 2.5 percent per year in real terms from its 2010 value of $65 trillion. Thus, the damage from global warming reaches about $40 trillion per year in 2110. The

## TABLE 18.3 Reducing GHG Emissions

| | "Business as Usual" | | | | Emissions Reduced by 1% per Year | | | | | |
|---|---|---|---|---|---|---|---|---|---|---|
| Year | $E_t$ | $S_t$ | $\Delta T_t$ | Damage | $E_t$ | $S_t$ | $\Delta T_t$ | Damage | Cost | Net Benefit |
| 2010 | 50 | 430 | 0° | 0 | 50 | 430 | 0° | 0 | 0.65 | −0.65 |
| 2020 | 55 | 460 | 0.5° | 0.54 | 45 | 460 | 0.5° | 0.43 | 0.83 | −0.72 |
| 2030 | 62 | 490 | 1° | 1.38 | 41 | 485 | 1° | 1.11 | 1.07 | −0.79 |
| 2040 | 73 | 520 | 1.5° | 2.66 | 37 | 510 | 1.4° | 2.13 | 1.36 | −0.83 |
| 2050 | 85 | 550 | 2° | 4.54 | 33 | 530 | 1.8° | 3.63 | 1.75 | −0.84 |
| 2060 | 90 | 580 | 2.3° | 6.77 | 30 | 550 | 2° | 5.81 | 2.23 | −1.27 |
| 2070 | 95 | 610 | 2.7° | 9.91 | 27 | 550 | 2° | 7.44 | 2.86 | −0.38 |
| 2080 | 100 | 640 | 3° | 14.28 | 25 | 550 | 2° | 9.52 | 3.66 | 1.10 |
| 2090 | 105 | 670 | 3.3° | 20.31 | 22 | 550 | 2° | 12.18 | 4.69 | 3.44 |
| 2100 | 110 | 700 | 3.7° | 28.59 | 20 | 550 | 2° | 15.60 | 6.00 | 7.00 |
| 2110 | 115 | 730 | 4° | 39.93 | 18 | 550 | 2° | 19.97 | 7.68 | 12.28 |

*Notes:* $E_t$ is measured in gigatonnes (billions of metric tons) of $CO_2$ equivalent ($CO_2$e), $S_t$ is measured in parts per million (ppm) of atmospheric $CO_2$e, the change in temperature $\Delta T_t$ is measured in degrees Celsius, and costs, damages, and net benefits are measured in trillions of 2007 dollars. Cost of reducing emissions is estimated to be 1 percent of GDP each year. World GDP is projected to grow at 2.5% in real terms from a level of $65 trillion in 2010. Damage from warming is estimated to be 1.3% of GDP per year for every 1°C of temperature increase.

---

[16]See, for example, the 2007 *Assessment Report of the Intergovernmental Panel on Climate Change*, Cambridge University Press or online at **http://www.ipcc.ch**; and the U.K. Government's Stern Review, online at **http://www.hm-treasury.gov.uk/independent_reviews/stern_review_economics_climate_change/**.

second scenario is one in which the GHG concentration is stabilized so that the temperature increase is limited to only 2 degrees Celsius, which is reached in 2060. To achieve this, GHG emissions must be reduced by 1 percent per year starting in 2010. The annual cost of this emissions reduction policy is estimated to be 1 percent of world GDP.[17] (Because world GDP is assumed to increase each year, so too does the cost of this policy.) Also shown in Table 18.3 is the annual net benefit from the policy, which equals the damage under the "business as usual" scenario minus the (smaller) damage when emissions are reduced minus the cost of reducing emissions.

Does this emissions-reduction policy make sense? To answer that question, we must calculate the present value of the flow of net benefits, which depends critically on the discount rate. A review conducted in the United Kingdom recommends a social rate of discount of 1.3 percent. With that discount rate, the NPV of the policy is $21.3 trillion, which shows that the emissions-reduction policy is clearly economical. The NPV is smaller but still positive ($1.63 trillion) if we use a discount rate of 2 percent. But with a discount rate of 3 percent, the NPV is −$9.7 trillion; with a discount rate of 5 percent, the NPV is −$12.7 trillion.

We have examined a particular policy—and a rather stringent one at that—to reduce GHG emissions. Whether that policy or any other policy to restrict GHG emissions makes economic sense clearly depends on the rate used to discount future costs and benefits. Be warned, however, that economists disagree about what rate to use, and as a result, they disagree about what should be done about global warming.[18]

## 18.4 EXTERNALITIES AND PROPERTY RIGHTS

We have seen how government regulation can deal with the inefficiencies that arise from externalities. Emissions fees and transferable emissions permits work because they change a firm's incentives, forcing it to take into account the external costs that it imposes. But government regulation is not the only way to deal with externalities. In this section we show that in some circumstances, inefficiencies can be eliminated through private bargaining among the affected parties or by a legal system in which parties can sue to recover the damages they suffer.

### Property Rights

**Property rights** are the legal rules that describe what people or firms may do with their property. If you have property rights to land, for example, you may build on it or sell it and are protected from interference by others.

• **property rights** Legal rules stating what people or firms may do with their property.

---

[17]This policy is the one recommended by the Stern Review, which was commissioned by the U.K. government. The cost estimate of 1 percent of GDP is from the Stern Review. The estimate of the damage from higher temperatures (1.3 percent of GDP for each 1 degree Celsius increase) is an amalgam of estimates from the Stern Review and the IPCC Report.

[18]This disagreement over the discount rate and its crucial role in assessing policies to reduce GHG emissions is spelled out quite nicely in Martin Weitzman, "The Stern Review of the Economics of Climate Change," *Journal of Economic Literature* (September 2007). Also, there are many uncertainties about the size of possible future temperature increases and their social and economic impact. Those uncertainties can have implications for policy but have been ignored in this example. See, for example, R. S. Pindyck, "Uncertainty in Environmental Economics," *Journal of Environmental Economics and Policy* (Winter 2007).

To see why property rights are important, let's return to our example of the firm that dumps effluent into the river. We assumed both that it had a property right to use the river to dispose of its waste and that the fishermen did not have a property right to "effluent-free" water. As a result, the firm had no incentive to include the cost of effluent in its production calculations. In other words, the firm *externalized* the costs generated by the effluent. But suppose that the fishermen had a property right to clean water. In that case, they could demand that the firm pay them for the right to dump effluent. The firm would either cease production or pay the costs associated with the effluent. These costs would be *internalized* and an efficient allocation of resources achieved.

## Bargaining and Economic Efficiency

Economic efficiency can be achieved without government intervention when the externality affects relatively few parties and when property rights are well specified. To see how, let's consider a numerical version of our effluent example. Suppose the steel factory's effluent reduces the fishermen's profit. As Table 18.4 shows, the factory can install a filter system to reduce its effluent, or the fishermen can pay for the installation of a water treatment plant.[19]

The efficient solution maximizes the joint profit of the factory and the fishermen. Maximization occurs when the factory installs a filter and the fishermen do not build a treatment plant. Let's see how alternative property rights lead these two parties to negotiate different solutions.

Suppose the factory has the property right to dump effluent into the river. Initially, the fishermen's profit is $100 and the factory's $500. By installing a treatment plant, the fishermen can increase their profit to $200, whereby the joint profit, without cooperation, is $700 ($500 + $200). Moreover, the fishermen are willing to pay the factory up to $300 to install a filter—the difference between the $500 profit with a filter and the $200 profit without cooperation. Because the factory loses only $200 in profit by installing a filter, it will be willing to do so because it is more than compensated for its loss. In this case, the gain to both parties by cooperating is equal to $100: the $300 gain to the fishermen less the $200 cost of a filter.

Suppose the factory and the fishermen agree to split this gain equally by having the fishermen pay the factory $250 to install the filter. As Table 18.5 shows, this bargaining solution achieves the efficient outcome. Under the column "Right to Dump," we see that without cooperation, the fishermen earn a profit of $200 and the factory $500. With cooperation, the profit of both increases by $50.

| TABLE 18.4 Profits under Alternative Emissions Choices (Daily) | | | |
|---|---|---|---|
| | Factory's Profit ($) | Fishermen's Profit ($) | Total Profit ($) |
| No filter, no treatment plant | 500 | 100 | 600 |
| Filter, no treatment plant | 300 | 500 | 800 |
| No filter, treatment plant | 500 | 200 | 700 |
| Filter, treatment plant | 300 | 300 | 600 |

[19]For a more extensive discussion of a variant of this example, see Robert Cooter and Thomas Ulen, *Law and Economics* (Reading, MA: Addison Wesley Longman, Inc., 2000), ch. 4.

| TABLE 18.5 Bargaining with Alternative Property Rights | | |
|---|---|---|
| **No Cooperation** | **Right to Dump ($)** | **Right to Clean Water ($)** |
| Profit of factory | 500 | 300 |
| Profit of fishermen | 200 | 500 |
| **Cooperation** | | |
| Profit of factory | 550 | 300 |
| Profit of fishermen | 250 | 500 |

Now suppose the fishermen are given the property right to clean water, which requires the factory to install the filter. The factory earns a profit of $300 and the fishermen $500. Because neither party can be made better off by bargaining, having the factory install the filter is efficient.

This analysis applies to all situations in which property rights are well specified. *When parties can bargain without cost and to their mutual advantage, the resulting outcome will be efficient, regardless of how the property rights are specified.* The italicized proposition is called the **Coase theorem,** after Ronald Coase who did much to develop it.[20]

• **Coase theorem** Principle that when parties can bargain without cost and to their mutual advantage, the resulting outcome will be efficient regardless of how property rights are specified.

## Costly Bargaining—The Role of Strategic Behavior

Bargaining can be time-consuming and costly, especially when property rights are not clearly specified. In that case, neither party is sure how hard to bargain before the other party will agree to a settlement. In our example, both parties knew that the bargaining process had to settle on a payment between $200 and $300. If the parties are unsure of the property rights, however, the fishermen might be willing to pay only $100, and the bargaining process would break down.

Bargaining can break down even when communication and monitoring are costless if both parties believe they can obtain larger gains. For example, one party might demand a large share and refuse to bargain, assuming incorrectly that the other party will eventually concede. Another problem arises when many parties are involved. Suppose, for example, that the emissions from a factory are adversely affecting hundreds or thousands of households who live downstream. In that case, the costs of bargaining will make it very difficult for the parties to reach a settlement.

## A Legal Solution—Suing for Damages

In many situations involving externalities, a party who is harmed (the victim) by another has the legal right to sue. If successful, the victim can recover monetary damages equal to the harm that it has suffered. A suit for damages is different from an emissions or effluent fee because the victim, not the government, is paid.

To see how the potential for a lawsuit can lead to an efficient outcome, let's reexamine our fishermen–factory example. Suppose first that the fishermen are given the right to clean water. The factory, in other words, is responsible for

---

[20]Ronald Coase, "The Problem of Social Cost," *Journal of Law and Economics* 3 (1960): 1–44.

harm to the fishermen *if* it does not install a filter. The harm to the fishermen in this case is $400: the difference between the profit that the fishermen make when there is no effluent ($500) and their profit when there is effluent ($100). The factory has the following options:

1. Do not install filter, pay damages:    Profit = $100 ($500 − $400)
2. Install filter, avoid damages:    Profit = $300 ($500 − $200)

The factory will find it advantageous to install a filter, which is substantially cheaper than paying damages, and the efficient outcome will be achieved.

An efficient outcome (with a different division of profits) will also be achieved if the factory is given the property right to emit effluent. Under the law, the fishermen would have the legal right to require the factory to install the filter, but they would have to pay the factory for its $200 lost profit (not for the cost of the filter). This leaves the fishermen with three options:

1. Put in a treatment plant:    Profit = $200
2. Have factory put in a filter but pay damages:    Profit = $300 ($500 − $200)
3. Do not put in treatment plant or require a filter:    Profit = $100

The fishermen earn the highest profit if they take the second option. They will thus require the factory to put in a filter but compensate it $200 for its lost profit. Just as in the situation in which the fishermen had the right to clean water, this outcome is efficient because the filter has been installed. Note, however, that the $300 profit is substantially less than the $500 profit that the fishermen get when they have a right to clean water.

This example shows that a suit for damages eliminates the need for bargaining because it specifies the consequences of the parties' choices. Giving the party that is harmed the right to recover damages from the injuring party ensures an efficient outcome. (When information is imperfect, however, suing for damages may lead to inefficient outcomes.)

---

**EXAMPLE 18.6**    The Coase Theorem at Work

As a September 1987 cooperative agreement between New York City and New Jersey illustrates, the Coase theorem applies to governments as well as to people and organizations.

For many years, garbage spilling from waterfront trash facilities along New York harbor had adversely affected the quality of water along the New Jersey shore and occasionally littered the beaches. One of the worst instances occurred in August 1987, when more than 200 tons of garbage formed a 50-mile-long slick off the New Jersey shore.

New Jersey had the right to clean beaches and could have sued New York City to recover damages associated with garbage spills. New Jersey could have also asked the court to grant an injunction requiring New York City to stop using its trash facilities until the problem was removed.

But New Jersey wanted cleaner beaches, not simply the recovery of damages. And New York wanted to be able to operate its trash facility. Consequently, there was room for mutually beneficial exchange. After two weeks of negotiations, New York and New Jersey reached a settlement. New Jersey agreed not to bring a lawsuit against the city. New York City agreed to use special boats and other flotation devices to contain spills that might originate from Staten Island and Brooklyn. It also agreed to form a monitoring team to survey all trash facilities and to shut down those failing to comply. At the same time, New Jersey officials were allowed unlimited access to New York City trash facilities to monitor the program's effectiveness.

# 18.5 COMMON PROPERTY RESOURCES

Occasionally externalities arise when resources can be used without payment. **Common property resources** are those to which anyone has free access. As a result, they are likely to be overutilized. Air and water are the two most common examples. Others include fish, animal populations, mineral exploration, and extraction. Let's look at some of the inefficiencies that can occur when resources are common property rather than privately owned.

• **common property resource** Resource to which anyone has free access.

Consider a large lake with trout to which an unlimited number of fishermen have access. Each fisherman fishes up to the point at which the marginal revenue from fishing (or the marginal value, if fishing is for sport instead of profit) is equal to the cost. But the lake is a common property resource, and no fisherman has the incentive to take into account how his fishing affects the opportunities of others. As a result, the fisherman's private cost understates the true cost to society because more fishing reduces the stock of fish, making less available for others. This leads to an inefficiency—too many fish are caught.

Figure 18.11 illustrates this situation. Suppose that because the catch is sufficiently small relative to demand, fishermen take the price of fish as given.

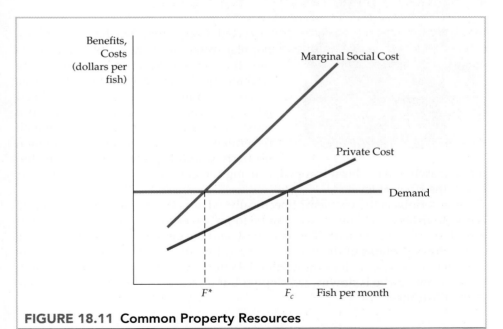

**FIGURE 18.11** Common Property Resources

When a common property resource, such as a fishery, is accessible to all, the resource is used up to the point $F_c$ at which the private cost is equal to the additional revenue generated. This usage exceeds the efficient level $F^*$ at which the marginal social cost of using the resource is equal to the marginal benefit (as given by the demand curve).

Suppose also that someone can control the number of fishermen with access to the lake. The efficient level of fish per month $F^*$ is determined at the point at which the marginal benefit from fish caught is equal to the marginal social cost. The marginal benefit is the price taken from the demand curve. The marginal social cost shown in the diagram includes not only the private operating costs but also the social cost of depleting the stock of fish.

Now compare the efficient outcome with what happens when the lake is common property. In this case, the marginal external costs are not taken into account, and each fisherman fishes until there is no longer any profit to be made. When only $F^*$ fish are caught, the revenue from fishing is greater than the cost, and there is a profit to be earned by fishing more. Entry into the fishing business occurs until the point at which the price is equal to the marginal cost, point $F_c$ in Figure 18.11. At $F_c$, however, too many fish will be caught.

There is a relatively simple solution to the common property resource problem—let a single owner manage the resource. The owner will set a fee for use of the resource that is equal to the marginal cost of depleting the stock of fish. Facing the payment of this fee, fishermen in the aggregate will no longer find it profitable to catch more than $F^*$ fish. Unfortunately, because single ownership is not always practical, most common property resources are vast. In such cases government ownership or direct government regulation may be needed.

---

**EXAMPLE 18.7**  Crawfish Fishing in Louisiana

In recent years, crawfish have become a popular restaurant item. In 1950, for example, the annual crawfish harvest in the Atchafalaya River basin in Louisiana was just over 1 million pounds. By 1995, it had grown to over 30 million pounds. Because most crawfish grow in ponds to which fishermen have unlimited access, a common property resource problem has arisen: Too many crawfish have been trapped, causing the crawfish population to fall far below the efficient level.[21]

How serious is the problem? Specifically, what is the social cost of unlimited access to fishermen? The answer can be found by estimating the private cost of trapping crawfish, the marginal social cost, and the demand for crawfish. Figure 18.12 shows portions of the relevant curves. Private cost is upward-sloping: As the catch increases, so does the additional effort that must be made to obtain it. The demand curve is downward sloping but elastic because other shellfish are close substitutes.

---

[21]This example is based on Frederick W. Bell, "Mitigating the Tragedy of the Commons," *Southern Economic Journal* 52 (1986): 653–64.

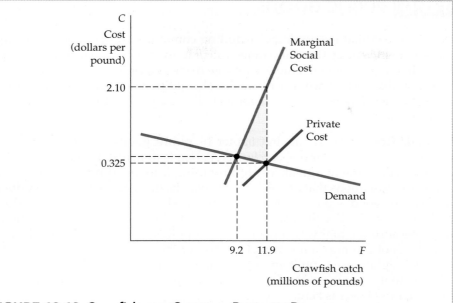

**FIGURE 18.12 Crawfish as a Common Property Resource**

Because crawfish are bred in ponds to which fishermen have unlimited access, they are a common property resource. The efficient level of fishing occurs when the marginal benefit is equal to the marginal social cost. However, the actual level of fishing occurs at the point at which the price for crawfish is equal to the private cost of fishing. The shaded area represents the social cost of the common property resource.

We can find the efficient crawfish catch both graphically and algebraically. Let $F$ represent the catch of crawfish in millions of pounds per year (shown on the horizontal axis), and let $C$ represent cost in dollars per pound (shown on the vertical axis). In the region where the various curves intersect, the three curves in the graph are as follows:

| | |
|---|---|
| Demand: | $C = 0.401 - 0.0064F$ |
| Marginal social cost: | $C = -5.645 + 0.6509F$ |
| Private cost: | $C = -0.357 + 0.0573F$ |

The efficient crawfish catch of 9.2 million pounds, which equates demand to marginal social cost, is shown as the intersection of the two curves. The actual catch, 11.9 million pounds, is determined by equating demand to private cost and is shown as the intersection of those two curves. The yellow-shaded triangle in the figure measures the social cost of free access. This figure represents the excess of social cost above the private benefit of fishing summed from the efficient level (where demand is equal to marginal social cost) to the actual level (where demand is equal to private cost). In this case, the social cost is approximated by the area of a triangle with a base of 2.7 million pounds (11.9 − 9.2) and a height of $1.775 ($2.10 − $0.325), or $2,396,000. Note that by regulating the ponds—limiting either access or the size of the catch—this social cost could be avoided.

## 18.6 PUBLIC GOODS

We have seen that externalities, including common-property resources, create market inefficiencies that sometimes warrant government regulation. When, if ever, should governments replace private firms as a producer of goods and services? In this section we describe a set of conditions under which the private market either may not provide a good at all or may not price it properly once it is available.

**Nonrival Goods** As we saw in Chapter 16, **public goods** have two characteristics: They are *nonrival* and *nonexclusive*. A good is **nonrival** if for any given level of production, the marginal cost of providing it to an additional consumer is zero. For most goods that are provided privately, the marginal cost of producing more of the good is positive. But for some goods, additional consumers do not add to cost. Consider the use of a highway during a period of low traffic volume. Because the highway already exists and there is no congestion, the additional cost of driving on it is zero. Or consider the use of a lighthouse by a ship. Once the lighthouse is built and functioning, its use by an additional ship adds nothing to its running costs. Finally, consider public television. Clearly, the cost of one more viewer is zero.

Most goods are rival in consumption. For example, when you buy furniture, you have ruled out the possibility that someone else can buy it. Goods that are rival must be allocated among individuals. Goods that are nonrival can be made available to everyone without affecting any individual's opportunity for consuming them.

**Nonexclusive Goods** A good is **nonexclusive** if people cannot be excluded from consuming it. As a consequence, it is difficult or impossible to charge people for using nonexclusive goods; the goods can be enjoyed without direct payment. One example of a nonexclusive good is national defense. Once a nation has provided for its national defense, all citizens enjoy its benefits. A lighthouse and public television are also examples of nonexclusive goods.

Nonexclusive goods need not be national in character. If a state or city eradicates an agricultural pest, all farmers and consumers benefit. It would be virtually impossible to exclude a particular farmer from the benefits of the program. Automobiles are exclusive (as well as rival). If a dealer sells a new car to one consumer, then the dealer has excluded other individuals from buying it.

Some goods are exclusive but nonrival. For example, in periods of low traffic, travel on a bridge is nonrival because an additional car on the bridge does not lower the speed of other cars. But bridge travel is exclusive because bridge authorities can keep people from using it. A television signal is another example. Once a signal is broadcast, the marginal cost of making the broadcast available to another user is zero; thus the good is nonrival. But broadcast signals can be made exclusive by scrambling the signals and charging for the codes that unscramble them.

Some goods are nonexclusive but rival. An ocean or large lake is nonexclusive, but fishing is rival because it imposes costs on others: the more fish caught, the fewer fish available to others. Air is nonexclusive and often nonrival; but it can be rival if the emissions of one firm adversely affect the quality of the air and the ability of others to enjoy it.

Public goods, which are both nonrival and nonexclusive, provide benefits to people at zero marginal cost, and no one can be excluded from enjoying them.

---

• **public good**  Nonexclusive and nonrival good: the marginal cost of provision to an additional consumer is zero and people cannot be excluded from consuming it.

• **nonrival good**  Good for which the marginal cost of its provision to an additional consumer is zero.

• **nonexclusive good**  Good that people cannot be excluded from consuming, so that it is difficult or impossible to charge for its use.

The classic example of a public good is national defense. Defense is nonexclusive, as we have seen, but it is also nonrival because the marginal cost of providing defense to an additional person is zero. The lighthouse is also a public good because it is nonrival and nonexclusive; in other words, it would be difficult to charge ships for the benefits they receive from it.[22]

The list of public goods is much smaller than the list of goods that governments provide. Many publicly provided goods are either rival in consumption, exclusive, or both. For example, high school education is rival in consumption. Because other children get less attention as class sizes increase, there is a positive marginal cost of providing education to one more child. Likewise, charging tuition can exclude some children from enjoying education. Public education is provided by local government because it entails positive externalities, not because it is a public good.

Finally, consider the management of a national park. Part of the public can be excluded from using the park by raising entrance and camping fees. Use of the park is also rival: because of crowded conditions, the entrance of an additional car into a park can reduce the benefits that others receive from it.

## Efficiency and Public Goods

The efficient level of provision of a private good is determined by comparing the marginal benefit of an additional unit to the marginal cost of producing it. Efficiency is achieved when the marginal benefit and the marginal cost are equal. The same principle applies to public goods, but the analysis is different. With private goods, the marginal benefit is measured by the benefit that the consumer receives. With a public good, we must ask how much each person values an additional unit of output. The marginal benefit is obtained by adding these values for *all* people who enjoy the good. To determine the efficient level of provision of a public good, we must then equate the sum of these marginal benefits to the marginal cost of production.

Figure 18.13 illustrates the efficient level of producing a public good. $D_1$ represents the demand for the public good by one consumer and $D_2$ the demand by a second consumer. Each demand curve tells us the marginal benefit that the consumer gets from consuming every level of output. For example, when there are 2 units of the public good, the first consumer is willing to pay $1.50 for the good, and $1.50 is the marginal benefit. Similarly, the second consumer has a marginal benefit of $4.00.

To calculate the sum of the marginal benefits to *both* people, we must add each of the demand curves *vertically*. For example, when the output is 2 units, we add the marginal benefit of $1.50 to the marginal benefit of $4.00 to obtain a marginal social benefit of $5.50. When this sum is calculated for every level of public output, we obtain the aggregate demand curve for the public good $D$.

> In §4.3, we show that a market demand curve can be obtained by summing individual demand curves horizontally.

The efficient amount of output is the one at which the marginal benefit to society is equal to the marginal cost. This occurs at the intersection of the demand and the marginal cost curves. In our example, because the marginal cost of production is $5.50, 2 is the efficient output level.

To see why 2 is efficient, note what happens if only 1 unit of output is provided: Although the marginal cost remains at $5.50, the marginal benefit is approximately

[22]Lighthouses need not be provided by the government. See Ronald Coase, "The Lighthouse in Economics," *Journal of Law and Economics* 17 (1974): 357–76, for a description of how lighthouses were privately funded in nineteenth-century England.

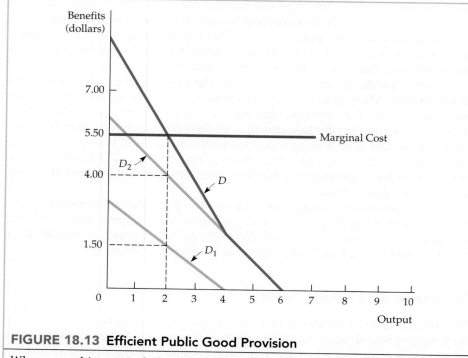

**FIGURE 18.13 Efficient Public Good Provision**

When a good is nonrival, the social marginal benefit of consumption, given by the demand curve $D$, is determined by vertically summing the individual demand curves for the good, $D_1$ and $D_2$. At the efficient level of output, the demand and the marginal cost curves intersect.

$7.00. Because the marginal benefit is greater than the marginal cost, too little of the good has been provided. Similarly, suppose 3 units of the public good have been produced. Now the marginal benefit of approximately $4.00 is less than the marginal cost of $5.50; too much of the good has been provided. Only when the marginal social benefit is equal to the marginal cost is the public good provided efficiently.[23]

## Public Goods and Market Failure

Suppose you want to offer a mosquito abatement program for your community. You know that the program is worth more to the community than the $50,000 it will cost. Can you make a profit by providing the program privately? You would break even if you assessed a $5.00 fee to each of the 10,000 households in your community. But you cannot force them to pay the fee, let alone devise a system in which those households that value mosquito abatement most highly pay the highest fees.

Unfortunately, mosquito abatement is nonexclusive: There is no way to provide the service without benefiting everyone. As a result, households have no incentive to pay what the program really is worth to them. People can act as **free riders**, who understate the value of the program so that they can enjoy the benefit of the good without paying for it.

• **free rider** Consumer or producer who does not pay for a nonexclusive good in the expectation that others will.

[23]We have shown that nonexclusive, nonrival goods are inefficiently provided. A similar argument would apply to nonrival but exclusive goods.

With public goods, the presence of free riders makes it difficult or impossible for markets to provide goods efficiently. Perhaps if few people were involved and the program were relatively inexpensive, all households might agree voluntarily to share costs. However, when many households are involved, voluntary private arrangements are usually ineffective. The public good must therefore be subsidized or provided by governments if it is to be produced efficiently.

**EXAMPLE 18.8**  The Demand for Clean Air

In Example 4.5 (page 134), we used the demand curve for clean air to calculate the benefits of a cleaner environment. Now let's examine the public-good characteristics of clean air. Many factors, including the weather, driving patterns, and industrial emissions, determine a region's air quality. Any effort to clean up the air will generally improve air quality throughout the region. As a result, clean air is nonexclusive: It is difficult to stop any one person from enjoying it. Clean air is also nonrival: My enjoyment does not inhibit yours.

Because clean air is a public good, there is no market and no observable price at which people are willing to trade clean air for other commodities. Fortunately, we can infer people's willingness to pay for clean air from the housing market—households will pay more for a home located in an area with good air quality than for an otherwise identical home in an area with poor air quality.

Let's look at the estimates of the demand for clean air obtained from a statistical analysis of housing data for the Boston metropolitan area.[24] The analysis correlates housing prices with the quality of air and other characteristics of the houses and their neighborhoods. Figure 18.14 shows three demand curves in which the value put on clean air depends on the level of nitrogen oxides and on income. The horizontal axis measures the level of air pollution in terms of parts per hundred million (pphm) of nitrogen oxide in the air. The vertical axis measures each household's willingness to pay for a one-part-per-hundred-million reduction in the nitrogen oxide level.

The demand curves are upward-sloping because we are measuring pollution rather than clean air on the horizontal axis. As we would expect, the cleaner the air, the lower the willingness to pay for more of the good. These differences in the willingness to pay for clean air vary substantially. In Boston, for example, nitrogen oxide levels ranged from 3 to 9 pphm. A middle-income household would be willing to pay $800 for a 1 pphm reduction in nitrogen oxide levels when the level is 3 pphm, but the figure would jump to $2200 for a 1 pphm reduction when the level is 9 pphm.

Note that higher-income households are willing to pay more than lower-income households to obtain a small improvement in air quality. At low nitrogen oxide levels (3 pphm), the differential between low- and middle-income households is only $200, but it increases to about $700 at high levels (9 pphm).

[24]David Harrison, Jr., and Daniel L. Rubinfeld, "Hedonic Housing Prices and the Demand for Clean Air," *Journal of Environmental Economics and Management* 5 (1978): 81–102.

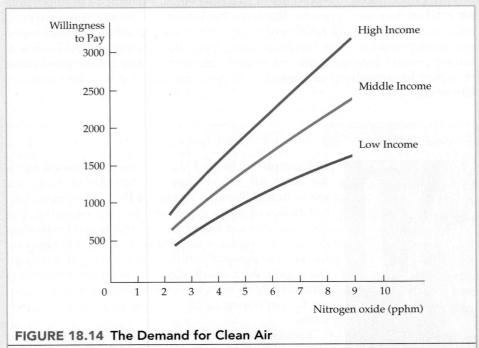

**FIGURE 18.14 The Demand for Clean Air**

The three curves describe the willingness to pay for clean air (a reduction in the level of nitrogen oxides) for each of three different households (low income, middle income, and high income). In general, higher-income households have greater demands for clean air than lower-income households. Moreover, each household is less willing to pay for clean air as the level of air quality increases.

With quantitative information about the demand for clean air and separate estimates of the costs of improving air quality, we can determine whether the benefits of environmental regulations outweigh the costs. A study by the National Academy of Sciences of regulations on automobile emissions did just this. The study found that controls would lower the level of pollutants, such as nitrogen oxides, by approximately 10 percent. The benefit of this 10-percent improvement to all residents of the United States was calculated to be approximately $2 billion. The study also estimated that it would cost somewhat less than $2 billion to install pollution control equipment in automobiles to meet emissions standards. The study concluded, therefore, that the benefits of the regulations did outweigh the costs.

# 18.7 PRIVATE PREFERENCES FOR PUBLIC GOODS

Government production of a public good is advantageous because the government can assess taxes or fees to pay for it. But how can government determine how *much* of a public good to provide when the free rider problem gives people an incentive to misrepresent their preferences? In this section we discuss one mechanism for determining private preferences for government-produced goods.

Voting is commonly used to decide allocation questions. For example, people vote directly on some local budget issues and elect legislators who vote on others. Many state and local referenda are based on *majority-rule voting*: Each person has one vote, and the candidate or the issue that receives more than 50 percent of the votes wins. Let's see how majority-rule voting determines the provision of public education. Figure 18.15 describes the preferences for spending on education (on a per-pupil basis) of three citizens who are representative of three interest groups in the school district.

Curve $W_1$ gives the first citizen's willingness to pay for education, minus any required tax payments. The willingness to pay for each spending level is the maximum amount of money the citizen will pay to enjoy that spending level rather than no spending at all.[25] In general, the benefit from increased spending on education increases as spending increases. But the tax payments required to pay for that education increase as well. The willingness-to-pay curve, which represents the net benefit of educational spending, initially slopes upward because the citizen places great value on low spending levels. When spending increases beyond $600 per pupil, however, the value that the household puts on education increases at a diminishing rate. The net benefit, therefore, actually declines. Eventually, the spending level becomes so great (at $2400 per pupil) that the citizen is indifferent between this level of spending and no spending at all.

Curve $W_2$, which represents the second citizen's willingness to pay (net of taxes) is similarly shaped but reaches its maximum at a spending level of $1200 per pupil. Finally, $W_3$, the willingness to pay of the third citizen, peaks at $1800 per pupil.

The dark line labeled AW represents the aggregate willingness to pay for education—the vertical summation of the $W_1$, $W_2$, and $W_3$ curves. The AW

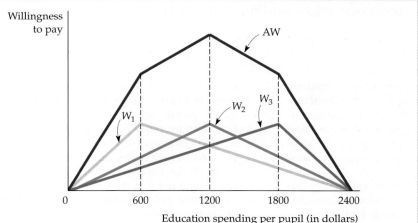

**FIGURE 18.15 Determining the Level of Educational Spending**

The efficient level of educational spending is determined by summing the willingness to pay for education (net of tax payments) of each of three citizens. Curves $W_1$, $W_2$, and $W_3$ represent their willingness to pay, and curve AW represents the aggregate willingness to pay. The efficient level of spending is $1200 per pupil. The level of spending actually provided is the level demanded by the median voter. In this particular case, the median voter's preference (given by the peak of the $W_2$ curve) is also the efficient level.

---

[25]In other words, the willingness to pay measures the consumer surplus that the citizen enjoys when a particular level of spending is chosen.

curve measures the maximum amount that all three citizens are willing to pay to enjoy each spending level. As Figure 18.15 shows, the aggregate willingness to pay is maximized when $1200 per pupil is spent. Because the AW curve measures the benefit of spending net of the tax payments required to pay for that spending, the maximum point, $1200 per pupil, also represents the efficient level of spending.

Will majority-rule voting achieve the efficient outcome in this case? Suppose the public must vote whether to spend $1200 or $600 per pupil. The first citizen will vote for $600, but the other two citizens will vote for $1200, which will then have been chosen by majority rule. In fact, $1200 per pupil will beat any other alternative in a majority-rule vote. Thus, $1200 represents the most preferred alternative of the *median voter*—the citizen with the median or middle preference. (The first citizen prefers $600 and the third $1800.) *Under majority rule voting, the preferred spending level of the median voter will always win an election against any other alternative.*

But will the preference of the median voter be the efficient level of spending? In this case yes, because $1200 is efficient. But the preference of the median voter is often *not* the efficient spending level. Suppose the third citizen's preferences were the same as the second's. In that case, although the median voter's choice would still be $1200 per pupil, the efficient level of spending would be less than $1200 (because the efficient level involves an average of the preferences of all three citizens). In this case, majority rule would lead to too much spending on education. If we reversed the example so that the first and second citizens' preferences were identical, majority rule would generate too little educational spending.

Thus, although majority-rule voting allows the preferences of the median voter to determine referenda outcomes, these outcomes need not be economically efficient. Majority rule is inefficient because it weighs each citizen's preference equally: The efficient outcome weighs each citizen's vote by his or her strength of preference.

# SUMMARY

1. An externality occurs when a producer or a consumer affects the production or consumption activities of others in a manner that is not directly reflected in the market. Externalities cause market inefficiencies because they inhibit the ability of market prices to convey accurate information about how much to produce and how much to buy.

2. Pollution is a common example of an externality that leads to market failure. It can be corrected by emissions standards, emissions fees, marketable emissions permits, or by encouraging recycling. When there is uncertainty about costs and benefits, any one of these mechanisms can be preferable, depending on the shapes of the marginal social cost and marginal benefit curves.

3. Sometimes it is the accumulated stock of a pollutant, rather than current level of emissions, that causes damage. An example of such stock externality is the buildup of greenhouse gases, which may lead to global warming.

4. Inefficiencies due to market failure may be eliminated through private bargaining among the affected parties. According to the Coase theorem, the bargaining solution will be efficient when property rights are clearly specified, when transactions costs are zero, and when there is no strategic behavior. But bargaining is unlikely to generate an efficient outcome because parties frequently behave strategically.

5. Common property resources are not controlled by a single person and can be used without a price being paid. As a result of free usage, an externality is created in which current overuse of the resource harms those who might use it in the future.

6. Goods that private markets are not likely to produce efficiently are either nonrival or nonexclusive. A good is nonrival if for any given level of production, the marginal cost of providing it to an additional consumer is zero. A good is nonexclusive if it is expensive or impossible to exclude people from consuming it. Public goods are both nonrival and nonexclusive.

7. A public good is provided efficiently when the vertical sum of the individual demands for the good is equal to the marginal cost of producing it.

8. Majority-rule voting is one way for citizens to voice their preference for public goods. Under majority rule, the level of spending provided will be that preferred by the median voter. This level need not be the efficient outcome.

# QUESTIONS FOR REVIEW

1. Which of the following describes an externality and which does not? Explain the difference.
   a. A policy of restricted coffee exports in Brazil causes the U.S. price of coffee to rise—an increase which in turn also causes the price of tea to rise.
   b. An advertising blimp distracts a motorist who then hits a telephone pole.
2. Compare and contrast the following three mechanisms for treating pollution externalities when the costs and benefits of abatement are uncertain: (a) an emissions fee, (b) an emissions standard, and (c) a system of transferable emissions permits.
3. When do externalities require government intervention? When is such intervention unlikely to be necessary?
4. Consider a market in which a firm has monopoly power. Suppose in addition that the firm produces under the presence of either a positive or a negative externality. Does the externality necessarily lead to a greater misallocation of resources?
5. Externalities arise solely because individuals are unaware of the consequences of their actions. Do you agree or disagree? Explain.
6. To encourage an industry to produce at the socially optimal level, the government should impose a unit tax on output equal to the marginal cost of production. True or false? Explain.
7. George and Stan live next door to each other. George likes to plant flowers in his garden, but every time he does, Stan's dog comes over and digs them up. Stan's dog is causing the damage, so if economic efficiency is

to be achieved, it is necessary that Stan pay to put up a fence around his yard to confine the dog. Do you agree or disagree? Explain.

8. An emissions fee is paid to the government, whereas an injurer who is sued and held liable pays damages directly to the party harmed by an externality. What differences in the behavior of victims might you expect to arise under these two arrangements?
9. Why does free access to a common property resource generate an inefficient outcome?
10. Public goods are both nonrival and nonexclusive. Explain each of these terms and show clearly how they differ from each other.
11. A village is located next to 1000 acres of prime grazing land. The village presently owns the land and allows all residents to graze cows freely. Some members of the village council have suggested that the land is being overgrazed. Is this likely to be true? These same members have also suggested that the village should either require grazers to purchase an annual permit or sell off the land to the grazers. Would either of these be a good idea?
12. Public television is funded in part by private donations, even though anyone with a television set can watch for free. Can you explain this phenomenon in light of the free rider problem?
13. Explain why the median voter outcome need not be efficient when majority-rule voting determines the level of public spending.

# EXERCISES

1. A number of firms have located in the western portion of a town after single-family residences took up the eastern portion. Each firm produces the same product and in the process emits noxious fumes that adversely affect the residents of the community.
   a. Why is there an externality created by the firms?
   b. Do you think that private bargaining can resolve the problem? Explain.
   c. How might the community determine the efficient level of air quality?
2. A computer programmer lobbies against copyrighting software, arguing that everyone should benefit from innovative programs written for personal computers and that exposure to a wide variety of computer programs will inspire young programmers to create even more innovative programs. Considering the marginal social benefits possibly gained by this proposal, do you agree with this position?
3. Assume that scientific studies provide you with the following information concerning the benefits and costs of sulfur dioxide emissions:

| | |
|---|---|
| Benefits of abating (reducing) emissions: | $MB = 500 - 20A$ |
| Costs of abating emissions: | $MC = 200 + 5A$ |

where $A$ is the quantity abated in millions of tons and the benefits and costs are given in dollars per ton.
   a. What is the socially efficient level of emissions abatement?
   b. What are the marginal benefit and marginal cost of abatement at the socially efficient level of abatement?
   c. What happens to net social benefits (benefits minus costs) if you abate one million more tons than the efficient level? One million fewer?
   d. Why is it socially efficient to set marginal benefits equal to marginal costs rather than abating until total benefits equal total costs?
4. Four firms located at different points on a river dump various quantities of effluent into it. The effluent adversely affects the quality of swimming for homeowners who live downstream. These people can build swimming pools to avoid swimming in the river, and

the firms can purchase filters that eliminate harmful chemicals dumped in the river. As a policy adviser for a regional planning organization, how would you compare and contrast the following options for dealing with the harmful effect of the effluent:

**a.** An equal-rate effluent fee on firms located on the river.

**b.** An equal standard per firm on the level of effluent that each can dump.

**c.** A transferable effluent permit system in which the aggregate level of effluent is fixed and all firms receive identical permits.

**5.** Medical research has shown the negative health effects of "secondhand" smoke. Recent social trends point to growing intolerance of smoking in public areas. If you are a smoker and you wish to continue smoking despite tougher anti-smoking laws, describe the effect of the following legislative proposals on your behavior. As a result of these programs, do you, the individual smoker, benefit? Does society benefit as a whole?

**a.** A bill is proposed that would lower tar and nicotine levels in all cigarettes.

**b.** A tax is levied on each pack of cigarettes.

**c.** A tax is levied on each pack of cigarettes sold.

**d.** Smokers would be required to carry government-issued smoking permits at all times.

**6.** The market for paper in a particular region in the United States is characterized by the following demand and supply curves:

$$Q_D = 160,000 - 2000P \quad \text{and} \quad Q_S = 40,000 + 2000P$$

where $Q_D$ is the quantity demanded in 100-pound lots, $Q_S$ is the quantity supplied in 100-pound lots, and $P$ is the price per 100-pound lot. Currently there is no attempt to regulate the dumping of effluent into streams and rivers by the paper mills. As a result, dumping is widespread. The marginal external cost (MEC) associated with the production of paper is given by the curve MEC = $0.0006Q_S$.

**a.** Calculate the output and price of paper if it is produced under competitive conditions and no attempt is made to monitor or regulate the dumping of effluent.

**b.** Determine the socially efficient price and output of paper.

**c.** Explain why the answers you calculated in parts (a) and (b) differ.

**7.** In a market for dry cleaning, the inverse market demand function is given by $P = 100 - Q$ and the (private) marginal cost of production for the aggregation of all dry-cleaning firms is given by MC = $10 + Q$. Finally, the pollution generated by the dry cleaning process creates external damages given by the marginal external cost curve MEC = $Q$.

**a.** Calculate the output and price of dry cleaning if it is produced under competitive conditions without regulation.

**b.** Determine the socially efficient price and output of dry cleaning.

**c.** Determine the tax that would result in a competitive market producing the socially efficient output.

**d.** Calculate the output and price of dry cleaning if it is produced under monopolistic conditions without regulation.

**e.** Determine the tax that would result in a monopolistic market producing the socially efficient output.

**f.** Assuming that no attempt is made to monitor or regulate the pollution, which market structure yields higher social welfare? Discuss.

**8.** Refer back to Example 18.5 on global warming. Table 18.3 (page 668) shows the annual net benefits from a policy that reduces GHG emissions by 1 percent per year. At what discount rate is the NPV of this policy just equal to zero?

**9.** A beekeeper lives adjacent to an apple orchard. The orchard owner benefits from the bees because each hive pollinates about one acre of apple trees. The orchard owner pays nothing for this service, however, because the bees come to the orchard without his having to do anything. Because there are not enough bees to pollinate the entire orchard, the orchard owner must complete the pollination by artificial means, at a cost of $10 per acre of trees.

Beekeeping has a marginal cost MC = $10 + 5Q$, where $Q$ is the number of beehives. Each hive yields $40 worth of honey.

**a.** How many beehives will the beekeeper maintain?

**b.** Is this the economically efficient number of hives?

**c.** What changes would lead to a more efficient operation?

**10.** There are three groups in a community. Their demand curves for public television in hours of programming, $T$, are given respectively by

$$W_1 = \$200 - T$$
$$W_2 = \$240 - 2T$$
$$W_3 = \$320 - 2T$$

Suppose public television is a pure public good that can be produced at a constant marginal cost of $200 per hour.

**a.** What is the efficient number of hours of public television?

**b.** How much public television would a competitive private market provide?

**11.** Reconsider the common resource problem given in Example 18.7. Suppose that crawfish popularity continues to increase, and that the demand curve shifts from $C = 0.401 - 0.0064F$ to $C = 0.50 - 0.0064F$. How does this shift in demand affect the actual crawfish catch, the efficient catch, and the social cost of common access? (*Hint:* Use the marginal social cost and private cost curves given in the example.)

**12.** The Georges Bank, a highly productive fishing area off New England, can be divided into two zones in terms of fish population. Zone 1 has the higher population per square mile but is subject to severe diminishing returns to fishing effort. The daily fish catch (in tons) in Zone 1 is

$$F_1 = 200(X_1) - 2(X_1)^2$$

where $X_1$ is the number of boats fishing there. Zone 2 has fewer fish per mile but is larger, and diminishing returns are less of a problem. Its daily fish catch is

$$F_2 = 100(X_2) - (X_2)^2$$

where $X_2$ is the number of boats fishing in Zone 2. The marginal fish catch MFC in each zone can be represented as

$$MFC_1 = 200 - 4(X_1)$$

$$MFC_2 = 100 - 2(X_2)$$

There are 100 boats now licensed by the U.S. government to fish in these two zones. The fish are sold at $100 per ton. Total cost (capital and operating) per boat is constant at $1000 per day. Answer the following questions about this situation:

a. If the boats are allowed to fish where they want, with no government restriction, how many will fish in each zone? What will be the gross value of the catch?

b. If the U.S. government can restrict the number and distribution of the boats, how many should be allocated to each zone? What will be the gross value of the catch? Assume the total number of boats remains at 100.

c. If additional fishermen want to buy boats and join the fishing fleet, should a government wishing to maximize the net value of the catch grant them licenses? Why or why not?

# APPENDIX

## The Basics of Regression

This appendix explains the basics of **multiple regression analysis**, using an example to illustrate its application in economics.[1] Multiple regression is a statistical procedure for quantifying economic relationships and testing hypotheses about them.

In a **linear regression**, the relationships are of the following form:

$$Y = b_0 + b_1 X_1 + b_2 X_2 + \cdots + b_k X_k + e \qquad \textbf{(A.1)}$$

Equation (A.1) relates a *dependent* variable $Y$ to several *independent* (or *explanatory*) variables, $X_1, X_2, \ldots$ For example, in an equation with two independent variables, $Y$ might be the demand for a good, $X_1$ its price, and $X_2$ income. The equation also includes an *error term e* that represents the collective influence of any omitted variables that may also affect $Y$ (for example, prices of other goods, the weather, unexplainable shifts in consumers' tastes, etc.). Data are available for $Y$ and the $X$s, but the error term is assumed to be unobservable.

Note that equation (A.1) must be linear in the *parameters*, but it need not be linear in the variables. For example, if equation (A.1) represented a demand function, $Y$ might be the logarithm of quantity (log $Q$), $X_1$ the logarithm of price (log $P$), and $X_2$ the logarithm of income (log $I$):

$$\log Q = b_0 + b_1 \log P + b_2 \log I + e \qquad \textbf{(A.2)}$$

Our objective is to obtain *estimates* of the parameters $b_0, b_1, \ldots, b_k$ that provide a "best fit" to the data. We explain how this is done below.

## AN EXAMPLE

Suppose we wish to explain and then forecast quarterly automobile sales in the United States. Let's start with a simplified case in which sales $S$ (in billions of dollars) is the dependent variable that will be explained. The only explanatory variable is the price of new automobiles $P$ (measured by a new car price index scaled so that 1967 = 100). We could write this simple model as

$$S = b_0 + b_1 P + e \qquad \textbf{(A.3)}$$

- **multiple regression analysis** Statistical procedure for quantifying economic relationships and testing hypotheses about them.

- **linear regression** Model specifying a linear relationship between a dependent variable and several independent (or explanatory) variables and an error term.

---

[1] For a textbook treatment of applied econometrics, it's hard to think of a better reference than R. S. Pindyck and D. L. Rubinfeld, *Econometric Models and Economic Forecasts*, 4th ed. (New York: McGraw-Hill, 1998).

In equation (A.3), $b_0$ and $b_1$ are the parameters to be determined from the data, and $e$ is the random error term. The parameter $b_0$ is the intercept, while $b_1$ is the slope: It measures the effect of a change in the new car price index on automobile sales.

If there is no error term, the relationship between $S$ and $P$ would be a straight line that describes the systematic relationship between the two variables. However, because not all the actual observations fall on the line, the error term $e$ is required to account for omitted factors.

## ESTIMATION

In order to choose values for the regression parameters, we need a criterion for a "best fit." The criterion most often used is to *minimize the sum of squared residuals* between the actual values of $Y$ and the *fitted* values for $Y$ obtained after equation (A.1) has been estimated. This is called the **least-squares criterion**. If we denote the estimated parameters (or *coefficients*) for the model in (A.1) by $\hat{b}_0$, $\hat{b}_1$, . . . , $\hat{b}_k$, then the *fitted* values for $Y$ are given by

$$\hat{Y} = \hat{b}_0 + \hat{b}_1 X_1 + \cdots + \hat{b}_k X_k \tag{A.4}$$

Figure A.1 illustrates this for our example, in which there is a single independent variable. The data are shown as a scatter plot of points with sales on the vertical axis and price on the horizontal. The fitted regression line is drawn through the data points. The fitted value for sales associated with any particular value for the price values $P_i$ is given by $\hat{S}_i = \hat{b}_0 + \hat{b}_1 P_i$ (at point $B$).

For each data point, the regression *residual* is the difference between the actual and fitted value of the dependent variable. The residual, $\hat{e}_i$, associated with data point $A$ in the figure, is given by $\hat{e}_i = S_i - \hat{S}_i$. The parameter values are chosen so that when all the residuals are squared and then added, the resulting sum is minimized. In this way, positive errors and negative errors are treated symmetrically; large errors are given a more-than-proportional weight.

• **least-squares criterion**
Criterion of "best fit" used to choose values for regression parameters, usually by minimizing the sum of squared residuals between the actual values of the dependent variable and the fitted values.

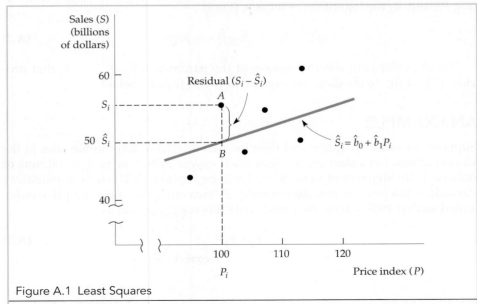

Figure A.1  Least Squares

The regression line is chosen to minimize the sum of squared residuals. The residual associated with price $P_i$ is given by line $AB$.

As we will see shortly, this criterion lets us do some simple statistical tests to help interpret the regression.

As an example of estimation, let's return to the two-variable model of auto sales given by equation (A.3). The result of fitting this equation using the least-squares criterion is

$$\hat{S} = -25.5 + 0.57P \tag{A.5}$$

In equation (A.5), the intercept −225.5 indicates that if the price index were zero, sales would be $ − 225.5 billion. The slope parameter indicates that a 1-unit increase in the price index for new cars leads to a $0.57 billion increase in auto sales. This rather surprising result—an upward-sloping demand curve—is inconsistent with economic theory and should make us question the validity of our model.

Let's expand the model to consider the possible effects of two additional explanatory variables: personal income $I$ (in billions of dollars) and the rate of interest $R$ (the three-month Treasury bill rate). The estimated regression when there are three explanatory variables is

$$\hat{S} = 51.1 - 0.42P + 0.046I - 0.84R \tag{A.6}$$

The importance of including all relevant variables in the model is suggested by the change in the regression results after the income and interest rate variables are added. Note that the coefficient of the $P$ variable has changed substantially, from 0.57 to −0.42. The coefficient −0.42 measures the effect of an increase in price on sales, *with the effect of interest rates and income held constant*. The negative price coefficient is consistent with a downward-sloping demand curve. Clearly, the failure to control for interest rates and income leads to the false conclusion that sales and price are positively related.

The income coefficient, 0.046, tells us that for every $1 billion increase in personal income in the United States, automobile sales are likely to increase by $46 million (or $0.046 billion). The interest rate coefficient reflects the fact that for every one percentage point increase in the rate of interest, automobile sales are likely to fall by $840 million. Clearly, automobile sales are very sensitive to the cost of borrowing.

## STATISTICAL TESTS

Our estimates of the true (but unknown) parameters are numbers that depend on the set of observations that we started with—that is, with our **sample**. With a different sample we would obtain different estimates.[2] If we continue to collect more and more samples and generate additional estimates, the estimates of each parameter will follow a probability distribution. This distribution can be summarized by a *mean* and a measure of dispersion around that mean, a standard deviation that we refer to as the *standard error of the coefficient*.

Least-squares has several desirable properties. First, it is *unbiased*. Intuitively, this means that if we could run our regression over and over again with different samples, the average of the many estimates that we obtained for each coefficient would equal the true parameter. Second, least-squares is *consistent*. In other words, if our sample were very large, we would obtain estimates that came very close to the true parameters.

In econometric work, we often assume that the error term, and therefore the estimated parameters, are normally distributed. The normal distribution has

• **sample** Set of observations for study, drawn from a larger universe.

---

[2]The least-squares formula that generates these estimates is called the *least-squares estimator*, and its values vary from sample to sample.

the property that the area within 1.96 standard errors of its mean is equal to 95 percent of the total area. With this information, we can ask the following question: Can we construct an interval around $\hat{b}$ such that there is a 95-percent probability that the true parameter lies within that interval? The answer is yes, and this 95-percent *confidence interval* is given by

$$\hat{b} \pm 1.96 \text{ (standard error of } \hat{b}) \tag{A.7}$$

Thus, when working with an estimated regression equation, we must not only look at the *point* estimates but also examine the standard errors of the coefficients to determine bounds for the true parameters.[3]

If a 95-percent confidence interval contains 0, then the true parameter $b$ may actually be zero (even if our estimate is not). This result implies that the corresponding independent variable may *not* really affect the dependent variable, even if we thought it did. We can test the hypothesis that a true parameter is actually equal to 0 by looking at its *t-statistic*, which is defined as

$$t = \frac{\hat{b}}{\text{Standard error of } \hat{b}} \tag{A.8}$$

If the *t*-statistic is less than 1.96 in magnitude, the 95-percent confidence interval around $\hat{b}$ must include 0. This means that we cannot reject the hypothesis that the true parameter $b$ equals 0. We therefore say that our estimate, whatever it may be, is *not statistically significant*. Conversely, if the *t*-statistic is greater than 1.96 in absolute value, we reject the hypothesis that $b = 0$ and call our estimate *statistically significant*.

Equation (A.9) shows the multiple regression for the auto sales model (equation A.6) with a set of standard errors and *t*-statistics added:

$$
\begin{array}{ccccc}
\hat{S} = & 51.1 & -0.42P & +0.046I & -0.84R \\
 & (9.4) & (0.13) & (0.006) & (0.32) \\
t = & 5.44 & -3.23 & 7.67 & -2.63
\end{array}
\tag{A.9}
$$

The standard error of each estimated parameter is given in parentheses just below the estimate, and the corresponding *t*-statistics appear below that.

Let's begin by considering the price variable. The standard error of 0.13 is small relative to the coefficient −0.42. In fact, we can be 95 percent certain that the *true* value of the price coefficient is on the interval given by −0.42 plus or minus 1.96 standard deviations (i.e., −0.42 plus or minus [1.96][0.13] = −0.42 ± 0.25). This puts the true value of the coefficient between −0.17 and −0.67. Because this range does not include zero, the effect of price is both significantly different from zero and negative. We can also arrive at this result from the *t*-statistic. The *t* of −3.23 reported in equation (A.9) for the price variable is equal to −0.42 divided by 0.13. Because this *t*-statistic exceeds 1.96 in absolute value, we conclude that price is a significant determinant of auto sales.

Note that the income and interest rate variables are also significantly different from zero. The regression results tell us that an increase in income is likely to have a statistically significant positive effect on auto sales, whereas

---

[3]When there are fewer than 100 observations, we multiply the standard error by a number somewhat larger than 1.96.

an increase in interest rates will have a statistically significant negative effect.

## GOODNESS OF FIT

Reported regression results usually contain information that tells us how closely the regression line fits the data. One statistic, the **standard error of the regression (SER)**, is an estimate of the standard deviation of the regression error term $e$. Whenever all the data points lie on the regression line, the SER is zero. Other things being equal, the larger the standard error of the regression, the poorer the fit of the data to the regression line. To decide whether the SER is large or small, we compare it in magnitude with the mean of the dependent variable. This comparison provides a measure of the *relative* size of the SER, a more meaningful statistic than its absolute size.

**R-squared ($R^2$)** the percentage of the variation in the dependent variable that is accounted for by all the explanatory variables, measures the overall goodness-of-fit of the multiple regression equation.[4] Its value ranges from 0 to 1. An $R^2$ of 0 means that the independent variables explain none of the variation of the dependent variable; an $R^2$ of 1 means that the independent variables explain the variation perfectly. The $R^2$ for the sales equation (A.9) is 0.94. This tells us that the three independent variables explain 94 percent of the variation in sales.

Note that a high $R^2$ does not by itself mean that the variables actually included in the model are the appropriate ones. First, the $R^2$ varies with the types of data being studied. Time series data with substantial upward growth usually generate much higher $R^2$s than do cross-section data. Second, the underlying economic theory provides a vital check. If a regression of auto sales on the price of wheat happened to yield a high $R^2$, we would question the model's reliability. Why? Because our theory tells us that changes in the price of wheat have little or no effect on automobile sales.

The overall reliability of a regression result depends on the formulation of the model. When studying an estimated regression, we should consider things that might make the reported results suspicious. First, have variables that should appear in the relationship been omitted? That is, is the *specification* of the equation wrong? Second, is the functional form of the equation correct? For instance, should variables be in logarithms? Third, is there another relationship that relates one of the explanatory variables (say $X$) to the dependent variable $Y$? If so, $X$ and $Y$ are jointly determined, and we must deal with a two-equation model, not one with a single equation. Finally, does adding or removing one or two data points result in a major change in the estimated coefficients—i.e., is the equation *robust*? If not, we should be very careful not to overstate the importance or reliability of the results.

## ECONOMIC FORECASTING

A forecast is a prediction about the values of the dependent variable, given information about the explanatory variables. Often, we use regression models to generate *ex ante forecasts*, in which we predict values of the dependent variable beyond the time period over which the model has been estimated. If we know the values of the explanatory variables, the forecast is *unconditional*;

* **standard error of the regression** Estimate of the standard deviation of the regression error.

* **R-squared ($R^2$)** Percentage of the variation in the dependent variable that is accounted for by all the explanatory variables.

---

[4]The variation in $Y$ is the sum of the squared deviations of $Y$ from its mean. $R^2$ and SER provide similar information about goodness of fit, because $R^2 = 1 - SER^2/Variance\ (Y)$.

if they must be predicted as well, the forecast is *conditional* on these predictions. Sometimes *ex post* forecasts, in which we predict what the value of the dependent variable would have been if the values of the independent variables had been different, can be useful. An *ex post* forecast has a forecast period such that all values of the dependent and explanatory variables are known. Thus *ex post* forecasts can be checked against existing data and provide a direct means of evaluating a model.

For example, reconsider the auto sales regression discussed above. In general, the forecasted value for auto sales is given by

$$\hat{S} = \hat{b}_0 + \hat{b}_1 P + \hat{b}_2 I + \hat{b}_3 R + \hat{e} \qquad \textbf{(A.10)}$$

where $\hat{e}$ is our prediction for the error term. Without additional information, we usually take $\hat{e}$ to be zero.

Then, to calculate the forecast we use the estimated sales equation:

$$\hat{S} = 51.1 - 0.42P + 0.046I - 0.84R \qquad \textbf{(A.11)}$$

We can use (A.11) to predict sales when, for example, $P = 100$, $I = \$1$ trillion, and $R = 8$ percent. Then,

$$\hat{S} = 51.1 - 0.42(100) + 0.046(1000 \text{ billion}) - 0.84(8\%) = \$48.4 \text{ billion}$$

Note that $48.4 billion is an *ex post* forecast for a time when $P = 100$, $I = \$1$ trillion, and $R = 8$ percent.

To determine the reliability of *ex ante* and *ex post* forecasts, we use the *standard error of forecast (SEF)*. The SEF measures the standard deviation of the forecast error within a sample in which the explanatory variables are known with certainty. Two sources of error are implicit in the SEF. The first is the error term itself, because $\hat{e}$ may not equal 0 in the forecast period. The second source arises because the estimated parameters of the regression model may not be exactly equal to the true parameters.

As an application, consider the SEF of $7.0 billion associated with equation (A.11). If the sample size is large enough, the probability is roughly 95 percent that the predicted sales will be within 1.96 standard errors of the forecasted value. In this case, the 95-percent confidence interval is $48.4 billion ± $14.0 billion, i.e., from $34.4 billion to $62.4 billion.

Now suppose we wish to forecast automobile sales for some date in the future, such as 2007. To do so, the forecast must be conditional because we need to predict the values for the independent variables before calculating the forecast for automobile sales. Assume, for example, that our predictions of these variables are as follows: $\hat{P} = 200$, $\hat{I} = \$5$ trillion, and $\hat{R} = 10$ percent. Then, the forecast is given by $\hat{P} = 51.1 - 0.42(200) + 0.046(5000 \text{ billion}) - 0.84(10) = \$188.7$ billion. Here $188.7 billion is an *ex ante* conditional forecast.

Because we are predicting the future, and because the explanatory variables do not lie close to the means of the variables throughout our period of study, the SEF is equal to $8.2 billion, which is somewhat greater than the SEF that we calculated previously.[5] The 95-percent confidence interval associated with our forecast is the interval from $172.3 billion to $205.1 billion.

---

[5]For more on SEF, see Pindyck and Rubinfeld, *Econometric Models and Economic Forecasts*, ch. 8.

## EXAMPLE A.1    The Demand for Coal

Suppose we want to estimate the demand for bituminous coal (given by sales in tons per year, COAL) and then use the relationship to forecast future coal sales. We would expect the quantity demanded to depend on the price of coal (given by the Producer Price Index for coal, PCOAL) and on the price of a close substitute for coal (given by the Producer Price Index for natural gas, PGAS). Because coal is used to produce steel and electricity, we would also expect the level of steel production (given by the Federal Reserve Board Index of iron and steel production, FIS) and electricity production (given by the Federal Reserve Board Index of electric utility production, FEU) to be important demand determinants.

Our model of coal demand is therefore given by the following equation:

$$COAL = b_0 + b_1 \, PCOAL + b_2 \, PGAS + b_3 \, FIS + b_4 \, FEU + e$$

From our theory, we would expect $b_1$ to be negative because the demand curve for coal is downward sloping. We would also expect $b_2$ to be positive because a higher price of natural gas should lead industrial consumers of energy to substitute coal for natural gas. Finally, we would expect both $b_3$ and $b_4$ to be positive because the greater the production of steel and electricity, the greater the demand for coal.

This model was estimated using monthly time-series data covering eight years. The results (with $t$-statistics in parentheses) are

$$COAL = 12{,}262 + 92.34 \, FIS + 118.57 \, FEU - 48.90 \, PCOAL + 118.91 \, PGAS$$
$$\quad\;\;(3.51)\quad\;\;(6.46)\quad\quad\;\;(7.14)\quad\quad\;\;(-3.82)\quad\quad\quad\;\;(3.18)$$

$$R^2 = 0.692 \quad SER = 120{,}000$$

All the estimated coefficients have the signs that economic theory would predict. Each coefficient is also statistically significantly different from zero because the $t$-statistics are all greater than 1.96 in absolute value. The $R^2$ of 0.692 says that the model explains more than two-thirds of the variation in coal sales. The standard error of the regression SER is equal to 120,000 tons of coal. Because the mean level of coal production was 3.9 million tons, SER represents approximately 3 percent of the mean value of the dependent variable. This suggests a reasonably good model fit.

Now suppose we want to use the estimated coal demand equation to forecast coal sales up to one year into the future. To do so, we substitute values for each of the explanatory variables for the 12-month forecasting period into the estimated equation. We also estimate the standard error of forecast (the estimate is 0.17 million tons) and use it to calculate 95-percent confidence intervals for the forecasted values of coal demand. Some representative forecasts and confidence intervals are given in Table A.1.

### TABLE A.1    Forecasting Coal Demand

|  | Forecast | Confidence Interval |
| --- | --- | --- |
| 1-month forecast (tons) | 5.2 million | 4.9–5.5 million |
| 6-month forecast (tons) | 4.7 million | 4.4–5.0 million |
| 12-month forecast (tons) | 5.0 million | 4.7–5.3 million |

# SUMMARY

1. Multiple regression is a statistical procedure for quantifying economic relationships and testing hypotheses about them.

2. The linear regression model, which relates one dependent variable to one or more independent variables, is usually estimated by choosing the intercept and slope parameters that minimize the sum of the squared residuals between the actual and predicted values of the dependent variable.

3. In a multiple-regression model, each slope coefficient measures the effect on the dependent variable of a change in the corresponding independent variable, holding the effects of all other independent variables constant.

4. A $t$-test can be used to test the hypothesis that a particular slope coefficient is different from zero.

5. The overall fit of the regression equation can be evaluated using the standard error of the regression (SER) (a value close to zero means a good fit) or $R^2$ (a value close to one means a good fit).

6. Regression models can be used to forecast future values of the dependent variable. The standard error of forecast (SEF) measures the accuracy of the forecast.

# GLOSSARY

## A

**absolute advantage** *(page 606)* Situation in which Country 1 has an advantage over Country 2 in producing a good because the cost of producing the good in 1 is lower than the cost of producing it in 2.

**accounting cost** *(page 222)* Actual expenses plus depreciation charges for capital equipment.

**actual return** *(page 178)* Return that an asset earns.

**actuarially fair** *(page 173)* Characterizing a situation in which an insurance premium is equal to the expected payout.

**adverse selection** *(page 620)* Form of market failure resulting when products of different qualities are sold at a single price because of asymmetric information, so that too much of the low-quality product and too little of the high-quality product are sold.

**advertising elasticity of demand** *(page 426)* Percentage change in quantity demanded resulting from a 1-percent increase in advertising expenditures.

**advertising-to-sales ratio** *(page 426)* Ratio of a firm's advertising expenditures to its sales.

**agent** *(page 631)* Individual employed by a principal to achieve the principal's objective.

**amortization** *(page 226)* Policy of treating a one-time expenditure as an annual cost spread out over some number of years.

**anchoring** *(page 188)* Tendency to rely heavily on one prior (suggested) piece of information when making a decision.

**antitrust laws** *(page 381)* Rules and regulations prohibiting actions that restrain, or are likely to restrain, competition.

**arbitrage** *(page 8)* Practice of buying at a low price at one location and selling at a higher price in another.

**arc elasticity of demand** *(page 39)* Price elasticity calculated over a range of prices.

**asset** *(page 177)* Something that provides a flow of money or services to its owner.

**asset beta** *(page 566)* A constant that measures the sensitivity of an asset's return to market movements and, therefore, the asset's nondiversifiable risk.

**asymmetric information** *(page 618)* Situation in which a buyer and a seller possess different information about a transaction.

**auction markets** *(page 509)* Markets in which products are bought and sold through formal bidding processes.

**average expenditure curve** *(page 530)* Supply curve representing the price per unit that a firm pays for a good.

**average expenditure** *(page 374)* Price paid per unit of a good.

**average fixed cost (AFC)** *(page 228)* Fixed cost divided by the level of output.

**average product** *(page 199)* Output per unit of a particular input.

**average total cost (ATC)** *(page 227)* Firm's total cost divided by its level of output.

**average variable cost (AVC)** *(page 228)* Variable cost divided by the level of output.

## B

**bad** *(page 77)* Good for which less is preferred rather than more.

**bandwagon effect** *(page 136)* Positive network externality in which a consumer wishes to possess a good in part because others do.

**barrier to entry** *(page 368)* Condition that impedes entry by new competitors.

**Bertrand model** *(page 456)* Oligopoly model in which firms produce a homogeneous good, each firm treats the price of its competitors as fixed, and all firms decide simultaneously what price to charge.

**bilateral monopoly** *(page 380)* Market with only one seller and one buyer.

**block pricing** *(page 396)* Practice of charging different prices for different quantities or "blocks" of a good.

**bond** *(page 556)* Contract in which a borrower agrees to pay the bondholder (the lender) a stream of money.

**budget constraints** *(page 83)* Constraints that consumers face as a result of limited incomes.

**budget line** *(page 83)* All combinations of goods for which the total amount of money spent is equal to income.

**bundling** *(page 413)* Practice of selling two or more products as a package.

## C

**Capital Asset Pricing Model (CAPM)** *(page 565)* Model in which the risk premium for a capital investment depends on the correlation of the investment's return with the return on the entire stock market.

**cardinal utility function** *(page 81)* Utility function describing by how much one market basket is preferred to another.

**cartel** *(page 444)* Market in which some or all firms explicitly collude, coordinating prices and output levels to maximize joint profits.

**chain-weighted price index** *(page 104)* Cost-of-living index that accounts for changes in quantities of goods and services.

**Coase theorem** *(page 671)* Principle that when parties can bargain without cost and to their mutual advantage, the resulting outcome will be efficient regardless of how property rights are specified.

**Cobb-Douglas production function** *(page 267)* Production function of the form $q = AK^{\alpha}L^{\beta}$, where $q$ is the rate of output, $K$ is the quantity of capital, and $L$ is the quantity of labor, and where A, $\alpha$, and $\beta$ are constants.

**Cobb-Douglas utility function** *(page 153)* Utility function $U(X,Y) = X^a Y^{1-a}$, where $X$ and $Y$ are two goods and $a$ is a constant.

**common property resource** *(page 673)* Resource to which anyone has free access.

**common-value auction** *(page 510)* Auction in which the item has the same value to all bidders, but bidders do not know that value precisely and their estimates of it vary.

**company cost of capital** *(page 566)* Weighted average of the expected return on a company's stock and the interest rate that it pays for debt.

**comparative advantage** *(page 606)* Situation in which Country 1 has an advantage over Country 2 in producing a good because the cost of producing the good in 1, relative to the cost of producing other goods in 1, is lower than the cost of producing the good in 2, relative to the cost of producing other goods in 2.

**complements** *(page 24)* Two goods for which an increase in the price of one leads to a decrease in the quantity demanded of the other.

**completely inelastic demand** *(page 35)* Principle that consumers will buy a fixed quantity of a good regardless of its price.

**constant returns to scale** *(page 215)* Situation in which output doubles when all inputs are doubled.

**constant-cost industry** *(page 299)* Industry whose long-run supply curve is horizontal.

**Consumer Price Index** *(page 12)* Measure of the aggregate price level.

**consumer surplus** *(page 132)* Difference between what a consumer is willing to pay for a good and the amount actually paid.

**contract curve** *(page 593)* Curve showing all efficient allocations of goods between two consumers, or of two inputs between two production functions.

**cooperative** *(page 275)* Association of businesses or people jointly owned and operated by members for mutual benefit.

**cooperative game** *(page 480)* Game in which participants can negotiate binding contracts that allow them to plan joint strategies.

**corner solution** *(page 90)* Situation in which the marginal rate of substitution of one good for another in a chosen market basket is not equal to the slope of the budget line.

**cost function** *(page 256)* Function relating cost of production to level of output and other variables that the firm can control.

**cost-of-living index** *(page 101)* Ratio of the present cost of a typical bundle of consumer goods and services compared with the cost during a base period.

**Cournot equilibrium** *(page 452)* Equilibrium in the Cournot model, in which each firm correctly assumes how much its competitor will produce and sets its own production level accordingly.

**Cournot model** *(page 451)* Oligopoly model in which firms produce a homogeneous good, each firm treats the output of its competitors as fixed, and all firms decide simultaneously how much to produce.

**cross-price elasticity of demand** *(page 36)* Percentage change in the quantity demanded of one good resulting from a 1-percent increase in the price of another.

**cyclical industries** *(page 42)* Industries in which sales tend to magnify cyclical changes in gross domestic product and national income.

## D

**deadweight loss** *(page 313)* Net loss of total (consumer plus producer) surplus.

**decreasing returns to scale** *(page 215)* Situation in which output less than doubles when all inputs are doubled.

**decreasing-cost industry** *(page 302)* Industry whose long-run supply curve is downward sloping.

**degree of economies of scope (SC)** *(page 250)* Percentage of cost savings resulting when two or more products are produced jointly rather than individually.

**demand curve** *(page 23)* Relationship between the quantity of a good that consumers are willing to buy and the price of the good.

**derived demand** *(page 522)* Demand for an input that depends on, and is derived from, both the firm's level of output and the cost of inputs.

**deviation** *(page 161)* Difference between expected payoff and actual payoff.

**diminishing marginal utility** *(page 96)* Principle that as more of a good is consumed, the consumption of additional amounts will yield smaller additions to utility.

**discount rate** *(page 561)* Rate used to determine the value today of a dollar received in the future.

**diseconomies of scale** *(page 246)* Situation in which a doubling of output requires more than a doubling of cost.

**diseconomies of scope** *(page 250)* Situation in which joint output of a single firm is less than could be achieved by separate firms when each produces a single product.

**diversifiable risk** *(page 564)* Risk that can be eliminated either by investing in many projects or by holding the stocks of many companies.

**diversification** *(page 170)* Practice of reducing risk by allocating resources to a variety of activities whose outcomes are not closely related.

**dominant firm** *(page 468)* Firm with a large share of total sales that sets price to maximize profits, taking into account the supply response of smaller firms.

**dominant strategy** *(page 482)* Strategy that is optimal no matter what an opponent does.

**duality** *(page 154)* Alternative way of looking at the consumer's utility maximization decision: Rather than choosing the highest indifference curve, given a budget constraint, the consumer chooses the lowest budget line that touches a given indifference curve.

**duopoly** *(page 450)* Market in which two firms compete with each other.

**Dutch auction** *(page 510)* Auction in which a seller begins by offering an item at a relatively high price, then reduces it by fixed amounts until the item is sold.

## E

**economic cost** *(page 222)* Cost to a firm of utilizing economic resources in production, including opportunity cost.

**economic efficiency** *(page 315)* Maximization of aggregate consumer and producer surplus.

**economic rent** *(page 297)* Amount that firms are willing to pay for an input less the minimum amount necessary to obtain it.

**economies of scale** *(page 246)* Situation in which output can be doubled for less than a doubling of cost.

**economies of scope** *(page 250)* Situation in which joint output of a single firm is greater than output that could be achieved by two different firms when each produces a single product.

**Edgeworth box** *(page 591)* Diagram showing all possible allocations of either two goods between two people or of two inputs between two production processes.

**effective yield (or rate of return)** *(page 558)* Percentage return that one receives by investing in a bond.

**efficiency wage** *(page 640)* Wage that a firm will pay to an employee as an incentive not to shirk.

**efficiency wage theory** *(page 639)* Explanation for the presence of unemployment and wage discrimination which recognizes that labor productivity may be affected by the wage rate.

**efficient (or Pareto efficient) allocation** *(page 590)* Allocation of goods in which no one can be made better off unless someone else is made worse off.

**elasticity** *(page 34)* Percentage change in one variable resulting from a 1-percent increase in another.

**emissions fee** *(page 653)* Charge levied on each unit of a firm's emissions.

**emissions standard** *(page 652)* Legal limit on the amount of pollutants that a firm can emit.

**endowment effect** *(page 186)* Tendency of individuals to value an item more when they own it than when they do not.

**Engel curve** *(page 116)* Curve relating the quantity of a good consumed to income.

**English (or oral) auction** *(page 510)* Auction in which a seller actively solicits progressively higher bids from a group of potential buyers.

**equal marginal principle** *(page 97)* Principle that utility is maximized when the consumer has equalized the marginal utility per dollar of expenditure across all goods.

**equilibrium (or market-clearing) price** *(page 25)* Price that equates the quantity supplied to the quantity demanded.

**equilibrium in dominant strategies** *(page 483)* Outcome of a game in which each firm is doing the best it can regardless of what its competitors are doing.

**excess demand** *(page 596)* When the quantity demanded of a good exceeds the quantity supplied.

**excess supply** *(page 596)* When the quantity supplied of a good exceeds the quantity demanded.

**exchange economy** *(page 590)* Market in which two or more consumers trade two goods among themselves.

**expansion path** *(page 241)* Curve passing through points of tangency between a firm's isocost lines and its isoquants.

**expected return** *(page 178)* Return that an asset should earn on average.

**expected utility** *(page 165)* Sum of the utilities associated with all possible outcomes, weighted by the probability that each outcome will occur.

**expected value** *(page 161)* Probability-weighted average of the payoffs associated with all possible outcomes.

**extensive form of a game** *(page 495)* Representation of possible moves in a game in the form of a decision tree.

**extent of a market** *(page 9)* Boundaries of a market, both geographical and in terms of range of products produced and sold within it.

**externality** *(pages 315, 646)* Action by either a producer or a consumer which affects other producers or consumers, but is not accounted for in the market price.

## F

**factors of production** *(page 196)* Inputs into the production process (e.g., labor, capital, and materials).

**first-degree price discrimination** *(page 393)* Practice of charging each customer her reservation price.

**first-price auction** *(page 510)* Auction in which the sales price is equal to the highest bid.

**fixed cost (FC)** *(page 224)* Cost that does not vary with the level of output and that can be eliminated only by shutting down.

**fixed input** *(page 198)* Production factor that cannot be varied.

**fixed-proportions production function** *(page 211)* Production function with L-shaped isoquants, so that only one combination of labor and capital can be used to produce each level of output.

**fixed-weight index** *(page 103)* Cost-of-living index in which the quantities of goods and services remain unchanged.

**free entry (or exit)** *(page 272)* Condition under which there are no special costs that make it difficult for a firm to enter (or exit) an industry.

**free rider** *(page 678)* Consumer or producer who does not pay for a nonexclusive good in the expectation that others will.

## G

**game** *(page 480)* Situation in which players (participants) make strategic decisions that take into account each other's actions and responses.

**general equilibrium analysis** *(page 586)* Simultaneous determination of the prices and quantities in all relevant markets, taking feedback effects into account.

**Giffen good** *(page 122)* Good whose demand curve slopes upward because the (negative) income effect is larger than the substitution effect.

## H

**Hicksian substitution effect** *(page 157)* Alternative to the Slutsky equation for decomposing price changes without recourse to indifference curves.

**horizontal integration** *(page 636)* Organizational form in which several plants produce the same or related products for a firm.

**human capital** *(page 570)* Knowledge, skills, and experience that make an individual more productive and thereby able to earn a higher income over a lifetime.

## I

**ideal cost-of-living index** *(page 102)* Cost of attaining a given level of utility at current prices relative to the cost of attaining the same utility at base-year prices.

**import quota** *(page 331)* Limit on the quantity of a good that can be imported.

**income effect** *(page 121)* Change in consumption of a good resulting from an increase in purchasing power, with relative prices held constant.

**income elasticity of demand** *(page 36)* Percentage change in the quantity demanded resulting from a 1-percent increase in income.

**income-consumption curve** *(page 114)* Curve tracing the utility-maximizing combinations of two goods as a consumer's income changes.

**increasing returns to scale** *(page 215)* Situation in which output more than doubles when all inputs are doubled.

**increasing-cost industry** *(page 300)* Industry whose long-run supply curve is upward sloping.

**indifference curve** *(page 70)* Curve representing all combinations of market baskets that provide a consumer with the same level of satisfaction.

**indifference map** *(page 72)* Graph containing a set of indifference curves showing the market baskets among which a consumer is indifferent.

**individual demand curve** *(page 113)* Curve relating the quantity of a good that a single consumer will buy to its price.

**infinitely elastic demand** *(page 35)* Principle that consumers will buy as much of a good as they can get at a single price, but for any higher price the quantity demanded drops to zero, while for any lower price the quantity demanded increases without limit.

**interest rate** *(page 553)* Rate at which one can borrow or lend money.

**intertemporal price discrimination** *(page 403)* Practice of separating consumers with different demand functions into different groups by charging different prices at different points in time.

**isocost line** *(page 236)* Graph showing all possible combinations of labor and capital that can be purchased for a given total cost.

**isoelastic demand curve** *(page 128)* Demand curve with a constant price elasticity.

**isoquant** *(page 208)* Curve showing all possible combinations of inputs that yield the same output.

**isoquant map** *(page 209)* Graph combining a number of isoquants, used to describe a production function.

## K

**kinked demand curve model** *(page 465)* Oligopoly model in which each firm faces a demand curve kinked at the currently prevailing price: at higher prices demand is very elastic, whereas at lower prices it is inelastic.

## L

**labor productivity** *(page 205)* Average product of labor for an entire industry or for the economy as a whole.

**Lagrangian** *(page 150)* Function to be maximized or minimized, plus a variable (the *Lagrange multiplier*) multiplied by the constraint.

**Laspeyres price index** *(page 102)* Amount of money at current year prices that an individual requires to purchase a bundle of goods and services chosen in a base year divided by the cost of purchasing the same bundle at base-year prices.

**law of diminishing marginal returns** *(page 202)* Principle that as the use of an input increases with other inputs fixed, the resulting additions to output will eventually decrease.

**learning curve** *(page 252)* Graph relating amount of inputs needed by a firm to produce each unit of output to its cumulative output.

**least-squares criterion** *(page 688)* Criterion of "best fit" used to choose values for regression parameters, usually by minimizing the sum of squared residuals between the actual values of the dependent variable and the fitted values.

**Lerner Index of Monopoly Power** *(page 363)* Measure of monopoly power calculated as excess of price over marginal cost as a fraction of price.

**linear demand curve** *(page 35)* Demand curve that is a straight line.

**linear regression** *(page 687)* Model specifying a linear relationship between a dependent variable and several independent (or explanatory) variables and an error term.

**long run** *(page 198)* Amount of time needed to make all production inputs variable.

**long-run average cost curve (LAC)** *(page 245)* Curve relating average cost of production to output when all inputs, including capital, are variable.

**long-run competitive equilibrium** *(page 296)* All firms in an industry are maximizing profit, no firm has an incentive to enter or exit, and price is such that quantity supplied equals quantity demanded.

**long-run marginal cost curve (LMC)** *(page 245)* Curve showing the change in long-run total cost as output is increased incrementally by 1 unit.

**loss aversion** *(page 187)* Tendency for individuals to prefer avoiding losses over acquiring gains.

## M

**macroeconomics** *(page 4)* Branch of economics that deals with aggregate economic variables, such as the level and growth rate of national output, interest rates, unemployment, and inflation.

**marginal benefit** *(page 88)* Benefit from the consumption of one additional unit of a good.

**marginal cost** *(pages 88, 227)* Cost of one additional unit of a good.

**marginal expenditure** *(page 374)* Additional cost of buying one more unit of a good.

**marginal expenditure curve** *(page 530)* Curve describing the additional cost of purchasing one additional unit of a good.

**marginal external benefit** *(page 648)* Increased benefit that accrues to other parties as a firm increases output by one unit.

**marginal external cost** *(page 647)* Increase in cost imposed externally as one or more firms increase output by one unit.

**marginal product** *(page 199)* Additional output produced as an input is increased by one unit.

**marginal rate of substitution (MRS)** *(page 75)* Maximum amount of a good that a consumer is willing to give up in order to obtain one additional unit of another good.

**marginal rate of technical substitution (MRTS)** *(page 210)* Amount by which the quantity of one input can be reduced when one extra unit of another input is used, so that output remains constant.

**marginal rate of transformation** *(page 602)* Amount of one good that must be given up to produce one additional unit of a second good.

**marginal revenue** *(pages 276, 350)* Change in revenue resulting from a one-unit increase in output.

**marginal revenue product** *(page 522)* Additional revenue resulting from the sale of output created by the use of one additional unit of an input.

**marginal social benefit** *(page 649)* Sum of the marginal private benefit plus the marginal external benefit.

**marginal social cost** *(page 647)* Sum of the marginal cost of production and the marginal external cost.

**marginal utility (MU)** *(page 96)* Additional satisfaction obtained from consuming one additional unit of a good.

**marginal value** *(page 374)* Additional benefit derived from purchasing one more unit of a good.

**market** *(page 7)* Collection of buyers and sellers that, through their actual or potential interactions, determine the price of a product or set of products.

**market basket (or bundle)** *(page 69)* List with specific quantities of one or more goods.

**market definition** *(page 8)* Determination of the buyers, sellers, and range of products that should be included in a particular market.

**market demand curve** *(page 125)* Curve relating the quantity of a good that all consumers in a market will buy to its price.

**market failure** *(page 315)* Situation in which an unregulated competitive market is inefficient because prices fail to provide proper signals to consumers and producers.

**market mechanism** *(page 25)* Tendency in a free market for price to change until the market clears.

**market power** *(page 350)* Ability of a seller or buyer to affect the price of a good.

**market price** *(page 8)* Price prevailing in a competitive market.

**market signaling** *(page 623)* Process by which sellers send signals to buyers conveying information about product quality.

**maximin strategy** *(page 487)* Strategy that maximizes the minimum gain that can be earned.

**method of Lagrange multipliers** *(page 150)* Technique to maximize or minimize a function subject to one or more constraints.

**microeconomics** *(page 4)* Branch of economics that deals with the behavior of individual economic units—consumers, firms, workers, and investors—as well as the markets that these units comprise.

**mixed bundling** *(page 418)* Selling two or more goods both as a package and individually.

**mixed strategy** *(page 488)* Strategy in which a player makes a random choice among two or more possible actions, based on a set of chosen probabilities.

**monopolistic competition** *(page 444)* Market in which firms can enter freely, each producing its own brand or version of a differentiated product.

**monopoly** *(page 350)* Market with only one seller.

**monopsony** *(page 350)* Market with only one buyer.

**monopsony power** *(page 374)* Buyer's ability to affect the price of a good.

**moral hazard** *(page 628)* When a party whose actions are unobserved can affect the probability or magnitude of a payment associated with an event.

**multiple regression analysis** *(page 687)* Statistical procedure for quantifying economic relationships and testing hypotheses about them.

**mutual fund** *(page 171)* Organization that pools funds of individual investors to buy a large number of different stocks or other financial assets.

## N

**Nash equilibrium** *(page 450)* Set of strategies or actions in which each firm does the best it can given its competitors' actions.

**natural monopoly** *(page 372)* Firm that can produce the entire output of the market at a cost lower than what it would be if there were several firms.

**negatively correlated variables** *(page 171)* Variables having a tendency to move in opposite directions.

**net present value (NPV) criterion** *(page 560)* Rule holding that one should invest if the present value of the expected future cash flow from an investment is larger than the cost of the investment.

**network externality** *(page 136)* Situation in which each individual's demand depends on the purchases of other individuals.

**nominal price** *(page 12)* Absolute price of a good, unadjusted for inflation.

**noncooperative game** *(pages 462, 480)* Game in which negotiation and enforcement of binding contracts are not possible.

**nondiversifiable risk** *(page 564)* Risk that cannot be eliminated by investing in many projects or by holding the stocks of many companies.

**nonexclusive good** *(page 676)* Good that people cannot be excluded from consuming, so that it is difficult or impossible to charge for its use.

**nonrival good** *(page 676)* Good for which the marginal cost of its provision to an additional consumer is zero.

**normative analysis** *(page 7)* Analysis examining questions of what ought to be.

## O

**oligopoly** *(page 444)* Market in which only a few firms compete with one another, and entry by new firms is impeded.

**oligopsony** *(page 374)* Market with only a few buyers.

**opportunity cost** *(page 222)* Cost associated with opportunities that are forgone when a firm's resources are not put to their best alternative use.

**opportunity cost of capital** *(page 561)* Rate of return that one could earn by investing in an alternate project with similar risk.

**optimal strategy** *(page 480)* Strategy that maximizes a player's expected payoff.

**ordinal utility function** *(page 80)* Utility function that generates a ranking of market baskets in order of most to least preferred.

## P

**Paasche index** *(page 103)* Amount of money at current-year prices that an individual requires to purchase a current bundle of goods and services divided by the cost of purchasing the same bundle in a base year.

**parallel conduct** *(page 382)* Form of implicit collusion in which one firm consistently follows actions of another.

**partial equilibrium analysis** *(page 586)* Determination of equilibrium prices and quantities in a market independent of effects from other markets.

**payoff** *(pages 161, 480)* Value associated with a possible outcome.

**payoff matrix** *(page 462)* Table showing profit (or payoff) to each firm given its decision and the decision of its competitor.

**peak-load pricing** *(page 403)* Practice of charging higher prices during peak periods when capacity constraints cause marginal costs to be high.

**perfect complements** *(page 77)* Two goods for which the MRS is zero or infinite; the indifference curves are shaped as right angles.

**perfect substitutes** *(page 77)* Two goods for which the marginal rate of substitution of one for the other is a constant.

**perfectly competitive market** *(page 8)* Market with many buyers and sellers, so that no single buyer or seller has a significant impact on price.

**perpetuity** *(page 556)* Bond paying out a fixed amount of money each year, forever.

**point elasticity of demand** *(page 37)* Price elasticity at a particular point on the demand curve.

**positive analysis** *(page 6)* Analysis describing relationships of cause and effect.

**positively correlated variables** *(page 171)* Variables having a tendency to move in the same direction.

**predatory pricing** *(page 382)* Practice of pricing to drive current competitors out of business and to discourage new entrants in a market so that a firm can enjoy higher future profits.

**present discounted value (PDV)** *(page 553)* The current value of an expected future cash flow.

**price discrimination** *(page 393)* Practice of charging different prices to different consumers for similar goods.

**price elasticity of demand** *(page 34)* Percentage change in quantity demanded of a good resulting from a 1-percent increase in its price.

**price elasticity of supply** *(page 37)* Percentage change in quantity supplied resulting from a 1-percent increase in price.

**price leadership** *(page 466)* Pattern of pricing in which one firm regularly announces price changes that other firms then match.

**price of risk** *(page 180)* Extra risk that an investor must incur to enjoy a higher expected return.

**price rigidity** *(page 465)* Characteristic of oligopolistic markets by which firms are reluctant to change prices even if costs or demands change.

**price signaling** *(page 465)* Form of implicit collusion in which a firm announces a price increase in the hope that other firms will follow suit.

**price support** *(page 324)* Price set by government above free-market level and maintained by governmental purchases of excess supply.

**price taker** *(page 272)* Firm that has no influence over market price and thus takes the price as given.

**price-consumption curve** *(page 113)* Curve tracing the utility-maximizing combinations of two goods as the price of one changes.

**principal** *(page 631)* Individual who employs one or more agents to achieve an objective.

**principal-agent problem** *(page 631)* Problem arising when agents (e.g., a firm's managers) pursue their own goals rather than the goals of principals (e.g., the firm's owners).

**prisoners' dilemma** *(page 462)* Game theory example in which two prisoners must decide separately whether to confess to a crime; if a prisoner confesses, he will receive a lighter sentence and his accomplice will receive a heavier one, but if neither confesses, sentences will be lighter than if both confess.

**private-value auction** *(page 510)* Auction in which each bidder knows his or her individual valuation of the object up for bid, with valuations differing from bidder to bidder.

**probability** *(page 160)* Likelihood that a given outcome will occur.

**Producer Price Index** *(page 12)* Measure of the aggregate price level for intermediate products and wholesale goods.

**producer surplus** *(page 291)* Sum over all units produced by a firm of differences between the market price of a good and the marginal cost of production.

**product transformation curve** *(page 249)* Curve showing the various combinations of two different outputs (products) that can be produced with a given set of inputs.

**production function** *(page 197)* Function showing the highest output that a firm can produce for every specified combination of inputs.

**production possibilities frontier** *(page 601)* Curve showing the combinations of two goods that can be produced with fixed quantities of inputs.

**profit** *(page 276)* Difference between total revenue and total cost.

**property rights** *(page 669)* Legal rules stating what people or firms may do with their property.

**public good** *(pages 613, 676)* Nonexclusive and nonrival good: the marginal cost of provision to an additional consumer is zero and people cannot be excluded from consuming it.

**pure bundling** *(page 418)* Selling products only as a package.

**pure strategy** *(page 488)* Strategy in which a player makes a specific choice or takes a specific action.

## R

**rate-of-return regulation** *(page 373)* Maximum price allowed by a regulatory agency is based on the (expected) rate of return that a firm will earn.

**reaction curve** *(page 452)* Relationship between a firm's profit-maximizing output and the amount it thinks its competitor will produce.

**real price** *(page 12)* Price of a good relative to an aggregate measure of prices; price adjusted for inflation.

**real return** *(page 178)* Simple (or nominal) return on an asset, less the rate of inflation.

**reference point** *(page 186)* The point from which an individual makes a consumption decision.

**rent seeking** *(page 370)* Spending money in socially unproductive efforts to acquire, maintain, or exercise monopoly.

**rental rate** *(page 236)* Cost per year of renting one unit of capital.

**repeated game** *(page 490)* Game in which actions are taken and payoffs received over and over again.

**reservation price** *(page 393)* Maximum price that a customer is willing to pay for a good.

**return** *(page 178)* Total monetary flow of an asset as a fraction of its price.

**returns to scale** *(page 215)* Rate at which output increases as inputs are increased proportionately.

**risk averse** *(page 167)* Condition of preferring a certain income to a risky income with the same expected value.

**risk loving** *(page 167)* Condition of preferring a risky income to a certain income with the same expected value.

**risk neutral** *(page 167)* Condition of being indifferent between a certain income and an uncertain income with the same expected value.

**risk premium** *(pages 167, 564)* Maximum amount of money that a risk-averse individual will pay to avoid taking a risk.

**riskless (or risk-free) asset** *(page 178)* Asset that provides a flow of money or services that is known with certainty.

**risky asset** *(page 177)* Asset that provides an uncertain flow of money or services to its owner.

**R-squared ($R^2$)** *(page 691)* Percentage of the variation in the dependent variable that is accounted for by all the explanatory variables.

## S

**sample** *(page 689)* Set of observations for study, drawn from a larger universe.

**sealed-bid auction** *(page 510)* Auction in which all bids are made simultaneously in sealed envelopes, the winning bidder being the individual who has submitted the highest bid.

**second-degree price discrimination** *(page 396)* Practice of charging different prices per unit for different quantities of the same good or service.

**second-price auction** *(page 510)* Auction in which the sales price is equal to the second-highest bid.

**sequential game** *(page 494)* Game in which players move in turn, responding to each other's actions and reactions.

**shirking model** *(page 640)* Principle that workers still have an incentive to shirk if a firm pays them a market-clearing wage, because fired workers can be hired somewhere else for the same wage.

**short run** *(page 198)* Period of time in which quantities of one or more production factors cannot be changed.

**short-run average cost curve (SAC)** *(page 245)* Curve relating average cost of production to output when level of capital is fixed.

**shortage** *(page 26)* Situation in which the quantity demanded exceeds the quantity supplied.

**Slutsky equation** *(page 156)* Formula for decomposing the effects of a price change into substitution and income effects.

**snob effect** *(page 137)* Negative network externality in which a consumer wishes to own an exclusive or unique good.

**social rate of discount** *(page 667)* Opportunity cost to society as a whole of receiving an economic benefit in the future rather than the present.

**social welfare function** *(page 598)* Measure describing the well-being of society as a whole in terms of the utilities of individual members.

**specific tax** *(page 336)* Tax of a certain amount of money per unit sold.

**Stackelberg model** *(page 455)* Oligopoly model in which one firm sets its output before other firms do.

**standard deviation** *(page 162)* Square root of the weighted average of the squares of the deviations of the payoffs associated with each outcome from their expected values.

**standard error of the regression** *(page 691)* Estimate of the standard deviation of the regression error.

**stock of capital** *(page 206)* Total amount of capital available for use in production.

**stock externality** *(page 664)* Accumulated result of action by a producer or consumer which, though not accounted for in the market price, affects other producers or consumers.

**strategic move** *(page 491)* Action that gives a player an advantage by constraining his behavior.

**strategy** *(page 480)* Rule or plan of action for playing a game.

**subsidy** *(page 339)* Payment reducing the buyer's price below the seller's price; i.e., a negative tax.

**substitutes** *(page 24)* Two goods for which an increase in the price of one leads to an increase in the quantity demanded of the other.

**substitution effect** *(page 121)* Change in consumption of a good associated with a change in its price, with the level of utility held constant.

**sunk cost** *(page 222)* Expenditure that has been made and cannot be recovered.

**supply curve** *(page 22)* Relationship between the quantity of a good that producers are willing to sell and the price of the good.

**surplus** *(page 26)* Situation in which the quantity supplied exceeds the quantity demanded.

## T

**tariff** *(page 331)* Tax on an imported good.

**technical efficiency** *(page 600)* Condition under which firms combine inputs to produce a given output as inexpensively as possible.

**technological change** *(page 206)* Development of new technologies allowing factors of production to be used more effectively.

**theory of consumer behavior** *(page 68)* Description of how consumers allocate incomes among different goods and services to maximize their well-being.

**theory of the firm** *(page 196)* Explanation of how a firm makes cost-minimizing production decisions and how its cost varies with its output.

**third-degree price discrimination** *(page 397)* Practice of dividing consumers into two or more groups with separate demand curves and charging different prices to each group.

**tit-for-tat strategy** *(page 490)* Repeated-game strategy in which a player responds in kind to an opponent's previous play, cooperating with cooperative opponents and retaliating against uncooperative ones.

**total cost (TC or C)** *(page 224)* Total economic cost of production, consisting of fixed and variable costs.

**transfer prices** *(page 433)* Internal prices at which parts and components from upstream divisions are "sold" to downstream divisions within a firm.

**tradeable emissions permits** *(page 656)* System of marketable permits, allocated among firms, specifying the maximum level of emissions that can be generated.

**two-part tariff** *(page 406)* Form of pricing in which consumers are charged both an entry and a usage fee.

**tying** *(page 423)* Practice of requiring a customer to purchase one good in order to purchase another.

# U

**user cost of capital** *(page 234)* The annual cost of owning and using a capital asset, equal to economic depreciation plus forgone interest.

**user cost of production** *(page 576)* Opportunity cost of producing and selling a unit today and so making it unavailable for production and sale in the future.

**utility** *(page 79)* Numerical score representing the satisfaction that a consumer gets from a given market basket.

**utility function** *(page 79)* Formula that assigns a level of utility to individual market baskets.

**utility possibilities frontier** *(page 598)* Curve showing all efficient allocations of resources measured in terms of the utility levels of two individuals.

# V

**value of complete information** *(page 174)* Difference between the expected value of a choice when there is complete information and the expected value when information is incomplete.

**variability** *(page 161)* Extent to which possible outcomes of an uncertain event differ.

**variable cost (VC)** *(page 224)* Cost that varies as output varies.

**variable profit** *(page 393)* Sum of profits on each incremental unit produced by a firm; i.e., profit ignoring fixed costs.

**vertical integration** *(page 636)* Organizational form in which a firm contains several divisions, with some producing parts and components that others use to produce finished products.

# W

**welfare economics** *(page 597)* Normative evaluation of markets and economic policy.

**welfare effects** *(page 311)* Gains and losses to consumers and producers.

**winner's curse** *(page 512)* Situation in which the winner of a common-value auction is worse off as a consequence of overestimating the value of the item and thereby overbidding.

# Z

**zero economic profit** *(page 294)* A firm is earning a normal return on its investment—i.e., it is doing as well as it could by investing its money elsewhere.

# ANSWERS TO SELECTED EXERCISES

## CHAPTER 1

**1. a.** *False.* There is little or no substitutability across geographical regions of the United States. A consumer in Los Angeles, for example, will not travel to Houston, Atlanta, or New York for lunch just because hamburger prices are lower in those cities. Likewise, a McDonald's or Burger King in New York cannot supply hamburgers in Los Angeles, even if prices were higher in Los Angeles. In other words, a fast-food price increase in New York will affect neither the quantity demanded nor the quantity supplied in Los Angeles or other parts of the country.

**b.** *False.* Although consumers are unlikely to travel across the country to buy clothing, suppliers can easily move clothing from one part of the country to another. Thus if clothing prices were substantially higher in Atlanta than Los Angeles, clothing companies could shift supplies to Atlanta, which would reduce the price there.

**c.** *False.* Although some consumers might be die-hard Coke or Pepsi loyalists, there are many consumers who will substitute one for the other based on price differences. Thus there is a single market for colas.

## CHAPTER 2

**2. a.** With each price increase of $20, the quantity demanded decreases by 2. Therefore, $(\Delta Q_D/\Delta P)$ = $-2/20 = -0.1$. At $P = 80$, quantity demanded equals 20 and $E_D = (80/20)(-0.1) = -0.40$. Similarly, at $P = 100$, quantity demanded equals 18 and $E_D = (100/18)(-0.1) = -0.56$.

**b.** With each price increase of $20, quantity supplied increases by 2. Therefore, $(\Delta Q_S/\Delta P) = 2/20 = 0.1$. At $P = 80$, quantity supplied equals 16 and $E_S = (80/16)(0.1) = 0.5$. Similarly, at $P = 100$, quantity supplied equals 18 and $E_S = (100/18)(0.1) = 0.56$.

**c.** The equilibrium price and quantity are found where the quantity supplied equals the quantity demanded at the same price. From the table, the $P^* = \$100$ and the $Q^* = 18$ million.

**d.** With a price ceiling of $80, consumers want 20 million, but producers supply only 16 million, for a shortage of 4 million.

**3.** If Brazil and Indonesia add 200 million bushels of wheat to U.S. wheat demand, the new demand curve will be $Q + 200$, or $Q_D = (3244 - 283P) + 200 = 3444 - 283P$.

Equate supply and the new demand to find the new equilibrium price. $1944 + 207P = 3444 - 283P$, or $490P = 1500$, and thus $P = \$3.06$ per bushel. To find the equilibrium quantity, substitute the price into either the supply or demand equation. Using demand, $Q_D = 3444 - 283(3.06) = 2578$ million bushels.

**5. a.** Total demand is $Q = 3244 - 283P$; domestic demand is $Q_D = 1700 - 107P$; subtracting domestic demand from total demand gives export demand $Q_E = 1544 - 176P$. The initial market equilibrium price (as given in example) is $P^* = \$2.65$. With a 40-percent decrease in export demand, total demand becomes $Q = Q_D + 0.6Q_E = 1700 - 107P + 0.6(1544 - 176P) = 2626.4 - 212.6P$. Demand is equal to supply. Therefore:

$$2626.4 - 212.6P = 1944 + 207P$$
$$682.4 = 419.6P$$

So $P = \dfrac{682.4}{419.6} = \$1.626$ or $\$1.63$. At this price, $Q = 2281$. Yes, farmers should be worried. With this drop in quantity and price, revenue goes from $6609 million to $3718 million.

**b.** If the U.S. government supports a price of $3.50, the market is not in equilibrium. At this support price, demand is equal to $2626.4 - 212.6(3.5) = 1882.3$ and supply is $1944 + 207(3.5) = 2668.5$. There is excess supply ($2668.5 - 1882.3 = 786.2$) which the government must buy, costing $\$3.50(786.2) = \$2751.7$ million.

**8. a.** To derive the new demand curve, we follow the same procedure as in Section 2.6. We know that $E_D = -b (P^*/Q^*)$; substituting $E_D = -0.75$, $P^* = \$2$, and $Q^* = 12$ gives $-0.75 = -b(2/12)$ so that $b = 4.5$. Substituting this value into the equation for the linear demand curve, $Q_D = a - bP$, we have $12 = a - 4.5(2)$. So $a = 21$. The new demand curve is $Q_D = 21 - 4.5P$.

**b.** To determine the effect of a 20-percent decline in copper demand, we note that the quantity demanded is 80 percent of what it would be otherwise for every price. Multiplying the right-hand side of the demand curve by 0.8, $Q_D = (0.8)(21 - 4.5P) = 16.8 - 3.6P$. Supply is still $Q_s = -6 + 9P$ and demand is equal to supply. Solving, $P^* = \$1.81$ per pound. A decline in demand of 20 percent, therefore, entails a drop in price of 19 cents per pound, or 9.5 percent.

**10. a.** First, considering non-OPEC supply: $S_C = Q^* = 20$. With $E_S = 0.10$ and $P^* = \$50$, $E_S = d(P^*/Q^*)$ implies $d = 0.04$. Substituting for $d$, $S_C = 20$, and $P = 50$ in the supply equation gives $20 = c + (0.04)(50)$, so that $c = 18$. Hence, the supply curve is $S_C = 18 + 0.04P$. Similarly, since $Q_D = 34$, $E_D = -b(P^*/Q^*) = -0.05$ and $b = 0.03$. Substituting for $b$, $Q_D = 34$, and $P = 50$ in the demand equation gives $34 = a - (0.03)(50)$, so that $a = 35.5$. Hence $Q_D = 35.5 - 0.03P$.

**b.** The long-run elasticities are: $E_S = 0.4$ and $E_D = -0.4$. As above, $E_S = d(P^*/Q^*)$ and $E_D = -b(P^*/Q^*)$, implying 0.4 $= d(50/20)$ and $-0.4 = -b(50/34)$. So $d = 0.16$ and $b = 0.27$. Next solve for $c$ and $a$: $S_C = c + dP$ and $Q_D = a - bP$, which implies that $20 = c + (0.16)$ (50) and $34 = a - (0.27)(50)$. Therefore, $c = 12$ and $a = 47.5$.

**c.** The discovery of new oil fields will increase OPEC supply by 2 bb/yr, so $S_C = 20$, $S_O = 16$, and $D = 36$. The new short-run total supply curve is $S_T = 34 + 0.04P$. Demand is unchanged: $D = 35.5 - 0.03P$. Since supply equals demand, $34 + 0.04P = 35.5 - 0.03P$. Solving, $P = \$21.43$ per barrel. An increase in OPEC supply entails a drop in price in \$ 28.57 or 57% in the short-run.

To analyze the long-run, use the new long-run supply curve, $S_T = 28 + 0.16P$. Setting this equal to the long-run demand gives: $28 + 0.16P = 47.5 - 0.27P$, so that $P = \$45.35$ per barrel, only \$4.65 per barrel (9%) less than the original long-run price.

## CHAPTER 3

**3.** Not necessarily true. Suppose that she has convex preferences (a diminishing marginal rate of substitution), and has a lot of movie tickets. Even though she would give up movie tickets to get another basketball ticket, she does not necessarily like basketball better.

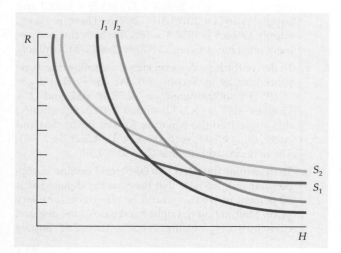

Figure 3(a)

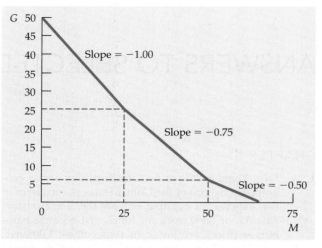

Figure 3(b)

**6. a.** See Figure 3(a), where $R$ is the number of rock concerts, and $H$ is the number of hockey games.

**b.** At any combination of $R$ and $H$, Jones is willing to give up more of $R$ to get some $H$ than Smith is. Thus Jones has a *higher* MRS of $R$ for $H$ than Smith has. Jones' indifference curves are steeper than Smith's at any point on the graph.

**8.** In Figure 3(b) we plot miles flown, $M$, against all other goods, $G$, in dollars. The slope of the budget line is $-P_M/P_G$. The price of miles flown changes as number of miles flown changes, so the budget curve is kinked at 25,000 and 50,000 miles. Suppose $P_M$ is \$1 per mile for $\leq$ 25,000 miles, then $P_M = \$0.75$ for $25,000 < M \leq 50,000$, and $P_M = \$.50$ for $M > 50,000$. Also, let $P_G = \$1$. Then the slope of the first segment is $-1$, the slope of the second segment is $-0.75$, and the slope of the last segment is $-0.5$.

## CHAPTER 4

**9. a.** For computer chips, $E_P = -2$, so $-2 = \%\Delta Q/10$, and therefore $\%\Delta Q = -20$. For disk drives, $E_P = -1$, so a 10 percent increase in price will reduce sales by 10 percent. Sales revenue will decrease for computer chips because demand is elastic and price has increased. To estimate the change in revenue, let $TR_1 = P_1Q_1$ be revenue before the price change and $TR_2 = P_2Q_2$ be revenue after the price change. Therefore $\Delta TR = P_2Q_2 - P_1Q_1$, and thus $\Delta TR = (1.1P_1)(0.8Q_1) - P_1Q_1 = -0.12P_1Q_1$, or a 12 percent decline. Sales revenue for disk drives will remain unchanged because demand elasticity is $-1$.

**b.** Although we know the responsiveness of demand to change in price, we need to know the quantities and the prices of the products to determine total sales revenues.

**11. a.** With small changes in price, the point elasticity formula would be appropriate. But here, the price of food increases from \$2 to \$2.50, so arc elasticity should be used: $E_p = (\Delta Q/\Delta P)(\overline{P}/\overline{Q})$. We know that $E_p = -1$, $P = 2$, $\Delta P = .50$, and $Q = 5000$. So, if there is no change in income, we can solve for $\Delta Q$: $-1 = (\Delta Q/.50)\,[((2 + .50)/2)/(5000 + \Delta Q/2)] = (\Delta Q \cdot 2.50)/(10,000 + \Delta Q)$. We find that $\Delta Q = -1000$: she decreases her consumption of food from 5000 to 4000 units.

**b.** A tax rebate of $2500 implies an income increase of $2500. To calculate the response of demand to the tax rebate, we use the definition of the arc income elasticity: $E_I = (\Delta Q / \Delta I)(\overline{I}/\overline{Q})$. We know that $E_I = 0.5$, $I = 25,000$, $\Delta I = 2500$, and $Q = 4000$. We solve for $\Delta Q$: $0.5 = (\Delta Q/2500)[((25,000 + 27,500)/2)/(4000 + (\Delta Q/2)]$. Since $\Delta Q = 195$, she increases her consumption of food from 4000 to 4195 units.

**c.** Felicia is better off after the rebate. The amount of the rebate is enough to allow her to purchase her original bundle of food and other goods. Recall that originally she consumed 5000 units of food. When the price went up by fifty cents per unit, she needed an extra $(5000)(\$0.50) = \$2500$ to afford the same quantity of food without reducing the quantity of the other goods consumed. This is the exact amount of the rebate. However, she did not choose to return to her original bundle. We can therefore infer that she found a better bundle that gave her a higher level of utility.

**13. a.** The demand curve is a straight line with a vertical intercept of $P = 15$ and a horizontal intercept of $Q = 30$.

**b.** If there were no toll, the price $P$ would be 0, so that $Q = 30$.

**c.** If the toll is $5, $Q = 20$. The consumer surplus lost is the difference between consumer surplus when $P = 0$ and consumer surplus when $P = 5$, or $125.

## CHAPTER 4—APPENDIX

**1.** The first utility function can be represented as a series of straight lines; the second as a series of hyperbolas in the positive quadrant; and the third as a series of "L"s. Only the second utility function meets the definition of a strictly convex shape.

**3.** The Slutsky equation is $dX/dP_X = \partial X/\partial P^*|_{U=U^*} - X(\Delta X/\Delta I)$, where the first term represents the substitution effect and the second term represents the income effect. With this type of utility function the consumer does not substitute one good for the other when the price changes, so the substitution effect is zero.

## CHAPTER 5

**2.** The four mutually exclusive states are given in Table 5 below.

**4.** The expected value is $EV = (0.4)(100) + (0.3)(30) + (0.3)(-30) = \$40$. The variance is $\sigma^2 = (0.4)(100 - 40)^2 + (0.3)(30 - 40)^2 + (0.3)(-30 - 40)^2 = 2,940$.

**8.** Calculate the expected utility of wealth under the three options. Wealth is equal to the initial $250,000 plus whatever is earned on growing corn, or investing in the safe financial asset. Expected utility under the safe option, allowing for the fact that your initial wealth is $250,000, is: $E(U) = (250,000 + 200,000(1 + 0.5))^{.5} = 678.23$. Expected utility with regular corn is:

$E(U) = .7(250,000 + (500,000 - 200,000))^{.5} + .3(250,000 + (50,000 - 200,000))^{.5} = 519.13 + 94.87 = 614$

Expected utility with drought-resistant corn is:

$E(U) = .7(250,000 + (500,000 - 250,000))^{.5} + .3(250,000 + (350,000 - 250,000))^{.5} = 494.975 + 177.482 = 672.46$

The option with the highest expected utility is the safe option of not planting corn.

## CHAPTER 6

**2. a.** The average product of labor, AP, is equal to $Q/L$. The marginal product of labor, MP, is equal to $\Delta Q/\Delta L$. The relevant calculations are given in the following table.

| L | Q | AP | MP |
|---|---|----|----|
| 0 | 0 | – | – |
| 1 | 10 | 10 | 10 |
| 2 | 18 | 9 | 8 |
| 3 | 24 | 8 | 6 |
| 4 | 28 | 7 | 4 |
| 5 | 30 | 6 | 2 |
| 6 | 28 | 4.7 | –2 |
| 7 | 25 | 3.6 | –3 |

**b.** This production process exhibits diminishing returns to labor, which is characteristic of all production functions with one fixed input. Each additional unit of labor yields a smaller increase in output than the last unit of labor.

### TABLE 5

| | Congress Passes Tariff | Congress Does Not Pass Tariff |
|---|---|---|
| **Slow growth rate** | State 1: Slow growth with tariff | State 2: Slow growth without tariff |
| **Fast growth rate** | State 3: Fast growth with tariff | State 4: Fast growth without tariff |

c. Labor's negative marginal product can arise from congestion in the chair manufacturer's factory. As more laborers are using a fixed amount of capital, they get in each other's way, decreasing output.

6. No. If the inputs are perfect substitutes, the isoquants will be linear. However, to calculate the slope of the isoquant, and hence the MRTS, we need to know the rate at which one input may be substituted for the other. Without the marginal product of each input, we cannot calculate the MRTS.

9. a. Let $Q_1$ be the output of DISK, Inc., $Q_2$ be the output of FLOPPY, Inc., and $X$ be equal amounts of capital and labor for the two firms. Then, $Q_1 = 10X^{0.5}X^{0.5} = 10X^{(0.5+0.5)} = 10X$ and $Q_2 = 10X^{0.6}X^{0.4} = 10X^{(0.6+0.4)} = 10X$. Because $Q_1 = Q_2$, they both generate the same output with the same inputs.

b. With capital fixed at 9 machine units, the production functions become $Q_1 = 30L^{0.5}$ and $Q_2 = 37.37L^{0.4}$. Consider the following table:

| L | Q Firm 1 | MP Firm 1 | Q Firm 2 | MP Firm 2 |
|---|---|---|---|---|
| 0 | 0 | – | 0 | – |
| 1 | 30.00 | 30.00 | 37.37 | 37.37 |
| 2 | 42.43 | 12.43 | 49.31 | 11.94 |
| 3 | 51.96 | 9.53 | 57.99 | 8.69 |
| 4 | 60.00 | 8.04 | 65.07 | 7.07 |

For each unit of labor above 1 unit, the marginal product of labor is greater for DISK, Inc.

## CHAPTER 7

4. a. Total cost, TC, is equal to fixed cost, FC, plus variable cost, VC. Since the franchise fee, FF, is a fixed sum, the firm's fixed costs increase by the fee. Then average cost, equal to (FC + VC)/Q, and average fixed cost, equal to (FC/Q), increase by the average franchise fee (FF/Q). Average variable cost is unaffected by the fee, as is marginal cost.

b. When a tax $t$ is imposed, variable costs increase by $tQ$. Average variable cost increases by $t$ (fixed cost is constant), as does average (total) cost. Because total cost increases by $t$ with each additional unit, marginal cost increases by $t$.

5. It is probably referring to accounting profit; this is the standard concept used in most discussions of how firms are doing financially. In this case, the article points to a substantial difference between accounting and economic profits. It claims that, under the current labor contract, automakers must pay many workers even if they are not working. This implies that their wages are *sunk* for the life of the contract. Accounting profits would subtract wages paid; economic profits

would not, since they are sunk costs. Therefore automakers may be earning economic profits on these sales, even if they have accounting losses.

10. If the firm can produce one chair with either 4 hours of labor or 4 hours of machinery or any combination, then the isoquant is a straight line with a slope of –1 and intercepts at $K = 4$ and $L = 4$. The isocost line, $TC = 30L + 15K$, has a slope of –2 and intercepts at $K = TC/15$ and $L = TC/30$. The cost-minimizing point is a corner solution, where $L = 0$ and $K = 4$, and $TC = \$60$.

## CHAPTER 7—APPENDIX

1. a. Returns to scale refers to the relationship between output and proportional increases in all inputs. If $F(\lambda L, \lambda K) > \lambda F(L,K)$, there are increasing returns to scale; if $F(\lambda L, \lambda K) = \lambda F(L,K)$, there are constant returns to scale; if $F(\lambda L, \lambda K) < \lambda F(L,K)$, there are decreasing returns to scale. Applying this to $F(L,K) = K^2L$, $F(\lambda L, \lambda K) = (\lambda K)^2(\lambda L) = \lambda^3 K^2 L = \lambda^3 F(L,K) > \lambda F(L,K)$. So, this production function exhibits increasing returns to scale.

b. $F(\lambda L, \lambda K) = 10\lambda K + 5\lambda L = \lambda F(L,K)$. The production function exhibits constant returns to scale.

c. $F(\lambda L, \lambda K) = (\lambda K \lambda L)^{0.5} = (\lambda^2)^{0.5} = (KL)^{0.5} = \lambda(KL)^{0.5} = \lambda F(L,K)$. The production function exhibits constant returns to scale.

2. The marginal product of labor is $100K$. The marginal product of capital is $100L$. The marginal rate of technical substitution is $K/L$. Set this equal to the ratio of the wage rate to the rental rate of capital: $K/L = 30/120$ or $L = 4K$. Then substitute for $L$ in the production function and solve for a $K$ that yields an output of 1000 units: $1000 = 100K \cdot 4K$. So, $K = 2.5^{0.5}$, $L = 4 \cdot 2.5^{0.5}$, and total cost is equal to $\$379.20$.

## CHAPTER 8

4. a. Profit is maximized where marginal cost (MC) is equal to marginal revenue (MR). Here, MR is equal to $\$100$. Setting MC equal to 100 yields a profit-maximizing quantity of 25.

b. Profit is equal to total revenue ($PQ$) minus total cost. So profit $= PQ - 200 - 2Q^2$. At $P = 100$ and $Q = 25$, profit $= \$1050$.

c. The firm produces in the short run if its revenues are greater than its variable costs. The firm's short-run supply curve is its MC curve above minimum AVC. Here, AVC is equal to variable cost, $2Q^2$, divided by quantity, $Q$. So, AVC $= 2Q$. Also, MC is equal to $4Q$. So, MC is greater than AVC for any quantity greater than 0. This means that the firm produces in the short run as long as price is positive.

11. The firm should produce where price is equal to marginal cost so that: $P = 115 = 15+4q = MC$ and $q = 25$.

Profit is $800. Producer surplus is profit plus fixed cost, which is $1250.

**14. a.** With the imposition of a $1 tax on a single firm, all its cost curves shift up by $1.

   **b.** Because the firm is a price taker, the imposition of the tax on only one firm does not change the market price. Given that the firm's short-run supply curve is its marginal cost curve (above average variable cost), and that the marginal cost curve has shifted up (or inward), the firm supplies less to the market at every price.

   **c.** If the tax is placed on a single firm, that firm will go out of business unless it was earning a positive economic profit before the tax.

## CHAPTER 9

**1. a.** In free-market equilibrium, $L^S = L^D$. Solving, $w = \$4$ and $L^S = L^D = 40$. If the minimum wage is $5, then $L^S = 50$ and $L^D = 30$. The number of people employed will be given by the labor demand. So employers will hire 30 million workers.

   **b.** With the subsidy, only $w - 1$ is paid by the firm. The labor demand becomes $L^{D*} = 80 - 10(w - 1)$. So $w = \$4.50$ and $L = 45$.

**4. a.** Equating demand and supply, $28 - 2P = 4 + 4P \cdot P^* = 4$ and $Q^* = 20$.

   **b.** The 25-percent reduction would imply that farmers produce 15 billion bushels. To encourage farmers to withdraw their land from cultivation, the government must give them 5 billion bushels that they can sell on the market. Since the total supply to the market is still 20 billion bushels, the market price remains at $4 per bushel. Farmers gain because they incur no costs for the 5 billion bushels received from the government. We calculate these cost savings by taking the area under the supply curve between 15 and 20 billion bushels. The prices when $Q = 15$ and when $Q = 20$ are $P = \$2.75$ and $P = \$4.00$. The total cost of producing the last 5 billion bushels is therefore the area of a trapezoid with a base of $20 - 15 = 5$ billion and an average height of $(2.75 + 4.00)/2 = 3.375$. The area is $5(3.375) = \$16.875$ billion.

   **c.** Taxpayers gain because the government does not have to pay to store the wheat for a year and then ship it to an underdeveloped country. The PIK Program can last only as long as wheat reserves last. But PIK assumes that the land removed from production can be restored to production at such time as the stockpiles are exhausted. If this cannot be done, consumers may eventually pay more for wheat-based products. Finally, farmers enjoy a windfall profit because they have no production costs.

**10. a.** To find the price of natural gas when the price of oil is $60 per barrel, equate the quantity demanded and quantity supplied of natural gas, and solve for $P_G$. The relevant equations are: *Supply:* $Q = 15.90 +$

$0.72P_G + 0.05 P_O$, *Demand:* $Q = 0.02 - 1.8P_G + 0.69P_O$. Using $P_O = \$60$, we get: $15.90 + 0.72P_G + 0.05(60) = 0.02 - 1.8P_G + 0.69(60)$, so the price of natural gas is $P_G = \$8.94$. Substituting into the supply or the demand curve gives a free-market quantity of 25.34 Tcf. If a maximum price of natural gas were set at $3, the quantity supplied would be 21.06 Tcf and the quantity demanded would be 36.02 Tcf. To calculate the deadweight loss, we measure the area of triangles $B$ and $C$ (see Figure 9.4). To find area $B$ we must first determine the price on the demand curve when quantity equals 21.1. From the demand equation, $21.1 = 41.42 - 1.8P_G$. Therefore, $P_G = \$11.29$. Area $B$ equals $(0.5)(25.3 - 21.1)(11.29 - 8.94) = \$4.9$ billion, and area $C$ is $(0.5)(25.3 - 21.1)(8.94 - 3) = \$12.5$ billion. The deadweight loss is $4.9 + 12.5 = \$17.4$ billion.

   **b.** To find the price of oil that would yield a free market price of natural gas of $3, we set the quantity demanded equal to the quantity supplied, use $P_G = \$3$, and solve for $P_O$. Therefore, $Q_S = 15.90 + 0.72(3) + 0.05P_O = 0.02 - 1.8(3) + 0.69P_O = Q_D$, or $18.06 + 0.05P_O = -5.38 + 0.69P_O$, so that $0.64P_O = 23.44$ and $P_O = \$36.63$. This yields a free market price of natural gas of $3.

**12.** First, equate supply and demand to determine equilibrium quantity: $50 + Q = 200 - 2Q$, or $Q_{EQ} = 50$ (million pounds). Substitute $Q_{EQ} = 50$ into either the supply or demand equation to determine price: $P_S = 50 + 50 = 100$ and $P_D = 200 - (2)(50) = 100$. Thus, the equilibrium price $P$ is $1 (100 cents). However, the world market price is 60 cents. At this price, the domestic quantity supplied is $60 = 50 - Q_S$ or $Q_S = 10$, and domestic demand is $60 = 200 - 2Q_D$ or $Q_D = 70$. Imports equal the difference between domestic demand and supply, or 60 million pounds. If Congress imposes a tariff of 40 cents, the effective price of imports increases to $1. At $1, domestic producers satisfy domestic demand and imports fall to zero.

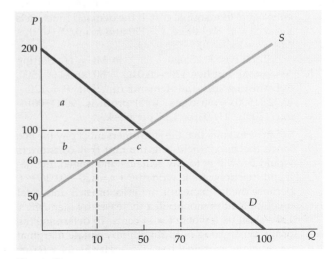

Figure 9

As shown in Figure 9, consumer surplus before the tariff is equal to area $a + b + c$, or $(0.5)(200 + 60)(70) = 4,900$ million cents or $49 million. After the tariff, the price rises to $1.00 and consumer surplus falls to area $a$, or $(0.5)(200 − 100)(50) = \$25$ million, a loss of $24 million. Producer surplus increases by area $b$, or $(100 − 60)(10) + (0.5)(100 − 60)(50 − 10) = \$12$ million. Finally, because domestic production is equal to domestic demand at $1, no hula beans are imported and the government receives no revenue. The difference between the loss of consumer surplus and the increase in producer surplus is deadweight loss which is $12 million.

**13.** No, they would not. The clearest case is where labor markets are competitive. With either design of the tax, the wedge between supply and demand must total 12.4 percent of the wage paid. It does not matter whether the tax is imposed entirely on the workers (shifting the effective supply curve up by 12.4 percent) or entirely on the employers (shifting the effective demand curve down by 12.4 percent). The same applies to any combination of the two that sums to 12.4 percent.

## CHAPTER 10

**2.** There are three important factors: (1) How similar are the products offered by Caterpillar's competitors? If they are close substitutes, a small increase in price could induce customers to switch to the competition. (2) What is the age of the existing stock of tractors? A 5-percent price increase induces a smaller drop in demand with an older population of tractors. (3) As a capital input in agricultural production, what is the expected profitability of the agricultural sector? If expected farm incomes are falling, an increase in tractor prices induces a greater decline in demand than one would estimate with information on past sales and prices.

**4. a.** Optimal production is found by setting marginal revenue equal to marginal cost. If the demand function is linear, $P = a − bQ$ (here, $a = 120$ and $b = 0.02$), so that $MR = a − 2bQ = 100 − 2(0.02)Q$.

Total cost $= 25,000 + 60Q$, so $MC = 60$. Setting $MR = MC$ implies $120 − 0.04Q = 60$, so $Q = 1500$. Substituting into the demand function, $P = 120 − (0.02)(1500) = 90$ cents. Total profit is $(90)(1500) − (60)(1500) − 25,000$, or $200 per week.

**b.** Suppose initially that the consumers must pay the tax. Since the price (including the tax) that consumers would be willing to pay remains unchanged, the demand function can be written $P + t = 120 − 0.02Q − t$. Because the tax increases the price of each unit, total revenue for the monopolist increases by $t$, so $MR = 120 − 0.04Q − t$, where $t = 14$ cents. To determine the profit-maximizing output with tax, equate marginal revenue and marginal cost: $120 − 0.04Q − 14 = 60$, or $Q = 1150$ units.

From the demand function, average revenue $= 120 − (0.02)(1150) − 14 = 83$ cents. Total profit is 1450 cents or $14.50 per week.

**7. a.** The monopolist's pricing rule is: $(P − MC)/P = −1/E_D$, using $−2$ for the elasticity and 40 for price, solve to find $MC = 20$.

**b.** In percentage terms, the mark-up is 50%, since marginal cost is 50% of price.

**c.** Total revenue is price times quantity, or $(\$40)(800) = \$32,000$. Total cost is equal to average cost times quantity, or $(\$15)(800) = \$12,000$, so profit is $20,000. Producer surplus is profit plus fixed cost, or $22,000.

**10. a.** **Pro:** Although Alcoa controlled about 90 percent of primary aluminum production in the United States, secondary aluminum production by recyclers accounted for 30 percent of the total aluminum supply. It should be possible for a much larger proportion of aluminum supply to come from secondary sources. Therefore the price elasticity of demand for Alcoa's primary aluminum is much higher than we would expect. In many applications, other metals, such as copper and steel, are feasible substitutes for aluminum. Here, the demand elasticity Alcoa faces may be lower than we would otherwise expect.

**b.** **Con:** The stock of potential supply is limited. Therefore, by keeping a stable high price, Alcoa could reap monopoly profits. Furthermore, since Alcoa had originally produced the metal reappearing as recycled scrap, it would have taken into account in its output decisions the effect of scrap reclamation on future prices. Hence, it exerted effective monopolistic control over the secondary metal supply.

**c.** Alcoa was not ordered to sell any of its U.S. production facilities. Rather, (1) it was barred from bidding for two primary aluminum plants constructed by the government during World War II; and (2) it was ordered to divest itself of its Canadian subsidiary, which became Alcan.

**13.** No, you should not. In a competitive market, a firm views price as being horizontal and equal to average revenue, which is equal to marginal revenue. If Connecticut's marginal cost increases, price will still be equal to Massachusetts's marginal cost, total marginal cost, and marginal revenue. Only Connecticut's quantity is reduced (which, in turn, reduces overall quantity), as shown in Figure 10.

## CHAPTER 11

**1. a.** The Saturday-night requirement separates business travelers, who prefer to return home for the weekend, from tourists, who travel on the weekend.

**b.** By basing prices on the buyer's location, sorting is done by geography. Then prices can reflect transportation charges, which the customer pays for whether

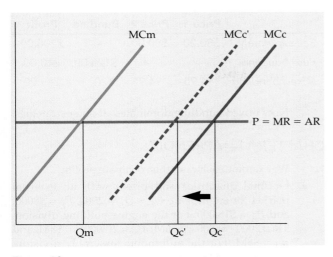

MCm    MCc'  MCc

P = MR = AR

Qm          Qc'  Qc

Figure 10

delivery is received at the buyer's location or at the cement plant.

c. Rebate coupons with food processors separate consumers into two groups: (1) customers who are less price sensitive (those who have a lower elasticity of demand) do not request the rebate; and (2) customers who are more price sensitive (those who have a higher demand elasticity) request the rebate.

d. A temporary price cut on bathroom tissue is a form of intertemporal price discrimination. Price-sensitive customers buy more tissue than they would otherwise during the price cut, while non-price-sensitive consumers buy the same amount.

e. The plastic surgeon can distinguish a high-income patient from a low-income patient by negotiation. Arbitrage is no problem because plastic surgery cannot be transferred from low-income patients to high-income patients.

8. a. A monopolist with two markets should pick quantities in each market so that the marginal revenues in both markets are equal to one another and equal to marginal cost. Marginal cost is the slope of the total cost curve, 40. To determine marginal revenues in each market, we solve for price as a function of quantity. Then we substitute this expression for price into the equation for total revenue. $P_{NY} = 240 - 4Q_{NY}$, and $P_{LA} = 200 - 2Q_{LA}$. Then total revenues are $TR_{NY} = Q_{NY}P_{NY} = Q_{NY}(240 - 4Q_{NY})$, and $TR_{LA} = Q_{LA}P_{LA} = Q_{LA}(200 - 2Q_{LA})$. The marginal revenues are the slopes of the total revenue curves: $MR_{NY} = 240 - 8Q_{NY}$ and $MR_{LA} = 200 - 4Q_{LA}$. Next, we set each marginal revenue to marginal cost (=40), implying $Q_{NY} = 25$ and $Q_{LA} = 40$. With these quantities, we solve for price in each market: $P_{NY} = 240 - (4)(25) = \$140$ and $P_{LA} = 200 - (2)(40) = \$120$.

b. With the new satellite, Sal can no longer separate the two markets. The total demand function is the

horizontal summation of the two markets. Above a price of \$200, the total demand is just the New York demand function. Below a price of \$200, we add the two demands: $Q_T = 60 - 0.25P + 100 - 0.50P = 160 - 0.75P$. Sal maximizes profit by choosing a quantity so that MR = MC. Marginal revenue is $213.33 - 2.67Q$. Setting this equal to marginal cost implies a profit-maximizing quantity of 65 with a price of \$126.67. In the New York market, quantity is equal to $60 - 0.25(126.67) = 28.3$, and in the Los Angeles market, quantity is equal to $100 - 0.50(126.67) = 36.7$. Together, 65 units are purchased at a price of \$126.67.

c. Sal is better off in the situation with the highest profit, which occurs in part (a) with price discrimination. Under price discrimination, profit is equal to $\pi = P_{NY}Q_{NY} + P_{LA}Q_{LA} - [1000 + 40(Q_{NY} + Q_{LA})]$, or $\pi = \$140(25) + \$120(40) - [1000 + 40(25 + 40)] = \$4700$. Under the market conditions in part (b), profit is $\pi = PQ_T - [1000 + 40Q_T]$, or $\pi = \$126.67(65) - [1000 + 40(65)] = \$4633.33$. Therefore, Sal is better off when the two markets are separated. Under the market conditions in (a), the consumer surpluses in the two cities are $CS_{NY} = (0.5)(25)(240 - 140) = \$1250$, and $CS_{LA} = (0.5)(40)(200 - 120) = \$1600$. Under the market conditions in (b), the respective consumer surpluses are $CS_{NY} = (0.5)(28.3)(240 - 126.67) = \$1603.67$, and $CS_{LA} = (0.5)(36.7)(200 - 126.67) = \$1345.67$. New Yorkers prefer (b) because their price is \$126.67 instead of \$140, giving them a higher consumer surplus. Customers in Los Angeles prefer (a) because their price is \$120 instead of \$126.67, and their consumer surplus is greater in (a).

10. a. With individual demands of $Q_1 = 10 - P$, individual consumer surplus is equal to \$50 per week, or \$2600 per year. An entry fee of \$2600 captures all consumer surplus, even though no court fee would be charged, since marginal cost is equal to zero. Weekly profits would be equal to the number of serious players, 1000, times the weekly entry fee, \$50, minus \$10,000, the fixed cost, or \$40,000 per week.

b. When there are two classes of customers, the club owner maximizes profits by charging court fees above marginal cost and by setting the entry fee equal to the remaining consumer surplus of the consumer with the smaller demand—the occasional player. The entry fee, $T$, is equal to the consumer surplus remaining after the court fee is assessed: $T = (Q_2 - 0)(16 - P)(1/2)$, where $Q_2 = 4 - (1/4)P$, or $T = (1/2)(4 - (1/4)P)(16 - P) = 32 - 4P + P^2/8$. Entry fees for all players would be $2000(32 - 4P + P^2/8)$. Revenues from court fees equals $P(Q_1 + Q_2) = P[1000(10 - P) + 1000(4 - P/4)] = 14,000P - 1250P^2$. Then total revenue = TR = $64,000 + 6000P - 1000P^2$. Marginal cost is zero and marginal revenue is given by the slope of the total revenue curve: $\Delta TR/\Delta P = 6000 - 2000P$. Equating marginal revenue and marginal cost implies a price of $3.00 per hour. Total revenue is equal to $73,000. Total cost is equal to fixed costs of $10,000. So profit is $63,000 per week, which is greater than the $40,000 when only serious players become members.

c. An entry fee of $50 per week would attract only serious players. With 3000 serious players, total revenues would be $150,000, and profits would be $140,000 per week. With both serious and occasional players, entry fees would be equal to 4000 times the consumer surplus of the occasional player: $T = 4000(32 - 4P + P^2/8)$. Court fees are $P[3000(10 - P) + 1000(4 - P/4)] = 34,000P - 3250P^2$. Then TR $= 128,000 + 18,000P - 2750P^2$. Marginal cost is zero, so setting $\Delta TR/\Delta P = 18,000 - 5500P = 0$ implies a price of $3.27 per hour. Then total revenue is equal to $157,455 per week, which is more than the $150,000 per week with only serious players. The club owner should set annual dues at $1053, charge $3.27 for court time, and earn profits of $7.67 million per year.

11. Mixed bundling is often the ideal strategy when demands are only somewhat negatively correlated and/or when marginal production costs are significant. The following tables present the reservation prices of the three consumers and the profits from the three strategies:

| Reservation Price | | | |
|---|---|---|---|
| | For 1 | For 2 | Total |
| Consumer A | $ 3.25 | $ 6.00 | $ 9.25 |
| Consumer B | 8.25 | 3.25 | 11.50 |
| Consumer C | 10.00 | 10.00 | 20.00 |

| | Price 1 | Price 2 | Bundled | Profit |
|---|---|---|---|---|
| Sell separately | $ 8.25 | $6.00 | — | $28.50 |
| Pure bundling | — | — | $ 9.25 | 27.75 |
| Mixed bundling | 10.00 | 6.00 | 11.50 | 29.00 |

The profit-maximizing strategy is to use mixed bundling.

15. a. For each strategy, the optimal prices and profits are

| | Price 1 | Price 2 | Bundled | Profit |
|---|---|---|---|---|
| Sell separately | $80.00 | $80.00 | — | $320.00 |
| Pure bundling | — | — | $120.00 | 480.00 |
| Mixed bundling | 94.95 | 94.95 | 120.00 | 429.00 |

Pure bundling dominates mixed bundling because with marginal costs of zero, there is no reason to exclude purchases of both goods by all customers.

b. With marginal cost of $30, the optimal prices and profits are

| | Price 1 | Price 2 | Bundled | Profit |
|---|---|---|---|---|
| Sell separately | $80.00 | $80.00 | — | $200.00 |
| Pure bundling | — | — | $120.00 | 240.00 |
| Mixed bundling | 94.95 | 94.95 | 120.00 | 249.90 |

Now mixed bundling dominates all other strategies.

## CHAPTER 11—APPENDIX

1. We examine each case, then compare profits.

a. Optimal quantities and prices with no external market for engines are $Q_E = Q_A = 2000$, $P_E = \$8000$, and $P_A = \$18,000$. For the engine-building division, TR $= 2000 \cdot \$8000 = \$16M$, TC $= 2(2000)^2 = \$8M$, and $\pi_E = \$8M$. For the automobile-assembly division, TR $= 2000 \cdot \$18,000 = \$36M$, TC $= \$8000 \cdot 2000 + 16M = \$32M$, and $\pi_A = \$4M$. Total profits are $12M.

b. Optimal quantities and prices with an external market for engines are $Q_E = 1500$, $Q_A = 3000$, $P_E = \$6000$, and $P_A = \$17,000$. For the engine-building division, TR $= 1500 \cdot \$6000 = \$9M$, TC $= 2(1500)^2 = \$4.5M$, and $\pi = \$4.5M$. For the automobile-assembly division, TR $= 3000 \cdot \$17,000 = \$51M$, TC $= (8000 + 6000)3000 = \$42M$, and $\pi = \$9M$. Total profits are $13.5M.

c. Optimal quantities and prices with a monopoly market for engines are $Q_E = 2200$, $Q_A = 1600$, $P_E = \$8800$, and $P_A = \$18,400$, with 600 engines sold in the monopolized market for $9400. For the engine-building division, TR $= 1600 \cdot \$8800 + 600 \cdot 9400 = \$19.72M$, TC $= 2(2200)^2 = \$9.68M$, and $p = \$10.04M$. For the automobile-assembly division, TR $= 1600 \cdot \$18,400 =$ TR $= 1600 \cdot \$18,400 = \$29.44M$, TC $= (8000 + 8800)1600 = \$26.88M$, and $p = \$2.56M$. Total profits are $12.6M.

The upstream division, building engines, earns the most profit when it has a monopoly on engines. The downstream division, building automobiles, earns the most when there is a competitive market for engines. Given the high cost of engines, the firm does best when engines are produced at the lowest cost with an external, competitive market for engines.

## CHAPTER 12

1. Each firm earns economic profit by distinguishing its brand from all other brands. If these competitors merge into a single firm, the resulting monopolist would not produce as many brands as would have been produced before the merger. But, producing several brands with different prices and characteristics is one method of splitting the market into sets of customers with different price elasticities.

3. a. To maximize profit $p = 53Q - Q^2 - 5Q$, we find $\Delta p/\Delta Q = -2Q + 48 = 0$. $Q = 24$, so $P = 29$. Profit is equal to 576.

b. $P = 53 Q_1 - Q_2$, $p_1 = PQ1 - C(Q) = 53Q1 - Q_1^2 - Q_1Q_2 - 5Q_1$ and $p_2 = PQ_2 - C(Q_2) = 53Q_2 - Q_1Q_2 - Q_2^2 - 5Q_2$.

**c.** The problem facing Firm 1 is to maximize profit, given that the output of Firm 2 will not change in reaction to the output decision of Firm 1. Therefore, Firm 1 chooses $Q_1$ to maximize $\pi_1$, as above. The change in $\pi_1$ with respect to a change in $Q_1$ is $53 - 2Q_1 - Q_2 - 5 = 0$, implying $Q_1 = 24 - Q_2/2$. Since the problem is symmetric, the reaction function for Firm 2 is $Q_2 = 24 - Q_1/2$.

**d.** Solve for the values of $Q_1$ and $Q_2$ that satisfy both reaction functions: $Q_1 = 24 - (1/2)(24 - Q_1/2)$. So, $Q_1 = 16$ and $Q_2 = 16$. The price is $P = 53 - Q_1 - Q_2 = 21$. Profit is $\pi_1 = \pi_2 = P \cdot Q_i - C(Q_i) = 256$. Total profit in the industry is $\pi_1 + \pi_2 = 512$.

**5.** *True.* The reaction curve of Firm 2 will be $q_2 = 7.5 - 1/2q_1$ and the reaction curve of Firm 1 will be $q_1 = 15 - 1/2q_2$. Substituting yields $q_2 = 0$ and $q_1 = 15$. The price will be 15, which is the monopoly price.

**7. a.** (i) In a Cournot equilibrium, when firm A has an increase in marginal cost, its reaction function shifts inwards. The quantity produced by firm A will decrease and the quantity produced by firm B will increase. Total quantity produced will decrease and price will increase. (ii) In a collusive equilibrium, the two firms will collectively act like a monopolist. When the marginal cost of Firm A increases, Firm A will reduce its production to zero, because Firm B can produce at a lower marginal coat. Because Firm B can produce the entire industry output at a marginal cost of $50, there will be no change in output or price. However, the firms will have to come to some agreement on how to share the profit earned by B. (iii) Because the good is homogeneous, both produce where price equals marginal cost. Firm A increases price to $80 and firm B raises its price to $79.99. Assuming firm B can produce enough output, it will supply the entire market.

**b.** (i) The increase in the marginal cost of both firms shifts both reaction functions inwards. Both firms decrease output, and price will increase. (ii) When marginal cost increases, both firms will produce less and price will increase, as in the monopoly case. (iii) Price will increase and quantity produced will decrease.

**c.** (i) Both reaction functions shift outwards and both firms produce more. Price will increase. (ii) Both firms will increase output, and price will also increase. (iii) Both firms will produce more. Because marginal cost is constant, price will not change.

**11. a.** To determine the Nash equilibrium we calculate the reaction function for each firm, then simultaneously solve for price. *Assuming marginal cost is zero*, profit for Firm 1 is $P_1 Q_1 = P_1(20 - P_1 + P_2) = 20P_1 + P_1^2 + P_2 P_1$. $MR_1 = 20 - 2P_1 + P_2$. At the profit-maximizing price, $MR_1 = 0$. So, $P_1 = (20 + P_2)/2$. Because Firm 2 is symmetric to Firm 1, its profit-maximizing price is $P_2 = (20 + P_1)/2$. We substitute Firm 2's reaction function into that of Firm 1: $P_1 = [20 + (20 + P_1)/2]/2 = 15 +$ $P_1/4$. $P_1 = 20$. By symmetry $P_2 = 20$. Then $Q_1 = 20$, and by symmetry $Q_2 = 20$. Profit for Firm 1 is $P_1 Q_1 = 400$, and profit for Firm 2 is also 400.

**b.** If Firm 1 sets its price first, it takes Firm 2's reaction function into account. Firm 1's profit is $\pi_1 = P_1[20 - P_1 + (20 + P_1)/2]$. Then, $d\pi_1/dP_1 = 20 - 2P_1 + 10 + P_1$. Setting this expression equal to zero, $P_1 = 30$. We substitute for $P_1$ in Firm 2's reaction function, $P_2 = 25$. At these prices, $Q_1 = 20 - 30 + 25 = 15$ and $Q_2 = 20 + 30 - 25 = 25$. Profit is $\pi_1 = 30 \cdot 15 = 450$ and $\pi_2 = 25 \cdot 25 = 625$.

**c.** Your first choice should be (iii), and your second choice should be (ii). Setting prices above the Cournot equilibrium values is optional for both firms when Stackelberg strategies are followed. From the reaction functions, we know that the price leader provokes a price increase in the follower. But the follower increases price less than the price leader, and hence undercuts the leader. Both firms enjoy increased profits, but the follower does best, and both do better than they would in the Cournot equilibrium.

## CHAPTER 13

**1.** If games are repeated indefinitely and all players know all payoffs, rational behavior will lead to apparently collusive outcomes. But, sometimes the payoffs of other firms can only be known by engaging in extensive information exchanges.

Perhaps the greatest problem to maintaining a collusive outcome is exogenous changes in demand and in the prices of inputs. When new information is not available to all players simultaneously, a rational reaction by one firm could be interpreted as a threat by another firm.

**2.** Excess capacity can arise in industries with easy entry and differentiated products. Because downward-sloping demand curves for each firm lead to outputs with average cost above minimum average cost, increases in output result in decreases in average cost. The difference between the resulting output and the output at minimum long-run average cost is excess capacity, which can be used to deter new entry.

**4. a.** There are two Nash equilibria: (100,800) and (900,600).

**b.** Both managers will follow a high-end strategy, and the resulting equilibrium will be (50,50), yielding less profit to both parties.

**c.** The cooperative outcome (900,600) maximizes the joint profit of the two firms.

**d.** Firm 1 benefits the most from cooperation. Compared to the next best opportunity, Firm 1 benefits by $900 - 100 = 800$, whereas Firm 2 loses $800 - 600 = 200$ under cooperation. Therefore, Firm 1 would need to offer Firm 2 at least 200 to compensate for Firm 2's loss.

**6. a.** Yes, there are two: (1) Given Firm 2 chooses $A$, Firm 1 chooses $C$; given Firm 1 chooses $C$, Firm 2 chooses $A$.

(2) Given Firm 2 chooses $C$, Firm 1 chooses $A$; given Firm 1 chooses $A$, Firm 2 chooses $C$.

b. If both firms choose according to maximin, Firm 1 will choose Product $A$ and Firm 2 will choose Product $A$, resulting in $-10$ payoff for both.

c. Firm 2 will choose Product $C$ in order to maximize payoffs at 10, 20.

12. Although antique auctions often have private-value elements, they are primarily common value because dealers are involved. Our antique dealer is disappointed in the nearby town's public auction because estimates of the value of the antiques vary widely and she has suffered from the winner's curse. At home, where there are fewer well-informed bidders, the winner's curse has not been a problem.

# CHAPTER 14

2. With the new program, the budget line shifts up by the $5000 government grant when the worker does no work at all and takes the maximum amount of leisure hours. As the number of hours worked increases (i.e., leisure decreases), the budget line has half the slope of the original budget line because earned income is taxed at 50 percent. When the after-tax income is $10,000, the new budget line coincides with the original budget line. The result is that the new program will have no effect if the worker originally earned more than $10,000 per year, but it will probably reduce the amount of time worked (i.e., increase leisure) if the worker earned less than $10,000 originally.

6. The demand for labor is given by the marginal revenue product of labor; $MRP_L = MR \cdot MP_L$. In a competitive market, price is equal to marginal revenue, so $MR = 10$. The marginal product of labor is equal to the slope of the production function $Q = 12L - L^2$. This slope is equal to $12 - 2L$. The firm's profit-maximizing quantity of labor occurs where $MRP_L = w$, the wage rate. If $w = 30$, solving for $L$ yields 4.5 hours per day. Similarly, if $w = 60$, solving for $L$ yields 3 hours per day.

8. The equilibrium wage is where the quantity of labor supplied is equal to the quantity of labor demanded, or $20w = 1,200 - 10w$. Solving, $w = \$40$. Substituting into the labor supply equation, for example, the equilibrium quantity of labor is: $L_S = (20)(40) = 800$. Economic rent is the difference between the equilibrium wage and the wage given by the labor supply curve. Here, it is the area above the labor supply curve up to $L = 800$ and below the equilibrium wage. This area is $(0.5)(800)(\$40) = \$16,000$.

# CHAPTER 15

3. The present discounted value of the first $80 payment one year from now is $PDV = 80/(1 + 0.10)^1 = \$72.73$. The value of all these coupon payments can be found

the same way: $PDV = 80[1/(1.10)^1 + 1/(1.10)^2 + 1/(1.10)^3 + 1/(1.10)^4 + 1/(1.10)^5] = \$303.26$. The present value of the final payment of $1000 in the sixth year is $1000/1.1^6 = \$564.47$. So the present value of this bond is $303.26 + \$564.47 = \$867.73$. With an interest rate of 15 percent, $PDV = \$700.49$.

5. Using $R = 0.04$, we can substitute the appropriate values into Equation 15.5. We find that $NPV = -5 - 4.808 - 0.925 - 0.445 + 0.821 + 0.789 + 0.759 + 0.730 + 0.701 + 0.674 + 0.649 + 0.624 + 0.600 + 0.577 + 0.554 + 0.533 + 0.513 + 0.493 + 0.474 + 0.456 + 0.438 + 0.456 = -0.338$. The investment loses $338,000 and is not worthwhile. However, were the discount rate 3%, the $NPV = \$866,000$, and the investment would be worth undertaking.

9. a. If we buy a bottle and sell it after $t$ years, we pay $100 now and receive $100t^{0.5}$ when it is sold. The NPV of this investment is $NPV = -100 + e^{-rt}100t^{0.5} = -100 + e^{-0.1t}100t^{0.5}$.

   If we do buy a bottle, we will choose $t$ to maximize the NPV. The necessary condition is $d\text{NPV}/dt = e^{-0.1t}(50 - t^{-0.5}) - 0.1e^{-0.1t} \cdot 100t^{0.5} = 0$. Solving, $t = 5$. If we hold the bottle 5 years, the NPV is $-100 + e^{-0.1 \cdot 5}100 \cdot 5^{0.5} = 35.62$. Since each bottle is a good investment, we should buy all 100 bottles.

   b. You are offered $130 for resale, so you would make an immediate profit of $30. However, if you hold the wine for 5 years, the NPV of your profit is $35.62 as shown in part (a). Therefore, the NPV if you sell immediately rather than hold for 5 years is $30 - 35.62 = -\$5.62$, and you should not sell.

   c. If the interest rate changes from 10 percent to 5 percent the NPV calculation changes to $NPV = -100 + e^{-0.05t} \cdot 100t^{0.5}$. If we hold the bottle 10 years, the maximum NPV is $-100 + e^{-0.05 \cdot 10} \cdot 100 \cdot 10^{0.5} = \$91.80$.

11. a. Compare buying the car to leasing the car, with $r = 0.04$. The present value net cost of buying is $-20,000 + 12,000/(1 + 0.04)^6 = -10,516.22$. The present value cost of leasing the car is $-3600 - 3600/(1 + 0.04)^1 - 3600/(1 + 0.04)^2 = -10,389.94$. You are better off leasing the car if $r = 4$ percent.

   b. Again, compare buying to leasing: $20,000 + 12,000/(1 + 0.12)^6 = -13,920.43$ with buying, versus $-3600 - 3600/(1 + 0.12)^1 - 3600/(1 + 0.12)^2 = -9,684.18$ with leasing. You are better off leasing the car if $r = 12$ percent.

   c. Consumers will be indifferent when the present value cost of buying and later selling the car equals the present value cost of leasing: $-20,000 + 12,000/(1 + r)^6 = -3600 - 3600/(1 + r)^1 - 3600/(1 + r)^2$. This is true when $r = 3.8$ percent. You can solve this equation using a graphing calculator or computer spreadsheet, or by trial and error.

# CHAPTER 16

6. Even with identical preferences, the contract curve may or may not be a straight line. This can easily be

shown graphically. For example, when both individuals have utility functions $U = x^2y$, the marginal rate of substitution is given by $2y/x$. It is not difficult to show that the MRS's of both individuals are equal for all points on the contract curve $y = (Y/X)x$, where $X$ and $Y$ are the total quantities of both goods. One example in which the contract curve is not a straight line is when the two individuals have different incomes and one good is inferior.

7. The marginal rate of transformation is equal to the ratio of the marginal costs of producing the two goods. Most production possibilities frontiers are "bowed outward." However, if the two goods are produced with constant returns to scale production functions, the production possibilities frontier is a straight line.

10. A change from a constant-returns-to-scale production process to a sharply-increasing-returns-to-scale process does not imply a change in the shape of the isoquants. One can simply redefine the quantities associated with each isoquant such that proportional increases in inputs yield greater than proportional increases in outputs. Under this assumption, the marginal rate of technical substitution would not change, and there would be no change in the production contract curve.

## CHAPTER 17

5. **a.** In the recent past, American automobiles appeared to customers to be of low quality. To reverse this trend, American companies invested in quality control, improving the potential repair records of their products. They signaled the improved quality of their products through improved warranties.

   **b.** Moral hazard occurs when the party to be insured (the owner of an American automobile with an extensive warranty) can influence the probability or the magnitude of the event that triggers payment (the repair of the automobile). Covering all parts and labor associated with mechanical problems reduces the incentive to maintain the automobile. Hence, a moral hazard problem is created with extensive warranties.

7. Moral hazard problems arise with fire insurance when the insured party can influence the probability of a fire. The property owner can reduce the probability of a fire or its impact by inspecting and replacing faulty wiring, installing warning systems, etc. After purchasing complete insurance, the insured has little incentive to reduce either the probability or the magnitude of the loss, so the moral hazard problem can be severe. In order to compare a $10,000 deductible and 90 percent

coverage, we need information on the value of the potential loss. Both policies reduce the moral hazard problem of complete coverage. However, if the property is worth less (more) than $100,000, the total loss will be less (more) with 90 percent coverage than with the $10,000 deductible. As the value of the property increases above $100,000, the owner is more likely to engage in fire prevention efforts under the policy that offers 90 percent coverage than under the one that offers the $10,000 deductible.

## CHAPTER 18

4. One needs to know the value to homeowners of swimming in the river, and the marginal cost of abatement. The choice of a policy tool will depend on the marginal benefits and costs of abatement. If firms are charged an equal rate effluent fee, the firms will reduce effluent to the point where the marginal cost of abatement is equal to the fee. If this reduction is not high enough to permit swimming, the fee could be increased.

   The setting of a standard will be efficient only if the policy maker has complete information regarding the marginal costs and benefits of abatement. Further, the standard will not encourage firms to reduce effluent further if new filtering technologies become available. A transferable effluent permit system still requires the policymaker to determine the efficient effluent standard. Once the permits are distributed, a market will develop and firms with a higher cost of abatement will purchase permits from firms with lower abatement costs. However, unless permits are sold initially, no revenue will be generated.

9. **a.** Profit is maximized when marginal revenue is equal to marginal cost. With a constant marginal revenue of $40 and a marginal cost of $10 + 5Q$, $Q = 6$.

   **b.** If bees are not forthcoming, the farmer must pay $10 per acre for artificial pollination. Since the farmer would be willing to pay up to $10 to the beekeeper to maintain each additional hive, the marginal social benefit of each is $50, which is greater than the marginal private benefit of $40. Equating the marginal social benefit to the marginal cost, $Q = 80$.

   **c.** The most radical change that would lead to more efficient operations would be the merger of the farmer's business with the beekeeper's business. This merger would internalize the positive externality of bee pollination. Short of a merger, the farmer and beekeeper should enter into a contract for pollination services.

# PHOTO CREDITS

| 515 | David Young-Wolff | PhotoEdit Inc. |
| 528 | | Corbis Digital Stock |
| 537 | Stock Montage | Photolibrary.com |
| 541 | Mark Peterson | © Mark Peterson/Corbis/SABA. |
| 542 | Spencer Grant | PhotoEdit Inc. |
| 547 | Dennis MacDonald | PhotoEdit Inc. |
| 559 | | BellSouth Advertising & Publishing |
| 566 | Michael Newman | PhotoEdit Inc. |
| 569 | Mark Antman | The Image Works |
| 572 | | Images.com |
| 576 | Grahame McConnell | Photolibrary.com |
| 588 | James Shaffer | PhotoEdit Inc. |
| 609 | Voisin | Photo Researchers, Inc. |
| 622 | Mike Powell | Getty Images, Inc. – Allsport |
| 627 | Ken Fisher | Getty Images, Inc. – Stone Allstock |
| 630 | E.R. Degginger | Animals Animals/Earth Sciences |
| 634 | Doug Martin | Photo Researchers, Inc. |
| 641 | | Getty Images, Inc. - Liaison |
| 657 | EyeWire Collection | Getty Images – Photodisc |
| 662 | Paul Kern | Omni-Photo Communications, Inc. |
| 667 | Howie Garber | Creative Eye/MIRA.com |
| 674 | Kelvin Aitken | Peter Arnold, Inc. |
| 679 | Jeff Greenberg | PhotoEdit Inc. |

# INDEX